A Portrait of the Hindus

LES HINDOUS,

PAR F. BALTAZARD SOLVYNS.

TOME QUATRIÈME.

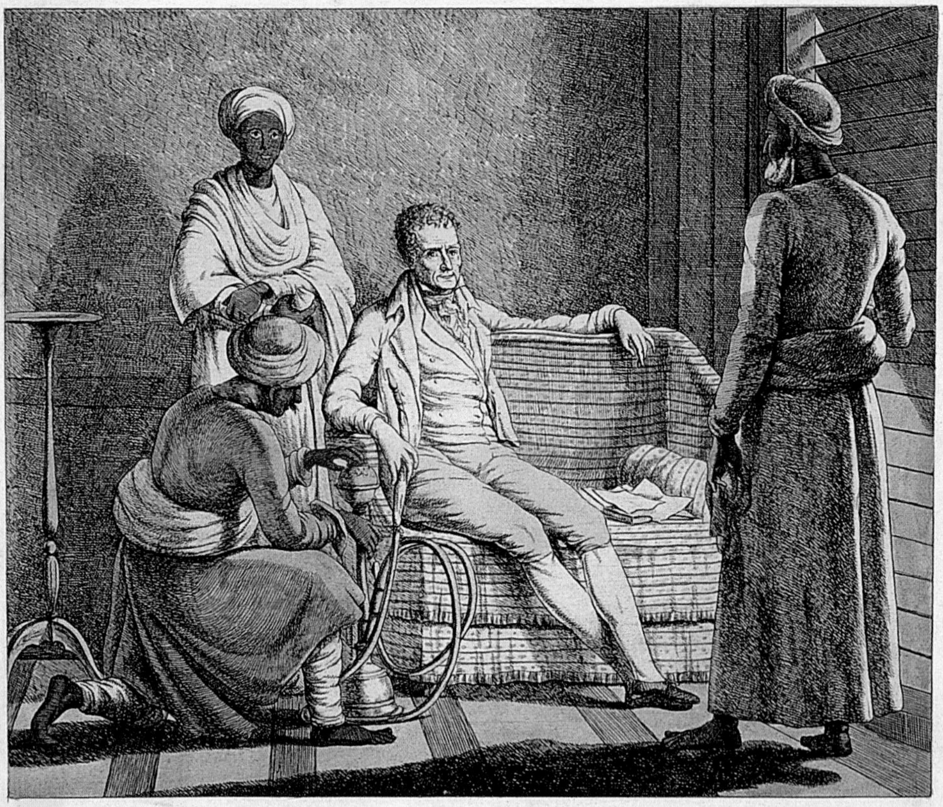

PARIS,
CHEZ L'AUTEUR, RUE DE BEAUNE, FAUBOURG SAINT-GERMAIN, N° 2.

DE L'IMPRIMERIE DE MAME FRÈRES.

1812.

A Portrait of the Hindus

Balthazar Solvyns & the European Image of India 1760-1824

Robert L. Hardgrave, Jr.

OXFORD
UNIVERSITY PRESS
in association with
MAPIN
Publishing

First published in India
in 2004 by
Mapin Publishing Pvt. Ltd.
Ahmedabad 380013
Tel: 91-79-755-1833 / 755-1793 • Fax: 79-755-0955
email: mapin@icenet.net • www.mapinpub.com

Simultaneously published in the United States of America
in 2004 by
Oxford University Press
198 Madison Avenue, New York, NY 10016-4314
by arrangement with
Grantha Corporation
77 Deniele Drive, Hidden Meadows
Ocean Township, NJ 07712

Distributed world-wide by
Oxford University Press
Except in the Indian Subcontinent by
Mapin Publishing

ISBN: 81-88204-15-3 (Mapin)
ISBN: 1-890206-52-0 (Grantha)
ISBN: 0-19-522041-2 (OUP)
LC: 2002115389

Design by: Paulomi Shah / Mapin Design Studio
Processed by Reproscan, Mumbai
Printed by Tien Wah Press, Singapore

Photographic Credits
Credit for reproduction is included with the plate as appropriate. Where "Private Collection" is indicated, permission has been secured from the current owner. For Pls. I.11 and I.20, the photographs, with permission to reproduce, were supplied by the previous (private) owners. Otherwise, where no credit is noted, as for the plates of Solvyns's etchings, the reproduction is from the author's own collection.

Captions
Front jacket: Hindu Rājā. See Pl. II.18, page 164.
Back jacket: Bisarjan. See Pl. II.190, page 391.
Spine: Goālā, cow-herd. See Pl. II.47, page 205.
Page 2: Pl. 1.1 Solvyns portrays himself, attended by servants, in Calcutta. Title Page *Les Hindoûs*, Vol. IV.
Page 5: Bālāk. Dancing Boy. See Pl. II.96, page 267.
Page 6: Ḍhāk. See Pl. II.156, page 349.
Page 127: Aghori. Female Ascetic. See Pl. II.91, page 258.

SOUTH ASIA RESEARCH

SERIES EDITOR
Patrick Olivelle

A Publication Series of
The University of Texas Center for Asian Studies
and
Oxford University Press

OXFORD
UNIVERSITY PRESS
Oxford • New York
Auckland • Bangkok • Buenos Aires • Cape Town
Chennai • Dar es Salaam • Delhi Hong Kong • Istanbul
Karachi • Kolkata • Kuala Lumpur • Madrid • Melbourne
Mexico City • Mumbai • Nairobi
Sao Paulo • Shanghai • Taipei • Tokyo • Toronto

Note to Readers on Spelling, Transliteration, Measurements, Cross-references, Endnotes, &c.

- Eighteenth century spelling was idiosyncratic, and in his descriptive text for the etchings, Solvyns often spells the same word in different ways. Solvyns's text is quoted as originally published, with idiosyncratic and varied spellings and punctuation; what are clearly typographical errors have been corrected.
- In transliteration of Sanskrit, Bengali, and Hindustani (Hindi/Urdu) words, diacritical marks follow usage by the Library of Congress.
- In the text, where sources use miles, feet, etc., non-metric measurements have been retained.
- Dimensions for the paintings and prints reproduced in *A Portrait of the Hindus* are given in metric measurements only. Dimensions for intaglio prints are to the impression.
- Cross-references to a Solvyns's etching or to material in the accompanying text and Commentary are to the Plate. Pl. II.194, for example, would refer the reader to the etching and discussion of Durgā Pūjā.
- References to the original plate numbers in the Calcutta edition of the etchings are by Section and Number, and for *Les Hindoûs*, they are by Volume, *Livraison* (Section), and Number. Thus, for Durgā Pūjā, they would be, respectively, Calcutta: Sec. XII. No. 4, and Paris: II.3.1.
- Endnotes use shortened references to the sources cited, referring the reader to the Bibliography.
- The term "Anglo-Indian" as used here refers to the British in India, not to its other usage as "Eurasian," unless otherwise noted.

Contents

Part I.
François Balthazar Solvyns Life and Work

Part II.
A Portrait of the Hindus

Acknowledgments

Over the course of my research on François Balthazar Solvyns, a great many people have given me assistance in pursuit of elusive words and images, in ferreting out information, resolving anomalies, and in finding the correct Bengali, Hindustani, Sanskrit, or Persian word for what in Solvyns's description was by no means always clear. I shall be forever grateful for their help, without which this work could never have been completed. Because of their number, I list them by country and alphabetically. I offer my apologies to any persons I may have inadvertently left out, for I am no less grateful for their assistance. If I have made errors in fact or judgment, they are wholly my own. I only pray they are not egregious. My thanks go to:

In India: Hena Basu, Falguna Sakha Bose, Hiren Chakrabarti, Ramakanta Chakrabarty, Niladri Chatterjee, Shubha Chaudhuri, Uma Dasgupta, Barun De, Pheroza Godrej, H. C. Gupta, the late R. P. Gupta, Jyotindra Jain, T. N. Madan, Jagmohan Mahajan, Somendra Chandra Nandy, Pran Nevile, the late Nisith Ranjan Ray, Nikhil Sarkar, Sandip Sarkar, Aditi Sen, Pradip Sinha.

In the United Kingdom: Mildred Archer, Christopher Bayly, Hugh Bett, Richard Bingle, T. Richard Blurton, Robert Blyth, Anne Bulley, the late Nirad Chaudhuri, Rosemary Creel, Giles Eyre, Rupert Featherstone, Irving Finkel, Basil Greenhill, Charles Greig, Niall Hobhouse, Richard E. Kossow, Roger Knight, Andrew Lambert, Brian Lavery, Jerry Losty, Peter Marshall, George Michell, Elizabeth Miller, Desmond McTernan, Graham Parlett, Jonathan P. Parry, Hugh Popham, Roger Quarm, C. William Radice, Robin Reilly, Pauline Rohatgi, Deborah A. Swallow, Graham Shaw, Giles H. R. Tillotson, Theon Wilkinson.

In Belgium: Norbert Hostyn, Alok Nandi, Bart De Prins, Eddy Stols, Ernest Vanderlinden.

In France: Deben Bhattacharya, Arsène Bonafous-Murat, André Jammes, Paul Prouté, Marie-José Segala.

In Germany: Hermann Kulke, Claus Peter Zoller.

In the Netherlands: Joep Bor, Ron Brand, L. B. Holthluis, Dirk H. A. Kolff, Joost Schokkenbroek, Elisabeth Spits.

In New Zealand: Hew McLeod.

In Australia: Barbara Hall, Geoffrey Oddie, Asim Roy.

In Mexico: Ishita Banerjee Dube.

In Canada: W. McAllister Johnson.

In the United States: Frederick M. Asher, Susan Bean, Jonathan Bober, Merry Burlingham, Garland Cannon, Amalendu Chakraborty, Michael Charlesworth, Paul B. Courtright, Robert J. Del Bontà, Neil De Marchi, Madhav Deshpande, Daniel Finamore, Malia E. Finnegan, Sumit Ganguly, Carl Gans, Pika Ghosh, Stuart Gordon, Kathryn Hansen, Brian Hatcher, Andrew Henderson, Francis G. Hutchins, the late Ali Jazayery, Brian Kensley, Joanna Kirkpatrick, Frank Korom, Richard Lariviere, Janice Leoshko, William Loos, Philip Lutgendorf, R. B. Manning, Rebecca Manring, Rachel McDermott, Michael W. Meister, Patrick Olivelle, Akos Östör, Pratapaditya Pal, Ludo Rocher, Rosane Rocher, Suchitra Samanta, Suchismita Sen, Anita Slawek, Stephen M. Slawek,

Brian K. Smith, Frederick M. Smith, Tony K. Stewart, Michael H. Styles, George Swartz, Joanna Williams, Anand Yang.

I wish to express my thanks to friends and colleagues who have assisted me with translations from French, Dutch, German, and Italian: Robert Dawson, Benjamin Gregg, Lawrence Haley, John R. J. Ike, François Lagarde, Kevin Lemoine, Jean-Luc Mazet, Richard Mills, Gail Minault, James Stephens, Herman Van Olphen, Maria Wells.

Special acknowledgment and thanks go to Sagaree Sengupta. From the beginning of the project, she has, with patience and enthusiasm, helped me in puzzling out Solvyns's idiosyncratic spellings of Bengali and Hindustani words, and her help with transliteration and diacritical marks has been indispensable.

I am grateful as well for the assistance provided by the staff of the Center for Asian Studies at the University of Texas and particularly to Anne Alexander for the many times she came to my rescue in the face of some software malfunction or computer glitch.

Photographs of the Solvyns etchings and other prints from my collection are by Eric Beggs and Richard Hall, and the map of "Solvyns's Calcutta" is by John V. Cotter, cartographer.

I want also to express my thanks to the American Institute of Indian Studies and to the University Research Institute of the University of Texas at Austin for funding portions of my research in India and in Europe. And I am grateful to the Victoria Memorial Hall, Calcutta, with which I was affiliated as an A.I.I.S. Fellow, and to Hiren Chakrabarti, who then served as the Victoria Memorial's Secretary and Curator.

My gratitude goes to publisher Bipin Shah at Mapin for his unwavering commitment to the Solvyns project and to Mapin Art Director Paulomi Shah for her care in bringing this book to publication. I am honored that *A Portrait of the Hindus* has been selected for inclusion in the Oxford University Press "South Asia Research" series.

Finally, and with the greatest appreciation, I thank members of the Solvyns family for their interest and help as I pursued this project: the Baroness Solvyns and Madame Henri de Wouters d'Oplinter née Marie-Louise Solvyns in Belgium and Laurence Solvyns and John Solvyns in Australia.

Robert L. Hardgrave, Jr.
Austin, Texas, August 2003

Introduction

The Flemish artist François Balthazar Solvyns (1760-1824), who lived in Calcutta (Kolkata) from 1791 to 1803, is little known, but his collection of etchings of the Hindus constructs a rich and compelling image of India two hundred years ago. These prints, depicting the people of Bengal in their occupations, festivals, and daily life, and the accompanying descriptive text, have rarely been referred to by historians of India. Indeed, for most historians, Solvyns was apparently unknown—or at least "unseen"—and no systematic use of his work had been made until, in the late 1980s, I initiated the current project with a long article, co-authored by a colleague in ethnomusicology, on Solvyns's portrayal of musical instruments.

Solvyns was born in Antwerp in 1760, of a prominent merchant family, and had pursued a career as a marine painter until political unrest in Europe and his own insecure position led him to seek his fortune in India. Following his arrival in Calcutta in 1791, Solvyns worked as something of a journeyman artist, but in 1794, he announced his plan for *A Collection of Two Hundred and Fifty Coloured Etchings: Descriptive of the Manners, Customs and Dresses of the Hindoos*. The collection was published in Calcutta in a few copies in 1796, and then in greater numbers in 1799. Divided into twelve parts, the first section, with 66 prints, depicts "the Hindoo Casts, with their professions." Following sections portray servants, costumes, means of transportation (carts, palanquins, and boats), modes of smoking, fakirs, musical instruments, and festivals.

The project proved a financial failure. The etchings, by contemporary European standards, were rather crudely done, and they did not appeal to the vogue of the picturesque. In 1803, Solvyns left India for France and soon redid the etchings for a folio edition of 288 plates, *Les Hindoûs,* published in Paris between 1808 and 1812 in four volumes. Even these sumptuous volumes failed commercially, victim to the unrest of the Napoleonic Wars and to the sheer cost of the publication. When the Kingdom of the Netherlands was formed in 1814, Solvyns returned to his native Antwerp, where William I appointed him Captain of the Port in recognition of his accomplishments as an artist. Solvyns died in 1824.

Solvyns's life is itself fascinating, and his portrayal of India constitutes an unrivaled visual account of the people of Bengal in the late eighteenth century. The prints in themselves are of importance in a tradition reaching back to the early seventeenth century, and even earlier, with encyclopedic efforts to represent systematically both the unfamiliar, as in costumes of foreign lands, and the familiar, as in the typologies of peasants, craftsmen, and street vendors. In portraying the Hindus, however, Solvyns is not simply recording ethnographic types. He gives his figures individual character and places them in time and space, with narrative interest, and in doing so, he provides the viewer intimate access. This separates him from purely encyclopedic interest, for with artistic purpose he combines the ethnographic and the aesthetic. He conveys "art as information."

As an artist, Solvyns provided a prototype for the genre of "Company School" paintings of occupations, done by Indian artists for the British, that became popular in the early nineteenth century. But more significantly from an historical and social perspective, Solvyns's work, with its accompanying descriptions, constitutes "the first great ethnographic survey of life in Bengal."[1] Moreover, in his ordered, hierarchical portrayal of Hindu castes in Bengal, however problematic it may be, Solvyns may well be the first European to provide a systematic ranking of castes. Yet this contribution has never been recognized, and historians and anthropologists have rarely drawn upon Solvyns for an understanding of society in Bengal in the late eighteenth century.

A Portrait of the Hindus: Balthazar Solvyns & the European Image of India, 1760-1824, is organized in two parts. In Part I, the first two chapters draw on primary sources and the few, often contradictory and frequently incorrect biographical profiles to provide an account of the life and work of Solvyns. The focus is on his work as an artist—his paintings and, most importantly, the Calcutta and Paris etchings. In these chapters, the fifteen Solvyns paintings known to survive are reproduced. A decade ago, only the four paintings in museums were known, but over the past ten years, I have been able to locate eleven other privately-owned Solvyns paintings. Of these, one has since come into a museum collection and two are with the Solvyns family.

In Chapter Three, I examine Solvyns as artist and Orientalist. I place Solvyns within the European print tradition and discuss the character, style, and technique of the etchings, with particular attention to differences between the Calcutta and Paris editions. I also examine and reproduce several Solvyns drawings that were not used for the etchings and copies of Solvyns's work by other artists, both European and Indian, and I look at Solvyns's influence on Indian artists of the Company School in their portrayal of Indian caste occupations.

Chapter Four reprints Solvyns's "Preliminary Discourse" to *Les Hindoûs*, Volume I (1808), with detailed annotations.

Part II presents Solvyns's portrayal of the Hindus, with 300 subjects in plates of the etchings from the Paris and Calcutta editions. For each subject, I include the texts from Solvyns's 1799 quarto *Catalogue* and from the Paris edition and provide a detailed Commentary on what Solvyns portrays and describes.

An appendix, "Solvyns in Libraries," lists libraries around the world holding Solvyns volumes.

A Portrait of the Hindus is fundamentally a scholarly book, but it is not intended as an "intervention" in current academic post-colonial, post-modern debates about the representation of "the other." These theoretical contributions have an important role in advancing our critical understanding of the production of knowledge, but they have no place in what is intended to be the basic reference work on Solvyns that will stand long after the dust has settled on current debates and as new issues are engaged.

Sources on the Life of Solvyns

There is comparatively little material on Solvyns's life. The earliest published biographical accounts of Solvyns are the entry in the *Biographie nouvelle des contemporains*, prepared just before his death in 1824 (though published only in 1825),[2] and an essay on Solvyns by Philibert Lesbroussart, a member of the Royal Society of Fine Arts in Ghent, published in Brussels in 1824, possibly as an obituary.[3] Copies of the original Lesbroussart article are apparently lost, but it was included in the Royal Society's annual publication in 1826,[4] with extensive quotations from Solvyns's Introduction to

Les Hindoûs that may not have been included in the original publication. The obituary for Solvyns in the British *Annual Register* for 1824 draws from Lesbroussart, often in word for word translation.[5]

Georges-Bernard Depping, a celebrated Paris intellectual, wrote the entry on Solvyns for *Biographie universelle, ancienne et moderne*, published in 1825.[6] Although Depping had known Solvyns in Paris and had a major hand in writing the introductions to each of the four volumes of *Les Hindoûs*,[7] he seems to have relied upon Lesbroussart—errors included—for much of his account of Solvyns's life, citing him at the end of the article.

Most subsequent biographical accounts of Solvyns draw upon one of these early sources—often verbatim—or from each other,[8] and in doing so, they perpetuate inaccuracies that first appeared there. The *Biographie nouvelle des contemporains*, for example, has Solvyns accompanying his Austrian patron, the Archduchess Maria Christina, to Vienna in 1789 and remaining there in her service until her death, whereupon he undertakes his voyage to the East. The Archduchess, however, died in 1798, and Solvyns sailed for India in 1790. The *Biographie* also erroneously credits Solvyns with mapping the coasts of the Red Sea on a voyage with Sir Home Popham. Solvyns sailed with Popham to India, arriving there in 1791, but they did not go by way of the Red Sea—and Popham's charts of the Red Sea were prepared on a subsequent voyage in 1801-1802, while Solvyns was in Calcutta.[9] The mistakes appear both in the Solvyns entry in *Biographie nouvelle des contemporains* and in Lesbroussart's article, but Lesbroussart adds another inaccuracy, placing Solvyns with Lord Cornwallis in the Mysore wars at Seringapatam in 1792—a mistake apparently arising from Solvyns's involvement in decorating the palanquins commissioned by Cornwallis for the hostage sons of Tipu Sultan.[10] The three errors, incorporated by Depping, appear in nearly all later accounts of the life of Solvyns.

---

1 Mildred and William G. Archer, "Francois Baltazard Solvyns: Early Painter of Calcutta Life," 10. The term *ethnographic*, introduced only in the 1830s, would, of course, have been unknown in Solvyns's time, but the Archers use the term in the sense of a systematic, descriptive account of a specific culture, here that of the Bengali Hindu, portrayed in a collection of etchings with accompanying text.

2 19:243-44. The dictionary was published in 1825, but the entry uses the present tense in referring to Solvyns's last projects and makes no mention of his death. The author of the entry in the *Biographie* is not identified and could well have been Lesbroussart.

3 Depping, "Solvyns" (1825), relied on the article for his biographical sketch and cites it as published in Brussels. The Depping entry on Solvyns in *Biographie universelle ancienne et moderne*, rev. ed., adds the date 1824 for Lesbroussart's article.

4 "Notice biographique sur François-Balthazar Solvyns, auteur des Hindous," in *Messager des sciences et des arts.*

5 Appendix to Chronicle, 234-36.

6 43:62-63.

7 See pp. 65-67 below for discussion of the Solvyns-Depping relationship.

8 See, for example, Gorton (1828), 2:926; Staes (1884); George C. Williamson (1903), 5:101; Spooner (1865), 2:908; Borchgrave (1921-24), 23:134-38; Foster, "Some Foreign European Artists in India," 94-98; and Hostyn, "Solvyns, Frans-Balthasar," *National Biographish Woordenbook* (1983), 10:595-99.

9 See discussion the Red Sea charts below, pp. 17-18 .

10 See below, pp. 30-31.

Chapter One

From Antwerp to Calcutta: A Flemish Artist in India

Calcutta in the late eighteenth century was an unlikely place for a Flemish marine artist, born to a prominent Antwerp merchant family, but for François Balthazar Solvyns (1760-1824), it was to be his home for thirteen years, and the product of his work there, a portrait of the Hindus in a collection of more than 250 etchings, would consume his life. With commitment to faithful representation and the sensibilities of an astutely observant artist, Solvyns combined the informational and the aesthetic in an unrivaled visual account of the people of India two hundred years ago. The account that follows, based on the limited information on Solvyns's life, provides us with some sense, however conjectural, of how this young man, trained as a marine artist, came to go to India and to take up his great project in portraying the Hindus.

Formative Years: Family, Education, and Patronage

François Balthazar Solvyns was born in Antwerp in 1760, the youngest child of Maximilien Solvyns (1703-1773) and Marie Elisabeth Abeloos (1717-1797). He was baptized in the Antwerp cathedral of Notre Dame on July 6, as Franciscus Balthazar Solvijns.[1] Until the twentieth century most people in the Low Countries had Latinized first names, but these names were never used except on birth, death, and marriage certificates. In addition, in Belgium many Flemings used two given names, as with Solvyns—one Dutch, Frans, and one French, François. Solvyns used the French form of his name and usually omitted his first name, François, or simply gave the initial F. His middle name appears in two forms, Balthazar, by which he was baptized and which appears on both his marriage and death certificates, and as Baltazard, which appears on the title pages of *Les Hindoûs*.[2] Frequently, he abbreviated it, "Balt.", as on the title page of the Calcutta edition of the etchings. The name on his death certificate, October 10, 1824, is Franciscus Balthazar Solvyns.

Balthazar had a sister, Marie Catherine Barbe (1754-1806),[3] and two older brothers, Pierre Jean (1756-1810) and Laurent Maximilien (1758-1828). Their father Maximilien was among Antwerp's leading merchants, the "wool king" of the city, and an outfitter of ships. Upon his father's death, Pierre Jean, a lawyer, took over the family business, and emerged, in his own right, as a leading figure in Antwerp, with an active and controversial political life.[4]

A partisan of the French Revolution of 1789, Pierre Jean (or simply Jean, as his name appears on official documents) served as deputy mayor of Antwerp and as adjunct treasurer for a period after the French took control of Belgium in 1792. He later served as a Prefect Counselor and as Judge of the Trade Tribunal, and in that capacity, he attended the arrival of Napoleon and Josephine in Antwerp in 1803.[5] Pierre Jean became increasingly involved in shipping from Ostend and suffered serious losses at sea during the Napoleonic Wars. His son Pierre Charles made a trip to the Indies as supercargo on a ship he outfitted and, on its return voyage, the English seized the ship and held Pierre Charles prisoner for several years. He was released only in 1812 through the efforts of his aunt, Marie Anne Greenwood Solvyns, Balthazar's English-born wife. Pierre Jean had three children, and it is through them that one branch of the present Solvyns family descends.[6]

The middle brother, Laurent, to whom Balthazar was closest, was an insurance agent and a leading Antwerp merchant, serving as president of Antwerp's Tribunal of Commerce in 1810. He never married.[7]

The Solvyns—Solvijns, in Dutch—family had come to Antwerp in the early 1700s from Steenhuyse, near Oudenaarde, and were soon established as prosperous merchants. Frans Solvyns was the first to arrive, and he was soon followed by his two cousins, Laurent and Maximilien, Balthazar's father.

Laurent (1699-1753), like his younger brother, became a prominent Antwerp merchant. One of his ten children, Laurent Pierre (1732-1793), in the 1760s, purchased the house of the great painter Jakob Jordaens (1593-1678), with its magnificent ceiling panels of paintings by the master. An architect and one of the directors of the Austrian Company of the East Indies, Laurent used the house as his place of business. The house was sold in 1823, when the family suffered financial reverses.[8]

The position of the Solvyns family in Antwerp in the late eighteenth and early nineteenth century is also suggested in the attainments of Laurent's grandson, Maximilien ("Max") Emanuel Solvyns (1751-1801). Max, like his cousin Pierre Jean, had supported the arrival of the French in 1792, and as other members of the Solvyns family, he served in the Antwerp municipal administration under the French. He became the director of the new Bureau of Trade, and in 1796, he was appointed as the first Captain of the Port of Antwerp, with the responsibility of opening the heavily silted harbor. Although more a merchant than a man of the sea, he held the position until just before his death in 1801.[9] Balthazar was later to serve as Captain of the Port, from 1815 until his death in 1824.

A family anecdote relates that during the time Balthazar lived in India, he unexpectedly encountered his cousin, Maximilien Emanuel, on the streets of Calcutta. "What on earth are you doing here?" the artist blurted out in Dutch. But Max, presumably there for commerce, was equally surprised, apparently having no idea that Balthazar was in India.[10]

In the Flemish provinces of the Austrian Netherlands, Dutch was spoken by the common people, but French was the language of the nobility and upper-middle classes, and it was the language of the Solvyns family. It had become, writes historian E. H. Kossmann, "the fashionable language, the language of social and cultural prestige, the language of the élite [and] Belgium assimilated the Enlightenment through the medium of French."[11]

Although from a mercantile family background, Balthazar Solvyns grew up in a city with the rich artistic tradition of Rubens, Jordaens, and Van Dyck, and at an early age, he began instruction in art as a pupil of André-Bernard de Quertenmont (1750-1835). Quertenmont became a professor at Antwerp's Académie des Beaux-Arts in 1771, at the age of 21, and in 1778 became one of the directors.[12] Solvyns apparently accompanied his teacher to the Académie, for in 1772, then only 11 or 12 years old,[13] Solvyns received the first prize in drawing at the Académie. There the young artist pursued the new Neo-classical curriculum established by André-Corneille Lens (1739-1822),[14] with study of anatomy using live models and plaster casts of classical sculpture. As director of the Académie, 1768-1781, Lens was a forceful advocate for Neo-classicism and secured close ties to the nobility, for whom he decorated their grand houses. His most important commission was for the decoration of Laeken, the palace of the Austrian governors in Brussels. Some early accounts of Solvyns's life suggest that Balthazar may have assisted Lens in the Laeken project, and it may well have been through Lens that Solvyns first came to the attention to the Austrian court.

Early biographical accounts relate that Solvyns's talent was recognized with patronage, and while he was a student at the Académie, in 1775, at the age of 15, he received a commission from the Austrian government in Brussels to paint a view of the harbor of Antwerp.[15] Lesbroussart—the apparent source of many subsequent biographical entries for the artist—describes Solvyns's early success: "Applying himself incessantly to all the various modes of execution, he soon acquired equal dexterity in the management of the pencil, the painting brush, and the graver. The residence of his youth doubtless gave the peculiar direction to his talent in which it first displayed itself, his earlier productions being almost exclusively sea-pieces, and views of sea-ports, subjects in which he excelled. . . ."[16]

Solvyns went to Paris in 1778 to study under François-André Vincent (1746-1816),[17] one of the major artists of the Neo-classical movement. Vincent, a member of the Académie royale, was a "history" painter and portraitist, and years later, when Solvyns, back from India, was at work in Paris on *Les Hindoûs*, Vincent painted his portrait. As Vincent's student, Solvyns remained in Paris for perhaps a year or more, and in 1780, his name reappears in the registry of the Académie in Antwerp.

Soon after the young artist's return, in 1780, the Governor-General commissioned Solvyns to paint the port of Ostend. Solvyns sought to combine harbor and cityscape in the painting, a difficult task, but "the result was masterful."[18] The painting (along with a possible companion view of the port of Antwerp) is now lost, but an engraving of the picture, "View of the City and Port of Ostend," was made by Robert Daudet (1737-1824)[19] in Paris and published there in 1784 (Pl. I.2). In the print, below the picture, on the left, it is signed "F. Balthazar Solvyns, pinxit," and on the right, "R. Daudet, sculsit." The engraving is "Dedicated to their Royal Highnesses, Madame Marie-Christine, Royal Princess of Hungary and Bohemia, Archduchess of Austria, Duchess of Burgundy, Lorrain and Saxe-Teschen, and Monseigneur Albert-

Casimir, Prince Royal of Poland and Lithuania, Duke of Saxe-Teschen, Grand Cross of the Royal Order of the Marshall of the Armies of His Majesty the Emperor and King of the Holy Roman Empire, Lieutenants, Governors, and Captains General of the Low Country, Etc., Etc., Etc., by their very humble and very obedient and loyal servant, F. Balthazar Solvyns." The cartouche, at the bottom, is by Pierre-Philippe Choffard (1731-1809), who specialized in such embellishments.[20]

The inscription at the bottom left establishes that Solvyns was then resident in Ostend: "It is sold in Ostend at Chez Solvyns and in Paris at the principal print merchants."

Pl. I.2. "View of the City and Port of Ostend" ("Vue de la Ville et du Port d'Ostende").
Copper engraving by R. Daudet, after the painting by Solvyns. 1784. 37.5 x 58 cm. Courtesy, Stadsarchief, Stadhuis, Ostend.

The engraving provides us with a good sense of the painting, but there is nothing to record Solvyns's treatment of Antwerp, thought to have been commissioned at about the same time as the Ostend painting. Solvyns's view of Ostend is of Neo-classical style, reflecting his Académie training. Ostend Museum curator Norbert Hostyn notes that the view gives a greater sense of grandeur than reality because of the widened perspective, as if by fish-eye lens, but the details are true to the port of the time.[21] The print portrays a tranquil scene below a clouded sky. Quiet waters pick up the reflections of the boats and ships that, with light wind, carry sail as they come into harbor. The view of the city shows the spire of St. Peter's, the city hall, and the lighthouse.

Solvyns's portrayal of Ostend, described as "a textbook example of Neoclassical marine painting,"[22] provided the prototype for four paintings of the same subject by other artists.[23]

At some point in the 1780s, Solvyns drew the attention of the Archduchess Maria Christina (1742-1798),[24] daughter of Maria Theresa and sister of Emperor Joseph II. What is now Belgium had been under Austrian Hapsburg rule from 1713, and in 1780, Joseph II, in conformity with the wishes of their mother, the late Empress, named Maria Christina and her husband, Albert of Saxe-Teschen, governors-general of the Low Countries. The Archduchess, impressed by his talent, appointed Solvyns to a post in the Laeken palace on the outskirts of Brussels, an honorary position "by which means he was enabled to devote himself in that charming retreat to the cultivation of his favourite pursuits."[25]

The French marine painter Claude Joseph Vernet (1714-1789), who had been commissioned by Louis XV to paint a series of ports of France, was a model for Solvyns, and, indeed, Solvyns might be regarded as the Belgian Vernet for the commissions he received to paint the ports of Ostend and Antwerp in the Austrian Netherlands. The paintings first hung at the Laeken palace, but when Maria Christina and Albert fled for Vienna in the upheaval of 1789, they took the paintings—or at least the painting of Ostend—with them. At the time of Solvyns's death in 1824, Lesbroussart referred to the Ostend painting as "now in the Imperial Palace at Vienna."[26] According to an administrator of Vienna's Museum of Fine Arts, the Solvyns painting was not in the Hofburg, but in the neighboring palace of Maria Christina and Albert, the present-day Albertina. In 1919, heirs of the Archduchess sold the contents of the Albertina, including the painting of Ostend (and perhaps that of Antwerp), and its whereabouts is unknown.[27]

Although Solvyns had embarked on a career as an artist, in 1786, he accepted the commission as captain of the royal corvette stationed on the Sheldt River at Fort Lillo, near Antwerp. As specified in the detailed commission document, the appointment was made on the resolution of their Royal Highnesses, Maria Christina and Albert. The government, "trusting fully in his loyalty, respectability, and diligence," named Solvyns to the post on the basis of "his capacities and intelligence concerning navigation" and conferred upon him "full powers, authority, and command." The appointment was clearly more than a sinecure, for it carried substantial responsibilities. As captain of the corvette, Solvyns was to ensure that any vessel coming down the Sheldt into the port of Antwerp pay all customs duties and that they be collected and duly recorded.[28] The position provided him a secure income and, at the same time, afforded him the opportunity, aboard a ship under his own command, to pursue his work as a marine painter.

In 1788, Solvyns joined in forming the Société des Beaux-Arts, with "For Utility, Benefit and Service" as its motto. The group had met informally for two years, but now on more formal terms, the artists gathered once a week at the "De Stad Oostende" ("The City of Ostend"), and later at "De Gulden Poort" ("The Golden Gate"), Antwerp taverns, where one or two works of a member would be shown and discussed. With the intent to hold a public exhibition each year, the association opened its first show in September 1789 in a room at No. 30 Schermersstaat, the guild house of the fencing school. It was the first public exhibition of paintings ever held in Antwerp, and among the 88 exhibits were 69 paintings and drawing. Four were by Solvyns: three oil paintings—"A View of the Schelde River with Ships," "View of Vlissingen [Flushing] on Rough Sea," and "Ships Saluting Each Other With Cannons"— and a drawing, "View of the Gorée Estuary Opposite the Port of Hellevoet."[29] The whereabouts of these pictures—or whether they have survived—is today unknown.

Only one painting by Solvyns before he left for India in 1790 is known to survive, "Ships on the Roadstead of a Dutch Harbor" ("Schepen op de rede van een Nederlandse haven," 1787), in Antwerp's Maritime Museum (Pl. I.3). Indeed, it is the only Solvyns painting in a Belgium museum. There is no record of the provenance of the painting, but the Maritime Museum acquired the painting in 1954 as part of the Chauveau collection from Brussels.[30] It was restored in 1995.

The painting demonstrates Solvyns's technical skill as a marine painter.[31] The port in the background is not identified, but the ships fly Dutch flags and more than half a dozen windmills may be seen in the distance along the coast to the right of the harbor. To the center left, at the entrance to the harbor, a state yacht is sailing in; to the right a large, full-rigged ship goes out to open sea. In the center foreground is a small fishing boat manned by a bearded sailor in a red hat. Solvyns signed the painting on a piece of driftwood in the lower right.

Pl. I.3. "Ships on the Roadstead of a Dutch Harbor."
Oil on oak panel. 1787. 53 x 72.5 cm. Nationaal Sheepvaartmuseum (National Maritime Museum), Het Steen, Antwerp. Inventory No. A.S. 54.11.76.

Political unrest had been brewing in the Austrian Netherlands from 1781, with the introduction of various reforms that culminated, in 1787, in the abolition of a host of traditional political institutions and privileges. Protest and resistance grew, and the movement to overthrow the foreign—albeit "enlightened"—absolutism centered in the province of Brabant. In the Brabant Revolution of 1789, as the revolt is termed, Belgian "Patriots," recruited on foreign soil, invaded the country, and the Austrian rulers were compelled to flee. According to early biographical sources, Solvyns, finding himself on the wrong side, accompanied his patron, the Archduchess, to Vienna in November 1789. If correct—and these sources are not reliable—within a short time, Solvyns left Vienna, returning to an uncertain political situation in the Low Countries and his departure for India in July 1790. In 1790, Austrian troops invaded, and Brussels was retaken in December. Maria Christina and her husband returned in June 1791. The international Treaty of the Hague, in 1790, had restored Austrian rule, though two years later, invasion by France finally displaced the Hapsburgs from the Low Countries.

With extensive trade between the free port of Ostend and the East, Solvyns had surely heard that fortunes were to be made in India, but he does not tell us when he made the decision that was to change his life. It seems unlikely, as suggested by Lesbroussart, that the plan had been "long formed."[32] The unrest in Europe and his own insecure situation as an artist, without his former patronage, may well have been the formative factors in his decision. But whatever led Solvyns to his decision, he left Europe at the age 30 for India and the city of Calcutta.

The Lure of Calcutta, "City of Palaces"

Calcutta, in 1790, was already a "city of palaces." It was the seat of British government in India, a center of commerce and wealth.[33] The Count de Granpré, who had visited the city in 1789, described it as "not only the handsomest town in Asia, but one of the finest in the world."[34]

From the 1760s, India, and Calcutta particularly, had begun to attract European professional artists.[35] By 1791, when Solvyns arrived in Calcutta, a number of painters, of varying talents, had already spent time in Calcutta and several had established residence. "The magnet that drew so many to India," writes Sir William Foster in his essay on British artists in India, "was the same as attracted thither a large number of their compatriots, namely, the hope that in the land of the pagoda-tree Fortune might prove kinder than in the crowded markets at home."[36] Solvyns must have gotten word in Ostend that artists—Kettle and Zoffany most prominently—had successfully shaken the "pagoda tree," with handsome return in gold coin ("pagodas").[37]

Tilly Kettle (1740-1786), the first important professional artist to go to India, "reaped a good harvest" as a portrait painter, notably in the court of Awadh (Oudh) in Lucknow,[38] and his success provided an impetus for other artists to seek their fortunes in India. John Zoffany (1733-1810) arrived in India in 1783, and like Kettle, painted in the court of the Nawab of Lucknow. Perhaps the best known European painter to work in India, Zoffany was reputed to have amassed a fortune of £10,000, a stupendous amount for the period, by the time he returned to England in 1789.[39]

For William Hodges (1744-1797), the Romantic even more than money provided the attraction to India. Hodges, who earlier had sailed with Captain Cook in the Pacific,[40] traveled in India from 1780 through 1783, principally as a landscape painter. He produced a number of oil paintings and two volumes of aquatints and engravings, *Select Views of India* (1785-88), that Solvyns's may well have seen in Belgium, and *Travels in India* (1793).[41]

It was both the prospect of fortune and the vision excited by Hodges's aquatints that led Thomas Daniell (1749-1840) and his nephew William (1769-1837) to India in 1786. Thomas soon published a collection of twelve etchings, *Views of Calcutta* (1786-88). The Daniells then embarked on extensive travels through north and south India, producing numerous drawings in preparation for a series of prints, as well as scores of paintings portraying landscapes, monuments, and scenes of Indian life. Following their return to England in 1793, Thomas and William Daniell brought out their elaborate *Oriental Scenery* (1795-1808), 144 aquatints that were to become the most famous of all European representations of India.[42]

Hodges and the Daniells came to India in search of the "picturesque,"[43] though they expressed their visions in very different ways—Hodges as a forerunner of the Romantic movement and the Daniells grounded in Neo-classicism.[44] Where Kettle and Zoffany largely pursued portraiture in painting nabobs and nawabs, British merchant-officials and Indian princes, Hodges and the Daniells portrayed India in its natural beauty and "scenic splendors." It was for Solvyns to portray *Indians*, the people of this fabled land in their customs, manners, and dress, in their occupations and festivals. But in going to India, the young marine artist from Antwerp could never have anticipated that his life would soon be consumed in a great project to portray the Hindus.

The Voyage to Calcutta: Captain Home Popham and the *Etrusco*

The voyage to India usually took some four to eight months, depending on the time of year, prevailing trade winds, and possible mishap—with the return voyage typically taking somewhat longer.[45] Solvyns set sail from Ostend in July 1790 and arrived in Calcutta eight months later, in March 1791.[46] His ship was the *Etrusco*, owned and under the command of Captain Home Popham (1762-1820), whose later career in the Royal Navy, as he rose to the rank of rear admiral, was marked by controversy.[47]

Popham had taken leave of absence from the Royal Navy in 1787 to go to the East Indies to pursue what he termed his "private affairs." Hoping to make his fortune, he was engaged for the next six years in mercantile enterprise from Ostend, then a free port and base for British merchants and captains in trade with India, contravening the monopoly of the East India Company under the flags of the Austrian Empire, Leghorn, and Tuscany.[48] The Company then enjoyed an official monopoly of British trade with the East, and it was not until 1793 that other British merchants were allowed to trade in its preserves. By a parliamentary act of 1784, British subjects trading in India "under the authority of a foreign Prince of State" could be fined, and the Company was authorized to seize any British subject trading independently or under the auspices of foreign companies. There was, however, no want of those, like Popham, who sought to make a profit by taking services with the Company's foreign rivals or "by employing the fiction of sailing under a foreign flag."[49]

Popham's first trip to India was in 1787. Though in violation of his own country's laws (for by his own testimony, his ship had a "Foreign Flag"), Popham was received in Calcutta by Lord Cornwallis, then Governor-General of Bengal. The voyage was a financial success. Back in Ostend, in 1790, Popham acquired a ship of his own, *L'Etrusco*, and secured permission from the Austrian Emperor, who among his many titles was Grand Duke of Tuscany, to sail under the Tuscan flag. "To such labyrinthine legal dodges were merchants and shipowners driven in their determination to evade the monopoly of the East Indies Company," Popham's biographer writes.[50] Even as authorities in Bengal might wink at such activities, the trade was not without risk. "If his legal fiction were exposed and *L'Etrusco* judged to be a British ship under false colours, he would be liable to arrest and deportation."[51] Before he left Ostend, Captain Popham received a cautionary letter from his brother William[52] in India, advising him that while he—William—would "attend to the necessary ceremonies respecting the flag you sail under. . . ; orders are positively sent to India to be very strict with respect to foreign ships, and yours, I have reason to believe, will be particularly marked."[53]

Popham, nevertheless, was prepared to take the risk. He had friends in the Bengal government, and evasion of the law was widespread, with endemic corruption and an interest among Company servants in sustaining the clandestine connection, for it was by foreign ships that they could send home their "ill-gotten gains."[54]

Outfitted by the house of Robert Charnock & Co. of Ostend, Captain Popham loaded "a cargo of masts, spars, iron, lead, copper, marble and bale goods," and the *Etrusco*, nominally commanded by Francisco Coppi, an Italian, and with Balthazar Solvyns aboard, set sail for India in July 1790. The *Etrusco* followed the most common route, with its first port of call at Funchal, on the Portuguese island of Madeira, where it took on supplies of fresh meat and vegetables and a cargo of wine, for which there was a ready market in India. The ship then called at Cape Town and picked up extra hands. The usual route brought ships to the Comoro Islands, in the Mozambique Channel, to pick up supplies, and it was in the channel that the *Etrusco* struck rocks. Damaged but fit to sail, it proceeded to Bombay for repairs, then to Madras, and on to Calcutta.[55]

As the *Etrusco* made its way up the Hugli river to Calcutta, the *Calcutta Gazette*, in March 1791, carried an advertisement of the ship's impending arrival and the sale of its cargo at which "the public will have an opportunity of being supplied with a great variety of articles, all of the best kind." The ad listed fine wines, including "a small quantity of very high flavoured Chatteaux [sic] Margaux," burgundies, hoc, and Madeira; gin and beer; perfumes and powders; boots and shoes; hats and hosiery. Various staples were offered, consisting of copper for sheathing, canvas, iron bars, pig lead, nails, oil paint, gunpowder, and glasswares.[56] The auction of "Europe Goods, just landed from the ship LE ETRUSCO" was held on April 12, 1791.[57]

On Popham's arrival in Calcutta, for all his confidence in evading scrutiny, legal action was taken against him as owner and commander of the *Etrusco*, and he was fined 500 pounds for acting under a foreign flag in trade with the East Indies. The Company in Calcutta decided that it was inadvisable to pursue action against Popham for the recovery of any other penalty, as it feared the risk of "defeat in any attempt made to enforce a penal statute enacted for the protection of the Company's exclusive trade."[58]

In early biographical accounts of Solvyns, he is associated with Captain Popham in another context—in reconnoitering and mapping the coasts of the Red Sea. The obituary for Solvyns in the *Annual Register*, following Lesbroussart, relates that Solvyns "accompanied Sir Home Popham in a voyage to the East, in the course of which he made charts of the greatest exactness. This excursion served to stimulate him to engage in further and more important researches, and he resolved to visit Hindostan, and to remain there until he had become thoroughly acquainted with that interesting ancient territory, with its monuments, with its civil and religious institutions, and with the character of its inhabitants."[59] The account, repeated in subsequent biographical entries on Solvyns, is clearly misinformed, for Popham's involvement with the Red Sea came a decade later. Popham was on commission of the Admiralty for eighteen months in the Red Sea, 1801-1802, and during this period, at his own initiative, he prepared a detailed survey chart, published in 1804.[60] Popham visited Calcutta in August 1801, but in all the materials relating to the Red Sea chart, nothing suggests any connection with Solvyns.[61]

Solvyns Settles in Calcutta

Just as Popham had brought the *Etrusco* to Calcutta in 1791 in violation of the law, Solvyns arrived without having first secured permission from London, as the law required. "A feature of the East India Company's monopoly was its policy of forbidding Europeans other than Crown or Company servants to reside in India without a license from the Court of Directors. . . ."[62] The hostility of the Directors in London to the settlement of non-official Europeans in India in the 1790s was intense, and

> no subject is more frequently reiterated in the dispatches of the India House than the unalterable determination of the Directors to prevent the intrusion of interlopers, and to keep their own countrymen aloof from their dominions. Licenses were granted with great caution and reserve; the immigrant was required to state directly the occupation he intended to follow, and local authorities were instructed to send him back if he was found to have deviated to any other vocation. In 1793 the Court renewed their orders for the expulsion of all unlicensed persons. "If any person," they say in their dispatch, "presume to go to India, and they appear within your jurisdiction without a license, we require you forthwith to deal with him . . . and send him home . . . ." Still, there were hundreds of Europeans residing in the interior of the country without a license, and any attempt to send them back to England would have brought an overwhelming storm of obloquy on the India House. . . . It is due to the Company and to the government of India to state that the extraordinary powers with which they were thus armed were used with the most exemplary moderation, and that during the next ten years, only two Europeans were sent out of the Country, and they were men of the most turbulent disposition.[63]

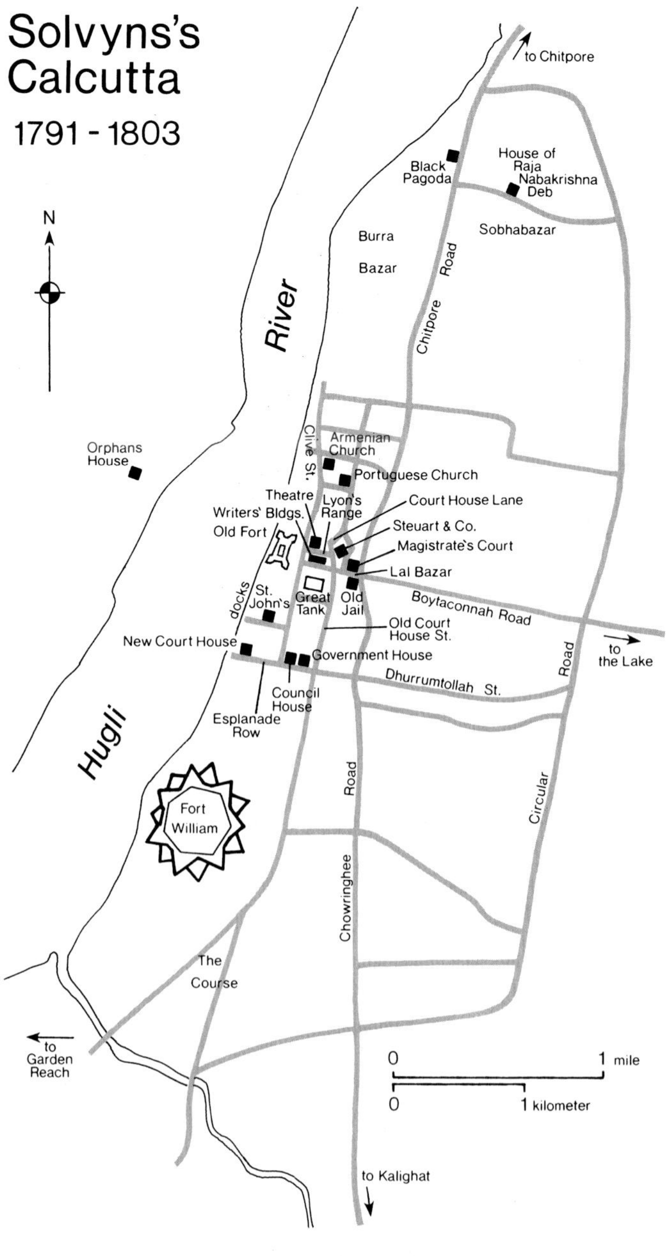

So it was that Solvyns, unlicensed interloper and a foreigner at that, established residence in Calcutta with apparently little, if any, difficulty. In the register of Europeans residing in Calcutta for the year 1794, Solvyns is listed among 585 non-officials (men only, as women were not recorded). His country of origin is given as "Antwerp" (with three others listed as "Flemish"). He is shown with two years' residence in Calcutta, living at Tank Square, and with occupation as a "Limner," that is, a painter.[64] He makes his first appearance in the published *Bengal Kalendar and Register* in 1794, listed as "Solwyns, Belthasar" [sic], "painter," and, giving the ship and date of arrival, "Le Etrusco, 1791."[65]

On his arrival in India, Solvyns, by his own account, inhabited a "country house" near the river Hugli.[66] Over the next twelve years, he moved several times, but all within the area of central Calcutta, not far from his early residence on Tank Square. By this time, the British in Calcutta were moving from this congested area of government and commercial buildings to the airy suburbs of Garden Reach and Chowringhee. Solvyns, however, remained in the center, with the Indian quarter, "Black Town," just to the North. As evidenced by advertisements he had taken in Calcutta newspapers, by February 1794, he had shifted to Old Court Lane, a narrow, short street, northwest of the Tank and behind the premises of Steuart & Co., coachmakers, where Solvyns was for a time employed as a decorator. By October 1794, he had moved to No. 27 Dhurrumtollah (Dharamtala) Street. Dhurrumtollah (renamed Lenin Sarani in 1969),[67] the eastward extension of Esplanade Row, was the site of an extensive bazaar established in 1794.[68]

In December 1795, Solvyns was in Cossitollah Street (today's Bentinck Street), which ran north from Chowringhee, leading from Dhurrumtollah to Lal Bazar, where, entering the Indian quarter, it became the Chitpore Road. Cossitollah took its name from the *kasāi*, or butchers, who once occupied the quarter. The street had developed in the 1780s with a variety of establishments, including two taverns, stables, undertakers, and a school.[69] Solvyns identified his residence on Cossitollah as "behind the Old Jail," which was located on the southwest corner of Lal Bazar at Cossitollah, and it was from this intersection that, looking westward, he set his view of "European Buildings in Calcutta" (Pl. II.1).

In 1797, Solvyns gave his address as the "Old Library, near the Bank of Hindostan."[70] The library was on Old Court House Street (now Hemanta Basu Sarani) and is the building with the apse on its side in Thomas Daniell's 1788 etching in *Views of Calcutta* (Pl. I.4). Solvyns is last recorded, in 1802,[71] as again residing in Cossistollah at "Emaumberry" (Imambarah), a Shiite building associated with the celebration of Muharram. There must have been such a building in the area, for Wood's "Plan of Calcutta," 1784-85, shows an Emambarry Lane off Cossitollah, on the east side about half way between Durrumtollah and Lal Bazar, but, used as Solvyns's address, the building, though still known as "Emaumberry," must have been converted to residential use.

Pl. I.4. "Old Court House Street Looking South."
Thomas Daniell, *Views of Calcutta*, No. 9. Etching, 1788. 40 x 51.4 cm. Oriental and India Office Collections, British Library, P284. By Permission of the British Library.

The Durrumtollah-Cossitollah area, at the edge of the native quarter, became increasingly mixed as the British began to move south. In Solvyns's time, it was probably a mix of Europeans from any number of countries, Armenians, "Portuguese" (a term loosely used to include Indian Roman Catholics as well as Indians of mixed Portuguese descent),[72] Indians of various types, and others in Calcutta's cosmopolitan mélange. Indeed, Solvyns seemed to gather them all altogether, placing himself right in the center, for his portrayal of the "Nations Most Known in Hindoostan" (Pl. II.7).

Bishop Reginald Heber would write of the area in 1823 that "the Durrumtollah and Cossitollah are pretty equally divided between the different nations, and . . . [to the north, beyond Lal Bazar,] is a vast town, composed of narrow crooked streets, brick bazaars, bamboo huts, and here and there the immense convent-like mansions of some of the more wealthy 'Babos' (the name of the native Hindoo gentleman, answering to our Esquire) or Indian merchants and bankers. . . ."[73]

Early Years in Calcutta: Solvyns's Struggle for Recognition as an Artist

The area of Calcutta in which Solvyns lived, between the European and native quarters of the city, was "marginal," and so too was Solvyns, despite his education and the respected position of his family in Antwerp. His "Belgian-French" culture, at a time of Anglo-French hostilities, may also have been a source of antipathy,[74] but most crucially, Solvyns—unlike Hodges, Zoffany, and, in all probability, the Daniells—came without letters of introduction to the Governor-General or high East India Company officials. As a "foreigner," without formal introduction and often pressed by financial need to pursue work, Solvyns was unable to secure entry into Calcutta society. And perhaps most galling was this failure to gain membership in the Asiatic Society of Bengal.

The Asiatic Society had been established in 1784, in the words of Sir William Jones (1746-1794), "for Inquiring into the History, Civil and Natural, the Antiquities, Arts, and Sciences, and Literature of Asia."[75] Jones, who had come to Calcutta in 1783 to assume the position of judge on the Supreme Court, was already a distinguished linguist and was to become the greatest of all British Orientalists.[76] With a group of East India Company officers who were keenly interested in Oriental studies, Jones was instrumental in founding the Society and its distinguished publication, *Asiatic Researches*. From its beginnings in 1784, membership—largely Company officials—increased from 30 to 110 at about the time Solvyns arrived in Calcutta.[77] The artist John Zoffany was elected to the Society in 1784, and, nominated by Jones, Thomas Daniell was elected in 1788. In 1790, Jones seconded the nomination of Arthur William Devis (1762-1822), who was to paint Jones's portrait.[78] Devis later worked with Solvyns in festivities honoring Lord Cornwallis, but there is no record of Solvyns as a member of the Asiatic Society nor of his even having attended a meeting in all his years in Calcutta.[79] Membership might have been prohibitively expensive for Solvyns, but his apparent exclusion from the Society's meetings suggests an isolation from the company of those who most closely shared his fascination with India and its peoples. Solvyns had occasional contact with Sir William Jones,[80] a man he greatly admired, but there is no basis for the notion that Solvyns's great project of portraying the Hindus "was originally undertaken at the instigation and under the patronage of the late Sir William Jones"[81]

Prospects for artists in Calcutta were not as Solvyns had hoped. In 1793, William Baillie (1753-1799),[82] an artist and publisher in Calcutta, wrote, "A little money may yet be picked up here by executing views in this Country and selling them at such easy prices as will ensure a profit to those who carry them home, but Landscape paintings will never do. Daniel [sic] found it a very discouraging pursuit with all his merit. Nothing but portrait has any chance, and even for that here is no great Rage at present." [83]

The high prices paid—or at least sought by artists—for portraits is suggested by an advertisement by a "Mr. Morris," who had set himself up in Calcutta in 1798 as a portrait painter. For ladies and gentlemen "inclined to favor him with their sittings," he was ready to paint them—15 gold mohurs (240 rupees) for the head only; 640 rupees for half length; and 1280 rupees for a "whole length" portrait.[84] But by the time Solvyns arrived in India, as Baillie notes, even portraiture was in trouble—and that was by no means Solvyns's forte. Although the general scale of remuneration for paintings might be higher in India than in England, William Foster wrote in his essay on British artists in India, expenses were also very high, and "the market, at the best of times, was a limited one. . . . In the early days, when fortunes were easily made, the East India Company's servants were munificent patrons; but, as time went on, incomes declined and an increasing disposition was shown to defer an outlay of this character until the days of retirement."[85]

In December 1792, Calcutta merchant Gavin Hamilton wrote of Solvyns to the artist Ozias Humphry (1742-1810),[86] who had lived in India from

1785 to 1787 and after his return to London maintained a correspondence with friends in Calcutta. Solvyns, Hamilton related, is "a tolerable good sea painter. . . and has some tolerable good views of Calcutta on the river side, extremely exact, but rather deficient in point of airiness and natural colouring."[87] A year later William Baillie mentions Solvyns in a letter to Humphry: "There is a Fleming a Mr. Solwyns [sic] who arrived about two years ago. He paints shipping extremely well—his skies all in an uproar however." But here and in later letters, Baillie expresses antipathy for Solvyns. "He is an able artist as a painter of seapieces: further this Desponent Saith not."[88] He did say more in 1795, when he wrote to Humphry, "I know him [Solvyns] but for these three years past have had no communications with him. I like to see liberality in Artists, but it was not be found with Mr. S. He would not tell me the least part of his *Mechanical* knowledge of painting, even the composition of a varnish he had."[89]

Solvyns's Paintings in India.

Only eleven oil paintings are known to survive from among those Solvyns did during his residence in India. These include seven marine paintings,[90] his specialty, and four landscape portrayals of the country homes of East India Company officials. Solvyns probably did some portraits as well, but none have yet surfaced. The only record of a portrait attributed to Solvyns while he was in India is in the journal *Bengal Past and Present* in 1933, and where the picture might be today, if it survives, is not known.[91] Of the Solvyns India paintings, nine are on panel, two on canvas. The titles of the India paintings are descriptive and were bestowed by their various owners.

Other paintings perhaps exist in private collections and may yet come on the market or in bequests to museums. Indeed, as late as the 1970s, only four Solvyns paintings were documented, each in a museum collection—"Ships on the Roadstead of a Dutch Harbor" (1787, before he left for India), in Antwerp's Nationaal Sheepvaartmuseum; "The Charlotte of Chittagong" (1792), in the National Maritime Museum, Greenwich; "Unidentified East Indiaman off Calcutta" (1794), in the Peabody Essex Museum, Salem; and "The Residence of Richard Goodlad at Barrypore near Calcutta" (1793), in the Victoria Memorial, Calcutta.

In painting, Solvyns's technique and style are Flemish, reflecting the tradition of seventeenth century marine painting. He worked principally on wooden panel rather than canvas, again following Flemish tradition. He chose fine mahogany, when available, and prepared his panels extremely well, as evidenced by the remarkably good condition of the painting in Calcutta's Victoria Memorial. Panels rarely fare so well under Bengal's climatic conditions. Employing impasto, Solvyns built up his paint in a highly professional manner. With imported oils or those he brought with him, he used a highly individual, broad palate, with strong primary colors.

"The *Charlotte of Chittagong*"

Pl. I.5. "The *Charlotte of Chittagong*."
Oil on panel. Signed bottom right: "B. Solvyns 1792".
53.5 x 61 cm. Courtesy National Maritime Museum, Greenwich.
Acquired 1958. © National Maritime Museum, London.

Solvyns painted "The *Charlotte of Chittagong*" in 1792, and Britain's National Maritime Museum, Greenwich, purchased the painting from a London dealer in 1958.[92] The ship is seen at anchor, lying in the Hugli river off Calcutta. The *Charlotte* is a "snow," a brig-like vessel with a main and fore mast and rigged mainly with square sails. The main mast is rigged with a large lateen sail for greater maneuverability. The figurehead at the prow is a woman. Following convention in marine painting,

Solvyns portrays the ship in another view, on the left, looking toward the ship's stern. The name *Charlotte of Chittagong* is painted above the windows. In the background to the right is another, smaller snow.[93]

The *Charlotte* flies the red ensign from the stern, the standard flag for British merchant vessels, and a commissioning pennant hangs from the main mast. It is not a Company ship, but likely one for private trade. According to the museum's descriptive note, "Vessels like the *Charlotte* were built in India and owned by Asian and European merchants. They were used in the 'country trade' to carry textiles, spices, opium and porcelains between Asian ports. The trade was more profitable than between Britain and India." Snow-rigged vessels of this type, with large passenger accommodation, were also used by the East India Company as dispatch vessels and to carry Company servants along the coasts and up the great rivers of India. Such ships were often described as Company yachts.

In the painting, native sailors or coolies on the deck of the *Charlotte* engage in various activities under the supervision of a European. Someone looks out from a cabin toward the viewer, an artistic convention. In the background, Solvyns portrays work on the docks.

"View of Calcutta, from below Fort William"

Pl. I.6. "View of Calcutta, from below Fort William, looking north with shipping."
Oil on canvas. c. 1792. 50.8 x 62.3 cm. Private Collection.[94]

In 1792, Solvyns painted a view of shipping on the Hugli river, looking north from below Fort William, with buildings of Calcutta along the shore. Spink & Son, London, offered the painting for sale in 1950, with an advertisement in *The Burlington Magazine* that illustrated the picture, 19.5 x 42 inches, signed and dated 1792, under the title "Men-o'-war and other craft off Calcutta."[95] The painting was seriously damaged in shipment to Canada for prospective sale, and, taken by the insurance company, was apparently destroyed.

In 1996, Spink included a smaller, unsigned version of the picture (Pl. I.6), apparently copied by Solvyns from the painting on board, in its sale, "A Journey Through India: Pictures by British Artists."[96] Unsold, it was placed for auction with Christie's for its annual "Visions of India" sale in 1999[97] and is now in a private collection. The view looks north to the Armenian Church on the right and the Military Orphan House, with its four towers visible, on the opposite Howrah side.

In the center is a fully-rigged ship with three masts and square sails, an East Indiaman, possibly a naval sloop or small frigate. The flag at the stern is the red ensign.

Solvyns adapted the scene for his later etching of the North-Wester (Pl. II.260).

"View of Calcutta, with Country Boats on the River Hugli"

In a painting, probably dating from 1792 or 1793, Solvyns portrayed a view of Calcutta with native boats (Pl. I.7) that he sketched for his collection of etchings. The painting, one of two known oils on canvas done by Solvyns while in India, had long been in the collection of the Hong Kong and Shanghai Bank with the title "Calcutta Harbour." The bank's curator's had attributed the picture, neither signed nor dated, to George Chinnery (1774-1852). Chinnery had lived in India before coming to China, and in his years in Bengal, 1808-1825, he often included Indian boats in his scenes of rural life. But the painting of Calcutta harbor is in no way characteristic of Chinnery's style,[98] and, in 1998, when shown a photograph of the painting by a restorer who had worked with the bank's collection, London dealer Charles Greig, a leading specialist on the paintings of British India, immediately recognized it as Solvyns and was able to negotiate its purchase for a British collector.

Pl. I.7. "View of Calcutta, with Country Boats on the River Hugli."
Oil on canvas. Unsigned, c. 1792. 45.7 x 61 cm. Private British Collection.

The painting is typical of Solvyns's work in the use of a series of horizontal planes, and its dramatic monsoon sky is a distinctive feature of most Solvyns oils, as in the strikingly similar sky of his other "View of Calcutta." Against the sky, the ship with white sails is Indian, but with unusual European rigging, characteristic of an earlier period. It is ketch-rigged with two masts, that is, the fore mast is larger than the after mast. It flies the red ensign as a merchant ship, probably with Anglo-Indian capital, an Indian crew, and likely a British officer. On the left is a ship fitted with sheer legs to hoist the mast into position. To the right, in the cloud's shadow, is an Indian country boat, possibly a paṭuā (Pl. II.234), and the small boat in the center is a ferry, or gudārā (Pl. II.259).

"The *Marquis Cornwallis*"

The *Marquis Cornwallis* was a three-masted, square-rigged ship, the standard for the vast majority of ocean-going ships of the time. With three decks and weighing 654 tons, it had a length of 104 feet and a breadth of 34 feet. On his first visit to Calcutta, Michael Hogan, an Irishman who had left the Royal Navy for private commerce, purchased the ship while it was under construction in 1791 from the firm of Gillett, Lambert & Ross. Registered initially as *Il Netunno* under the Genoese flag to avoid running afoul of the East India Company monopoly, the ship made its first voyage to Ostend.[99] Upon his return to Calcutta in 1793, Hogan commissioned Solvyns to paint the *Netunno,* and the artist did so in two versions, which today are identified by the ship's later name, the *Marquis Cornwallis*. One (Pl. I.8) portrays the ship under sail,[100] with what is possibly a small pilot cutter to the left. In the other painting (Pl. I.9), the ship is anchored, with sails furled. The Bengal country boat in the left foreground is a bhur, used for loading and unloading ships, later portrayed in an etching by Solvyns (Pl. II.256); in the background to the right is an ulāk (Pl. II.250). Curiously, both

Pl. I.8. The *Marquis Cornwallis* under sail.
Oil on panel. Signed: "B. Solvyns 1793". 39.4 x 61.6 cm. Private Collection. Courtesy of Franklin Brooke-Hitching, London.

Pl. I.9. The *Marquis Cornwallis* at anchor.
Oil on panel. Signature and date barely discernible, but clearly Solvyns and probably 1793. 43.2 x 61 cm. Private Collection.

paintings show the ship with the red ensign of a British merchant vessel, although it was not until 1794 that Hogan registered the ship under the British flag as the *Marquis Cornwallis*.[101] It may have been that Hogan chose not to have a flag of convenience, that of Genoa, portrayed, with its taint of illicit trade, but favored for the paintings the red ensign in the ship's British home port of Calcutta.

With its new name, the *Marquis Cornwallis* ended its private India trade, and in 1795, Hogan found a new client—the British government for the transport of Irish convicts to New South Wales. Captain Hogan sailed from Portsmouth to Cove, the port for Cork in Ireland, to pick up prisoners sentenced to "transportation." The *Marquis Cornwallis* was one of the first convict ships to carry political prisoners from Ireland to Australia, and on route, there was a mutiny that became a cause célèbre. As soon as the ship left Cove, the convicts (168 male and 76 female), instigated—or at least abetted—by one of the Irish soldier guards, began to plot mutiny. Informers disclosed the plan to Captain Hogan, who had forty-two men and eight women summarily flogged. Seven of the convicts died from their wounds, and their leader, the mutinous guard, died in irons. On the ship's arrival in Australia, the prisoners—many of whom were radical "Irish Defenders"—won support among the non-political Irish convicts already in New South Wales, and the ship entered Australian history.[102]

"Unidentified East Indiaman off Calcutta"

In his painting of an "Unidentified East Indiaman off Calcutta" (Pl. I.10), Solvyns portrays a small, full-rigged ship at anchor in the Hugli river. From the stern, it flies the red-and-white stripped Company ensign, with the Union flag in the corner. The figurehead on the prow is a robed figure bearing a scepter and an orb surmounted by a cross, symbols of kingly power. Like the *Charlotte*, it appears to be a passenger ship, suggested by the awnings and ports. Armed, such ships could serve as a cruiser in escorting merchant vessels against the threat of piracy.

Solvyns includes a variety of native craft in the foreground. To the left is a morpaṅkhī (Pl. II.231), a pleasure boat with a peacock prow. In the center, a European in a top hat is being transported to the ship in a dinghy (ḍiṅgi, Pls. II.236, II.237). To the right is a ḍiṅgi of another type, with a standing boatman looking toward the viewer. European buildings of Calcutta stretch along the horizon below the warm colors of the sky.

The painting is in the Peabody Essex Museum, Salem, Massachusetts.[103] Its provenance is unknown.

Pl. I.10. "Unidentified East Indiaman off Calcutta."
Oil on panel. Signed bottom right, "Solvyns Calcutta". 1794. 67.3 x 121.5 cm. Peabody Essex Museum, Inventory No. M13461. Acq., 1968, Fellows and Friends Fund. Photograph courtesy Peabody Essex Museum, Salem, Mass.

"The Launching of Gabriel Gillett's Armed Merchantman in Calcutta Harbor"

Of the paintings Solvyns did in India, the finest is "The Launching of Gabriel Gillett's Armed Merchantman in Calcutta Harbor" (Pl. I.11), done in 1798 or 1799 on commission by the ship's owner. We can only surmise the identity of the ship. Based on a note appearing in the *Calcutta Gazette*, the painting has been thought to be of the *Cuvera* (Kubera, the Indian god of wealth), launched on September 26, 1798, from the yard of Edwards, Gillett, and Hawkins, just west of St. John Church on Church Lane.[104] But the weight of the *Cuvera*, 930 tons, seems substantially greater than the ship portrayed in the painting. Alternatively, it could be the 818-ton *Bengal*, the first ship listed under Gillett's name as principal managing owner in the *Register of Ships, Employed in the Service of the East India Company*.[105] The *Bengal*, however, is described as having three decks, while the ship in the painting has two decks with a raised quarter deck. The *Cuvera*'s maiden voyage was to England; the *Bengal* was employed in coastal trade and in the Bay of Bengal.

The painting portrays the moment of launching, with the crowd cheering and waving. The wooden scaffolding and platforms show where the ship was built, and Solvyns here seeks to portray action as the ship goes down the shipway into the river—but, oddly, without a launching cradle. That the cradle is not portrayed suggests that Solvyns had sketched the ship before the actual launching and then returned to capture the excitement of the crowd at the launching itself. In the foreground, Solvyns depicts himself, sketchbook in hand, standing on a cradle in the yard, drawn presumably before (or after) the launching.

The ship appears to be modeled on a naval frigate, probably with 32 guns. It flies a red ensign from the stern and a Union Jack from the bowsprit. A pennant flies from a pole on the ship. It is likely emblazoned with Gillett's emblem or possibly a celebratory message for the launching. Its three masts will be raised only after launching, the last stage after getting the ship into the water.

In a rich portrayal of the docks, Solvyns fills the crowd assembled for the launching with many of the figures he had drawn for his etchings published two years before in 1796. The varieties of people—Hindu, Muslim, Chinese, Armenian, European—reflect Calcutta's cosmopolitan character, portrayed in Solvyns's later etching, "Of the Nations Most Known in Hindoostan" (Pl. II.7), for the Paris edition, *Les Hindoûs*.

The ship's owner, Gabriel Gillett (1760-1848), in the center, stands under a parasol held by his

Pl. I.11. "The Launching of Gabriel Gillett's Armed Merchantman in Calcutta Harbor." Oil on panel. c. 1798/1799. 67 x 120.5 cm. Peabody Essex Museum, Salem, Mass. Inventory No. M-26444.

servant. Gillett, of a merchant family engaged in non-official "country trade," headed one of Calcutta's largest and most successful shipbuilding firms.[106] The painting remained within the Gillett family until 1980,[107] when it came on the market. The painting, unsigned, was wrongly attributed by Sotheby's to Robert Home (1752-1834) at the time of the sale.[108] Home, who arrived in India in 1791, was Calcutta's most prominent painter in the years from 1794 until his departure in 1814. He painted portraits of leading merchants and officials, with several paintings of the Governor-General, the Marquis Wellesley.[109] Home's Sitters Book records that he painted a portrait of Gabriel Gillett in 1795, thus providing the tie for attributing "The Launching" to Home. London dealers Giles Eyre and Niall Hobhouse, who purchased the painting, were convinced it was by Solvyns. Eyre had long been interested in Solvyns and, with an exhibition and sale of selected etchings in 1978, was the first to show Solvyns's work in London.[110] In looking at the painting, he recognized both the style and figures portrayed as distinctively Solvyns. Eyre & Hobhouse sold the painting to a private collector, and the Peabody Essex Museum acquired the painting in 1994.[111]

The Gillett family, aside from commissioning the painting, subscribed to Solvyns's collection of etchings portraying the Hindus, and the copy of the 1799 edition now in London's Wellcome Institute collection bears the signature of its first owner, J. Gillett, presumably Jonathan, Gabriel's partner in shipbuilding.[112]

Unidentified Landscape

In addition to marine subjects, Solvyns also accepted commissions for landscape portrayals of country houses belonging to British East India Company officials and to senior merchants. The earliest (Pl. I.12), dated 1792, portrays a now unidentified house in the distance, with two European gentlemen in the foreground, attended by Indian servants who trail behind. Solvyns elongates the figures in the mannerist style characteristic of his etchings. In the background and to the left is a bullock and, beyond, cattle graze. To the right, in the distance, a European rides from the house in a cart, with four Indian servants running alongside.

The painting had long been in a private collection in Belgium and may have been brought back from India by Solvyns when he returned to Europe in 1804.

Pl. I.12. Unidentified Landscape near Calcutta.
Oil on panel. Signed, "B. Solvyns 1792". 43.2 x 61 cm. Private Collection, Belgium.

"The Residence of Richard Goodlad"

Solvyns's "The Residence of Richard Goodlad at Baruipur, Bengal" (Pl. I.13), in the collection of the Victoria Memorial in Calcutta, is the only known Solvyns painting in India. Goodlad is listed under "senior merchants" in the *Bengal Almanack* for 1796 as salt agent[113] for the districts of 24 Purganas and Roymungal. He was a member of the Asiatic Society. His fine Palladian house was at Baruipur, some 15 miles southeast of Calcutta, in 24 Purganas.

Over the years, the painting survived Calcutta's climate remarkably well. It is the only oil painting in the Victoria Memorial collection that is on a wooden panel. Rupert Featherstone, who directed the restoration of the picture in the mid-1990s, writes that "Solvyns was from Antwerp where the long-established tradition of painting on wood may explain his selection of this support" for this and other paintings he did in India. Although Solvyns was not alone among artists in India in using panel, Featherstone notes that it was an unusual choice for the end of the eighteenth century. "Wood panels are notoriously responsive to changes in relative humidity, and will flex and curve as moisture is absorbed or desorbed by the panel. Such dimensional changes often lead to flaking of the paint, and although this

Pl. I.13. "The Residence of Richard Goodlad at Baruipur, Bengal." Signed and dated "Balthazar Solvyns 1793". Oil on Panel. 70 x 95 cm. Victoria Memorial Hall. R 2185.

painting is generally in a fine state of preservation, it showed evidence of minute paint losses in the past."[114]

The Solvyns's painting of the Goodlad house, along with nine oils by the Daniells among other works, came to the Victoria Memorial in 1932 as part of the important collection of George Lyell, a British businessman who headed the Calcutta firm of Macneill & Co.[115] On Solvyns's typical horizontal and with his dramatic skies, the picture portrays the Goodlad house in the distance, with a boy, shaded by an umbrella (*chātā*), tending cattle in the foreground and an Indian figure, attended by an umbrella bearer, looking toward the house.

"Views of the Country Residence of William Farquharson"

In 1979, two unsigned paintings came to auction at Christie's in London. Identified only as English School, circa 1790, they were described as "A View on the Hooghley River at Garden Reach with sailing vessels in the foreground" and "A View of a House at Garden Reach with elegant figures in a formal garden."[116] The paintings, which were with the Farquharson family in England, did not sell, and in 1997, they were again on the block at Christie's in the annual "Visions of India" sale.[117] In the meantime, Charles Greig had established Solvyns as the artist. Greig was also able to identify the subject, for James Moffat, Solvyns's contemporary in Calcutta, had copied one of the paintings (without acknowledging Solvyns) for his 1800 aquatint, "View on the Banks of the Houghly near Calcutta, the Country Residence of William Farquharson, Esqr."[118]

William Farquharson (1758-1830) arrived in India in 1776 to join the service of the East India Company and became, in his later life, one of Calcutta's leading merchants. In about 1789, when Farquharson was Military Paymaster General, Arthur Devis painted his portrait, with the house in the background.[119]

Pl. I.14 (above) and I.15.
"Views of the Country Residence of William Farquharson Esq., at Garden Reach on the Banks of the Hooghly River, near Calcutta." Oil on panel. Balthazar Solvyns, unsigned, c. 1793. Each 48 x 77 cm. Private British Collection.

The Farquharson house was some five miles down river from Calcutta at Garden Reach. The Solvyns paintings, probably done about the same time as the Goodlad house painting, 1793, depict the house from two sides. One (Pl. I.14) portrays the house in a view from the river (the painting copied by Moffat). In the river, immediately in front of the house is a morpaṅkī, a long pleasure boat with a peacock's bow that Solvyns portrayed in his collection of etchings (Pl. II.231). Solvyns depicts a paṭuā (Pl. II.234) on the left; to the right a brig (Pl. II.249), flying the red ensign, is at sail and beyond is a full-rigged ship.

In the second view (Pl. I.15), with the house in the distance, Farquharson and his wife are seen riding. Mrs. Farquharson is accompanied by an umbrella-bearer and Mr. Farquharson is followed by his syce (depicted in the series of Solvyns's etchings of domestic servants, Pl. II.118). To the right is the ḍoriyā (Pl. II.121), the dog-keeper with the dogs, and beyond a bhīstī, or water-carrier (Pl. II.111).

Garden Reach, on the east bank of the Hugli below Calcutta, was favored for its cool breezes by high East India Company officials, and here they built stately country residences. Mrs. Eliza Fay, in a letter soon after arriving with her husband in Calcutta in May 1780, described seeing Garden Reach as their boat approached Calcutta. "The banks of the river are . . . absolutely studded with elegant mansions, called here as at Madras, garden-houses. These houses are surrounded by groves and lawns, which descend to the waters-edge, and present a constant succession of what can delight the eye, or bespeak wealth and elegance in the owners."[120]

The Andaman Drawings

Sometime in 1792, Solvyns prepared a watercolor drawing of two Andaman Islanders (Pl. I.16), along with copies of several watercolors by other artists, for the East India Company. In the British search for suitable new naval harbors in the Bay of Bengal, Lieutenant Archibald Blair was commissioned in 1788 to survey the Andaman and Nicobar Islands, where he was joined in 1789-1790 by Captain Alexander Kyd,[121] Surveyor-General, with his assistants, Lieutenants Robert H. Colebrooke[122] and J. Wales. In preparing the report for London, Kyd collected various accounts of the Andamans, illustrating them with copies of watercolors by Colebrooke, Wales, and Blair. In a letter to Earl Cornwallis, Kyd wrote that "To the very imperfect sketch [of the islands] I have annexed a drawing of the two natives brought here by Lieut. Blair."[123] The drawing and at least some of the copies of the watercolors were made by Solvyns. Mildred Archer, long the curator of Prints and Drawings at the India Office Library, writes that Solvyns, like Arthur Devis, "was finding it difficult to earn a living in India, and it seems probable that Colebrooke, whom he knew, obtained for him this small commission to make drawings illustrating Kyd's account of the Andaman and Nicobar Islands."[124] They had probably met soon after Colebrooke's return to Calcutta from the war against Tipu Sultan in Mysore. A few months later, in February 1793, Solvyns painted several large

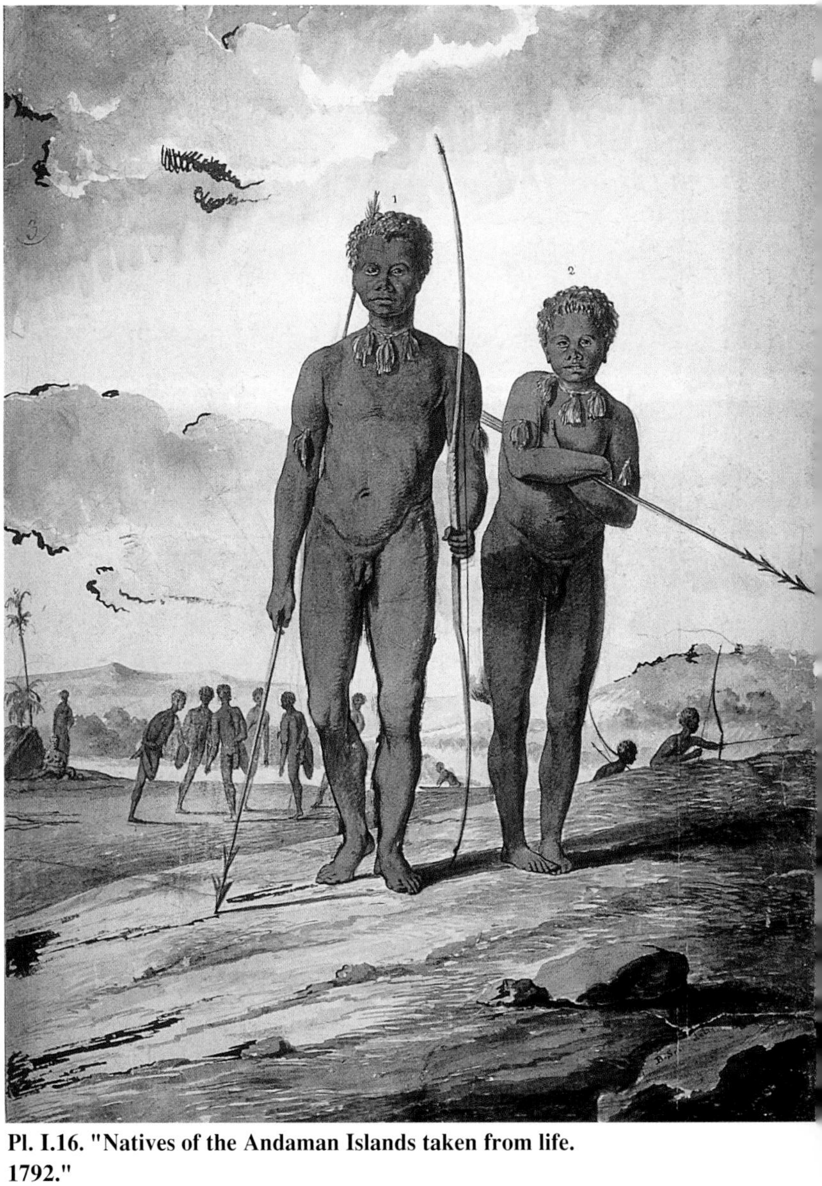

Pl. I.16. "Natives of the Andaman Islands taken from life. 1792."
1. Otta Caggy Yuka. 2. Tytahee. B. Sol. del. Watercolor, 42 x 28 cm. Oriental and India Office Collections, MSS.Eur. F. 21/2. By Permission of the British Library.

transparencies from drawings by Colebrooke for a celebration of the Cornwallis victory in Mysore.

Solvyns's drawing of the Andaman Islanders is perhaps the earliest portrayal of these people. A preliminary sketch was among the drawings included in an album assembled by Solvyns widow.[125] In the finished watercolor, the title is inscribed in ink below the drawing, and the names of the two islanders appear at the top. The Kyd report described the two islanders as adult males, 4 ft. 7 in. and 4 ft. 2 in. in height, making them "among the lowest in stature of the human race." [126] In the drawing, they each hold a spear, and the taller figure holds a bow. In the background, Solvyns portrays other islanders, as he imagined them, in what appears to be some sort of game or dance as they run, each with one leg in the air, in a circle.

Solvyns's portrayal of the islanders probably drew on Colebrooke's notes or on conversations with him. Colebrooke, in his later published account, "On the Andaman Islands" (1795), wrote, "The *Andaman Islands* are inhabited by a race of men the least civilized, perhaps, in the world; being nearer to a state of nature than any people we read of. Their colour is of the darkest hue, their stature in general small, and their aspect uncouth. Their limbs are ill formed and slender, their bellies prominent, and, like the *Africans*, they have wooly heads, thick lips, and flat noses. They go about quite naked. . . . [They are hunters and gatherers], and their bows are remarkably long, and of an uncommon form; their arrows are headed with fish-bones, or the tusks of wild hogs; sometimes merely with a sharp bit of wood, hardened in the fire. . . ."[127]

The materials collected by Kyd for dispatch to London—now in the India Office Library[128]—include a map by Blair and fourteen drawings and watercolors. Two are by Solvyns—the portrait of the two Andaman Islanders and a rather muddy and uninteresting watercolor of a waterfall on Penang from a sketch by James MacDonald done in 1792. The others are copies, perhaps by Solvyns, of watercolor views of the Andaman and Nicobar Islands by Colebrooke, Wales, and perhaps Blair.[129]

Steuart & Co.

With insecure prospects for painting commissions, Solvyns, soon after his arrival in Calcutta in 1791, took employment with Steuart & Co., Coachmakers. Established in 1775 under another name, the firm took the Steuart name in 1783, when purchased by James Steuart, who was soon joined in Calcutta by his brother Robert and other members of the family. Located at No. 8 Old Court House Corner, it was Calcutta's leading builder of palanquins and carriages.[130] In Solvyns's time, "J. & R. Steuart" advertised in the *Calcutta Gazette* offering "Chariots, Phaetons, Buggies, and Palanquins."[131]

From 1783, Steuart & Co. employed Indian artists "to assist British craftsmen in painting and decorating not only carriages, palanquins and sedan chairs but ceremonial elephant housings."[132] Solvyns may have been the first European artist, as such, employed by the firm. (Coincidentally, Thomas Daniell as a young artist had similarly worked as a coach painter in England.[133]) There is no record of the dates of Solvyns's employment by Steuart & Co., but Solvyns in 1792 or 1793, Solvyns decorated two magnificent palanquins commissioned by Lord Cornwallis for the hostage sons of Tipu Sultan (1750-1794), ruler of Mysore. William Baillie, in a letter of October 4, 1795, to fellow artist Ozias Humphry, writes that Solvyns had "picked up a good deal of money I believe from Stewart [sic] the coachmakers for embellishing palankeens, &c. I do not mean common ones, but some that he has made for the country princes. The two first were ordered by Lord Cornwallis for the Mysore Princes, and were valued each at about 6 or 7,000 Rs. The ornamental painting did Solvyns much credit, in one colour only on a gold ground. You can conceive nothing superior to the workmanship of these Palankeens—all the metal with feet &c. overlaid with silver and in some parts solid silver, the lining velvet with rich silver or gold Embroidery and fringe. Stewart has lately made two for the King of Tanjore's sons, which, it is said, will cost near 10,000 Rs. each."[134]

Whether Solvyns was involved in decorating the Tanjore palanquins in 1795 is not known, but he did decorate the palanquins for the Mysore hostage princes (Pl. I.17), and the money he earned may well have been initial capital that enabled him to undertake his great project in portraying the Hindus in 250 etchings. There is no record as to the date when Cornwallis commissioned the palanquins from Steuart & Co. or of their delivery to Madras, where the princes were held, but the first published reference to the palanquins is made in an account of the return of the princes to their father in March 1794. At the ceremony, Captain Doveton, who escorted the boys, presented gifts for Tipu, "and the palanquins that the Marquis Cornwallis had given to the Princes [were] exposed to view; on seeing them, the Sultan was pleased to say 'that, where friendship subsisted, there was no need of presents.'"[135] At the time of Tipu's death in 1799, the two presentation palanquins were found at Seringapatam, but "they appeared never to have been unpacked."[136]

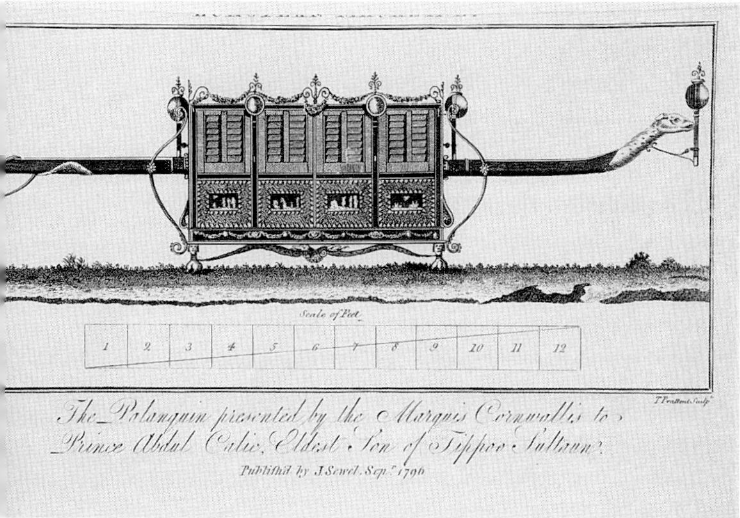

Pl. I.17. "The Palanquin presented by the Marquis Cornwallis to Prince Abdul Carlic, Eldest Son of Tippoo Sultaun." Engraving by T. Prattent, published by J. Sewell, London, 1796. 11.7 x 19.2 cm. Yale Center for British Art, Paul Mellon Collection.[137]

Facing defeat by British forces in the Third Anglo-Mysore War, Tipu Sultan secured peace on February 6, 1792, by submitting to the terms of the Treaty of Seringapatam by which he was compelled to surrender half his dominions, pay substantial indemnity, and deliver his two sons, aged 8 and 10, to the British as hostages pending fulfillment of treaty obligations. The princes, bejeweled and mounted with dignity on richly caparisoned elephants, left their father and, accompanied by a trusted *vakīl*, were received by Lord Cornwallis, assured of his "paternal protection," on February 26, 1792.[138] They were returned to their father in March 1794, only to again be taken prisoner after Tipu's defeat and death in the Fourth Mysore War in 1799. The princes lived out their last days as celebrated residents of Calcutta.

Lesbroussart[139] (and subsequent biographical entries relying on his account) mistakenly places Solvyns at Seringapatam, Tipu's capital, in 1792. Robert Home, official artist of the Third Mysore War, was the only artist with Cornwallis when he received the hostage princes.[140] In the summer of 1793, Arthur William Devis went from Calcutta to Madras to make sketches for a large painting of the surrender of the princes,[141] prompting Home to portray the event he had witnessed in "The Reception of the Mysorean Hostage Princes by Marquis Cornwallis"[142] The subject —indeed, everything associated with the defeat of Tipu—became enormously popular among European artists.[143] George Carter, who had earlier worked in India, in 1792 painted a portrait of the transfer of the young princes as he envisioned it from hearsay,[144] and artists such as Mather Brown, Henry Singleton, and Thomas Stothard, who had never been to India, drew upon their imaginations to portray the scene.[145]

The Cornwallis Illuminations

In April 1792, soon after British forces in Mysore secured the submission of Tipu Sultan, Calcutta celebrated Cornwallis's victories, and the festivities brought Solvyns his first public recognition in Calcutta as a newly established artist. Under the headline "Grand Gala," the *Calcutta Gazette* reported that throughout the city, everyone was "vying with each other for the beauty and elegance of their illuminations," painted transparencies, done on sheer cloth, stretched within a frame and illuminated from behind. Often used in stage design, illuminations were a popular eighteenth century decor for balls and celebrations.[146] The newspaper described the decorations for the Cornwallis gala as impressive for their "splendor and magnificence" and noted that "The illuminations of the houses of the Armenians and the Natives were almost equal to our own."

> The Government house was on the whole the most splendid—The lights were disposed with infinite taste, and being of different colours, the effect was extremely beautiful—a very large transparent painting was placed in the center of the house, 32 by 27—On the top Fame with her Trumpet covering the Bust of Lord Cornwallis—underneath the Figure of Britannia, receiving the Treaty from Tippoo's sons attended by a Vakeel—a Hercules was placed behind Britannia, and in the background a View of

Seringapatam—Great pains had evidently been taken with this piece, displayed great skill and was executed in a masterly manner, by Mr. Salvyns [*sic*], an eminent Artist lately arrived, who had only six days to complete this capital Painting. The Centinels at the Gateways were a most excellent addition.[147]

The World, a Calcutta weekly, in its brief description of the celebration, identified Arthur Devis as executing a "fine representation of the memorable action of the 6th of February 1792," but made no reference to Solvyns.[148]

In February of the following year, Calcutta celebrated the first anniversary of the British triumph in Mysore with a grand ball attended by Lord Cornwallis himself. The Theatre,[149] where the fete was held, was illuminated outside with a profusion of lights and was decorated inside with banners, helmets, and military trophies. Facing the front was a large illuminated transparent painting by Devis that portrayed the storming of Bangalore by British troops on the night of March 21, 1791. In front of the eastern door was a "grand transparent view of Seringapatam, by Messrs. Devis and Solwyns [sic], from a Drawing of Lieutenant Colebrooke. Over the Windows were light transparent Views of the principal Forts taken from the enemy . . . , painted by Mr. Solwyns, from Drawings of Lieutenant Colebrooke."[150] Colebrooke, who had probably helped Solvyns a few months earlier in securing the commission for the Andaman Island pictures (discussed above), published his *Twelve Views of Places in the Kingdom of Mysore* in 1794.

In October 1794, Solvyns advertised "*Just Published*, A Portrait of Marquis Cornwallis, etched from a pencil sketch taken from life, to be had on application to Mr. Solvyns, Dhurrumtollah, No. 27; price six Sicca Rupees. Calcutta."[151] If it was published, no copies of the print are known to survive, but Solvyns may have decided to abandon the project with the publication in Calcutta that year of a mezzotint engraving of Cornwallis after an oil painting by Devis.[152]

Solvyns may have again been involved in 1803, his last year in Calcutta, in painting transparencies for "a most splendid entertainment" celebrating Tipu's defeat and the conclusion of peace. The ball, attended by some eight hundred ladies and gentlemen, including distinguished natives and foreign dignitaries, was held in Lord Wellesley's imposing new Government House, and a variety of illuminated transparencies were exhibited, but accounts mention no artist by name.[153]

John Alefounder and the Steuart & Co. Painting

Solvyns's association with Steuart & Co. may have secured the commission for a portrait of a young man, thought to be William Steuart. Attributed to Solvyns, the apparently unsigned painting, on mahogany panel, hung in the office of the firm as late as 1933, when it was dimly reproduced in *Bengal Past and Present* in an article on the history of the firm.[154] Its whereabouts today is unknown.

Another unsigned painting (Pl. I.18), portraying the premises of Steuart & Co., was once presumed to be by Solvyns, but Giles Eyre and Charles Greig, London dealers specializing in European paintings of India, believe it to be by John Alefounder (1758-1794). The painting, done between 1792 and 1794, was engraved in a colored aquatint version and published in London in 1795 by Francis Jukes.[155] The print carries an inscription dedicating "this view of a House, Manufactory, and Bazar, in Calcutta" to the chairman and directors of the East India Company," with a note that the original picture was in the possession of James Steuart. The engraving would have been based on a drawing (now lost), after the painting, sent from Calcutta to London. The painting likely remained in Calcutta in the offices of Steuart & Co., perhaps as late as 1907, when the building was torn down, but in his history of the firm, Sir Evan Cotton, in 1933, refers to having seen only the engraving and writes that "the picture [which he thought to be by Solvyns] cannot be traced."[156] The painting was acquired by Eyre & Greig in 1991 when it appeared—without attribution—on sale in Denmark. Its provenance is unknown, and it is now in an important British private collection.

Steuart & Co. was located on Old Court House Street, just to the northeast of Tank Square. (See map, p. 18.) It stood behind the Old Court House until the decaying building—serving in its last years as a place of public entertainments—was torn down in 1792.[157] Its demolition opened the view of the coachmaker's firm presented in the painting.

Pl. I.18. "View of a House, Manufactory, and Bazar, in Calcutta" (Steuart & Co., Coachmakers).
Unsigned, attributed to John Alefounder, c. 1792-94. Oil on canvas, 40.6 x 82.6 cm. Private British Collection.

The painting and the print portray the building's curved facade in the same perspective, but there are differences between the two. To the far left, there is a view down Lyon's Range, the street behind the Writers' Buildings, that leads west to the walls of the Old Fort and the Customs Master's House within. In the Jukes print, the masts of ships rise above the far wall, where they are not to be seen in the painting—and, indeed, could not have been seen from Steuart & Co. Various other changes are also evident as well in the print, most notably the more dramatic sky and the adjutant stork (Pl. II.289) in flight and another perched atop the building behind Steuart & Co. These were likely added by the artist—presumably Alefounder—to the drawing sent to Jukes for engraving, but could have been embellishments by Jukes himself.

The gated entrance to the courtyard, to the right, provides a background for Solvyns's portrayal of the long palanquin (Pl. II.226) in his series of etchings.

The foreground of the Steuart & Co. picture includes the passage of a long palanquin and a waiting carriage by the gate, with people representing various caste occupations and trades. "A Key to a View in Calcutta," published with Jukes's engraving, provides a guide to the subjects portrayed.[158] The spellings are notably different from those used by Solvyns for his etchings.

The portrayal of the firm (Solvyns's employer), the inclusion of people in their caste occupations (the principal subject of Solvyns's etchings), and the elongated form of the figures surely suggest Solvyns as the artist. And the figure of the watercarrier (bhīstī) in the center foreground is very similar to Solvyns's later etching (Pl. II.111) When Eyre & Greig acquired the Steuart & Co. painting in 1991, Greig was confident that it was by Solvyns, but on close examination after the picture was cleaned, he had serious doubts. Then in placing it next to Solvyns's "The Launching of Gabriel Gillett's Armed Merchantman in Calcutta Harbor" (Pl. I.11) and later beside Solvyns's two paintings of the Farquharson house (Pls. I.14 and I.15), it was, Greig relates, "immediately apparent that they could not possibly be by the same hand." On the basis of his very limited surviving work, John Alefounder seemed to Greig the most likely painter of the Steuart & Co. picture.[159]

A number of factors led Greig to this judgment, but the technique and style of the painting also aroused his suspicions. The painting is composed on a diagonal, reflecting the training that Alefounder had in England, while Solvyns would likely have approached it with the use of horizontal planes that characterize his style. The sky is weak in comparison with Solvyns's known work. The perspective of the building is peculiar, as the artist had difficulty in portraying its curved facade, and from the one surviving painting by Alefounder (a portrait of Mrs. Graham of Kinross, 1786),[160] Greig contends, we know he had considerable difficulty with perspective. The palette in the Steuart & Co. picture, though similar to that of Solvyns, is much closer to the Alefounder picture; indeed, with the two pictures compared side-by-side, Greig was convinced that they were by the same hand. And though the elongated figures are again similar to Solvyns's style, the outline of the figures is much harder than in Solvyns's paintings.

Another factor in the attribution of the painting relates to the print. Even if Solvyns had not signed the painting, he would surely have included his name as the artist on the Frances Jukes aquatint, as he did on the 1784 engraving of the port of Ostend (Pl. I.2). And had Jukes appropriated the painting for the engraving without Solvyns's permission, Solvyns would not have let it go without comment—as we know by his later attacks on the pirated edition of his work brought out in London by Edward Orme. By the time Jukes published the engraving, Alefounder was dead.

Solvyns and Alefounder knew each other and, at least in 1794, they shared rooms in a building close to Steuart & Co. They also shared an interest in portraying Indian life around them. Indeed, as Mildred Archer writes, Alefounder was the first European artist in India to "actually publish a scheme of pictures dealing with the social scene."[161] Encouraged by a civil servant of the East India Company to give up his unsuccessful pursuit of portrait commissions and to paint the manners and customs of the natives, Alefounder, after initially rejecting the idea, announced in July 1788 a plan for 28 pictures that included the hook-swinging festival (Caṛak Pūjā), a fakir, a bearer, "A Native Girl," and "A Hindoostanee Lady." Three months later, he advertised another plan for 36 paintings—12 of nawabs and men of importance ("remarkable characters"), 12 of Indian figures, presumably to illustrate different costumes, and 12 of customs and ceremonies. Drawings of the paintings were to be sent to England for engravings, but nothing more was heard of the project, and it is assumed that "the scheme failed for want of support." Whether the few pictures Alefounder managed to send back for exhibition at the Royal Academy were from these proposed series is not known.[162]

In the early 1790s, Alefounder etched frontispieces for several issues of the *Calcutta Monthly Register*. Among these is a portrayal of a "A Balasore Bearer" (Pl. I.19), the most prominent of the palanquin carriers in Calcutta. These bearers, from Orissa, were also portrayed by Solvyns (Pl. II.43).

Alefounder had arrived in Calcutta in October 1785 "with no securities, no introductions, no friends

Pl. I.19. "A Balasore Bearer."
Etching by John Alefounder. Frontispiece, *Calcutta Monthly Register,* Vol. II, No. 8 (June 1791). Private Indian Collection.

and little charm,"[163] and, with no prospects, he had, in Ozias Humphry's words, "gone melancholy mad and neither knows any person nor can do in his profession the smallest thing."[164] In January 1786, Alefounder tried to hang himself—an apparently frequent response among Europeans in Calcutta to loneliness and depression.[165] Arthur Devis tried to help him, but to no avail, and Alefounder publicly accused Devis of selling his pictures and materials without his knowledge.[166] Alefounder recovered his spirits sufficiently to propose his plans for the series of paintings, but, as Archer writes, "as with so many of his schemes it came to nothing."[167] In 1793, Alefounder announced his intention to return to England, but, delaying his departure, in February 1794, he advertised a sale of paintings that could be viewed at Solvyns's house on Old Court Lane, behind Steuart & Co.[168] Alefounder was then living with Solvyns, who had befriended him, but with growing desperation and increasingly despondent, Alefounder, with a penknife to his neck, committed suicide December 20, 1794.[169]

Solvyns shared much with Alefounder, including the difficult prospects for an artist in Calcutta at a time when the market had been largely sated. But Solvyns, for all his difficulties, persevered with obsessive determination.

Arthur William Devis, the Daniells, and Other Artists

Arthur Devis came to India more by accident than intent, the result of mishap and opportunity on a circuitous journey to China. Rather than return to England, he chose to go to India, arriving in Calcutta in 1784. He remained in India for a little more than ten years. Solvyns worked with him on the Cornwallis illuminations in 1792 and 1793, and the two had sought to help Alefounder. There is no reference to Solvyns in accounts of Devis in India,[170] but Devis, with Alefounder, may well have been instrumental in drawing Solvyns's interest to the portrayal of the Hindus, the project that was to distinguish his life and work.

By 1792, Devis had already begun work on a series of paintings depicting native occupations. On October 18, 1792, the *Calcutta Gazette* announced that "Mr. Devis is at present at Santipore [about 60 miles north of Calcutta] busily employed in the execution of his paintings from which the engravings of the arts and manufactures of Bengal will be taken . . . ." In a letter in October 1795 to Ozias Humphry, who had once hoped to pursue such a project himself,[171] Baillie mentions a series of thirty paintings by Devis representing the manufactures of the country, which upon his return to England, Devis intended to have "engraved and painted in colours under his own inspection. . . ." Baillie singles out "the Pottery" (Pl. I.20) for praise as "a charming little picture," but writes that he saw only four or five of the pictures and that as far as he could learn, only a few pictures of the series had been finished before Devis left India in January 1795.[172]

The series, which Devis proposed to call "The Economy of Human Life," was never completed. After his return to England, Devis exhibited five paintings from the "occupations" project at the Royal Academy, London, including his portrait of the potter, but Devis's financial problems and mounting debt undermined his efforts to bring it all to fruition.[173] He did, however, complete at least nineteen paintings in the series.[174] Of these, apparently only two, the pottery and the loom, were engraved and published.[175]

Devis's project, as Alefounder's proposals to depict the manners and customs of the Indians and later Solvyns's portrayal of the Hindus, drew little interest and failed financially. Thomas Hickey (1741-1824) fared no better. In 1804, he petitioned the East India Company to appoint him as its "historical and portrait painter," and, perhaps inspired by Solvyns's etchings, he proposed to visit the regions under Company rule to make "pictures of the inhabitants, their characteristics, castes and costumes." The Company declined, and he was informed that this "must be left to the exertions of voluntary enterprise and encouragement of private patronage."[176] He received no encouragement.

Most Europeans preferred a romanticized India to the one they observed in everyday life. The Daniells were more to their liking. Thomas Daniell and his nephew William, who traveled in India from 1786 to 1794, surely wanted to portray the "real" India, but they saw it through the lens (or, perhaps more accurately, the camera obscura) of the picturesque, and the essentially classical compositions of their *Oriental Scenery* were enormously successful.[177]

Solvyns makes no mention of the Daniells, and in their various journals and letters, they say

Pl. I.20. "The Pottery." Arthur William Devis.
Oil on canvas laid on board. c. 1792. 43.5 x 59 cm. Oriental and India Office Collections, British Library. F980.

nothing of Solvyns. They likely had some contact with each other in Calcutta, but there is no evidence to support the assertion by German art historian Fiorillo, in 1808, that Solvyns had assisted the Daniells in preparation of drawings for their *Oriental Scenery*.[178] Nagler, in the *Neues allgemeines künstler-lexikon*, repeats the Fiorillo account and adds that the Daniell prints gave Solvyns the impetus to produce his work on India, with the notable difference that Solvyns paid great attention to the mores and costumes of the people.[179]

Soon after his arrival in India in 1786, Thomas Daniell began work on his *Views of Calcutta* (1786-88). The series of twelve aquatints, the first set of prints protraying the city, took sixteen months to complete.[180] (See Pl. I.4). The buildings depicted are principally those of European Calcutta, although one etching is of a "Gentoo Pagoda and House" along Chitpore Road. The streets bustle with life, with carriages, palanquins, carts, camels and elephants, and Europeans and Indians alike are seen in various activities—at work and leisure and, for the Indians, in religious procession and at the bathing ghāts along the river. In Thomas and William Daniells' later *Oriental Scenery* (1795-1808), people provide little more than scale for great buildings, romantic ruins, and panoramic scenery. In the *Views of Calcutta*, the human context is more important, providing an essential vitality, but the dominant impression is one of bricks-and-mortar. Daniell's interest was not fundamentally in the *people* of India, and here Solvyns stands in stark contrast.

In 1794, William Baillie, who had known the Daniells, brought out his own *Twelve Views of*

Calcutta. Like his earlier etching of Fort William (1791), Baillie's *Views* portray a Calcutta with virtually no people or activity of any kind. Their sterility could hardly have been in sharper contrast to the vibrant reality of Calcutta's life or to the subjects Solvyns's engaged in his portrayal of the Hindus.[181]

We know little of Solvyns's association with other artists in Bengal. He had worked with Devis in the illuminations and had shared rooms with John Alefounder. He had encountered William Baillie, though apparently in mutual antipathy, and amateur artist Lt. Robert H. Colebrooke helped Solvyns secure the commission to draw the Andaman Islanders. There is reference to Francesco Renaldi (1755-c.1799) visiting Solvyns's house in 1796,[182] and Solvyns's name appears on the subscription list for a collection of etchings by Robert Mabon (d. 1798),[183] but beyond these few recorded contacts, there is nothing to give us a sense of Solvyns's ties to artists, professional and amateur, living in Calcutta or to those passing through the city.

A Collection of 250 Etchings Descriptive of the Hindus

Sometime in 1793, though possibly earlier, Solvyns began work on what was to become his life consuming project, a collection of etchings portraying the Hindus in their costumes, occupations, and cultural life. In November 1793, William Baillie wrote to his friend Ozias Humphry in London, mentioning that Solvyns "is now engaged in executing a sett [sic] of 250 prints, etchings, of the natives in their various dresses & employments."[184]

In February 1794, Solvyns announced the project in an advertisement in the *Calcutta Gazette*.[185] It was the most ambitious publishing venture yet undertaken in India. In advertising the *Collection*, Solvyns refers to the prints as "engravings," a term that was then used inclusively.[186] The studies of costume so popular in the eighteenth century were almost invariably etched, though typically described as "engravings." In specifying that the prints would be "engraved in *Aqua Fortis*," however, Solvyns conveys that they are to be etchings, and when finally published, the title page so described them: *A Collection of Two Hundred and Fifty Coloured Etchings: Descriptive of the Manners, Customs, and Dresses of the Hindoos*.

The etchings were organized in twelve sections, with all but one preceded by a large double-plate. In preparing the etchings for publication, Solvyns stayed largely with the advertised plan, varying only in the placement of double-plates and in the substitution, for the large etching preceding Section X, of a view of Calcutta's Black Town for the originally intended Hindu mode of playing games.[187]

PROPOSALS for Publishing, By Subscription,
An interesting and valuable collection of
TWO HUNDRED AND FIFTY ENGRAVINGS,
eleven of which will be executed on a larger scale
than the others;
one large engraving to be affixed to each section,
except the last.
DESCRIPTIVE OF THE MANNERS, CUSTOMS, & DRESSES,
OF THE NATIVES OF BENGAL:
particularizing every character in the different casts,
with the peculiar attribute of each.
By BALT. SOLVYNS.
*****

The Collection is intended to be divided into twelve Sections; one of each section to be delivered immediately to every Subscriber, with an explanatory List of all the Subjects.

In this first Attempt to present to the Public such an interesting and valuable Collection, the Proprietor hopes to receive the Patronage and Support of Gentlemen resident in India, in order to enable him to complete so splendid a Design, pledging himself that no Exertions shall be spared on his Part to render it worthy their Attention.

To Gentlemen to whom the whole of the Scenes, Characters, &c., intended to be represented may be familiar, and may be about to return to their native Country, a Work of this Nature cannot but be particularly pleasing, and must, no Doubt, prove a valuable and desirable Acquisition.

The Proprietor, encouraged by these Considerations, and hoping to receive the general Approbation of the Public, means hereafter to undertake another Publication descriptive of the Scenery throughout Bengal, Behar, and Orissa.

The whole of the Drawings of the present Publication are in the possession of BALT. SOLVYNS, Old Court Lane; where one Engraving of each Section is exhibited:—The first Section before delivery will be equally exposed, as will those of the other Sections in the same Manner. All Letters addressed to Mr. SOLVYNS, will be punctually answered, Orders received, and the Engravings forwarded according to the directions of the Subscribers.

The Engravings will be equal to the original Drawings, taken from Nature, being all engraved in *Aqua Fortis*, and afterwards colored by B. Solvyns, upon *Royal Paper*.[188]

The Size of the Engravings to be 15 inches by 11, at one Sicca Rupee each; the Total Amount of the Subscription being 250 Sicca Rupees; to be paid at the Time of subscribing.

The Subscriptions will be received by Messrs. BARBER and PALMER,[189] who will be responsible for the Delivery of the whole, or return the Amount should any unforeseen Accident prevent the Proprietor from completing so great and laborious an Undertaking.

THE FIRST SECTION will contain 66 Subjects, representing the various Bengallee Casts, with their respective Professions. The large Engraving, a general View of Calcutta, taken from Kidderpore Bridge.

THE SECOND SECTION will contain 35 Engravings, of the Servants employed in the Domestic Concerns of European Families; and the only Section in which the Moor Cast will be introduced: The large Engraving, a View of the European Buildings in Calcutta.

THE THIRD SECTION will contain 8 Engravings, descriptive of as many Dresses worn by Bengallee men: The large Engraving, a View of Bengal Buildings.

THE FOURTH SECTION will contain 8 Engravings, Dresses of Bengallee Women: The large engraving, a Bengallee Nautch.

THE FIFTH SECTION will contain 8 Engravings, representing Vehicles drawn by Horses, Bullocks, &c., according to the Purposes for which they are intended, as practiced by the Natives. The large Engraving, a Public Bengallee Road.

THE SIXTH SECTION will contain 8 Engravings of Palanquins. The large Engraving, the Mode of driving Elephants and Camels.

THE SEVENTH SECTION will contain 10 Engravings of Faquirs. The large Engraving, a View of Callee Ghaut Pagoda.

THE EIGHTH SECTION will contain 13 Engravings of Pleasure boats. The large Engraving, a representation of the coming in of the Bhaun or Bhore in Sight of Garden Reach.

THE NINTH SECTION will contain 17 Engravings of Boats of Lading. The large Engraving descriptive of a North-Wester off Calcutta.

THE TENTH SECTION will contain 8 Engravings of the various Modes of Smoking with the Hookah, &c. The large Engraving, the Mode of playing their Games.

THE ELEVENTH SECTION will contain 36 Engravings of Musical Instruments. The large Engraving a Sharack [Caṛak Pūjā].

THE TWELFTH SECTION will contain 22 Engravings, representing the Public Festivals, Funeral Ceremonies, &c. &c of the Natives.

Calcutta, Feb. 1, 1794.

A month later, Solvyns took another advertisement in the *Gazette*:[190]

Engravings. Mr. Solvyns being obliged to fix the 18 of April next, as the time to close receiving Subscriptions for his Collection of 250 ENGRAVINGS, he begs the favor of these Ladies and Gentlemen who have already promised, and those who intend to Subscribe, to honor him by sending their names before this time. He further informs them, that all the Engravings will be ready for delivery before that period twelve months, unless any unforeseen accident should cause a delay.

Calcutta, March 1, 1794.

For some time, Solvyns had wandered with his sketchbook through Calcutta and its environs, drawing Indians in their occupational pursuits, their festivals, and the rich diversity of their cultural lives. He drew their musical instruments, their boats, their carts, and their modes of smoking. With genuine curiosity and a keenly observant and sympathetic eye, Solvyns recorded an India few Europeans *really* saw. His commitment was to faithfully portray the Hindus in their manners, customs, and costumes. As he sketched, Solvyns made notes as to the caste names of the people and of words for the various activities and objects he portrayed. He would surely have been one of the few Europeans of his time to know "Black Town" with any intimacy, and he must have become a familiar figure among Indians as he filled his sketchbooks and asked questions about aspects of life in Bengal.

An early account of Solvyns states that, "[f]illed with enthusiasm and determined to overcome every obstacle, he soon acquired such knowledge of the indigenous language" as to enable him to converse with the Brahmin Pundits and thus "make himself master of that knowledge with which he afterwards enriched Europe."[191] Solvyns surely did not learn Sanskrit, but he likely acquired some knowledge of Hindustani and Bengali. Whatever fluency Solvyns attained, however, his command of the language was limited, as evidenced by his occasional confusion in correctly identifying what he portrays. In the 1799 *Catalogue* for the Calcutta etchings, he acknowledges "a gentleman, who had made the native languages his study," as his source for the names he gave to the various subjects of his etchings. Solvyns surely relied on Indians as well for names of what he observed, but his ear sometimes failed him as he sought to transliterate it. Moreover, Solvyns's romanized spellings of the same word are sometimes variable. The result is that finding the correct name or word for what Solvyns describes becomes something of a detective job—a search for the solution to a puzzle—and in some cases, the word remains elusive.

Solvyns had likely supported himself while preparing the drawings for the project with money earned in decorating palanquins, as those for the Mysore princes, and carriages for Steuart & Co. There is no record of the number of subscriptions Solvyns might have gotten in response to his advertisements for the collection of etchings, but by the fall 1794, Solvyns may well have been pressed for money, as he was so often in the course of his life. Baillie, in a letter to Humphry in 1795, refers to Solvyns cleaning pictures and of receiving a reported Rs. 100 each for cleaning "a great number of Mr. Daniel's [sic] pictures" owned by East India Company official Peter Speke. Solvyns, Baillie wrote, "is a true Dutchman, for he turns everything to advantage." According to Baillie, Solvyns was "going home this season having picked up, he says about forty thousand [rupees]."[192] Baillie surely had it wrong, for everything suggests that Solvyns was in financial straits and, with the etching project still underway, in no way prepared to return to Europe.

In his letter to Humphry, Baillie again refers to Solvyns. "His forte is shipping. His Landscapes I do not admire. His trees are *riggled* too much like China painting." Baillie then commented on Solvyns's project, which he had first mentioned to Humphry in 1793: "He is executing now a Sett of 250 Etchings, coloured, representing the Trades, characters, occupations &c of the natives. I have not seen any of them. They are not however published yet but are promised in Dec. He executes them at the low rate of 250 Rs the Sett, or one rupee each print. I have been told that the etching is extremely rough and at the same time slight."[193]

Baillie judges Solvyns's price low compared to the 5 gold mohurs (80 rupees) he sought for his own set of etchings, *Twelve Views of Calcutta*, published in 1794,[194] but W. H. Carey, writing nearly one hundred years later in *Good Old Day of the Honorable John Company*, thought Baillie's price of Rs. 80 for the Calcutta prints an indication of "the extravagant prices that in 1794 were charged by engravers for reproductions of their work."[195] Thomas Daniell's *Views of Calcutta* (1786-88), with 12 colored aquatints, sold in India for the princely sum of 12 gold mohurs—192 rupees.[196] Compared to these prices, Solvyns's one rupee per print was a bargain indeed.

Baillie's expressed dislike for Solvyns may have been rooted in jealousy, and in June 1796, he solicited subscriptions for a proposed collection of etchings, a "Compendium of Arts and Manufacture," that pilfered Devis's title and would compete with Solvyns in portraying life in Bengal.[197] Four months later, in the *Calcutta Gazette*, Baillie announced "that on account of very slender encouragement hitherto received, he is under the necessity of relinquishing all hopes of being able to publish that Work." In another advertisement that he took in the same issue of the paper, however, Baillie proposed "a set of twelve views in Bengal," as a companion to his earlier views of Calcutta. The subscription price was 50 rupees for the set.[198] They were never published.

By contrast, Solvyns persevered. In his search for income, Solvyns apparently offered his not yet fully-honed skills in etching to other artists. Thomas Anburey (1759-1840), an amateur artist in the Bengal Engineers, had in 1793 advertised his intention to publish a collection of prints based on original sketches he had done on his survey travels. But a year later, in October 1794, Anburey announced in the *Calcutta Gazette* that he found himself "under the necessity of relinquishing his original proposition of sending his VIEWS to England to be engraved in Aqua Tinta, and having had the most satisfactory proofs of the abilities of MR. SOLVYNS, has engaged him to etch and finish them in Water Colours. . . ." He advised the public that "Specimens of the work will be ready for exhibition on the 1st of the ensuing month, and may be seen on application at Mr. Solvyns or Mr. Devis's."[199] We know nothing more, but Anburey's views were ultimately published in London as *Hindoostan Scenery* in 1799, with its twelve colored aquatints etched by Francis Jukes.[200]

Solvyns, in his various enterprises, also engaged in the sale of art. Although perhaps for his own collection, Solvyns's purchase of a painting by George Farington (1752-1788) was likely for resale. Solvyns bought the picture—a depiction of the Murshidabad Nawab's durbar—from the estate sale of Robert Pott, the British Resident at Murshidabad, who as a patron of European artists in Bengal had built a fine collection.[201]

Whether diverted by other work or in struggling to gain mastery of printmaking in what were surely difficult conditions, Solvyns did encounter "unforeseen" delay in completing his collection of etchings. He may well have had difficulty in securing the copper plates, a substantial expense to which Solvyns makes no reference, and he perhaps waited months for their shipment from Europe. Moreover, the Calcutta climate, especially during the monsoon season, posed a daunting challenge for such an ambitious printing project. Solvyns had to secure the copper plates from risk of oxidation, and paper and inks were also vulnerable to dampness and humidity. Nearly six months after the expected date of delivery, he advertised:

> MR SOLVYNS Begs leave to acquaint the Subscribers to his ENGRAVINGS, that they will be ready for delivery by the 1st December next.—Mr. S. is sorry that from unavoidable occurrences, they could not be completed at the time he first promised, and begs to apologise to his Subscribers for the delay.
>
> Calcutta, Aug. 19, 1795.[202]

That next December, instead of delivering the completed prints to his subscribers—it would be yet another year before they received them—Solvyns announced a new project with an advertisement on the first page of the *Calcutta Gazette*:[203]

> MR. SOLVYNS Respectfully informs the Public, he proposes to publish a COLLECTION OF HEADS, ETCHED AND COLOURED by himself, exhibiting the NATIVE and various other INHABITANTS of INDIA, etc., etc. The whole forming a curious and interesting collection of three hundred different Heads, to be published in Numbers Monthly, to begin in January 1796, containing Twenty-five coloured Etchings each.
>
> To be had of MR. SOLVYNS only, at his house in Cassitollah Street behind the Old Jail, at Sicca Rupees Sixteen each number; and all letters or orders addressed to him as above, will be punctually attended to.
>
> Gentlemen wishing to subscribe for the Collection complete, may have it forwarded to them at Sicca Rupees 168; one half to be paid on delivery of the first number, and the remainder when the work is finished.
>
> The Drawings of the whole Collection, taken partly from Nature and partly from Original Paintings in the possession of Gentlemen in India.
>
> MR. SOLVYNS begs leave to intimate, that this has no connection whatever with the work he is now publishing Descriptive of the Manners, Customs, and

Dresses of the Natives of Bengal; as it only comprises such part of that work as from the nature of it, must necessarily be introduced. The great variety in Nature, and Dress characteristick of the Natives and other Inhabitants of India naturally attracts the attention of an Artist, and first induced by Mr. S. to attempt this collection. The whole has been executed with considerable care, as opportunities offered; how far he has succeeded in rendering it worthy of attention and approbation; he leaves a liberal and discerning public to determine.

Calcutta, December 1795.

Almost surely for want of subscribers, the proposed "Collection of Heads" was never published, and no drawings survive—though perhaps the twelve heads Solvyns included in the fourth volume of *Les Hindoûs* (IV.12.1-6), published in Paris in 1812, were from drawings originally prepared for this project. Solvyns had apparently abandoned the idea, mentioned in his 1794 advertisement, for etchings "descriptive of the scenery throughout Bengal, Behar, and Orissa." But that Solvyns advertised for subscriptions for this new collection of prints before completing his delayed Bengal etchings suggests that he was unrealistically ambitious or financially pressed.

For whatever reasons, it was not until nearly a year later, in November 1796, that Solvyns completed the etchings and announced delivery to subscribers.[204]

CARD. MR. SOLVYNS respectfully informs the Subscribers to his collection of PRINTS descriptive of the Manners, Customs, and Dresses of the *Indians*, that the work, being finished, will be delivered in all December, according to priority of subscription; agreeable to his former intimation.

Calcutta, November 13, 1796.

There were apparently few initial subscribers to the collection of etchings, for copies of the edition bearing the 1796 imprint on the title page are very rare.[205] After the first issue, however, Solvyns, with the aid of native assistants, continued to print and color etchings, and in 1799, he changed the date on original title page from "1796" to "1799"—the date that appears on most copies of the Calcutta edition.[206]

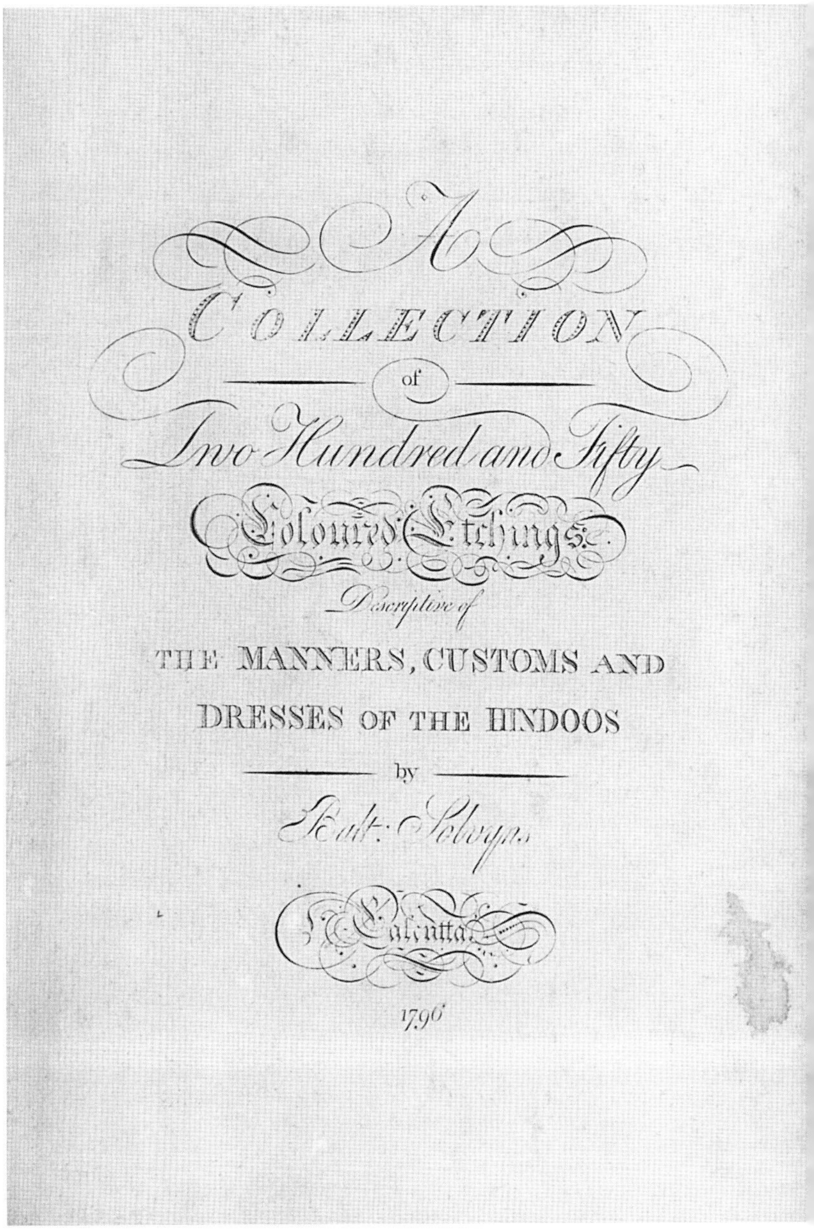
A Collection of Two Hundred and Fifty Coloured Etchings Descriptive of THE MANNERS, CUSTOMS AND DRESSES OF THE HINDOOS by Balt. Solvyns

Calcutta

1796

Pl. I.21. Title page of the 1796 imprint of Solvyns's *Les Hindoûs*. Courtesy Bibliothèque nationale de France.

The title page was engraved by Francis Dormieux, established in Bow Bazar as an accomplished silversmith and the best engraver in Calcutta at that time.[207] This may have been Dormieux's first commission of this sort, but he went on to engrave title pages for other books published in Calcutta,[208] and in 1805 published his own book of "Hindoostany Characters," with engravings of Indian "types" from Company School paintings by Indian artists.[209] The title page for Solvyns's 1796 printing, though without Dormieux's name, is in the engraver's style, as clearly evident in the distinctive "Calcutta" at the bottom of the page. Curiously, however, the engraver's name, "F. Dormieux Scripsit," appears in tiny letters at the lower left on the title page bearing the 1799 date in a few volumes of the *Collection*, but, perhaps reflecting conflict over payment, it is omitted on most copies.[210]

The availability of materials—copper plates, pigments, and paper—imposed serious constraints on any artist working in India. We have no record as to how Solvyns secured the more than 250 copper plates needed for the project, but he must have ordered them from Europe at enormous expense, and the lapse of time for the long voyages each way may well have accounted, in part, for delays in publication. Imported pigments for watercolor, as for oil painting, were more readily available. Although Indian-made paper was of good quality, paper was in short supply. Solvyns is reported to have made his own paper for the etchings,[211] although the sheets on which the tissue-thin etchings are mounted are, in most copies, European imports.

Solvyns often worked from his lodgings, but we have no information as to whether he had a separate studio for etching the copper plates, printing, and coloring. His space requirements would have been considerable. At least for a period, Solvyns had a European assistant, a Mr. J. Johnson, of whom we know only his name,[212] and he clearly employed Indian assistants in coloring the etchings. Baillie had used native artists in preparing his etchings, as had Daniell for coloring *Views of Calcutta*.[213]

Solvyns's *Collection of Two Hundred and Fifty Coloured Etchings* was "by far the largest, costliest, and most ambitious book to have been printed in Calcutta before 1800."[214] Indeed, it was the most ambitious printing project undertaken in all India to that time. Thomas Daniells, of course, had printed his *Views of Calcutta* a decade earlier, but the collection included only 12 aquatint engravings; Solvyns published 250 prints, a staggeringly difficult undertaking for the period.

Solvyns provides a description of how he came to undertake the project in a handwritten preface to the set of watercolors from which the Calcutta etchings were made.[215] Dated December 1798, it was apparently a draft for the text of the *Catalogue* that would appear the following year. With his idiosyncratic and inconsistent spellings and punctuation, he wrote,

> On my arrival in India, I was like most strangers highly pleased and entertained with the novelty of the objects, and scenes around me, and I recollect expressing my surprise that in a country where so many gentlemen from their local knowledge and abilities, were eminently qualified for the task, none had hitherto attempted a Collection of Drawings descriptive of the Manners, Customs and Dresses of the Hindoos, on a plan something similar to that which I have now the Honor of laying before the public.
>
> I conceived that to many, who never could have an oportunity of visiting India, but who from their connexions would feel interested in every thing that concerned it, a work of this kind must be peculiarly edifiing and amusing: nor did I think it would be less acceptable to others who having spent a great portion of their lives in India must be gratified by the representation of objects and scenes familiar to them in their earlier years.
>
> The difficulty of acquiring the requisite information, the magnitude of the Collection it self, and the arrangement necessary in a work of this kind may be easily conceived: but I must candidly own, when I first adopted the Design I was neither aware of the expenses, nor labor which has attended it.
>
> It will be readily perceived that in my original Drawings I have made choice of the most characteristick objects and such as are most frequently to be met with in Bengal, but at the same time no opportunity escaped me of adding to my Collection whatever I conceived curious or interesting from other parts of India.
>
> I have to express my sincere acknowledgements to several gentlemen for their information on a variety of points they kindly afforded me, and without which in many instances, I must have been at a loss.
>
> My Subscribers are also entitled to my warmest thanks for their liberality and indulgence, during the delays which have attended my publication which had it been in my power, inclination no less than interest would have prompted me to avoid.
>
> Whatever may be the opinion of my Subscribers and the Public of the stile in

which this work is executed: I trust some merit will be allowed me, for the industry and perseverance I have evinced in so intensive and arduous an undertaking: and I can affirm no pains have been spared on my part, to render it worthy of their approbation.

I trust the liberal support and encouragement I have experienced, will induce others of superior abilities to come forward, and that the Public will soon be in possession of a Collection as splendid as the design will admit.

In 1799, when Solvyns prepared the new title page for the *Collection*, he published *A Catalogue of 250 Coloured Etchings: Descriptive of the Manners, Customs, Character, Dress, and Religious Ceremonies of the Hindoos*, a 28-page brochure in quarto that listed each of the etchings with brief descriptions. The *Catalogue* was printed by the Mirror Press, at the time one of nine, possibly more, presses in Calcutta. Their principal output was newspapers, with almanacs and calendars accounting for the largest of a limited number of books.[216]

The *Catalogue* begins with Solvyns's dedication to the Governor-General, Richard (later Marquess) Wellesley (1760-1842):

This attempt to delineate the manners, customs, character, and religious ceremonies of the natives of Hindostan, can no where be dedicated with so much propriety as to the Right Hon'ble Richard, Earl of Mornington, Knight of the most illustrious Order of St. Patrick, Governor General of all the British possessions in India, &c. &c.

From whose virtues, talents, and energy—they, in common with the other inhabitants of the country, enjoy every blessing dependent on a firm, equitable, and wise administration,—and expect, with confidence, victory, peace and security, to terminate the present critical and arduous juncture, in the future happiness, prosperity, and glory of the empire.

As the benignity and liberality of his Lordship give hope of protection to every industrious endeavour, so his celebrity as a liberal connoisseur, and his acknowledged eminence in the sister arts,—in accomplishments and learning, alike elegant, and extensive, encourage the humble artist to presume on his patronage.—on these considerations, the honor of prefixing his Lordship's name to this work, has been humbly solicited with every sentiment of respect, by his Lordship's most obedient humble servant, The Author, Calcutta, 1st January, 1799.

In the Preface, entirely changed from his earlier draft and less personal, Solvyns describes his purpose, in part, as to provide Europeans in India with a visual memento of their experiences, something they might share with friends and family upon their return home, as photographs were later used, but Solvyns had a more serious commitment in his portrayal of the Hindus. He sought to provide a faithful and systematic account of the people among whom he lived and thereby secure recognition as both artist and Orientalist in extending European knowledge of India.

The work was undertaken under the Idea, that a delineation from Nature of such objects in Hindostan, as are interesting from their beauty or novelty to an European, or any way elucidatory of the habits, manners, and features of the various tribes, which inhabit the Country, would be acceptable to the Public; and that it would be particularly interesting to those who had resided many years in India,—as a help to them, on their retreat to their native Country,—to recall to their recollection, occurrences of their youth and scenes formerly familiar to them; at the same time that it would serve to illustrate to their friends in Europe, their observations and descriptions of the character, customs and manners, the persons, and dresses, of the inhabitants of Hindostan, their implements of Husbandry, manufacture, and war—their modes of conveyance by land and water—the various sectaries of religion with their peculiar ceremonies, and the appearance of the face of the Country.

With these hopes I formed my plan, and conceive, that a linear representation will be desirable, to convey an idea of those subjects relative to the Country, which can hardly be described by any other means.

As, in the present race of Hindoos, we see, perhaps with little change, the Customs, features and character—the religious Mysteries, and public amusements of their ancestors at an age, when the inhabitants of few other parts of the globe, were in a state of civilization, (their attachment to their ancient religion having preserved to them their primitive manners, amidst the influence of commerce with foreigners, and the fanatic Tyranny of their Mahometan Conquerors;) a faithful representation of them cannot but be acceptable to every enquiring mind.

The valuable discoveries made, through the acquisition of the Shanscrit Language by Europeans, of the allegorical and enigmatical Language of the Religion, and concerning the Arts, Sciences, and History of this ancient people, cannot but excite the curiosity of all Europe,—the mythology has been proved to be the same, as that of the Egyptians, Greeks and Romans—and its trivial and frivolous rites, the external of moral and political institutions; introduced under the character of sanctity, to render their observance more certain and easy: as the mysterious ceremonies of their religion, are discovered to be enveloped in darkness, purposely to elude discovery and to chain superstition and fanaticism.

Solvyns concludes his Preface with an appreciation of the Orientalists from whom he had long sought acceptance.

Should the work excite a desire for an acquaintance with the symbolical Mythology of the Hindoos, I presume a better source of information cannot be referred to, than the transactions of the Asiatic Society, and the translates and writings on the subjects, by the late Sir William Jones, and Mr. Charles Wilkins.[217]

At the end of the *Catalogue*, following the descriptive list of the 250 etchings, Solvyns writes,

It is perhaps to lamented that I prefixed the names, supplied me by a gentleman, who had made the native languages his study, to the Plates, before I had an opportunity of availing myself of the orthography of the late Sir William Jones.—I am told that my present plan will be more acceptable to the generality of readers, as the other can be digested by those only who have, in some measure, made the Shanscrit Language their study; but the adoption of it would have attended with the advantage of preventing the errors of the present arbitrary pronunciation, and have referred to a standard.

I had once attempted to collect materials to insert in my list, a general Sketch of the Practical Religion of the Hindoos, and the peculiarities of the Customs and Ceremonies of each Sect and Country; but I soon found the information I was able to obtain, to be so contradictory, that it became prudent to confine my remarks to the Plates, and to refer to such authority as is established.

It is not probable, that the choice of the figures to represent the different sects and professions, can give general satisfaction, as almost every person is inclined to form his ideas of Characters from the particular objects, to which he has been familiarized,—but a better plan has not occurred to me than the one I have adopted, of copying every object from Nature.

The arrangement of the Numbers, and the execution of the Work, I am confident, requires an apology, and perhaps, the best I can offer is to submit myself, with a consideration of the whole to the indulgence of the Public.

Last Years in Calcutta

We have almost nothing as to how Solvyns's etchings were received in Calcutta. William Baillie had referred to them as "extremely rough," and the brief obituary for Solvyns that appeared in the Calcutta *Gazette* in 1826, two years after his death, may have reflected earlier Anglo-Indian judgment: "His sketches, though not very picturesque, are very faithful delineations, and he must have been a man of very laborious and observant research. The engravings, executed by himself and published in Calcutta are very rude. . . ."[218] Solvyns's etchings, "by contemporary European standards," were deemed "monotonous and unattractive," as Mildred Archer notes. "The fashionable British public at the end of the eighteenth century was becoming used to aquatints of superb quality with soft colouring and subtle gradations of tone, such as those by the Daniells. Solvyns' pictures, with their elongated figures, rough hatching, fuzzy shading and flat washes of sombre colour were, as the obituary observed, 'rude' and 'not picturesque.'"[219] But Solvyns's "faithful delineations" may have been disturbing as well. "Nowhere is there any concession to conventional 'sensibility' or to contemporary taste," Giles Eyre comments, "and his drawings must have sent a shudder down the spine of fashionable people serving their dishes of tea, disdainful of the real Bengali world around them."[220]

There are no records as to the number of sets Solvyns printed and sold, but the etchings brought Solvyns little financial reward for his great effort. Less than a year after he delivered the 1796 printing to his subscribers, Solvyns placed two advertisements in the *Calcutta Gazette*:[221]

> PAINTINGS, Cleaned, repaired, and varnished, on application to Mr. B. Solvyns, or his Assistant Mr. J. Johnson, at his House, called the Old Library, near the Bank of Hindostan, where PAINTINGS, DRAWINGS, and PRINTS, are bought and sold on Commission.
>
> A CARD. MR. BALT. SOLVYNS begs leave to inform the Public, he has it now in his power to instruct any Lady or Gentleman in the Art of Oil Painting, Drawing in Water Colors, Chalks, etc. etc. after nature or copying.

The 1799 printing of etchings, with its accompanying *Catalogue,* fared little better financially, and by October 1802, Solvyns again advertised "Lessons in Drawing, Painting, &c. &c at his house or abroad on reasonable terms. Mr. S. also Cleans, Repairs, and Restores all kinds of paintings."[222] But even as he sought compensation by other means, Solvyns continued to prepare copies of the etchings for subscribers, with the last recorded delivery less than two months before he left India.[223]

Sometime in 1803, or before, Solvyns determined that his years in India had run their course without the recognition and recompense that was his due. He never attained the social acceptance in the closed British society of Calcutta that might rightly have been his by reason of his family and background. For all his intellect and curiosity in things Indian, Solvyns never gained membership in the Asiatic Society. He had worked desperately hard, but was almost away strapped for money. And the great project that had consumed his life, the portrayal of the Hindus in 250 colored etchings, had failed financially and been judged "rude" and, in its somber hues, unattractive.[224] In all of this, a lesser man might have been defeated, as Solvyns's friend Alefounder had been driven to suicide, but by strength of character, Solvyns persisted with dogged determination. Now, after twelve years in Calcutta, he prepared for the costly return voyage to Europe.[225]

---

1 *Registrum Baptismale Ecclefice Cathedralis Beatæ Mariæ Virginis Ad Boream Antverpiæ* [Parish Book, baptisms], No. 39, p. 118, Notre Dame du Nord. Stadsarchief, Antwerp. His godparents are listed as Franciscus Emmanuel Maria Solvijns and Maria Catharina Lucia Solvijns. The Notre Dame parish was large and had been divided into North and South. The Bisschops and Donnet genealogical notes in the Stadsarchief, Antwerp, include files on the Solvyns family, with several entries for François Balthazar and his immediate relations.

2 In some documents, he uses the variant spelling Balthazard.

3 She married in 1797 in Antwerp to François Léopold de Backer, an apothecary. They had no children.

4 "Généalogie de la famille baronniale Solvyns," unpublished family record; Prims, "Max en Jean-Pierre Solvyns;" and Prims, "Pierre Jean Solvyns," n.p.

5 Prims, "Pierre Jean Solvyns," n.p. The Antwerp artist Mathieu-Ignace Van Brée (1773-1839) portrayed the scene in a painting, "L'Entée de Bonaparte premier consul à Anvers, le 18 juin 1803." In the collection at Versailles, the painting is reproduced in Coekelberghs and Loze, 150, and in Suykens, 276-77.

6 "Généalogie de la famille baronniale Solvyns," unpublished family record.

7 Hostyn, "Solvyns, Frans-Balthasar," *National Biographish Woordenbook*, 10:594-95. Laurent served as president of Antwerp's Tribunal of Commerce in 1810. Beterams, 88.

8 Généalogie de la famille baronniale Solvyns," unpublished family record, and information provided by Ernest Vanderlinden, Berlaar, Belgium. The sale of the Jordaens house is described in Tijs.

9 Frison, 9-23; Généalogie de la famille baronniale Solvyns," unpublished family record. Boumans, 684-85, relates that Maximilien secured the appointment without the rank of a French naval officer, as the law required. Because of this, at the behest of the new Prefect, he was replaced in 1801, prior

to the end of his six-year term. Also see, Prims, "Max en Jean-Pierre Solvyns," and Prims, *Antwerpiensia 1929*, 357.

10 "Généalogie de la famille baronniale Solvyns," unpublished family record.

11 55.

12 Hymans, "Quertenmont," in *Biographie nationale . . . de Belgique*, 18:262-63.

13 Sources vary on Solvyns's age at the time he won the prize. The *Biographie nouvelle des contemporains*, 243, gives his age as 11; Lesbroussart, 68, has him taking the prize at 12.

14 On Lens, see Jacobs, *The Dictionary of Art*, 19:165-66, Loze, 67-89, and Hymans. On Neo-classicalism, see Wilton-Ely, *The Dictionary of Art*, 22:734-42.

15 Hostyn, "Solvyns, Frans-Balthasar," *National Biographish Woordenbook*, 10:595.

16 68, as translated in *Annual Register, 1824*, Appendix to Chronicle, 234-35

17 See Cuzin., *The Dictionary of Art*, 32-584-85.

18 Hostyn, "Solvyns, Frans-Balthasar," *National Biographish Woordenbook*, 10:595.

19 On Daudet, see Roux, 6:47-48. Roux, 6:51, lists the print among Daudet's work in the Bibliothèque nationale, Cat. No. Vc.78. In Belgium, copies of the print are in the Stadsarchief, Ostend (V.373), and in the Cabinet des estampes, Bibliothèque royale Albert I, Brussels (S.II. 40651).

20 The faintly discernible signature below the cartouche reads "P. P. Choffard fecit 1784." On Choffard, see Roux, 4:370.

21 Interview with Hostyn, Ostend, May 31, 1991.

22 Hostyn, "Solvyns, Frans-Balthasar," *National Biographish Woordenbook*, 10:596.

23 The paintings are the subject of Hostyn, "Omtrent een Gezicht op de Haven van de Stad Oostende."

24 *Biographie nationale . . . de Belgique*, 13:722-27.

25 Lesbroussart, 69, as translated in *Annual Register, 1824*, Appendix to Chronicle, 234-35.

26 69; also Solvyns's obituary, *Annual Register, 1824*, Appendix to Chronicle, 234.

27 Hostyn, "Omtrent een gezicht op de haven van de stad Oostende," 116. In a letter to Mr. Hostyn, Dr. Karl Schutz of the Kunsthistorishches Museum, Vienna, September 23, 1980, provided information on the Solvyns painting. The print collection was the only part of the Albertina inventory that was not sold, and it became property of the state.

28 Archives générales du Royaume. Chambre des Comptes. Registre aux patentes de 1775 à 1786, No. 374, folio 292 verso. Commission de Capitaine de la corvette Royale qui est de station sur l'Escaut, en faveur de Balthazar SOLVYNS. 23 August 1786.
Biographical sources on Solvyns's life are surely incomplete and often inconsistent or simply wrong, as evidenced here. Most accounts, probably repeating Lesbroussart's mistake, 69, state that at the age of 16, Solvyns was appointed captain of Fort Lillo. Burbane, 46, without giving his source, writes that Solvyns was 18 when he accepted the charge as captain at Fort Lillo. De Paepe, 84, describes Solvyns as a young officer in the corps of engineers and gives his age as 20 when he was named "commandant" of Fort Lillo. The Solvyns family genealogical records, by contrast, correctly state that on August 23, 1786, at the age of 26, Balthazar was made captain of a "corvette royale" at Fort Lillo. "Généalogie de la famille baronniale Solvyns," unpublished family record.

29 Van den Branden, 3:269-70; Génard, 2:600-01; Persoons, 5; Hostyn, "Solvyns, Frans-Balthasar", 597.

30 The painting came to the museum when the Friends of the National Maritime Museum bought the collection of the Musée Folklorique de la Marine, Brussels, a private museum belonging to the Chauveau family of antique dealers. The collection included ship models, nautical instruments, and among various pictures, the Solvyns painting, described in the inventory simply as a marine painting, oil on panel.

31 Hostyn, curator of the Ostend museum, discusses the painting in "Schilders van de zee."

32 69; also *Annual Register, 1824*, Appendix to Chronicle, 235.

33 Of the many books on Calcutta, see especially: Losty, *Calcutta: City of Palaces*; Sukanta Chaudhuri, ed., *Calcutta: The Living City*: Pratapaditya Pal, *Changing Visions, Lasting Images: Calcutta through 300 Years*; Pradip Sinha, *Calcutta in Urban History*: and Nisith Ranjan Ray, *Calcutta: The Profile of a City*. P. Thankappan Nair provides selections from early accounts of the city in his volumes on Calcutta in the 18th and 19th centuries.

34 2:2.

35 From 1769, when Tilly Kettle arrived in Madras, until 1820, some 60 professional artists went to India. Mildred Archer and W. G. Archer, *Indian Painting for the British 1770-1880*, 10.

36 "British Artists in India, 1760-1820," 1.

37 The phrase "pagoda tree" referred to the opportunity for rapid fortune. *Hobson-Jobson*, 657.

38 Milner, 74. Although principally a portrait painter, he also did several paintings depicting Indian life, notably his Madras scenes of ordinary people at a temple, of dancing girls, and of suttee. On Kettle, see Mildred Archer, *India and British Portraiture*, 66-97.

39 K. Chakrabarti, 19-20. On Zoffany, see Mildred Archer, *India and British Portraiture*, 130-77.

40 On Hodges's voyage with Captain Cook, see Joppien and Smith, Vol. 2, and Bernard Smith, 111-34.

41 On Hodges, see Stuebe; Tillotson, *The Artificial Empire*; and Leoshko and Charlesworth.

42 Of the considerable literature on the Daniells, see, notably, Thomas Sutton; Mildred Archer, *Early Views of India*; Shellim, *India and the Daniells*; Mahajan, *Picturesque India*; and Martinelli and Michell.

43 See Chapter Three, pp. 90-91.

44 Michell contrasts the artists in his discussion of "The Daniells as Artists," in Martinelli and Michell, 19-26.

45 See Evan Cotton, *East Indiamen*, 119-120. For a description of the voyage and accommodations for passengers, see Russell Miller, 122-45. William Hickey, in his *Memoirs* (1749-1809), provides rich descriptions of the voyages to and from India.

46 Some early biographical entries for Solvyns mistakenly have him sailing to India in 1789.

47 The account of Home Popham below draws principally upon the biography by his descendant Hugh Popham and the entry in *The Dictionary of National Bibliography*, 16:143-46. I am grateful to Hugh Popham for his assistance in gathering material relating to the India voyage.

48 Popham, 29-30.

49 Ibid., 33. The British Consul in Ostend estimated the illicit Ostend trade with India at £100,000 a year. Furber, 140. On the clandestine trade generally, see Furber, 110-59.

50 Ibid., 32.

51 Ibid., 33.

52 William Popham (1740-1821), an officer in the Bengal Army, served under Cornwallis in the sieges of Seringapatam,

1791-92, in the Third Mysore War. Another brother, Stephen, was the East India Company's solicitor in Madras.

53 Quoted in Popham, 32.

54 Popham, 33. Years later, in a speech in the House of Commons, Popham defended himself against the charge that he had engaged in illegal trade, arguing that he believed the ban to have been relaxed. Cornwallis knew at the time he was a British subject in command of a foreign ship, Popham said, but "that Noble Lord . . . *abstained from noticing* the trade" in which he had been engaged. Popham, 34.

55 Ibid., 34.

56 March 3, 1791 (Vol. 15, No. 366), 3.

57 Advertised in the *Calcutta Gazette*, April 7, 1791 (Vol. 15, No. 371), 3. In the months after arriving in Calcutta, Popham employed the *Etrusco* in coastal trade for the East India Company, with calls at Prince of Wales Island (Penang) and Bombay. *The World* (Calcutta weekly), October 29, 1791 (Vol. 1, No. 3), 3, and November 5, 1791 (Vol. I, No. 4), 3. In January 1792, as advertised in *The World*, December 31, 1791 (Vol. 1, No. 12), 1, the *Etrusco*, "Burden about 8500 bags of rice, a primesailer, remarkably strong," was sold at public auction in Calcutta.

58 Secret Letter dated April 27, 1792. National Archives of India, *Fort William-India House Correspondence*, 17:460. Popham's legal difficulties were not over, for with a new ship that he named "Etrusco," perhaps for luck, Popham continued to engage in trade in violation of the Company charter. On his return to Ostend in 1793, the ship was seized by a British frigate, and in a case that dragged on long after his return to the Royal Navy, Popham was finally compensated for his loss. *The Dictionary of National Biography*, 16:144. Popham was promoted the rank of Rear Admiral in 1814.

59 *Annual Register, 1824*, Appendix to Chronicle, 235; Lesbroussart, 69. Also see *Biographie nouvelle des contemporains*, 19:243.

60 Home Popham's chart of the Red Sea was published in London by W. Faden, "geographer to the King," July 13, 1804. A copy is in the British Library, Maps 49110.(10.).

61 See Popham, 89-99. Depping, "Solvyns" (1825), 43:62, writes of the Red Sea maps that "we do not know where they are located. They were searched for in vain in the collection of Labanoff." Prince Alexandre Labanof (b. 1788) was a Russian savant and bibliophile. Why Depping would have believed the charts to be in Labanof's collection is not evident. On Labanof, see *Nouvelle biographie générale*, 28:322.

62 India Office Records, *Handbook. Biographical Series,* 18.

63 Marshman, *The Life and Times of Carey, Marshman, and Ward*, 1:73-75.

64 *Bengal, European Inhabitants, 1783 to 1807*. India Office Records 0/5/26.

65 Solvyns was similarly listed the following year for the first time in the *East India Kalendar*, 96. During the time he was resident in Calcutta, he was also listed, irregularly, in the *Bengal Directory and Almanak*.

66 Text for Pl. II.279.

67 See Nair, *A History of Calcutta's Streets*, 518-20.

68 The east end of Esplanade Row and Dhurrumtollah Bazar is portrayed in a lithograph by William Wood, reproduced in Losty, *Calcutta: City of Palaces*, Fig. 27.

69 See Nair, *A History of Calcutta's Streets*, 198-99.

70 Advertisement, *Calcutta Gazette*, October 19, 1797 (Vol. 18, No. 712), p. 3.

71 Advertisement, *Calcutta Gazette*, October 14, 1802 (Vol. 38, No. 972), p. 1.

72 See Commentary for Pl. II.6.

73 Quoted in Losty, *Calcutta: City of Palaces*, 95. Also see Losty, 93.

74 The British had long cultivated a dislike of the French and of French culture. Sir William Jones's intense dislike for the French Orientalist Anquetil-Duperron came, in part, from his disdain for "the French nation." S. N. Mukherjee, *Sir William Jones*, 23.

75 Sir William Jones, *A Discourse on the Institution of a Society* . . . . Originally the Asiatick Society, the name was changed in 1825 to the Asiatic Society. On the history of the Society, see Kejariwal.

76 Of the many books on Jones, see Cannon for the major biography.

77 S. N. Mukherjee, *Sir William Jones*, 78.

78 Reproduced in Mildred Archer, *India and British Portraiture*, 250, Pl. 174.

79 See Sibadas Chaudhuri on the proceedings of the Asiatic Society.

80 Solvyns writes of his presence in conversations Jones had with a Daṇḍī ascetic (Pl. II.136).

81 In an advertisement for the Paris edition of Solvyns's etchings, *Les Hindoûs*, that appeared in London's *Quarterly Review* in 1813, the bookseller stated that "This Work was originally undertaken at the instigation and under the patronage of the late Sir William Jones." Bohn, *Catalog of Books* (1847), quoted in Abbey, 381, repeats it, and following from this, Mildred Archer, in "Baltazard Solvyns and the Indian Picturesque," 13, writes that in 1794, Solvyns had, "with the encouragement of the orientalist, Sir William Jones," announced his scheme for the 250 etchings descriptive of the Hindus. Solvyns was surely inspired by the work of the great Orientalist, but nothing supports any involvement by Jones in Solvyns's decision to undertake the project.

82 Joining the Bengal Army in 1777, Baillie served with the Bengal Engineers until 1785, when he started the *Calcutta Chronicle* weekly. In 1792, he published a "Plan of Calcutta," from the original by Lt. Col. Mark Wood. His *Twelve Views of Calcutta* appeared in 1794. Six of the Baillie *Views* are reproduced in Losty, *Calcutta: City of Palaces*.

83 Letter from William Baillie, Calcutta, to Ozias Humphry, London, November 23, 1793, Ozias Humphry Papers, HU/4/88-89, Royal Academy of Arts, London, reprinted in Evan Cotton, "Letters from Bengal," 127.

84 W. H. Carey, *Good Old Days*, 2:185. Morris does not appear in Mildred Archer, *India and British Portraiture*.

85 “British Artsists in India,” 1.

86 See Mildred Archer, *India and British Portraiture*, 184-203.

87 Letter, December 12, 1792. Ozias Humphry Papers, HU/2/130, Royal Academy of Arts, London.

88 Letter, November 23, 1793. Ozias Humphry Papers, HU/4/88-89, Royal Academy of Arts, London. Baillie's enmity toward Solvyns may be, in part, a matter of envy, for, despite Solvyns's own struggle to making a living from art, Baillie, with few commissions, was compelled to become Superintendent of the Free School in order to support himself. See Godrej and Rohatgi, *Scenic Splendors*, 30-31.

89 Letter of October 4, 1795. Ozias Humphry Papers, HU/4/112-117, Royal Academy of Arts, London.

90 I am grateful to the following specialists in marine painting and history for assistance in identifying ships and for descriptive detail in Solvyns's paintings of ships in India:

Daniel Finamore and George Schwartz of the Peabody Essex Museum, Salem, Massachusetts; Brian Lavery and Robert Blyth at the National Maritime Museum, Greenwich; and Andrew Lambert, King's College, London.

91 The portrait, thought to be of William Steuart, is discussed on pp. 32.

92 The picture is illustrated in the National Maritime Museum, *Concise Catalog*, 368; in Archibald, Pl. XXII; and in Kemp and Ormond, Pl. 59.

93 I am grateful to Brian Lavery, curator and naval historian, at the National Maritime Museum, for his insight in examination of the painting.

94 Reproduced with the permission of Spink and Son Limited, London.

95 92 (March 1950): iv.

96 Spink, Lot 36, "Calcutta from below Fort William looking north," p. 38, with color reproduction.

97 Christie's, Lot 57, with color reproduction, *Visions of India* (catalog for the auction of October 5, 1999), 50.

98 Conner, in his superb book on Chinnery, includes several Chinnery sketches and watercolors of Indian boats (Color Pl. 46, Pls. 88 and 89), but, although illustrating several Chinnery paintings from China in the collection of the Hong Kong and Shanghai Bank, he does not include the painting of Calcutta harbor.

99 Styles, unpublished ms., Chap. 2, based on the Michael Hogan Family Papers. The tonnage is from the Public Records Office, London, BT/111/1.

100 The painting of the *Marquis Cornwallis* under sail, together with the ship's log, came onto the market in the 1980s and is now in a private collection. A copy of the painting, on canvas, done sometime in the nineteenth century, remained with the family and is now in the collection of Michael Styles, an American descendant of Michael Hogan. Styles has done extensive research on the captain and the ship for a book, *Captain Hogan: Sailor, Merchant and Diplomat on Six Continents*, awaiting publication.

101 The registry (September 23, 1794, in London) is recorded in Public Records Office, London, BT/111/1.

102 Syles, Chapter 3; Hughes, 183-84; and Bateson, 131-34. For a full chronicle of the mutiny, see Hall.

103 Peabody Essex catalog entry, No. 2149, Philip C. F. Smith, 61.

104 *The Calcutta Gazette*, September 27, 1798, carried a note on the launching of a "large new ship, . . . named *Cuvera*, the Indian Plutus." In a correction of its described weight, the *Gazette*, a week later, gave its weight as 930 tons. Farrington, 245, lists the *Cuvera* at 935 tons, but gives the date of its construction incorrectly as 1796. The India Office Library has a log for the *Cuvera*'s maiden voyage to England, on charter to the Company, embarking November 19, 1798. IOR: L/MAR/B/369A.

105 Farrington, 55. The *Bengal* is the only ship listed under Gillett's name by Farrington for the period Solvyns was in Calcutta. Hardy, 202, 218, 235, lists three voyages for the *Bengal*.

106 Phipps, in his 1840 account of shipbuilding in India, refers to Gillett's as "a large and successful Ship building establishment" in the 1790s (vii). In the late eighteenth century, India was an important source of ships for the British fleet. Jean Sutton, 49.

107 On a sheet of paper pasted to the back of the painting, Mary H. Trotter, October 1, 1924, describes the picture and identifies Gabriel Gillett as her grandfather. The painting was sold by the executors of the estate on the death of Arthur Malcolm Gillett Trotter.

108 Sotheby's, Lot 116, Catalog for the sale of March 12, 1980.

109 See Mildred Archer, *India and British Portraiture*, 298-332.

110 On Eyre's involvement with Solvyns, see pp. 32, 79-85, 100-01.

111 Soon after the museum acquired the painting, it was featured on the cover of *The American Neptune: Maritime History & Arts*, 55 (Winter 1995), published by the Peabody Essex. Relying on Kemp and Osmond, Pl. 59, the note to the cover illustration, 2, incorrectly characterized Solvyns as ending his career as "a dock worker in Antwerp." He was, in fact, Captain of the Port. See pp. 68-69.

112 See Appendix, "Solvyns in Libraries," pp. 538-40.

113 The salt trade, like opium, was a Company monopoly and an important source of revenue.

114 76. The painting (previously titled "The Residence of Richard Goodlad at Barypore near Calcutta") is illustrated, 77, in color as Fig. 12. It is also included, in Eyre and Greig, 54, with a color reproduction on the inside back cover of the catalog.

115 See Nitisth R. Ray, "George Lyell Collection."

116 Christie's, *Important English Pictures* (catalog for the sale of June 22, 1979), Lots 35 and 36, illustrated in black-and-white.

117 Christie's, *Visions of India* (catalog for the sale of June 10, 1997), Lot 84, illustrated in color. The painting of the Farquharson's residence is reproduced in Wild, 56, without attribution.

118 The aquatint with soft-ground etching, Calcutta, 1800, is reproduced in Losty, *Calcutta: City of Palaces*, 77, fig. 41. On another Moffat copy after Solvyns, see pp. 106-07.

119 "Mr. and Mrs. William Farquharson outside their house near Calcutta on the Hoogly River," c. 1789, oil on canvas, in a private British collection.

120 Letter XV, Calcutta, May 22, 1780, in Fay, 171-72; reprinted in Nair, Calcutta in the 18th Century, 191. For descriptions of Garden Reach and its fine houses, see Losty, *Calcutta: A City of Palaces*.

121 Alexander Kyd (1754-1826) was the nephew of Robert Kyd (1746-1793), founder of the Botanic Gardens near Calcutta. On inheriting the gardens, Alexander transferred them to the East India Company in 1794. Mildred Archer, *British Drawings in the India Office Library*, 2:468. See reference to the gardens in Commentary for Pl. II.261.

122 An officer in the Bengal Infantry, Colebrooke (1762-1808) served as a surveyor in the Second Mysore War, 1781-85, and conducted surveys during the Mysore campaigns in 1791 and 1792. His *Twelve Views of Places in the Kingdom of Mysore* was published in 1794. He accompanied Kyd in surveying the newly acquired island of Penang in 1787 and was with Kyd in the Andaman and Nicobar Islands from November 1789 to April 1790. He succeeded Kyd as Surveyor-General, serving from 1800 to his death in 1808. Mildred Archer, *British Drawings in the India Office Library*, 1:142-43; Godrej and Rohatgi, 109-10; Phillimore, 1:328.

123 India Office Library, MSS. EUR. F21/I [Calcutta, November 8, 1792], Capt. Kyd. *Account of the Andamans*, 6.

124 *British Drawings in the India Office Library*, 1:31-32.

125 On the album, see pp. 83-85.

126 India Office Library, MSS. Eur. F21 (Kaye No. 150)/I, Capt. Kyd. *Account of the Andamans*, 7. In his history of British relations with the Andamans, Portman refers to the two islanders taken by Blair, 86, and discusses Blair's activities more generally, 80-115.

127 389-92. The description is almost identical to that of Lt. Col. Symes's "An Account of the Andaman Islands," 91-92. Symes may have seen Colebrooke's unpublished report, though (less likely) Colebrooke may have borrowed from Symes to supplement his own eye-witness account.

128 MSS. Eur. F21 (Kaye No. 150).

129 Milded Archer lists and describes each in *British Drawings in the India Office*, 2:470-72. Two are reproduced in plates: No. 3, "Inhabitants of the Andaman Islands," by Solvyns (Pl. 105); and, No. 12, "Village huts on Nancowry," a watercolor that Archer describes as a copy "probably" done by Solvyns (Pl. 106).

130 Evan Cotton, "A Famous Calcutta Firm. The Story of Steuart & Co." Steuart & Co. remained the established coachmaker until well into the twentieth century. See Ranabir Ray Choudhury, 55 and 183, for Steuart & Co. advertisements from Calcutta newspapers in 1885 and 1890. The building, on the street now called Hemanta Basu Sarani, was torn down in 1907. "The Editor's Note Book," *Bengal Past and Present*, 49 (1935): 142.

131 E. g., September 22, 1791.

132 Mildred Archer, *Company Drawings in the India Office Library*, 73.

133 Mildred Archer, *Early Views of India*, 10.

134 Ozias Humphry Papers, HU/4/112-117, Royal Academy of Arts, London. The letter is reproduced in Evan Cotton, "Letters from Bengal," 128-32, and, in part, in Evan Cotton, "A Famous Calcutta Firm," 70. On the Tanjore palanquins, see Solvyns's portrayal of the miyāna palanquin, Pl. II.225.

135 *Calcutta Gazette*, May 1, 1794, in Seton-Karr, 2:387.

136 (Anon) *Narrative Sketches of the Conquest of Mysore* (1800), 98, quoted in Buddle, "The Tipu Mania," 58.

137 The engraving is also reproduced in Buddle, "The Tipu Mania," 58, Pl. 4, without note of the Solvyns association.

138 Both the artist Robert Home and Major Alexander Diron were present at the ceremony at which Cornwallis received the princes. See Home, *A Description of Seringapatam*, quoted in Mildred Archer, *India and British Portraiture*, 300, and Diron, 224, quoted in Telsche, 248. Also see Cornwallis, 2:138, 151, and Bowring, 170-73. Teltscher, 248-51, analyzes the symbolism of its portrayal. A *vakīl* (Anglo-Indian, vakeel) is an authorized representative or ambassador, as here, or an attorney. On the hostage princes, see Buddle, *The Tiger and the Thistle*, 31-33.

139 71; also *Annual Register, 1824*, Appendix to Chronicle, 235. The mistake was likely based on knowledge of Solvyns's connection to the palanquins Cornwallis commissioned for the princes.

140 In addition to a number of fine paintings, Home also published two volumes of prints, *Select Views in Mysore* and *A Description of Seringapatam*. On Home, see Mildred Archer, *India and British Portraiture*, 298-332, and Godrej and Rohatgi, *Scenic Splendours*, 112-14. Another artist, Robert H. Colebrooke, as noted earlier (See fn. 122), had been in Mysore as a surveyor and produced his own collection of *Views*. Colebrooke's drawings were used for illuminated transparent paintings by Solvyns and Devis at a 1793 celebration of Cornwallis's victory. See below.

141 See Evan Cotton, "Letters from Bengal," 111, 129. The painting, "The Reception of the Hostage Princes of Mysore before Seringapatnam by Marquess of Cornwallis," was completed in London and exhibited at the Royal Academy in 1802. Now in the collection of Lord Biddulph, it is reproduced in Mildred Archer, *India and British Portraiture*, Pls. 187. (Devis also did a larger version of the painting, Archer, Pl. 188.) Devis, in an advertisement in the *Calcutta Gazette*, Feb. 6, 1794 (Seton-Karr, 2:574), proposed a print from the painting and offered it by subscription at the substantial price of 80 Sicca Rupees. W. H. Carey, writing in 1882, describes Devis's paintings in *The Good Old Days of the Honorable John Company*, 2:209-211, and refers to the engraving: "[W]e still find the 'Sons of Tippoo' in the parlours of inns and other places where old prints linger."

142 Madras, 1793-95. Reproduced in Bayly, *The Raj*, 154-55, Pl. 157. It is also reproduced in Mildred Archer, *India and British Portraiture*, Pls. XIV and 213; in Buddle, *The Tiger and the Thistle*, Pl. 38; and in Guy and Boyden, 46. The painting was first exhibited at the Royal Academy, London, in 1797, and is today in the National Army Museum, London. Teltscher, 249-51, taking the painting as representative of the genre, examines it as an expression of British paternal dominance and emblematic of Cornwallis's achievement. Home did another painting, c. 1793, of the hostage princes leaving home, in Mildred Archer, *India and British Portraiture*, Pl. 214.

143 See Mildred Archer, *India and British Portraiture*, 218-19, 419-35; Pal and Dehejia, 50-55; and Buddle, who treats "Tipu Mania" in a full article.

144 Ibid., 279, Pl. 194.

145 On the "hostage paintings" generally, ibid., 420-27. The Singleton print is reproduced in color in Buddle, "The Tipu Mania," 56, Pl. 3.

146 Perhaps originally introduced from China, painted transparencies on linen, silk, gauze, and even paper, had long been done in Europe and were popular for "illumination nights." Their use in scene painting for the theater dates back at least to the seventeenth century, when Inigo Jones used transparencies in the scenery for "Oberon." See Rosenfeld, 55-59. Edward Orme, in *An Essay on Transparent Prints, and on Transparencies in General*, 49-51, describes two techniques: The first, apparently more usual, was done "with white wax and spirit of turpentine, mixed together hot, and put on by the fire. . . , [but the cloth thus waxed] is difficult to lay colours upon. . . ." Orme recommended a second technique: "The cloth must be first strained upon a frame. . . and well primed over, on both sides, with a good stout size, made of isinglass, with a small quantity of spirit of wine mixed in it, then strained through a rag. You should continue priming it over, till all the interstices in the cloth are filled up, and emit no little lights through. When the priming is hard, you may paint the transparency. . . ." Also see Ackermann, *Instructions for Painting Transparencies*. Both Orme (who pirated Solvyns's etchings for *Costumes of Indoostan*) and Ackermann published prints and developed techniques for making transparent prints for windows and fire-screens.

147 April 26, 1792 (Vol. 17, No. 426), 1. Old Government House, where Solvyns's transparency was exhibited, served both as official residence of the Governor-General and for government offices. Its small size had long been inadequate to the needs of state, and it was demolished in the late 1790s. In its place, on Esplanade Row, Wellesley's new Government House was erected as a monument to a new vision of empire. On old Government House, see Losty, *Calcutta: City of Palaces*, 58-60, with Thomas Daniell's 1788 etching, 59, Fig. 28. The Daniell etching is also included in Mildred Archer, *Early Views of India*, 32-33, Pl. 14.

148 April 28, 1792 (Vol. 1 No. 29), 2.

149 The Theatre, on Clive Street, served Calcutta from 1775 to 1808 with largely amateur productions, and its adjacent ballroom was a venue for balls, grand dinners, and state occasions.

150 *Calcutta Gazette*, February 7, 1793 (Vol. 18, No. 467), 4; in Seton-Karr, 2:361-63.

151 *Calcutta Gazette*, October 2, 1794 (Vol. 22, No. 553), 2, and October 13, 1794 (Vol. 22, No. 556), 2, the later in Seton-Karr, 2:584.

152 Both the Devis painting and the engraving (by H. Hudson) are reproduced in Mildred Archer, *India and British Portraiture*, 159-61, Pls. 184 and 185. Also see Rohatgi, *Portraits in the India Office Library and Records*, 49.

153 *Calcutta Gazette*, January 27, 1803; in Seton-Karr, 4:83-85. The fete was held on January 26, 1803. Also see H. E. A. Cotton, *Calcutta Old and New*, 128-29; and Valentia, 1:60-62, in Nair, *Calcutta in the 19th Century*, 2-4. Wellesley (1760-1842), brother of the Duke of Wellington, served as Governor-General of India from 1797 until 1805. He was made Marquess in 1799, in recognition of his services in the defeat of Tipu Sultan and the conquest of Mysore. The magnificent new Government House, on Esplanade Row, was erected on the orders of the Governor-General Marquess Wellesley and was first used officially in 1802. See Losty, *Calcutta: City of Palaces*, 71-76, with James Moffat's 1802 watercolor of Government House, 74, Pl. 11.

154 Evan Cotton, "A Famous Calcutta Firm," opp. p. 71. It is possible that a signature was obscured or perhaps concealed by the frame.

155 The print, 50.5 x 62.5 cm., was published May 1, 1795, by F. Jukes Engraver, Howland Street, and by Messrs. Colnaghi & Co., Pall Mall. Jukes (1745-1812) was a specialist in topographical prints and, along with the Daniells, "was one of the first to develop the process of hand-coloured aquatinting to a high degree of perfection." Godrej and Rohatgi, *Scenic Splendor*, 32. The print is reproduced in black and white in *Scenic Splendor*, 31, Fig. 10, and in color in Losty, *Calcutta: City of Palaces*, Pl. 9, with discussion, 66-67.

156 "A Famous Calcutta Firm," 70-71. Also see "The Editor's Note Book," with a reproduction of the print, *Bengal Past and Present* 49 (1935):142.

157 St. Andrew's Church, completed in 1818, now stands on the site of the Old Court House. Thomas Daniell portrayed the Old Court House in a 1786 etching from the "Views of Calcutta," reproduced in Mildred Archer, *Early Views of India*, 20-21, Pl. 5, and in Losty, *Calcutta: City of Palaces*, 51, Fig. 23.

158 A copy of the key, with the engraving, is in the India Office Library, Maps, K.Top.115.46.d.

159 Conversation with Charles Greig, London, April 12, 1994, and letter of February 13, 1999.

160 In a private collection. William Foster, writing in 1931, "British Artists in India," 7, notes that with this one exception, not a single canvas or miniature by Alefounder has been found.

161 *India and British Portraiture*, 271. On Alefounder, see 270-72.

162 The advertisements appeared in *The Calcutta Chronicle*, July 31, 1788, and October 2, 1788. See Foster, "British Artists in India," 6-7, and Mildred Archer, *India and British Portraiture*, 271.

163 Mildred Archer, *India and British Portraiture*, 270. On Alefounder's troubled life, also see Evan Cotton, "A Calcutta Painter."

164 Letter of December 29, 1785, quoted in ibid., 270.

165 On September 6, 1787, the *Calcutta Gazette* editorialized: "Scarce a week has elapsed for a considerable period past, that our newspapers have not announced one or more shocking instances of suicide, either among Europeans or Natives. To what cause to impute this melancholy disposition, we know not. . . ."

166 Devis had sold the materials to pay off Alefounder's debts and enable him to return to England, but Alefounder, in an advertisement in the *Calcutta Gazette*, September 21, 1786, denounced Devis's action and sought recovery of the items sold. See W. H. Carey, *Good Old Days*, 2:214-15.

167 *India and British Portraiture*, 271.

168 *Calcutta Gazette*, February 20, 1794. William Baillie, Calcutta, conveyed the news to Ozias Humphry in London, in a letter of October 4, 1795. Ozias Humphry Papers, HU/4/112, Royal Academy of Arts, London, quoted in Evan Cotton, "Letters from Bengal," 131; Foster, "British Artists in India," 7; and in Mildred Archer, *India and British Portraiture*, 272.

169 His death was announced in the *Calcutta Gazette*, December 25, 1794. By this time, Solvyns had shifted his lodging, shared with Alefounder, to Durrumtollah.

170 On Devis, see Mildred Archer, *India and British Portraiture*, 234-69; Pavière, 101-41; W. H. Carey, *Good Old Days*, 2:208-12; and Foster, "British Artists in India," 24-31.

171 Foster, "British Artists in India, 1760-1820," 52-53, quotes Humphry, in a letter from India in 1785: While in India, in 1785, Humphry expressed his desire "to collect materials, by drawing and painting the dresses and manners of the people, which I shall endeavor to convert both to profit and employment after by return to England." Humphry MSS, 3:50, Royal Academy, London, quoted in Mildred Archer, *India and British Portraiture*, 191. He never carried out his plan, but see his drawings of the Hicarrah and of Indian women in Archer, Pls. 121 and 124. Also see Foster, "British Artists in India, 1760-1820," 52-53.

172 Letter from William Baillie, Calcutta, to Ozias Humphry, October 4, 1795, in Evan Cotton, "Letters from Bengal," 129. In an earlier letter, November 23, 1793, Baillie had written of Devis's intention to go home, "but I believe not with a fortune: poor fellow, had he not been so liberal in spirit, he might have saved, I doubt not, a handsome sum of money." "Letters from Bengal," 125-26.

173 On the Devis paintings of "The Economy of Human Life," see Mildred Archer, *India and British Portraiture*, 264-69; Alexander; and Pal and Dehejia, 136-37. .

174 In 1979, from "The Property of a Deceased Estate," Sotheby's auctioned 24 Devis paintings, originally acquired by Devis's friend John Biddulph between 1802 and 1810. Of these 19 paintings were from the series portraying Bengal occupations. The paintings are illustrated in the Sotheby catalogue, 21 March 1979. "The Pottery" was included as Lot 42. Purchased by a private collector, the painting was sold at auction in 1999 to the India Office Library. Twelve paintings from the Devis sale were exhibited as "Arts and Manufactures of Bengal" by Eyre & Hobhouse, London, Sept. 15-Oct. 19, 1979.

175 The engravings, 1800, are reproduced in Mildred Archer, *India and British Portraiture*, 258, Pls. 182 and 183. Archer also illustrates four of the paintings, 256-57, Pls. 178-181. The engraving of the pottery is reproduced in Pal and

Dehejia, 136, Pl. 133; the loom (in color) in Rohatgi and Godrej, eds., *India: A Pageant of Prints*, 5, Pl. 4.

176 Quoted in Archer and Lightbrown, 13 and Mildred Archer, *India and British Portraiture*, 229-30. See Archer, *India and British Portraiture*, 204-33, for an account of Hickey's life and work.

177 See Mildred Archer, *Early Views of India: The Picturesque Journeys of Thomas and William Daniell 1786-1794*.

178 5:729.

179 7:48-49. Füssli, in the *Allegemeines künstlerlexikon* (1814), 2:1675, also relies on Fiorillo. Füssli and Nagler, following Fiorillo, also confuse Solvyns's Calcutta etchings with the Orme pirated edition, *The Costume of Indoostan*.

180 Rohatgi, "The India Office Library's Prints of Calcutta," 12. Mildred Archer, *Early Views of India*, 13-36, reproduces the Daniell etchings of Calcutta and discusses their production. On Daniell's difficulties with the Calcutta etchings, see Godrej and Rohatgi, 27-29. Diarist William Hickey made 12 drawings in 1789 after the Daniell prints that identify, with a key for each, the particular houses and buildings portrayed. See Rohatgi, "The Growth of Georgian Calcutta Seen through the Eyes of British Artists," and Nisith R. Ray, "Calcutta Houses and Streets in 1789."

181 Losty, in *Calcutta: City of Palaces*, reproduces several Baillie etchings: Figs. 13, 31-35.

182 Mildred Archer, *India and British Portraiture*, 125.

183 Mabon, who had worked as an assistant to the artist James Wales in western India, moved to Calcutta in 1796, where he etched and published 20 plates as *Sketches Illustrative of Oriental Manners and Costumes*. The etchings were rather cartoon-like renderings of his drawings from western India. "B. Solwyns, Esq." [sic] was among the 160 subscribers listed for the set, offered at 30 rupees. See Mildred Archer, *India and British Portraiture*, 349.

184 Letter from William Baillie, Calcutta, November 23, 1793. Ozias Humphry Papers, HU/4/88-89, Royal Academy of Arts, London. Reprinted in Evan Cotton, "Letters from Bengal," 126.

185 February 6, 1794 (Vol. 20, No. 519), 2, reprinted in Seton-Karr, 2:575-77.

186 In the eighteenth century, "engraving" had come to mean any intaglio process, including etching, whereas "line-engraving" referred specifically to the use of the burin.

187 The Calcutta etching for Sec. X is titled "A View of a Bengalee Road in Calcutta." In the Paris edition, it is "The Black Town at Calcutta" (Pl. II.6). Solvyns did not include an etching of Hindu games in the Calcutta *Collection*, but it is in the Paris edition as "Pounchys [pachisi] and Other Games" (Pl. II.10).

188 *Aqua fortis* is nitric acid, used in etching. Royal paper, according to the *OED*, is of a size measuring 24 by 19 in. (61 x 48.3 cm.) as used for writing and 25 by 20 in. (63.5 x 50.8 cm.) for printing. Solvyns here may use the term "royal paper" simply to convey a more luxurious folio size, for (except for the large format prints) the etchings themselves are trimmed to approximately 36 x 25 cm. and are mounted on larger sheets measuring from 41 x 27 to 53 x 36.5 cm. See the discussion of the Calcutta edition in Chapter Three, pp. 91-93.

189 Leading merchants of Calcutta, with John Palmer (1767-1836) as senior partner. Under his direction, the firm grew into the great Palmer & Co., and John Palmer became the richest of all Calcutta merchants up to his bankruptcy in 1830. See H. E. A. Cotton, *Calcutta Old and New*, 473, 597.

190 March 6, 1794 (Vol. 20, No. 523), 2.

191 *Annual Register*, 1824, Appendix to Chronicle, 235, translated from Lesbroussart, 70-71.

192 Letter dated October 4, 1795. Ozias Humphry Papers, HU/4/112-117. Royal Academy of Arts, London. Speke acquired the Daniell paintings in a lottery sale by the Thomas Daniell in Calcutta, referred to in an earlier Baillie letter, November 23, 1793, Ozias Humphry Papers, HU/4/88-89, Royal Academy of Arts, London. On Speke, see Evan's note 64 to the edited papers, "Letters from Bengal," 130.

193 Letter dated October 4, 1795. Ozias Humphry Papers, HU/4/112-117. Royal Academy of Arts, London. Reprinted in Evan Cotton, "Letters from Bengal," 129-30.

194 Baillie, letter to Humphry in London, November 23, 1793, Ozias Humphry Papers, HU/4/88-89, Royal Academy of Arts, London. Reprinted in Evan Cotton, "Letters from Bengal," 125. One gold mohur was valued at 16 rupees. *Hobson-Jobson*, 573. (Cotton gives 3 gold mohurs as the price, perhaps a misreading of the handwriting, for Baillie advertised the set at 5 gold mohurs in the *Calcutta Gazette*, May 29, 1794). Also see Godrej and Rohatgi, *Scenic Splendours*, 30-31.

195 2:185.

196 Mildred and William Archer, *Indian Painting for the British 1770-1880*, 12, note the substantial prices charged by the Daniells. They judge Thomas Daniell's proposed twenty-four "Views in Hindostan," advertised in the *Calcutta Gazette* in 1795 at 200 rupees (about £22), as "priced high." The Daniell's *Oriental Scenery* (1795-1808), 144 colored aquatints, was published in England at £210– Rs. 1890 at the exchange rate of roughly Rs. 9 per £1.

197 *Calcutta Gazette*, Vol. 25, No. 640 (June 1, 1796).

198 Vol. 26, No. 661 (October 27, 1796).

199 *Calcutta Gazette*, October 30, 1794 (Vol. 22, No. 557), 1.

200 On Sir Thomas Anburey, see Godrej and Rohatgi, *Scenic Splendours*, 111, 147.

201 Mildred Archer, *India and British Portraiture*, 125. The artist Francisco Renaldi viewed the painting at Solvyns's house in 1796. Farington, who lived in Bengal from 1783 until his death in 1788, had begun a series of drawings of Indian festivals, known today only through four copies by a Company School artist, illustrated in Archer, Pls. 78-81.

202 *Calcutta Gazette*, August 20, 1795 (Vol. 23, No. 599), 2.

203 December 31, 1795 (Vol. 24, No. 618), 1.

204 Advertisement, *Calcutta Gazette*, November 24, 1796 (Vol. 26, No. 665), 2. A "card" is a brief published statement or request. From the advertisements, it seems that Solvyns's original proposal to deliver the etchings in installments was not followed, but that the etchings were delivered only when the full collection was complete.

205 For the six libraries holding copies of the 1796 imprint, see Appendix, "Solvyns in Libraries."

206 The 1799 edition is listed in Abbey, Entry 421, 2:377-381.

207 Wilkinson, in *The Makers of Indian Colonial Silver*, 53-54, gives Dormieux's dates of residence in Calcutta as 1798 to 1821, but the 1796 printing of the Solvyns *Collection*, with its title by Dormieux, moves his time in Calcutta to an earlier date. Indeed, the Dormieux family (probably Huguenot) had long been in India, and Francis was likely born there.

208 See, for example, *Oriental Miscellany*, published in 1798, for which Dormieux also made engravings from various drawings.

209 See Kattenhorn's entry in the catalogue of British drawings in the India Office Library, 6-8. Kattenhorn, 6, writes that the subjects of "Hindoostany Characters" suggest that Dormieux had planned to produce a set similar to Solvyns's portrayal of the Hindus, but the engravings are small and there is no suggestion of an attempt to put together a systematic portrayal in the manner of Solvyns, nor is there a suggestion of any influence by Solvyns, either in form of the figures or in their treatment.

210 Of the various copies of the 1799 Calcutta edition that I have examined or about which I have specific information, only two (the copies in the New York Public Library and in the Buffalo and Erie County Public Library) bear the Dormieux name on the title page.

211 Lesbroussart, 71. For a detailed discussion of the mounting and the paper used, see Chapter Three, pp. 92-93.

212 There is reference to him in an advertisement that Solvyns placed in the *Calcutta Gazette*, October 19, 1797 (Vol. 28, No. 712), p. 3.

213 In a letter to Ozias Humphry in London, November 23, 1793, Baillie writes that he will employ native artists to assist in his preparing his "Twelve Views of Calcutta." "The native artists tho' totally incapable of taking advice themselves can copy extremely well. All Daniel's [sic] were stained principally by natives." Ozias Humphry Papers, HU/4/88-89, Royal Academy of Arts, London. Reprinted in Evan Cotton, "Letters from Bengal," 125. Also see Mildred Archer, *Early Views of India*, 15-16.

214 Shaw, 196.

215 The set of watercolors is in the Victoria and Albert Museum, London, Department of Prints, Drawings and Paintings, Acquisition number 8937.1-98, 8937.98a-247, Press mark S-20.

216 With nearly all printing equipment and materials imported from Europe, printing costs in late eighteenth century Calcutta were much higher than in London. On printing in Calcutta, see Shaw; also see Nikhil Sarkar, "Printing and the Spirit of Calcutta."

217 Wilkins (1749/1750-1836) was a founding member of the Asiatic Society and translator of the *Bhagavadgītā.*

218 *The Government Gazette* (Calcutta), May 18, 1826 (Vol. 41, No. 573), p. 4. Esthetic judgments of Solvyns's work are discussed in Chapters Two and Three.

219 "Baltazard Solvyns and the Indian Picturesque," 15.

220 Gallery notes for an exhibition of Solvyns etchings, Hartnoll & Eyre Ltd., London, July 18-28, 1978.

221 The advertisements appeared in the same issue, October 19, 1797 (Vol. 28, No. 712), p. 3.

222 *Calcutta Gazette*, October 14, 1802 (Vol. 38, No. 972), p. 1.

223 The copy of Solvyns's *Catalogue* for the Calcutta etchings (from the library of J. R. Abbey) in the Yale Center for British Art, New Haven, bears the handwritten note of the original owner: "These Etchings were begun by Mr Solvyns on a liberal subscription, viz 250 Rupees each set, in the year 1793, & the Copy to which this a Catalogue was delivered April 27th 1803–Mr S. has indeed been finishing & delivering Copies occasionally these three years past." Abbey, 381.

224 Mildred Archer, "India and the Illustrated Book," 13.

225 "The Captains of the homeward-bound Indiamen demand eight thousand rupees for the passage of a single person. . . . Forbes, as quoted in Goldsbourne, Notes, 354.

Chapter Two

Return to Europe: *Les Hindoûs*

Balthazar Solvyns sailed for Europe in 1803 on what was to be an ill-fated voyage. As with much in the accounts we have of Solvyns's life, information on his departure from India is incomplete and inconsistent. By one report, he departed from Calcutta in June 1803 aboard the *Phoenix*. This was a common name for ships, but a ship of that name did leave Calcutta for Rangoon at that time.[1] Rangoon would have been an unusual stop for a ship bound for Europe, as it was more typically a port of call on route to China. If this was, in fact, Solvyns's ship, it may have proceeded to Penang and, with likely calls at Madras and Bombay, on toward Europe. But then Solvyns may simply have been aboard another ship.

Solvyns provides no account of his voyage, but according to De Paepe, an advocate in Ghent who in 1837 published a biographical profile on Solvyns for *La Revue Belge*, his ship was seized by the French and taken to the Isle de France (Mauritius). The Peace of Amiens had just been broken: Britain and France were again at war and would remain so for twelve years.[2] In Mauritius, the French colonial militia, assuming Solvyns to be English, took him prisoner. Finally able to convince them of his citizenship and status as an artist and scientist, he was given permission to return home to Antwerp, which had by then come under Napoleon's rule. Solvyns sailed from Mauritius for France aboard a French ship. Off the coast of Spain, a violent storm wrecked his ship, and reports of his death had already spread when Solvyns, having escaped harm, arrived in Paris, where he became the object of flattering attention.[3]

In the earliest essay on Solvyns's life, Lebroussart, in 1824, wrote that in the storm, Solvyns abandoned everything else he possessed on board the ship in a successful effort to save his drawings and notes.[4] Lebroussart makes no reference to copies of the etchings that Solvyns surely would have brought with him. If Solvyns had brought the copper plates from Calcutta, they were evidently lost or destroyed. Nagler's *Neues sllgemeines künstler-lexikon* (1847), in the entry for Solvyns, states that the plates had become oxidized and could no longer be used. This was the reason, according to Nagler, that Solvyns prepared his new work on the Hindus.[5]

Marriage to Marie Anne Greenwood

Upon his return from India in 1804, Solvyns settled in Brussels, residing on the rue de la Liberté. Although members of the Solvyns family, including Balthazar's brother, Pierre Jean, served prominently as officials in Antwerp under Napoleon, Balthazar was placed briefly under police surveillance because of suspected sympathies for England—perhaps both for his years in Calcutta and because of his marriage to an English woman.[6]

Solvyns married Marie Anne (Mary Ann) Greenwood on November 15, 1804. Marie Anne, twenty years his junior, was born January 16, 1782, and, according to the marriage certificate, was then living in St. Omer (now in French Flanders) with her parents, Charles and Sara Greenwood. Her father, who later moved to Ghent, is identified as a *rentier*, of independent means. The banns were published both in St. Omer and in Antwerp, and the wedding, in Brussels, was conducted by the mayor in his capacity as the city's registrar. There were four witnesses—three *rentiers* and one merchant.[7]

In the marriage certificate, Solvyns is identified as a *négociant*, a merchant. Ten days before his marriage, Solvyns similarly identified himself as a *négociant* in a petition to obtain an exemption from the second publication of the banns for the marriage.[8] In seeking the exemption, he was, he wrote, "motivated upon the fact he was obligated to embark . . . immediately for the Isle de France [Mauritius], where major affairs of commerce call him." The dispensation was granted.

The document suggests that Solvyns, living in Brussels, had decided to abandon art and enter into some business venture that would take him to the Isle de France. The island had been settled by the French in 1722 and was both a major center for French commerce with the East Indies and an important way station for ships rounding the Cape of Good Hope in the voyage to India. (The British, who took the island in 1810, returned its name to Mauritius.) There is no record of what Solvyns's business might have been, but he did not go, for Solvyns, with Marie Anne, soon established residence in Paris,[9] where he was to take up the publication of *Les Hindoûs*.

Solvyns may have met Marie Anne through Greenwood family acquaintances in Ostend, where he had lived for a time before going to India. Ostend had a substantial British colony, many taking nationality of the Austrian Netherlands, and among them was a certain N. Greenwood, who served as an official by appointment of the Emperor Joseph II.[10] Solvyns is likely to have known him, and through him perhaps Marie Anne's parents—though, in 1790, when Solvyns left for Calcutta, Marie Anne would have been only eight years old. Solvyns might also have been introduced to Marie Anne's family through Calcutta connections, for there was an army officer named John Greenwood at Fort William, in Calcutta,[11] who Solvyns may have come to know. In any case, Solvyns's marriage to Marie Anne Greenwood was arranged very soon after his return from India.

Solvyns family records describe Marie Anne as "a kind and charming woman of strong character and diligence." In addition to securing the release of her husband's nephew as a prisoner of war in England, she was also responsible for the release of several English prisoners held in France. Intriguingly, but without supporting documents, the entry for Marie Anne in the Solvyns family genealogy album states that she was "a close friend of the Empress Josephine of France" and "made several voyages to and from England for various reasons on behalf of the Empress."[12]

Les Hindoûs

According to De Paepe's 1837 account of Solvyns's life,[13] soon after his return from India, Solvyns showed his drawings and prints of the Hindus to Joseph Van Praet (1745-1837),[14] a longtime friend and Flemish compatriot. Van Praet had attained great distinction as Conservator of Printed Books at the Bibliothèque nationale de France and, in 1814, was named to the Legion of Honor. Impressed by Solvyns's work, Van Praet urged him to prepare a more lavish edition of the etchings, and it may well have been through Van Praet that Solvyns was able to gain the attention of the Institut de France and secure favor of the officials who proved financially crucial to the completion of his enterprise.

Solvyns's decision to prepare a new set of etchings from his drawings of the Hindus was also prompted by the publication of a pirated copy of his work in London. In 1804-1805, the firm of Edward Orme brought out an edition of Solvyns's etchings, acknowledging him, but without his permission. Dedicated to "the Directors of the Honourable the United East India Company," the volume, *The Costume of Indostan,* with 60 plates, smaller in size than the originals, corresponded closely to a series of volumes on costumes published by William Miller.[15] Each Orme plate is accompanied by a descriptive text, in both English and French, usually an expanded (sometimes erroneous) paraphrase from Solvyns's 1799 *Catalogue*.

Orme published the pirated edition in parts in 1804 and 1805, with an undated title page: "The Costume of Indostan, elucidated by Sixty coloured Engravings; with Descriptions in English and French, taken in the years 1798 and 1799. By Balt. Solvyns, of Calcutta. Published by Edward Orme, Printseller to His Majesty and the Royal Family, 59 New Bond Street."[16] It was printed by W. Bulmer & Co., Cleveland-Row. The Orme edition was reissued in 1807 under the title *The Costume of Hindostan* and printed by J. Hayes, Dartmouth Street, Westminister. The price was £8.8s.

Solvyns was angered by the Orme publication, and in his introduction to the first volume of *Les Hindoûs*, published in 1808, he attributes his decision to bring out the Paris edition of the etchings in part to his desire to make amends for Orme. Solvyns "found himself in some sort obliged to publish the result of his long and scrupulous observations by the abuse which he saw made of his name and of his works to lead the public into error by giving authority to incorrect notations and mutilated descriptions. A Mr. Orme published in London, a piecemeal collection, a sort of counterfeit of a set of sketches which I had formerly published at Calcutta, and which even in the country itself were received with great applause."[17]

With the decision to abandon any consideration of a career in business, Solvyns now set about to re-establish himself as an artist and to begin preparations for what was to become his great work, *Les Hindoûs*. In the meantime, in 1806, he sent a painting for the art salon at Ghent—"The Strand at Flushing [Vlissingen] with Several Ships."[18] The whereabouts of the painting—or its survival—is unknown.

We have no record of when Balthazar and Marie Anne moved from Brussels, but in Paris, the Solvyns first lived on the rue du Lille in Faubourg Saint-Germain. By 1807, they had moved to Saint

André des Arcs,[19] No. 11, the address for "Chez Solvyns" on the title pages for the first three volumes of *Les Hindoûs*. The fourth volume, published in 1812, carried a new address, rue de Beaune, Faubourg Saint-Germain, No. 2, to which he moved sometime during the course of that year.[20]

Les Hindoûs Proposed

Solvyns had a "Prospectus" (in French)[21] for *Les Hindoûs* put out in 1807 by the bookseller H. Nicolle, whose premises, at 12, rue de la Seine, was a short walk from the artist's residence.

> The modern and commercial history of Hindostan has been the subject of research by several writers. Some have endeavored to reveal the mysteries of the sacred language of the Brahmins and to penetrate the antiquities of India. The Academy of Calcutta, otherwise known as the Asiatic Society, especially deserves the gratitude of Europe in these diverse respects.
>
> But the mores, the customs of the Hindus, their way of life in the civil order and under the powerful influence of their religion; the description of castes or diverse professions, of the costumes characterizing each of these castes, of the machines, tools, and instruments employed in industry, which serve the needs of life or its pleasures, has been illustrated by no one before: it is, however, we dare to think, one of the best ways of portraying the Hindus such as they have always existed.
>
> M. Solvyns, from Antwerp, has undertaken this description.
>
> During a sojourn of 15 years in Bengal,[22] he associated himself with pundits and brahmins, and he was able to acquire local knowledge and choose with discernment all the materials for such a work. M. Solvyns, also bringing the great advantage of having studied drawing and painting in Paris under one of our most able painters, M. Vincent, has faithfully drawn, in the presence of the subjects, everything that he saw and observed; he had no need for recourse to foreign hands and to draw, as is often the case, from mere tales or from notes.
>
> M. Solvyns undertook to publish in Calcutta, under the eyes of those who could judge his descriptions most reliably, the sketches of the work he is announcing today; and despite local difficulties of every kind, he produced a certain number of copies of his drawings, with a simple catalogue in English. An unsatisfactory edition was published in London based on one of these copies.
>
> The sketches published in Calcutta enjoyed great success: the translation done in London, though abridged, was no less well-received. M. Solvyns therefore dares flatter himself that the complete description of the Hindus executed in Paris under his direction and to a great degree by himself can be of interest; it will certainly be the only original and complete work on the Hindus.
>
> It is indeed not a purely mercantile speculation undertaken by the author, but it is rather that he takes great delight in proposing to describe a people and mores that he long observed and which must be of interest in so many aspects to scholars and to the curious. He hopes that they will reward him by an encouraging reception for the pains and sacrifices his work has cost him; through recourse to his own means, he has protected this undertaking from every kind of delay, and nothing can thwart its execution.
>
> The portfolio of M. Solvyns contains 252 drawings. They will form, with a summary explanation in French and English, which will be found facing each plate, four large volumes *in-folio* in *atlantique* format.[23]
>
> The first volume will contain the castes or professions of the Hindus, with their divisions and subdivisions, as they have been approximately established according to the laws of Menu [Manu], the legislator of the Hindus, and such as they exist in the hierarchy or degradation of status, from the Brahmins to the Sudras. These plates will also contain descriptions of machines, tools, and instruments in use among this people.
>
> The second volume will contain the dress of men and women, fakirs or religious beggars, the different ways of smoking the hookah, and the musical instruments.
>
> The third volume will contain the description of palanquins or sedan chairs, carriages harnessed to horses or dragged by oxen, pleasure or promenade barques, and boats of laden or transport.
>
> The fourth volume will contain domestics employed in the service of the grandees of the country and of Europeans or rich foreigners residing in Hindostan.

M. Solvyns, having wished to depict only Hindus and what concerns them exclusively, had to exclude with great care everything foreign to them. It is only in the last volume, in the section on domestics, that he introduced Mohammedans, because they alone are admitted into the service of the Hindus.

Each plate, being destined to represent a particular subject, will offer in the foreground a principal figure and, behind, accessory figures relating to the subject so that one can find and easily distinguish, according to the profession or occupation illustrated, all the attributes, furniture, tools, acts or operations that characterize it and develop it completely. There will be at the head of each installment, except for the last volume, a double-sized plate that will represent the grouping of several subjects. These plates will all relate to general views of the country, to phenomena or scenes of nature proper to Hindostan; to festivities, expiations, and religious ceremonies of the Hindus.

A Preliminary Discourse will be found at the head of the work, with an illustrated frontispiece; and at the end a vocabulary or explanation of words of the language of the country.

The execution, in all, will be in keeping with the importance and interest of the work. The subjects, sketched after nature and engraved by M. Solvyns, will be colored by the most competent printers on vellum grand colombier.

The four volumes will be set forth in 42 installments of 6 plates each. The price of each installment is 36 f.

In April 1808, *Le Moniteur*, the official government newspaper under Napoleon, published an unsigned article under the heading "Histoire-Beaux-Arts," about *Les Hindoûs*. It was, in fact, Solvyns's own "Prospectus," word-for-word, save for a few changes at the end. It noted that eight installments, *livraisons*, had thus far been issued and that their "execution is an indication of the importance and interest of the work."[24]

As originally conceived, *Les Hindoûs, ou description e leurs mœurs, coutumes et cérémonies,* was to appear in 42 installments, in large folio, each with six plates, including one double-plate. The price per installment was 36 francs, or 1512 fr. for the entire work—a staggering price. Although Solvyns subsequently added six installments for a total of 48, with 288 plates, the "Prospectus" provided a detailed description of the project that was to consume Solvyns for the next five years. Only one element of the projected work was never realized: the glossary of Indian words, promised for the end of the last volume, was not included in the completed publication.

According to the plan, two installments were to be published each month, the first appearing in 1807.[25] Each installment of six prints, with explanatory text, was accompanied by a title page in French, with the number of the *livraison* handwritten in ink. The earliest of two title pages used for the installments is dated 1807 and gives Crapelet as the publisher. Charles Crapelet (1762-1809) headed an established Paris firm, but within a fairly short time, perhaps under pressures of the French publishing "crisis" that brought many firms to bankruptcy or simply because the magnitude of the project was beyond the firm, Crapelet gave up the publication of *Les Hindoûs* to Mame Frères. Mame, a distinguished publishing house in Tours, was then just starting in Paris and likely saw *Les Hindoûs* as a way to bring visibility and prestige to the new Paris venture. Although Solvyns continued to use the "Crapelet" title page indiscriminately with some later installments,[26] he prepared a new title page to include reference to his dedication of the work to the Institut de France and his new publisher, Mame Frères. The first volume of *Les Hindoûs*, dated 1808, carries the imprint "De l'Imprimerie de Mame Frères."

The new installment title page, as translated from the French, reads:

The Hindus
Description of their Manners, Customs, and Ceremonies, etc.
drawn according to nature in Bengal
and represented in 252 plates.
By F. Balthazard Solvyns;
Engraved with acid and completed by himself.
The work is dedicated to the Institut de France.

There follows the *livraison* number (by hand), Solvyns's address at the Place Saint-André-des-Arcs, bookseller H. Nicolle, publisher Mame Frères, and year.

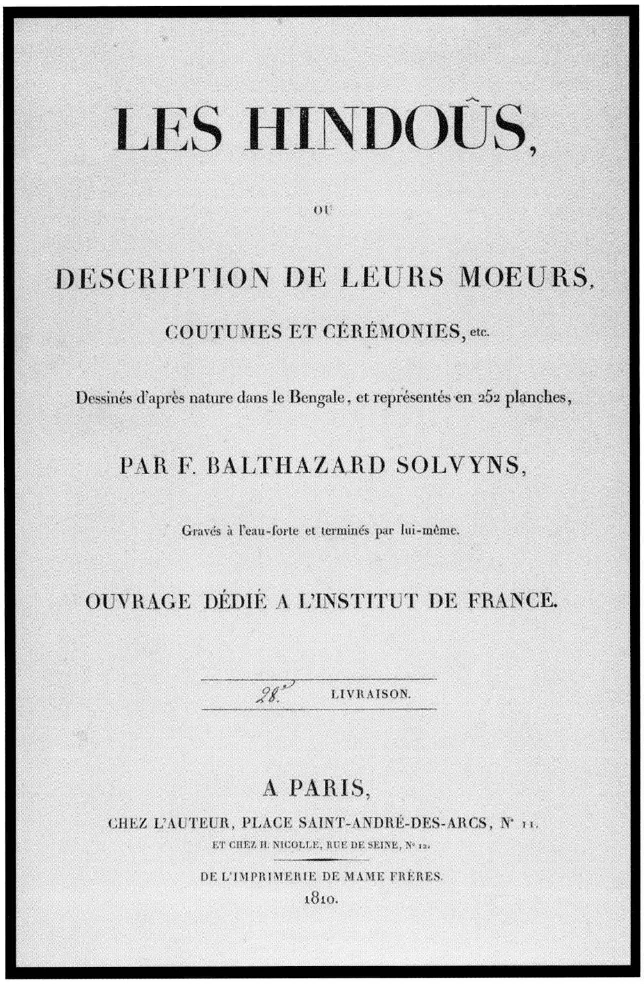

LES HINDOÛS,

OU

DESCRIPTION DE LEURS MOEURS,

COUTUMES ET CÉRÉMONIES, etc.

Dessinés d'après nature dans le Bengale, et représentés en 252 planches,

PAR F. BALTHAZARD SOLVYNS,

Gravés à l'eau-forte et terminés par lui-même.

OUVRAGE DÉDIÉ A L'INSTITUT DE FRANCE.

28.e LIVRAISON.

A PARIS,

CHEZ L'AUTEUR, PLACE SAINT-ANDRÉ-DES-ARCS, N° 11.

ET CHEZ H. NICOLLE, RUE DE SEINE, N° 12.

DE L'IMPRIMERIE DE MAME FRÈRES.

1810.

Pl. I.22. Title page for *Livraison* 28.
Courtesy Partha Mitter.

In the original "Prospectus," Solvyns announced the publication of *Les Hindoûs* with 252 plates in 42 installments, and the title pages for the installments continued to bear the number 252 even after Solvyns had decided to expand the edition to 288 plates in 48 installments—a decision that must have come some time before the publication of the first volume in 1808.[27] For the 252 plates initially projected for the Paris edition, Solvyns incorporated most of the subjects portrayed in the Calcutta *Collection*, with new etchings corresponding, more or less closely, to the originals. Inexplicably, he omits several subjects from the earlier edition and adds new ones. The 36 etchings of the additional six installments constitute the last half of Volume IV, published in 1812, and have no basis in the earlier Calcutta edition. They include 30 prints depicting plants and animals and a final section of 6 prints (to which Solvyns refers in the Preliminary Discourse to Volume I) portraying the heads of Indians "with characteristic features."[28]

The Preliminary Discourse and the title page for Volume I were issued only as the final installments for the first volume were completed in 1808. The twelve installments for Volume II were completed, with its Introduction and title page, two years later, in 1810. Those for Volume III followed in 1811 and for Volume IV in 1812.

The first page of each volume bears the title, *Les Hindoûs, ou Description de leurs moeurs, coutumes et cérémonies* [*The Hindus, or a Description of their Mores, Customs, and Ceremonies*]. The formal title page then follows, with an etching depicting a scene of life in Bengal.

The etching on the title page of Volume I (Pl. I.23) portrays a brahmin priest on his way to perform *pūjā*, worship. He carries a śaṅkh, or conch shell, and ghaṇṭā, bell, used in religious ritual. Solvyns portrays the śaṅkh and ghaṇṭā in his series of etchings of musical instruments (Pl. II.146). In the water behind the priest, Hindus engage in their ablutions. The boats are a peacock-headed morpaṅkhī and, to its left, a

LES HINDOÛS,

PAR F. BALTAZARD SOLVYNS.

TOME PREMIER.

PARIS,

CHEZ L'AUTEUR, PLACE SAINT-ANDRE-DES-ARCS, N° 11,

Et chez H. NICOLLE, rue de Seine, n° 12, à la librairie stéréotype.

DE L'IMPRIMERIE DE MAME FRÈRES.

1808.

Pl. I.23. Title Page, *Les Hindoûs*, Vol. I.

Pl. I.24. Etching from the title page *Les Hindoûs*, Vol. II.

pinnace, a native yacht. Solvyns portrays each boat in separate etchings (Pls. II.231 and II.229).

The etching on the title page of Volume II (Pl. I.24) depicts a woman, among other figures, at Calcutta's famous Kālīghāṭ temple (Pl. II.4). The etching on the title page of Volume III (Pl. I.25) portrays an Indian at leisure smoking one of the many varieties of the kaliyūm hukā (Pl. II.210). In the etching on the title page for Volume IV (Frontispiece, Pl. I.1), Solvyns portrays himself, attended by three servants, one of whom prepares the snake hukā (Pl. II.208) enjoyed by European gentlemen in India.

Three hundred copies of *Les Hindoûs* were printed.[29] They were printed in folio, measuring 57 x 41.5 cm., on high quality, off-white wove paper, described by Solvyns as "*vélin grand colombier*."[30] There is no record as to the number of subscribers who received the installments as they were issued, but, as in the general practice of the time, most sales were made for bound volumes. But even those receiving the individual installments would have had them bound, as bindings typically were ordered separately according to the taste and pocketbook of the subscriber.[31] Indeed, very few examples of the Paris etchings exit in their original, unbound *livraisons*. Bindings for *Les Hindoûs* varied enormously, from simple boards to the finest tooled leather.

The publication of *Les Hindoûs,* according to De Paepe, was a "sensation." "No author had before published by his own resources a work of such importance, with such luxurious abundance of engravings. . . . Works of this achievement had only been published with the cooperation of the government." Solvyns counted the most famous people in science, government, and diplomacy as his subscribers. They were, De Paepe relates, the only subscribers he could expect, for the expense of the work made it inaccessible to those with lesser fortunes. "Its format permitted it to take its place only in vast libraries."[32]

Pl. I.25. Etching from the title page *Les Hindoûs*, Vol. III.

As others earlier had been dependent upon government support for such lavish publications, Solvyns, soon after beginning the project, sought official support and subvention. He turned to the Institut de France. In November 1806, the Institut's division of fine arts (*la classe des beaux-arts*) appointed a commission to examine Solvyns's original drawings and the newly published etchings. Three of France's leading artists were charged with the responsibility: the great Neo-classical painter Jacques Louis David (1748-1825); Nicholas-Antoine Tauney (1755-1830), who had received many commissions from Napoleon for battle paintings; and François-André Vincent (1746-1816), Solvyns's teacher in Paris in 1778.[33] They reported favorably, and on December 10, 1806, the Perpetual Secretary for the Institut's section on fine arts advised Solvyns that the illustrious body had accepted the publication of this work under its patronage. In his letter to Solvyns, the Secretary wrote that the Institut had received the first installment of the "Description of the Hindus" and the attached prospectus and that they had been presented to the four sections of the Institut. The work was welcomed with interest and esteem. "It was observed especially, as a particular merit, the character of faithfulness to local detail that is lacking in almost all engravings of picturesque travels." The Secretary concluded his letter by thanking Solvyns in the name of the Institut for the dedication and congratulating him for his work.[34]

Solvyns expressed his gratitude in an effusive dedication to the Institut de France, printed in French only, following the title page to the first volume of *Les Hindoûs*. "I beseech you, gentlemen," he concluded, "to accept the homage as well as the respect with which I have the honor of being your very humble and very obedient servant. F. Balthazard Solvyns, Author, Engraver, and Publisher of the Description of the Hindus."

Even as he was working to bring out the first volume of the great folio edition of *Les Hindoûs*, Solvyns announced, in 1808, a quarto edition to be published with 252 plates. The "Prospectus" reprinted the description of the project that he had earlier published, but in an addendum, Solvyns justified the quarto edition by explaining that "a large number of collectors have expressed regret that in its present form and price [*Les Hindoûs*] was destined only for the libraries of rich patrons of the arts when, however, it is indispensable to all who would like to acquire special knowledge of the Hindus." Issued in installments, this less expensive collection would be accompanied by explanatory text in French, English, and German. The price for each installment of six uncolored etchings was 10 francs.

On April 1, 1808, Solvyns sent a printed letter to booksellers briefly describing his undertaking. "I forward to you the Prospectus as a means of becoming acquainted with the work and of collecting subscriptions. You will enjoy the customary discount." He concluded by announcing that the first installment in quarto would be placed on sale "in the course of this month."[35]

Solvyns soon issued seven installments, with a total of 42 plates, but the quarto edition was never continued.[36] Solvyns did the etchings himself, working either from his original drawings or the Calcutta etchings, to which they correspond more closely in detail and background than to the new folio prints.[37] Solvyns's obituary in the *Annual Registrar* for 1824 judged the quarto etchings, both in "actual beauty" and in "the execution of the plates, . . not inferior to the large edition."[38]

French Government Support

As Solvyns began work on the etchings for the grand folio edition of *Les Hindoûs*, he faced mounting expenses. With the aid of well-connected friends in Paris, he sought a subvention from the French government to enable him to move forward in the ambitious publishing venture. Under Napoleon, France sought the expansion of both imperial power and knowledge. In his military expedition to Egypt in 1799, Napoleon brought an array of scientists, scholars, and artists to record every aspect of its land and civilization and, by his order, initiated publication of the monumental *Description de l'Egypte*. With Napoleon's dream of conquering India, the French government might well be disposed to supporting so grand a publication as Solvyns proposed for the portrayal of the Hindus.

On December 24, 1807, the Chief of the Bureau of Fine Arts, B. Neuville, prepared a report to the Minister of the Interior, Joseph Fouché,[39] recommending that the government support Solvyns's project for the publication of *Les Hindoûs*, noting that the commission charged by the division of fine arts of the Institut de France to examine the work had praised it highly. He urged that the government subscribe to "this fine enterprise, all the more so because the author is in need of some encouragement."

The work, Neuville wrote, would have 42 installments of six prints each. Each installment would cost 36 francs, and the complete set cost 1512 fr. Neuville proposed that the government subscribe to six copies, for a sum of 9072 fr., to be paid as the installments are issues. "Thus far this year," he wrote, "only 216 fr are to be paid for the first installments that have already appeared."[40]

The French bureaucracy moved slowly, for it was not until June 30, 1808, that the Minister wrote to Solvyns that he would subscribe for six sets of the work. "You will please deposit at the archives of the Ministry the installments of this work as they appear, each installment getting you 36 fr."[41] By this time, Solvyns had decided to increase the number of installments from 42 to 48, but throughout the correspondence on the subvention, the cost per set remained at 1512 fr., rather than at the new price of 1728 fr.

In any case, the subsidy was in no way sufficient to meet the costs of the project, and over the next three years, Solvyns repeatedly sought additional support.[42] On May 2, 1809, Neuville reported to the Minister of the Interior that "Mr. Solvyns has said, given his present circumstances, that he would be unable to continue publishing his work if the government did not help him." Neuville requested that the Ministry's subscription be increased to 15 sets. He expressed his personal support for the project, characterizing *Les Hindoûs* as offering a "truth and originality rare in works of this type." The Institut de France, he wrote, had urged Solvyns to publish the work and had accepted its dedication. The Solvyns project had secured support from the highest levels, for Neuville then adds, "His Highness the Prince of Bénévent [the ubiquitous Talleyrand][43] reminds you of the promise made to the artist and asks you to support his enterprise more efficaciously."

A week later, with heightened urgency, Neuville again wrote to the Minister, explaining that because expected library subscriptions had not been forthcoming, Solvyns was financially pressed and had been unable to produce and deliver the installments as scheduled. It was thus all the more important that the Ministry increase its subscription.[44] The Minister agreed and so advised the artist. Solvyns responded in a letter to Fouché, dated August 10, 1809, in which he expressed his gratitude for the support and encouragement offered through the subscriptions. He wrote that he had thus far published one and one-half volumes of *Les Hindoûs*, but that "Despite favorable reviews, the circumstances of libraries renders my work difficult. . . ."

Solvyns and his friends in the Ministry continued to push for enhanced support, and in late August 1809, the Minister of the Interior agreed to increase the subscription to 35 sets, bringing the total subsidy to 52,920 fr.—a very substantial amount, though paid out only as each installment was completed. On January 12, 1811, as Solvyns was in the midst of work on the third volume, he wrote to the Minister that the publisher was experiencing losses and delays because of the bad state of finances of several book dealers. He requested that the Ministry provide an advance of one half of what it would owe him for the remaining installments of the third volume—thus enabling him to finish the work on schedule. The request was approved, and in July 1811, Solvyns requested a similar advance for the fourth volume. This too was approved, and the last volume of *Les Hindoûs* was published in 1812.

A "Prospectus" for the Completed Work

On January 1, 1812, Solvyns published a "Prospectus" providing a full description of the complete work,[45]

> *Les Hindoûs,* or a Description of their mores, costumes, ceremonies, etc., etc., sketched after nature in Bengal and represented in 292 plates, with [including] four frontispieces, by F. Balthazard Solvyns, engraved and completed by him. Four volumes grand in-folio, on *vélin grand colombier* [a fine wove paper], the subjects printed in color, the text in French and in English.
>
> The purpose of this work is to give a satisfying idea of the mores, customs, and way of life of the Hindus, according to the observations the author had the opportunity to make in this respect during his long sojourn in the midst of this people. The details one finds in the accounts of other travelers, far from satisfying the curiosity of the public merely excited it all the more, and for a long time one has felt the need of having a complete description of everything concerning this singular nation. To do so required a combination of favorable circumstances that the author was happy enough to realize; that is what stirred him, as soon as he returned to Paris, to engrave the sketches he had made in India and to accompany them with an explanatory text facing the engraving.
>
> Here in general is the distribution of the materials contained in this work.
>
> The first volume includes a detailed description of the castes and subdivisions of classes among the Hindus; first, the religious castes; the brahmins, their diverse sects, superstitions, customs, function, costumes, etc.; second, the warrior caste; details on the military class, on the princes and grandees of this country, their authority, ornaments, privileges, etc.; third, the merchant caste; the objects of trade in India, their industrial practices, traffic, and speculations; fourth, the working and servant class; that embraces all the professions and all the trades, and sometimes singular mores and customs of the Hindu people; the plates which represent the individuals of this caste also contain the machines, tools, and instruments which they utilize in their diverse occupations. The large prints in this volume represent religious festivals, processions, expiations of the Hindus, objects of mythology, etc.
>
> The second volume contains subjects as various as those of the preceding one; they are the costumes and the adornment of Hindu men and women, the description of the way of life, their amusements. The class of fakirs or devotees is described there in great detail, each sect of this class being represented in a single print, accompanied by an account of their strange customs and pious follies. The music of the Hindus also occupies a great part of this volume; all the instruments the Hindus use, whether in their public ceremonies or special celebrations, are represented there and described with the greatest possible precision. In the large prints of this volume, one

sees, as in the preceding one, several ceremonies and solemn religious occasions; the last four are reserved for the description of ceremonies performed by the women who burn themselves with the bodies of their husbands. This custom, which has never been faithfully represented, is seen in the prints just as the author observed and sketched it on the very spot.

The third volume includes all sorts of subjects relating to the costumes of the Hindus; we find there, among others, the descriptions of their palanquins or sedan chairs, carriages harnessed to horses and oxen, and boats for pleasure, cargo, and transport. Everything concerning the construction of vessels or naval architecture among the Hindus is treated extensively in this volume. The large prints of the third volume represent some remarkable phenomena and views of Hindustan and of the other parts of India that the author visited.

The fourth volume contains the numerous class of domestics employed in the service of the grandees of India and of Europeans or other rich foreigners residing in this country. As already announced, there are no large prints in this volume, but one does find there trees, plants, animals, insects, birds, and the best known fish in the land of the Hindus. To complete this last volume, the last installment contains rather large heads to acquaint people perfectly with the physiognomy of each caste with its subdivisions.

At the head of each volume there is a frontispiece and a preliminary discussion, and at the end a list of objects contained in each volume.

The execution of the calcographical and typographical parts respond in every way to the importance of the work. The subjects, all sketched from nature and engraved by the author himself, are colored and printed with the greatest care.

Solvyns here refers to his dedication of *Les Hindoûs* to the Institut de France, and he quotes, in full, the letter of the Perpetual Secretary praising the work. Solvyns then provides a price list:

Price for the complete work in 48 installments	1,728fr.
Four unbound volumes	1,760
Bound in calf leather	1,808
There are several copies retouched by the author	2,600

A Matter of Money

In the "Prospectus," Solvyns offers copies hand-colored (*retouchés*) by himself, but among various copies of *Les Hindoûs* examined, there is no discernible difference in coloring. The plates are printed in color *à la poupée*, with additional color wash applied by hand.[46] Whether Solvyns or, more likely, a colorist employed by the publisher applied the wash is unknown, but the applications are uniform from copy to copy, and nothing suggests differences that would warrant the price differential. What is clear, however, is that 2600 francs,—or, indeed, 1728 fr.—was a very substantial amount of money, and there may well have been no subscribers for the much more expensive offering. The cost of *Les Hindoûs* was enormous by any standard: In 1812, for the price of the four unbound volumes, at 1760 fr., one could have purchased a good house in the Paris suburbs. Clearly, these were volumes only for great libraries and the wealthiest collectors.

Les Hindoûs was published with the highest standard of quality in paper and printing, but it was by no means unique. The finest books of the period were those published by Pierre Didot, and the most magnificent—just a few years after *Les Hindoûs*—was Joseph Redouté's *Les Roses*, containing 170 prints, published in folio in three volumes, 1817-1824, at a cost of 1200 francs.[47]

Solvyns, with his French and English text, envisioned a market for *Les Hindoûs* in Great Britain despite ongoing war.[48] As much as Solvyns despised the Orme pirated edition of his work, it had done well commercially and had served to introduce his name and work across the channel. Moreover, the success of the Daniells' sumptuous *Oriental Scenery*—priced at 200 guineas (£210)—gave ample evidence of British interest in the portrayal of India. *Les Hindoûs* was priced in Great Britain at 100 guineas[49]—half the cost of the Daniells' 144 aquatints, but still a substantial price. In the United States, *Les Hindoûs* is reported to have been priced at $500.[50]

An advertisement for *Les Hindoûs* appeared in London's *Quarterly Review* in 1813. After describing the set of four volumes, the bookseller stated that "There are only 300 Copies, one half of which have been subscribed for the Continent by the different crowned heads, public institutions, and distinguished literati, from all of whom it has met with unqualified approbation. The remaining 150 Copies have been purposely reserved for this Country, to which it is presumed that a Work of this nature must be peculiarly interesting. It has met with the entire approbation of Sir Joseph Banks, and other distinguished literary and scientific persons in England; and the Author ventures to presume, that from the accuracy and fidelity of his Delineations, his Work will be found worthy of a place in every distinguished Collection, both public and private, in the British dominions."[51]

The expense of producing *Les Hindoûs* had taxed Solvyns's every resource and had exhausted his wife's fortune. His hopes of compensation, however, were frustrated by the deepening economic and political crisis that attended the completion of the project and release of the final volume in 1812. The whole enterprise had been pursued in the course of the Napoleonic Wars, with much of Europe in turmoil and with France itself under increasing strain. "[I]t was truly a poorly chosen moment for the publication of such costly works. . . ."[52]

The high price for *Les Hindoûs* necessarily limited sales to the wealthiest collectors, but the book market was in crisis, and numerous dealers went bankrupt. The library purchases and the market response that Solvyns had hoped for—and expected—were not forthcoming. Many of the copies taken on subscription by the government, as subvention for the project, were presented as diplomatic gifts to major European libraries[53]—thus, ironically, further undermining sales that Solvyns might otherwise have been able to secure.

Early biographical accounts of Solvyns's life underscore the financial disaster that brought him near ruin. *Les Hindoûs* had consumed his energy and his wealth. Lesbroussart lamented that of "all the problems and worries that were born from this undertaking, . . . the only profit for this author seemed to be the glory of having done it."[54] In its obituary for Solvyns, the *Annual Review* for 1824 wrote that for all his perseverance, "Solvyns was not destined to reap the pecuniary advantages which he might justly have anticipated; for political events that were productive of ruin to so many individuals, affected him also. . . ." [55]

In its entry for Solvyns, the *Biographie nouvelle des contemporains* (1825) noted that *Les Hindoûs* "required considerable advances, and far from enriching the author, as it should have, became for him a source of hardship due to the bankruptcy of various booksellers and to the political turmoil of that epoch."[56] The early nineteenth century witnessed a major crisis in French publishing, with numerous bankruptcies among publishers, printers, and booksellers,[57] and Solvyns's own dealer, Nicolle, went bankrupt, gravely compromising the artist's position. The title pages of the first two volumes of *Les Hindoûs* had carried the name of chez H. Nicolle, through which the publication was sold, but sometime soon after 1810, the bookseller was out of business.[58]

George-Bernard Depping, who had assisted Solvyns in writing the introductory essays for *Les Hindoûs*, reflected on his association with Balthazar and Marie Anne: "This vast enterprise executed in the midst of the recent wars engulfed the fortune of his wife and threw him into great embarrassment, which he felt for the rest of his life."[59]

Reviews

In April 1808, the *Journal de l'empire*, Paris, published a two-part article on *Les Hindoûs*, with extracts from Solvyns's Preliminary Discourse.[60] A year later, the *Journal* published a review of *Les Hindoûs*. The first volume was now complete, and the reviewer, author of the earlier articles and identified only as "A.", judged it "magnificent." Its *atlantique* format, fine paper, superb lettering, etching, and color unite, he wrote, "to erect one of those literary monuments in which luxury likes to spread all its wealth." But this, he emphasizes, is not useless luxury, for Solvyns is a patient and enlightened observer, precise and faithful to the task he sets for himself in portraying the Hindus.[61] In his later review of Volume II, "A" wrote of Solvyns's "passion for work" and again richly praised the etchings as "precise and faithful." In doing so, however, the reviewer seized on Solvyns's portrayal of fakirs and of suttee to deplore Hindu superstition and cruelties—pronouncements at odds with Solvyns's own more considered judgment and sympathy.[62]

The distinguished *Mercure de France* reviewed the first volume of "this most interesting and truest work on Hinduism."[63] The reviewer ("L.B.") describes the project more generally and the contents of Volume I, praising Solvyns for his faithfulness to the subject and for the clarity of the text. The reviewer gives Solvyns's portrayals special importance given the changes in Hindu culture, already evident under Muslim influence, and increasing with the European presence in India. "We will soon no longer be able to study [the Hindu nation] directly, and perhaps this picturesque description [*Les Hindoûs*], which is the first that has been made, will be the last."

A few months later, again the pages of the *Mercure de France*, the reviewer extended his remarks with a discussion of the Preliminary Discourse and Solvyns's overall plan for *Les Hindoûs*.[64] In judgment of the first volume, he writes that Solvyns "has attained his objective with great simplicity, clarity, and precision. . . ."

Langlès's Review

In the Preliminary Discourse of the first volume *Les Hindoûs*, Solvyns expressed the hope that the public reception of his work would prove worthy of the labor and expense of its execution. He surely did not receive monetary reward, but he could take satisfaction in what Lesbroussart had called the "glory" of having produced it. *Les Hindoûs* was a magnificent work.

In November 1809, the French Orientalist Louis Matthieu Langlès (1763-1824) wrote a lengthy review of the first volume of *Les Hindoûs* for the official newspaper, *Le Moniteur*.[65] Langlès, Keeper of Oriental manuscripts at the Bibliothèque nationale de France, was a member of the Institut de France, to which Solvyns dedicated the work, and, according to Depping, was among those who regularly visited Solvyns's home—or salon, as it might well be called. Partha Mitter, in *Much Maligned Monsters*,[66] wrote of Langlès that "there was not a single important account of Indian antiquities that did not find a place in his work." Langlès did the heavily annotated French translations of the religion, philology, and history sections from the first two volumes of the journal of the Asiatic Society of Bengal, *Asiatick Researches*,[67] and among numerous books, he translated William Hodges's *Travels in India*, and the travel journal of the Daniells. Langlès reproduced a number of the Daniell aquatints in his own volume on monuments of India.[68]

In the notes to his translation of Hodges, published in 1805, Langlès refers to Solvyns's 1799 Calcutta etchings as "interesting and invaluable." The artist, he wrote, "combines with a truly distinguished talent a quality that is very rare among modern painters—great precision and the courage to sacrifice all the expected charm to austere truth." Langlès notes that copies of the *Collection* are quite rare, but that he is happy to possess one.[69]

Four years later, writing for *Le Moniteur*, Langlès begins his review of *Les Hindoûs* with extensive quotations from Solvyns's commentaries on brahmins and other subjects portrayed in the etchings. Commending the work to scholars, he emphasizes the accuracy with which Solvyns treats his subjects and praises his treatment of their way of life—especially important, he notes, for this will surely change under European influence. The etchings and the explanations accompanying them, Langlès writes, reflect both Solvyns's many years in India and an intimacy with the natives inspired "by the gentleness and loyalty of his character."

Langlès describes Solvyns as working "with inconceivable activity" and notes that with each installment the etchings have steadily improved. He has high praise for the typography, stating that with *Les Hindoûs*, the publishers, the Mame brothers, prove that "it is only in Paris that the celebrated Didots can find, if not their equals, at least worthy imitators. . . ."

Of Solvyns, Langlès concludes, "This estimable and indefatigable artist is entitled to expect for his undertaking the most useful encouragement." Solvyns received deserving support in the Institut's acceptance of the dedication of *Les Hindoûs* and in public praise for the work by the Perpetual Secretary of the Institut's section on fine arts. Moreover, he writes, another member of the Institut, François-André Vincent, "formerly his teacher, today his friend," had shown keen interest in Solvyns "as commendable for the strength of his character as for the superiority of his talent."

The Vincent Portrait

While Solvyns was working on *Les Hindoûs*, or soon after completing it, Vincent, with whom he had studied as a youth, did Solvyns's portrait. Whether it was an oil or drawing is unknown, for there is no record of the original,[70] but it survives as a lithograph (Pl. I.26) by Léopold Boëns (1795-1837), published in Brussels.[71]

Pl. I.26. "F. B. SOLVYNS, *Auteur des Hindoûs*."
By Léopold Boëns, after François-André Vincent. Lithograph, de Burggraaff, rue des Chandeliers 343, Brussels. No date. 36 x 27 cm. Solvyns Family Collection, Brussels.

Langlès's Reprise

In April 1811, a year-and-a-half after his review of the first volume of *Les Hindoûs*, Langlès again gave Solvyns high praise in the pages of *Le Moniteur*.[72] In a review of the second volume, Langlès describes with enthusiasm and clear delight the subjects portrayed. In both its visual and textual presentation, this is a work he truly enjoys. Solvyns, he writes, "leaves nothing to desire as far as the exactitude of his figures and the simplicity and truthfulness of his descriptions. This assertion is based on the unanimous and spontaneous testimony of those Europeans who have visited India and observed the Hindus."

Langlès is impressed by the quality of production evident in the second volume. "As opposed to most works of this type that are published in installments, this one continues to perfect itself. There is a noticeable improvement in the technique of engraving and coloring. We cannot say the same for the typography because it is difficult to bring it to a higher degree of perfection. Since the beginning of this work, M. Crapelet and Mame have consistently employed an elegant font, nourished and drawn with a beautiful black on vellum paper, that proves that this type of enterprise, as in almost all others, we [the French] need fear competition from no other nation."

Depping and the Introductions to *Les Hindoûs*

In the great *Biographie universelle, ancienne et moderne*, published in 1825, Georges-Bernard Depping (1784-1853) wrote the entry for Solvyns. In his discussion of *Les Hindoûs,* he asserts that "The preliminary discourses heading each of the four volumes were written in great part by the author of this article," that is, by Depping himself.[73] Depping's entry on Solvyns was then appropriated in 1829 by Mathieu Guillaume Delvenne (1778-1843) for inclusion in his *Biographie du royoume des Pays-Bas*.[74] He omitted Depping's initials, "D-g.", at the end of the article, and with the entry otherwise intact, readers assumed that it was Delvenne who claimed authorship of the introductions to *Les Hindoûs*. Thus, nearly one hundred years later, Borchgrave, in the entry for Solvyns in the *Biographie nationale . . . de Belgique*, writes that Delvenne claimed paternity of the Preliminary Discourse.[75] The British Library catalogue entry for *Les Hindoûs* notes that "The preliminary discourses generally, and part of the text occasionally [are] attributed to G. B. Depping. . . . Authorship of the preliminary discourses [is] also claimed by M. G. Delvenne."

Depping was a celebrated French intellectual of German origin and came to France in 1803. He collaborated in founding the journal *Annales des voyages* and wrote various works on travels and geography. According to the *Nouvelle biographie générale*, Solvyns, beginning work on the luxury edition of *Les Hindoûs*, charged Depping with writing text, a task similar to one he later assumed for a book on Russia.[76] The biographical entry indicates that Depping also wrote on France and Germany—but nothing in his life or work indicates any knowledge of Asia. The *Dictionnaire de biographie française* later suggested Depping spread himself thinly, "writing on all subjects with equal incompetence. . . ." [77]

It is surely plausible that Depping wrote the greater part of the Preliminary Discourse to Volume I and portions of the introductions to subsequent volumes that refer to and draw from various European accounts of India and translations of Hindu texts, but the discussions of the artist's purpose and of the prints themselves are surely by Solvyns himself.

In his reminiscences of his life in Paris, Depping provides the only first-hand account of Solvyns and his wife, Marie Anne, as he describes his association with them. In these passages, Depping's claim to the authorship of at least portions of the introductions to each of the four volumes of *Les Hindoûs* is made with modesty and substantial credibility—and with no evidence of resentment for Solvyns's failure to acknowledge his contribution. The account, written with sympathy and respect, merits extended quotation.

Depping met Solvyns as the artist was completing the first volume of *Les Hindoûs.* Solvyns had been helped in the publishing project, Depping writes, by an old friend in Paris (unnamed, but probably Van Praet). He describes Solvyns as "a very hard-working man, working from morning to evening," and as "fully redeeming his promise to the public in producing the four folio volumes."

> But to bring this project to completion, especially in the terrible war years, he [Solvyns] had to make great sacrifices and thereby later came into great difficulties and lost the peace of his life.
>
> If he had only allowed himself to be advised by a friend wise in the business aspects of publishing as to the monstrous costs of such an undertaking and what little return one can expect from these sumptuous works, then perhaps he would have reduced this work by half or even three-quarters. Then he would have been rewarded for his great effort and, indeed, might have been richly remunerated.[78]

Depping suggests that Solvyns's problems came, in part, because of his commitment to fidelity rather than to the beauty of the composition. Solvyns "gave the public an extremely accurate representation, an accuracy seldom found in copper engravings." "This man sacrificed everything for truth, but the great public cannot well judge this merit, preferring to emphasize that which is pleasant."[79]

By contrast, the financially successful pirated edition of Solvyns's work, published by Orme in London, with its soft lines and warm pastel colors, gave, in Depping's words, "a pleasing aspect." Solvyns, however, "could never bring himself to look at these plates because they were so far removed from reality."

> Unfortunately, he was not a poetic spirit and made his drawings all too prosaic. For example, when he stood before a Hindu he was drawing and observed an empty wall, an old mat, or similar common things, he would depict these in his drawings most accurately—even when they reappear twenty times. Here a poetic choice among the objects would have been in better taste and more pleasing to the eye, and yet he did not wish to depict things other than as he found them.[80]

Depping then goes on to describe his association with Solvyns and his involvement in writing the introductions for *Les Hindoûs.* The warmth and lively intellectual life of the Solvyns household in Paris is fully evident, as is the charm, devotion, and strong character of Marie Anne Solvyns.

> When Maltebrun[81] took me to him, the first volume [of *Les Hindoûs*] was about finished and was missing the introduction, which was to serve [as an overview of the full set of four volumes]. But because [Solvyns] was not able to do the introduction himself, he proposed that I do it. Therefore, I took over the introduction as well as those for the following volumes and also the overview of the text [for each plate], which Solvyns wrote down briefly in a very simple style because he never wanted to report something which he had not personally seen or heard. The text [accompanying the plates] is thus limited, but nevertheless contains many facts and has the merit that it reports only Solvyns's own observations.
>
> From now on, I ate once a week at Solvyns's place, and his house became for me one of the most pleasant places in Paris. He had enjoyed India so much that he took on Indian characteristics; instead of sending his maid to the market, he ordered her to go to the bazaar. The copper etchings in his house were of India. His furniture was, in part, in the Indian style.
>
> He had taken to wife an extremely lively and active English woman, who out of love for her husband acquainted herself well with the Hindus and appeared to have made her husband's undertaking the main activity of her life. She was especially gracious to all persons who praised her

husband's work and who encouraged him; but woe to those who expressed the slightest criticism. They [critics] exposed themselves to the wrath of the beautiful and lovely wife.

• • • •

Everyone in the house and friends were in good spirits and very happy. Here I saw many Englishmen and Flemings and several Parisian scholars, such as Van Praet, the most famous conservator of the great library [Bibliothèque nationale de France], who gave me permission to take home books from this very library (a favor that was very important to me) and who for 28 years was always the first and last person I saw at the library; Langlès, a professor of Persian, . . . who very kindly loaned me from his precious library new English travel books that I used for *Annales des voyages* [Depping's journal]; and [Charles-Marie] Feletz,[82] one of the most intelligent contributors to the *Journal de l'empire*, and who later became a university inspector, librarian, and academic, but who never published anything other than what he wrote for the *Journal*.

One of the most cheerful residents [in the Solvyns house] was a banker, a friend from Solvyns's youth, who was wise in the ways of the world and who in conversation liked to talk about his youthful follies. . . . In this house, one story would lead to another, and others offered stories of their own.

When my introduction for this valuable work on the Hindus was finished, it was read at the Solvyns's home in a circle of scholars and, aside from several remarks that Maltebrun made to me, it was greeted with approval and was thereupon printed in the same magnificent style as the rest of the work.

I can no longer, however, consider this introduction to be a good work. In those days we still did not have the works of a Ward, a Buchanan, a Dubois about the Hindus, and even then perhaps much was missing that would have been necessary to depict this remarkable people accurately. Without a more precise and accurate knowledge and appreciation of their character, religion, artistic achievements, and literature, one cannot make a comprehensive and well-founded judgment. A philosophical overview of the past and present condition of the Hindus at the beginning of a great work, such as that of Solvyns, that depicted all the conditions of their life and religion would be a great contribution if it could be paired with expert knowledge and lack of bias. But I now recognize better than then the difficulty of such a task.

Depping describes Marie Anne's commitment to her husband's project but makes no reference to her having translated the French text of the introductions to the four volumes of *Les Hindoûs*, as well as the descriptions accompanying each plate, into English. *La France littéraire* (1838), however, states that the English text was Madame Solvyns's translation,[83] and, given Marie Anne's support for her husband in the project, this would not be surprising. Certain oddities in the translation, such as misspelled words and the occasional use of a French word instead of the English, might suggest a native French-speaker as the translator, but Marie Anne had lived nearly all her life in France.

Solvyns's Perseverance: A New Proposal

At the end of the Introduction to *Les Hindoûs*, Vol. IV, Solvyns provides his readers a brief reflection on his great project:

> I could not give a greater extent to these observations without extending at the same time the reasonable limits of a work already so voluminous. Perhaps I may on future occasion offer to the public what remains for me yet to say upon a subject to which the principal employment of my life and fortune has been devoted. It will depend upon the judgement they pass upon this first fruit of my long labours, whether I shall again resume the graver and the pen, and endeavour to retrace the objects which struck me most in a country where so many years of my life have been spent, and to communicate the pleasing remembrances they have left.[84]

For all the financial difficulties that the publication of *Les Hindoûs* had imposed upon him, Solvyns was, in fact, eager to begin another project. In the 1812 "Prospectus" for *Les Hindoûs*, after describing its four volumes, Solvyns announced that he was occupying himself with a new book, *Voyage pittoresque aux Indes orientales et en Chine* (A

Picturesque Voyage to the East Indies and China), which he described as "in 200 plates, with an explanatory text, nautical maps, the daily course of the ships, and astronomical observations made during his travels." It would be in "two volumes, in quarto on vellum paper, with the plates engraved in aquatint, imitating watercolor, and printed in color, the whole being executed by the author according to the specimen print that will shortly accompany a detailed prospectus."

Solvyns had never been to China and apparently planned to undertake the voyage so that he might portray the experience in etchings and text. Perhaps he intended to take subscriptions for the volumes to finance his travels. Solvyns surely never lacked for ambition, but he never made the voyage. The promised prospectus may have come out in 1814, but *Voyage pittoresque* was never published.[85]

Return to Antwerp

The fourth volume of *Les Hindoûs* was published in 1812, just as the French Empire, after years of war and expansion, was shaken by Napoleon's humiliating withdrawal from Russia. The French hold over Europe was broken by a succession of military defeats, and in March 1814, Czar Alexander and Prussian King Friedrich Wilhelm III led allied troops into Paris. A month later, Napoleon abdicated.

Napoleon's defeat ended French domination of the Belgians, but, as they had in 1790, foreign powers were to decide the political status of the country. Pursuant to the Treaty of Paris, May 30, 1814, with the aim of containing France in the north, the London protocols, signed by the Prince of Orange on June 21, 1814, united Belgium and Holland as the Kingdom of the Netherlands under a single sovereign. On July 31, the Belgium provinces were formally handed to Prince of Orange, to be crowned a year later as King William I.

Burdened by financial problems and worry over the failure of *Les Hindoûs* to secure the sales he had anticipated, Solvyns, sometime in 1814, returned to Antwerp. He and Marie Anne took up residence at 7 Schipstraat (rue des Bateaux), the family house on the Schedt River, where Solvyns had grown up.[86]

Soon after returning, Solvyns exhibited a painting, "Rough Sea with a Gunboat, a Frigate and Other Vessels," along with a copy of his newly published *Les Hindoûs* at the Ghent Salon of 1814. The catalog described Solvyns as "artist-draftsman of Antwerp and corresponding member of the Société des Arts à Gand."[87] The etchings made a particularly favorable impression, for the Academy of Ghent, on August 1, 1814, awarded its metal of honor to Solvyns for *Les Hindoûs*.[88]

Solvyns's Appointment as Captain of the Port of Antwerp

In the fall of 1814, in recognition of Solvyns's artistic achievements and with concern for the artist's difficult financial position, William I, bearing the provisional title of Sovereign Prince, named Solvyns "to the honorable and lucrative position" of Captain of the Port of Antwerp and of the waters of the Schedt River.[89] Solvyns assumed the position, once held by his cousin Maximilien, in 1815 and retained it until his death in 1824. The post carried an annual salary of 3,000 florins, a comfortable income, though modest compared to his brother Laurent's income of 15,000 florins as a merchant.[90]

Under the United Kingdom, with an opening of trade between the southern and northern Netherlands, the port of Antwerp handled increased tonnage,[91] and as harbormaster, Solvyns assumed considerable responsibility. Reflecting the French culture of the Antwerp upper classes, Solvyns referred to himself as "Capitaine du port et des Eaux d'Anvers," although all official documents were in Dutch. His specific duties changed over his nine years of service, in part the product of growing tensions between the Belgians and their Dutch overlords. In 1816, a royal decree created the new position of "Water Scout" (*Waterschout*), and many of the duties formerly invested in the harbormaster were given to the new appointee, a Dutchman. In 1820, another decree reduced the responsibilities of the Captain of the Port to assigning ships to specific docks or anchorage. The City of Antwerp resented the imposition of central authority and especially the cost of paying a second harbor official, but, defending Solvyns as one of their own, city officials resisted pressure to abolish the post of harbormaster.[92]

Soon after appointing Solvyns to the position of Captain of the Port of Antwerp, in November 1814, William I presented a magnificent morocco-bound set of *Les Hindoûs* to the library of Brussels—the volumes now in the collection of the Bibliothèque royale Albert I.

The Brussels newspaper *L'Oracle*, in reporting the gift, lavished praise both on the new king, for his support of the arts, and on Solvyns, for the importance of his contribution. The article recounted Solvyns's work in India and his devotion, sparing no effort, to presenting a detailed and truthful portrayal of the people of India.[93]

As Captain of the Port, Solvyns held a position of respect in the city of Antwerp. On July 26, 1815, he signed the request which the Society for the Promotion of the Fine Arts in Antwerp directed to King William as an intermediary for the return of artworks stolen by the French from Antwerp during the Revolution.[94] We know little of Solvyns's life and activities during the time of his service as harbormaster, but he did continue to paint.

"The Entry of William I, King of Holland, on His Yacht in the Port of Antwerp."

In 1818, Solvyns completed a canvas portraying "the entry of William I, King of Holland, on his yacht in the port of Antwerp" (Pl. I.27).[95] It was his largest work, and one of only two or possibly three paintings known to survive from his years as Captain of the Port. The painting, which he exhibited in Brussels to great success, depicts the king and his two sons on the royal yacht as they arrived in Antwerp on August 12, 1817.[96] The city's civil and military authorities welcomed the king with brilliant festivities, the volley of cannon, and the ringing of bells. More than 400 ships and boats, decorated and flying diverse flags, had gathered in the port, a feat of management in which Solvyns, as Captain of the Port, likely played the major role.[97] In the painting, Solvyns portrays himself in the small boat in the foreground. Standing, as he holds his son's hand, Solvyns waves his greeting to the king. Solvyns's wife Marie Anne, wearing a bonnet and a shawl over her shoulders, sits behind them in the boat. The signature, "Balt Solvyns Antwerpen 1818," is painted on a buoy in the lower right.

The painting is with the branch of the Solvyns family now resident in Australia, descendants of Balthazar's brother Pierre Jean. Its provenance is unclear, however, for in 1843, Solvyns's widow, Marie Anne, included the painting among five items offered for sale by lottery (discussed below). The family has no records as to whether the painting was acquired by the luck of a winning lottery ticket or later purchased to bring it back into the Solvyns family.

Pl. I.27. "The Entry of William I, King of Holland, on His Yacht in the Port of Antwerp."
Oil on canvas. Signed "Balt Solvyns Antwerpen 1818". 125 x 190 cm. Solvyns Family, Australian Branch, Collection.

Solvyns's Self-portrait

Another oil is probably from about the same time, an unsigned self-portrait, on canvas, still within the Solvyns family (Pl. I.28), but with no information as to its provenance.

Pl. I.28. F. Balthazar Solvyns.
Oil on canvas. Unsigned. 60 x 48 cm. Solvyns Family Collection, Belgium.

A Curiosity

A curious painting (Pl. I.29) in a private collection in Belgium bears the signature "SOLVYNS Antwerpen," and although the treatment of the ship, boats, and figures is characteristic of neither Solvyns's style nor competence, it seems unlikely that such a picture would be forged. The painting is undated and could be an immature work from the artist's youth, but the Dutch flag suggests that it was probably done after Solvyns's return to Antwerp when Belgium and Holland were united under King William I of the Netherlands. What is especially odd about the picture is that the ship, with the appearance of what might be a royal yacht, is a construction of fantasy, an amalgamation of several ship types that bears no resemblance to any real ship of the time.[98]

Pl. I.29. Painting of a Ship with Dutch Flag.
Oil on board. Signed "Solvyns Antwerpen". 30 x 40 cm. Private Belgium Collection.

New Etchings

Solvyns may also have done some etchings after his return to Antwerp. In the print collection of the Plantin-Moretus Museum in Antwerp, there is a small, undated etching (Pl. I.30) of a ferry boat in a Low Countries setting that is attributed to Solvyns.[99] The sky is characteristic of Solvyns's work, as is the line for the waters, but the figures in the boat are rendered with a proportion that contrasts with Solvyns's elongated figures characteristic of his Indian portrayals. Below the print, handwritten, but not in Solvyns's hand, it reads: "F. Solvyns, fecit". The print came to the museum from a private collection, its provenance unknown.

There is also reference to a Solvyns etching in the catalog of the city of Antwerp's Ter Bruggen

Pl. I.30. A Ferry Boat.
Copper etchings attributed to Solvyns. 15.5 x 24 cm. Museum Plantin-Moretus/ Stedelijk Prentenkabinet, Antwerp.

collection—"Le débarguement des officers d'un navire en rade" (disembarkation of naval officers in the roads),[100] but its whereabouts is unknown.

Last Years and Death

In 1819, Solvyns announced a lottery for the numerous remaining copies of *Les Hindoûs*. The raffle never took place, and we have no record as to how, if at all, Solvyns finally disposed of them,[101] but the proposed lottery in no way represented a closure to the artist's absorption with India. According to his contemporaries, until his death in 1824, Solvyns remained "inexhaustibly as well as very instructively conversant" about the Hindus and the time he spent in India.[102]

On October 10, 1824, Solvyns died of a stroke. In a notice published in the Antwerp newspaper, "Madame Solvyns-Greenwood" announced to the public the death of her husband, François Balthazar Solvyns, Captain of the Port of the City, at the age of 64 years and 3 months. The funeral was conducted in the church of Notre-Dame, where Solvyns had been baptized as an infant.[103]

In its obituary, the *Annual Review*, published in London, captured the vital force of Solvyns's life—the zeal with which he had pursued his great project to portray the Hindus: "No difficulty, no obstacles, no expense could check his perseverance, or cool his enthusiasm."[104] But for all his work, neither the *Collection of Two Hundred and Fifty Coloured Etchings* from Calcutta nor *Les Hindoûs* brought Solvyns the recognition and reward that he had sought.

In March 1826, Calcutta learned of his death. Of Solvyns, the *Gazette* wrote that "His Sketches, though not very picturesque, are very faithful delineations, and he must have been a man of very laborious and observant research. The Engravings executed by himself, and published in Calcutta, are very rude; but they are highly prized on the Continent, and we know an instance in which 100 guineas were given for a copy."[105]

Interest in Europe was reflected perhaps in Depping's report, just a year after Solvyns died, that someone was beginning a Leipzig edition of the etchings, with text by Dr. Bergk, but Depping described it as "a feeble imitation of the great work" on the Hindus. "We do not know if it was continued."[106] The Leipzig etchings were not for a pirated German edition of Solvyns's work, but were copies of various Solvyns Calcutta etchings used as illustrations for Bergk's *Asiatisches Magazine*.[107]

In 1829, five years after his death, friends and admirers sought to erect "a simple and modest" memorial for Solvyns in one of the chapels of the Notre-Dame Cathedral in Antwerp. The artist Mathieu-Ignace Van Brée (1773-1839),[108] then director of the Académie des Beaux Arts in Antwerp, was to draw a symbolic figure, *India Unveiled by the Genius of Art*, that would then to be sculpted by Philippe Parmentier (1787-1851). According to the *Journal d'Anvers*, funding for the monument would be raised by public subscription. The article described the difficulties Solvyns had encountered in bringing out *Les Hindoûs*. The work was of such immense cost that only very rich connoisseurs and great libraries could afford the price. Moreover, the political upheaval at the end of the Napoleonic Wars brought ruin to a great many booksellers who sold the work, resulting in serious financial loss to the author. "All of his work and great sacrifices were lost, " the *Journal* related, "but [Solvyns] still had the glory of adding his name to the famous men who have honored their country."[109]

The proposal for the monument, however, came to nothing, for as so often in the course of Solvyns's life—even now in death—political events intervened, here with the disturbances that led to the Revolution of 1830 and the establishment of the Kingdom of Belgium.[110] In 1868, the City of Antwerp named a street after the artist: Solvijinsstraat.

Survivors

Balthazar and Marie Anne had three children. The eldest, Charles Balthazar, was born in Paris in 1811. In 1833, Charles, a second lieutenant in the Belgium army corps of engineers, died at Ft. Lillo—where Balthazar had served as a young man—while working on the fortification of nearby Fort Lacroix. A gravestone in the cemetery of the village of Vorderen expresses the gratitude of the villagers to the courageous young officer who saved them from flood at the price of his own life.[111]

Solvyns's second son, Ignace Henri Stanislas (1817-1894), ennobled with the title of Baron in 1875, had a distinguished diplomatic career. At the time of his death in 1894, he served as Belgium's ambassador in London—Envoy Extraordinary and Minister

Plenipotentiary, a position he held for more than twenty years. Earlier, he served as Secretary of the Belgium Legation in Washington, and, while in the United States, he married, in 1855, Henriette Livingston-Brown of New York; they had no children.[112]

Solvyns's youngest child was a daughter, Marie Anne Catherine (1820-1863), who married Antoine Alexandre de Froëlich (1804-1847), a Polish officer who had been admitted to the newly-formed Belgium army. They had two children, both boys, Solvyns's only grandchildren, but each died young, unmarried and without children.[113] Thus, Balthazar Solvyns left no direct descendants.

Solvyns's widow, Marie Anne, remarried in 1825. Her new husband, Pierre Joseph Marie Colette de Ryckere (1793-1863), eleven years her junior, was a diplomat and professor of law at the University of Ghent. Marie Anne died in Ghent on August 31, 1844, and was buried in the cemetery there next to her parents, Charles and Sara Greenwood.[114]

We have little information as to the contents and survival of Solvyns's personal collection of his own work. On March 6, 1829, Solvyns's children presented a fine set of *Les Hindoûs* to Antwerp's Stadsbibliotheek in memory of their father. That same year, Marie Anne presented a bound album of 41 of her late husband's drawings from India as "a souvenir from the hand of he who drew them and who always wanted to present them himself" to a gentleman whose name in her inscription is now unfortunately indistinct.[115]

The drawings in the album were among those that Solvyns had saved from the shipwreck on his return from India. These were mainly sketches taken in the field, but Solvyns had also saved the fully-developed drawings from which the 250 Calcutta etchings were made. Solvyns used these drawings for the new etchings of the Paris edition, *Les Hindoûs*, but we know nothing of their whereabouts until April 1883, when the South Kensington Museum in London —today's Victoria and Albert Museum—acquired, from a London dealer, a collection of 248 watercolor paintings executed by Balthazar Solvyns in Bengal.[116]

The Lottery

The year before she died, Marie Anne offered some of her husband's work in a lottery. In 1843, *La Revue Belge* (Liège)[117] carried the announcement of "A sale [*vente per actions*, sale by shares or lottery] of a copper plate and four magnificent seascapes by Balthazard Solvyns of Antwerp." Comparing Solvyns with Claude Vernet, the great painter of seascapes and the ports of France, the notice described the items to be raffled:

The most important work was a painting described as "The arrival of William of Nassau in 1814, coming to take possession of Belgium, by virtue of the articles signed in London. This painting of great dimension represents the king and his two sons on the royal yacht, *The City of Antwerp*, and all the consuls on their respective ships." The painting, however, is wrongly described, for it depicts the King's entry into the Port of Antwerp in 1817, not in 1814. And as noted earlier, the painting (Pl. I.27) remains today within the Solvyns family.[118]

Three other paintings are identified as "A cutter entering the port"; "The meeting of the fleet on high sea"; and "A ship that has broken down." "These later subjects are rendered with truth that merits the character of the artist."

The fifth item for the lottery is identified in the notice as "A copper plate etched by the best masters of the period, representing the *View of the Port of Ostend*. The picture was painted by Solvyns when he was at the castle of Laeken, captain in the service of Maria Christina. During his [Solvyns's] voyage to India, the Duke of Saxe-Tesschen had an engraving made of it, and on the death of Solvyns, he sent the plate to his widow." The print (Pl. I.2, discussed, pp. 13-14.) was, in fact, engraved in 1784, six years before Solvyns's departure for India, and was dedicated by Solvyns to his patrons, Maria Christina and her husband Albert, Duke of Saxe-Tesschen.

The fate of the three smaller paintings and of the copper plate is unknown.

The items for the lottery were placed on view at the Hotel de la Poste, 25 Place d'Armes, in Ghent, "where one can see them and subscribe every day."

The *La Revue Belge* announcement gave the details on the manner by which the lottery would be conducted. Each subscriber would receive a copy of the Port of Ostend engraving. The number of shares (tickets) was fixed at 8000, with each share priced at 10 francs. If the full complement of shares were sold, the receipt would be an impressive 80,000 francs—far more than the items could possibly have yielded at sale or auction. The notice stated that His Majesty King Leopold had taken the first hundred shares.

The announcement specified that the shares "will be numbered, counter-signed by the widow of Solvyns, will be taken from a counterfoil book, will remain at the *Hotel de la Poste* until the drawing which will take place on January 6, 1844, at 10:00 in the morning, by a commission named by and among the bearers of the present shares. This operation will take place by means of two drums, one of which will contain the numbers of the shares; the other an equal number of white blank tickets less five tickets designating by category each of the paintings and the plate placed on sale."

In the eighteenth and early nineteenth century, lotteries were immensely popular in Europe and Great Britain. Lotteries consisted of "all sorts of schemes," as for the disposal of art collections, jewelry, houses, and land, but most lotteries involved money prizes. "India was by no mean free of the excitement," writes W. H. Carey, and the papers were full of such offerings.[119] In 1792, in Calcutta, soon after Solvyns's arrival, Thomas Daniell held a lottery for the "speedy sale" of pictures that he had made on his tour of Upper India. "The scheme was 150 chances at 150 rupees a chance. Each ticket to draw a prize, the highest prize being a picture valued at 1,200 rupees and the lowest at 250 rupees."[120] A year later, in Madras, the Daniells held another lottery of paintings and drawings.

In Europe, lotteries were held for all sorts of things. In the Low Countries, lotteries for paintings go back at least to the mid-seventeenth century in Haarlem,[121] but they seem to have been comparatively rare for art, as serious collectors preferred to bid directly on the object desired. But for the seller, as for Marie Anne Solvyns de Ryckere, it was often a way of assuring profit.

The typical procedure involved two barrels, one with tickets bearing the number (or name of the lot-holder), the other with bits of paper that were either blank or indicating the prize won. One person drew the numbers and another drew the prize slips.[122] Such a procedure is portrayed by Hogarth in his 1724 engraving, "The Lottery," and it seems that this is the way Solvyns's widow raffled off the five items.

The lottery symbolizes Solvyns's virtual eclipse as a recognized artist. Volumes of the Calcutta etchings and of *Les Hindoûs* occasionally came onto the market, but at a fraction of their original prices, and over time, his work was largely forgotten. In accounts of European artists in India, Solvyns received only passing mention, if acknowledged at all. And, with few exceptions, even among specialists on Indian social history and ethnography, Solvyns's portrait of the Hindus was wholly unknown. It was not until the late 1960s that interest was awakened in Solvyns as an artist and Orientalist.

---

1 The only source for the ship that Solvyns took is an editor's note in *Bengal Past and Present*, 49 (1935): 142, that "Solvyns sailed from Calcutta in the *Phoenix* in June 1803. . . " No further detail or source is provided. The *Calcutta Gazette*, on March 24, 1803 (Vol. 39, No. 995), carried an advertisement for the sale of "the Good Ship Phoenix," and on May 5 (Vol. 39, No. 1001), another ad announced "Freight for Rangoon, the ship Phoenix, will sail in all this month for Rangoon. . . ."

2 With the resumption of war, any British ship would have risked seizure by the French. *Lloyd's List,* providing twice-weekly reports of British ships lost or captured, makes no mention of the *Phoenix*, but reported (October 12, 1804) that the *Althea*, on route from Bengal to London, was taken by the French and taken to Mauritius in May 1804. The *Admiral Alpin*, bound from Portsmouth for India, was seized by the French near Mauritius in January 1804. Farrington, 3.

3 De Paepe, 85-86.

4 72.

5 7:48-49.

6 "Généalogie de la famille baronniale Solvyns," unpublished family record.

7 Acte de mariage, Archives de Bruxelles, No. 72, in Sagala (Unpublished), Catalogue des pieces justificatives, Vb1. The document is of the French Republic, for Belgium was then under Napoleon's rule.

8 Archives de Bruxelles, No. 72, petition, dated 15 Brumaire XIII (November 5, 1804), in Sagala (Unpublished), Catalogue des pieces justificatives, Vb2.

9 As indicated in wills, executed by Solvyns and his wife in October 1805 (3 Brumaire XIV), they were residing in Paris, rue de Lille, Faubourg St. Germain, No. 67. In their wills, each bequeaths all goods and property to the other. Archieves nationales (Paris), minutier central (Meuble C8.SI), ET/IX/889, in Sagala (Unpublished), Catalogue des pieces justificatives, VIa.

10 Verbanck, 5; Borchrave, 23:136.

11 John Greenwood, listed at Fort William, was married in Calcutta in 1796. *Bengal Past and Present* 21 (July-December 1920): 122.

12 "Généalogie de la famille baronniale Solvyns," unpublished family record.

13 86.

14 Gergmans, "Praet," in *Biographie nationale . . . de Belgique*, 18:154-63. In his history of the Bibliothèque nationale de France, Balayé discusses Van Praet extensively. Van Praet served the library with his expertise from 1784 until his death in 1837.

15 See discussion of the Orme edition in Chapter Three, p. 106.

16 For publishing detail on the Orme edition, see Abbey, Entry 429, 2:393-94; Tooley (No. 461), 369-71, and Hardie, 132.

17 *Les Hindoûs*, 1:29, reprinted in Chapter Four, p. 125.

18 The painting measured 42 x 53.5 cm. The entry for the picture in the exhibition catalogue describing Solvyns as "now a painter at the English Factory at Calcutta in Asia" is surely odd, for Solvyns had returned to Europe in 1804. Hostyn, "Solvyns, Frans-Balthasar," 597-98.

19 The street is today called St. André des Arts. No. 11 is located at Place St. Michel.

20 In the *Les Hindoûs* prospectus, dated January 1, 1812, Solvyns still gives his address as Saint André des Arcs.

21 No copies of the original Prospectus are known to survive, but the full text, from the original typeface, was reprinted in 1808, with an addendum announcing the publication of a quarto edition. A copy of this Prospectus is in the Newberry Library, Chicago.

22 The period is from his departure from Ostend in 1790 through his return to Europe in 1804, but Solvyns's actual time in Bengal amounted to a little more than twelve years.

23 *Atlantique* refers to the large format paper size, like atlas or elephant folio.

24 *Gazette nationale, ou, Le Moniteur universel*, April 14, 1808.

25 Füssli, 2:1675.

26 Bibliothèque nationale de France has a copy of one of the separate *livraison*. (Od.32a. tomes 1 et 2. Fol.). It carries the original "Crapelet" title page, but the installment, the 29th *livraison*, is for the six prints of the Fifth Number in Vol. III, published by Mame in 1811. On the publishing crisis, see Hesse, 205-10.

27 Oddly, the installments continued to be issued with reference to 252 plates on the title page even as late as the 44th installment, which contained the six plates of the tenth section for Volume IV—etchings 271-276. Item No. 2832, *Bibliographie de l'empire Français*, 2:426.

28 Details of publication in Abbey, Entry 430, 2:394-98.

29 *Bibliographie nouvelle des contemporains,* 19:244. The listing in the *Bibliographie de l'empire* for the years 1811-12 has an entry for installments 41 and 42 and gives 500 as the number printed. (Entry No. 2373, 2:353-54.) This is possibly a typographical error, for the entries for installments 43-46 indicate that 300 were printed. (Entry No. 2692, 2:402; No. 2832, 2:426.)

30 "Prospectus," January 1, 1812.

31 Publishers offered their recommendation for binding. In the copy of *Les Hindoûs* in the Victoria Memorial, Calcutta, a small printed notice, *Avis*, is pasted on the title page, advising collectors that the publisher's binder is Tessier, known for its care of great works. Tessier is identified as the binder and gilder for the Treasury, the Bureau of War, and the "Calcographie Piranesi," and the address is given as rue de la Harpe, No. 45, vis-à-vis calle des Deux Portes, à Paris.

32 86-87.

33 David, Taunay, and Vincent were appointed on November 22, and turned in their oral report on November 29, 1806, according to Institut records. Bonnaire, 3:57-58. Schnapper and Serullaz, 608, in the exhibition catalogue *Jacques Louis David*, list the appointment in the "Chronologie" of David's life.

34 Solvyns quotes the letter in its entirety in his January 1, 1812, "Prospectus" for *Les Hindoûs*. Also see De Paepe, 87.

35 A copy of the letter, together with the "Prospectus" for the quarto edition, is in the Newberry Library, Chicago. The review of *Les Hindoûs* in *Mercure de France*, March 4, 1809, notes that Solvyns was publishing an edition "in quarto on double *grand-raisin* paper," with engravings that are not colored, "but which are also executed by him with much care."

36 *Les Hindoûs, ou description de leurs mœurs, costumes, cérémonies, etc., etc., dessinés d'après nature dans le Bengale, et représentés en 252 planches par F. Balthazar Solvyns, gravés à l'eau-forte, et terminés par liu-même*. Paris: Frères Mame, 1808. The quarto edition etchings measure 19 x 23 cm. Bibliothèque nationale de France, 4-02K.128. See Colas, No. 2768, p. 2:985.

37 The portrayal of "Tantys" (Tā̃tis), weavers, Pl. 26 in the quarto edition, for example, has a thatched door open in the background and a religious image in a niche in the wall at the top center—both of which are in the Calcutta etching, but not in the Paris folio print (Pl. II.33).

38 Appendix to Chronicle, 235. The obituary incorrectly assumed the edition to have been announced only shortly before Solvyns's death and that its posthumous completion could be expected. Depping, "Solvyns" (1825), 43-62-63, however, correctly writes that "During the printing of *Les Hindoûs*, he undertook another edition in quarto, engraving the etchings himself, but only published a few installments."

39 Fouché (1759-1820) had enormous power as Minister of Police, a position which he held almost continuously from 1799 to 1815.

40 Archives nationales (Paris), correspondences générale (An XIII-1817), Côte:F/21/707.

41 Letter from Robillard Perouville to Balthazard Solvyns, Paris, January 30, 1808, Archives nationales, correspondences générale (An XIII-1817), Côte:F/21/707.

42 The correspondence, here cited, is in Archives nationale, indemnités littèraires, Côte:F/17/3224—documents, Dossier Solvyns (Baltazar), 1811. I am grateful to Marie-José Sagala for providing me photocopies of the documents in the appendix to her thesis.

43 The statesman Charles-Maurice de Talleyrand-Périgord (1754-1836) was named Prince of Bénévent (Benevento, a city in southern Italy) in 1806 as part of Napoleon's efforts to consolidate his control over Italy.

44 Letter, May 9, 1809.

45 Here translated from the French. The "Prospectus" is in the Solvyns family collection, Brussels.

46 See Chapter Three, p. 94, for a discussion of *à la poupée* technique and the coloring of the Paris edition.

47 On *Les Roses*, Brunet, 4:1175-76, and Gordon N. Ray, *The Art of the French Illustrated Book*, 1:147-48. On the firm of Pierre Didot, see Ray, 1:120-27.

48 During the Napoleonic Wars, there was a British embargo against French goods, but books, as other items, were easily smuggled, usually via Holland.

49 White, Cochrane & Co., booksellers in Fleet Street, London, advertised *Les Hindoûs* at £105 in boards. *The Quarterly Review*, No. 18 (July 1813), 3-4. London book dealer Henry Bohn, *Catalog of Books* for 1841, 4:1791, notes that *Les Hindoûs* was originally priced in Britain at 100 guineas. Also see Abbey, 1:398. At the prevailing rate of exchange, the

British price was roughly equivalent to the price in French francs.

50 Spooner, 908.

51 Advertisement by White, Cochrane & Co., *The Quarterly Review*, No. 18 (July 1813), 3-4. The great British naturalist Sir Joseph Banks (1744-1820) was the president of the Royal Society.

52 Staes, *Antwerpsche reizigers*, 201.

53 De Paepe, 87.

54 76.

55 Appendix to Chronicle, 235.

56 19:244,

57 Hesse, 205-10.

58 Burbure, 47.

59 "Solvyns" (1825), 43:63. Spooner, 908, and George C. Williamson, in *Bryan's Dictionary of Painters and Engravers*, 5:101, refer to the Solvyns's "pecuniary embarrassment."

60 April 8, 1808, 3-4, and April 13, 1808, 3-4.

61 June 15, 1809, 1-4.

62 *Journal de l'empire*, February 8, 1811, 1-4.

63 March 4, 1809, 408-11.

64 July 8, 1808, 74-79. The reviewer also discusses at some length the first two installments of Volume II and their portrayal of women, noting the unhappy condition of Hindu women, "at least those of inferior condition."

65 *Gazette nationale, ou, Le Moniteur universel*, No. 509 (November 5, 1809):1224-26. A German translation of Langlès's article was published in the *Tübingen Morgenblatt*, a "morning newspaper for the educated classes," April 18, 1810, 369-70.

66 180.

67 Published as *Recherches asiatiques; au, Mémoires de la société établie au Bengale* in Paris, 1805.

68 *Monuments anciens et modernes de l'Hindoustan.*

69 *Voyage pittoresque de l'Inde*, 2: 148. In his notes to the Hodges volume, Langlès refers several times to Solvyns's Calcutta etchings, underscoring their value. The Solvyns volumes in Langlès's personal library (listed in Langlès, *Catalogue des Livres*, numbers 3326-29) are now in the Bibliothèque national, Paris: the 1799 *Collection* and *Catalogue*, *Costume of Hindostan* (1807), and the first two volumes of *Les Hindoûs*.

70 In his last years, in declining health, Vincent devoted himself largely to portraiture. In the documentation on Vincent in the Départment des peintures, Musée du Louvre, there is no reference to the portrait of Solvyns.

71 A copy of the print is in the Cabinet des estamps, Bibliothèque royale Albert I, Brussels, Cat.. No. S.II.87402;

72 *Gazette nationale, ou, Le Moniteur universel*, April 26, 1811.

73 "Solvyns" (1825), 43:62.

74 417-18. On Delvenne, see *Biographie nationale . . . de Belgique*, 5:506.

75 23:236. Staes, in *Antwerpsche reizigers* (c. 1884), 198, wrote that each volume of *Les Hindoûs* opens with an introduction by Solvyns, "apparently with the collaboration of a certain Mr. Delvenne."

76 "Depping, Georges-Bernard [George Bernhard]. *Nouvelle biographie général*. 13:702-05.

77 10:1108.

78 192-93. Quoted passages here and below are translated from the German.

79 193.

80 193. In his 1825 biographical entry on "Solvyns," 43:62, Depping judged the etchings as bad artistically, but "notable for their fidelity."

81 The *Nouvelle biographie générale*, 33:104-08, lists him as "Malte-brun (Malte-Conrad Bruun)," 1775-1826, a Danish geographer resident in Paris and associate of Depping.

82 On Feletz (1767-1850), see Jadin.

83 Quèrard, 9:207-08. The catalog entry for the volumes in the British Library gives "Mary A. G. Solvyns" as having translated the French into English.

84 4:10.

85 Depping, "Solvyns" (1825), 43:63, writes that the book was announced but never published. Quèrard, 9:207-08, states that Solvyns printed a prospectus for *Voyage pittoresque* in 1814, but that the book never came out. Probably mistaking the prospectus for the book, the entry for Solvyns in *Bibliographie nouvelle des contemporains* (1825), 19:244, states that Solvyns published *Voyage pittoresque* in 1814. According to the Thieme-Becker *Künstler-Lexikon*, 37:260, Solvyns engraved 200 plates for a work that remained unpublished.

86 The street was destroyed in the "rectification of the quais," 1883-1888, when the banks of the Scheldt were straightened to accommodate boat moorings below the Steen fortress (where the Maritime Museum is now located). Information provided by Ernest Vanderlinden, Berlaar, Belgium. At some point, Solvyns moved to 14 Burchtplein, where he resided at the time of his death in 1824, as recorded (Sect. No. 157) on his death certificate.

87 Hostyn, "Solvyns, Frans-Balthasar," 598.

88 *L'Oracle* (Brussels), August 4, 1814 (No. 215): 3. Also see Claeys, 46.

89 *L'Oracle* (Brussels), November 26, 1814 (No. 329): 4. The newspaper described the appointment as compensation to Solvyns by the prince "in the most noble and generous manner" for the artist's great effort in producing his portrayal of the Hindus. Archibald, in *Dictionary of Sea Painters*, 200, suggests that Solvyns's "financial embarrassment . . . may have been the reason for his taking a job in the Antwerp docks. . . ." But Solvyns, with the prestigious position of Captain of the Port, was hardly "a dock worker," as he was characterized (probably from Archibald) in the note to the cover illustration of the painting, "The Launching of Gabriel Gillett's Armed Merchantman in Calcutta Harbor," *The American Neptune* 55 (Winter 1995):2.
Boumans, 685, and Prims, *Antwerpiensia 1929*, 359-60 (perhaps relying on Boumans), state that Solvyns was appointed in 1812 to succeed J. B. Hoest, who had served as harbor master, following Maximilien Solvyns, from 1801 to 1812. But Balthazar was in Paris in 1812, and it was not until 1814 that King William secured rule over Antwerp. Boumans and Prims oddly take no account of the fall of Napoleon and the change of regime in Belgium.

90 Beterams, 88, 135.

91 On the history of the port in this period, see Veraghtert.

92 Prims, *Antwerpiensia 1929*, 360-61. When Solvyns died in 1824, the city government, after considerable debate, decided to retain the position of Captain of the Port.

93 *L'Oracle*, November 26, 1814 (No. 329):3-4.

94 Hostyn, "Solvyns, Frans-Balthasar," 598.

95 As described in "Généalogie de la famille baronniale Solvyns," unpublished family record. Lesbroussart, 69, makes passing reference to the painting, but gives neither title nor date of the subject portrayed. Staes, 202, gives the same title that appears in the Solvyns family records, but provides no

detail. Woussen, 304, providing the date of the scene depicted, gives the title as "The Arrival of H. M. the King of the Low Countries at the Port of Antwerp on 12 August 1817."

96 *La Revue Belge* 23 (January-April 1843):190, in Marie Anne Solvyns's notice of sale, incorrectly describes the scene portrayed as "the arrival of William of Nassau in 1814 to take possession of Belgium." The date given in *La Revue Belge* perhaps led Staes, 202, to write that it was on the basis of this painting that Solvyns "secured the favor of the monarch and was appointed harbormaster of Antwerp." The port of Antwerp, however, was occupied by the French fleet until the end of August 1814, and William I visited the city for the first time on March 28, 1815.
A publication in the Stadsarchief, Antwerp, "Aentekeningen van sommige merkeerdige zaken te Antwerpen voorgevallen tusschen 1792 en 1830" ("Comments on a Few Notable Things at Antwerp that Occurred between 1792 and 1830"), notes that "On 12 August 1817, William I went along the Scheldt on his yacht and arrived in Antwerp. The new mayor, F. Van Ertborn, and his councilmen went to congratulate the king." I am grateful to Bart De Prins, University of Leuven, and to the Stadsarchief for assisting me in confirming the date of the scene portrayed.

97 Antwerp newspapers described the king's arrival and the city's festivities. In the evening the city was illuminated, and the cries of "Long Live the King" could be heard on every side. The following day, the king proceeded to Laeken, the royal palace in Brussels. See *Journal constitutionnel, commercial et litteraire de la province d'Anvers*, August 14, 1817, and August 15, 1817, and *Antwerpsche nieuwsblad*, August 14,1817.

98 In confronting this puzzle, I am grateful to Joost Schokkenbroek, Curator of Material Culture, and to Elizabeth Spites, Assistant Curator for Ship Models, at the Scheepvaartmuseum, Amsterdam.

99 Stedelijk Prentenkabinet Cat.. No. II/S.411.

100 The print is listed as No. 1343 in Ter Bruggen, 2:201, with a handwritten number, 3982, beside the entry in the volume in the Stedlijk Prentenkabinet, Antwerp.

101 *Biograpahie nouvelle des contemporains*, 19:244; Depping, "Solvyns" (1825), 43:63; Staes, 202; and Burbure, 47.

102 Staes, 202-03.

103 The death certificate records his name as he was baptized: Franciscus Balthazar Solvyns. His brother Laurent registered the death and signed the document, recorded for the City of Antwerp, 1st District, on October 12, 1824.

104 *Annual Review*, 1824, Appendix to Chronicle, 235.

105 *The Government Gazette* (Calcutta), May 18, 1826 (Vol. 41, No. 573), p. 4.

106 Depping, "Solvyns" (1825), 43:63. The reference is to Johann Adam Bergk (1769-1834) of Leipzig, publisher of the *Asiatisches Magazine* and author of several books relating to Asia.

107 The Leipzig copies are discussed in Chapter Three, p. 107.

108 On Van Brée's life and work, see Coekelbergs and Loze, 148-54.

109 "Monument à élever dans l'eglise de Notre-Dame à Anvers, A la mémoire de Balthasar Solvyns de cette ville, auteur d'un grand ourage sur l'Inde." *Journal d'Anvers*, March 22, 1829, pp. 2-3.

110 Staes, 202-03.

111 De Paepe, 84

112 "Généalogie de la famille baronniale Solvyns," unpublished family record. Baron Solvyns had served as the minister to the courts of Portugal, Sweden, Turkey, and Italy between 1858 and 1873, and had been ambassador in London from 1873 until his death in 1894. Boase, 3:665. His obituary, with a picture, appeared in *The Times* of London January 4, 1894, p. 5, and January 9, 1894, p. 6.

113 "Généalogie de la famille baronniale Solvyns," unpublished family record.

114 "Généalogie de la famille baronniale Solvyns," unpublished family record.

115 For a discussion of the album, see Chapter Three, pp. 83-85.

116 See Chapter Three, pp. 81-83, for a discussion of the drawings used for the etchings. One of the original drawings (the Āhir, Pl. I.42) is reproduced for comparison with the Calcutta and Paris etchings.

117 23 (January-April 1843), 190-91.

118 See discussion of the painting, p. 69.

119 *Good Old Days*, 2:2-3.

120 Mildred Archer, *Early Views of India*, 104; W. H. Carey, *Good Old Days*, 2:5.

121 See De Marchi, 214-19, on the role of lotteries in the seventeenth century art market in Holland.

122 I am grateful to Neil De Marchi for his clarification of the procedure.

Chapter Three

Balthazar Solvyns, Artist and Orientalist

In the years after his death in 1824, Solvyns came largely to be forgotten. In brief biographical entries or in occasional references, his etchings of the Hindus were described as crude, albeit faithful to his subject, and when they were copied, it was usually without attribution. Few scholars of Indian culture knew of Solvyns's work; fewer still had ever seen his etchings or read his accompanying descriptive text. Histories of Calcutta and studies of Bengali culture were published without drawing upon the rich sources of Solvyns's portrait of the Hindus. For nearly 150 years, in studies of European artists in India, Solvyns received only passing mention, if at all. It was not until 1969, through an article by Mildred Archer, the leading authority on European artists in India and the art of the British Raj, that Solvyns's work began to gain recognition.

In recent years, several books and articles on India have reproduced etchings by Solvyns as illustrative of Calcutta two hundred years ago, but few have drawn substantively on these portrayals or on Solvyns's text. Solvyns's work has been included in exhibitions and collectors seek his etchings or the rare oil painting that may come onto the market, but Solvyns, even today, has not attained the recognition as an artist and Orientalist he had sought in his own lifetime. Comparatively few academic specialists on India are familiar with Solvyns and his portrait of the Hindus, and among the larger audience of those interested in India, its peoples and cultures, Solvyns remains almost entirely unknown.

The preceding pages provide an account of Solvyns's life and his great project to portray the Hindus. We now turn to a closer consideration of the artistic and print traditions to which his etchings relate and the influences that shaped the character of his work. In examining his style and technique, we compare the Calcutta and Paris editions of the prints and the format and organization of the volumes. We look, as well, at Solvyns's impact on the Company School of Indian painting and at the copies made after Solvyns's etchings by both Indian and European artists.

Critical Judgment and Market Value

In one of the earliest judgments of Solvyn's work, Louis Langlès, in 1805, described the *Collection* of Calcutta etchings as "invaluable," combining "a truly distinguished talent" with rare precision in commitment to "austere truth."[1] Johann Fiorillo, in his history of art, published in Germany in 1808, judged Solvyns's Calcutta etchings notable for their "accuracy and beauty."[2] Soon after Solvyns's death, however, Depping described the etchings—both Calcutta and Paris editions—as bad artistically, but "notable for their fidelity."[3] Quèrard, in *La France littéraire,* echoed the judgment.[4]

The distinguished Orientalist Horace H. Wilson (1786-1860), who served in Calcutta as Secretary to the Asiatic Society of Bengal and later, in London, as the Director of the Royal Asiatic Society, recognized Solvyns for the "comprehensive scale" of his work. "The drawings of Solvyns, originally etched and published by himself in Calcutta, represent Hindus of various castes and avocations, with very commendable fidelity, but with little of picturesque effect." He notes that the series was "re-engraved" in Paris, and writes, "The engravings are of course much superior to the etchings printed in Calcutta, but they necessarily retain the stiffness and hardness of the original designs."[5]

Ebert's biographical dictionary, first published in German in the 1820s, described the prints of *Les Hindoûs* as "distinguished by a rare fidelity and truth of representation."[6] The emphasis on fidelity was recurrent in descriptions of Solvyns's work in the years that followed, but more often than not, the etchings were disparaged for want of picturesque beauty and technical skill. Brunet's guide to rare book sales, for example, describes *Les Hindoûs* as "a curious work whose colored prints are remarkable more for their character of truth than for their execution, which, to tell the truth, from an artistic point of view, is less than mediocre."[7]

Baron Jules Saint-Genois, in 1847, wrote of Solvyns's work that "if the prints do not have irreproachable execution, they have at least scrupulous exactitude."[8] And Josef Staes, in his 1884 account of Antwerp travelers, emphasizes Solvyns's veracity: "Regarded from an artistic point of view the illustrations are certainly not what one would call beautiful; yet we do not doubt the fact that they are faithful to the truth. The text is short and mostly rather dry and stiff; yet the writer records nothing save what he has seen with his own eyes."[9]

Solvyns had failed financially in his *Collection of Two Hundred and Fifty Coloured Etchings*, published in Calcutta, and the French edition, *Les Hindoûs,* brought him close to bankruptcy. For much of the next 150 years, Solvyns's works, as they occasionally came onto the rare book market, fared poorly. *Les Hindoûs* and the rarer Calcutta edition were offered for a fraction of the price Solvyns originally sought. *Les Hindoûs* had been advertised in Britain in 1813 at 100 guineas, but by 1817, "Ackermann's Library" offered copies of the set at £84 in boards.[10] In 1841, London dealer Henry Bohn's *Catalog of Books* listed three sets of *Les Hindoûs,* priced from 12 to 20 guineas, depending on the binding.[11] In 1847, Bohn again listed the more expensive set—four volumes "bound in russia extra, gilt edges, by Straggemeier"—at 20 guineas, the value (the dealer noted) of the binding alone. A volume containing 150 etchings of the original Calcutta edition was offered at 4 guineas.[12]

Brunet's manual for rare books (1860-65) records French sales of *Les Hindoûs* well below the original price of 1760 francs for the unbound volumes. Over the previous two decades, bound sets of the four volumes had sold in a range from 100 to 376 francs. Brunet also notes that the 1799 Calcutta edition, which had first sold in France at 600 francs, had also seen declining value.[13]

Solvyns Rediscovered

In the late 1960s, in the course of her work on European artists in India, Mildred Archer, then curator of prints and drawings at the India Office Library in London, was drawn to the study of "the life and work of a Flemish artist whose experiences in India caused him to play no mean part in the education of Europe in Indian life."[14] With her husband, William G. Archer, for many years Keeper of the India Section of the Victoria and Albert Museum, she wrote "Francois Baltazard Solvyns: Early Painter of Calcutta Life" for a 1968 festschrift honoring the Bengali scholar Humayun Kabir. It was the first article on Solvyns, beyond brief entries in biographical dictionaries, since Lesbroussart's 1826 paper following the artist's death. The article repeats some of the inaccuracies of early biographical accounts, but Mildred Archer, through close examination of the *Calcutta Gazette* in the years of Solvyns's residence in India, fills in details of Solvyns's work in Calcutta and his proposal to publish *A Collection of Two Hundred and Fifty Coloured Etchings: Descriptive of the Manners, Customs and Dresses of the Hindoos.* Moreover, she places Solvyns in the context of other European artists working in India and is the first to recognize Solvyns's influence on Indian artists of what came to be called the Company School, the genre of paintings of Indian life—costumes, occupations, festivals—produced principally for Europeans in India.

In embarking on his "great scheme" to portray the Hindus, the Archers write that Solvyns, though without training in print-making, made the etchings himself, and "the result by contemporary European standards was monotonous and unattractive. . . . Solvyns's pictures, with their elongated figures, fuzzy hatching and flat washes of sombre colour were, as [his *Calcutta Gazette*] obituary observed, 'rude' and 'not very picturesque.'"[15] "At the same time," they conclude, "his pictures with their careful detail, not only of dress, but of crafts, tools and environment, convey a wealth of information concerning caste, costume, technology and a way of life that is fast disappearing in India today. They are, in fact, the first great ethnographic survey of life in Bengal . . . ."[16]

The Kabir festschrift had a limited reach, but in January 1969, Mildred Archer published "Baltazard Solvyns and the Indian Picturesque" for *The Connoisseur* magazine. The widely-read article varied only slightly from the earlier version and included additional plates illustrating Solvyns's work as well as copies after Solvyns and paintings of the Company School.

The Archer articles awakened interest in Solvyns, and works on Bengali history, society, and culture began to recognize Solvyns's contribution. Occasional references to Solvyns had appeared in earlier years, as in the pages of *Bengal Past and Present*, and in the 1930s, a series of volumes of extracts from old newspapers, in Bengali, included nine plates redrawn from Solvyns etchings.[17] Calcutta historian Pradip Sinha, writing in the 1960s, recognized the importance of Solvyns, along with the Daniells and others, in providing "a graphic and still largely unexplored view of the social life of the

Indians and English in Bengal."[18] But with the Archer articles, Solvyns gained wider recognition. In 1978, Somendra Chandra Nandy, in his biography of "Cantoo Baboo," reproduced fifteen Solvyns plates. The Tollygunge Club's *Calcutta 200 Years,*[19] published in 1981, included nine Solvyns plates among its many illustrations, but did not draw on Solvyns more substantively in discussing Calcutta society. *Calcutta: The Living City,*[20] a richly illustrated two-volume 1990 portrait of the city commemorating its 300th anniversary, makes extensive use of Solvyns, but again more by way of illustration that as an ethnographic source. And *Naari,*[21] a tribute to the women of Calcutta, 1690 to 1990, includes eight color plates from *Les Hindoûs.* Calcutta's tricentennial was also the occasion for the publication of "A Portrait of "Black Town: Baltazard Solvyns in Calcutta, 1791-1804,"[22] a precursor to *A Portrait of the Hindus.*

Solvyns reproductions appeared in various books on India and on its representation by European artists,[23] and etchings by Solvyns were included in important exhibitions on the art of the Raj. The 1982 exhibition, "India Observed," organized by the Victoria and Albert Museum as a part of Britain's Festival of India, included two Solvyns etchings.[24] Four years later, Solvyns was among the artists represented in "From Merchants to Emperors: British Artists and India, 1757-1930" at the Morgan Library in New York and the Los Angeles County Museum of Art,[25] as he was in exhibitions from the Max Allen and Peter Allen Collection,[26] and the Ehrenfeld Collection.[27] "The Raj: India and the British 1600 - 1947," the stunning exhibition mounted at London's National Portrait Gallery in 1990-1991, included an original watercolor by Solvyns, preparatory to his etching of a *chilim* smoker (Pl. II.207).[28]

Works by Solvyns, both etchings and oil paintings, also came onto the market at auction. Over the years, Sotheby's and Christie's in London periodically offered Solvyns material, as well as copies after Solvyns by both Indian and European artists, and from the mid-1990s, Christie's annual "Visions of India" sales regularly included Solvyns, giving increased visibility to the artist. Among galleries, Spink & Son, long-established London dealers in Asian art, occasionally handled Solvyns, but it was Giles Eyre, beginning with a 1978 exhibition of 26 etchings from *Les Hindoûs,* who gave Solvyns the attention his work deserved.[29]

Solvyns's Sympathy for India

It was Solvyns's sympathetic and realistic portrayal of ordinary Indians that drew Eyre to Solvyns. In his note for the 1978 exhibition, Eyre wrote that Solvyns "wandered all over [Calcutta] drawing men and women of every conceivable caste and calling, not just the servants employed in European households, such as the hookah-bearer, dog-boy and wine-cooler. He delineated every kind of musical instrument, methods of transport, boats on the river and the stranger scenes in the countryside."

Europeans in late eighteenth century Bengal, for the most part, associated fairly easily with Indians. With exceptions surely, they were generally free of the evangelical and utilitarian judgments that, with the sense of racial superiority, came only a few years later to dominate European attitudes toward India and Indians. Solvyns arrived in India as the social distance between European and Indian began to increase,[30] but tolerance remained the prevailing attitude, and if Hinduism was burdened by "superstition," so too, from an Enlightenment perspective, was Christianity. Nevertheless, for the Orientalists, India was in a condition of decay, its religion and culture having declined from a golden Hindu antiquity.[31] No Indians were members of the Asiatic Society in its early years, and while Sir William Jones accepted Indians of the upper class as equals, he had little sympathy for ordinary Indians.[32] But the Orientalists' India was not wholly one of a constructed past. Members of the Asiatic Society like H. T. Colebrooke investigated aspects of contemporary society, albeit with a concern for their origins as revealed in ancient Sanskrit texts.[33]

Solvyns, though not a member of the Asiatic Society, shared much of the Orientalists' perspective and aspired to be recognized among them, but his India was clearly the one in which he lived. He was closely observant, curious, and, even in a time of tolerance, less judgmental of Indian customs than most Europeans of his day. Indeed, he often finds Indian culture and thought superior to much of what was to be found in Europe. Perhaps, in part, as a result of his own "marginality," Solvyns reached out to the India around him, and his etchings reveal a sympathy with the Indians he portrays. No other artist entered the

Indian's world as Solvyns penetrated the heart of Calcutta's 'Black Town."

What is most striking about Solvyns is his genuine interest in the people of India. European artists in India, following the market, were drawn principally to commissioned portraits and landscape. When ordinary Indians were portrayed by such accomplished painters as Tilly Kettle and John Zoffany, they were usually romanticized. In the aquatints of the Daniells' *Oriental Scenery*, human figures provide little more than scale for monuments and landscape. They are almost entirely absent in William Baillie's etchings of Calcutta.

Other than Arthur Devis and, though less important, John Alefounder, Solvyns is the only European artist in the late eighteenth century Bengal who sought to portray Indians in their daily lives. He had a singular understanding of Bengali life and character, and he portrayed his subjects as individuals. No doubt, British residents in Calcutta may have thought Solvyns's interest in Indians somewhat peculiar, for despite the curiosity of the Orientalists, most Europeans regarded Indians as little more than "background" to their own commercial and social activities. As we saw earlier, Solvyns's "marginality" to British society in Calcutta opened him to the experience of Bengali life and made him more sensitive to the ordinary Indian, more sympathetic with Indian culture. Giles Eyre is convinced that no one had his sensitivity. George Chinnery (1774-1832), a decade after Solvyns in Bengal, had what Eyre calls "an amazing antenna for the woodsmoke and cowdung of India, but," he says, "nothing compares with Solvyns."[34]

In his 1978 gallery notes, Eyre wrote, "Adversity sharpened [Solvyns's] observation. . . . Nowhere is there any concession to conventional 'sensibility' or to contemporary taste. Neither the cockroach nor the white-ant is missing; and his drawings must have sent a shudder down the spine of fashionable people serving their dishes of tea, disdainful of the real Bengali world around them."[35] The late Nisith Ranjan Ray, historian of Calcutta and curator of the Victoria Memorial, agreed. In a brief pictorial monograph on Calcutta that reproduced a number of Solvyns etchings, Ray wrote that most European artists in India in the late eighteenth century "preferred to present visual studies of the landscapes, scenes, houses, buildings and streets in and around the official and European residential areas in Calcutta to the exclusion of their Indian counter-parts. . . . Balt. Solvyns is a notable exception. He has left for posterity vivid studies in pictures of the life and living of the people in Calcutta. . . ."[36]

At the time Solvyns was in Calcutta preparing his portrait of the Hindus, Captain Charles Gold (d. 1842), an officer of the Royal Artillery, was pursuing something very similar in South India. Between 1791 and 1798, Gold made a number of sketches of native life that were published after his return to England as *Oriental Drawings* in 1806.[37] The fifty colored etchings depict people, places, and various activities, with a descriptive text accompanying each plate. (See Pl. I.31)

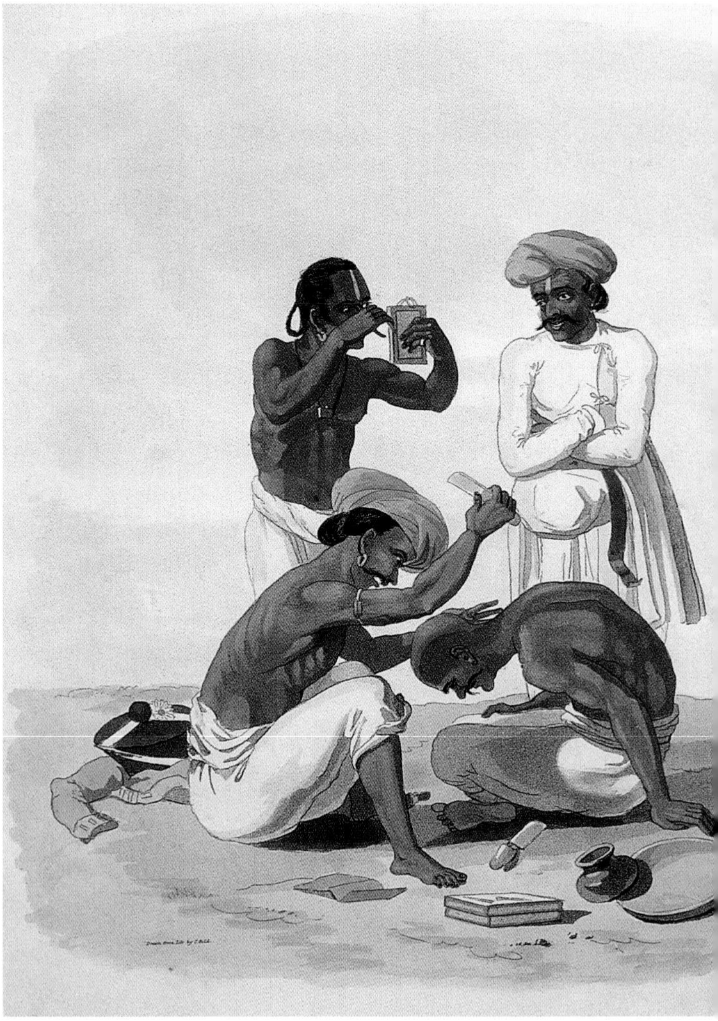

Pl. I.31. "Barbers."
Hand-colored etching by Charles Gold, from *Oriental Drawings* (Pl. 17), 1806. 32 x 25 cm. (sheet). Robert J. Del Bontà Collection, San Francisco.

In his Introduction, Gold writes that "the dresses are minutely attended to, and characters strictly preserved. . . ." He makes no attempt to provide a systematic portrayal comparable to Solvyns's etchings of Bengal, and although he includes some of the same subjects treated by Solvyns—people in their caste occupations, religious penitents (Pl. II.140), and hook-swinging (Pl. II.193)—there is no suggestion that he had used Solvyns's work as a model nor that he had even seen the Calcutta etchings.

Solvyns's Commitment to Truth

From his first announcement of his project to portray the Hindus, Solvyns emphasized his commitment to "truth," to the portrayal of only what he personally observed and to the description of only what he could verify first hand. In the Preliminary Discourse to the first volume of *Les Hindoûs*, he writes that "The drawings from which are engraved the numerous plates with which this work is enriched, were taken by myself upon the spot. Instead of trusting to the works of others, or remaining satisfied with the knowledge contained in preceding authors, I have spared neither time, nor pains, nor expence, to see and examine with my own eyes, and to delineate every object with the most minute accuracy. . . . Truth, perspicuity and precision were the ends at which I constantly aimed." [38]

In his Introduction to *Les Hindoûs*, Vol. II, Solvyns expresses satisfaction that his "exactness" in portraying the Hindus in the first volume

> has met with the approbation of the public, who are sensible that truth is the first quality of a traveller who attempts to give a knowledge of foreign nations, and to draw the attention to subjects till then but little known. Those who are of opinion that a part of this scrupulous fidelity should have been sacrificed to a more pleasing effect in the execution, are not acquainted with the end which I proposed to myself in publishing this work; their number besides is too inconsiderable to render it necessary to enter into a long discussion to convince them of their error. I will not even attempt to conceal from them that the prints in this second volume, and those which are to follow, bear the same distinctive character as those of the first: truth is their predominant quality, and that by which they chiefly endeavour to attract and merit notice.[39]

Solvyns seeks to portray the Hindus with accuracy and truth and, in doing so, provides an unrivaled ethnographic account of Bengal in the late eighteenth century. In a few instances, however, Solvyns fails to adhere to his standard of portraying only what he observed. In "Rājā in Full Dress" (Pl. II.19), he copied an Indian miniature painting, with all its conventions, and in "Vessels of All Sorts" (Pl. II.263), one of the ships (of seventeenth century design) was likely copied from a painting after his return from India. Both prints appear only in the Paris edition. In another print, in both the Calcutta and Paris editions, Solvyns apparently succumbed to the fanciful—or at least to exaggeration—in portraying what he describes as an "Ourang-Outang" (Pl. II.279). But such lapses are exceptional, and Solvyns's fidelity to his subject is his hallmark.

Solvyns's Style: The Drawings[40]

In about 1793, Solvyns began work for his *Collection of Two Hundred and Fifty Coloured Etchings: Descriptive of the Manners, Customs and Dresses of the Hindoos*. He prepared his etchings from drawings that he made from life in and around Calcutta. In some instances, Solvyns invited his subject to model at his house, as he did in portraying the hijrā (Pl. II.94). But whether "in the field" or in the studio, his commitment was to a faithful portrayal of what he observed. He portrays them with sympathy, but without sentimentality. The etchings, he wrote in his introduction to *Les Hindoûs*, "are meerly representations of the objects such as they appeared to my view, and such as they would appear at this hour to the reader, if he could be suddenly transported into the midst of them."[41] Solvyns provides a sense of immediacy, as his images often appear to capture action, like a freeze-frame from a motion picture, with someone just emerging from a doorway (Pl. II.191) or the fleeting glimpse of a man leaving the room (Pl. II.160).

Solvyns was academically trained in Neo-classicism, but his etchings, and the drawings from which they were made, have a "primitive" character and lack the classical form so evident in Devis, whose technique descended from England's great portrait painters.[42] Moreover, in contrast to Devis, Solvyns used a series of horizontal planes. To alter and soften the rigidity of these horizontal planes, Solvyns gave his pictures distinctively dramatic skies, seen in the etchings as well as in his oil paintings.

The etchings, with their somber hues, however, stand in notable contrast to Solvyns's oils, with their strong primary colors. Avoiding the bright (and to European eyes, gaudy) gouaches of Indian artists, in coloring the etchings, Solvyns was limited by the few washes that were available in Calcutta. But the etchings are distinct in style as well. Solvyns was trained as a marine artist, and although as a youth at the Académie in Antwerp he won prizes for his drawings of the plaster casts of classical sculpture, he was not accomplished in portraiture or in representing the human figure from nature. In approaching the subjects that were to constitute his portrait of the Hindus, Solvyns, schooled principally as a marine painter, had little experience to draw upon. When Solvyns put his hand to figure and landscape painting, Solvyns was virtually training himself.[43]

From his sketches, Solvyns prepared the watercolor drawings from which the 250 Calcutta etchings were made. In these drawings, the figures are softer, more individualized in portrayal than in the etchings. This is not surprising given Solvyns's inexperience in working with the needle and the constraints it imposed, but the elongated figures, with their disproportionately long legs and oversized feet, are true to the original drawings. With Solvyns's Académie training and the prizes he won as a student in Antwerp, he knew how to draw (whatever limitations he may have had), and the stylized figures, with their "mannered" elegance were clearly intended.

In the use of mannerist proportions, Solvyns was in the company of many eighteenth century artists who elongated the human figure for effect, as Gainsborough did in his portraits. In India, it is seen, among others, in the work of Hodges, Alefounder, and in drawings by an amateur artist, a contemporary of Solvyns in Calcutta, identified only as "Colonel Green" (Pl. I.32).[44]

Bernard Smith, in *Imagining the Pacific*, a study of the artists who sailed with Captain Cook, refers to the elongated figures by John Webber (1751-1793), who he describes as "Europe's first serious ethnographic artist."[45] "[M]annerist proportions would have given Webber's portrayal of Pacific people elegance and dignity." Webber, Smith writes, "may have believed that the people he encountered possessed an innate human

Pl. I.32. Balasore Palanquin Bearers, by "Colonel Green." Pencil, ink, and watercolor, c. 1790s. Cover illustration for the gallery exhibition catalog, "Records of a Western Response to India 1785-1885," July 20-Aug. 6, 1982. Courtesy Eyre & Hobhouse Ltd.

dignity and sought to make that dignity visible."[46] However odd Solvyns's elongated figures may appear to us, they convey, as do Webber's portrayals, the artist's respect and sympathy for his subject.

Although taken from life, as art historian Malia Finnegan observes, Solvyns's images follow a standard compositional format. In a highly perceptive Master's thesis on Solvyns, using the Paris etchings for her analysis, she describes the constants in format that are also present in the original drawings: "a principal subject who is close to the picture plane and who occupies two-thirds to three-fourths of the vertical picture space, a setting that is associated with the individual, and a composition that takes up all the picture space." Finnegan then describes selected etchings. Of Oriya Brahmin (Pl. II.17), for example, she writes: "By making the Brahmin the composition's central focal point and bringing him close to the picture plane, the artist commands the viewer's attention to the figure and enables him to read the ethnographic details of costume and adornment, facial expression, and physical features."[47] The formula is repeated with variation in subject, pose, and setting.

The collection of Solvyns's original drawings for the etchings are now in the Victoria and Albert Museum. The set consists of 248 drawings, two short of being complete.[48] A title page, hand-lettered in black ink on blue-gray paper, reads: "A Collection of Two Hundred and Fifty Drawings Descriptive of the Manners, Customs and Dresses of the Hindoos by Balt: Solvyns. Calcutta." There is no date. The lettering is in the same style and form as the engraved title page for the *Collection* of etchings, and the flourish of "Calcutta" indicates that it is by the hand of the engraver Francis Dormieux,[49] perhaps provided to Solvyns as a sample of his work.

The drawings, in pencil and watercolor, are organized into twelve sections, corresponding to the order of the etchings in the *Collection*. Those prepared for the standard plates vary slightly in size, but are approximately 37 x 25 cm.; drawings for the eleven large "double" plates preceding Sections II-XII measure roughly 35 x 57.5 cm. The drawings are pasted on sheets of blue-gray paper trimmed to the same size. For each, on the back (verso) of the previous drawing and facing the drawing described, Solvyns lettered in the name of the subject and, on most, the section and drawing (plate) number. These inscriptions are in pencil, with a few completed in ink; most are unfinished.

In December 1798, more than two years after the drawings had been completed and the collection assembled, Solvyns, in a fine hand (clearly learned from copy books), inscribed the pages with a dedication, preface, and a description for each of the 250 drawings. Together, these constitute a draft for what was to appear the following year in the *Catalogue of 250 Coloured Etchings; Descriptive of the Manners, Customs, Character, Dress, and Religious Ceremonies of the Hindoos.*

On the back of the title page in the collection of drawings, Solvyns wrote the draft of the dedication to Lord Wellesley, the Governor General, that was published with greater embellishment in the 1799 *Catalogue*. Solvyns's preface, without title, then follows on the next page, again in his hand, but it bears only fleeting similarity to the published Preface of the *Catalogue*.[50] For each drawing, on the back of the preceding drawing, where he had earlier inscribed the name and number, Solvyns wrote in script a brief description that corresponds closely to the later text of the *Catalogue*.[51]

An Album of Drawings

For at least some of the subjects, Solvyns did more than one copy of the watercolor in preparation for the etchings, for in addition to the drawings in the Victoria and Albert Museum, an album that Solvyns's widow, Marie Anne, presented in 1829 to a friend or patron of her husband contained a number of drawings, at various stages of completion, that were later fully realized in the etchings. The album, "Desseins originaux faits dans l'Inde par François Balthazard Solvyns," contained 41 drawing, some fully complete and watercolored; others were pencil sketch studies. In 1929, the London bookseller Francis Edwards sold the album to a collector in Bombay,[52] and in the mid-1980s, London art dealers Eyre & Hobhouse acquired the album, and soon after the partnership was dissolved, Hobhouse included a watercolor drawing from the album in an exhibition associated with European travels.[53] In 1986, the India Office Library purchased four drawings from the album,[54] and Hobhouse subsequently sold the album to Maggs Bros., London rare book dealer, which offered the collection for sale.[55] The India Office Library purchased another five drawings from Maggs;[56] others were purchased by various private collectors.[57]

The drawings vary in size, with most in a fairly close range of 37 x 26 cm. Two of the 41 drawings are signed "B. Solvyns" on the lower left below the picture. Most are reasonably complete watercolors preparatory to the etchings, and, as those in the Victoria and Albert Museum collection, are reverse images of the Calcutta etchings. (The "reversals" are discussed below in addressing the Calcutta edition.) A few are preliminary drawings, studies not yet fully worked up for the etching. Of these, the most interesting, now in the collection of the India Office Library, is a study of the Kālīghāṭ temple (Pl. II.4) that shows architectural detail and notes on color (Pl. I.33). Another preliminary study, with penciled notes, is of the "Rajah Hindoo at his Prayers" (Pl. I.34) that appeared as an etching only in the Paris edition (Pl. II.18). Nine of the drawings do not correspond to etchings of either the Calcutta or Paris editions. Of these, one is a preliminary drawing for the watercolor that Solvyns did of two Andaman Islanders in 1792 (Pl. I.16).[58] Two are of Hindu ascetics (Pls. I.35 and 36) that for some reason Solvyns chose not to etch and include in the series of "Faquirs and Holy Mendicants." Another drawing that never appeared as an etching portrays a standing man spinning cotton, with another man weaving at a loom (Pl. I.37).

Pl. I.33. Kālīghāṭ temple.
Oriental and India Office Collections. WD 4268.
Pencil, 28.2 x 41.8 cm. Courtesy Maggs Bros Ltd., London.

Pl. I.34. Rajah.
Pencil and watercolor. 39 x 28 cm. Courtesy Niall Hobhouse.

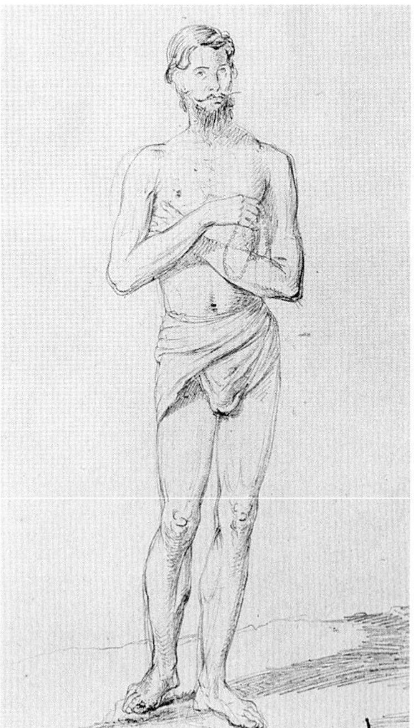

Above left:
Pl. I.35. Standing ascetic wearing a sword and carrying a small staff.
Oriental and India Office Collections. WD 4315.
Pencil. 37 x 25 cm. Courtesy Maggs Bros Ltd., London.

Above right:
Pl. I.36. Standing ascetic holding a rosary.
Oriental and India Office Collections. WD 4316.
Pencil. 37 x 25 cm. Courtesy Maggs Bros Ltd., London.

Pl. I.37. A man spinning cotton, another weaving at the loom.
Oriental and India Office Collections, British Library, WD 4125.
Pencil. 26.9 x 40 cm. By Permission of the British Library.

The album included an especially good watercolor drawing of two hunters, *shikārīs* (Pl. I.38), that was never etched and thus appears in neither the Calcutta nor Paris editions. The Calcutta edition (Sec. I, No. 64), however, contains an anomaly in Solvyns's mislabeling the etching of a Mārāṭha (Pl. II.52) as "A Shikaury," and the error was compounded in the 1799 *Catalogue*, where he described the etching as "Shikaury,—Hunters; with their arms, their method of taking their game, and shooting poisoned arrows at wild beasts." He caught his mistake for *Les Hindoûs*, where it is there correctly identified as portraying a Mārāṭha. Solvyns's *Catalogue* entry describes the drawing illustrated here. A shikārī stands with his bow and arrows, and, behind him, we see the upper portion of another hunter carrying a spear.

Native shikārīs were usually lower caste Hindus "who gain their livelihood entirely by catching birds, hares, and all sorts of animals."* Europeans in India used the Hindustani word *shikārī* both for "a native expert, who either brings in game on his own account, or accompanies European sportsmen as guide and aid," and for the European sportsman himself.** With the European love of hunting, there is an enormous literature on the *shikār*, and it was a favored subject by European artists in India. Among the most famous collections of prints–and one to which Solvyns refers in the text for the Paris edition (Pl. II.281)–is Thomas Williamson and Samuel Howett, *Oriental Field Sports*, with 40 colored engravings, first published in 1807 by Edward Orme–the same Orme who had pirated Solvyns's Calcutta etchings for *The Costume of Indostan*.

* Daniel Johnson (1822), 25, in *Hobson-Jobson*, 827.

** *Hobson-Jobson*, 827-28.

Pl. I.38. Shikārīs, Hunters.
Pencil and watercolor. 36.8 x 25 cm. Courtesy Erye and Greig, Ltd.

The Peabody Essex Watercolor

What is almost surely an original watercolor drawing by Solvyns of Jhāpān, the snake festival, is included among the unbound Calcutta etchings in the collection of the Peabody Essex Museum.[59] The section and numbers are written in at the top, with the title (later trimmed) below the picture. The watercolor corresponds to the composition of the Calcutta etching and was apparently copied from the print, for it is the reverse image of the original drawing (in the Victoria and Albert Museum) from which the etching was made. One can only speculate as to why Solvyns did the watercolor. Perhaps, in assembling a collection for a buyer, he did not have a copy of the Jhāpān print on hand and simply prepared the watercolor as a substitute, inserting it in its appropriate place among the etchings. Another copy of Solvyns's Jhāpān is by an Indian artist (see below, Pl. I.51).

The Solvyns Etchings: Calcutta and Paris Editions

Print Traditions

Etching served Solvyns well in what he sought to do and to convey as an artist. He had no training in engraving, and his skills in etching were rudimentary and almost surely self-taught, but Solvyns found in etching an almost direct translation of the original drawing. The free trace of the etching has the fluency of drawing in contrast to the precision and clarity of the engraved line. Solvyns's work on the copper plate lacks finesse—indeed, it was dismissed by his critics as crude—but he brings to the print an immediacy that reduces the distance between the viewer and the subject. Thus, ironically, Solvyns's limited skill in working with the medium served his artistic purpose.

For all Solvyns's commitment to "truthfulness" in the portrayal of what he saw, the etchings are not simply ethnographic representations of costumes and customs. Solvyns *interprets* India as he experienced it. He seeks to represent the Hindus, not in the picturesque or romantic, but, nevertheless, in an artist's vision, presented artistically.

That Solvyns was bringing artistic sensibility to what he observed and then portrayed in the etchings is evident in his use of various conventions from European traditions. In many prints, for example, he includes elements of recognized genre, as the woman and child in the background of the portrayal of the Pod laborer (Pl. II.69)—scenes of ordinary people and everyday life with social concern. In another print, Bisarjan (Pl. II.190), depicting the immersion of the goddess Kālī, Solvyns (in the Paris etching only) includes a figure in the boat who looks out at us, a European convention to draw the viewer into the picture.

In preparing the Calcutta etchings, Solvyns drew upon eighteenth century artistic conventions in European drawing and watercolor, and he wanted to convey to the viewer the intimacy and the immediacy of drawings. In format, Solvyns reduced the "printness" of the etchings to an absolute minimum. He trimmed the etched sheet *within* the intaglio platemark to give it the appearance of a drawing rather than a print, and he mounted the etching on a larger paper, placing a border around the picture in the manner of a deluxe presentation of a drawing. Moreover, Solvyns intended that, as a collection, the etchings provide the pleasure, both in ownership and in examination, of an album of watercolors—an impression further enhanced by hand-coloring.

In producing what might be described as multiple drawing albums, Solvyns responded to a European taste for collecting affordable surrogate drawings, that is, prints that reproduce, recreate, and give to the purchaser the appearance of drawing. Etchings presented in this form date from the sixteenth century, and they reach their apogee in the late eighteenth century. The aquatint, for example, introduced in the mid-eighteenth century, provides a particularly effective way of reproducing wash drawings and, with the addition of colors by hand, gives a "spontaneity and natural effect not seen in other forms of engraving."[60] Paul Sandby (1725-1809) did exactly that in affecting a set of watercolor landscapes in his views of Wales (1775),[61] the first great English project in aquatint. Thomas and William Daniell followed some years later with their magnificent aquatints of India, *Oriental Scenery*. Collections of aquatints, as illustrated travel books, were enormously popular well into the 1830s, when they were overtaken by the new process of lithography.[62]

In the eighteenth century, prints were only occasionally framed and hung on the wall. Instead, collectors placed their prints and drawings in large, bound albums. Such albums were typically organized by subject—one for landscapes, another for portraits—though major artists might command separate albums for their various works. Artists responded by preparing their own albums, collections of engravings or etchings on a particular theme or subject.

Solvyns, from his studies in Antwerp and Paris, would have been familiar with such albums, and he would surely have seen some of the most popular collections of prints portraying genre scenes of everyday life, street criers, and working people and prints of the costumes of exotic lands—subjects that closely correspond to his portrayal of the Hindus.

Sets of prints portraying costume date from as early as the mid-sixteenth century, and by the eighteenth century, they are among the most popular subjects in the growing market for collections of prints.[63] The engravings in Nicholas de Nicolay's account of his travels in Turkey provide a prototype for books on costume.[64] The Nicolay plates depict Turkish men and women as "types," engaged in various trades and with their distinctive costumes. The Ottoman Empire, especially after the 1683 siege of Vienna, excited considerable European interest, and illustrated books depicted the manners, customs, and costumes of the Turks and their subject peoples. The Flemish artist Jean-Baptiste Vanmour (1671-1737) settled in Constantinople, where he was patronized by both Turks and Europeans. His most important commission, by the French ambassador, Charles de Ferriol, was for a series of 100 paintings of Levantine costumes that were engraved, after Vanmour drawings, for the famous *Recueil de cent estampes représentant différentes nations du Levant*, published in 1714 by Jacques Le Hay.[65] A German translation soon followed, and pirated editions were brought out in Italian and Spanish. Most of the engravings focus on a central figure as a "type," posed, and modeling a costume. (See Pl. I.39) In the format of its presentation, the Le Hay collection became a model for the genre, and Solvyns would likely have seen it as a student in Antwerp or Paris. Indeed, this could well have been a prototype for Solvyns's Calcutta etchings, for the figures are similar in form, though not in the character of artistic expression.

Pl. I.39. "Barbier Ambulant" (Itinerant Barber).
No. 58, Jacques Le Hay, *Recueil de cent estampes représentant différentes nations du Levant*, 1714. Engraving by G. Scotin. Courtesy Maggs Bros Ltd., London.

Jean-Baptiste Le Prince (1734-1781), often credited as the inventor of the aquatint process, produced several series of enormously popular prints depicting the peoples and costumes of various nations, the most famous of which portray Russia.[66] The Le Prince aquatints vary in subject from a single figure to more complex genre scenes of common life, presented with great virtuosity in technique.[67] Among the most comprehensive volumes of costume prints was Thomas Jefferys's *Collection of the Dresses of Different Nations* (1752-1772), with 480 plates, copies of work by other artists, including Le Prince.[68] Pierre Duflos's folio collection of 264 hand-colored engravings (1780) was among the most sumptuous published in the late eighteenth century. The prints portray single figures rather fancifully costumed, with no background, representing all nations.

These artists, following Le Hay, generally placed their central figure in a setting that suggests context (albeit minimally), but costume studies and collections of fashion plates often portrayed the subject against little more than the white background of the page itself. The various costume books published by William Miller in London, for example, are of this character, as is *The Costume of Indostan*, Orme's pirated edition of Solvyns's etchings.[69]

Solvyns, by contrast, is concerned with context, and though most figures stand in poses similar to those in which Le Hay, among others, positioned his subjects, he provides a background that relates directly to what they do in life. But in this too, Solvyns comes out of an established tradition. From the early seventeenth century, with its concern for greater naturalism and for the representation of the subject in the context of a particular time and space, it was conventional to portray the figure against a background that suggested his or her work or activities. Sets of prints depicting street criers were especially popular, selling in the thousands.[70] Notable is the famous set of 80 prints, after drawings by Annibale Carracci, portraying the trades of Bologna. The original drawings probably date from the 1590s, but Simon Guillain (1589-1658), a Frenchman, etched them in the mid-seventeenth century.[71] Each print depicts a single figure as representative of an occupation, in a format very similar to Solvyns's presentation.

The wonderfully evocative "Cries of Paris" (1737-46), sixty etchings after drawings by sculptor Edmé Bouchardon (1698-1762), portrays various trades and occupations of Paris.[72] Wheatley's *The Cries of London*, with genre scenes focusing on street criers, enjoyed great popularity through various editions.[73] Another set, *Divers portraits* (1775), is by Giovanni David (1743-1790), a Genoese painter, occasional etcher, and one of the pioneers of aquatint in Italy. The series of twelve prints of Italian genre types shows people from different walks of life.[74] One print portrays a fisherwoman of Palestrina, with a rod over her arm and against a background suggesting her work (Pl. I.40). She is an archetype, but not without individual personality. The character of the print, as in the use of the line, cross-hatching, and the way the sky is handled, is similar to Solvyns in many ways, and it is possible that he might have seen David's work while he was in Paris as a student. He was, in any case, almost surely familiar with the genre.

Pl. I.40. 'Femme de Palestrina."
Etching and aquatint, Giovanni David, 1775. 24.2 x 16.9 cm. Jack S. Blanton Museum of Art, The University of Texas at Austin. Gift of Julia and Stephen Wilkinson 1993.

In representing the Hindus in their various occupations and pursuits, Solvyns's etchings are clearly in the tradition of the systematic portrayal of costumes and trades, but his prints depicting festivals and religious ritual draw on another tradition in printmaking: the schematic rendering of the ethnographic, the curious, and the exotic. Fascination with the unfamiliar has always been present in art, and in the graphic arts, we find it in prints of the fantastic during the Middle Ages. With the voyages of discovery, we get efforts to provide systematic visual records of new found lands and peoples, of which the engravings by Theodor de Bry (1528-1598), after John White's watercolors of Native Americans in Virginia, are a superb example.[75]

Closer to Europe, the Ottoman Empire exerted its fascination through various accounts and portrayals that continued, in "the Oriental obsession," well into the nineteenth century.[76] Cornelis de Bruyn

(1652-1726), a Dutch traveler and painter, published his *A Voyage to the Levant*, with 210 engravings, to great popularity. First in Dutch in 1698, it was then published in French (1700) and in English (1702), and went through numerous editions. Another volume, first published in French in 1718, illustrated Bruyn's *Travels into Muscovy, Persia, and Parts of the East-Indies*. Its 320 plates portray peoples, costumes, cities, architectural monuments, modes of transport, fauna, and flora in an encyclopedic survey.[77]

Among the most lavish travel collections from the late sixteenth and early seventeenth centuries were those of the Dutch voyager Linschoten (1563-1611)[78] and of Bry.[79] Both include accounts of India that are notable for their impressive engravings. Although European books on India often included engravings of the exotic—frequently fanciful, sometimes fantastic, representations based on travelers' accounts and tales—Linschoten and Bry seek to provide a realistic and credible portrayal. The books by the Dutch traveler Philippus Baldaeus (1632-1672) include engravings of the "gods and monsters" variety, but the prints in his *Naauwkeurige beschyvinge* (Amsterdam, 1672) are remarkably faithful to their subject. Indeed, his scenes of life in South India and Ceylon are not unlike those portrayed by Solvyns more than a century later.[80] The engravings in Robert Knox's *An Historical Relation of the Island Ceylon in the East Indies* (London, 1681) reflect an intended fidelity to the subject that Solvyns would have appreciated.[81] And the 1704 engraving of the snake-charmer of Malabar (Pl. I.41), illustrating the travels of Johannes Nieuhof (1618-1672), might have been by Solvyns himself but for the wildly fanciful cobras.[82]

It is unlikely that Solvyns would have seen either the Knox prints of Ceylon or the Malabar engraving, but he was surely familiar with the more favored depiction of the images of gods and monsters, of tortured religious austerities, and of suttee.[83] Bernard Picart (1673-1733), a French artist and engraver and perhaps the leading illustrator of the early eighteenth century, portrayed religious practice in India in an enormously popular series of engravings that went into many editions.[84] (See Pl. I.42.) In his "Introductory Discourse" to *Les Hindoûs*, Solvyns expressed disdain for renderings of an imaginary India and promised his reader to portray the Hindus, as he observed them, with "fullness, truth and spirit to the resemblance." But Solvyns by no means ignores the "exotic," as is clearly evident in his series of "Fakirs and Holy Mendicants" (Pls. II.135-45) and in the etchings of suttee (Pls. II. 199-202) and the expiatory rite of Caṛak Pūjā, "hook-swinging" (Pl. II.193).

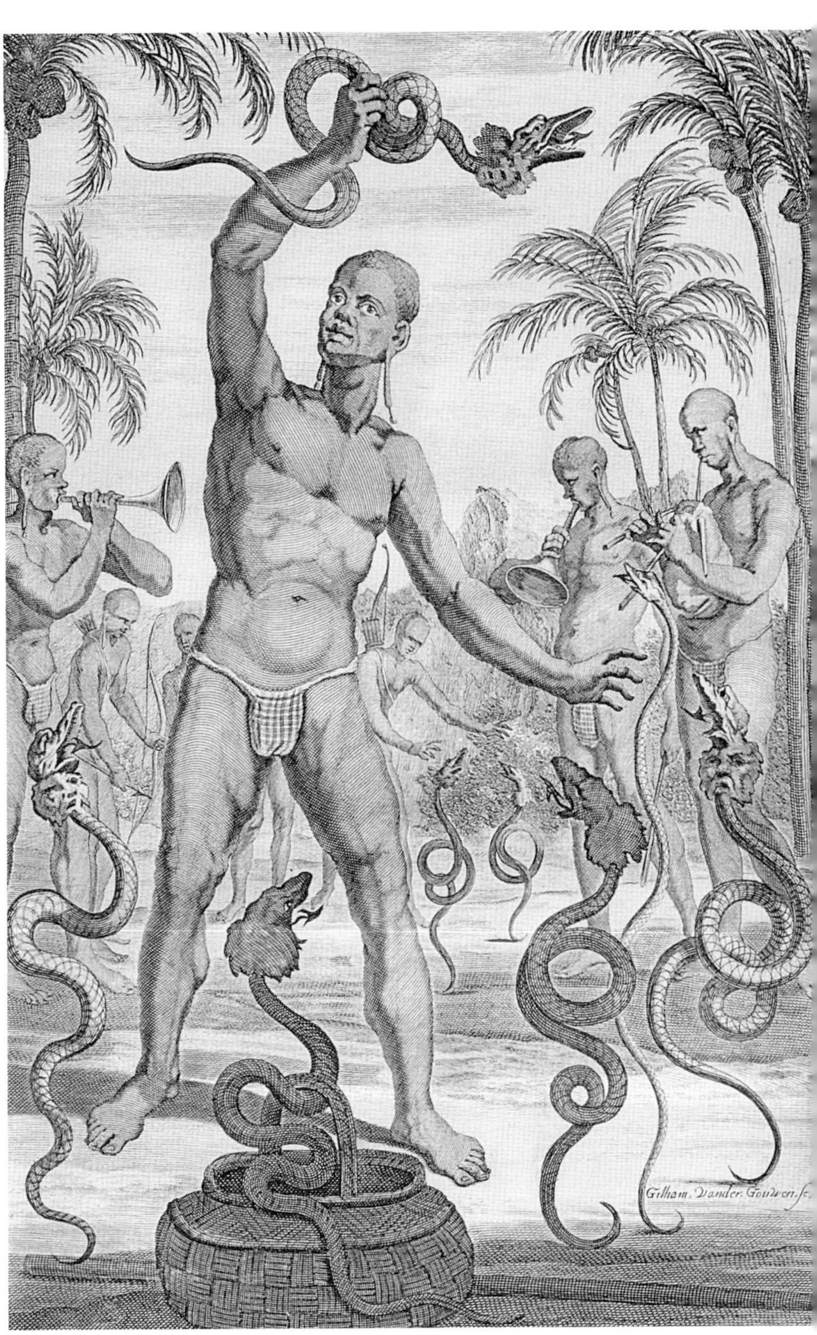

Pl. I.41. "A Malabar Shewing tricks with Serpents."
Engraving from *A Collection of Voyages and Travels*, 2nd. ed. London, 1732 [1704]. 28 x 18.4 cm. Robert J. Del Bontà Collection, San Francisco.

Solvyns's etchings of the Hindus reflect printmaking traditions in the portrayal of costumes, trades, and the exotic, but Solvyns is not simply recording ethnographic types. He gives his figures individual character and places them in time and space, with narrative interest—as, for example, in his

Pl. I.42. "Divers Pagods and the Penitence of the Faquirs."
Engraving, Bernard Picart, c. 1730. 33.8 x 41.7 cm.

inclusion of a partially seen figure leaving the room (Pl. II.160). There is a story, and Solvyns provides the viewer intimate access. This separates him from purely encyclopedic interest, for with artistic purpose he combines the ethnographic and the aesthetic. He conveys "art as information."[85]

In the Calcutta etchings, especially the more complex scenes of the double-plates, Solvyns's free line, his roughness and directness of touch, suggest another source of influence in the English satirical prints of James Gillray (1756-1815) and Thomas Rowlandson (1756-1827), with their pronounced rudeness in line work. There is nothing of the satirical in Solvyns's portrayals—as there is in some later work by European artists in India[86]—and Solvyns does not have the boldness and marvelously expressive physiognomies of Gillray and Rowlandson, but he surely would have known the prints from their circulation in Calcutta. Gillray and Rowlandson frequently directed their scorn at the East India Company and the British in India.[87] Influence may have gone in the other direction as well, with British satirists drawing upon Solvyns. Rowlandson's "The Burning System,"[88] for example, with its central scene of suttee, along with musicians and hook-swinging, suggests that Rowlandson might well have seen Solvyns's etchings, though the subjects were also portrayed by other artists in India.

The Picturesque

Solvyns drew upon various print traditions, but his commitment to a gritty ethnographic realism, albeit with artistic purpose, separated him from the vogue for the picturesque. From the 1780s, books by William Gilpin (1724-1804) popularized what came to be known as the "picturesque."[89] Theorists of the picturesque recommended "irregularity, variation, decay and wildness in 'natural' appearance as sources of aesthetic pleasure."[90] The artist who observed nature through the lens of the picturesque might thus "improve" the landscape in its representation. Favored subjects included gnarled trees with rough foliage, craggy cliffs, waterfalls, rustic bridges, rude cottages, and ruins. In contrast to the earlier aesthetic category of the sublime, characterized by vastness and grandeur and evoking awe, the picturesque conveyed an atmosphere of nostalgia and melancholy.[91]

By the late eighteenth century, the sketchbook had become an essential accessory of travel—as the camera is today—and most travelers either made sketches themselves or took professional artists with them to depict what they saw.[92] Professional artists, like William Hodges and William and Thomas Daniell, themselves became travelers "in search of the picturesque," of rough and irregular landscapes and the pleasure of ruins.[93] And for those at home there was the delight in richly illustrated books of travel—"the picturesque voyage"—and collections of "views" in lavish folio editions of engravings, etchings, and aquatints.[94] Hodges, with the publication of *Select Views of India* (1785-1788), was the first professional artist to illustrate his travels in India in a collection of prints. The Daniells, with the 144 colored aquatints of *Oriental Scenery* (1795-1808), were among the many to follow.[95]

Solvyns's aesthetic, however, did not conform to the standards of the "picturesque" that shaped the representation of the unfamiliar in illustrated books of travel at the end of the eighteenth century. Solvyns's etchings, as we have noted, were disparaged for their want of the picturesque. But criticism was directed, as well, at the "crudeness" of his style and technique. Bruhn, in his catalog for the prints of the Max and Peter Allen Collection, writes of the Calcutta edition that Solvyns's "etching is technically and stylistically crude, and he handles the needle in a squiggly, unsure fashion. The coloring is thin and at times almost washed out. But the work shows such a cumulative energy, as the pages are turned, that these shortcomings become altogether minor. The figures have an immediacy that only an observant person could give them, and Solvyns imparts a sympathetic and monumental aspect to each subject by making it dominate the background and the full page."[96]

The Calcutta Etchings[97]

Etching underscores the identification of the print with drawing, and, more than any technique until lithography, it is a medium that allows the artist great freedom and that demands little training. You cannot simply enter into the practice of engraving and teach yourself, but if you know how to draw, as Solvyns did, all you need is a grounded plate and you can translate your drawing style to its surface.

In terms of the individual images of the Calcutta etchings, Solvyns understands that there are conventional ways of making shapes plausible in three dimensions by variation in shading, hatching, cross-hatching, and so on, but he does not bring it off very well. The line is scratchy, and his handling of space is awkward. The spatial problem is seen, for example, in the odd—almost disorienting—perspective of the carpet on which the Jamādār (Pl. II.101) stands—clearly evident in the Calcutta etching, but, by coloration, even more pronounced in the Paris edition. Although his elongated figures are clearly intentional, his treatment of human proportions are not quite right, and he has problems with foreshortening. He understands that shading is a way of defining volume in human anatomy, but he does not know how to lay the lines to make it effective. On the other hand, Solvyns is accomplished, even subtle, in how he disposes line across a larger, more abstract area, as in his treatment of the draperies in the costumes he portrays.

In his etching technique, he uses only one needle, or point, for the whole etching. It is a single bite, that is, it is produced by a single, relatively short immersion of the copper plate in acid, giving fairly shallow depth. The Calcutta etchings, however, vary considerably in line from plate to plate. In some, the line is very thin and light; in others, it is wide and dark. This difference results from variation in the length of time these plates were bitten in acid. A brief exposure would have produced the lighter effect, a longer one the darker effect. There is no indication of foul-biting, that is, of any unintended biting where the ground was not laid in efficiently or gave way unexpectedly during the biting.

Solvyns's work on the plates is not refined. In the Calcutta etchings, he is really improvising—and under difficult conditions—but he understands enough to make it work. Solvyns knows, for example, that he does not have to lay the lines in too closely because he will be coloring them by hand. Thus, when he wants deeper shadow, he need not worry about having to make the lines dense. He relies on color, as he does in sometimes finishing a line, as in one print where the etched line of a tree was not drawn to the ground—as if the tree hangs in space—but Solvyns grounds it with color. Similarly, he paints clouds in where there may be unetched sky. In what may have been an afterthought, in his Calcutta etching of the ḍoṅga (Pl. II.243), a dug-out boat, a bold sunset is wholly painted in. (The sunset is in neither the original drawing nor the Paris etching.)

With unetched lines, Solvyns may well have acted with purpose, for the overall effect is confirmation that he intended his *Collection of Two Hundred and Fifty Coloured Etchings* to be a drawing album. He knows from the beginning that they are to be presented as drawings. Solvyns gives us not simply an ethnographic record of "the manners, customs, character, dress, and religious ceremonies of the Hindoos," but an artistic interpretation—as Le Hay, Le Prince, and others did earlier with ethnographic material. Solvyns, though perhaps not consciously, comes out of that tradition, but the Calcutta etchings lack technical artistic accomplishment and met poor reception.

The title page for the *Collection* was engraved by Dormieux (discussed in Chapter One),[98] but the section pages and titles appear to be by a different, less skilled hand, perhaps by Solvyns himself. The section pages are engraved in the same style as the names and numbers that label each etching. The style is that of an "alphabet book," a printed pattern book of characters and calligraphy used as a model for draftsman or in learning penmanship.

Differences Among Copies of the Calcutta Edition

There is nothing to suggest the number of copies Solvyns may have made of the Calcutta etchings. They were first issued with an engraved title page bearing the date 1796, but only six copies of the 1796 imprint are known to survive; other copies with a title page bear the date 1799. Every copy of the Calcutta etchings varies in one way or another. Solvyns sold *The Collection of Two Hundred and Fifty Coloured Etchings* unbound, and, reflecting the taste of the individual subscribers or later collectors, there is considerable variation in binding. A few copies today are in one-volume original Calcutta leather bindings; some are in Calcutta bindings of two volumes; others have been bound (or rebound) in Europe. Bound volumes are not always complete, some lacking one or two prints; others missing substantially more, occasionally whole sections. And although most etchings are bound in Solvyns's numbered order, a few volumes mix them up.

Some collections of etchings were never bound at all. The Wellcome Institute Library, London, has in its print collection, for example, a number of individual Solvyns etchings.[99] A few are from the Paris edition, but most are Calcutta etchings, colored and pasted on paper, with ink ruled borders and the title pasted below. Uniquely, however, the Wellcome collection also includes a few Calcutta etchings, uncolored or partially colored, that were never affixed to the folio pages, that is, pasted on the larger sheets of paper that provide both border and backing. These are among the few copies of the etchings—on their almost tissue-thin paper, possibly made by Solvyns himself—that are unmounted.

There is considerable variation among copies of the Calcutta etchings in format, titling, textual accompaniment, and coloration. (See Pl. I.44 for standard format.) The size of the papers on which the etchings are mounted also varies, from roughly 41 to 53 cm. in height and 27 to 36.5 cm. in width. Those bearing the 1796 imprint are on the smaller sheets, but there is no uniformity in size even here.[100] No two copies of either the 1796 or 1799 imprints are, in fact, exactly alike, and the variation is often substantial.

The copy of the rare 1796 Calcutta printing in the Departement des Estampes, Bibliothèque nationale, Paris, is 43 x 32 cm. in size, and the paper on which the etchings are pasted is of cream color (the case for most copies of the Calcutta *Collection*). Each etching is framed by four lined borders in black ink, with a light blue wash on the outside and a darker blue wash in the inner border. The engraved labels for Section and Number are pasted in at the top on the left and right, respectively, and the title is pasted below the etching—all within the inner border and are colored in blue wash. The etchings are in two volumes, bound in rich, tooled morocco, with the title "Costumes des Indous par Solvyns" on the spine. The pages are gilt-edged.

The copies of the 1796 imprint in the Buffalo and the University of Texas libraries contrast with the Paris copy in a number of ways, most notably in that the etchings in both are mounted on blue paper.[101] Neither copy has the complete 250 etchings, and in the Texas copy, many of the etchings are either uncolored or only partially colored. Although organized according to Solvyns's scheme, the etchings in the Buffalo and Texas copies lack his engraved titles and numbers, and at some later time, they were written in by hand.[102] These copies must surely have been among of the first to be assembled, but it seems odd that Solvyns would have allowed copies so unfinished to leave his studio. Even in copies bearing the 1799 title page, however, a few etchings may lack the engraved title and number labels and have instead hand-lettered titles and numbers, either in pencil or ink, that Solvyns did himself—and even these are sometimes unfinished. In a few instances the titles and/or numbers are altogether absent. In most copies, Solvyns drew a double-lined border, though even here there is some variation from copy to copy.

One of the most pronounced differences among copies of the Calcutta etchings is in coloration. Although some volumes contain a few etchings that are uncolored or only partially colored, most prints are colored, but with variation. Solvyns relied heavily on Indian assistants under his supervision to color the etchings in accordance with the original drawings, but sets were printed and colored over a period of several years, with variation in shade and thickness of the watercolors used. When a printing of a particular etching was ready for coloration, the copies might either be colored wholly by one person or, possibly, several assistants may have been employed in an "assembly line," each applying one color and then passing the print on to the next assistant for another color. But all copies of a print were not colored at the same time. New impressions of the print may have been done later or, alternatively, all copies of the same impression were not colored at the same time. Some copies appear to have an expanded palette, with richer color and bolder range; others, a more limited palette, with colors that seem especially somber. Variations in the skill with which the color is applied is also evident, indicating that all prints were not colored by the same person. Perhaps the finest applications are by Solvyns himself. In some etchings, the shading gives the figure better form, more modeling and muscle tone.

A further variation involves the textual accompaniment to the Calcutta etchings. Solvyns issued the prints bearing only the title below the etching and without descriptive text. To provide a brief description of each print, in 1799, Solvyns published *A Catalogue of 250 Coloured Etchings; Descriptive of the Manners, Customs, Character, Dress, and Religious Ceremonies of the Hindoos*. In a few copies of the *Collection*, these descriptions have been written in by hand on the back of the preceding page to face the etching. At some point after a number of copies had been sold and delivered, perhaps to stimulate further sales, Solvyns had a large-type copy of the *Catalogue* descriptions printed. These were then cut and pasted opposite each plate on the back of the preceding page.[103]

For all his effort, as we have seen, the Calcutta edition was a financial failure. In leaving India, Solvyns probably intended to leave the Hindus behind, but within two years after his return to Europe, he was again at work on a new set of etchings, *Les Hindoûs*, based on his drawings from Bengal.

The Paris Etchings

In *Les Hindoûs*, Solvyns brings a surer and more disciplined hand. He has studied what makes "successful" prints work and was surely affected by the commercial success of the Orme prints (see below), even as he damned them. In the Paris edition, Solvyns seeks to present a cleaner, more finely executed work, one that appeals in beauty even as ethnographic fidelity remained his paramount concern. He brings to the new Paris etchings greater skill and more control, but at the cost of the freedom that the crudeness of his line reflected in the Calcutta etchings. In the Paris etchings, he lays the line more carefully; it is more deliberate, truer to graphic conventions. In doing so, Solvyns suppresses his own personality, and as the etchings lose some of their—and his—eccentricities, the directness, immediacy, and spontaneity of the Calcutta etchings are diminished.

Solvyns may have intended that the Paris etchings appear less confrontational to the viewer, as he distances the subject both physically and conceptually. He sets the central figures back from the foreground of the Calcutta etchings to the middle ground in *Les Hindoûs*, with the figures reduced in size relative to the setting. As devices for conquering the spatial awkwardness evident in the Calcutta prints, Solvyns not only distances his figures from the viewer, but builds up the articulation of the background so that the figures are more anchored and meld in more effectively.

In etching the Paris plates, Solvyns used multiple tips, but in a single, shallow bite. Lines do not have a deeper bite than those of Calcutta, but for the darker line, Solvyns seems to have used a broader tip on the needle. As in the Calcutta etchings, the Paris plates have a single immersion.

In the Calcutta etchings, each print was colored by hand, and every print varies in coloration. The Paris prints, by contrast, are etchings with aquatint, colored *à la poupée*, with hand-coloring.[104] Coloration is principally by hand, but there is extensive color *à la poupée*. The technique is superb, and the prints of *Les Hindoûs* hold their own in the quality of printing. A number of elaborate folio collections of prints published in France in the early nineteenth century were done *à la poupée*, of which Redouté's flowers stand as perhaps the finest.[105]

Beyond hand-coloring, there were two ways to color prints in this period, and the French were the masters of both. One used multiple plates, much as color printing today. Typically three, four, or sometimes even six plates were employed, with careful registration that blended the colors effectively, making the individual plates difficult to distinguish. The other technique was *à la poupée*.[106] The *poupée* is a little "doll," what the French printers call their bunched cloth instrument for dabbing on colors. A print colored *à la poupée* means that rather than using multiple plates, the different colors are all applied on one plate. The artist or publisher determines the colors, and the professional printer—required for uniformity—dabs the colors on the plate. The process requires a fresh dabbing for each strike, and this is both slow and expensive—a factor contributing to the high cost of *Les Hindoûs*. The result is a true color print, but Solvyns also used wash—what he refers to in his Prospectus as *retoucher*—applied by hand.

Solvyns almost surely relied on colorists employed by the publisher for the hand-coloring, but those that may have been colored by his own hand (*retouche*) are not distinguishable. The coloration is remarkably consistent, with little or no discernible variation among different copies of the same print. Colored washes are used to fill in space within the etched line and in such expansive areas as the sky, but hand-coloring is particularly notable where the color itself takes the place of the etched line, as seen in a number of the prints portraying household servants. The pattern in the pants worn by the Darzi (Pl. II.115) and by Baulber (Pl. II.125), for example, is almost wholly painted in.

Solvyns has considerable ambition for *Les Hindoûs*, and his model is the classic line engraving, with all its conventions. He moves away from the appearance of a drawing made on the spot so evident in the spatial and temporal immediacy of the Calcutta etchings, and he seeks to convey more the look of an engraving, as in the way he covers the figures with line so as to appear engraved. The figures are more refined, less personalized and idiosyncratic.

Differences between the Calcutta and Paris Editions

There are any number of differences between the Calcutta and Paris etchings and in the format of the two editions, and the reversed images of the subjects portrayed are among the most readily apparent. The Calcutta etchings are nearly all mirror images of the original drawings that are now in the Victoria and Albert Museum. The reversed images resulted from the way in which Solvyns transferred the drawing to the plate. We do not know Solvyns's method, but from the sixteenth century, a standard procedure to transfer the image has been to use an intermediary sheet that is completely rubbed with chalk or graphite on one side. This marked side is placed face down on the grounded plate, and the drawing is placed on top. The artist then traces over the lines of the drawing with a stylus or whatever will get the design down. The printed image is the reverse, or mirror, image of the drawing, as we see in Solvyns's Calcutta etchings.

In the etchings for *Les Hindoûs*, Solvyns restored the composition of the original drawings. The Paris prints, however, are not simply newly etched transfers of the drawings Solvyns brought back from Calcutta. What seems likely is that, rather than preparing new drawings for transfer, Solvyns—using the Calcutta prints as models—drew directly on the grounded copper plates. This would account for the return to the composition of the original drawings.

The prints of *Les Hindoûs* correspond more or less closely to the Calcutta etchings in portraying the same subjects, but the printed images in the Paris edition are slightly smaller, with the size of the subject reduced accordingly, but also with variation in detail. The Calcutta etchings are trimmed to the image and measure approximately 36 x 25 cm. for the standard plate, with variations of as much as a centimeter or more from print to print. Double-plates of the Calcutta edition are roughly 34 x 49 cm. The intaglio impressions of the Paris prints (with variations from print to print within a range of one or two centimeters) measure 36 x 25 cm. and, for double-plates, 36 x 49 cm., and the images themselves, 34.5 x 24 and 34.5 x 48, are slightly smaller than those of Calcutta, but again with minor variations.

Solvyns, as we have seen, brings a greater refinement and technical skill to the Paris etchings, but at the cost of the immediacy that corresponds to the original drawings. In the Calcutta edition, the figures often appear dour, sullen, but they are treated sympathetically and emerge as individuals, not simply as "types." Something of this artistic individuality is lost in the Paris etchings, as Solvyns, with less the character of the original drawing, gives a more idealized representation, but the subjects remain real people, the actual persons who posed for the artist.

There are, as well, differences in composition, as Solvyns moves the figures further back in the Paris etchings, distancing the viewer from the subject. But beyond the overall differences in the character of the Calcutta and Paris etchings, there are differences in what is portrayed in individual prints. Such differences from the original Calcutta to the Paris etchings are usually in the treatment of the background or in matters of detail, as, for example, in the disappearance of the keys that hang from the cummerbund of the Rawāni bearer (Pl. II.44) and in the omission of the framed picture on the wall and changes in the moldings in the portrayal of the banian (Pl. II.99). A few are more striking, as Solvyns's taking down the mast of the "bangles" in the Paris etching (Pl. II.245), while the boat is portrayed in the earlier Calcutta print with its mast up, and Solvyns's portrayal of the ascetic avadhūta (Pl. II.141), where in the Calcutta etching he wears a loin cloth, but stands naked in the Paris edition.

For *Les Hindoûs*, Solvyns prepared new etchings of the subjects portrayed in the Calcutta edition, but for whatever reasons, he did not include the subjects of twelve prints that appear in the earlier *Collection of Two Hundred and Fifty Coloured Etchings*. He also makes substantial modification in the presentation of three subjects. The udbāhu, a fakir, who is portrayed separately in the Calcutta etchings, is placed in a scene with other religious ascetics in the Paris edition (Pl. II.140). And the horse and tatoo that appear separately in the Calcutta etchings are combined in a single Paris etching (Pl. II.215).

Of the 288 etchings in *Les Hindoûs*, 51 portray new subjects. As discussed earlier,[107] Solvyns had initially proposed 252 prints for the Paris edition, but soon after getting under way, he decided to expand their number by adding six sections containing 36 plates depicting flora and fauna and Indian "heads" as physiognomic types. But, in addition to the etchings for the new sections, another 15 new etchings portray a variety of subjects, as, for example, the "Rajah Hindoo Prince at his Prayers" (Pl. II.18) and the "Rajah in Full Dress" (Pl. II.19) that were not included in the Calcutta edition. Of the 51 new subjects, only one drawing, "Raja," is known to survive (Pl. I.34).

The flavor of the differences between the Calcutta and Paris etchings may be seen in the comparison of Solvyns's portrayal of the Āhir milk-seller (Pls. I.44 and I.46), here shown with the original drawing (Pl. I.43) from which the Calcutta etching was taken and the Orme copy (Pl. I.45) in *The Costume of Indostan*, discussed below. The Āhir, in the Paris etching, is also included with descriptive text and commentary in Part II (Pl. II.28).

Text, Format, and Organization: Calcutta and Paris

When Solvyns first published the Calcutta etchings in 1796, there was no textual description to accompany his portrayals. Each print was simply labeled with a name. Even for Europeans in Calcutta familiar with the castes and customs of Bengal, this was hardly sufficient, and it was wholly inadequate for those back in Britain who had never been to India and for whom the figures and scenes depicted would be largely meaningless. Solvyns responded with the

The Āhir Milk-seller

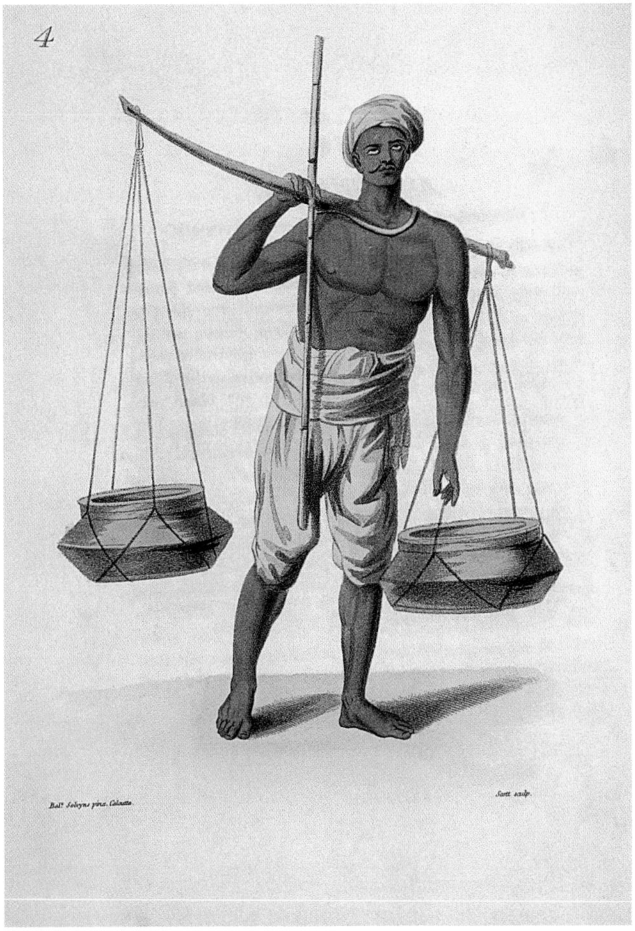

Pl. I.44. Calcutta etching: Sec. I, No. 20. 37.3 x 25 cm. (trimmed to image).

Opposite page:
Pl. I.43. Solvyns's original drawing, No. 20, 37 x 25 cm. From "A Collection of Two Hundred and Fifty Drawings Descriptive of the Manners Customs and Dresses of the Hindoos by Balt. Solvyns. Calcutta."
By courtesy of the Board of Trustees of the Victoria and Albert Museum, London.

Right, top:
Pl. I.45. Copy after Solvyns, *The Costume of Indostan*, No. 4. 34 x 25 cm. (sheet).

Right, bottom:
Pl. I.46. Paris etching: I.4.2. 36 x 24.7 cm.

publication of the quarto *Catalogue* as a companion to the 1799 printing. A few subscribers copied the *Catalogue* descriptions by hand onto the pages of the *Collection*, and at some point, to stimulate sales, Solvyns had the descriptions printed in large type and pasted them in to face each etching. But the descriptions were brief and unlikely to satisfy those unfamiliar with India. Indeed, the inadequacy of descriptive text for the Calcutta edition may have been one factor in its lack of commercial success.

When Orme brought out his pirated edition of the Solvyns etchings, he accompanied each plate with a description in both English and French. The text enhanced interest and accessibility and contributed to the success of *The Costume of Indostan*. Solvyns condemned the "counterfeit" images and "mutilated descriptions" of the Orme volume, but Orme's text may well have served as the stimulus, if not the model, for Solvyns's inclusion of detailed descriptions for the etchings of *Les Hindoûs*. For the Paris edition, Solvyns knew that in the representation of the unfamiliar, there had to be textual accompaniment. For each etching, he provides descriptive text, in both French and English, ranging from a few sentences to several paragraphs. Solvyns emphasizes that he includes only what he observed or had learned personally from credible informants.

Solvyns organized the 250 etchings of the Calcutta edition in 12 sections according to subject.[108] Sections 2 through 12 are preceded by large double-plates. The engraved pages for the sections read:

> Section 1st. 66 Prints, of the Hindoo Casts, with their respective professions.
>
> Section 2nd. 35 Prints, of the Servants employed in the domestic Concerns of European Families: and the only Section in which Mahometans are introduced.
>
> Section 3rd. 8 Prints, Dresses of Hindoo Men.
>
> Section 4th. 8 Prints, Dresses of Hindoo Women.
>
> Section 5th. 8 Prints, of Vehicles, Horses and Bullocks, as practiced by the Natives.
>
> Section 6th. 8 Prints, of Palanquins.
>
> Section 7th. 8 Prints, of Faquirs.
>
> Section 8th. 13 Prints, of pleasure Boats.
>
> Section 9th. 17 Prints, of Boats of Lading.
>
> Section 10th. 8 Prints, of the Various Modes of Smoking, with the Hooka &c.
>
> Section 11th. 36 Prints, of Musical Instruments.
>
> Section 12th. 22 Prints, of public Festivals, Funerals, Ceremonies &c.

In addition to expanding the number of prints in the Paris edition, Solvyns also organized them in a different way. As we saw in Chapter Two, in the history of the publication, the 288 etchings of *Les Hindoûs* were issued in 48 installments, or *livraisons*, each with six prints and letterpress sheets bearing the descriptive text in both French and English. These, in turn, were organized into four volumes of 12 *livraisons*. Each volume opens with a title page bearing an etching; an introductory essay, in both French and English, then follows with a discussion of the subjects portrayed. The Preliminary Discourse of Volume I (reprinted here in Chapter Four) embodies an account of European scholarship on India and was largely written (though without acknowledgment) by Georges-Bernard Depping.[109] Depping may also have had a hand in writing portions of the introductions to the subsequent volumes, but these essays principally provide an overview of the various subjects treated and do so from Solvyns's perspective.[110] In the first three volumes of *Les Hindoûs*, the first print of each section (*livraison*) is a double-plate, many depicting the festivals and ceremonies that are grouped together in the last section of the Calcutta edition. Save for the double-plates, subjects remain grouped in the Paris edition, though without section titles and in a somewhat different order. Thus, in Volume I of *Les Hindoûs*, the etchings portraying the various castes, identified by their profession, are grouped together. Similarly, fakirs and musical instruments are together in Volume II, boats in Volume III, household servants in Volume IV, and so on. For each volume, Solvyns provides a "List of the Subjects," placed either at the end or, in a few copies, immediately following the title page.

Hierarchy in Portrayal of Subjects

In both the Calcutta and Paris edition, Solvyns organizes his subjects in a very Hindu way—by what he understands to be the hierarchy of rank or of quality. Thus, in first section of the Calcutta edition, the 66 castes portrayed are ordered (with some inconsistency) from the highest to the lowest. Solvyns begins with the four *varnas*, or classes of Hindu society: five plates devoted to brahmin castes, followed by plates depicting the kṣatriya, vaiśya, and śūdra. With respect to the hierarchy of specific castes (*jāti*), he writes in the 1799 *Catalogue* that "strict regard not being now paid to the ordinances of their religion, prescribing the duties of each, I have not been able to follow much order in the arrangement." But, despite his caveat about the fluidity in ranking, his portrayal of people by their occupation is almost entirely by caste and, most significantly, is organized, albeit with a few anomalies, according to traditional Hindu notions of ritual purity and pollution. The last occupational castes depicted are those of the lowest rank, such as the Kāorā, the swineherd (Pl. II.73). Solvyns similarly organizes the section on household servants by rank, from the high caste "banian," agent or overseer (Pl. II.99), to the low caste methar, the "sweeper" or scavenger (Pl. II.129). Even musical instruments and boats are presented with some sense of hierarchy in purity or prestige.

In the "Prospectus" for *Les Hindoûs*, Solvyns writes: "The first volume will contain the castes or professions of the Hindus, with their divisions and subdivisions, as they have been approximately established according to the laws of Menu [Manu], the legislator of the Hindus, and such as they exist in the hierarchy or degradation of status, from the Brahmins to the Sudras." Although there is some reorganization in the Paris edition and subjects are no longer divided into titled sections, he generally follows the same order for each grouping as in the Calcutta edition, reflecting the *homo hierarchius* of the Hindu world. Where etchings are reordered, it may well be that Solvyns, with another ten years' experience in India after devising the organization for the Calcutta prints, sought to correct what he deemed mistakes in his earlier ranking. Thus, for example, the "untouchable" Hāṛi, scavenger (Pl. II.71), is lowered in rank to third from the bottom.

In his ordered portrayal of Hindu castes in Bengal, however problematic it may be, Solvyns may well be the first European to provide a systematic ranking of castes. Even with some indeterminacy of status, however, there are a few notable mistakes, as in his placement of those bearing arms—such as the Rājput (Pl. II.48)—among the middle ranking castes rather than among those of higher status. In ordering the subjects portrayed, Solvyns probably relied on high caste Bengali informants, but that he chose to present his portrait of the Hindus as a mirror of hierarchy in Indian society underscores Solvyns's pioneering role as an ethnographic artist.

Solvyns's Distaste for Muslims and Sympathy for Hindus

In his portrayal of the peoples of India, Solvyns draws sharp distinction between Hindu and Muslim and contrasts Hindu civilization with what he describes in his 1799 *Catalogue* as "the fanatic Tyranny of their Mahometan Conquerors." At various points in the Paris edition, *Les Hindoûs*, he expresses a distaste for Muslims that reflected an Orientalist prejudice that, in dichotomizing Hindu and Muslim cultures, exalted Hindu, Sanskritic civilization and deemed the Muslim presence in India a foreign and corruptive incursion. Moreover, as Rosane Rocher writes, "British sympathies tended to be on the side of the Hindus against Muslims in the eighteenth century . . . . Not only had Europeans a heavy baggage of fear of, and hostility toward, Muslims that went back to the struggle for Spain and the Crusades, in India the British were primarily displacing Muslim powers."[111]

Solvyns includes Muslims in only a few etchings, as indicated by his note on the title page to Section 2 of the Calcutta edition, portraying household servants. It is, he tells us, "the only Section in which Mahometans are introduced." In the Preliminary Discourse for *Les Hindoûs*, he explains, "I began by declaring that it was my intention to paint only the Hindoos and what related exclusively to them; but the picture of their domestic life would not have been complete if I had left out their servants, who are very deserving of a place, though mostly of Mahometan extraction."

It is the Hindus, Solvyns tells his reader, that he principally portrays in his etchings. Although he occasionally joins Christian condemnation of "debauchery" in various Hindu festivals, as in his description of Rās Yātrā (Pl. II.185), of expiatory "cruelties," as in Caṛak Pūjā, hook-swinging (Pl. II.193), or of "superstition" more generally, Solvyns is generally sympathetic to Hinduism, expressing admiration for its sublime conceptions of the deity, and, in contrast to the views of "benighted" India that came to dominate European attitudes in the nineteenth century, he is remarkably non-judgmental in his account of the Hindus. His India is not the idealized antiquity of the Orientalists but the daily life of India as he observed and experienced it. The task he sets for himself is to provide an accurate and "faithful" portrayal of a people who have been inadequately represented in European descriptions of India.

Solvyns's Influence

Solvyns and the Company School

In the late eighteenth century, Indian artists began to paint for Europeans in India, combining European and Indian styles in what came to known as the "Company School." Mildred Archer, who has written extensively on Company School painting, was the first to connect Solvyns with the genre. Indian artists were employed by the East India Company as draftsmen and instructed in European techniques; others worked as assistants to European artists, like Solvyns; and many had the opportunity to see, study, and copy European prints that were sold in the shops and bazaars of Calcutta and other urban centers. Of the European artists in India, Hodges and Solvyns exercised the greatest influence on the character of Company painting in Bengal. In 1788, Thomas Daniell observed that the "commonest bazaar [in Calcutta] is full of prints—and Hodges' *Indian Views* are selling off by cart loads."[112] Hodges' influence is evident in the work of several Calcutta and Murshidabad artists, but they had only his prints to study. Solvyns provided some artists "a more direct association." He employed Indians as assistants in coloring and printing his massive work, and his collection of etchings provided something of a prototype in both subject and format.[113]

Company painting developed local styles, but, as Archer writes, "artists gradually adjusted their style and subject-matter to suit British taste." The subjects favored by patrons were costumes; occupations and trades (each shown with its identifying attributes—a weaver at his loom; a potter at his wheel); domestic servants; ascetics; modes of transport; and festivals. Such subjects—often presented as "types"—were arranged in sets that provided "a conspectus of social life in India."[114]

In Solvyns's *Collection of Two Hundred and Fifty Coloured Etchings*, Indian artists found the very subjects that, as they had already come to realize, appealed to Europeans. Moreover, Solvyns's format and style are reflected in a number of Company School paintings. It is no coincidence, Archer argues, that many sets of paintings made in Calcutta in the first decades of the nineteenth century employ idioms distinctive of Solvyns's work—"tall brooding figures, sombre colours and heavy black borders."[115] Influenced by Solvyns, Company School artists "adopted similar types of composition, setting a figure against a low horizon or showing him surrounded by the implements of his trade. Types of subjects depicted by Solvyns were also used for stereotyped sets—occupations, costumes, transport, festivals. . . ."[116]

In the Company School holdings of the India Office Library, for example, a collection of "Drawings illustrating the Manners and Customs of the Natives of India" includes a number of watercolor paintings that bear the distinctive characteristics of Solvyns's influence.[117] The paintings, c. 1798-1804, are by an unknown Calcutta artist, perhaps from Murshidabad. Among them is a watercolor portraying the worship at a Kālī temple at Titaghar, near Calcutta.[118] Solvyns's influence on the artist is clearly evident, and it bears similarity to Solvyns's depiction of the Kālīghāṭ temple in Calcutta (Pl. II.4), but this is no copy. In commenting on the painting, Pratapaditya Pal rightly notes that "while his elongated figures, his sombre tones, and colouring may reflect the awareness of Solvyns's style, the spontaneity of the picture indicates that the artist may have worked from a sketch made on the spot."[119]

London art dealer Giles Eyre, in the notes prepared for a 1978 sales exhibition of 26 etchings from *Les Hindoûs*, recognized Solvyns's influence on Company School painting in Calcutta and Murshidabad.[120] And, in the 1970s, Hartnoll & Eyre sold a set of *Les Hindoûs* in which watercolors by a Company artist had been pasted on the flyleaves of each volume. When the volumes came again onto the market some years later, there was some thought that the watercolors were by Solvyns himself, but they are clearly Company paintings, probably Patna School, c. 1820.[121] Although lacking the characteristic border of

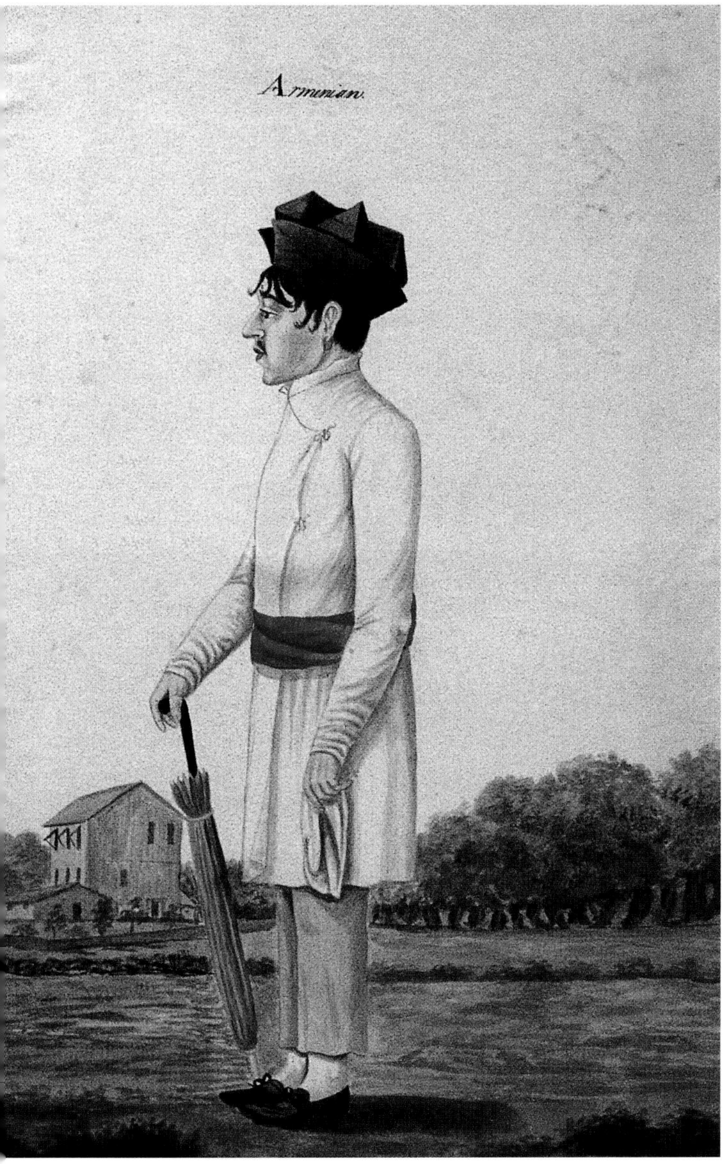

Pl. I.47. An Armenian. Watercolor, Company School, Patna, c. 1820. 36.4 x 27 cm.
Courtesy Bernard Shapero Rare Books, London.

the Company pictures by the Calcutta artists influenced by Solvyns, the positioning of the figure and the treatment of the background, as in the portrayal of an Armenian (Pl. I.47), suggest a likely Solvyns influence.

Over the years, Eyre & Hobhouse handled a number of Company School paintings that reflected Solvyns's influence, none more so than the "Madrass Dubash" (Pl. I.48), by an Indian artist Hobhouse identified as "in the circle of Solvyns."[122] *Dobāshī* (literally man of two languages) was originally the name for an interpreter, but the word came to refer to the chief servant in a European household or firm, comparable to the banian (Pl. II.99) in Bengal.[123]

The Fraser Collection

One of the most intriguing "Company School" works associated with Solvyns is the collection of his Calcutta etchings painted over by an Indian artist in bright colors. The collection of 248 pictures, now in Harvard's Houghton Library, is bound in leather in two volumes, and inscribed, by hand, "Portraits of East Indians by C. C. Fraser after the plan and manner of Solvyns. Calcutta 1805."[124] Major Charles Collins Fraser (1760-1837), aide-de-camp to Governor General Marquess Wellesley from 1803 to 1805, was not, of course, the artist, but the original owner. The artist was Bengali, a painter of the Company School.

In the Fraser collection, the etchings (trimmed to the image, as Solvyns did in his own presentation) are pasted on larger sheets of watermarked paper (J. Whitman 1794), with a wide border in black ink on the paper around the etching. Within the border, on the left below each etching, a small space is left uncolored for the title, written in Bengali script and corresponding in most cases to Solvyns's term or description. In the pictures, Solvyns's etched lines are usually visible, but the watercolor is heavier—and brighter—than Solvyns's own washes and some are opaque gouache. The etched lines, as Mildred Archer notes in her discussion of the pictures, "are often reinforced by pen-and-ink and brush strokes." [125] In painting over the etchings, the artist fills in detail that Solvyns's omitted, especially in the backgrounds, which are sometimes quite different. He adds things of his own liking, appropriate to the subject portrayed, such as a caste-mark on the forehead of a figure, a sacred thread, a necklace, or, as Archer observed, Bengali inscriptions on an amulet. The Indian artist thus gives the pictures a distinct character that led viewers to assume that these were copies, as the inscription reads, "after the plan and manner of Solvyns." Indeed, Mildred Archer wrote that the Fraser collection "includes a number of pictures that are not engravings but water-colour versions of the original Solvyns plates."[126] All of the pictures, however, are painted over Solvyns's etchings, including the portrayal of a subject, the *cākarāni*, a female servant, that Solvyns himself does not include among his 250 etchings "descriptive of the manners, customs and dresses of the Hindoos."

Overleaf:
Pl. I.48. "Madrass Dubash." Watercolor and gouache, Company School, c. 1800. 18 x 12.7 cm.
Courtesy of Eyre & Hobhouse Ltd.

Madrass Dubash
55

The cākarāni is, in fact, Solvyns's "Woman of Inferior Rank," but presented in an entirely different context, as evident in the comparison of the two pictures (Pls. I.49 and I.50). (For the Paris etching of "A Woman of Inferior Rank," see Pl. II.88.) The Indian artist of the Fraser collection gives her a new persona: the figure is the same, but she is now a kitchen servant, portrayed against a background of cooking implements instead of the mats and thatched roof of Solvyns's original depiction.

The Fraser collection surely stands as a curiosity, and Archer speculates as to its history. Fraser's association with Governor-General Wellesley may have been the key.

Wellesley himself was keenly interested in 'men and manners' and was building up a large collection of paintings by Indian artists. . . . He was surrounded by a group of sophisticated young men who shared his interests and enthusiasms. Benjamin Sydenham and John Ritso, both keen amateur artists, were on his staff. Dr. [Francis] Buchanan, the great naturalist, ethnologist, and antiquarian, was Wellesley's surgeon and, throughout his career, had employed Indian artists to illustrate

Pl. I.49. Cākarāni.
Gouache over Solvyns etching, by an Indian artist. From "Portraits of East Indians by C. C. Fraser after the plan and manner of Solvyns. Calcutta 1805," Vol. I, No. 27. Widener Library, Harvard University. Courtesy President and Fellows of Harvard College.

Pl. I.50. "A Woman of Inferior Rank,"
Sec. IV, No. 2, from *A Collection of Two Hundred and Fifty Coloured Etchings: Descriptive of the Manners, Customs and Dresses of the Hindoos*, Etching by Solvyns, Calcutta, 1799.

his reports and surveys. Major Fraser was probably 'caught up' in the general cultural atmosphere of Government House with its interest in 'men and manners'. It seems likely that after Solvyns had left India in 1803 or 1804 Fraser had acquired an incomplete set of uncolored etchings which Solvyns had left unfinished in Calcutta. Fraser, wishing to complete them, may then have employed an Indian artist to colour and finish the set.

Relating the Fraser artist to Solvyns's influence on Company School painting in Calcutta, Archer writes,

> Indian artists lived in colonies in the bazaar and were usually castemen and related. If in 1805 one of the members was laboriously colouring this huge work, nothing is more probable than that his friends and relations continually came to watch him and examine the original with great care. They would almost certainly have copied from it and taken hints. These two volumes . . . may be a clue to one of the ways in which British influence came to bear on Indian artists and may explain how so many idioms characteristic of Solvyns' work appear in paintings by Indian artists at Calcutta and Murshidabad.[127]

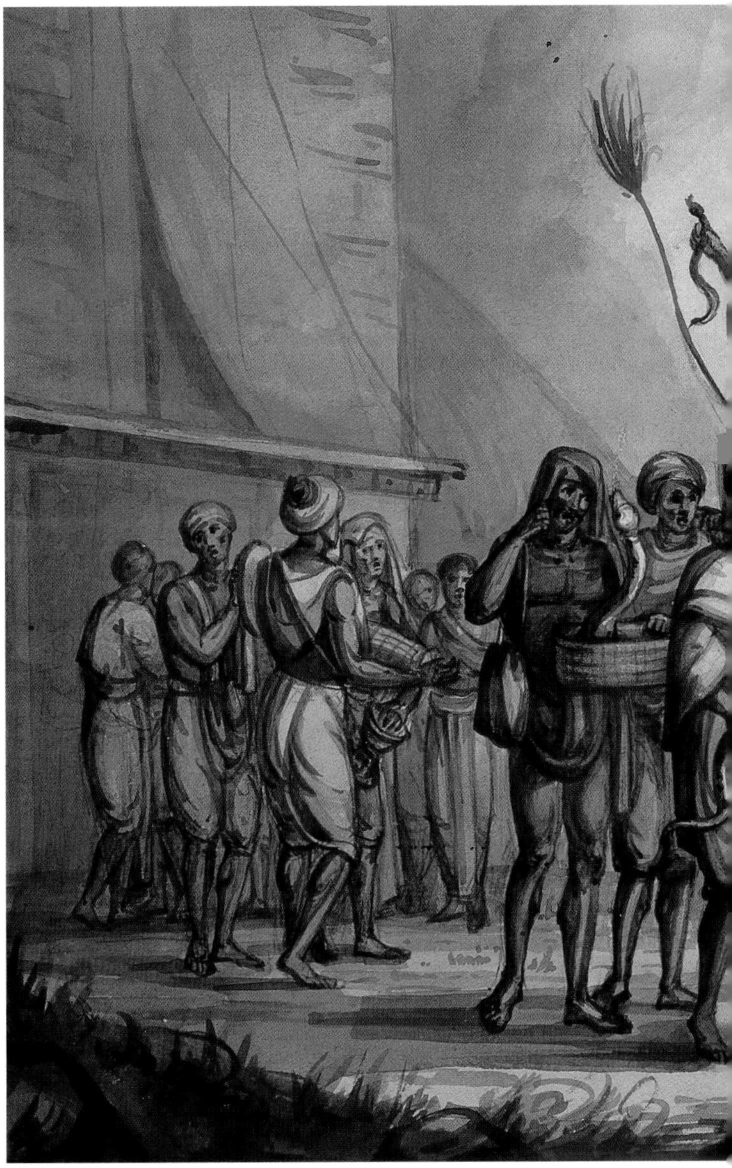

Pl. I.51. Jhāpān, festival of snakes.
Copy after Solvyns by an Indian artist, c. 1800. 33.5 x 46 cm. Private collection.[133]

Copies after Solvyns by Indian Artists

In 1979, Sotheby's auctioned "a folio of watercolours of Hindu figures, customs and musical instruments" identified as by Solvyns.[128] Purchased by New York collector Paul F. Walter, the eight watercolors were included in the Christie's "Visions of India" sale from his collection in 1995.[129] The pencil and watercolor drawings are not, in fact, by Solvyns, but by an Indian artist copying Solvyns's Calcutta etchings. One is a copy of Solvyns's etching of Jhāpān, the festival of snakes (Pl. II.196). The watercolor (Pl. I.51) is not a tracing, for the figures are slightly smaller and vary somewhat in placement, though in overall composition, it is very similar to the etching from which it was copied. Other watercolors in the collection are composites that combine several figures from Solvyns's etchings. One, for example, brings together three household servants—a sarkār, khānsāma, and darzī (tailor)—with a palanquin and bearers, adapted freely from Solvyns's images, in the background.[130] Another combines three drummers that Solvyns had portrayed individually,[131] and one depicts a hukābardār (Pl. II.108) together with two figures from his series of etchings portraying the *hukā*.[132]

Among the most intriguing works by Calcutta artists influenced by Solvyns are two composite drawings of "different Indian types" based on figures portrayed individually by Solvyns and arranged to create scenes of Indian life. Included in an exhibition by Hobhouse in 1985,[134] the drawings—pen and ink with watercolor—are now in the India Office Library. One (Pl. I.52) depicts five figures copied, apparently by tracings, from Solvyns's work. The central, seated figure is a daibik, or astrologer, with a sloop in the background.[135] The artists adds his own touch with

the figure leaning on the balcony and the rowboat near the shore. The second drawing (Pl. I.53) brings together nine figures from Solvyns, six from the series of servants and three from his portrayal of musical instruments.[136]

In both drawings (in contrast to the eight watercolors from the Walter Collection), the figures are positioned as in Solvyns's original drawing and not in the reversed image of the Calcutta etchings. (The exception is the woman sweeper, the methrānī, peering through the door, who appears as in the etching.) The drawings could have been based on the etchings, with tracings done to produce a reversal and thus a return to the composition of Solvyns's original drawings. But Jerry Losty, curator of prints and drawings at the India Office Library, believes that

> A more likely explanation is that . . . the artist, whom we must suppose assisted Solvyns in the preparation of the plates and therefore had access to Solvyns' original drawings, made *charboys* or tracings from them direct. The sharpness of detail in the Calcutta harbour scene, especially in the faces, contrasts with the poorly executed line and faces in the etchings, and suggests that the unknown artist has been truer to Solvyns' original intentions through working closely with the original drawings. It is impossible not to admire the skill with which he has placed his figures, when through the nature of the charboy he was unable to adjust the height or stance of any of them, and added extra interest to . . . his composition through discreet additions.[137]

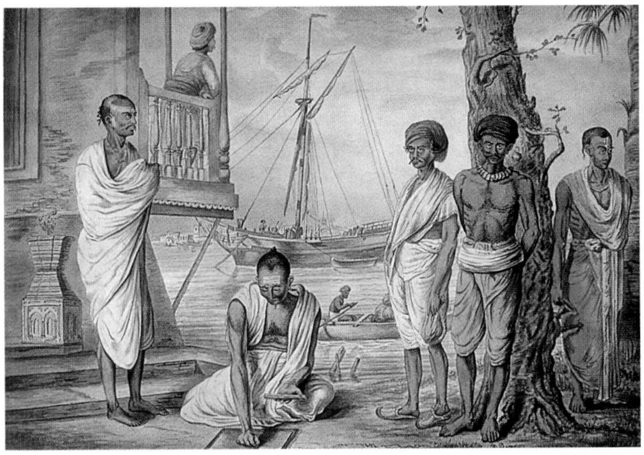

Pl. I.52. Watercolor drawing after Solvyns, Calcutta, c. 1800. 42.6 x 60.3 cm.
Oriental and India Office Collections, British Library, Add.Or.4307. By Permission of the British Library.

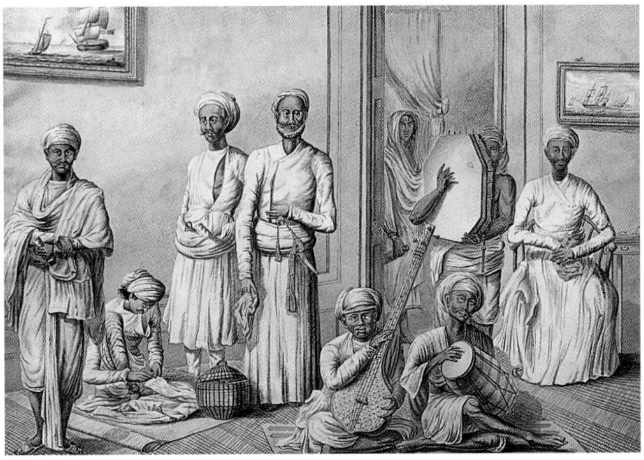

Pl. I.53. Watercolor drawing after Solvyns, Calcutta, c. 1800. 42.4 x 60 cm.
Oriental and India Office Collections, Add.Or.4663. By Permission of the British Library.

The circumstances under which these composite watercolor drawings were likely made, as well as the palette that so closely reflects Solvyns's own, suggest they may have been done under Solvyns's supervision.

European Copies after Solvyns: Orme, et al.

Solvyns influenced Indian artists in the development of the Company School, and, as in the composites, his images were sometimes copied directly, but over the century that followed his work in Calcutta, Solvyns's portrayals of the Hindus were to be copied many times in European publication, often without attribution. Most prominent was *The Costume of Indostan* (1804-05), Edward Orme's pirated edition of Solvyns's etchings.[138] Orme credits Solvyns on the title page, but without the artist's knowledge or permission, and Solvyns took the publication as an abuse of his work.

The prints in *The Costume of Indostan* contrast dramatically with the Calcutta etchings from which they were copied. For the edition, Edward's brother, William Orme, made watercolor copies of figures from Solvyns's etchings.[139] The prints, after the Orme watercolors, are etchings using a grounded copper plate, but with a stipple engraving technique that gives the appearance of a conventional engraving.[140] After the initial ground was cleared, the engravers—"Scott" and "T. Vivares"—used a burin, the cutting tool, directly on the plate. In contrast to Solvyns's affect of drawing, the Orme pictures are clearly prints, for with stipple engraving, the purpose is to transmit design with clarity and purity. With the warm colors, applied by hand, the prints convey an impression akin to English portrait miniature painting. Each Orme plate is accompanied by a descriptive text, usually an expanded, not always accurate, paraphrase of Solvyns's 1799 *Catalogue* description.

In format and style, Orme's *Costume of Indostan* corresponds almost identically to earlier volumes on the costumes of China and Turkey, published by William Miller in London. Both Orme and Miller used the same printer, W. Bulmer & Co. Miller's establishment, on Old Bond Street, was close to Edward Orme, and they surely knew each other as competitors, if not as friends. The Miller volumes included China and Turkey, though not India. The China engravings are dated 1799; those for Turkey, 1802.[141] Each volume contained 60 hand-colored engravings, done with soft-line and pastel colors, and the figures are portrayed alone, abstracted from their context or background. This is precisely the format for the later Orme prints.

The page layout in *The Costume of Indostan*, with the figures removed from their surrounding environment, is elegant, but, together with use of stipple engraving, suppresses the artist's personality and the character of his hand. Solvyns is not present here nor does the subject command the immediacy that gives to the viewer a sense of being there, and that, ironically, may be the very reason the Orme edition was successful. Mildred Archer writes that William Orme's drawing for the pirated edition "was more professional and the coloring more attractive, with pinks, mauves, and greens replacing the sepia of Solvyns' plates. Yet Solvyns' prints," she contends, "give a far more comprehensive survey of the subject, and his drab figures, conveying a sense of sadness. . . , are a far more realistic and moving record of the Bengal villager and city-dweller than Orme's prettified version."[142] Orme tames the roughness of Solvyns and renders the images less personal and more appealing. The subject becomes more accessible by being less ethnographic.

Solvyns denounced Orme's appropriation of his Calcutta etchings, but even before the Orme volume, Tenant's *Indian Recreations* (1803) included three prints copied from Solvyns. They were engraved by R. Scott,[143] who also engraved a number of the prints for *Costumes of Indostan.*

We have no record of Solvyns's knowledge of the Tenant copies or of the particularly interesting appropriations of his work by the Calcutta artist James Moffat (1775-1815). From 1798 into the first decade of the nineteenth century, Moffat engraved and issued some 50 aquatints that included many views of Calcutta and its environs as well as scenes from "up country." Most of these were from his own drawings, but some were after unidentified artists.[144] Among these prints is a view of Banaras depicting the immersion of the goddess Kālī against the backdrop of the ghats (Pl. I.54). The central image of the terracotta goddess being thrown into the water is copied directly from Solvyns's Bisarjan (Pl. II.190), but the scene is transported from Calcutta to Banaras.

Another Moffat aquatint, again without acknowledgment, is a copy of an oil painting by

Pl. I.54. "View at Benares, with a representation of the Callee Poojah, a Hindoo Holiday. Exhibiting the ceremony attending the throwing of the image of their Gods and Goddesses into the Water. Drawn & Engraved by J. Moffat, Calcutta." c. 1802.
Aquatint with soft-ground etching. After Solvyns in part, without acknowledgment. 33 x 50 cm. Photograph courtesy Peabody Essex Museum, Salem, Mass. Inventory No. M3203b.

Solvyns, "View of the Country Residence of William Farquharson Esq., at Garden Reach on the Banks of the Hooghly River, near Calcutta" (c. 1793), discussed earlier.[145] The Farquharson family apparently permitted Moffat to make a drawing of the painting, which he used then in preparing the print, published in Calcutta in 1800. Solvyns probably saw the print, but whatever displeasure—or outrage—he expressed did not prevent Moffat from issuing the Bisarjan copy two years later.

Soon after the first printing of Orme's *Costume of Indostan* (1804-05), Johann Adam Bergk appropriated Solvyns's images for use as illustrations in his *Asiatisches Magazine*, published in Leipzig. The quarterly magazine first appeared in 1806 and continued publication erratically at least until 1811.[146] Each issue contained hand-colored etchings copied from the work of various artists, including Charles Gold as well as Solvyns. In the first nine issues (1806-1811), there are nine prints copied from Solvyns's Calcutta etchings. Several are composites of figures that Solvyns portrayed individually, as in the three prints that portray musicians with their instruments.

At about the same time, Sir Richard Phillips published a popular geography book, "for the use of schools, and young persons," that included (without attribution) four small engravings after Solvyns. Of the four plates, dated 1806 and 1809, two were copies of Solvyns's depiction of suttee—a curious choice for impressionable young minds.[147] With a copy of his portrayal of sādhus (Pl. II.140b), Solvyns appeared in another book for children, *Bilderbuch für Kinder*, published in Weimar in the early nineteenth century in both German and French.[148]

In 1809, Solvyns's portrayal of "A Woman of Distinction" (Pl. II.87) was freely copied for inclusion in a print of "A Smoking Party in the Province of Bengal" (Pl. I.55). The two smokers seated below the woman are taken from another source.

Pl. I. 55. "A Smoking Party in the Province of Bengal."
John Chapman, engraver. 23.7 x W: 18.8 cm. London, Published Dec. 23, 1809, by J. Wilkes. Robert J. Del Bontà Collection, San Francisco.

Among the most attractive and successfully conceived copies of Solvyns's work were those in Giulio Ferrario's *Il Costume antico e moderno*, an extraordinary collection of colored etchings portraying costumes of the world. Of the eighteen volumes in the first series, published in Milan, one—published in 1816—is devoted largely to India.[149] In the Preface, Ferrario lauds Solvyns for unrivaled accuracy, precision, and clarity in portraying the Hindus. With "truth as his guide," Solvyns presents his subjects "so that the reader sees them as if he were transmitted into their midst." In portraying this nation so worthy of our curiosity, Ferrario writes, Solvyns deserves our esteem and gratitude.[150] With 313 pages of text (in Italian), drawing extensively upon Solvyns's descriptions in *Les Hindoûs*, the section on India includes 63 plates, 33 of which are copied from Solvyns's Paris etchings. Some are very close copies, but others are adapted freely, sometimes adding figures or changing the composition, as in the Rath Yātrā (Pl. I.56, after Solvyns's Pl II.188), where the copy adds a throng of celebrants to pull the chariot and a devotee is shown being crushed under a wheel of Jagannātha—not in the Solvyns original. Many of the Ferrrario prints are composites, grouping several Solvyns figures together. Each plate is numbered, and most include the name of the artist who did the etching after Solvyns. (Four different artists were employed in preparing the copies.)

Pl. I.56. Rath Yātrā.
Hand-colored aquatint by Gaetane Zancon after Solvyns, 18.2 x 26.1 cm., from Ferrario, *Il Costume antico e moderno, Asia,*Vol. II, No. 24, 1816.

Some years later, probably about 1840, an Italian artist copied (at least) two of the prints from the Ferrario collection in hand-colored lithographs. As with many early lithographs, they attempt to achieve the granular effect of a soft-ground etching. Although similar to the Ferrario plates, they are distinct and were probably issued as separate prints rather than as part of a book. In portraying the nautch, the Ferrario print (No. 51) is a close copy of Solvyns's etching in *Les Hindoûs* (Pl. II.195), but the lithograph copy (Pl. I.57) changes the composition, moving the dancers to the center and the musicians on the right to the back. For balance, the artist adds a small audience on the left. In place of the standing figures under the arch in the background, the lithograph has an open space, with a guard peering in to watch. The lithograph of the musicians (Pl. I.58), like the Ferrario print from which it was copied (No. 50), is a composite of musicians that (but for one) Solvyns portrayed individually in separate etchings.[151] The lithograph portrays the same musicians as in the Ferrario print, but rearranges the figures and makes various changes in detail, as in adding a platform for the seated drummer—the one figure that, oddly, is not directly based on Solvyns's portrayals.

Pl. I.57. Costumi dell' Asia. "Danza delle Ram-genve ossieno ballerine" [Dance of the *Rāmjanīs* or Dancers].
Italian hand-colored lithograph, c. 1840. 18.8 x 28.6 cm.

Pl. I.58. Costumi Indiani. "Instrumenti Musicali."
Italian hand-colored lithograph, c. 1840. 18.8 x 28.8 cm.

Other Italian copies after Solvyns, from an unidentified volume, include his Hindu Buildings (Pl. II.3) and a grouping of four figures that Solvyns had portrayed in separate etchings.[152] Solvyns images appear in a number of publications in the early nineteenth century. The frontispiece for Volume I of *Historical and Descriptive Account of British India* (1832),[153] for example, has an engraving of a "Group of Figures" in which the "Cshatrya" is directly copied from Solvyns (Kṣatriya, Pl. II.20)), as is the "Tantee, or Weaver at his Loom" (Pl. II.33) in Volume II.[154] Knight's *The Hindoos* (1834) has eight plates taken from Solvyns—identified as "from drawings by W. Westall," with no reference to Solvyns.[155] Solvyns's portrayal of Gaṅgā yātrā, Hindus dying (Pl. II.198), is copied, without attribution, in a collection of 150 colored prints entitled *L'Inde française* (1827-35),[156] and several other prints, while not direct copies, are modeled after Solvyns. *Voyage pittoresque autour du monde* (1834), by Dumont d'Urville (1790-1842), includes copies of two Solvyns etchings, Bisarjan (Pl. II.190) and his portrayal of suttee (Pl. II.201).[157] Four copies after Solvyns appear, unattributed, among the colored prints of August Wahlen's *Moeurs, usages et costumes de tours les peuples du mond* (1843).[158]

In the nineteenth century, illustrations for books and magazines were often freely "borrowed." Among those copying Solvyns, portrayals of Hindu festivals and especially of suttee were favored. Shoberl's *Hindostan* (1822), in the popular "World in Miniature" series, has four small colored engravings copied from Solvyns, including the dramatic image of the widow leaping onto the pyre of her husband (Sahagamana, Pl. II.201).[159] Of all Solvyns's etchings, this was the one most frequently copied and reproduced. The *Missionary Papers* of the Church Missionary Society in 1823 and 1824 included it, along with another suttee image, "The Burying of a Hindoo Widow Alive" (Pl. II.202), among four wood engravings copied from Solvyns's etchings.[160] Solvyns's representation of suttee again appears in the Rev. William Ward's *A View of the History, Literature, and Religion of the Hindoos* (1824), with "Gentoo Window Going to be Burnt with her Dead Husband" (Pl. II.199) and the recurrent image of widow leaping into the flames.[161] *India's Cries to British Humanity* (1830), a book denouncing suttee and other Hindu practices, reproduces Solvyns's portrayal of the "Exposure of the Sick on the Banks of the Ganges" (Pl. II.198) and "Burying Alive a Hindoo Widow."[162] Julia Corner's *History of India: Pictorial and Descriptive* (1846), among plates after various artists, includes "Ceremony of burning a Hindu Widow with the Body of her late Husband. Painted by B. Solwyn [sic]."[163]

Surely the most unusual copy of Solvyns's work appears on a nineteenth century gold-plated silver snuff box. The relief on the top of the box (Pl. I.59) depicts the woman leaping into the flames to the corpse of her husband, copied from Solvyns's Calcutta etching; the relief on the bottom (Pl. I.60) is of Solvyns's portrayal of "hook-swinging," Caṛak Pūjā (Pl. II.193). The box, in the Peabody Essex Museum, Salem, Mass., carries the mark "P," for a Chinese silversmith in Canton in the second quarter of the

Pl. I.59. A Woman Leaping into the Flames to the Corpse of her Husband.
Top Relief on Gold-plated Silver Snuff Box. Second Quarter of the 19th Century, Canton. Height 2 x width 7.3 x depth 6 cm. Photograph courtesy Peabody Essex Museum, Salem, Mass. Inventory No. E85229.

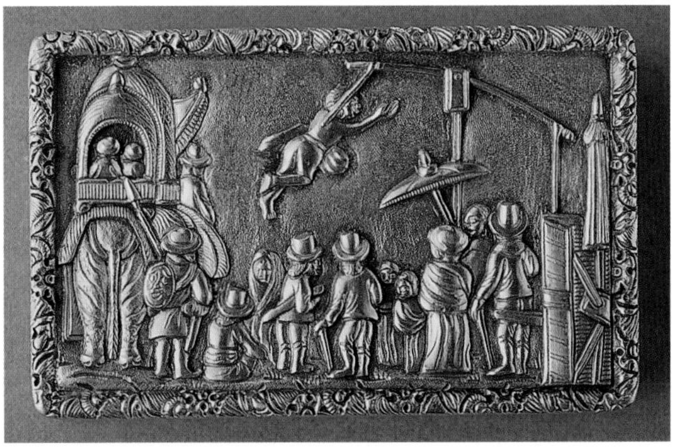

Pl. I.60. Hook-Swinging, Caṛak Pūjā.
Bottom Relief on Gold-plated Silver Snuff Box. Second Quarter of the 19th Century, Canton. Height 2 x width 7.3 x depth 6 cm. Photograph courtesy Peabody Essex Museum, Salem, Mass. Inventory No. E85229.

nineteenth century. Although of Chinese manufacture, with decorative borders and construction that are distinctively Chinese, the box was made for the Anglo-Indian market.[164] Similar boxes (although entirely silver) with the Solvyns reliefs have come onto the market from time to time.[165] A silver match case, also of Chinese manufacture, provides a companion to the snuff box. On one side, the match case has a compressed scene of Solvyn's suttee, with the woman leaping onto the pyre; on the other side is the Paramhaṃsa from Solvyns's series of religious ascetics (Pl. II.135).[166]

As a postscript to the discussion of copies after Solvyns, note should be made of a album of watercolors by an unidentified European artist that came onto the market in London in 1997. Inscribed "The Costume of Hindostan from drawings by Balt. Solvyns," with the initials WB and dated 1811, the album contains forty beautifully executed watercolors copied from the Orme prints after Solvyns.[167]

Solvyns, as an ethnographic artist and Orientalist, provides a window into the world of Calcutta more than two hundred years ago. In his portrayal of the various castes, distinguished by their profession, of household servants, religious mendicants, musical instruments, boats, carts, and palanquins, modes of smoking, and religious ceremonies and festivals, Solvyns gives us unique access to the life and culture of Bengal.

---

1 On Langlès's judgment of Solvyns's work, see Chapter Two, pp. 64-65.
2 5:729-30.
3 "Solvyns" (1825), 43:62. On Depping and his relationship with Solvyns, see Chapter Two, pp. 65-67.
4 9:207-08.
5 Preface to Thomas Bacon, *The Oriental Portfolio*, 1.
6 4:1749. See Kejariwal on Wilson's life and work.
7 5:432.
8 1:190-91. Also, see 1:186.
9 198.
10 Abbey, 2:398.
11 4:1791.
12 *Catalog of Books,* 1:89-90.
13 5:433-34.
14 Mildred and William G. Archer, "Francois Baltazard Solvyns: Early Painter of Calcutta Life," 1.
15 Ibid., 6. Also, Mildred Archer, "Baltazard Solvyns and the Indian Picturesque," 15.
16 Mildred and William G. Archer, "Francois Baltazard Solvyns: Early Painter of Calcutta Life," 10.
17 Brajendranath Bandyopadhyay. The Solvyns copies appear in Vol. III (1935) and were engraved and printed by the Bharat Phototype Studio, Calcutta.
18 "Printed Sources for 18th and 19th Century Studies," 61.
19 Edited by Nayak.
20 Edited by Sukanta Chaudhuri.
21 Edited by Tharoor.
22 Hardgrave, in Pratapaditya Pal, *Changing Visions, Lasting Images: Calcutta Through 300 Years.*
23 In 1991, Okada and Isacco, for example, include Solvyns, with a number of handsome color plates, in their book on images of India in the nineteenth century.
24 Archer and Lightbrown, catalog entries 100 and 101.
25 See Pratapaditya Pal and Dehejia for the book published in connection with the exhibition. Two Solvyns etchings are reproduced, Pls. 26 and 178, as are two watercolor (pen and ink and wash) copies of Solvyns's work by an Indian artist, "Hookah-bearer" (Pl. 129) and "Snake Festival" (Pl. 130), both incorrectly attributed to Solvyns himself. I discuss the watercolors, with a reproduction of the "Snake Festival" (Pl. I.51), pp. 104-05.
26 "A Journey to Hindoostan." Bruhn, catalog, Pls. 55 and 56.
27 "Interaction of Cultures: Indian and Western Painting, 1780-1910." The two drawings included are handsomely reproduced, with detailed descriptions, in the catalog. Bautze, Pls. 3 and 80. I discuss the drawings, from an album assembled by Solvyns's widow, on pp. 83-85. See fn. 57 below.
28 Illustrated in Bayly, *The Raj*, Pl. 262. The watercolor, loaned by Eyre & Greig, is from the album assembled by Solvyns's widow, discussed below.
29 The gallery, Hartnoll & Eyre, in St. James, London, with exhibitions of such painters as Hodges, the Daniells, Zoffany, and Devis, had come to specialize in European artists' portrayal of Indian subjects. Rechristened Eyre & Hobhouse in the late 1970s, it handled various Solvyns items, including composite copies of Solvyns's subjects by Indian artists and, most notably, an album of Solvyns's drawings from Calcutta assembled by his widow. In 1985, Eyre formed a partnership with Charles Greig, who shared his enthusiasm for Solvyns, and the firm handled several previously unknown–or unrecognized–Solvyns paintings from his time in India.
30 Spear discusses the onset of these changes in "racial relations" in *The Nabobs: A Study of the Social Life of the English in Eighteenth Century India*. 126-45.
31 See Rocher, "British Orientalism in the Eighteenth Century." Since the publication of Said's influential book, Orientalism has been under attack, and such post-modern critics of Orientalism as Dirks have implicated European artists in India as complicit in the "colonial project." Teltsher, 129-31, argues that Solvyns's "painstaking project to chart the Hindu people" renders them "interpretable" within the language of the colonizer, thereby facilitating "mastery over a mass of people." For a defense of the Orientalists in India, see Kopf, "European Enlightenment, Hindu Renaissance and the Enrichment of the Human Spirit."
32 S. N. Mukherjee, *Sir William Jones*, 125.
33 Kejariwal, 83.
34 Conversations with Charles Greig and Giles Eyre, London, April 4, 1994.
35 Exhibition notes, Hartnoll & Eyre, Ltd., London, July 28, 1978.
36 *The City of Job Charnock*, 30.
37 See Mildred Archer and Lightbrown, 84-85, and the entry for Gold in Abbey, 2:392-93.
38 21. The Preliminary Discourse is reproduced in Chapter Four, where Solvyns discusses his commitment of fidelity. See pp. 117, 122, 125.

39 2:11.

40 I am indebted to Jonathan Bober, Curator of Prints, Drawings, and European Paintings at the Blanton Museum of Art, The University of Texas at Austin, for his insights and suggestions relating to Solvyns's style, to print traditions, and an array of technical issues in examination of Solvyns's etchings.

41 1:21. See Solvyns's Preliminary Discourse, reprinted in Chapter Four, p. 115-26.

42 On Devis, see Mildred Archer, *India and British Portraiture*, 232-69, and Pavière, 101-41.

43 In this discussion of Solvyns's style and technique, I am indebted to extended conversations with Charles Greig and Giles Eyre.

44 Mildred Archer, *British Drawings in the India Office Library*, 2:622, suggests that he might be Christopher Green, who died a Major-General in 1805. A similar Green drawing, "*Hurcurra* (messenger) exchanging a letter, on a street in Calcutta," was auctioned at Christie's "Visions of India" sale, September 21, 2000, Lot 340, with catalog illustration. Green also did a watercolor of Bengal sepoys, referred to in the Commentary on Solvyns's portrayal of the sepoy (Pl. II.95), fn. 9.

45 184. Webber sailed with Cook on the third voyage. Smith, 74, writes that "What Cook and Webber were engaged in . . . was nothing less than a well-thought-out programme to provide a systematic ethnographic account of the peoples encountered in the Pacific." On Webber, see Joppien and Smith, Vol. 3. Also see Joppien and Smith, 1:3-9, for a discussion of conventions for drawing non-European peoples.

46 75.

47 21-22. Never published, Finnegan's University of Maryland thesis (1991), with a brief 55 pages of double-spaced text, is filled with insight and written with style.

48 Department of Prints, Drawings and Paintings, Accession numbers 8937.1 to 98 and 8937.98a to 247. Press mark S-20. The drawings for the etchings of "Elephants and Camels," the double-plate before Section V, and "A Bengali Road," double-plate before Section VI, were missing when the collection was acquired in 1883. Staes, 197, in 1884, refers to the acquisition, but incorrectly gives the number of drawings as 238.

49 See Chapter One, pp . 41-42.

50 See Chapter One, pp. 42-44, for the *Catalogue* dedication and both the draft and published preface.

51 Pauline Rohatgi and Graham Parlett's forthcoming *The British Artist in India: A Catalogue of the Collections at the Victoria & Albert Museum*, will include the text of Solvyns's descriptive notes. As in Mildred Archer's catalogs for holdings of drawings in the India Office Library, the category "British" includes other European artists in India. Where Solvyns's notes for the original drawings provide information that is not included in either his 1799 *Catalogue* description or in the text for *Les Hindoûs*, I have incorporated it in my Commentaries on the etchings.

52 Charles Greig, conversation, April 12, 1994. William Foster, "Some Foreign European Artists in India," 97-98, refers to Edwards' sale of the album but not to the buyer.

53 The drawing, "A Hooka Snake," is illustrated, No. 24, in the exhibition catalog, *Aa to Zywiec*, Summer 1985.

54 Kattenhorn, 294, lists the India Office Library acquisitions in the Prints and Drawings collection by catalog number: WD 4123: Avadhūta, watercolor (Pl. II.141); WD 4124: A sloop, watercolor, illustrated as Pl. 48 (Pl. II.254); WD 4125: A standing man spinning cotton, another at a loom with huts beyond, pencil; and WD 4126: A camel, pencil. The last two drawings do not correspond to etchings included in either the Calcutta or Paris editions. Losty, curator of prints and drawings at the India Office Library, discusses the acquisitions in "The Belgian Artist F. B. Solvyns and his Influence on Company Painting," with illustrations of the Avadhūta and the sloop.

55 See listings and illustrations in Maggs's catalogs No. 1092, *Travel Books* (1989), and No. 1123, *Voyages and Travels* (1991).

56 Kattenhorn, 294, catalogue listings: WD 4268: The Kālīghāṭ temple, pencil (Pl. II.4); WD 4313: A sannyāsī, watercolor (Pl. II.137); WD 4314: Two standing figures, one with a bow and arrow, pencil; preliminary study for Solvyns's watercolor of the Andaman Islanders; WD 4315; Standing ascetic wearing a dagger and carrying a small staff, pencil; WD 4316: Standing ascetic holding a rosary, pencil. The two ascetics are not included among the etchings.

57 Two drawings, now in the Ehrenfeld Collection, "An Urdhvabahu or Man with Raised Arm," Pl. 3, and a "Kose," Pl. 80, are illustrated in Bautze. For Solvyns's etchings of the subjects see, respectively, Pls. II.140 and II.251.

58 See pp. 29-30.

59 Jhāpān is illustrated in the Paris etching (Pl. II.196), with text and commentary.

60 Prideaux, 1.

61 *Twelve Views in Aquatinta from Drawings Taken on the Spot in South-Wales.*

62 Ronald Russell, 79. Also see Godrej and Rohatgi, 23.

63 Mayor, in discussing prints portraying "Man's variety," Pls. 383-87, writes, "In the 1550s the earliest series of costume prints of various peoples surveyed Europe and the Near East in some 100 Italian engravings. The first of the innumerable books of the costumes of the New World as well as the Old was issued in Paris in 1562. . . ." See Davenport, Vol. 2, for a sampling of European costume prints. Prideaux, 317, discusses the popularity of costume prints in the late 18th and early 19th centuries.

64 French and Dutch editions were published in Antwerp in 1576; an Italian translation followed in 1577; and an English translation was published in London in 1785.

65 The Le Hay prints are sometimes listed under Ferriol. On the publishing history and various editions of the Le Hay collection, see Navari, 128; Sweetman, 61-62; and Colas, 1:677-78. Jerome I. Smith, with 10 reproductions of the prints, discusses the Le Hay prints and their impact on European taste and fashion. Sweetman, 44-72, discusses "the Oriental obsession" in the European fascination for Turkish themes, *turqueries*, especially in early 18th century France.

66 See Colas, 1:684-87, for a listing of the print albums by Le Prince. On Le Prince, see Hédou.

67 Gordon Ray, 1:76, writes that "Expert and charming though Le Prince may be, it must be admitted that his continuing insistence on the same figures, costumes, and scenes at last becomes somewhat monotonous."

68 Most plates are uncolored and portray a single figure with no background. In Vol. III, Pls. 35-43 depict Indian figures copied from Indian miniatures or, as Pl. 43, "A Merchant of India," copied from Le Hay.

69 See discussion below of the Orme volume. For publishing details on the Miller and Orme volumes, as well as other costume books published in England, see Tooley.

70 Mayor briefly discusses these "hawkers and walkers," reproducing several examples, Pls. 201-205. He writes that

"During the centuries when street criers posed unconsciously for artists, some 300 sets of prints recorded the noisy life of Bologna, Rome, Venice, Paris, Vienna, London, Saint Petersburg, and New York."

71 *Diverse figure al numero di ottanta* (1646). See Mayor, 203.

72 See Mayor, 204, and Davenport, 2: Pls. 1806-09.

73 Francis Wheatley (1747-1801). The first edition, 1775, with 62 woodcut plates, minimized context, but in the 1804 and later editions, the criers were presented in 48 engravings, embellished with additional figures and street activity.

74 See Boerner, 3-5, with reproductions of seven prints from *Divers portraits*.

75 See Bry, *Discovering the New World*.

76 Said has famously examined "Orientalism" as a phenomenon relating to the European perception and "construction" of the Middle East, and his arguments have been extended to India by Dirks among others. Tillotson, *The Artificial Empire*, 105-16, provides a note of caution in applying Said's critique of Orientalism to European artists' portrayal of India. For a major critique of the Saidian approach, see MacKenzie.

77 Among them is a print of a Hindu baniā, or merchant, from a sketch drawn in 1704 in Isphahan, where a number of Indians lived as merchants. R. P. Gupta, "Some British & European Painters in India 1760-1820," n.p., discusses the Bruyn print.

78 Linschoten lived in India from 1583 to 1589. See Lach, 198-204. The engraving of suttee in Linschoten, discussed in the introduction to Solvyns's etchings of satī, Pt. II, p. 422 , is among the earliest portrayals of the rite.

79 Theodor de Bry was an engraver and publisher in Frankfurt, specializing in travel collections in two series, *Grands voyages* and *Petits voyages*, published in Latin and German between 1598 and 1628. His *India orientalis*, in several parts, is part of the series of *Petits voyages*. The collections were reprinted under various titles and in translation. See Lach, 216.

80 See reproductions of the Baldaeus prints in Lach and Van Kley, Pls. 173, 184, 185, and 189. It is unlikely that Solvyns would have seen either the Baldaeus or Knox volumes.

81 Lach and Van Kley include several plates from Knox that aptly illustrate what they describe, 956, as "one of the most informative and reliable accounts of an Asian society published in the seventeenth century." See, notably, Pls. 286, 187, and 193.

82 The account of Nieuhof's "Remarkable Voyages and Travels into the East Indies," translated from the Dutch, is in *A Collection of Voyages and Travels*, edited by Awnsham Churchill and John Churchill. The print, by the Dutch engraver Gilliam (Willem) van der Gouwen, is in Vol. II of the 1st edition (London, 1704), between pages 280 and 181, and in the 2nd edition, Vol. II., between 242 and 243.

83 For a sampling of the portrayal of the Indian exotic in early books, see Mitter, *Much Maligned Monsters*, and Lach and Van Kley, *Asia in the Making of Europe*, Vol.. III, Book Two. In my discussion of Solvyns's depiction of fakirs, p. 309, I discuss early portrayals; and on the portrayal of suttee, see my discussion in relation to Solvyns's etchings, p. 422.

84 Picart's engravings of India are included in *Cérémonies et coutumes religieuses des tous les peuples du monde* (1723-1743). I discuss Picart's print of the gathering of sādhus, reproduced here, on pp. 309 and 324.

85 The phrase is Bernard Smith's. See his discussions of "art in the service of science and travel," in *Imagining the Pacific*, 1-39, and of the wedding of the esthetic and ethnographic, 51-76.

86 See, for example, Charles D'Oyly's watercolor, "The Emporium of Taylor & Co. in Calcutta," c. 1825-28, reproduced in Bayly, *The Raj*, 187, Pl. 220, and the enormously popular *Curry & Rice* by Atkinson, first published in 1859 and reprinted in many editions.

87 See satirical prints reproduced in Pal and Dehejia, 58-64.

88 Reproduced in Bayly, *The Raj*, 222, Pl. 179.

89 See especially *Three Essays on Picturesque Beauty* (1792). Also see Uvedale Price, *An Essay on the Picturesque* (1794). For a brief overview of the picturesque, see Hunt. Also see Tillotson, "The Indian Picturesque." In *The Artificial Empire*, 11-36, Tillotson discusses the picturesque in terms of aesthetic theory, especially as it related to William Hodges.

90 Copley and Garside, "Introduction," 3.

91 See Godrej and Rohatgi, eds., *Scenic Splendours: India Through the Printed Image*, 2.

92 On the genre of illustrated travel books, see Prideaux, 215-57.

93 Although with very different styles, both Hodges and the Daniells were identified with the "picturesque." Hodges brought a Romantic vision, while, as Mildred Archer writes in "British Painters of the Indian Scene, 1770-1825," 4, Thomas Daniell "employed a style of cool and limpid realism, endowing his scenes with calm majesty and, with the accepted conventions of the picturesque, contrived to express a sense of serene and classical order." For a comparison of Hodges and the Daniells in the context of the picturesque, see Archer and Lightbrown, 8-11, and Leoshko and Charlesworth.

94 See Ronald Russell, 55-59.

95 Abbey, Vol. 2, provides a bibliographical catalog for India of "travel in aquatint." Among the many books on European prints, see especially those by Mildred Archer, Pal and Dehejia, Godrej and Rohatgi, Rohatgi and Godrej, and Mahajan.

96 60.

97 I am grateful to Jonathan Bober, Janice Leoshko, and Michael Charlesworth for their help with technical aspects of Solvyns's etching technique.

98 Pp. 41-42.

99 No. IVC 51057-51080.

100 Both the Buffalo and Texas copies of the 1796 imprint are 41 x 27 cm. By contrast, the Buffalo copy of the 1799 imprint measures 52.5 x 36.5 cm., the largest of any listed copies of the Calcutta edition. See Appendix, "Solvyns in Libraries."

101 Blue paper, made from blue rags, was in widespread use, and was used for drawings, among other things. Krill, 56-61.

102 The Texas volume, in the collection of the Harry Ransom Humanities Research Center, is in very poor condition, and the etchings have worm holes, suggesting that it may have remained in India for many years. At some point, someone crudely lettered the numbers and titles on orange colored labels and pasted them onto the pages. In the copy at the Grosvenor Rare Book Room of Buffalo and Erie County Public Library, the numbers and titles are handwritten in pencil.

103 The copies of the Calcutta etchings in the Arents Collection of the New York Public Library and in the Buffalo and Erie County Public Library have the large type format *Catalogue* descriptions.

104 The entry for *Les Hindoûs* in Abbey, *Travel in Aquatint and Lithography*, 2:398, incorrectly notes that "The method of printing seems to be that at least two plates have been used to give a basic chiaroscuro, while more than one colour is sometimes applied by each of these plates." A close examination of the prints indicates the use of a single plate.

105 Most notably, *Les roses* (1817-1814), with 170 prints.
106 The technique dates from the 1770s. Mayor, 347.
107 Chapter Two, pp. 55-57.
108 Solvyns used Arabic numbers for the sections in *Collection* of etchings, but Roman numerals in the *Catalogue*. Solvyns's *Catalogue* description of each section also varies slightly from the section title pages in the *Collection*.
109 See discussion of Depping's role in Chapter Two, pp. 65-67.
110 Portions of the introductions are included in Part II in the openings to the relevant sections into which the etchings are organized.
111 "British Orientalism in the Eighteenth Century," 222.
112 Quoted in Pratapaditya Pal, "Indian Artists and British Patrons," 130.
113 Pratapaditya Pal, "Indian Artists and British Patrons," 130. Also see Mildred Archer, *Company Drawings in the India Office Library*, 1-10.
114 Mildred Archer, *Company Drawings in the India Office Library*, 7-8. On the Company School, also see Mildred Archer and W. G. Archer, *Indian Painting for the British 1770-1800*.
115 *Company Drawings in the India Office Library*, 75. Also see Losty, "The Belgian Artist F. B. Solvyns and his Influence on Company Painting."
116 Mildred Archer, "Baltazard Solvyns and the Indian Picturesque," 17.
117 Add. Or. 1127-1174. These are listed in Archer, *Company Drawings in the India Office Library*, 77-78. The Murshidabad and Calcutta drawings in the India Office Library are listed, 59-95.
118 India Office Library No. Add. Or. 1128. Illustrated in Archer, *Company Drawings in the India Office Library*, Pl. 24. Solvyns's influence is seen in another black-bordered painting illustrated in Archer, Pl. 26, "Armed retainers."
119 "Indian Artists and British Patrons," 133. The painting is reproduced, Fig. 9.
120 Notes for sale, July 18-28, 1978, Hartnoll & Eyre Ltd, 39 Duke Street, St. James, London.
121 That they may be Patna School is suggested, for example, by their similarity to the Patna paintings of Indian men in Christie's *Visions of India* sale, 21 September 2000, Lot 315.
122 The painting was illustrated, No. 27, in the exhibition catalog, *Aa to Zywiec*, Hobhouse Limited, Summer 1985.
123 On the "dubash," see *Hobson-Jobson*, 328.
124 The Fraser volumes were part of the original Harry Elkins Widener collection acquired by Harvard after Widener's death in the sinking of the Titanic in 1912.
125 "Baltazard Solvyns and the Indian Picturesque," 17.
126 *Company Drawings in the India Office Library*, 75.
127 "Baltazard Solvyns and the Indian Picturesque," 17-18. Also see Mildred and W. G. Archer, "Francois Baltazard Solvyns: Early Painter of Calcutta Life," 6-9.
128 Sotheby Parke Bernet, London, Sale, November 22, 1979, Lot 64, "The Property of a Lady."
129 Sale of May 25, 1995, Lots 23-26. Three of the watercolors are illustrated in the catalog.
130 This watercolor is reproduced in the Sotheby sale catalog, November 22, 1979, Lot 64.
131 Illustrated in the Christie's catalog, Lot 26.
132 Reproduced in Pratapaditya Pal and Dehejia, Pl. 129.
133 Reproduced with permission. The watercolor, Lot 23, is illustrated in the Christie's catalog. It was included in the 1986 "From Merchants to Emperors" exhibition and is reproduced (with an incorrect attribution to Solvyns himself) in the volume published in connection with the exhibition. Pratapaditya Pal and Dehejia, Pl. 130.
134 Illustrated in the catalog, *Aa to Zywiec*, Summer 1985, Nos. 25 and 26.
135 From left to right, the figures are Solvyns's Kanaujī brahmin (Pl. II.14); daibik (Pl. II.23); kharacbardār (Pl. II.109); Rājput (Pl. II.48); and Śūdra (Pl. II.22), with a sloop (Pl. II.254) in the background.
136 Of the nine figures, the four on the left are Solvyns's sarkār (Pl. II.100); darzī (Pl. II.115); barber (Pl. II.125); and jamādār (Pl. II.101). On the right, in the foreground, are Solvyns's tambūrā (Pl. II.148) and ḍholak (Pl. II.159), and, in the background, his methrānī (Pl. II.134, ḍamphā (Pl. II.166), and banian (Pl. II.99).
137 "The Belgian Artist F. B. Solvyns and his Influence on Company Painting," 9.
138 See discussion of the Orme edition, Chapter Two, p. 54. Orme was, after Ackermann, the most important London publisher of volumes of prints. See Prideaux, 242-43. On the business of prints and illustrated books in London, see Ford's history of the Ackermann firm.

Orme may also have planned a volume of prints copied from the work of Indian artists of the Company School. Gold, in his *Oriental Drawing*, text for Pl. 40, writes that "On the suggestion of Europeans, some of the country artists have been induced to draw a series of the most ordinary casts or tribes representing a man and wife. . . . These drawings . . . do credit to the uninstructed authors of them; and the world is about to be gratified with a series of coloured engravings from them, under the title of THE COSTUME OF INDIA, which, when revised by the hand of an able European artist, will certainly merit notice and encouragement from their novelty. They are published by Orme. . . ." Such a volume never appeared, but it is possible that Gold mistook the announcement of *The Costume of Indostan* for a forthcoming collection of prints based on the work of Indian artists.
139 The William Orme watercolors are in the Department of Prints, Drawings, and Paintings of the Victoria and Albert Museum, London, Press Mark 0 7 d, Accession Numbers 6785. 1-59. The drawing for Pl. 7, "Baut" (Bhāt), *The Costumes of Indostan*, is missing. In addition to the watercolors after Solvyns, Orme also copied paintings by Thomas Daniell and Francis Swain Ward for *Twenty-four Views in Hindostan*, published by Edward Orme in 1805. The collection is sometimes bound with Blagdon. See Abbey, Entries 424 and 425, 2:382-89.
140 This was the technique, for example, used by Francesco Bartolozzi (1727-1815), an Italian who was active and very popular in England in the 1790s.
141 The China prints were engraved for Miller by Dadley after paintings by Lt. Col. George Henry Mason from the original drawings of Peu Qua of Canton. See Mason, *The Costume of China* (1800). The Turkey prints were engraved by Dadley after drawings by Octavian Dalvimart. See Dalvimart, *The Costume of Turkey* (1804).
142"India and the Illustrated Book," 13. Also see Archer, "Baltazard Solvyns and the Indian Picturesque," 15-16.
143 The three engravings are "A Tauntee," opp. 1:299; "The Oil Mill of the Hindoos," opp. 2:139; and "The Thrashing Floor of a Ryut," opp. 2:313.
144 On Moffat's work, see Godrej and Rohatgi, 32-34. They provide a list of Moffat prints, 157, but does not include the

Solvyns's Bisarjan copy. On Moffat, also see Losty, *Calcutta: City of Palaces*, 74, 76-79.

145 See pp. 27-29 for a discussion of the painting. Losty, *Calcutta: City of Palaces*, 77, Fig. 41, reproduces the print.

146 The last issue of the periodical held by the British Library is Vol. III, No. 1, for 1811. We have no information as to whether it continued publication. Depping thought the Leipzig prints were to be a German pirated edition of Solvyns's work. See Chapter Two, p. 71.

147 Phillips's *Geography* went through many editions. The Solvyns copies in the 5th ed. are "An Hindoo Market in Bengal" (Pl. 32, opp. p. 398); "A School among the Hindoos" (Pl. 33, opp. p. 402); "An Hindoo Woman throwing herself on the funeral Pile of her Husband" (Pl. 34, opp. p. 406); and "An Hindoo Woman about to be buried in the grave of her Husband" (Pl. 34, opp. p. 408). A fifth copy after Solvyns, "A Gentoo Woman burning herself on the funeral pile of her husband," is listed in a description of plates at the end of the book, but it does not appear in the volume.

148 Bertuch, Pl. CCXXXII.

149 *Asia*, Vol. II.

150 Trans. from the Italian, ibid., 9-10.

151 The musical instruments portrayed, from left to right, correspond–not always very accurately–to Solvyns's śaṅkh and ghaṇṭā (Pl. II.146); bā̃śi (Pl. II.180); ḍhāk (Pl. II.156); ḍholak (Pl. II.159); surmaṇḍal (Pl. II.169); kartāl (Pl. II.171); the unidentified drummer; and jagajhampa (Pl. II.168).

152 Robert J. Del Bontà Collection, San Francisco.

153 Hugh Murray, et al.

154 2:450.

155 Plates copied from Solvyns are 1:8,1:12, 1:113, 1:250; 2:45, 2:95; 2:165, and 2:319. William Westall provided illustrations of many topographical books on India, notably Grindlay's *Scenery*.

156 Burnouf and Jacquet, "Indien agonisant porté sur les bords du Gange," Vol. II, Sec. 21, Pl. 6.

157 The plates, without attribution to Solvyns, are in Vol. I: Pl. XVII, 1 ("Procession sur l'eau de la Kaly Déesse"), opp. p. 131, and Pl. XVII, 3 ("Veuve se jetant dans le bûcher"), opp. p. 134.

158 The copies, in Vol. I, *Asia*, are of single figures: Solvyns's portrayals of a soldier (*havildār*) in traditional Indian military dress (Pl. II.95); a bālak (Pl. II.96)'; the pināk (Pl. II.150); and a free adaptation of the Rājput (Pl. II. 48). The volume, with the prints, appeared in Italian translation in 1844.

159 Pl. 40, "A Hindoo Widow burning herself with the corpse of her husband," Vol. 3, opp. 99. The other prints are No. 28, Vol. 2, opp. 252; Pl. 29, Vol. 3, opp. 1; and Pl. 35, Vol. 3, opp. 44. Shoberl, 3:129, acknowledges Solvyns as the source for the suttee print. See the discussion of the representation of suttee in the introduction to Solvyns's etchings of satī, pp. 421-26, and in the commentaries for the four satī prints (Pls. II.199-202).

160 The sati prints appeared in Vol. 34 (Midsummer 1824) and Vol. 32 (Christmas 1823). The other prints were "Water Procession of the Image of Kalee" (Pl. II.190), Vol. 33 (Lady, Day, 1824), and "Death of Hindoos on the Banks of the River Ganges" (Pl. II.198), Vol. 29 (Lady Day, 1823). The prints were collected and published in *The First Ten Years' Quarterly Papers of the Church Missionary Society* (1826).

161 The sati prints appear opp. 375 and 392. Ward also includes a copy of Solvyns's portrayal of "Hindu Fakirs" (Pl. II.140), opp. 371.

162 Peggs, 303 and 77, respectively.

163 Pl. 5.

164 I am grateful to Paul Courtright for first drawing my attention to the item and to Susan Bean of the Peabody Essex Museum for further information. The museum's silver specialist Crosby Forbes linked the box to the Chinese silversmith. Bean portrays the box in *Yankee India*, 190 (Figs. 11.22-23).

165 Some of these, as the box in Charles Greig's collection, appear to be silver cast copies made in India from a Chinese original.

166 The match case, of a wedge shape approximately 5 x 4 cm., is in the collection of Charles Greig.

167 The album was listed by Bernard Shapero Rare Books, London, in his catalog *World Travel V*, item 243, with an illustration of the watercolor of the "D'haul" (ḍhāk, Pl. II.156). The album sold at auction, Lot 129, in Christie's "Visions of India" sale, June 10, 1997. The watercolor "A Hooka Burdar" (hukābardār, Pl. II.108), is reproduced in color in the catalog.

Les Hindoûs: Preliminary Discourse

The Preliminary Discourse to Volume I of *Les Hindoûs* is reproduced here with only minor omissions. The text retains the idiosyncratic and varied spellings as well as the punctuation of the original. Solvyns's footnotes are here placed within the text in brackets.

Solvyns acknowledges no assistance in the authorship of the Preliminary Discourse and the Introductions to the subsequent volumes, but, as discussed in Chapter Two (pp. 65-66), those portions of the text that refer to and draw from European accounts of India and translations of Hindu texts are probably by Georges-Bernard Depping. Discussions of the artist's intent, as his commitment to truth in portrayal, and of the prints themselves are by Solvyns.

As most of the text in the Introductions to volumes II, III, and IV relates directly to the subjects portrayed, relevant portions are included in the discussions opening each section into which Solvyns's etchings have been organized for *A Portrait of the Hindus*. Thus, for example, Solvyns's general discussion of Indian music in the Introduction to Volume II, opens the section on musical instruments. In two instances, the discussion in the Introduction is included within the Commentary on the prints (Pls. II.10 and II.198).

Preliminary Discourse[1]

The vast Country whose population is the subject of this work, is that delightful region known to the moderns by the name of Hindoostan or Hindostan, and which, from the fertility of its soil, the amenity of its climate, and the abundance of everything necessary to the wants or even to the pleasures of life, the ancients had distinguished by the title of Paradise of the World. But more celebrated than known, this happy spot, from the earliest ages till the two last centuries, has been an object of exaggerated admiration to other nations, whose credulity was without limits for a country whose beauties in reality surpassed the ordinary gifts of nature. From Herodotus, who, to some interesting notions of Hindoostan has added many absurd fables, such, for example, as that of a species of ant as large as dogs [Lib. iij, 102.],[2] whose instinct discovered to the natives the treasures buried in the sands, down to Marco Paolo and Monteville [Mandeville],[3] to whom this country appeared a paradise glowing with gold and silver, shaded with the tree of life, and rich with an endless variety of wonderful objects, India has been the most fertile field for the inventive imagination of the poet and the scarce less inventive fancy of the traveller.

But while the vulgar listened with stupid astonishment to these ridiculous tales and marvellous accounts, some less superficial minds extending their view beyond these objects of common admiration, studied the manners and native character of the Indian people; and were perhaps not less astonished to discover in the Hindoos a portion of mankind exempt from ambition, from vanity, from curiosity, satisfied in the enjoyment of what nature bestowed, and possessing in their mild and calm disposition that happiness which they themselves had pursued so long in vain, through the mazes of philosophy and science. Apollonius Tyanaeus,[4] so highly famed for his knowledge, his actions and his travels, after traversing the most celebrated countries of the globe, bears this noble testimony of the Hindoos, as we have it from his historian Philostratus.[5] [De vitâ Apoll. Tyan., lib. iij.] There, he says, I found a race of mortals living upon the earth, but not adhering to it, inhabiting cities, but not being fixed to them, possessing every thing, but possessed by nothing. Supposing even the travels of Pythagoras in India fictitious,[6] they still hold out a proof of the high opinion which the ancients had of the morality of the Hindoos, and of the priority of their civilisation. Happy had they attracted notice by these advantages only. The richness of their country soon awakened the avarice of numerous invaders, to whom their mild and easy temper could oppose but a weak and useless resistance. Subdued at different periods by Darius Hidaspes, by Alexander the Great, by the Parsis or Guebres,[7] by the Mahometans, by the Moguls and Tartars, etc., they were obliged to give up a great part of their establishments to their enemies, and to receive in some sort the laws and political constitutions of their conquerors. But while the influence of these revolutions was perceived in their political existence and in their population, the native character, the moral and religious system retained all its primitive purity, and was neither undermined by the slow operation of time, nor overthrown by the violence of man. In the course of the two last centuries, it is true, the closer connection of Europeans with this country seems to have made some impression upon the primitive character of the Hindoo nation. Not only are their numbers considerably lessened, but many of them have been insensibly incorporated with other nations, new manners and new forms of worship have been introduced, where formerly the name of Brahma only was revered. But it will not escape the attentive observer, that different changes which the country underwent, by the introduction of a new people, foreign to all their ancient habits, never reached the genuine race of Hindoos; diminished indeed in its numbers and extent, but still unaltered, still constant in its manners, its opinions and its belief. It is now considerably more than twenty centuries, that history represents the Hindoos as we see them in our present days. All around them has submitted to the revolutions of this globe; of cities once great and flourishing we scarce can explore the ruins beneath the sand of the desert; the barren wilderness is covered with magnificent towns, and alive with a numerous population; lakes and rivers have yielded their beds to the productive soil; the boundaries of the Ocean have advanced or retreated; inundations, volcanic eruptions and earthquakes have excavated the abyss, buried or raised up the mountain; but amidst these vicissitudes of nature and of man, the character of the Hindoo remains the same.

The history of Arrian[8] is the description of the life and manners of the Indians of our own time. What spectacle more interesting or more deserving of our attention, than the remains of a celebrated nation inhabiting one of the most delightful countries of Asia, and treasuring up as a sacred deposit, the simplicity of its antique virtues, in the midst of universal corruption and the refinements of foreign civilization?

Since the revival of science and of letters in Europe has awakened in its inhabitants the noble ambition of enlarging the boundaries of human knowledge, and extended their relations and their power over the whole surface of the earth, the country of the Hindoos has been one of the chief objects of their researches. While avarice and every meaner passion was gratified with an ample range, a fruitful mine was not wanting in this interesting country, to reward the labours of science. The English and French especially, have enriched the litterature of Europe with many valuable works that may serve to dispel the darkness which enveloped the geography and history of India, and more especially of Hindoostan, until they appeared, as may be seen by the ample bibliographical list which we owe to Mr. Wahl,[9] the continuator of Busching's geography.[10] Anquetil Duperron,[11] Fra Paolino,[12] Jones[13] and others have made known their religion; Rennell[14] and Tiefenthaler,[15] the geography; Dow,[16] Orme,[17] Holwell,[18] the history; Gough,[19] Daniel[20] and Hodges,[21] the monuments; the society of Calcutta, the authors of the Asiatic Register[22] and Researches[23] the litterature, the natural history; the mythology and other interesting objects.—We are now, in short, well acquainted with the soil, the riches, the curiosities of Hindoostan; its inhabitants alone have not yet been observed nor represented with that accuracy which is necessary to make them perfectly known; for we cannot surely take the unconnected details given by different travellers, though men of excellent information, such as Crawford,[24] Sonnerat,[25] Hamilton,[26] Mackintosh,[27] Forster,[28] Le Gentil,[29] and many others, for a complete and satisfactory delineation.

It is true that to fulfil such a task requires a coincidence of circumstances which seldom falls to the lot of a traveller, and which few of any description are happy enough to unite. It was, in the first place, necessary to reside among this people a sufficient time to have opportunities of observing them in all their habits of life, their customs, domestic manners, daily occupations, civil and religious ceremonies, amusements, feasts, games, etc.; for it is in all these that the Hindoos are truly an original people differing essentially from all others.

Customs (says Mr. Rennell), which in every country acquire a degree of veneration, are here rendered sacred by their connexion with religion: the rites of which are interwoven with the ordinary occurrences of life.

Now when we find that everything in India, down to the form of their household furniture, and their tools, is handed down to them from the most remote antiquity, and that their domestic life is a continued exercise of their ancient worship, we shall feel no difficulty in agreeing that to acquire a true knowledge, and form a proper judgment of this people, it is not only necessary to have resided long among them, but to have also had an opportunity of following them through all their actions, with a sufficient power of observation, to discern the primitive and pure casts, from the mixed tribes, which are now so frequent in many parts of India.

It is owing to not having fulfilled these necessary conditions, that the greater number of travellers have brought back to Europe such imperfect or false notions of the Hindoos, and disgraced their works by such strange ideas and such ridiculous mistakes. Another obstacle which has hitherto stood in the way of acquiring clear and accurate ideas upon these subjects, is, that those who have had an opportunity of obtaining such ideas upon the spot, being unused to handle the pencil, were obliged, in order to transmit them, to have recourse to artists to whom they were totally new; or if they thought themselves capable of tracing them with the pencil or the graver, it was oftener with the talent of an amateur than of an artist. Besides, all the prints which I have seen given with the accounts of travels in this country, are on so small a scale, that the lesser details are confused and offer only vague and undetermined objects.

From such a view of the imperfect and erroneous state of our information upon India, and under the foregoing consideration, I might reasonably flatter myself that a work where nothing was neglected which might rectify accredited error, or supply omission in these interesting subjects, would meet with a favourable reception. I have presumed to offer with confidence to the public the result of a long and uninterrupted study of this celebrated nation in its own territory, during a residence of fifteen years.[30] The drawings from which are engraved the numerous plates with which this work is enriched, were taken by myself upon the spot. Instead of trusting to the works of others, or remaining satisfied with the knowledge contained in preceding authors, I have spared neither time, nor pains, nor expence, to see and examine with my own eyes, and to delineate every object with the most minute accuracy; which will easily be felt by whoever will take the trouble of considering with some attention these fruits of long and painful application.

Henceforth the public will not be exposed to admit false or confused ideas upon a subject so interesting to curiosity and so well deserving of attention, nor led astray in the track of authors more disposed to the chimeras of system, than to strictness of observation, and severity of truth.

These alone have been my constant guides, my ultimate objects in this work. I admitted nothing as certain but upon the proof of my own observation, or upon such testimony as I knew to be incontrovertible. I have wholly neglected the testimony of authors who have treated these subjects before me, and have given only what I have seen, or what I have myself heard from the mouth of the natives the best informed and most capable of giving me true instructions upon the subject of my enquiries. I might no doubt have enlarged the text which is annexed to the plates, with the help of the numerous works which have already been written upon India, but I could no longer have answered for the truth of it, and I flatter myself that the public will not condemn this motive for abridging it. Truth, perspicuity and precision were the ends at which I constantly aimed. With respect to the first I apprehend no contradiction; for the others, I must await the judgment of the impartial reader.

What I have said of this text, may also in some degree be applied to the prints themselves, in which I have purposely avoided all sort of ornament or embellishment; they are merely representations of the objects such as they appeared to my view, and such as they would appear at this hour to the reader, if he could be suddenly transported into the midst of them. This circumstance did not escape the sagacity of the members of the Institut de France, that illustrious society which has had the goodness to accept the dedication of this work, and whose approbation is for me an encouragement and favourable omen of public favour. It is not for me to say more upon the merits of my work, and the qualities by which I may hope it will be distinguished from all others of the kind, if indeed the fragments which modern travellers have published may be at all placed in the same class. But before I communicate my own observations upon the Hindoos, I believe it will not be inexpedient to submit some general reflexions, which may form as it were a supplement to the briefness of the text, and present to such as have but a superficial knowledge of this remarkable people, an abridgment of all which relates to it. Perhaps even men of deeper information may not be averse to take with me a cursory view of the subject, and thus recall of their minds what has been the object of more serious application. I think it proper also to lay before the public the plan I have followed, which I shall have an opportunity of doing in the course of this analysis.

The fertile and delightful soil of Hindoostan is traversed by several chains of lofty mountains, whose summits, bare of every sort of vegetation, rear into the clouds heaps of rocks, or plains of barren sand, out of which again covered with eternal snows and ice start up some more elevated points. Nothing can be more pleasingly striking than the contrast between these dreary masses and the delicious plains which unfold themselves from the foot of the mountain, refreshed and watered by numerous rivers, in all the richness of vegetation. This contrast of nature has its effect on the temper of the inhabitants. Those of the sterile mountain and its gloomy crevices, are savage and warlike, while those of the happy plain below are mild and gentle as their soil and climate. Nevertheless, a variety so remarkable in these different branches of the same people, has not effaced the original stamp of national character, which through every age has distinguished the physical and moral nature of the Hindoo; that peculiar cast of feature that keeps them distinct from every other nation which has settled in India. Simplicity and temperance are virtues common to the whole race, and are remarked in every part of Hindoostan which has escaped the fatal influence of European manners. To these two qualities, add that the happy temperature of climate, milder here than in the other provinces of India, strengthens the nervous system, and gives a solidity to the body not to be impaired by the fatigues of life, and you will conceive why of all mankind the Hindoo possesses in the highest degree the means of happiness in the enjoyment of his existence. Indifferent to the treasures which lye concealed in the bosom of his mountains, he is satisfied with a frugal diet and a simple hut, and a stripe of cloth suffises for his garment. Such was his mode of life more than two thousand years ago, such it is to day wherever art has not intervened to efface the traces of nature. . . .

The mother tongue, whence all the other idioms derive which are spoken in India, particularly in Hindoostan, with the exception of those introduced by foreign nations, is the Ssamsskrida or Samsskret, which the Europeans write and pronounce Sanscrit. We owe to the labours of modern men of science, more especially the English, that this beautiful language, remarkable for its copiousness and extraordinary pliancy, is becoming every day more and more known. In this perfect idiom are written the sacred books of the Hindoos; as well as all the ancient works and monuments of the Indian history and litterature. It remains the language of the Brahmuns, who possess it to this day, while the other Hindoos know only the living language of their own provinces, which, derived from this common source, are again frequently subdivided into different dialects. In this manner the Hindoostan language, derived from the Sanskrit, has in its turn given rise to the dialects of Pendchab,[31] of Gudchurat,[32] of Nepal, of Bengal, etc.; all taking their names from the provinces where they are spoken. The true Hindoostan language is now to be met with only at Benares, in the kingdom of Potna[33] and in some separate districts throughout Hindoostan. The letters in use among the different nations of India are as various as their dialects; but it is not difficult to trace in all of them the character of the ancient Sanskrit. The description and names of the several nations who have occupied Hindoostan have varied at different periods; the Greeks and Romans, but little acquainted with the language of the country, had but confused and often very false notions of them: it would consequently be an useless trouble to seek among the present inhabitants the nations whom ancient authors have described under many different appellations. We are not less in the dark upon the constitution of the primitive states of that country; there is however every reason to believe that in the more remote periods the patriarchal government existed here as well as in the greater part of Asia. Each separate family which are generally very numerous, was under the government of a chief, with absolute power of life and death over all the members of that community. Some of these heads of families, more powerful than their neighbours, subdued them; and in this manner became masters of vast extents of country over which in time they assumed the title of king; others were under the necessity of submitting to the power of a conqueror, and forced to acknowledge the authority of a foreigner; so that, by degrees, the patriarchal form gave way to a sort of feudal system not unlike what was established in Europe in the middle ages. Thus in the time of Alexander, part of the Indian states were under the vassallage of the Persians, or even of some more powerful prince of their own nation, while others remained independent and free from all foreign interference. Some of these states found means to maintain their independence during a long succession of ages, and even to this day there remain a few who have a government of their own, while all the provinces that surround them are under the servile yoke of foreign or of native masters.

Of the Indian nations we have no complete history. The historical narrations written by the natives themselves are very imperfect, especially when they relate to periods anterior to the invasion of the Mahometans. But were we even in possession of such monuments, I would not exercise the patience of my reader by offering them to his notice. It has already been but too often experienced, that little interest can arise from history, where all is oppression and cruelty on one side, and on the other a melancholy example of extreme weakness. Let us rather for a moment turn our eyes to the religious and civil institutions of the Indians, much more interesting and more celebrated than all the rest of their history. I put under one head the religious and civil system; among the Hindoos it is well known that they are united and inseparable. The origin of their religion is enveloped in impenetrable darkness. All that we know about it is that it ascends to the most remote antiquity. Here then we may discover the source from whence in our days have flowed those hypothesis, unsatisfactory at least, if not quite unfounded, those strange comparisons between the Hindoo religion and that of the Christians, by which it would seem to be inferred that the latter being less ancient and bearing some resemblance to the former in many of its most essential dogmas, has evidently been copied from it: that the Christians were but imitators of the Hindoos, who in their turn did no more than borrow their theological principles from the religion of Mithra. Perhaps such rash opinions would from their first appearance have fallen into oblivion along with their authors, if in the number had not been found some brilliant writers, who by the charms of their style seduce their readers, and lead away their judgment by the authority of their names, and even by the boldness and novelty of their systems. From such men as these, conjectures at best but slenderly supported, and which a little deeper research guided by candour and sincerity would probably be sufficient to destroy, have acquired a sort of consistency. If in reality there exists any resemblance between the dogmas of the Christian religion and that of the Hindoos, it is in my opinion much more simple to suppose with Thomas Maurice[34] and other authors, that these dogmas being already as it were contained or implied in the religious code or in the patriarchal history of Moses, beyond which no history reaches, were from thence spread with more or less embellishment of oriental fancy over the nations not only of India but of all Asia. What adds still more probability to this reasonable opinion, are the historical proofs which have been lately acquired, that these same dogmas have existed at a very remote period in the most northern regions of Asia, where no Hindoo had probably ever thought of penetrating. The only example which I shall cite is the medal representing the Divinity under a triple form, found in the most remote part of Siberia. [Indian antiquities, London, 1801.][35] But without entering into further particulars which would lead me too far away from my subject, I will proceed to give some idea of the religion of the Hindoos, and pay no further attention to any system to which it may give rise.

From time immemorial this people is in possession of a code at once civil and religious, which they attribute to their legislator Menu[36] by some authors supposed to be Noah, whom the Indians have named Nuh. It appears that, at first, this code was not committed to writing, but preserved in the memory of the Brahmuns, who on occasions of difficulty were consulted by their princes. By the laws of Menu all the Hindoos are, as we know, divided into four classes or casts, each of which is again subdivided into an infinite number of other classes distinguished by their occupations, their professions and the prerogatives which they enjoy exclusively, and which the others can by no means acquire. On this foundation rests the whole religious and civil system of the Hindoos: each individual has from the hour of his birth a rank and situation which he can never change; all the functions of his life are traced out to him by the constitutions of his cast; every particular, even the different sorts of food which he may use, is regulated by the code. It has not been in the power of twenty centuries to obliterate these rigorous distinctions; and to this day the true Hindoos observe them with the most scrupulous exactness. Institutions of this nature, tending to fetter the genius and extinguish the spirit of emulation and that happiness of natural disposition which might raise an obscure Hindoo to the rank of a great man in another class, may without doubt be very justly censured; but on the other hand, plausible reasons are not wanting in their defence; and it is certain that in India at least they are not in the way of private happiness or of civil government. This Mr. Maurice has very ably demonstrated in the work above cited.

> "By this arrangement it should be remembered the happiness and security of a vast empire was preserved inviolate during a long series of ages under their early sovereigns; by moderating the fiery spirits of ambitious individuals, intestine feuds were in a great measure prevented; the wants of an immense population were amply provided for by the industry of the labouring classes, and the several branches of trade and manufactures were carried to the utmost degree of attainable perfection. Though the stern ferocity of Mahometan despotism violently insulted their religion and overturned their government, yet they have not been able to wrest from them the superior palm of excellence to which the curious productions of the India loom are so highly entitled, and the exquisite work in gold and jewellery that passes through the pliant fingers of the Indian artist, remain still unrivalled in any commercial region of the earth."[37]

I shall have occasion to speak again upon this last article in the course of this dissertation. Let us for a moment longer confine our attention to the religious constitution given to this people by their legislator Menu.

The first and most noble cast is that of the Brahmuns:[38] by them therefore it was proper that my description should begin: the order which seemed to me the most natural, was to represent each class and each subdivision, as well in the Brahmun cast as in the three others, in separate plates, that the reader might have it in his power to judge of their difference by the costume and the occupation of the individuals who fill them. In the text will always be found the denomination under which each of these classes is distinguished by the natives. In common with all the worships of the east, that of the Hindoos enjoins a great number of ceremonies, of festivals and rites, which, to be agreeably and distinctly represented to the eye, required a larger scale than the other prints: and as it entered into my first plan to place at the head of each number a plate of double the size of the others, I have in general reserved them for the representation of these religious feasts and assemblies. I might have placed all these together in one volume; but the present arrangement appeared preferable as affording more variety to the work.[39] Among these ceremonies are many which seem to be strongly in contrast with the mild and humane manners that I have attributed to the Hindoos in the beginning of this discourse. We shall be astonished to behold their cruel expiations, their painful penances, the horrid death of their widows, and other superstitious practices of the same sort. No doubt it is not easy to reconcile these instances with the universal mildness of character of this people, which they carry so far as to avoid shedding the blood even of animals [*See Esp. des Lois, chap. 3, liv. 14*, for an explanation of this opposition between the timidity and mildness of their disposition and the ferocity of some of their customs.[40]], who are to them objects of the greatest pity. But in the observing mind, the astonishment arising from this opposition will subside with the reflection, that the history of human nature offers similar examples at every period and among every people. Moreover the religion of the Hindoos dates probably from a period when the inhabitants of Asia, but little advanced in civilisation, mingled with their worship these barbarous and sanguinary customs. The history of India itself contains sufficient proofs that at an early period human sacrifices were performed; even to this day the horrid practice exists in certain districts, as I myself have witnessed. The institutions of Menu, in other respects so mild and humane, authorise in unequivocal terms certain modes of suicide as acts agreeable to the divinity in expiation of sin,[41] and denounce on some occasions the most severe punishments for the slightest faults, as may be seen in the Hindoo laws published lately by some scientific men in England. It would be foreign to my present purpose, besides to inquire here whether what is harsh and cruel in these laws derives in reality from Menu, or whether it proceeds not rather from the despotism whose iron sceptre weighed down India as well as the rest of Asia. The Brahmun cast is not subjected to all these laws; their crimes even are not ever punished with severity. This is one of the many privileges which this cast enjoys, as the most noble and most respectable. All religious matters come under its jurisdiction. The sovereign himself has but a deliberative voice in the ecclesiastical council. In their department also are the sciences in all their branches, the elements of which they teach in a sort of academies very common throughout Hindoostan. Young persons are admitted into them after being instructed in the first rudiments of writing, reading and arithmetic, in smaller schools kept generally in the open air, before the house of the Brahmun appointed for this purpose, as will be seen in the tenth number, vol. 3.[42] Once initiated in the sacred knowledge of the Brahmuns, they are enjoined to keep a strict silence till a certain age, as in the school of Pythagoras. The young Brahmun begins from his earliest age to accustom himself to the sacred rites, and the precepts of the Veda. All that concerns his education has been prescribed in a particular chapter of the Institutions of Menu. Although all the Brahmuns form a part or the sacerdotal cast, there are nevertheless but a certain number of them who devote themselves to the service of the temples, the sacrifices and public instruction. These enjoy constantly the revenues of the lands attached to each temple or pagoda from time immemorial. The other Brahmuns take different employments, or apply themselves to the sciences. Notwithstanding all the efforts of the missionaries, no Brahmun has ever yet been known to embrace the christian religion; and in general, though the Hindoos have been subdued by many different peoples, they never adopted the religion of any of their conquerors, nor ever sought to spread their own into the neighbouring countries. The faquirs are a particular class of men among the Hindoos, whose superstitious fanaticism and singularity of rites deserve particular notice. I have therefore set apart several plates of the second volume[43] to represent them in the exercise of all their extraordinary practices, which renders it unnecessary to speak of them here.

The second cast of the Hindoos is that of the K'huttrys,[44] who give themselves the title of children of the kings,[45] because they look upon themselves as descendants of the ancient kings of India, distinguished by the name of children of the Sun and Moon. From this cast must descend all the princes of India, if they are not of the first cast; for there are examples of Brahmun families upon the throne.

By the ancient statutes of India, says Paolino, the king is the first soldier of the empire: and from this cast also are taken the warriors who are to defend the State. Nevertheless, since the Indians have begun to adopt the military system of Europe, and to take foreign troops into their pay, they take a great number of soldiers from the inferior casts; but the command is always given to the K'huttrys. As defenders of the State, they enjoy great privileges which place them much above the other casts, and give them in their eyes something like the authority of the patricians at Rome. Entirely devoted to the military service and without fixed establishments, they are always ready to take the field; and by this political institution an Indian prince can in a few hours set on foot a formidable army with very little cost to the State, the Indian soldier being naturally sober and satisfied with the most frugal diet.

The third class, that of the Byces,[46] Husbandmen, farmers and Merchants, is perhaps the most useful to the State, in providing for the public expences by the tax which it pays for the land, the cultivation of which is its chief occupation. Every farmer pays about the sixth part of the revenue of his land; and after paying this tribute, he and his family enjoy in peace the fruits of their labour, and dispose of them as they please. We cannot praise too highly the wisdom of the legislator, who having placed all the honors and all the authority in the two superior casts, ordained that the Merchant and the Farmer should live in peace under the protection of the government, and never feel the pressure of civil or military charges; so that even in the midst of war, these estimable and useful members of society may follow quietly their several professions. Whether the laws of Menu in this respect are the effect of his deep political views, or that they are the dictates of humanity, it is not less true that they may serve as a model to some part of our civilized Europe. [*Meherculè non est quod Europaei homines his gentibus insultant easque barbaras vocitent, quandò verum Europeaenum legale systema praestantiam illius non attingit; nunc ruit, nunc attollitur: simplici et salubri illarum gentium institutione jam à tribus mille et ampliùs annis certâ, intactâ, tectâ, incolumi et immortabili persistente. Quis igitur non dicat praestare inter gentiles vivere quàm stultis non-nullorum Europaeorum novatorum ineptis legibus et institutis perpoliri?* Pag. 230, fol. 2, *Paullini systema Brachmanicum, Româ,* 1791.[47] ("My god, there is no reason for Europeans to scoff at these people and call them barbarian, when, in fact, the

European legal system does not come close to the excellence of theirs. Whereas the European system constantly goes through peaks and valleys, for over 3,000 years now the plain and wholesome principles of these people have been fixed, left undisturbed, unblemished, and forever steady. Who would not say, therefore, that it is better to live among the Hindus than to be furbished by the inane and inept laws and principles of a series of European innovators?"[48])]

The same paternal protection is extended by the Hindoo institutions to the fourth case, that of the Soodders[49] or Mechanics, in less consideration than the three others, and divided, according to their respective trades, into different tribes or corporations, each of which is distinguished by their particular dress, hieroglyphical marks, pretentions, customs, and even their tutelar divinities. I shall take care to enter sufficiently into details of the principal employments of each of them, to shew the characteristic marks which distinguish them, and to which are attached the different degrees of respect or of contempt with which they are treated. In many of the engravings hieroglyphic signs will be remarked on the forehead of some Hindoos, by which they are known in the first place as Hindoos, and secondly as members of the particular sect to which they have devoted themselves. I have represented the very persons themselves whom I saw on the spot.

The reader would have but an imperfect idea of the Hindoos if he confined himself to a knowledge of their worship, their customs and their particular employments. I have therefore taken pains to collect all the objects which may tend to illustrate their manner of living, the state of their arts, their ordinary amusements, the occupations of their leisure hours, the interior of their houses, their furniture, instruments, etc. . . . A part of these objects are already in the plates which represent the individuals of each cast, as I always endeavoured to introduce into the drawing all the circumstances of the spot in which I took them.

Quiet is the happiest state of life to the peaceable Hindoo: as soon consequently as his business is done, and that he can gave himself up to his natural indolence and smoke his houka in repose, he enjoys his utmost notion of happiness, and remains hours together without stirring from his place or changing his attitude, which to us Europeans would be a very uneasy one. The postures of the Hindoo at rest and smoking are indisputably very original, and I thought myself under an obligation to bring them into the pictoresque description of this people. Their very mode of smoking differs materially from that of Europeans. As it has never been faithfully represented in the prints yet published, it appeared to me to require great exactness in the drawings that I took, which give even the most minute circumstances.[50]

Though the Hindoo esteems quiet above all other enjoyments, he is no enemy to arts and letters, and it is of consequence to shew our proud Europeans that he cultivates them with success.

With respect to architecture, many English artists, as I have already said, have given specimens of the fine monuments spread over Hindoostan: I have nevertheless given several of them in my drawings, to prove that if the Hindoos cannot attain in their works the sublime severity of the Greek and Roman stile, they have at least raised monuments which are master-pieces of boldness, solidity, taste, and even grandeur. This must be understood of some of their temples, the facades of which are really fine, and the interior grand and magnificent. But the taste of their private buildings is totally different from those of Europe, for the simple reason that the climate of India is very different from that of Greece or Italy, and still more from the temperature of the northern parts of our continent. Nothing can be more simple than the habitation of an Hindoo of the poorer cast; a few branches of the palm-tree, a few bamboos, a little mud and straw, are all the materials necessary to raise a protection against the heat. The rich alone copy the luxuries of Europe, if that of the great men of the cast does not even surpass our own.

Their sculpture is necessarily inferior; consecrated entirely to their worship, even when destined to other use, it must have the same model in view, from which the slightest deviation is not allowed. Almost all the statues of their divinities are hideous figures, shapeless and deformed; but the artist would subject himself to very severe punishment if he presumed to give them a more regular form. Music is very generally cultivated among the Hindoos, especially as it is subservient to dancing, one of their favourite diversions. We may form a judgment of the character of this art in Hindoostan, from the specimens published by Will. Jones,[51] Hamilton Bird,[52] and the baron d'Alberg.[53] Drawings also of several of their musical instruments have been published, but in a very imperfect manner; in the first place, they do no more than represent the instrument, without giving an idea of the manner in which it is played, which is not easy to conceive without having it under the eye: the figures too are so small, that it is not possible to guess the parts of which they are composed, and still less to make one after them. The manner in which I have drawn these different instruments in my collection[54] is not, if I am not much mistaken, liable to any of these objections.

To pass from the pleasing to the useful arts, we may perceive at first sight that the Hindoos might in many things give lessons to the ablest Europeans, which in reality they may boast to have done. It is scarcely necessary to make particular mention of their famous stuffs, which, under the name of musslins, chintzes, cachemirs, etc., are in such great repute in most parts of the world. The same may be said of their jewellry and gold and silver work, their varnish, their dyes, and numberless other articles of luxury or necessity.

But the process which they employ in their manufactories and fabricks is transmitted from father to son since time immemorial, without their ever attempting any improvement or more extensive application. With them, as in China, the arts and sciences have never risen beyond a certain degree of perfection. It is evident that they stopped where there was no immediate use in going further. As they had never copied any of the neighbouring nations, they were not more inclined to adopt any new process invented by strangers; the means which they employ are besides so simple that it would be very difficult to attain any greater degree of perfection at the same cost, and with the same instruments, and their obstinate attachment to the methods employed by their fathers is even one great cause of their excelling in all the trades to which they apply.

Mr. Mackintosh observes that the natives of Europe have a love of novelty and an ardent desire of perfection, which makes them despise the past, and esteem the present only as worthy of their attention. In Asia on the contrary, and especially in India, on both sides of the Ganges, ancient customs and manners are most scrupulously adhered to. There, the object of emulation is not to invent new things, but to preserve in all their original purity the practices and documents of the remotest antiquity. There may perhaps be perceived some connection between this turn of mind and the taste which prevails in India not for invention or speculation but for imitation. In this art the Indians excell to such a degree that whether in cloth, earthen ware, metal, wood or stone, the copy is not to be distinguished from the original. They seem particularly fitted for works of imitation, by that perseverance which they so eminently possess, and that other faculty by which their whole attention is absorbed in the object of their occupation. Nothing can cause the slightest distraction in their ideas or imagination. The whole force of their mind is by this steady attention concentrated in one single object. By this perseverance and extreme application they preserve an equability of temper which may sometimes perhaps be raised by the use of opium or of some intoxicating herb, but is never depressed by labour unsuited to their frame or constitution.—The calm of their mind, even under the most afflicting circumstances, is seen through the pleasing smile which never leaves their countenance.

A slight view of the prints representing the Soodder cast will be sufficient to convince us of the simplicity of their machinery and of their tools. What it said here of their mechanical instruments may be equally applied to those of agriculture, which require to be the less complicated as the soil of Hindoostan needs but to be slightly stirred to produce in the greatest abundance rice and other vegetables, which are the food of the inhabitants of this happy country. Since the arrival of the Europeans, the Hindoos have little by little become familiar with their arts and inventions, and have imitated some of them pretty successfully. But there are still parts of the country where every thing is done after the manner of the ancient Indians, and where scarce any innovation has been yet admitted.

The trade of Hindoostan, so famous in every period of time, is naturally divided into the two branches, of home and foreign. The home trade is generally carried on in large market places called bazars. It was not without difficulty that I have been able to obtain a representation of one of them for this work, for though these markets are held in every part of Hindoostan, they are almost all frequented indiscriminately by Musselmans and other strangers. But that which will be found in the third volume[55] is a true Hindoo bazar.

For the foreign trade the Indians transport their goods by land or by sea. By land they use carriages of various forms of which an exact representation will be found in the third volume,[56] where also I have given the manner of travelling in India, especially that of being carried in litters called palanqueens, of which there are also many different sorts, none of which, at least of all those which I met as I travelled, are I believe omitted.

An object indisputably of greater curiosity than their carriages or palanqueens, are their ships and boats whether for freight or pleasure. In ancient times the Indians excelled in the art of constructing vessels, and the present Hindoos can in this respect still offer models to Europe; so much so that the English, attentive to every thing which relates to naval architecture, have borrowed from the Hindoos many improvements which they have adapted with success to their own shipping. This was a very particular object of my attention during my residence in India, and I dare hope that the drawings which I give in the third volume[57] will be looked upon as what is most complete upon that subject. On examining them it will without difficulty be agreed that the Indian vessels unite elegance and utility, and that they are models of patience and fine workmanship.

If hitherto I have not spoken of the Hindoo women, the truth is, that the part which they act among that people is so little interesting, and they are so seldom to be met with in the public places of Hindoostan, that it is not to be wondered at that I have confined myself generally to the representation only of the men.

In the code of Menu, in other respects replete with precepts of wisdom, it is declared with great harshness, that women are incapable of independence, and it even seems to be insinuated that they are beings of an inferior order, to whom on that account the texts of the Vedas or sacred books cannot be applied. Shut up in their separate apartments, the Hindoo women are seen only by their nearest relations, and when they appear in public, it is never without a veil upon their face. This, as may be supposed, does not extend to the lower classes, whose women appear in public and frequent assemblies without reserve. This distinction may be easily remarked in the plates which represent any feast or ceremony.

Although the women of the higher casts are never exposed to the eyes of the public, they are here as in Europe and everywhere else, very fond of dress, but with this difference, that fancy and fashion make a great part of the value of the ornaments of an European woman, while those of the Hindoo woman have all their intrinsic worth, and join solidity to shew. The particulars of their different costumes, which are not constantly changing as in Europe, are given collectively in the second volume.

Other subjects, such as their marriage ceremonies, funerals, etc., requiring as well as the feasts and religious ceremonies a larger plate, have been distributed among the different numbers.

I began by declaring that it was my intention to paint only the Hindoos and what related exclusively to them; but the picture of their domestic life would not have been complete if I had left out their servants, who are very deserving of a place, though mostly of Mahometan extraction. I have reserved the greater part of the fourth volume to represent them in their different dresses and employments.[58] At the end of this volume, I have thought it proper to add a suit of heads, with the characteristic features of all the Indian nations whom I have met in my travels in the interior of India and the adjacent islands.[59]

I presume to think, that the public will receive this original collection the more favourably as it is the first of the kind, and that in all engravings of Indians which have hitherto appeared, the original traits and particular physiognomy of the different individuals of this people are not sufficiently distinguished. It is not even uncommon to find in the accounts published by travellers, figures whose costume indeed is Indian, but whose shape, complexion and countenance are entirely European. These are faults, it will be allowed, which a traveller whose credit rests upon veracity and exactness ought to endeavour particularly to avoid.

To complete the collection of all that struck me most forcibly in my travels, I have added some of the most remarkable natural beauties of the country, gardens, highroads and pictoresque scenes on the continent or in the neighbouring islands, and to conclude, two extraordinary phenomenas of nature, one occasioned by the north-west wind,[60] the other by the tide in the river Ougli.[61]

Such are the outlines of the people which I have endeavoured to paint, and such the researches and studies which I made, in order to give fullness, truth and spirit to the resemblance. When the first numbers of this work were published, it was remarked that, not only it was the first of the kind that had appeared upon India, but that, in all probability, it must be the last. Nor will this conjecture appear unfounded, when we reflect upon the concourse of circumstances more difficult now than ever to unite, and which are yet all of them indispensably necessary to produce an exact and animated pictoresque description of that remote country upon so general and extensive a plan.—The author may then not unreasonably flatter himself that his work will stand original and alone, and that it is well calculated to diffuse the knowledge of so interesting a country, which so long a years residence gave him an opportunity of acquiring.

He found himself in some sort obliged to publish the result of his long and scrupulous observations by the abuse which he saw made of his name and of his works to lead the public into error by giving authority to incorrect notions and mutilated descriptions.—A Mr. Orme published in London, a piecemeal collection, a sort of counterfeit of a set of sketches which I had formerly published at Calcutta, and which even in the country itself were received with great applause.[62] They were however no more than a rough outline of some part of what I now publish. An early and regular education in the imitative arts in the school of a most celebrated master: painful journeys, continued absence from my native country, long residence in a foreign climate, care, fidelity, study and expence, I have spared none of these to acquire true and ample information, and render my work as interesting and meritorious as the subject would admit. May the reception which it meets with from the public prove that the execution is not unworthy of the labour and expence!

---

1 I am grateful to Rosane Rocher, Patrick Olivelle, and Richard Lariviere for their assistance in identifying various references and passages in Manu and the *Bhagavadgītā* and in sorting out anomalies in this account of Hinduism.

2 The reference is to *The Histories*, Book Three, where Herodotus recounts the tale of near dog-size ants that were used in India to dig for gold.

3 Sir John Mandeville, described by Samuel Purchas in 1625 as "the greatest Asian Traveller that ever the World had," may well have been a complete fraud. His *Travels*, first published in French in 1366, was a mix of fact, fancy, and the fantastic, and, like *The Travels of Marco Polo*, was widely read.

4 Apollonius of Tyana, first century, Greek Neopythagorean philosopher, traveled to India.

5 Flavius Philostratus (c.170-c.245), a Greek sophist, is best known for his *Life of Apollonius of Tyana*, a work that has been both dismissed as fabulous and untrustworthy and praised as a largely reliable account of Apollonius's travels and observations in India.

6 Although his disciples in second century Alexandria promoted the story, there is no evidence that Pythagoras, the sixth century BCE Greek philosopher and mathematician, ever travelled to India. Woodcock, 150.

7 Another name for the Parsis or Zoroastrians.

8 Arrian (Flavius Arrianus), c.95-180, Greek historian and author of *Indike*, an account of India from Megasthenes and Nearchus.

9 Samuel Friedrich Günther Wahl (1760-1834), *Erdbeschreibung von Ostindien . . . in Nachträgen zu der von M. C. Spengel angefangenen Fortsetzung von D. A. F. Busching's Erdbeschreibung Asiens* (1805).

10 Anton Friedrich Büsching (a.k.a. Anthony F. Busching), 1724-1793, a German geographer, was best known for his *Neu Erdbeschreibung* (1754-92), a portion of which was translated into English in six volumes as *A New System of Geography* (1762).

11 The French Orientalist Abraham Hyacinthe Anquetil-Duperron [du Perron], 1731-1805, went to India as a private soldier in 1754. Returning to France in 1761, he was elected to the French Academy. His works include *Recherches historique et chronologiques sur l'Inde* and *L'Inde en rapport avec l'Europe*, and a translation of the Persian version of the *Upanishads* into Latin. On the life and work of Anquetil-Duperron, see Waley and Kieffer. On Anquetil-Duperron and other European savants, also see Partha Mitter, *Much Maligned Monsters*; Schwab; and Lach and Van Kley. In the text, Solvyns makes a typographical error (corrected here) in placing a comma between Anquetil and Duperron.

12 Paulinus (Paolino) a S. Bartholomaeo, 1748-1806, was a Carmelite monk who worked as a missionary in Malabar for thirteen years, from 1776 to 1789. Upon his return to Europe, he published a Sanskrit grammar, *Dissertation on the Sanskrit Language*, and a treatise on Hinduism, *Systema Brahmanicum*, from which Solvyns later quotes. His *Viaggio alle Indie Oriental*, collected from his observations in India, was published in various translations. The English edition, *A Voyage to the East Indies* was translated from the German.

13 Sir William Jones (1746-1794). See, Chapter One, p. 20.

14 Major James Rennell (1742-1830), of the Bengal Engineers, known as "the father of Indian geography," became Surveyor-General of Bengal in 1764. With various editions, his *Bengal Atlas* was published in 1779 and *Memoir of a Map of Hindostan* in 1783. On Rennell's work, see Edney.

15 Father Joseph Tief(f)enthaler, S.J. (1710-1785), a Tyrolean missionary and geographer of India.

16 Alexander Dow (1735 or 1736-1779) was an English scholar of Persian. His *History of Hindostan* purports to be a translation of the seventeenth century historian Firishta, but, notes Peter J. Marshall, *The British Discovery of Hinduism*, 6-7, the translation is virtually indistinguishable from Dow's own glosses. Dow's work, also in French translation, includes his dissertation on the Hindus.

17 Robert Orme (1728-1801) served as official historian of the British East India Company. His major work was *A History of Military Transactions of the British Nation in Indostan from the Year 1745*.

18 John Zephaniah Holwell (1711-1798), incarcerated in the Black Hole of Calcutta, served briefly as Governor of Bengal before leaving India in 1760. His works include *Interesting Historical Events Relative to the Provinces of Bengal and the Empire of Indostan* and *India Tracts*, with an account of the Black Hole incident. Peter Marshall, *The British Discovery of*

Hinduism, 5-6, describes his writings as eccentric and polemical.

19 Richard Gough (1735-1809), *A Comparative View of the Antient Monuments of India.*

20 Painters Thomas Daniell (1749-1840) and William Daniell (1769-1837). See pp. 16, 36, 91.

21 Painter William Hodges (1744-1797). See pp. 16, 91.

22 *The Asiatic Annual Register* was published in London, beginning in 1799, as virtually the official organ of the East India Company.

23 *Asiatic Researches,* the journal of the Asiatic Society of Bengal, Calcutta, began publication in 1788.

24 Quintin Craufurd (1743-1819), *Sketches Chiefly Relating to the History, Religion, Learning, and Manners of the Hindoos* (1790 and 1792).

25 Pierre Sonnerat (1749-1814), a French Orientalist sent by Louis XVI to India, provided an account of his travels, 1774-1781, and observations in *Voyage aux Indes Orientales et à la Chine* (translated into English as *A Voyage to the East-Indies and China*). On the life of Sonnerat, see Ly-Tio-Fane.

26 Solvyns's reference is to Captain Alexander Hamilton, who sailed and traded in the Indies from 1688 to 1723 as "one of the 'Interlopers' condemned in the Company records." Losty, *Calcutta, City of Palaces,* 16. See Hamilton's *A New Account of the East-Indies.* On Hamilton, see Nair, *Calcutta in the 18th Century,* 1-2.

Another Alexander Hamilton (1762-1824) also figured significantly among Orientalists in Bengal. The later Hamilton served in the Bengal Army, taking up the study of Indian languages, principally Sanskrit, and was among the early members of the Asiatic Society. He later became a professor at the newly-founded East India College in 1806, where he was, as Rosane Rocher states, "the first man to teach Sanskrit effectively and regularly in Europe." The College, moved to Haileybury in 1809, had been established for the instruction of future civil servants of the East India Company. Rocher, *Alexander Hamilton (1762-1824),* 66.

27 William Mackintosh, *Travels in Europe, Asia, and Africa* (1782). Nair, *Calcutta in the 18th Century,* 180-81, writes that there is internal evidence that the work was "revised and augmented," if not written, by Philip Francis, and "it was an open secret at that time, that the *Travels* was printed at the expense of Philip Francis as part of his scheme to asperse the character and compass the overthrow of Governor-General Warren Hastings."

28 George Forster (1751-1792), a civil servant with the East India Company, wrote *Sketches of the Mythology and Customs of the Hindoos* (1785) and *A Journey from Bengal to England* (1798), an account of his overland journey in 1782. An earlier edition of the work was apparently published in Calcutta in 1790 by the Honorable Company's Press, but no copies survive.

29 The Frenchman Guillaume Joseph H. J. B. Le Gentil de la Galaisière (1725-1792) first went to India as a soldier in 1752. Later, a member of the French Academy of Sciences, he provided the most detailed of the early accounts of Indian astronomy. He recounts his voyage and travels in India, 1761 to 1769, in *Voyage dans les mers de l'Inde.*

30 Solvyns includes his time at sea, from his departure from Antwerp in 1790 until his return to France in 1804.

31 Punjab. In the English text, this is printed as "Pendshal," a typographical error. The French text rendered it "Pendchab."

32 Gujarat.

33 Patna.

34 Thomas Maurice (1754-1824), a cleric who never set foot in India, compiled works by Orientalists. His seven volume *Indian Antiquities,* in various editions, is a miscellany of history, geography, and religion. He also compiled *The History of Hindostan* and wrote *Memoirs of an Author of Indian Antiquities.*

35 The reference is to "an account of the celebrated medal found in the deserts of Siberia" in Maurice's "A Dissertation on the Pagan Triads of Deity," in *Indian Antiquities,* 5:9-12.

36 Manu is the legendary law-giver of Indian antiquity. The *Manusmṛiti* (or *Mānava -Dharmaśāstra*) the compendium of Hindu law that bears his name, gained "authoritative" status among Europeans through Sir William Jones's translation, *Institutes of Hindu Law; or, The Ordinances of Menu* (1794), among the earliest Sanskrit works to be translated into English. On Manu, see Lingat, 73-96.

Nathaniel Halhed (1751-1830), commissioned by Warren Hastings, published *A Code of Gentoo Laws,* in translation from the Persian, in 1776. Jones and Colebrooke took a critical view of the compendium. See Rocher's life of Halhed, *Orientalism, Poetry, and the Millennium,* and her "British Orientalism in the Eighteenth Century," 220-25.

37 Maurice, *Indian Antiquities,* 7:802-03.

38 Pls. II.13-17.

39 In the Calcutta edition, etchings depicting festivals and religious ceremonies are grouped together in Section XII. On the difference in the organization of prints in the Calcutta and Paris editions, see pp. 95-98.

40 The reference is to Montesquieu's *Spirit of the Laws* (1748), Part 3, Book 14, Chapter 3.

41 See, for example, Manu, 11.74, 11.80, 11.91-92, and 11.105.

42 Pl. II.11.

43 Pls. II.135-45.

44 kṣatriyas, Pl. II.20.

45 *Rājaputra.*

46 vaiśyas, Pl. II.21.

47 Paulinus, *Systema Brahmanicum.* See fn. 12.

48 I am indebted to Rosane and Ludo Rocher for helping me with this translation.

49 śūdras, Pl. II.22.

50 Pls. II.203-212.

51 "On the Musical Modes of the Hindoos."

52 William Hamilton Bird, *The Oriental Miscellany: Being a Collection of the Most Favourite Airs of Hindoostan* (1789).

53 Baron Johann Friedrich Hugo von d'Alberg (Dalberg), *Ueber die musik der Indier. Eine abhandlung des Sir William Jones. Aus dem Englischen übersetzt mit erläuternden anmekungen und zusätzen begleitet von F. H. v. Dalberg.* (Erfurt: Beyer und Mring, 1802). This is a German translation of Jones's "On the Musical Modes of the Hindoos" and includes plates depicting musical instruments.

54 Pls. II.146-81.

55 Pl. II.5.

56 Pls. II.213-228.

57 Pls. II.229-64.

58 Pls. II.99-134.

59 Pls. II.295-300.

60 Pl. II.260.

61 Hugli. Pl. II.261.

62 *The Costume of Indostan.* For a discussion of this pirated edition, see p. 106.

Part II

Part II

A Portrait of the Hindus

Contents

Etchings from the Calcutta edition not included in *Les Hindoûs*

97. Brajbāsī in Military Accoutrement
98. Fisherwoman

Servants of the European Household in Calcutta

99. Banian. Chief Servant Comptroller
100. Sarkār. Steward
101. Jamādār. Head Servant
102. Chobdār or Āṣā-soṭābardār. Mace-bearer
103. Soṭābardār. Staff-Carrier
104. Khānsāma. House Steward
105. Dwārbān. Porter
106. Sardār. Valet
107. Khidmatgār. Table Servant
108. Hukābardār. Hukā-bearer
109. Kharacbardār. Marketing Servant
110. Chauṅrībardār. Whisk-Bearer
111. Bhīstī. Water-Carrier
112. Dhobī, Dhobā. Washerman
113. Mākhanwālā. Butter-Man
114. Rotīwālā. Bread-Maker
115. Darzī. Tailor
116. Khālāsi. Sailor, Workman
117. Coachman
118. Sāis. Groom
119. Ghāsyārā. Grass-Cutter
120. Maśālcī. Torch-Bearer
121. Ḍoriyā. Dog-Keeper
122. Caukīdār. Watchman
123. Harkārā. Messenger
124. Peyādā. Footman
125. Baulber. Barber
126. Hajām. Barber
127. Ābdār. Cooler of Drinks
128. Bāwarchī. Cook
129. Methar. Male Sweeper
130. Koṛābardār. Lash-Bearer
131. Ayah. Nursery Maid
132. Ayah. Ladies' Maid
133. Dāi. Wet-Nurse
134. Methrānī. Female Sweeper

Fakirs or Religious Mendicants

135. Paramhaṃsa
136. Daṇḍī
137. Sannyāsī
138. Baiṣṇab, Vaiṣṇava
139. Nānak Panthī
140. Udbāhu, Ūrdhvabāhu
141. Avadhūta
142. Rāmānandī
143. Brahmacārī
144. Nāga
145. A Fakir at his Prayers

Musical Instruments

146. Śaṅkh and Ghaṇṭā
147. Kā̃sar
148. Tambūrā
149. Kuplyans or Bīn
150. Pināk
151. Sitār
152. Sāraṅgī
153. Sārindā
154. Amṛti (Omerti)
155. Oorni
156. Ḍhāk
157. Ḍhol
158. Khol
159. Ḍholak
160. Tablā
161. Joorghaje
162. Ṭikārā
163. Pakhāvaj
164. Nagāṛā
165. Kāṛā
166. Ḍamphā
167. Doira
168. Jagajhampa
169. Surmaṇḍal
170. Khanjari
171. Kartāl
172. Kā̃si
173. Jaltaraṅg
174. Manjīrā
175. Jhā̃jhari
176. Rāmśiṅgā
177. Bā̃k
178. Surnāī
179. Tobrie
180. Bā̃śi
181. Bhoraṅga [Etching from Calcutta collection]

Festivals and Ceremonies

182. Mahābhārata Sabhā
183. Rāmāyan Gāyan
184. Hari Saṅkīrtan
185. Rās Yātrā
186. Jhulan Yātrā
187. Snān Yātrā
188. Rath Yātrā
189. Dol Yātrā
190. Bisarjan
191. Jhā̃p
192. Nīla Pūjā
193. Caṛak Pūjā
194. Durgā Pūjā
195. Nautch
196. Jhāpān
197. Bibāha. Marriage
198. Gaṅga Yātrā

Satī

199. Sahagamana
200. Anumaraṇa, Anumṛtā
201. Sahagamana
202. Sahagamana

Modes of Smoking, &c.

203. Nārikel
204. Nārikel
205. Nārikel
206. Nārikel
207. Chilim
208. Snake Hukā
209. Gaṛgarā
210. Kaliyūm
211. Cheroot
212. Pān

Modes of Conveyance

213. Elephants and Camels
214. Lādū Bail
215. Horse and Ṭaṭu
216. Rath
217. Gāṛi
218. Ekkā
219. "Rahhoo"
220. Hackery

Palanquins

221. Copālā Pālki
222. Jhālidār Pālki
223. Mahāpā
224. Dulī
225. Mīyāna
226. Long Palanquin
227. Bochā
228. Chair Palanquin

Boats of Bengal

229. Pinnace
230. Fīlcehrā
231. Morpañkhī
232. Bājrā
233. Bhāuliyā
234. Paṭuā
235. Pānsi
236. Khelā or Lāl Ḍiṅgi
237. Ḍiṅgi
238. Magarcehrā
239. Donī
240. Jāliyā Ḍiṅgi
241. Saraṅgā
242. Ekṭhā
243. Ḍoṅga
244. Grab
245. Bangles
246. Pāṭeli
247. Katrā
248. Bālām
249. Brig
250. Ulāk
251. Kośā
252. Palwār
253. Holā
254. Sloop
255. Towboat
256. Bhur
257. Iṭā Ḍiṅgi
258. Gudārā
259. Gudārā
260. North-Wester
261. Bore
262. Balasore Roads
263. Vessels of All Sorts
264. Penang

Natural History: Plants and Animals

265. Tamarind
266. Mango
267. Jackfruit
268. Coconut and Other Palms
269. Banana
270. Bamboo
271. Rice
272. Sugar Cane
273. Mustard
274. Cotton
275. Indigo
276. Cochineal
277. Buffalo
278. Tiger
279. Hoolock Gibbon (?)
280. Hanuman Langur
281. Jackal
282. Bengali Dog
283. Crocodile
284. Cobra
285. Tryphlops, a Serpent
286. Centipede
287. Muskrat
288. Tapsī Māch
289. Adjutant Stork
290. Vulture
291. Black Kite
292. Flying Fox
293. Cockroach
294. White Ant, Termite

Indian Heads

295. Brahmins
296. Kṣatriyas
297. Vaiśyas
298. Śūdras
299. Hindus of Upper India
300. Mughals

A Note on Format and Commentaries

Part II of *A Portrait of the Hindus* makes no attempt to present a facsimile of either *A Collection of Two Hundred and Fifty Coloured Etchings* or *Les Hindoûs*, the Calcutta and Paris editions of Solvyns's etchings, and I have taken a certain liberty in the organization of plates to provide greater coherence. The plates are organized by subject matter generally following Solvyns's division of sections in the Calcutta edition and the groupings into which the etchings are ordered in *Les Hindoûs*. Departing from Solvyns's organization of plates, however, "Solvyns's Calcutta" includes some of the double-plates that divide the various sections in both the Calcutta and Paris editions as well as other etchings that portray life in the city but do not fit logically in Solvyns's subject groupings. The etchings for "Festivals and Ceremonies" and "Sati" are double-plates in the Paris edition, which Solvyns does not group together, but distributes through the first three volumes of *Les Hindoûs* as the first print of each *livraison* (installment or section).

The plates for *A Portrait of the Hindus* are from *Les Hindoûs*, supplemented with Calcutta etchings for those subjects not included in the Paris edition. In a few instances where the Paris and Calcutta prints are notably different, both are included. Within each subject grouping, the plates follow the order of the etchings in *Les Hindoûs*. The order takes on special importance in the portrayal of "Castes and Occupations" and of "Servants," as Solvyns sought to follow the traditional Hindu hierarchy of status and ritual purity, and he used such hierarchy even in ordering his presentation of boats and of musical instruments. (See Chapter Three, pp. 98-99, on hierarchy in portrayal of subjects.) Solvyns makes some adjustments from his original Calcutta ordering of prints for the Paris edition, perhaps reflecting a change in his judgment as to the "proper" rank for a few castes in the hierarchy. Rather than trying to insert the etchings that were not included in *Les Hindoûs* into Solvyns's order for the Paris edition, I have placed them at the end of the sections in which they would be grouped.

The plates in *A Portrait of the Hindus*, Part II, are numbered sequentially. As applicable, each subject is identified by its number in the Calcutta edition, the Orme pirated edition, and the Paris edition. Thus, for the Āhir, milkman (Pl. II.28), the Calcutta listing is by Section and Number (Calcutta: Sec. I, No. 20); for Orme, by plate number (Orme: 4); and for the Paris edition, by Volume, *Livraison*, and Number (Paris: I.4.2).

The description of the etching from Solvyns's *1799 Catalogue* follows the Calcutta number. Solvyns's text for each print in *Les Hindoûs* follows the Paris number and appears in a gray box.

For each subject, I provide a Commentary on Solvyns's etching and text to identify who and what is portrayed. I draw extensively from sources roughly contemporary with Solvyns, and provide detailed bibliographic notes to lead the reader to further material on the subject. Each Commentary is self-contained, with cross-references, as an entry in an encyclopedia.

Descriptions in the 1799 *Catalogue* closely follow Solvyns's notes for the drawings now in the Victoria and Albert Museum. In instances where Solvyns's original notes contain information that is not included in the Calcutta *Catalogue* or the Paris text, I have incorporated his comments into my Commentaries.

Solvyns's Calcutta

Calcutta, founded by the British in 1690, had grown by Solvyns's time into a cosmopolitan city of some 300,000 people.[1] Population estimates vary, and figures upwards of 600,000 likely included the city's environs as well as workers who came daily into Calcutta from outlying villages. Of the Indians, the greater number were Hindus, most of whom were Bengali, but Oriyas, Biharis, and others from various parts of India had found their way to the new center of power and commerce. Muslims accounted for about a third of the Indian population, and again most were Bengali, although there was a considerable presence of Muslims from western India. There were native Christians, Eurasians, Armenians, Persians, Arabs, and Chinese, among others, and some 4,000 Europeans.[2] Solvyns portrays the various peoples of Calcutta in his etching "The Nations Most Known in Hindoostan" (Pl. II.7).

Until about the time of Solvyns's arrival in Calcutta in 1791, Europeans were concentrated in the area around Tank Square and to the east along Lal Bazar and Boytaconnah roads and from Esplanade Row along Dhurrumtollah Street.[3] (See map of "Solvyns's Calcutta" in Chapter One, p. 18.) Mixed among them were Armenians (to the north of the Tank), native Christians, Eurasian "Portuguese," and some Indians. By the 1790s, wealthier Europeans were moving south in greater numbers to build fine new houses in Chowringhee, an area which only a few years before had been infested with tigers, wild boars, and dacoits (robbers).[4] Central Calcutta, with its government and commercial buildings, became increasingly mixed residentially, an intermediate "gray" area between the white European town and "Black Town" to the north.[5]

European Calcutta had been characterized as a "city of palaces" from the 1780s, and in 1789, the Count de Granpré described it as "not only the handsomest town in Asia, but one of the finest in the world."[6] The artist William Hodges was impressed: "The streets are broad; the line of buildings, surrounding two sides of the esplanade of the fort, is magnificent; and it adds greatly to the superb appearance, that the houses are detached from each other, and insulated in a great space. The buildings are all on a large scale, from the necessity of having a free circulation of air, in a climate the heat of which is extreme. The general approach to the houses is by a flight of steps, with great projecting porticoes, or surrounded by colonades or arcades, which give them the appearance of Grecian temples. . . ."[7]

In contrast to the open and spacious character of European Calcutta, Black Town was a crowded warren of houses, markets, and temples intermixed with patches of agricultural cultivation, giving it something of the character of "an agglomeration of villages."[8] With the rise of Calcutta, as Black Town developed, the British authorities formally divided the native area "into a number of quarters, allocating each quarter to one professional group or caste." Thus, with *ṭolā* and diminutive *ṭuli* referring to localities particular to an occupational caste, the Jāliyā fishing caste (portrayed by Solvyns in Pl. II.57) was concentrated in Jeliatola, the Kumārs (Pl. II.36), potters, in Kumartuli, and so on.[9] Even today, many of these neighborhoods retain their distinct character.

The poorer Indians lived in huts with thatched roofs and walls of woven mats, ever vulnerable to fire, or in mud huts with tile roofs. More prosperous artisans and merchants might have *pakkā* houses of clay brick,[10] one or two stories tall, as those depicted in Solvyns's etching of "Hindoo Buildings" (Pl. II.3). Scattered throughout the Black Town were the great houses of wealthy Hindus and Muslims, some outwardly undistinguished but richly adorned within, others grand statements of new wealth in Palladian style. (The distinctive interior design of the Hindu mansion is discussed in the Commentary for Mahābhārata Sabhā, Pl. II.182.) Such houses were typically surrounded by the servants' thatched huts.

For most Europeans, Black Town, with its "narrow crooked streets," was "deep, black and dingy." It was chaotic and dirty, filled with "villainous" smells and with the "constant clamour of voices" and an almost unceasing thumping and jingling of drums and cymbals.[11] Few Europeans ventured into the area, save perhaps at the invitation of a wealthy Hindu to attend a nautch party at a palatial house (see Pl. II.195). But for Solvyns, Black Town opened a world of compelling fascination, and, with his sketchbook, he entered it to portray the Hindus.

The plates grouped here as "Solvyns's Calcutta" are drawn from various sections of *Les Hindoûs*, save for one, "A View of Calcutta" (Pl. II.2), which was not included in the Paris edition and is from the collection of Calcutta etchings. Some are double-plates that begin each of the sections (*livraison*) into which the volumes of the Paris edition are divided; others are single plates that fit none of the groupings into which Solvyns organized the etchings. Together they illustrate aspects of the Calcutta in which Solvyns lived and worked.

---

1 Among the many books on the history of Calcutta and on its character in the late 18th and early 19th centuries, see especially: Sukanta Chaudhuri; Losty, *Calcutta: City of Palaces*; Pradip Sinha, *Calcutta in Urban History*; Nisith Ranjan Ray, *Calcutta: The Profile of a City*; S. N. Mukherjee, *Calcutta: Myths and History*; A. K. Ray; Cotton, *Calcutta Old and New*; Busteed; Blechynden; and Raja Binaya Krishna Deb. P. Thankappan Nair provides selections from early accounts of the city in his volumes on Calcutta in the 18th and 19th centuries.

2 On population, see, for example, James R. Martin, 41-44.

3 William Baillie distinguished the Indian and European quarters in his *Plan of Calcutta*, 1792, from the original map by Lt. Col. Mark, in 1784-85.

4 Cotton, *Calcutta Old and New*, 230.

5 See Pradip Sinha, *Calcutta in Urban History*, 7-13; Biswas, 110; Dhriti K. L. Choudhury, 159-60; and James Martin, 18.

6 2:2.

7 *Travels in India*, 15; reprinted in Nair, *Calcutta in the 18th Century*, 208.

8 Marshall, "The Company and the Coolies," 25. Also see S. N. Mukherjee, *Calcutta: Myths and History*, 86-108, and Milbourn, 255. See Sumanta Banerjee, 23-33, and Sreemani, 25-28, on the development of Black Town. The Governor-General, Marquess Wellesley, expressed concern for the dangers of fire and for poor sanitation in Black Town in a minute, June 16, 1803, on needs for civic improvement in Calcutta, in Montgomery Martin, ed., *The Dispatches, Minutes, and Correspondence of the Marquess Wellesley, K.G.*, Vol. IV, Appendix Q. 772-74. On town planning and architectural style, see King, *The Bungalow* and *Colonial Urban Development*.

9 Pradip Sinha, "Social Change," 387. Also see Sinha, *Calcutta in Urban History*, 13-61 and 241-44; Nair, "The Growth and Development of Old Calcutta;" A. K. Ray, 196-97; and Benoy Ghosh, 53.

10 In construction, the term *pakkā* is used for buildings of bricks and mortar. See "Pucka," *Hobson-Jobson*, 734.

11 Heber, 3:238-39, reprinted in Nair, *Calcutta in the 19th Century*, 403-04. Also see Mackintosh, 2:274, in Nair, *Calcutta in the 18th Century*, 181.

II.1. European Buildings in Calcutta

Pl. 11.1. European Buildings in Calcutta. Paris: III.12.1. Double-plate.
Calcutta: Before Sec. II. A representation of the Style of the European Buildings in Calcutta: the View taken from the four cross Roads, near the office of the Justices of the Peace.

Paris: III.12.1. EUROPEAN BUILDINGS AT CALCUTTA: This number will bring forward several objects which could not have been well placed in the preceding ones. This last large plate of the work has been employed to represent the houses of the Europeans in the capital of India. The view is taken from the meeting of four handsome streets. The house of the justices of peace and the one remarkable for the extensive sale rooms which it contains, forms a striking object. The European houses at Calcutta are always at some distance from each other, and have a very respectable appearance. They have all grand peristyles of different orders: the doors and windows are large, and the rooms very lofty, on account of the excessive heat, which would be insupportable in low and confined appartments. The walls are painted white, paper or tapistry are never used; they are sometimes hung with prints or pictures, but these are destroyed in a short time. Chimnies are seldom seen, the apartments are generally on the first story, but the dining-room is frequently on the groundfloor. The roofs are always flat and accessible by a staircase; it is a great enjoyment to breathe the morning and evening air upon these platforms. The walls are built of baked bricks, and the morter composed of lime and brickdust: this is covered first with a coat of sand and lime, and afterwards with powdered shells which give a dazzling white colour. The platforms are covered with pieces of wood, and afterwards with bricks of ten or twelve inches, which are covered first with a layer of Sulky [*surkhī*] or pounded bricks, and then with one of a finer Sulky mixed up with lime, *Gour* [*gur*] (sugar) and oil. After beating this composition during several days, it is finally covered with a thin coat of fine lime, which forms a solid surface, capable of resisting the temperature of all the different seasons.

In the background is seen the monument erected before the old fort, in commemoration of the black hole: where so many English prisonners perished in 1756, by the cruel orders of the Soubab Sarajah Douhla.

Commentary: Solvyns here portrays Lal Bazar looking westward at the crossing of Chitpore Road. The large colonnaded building to the right, at the intersection of the two streets and across from the jail, is the Court of the Justices of the Peace. To the left is the auction house of Burrell and Gould.[1] Some thirty years later, James Baillie Fraser depicted Lal Bazar, looking east toward Chitpore Road.[2]

In the distance is the Holwell Monument, an obelisk erected in 1760 on the northwest corner of Tank Square by John Zephaniah Holwell (1711-1798), one of the survivors, to commemorate those who died in the "Black Hole," the stifling cell into which a number of British were imprisoned by Siraj-ud-Daula, Nawab of Bengal, when he attacked Calcutta in 1756.[3] Thomas Daniell depicts the Holwell monument in one of his *Views of Calcutta* (1786).[4]

Lal Bazar was a street and locality, not a market as such, and was synonymous with the Calcutta police headquarters located there. The area was also famous for its "punch houses" and places of entertainment, kept mainly by "Portuguese [Eurasians], Italians, and other foreigners."[5] During his years in Calcutta, Solvyns lived at various locations within a short walk of the scene he portrays. The fine European buildings, many within separate walled compounds, are abutted by Indian shops, and the streets are filled with an array of vehicles—carriages, carts, and palanquins—and all variety of people, European and Indian. In the center foreground, the man and woman, standing with their backs to us, are likely "Portuguese" (the term used rather inclusively for Eurasians and native Roman Catholics). To their right, a proud European rides a horse as his attendant, the *chātā*-bearer, carries an umbrella to shade him from the sun.[6] A ḍoriyā, dogkeeper (Pl. II.121), has brought the hounds out for exercise, and before a doorway, an Armenian merchant, with his peaked black hat, is engaged in conversation with a bearded Muslim. Toward the left are clusters of people in various activities, three Europeans chatting together, two Indian women and a child, laborers, and household servants.

In his text, Solvyns provides a succinct description of the architecture and construction of European buildings in Calcutta—imposing buildings that appeared to Mrs. Eliza Fay, in 1780, as "palaces."[7] Thomas Twining, who arrived in Calcutta as a young man in 1792 to begin service as a "writer" (clerk) with the East India Company, recorded his first impressions of the " 'City of Palaces,' with its lofty detached flat-roofed mansions . . . ." He was impressed by the "magnificent buildings" along Esplanade Row, government offices and private residences of civil and military officers. "They were all white, their roofs invariably flat, surrounded by light colonnades, and their fronts relieved by lofty columns supporting deep verandahs. They were all separated from each other, each having its own small enclosure, in which, at a little distance from the house, were the kitchen cellars, store-rooms, etc., and large folding gate and porter's lodge at the entrance."[8]

The finest houses were typically two-storied, with pediments and classical columns of Palladian style. From the portico, stairs led up to the first floor and the deep veranda that afforded relief from the sun. On the balustraded flat roof, residents could enjoy the fresh air in the morning and evening, and in the hottest weather, they might have their beds taken up to sleep under the stars.[9]

Less grand were one-story bungalows, European adaptations from the Bengali house form, portrayed by Solvyns in Pl. II.44 and described in the accompanying Commentary. The bungalow was the principal house style for Europeans in rural India and in military cantonments.

The bright whiteness of the exterior walls of European houses, so often mentioned in descriptions of Calcutta, came from the application of *cūnā* (Anglo-Indian, *chunam*), the lime-based coating that Solvyns refers to above and in his portrayal of the Cunāri (Pl. II.60), who prepares the lime as his traditional occupation. *Cūnā* was a plaster made of shell-lime, sand or brick-dust (*surkhī*), molasses, and hemp.[10] It gave a polished white brilliance to the walls, both inside and out, of houses and buildings and had the durability of stone.[11] It was used as well for the ground floors and as mortar for bricks. The British first used *cūnā* for their buildings in Madras—indeed, it was sometimes described as "Madras Stucco"—but Mrs. Nathaniel Kindersley, in a letter of 1768, wrote that although the materials were mixed in the same way, the *cūna* in Calcutta lacked the "fine gloss" so much admired in Madras. She explained that "this is owing to all the water in Bengal partaking so much of the salt-petre with which the earth is in every part impregnated."[12] Perhaps *chunam* had not yet been successfully adapted to Bengal, for Roberdeau in 1805 wrote of its "dazzling appearance" in Calcutta.[13]

The interiors of the European houses were spacious, with high ceilings, and the walls were plastered and whitewashed. Toward the end of the eighteenth century, the monotonous whitewash was relieved by the introduction of color washes and by divided plaster wall panels in two tones, seen in many of Solvyns's etching portraying the servants of European households. Pictures too begin to appear on the walls.[14] There were no wooden wall panels, papers, or tapestries, for they would soon be eaten by white-ants, termites (Pl. II.294), the scourge of any household. The problem of insects accounted as well for minimal furnishings, and for protection, the legs of tables and chairs were often placed in small vases of water, as Solvyns portrays in an etching (Pl. II.285). The windows might be shuttered or covered with venetian blinds (usually painted green), and the veranda often had split bamboo or *ṭaṭṭī* screens that could be lowered to provide protection from the sun. *Ṭaṭṭīs*, when wet, also provided a cooling breeze, as Solvyns relates in his portrayal of the bhīstī, watercarrier (Pl. II.111). Floors were typically plastered and covered, if at all, with fine woven mats that were nailed down, although in Solvyns's etchings of servants, the flooring appears often to be wooden, and (as in Pl. II.101) colorful rugs add brightness to the room.

The fine houses of Company officers and senior merchants were notable for their size, "their whiteness and Palladian porticos, the loftiness of the rooms, and the scanty furniture," but striking too was "the manner in which the European houses are scattered, with few regular streets, but each with its separate court-yard and gateway, and often intermixed with miserable huts. . . ."[15] As the servants did not eat or sleep in their master's house and the Black Town was some distance away, they were permitted to put up huts in the compound or on the outside along the walls. Thus, "the most elegant mansions were environed with thatched mud huts. . . ."[16]

---

1 Losty, *Calcutta: City of Palaces*, 68-69, describes the scene and reproduces the etching from the Calcutta edition, Fig. 36. For Lal Bazar street , see Nair, *A History of Calcutta Streets*, 509-11.

2 "A View of Loll Bazaar from opposite the House of John Palmer Esq, 1819," Pl. 16 from *Views of Calcutta and its Environs*, reproduced in Losty, *Calcutta: City of Palaces*, Fig. 50.

3 Holwell, who served temporarily as Governor in 1760, wrote *A Narrative of the Black Hole*, recounting the incident in which, after the capture of old Fort William by Nawab Siraj-ud-daula in 1756, 123 English prisoners suffocated in the small room in which they were imprisoned.

4 The Old Fort, the Playhouse, Holwell's Monument," reproduced in Mildred Archer, *Early Views of India*, Pl. 4, and in Losty, *Calcutta: City of Palaces*, Fig. 24. Losty, 52, discusses the monument.

5 Report by the Justices of the Peace, Calcutta, to the Governor-General, January 31, 1800, in Sterndale, 57. The report recorded eleven licensed European punch houses. On the character of Lal Bazar, also see Long, *Calcutta in the Olden Time*, 21-22.

6 On the *chātā*, umbrella, see Pl. II.47.

7 131, letter from Calcutta, May 22, 1780; reprinted in Nair, *Calcutta in the 18th Century*, 192.

8 73-74, Journal entry for August 22, 1792; reprinted in Nair, *Calcutta in the 19th Century*, 277. Cotton, *Calcutta Old and New*, and Long, *Calcutta in the Olden Time*, provide detailed descriptions of the city's principal European buildings.

9 On the architectural style of the great European houses, see Mildred Archer, *India and British Portraiture*, 52-53; Spear, 49-50; and Nilsson, 178.

10 Marshman, "Notes on the Left or Calcutta Bank of the Hooghly," in Alok Ray, ed., *Calcutta Keepsake*, 181-82.

11 See entry in *Hobson-Jobson*, 218-19; Stavorinus, 1:514.

12 279; also in Nair, *Calcutta in the 18th Century*, 147.

13 In Nair, *Calcutta in the 19th Century*, 51.

14 Pearson, 141-42.

15 Heber, 3:225-26, in Nair, *Calcutta in the 19th Century*, 398.

16 Suresh Chandra Ghosh, 112.

II.2. A View of Calcutta

Pl. II.2. A View of Calcutta. Calcutta: Double-plate before Sec. 12.

Calcutta: Before Sec. 12: A View of Calcutta from the Road Leading to the Course

Commentary: Solvyns's "A View of Calcutta" is not included in *Les Hindoûs*. The etching in the Calcutta edition is the mirror image of the drawing, and as reproduced here, the image is reversed to return to the original perspective.

The double plate portrays a scene looking toward Esplanade Row from the south, with the masts of ships rising over the buildings and trees in the background. Solvyns describes the view as from the road leading to the Course on what is now the Maidan.[1]

The buildings themselves are barely discernible, but the large columned building in the center is the new Court House.[2] In the foreground, to the left, bearers rest beside a chair palanquin (Pl. II.228), and beyond, across the Hugli river, we see the towers of the Military Orphan School.[3] To the right, the picket fence may well be the one that surrounded the area of Fort William, as shown in William Baillie's etching, "South View of Calcutta, taken from the Glacis of Fort William" (1794).[4]

The Course, shown on the map of Solvyns's Calcutta (p. 18), was the main road across the Esplanade, the expanse of land cleared of jungle to provide Fort William's five-square kilometer parade ground. In Solvyns's time, as it had long been, the Course was favored for recreational rides and as the place to be seen. In 1768, Mrs. Kindersley wrote that "A little out of the town is a clear airy spot free from smoke or any encumbrances called the *Corse*, (because it is a road the length of a corse [coss] or two miles) in a sort of ring or rather angle, made on purpose to take the air in, which the company frequent in their carriages about sunset, or in the morning before the sun is up."[5]

1 In his 1794 advertisement for the proposed collection of etchings, *Calcutta Gazette*, February 6, 1794 (Vol. 20, No. 519), 2, reprinted in Seton-Karr, 2:575-77, Solvyns describes the print as "a general View of Calcutta, taken from Kidderpore Bridge," but this would have been at much greater distance and the buildings of Esplanade Row would have been obstructed by Fort William.

2 Thomas Daniell, in *Views of Calcutta*, depicts the Court House and, in another etching, buildings to the east along Esplanade Row. Reproduced in Mildred Archer, E*arly Views of India*, Pls. 8 and 13, and in Losty, *Calcutta: City of Palaces*, Pl. 7 and Fig. 29. For a key to the buildings in the Daniell prints, see Nisith R. Ray, "Calcutta Houses and Streets in 1789."

3 The school is the subject of an etching by William Baillie, reproduced in Losty, *Calcutta: City of Palaces*, Fig. 33. Baillie, looking across the Maidan, portrays a "View of Esplanade Row, Calcutta, from the River to the Council House" (1794), in Losty, Fig. 35.

4 No. 10, *Twelve Views of Calcutta*.

5 Letter LXV, Calcutta, June 1768, in Kindersley, 281; reprinted in Nair, *Calcutta in the 18th Century*, 148. It was still the place to go in 1805, by Roberdeau's description, 123-24; reprinted in Nair, *Calcutta in the 19th Century*, 51-53. Cotton, *Calcutta Old and New*, 119, notes that the Course was dusty and crowded, but in the evening, it was the "scene" in Calcutta.

II.3. Hindu Buildings

Pl. II.3. Hindu Buildings. Paris: II.1.1. Double-plate.

Calcutta: Plate before Sec. III. A View taken in the Chitpore Road, Calcutta; shewing the style of Architecture of the Natives Buildings, and the Hindoo Mundars [*mandirs*].

Paris: II.1.1. HINDOO BUILDINGS: A view of Calcutta seemed best calculated to convey an idea of the architecture of the Hindoos. Of this town, one of the largest and most magnificent of India, and every day increasing by the many sumptuous buildings erected especially in the residence of the English, a more particular description will be given hereafter. In the vast population of this capital the mixture of different nations is more striking than in the other towns of Hindoostan. This drawing represents the quarter inhabited chiefly by Hindoos, called the *Black Town*; it is taken from the road leading to Chitpore, a place almost exclusively peopled by the natives of the country. My intention was to give, as far as it could be done in a single drawing, a general idea of the distinctive character of the Hindoo architecture. The first striking difference is the conical form of all their pagodas or *mundars* in this capital, amidst the spherical domes of the Musselman mosques; which observation may be extended to their religious edifices all over Hindoostan. The private houses, both of the rich and poor, are generally surrounded at the first story by large covered balconies. Besides their use in keeping out the rays of the sun from the interior apartments, they serve as a place of repose to the indolent Hindoo, where he enjoys a cooler air and sleeps away the heat of the day, while his servants give a gentle motion to the air around him, with large fans called *pankas*. Here too he indulges in the phlegmatic pleasure of smoking the hooka[1] and frequently receives his visits. Although this plate was particularly destined to the Hindoo architecture, it has not been in my power to represent the interior of their habitations and religious buildings, which has been partly described in the foregoing plates [see Pl. II.182] and will again be noticed more minutely in the course of the work.

Commentary: The view is along Chitpore Road in the heart of Indian Calcutta, "Black Town," to the north of the area where Europeans lived. Chitpore Road, the oldest road in Calcutta, connected the town of Chitpur to the north with the famous Kālīghāṭ temple (Pl. II.4) in the environs of Calcutta to the south. From Lal Bazar north, it was the principal artery of Black Town, and along its route were large houses of the wealthy, huts of the poor, bazaars, and a number of temples, the most famous of which was the "Black Pagoda" (see Pl. II.6).

In Solvyns's etching, we see an intersection, at which stands a *pakkā* two-story house, with a veranda, a distinctive architectural feature that the British adopted for themselves.[2] The *pakkā-kachchā*, superior-inferior, distinction has many applications, but in construction, *pakkā* (Anglo-Indian, *pucka* or *pukka*) refers to buildings of brick and mortar; *kachchā* to thatched or mud huts.[3] Solvyns describes the construction of the mud hut in his text for Pl. II.35.

The temple behind the house is in the Bengali *āt-chālā* style. Made of brick, it is the form of a traditional hut with an arched thatched roof, one upon the other. Calcutta then, as now, had many such temples, built by wealthy Hindus to serve the neighborhood or often their own family alone.[4]

In the right foreground of the etching, an Indian sits beside a funerary post, *bṛṣo kaāh*, described in the Commentary for Solvyns's portrayal of the Vaidya (Pl. II.25).

In his Paris text (above), Solvyns refers to "large fans called *pankas*." The *pankhā* (or punkah in Anglo-Indian usage) is a fan constructed of a coarse cloth stretched over a rectangular frame of light wood and hung from the ceiling in the center of the room. Suspended some seven feet above the floor, it often extended nearly the full length of the room. The cloth was usually white-washed, and a linen fringe typically hung from the bottom. More elaborate *pankhās* were decorated with gilt frames, fluted silk, and gold beading, and some were embellished with paintings. The house "punkah-wallah" pulled the fan to and fro by a line attached to the center of the frame. With better *pankhās*, the line was covered with scarlet cloth for a more tasteful appearance.[5]

The *pankhā* probably dates in India at least from Mughal times, if not earlier, but it came into use in well-established Indian and European households in Calcutta sometime in the mid-1780s. It was not until the nineteenth century that they came to be widely used, and even then, the *pankhā* was often confined to the dining room, as seen in an illustration by Charles D'Oyly.[6] In earlier years, at least at more elegant dinners, a personal servant (a "kittysol-boy") with a palm leaf fan was positioned behind each chair.[7]

Solvyns does not depict the great houses of the "opulent" Hindus in his etching of "Hindoo Buildings," although he portrays their interior courtyards in his depiction of various festival occasions, as described in Pl. II.182. Many such houses, constructed of brick and with flat roofs, were enclosed within a gated compound, with several smaller houses, for servants, cooking, and other uses, within its walls.

---

1 See Solvyns's portrayal of the *hukā*, Pls. II.203-210.

2 The word *veranda* comes into English from India, but is probably originally from the Portuguese. *Hobson-Jobson*, 964-66. See Nilsson, 179.

3 *Hobson-Jobson*, 734. The widely used *pakkā* and *kachchā* are Hindi; the terms in Bengali are transliterated as *pākā* and *kā̃ca*.

4 See McCutchion, "Temples of Calcutta," and Amiya Kumar Banerji, "Temples in Calcutta and its Neighbourhood."

5 Among numerous European descriptions of the *pankhā*, see *Hobson-Jobson*, 742-44; D'Oyly and Williamson, Pl. 8; Roberts, *Scenes and Characteristics of Hindostan*, 2d. ed., 1:7. Colesworthy Grant, *Anglo-Indian Domestic Life*, 23-24; Dewar, 104-11; and Spear, *The Nabobs: A Study of the Social Life of the English in 18th Century India*, 96-98.

6 D'Oyly and Williamson, *The European in India*, Pl. VIII. The accompanying text (by Williamson) reads, "The Punkah . . . agitates the air greatly, and affords extreme refreshment to such as are seated under its line of action." H. E. A. Cotton writes that *pankhās* appear not to have been in general use even as late as 1808, when they were advertised in a Calcutta newspaper as a special attraction. *Calcutta Old and New*, 126. In the text for Pl. XVI, *The European in India*, Williamson discusses in detail the various kinds and sizes of *pankhās*.

7 Suresh Chandra Ghosh, 103-04.

II.4. Kālīghāṭ

Pl. II.4. Kālīghāṭ. Paris: II.4.1. Double-plate.
Calcutta: Plate before Section VII. A View of Calleegaut Pagoda or Mundar.

Commentary: The present Kālīghāṭ temple was completed in 1809, after seven to eight years' construction in renovating and enlarging the original seventeenth century building.[2] The temple is today a complex of buildings, with the main shrine, the temple of Kālī, in a walled enclosure and towering some 90 feet high in the traditional Bengali architectural style, with its distinctive curved cornices. In and around the enclosure are other, smaller temples, most dedicated to Śiva, and several flat-roofed buildings.[3]

Solvyns provides us with a view of the temple of Kālī and the adjacent flat-roofed pavilion—"incongruously built on English classical lines"[4]—before the renovations. But for an enlarged pavilion and the construction of other buildings in the complex, they appear in the etching very much as they do today.[5] What is most striking in Solvyns's portrayal, however, is the tranquillity of the scene, a contrast surely to congestion of today's Kālīghāṭ, with its throngs of worshippers and merchants selling trinkets and memorabilia.

The site at Kālīghāṭ (or at least its proximity) had seen earlier temples, for according to myth, it was here, beside the old course of the Hugli River (now called Tolly's Nullah), that a toe of the goddess Satī's right foot fell to earth as her body was dismembered by Viṣṇu's discus. It is in the horrific, destructive form of Kālī that the goddess, Śiva's *śakti*, his consort, is worshipped here.[6]

The word *ghāṭ* means a landing place on a river or body of water, thus giving the name to the most famous temple in all Calcutta. But however celebrated, the temple was not—as is often written—the source of Calcutta's name.[7]

The benign image of Kālī, as "Dakṣiṇākālī, resides inside the main temple. The image at Kālīghāṭ is not in the popular iconographic form depicting the goddess necklaced in skulls, as seen in Solvyns's print

Paris: II.4.1. A VIEW OF THE PAGODA OF CALLEEGAUT: In the first number of this volume I said a few words about the Hindoo Pagodas, in speaking of the architecture of this people in general:[1] the following description will clear all doubts which may yet remain, and give a clear and settled notion of this subject. With this intention, I did not choose for my engraving one of their most sumptuous and ornamented temples, nor one of the most simple; neither of which would have conveyed a true idea of the character of Hindoo architecture. The Pagoda of Calleegaut, two leagues from Calcutta, is in a just medium between these two styles, and may serve as a model.

The first view of this Pagoda shews that it consists of several distinct buildings; that which rises in a conical form above the body of the temple is the sanctuary. This part of the Pagoda contains the idol to whose worship it is dedicated: and here the Brahmuns only who serve the temple, have a right to enter. The building which preceedes this sanctuary may be properly called the church, where individuals meet to offer up their prayers and *poojahs*. Before it, is a court in which the animals destined to their sacrifices are put to death: which to a stranger gives it the appearance of a butcher's slaughterhouse. Their mode of killing their victims is very simple: the head of the animal is drawn between two pieces of wood fixed in the ground, and instantly separated from the body by the stroke of a large cutlass. The head only is carried into the sanctuary and offered to the divinity; the remainder serves to make a repast for the person who offers the sacrifice and his friends, if they are of the casts in which the use of animal food is allowed. To some it is entirely forbidden; others have a right to eat the flesh of goats only; animals with which this country abounds.

In the wall which surrounds the Pagoda are several doors: near the enclosure are many pools or reservoirs for bathing before the sacrifice. All these different accessory objects of the exterior of the edifice, are seen in the engraving: it will be remembered that views of the interior have been given in former prints, particularly one of the sanctuary of a Pagoda consecrated to the goddess Dourgah [Durgā, Pl. II.194.].

All these Pagodas, as may be imagined, have their particularities analogous to the divinity to whose worship they are devoted: but the architecture is nearly the same: that which I have represented is the most general in all the countries inhabited by the Hindoos, especially in Bengal. These public edifices, as well as the houses of private people of fortune, are built of baked earth; but what is most striking is, that even the ornaments are made of the same materials. The works of the Hindoos in this way are really surprising, and it were to be wished that some person would attend more particularly to them, and communicate their process to our European artists.

of Bisarjan (Pl. II.190) at Kālī Pūjā. Rather, as the Rev. Ward described it, "The image is a large black stone, to which a horrid face, partly cut and painted, has been given; there are neither arms nor legs, a cloth covering all the lower part which should be the body."[8] In the pavilion (Solvyns's "church"), there are daily readings recounting the exploits of the Goddess. Here too people may offer their prayers and *mantras* and, with Kālī as witness, gather for such important Hindu ceremonies as a child's first rice-feeding, the sacred threat investiture, and marriage.[9] Within the compound, as Solvyns describes, is the place of ritual sacrifice. Here the animals, principally goats, are decapitated with the heavy blade in a single stroke by the Kāmār (Pl. II.35), a blacksmith traditionally employed for the ritual slaughter.

The temple is a focus of festivities during Kālī Pūjā (Pl. II.190) in Calcutta. Maria Graham wrote in a letter of October 25, 1810, "This is the season of festivals; I hear the tomtoms, drums, pipes, and trumpets in every corner of town, and I see processions in honour of Kali going to a place two miles off, called Kali Ghaut, where there has long been a celebrated temple to this goddess. . . . In all the bazars, at every shop door, wooden figures and human heads, with the neck painted blood-colour, are suspended, referring, I imagine, to the human sacrifices formerly offered to this deity, who was, I believe the tutelary goddess of Calcutta."[10] Kālīghāṭ also sees great activity during Durgā Pūjā (Pl. II.194), with great numbers of goats sacrificed to the goddess. Part of the Kālīghāṭ complex, the temple to Śiva Nakuleśwar draws throngs of devotees during Śivarātrī, "Śiva's Night," held in February, and was in Solvyns's time, the scene of the Gājan festival's Jhā̃p (Pl. II.191), Nīla Pūjā (Pl. II.192), and Caṛak Pūjā (Pl. II.193). And at the Kālghāṭ's Shayam Ray temple, Dol Yātrā (Pl. II.189) celebrates the loves of Kṛṣṇa.

Kālīghāṭ is today in the heart of south Calcutta, a stop on the city's subway system, but in Solvyns's time, it was some distance from the town, reached by a pilgrim road through tiger-infested jungle. The temple, however, was a major center of religious devotion and was richly endowed by pious Hindus. Raja Nabakrishna Deb[11] was said to have spent 100,000 rupees on worship of the goddess in a single visit, with offerings of gold and silver, feasting, and "trifling" presents to the poor. In the eighteenth century, officials of the East India Company made contributions to the temple, perhaps to establish their good graces among the Hindus, but Ward relates several accounts of Europeans "expending thousands of roopees in offerings" to Kālī. One of his brahmin informants assured him "that very frequently European men presented offerings, soliciting some favour at the hands of the goddess, and that very lately a gentleman in the Hon. Company's service, who had gained a cause at law, presented thank-offerings to Kalee. . . ." And it was further affirmed that each month four or five hundred Muslims presented offerings to the goddess.[12]

Solvyns depicts bathing at Kālīghāṭ, as devotees purify ritually and enjoy themselves in the sacred waters that are a part of the Ganges river system. An Indian artist of the Company School painted a similar scene at another Kālī temple, at Titaghar, outside Calcutta. The subject, the manner in which it is treated, and the black border all suggest Solvyns. Indeed, Pratapaditya Pal writes that "Nowhere is Solvyns' influence more vividly perceptible than in the works of [this] unknown Calcutta artist, probably from Murshidabad, dated by Archer between 1798 and 1804." Although the watercolor is not a copy of Solvyns's print, the artist's "elongated figures, his sombre tones, and colouring may reflect awareness of Solvyns's style. . . ."[13]

Kālīghāṭ is, of course, associated with its own genre of painting. As Puṭuās (Pl. II.67), folk-painters, moved into the neighborhood of the temple in the nineteenth century, they developed the distinctive "Kālīghāṭ" style—fresh, lively, and colorful—that in its inexpensive and quickly-executed watercolors became enormously popular.[14]

Solvyns's preliminary sketch of the temple, made on the site, was included in the album of drawings compiled by his widow and is reproduced in Chapter Three (Pl. I.32).

---

1 See Pl. II.3, Hindu Buildings.

2 Indrani Roy, 3, and Kalyani Datta, 25.

3 McCutchinson, "Temples of Calcutta," 49. McCutchinson uses the term *āt-chālā* for the Bengali architectural style.

4 Losty, *Calcutta: City of Palaces*, 69. Losty, Pl. 4, reproduces Solvyns's etching of Kālīghāṭ from the Calcutta edition, which is a mirror image of the original drawing. Losty intended to correct the reversal in reproduction, as the plate carries the note, "*Reversed from original,*" but the plate, in fact, corresponds to the Calcutta etching. In the Paris etching, which we reproduce, Solvyns returned the image to that of the original drawing.

5 Pratapaditya Pal compares Solvyns etching of "Pagoda of Calleegaut" from the Paris edition with a photograph of the temple today. "Kali, Calcutta, and Kalighat Pictures," 110-111.

6 Cotton, *Calcutta: Old and New*, 973-74; Kalyani Datta, 24; and Stutley, 137. On accounts of the origin of the temple, see Bysack; Indrani Roy, 15-23, and C. R. Wilson, *The Early Annals of the English in Bengal*, 1:129-30.

7 The English name Calcutta comes from Kalikata, one of the three villages that formed the nucleus of the city. The origin of the word itself is disputed. See Sukanta Chaudhuri, 1:1; Nair, *Calcutta in the 17th Century*, 34-59, 467; and Jogendra Nath Bhattacharya, 247fn. On January 1, 2001, the Government of West Bengal officially changed the name of the city to Kolkata.

8 *A View of . . . the Hindoos*, 3:118.

9 Kalyani Dutta, 26.

10 134.

11 On Deb, see Commentary for Pl. II.182.

12 Ward, *A View of . . . the Hindoos*, 3:122-29. Also see Raja Binaya Krishna Deb, 64-66, and Kalyani Dutta, 25.

13 "Indian Artists and British Patrons in Calcutta," 133. Also see Mildred Archer, *Company Drawings in the India Office Library*, 79, Cat. No. 45, Pl. 24.

14 On Kālīghāṭ painting, see especially Jyotindra Jain; W. G. Archer, *Kalighat Paintings*; R. P. Gupta, "Art in Old Calcutta: Indian Style," 139-42; Pratapaditya Pal, "Kali, Calcutta, and Kalighat Pictures"; and Sumanta Banerjee, 130-37. Jain, 8-9, reproduces Solvyns's Paris etching of Kālīghāṭ.

II.5. Hindu Bazar

Pl. II.5. Hindu Bazar. Paris: III.11.1. Double-plate.

Calcutta: Sec. XII, No. 22. A Bazar, or Indian Market.

Paris: III.11.1. HINDOO BAZAR: There are at present in Hindoostan few Bazars frequented exclusively by Hindoos: this which the print represents is of that number. These Markets are generally held near the house of some great man who lets out the spot and levies a tax upon the merchants who expose their goods to sale, under sheds or mats or in shops. There are fixed days for them, but some days the affluence is greater, and they are frequented by women mostly of an advanced age. In the towns inhabited by Europeans, the Bazars are well supplied with all sorts of provisions: which is not the case in the country. The lowest current money of the Bazars is the shells or *cories*, whose value is specified in the 1st vol. no. 6 [Pl. II.38.]. In the interior of the country, the business is done by exchange. Rice for fish, cotton for rice, etc. Excellent butcher's meat, beef, mutton, kid, is sold cheap in the great towns inhabited by Europeans, as well as poultry, except turkeys which are very dear, and only brought up by the Portuguese.[1] An European who is satisfied with a simple diet may live very cheap in India, but once luxuries are admitted, the expence of the table becomes enormous, particularly respecting wines.

There are separate Bazars where the appearance of an European sets all the dealers to flight; the troops sometimes on changing quarters, take advantage of this terror to strip the shops abandoned by their masters.

Commentary: Solvyns here portrays a *hāṭ*, a market held on a particular day. Typically held once a week, it is a general market, of the sort found throughout India, offering various commodities for sale, from fish (seen on the far left) to fruits, vegetables, and spices. It has the character of a village market day, in contrast to the permanent bazaar, with its stalls and shops and daily activity. Walter Hamilton, in his 1820 *Description of Hindoostan*, describes "hauts or open markets [as] held on certain days only, and are resorted to by petty venders and traders. . . . They are usually established in open plains, where a flag is erected, to the vicinity of which, the farmer brings the produce of his lands, the mechanic that of his work shop, and the fisherman of his net. To carry on these operations a space of ground is reserved, divided by narrow paths into several plots. . . , each plot being occupied by two or three venders, and the whole transacted in the open air."[2] Solvyns identifies the *hāṭ* in the etching as a "Hindoo" market to distinguish it from cosmopolitan bazaars that brought a mixture of nationalities both as merchants and customers.

As with the weekly *hāṭ*, bazaars, large and small, were scattered throughout Calcutta. Some were extensive areas of the city, like Burra Bazar" ("Great Bazaar"), devoted to trade and commerce, with each specialty—yarn, spices, silks and brocades, copper implements, gold, whatever—in its particular locale. Others were markets devoted to a particular commodity.[3] Burra Bazar, "a vast and interlocking series of business zones," just to the north of the Armenian and Indo-Portuguese sections of central Calcutta (see map, p. 18), was "the historic nucleus" of the Indian Calcutta.[4] It was the mercantile heart of the native town, the central wholesale market area. Its trade was dominated by Bengali merchants, both Hindu and Muslim, but it had a substantial number of merchants from northern and western India, Armenians, and others, giving it a cosmopolitan character. Lal Bazar was the area within the "gray zone" where European goods were sold in shops run by Europeans of various nationalities, Eurasian Portuguese, and, no doubt, Indians as well. It was estimated that there were some 10,000 "native" shopkeepers in Calcutta in 1797-98.[5]

Solvyns's reference to certain markets where the appearance of a European sets the venders to flight is curious, but perhaps Solvyns writes of incidents that had recently occurred and would be familiar to his Calcutta audience. Although Europeans rarely penetrated the Indian town that Solvyns portrayed, few Indians in Calcutta would be unfamiliar with them. There may have been occasions, however, when European rowdies or lowlifes—and they were surely to be found in Calcutta—ventured into Black Town to make trouble. There may also have been incidents when British soldiers went out with a handful of Indian troops (sepoys, Pl. II.95), and on the venders' flight, the troops plundered the stores.

---

1 The term "Portuguese" referred principally to the mixed Indo-Portuguese and to Indian Roman Catholics. See Commentary for Pl. II.6.

2 *A Geographical, Statistical, and Historical Description of Hindoostan and Adjacent Countries*, 1:38.

3 On Calcutta's markets generally, see Sreemani, 67-98, and Raghab Bandyopadhyay. On the role of the bazaar in Indian cities, see Bayly, *Rulers, Townsmen and Bazaars.*

4 Pradip Sinha, *Calcutta in Urban History*, 54. On Burra Bazar also see Bunny Gupta and Jaya Chaliha; W. H. Carey, 2:104-13; and Nair, *British Social Life in Ancient Calcutta*, 106-08. Nair also describes some of the other major bazaars of late 18th century Calcutta.

5 Marshall, *Bengal: The British Bridgehead*, 162.

II.6. Black Town

Pl. II.6. Black Town. Paris: III.9.1. Double-plate. **Calcutta: Before Sec. X.** A View of a Bengalee Road in Calcutta.

Commentary: Solvyns here portrays the northern outskirts of Calcutta, on Chitpore Road, looking south toward the towers of the "Black Pagoda" in the center background. The Hugli river is to the right. The Black

Paris: III.9.1. THE BLACK TOWN AT CALCUTTA: Each nation at Calcutta has its particular quarter; so we have the English quarter, the Portuguese quarter, etc. . . . That which is inhabited by the natives, who, whether they are originally Hindoos or Mussulmans, differ from all the others by their complexion which is as dark as the Caffries, is called the *Black Town*. No European is to be seen there, and the construction of the houses is entirely different from ours: one part of it is represented in this print. The road on which are seen men of horseback, on foot, and in palanquins, is that which leads to Chitpore. As there is a considerable carriage of wood here, on account of the magazines and different buildings, the general employment of the neighbourhood is sawing planks for which they use small curved saws as in the print; and with these they do a great deal of work in the day, when they work on their own account: for they seem to undergo a total change as soon as they come under a master, and are as lazy as they were industrious.

In another print I will give a view of the whole principal street of Chitpore [Pl. II.3].

Pagoda, a brick temple in the Bengali pinnacled style dedicated to Śiva, had been built by the wealthy merchant Gobindram Mitter (Govinda Ram Mitra) in 1731. Although never fully completed, the "nine jeweled" (nine pinnacled) temple was the highest structure in Calcutta. It was heavily damaged in a terrible cyclone in 1737. Thomas Daniell portrayed the surviving towers of the temple in his *Views of Calcutta* and later in *Oriental Scenery*.[1] The pagoda collapsed some years after Solvyns's provided his distant view, with the main tower standing.

In the foreground, Solvyns depicts carpenters at the river's edge sawing timber. In another print, he portrays the carpenter (Chutār, Pl. II.54) in his workshop, with the different modes of sawing wood.

In referring to the Bengalis' complexion as "as dark as the Caffrees," Solvyns uses the term then current in Calcutta for black Africans. "Caffree" was a corruption of the Arabic *kāfir*, for infidel, and was picked up by Europeans in Bengal from Portuguese slavers. "Caffree boys" were sometimes employed as household slaves in eighteenth century Calcutta even in Solvyns's time.[2]

The "Portuguese" to whom Solvyns refers in his text are the Eurasian Indo-Portuguese, though the term was loosely extended to include Eurasians more generally as well as native Roman Catholics.[3] They were distinguished by their religion, names, and by their European dress and lifestyle. The pidgin Portuguese that was once a *lingua franca* of early Calcutta had declined substantially in use by Solvyns's time. Their quarter was Murghihatta, a name taken from the Bengali *murgi*, chicken, and *hāṭ*, market, for they were the only people in Calcutta who kept fowl.[4] The area was located to the north of Tank Square, very near the Armenian quarter and centered around the old Portuguese Church, which was torn down for the construction of the Catholic cathedral between 1797 and 1799. The new cathedral was built largely through the munificence of a wealthy Indo-Portuguese banking family.[5] Most "black Portuguese," as they were sometimes called, were poor, and they were generally viewed by Europeans as disreputable and dishonest.[6] Their unsavory reputation was rooted in the seventeenth and early eighteenth centuries, when they had been employed in the East India Company army. Called "topasses," "topas," or "topaz" (thought to be a corruption of the Persian *top-chī*, gunner, or from *topā*, hat, which they wore in European style),[7] they were regarded as unreliable, lazy, and degenerate. In Solvyns's day, the prejudice remained, though they were often employed as servants in European households, especially as ayahs, nursery maids (Pl. II.131), and Solvyns makes reference to them in various contexts.

---

1 The etching from *Views of Calcutta* (1787) is reproduced in Losty, *Calcutta: City of Palaces*, Fig. 22, and in Mildred Archer, *Early Views of India*, Pl. 7. The *Oriental Scenery* aquatint, from a drawing done in 1792, is reproduced in Losty, Pl. 3, and in Archer, Pl. 97. Losty, 48, discusses the Black Pagoda. McCutchion, "The Temples of Calcutta," 52-53, discusses its architectural style.

2 On "Caffree," see *Hobson-Jobson*, 140-42. Accounts of Calcutta in the 18th century often refer to slaves, as in W. H. Carey's discussion, *Good Old Days*, 1:465-73. On slavery in Bengal, see A. K. Chattopadhyay.

3 See Pradip Sinha, *Calcutta in Urban History*, 44-52; Hawkesworth, 48-52; Cotton, *Calcutta Old and New*, 204-06; and Suresh Chandra Ghosh, 56-91.

4 A. K. Ray, 196.

5 *Calcutta: City of Palaces*, 90.

6 Blechynden, 69, writes that "the proud Portugese names they had inherited [became] a byword through the land for all that was vicious, idle, and degrade." Also see Long, *Calcutta in the Olden Time*, 130.

7 *Hobson-Jobson*, 933-34.

II.7. The Nations Most Known in Hindoostan

Pl. II.7. The Nations Most Known in Hindoostan. Paris: III.12.5.

Paris: III.12.5. OF THE NATIONS MOST KNOWN IN HINDOOSTAN: To give the public an idea of the sight which an Indian town offers to a traveller, I have brought together in this print all the different costumes which are there met with. In the foreground is a Hindoo with his wife, a man of upper Hindoostan, a Mussulman, a Mogul, a Persian, an Arabian, a Mug, a Chinese, a Malay, an Armenian and some Europeans, Englishman[,] Dutchman and others, as different nearly from each other in their appearance, as they are from the Hindoos. It is proper to observe to the reader, that these costumes were drawn about 1790, so that some years hence this print, may not perhaps be so exact, on account of the constant changes in European fashions.

Commentary: William Tennant, in 1799, wrote that "The group of inhabitants that meets your eye in passing along the streets of Calcutta, is a multifarious mixture of adventurers of every complexion, and from almost every nation in the world. Even the mercantile part of the community consists of inhabitants from almost all the countries of Europe and Asia."[1] Solvyns here gathers together the peoples of various "nations" resident in the already cosmopolitan city of Calcutta. He lists figures in the foreground of the etching, but these do not readily match the subjects portrayed. Three figures correspond closely to Solvyns's portrayals in individual etchings: a Brajbāsi, armed with a dagger and sword (Pl. II.97), and a sepoy of the Bengal Army in the sun-dial hat (Pl. II.95), both at the far left, and, center-left and facing the viewer, a Rāmjanī, dancer (P. II.93). Behind the Rāmjanī is the "Dutchman," Solvyns himself. The woman with the uncovered head facing the artist may be another dancer or possibly an Indo-Portuguese woman.[2]

Solvyns stands under a *chātā*, as do the two Europeans, attended by their servants (one of whom may be a bearded Bengali Muslim), at the far right. The *chātā*—also called a "kittysol" or "roundel" by Europeans—umbrella was traditionally associated with high social status in India, a consideration enhanced by the practical need for protection from the sun. Europeans when outside were regularly accompanied by kittysol or roundel "boys," even when borne by a palanquin.[3] In the mid-eighteenth century, the Company enacted sumptuary laws forbidding junior clerks the use of roundel boys (as also the use of palanquins), and Clive ordered that these be strictly enforced[4]—perhaps with concern both that these young gentlemen not be overly-inflated in self-importance and that the status and dignity of high officials in no way be diminished.

The bear-chested man facing the viewer on the left is Hindu, perhaps an agriculturist, with a squatting woman tending a child to his left and a standing woman, possibly his wife, facing him. Behind the man, we see the bearded face of a North Indian Muslim. In the center, back, is a Chinese, with a queue and straw hat, in conversation with two figures, a Malay and possibly a Magh.[5] To their right is a Mughal (see Pl. II.300) talking with two Armenians in their distinctive hats. In describing this "highly respectable" community of merchants, Wallace, in 1823, wrote that the Armenian costume gives them "a remarkable appearance. . . . The cap is of black velvet, and triangularly shaped, and the frock is generally of the same materials, but embraces the neck closely, flowing down to the knee, something like a surtout [overcoat]."[6]

"The Armenians are the most respectable, and perhaps the most numerous body of foreign merchants in this capital," Tennant wrote. "They carry on an extensive trade from China, and most of the sea-ports to the eastward and to the west, as far as the Persian Gulph. Their information from all these quarters, is deemed the most accurate and minute of any body of men in their profession. They are attentive, regular, and diligent in business; and never think of departing from their line of life, and indulging in dissipation. . . . Their houses are, therefore, of old standing, and many of them are possessed of large capitals. As subjects, they are perhaps the most peaceable and loyal to be found in any country; as members of society, they are polite and inoffensive."[7]

In the center, seated on the ground, is a Bengali "babu," or gentleman, wearing a wide-brimmed *śāmlā*.[8] Opposite, the man wearing the peculiar cap is apparently an astrologer (see Pl. II.23) and may be reading the babu's fortune.

Who, among the figures portrayed, is the Arab, the Persian, or, indeed, the Magh, is undetermined.

---

1 *Indian Recreations*, 1:52. On Calcutta's ethnically diverse population see N. R. Ray, *City of Job Charnock*, 36-37, with Colesworthy Grant's picture of the cosmopolitan merchants of Barrabazar. The European population of Calcutta was itself cosmopolitan, with Italians, Portugese, Germans, Dutch, and others. See Furber, 256-57.

2 On the "Portuguese," see Commentary for Pl. II.6.

3 On the *chātā*, kittysol, and rondel, see fn. 3 in the introduction to Solvyns's portrayal of palanquins, p. 456, and on the *chātā*, also see Pl. II.47. Goldsborne, in *Hartly House*, 290, writes that the indoor function of "kittysol boys" was to wave fans or *chauṅrīs* of palm leaves behind their master's chair.

4 *Hobson-Jobson*, "Roundel," 771.

5 On the Chinese in Calcutta, see Sircar. On the Maghs, see Pl. II.251.

6 Wallace, 392, in Nair, *Calcutta in the 19th Century*, 329. See the portrayal of an Armenian, with his peaked hat, in a Company School painting influenced by Solvyns, Pl. I.47.

7 *Indian Recreations*, 1:52-53. The Armenian presence in Calcutta dates back to the founding of the city, and their church, built in 1724 on Armenian Street, is the oldest in Calcutta. See Chaliha and Gupta; Hawkesworth, 52-54; H. E. A. Cotton, *Calcutta Old and New*, 206; Deb, *The Early History and Growth of Calcutta*, 44; Blechynden, 19, and fn. 21, pp. 26-27.

8 The *śāmlā* turban is of Bengali style. It has a wide brim made of *śolā* (pith) and is covered with minute folds of muslin. The great Bengali reformer Ram Mohan Roy (1774-1833) is shown in some portraits wearing a *śāmlā*. The term "babu" (Bengali, *bābū*) was a term of respect for certain gentlemen, but among Anglo-Indians, it was often used with derision. See *Hobson-Jobson*, 44.

II.8. Hindu Conversations

Pl. II.8. Hindu Conversations. Paris: III.12.2.

Paris: III.12.2. HINDOOS CONVERSATIONS: The Hindoos take a particular delight in numerous meetings, for the sake of the conversation to which they give rise. This is the place to treat of marriages, money matters, and scandal; to cry up those whose entertainments have been the most brilliant, whose imprecations have been loudest against the images of the Gods, when they were thrown into the water:[1] to talk of those whose debaucheries were most excessive at the public festivals.[2] Such are the subjects of their conversations, which take place in the cool of the evening, and frequently in the night: tobacco and *Paun* [*pān*, Pl. II.212] are distributed here in great profusion, and women are absolutely excluded. The print represents one of these meetings. It must be observed that the Hindoos have a way of conversing by signs as well as by words. It would hardly be imagined that, while the two Hindoos, who occupy the foreground of the print seem to attend to the general conversation, are transacting some important commercial business, by the different manners in which they join their hands, under the folds of their cloths, and that they are perhaps agreeing upon the payment of many thousand pounds.

1 On the immersion of the images in the water, see Bisarjan, Pl. II.191.

2 On the "debaucheries," also see Commentary for Bisarjan, Pl. II.191.

II.9. Jugglers

Pl. II.9. Jugglers. Paris: III.12.3.

Paris: III.12.3. JUGGLERS: The dexterity and surprising feats of the Indian jugglers are well known. It would take up too much time to describe them all, therefore I shall confine myself to a few, which I saw and drew, upon the spot. In the foreground is a man who, with a sabre or a large flat sword, enters the throat to the abdomen: draws out the instrument which is often dripping with blood; asks for a glass of wine or spirits, and continues his tricks as if nothing had happened. Several English physicians have reasoned upon this fact, which has been so well attested, that the truth of it could not be called in question, and which seems notwithstanding in opposition to all the demonstrations of anatomy. For my part, I have been an eye witness of it, and consequently can admit of no doubt. Near this man is another, whose tricks are less perillous: they consist in throwing up with his hands, arms, feet and legs, a great number of hollow balls, or round bells. A third performs the same feats with two canon balls of thirty or forty pounds weight, which he throws up in the same manner from his legs, arms, and even his back, with astonishing suppleness and address. Farther off is a woman who lies flat, upon an iron plate which turns round upon a sharp point fixed on the top of a bambou. After having turned round for some time with the plate, without losing her equilibrium, she descends from the top of the bambou, to amaze the spectators by new performances.

Commentary: Solvyns's "jugglers" includes sword-swallowers and acrobats as well as jugglers. In India, these entertainers, like snake-charmers, typically wandered in bands and in Bengal were primarily drawn from such castes as the Bediyās,[1] whom Europeans likened to gypsies. They performed at fairs, festivals, and marketplaces and along the roadside with dancing bears, trained monkeys and goats, and as magicians, jugglers, and, especially with women and children, as acrobats.[2]

In his Introduction to Volume III of *Les Hindoûs*, Solvyns, refers to "the tricks and feats of strength of their Jugglers," and notes the astonishment of Europeans at their "wonderful dexterity and incomprehensible slight of hand."[3] There Solvyns mentions Colonel Gilbert Ironside's 1801 "Account of Feats of Strength, Activity, and Legerdemain, in Hindustan," describing balancing acts, rope-dancing, acrobatics, and various feats of strength.[4]

1 See discussion of the Māl snake-catchers (Pl. II.65) and Bediyā (Pl. II.78).

2 Benoy Bhattacharya, 51, and Risley, *Tribes and Castes of Bengal*, I:83. Also see Sherring's discussion of the Nats, who he describes as "a tribe of vagrants who live by feats of dexterity, sleight of hand, fortune-telling, and the like. . . ." 1:387. W. H. Carey, in *The Good Old Days of the Honorable John Company*, 1:369-76, in describing "Indian jugglers," relates their various feats.

3 3:3.

4 *The Asiatic Annual Register . . . for the Year 1801*. "Miscellaneous Tracts," 27-33. The following year, *The Asiatic Annual Register, for the Year 1802* carried Ironside's obituary. Born in 1737, he had come to Bengal in 1759 as an ensign in the Honorable Company's Army. "Characters," 43-44. Also see Hodson, 528.

II.10. Pachisi

Pl. II.10. Pachisi. Paris: III.12.4.

Paris: III.12.4. POUNCHYS AND OTHER GAMES: The game of *Pounchys,* with all its simplicity and monotony, is more interesting to the Hindoos, than either chess or draughts, which, as is well known, come also originally from their country. Men, women and children play at *Pounchys;* and perhaps the chief attraction is, that it requires no effort either of memory or judgement. All that is requisite, is to throw five oblong dice, or pieces of ivory with various marks, which are to be observed as they fall to the ground. This game is sometimes also played with the *Courries* [cowrie, or *kauṛī*] or small shells, which as we have often had occasion to remark [Pl. II.38], are the current money of India. The Hindoos are not in general so much addicted to gaming as other asiatic nations, such as the Chinese, or Malays. It is not with them a passion in which their whole fortunes are squandered. If some few individuals give way to it to excess, they do it in private, and avoid the eye of the public. The Hindoos instead of losing their money in this manner, prefer spending it in brilliant feasts, in constructing temples, or public stairs leading to the river.

Commentary: Pachisi—*pacisī*, literally "twenty-five," for the highest throw of the dice—is played on an embroidered cloth "board" in the shape of a cross. There are typically four players, two for each side (though two alone may play), and cowrie shells are used as the dice. The winning side gets all its "men" into the center first according to the throw of the dice. A variation of the game was introduced into the United States in the 1860s as "parcheesi."[1]

Solvyns depicts two games—a game of chess to the right and to the left center the game he describes as "pounchys," but which is shown played by two persons on a square board and not on the distinctive four-armed cruciform of pachisi. He refers to and depicts the use of oblong dice—a dice form that dates back to the Indus civilization—that are used in *chausar*, a game similar to pachisi also played on a cruciform board, but with three oblong dice rather than cowries, as in pachisi.[2] The use of dice may well have been adapted to pachisi, but the square board Solvyns's depicts suggests another game entirely.

In his "Introduction" to *Les Hindoûs*, Vol. III, Solvyns writes more generally that

> One cannot help blaming the Hindoos, for losing more than half their time, in an amusement which is at best, but flattering to

the grossest senses; but on the other hand, who can envy them this simple enjoyment, when he reflects, that they do not like so many others, squander their time and fortunes at play, which if we except chess, and the innocent pastime of Pounchys . . . , has but little attraction for them: while with their neighbours the Chinese and other Asiatics, the love of gaming becomes a passion, and even a sort of rage. The wise laws of Minou [Manu] condemns this taste, as most prejudicial to the welfare of the state [Manu 7.47, 7.50], and enjoins all sovereigns to treat gamesters as robbers, and bannish them from their dominions as dangerous subjects [Manu 9.225].[3]

1 The game is described in Henry Grant and Colebrooke, 230; Brown, "The Indian Games of Pachisi, Chaupar, and Chausar," 296-302; Falkener, 256-63; Murray, 135; and Crooke, *Things India*, 97.

2 Brown, 297-302; Murray, 134; and Falkener, 263-64..

3 3:3.

II.11. School

Paris: III.10.1. SCHOOL: The schools, in India, are kept in the open air, before the house of the Brahmun who teaches. The scholars pay nothing if the master is in easy circumstances, and are taught to read and write in the vulgar tongue of the country and the Sanscrit. The manner of teaching is very simple. For reading, one of the scholars pronounces a letter or a syllable, which is repeated by all the class, in chorus and with a sort of melody. For writing, the letters or characters are traced in the sand: those who are a little more forward, write with reeds cut in the form of a pen, and ink, upon green banana leaves, or grave with either pointed or round instrument upon the dry leaves of the palm-tree. The print represents all these different occupations of the school. The master in one hand holds his hooka or pipe, and in the other a small bambou which he uses as a ferula. It is remarkable that, though the use of paper has been long known in India, all the ancient documents are written, or rather graved, upon the dry leaves of the palm, which, when assembled together, are called *Poytas* [*pothī*]. In the first volume there are representations of these writings in the hands of the Rajahs praying [Pl. II.18], of the Astronomers [Pl. II.23], and of the Faquirs [Pl. II.136].

Pl. II.11. School. Paris: III.10.1. Double-plate.
Calcutta: Sec. XII, No. 21. A School.

Commentary: Many of India's rural schools today have changed little from that depicted by Solvyns, save that instead of palm leaves, pupils write on slates or boards. A good many villages in Bengal would have had such schools, but comparatively few children attended and then generally only those of the higher castes. The aims were to teach the children "how to form the letters in the Bengali alphabet and to keep the kind of accounts that would enable a cultivator to compete on more than totally unequal terms with merchant and tax assessor." But few children attained even these modest goals, and "the great mass of children simply did not go to school."[1]

1 Marshall, *Bengal: The British Bridgehead*, 30.

II.12. Bengali Road

Pl. II.12. Bengali Road. Paris: III.8.1. Double-plate.
Calcutta: Before Sec. VI. A Bengalee Road, to the North of Chitpore.

Commentary: Barrackpore, on the Hugli river, 17 miles north of Calcutta, took its name in 1772, when the East India Company first stationed troops there, and its pleasant situation provided the country residence of the Governor-General. Unhappy with the modest bungalow, Lord Wellesley, in 1804, ordered the construction of a magnificent palace at Barrackpore, but the Board of Directors in London suspended the project, leaving the foundations and unfinished arches "like an ancient ruin."[1]

Wellesley also projected a grand avenue that was to become the Barrackpur Trunk Road, but even at the time Solvyns portrayed the road, it was surfaced with *khoā* (wrongly identified by Solvyns as *surkhī*),[2] described in *Hobson-Jobson* as "a kind of concrete, of broken brick, lime, &c, used for floors and terrace roofs."[3] The use of *khoā* in road-construction in Bengal, from Solvyns's account, was apparently widespread.

The scene Solvyns portrays is dominated by a great banyan tree, the Indian fig tree (*Ficus indica* or *Ficus religiosa*), to which oddly he makes no specific

Paris: III.8.1. BENGALEE ROAD: The high roads in Bengal are in general less covered than this which the print represents; but I preferred it, in order to have an opportunity of bringing into my drawing the banana, and other Indian trees which are so often mentioned in the relations of travellers. This is part of the road from Calcutta to Baracpore. I have drawn it with the most scrupulous exactness, without omitting or adding the slightest circumstance. Like all the Bengal roads it is paved with bricks, with a layer of *sulky* [*surkhī*], or broken bricks, over them; which forms an excellent surface. The shade of the trees is a great comfort to travellers, and under it too they frequently meet shops of refreshments. The views which present themselves are often magnificent: on each side of the road immense fields extend as far as the eye can reach, where the white of the cotton is agreeably intermixed with the yellow flower of the mustard plant. But the scene alters in the rainy season, when all the low country is inundated and forms a vast lake.

Among the accessories of the print is seen a carriage of the country, and some loaded oxen.

reference, preferring to note the banana trees by the thatched hut in the center of the etching. In the Paris edition, where Solvyns includes a section of six plates depicting trees, he depicts the banana (Pl. II.269), but again no banyan, a striking omission in that this impressive tree was eulogized by poets, including Milton, and later likened to "a great cathedral, aisled and choired in wood."[4]

The banyan's temple-like character comes as its branches drop shoots to the ground that root and support the parent tree. Extended in this way, one tree may come to cover a vast expanse, as does the famous banyan in the Indian Botanic Garden at Shibpur across the Hugli from Calcutta. The garden—to which Solvyns makes no reference—was founded in 1787 at the suggestion of Lt. Col. Robert Kyd, military secretary to the Governor-General, Lord Cornwallis.

The word "banyan" is not Indian, but is derived from the name given by Europeans in the early seventeenth century to a particular tree under which Hindu traders—banians—gathered. It was later extended to other such trees and was taken as the English name for the species.[5] The Sanskrit name for the tree, sacred to Viṣṇu, is *nyagrodha*, meaning "growing down."[6]

---

1 H. E. A. Cotton, *Calcutta Old and New*, 807-11.

2 *Hobson-Jobson*, in its entry for "soorky," 854, states that in his description, Solvyns misuses the word. "The substance in question is khoa." On *surkhī*, used in the preparation of *cūnā*, the plaster of Calcutta buildings, see Pl. II.60.

3 480.

4 *Hobson-Jobson*, 65-66.

5 *OED*, 652; Lewis, 59-60. On the Hindu banian, see Pl. II.99.

6 Walker, 1:357-58.

Castes and Occupations

Section I of the Calcutta etchings, "Sixty-six prints of the Hindoo casts, with their professions," opens with the portrayal of the four *varṇas*, the classes of Hindu society: brahmin, priest (with five brahmin castes depicted); kṣatriya, warrior; vaiśya, merchant; and śūdra, the class that included the vast majority of Hindus and embraces castes of high status, such as the Vaidya, physician (Pl. II.25), and Kāyastha, writer (Pl. II.26), as well as numerous agricultural and craft castes.[1] The Preliminary Discourse for *Les Hindoûs*, Volume I (Chapter Four, pp. 115-26), describes the *varṇa* according to Manu, the legendary law-giver of Indian antiquity.

Solvyns, like many others, uses the term "caste" in reference both to *varṇa* and *jāti*, caste proper, but he understands that castes (*jāti*), by tradition, are endogamous, occupationally defined, and hierarchically ranked. He recognizes, as well, that caste distinctions are sometimes ambiguous and that ranked positions may be fluid and contested. It is clear, nevertheless, that in the organization of the etchings of castes and occupations, Solvyns attempts to present the Hindus in terms of what he understands to be the hierarchy of caste status and purity. The traditionally highest castes come first, while the "untouchable," ritually polluted castes that fall outside the four *varṇas* and below the śūdras are the last depicted.

In his ranking, Solvyns, as an ethnographic artist, is among the first Europeans to provide a systematic account of caste hierarchy.[2] He likely relied heavily on high caste Hindus, including brahmin pandits, for their judgments as to comparative status of the various castes, but even in traditional terms, Solvyns is sometimes very much off the mark. His comparatively low placement of the "warrior" castes and communities—Rājputs (Pl. II.48), Sikhs (Pl. II.51), Mārāṭhas (Pl. II.52)—in the order of presentation in both the Calcutta and Paris editions of the etchings, for example, does not accord with their higher status. There is some variation between the two editions in the order in which castes are portrayed, and Solvyns, in *Les Hindoûs*, may have attempted to correct misplacement in ranking, though it did not affect the position of the warrior castes. Moreover, new anomalies are introduced, as in the ranking—or at least the order of presentation—of the two weaver castes. In the Calcutta edition, Solvyns ranked the Jugi (Pl. II.27) below the Tā̃ti (Pl. II.33), reflecting the Jugi's traditionally lower status, but in the Paris edition, whether intended or not, he elevates the Jugi to a position substantially higher than the Tā̃ti.

There are some differences between the Calcutta and Paris editions in the subjects portrayed in the series of castes and occupations. Eight of the portrayals in the Calcutta edition do not appear in *Les Hindoûs*, and for the Paris edition, Solvyns adds two that had not appeared earlier. A possible explanation for the omissions is that it enabled Solvyns to include all of the etchings of castes and occupations in Volume I, but the logic here is undermined by Solvyns's inclusion of certain occupations in portraying the dresses of Hindu men and Hindu women (corresponding to sections III and IV in the Calcutta edition).

The presentation of Solvyns's etchings below follows the order of the Paris edition, with the additional Calcutta etchings ordered separately at the end.

Brahmins

In both the Calcutta and Paris editions, brahmins occupy the preeminent position in the order of presentation. The 1799 *Catalogue* includes a short description:

> It is universally known, that the Brahmuns are the Priests of the Hindoos; and that by the tenets of their religion, to them are assigned the duties of teaching and reading their sacred Books, of sacrificing, of assisting others to sacrifice, of giving Alms, if rich, and if indigent of receiving gifts; they are forbidden trade, service, and the performance of all menial offices.

The above mentioned Brahmuns, excepting the first, are all named from the countries or the sectaries to which they belong,—they all are held in respect and veneration by Hindoos of every part; yet the inhabitants of one country will not eat and drink from the hands of a Brahmun of a different Tribe.[3]

In his notes to the original drawings, Solvyns writes, "It may be necessary to observe that by the tenets of their religion, they [brahmins] are forbid Trade, Service, or performing any menial office: this however is little attended to."

In the Paris edition, Solvyns provides a brief introductory account of "Brahmuns, Philosophes or Indian Priests, Disciples of Brahma."

There are several classes of them. We shall take notice of the five most known; the *Sroterys* [Śrotriya], the *Kanoges* [Kanaujī], the *Drawers* [Drābiṛ], the *Brijbasis* [Brajbāsī] and the *Oorias* or *Orissas* [Oriyya, or Orissa].

The Brahmun is the first of the four original Hindoo casts; the K'huttry [kṣatriya], the Byce [vaiśya] and the Soodder [śūdra] are the three others, and are termed the sacerdotal; the military, the commercial and the servile; the origin with that of the creation, is described in the Institutes of their divine legislator *Menu* [Manu], as follows:

"The supreme Being having created the waters, placed in them a productive seed, which became an egg, and in it he was born himself in the form of Brahma, the great forefather of all spirits. After having remained a whole year inactive in the egg, he caused it to divide, and formed of its divisions the heavens and the earth; he then (after having produced the principle of the soul, consciousness, reason, the perceptions of sense, the organs of sensation, demi-gods, genius, etc. etc.) to multiply the human race, caused the Brahmun to proceed from his mouth, the K'huttry from his arm, the Byce from his thigh and the Soodder from his foot."[4]

The brahmins thus form the highest of the four classes, or *varṇas*, of Hindu society. The Sanskrit name for the class is *Brāhmaṇa* or *Brāhmaṇ*, but the terms are easily confused with, among other words, Brahma, the god; *brahman*, a magical force; Brahman, the "world spirit; and with *Brāhmaṇas*, the texts on sacrificial ritual. Thus, for clarity, we follow widespread usage in transliterating the class name as brahmin. It is the priestly class, and the name originally meant "one possessed of *brahman*," a magical force referred to in the *Ṛg Veda*, the hymns that are the oldest and most sacred of all Hindu texts.[5]

Brahmins are divided into a number of castes and subcastes, some denoting the geographic region of their origin. Of the five brahmin groups Solvyns portrays, four are regional—Kanaujī, from Kanauj in what is now Uttar Pradesh; Drābiṛ (Drāviḍa), from southern India; Brajbāsī, from Braja, an area around Mathura and Agra; and Oriyya, from Orissa. Śrotriya brahmins form a caste (or subcaste) defined by their study of the Vedas.[6]

---

1 On the *varṇas* and their distinction from caste (jāti), see Basham, 138-52.

2 See the discussion of Solvyns's ranking of the various subjects he portrays in Chapter Three, pp. 98-99.

3 2.

4 The passages from Manu, which Solvyns had earlier included in the 1799 *Catalogue*, 2-3, are from the creation story related in 1.8-9 and 11-15, and, for the four *varṇas* (classes), 1.31 (detailed in 1.87-91). The quotations are not from Sir William Jones's translation of Manu, *Institutes of Hindu Law* (1794), but could be Solvyns's paraphrase of Jones, with the artist's own spellings for the four *varṇas*. On the Jones's translation, see the Preliminary Discourse, Chapter Four, p.125, fn. 36. See p. 425, fn. 28, in the introduction to the section on Sati for a note on the quotations from Manu in *Les Hindoûs* and their translation into French, then back into English.

5 Basham, 140.

6 See Raychaudhuri and Raychaudhuri; Nripendra Kumar Dutt, 2:1-45; Risley, *The Tribes and Castes of Bengal,* 1:141-62; Wise, 227-50; Jogendra Nath Bhattacharya, 26-35; and John Wilson, 2:203-20.

II.13. Śrotriya Brahmin

Pl. II.13. Śrotriya Brahmin. Paris: I.1.2.

Calcutta: Sec. I. No. 1. Srotery Brahmuns of the Bengalees, performing their devotions; with the Garrah [*ghaṛā*],[1] and the Cossa [*kośā*], or Argah [*arghya*][2] utensils used by them in their offerings.—The Srotery is named from possessing seven goons [*guṇa*] or sciences,[3] as the Koleen [kulīn] is skilled in nine of their sciences.

Paris: I.1.2: SROTERYS BRAHMUNS. The principal figure represents a Brahmun at his prayers on the bank of the Ganges; near him are the *garrah,* the *cossah* or *argah,* vases appropriated to the *poujahs* [*pūjā*] or pious offerings; he makes various signs with his fingers. All these ceremonies are necessary parts of the act of prayer.

The *Srotery* properly speaking is known only in Bengal. He affects the first rank among the Brahmuns, and to derive his name from the possession of seven *gooms* or sciences. The Koleen, or first sect of *Sroterys,* assert their knowledge of nine sciences.

A string of cotton hanging from the shoulder half way down the thigh, is the general distinction of all the Brahmuns, who set a great value upon this mystical ornament.

This class or sect of Brahmuns is held in great veneration among the Hindoos. They are bound by a precept common to all Brahmuns, to teach publicly to read, and explain the sacred writings, and to perform *poujahs* or sacrifices. If rich they give alms; if poor they recieve them. They are forbidden to carry on any sort of trade or to act in any servile capacity.

The Brahmun in common with all the other Hindoos generally paints his forehead, his ears and his body, with all sorts of colours. Some imprint upon their skin the name of the god whom they adore, the munters [*mantras*] or texts of the sacred books, or some hieroglyphical emblem of their religion.

Commentary: A Śrotriya is one who studies the *Vedas*, the earliest and most sacred body of Hindu knowledge, made up of hymns transmitted orally in archaic Sanskrit. The term was originally used in Bengal to refer to any learned brahmin,[4] but came more specifically to designate those ranking below the kulīn, the highest class, among Rāḍhiya and Vārendra brahmins, who trace their ancestry to Kanauj.[5]

The Rāḍhiyas (also termed Rāṛhi or Rāṛhiya) are the largest of the Bengali brahmin castes and, with the Vārendras (Bārendras), are divided into two classes, kulīn and Śrotriya, each of which contains numerous subcastes. The distinction between the two classes provides clarification for Solvyns's reference to what he calls "*gooms* or sciences." The higher kulīn class, by tradition, was composed of those brahmins who possess nine qualities (Sk., *guṇa*) of merit or sacerdotal virtue: ceremonial purity; discipline; learning; reputation for purity; zeal in pilgrimage; piety; observance of legal marriages (specifically limiting kulīn girls to marriage within the kulīn class); penance; and charity. Brahmins of the Śrotriya class possess only eight of the qualifications—not the seven Solvyns indicates. Śrotriyas do not follow the strictures with regard to marriage of their daughters and thus occupy lower rank.[6] In order to improve their social position, however, Śrotriyas seek by means of substantial dowries to marry their daughters to kulīn brahmins.[7]

The "various signs" that Solvyns's Śrotriya makes with his fingers are *mudrās*, symbolic hand gestures of ritual meaning evoking the deity.

The figure wears the *tilak*, or sect mark on his forehead (barely distinguishable in the print) that identifies him as a Bengali Vaiṣṇava—two vertical lines joined at the lower end. The various Vaiṣṇava sects are distinguished by different *tilaks*, termed *ūrdhvapuṇḍra,* applied with sandalwood paste (or other prescribed substances) to the forehead and other parts of the body. The Śaivite *tilak*—called a *tripuṇḍra*—similarly varies in form for the distinct sects. Its characteristic three horizontal lines across the forehead are usually made with ashes from a ritual fire.[8] Throughout his portrait of the Hindus, Solvyns frequently depicts "clean" caste males with the *tilak* on the forehead and sometimes on the arms and upper body as well.

Solvyns portrays the heads of a Śrotriya man and woman (Pl. II.295) as representative of the brahmin caste and discusses the personalities reflected in their physiognomies.

---

1 The *ghaṛā* is a spherical metal pot used for carrying water and is described in detail by Ghosha, 22. The Anglo-Indian corruption of the word was typically rendered as *ghurra*. The Sanskrit is *ghaṭa*. With the spout, as depicted by Solvyns, it is for ritual use in *pūjā*.

2 The *kośā* is a vessel shaped like the long petal of a plantain flower. A small spoon of the same shape, called *kusi*, is used with it in religious ritual. The vessel is also called an *arghya pātra*, taking the name from the libation, *arghya*, it holds. The offering typically consists of water, unhusked rice-grains, *dūrvā* grass, and flowers. See T. N. Mukharji, 186; Ghosha, xxii; and Monier-Williams, 89.

3 Solvyns mistranslates *guṇa*, a quality, as a "science."

4 Raychaudhuri and Raychaudhuri, 52, and N. K. Dutt, 2:5.

5 See Solvyns, Kanaujī Brahmins, Pl. II.14. On the Rāḍhiya brahmins, also see J. N. Bhattacharya, 27-32; Wise, 227-38.

6 Raychaudhuri and Raychaudhuri, 27; Risley, *The Tribes and Castes of Bengal*, 1:145-46; and "Report of the Committee. . .," in Mitra, 211.

7 The high status kulīn brahmins came to be associated with an institutionalized system of hypergamy called "kulīnism," wherein brahmin families of lower rank would provide large dowries to marry their daughters to kulins. The bride would remain with her family, only to be visited occasionally by her kulīn husband as he made his marital rounds. Many a kulīn polygamist, who might have as many as a hundred wives, lived entirely by these means, and as the practice grew over the course of the eighteenth and nineteenth centuries, it was met by opposition from reformist Hindus and Europeans. See Raychaudhuri and Raychaudhuri, *passim*; Tapan Raychaudhuri, "Norms of Family Life and Personal Morality Among the Bengali Hindu Elite, 1600-1850," 13-25. The "evils" of kulīnism prompted inquiry by the government, "Report of the Committee appointed in 1866 by the Government of Bengal to report on the necessity of Legislation on the subject of Polygamy among the Hindus," reprinted in Asok Mitra, *The Tribes and Castes of West Bengal*, 210-14, and in Risley, *The People of India*, 431-40. Also see Risley, *The People of India*, 166-71. Basanta Coomar Bose's *Hindu Customs in Bengal* is devoted largely to the ritual life of the kulīn brahmin and includes an extended discussion of kulīnism, 29-44.

8 O'Malley, "The Insignia of Hindu Sects," in Asok Mitra, *The Tribes and Castes of West Bengal*, 272-74. Also see Walker, 1:208; and Bedi and Bedi, 14-19.

II.14. Kanaujī Brahmin

Pl. II.14. Kanaujī Brahmin. Paris: I.1.3.
Calcutta: Sec. I, No. 2. A Kanoge Brahmun—The shrub represented is the Tulsee [tulsī], held in great veneration by all Hindoos.

Paris: I.1.3: KANOGE BRAHMUN: These Brahmuns have no particular distinction, further than that they always perform their devotions and sacrifices near a heap of stones or hillock of earth upon which is planted a shrub called *tulsee*, which they hold in high veneration. They take their name from the country which they inhabit.

The *Kanoge* is less strict than the other Brahmuns of Bengal, Behar and Orissah. Numbers of them as well as of the *Brijbasis*, serve at present as seapoys or soldiers, even under the european standard, which is nevertheless strongly prohibited by the law of *Menu* [Manu], their legislator. Their native climate is not so warm, for which reason probably they are more cloathed.

The *Kanoge* bears on his forehead the distinguishing mark of his worship, and round his neck the *poitah* [*paitā*],[1] *mallah* [*mālā*][2] or beads which every Hindoo of both sexes, except widows and some few casts is bound to wear, as we shall have occasion to explain in the course of this work.

The signs which the principal figure appears to be making with his fingers under the drapery, have a mystical signification unknown to any but themselves. The stairs upon which the *Kanoge* Brahmun stands were erected by some rich Hindoo to descend to the river to bathe and perform his sacrifices. Nothing is esteemed more agreeable to the divinity of the Hindoos than to construct steps down to the rivers, as on their strands the greater part of their religious acts are performed.

Commentary: The Kanaujī (or Kānyakubja) brahmins take their name from the place of their origin, Kanauj, capital of an early empire, located to the east of Mathura. In his note to the original drawing, Solvyns wrote that "This was the original Race of Brahmuns, from whence all others are descended."

Kanaujīs form one of the five groups of Gaur brahmins of North India, and among various traditions accounting for their presence in Bengal is the story that they are descendants of five priests who came at the invitation of King Ādiśūra in the ninth century. These Kanaujīs are known by the caste names of Rāḍhiya (also Rāṛhi, Rāṛhiya) and Vārendra (Bārendra).[3] Tradition also relates that another group of brahmins from Kanauj—known as Vaidiks—came to Bengal in flight from the imposition of Muslim rule in their homeland in the eleventh century.[4] The three Kanaujī groups, Rāḍhiya, Vārendra, and Vaidik, form a majority of the brahmins in Bengal.[5]

Solvyns notes that many Kanaujīs served as sepoys [Pl. II.95]. Indeed, they formed a substantial portion of the Bengal Army well into the nineteenth century, but in growing unease to perceived threats to their caste purity and religious integrity, symbolized by the "greased cartridges," they figured prominently in the Mutiny of 1857. Risley writes that one of their titles, "Pānde, being originally a corruption of the word *paṇḍit*, a learned man, became, under the form of Pandy, the generic designation of the mutineers of 1857."[6]

The Kanaujī brahmin that Solvyns depicts is at his prayers on a bathing *ghāṭ,* the broad steps leading down to a river. Behind the figure, tulsī grows in a stone or earthenware urn, a setting that contradicts the artist's assertion that "they always perform their devotions . . . near a heap of stones or hillock of earth" upon which tulsī is planted. But Solvyns's portrayal in the etching is correct, for the tulsī (*Ocimum sanctum*), the basil plant sacred to Viṣṇu, is "frequently planted in a vase on a pedestal in the vicinity of a Hindu temple or a domestic shrine. . . ."[7] The planter is called a tulsī *mañca* (or *maṇḍap*) and is an object of veneration and daily ritual in most Bengali Hindu homes.[8]

A close examination of the etching shows the figure to be wearing, as indicated by Solvyns's text, both the sacred thread and a necklace. The necklace (*mālā*) appears to be a string from which an object or objects hang. Given the Kanaujī veneration for the tulsī, these are likely tulsī beads, made from the woody stem of the plant.

The sacred thread, *paitā*, is properly confined to males of the three highest "twice-born" classes. It is hung over the right shoulder and under the left arm and is worn next to the skin, without removal, from the time of the initiation ceremony. The cord is "of three threads, each of nine twisted strands, made of cotton, hemp, or wool, for brāhmaṇs, kṣatriyas, and vaiśyas respectively." "Its removal or defilement," writes Basham, "involves the owner in great humiliation and ritual impurity, which could only be expunged by rigorous penance."[9]

---

1 Solvyns's term, *poytah* (Anglo-Indian, *poita*), is a corruption of the Bengali word for "sacred thread," *paitā*. Solvyns also transliterates the word *paitā* as *poytah*. Solvyns's spellings vary throughout the manuscript, sometimes wrongly using the same transliteration for two different words, as in his use of *poitah* (Pl. II.182) and *poytah* (Pl. II.136) for a palm leaf manuscript (*pothī*).

2 *Mālā* refers to a necklace, beads, or a garland, and as beads may be used, like a rosary, in prayer and meditation. Beads are made of various objects, such as tulsī, sacred to Viṣṇu, and the dried berry called *rudrākṣa*, sacred to Śiva. For a discussion of *rudrākṣa*, see Pl. II.18.

3 Risley, *The Tribes and Castes of Bengal*, 1:144-53, 156-57; R. C. Majumdar, *The History of Bengal*, 1:625-26; and N. K. Dutt, 2:2-3, 13-15. Also see Sherring, 1:22-28; J. N. Bhattacharya, 26-34; 38-40.

4 Raychaudhuri and Raychaudhuri, 83-84.

5 For an extensive discussion of these divisions, see Raychaudhuri and Raychaudhuri, 1-87.

6 Risley, *The Tribes and Castes of Bengal*, 1:157. Also see J. N. Bhattacharya, 39.

7 Lewis, 240. Ashes of a deceased relative are sometimes preserved with the tulsī in such an urn. Ayurvedic physicians also use tulsī medicinally. Tulsī, writes B. A. Gupte, xxxix, "is a great purifier of the atmosphere. . . ."

8 Parks, writing in 1822, describes the "Pooja of the Toolsee," 1:42-43, with a lithographic plate, No. 7 facing p. 43, from her original sketch.

9 163.

II.15. Drābir̥ Brahmin

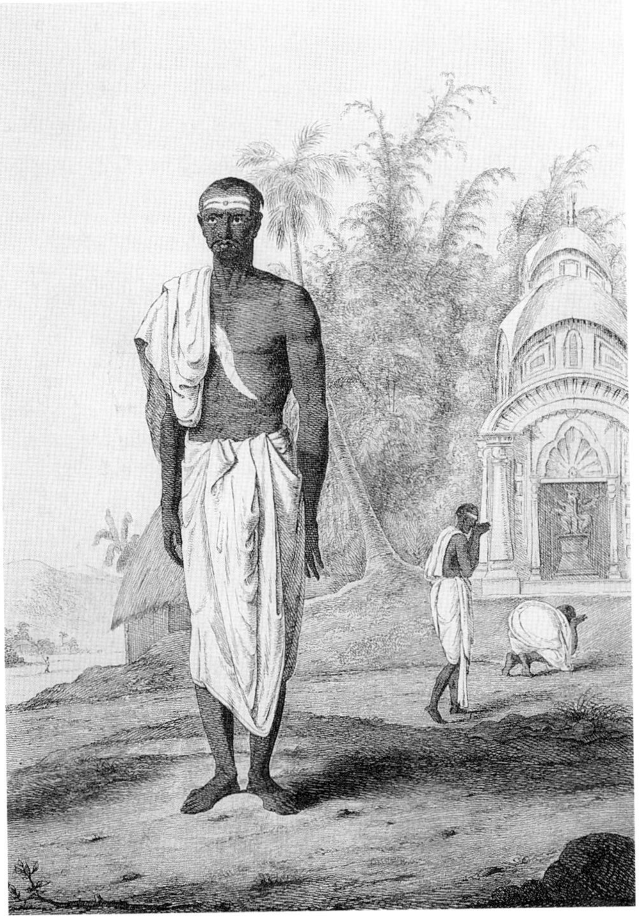

Pl. II.15. Drābir̥ Brahmin. Paris: I.1.4.
Calcutta: Sec. I, No. 3. Drawer Brahmuns—the back ground shewing the manner of the prostrating themselves in their Munders [*mandir*] or Pagodas.

Paris: I.1.4: DRAWERS BRAHMUNS: These differ totally from all other Brahmuns, and are seldom met with in the countries inhabited by Europeans. They have a peculiar idiom or jargon unknown to all the other sects of Brahmuns in Hindoostan. In a state nearly uncivilized, there can be few enlightened men among them. The country which they inhabit is mountainous. These which the plate represents were from Ewalwa [Malwa] or the Mahratta country.

The *Drawers* use fewer ablutions than the other Brahmuns; though they can not take any nourishment without bathing or washing their bodies. They adore the god *Ram,* and prostrate themselves in his temples as shewn in the plate. They paint their foreheads and their bodies like the other Brahmuns; but inviolably in the middle of their foreheads they bear a little rice.

In all my travels I have met but three or four individuals of this sect, and could never obtain any satisfactory account of their origin, their religion or its mysteries. Their language, as I have before observed, being known but to themselves. They are less corrupted than the other Brahmuns, and have preserved more of the purity of their primitive religion

Commentary: The name Drābir̥ is almost surely Drāviḍa, the term used to refer to brahmins south of the Vindhya Hills, consistent with the Śaivite sect mark across the forehead of Solvyns's figure. Risley, following H. H. Wilson, lists five classes of Dravida brahmins, distinguished by the linguistic region of their origin—Marathi, Gujarati, Kannada, Telugu, and Tamil, the later carrying the name Drāviḍa specifically.[1] He does not, however, describe such brahmins among those found in Bengal. Calcutta, nevertheless, was in Solvyns's time already a cosmopolitan city, and it is not surprising that some Drāviḍa brahmins were resident, having migrated from other parts of India.

Solvyns places their origin in the mountainous area of "Ewalwa or the Mahratta country." This is likely Malwa, an extensive plateau in the Vindhyan Hills of central India in what is now Madhya Pradesh. Although a Hindi-language area, it was under Mārāṭha control and Maharashtrian brahmins followed the expansion of Mārāṭha political power. Indeed, it was said that they "were the brains of the Maratha confederacy."[2] Even today, in Indore, in the heart of Malwa, Maharashtrian brahmins—there called "Decanni" brahmins—are the most numerous in the substantial brahmin community.[3] It would seem then that some Maharashtrian ("Drāviḍa") brahmins migrated from Malwa in the eighteenth century to Calcutta. But Solvyns's reference to the mystery of their origin and their language as "known but to themselves" suggests something more obscure, and his entry remains a puzzle.[4]

The temple portrayed is in the distinctive Bengali style of a brick "hut" with curved cornices and roof, and its similarity to the thatched curvilinear hut behind the central figure is notable. Such temples may have several stories, with "huts" stacked one upon the other.[5]

1 Risley, *The Tribes and Castes of Bengal*, 1:143.
2 Quoted in Shrivastav, 139-40.
3 Ibid.
4 I am grateful to Aditi Sen, Frank F. Conlon, and Kathryn G. Hansen for their help in identifying Drawer as Drābiṛ/Drāviḍa and Ewalwa as Malwa.

5 David McCutchion identifies such temples as in the *chālā* style, though the artists who designed and built these temples were surely freer in their expression than stylistic canon might suggest. On the "hut" or *chālā* style, see Michell, *Brick Temples of Bengal*, 20-24. On the Bengali curvilinear hut, see Nilsson, 186.

II.16. Brajbāsī Brahmin

Pl. II.16. Brajbāsī Brahmin. Paris: I.1.5.

Calcutta: Sec. I., No. 4. A Brijbasi Brahmun, in the act of repeating Munters [*mantras*] or incantations—the ceremony he performs under his cloaths, he, in common with all Hindoos, must keep inviolably secret.

Paris: I.1.5: BRIJBASIS BRAHMUNS: These Brahmuns also take their name from their country. They pray sitting or standing with their feet in water. They carry round their necks a collar of while shells, and wear more ornaments and juwels than any other Brahmuns. The piece of yellow cotton with which they sometimes cover their head and sometimes their shoulders, is kept always wet. Their head is always covered with a cool turban or *shawl* or some other rich stuff, arranged in a manner different from the Musselmen.

Of a more robust frame than the other Brahmuns, they count many warriors of their sect: who are taken into pay to make incursions into an enemies country and employed by merchants as guards on the transport of their goods. There is no instance of a *Brijbasi* having abandoned what has been trusted to him in this manner. He defends it at the peril of his life; and by these means this sect has acquired the reputation of great bravery and inviolable fidelity.

To the right of the principal figure is a *Brijbasi* seated in the water, performing his *poujahs* [*pūjā*] or sacrifices. In the back ground is represented a view of the Ganges or *Berampooter* [Brahmaputra], with *bangaloos* [bungalows],[1] pagodas, boats and trees of the country.

Commentary: The Brajbāsī brahmins originate in Braj, an area around Mathura and Agra, roughly corresponding to the region of Vr̥indāvan (Brindāban) associated with the god Kr̥ṣṇa, in what is today Uttar Pradesh. The region is associated with the Hindi dialect Braj Bhaṣā.

As in Solvyns's portrayal of the Kanaujī brahmin, the figure in the etching is in prayer and the symbolic hand gestures, *mudrās*, are concealed. In Tantric ritual, the *mudrās* are a language of magical power, and, just as the *mantras*—sacred formulas—are not be said aloud, the gestures are hidden to insure their efficacy.

Solvyns depicts the Brajbāsī as a guard in a separate etching (Pl. II.50), and we discuss that role in the accompanying commentary.

1 For a discussion of the bungalow house style, see Commentary to Pl. II.44.

II.17. Oriya, Orissa Brahmin

Pl. II.17. Oriya, Orissa Brahmin. Paris: I.1.6.
Calcutta: Sec. I, No. 5. An Ooria or Orissa Brahmun, offering his devotion to the sun; the back ground represents the style of the Architecture of the Munders [*mandir*, temple] of the sect.
Orme: 1.

Paris: I.1.6: OORIAHS OR ORISSAHS BRAHMUNS: Like the preceding and the greater part of Brahmuns, these also borrow their name from their country.

The *Ooriahs* or *Orissahs* Brahmun asserts that in the very country from which he takes his name the god *Brahma* descended to people the world.

These Brahmuns pray holding their string of cotton [sacred thread][1] in both their hands, and with their eyes turned to the sun.

To them is allotted the service of the famous pagoda of *Jaggernaut* at Ballassore. They are the neatest and best drest of all the Brahmuns.

The *Goallahs* (cowherds) and the *Bearers* or palanquin carriers dispersed through all the great towns are to this cast and come originally from the same country.

The *Ooriahs* or *Orissahs* Brahmuns preside in public assemblies and prescribe very rigourous laws and abstinences to the members of their cast.

The colour of the Hindoos of this cast or sect is more yellow and bordering upon the copper tint. I shall have occasion here after to enter into farther details concerning these Brahmuns.

The architecture of the pagoda or *Mundirah* [*mandir*] represented in the engraving is unworthy of the Hindoo stile of building; but it is faithfully copied from the object itself; as we have made it a rule never to embellish, or allow any sort of alteration.

Commentary: Solvyns portrays the Oriya brahmin in early morning ritual. Having taken the sacred thread from under his arm, but without removing it from his neck, he stretches it out between his two thumbs, and with a mantra of purification, washes it in water. The thread is then placed again over the right shoulder and under the left arm. The ritual should be performed, if possible, beside water and with eyes toward the sun.

The Oriya (or Utkala) brahmins are from Orissa and in Bengal served as itinerant priests and were often employed as cooks and in other comparatively menial jobs.[2] In the late eighteenth century, Raja Nabakrishna Deb sought to attract brahmins to Calcutta and offered them land, houses, and employment, and he is reputed to have introduced Oriya brahmins into Calcutta society as cooks.[3] Oriya brahmins were likely among the substantial numbers of palanquin bearers from Orissa (Pl. II.43), but it seems improbable that the Goālā cowherds (Pl. II.47) were brahmin, unless, in his portrayal, Solvyns uses the term generically rather than to refer to the Goālā caste as such, and this is not suggested by his text.

Sherring, however, does note the Oriya brahmin's willingness to take up a range of employment. He lists them as the fifth division of the five Gaur brahmin groups of northern India and writes: "Compared with the Brahmans of the North-Western Provinces, they are very lax in their habits, and by no means adhere with such strictness to caste rules as many others of their order. The truth is, they have more common sense, and far less pride, than Brahmans of Benares, and of similar places, in which caste prejudice is very powerful. . . . The Ooriya Brahmans not only engage in trade and agriculture, but employ themselves in the lowly occupations of brickmaking and bricklaying. Yet they are not all equally sensible and free from prejudice. There are some who pretend to greater purity than the rest, meaning thereby greater strictness and rigidity."[4] It is to the later, no doubt, that Solvyns refers in their "rigourous laws and abstinences."

Solvyns mentions the Oriya brahmins who serve the Jagannatha[5] temple at Balasore (Baleshwar). On the north coast of Orissa, 125 miles south of Calcutta, Balasore was in Solvyns's time a major anchorage for ships on their course to Calcutta, and Solvyns portrays it in his "View of Ballasore Roads" (Pl. II.262.). This is not, however, the location for Solvyns's depiction of the Oriya brahmin, as the temples in the background are Bengali in style—despite the 1799 *Catalogue* reference to the architectural style being that of the Oriya brahmin's "sect." The two side temples are of the nine-pinnacled or jeweled *navaratna* type; the central temple is a one-pinnacled *ekanatra*. Solvyns's comment that these temples are "unworthy of the Hindoo stile" is perhaps prompted by a perceptive eye to Islamic influence, for the *ratna* is rather like the *chhatri*, or dome, in the Islamic style, and McCutchion refers to the form as "Indo-Islamic."[6] Clusters of such temples, often within the walled compounds of zamīndārs, were common in Bengal.

---

1 The sacred thread (Bengali, *paitā*; Sk. *yajñopavīta*) is worn only by males of the three "twice-born" classes—brahmin, kṣatriya, and vaiśya—and is invested in the rite of *upanayana*, the second birth, as a boy becomes "a full member of his class and of society." The thread—"a cord of three threads, each of nine twisted strands, made of cotton, hemp or wool, from brāhmaṇs, kṣatriyas and vaiśyas respectively"—is hung over the right shoulder and under the left arm. It is worn throughout life, without removal. Basham, *The Wonder That Was India*, 162-63. In recent centuries, as a matter of practice, the sacred thread has been largely restricted to brahmins, although it has sometimes been appropriated as the "Sanskritized" symbol of claimed higher status by upwardly mobile non-brahmin castes.

2 Risley discusses the origin and social structure of the Oriya brahmins, but offers nothing on their position in Bengal. *The Tribes and Castes of Bengal*, 1:160-61. On the Oriya brahmins, also see J. N. Bhattacharya, 46-50.

3 Deb, *The Early History and Growth of Calcutta*, 49. On Raja Nabakrishna Deb, see Commentary for Pl. II.182.

4 1:73.

5 On the god Jagannātha, see Commentaries for Snān Yātrā, Pl. II.178, and Rath Yātrā, Pl. II.188. On Balasore brahmins, see O'Malley, *Bengal District Gazetteers; Balasore*, 60-62.

6 "The pinnacled or *ratna* design has the same lower structure as the *chālā* series—a rectangular box with curved cornice—but the roof is more or less flat (following the curvature of the cornice) and is surmounted by one or more towers or pinnacles called *ratna* (jewel). The simplest form has a single central tower (*eka-ratna*), to which may be added four or more at the corners. . . . By thus increasing the number of stories and corner turrets, the number of *ratnas* [may] be multiplied. . . up to a maximum of twenty-five." Michell, *Brick Temples of Bengal*, 24. On the *ratna* style, 24-29.

II.18. Hindu Rājā

Pl. II.18. Hindu Rājā. Paris: I.2.2.

Commentary: The rājā depicted is Ishwar Chandra of Nadia (1747-1802), who, like his grandfather, the famous Maharaja Krishna Chandra Roy, and many of the rājās of Nadia before him, was a Sanskrit scholar and patron of poets and religion. He became rājā in 1788 and resided in Krishnagar, then a center of Sanskrit learning, the capital of Nadia and located about 60 miles north of Calcutta on the Hugli river, about half way to Murshidabad.[1] Solvyns, in his discussion of Gangā Yātrā (Pl. II.198) also writes of the raja of Nadia in his near-death experience.

The bel, or bael, tree is the thorny Bengal quince (*Aegle marmelos*), sacred to Śiva. Also known as *sriphala*, its trifoliate leaves—said to represent the Hindu triad of Brahmā, Śiva, and Viṣṇu—are an essential element of Śaivite ritual and are also laid over the *liṅga*, symbolic representation of Śiva, to cool and refresh the deity. The tree, used for medicinal purposes and regarded as auspicious, is frequently planted in front of a house, as here depicted.[2]

The *pothī* (Solvyns's *poltars*) is the traditional unbound book, its pages here composed of palm leaves.

Śāstra has broad meaning, as sacred texts generally, but most frequently the term refers to codified texts of a specialized field of knowledge, such as the Dharmaśāstra (law), Arthaśāstra (politics), or Alamkaraśāstra (poetry). Here the reference is to sacred scripture, though not to a particular text.

The tiger skin upon which the rājā sits has both royal and divine association. Alain Daniélou writes that "the tiger is the vehicle of Śakti, the symbol of the power of Nature. . . . Śiva is beyond the power of Nature. He is its master and carries the skin of the tiger as a trophy."[3]

The rājā wears the ashen marks of the Śaivite on his forehead, arms, and body. The chaplets, or *mālā* (beads), he wears around his neck are *rudrākṣas*.

Paris: I.2.2. RAJAH HINDOO PRINCE AT HIS PRAYERS: The Rajahs are the Hindoo princes, as the *Nabobs* are the Musulman princes of Hindoostan, and their rank is the same. The Rajahs are generally of the Brahmun cast. The Rajah represented in this plate was the Rajah of Kisnagur, a *Cheroutery* [Śrotriya] *Brahmun*, and in high repute for his piety. When he prayed, his right arm and the hand was covered with a sort of glove or hanging sleeve. His head, his arms, and his body were decorated with a great number of chaplets and other ornaments. He consented to have his portrait taken by Mr. Solvyns, and as all the Hindoos attach the greatest importance to the minutest details of their religious dresses, he expressed the strange wish that the drawing of his person in front should offer also to the view the chaplets and ornaments which adorned his back.

He was seated on the skin of a royal tyger, under the shade of a Bel tree, which the Hindoos hold in great veneration. Before him stood a golden tripod, on which were placed some *poltars* [*pothī*] or palm leaves carved with the texts of the sacred books.

The more corpulent the Rajah, the greater consideration he enjoys in his sect; so that few of them are thin, or even of low stature. Their complexion is of a clearer yellow than that of most other Hindoos. They eat greater quantity of gui [ghee, *ghī*], or butter which they melt in milk, and which probably helps to encrease their bulk. Every sort of meat is forbidden for them, as well as for all other Brahmuns. They are very nice about the water which they drink; their scruples on this point go so far as not to allow it to be touched by any person, not even by a stranger Brahmun, even though he were of their own sect. All the casts, without excepting even the Soodders, who are the lowest, are extremely strict in this respect.

The Rajahs are particularly careful of the cleanliness of their persons: consequently they bathe frequently in the day, and before they enter in the bath, never fail to rub themselves with oil of mustard. To this friction they seem to attach something very mysterious, and while it is performing, recite *munters* [*mantras*] or texts of the *Shastah* [*śāstra*] or of some other sacred book.

Rudrākṣa berries are used to make Śaivite rosaries. The berries, their name meaning "Rudra's eye," are said to symbolize either the third eye of Śiva (also known as Rudra) or his tears on contemplating the final destruction of the world. The usual number of beads in the Śaivite *mālā* is 108. When worn, the *mālā* serves as an amulet, offering protection against evil, but its primary function is as a rosary, depicted here in its concealed use by the rājā.[4]

Solvyns writes that the rājā sits in prayer with his ritually-pure right arm and hand "covered with a sort of glove or hanging sleeve," but the print, from the Paris edition, depicts the left arm covered. Solvyns's original drawing, however, portrays the right arm covered, and the print simply reverses the drawing (Pl. I.33).[5] The "sleeve" is a *gomukhā*, a cloth bag (said to resemble a cow's head) that holds a *japamālā*, or rosary, and as the devotee fingers each bead inside the bag, he repeats the name of his deity. As with the concealed hand gestures, *mudrās*, of the Brajbāsī brahmin (Pl. II.16), the use of the rosary is hidden to insure its efficacy.[6]

---

1 On the rājās of Nadia, see, Hunter, *A Statistical Account of Bengal*, 2:142-65; J. H. E. Garrett, 149-63; "The Territorial Aristocracy of Bengal. No. II—The Nadiya' Ra'j," *Calcutta Review*, 109 (1872):85-118.

2 B. A. Gupte, xxxiii; Sankar Sen Gupta, "A Note on Soma and Bel-tree and their Presiding Deities—Chandra and Siva," 105-06.

3 216.

4 Hartsuiker, 90; Ghurya, *Indian Sadhus*, 91-92; Stutley, 254; and Walker, 2:217.

5 The original drawing was included in the album of drawings compiled by Solvyns's widow, discussed in Chapter Three, pp. 83–85. In most instances, because Solvyns prepared the Paris edition from the "reversed" etchings of the Calcutta edition and not from his original drawings, the Paris prints return the perspective to the original. The rājā, however, was not included in the Calcutta edition and the Paris print was etched from the original drawing, with the printed image thus reversed.

6 I am grateful to Frederick M. Smith and T. N. Madan for clarifying the significance of the covered hand. Personal communication. On the use of the *japamālā* and *gomukhā*, see Hartsuiker, 90, 92.

II.19. Rājā in Full Dress

Paris: I.2.3. RAJAH IN FULL DRESS: This Hindoo prince is represented sitting in his palace, and dressed in a long robe called *courti* [*kurtā*] or *jamma* [*jāma*]. This is not a mahometan dress, as the resemblance might lead us to imagine. It was used in Hindoostan before the conquest by Timur, or Tamerlan.

The scene which this *Rajah* occupies is faithfully copied. He sits on a carpet, with a flower in his hand, and near him are placed various preparations of betel leaves and of the finest essence of roses. He offers some of them, as well as the *houka* [*hukā*][1] or pipe, to the persons who are introduced to his presence. Behind the *Rajah* are his servants with *chouris* [*chauṅrī,* whisk] of peacock's feathers, to keep off the flies; but this is a service of more parade than use. Before him rises a small water-spout.

The luxuries of a *Rajah* are his women, his servants, his elephants, camels, and horses.

The prince whom Mr. Solvyns has represented here is the *Rajah* of Tanjor. He found his court composed of the native men of science, male and female dancers, singers, musicians, buffoons, and juglers.

His vast palace consists of several separate pavilions, with different courts or small squares. The beds are in the center of the rooms, surrounded with carpets, and ornamented with small looking glasses or little pictures frequently reversed or hanging crossways. The doors and windows are very small. The *Rajahs* prefer inhabiting the most elevated appartments and on the terraces which cover their palaces.

Pl. II.19. Rājā in Full Dress. Paris: I.2.3.

Commentary: This print is an anomaly for any number of reasons. First, it purports to be of the Rājā of Tanjore at his palace, yet there is no evidence that Solvyns ever visited Tanjore. The print is not included in the Calcutta edition, and, conceivably, Solvyns could have sailed from Calcutta in 1804, with a stop at Madras, affording him an opportunity to go down to Tanjore. This seems most unlikely, and Solvyns makes no reference to any such visit. The subject portrayed does not appear to be the Rājā of Tanjore at all, but rather a rājā of Bengal, suggested by style of dress and the presence of a sepoy in the background wearing the distinctive "sundial" hat of the Bengal Army.

Although Solvyns repeatedly emphasizes that he took his subjects from life and that his textual descriptions are from his personal observation, the prince is almost surely copied from an Indian painting. Solvyns's rājā bears close resemblance to a Company School portrait of a Bengali Muslim notable, c. 1785-1790, by a Murshidabad artist in the India Office Library collection.[2] The figure is seated on a small carpet and rests against a bolster. He sits in the same position as Solvyns's rājā and similarly holds a flower in his hand. The turban and costume are almost identical, and there is even likeness in the bearded profile of the two faces. The Company School painting depicts the notable alone, while Solvyns surrounds his rājā with various attendants.

It is unlikely that Solvyns copied this very portrait, but the picture represents the conventional form in Indian painting that would have been familiar to Solvyns through the many Murshidabad artists resident in Calcutta. The similarity of the two pictures indicates that here Solvyns did not portray his subject from life, but copied a painting, and the fashion situates it in the Muslim courts of Bengal.

In the description of the rājā's clothing, Solvyns mistakenly takes the *kurtā* and *jāma* as the same. The *kurtā* is a long shirt, while the *jāma,* or surcoat, is "a full-length cotton gown comprising a voluminous skirt gathered onto a fitted, side-fastening, cross-over bodice with narrow elongated sleeves." The accompanying sash is called a *paṭkā*.[3]

The object to the fore right appears to be a whisk of yak hair held upright in a stand.

1 Solvyns depicts various forms of *hukā*, Pls. II.203-210.
2 Mildred Archer, *Company Drawings in the India Office Library*, Pl. 19.
3 Catalog description, item 125, by Jayne Shrimpton in Bayly, *The Raj,* 110. On Solvyns's portrayals, see Pl. II.86 for a description of both the *kurtā* and *jāma.*

II.20. Kṣatriya

Pl. II.20. Kṣatriya. Paris: I.2.4.
Calcutta: Sec. I, No. 6. The K'huttry [kṣatriya]:—in eminence next to the Brahmun. At present they dress generally, as presented in the plate, like Mahometans.—By the Mogul Government they were employed in preference to the other Casts of Hindoos, and still they are connected with them more than with the sects of their own Religion—they are not so numerous in Bengal as in the Northern parts of Hindostan.—According to the precepts of their Religion, Princes, or Rajahs, Landlords, and Soldiers, should be of this Cast.
Orme: 2.

Paris: I.2.4. K'HUTTERY LANDHOLDER: The *K'hutterys* are the second of the four casts in which all the Hindoos are comprehended. This is the warriour cast, and is remarked for courage. Those who serve in the armies obey only the orders which are issued by their own cast.

They are less superstitious than the other Hindoos, and are in habits of greater familiarity with the Mahometans; which displeases to the other casts.

Many of the *K'hutterys* are robust and well made; the women of this cast, which is the least numerous of any, especially in Bengal, are handsome and of a strong form. In general a short residence in India is sufficient to be able to seize at first sight the distinguishing character of the individuals of each cast, and even of its subdivisions; and this holds good especially with respect to the *K'hutterys*.

Those who live in villages hold bazars or markets before their houses, out of which they raise considerable revenues. There are also frequently near their dwellings public temples or pagods in which festivals are celebrated. The *tannahs* [*thānā*] police or guard houses, are also in their neighbourhood, as are the kudgeries [*kacharī*], where the public revenues are received, and such causes heard as are not of sufficient importance to be carried before the chief council, or the high tribunals of the capital.

The *K'huttery* whom this plate represents is seated on a chair, and with the exception of the *packy* [*pāg*, *pāgaṛī*][1] or turban, is dressed nearly in the manner of a Rajah. In his ears, according to the general practice of Hindoos of his cast, he wears large rings with a big pearl or precious stone in the middle. They have also circles of gold or silver round their arms and legs.

In the foreground are columns, and in the distance other buildings of hindoo architecture.

Commentary: The kṣatriyas constituted the traditional ruling class in the Hindu hierarchy, and as "protectors," they both governed and served as warriors. In North India, they were substantial landowners, zamīndārs,[2] but they are not indigenous to Bengal and, as Solvyns rightly notes, are comparatively few in number.

Solvyns's "kuderie," also "kedgeree," is more typically rendered as "cutcherry" by the British in India. Derived from the Hindi, *kacharī* for hall or chamber of audience, the word in Bengal was applied to the office of a zamīndār, or landlord, as depicted here; to a caste tribunal; and, in British Indian usage, to an office of a revenue magistrate or to a court of justice.

Solvyns portrays the kṣatriya in his series of "Heads" (Pl. II.296), and describes physiognomical attributes.

1 The most common Indian word for a turban, made up of yards of material wound round the head. See Crill, 10-19.

2 In Bengal, the Hindustani-Persian term *zamīndār*—*jamidār* in Bengali—applied to a variety of people with rights to land and its revenue. Marshall, *Bengal: The British Bridgehead*, 53-54. Zamīndārs were formerly collectors of revenue from lands held by a number of cultivators, but in the "Permanent Settlement" of 1793, the British gave them effective ownership of the land.

II.21. Vaiśya

Pl. II.21. Vaiśya. Paris: I.2.5.

Calcutta: Sec. I, No. 7. A Byce, represented as a Merchant—The Byce [vaiśya] is the third Cast, and they are ordered by their sacred Books to be employed in merchandize and husbandry.

Paris: I.2.5. BYCE MERCHANT: The *Byces* form the third primitive cast. They are in general looked upon in a good right throughout Hindoostan; and being for the most part rich, are sumptuously cloathed and have a numerous attendance.

Seated with a careless air on a mat or carpet, constantly smoking the *houka* [*hukā*],[1] or chewing betel, and waving a fan not unlike a vane moving on its pivot, the Byce waits for his customers. When they appear he unfolds his merchandise; and what is bought is always paid for in ready money. I shall have elsewhere occasion to speak of the species used in these sales.

The number of *Byces* in the lower countries of the Ganges, as well as in Bengal is inconsiderable, as the strict observance of their religious practises precludes the facility of travelling. Nevertheless those of Bengal who are in habits of dealing with the Europeans have amassed large fortunes. They are a sort of traders by commission. They send their sircars [*sarkār*, Pl. II.100] or brokers to buy or bespeak the cotton stuffs or other produce of industry, which are afterwards, either forwarded to their warehouses, or loaded on boats to be shipped on board the trading vessels.

The *Byces* have other agents who travel into distant countries in search of shawls, Persian stuffs, silks and other articles of value.

These travelling clerks are for the most part born in the south of Hindoostan. There are among them many *Pharsies* [Parsis], especially at Bombay, as well as Armenians and Greeks.

Commentary: The vaiśyas, ranking third in the Hindu hierarchy, are the merchant class. There are no true Bengali vaiśyas, as the Bengali traders and bankers are primarily of the śūdra baṇik (baniā) castes (Pls. II.38 and II.41) and from such castes as the Tā̃tis (Pl. II.33), weavers, and Tilis (Pl. II.42), originally oil-pressers by profession.[2] Vaiśyas, such as the various Marwari castes, began to migrate from Rajasthan into Bengal in the early eighteenth century, most notably the family of Jagat Seth, bankers to the nawabs of Bengal. From a few families in Calcutta, their numbers and wealth increased over the course of the nineteenth century, assuming enormous power over the commerce and industry of the city, seen, for example, in the House of Birla.[3]

The fan held by one of the figures sitting in the background is likely made of palm leaf, bamboo, or *khas* (*khaskhas*) root, noted for its cooling fragrance when wet.[4]

Solvyns, in his series of "Heads" (Pl. II.297), discusses what he deems to be the "cunning" character of the vaiśyas, as reflected in their physiognomy.

1 Solvyns depicts various forms of *hukā*, Pls. II. 203-210.

2 See N. K. Dutt, 2:100, 127.

3 See Timberg.

4 T. N. Mukharji, 313, and *Hobson-Jobson*, 283-84.

II.22. Śūdra

Pl. II.22. Śūdra. Paris: I.2.6.

Calcutta: Sec. I, No. 8. A Soodder [śūdra], the fourth and last cast of the Hindoos—prescribed by their religion to serve the other Classes and to be engaged in handicraft and menial Offices—The print represents him as a servant to a priest.

Paris: I.2.6. SOODDER SERVANT: This is the lowest of the primitive casts, and the only one which furnishes workmen and servants.

The Soodder represented in this plate is the servant of a Brahman or rich Hindoo. He is carrying water in a vase called *garrah* [*ghaṛā*].[1]

A Soodder who behaves well, and practises exactly the religious rites of his cast, is pretty sure to conciliate the esteem of the other Hindoos with whom he has to do. There are even in this cast women of excellent characters, who seldom appear in public, and allow themselves fewer liberties than women of the highest casts. But unfortunately this does not always save the Soodder from being treated with a sort of contempt by the Hindoos of the three other casts; and those who exercise employments which are reputed base, such as swine-herds, grave-diggers, nightmen, oppose in vain their good conduct to the detestation and abhorrence of the other Hindoos.

These different inferiour professions will be described in their proper places; for, after the four original casts which comprehend all the natives of Hindoostan, there are subdivisions which are degradations of the small number of primitive casts which have been described.

It may not perhaps be superfluous to observe here that the Soodders ought not to be confounded with the *Parriahs* [pariah], as is generally the case. The term *Parriah* is a denomination which denotes in general every thing which is worst. A bad priest, who neglect his religious duties, is a *Parriah Brahmun*, as a bad house is a *Parriah gor* [*ghar*], a bad shoe *Parriah dutie* [*juti, jutā*], etc. There are *Parriahs* therefore in every cast, but there is no particular cast of *Parriahs*.

Commentary: Śūdras are the lowest class of the four *varṇas* of Hindu society—those who, by the laws of Manu, are to serve the three higher "twice-born" classes. The vast majority of Bengali Hindus are śūdra, identified by their various occupational castes or subcastes (*jāti*), many of which Solvyns depicts. Ranked in degrees of purity and pollution, the śūdra castes of Bengal include those, such as the Kāyastha (Pl. II.26) and Vaidya (Pl. II.25), that are ritually pure and of social status virtually equivalent to the brahmin. There are also the śūdra trading and banking castes, like the baṇik, with families of great wealth. Among the higher caste and wealthier śūdras who have brahminized their ritual life, some wear the sacred thread of the "twice-born." The larger number of śūdras are in the artisan and agricultural castes, and at a lower level are those śūdra castes that are degraded by their traditional occupations but distinguished from the ritually polluted castes below them in the social hierarchy, those groups identified in the Dharmaśāstras as *caṇḍāla*—"wild," outside the four *varṇas* classes and the lowest of all caste categories.[2]

Solvyns includes among the śūdras those castes "such as the swine-herds, grave-diggers, nightmen" that are usually classified as *caṇḍāla* or "untouchable" (a term introduced in the early twentieth century) and are regarded by "clean" Hindus as outside the pale of *varṇa*. These "outcastes" were widely termed "pariahs"—a usage Solvyns disputes. The word "pariah" is a corruption of *Paraiyan*, the name of a specific South Indian untouchable caste, but from the early sixteenth century in India, Europeans extended it mistakenly to refer to "untouchable" castes more generally and, with time, the word entered English and French to mean any social outcast.[3]

Solvyns is correct in identifying its usage among Europeans in India to include reference to the worst of almost anything—thus "pariah dog" (Pl. II.282) for an ownerless cur and "pariah arrack" for the poisonous native spirit sold to European soldiers and sailors.[4] But Solvyns is clearly wrong in saying "there is no particular caste of *Parriahs*" (although he would have been unlikely to encounter Paraiyans in Calcutta), and his statement that there are pariahs "in every cast" is at odds with the general use of the term to refer to the "unclean" castes below the śūdras later known as untouchables or, by government classification, as scheduled castes—those Mohandas Gandhi embraced as "Harijans," children of god, and who today prefer to be known as "dalits," the oppressed.

In his physiognomical series of "Heads," Solvyns portrays the śūdra (Pl. II.298). Although recognizing variation in character among the many śūdra castes, he concludes that "the general characteristic traits of the *Soodders* physionomy [sic] are application, meanness and stupid resignation."

1 See Pl. II.23, fn. 1.
2 On the position of the śūdras of Bengal and of the distinctions among them, see, among others, Risley, *The Tribes and Castes of Bengal*, Jogendra Nath Bhattacharya, and Asok Mitra, *The Tribes and Castes of West Bengal.*
3 *Hobson-Jobson,* 678-80.
4 Ibid., 681.

II.23. Daibik. Astrologer

Paris: I.3.2. DYBUCK, ASTRONOMER: According to Menu [Manu], the divine legislator of the Hindoos, the first Astronomers sprung from the rib of their father, of the Rajpoot [Rājput] cast, and from that of their mother, of the cast of Byces [vaiśya].

There are two sorts of Dybucks.

The one sedentary, who apply themselves to the observation of the stars and the phenomenons of the heavens, and are generally respected. Many of these have acquired a considerable share of knowledge, and calculate eclipses with exactness. Their prognostics of the change of weather and the variations of the atmosphere are received with great confidence. They pretend also to some insight into futurity, and the people have a blind faith in their knowledge in this respect.

The others travel over the country, particularly through the villages, to tell fortunes. They foretell future events by inspection of the hand and other parts of the body, and pretend to tell what has happened in the course of the life of whoever consults them. The greater part of these, being Brahmuns, find under that title an easy access to the interior of the houses. But they are no better than mountebancks, and many of them, by their dissolute behaviour, draw upon themselves the reproachful appellation of *Parriahs*.

He who is the subject of the plate is sitting before his house, calculating an eclipse. Before him are his tablets, and in his hand the chalk with which he writes on a blackened board. He was often consulted by the learned, even from Europe, and expressed himself with great accuracy and precision.

The Dybucks have a particular mode of calculation. See on this subject, and on their astronomical discoveries, the Memoirs of the Asiatic Society of Calcutta.

Pl. II.23. Daibik. Paris: I.3.2.

Calcutta: Sec. I, No. 13. Dybuck—An Astronomer and Astrologer, calculating an Eclipse,—he is the offspring of a Rajpoot father, and Byce mother.

Orme: 3.

Commentary: The Bengali word for astrologer, *daibik* (or *daibajña*)—transliterated by Solvyns as Dybuck—means "one who knows fate." Respected astrologers would be familiar with the position and movement of the planets, and their knowledge of astronomy was often profound. In the late eighteenth century, Europeans such as Le Gentil,[1] Bailly,[2] Playfair,[3] Craufurd,[4] and Bentley[5] provided detailed accounts of Hindu astronomy, and Solvyns refers to the article by Samuel Davis (1760-1819), "On the Astronomical Computations of the Hindus," in *Asiatick Researches*.[6]

The figure Solvyns depicts sits before his calculations holding a palm leaf book. In his note to the original drawing, Solvyns writes that "he is also a Calculator of future Events, and pretends to foretell lucky and unlucky days."

Jogendra Nath Bhattacharya, president of the Brahmin Sabha of Bengal in the late nineteenth century, wrote that "the astrologer castes of Bengal [in all probability] were Brahmans at one time, but have been degraded to a very low position. . . ."[7]

---

1 Guillaume Joseph H. J. P. Le Gentil de la Galasière (1725-1792). Member of the French Academy, astronomer and traveler, he chronicled his voyage, 1761-1769, to India.

2 Jean Sylvain Bailly (1736-1793), French astronomer and politician.

3 John Playfair (1748-1819) was a professor of mathematics at the University of Edinburgh.

4 Quintin Crawfurd (1742-1819) wrote on "Astronomy of the Brahmans," in *Sketches Chiefly Relating to the History, Religion, Learning, and Manners of the Hindoos*, 1:284-361.

5 John Bentley (d.1824), in *Asiatic Researches,* wrote on the *Sūrya Siddhānta*, an early Sanskrit work of astronomy that was subject to considerable controversy among Orientalists of the late eighteenth century. See Kejariwal, 87-89. For an overview of early European writings on Hindu astronomy, see "The Astronomy of the Hindus," *Calcutta Review* 1 (1844): 257-90.

6 2:175-226.

7 137.

II.24. Bhāt. Genealogist

Pl. II.24. Bhāt. Paris: I.3.3.

Calcutta: Sec. I, No. 40. B'haut a most extraordinary Tribe; whose profession it is to flatter and puff, and spread reports in commendation of those who employ them.

Orme: 7.

Paris: I..3.3. B'HAUT PUFFER, FLATTERER: The B'hauts, though of the Brahmun cast, are nevertheless looked upon as *Soodders* [śūdras], from the nature of their employment, which is somewhat domestic.

Their business is to give as much publicity as possible to every honorable or flattering circumstance which they know of their employers, and frequently to whatever their imagination can suggest in this way; for they do not pique themselves upon truth. They are distinguished by the abundance and extreme volubility of their language, and it is not uncommon to hear several of them rising with one another in exaggerations and fibs.

They frequent the houses of their master's acquaintance, where they sound his praises; and there are Hindoos who keep numbers of them in pay, and send them even to a great distance to promulgate, true or false, whatever may tend to encrease their honor or reputation. They run before the carriages and palanquins, publishing to the sound of the *caunsy* [kā̃śi, Pl. II.172] (a plate of brass which they beat pretty forceably) the name and qualities of their masters. It is a part of their functions also to wait at the entrance of the rich Hindoos's houses. Their pay is very considerable.

This practise is now wearing off. The Musulmans are those who employ them most, and they are to be found in greater number in the north than in the south of Hindoostan.

They are dressed like the Hindoos in general; but while they are sounding forth their flatteries; they cover their head with a cloth, as is represented in this plate, as if this adjustment added to their assurance.

Commentary: Even into the nineteenth century, rich Bengalis employed people to act as sycophants. Bhāts, of the caste of genealogists and family bards, were singers of praise of great men. Of disputed origin, as are most Indian castes, they claim descent from the brahmin eulogists of epic times. But those Bhāts so employed by Solvyns's time had fallen from the honor of their ancient profession. They had become notorious as "rapacious and conceited mendicants." During the marriage season in Bengal, Bhāts would be engaged by families to sing of their worth and renown. But, Risley quotes Dr. James Wise, the esteemed civil surgeon and ethnologist at Dhaka, that "They are met with everywhere when Hindu families celebrate a festival or domestic event, appearing on such occasions uninvited, and exacting by their noisy importunity a share of the food and charity that is being doled to the poor. . . . During Durga Puja they force their way into respectable homes and make such a horrid uproar by shouting and singing that the inmates gladly pay something to be rid of them."[1]

Bhāts were famed for their capacity to make poetry on the spur of the occasion, and on days of special importance, they would provide "in pompous language" the genealogical history of the family that had summoned them. But Bhāts were also "much dreaded by their employers on account of the power they have of distorting family history at public recitations, if they chose to do so, and of subjecting any member to general ridicule."[2]

Shoberl, in his account of Hindostan in *The World in Miniature*, writes that "there is among the Hindoos a particular class of public vocal performers, called Bhauts, who are most numerous in the province of Guzerat [Gujarat], and who, like the European minstrels and troubadours in the ages of chivalry, go about singing selections from the mythological legends of the Hindoos, or verses of their own composition, either to praise some renowned warrier, to commemorate a victory, to record a tragical event, or to panegyrise a present object."[3] It would seem that in Bengal, for Solvyns, their role was principally as the praise-singer of contemporary mortals.

In his note to the original drawing, Solvyns adds that Bhāts "also carry cards of Invitation, and attend as Durwans or porters" (Pl. II.105), but only those fallen on very hard times would likely take such a position.

---

1 Risley, *The Tribes and Castes of Bengal*, 1:102; 98-103 on the Bhāt caste. Also see R. V. Russell, 2:251-70.

2 Sherring, 1:271-72.

3 Shoberl, 3:34.

II.25. Vaidya. Physician

Commentary: The Vaidya caste, traditionally Ayurvedic physicians and comparatively small in numbers, is the highest ranked of the Bengali śūdras. Respected for their erudition in Sanskrit, Vaidyas (also known as Ambaṣṭhas) were the only non-brahmins admitted into the Sanskrit grammar schools of Bengal, although, not being brahmins, they were not permitted to study the Vedas and *Smṛiti* religious texts. Solvyns describes them solely as physicians, but they were also prestigious landowners, and in the nineteenth century, responding to new opportunities through Western education, they assumed prominence as lawyers, teachers, and managers. Family names among the Vaidyas include the familiar Gupta, Das Gupta, and Sen Gupta.[4]

The funerary post—*bṛṣo kāth*—is erected in the performance of the *śrāddha*, the ceremony, held several days after the cremation, that releases the soul of the deceased. Joguth Chunder Gangooly writes that "The invitations, through letters and by messengers, draw immense crowds of relatives, friends, priests, monks, and beggars. In an open spacious place . . . an earthen alter is erected, and *brisho kastō*, or funeral post, is placed near it. This post is carved out of a piece of wood, either *bale*, *nim*, or *jug-go doomur*, a kind of fig-tree. The priest marries a calf and a young bull before it, while it serves as a pole to which cords are fastened for the purpose of binding the queer bridegroom. . . . Three days after this ceremony, they all anoint themselves with yellow powder and oil, and for a long procession of singers, priests and relations,

Pl. II.25. Vaidya. Paris: I.3.4.

Calcutta: Sec. I, No. 11. A Byde [Vaidya]—or Physician sprung from a Brahmun on a Woman of the Byce Class. The Hindoos possess a system of Medicine transmitted by their sacred Books; consistent with their religion, they cannot acquire any knowledge of anatomy by dissection. The wooden carved device, called a Bursah-Caut [*bṛṣo kāth*], is erected in commemoration of the dead.

Paris: I.3.4. BYDE, PHYSICIAN: Menu gives the descent of Physicians from a Brahmun and a woman of the cast of Byces [vaiśya] or Merchants. Their age in general gains them the credit of experience, which ensures to them great respect. They pursue a system of medicine traced out in the sacred writings, and from which they are not allowed to depart. As they are deprived too of instruction by the inspection of dead bodies, they are totally deficient in anatomical knowledge.

Simples,[1] into the properties of which their experience gives them a tolerable insight, form the basis of the few medicines which they employ. When a physician visits his patient, he carries with him a box which contains his drugs, which he administers as he sees occasion, and generally gives them in the *paun* [*pān*][2] or betel leaves, which the Hindoos are in the habit of chewing. But he seldom fails to begin by prescribing the *congie*,[3] a beverage made with rice water.

As the Hindoos are under little apprehensions of death, and as soon as they are sick get themselves carried to the banks of a river, not to contaminate the whole family by dying in the house, they seldom have recourse to the assistance of a Physician.

The carved wood seen in the plate, and which is called *bursah-caut* is placed in commemoration of the dead before the houses, in the bazars or markets, on the high roads, near the pagods, or on the stairs which lead to the river, where the greater number of them are to be seen, because there the Hindoos prefer to terminate their career.

carry the funeral post on their shoulders, and stick it into the ground by the side of the river."[5] R. P. Gupta states that traditionally after the ceremony, the *bṛṣo kāth* is immersed in the Ganga or whatever river may be near.[6]

The Serampore missionary William Ward (1769-1823) described the *"Vrishu"* (*bṛṣo*) post: "Vrishu is the name for a bull. A rough image of one of these animals is carved in the middle of the post, which is afterwards set up at a public road till it rots or falls down. It is often full of rough carved figures."[7] The posts are typically six to seven feet tall, four-sided, tapering upwards, with several carved sections. In the lower half is the standing figure of the deceased, carved in the round. In the post depicted here by Solvyns and again in his view of Calcutta (Pl. II.3), a carved elephant is immediately above the figure and, above that, the bull, *vrsa* (*bṛṣo*), the vehicle of the god Śiva, from which the funeral post takes its name. This is then topped by a *cuṛā-mandir,* or temple.[8]

The posts are carved by the Kāmārs, or Karmakāras (Pl. II.35), and painted by Paṭuās (Chitrakāras) (Pl. II.67).

The hut portrayed in this and other Solvyns etchings is of a traditional Bengali form that reflects architectural style in eastern India that art historian Michael Meister traces to the Vedic period. In expression of both local identity and continuity, the form is imitated in mosques of the Sultanate period and in the brick temples built by Hindu landlords in the sixteenth and seventeenth centuries.[9]

---

1 Medicinal plants.
2 See Pl. II.212.
3 Anglo-Indian *congee*, from the Tamil *kañjī*, is the water in which rice has been boiled. It is used as a diet for the sick and also, by washermen, as a starch.
4 On Vaidyas, see, Risley, *The Tribes and Castes of Bengal*, 1:46-50; J. N. Bhattacharya, 126-36; N. K. Dutt, 65-81; and Wise, 199-207.
5 59-60. Gangooly converted to Christianity and came to the United States at the invitation of the Unitarians. He notes, 61, that the museum in Salem, Massachusetts—now the Peabody Essex Museum—had a *bṛṣo kāth*, and, indeed, it may be seen there today.
6 Letter to the author, April 29, 1993.
7 *A View of the History, Literature, and Mythology, of the Hindoos*, 3:357. Ajitcoomar Mookerjee, in *The Folk Art of Bengal*, 14-15, writes that "The installation of *Brisa-Kat* (Bull-posts) in memory of dead persons" are usually placed at the junction of three roads.
8 Perhaps more typical for the form above the lower figure is the carved image of Mahādeva (Śiva, as Great God) with his vehicle, the bull, and sometimes with a *liṅga*, phallic representation of procreative power. Above these figures, Rādhā and Kṛṣṇa may be depicted, topped by the *mandir*, with a *chakra*, or wheel, at the pinnacle. S. K. Ray, 330. Mookerjee, in *The Folk Art of Bengal*, includes three plates (figures 19-21) depicting the *bṛṣo kāth*, including one erected for a woman. The carved figure, standing nearly two-thirds the height of the post, is topped by a bull, *liṇga*, and temple.
9 Preface to his translation of Louis Renou's "The Vedic House." Illustrating the article, Meister reproduces several of Solvyns's etchings portraying the hut.

II.26. Kāyastha. Writer

Paris: I.3.5. CAUSTRO, WRITER: This cast is not numerous in Bengal. He who is drawn here wrote in one of the public offices, and was perhaps the only one in the town of Calcutta. But many of those who are employed as writers, either by government or by European or Armenian merchants, maintain that they are of this cast; which is a proof at least that it is in some repute. The number of Caustos is greater in the interior of the country, and especially in the north of Hindoostan.

They are assiduous but slow at their work. They write very well, even the languages of the foreign nations who trade in India, and are frequently employed as *sircars* [*sarkār*, Pl. II.100], store-keepers and house-stewards, as *cherofs* [*shroff*],[1] or bankers, and in all commercial relations.

They are humble with their masters, but insolent to their inferiors. Their countenance is in general interesting. Their dress is the *courti* [*kurtā*] or *jamma* [*jāma*].

Nothing is to be met with in any of the sacred books relating to this cast. The legislator Menu himself is silent in respect to them.

Pl. II.26. Kāyastha. Paris: I.3.5.

Calcutta: Sec. I, No. 12. A Causto—properly of the writer Cast—represented in his occupation in the service of an European.

Commentary: Ranked among śūdras in Bengal second only to the Vaidya, the Kāyasthas—the caste of writers, accountants, and clerks—are, in fact, numerous, and, in Solvyns's time, there were many in Calcutta with considerable influence. Dutt, in *Castes in Bengal*, proclaims that "Bengal is pre-eminently the land of Kayasthas."[2] James Wise writes that "The Kayath caste is the most intellectual, and the best educated in Bengal," and he describes them as having dominated financial and revenue offices under the Mughals. "Since the English occupation, [they have] almost secured the whole of the subordinate Government offices."[3]

Bhattacharya, in *Hindu Castes and Sects*, confirms this account: "The Kāyasthas have, from a very remote period of antiquity, been regarded as the class whose proper avocation is to serve as clerks and accountants. Brahmans excluded them from the study of the Sanskrit language and literature. But they learned the three R's with great care, and during the period of Moslem rule, mastered the Persian language with such assiduity as to make it almost their mother-tongue. . . . During the time of the Hindu kings, the Brahmans refrained from entering the public service, and the Kāyasthas had almost the monopoly of the subordinate appointments. Even under the Mohamedan kings, some of them attained very high positions. . . . Under British rule the Kāyastha element has been predominating in all the departments of public service."[4]

Europeans sometimes viewed clerks with considerable disdain, as in this description of a Bengali "quill driver": "though they profess to understand English and are tolerably correct in copying what is put before them, they do not understand the meaning of anything they write; a great convenience this to such as conduct affairs that require secrecy, since the persons employed cannot, if they are so disposed, betray their trust."[5]

Calcutta historian Pradip Sinha gives particular prominence to Kāyasthas in his list of the wealthy families of Calcutta in the late eighteenth century and writes that the leadership of society had passed into their hands. Various Kāyastha families—Mitra, Datta, Ghosh, and others—contended for influence, and out of this "severe contest . . . emerged Raja Nabakrishna[6] as the leading figure of the metropolitan community."[7]

Solvyns is correct that early sacred texts, including Manu, make no mention of the Kāyasthas, but there are "heated controversies" about the origin and status of the caste.[8]

---

1 The Anglo-Indian *shroff* is a corruption of the Arabic *ṣarrāf*, money-lender or money-changer.
2 58.
3 Wise, 309. See pp. 309-18 for discussion of Kāyasthas. Also see Risley, *The Tribes and Castes of Bengal*, 1:438-443, and Sherring, 1:305-13.
4 139-40. For the entry on Kāyastha, see pp. 139-48.
5 Quoted in Long, *Calcutta in the Olden Time: Its Localities & Its People*, 132.
6 On Raja Nabakrishna Deb, see Pl. II.182. For his role as a patron of Durgā Pūjā and the nautch, see Pls. II.194 and II.195.
7 Pradip Sinha, "Social Change," 392.
8 Kane, Vol. 2, Pt. 1: 75-77. Also see Risley, *The Tribes and Castes of Bengal*, 1:438, and Asok Mitra, *The Tribes and Castes of West Bengal*, 27-28.

II.27. Jugi. Weaver

Commentary: The Jugi (or Jugī) caste of weavers occupied a traditional status considerably below the Tā̃ti (Pl. II.33), the superior śūdra weaver caste of Bengal, but, anomalously (and at odds with his earlier ranking in the Calcutta collection), Solvyns gives Jugis a higher position in the order of the Paris etchings.

Bhattacharya writes that their origins are probably as descendants of Yogī (Jogi) mendicants who were once numerous across northern India. "The name of the caste, their usual surname of Nath, their practice of burying their dead, and the profession of lace and apron string selling" connect them with the ancient Jogis, who engaged in such practices.[1]

Solvyns makes no reference to their inferior status among śūdra castes, but Wise writes that the Jugis are "everywhere reviled by Hindus." Wise found, however, that the only grounds "offered by natives for abusing and ill-treating Jogis" was their use of inferior starch in weaving and the burial of their dead.[2] In the Hindu world of the pure and impure, starch made from boiled rice (*māṛ*), used by the Jugi, is deemed inferior to starch from parched rice (*khoi*), used by the Tā̃ti. Moreover, the Jugis differed from the Tā̃ti in using a more cumbersome loom, a distinct shuttle, and Jugis wove coarse material.[3]

Pl. II.27. Jugi. Paris: I.3.6.

Calcutta: Sec. I, No. 42. Joogee, properly a seller of Cloth, but now often engaged as a weaver.

Paris: I.3.6. JOOGEE, CLOTH MERCHANT, WEAVER: The Joogees, who were originally only sellers of the cloth which they brought into the bazars, undertook to manufacture them, and became weavers. They take commissions also for furnishing certain quantities of muslins and other cotton stuffs at stated times; they get them wove and never fail to deliver them according to their engagement.

The Hindoos of this cast are seldom met with but in the country; they are more numerous in Orissah than elsewhere. The women are industrious and very laborious. They spin the cotton for those fine muslins so much esteemed in Europe, of which the thread is so fine that to prevent its breaking it must be kept carefully moistened all the time they are working it.

The women of the Joogees are distinguished by a striking particularity. Instead of burning themselves along with the corpse of their husbands, as other widows do, they bury themselves alive with his dead body. This dismal ceremony will be hereafter described.

The Joogees are extremely clean in the inside of their houses, but their cleanliness is produced by means which may be allowed to call extraordinary. It is by rubbing and washing their apartments every morning with the dung and urine of cows.

Their merchandise is kept in large wooden boxes placed on four rollers, so as to be easily moved: a wise precaution in a country where the habitations being constructed with bamboo, and covered with straw, are liable to be frequently destroyed by fire.

During Solvyns's time in India, the Jugis were almost all weavers, but during the nineteenth century, the cloth they manufactured was displaced by English piece-goods, and the Jugis moved into agriculture and other occupations.

Solvyns is amazed by the "extraordinary" means of Jugi cleanliness, but for the Hindu, the cow is holy and both its dung and urine are pure and purifying. Indians daub the floors and hearth of their thatched or mud houses "with freshly-mixed cow-dung and earth to purify them and keep them clean."[4]

It was the practice of burial,[5] however, that distinguished the Jugi from orthodox Hindu castes, although it is not defiling as such. Burial is found among a few other castes, notably in South India, and among sādhus, holy men, such as the yogī mendicants to whom the Jugis link themselves in following the custom.[6] Solvyns in *Shoho-Gomon* (Pl. II.202) depicts a Jugi widow buried alive with her deceased husband.

1 J. N. Bhattacharya, 190. On Jugi origin and character, see Risley, *The Tribes and Castes of Bengal*, 1:355-60. On the yogī mendicants, see Briggs.

2 Wise, 290-91. Entry for Jogi, pp. 290-95.

3 Hossain, 47-48.

4 Walker, 1:257.

5 Risley, *The Tribes and Castes of Bengal*, describes Jugi burial practice, 1:359.

6 Briggs describes Yogi burial, 39-43. For a discussion of Jugi burial, see the Commentary on Solvyns's depiction of suttee burial, Pl. II.202.

II.28. Āhir. Milkman

Pl. II.28. Āhir. Paris: I.4.2.
Calcutta: Sec. I, No. 20. Auhheer or Seller of Milk, Curds, and Whey.
Orme: 4.

Paris: I.4.2. AUHHEER or NAUHYR. MILKSELLER, MILKMAN: Although the Milkmen are of the cast of Gwallahs (Cow-herds) [Goālā, Pl. II.47], they must not be confounded with them. These last feed the cows, and the others buy up the milk to retail it in the markets.

They are remarkable for their agility and dexterity, and are to be seen at break of day in numerous troops, walking one after another, and carrying each two large vases of very thin earthen ware, full of milk, hanging as it were to the beam of a scale balanced on one of their shoulders. They carry a stick, walk very fast, sometimes run, and change their load from one shoulder to another without ever stopping.

The Nauhyrs are distinguished by their wild look and yellow turban. They seldom intermarry with any other casts but those of the Cow-herds, Ploughmen, Gardeners, Treshers of rice, and such like inhabitants of the country, among whom the characteristic virtues of the Hindoos, mildness and simplicity, have been best preserved. They follow the same rites as the Oriah cast,[1] adore the divinity under the form of *Jaggernaut* [Jagannātha][2] and have some feasts and ceremonies peculiar to themselves.

Milk is consumed in great quantities. They drink it fresh, take it with sugar, use it in pastry; but it is employed chiefly in making *ghi* [*ghī*] a sort of melted butter which never corrupts, and is in general use among the Hindoos, who look upon it as very conducive to corpulence.

Commentary: The Āhir, or Ābhīra, is a pastoral caste, with origins in Bihar. (Solvyns's term "Nauhyr" is almost assuredly his mistranscription of Āhir.) Āhirs enjoy a comparatively high social position as śūdras from whose hands a brahmin will take water.[3] As sellers of milk, they claim superiority over the Goālā cowherds, but Wise notes that they "are degraded by making butter, curds, or clotted milk."[4]

In the print, the Āhir is depicted with a *bahangī*, the shoulder-yoke for carrying loads. The pole is typically made of stout yet pliant bamboo. The Anglo-Indian term was *bangy* or *banghy*, and those who bore loads by this means were called bangy-wallahs or bangy-bearers.[5]

The text for the plate in Orme's pirated edition of Solvyns states that "The milk is coagulated by vegetable acids, and generally boiled previous to that process, hence the curds, whey, and buttermilk differ much, both in taste and consistency, from the same articles in Europe. The natives are very fond of them, particularly the later, imagining that they are cooling as well as nutritious."

---

1 Reference to the Goālā, who were originally from Orissa.
2 See Pl. II.187, Snān Yātrā, and Pl. II.188, Rath Yātrā.
3 For entries on Āhir, see Crooke, *Tribes and Castes of North Western India*, 1:49-66; Elliot, *Memoirs on the History, Folk-lore, and Distribution of the Races of the North Western Provinces of India*, 1:2-6; R. V. Russell, 2:18-38. A photograph of an Āhir appears in Watson and Kaye, Vol. I, No. 13.
4 Wise, 196-97.
5 *Hobson-Jobson*, 60; Blechynden, 171; Colesworthy Grant, *Rural Life in Bengal*, 109.

II.29. Cāṣādhobā. Agriculturalist

Paris: I.4.3. CHASSA-DOBAS. RICE-THRESHERS: The business of the Rice-Thresher is no more than to lead the oxen round a bambou or post to which they are yoked, to separate the grain by treading under their feet a certain number of sheafs.

This process is known in Europe. But, with respect to the Hindoos, it gives rise to this reflection, that, in all their operations, they follow nature only, who points out to them the most simple means. Not that they want industry; but their dispositions, their manners, their religion, continually lead them back to nature. She is the mother whom they love, the power whom they obey, the divinity which they adore under so many different emblems. Neither the lapse of time nor the influence of foreigners can eradicate this caracteristic trait of a nation which ascends to the most remote antiquity, and whose population is immense.

The Chassa-Doba never does any work out of his profession. In this they are brought up from their infancy; and as they can aspire to no higher employment than that of leading their oxen, it is not to be wondered at that their understandings should be very much circumscribed, and that they should be considered as to represent the image of stupidity throughout India. From this they are so easily known, that the first look on their face, which is nearly the same in all, discovers the class to which they belong.

Pl. II.29. Cāṣādhobā. Paris: I.4.3.
Calcutta: Sec. I, No. 44. Chassa Doba, a thresher of Rice, Corn, &c. which is done by treading it under the Feet of Cattle.

Commentary: The name of the caste derives from *cāṣā*, farmer, and *dhobā*, washerman, and together the term denotes a caste of agriculturalists. Although various accounts exist among them for more exalted origins, Risley accepts the tradition that they are "probably a branch of Dhobās [washermen] who have taken to cultivation, and thus raised themselves so far above the parent caste that they now disown all connexion with it." In popular regard, however, the Cāṣādhobā retained the low social status of its dhobā origins.[1]

Nothing in Risley's description supports Solvyns's assertion that the Cāṣādhobā worked exclusively as rice-thrashers. Perhaps a sub-caste had so identified itself, but the caste generally engaged in cultivation and, at least by the end of the nineteenth century, if not in Solvyns's time, many had become carpenters and artisans and some had taken to trade, with prosperous grain merchants and money-lenders among them.[2]

1 Risley, *The Tribes and Castes of Bengal*, 1:194-95.
2 Ibid., 1:195.

II.30. Cāṣākaibarta. Agriculturalist

Paris: I.4.4. CHASSAH-KHYBERTS. GARDENERS: This is another agricultural cast; and the Chassah-Khyberts partake of the great respect which is attached to these casts. They would consequently consider themselves as degraded, if they did any other than garden work. In reality, such a dereliction of their rank would deprive them of it irrevocably; or at the least, after having thus sinked to the lowest stage of *Pariahs,* great expiations, and even pecuniary sacrifices, would be necessary to restore them to their cast. This is the condition to which all the Hindoos are subject.

The Chasah-Khybert who is the principal figure in this engraving carries on his shoulder the *kodali* [*kodāli*] or spade with which he stirs the earth. In the second distance are other gardeners at their work. The scene is a garden, or rather a groupe of trees of the country, and a ruined gateway; an object that often occurs in the hindoo landscapes, on account of the little solidity of their buildings which have frequently no other cement than mud.

The hindoo gardens are extensive and well furnished with fruit trees, such as cocos, mangoes, jacks, etc., which form a sort of orchard. The bettle-nut-tree, which attracts the eye most by its straitness and elevation, forms a beautiful avenue. The bambou is reserved for fences and the backs of ditches, where they grow into quick hedges.

These ditches are dry during nine months of the year, but during the rainy season they become little rivers. There are besides in all the gardens tanks, or reservoirs of water, for the use of the plantation, in which too they breed fish: of these they are very fond, and like to make presents of them among themselves.

The walks of these gardens are not very enticing, being infested with serpents, scorpions, and other dangerous reptiles, and great quantities of very troublesome insects.

Pl. II.30. Cāṣākaibarta. Paris: I.4.4.
Calcutta: Sec. I, No. 19. A Chassa, Khybert, or Gardener.

Commentary: Solvyns gives no recognition that the Cāṣākaibarta are a sub-caste of the fisher Kaibarta community who took to agriculture, but the concern for ritual purity Solvyns describes undoubtedly reflects their anxiety as to social status, for, as Wise writes, "while the fisher caste is invariably reckoned impure, the agricultural is not always so."[1] Indeed, by the early twentieth century, the caste had succeeded in changing its name for census designation to Māhiṣya to disassociate itself from the Kaibarta.[2]

The social status of the Kaibarta sub-castes vary considerably, and while the fishermen occupied a traditionally lower position, the cultivators enjoyed higher status. Bhattacharya, in *Hindu Castes and Sects*, states that the Cāṣākaibartas, who are quite numerous, may be reckoned among the rural aristocracy in Midnapore district and in other districts of Bengal as ranking next to the Kāyasthas (Pl. II.26).[3]

1 Wise, 299. Risley describes the Kaibarta as "a large fishing and cultivating caste of Bengal." See *The Tribes and Castes of Bengal*, 1:375-82.

2 Asok Mitra, *The Tribes and Castes of West Bengal*, 5, 21-22, 32-33, 73. Also see N. K. Dutt, 131-41.

3 222-23.

II.31. Āgari. Cultivator

Pl. II.31. Āgari. Paris: I.4.5.

Calcutta: Sec. I, No. 14. Augrees—or Ploughmen cultivating their lands,—the Plough is represented in the Plate, and their Harrow is a bush. The Augree is descended from a Rajpoot father, and Bhaat mother—if he wears the Poitah [*paitā*] or Thread round his neck, he cannot employ himself in handicraft.

Paris: I.4.5. AUGRYS. PLOUGHMEN: This is properly speaking the natural inhabitant of the country, *the man of the fields,* who, far from towns, has preserved all the simplicity of his forefathers.

The Angry seldom moves far from his cottage: he is not often to be seen even in the populous villages. Satisfied with little, he lives upon the produce of his labour. In the course of whole years perhaps no piece of money has passed through his hands, not even a *couries* [cowrie; H., *kauṛī*] a shell which supplies the place of the smallest coin. The Augrys offer this peculiarity, that, to apply to their labour, they quit the *poytah* or chaplet which the Hindoos wear as a point of their religion constantly round their neck. It would be difficult to give the true motif of this practice of the ploughmen. Let it suffice to observe that nothing can be inferred from it unfavourable to agricultural labour, which on the contrary is held in the highest estimation.

In the second distance of the drawing is an Augry guiding a plough drawn by two oxen. This plough has the shape of an anchor, the stock of which serves for the beam. One of the arms, covered with iron, makes the share; the other, held by the ploughman, gives the proper direction for opening the ground more or less. The Augry is often up to the middle in water, particularly in rice grounds.

At a greater distance is another labourer who breaks the clods which the plough has left, with one or more palm leaves, which produce nearly the same effect as our harrow.

To the right is a view of the ploughman's habitation.

The soil in general is arid from the long droughts; but the eye is amply repaid, and delighted even to admiration, when, in due season, the fields are enamelled with the lively and variegated colours of the cotton, indigo, poppies, mustard, etc.

Commentary: Nineteenth century ethnographers noted that the Āgaris claimed to be kṣatriyas, but were regarded by others as śūdras.[1] In Bengal, as in other parts of India, it was not unusual for śūdra castes aspiring to higher social status to assert kṣatriya rank, adopting the sacred thread and "Sanskritizing" their ritual life by emulating the practices of the higher castes.[2] This was especially true for castes that sought ritual validation for higher economic or political position already attained, as would have been the case for the Āgari as a dominant caste of rural Bengal.

Solvyns writes of the *paitā* as a "chaplet" that Hindus wear round the neck, but the *paitā* is the sacred thread, worn over the right shoulder and under the left arm.[3] The Āgari Solvyns depicts does not wear the *paitā*, and perhaps we can assume that, following Solvyns's text, he is at work and has taken it off. In the *Catalogue* for the Calcutta edition, Solvyns writes that "if he wears the Poitah or Thread round his neck, he cannot employ himself in handicraft." Solvyns rightly recognizes, however, that this is against the normal prescription that "twice-born" Hindus never remove the thread.

In the print, the figure is shown to wear a necklace, as distinct from the *paitā*. In the Calcutta edition, it is etched with no articulation of distinct beads, but in the Paris edition, it is clearly a string of beads, most probably rudrākṣa beads.[4]

The Rev. Lal Behari Day, in *Bengal Peasant Life*, an anthropological portrait of a Bengali village in the form of a novel, published in 1878, has an Āgari, or "Ugra-Kshatriya," as his hero. He writes that "amongst the peasantry of Western Bengal there is not a braver nor more independent class. . . . Somewhat fairer in complexion than Bengali peasants in general, better built, and more muscular in their corporeal forms, they are known to be a bold and somewhat fierce race, and less patient of any injustice or oppression that the ordinary Bengali rāiyat [cultivator]. . . ."[5]

Solvyns description of the plow is amplified by his contemporary William Ward: "A Bengali plough is the most simple instrument imaginable: it consists of a crooked piece of wood, sharpened at one end, and covered with a plate of iron which forms the plow-share. A wooden handle, about two feet long, is fixed to the other end crossways; and in the midst, a long straight piece of wood or bamboo, called the eecha, which goes between the bullocks, and falls on the middle of the yoke, to which it hangs by means of a peg, and is tied by a string. The yoke is a neat instrument, and lies over the necks of two bullocks, just before the hump, and has two pegs descending on the side of each bullock's neck, by means of which it is tied with a cord under the throat. There is only one man or boy to each plough, who with one hand holds the plough, and with the other guides the animals, by pulling them this or that way by the tail, and driving them forward with a stick."[6]

---

1 J. N. Bhattacharya, 124. Entry for Āgari, pp. 123-25.

2 M. N. Srinivas provides the classic analysis of the process in *Caste in Modern India and Other Essays*. The claims to kṣatriya status are analyzed in the context of a South Indian caste in Hardgrave, *The Nadars of Tamilnad: The Political Culture of a Community in Change*.

3 See discussion of the *paitā* in Pl. II.14.

4 On rudrākṣa beads, see Commentary for Pl. II.18.

5 278.

6 *A View. . .*, 1:101 fn.

II.32. Bārai. Betel Cultivator

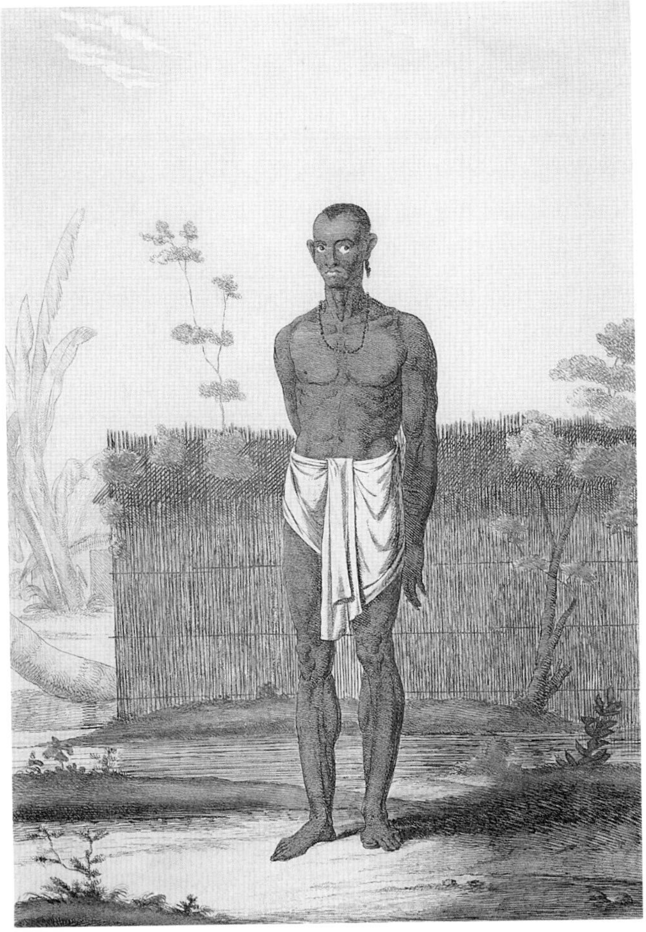

Pl. II.32. Bārai. Paris: I.4.6.

Calcutta: Sec. I, No. 15. A Berage—or Pawn planter, with a View of his Plantation which is enclosed and overlaid with sticks, to screen the plant from the intense heat of the Sun. The Pawn leaf with the beetle-nut, quick lime, and some aromatic seeds, is eaten by the Natives as a luxury, and given at their entertainments and feasts, as marks of friendship or favor.

Paris: I.4.6. BERAGE. CULTIVATOR OF PAWN: The Berage must also be classed among the simple and peaceable inhabitants of the country. He follows no other business than that which attends the cultivation of the pawn [*pān*]. One may form an idea of the strict separation of professions, and the exactness with which each one, to use the expression, minds his own business, by observing that the Berage does not go to sell the pawn he raises, even to the nearest markets. A merchant comes to deal with him for it, who has no other business than to buy and sell.

The pawn besides requires and deserves a great deal of care. It must be watched with an assiduity that frequently occupies both the day and the night. It must be preserved from insects, sheltered from the too great heat of the sun, and certain winds which, by destroying the plantation at once, would cause perhaps the total ruin of the proprietor, and deprive him of all revenue till a new plantation had produced leaves of a size fit for the market.

But if he succeeds, the Berage is amply repaid for his trouble; as nothing is more profitable than a good crop of pawn.

The Hindoos use large quantities of these leaves prepared with bettle-nuts, tobacco, all sorts of aromatic seeds, and quick-lime. To offer pawn with profusion is among them a mark of preference and a friendship, as well as the enjoyment of the luxury. Large quantities of it are consumed in their feasts and assemblies.

A pawn plantation is generally a square of greater or less extent, surrounded with a hedge of bambou as close as possible, to protect and shelter the plants.

Commentary: Solvyns gives to this caste the Bengali name, *baraj*, for the *piper betel* vine they cultivate as their traditional occupation. The correct name for the caste, however, is Bārai, though it is sometimes known as Bārui or Bāruji.[1]

In his notes with the original drawing of the Bārai, although not in the printed texts, Solvyns uses the word "soupiere" (*supuri*) for the betel nut. The aromatic betel (areca) leaf they grow is known as *pān* (Pl. II.212), as is the addictive chewing preparation wrapped in the leaf sold by the Tāmulī caste (depicted only in the Calcutta etchings, Pl. II.75).

Risley provides a detailed description of *pān* cultivation and notes that the *pān* garden is regarded as an almost sacred spot, entered by the Bārai only after bathing and with clean clothes.[2]

1 Risley, *The Tribes and Castes of Bengal*, 1:71-74; J. N. Bhattacharya, 232-33.

2 *The Tribes and Castes of Bengal*, 1:72-73.

II.33. Tā̃ti. Weaver

Paris: I.5.2. TANTYS. WEAVERS: We have already spoken of the weavers in the article of the Djougis [Jugi, Pl. II.27], and it would require many plates to give an adequate idea of the various means they use to bring their cotton cloaths to perfection; but we cannot avoid giving some notion of the simplicity of their contrivances.

The Tanty digs first a hole in the earth for his legs so as to be seated conveniently on the ground, into which he drives two strong bambous at a distance regulated by the breadth of his cloath, and near enough to a wall, to be held to it by other thinners bambous. The engraving represents this rustic loom so as to dispense with further details.

Seated here upon mat with his *houka* [*hukā*] or smoking piper, and his vase of water to quench his thirst and wash his hands and feet, the Tanty weaves with quiet indifference those cotton stuffs so highly valued in Europe. We have remarked before that to prevent the thread from breaking, it is necessary to keep it moist, we must add that the great fineness of the thread requires even sometimes that the loom should be kept under water.

All the family share in the work, the men weave, the children spin and the women after the business of the house is done come and take their part. The kitchen indeed does not occupy much of their time, so abstemious are the Hindoos. Rice is their chief food; and to dress it they dig a hole in the earth in which they place a *cudjery* [*khicuṛī*][1] or a pot made for this purpose, under which a few pieces of thin wood soon perform all their operations of cookery.

In the foreground of the plate is a Tanty standing up. His sandals are remarkable. They are of wood, and he holds them by a sort of button with his toes, which nevertheless does not prevent his walking with great ease and celerity.

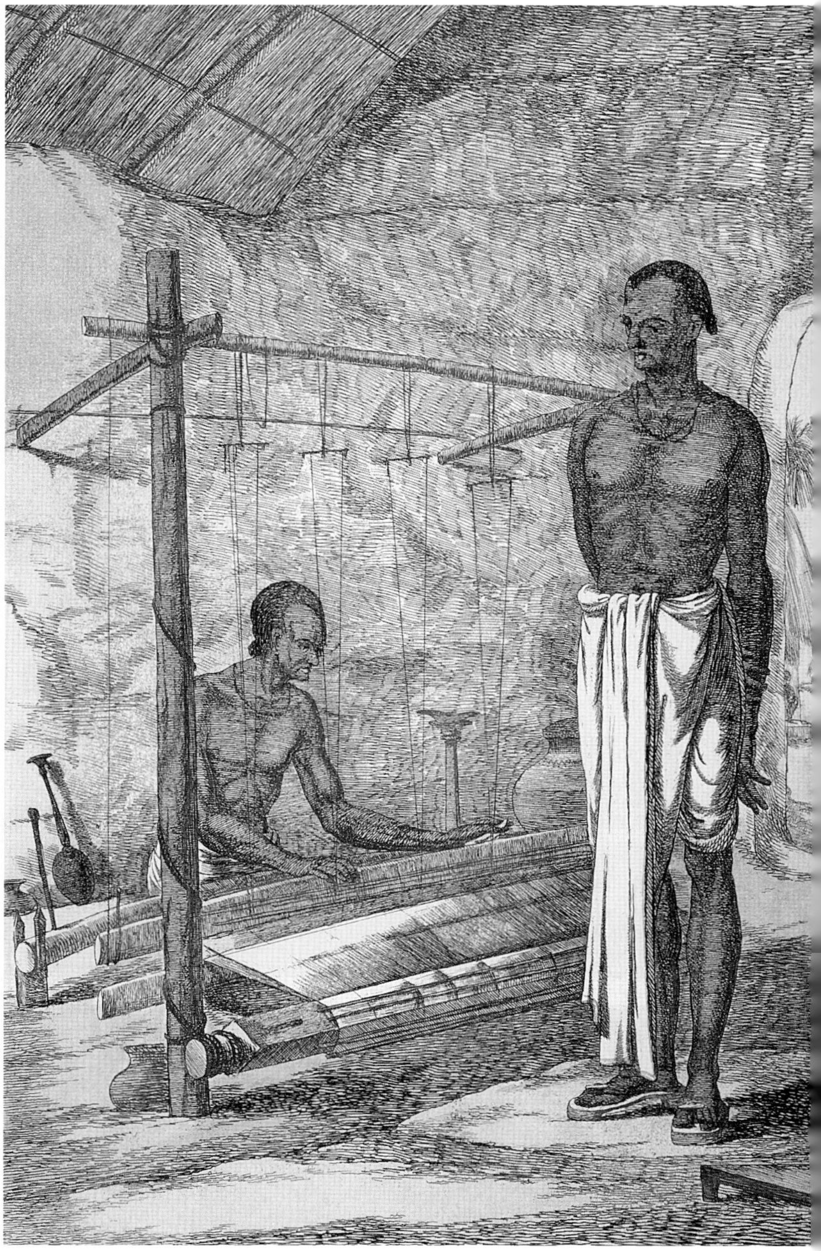

Pl. II.33. Tā̃ti. Paris: I.5.2.

Calcutta: Sec. I, No. 39. Tauntees or Weavers—with the manner of their working the loom—their women spin the thread.

Orme: 6.

Commentary: *Tā̃ti* (often transliterated Tānti) is sometimes used as a generic term for weavers, but the Tā̃tis (also Tantrabayas or Tantubāyas) in Bengal form a distinct caste.[2]

There are a number of Tā̃ti sub-castes, typically traceable in their distinctions to occupational differences, as in the particular fabric woven—cotton, silk, or coarser cloths.[3] The Tā̃tis here depicted are at their loom,[4] and Solvyns describes them as hardworking and abstemious. J. N. Bhattacharya shares this judgment, writing that they are "very industrious, thrifty, and sober. The only luxuries in which they indulge are fish, curry, and a porridge of black kidney beans. They never waste one moment of their time in idle talk or amusement. Their adult males are always at their looms, while their females devote themselves to dress and carding the yarn whenever they are not occupied with household work."[5] Working at the spinning wheel or with a hand-held device, women of many castes on a part-time basis prepared cotton thread for the weavers.[6]

The Tā̃tis are śūdras of comparatively high status, and Wise notes that "the purity of a Tanti depends on the quality of the starch used in weaving." The Tā̃ti prepares a starch (*khoi*) of parched rice boiled in water, in contrast to the impure Jugi who makes starch (*māṛ*) by merely boiling rice, "a process that is considered utterly abhorrent."[7]

In his study of the hierarchy and fluidity of caste in Bengal, Hitesranjan Sanyal writes that "The correlation between the levels of technology and ritual rank is . . . demonstrated by respective positions of the different castes of weavers in Bengal. The Tantu-bays produce coarse cloth but they are also proficient in manufacturing the finest varieties of cotton and silk textile. They are the most prosperous among the weavers and rank among the clean Sudras. The Jogis. . . are also traditional weavers. But the Jogis manufacture interior varieties of cloth, coarse blankets and ribbons."[8]

The Tā̃tis were among the earliest residents of the villages that became Calcutta, and they included both the weavers themselves and such prosperous merchant families as the Setts and Basāks (Bysacks). The rise of these wealthy Tā̃ti families represents what one scholar describes as "the most remarkable instance of upward economic mobility" in early eighteenth century Bengal.[9]

Textiles were exported to Europe and enriched Calcutta, but the decline of the cotton industry in Bengal was already evident by Solvyns's time. By the late eighteenth century, the spinning and weaving industries in Great Britain were securely established, and Indian piece goods faced increasing competition. "For the first time perhaps in the history of her trading relations with the West, India stood in the position of a buyer whose traditionally low cost products were being pushed out of both domestic and foreign markets by European products."[10] In the decade of the 1820s, export production of cotton goods collapsed in Bengal, throwing weavers and others involved in manufacture and trade out of work. By 1828, the British East India Company's Board of Trade reported that "a revolution so mighty and complete. . . is hardly to be paralleled in the history of commerce."[11]

During the course of the nineteenth century, many weaver families of Calcutta were able to retain prosperity, moving into business and the professions, but, as J. N. Bhattacharya writes, "the condition of their castemen in the interior. . . became indeed deplorable," as they were forced into menial service and agricultural labor.[12] Wise writes that while "the produce of their looms has been celebrated from the earliest historical times," "the weavers have suffered more from the vicissitudes of the last century than any other class."[13]

Solvyns's refers to the "remarkable" sandals worn by the standing figure and he includes them in three other prints (Pls. II.136, , II.149, and II.203). These strapless sandals, *pādukā*, are worn by gripping a peg between the toes.

1 A *khicuṛī* is a one-pot dish of rice, dal, and vegetables. It is often used in ritual offerings. In Anglo-Indian usage, "cudgerie" or "kedgeree" was a rice dish served at breakfast. *Hobson-Jobson*, 477. Solvyns uses the term for the pot itself.

2 Risley, *The Tribes and Castes of Bengal*, entry for Tānti, 2:295-304; J. N. Bhattacharya, entry, 184-86. Sukumar Sen, following the dominant tendency gives the name *Tā̃ti* as derived from the Sanskrit *tantravayanika*, those who weave on the loom, *tantra* meaning loom. But S. K. Ray, "The Tantubāyas or Tāntis (weavers)," 342, writes that "the word Tantu means natural 'fibre' (ansh)."

3 Hossain, 48. See this volume generally with regard to Tā̃tis.

4 The Reverend William Tennant, in his *Indian Recreation*, includes an etching of "A Tauntee" (opp. p. 301), that, while not a copy of Solvyns, bears striking resemblance. K. N. Chaudhuri, in *Asia Before Europe*, reproduces the Solvyns's etching from the Calcutta edition to illustrate the Indian treadle loom. Pl. 58, p. 315.

5 186.

6 Ward, *A View of . . . the Hindoos*, 1:125-26. Also see J. N. Bhattacharya, 186. Shoberl, 4:161-94, discusses "Cotton and Silk Manufactures" and includes eleven colored engravings depicting various processes.

7 381. Wise's entry for Tānti, 380-87.

8 20.

9 Sushil Chaudhury, 156.

10 K. N. Chaudhuri, *Economic Development of India Under the East India Co.*, 35. Also see Debrenda Bijoy Mitra and Sushil Chaudhury, 132-77.

11 Quoted in N. K. Sinha, *The Economic History of Bengal, 1793-1848*, 3:8.

12 182-86.

13 380.

II.34. Śā̃khāri. Conch Shell-Cutter

Pl. II.34. Śā̃khāri. Paris: I.5.3.

Calcutta: Sec. I, No. 21. A Sunkhaury, or maker of ornaments, of the sunk [*śaṅkha*, conch] shell worn by the women on their wrists. With a View of their method of cutting and grinding the shells.

Commentary: Śā̃khāri (often transliterated Śāṅkhārī; Sk., Śaṅkhakāra) is the caste of those who make and sell conch shell bangles, considered auspicious for Hindu married women.[1] Dealers of the caste are also called Śaṅkhabaniks, but many bangle dealers are Muslims who import the conch shells from South India, sell them to those Śā̃khāris working under them, and then retail the finished products.[2] As with other castes of craftsmen, they occupy their own neighborhood, or *ṭolā*, in Calcutta, centered in today's Jorasanko and Keshab Sen streets.

In their work, there is often a division of labor within the caste in producing the conch bangle. After cleaning and filing the shell, the Śā̃khāri, holding the conch obliquely between his feet, uses a three-foot long crescent-shaped saw known as a *śaṅkha-karāt* to slice the shell into rings. Typically Śā̃khāri specialists then polish and engrave the outer surface for the finished bangle.[3] Śā̃khāris also decorate intact conch-shells that are used as horns in Hindu ritual, depicted by Solvyns in his portrayal of musical instruments (Pl. II.146).

The conch shell bangle was traditionally used in Bengal by every married woman of the "respectable castes" and was symbolized as a sign of marriage (*sābitrī-śaṅkha*), just as the streak of red down the part of the hair. And, as Solvyns notes, the *sābitri-śaṅkhas* are red in color.

The traditional painter-bards of Bengal—the Paṭuā, or Chitrakāra (Pl. II.67)—sing of the origin of the conch-shell bangles: It seems that one day the goddess Durgā asked Śiva, her husband, for a pair of

Paris: I.5.3. TCHANKARYS, SUNKHAURYS. WORKERS OF SHELLS: All the Hindoo women wear ornament on their wrists. None of them would be seen without their bracelets, except after the death of a husband or some near relation, in which case all ornaments are forbidden.

There are casts who have their bracelets of beaten-iron, of brass or of silver; but those made with the *sunk*, shell, are looked upon as most suitable. The Hindoo woman who piques herself upon her strictness and who professes the *sastah* [*śāstra*] (sacred book) prefers them to bracelets of the richest metals. They are however dear, and form a considerable branch of trade. The poor wear a cheaper sort of laque-wax, or glass.

The address with which the Tchankary cuts the shells is remarkable. The instrument in the hands of the figure in the foreground is an iron saw without teeth, such as is used to saw marble. With this by continued friction the workman cuts at last through the *sunk* or shell, which he holds confined between his feet as is seen in the back ground. When the shells are cut, the form required is given by rubbing them upon a hard stone with sand and water. Rings are adjusted afterwards one with another and ornamented with gum-lacque or wax generally red, by which means also the joints are concealed.

The Tchankary is of a lighter colour than the generality of Hindoos; his cast is distinguished among the artisans.

conch-shell bangles. He said he was too poor to give them to her, and in dismay she went away to her father's house. There a Śãkhāri came to her, but the bangles broke as they were fitted on her arm. The Śãkhāri remarked that perhaps she was not faithful, and Durgā gave him a look of fire. The Śãkhāri survived to Durgā's astonishment and revealed himself to be her husband Śiva. He presented the bangles to her, which she then wore as the emblem of their marriage.[4]

1 See Risley, *The Tribes and Castes of Bengal*, entry, 2:221-23; Wise, entry, 364-67; Benoy Ghose, 56-74; S. K. Ray, "The Sankhakaras or Sankharis (Makers of Conch-Shell Bangles);" and, with color photographs, Prabhas Sen, *Crafts of West Bengal*, pp. 138-42.

2 S. K. Ray, "The Sankhakaras . . . ," 340.

3 The craft technique is detailed in Sukumar Sinha, and in R. P. Gupta, "Craftsmen at Work," 21.

4 G. S. Dutt, *Patua-Sangit*, as related in S. K. Ray, "The Sankhakaras . . . ," 340-41.

II.35. Kāmār. Blacksmith

Paris: I.5.4. KOUMARS. SMITHS (OR BLACKSMITHS): The Smith who is likewise called *Lahaur* [Lohār] works sitting on the ground; the favourite position of the Hindoos as often as the nature of his business will admit of it: close by his side are his coals and his anvil which is often but a stone or a bit of an anchor, so that he does his work without moving from his seat, unless it be of a large size. The bellows which he moves with feet is of the simplest construction.

In parts of Hindoostan and of the Malabar coast they work iron without fire, and give it by beating the degree of heat necessary to make it malleable. The Hindoos do not excell in this sort of work. Except their sabres, *crests* or poignards [daggers], and lances, they produce nothing remarkable.

The work-shop of the Smith is, as the plate represents it, a sort of shed, formed of mats joined together supported by bambous, and covered with straw. All the Hindoos cabins are nearly of the same construction, excepting in the countries where they are built of earth, which being naturally loamy is easily moulded up with water. The walls are raised, and holes cut in them afterwards for windows and doors, at an elevation of about five or six feet the bambous are fixed and crossed, upon which is thrown a roof of rice or any other straw; in other places they make use of reeds: such is the nature of an ordinary Hindoos habitation. Nothing more remains than to wash it religious by every day with cow-dung, to preserve it from unlucky accidents, as well as from the injuries of time.

Commentary: The smith in Bengal is called Kāmār, or Karmakāra, and works principally with iron but also with gold and other metals, thus combining the distinct crafts of the Lohār (iron) and the Soṇār (gold) found in other parts of North India. They occupy a social position among the higher śūdras.[1]

Only the men of the Kāmār caste engage in metal-working, and they do so traditionally in home workshops, as Solvyns describes. Their proverbial "hundred and eleven" manufactures include iron agricultural implements, domestic utensils, tools, weapons, and various kinds of fishing equipment.[2]

The Kāmārs play a distinct role in the religion of Bengal, to which Solvyns makes no reference. They are the authorized slaughterers of sacrificial animals, and for the service, the Kāmār receives either the head of the animal (usually a goat) or a monetary gratuity. Their role here arises from their manufacture of the *khāḍā*, the heavy blade used in ritual sacrifice.[3] And, although they engage in no other forms of carpentry, they carve the wooden funerary posts, *bṛṣo kāth*, depicted by Solvyns (Pls. II.25 and II.3).

The cow-dung wash, to which Solvyns refers, purifies the floor and the hearth of the mud hut. The dung of the cow, sacred to the Hindus, is ritually pure.

1 Risley, *The Tribes and Castes of Bengal*, 1:388-92; Wise, 300-01.

2 Their manufactures are detailed by S. K. Ray, "The Karmakaras (Ironsmiths)," and by Prabhas Sen, "Brass and Bell Metal," in *Crafts of West Bengal*, 82-92. For the techniques and economy of the craft, see K. B. Pal.

3 S. K. Ray, "The Karmakaras (Ironsmiths)," 330; J. N. Bhattacharya, 195.

Opposite page:

Pl. II.35. Kāmār. Paris: I.5.4.

Calcutta: Sec. I, No. 23. Kumaur or Lohaur—Blacksmiths, representing their simple method of blowing their bellows and working.

II.36. Kumār. Potter

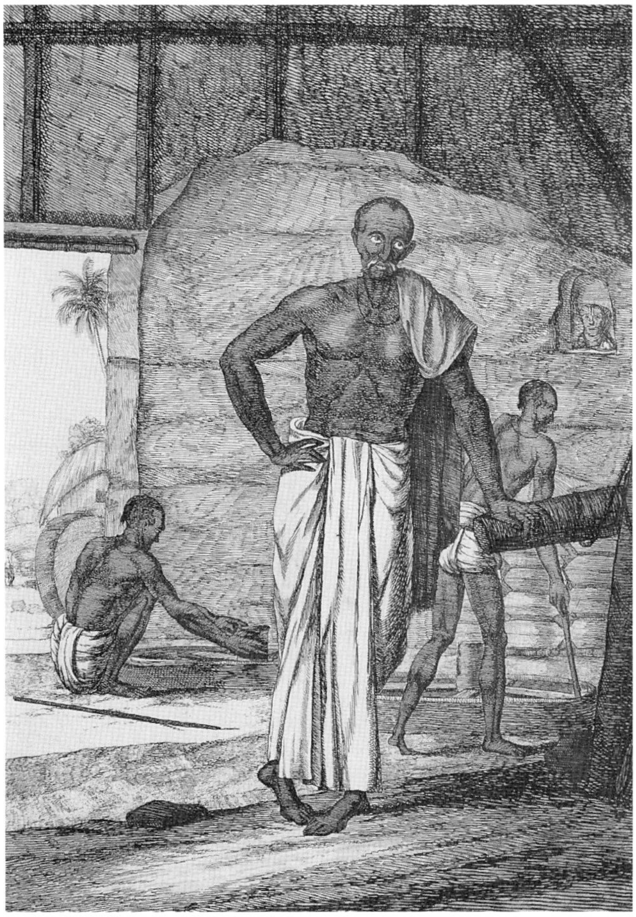

Pl. II.36. Kumār. Paris: I.5.5.
Calcutta: Sec. I, No. 16. Coomhar—or earthen pot-maker, with their simple and curious method of making their Pots, by the help of a revolving Wheel.

Paris: I.5.5. QOMARS, COOMARS. POTTERS: The *Qomars* are laborious, and notwithstanding their poverty form a cast that is esteemed.

Besides the principal figure which is a Potter standing up, the print represents several *Qomars* in different operations of their trade.

A wooden wheel fixed horizontally in the ground: in the midst of a sufficient quantity of prepared clay, the Potter sitted, putting his wheel into motion with extraordinary velocity by means of a stick which he darts very dextrously into the holes made to receive it, and giving at the same time to his vase either with his hand or with a bit of wood the form which he desires. Such is the picture of a Hindoos Potter at his work.

The vessel after having received its last form, is dried in the sun, which is sufficiently hot for several kinds of pottery; others require baking in the oven. In general they are so very thin that it is surprising to see them so well shaped.

Potter's-ware is much used in Hindoostan: the *cudgerie* [*khicuṛī*][1] or rice pot, frequently serves but once. The *Qomars* makes also tiles and bricks as well as the ornaments of the pagodas and houses of the richer Hindoos, the forms and relievos of which are always extraordinary and frequently obscene.

Commentary: The name Kumār is derived from the Sanskrit *kumbhakāra*, meaning literally maker of earthen jars, and the potter caste is known by both words, as well as by the name Kumhār. They occupy, as Solvyns notes, a social position as higher or "respectable" śūdras. There are numerous endogamous Kumār subcastes, distinguished by the area from which they originally came, by the quality of the clay they use, or by the particular items manufactured.[2]

The Kumārs make a wide range of earthenwares.[3] Pottery is made on the wheel (*cāk*) and often cast with the use of prepared molds of various sizes and shapes to produce ware for specific household, storage, and ritual uses. Kumārs also make, hand-modeled or cast, religious images and terracotta dolls and toys. Women and children join in the family craft, but only men work at the wheel and in shaping religious images.

In Calcutta, the potters are concentrated in Kumartuli, not far from Burra Bazar in the northern part of the city. The neighborhood is famous for its production of the clay images so essential to the religious life of Bengal, as in the celebrated Durgā and Kālī pūjās.[4] According to local tradition, Maharaja Krishnachandra (1710-1783) of Nadia popularized the worship of clay images in lower Bengal in the early eighteenth century. Under the rājā's patronage, Nadia became the center for clay-modeling, and it was from Nadia that many of the Kumartuli families came to Calcutta.[5]

The Kumār workplace, depicted by Solvyns, is described by Risley: "Beneath the same thatched roof are the kiln, storehouse, and dwelling-house, while at the door the clay is prepared. The kiln is called the *pan*, from the Sanskrit Pavana, that which purifies, and the hut the *panghar*. The kiln is divided into compartments in which the newly-made vessels are arranged, earth being heaped over all."[6] These potters' workplace is usually situated on the bank of a river, providing ready access to clay and the fuels used for low-temperature pottery firing, typically grass, reeds, bamboo, and sometimes twigs.[7]

In addition to the wooden wheel, described by Solvyns, the Kumārs use a wheel made of baked clay, weighted along the rim and revolving on a pivot cut from the heart of a tamarind tree. Wise notes that the neck and body of all globular vessels are made on the wheel, but the body is fashioned by hand, often by women. The most common earthenware of Bengal is red, but using the same laterite clay, a black pottery is produced by covering the kiln at a certain stage and adding oil-cake to the fire. The pottery is unglazed, but after baking, the Kumārs may paint or incise their work, often imparting a gloss by the use of egg white or oils. The images of gods may be further embellished with powdered mica sprinkled over them while the paint is wet.[8]

---

1 See Pl. II.33, fn. 1.
2 Risley, *The Tribes and Castes of Bengal,* 1:517-526; Wise, 332-36; and S. K. Ray, "The Kumbhakaras (Potters and Clay-Modelers)." For a rich portrayal of the living tradition of Bengali crafts in their full range, though especially strong on image-making, see Glassie.
3 On styles and techniques, see Prabhas Sen, "Pottery and Terracotta," in *Crafts of West Bengal*, 22-39, with numerous color photographs, and in his "Potters and Pottery of West Bengal." Also see Benoy Ghose, 16-55.
4 See Siddiqui and De. Prabhas Sen describes the modeling technique for clay images in "Festival Crafts," in *Crafts of West Bengal*, 162-73. In Bisarjan (Pl. II.190), Solvyns depicts the clay image of Kālī as it is about to be immersed in the water at the conclusion of the festival honoring her.
5 Benoy Ghose, 44-46; Pranab Bandhyopadyay, 112; and Prabhas Sen, "Potters and Pottery of West Bengal," 46.
6 Risley, *The Tribes and Castes of Bengal,* 1:525.
7 Prabhas Sen, "Potters and Pottery of West Bengal," 44.
8 Wise, 333; Risley, *The Tribes and Castes of Bengal,* 1:524-25. See also Saraswati and Behura.

II.37. Kā̃sārī. Coppersmith

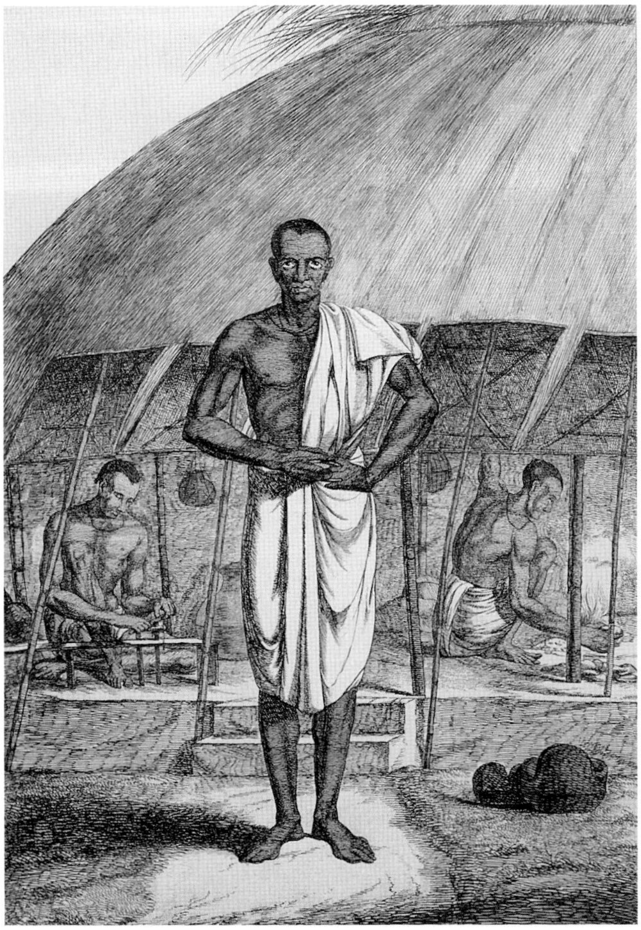

Pl. II.37. Kā̃sārī. Paris: I.5.6.
Calcutta: Sec. I, No. 22. A Causaury, or Thataree, a Brass and Copper-smith.

Paris: I.5.6. KANSAURIS. COPPER-SMITHS: The Hindoos use a great deal of copper, as well for domestic purposes, as in the ornaments of their pagodas, and even for the figures which represent their gods. The most devout among them prefer copper vases to silver, both for their private and for their sacrifices.

It is again wonderful by what simple means the *Kansaury* works up his copper, melts and mixes the different metals. His furnace is nothing more than a hole in the ground, accessible to the wind of a bellows which is itself no more than a skin well closed, except where a piece of bambou serves for a pipe. The workman always seated on the ground, with one hand moves his bellows which he confines by his feet. His crucibles are of earth prepared with wool or goats hair and suffise for the fusion of the hardest metals. The same composition with the addition of some oil of mustard to harden it in the fire serves for the moulds. To judge by the ornaments of the ancient idols, the use of the files and such like instruments reaches among the Hindoos to the highest antiquity. Their works moreover from the complicated variety of their details, and the uniform simplicity of their means serve as to many monuments of their extreme patience.

Commentary: The name of the caste, Kā̃sārī (often transliterated Kānsāri; Sk., Kāngsakāra) is derived from *kā̃sā* (*kānsā*) bell-metal, an alloy generally with 7 parts copper and either 1 or 2 parts tin. Solvyns describes the Kā̃sārī as a "copper-smith," but while at one time there were true copperworkers (Tāmāras) and traders (Tāmārabaniks) in Bengal, by Solvyns's time they had merged into the metal alloy maker and trader caste.[1] In the entry for the 1799 *Catalogue*, Solvyns also identifies the caste as "Thataree" (Ṭhāṭāri in Bengali, Thatherā in Hindi), a North Indian caste of metal workers corresponding to the Kā̃sārīs of Bengal. In Bengal, they are grouped with the Kā̃sārīs, but are sometimes distinguished as polishing and engraving utensils the Kā̃sārī supplies.[2]

Kā̃sārīs work both in manufacture and sales of brass, copper, and bronze objects. Centered in the Calcutta neighborhood of Kansaripara, they produce both ritual objects and utensils (made with copper, *tama*, a sacred metal) and domestic utensils (more typically of brass). Women are involved in the craft in preparing the molds (inner and outer) for casting.[3] Kā̃sārīs are "respectable" śūdras, and the merchants among them, some quite wealthy, are called Kansabaniks.[4]

1 Meera Mukherjee, 3-5, 11-16, 74. The book details metal-working techniques. Also see Prabhas Sen, "Brass and Bell Metal," in *Crafts of West Bengal*, pp. 92-97.

2 Risley, *The Tribes and Castes of Bengal*, 1: 419-20; and J. N. Bhattacharya, 199.

3 S. K. Ray, "The Kangsakaras (Makers of kangsa or kansha, an alloy)." For a description of the methods of casting, see Ajitcoomar Mookerjee, 20-22.

4 Risley, *The Tribes and Castes of Bengal*, 1:419-20; J. N. Bhattacharya, 199. On the social position of the Kā̃sārīs, see Smriti Kumar Sarkar.

II.38. Soṇār Bāniyā. Money-Changer

Commentary: The Soṇār Bāniyā—Subarnabanik in Bengali—is a money-lending and merchant caste of Bengal. The name is derived from *soṇār* (gold) and *bāniyā, bene, banik* (merchant). Although traditionally accorded comparatively low social status among the śūdra castes, Risley notes that they claim to be vaiśyas and that there is a "tolerably widespread feeling that the standing allotted to them by tradition is ludicrously incompatible with their wealth and abilities."[3] Their ostentatious display of wealth, described by Solvyns, may be taken, in part, as a visible assertion of their claim to higher caste status. A grand statement of their opulence remains today as "the Marble Palace" in North Calcutta, built in 1835 by Raja Rajendro Mallik.

The Subarnabaniks were largely itinerant gold merchants who took full advantage of new opportunities in Calcutta, with a rise in wealth as money-lenders and bankers, urban landlords, purveyors of goods, and as go-betweens in association with the European trading companies. By the late eighteenth century, during the time that Solvyns lived in the city, the Subarnabaniks contested for the

Pl. II.38. Soṇār Bāniyā. Paris: I.6.2.

Calcutta: Sec. I, No. 33. Sonaur Bunnya, or Shroffs, Money Changers, Bankers, &c.—The specie current in the country consists of the Gold Mohur, the Rupee of silver, Pice of Copper, and the shells called Couries.

Paris: I.6.2. SONAUR-BUNNYAS. MONEY-CHANGERS: The money changers who are also called *shroffs,*[1] are at the same time bankers. They are good calculators, and lend upon pledges at a very high interest. In general, their principal characteristic is their avidity and ostentatious luxury, which for their wives and children consists in being covered with a quantity of gold and silver jewels. They are, as stockholders, at the head of the most considerable trading houses of Hindoostan; which gives them that sort of respect which everywhere follows riches; as well as all that vanity and air of arrogance which we have endeavoured to express in the engraving.

They acquire also great importance from the power which they exercise in regulating every morning the price of exchange of notes (hourdies) [*huṇḍī*][2] and of coins, which determines that of every article in the bazars or markets, where their counting houses are established in the quarters where the circulation is most active. The different species of coin are placed in separate piles before them, to facilitate their transactions with their customers.

The current coins are, the *gold mohur*, worth 16 shillings and 8 pence; the silver *roupee* [rupee]; about 1 shilling 10 pence; (the *lack* [lakh] is one hundred thousand roupies); the *annas*, a copper coin, about the sixteenth part of a roupee; the *pice*, half of an *annas*; the couries [cowries] or shells, of which 120 are equal to a *pice*; so that it requires near 4000 to make a roupee. This last species of money was admitted in favour of the people, on account of the cheapness of provisions; a dozen of these shells suffise to buy as much fish, rice, and snuff as are necessary for one day.

leadership of Calcutta society, but, as Pradip Sinha relates, "their position in the caste hierarchy stood in the way," and they lost out to the Kāyasthas.[4]

A certain high caste disdain is evident in Bhattacharya, *Hindu Castes and Sects*, where he writes that the Subarnabaniks are believed to be "very hard-fisted, . . . but they never deny themselves any personal comfort consistent with their ideas of economy. Some of them live in palatial mansions, and keep splendid equipages. They do not invest much of their money for the benefit of their souls in the next world, and with the exception of a few of their wealthy members, they very seldom incur any expenditure by way of charity to the poor."[5] "The middle classes among them have generally *poddari* [exchange] shops in the large towns where they sell and buy gold and silver in the form of ingots, as well as in the shape of plate and jewelry."[6]

Walter Hamilton, in his *Description of Hindostan*, soon after Solvyns's time in India, writes that the *poddārs* (Hindustani for money-lender) often have no shop, but sit in the open market with heaps of cowries before them, exchanging them for silver. "In the morning the money changer usually gives 5760 cowries for a rupee, and in the evening he gives a rupee for 5920 cowries, which is a profit of one thirty-sixth part on every good mint rupee." In the country," Hamilton notes, "all minor transactions, and even some of considerable magnitude, are settled by cowries. . ."[7]

The money in circulation in Bengal in the late eighteenth and early nineteenth centuries included the gold mohur, equal to 16 sicca rupees. The silver sicca rupee was coined by the East India Company government in Bengal from 1793, and was valued at a premium over the standard rupee.[8] A coin to which Solvyns makes no reference was the South Indian "pagoda," equal to four rupees. The phrase "shaking the pagoda tree" was used by Europeans to suggest the wealth that was to be made in India.[9]

---

1 From the Arabic *ṣarrāf*, the word was used by Europeans in India (as well as in China) for money-lenders.

2 Traditional note of exchange; negotiable instrument.

3 Risley, *The Tribes and Castes of Bengal*, 2:261-66; also see Wise, 370-71, and Jogendra Nath Bhattacharya, 158. On the Subarnabaniks as bankers, see N. K. Sinha's discussion of "Indigenous Banking, 1793-1848," in *The Economic History of Bengal*, 3:73-87.

4 "Social Change," 392. Also see Pradip Sinha, *Calcutta in Urban History*, 70-75, and Nisith Ranjan Ray, *Calcutta: The Profile of a City*, 38-41.

5 159. For the Subarnabanik self-image, see N. N. Laha, *Subarnabanik Katha O Kirti* [Bengali]. vols. 1-3, cited in Pradip Sinha, *Calcutta in Urban History*, 71, fn.30.

6 Pradip Sinha, *Calcutta in Urban History*, 158.

7 *A Geographical, Statistical, and Historical Description of Hindostan and Adjacent Countries*,1:39-40. The value of the cowrie seems to have varied considerably. *A Glossary of Indian Terms*, 56, gives the number of cowries for a rupee as "from 2,500 to 5,000, according to circumstances."

8 On the equivalents of Indian coinage, see Milbourn; Grant and Colebrooke; and Furber, 348-49. On the sicca rupee, see Goldsborne, note by Cotton, 309.

9 *Hobson-Jobson*, 652-57.

II.39. Hālwāi. Confectioner

Pl. II.39. Hālwāi. Paris: I.6.3.
Calcutta: Sec. I, No. 41. Hulwye, a Pastry and Confectioner.

Paris: I.6.3. HULWYES. PASTRY-COOKS.: There are two classes of Pastry-cooks in Hindoostan, and they afford another proof of the strict separation of professions; the *Hulwyes* not being allowed to employ the same ingredients as the *Mayras*, whom we shall next describe [Pl. II.40]. The first must not use *gui* [*ghi*] nor oil in their pastry, which notwithstanding they find means to make very delicate with rice-flower and cocoa-nut rendered as white as snow. The rich consume great quantities of this pastry; but the primitive Hindoos prefer that of the *Mayras*: which confirms the idea that the pastry of the *Hulwyes* was introduced by the Musselmans; and they are accordingly in greater number and higher estimation in the countries which were formerly under the Musselman domination. Their dress also bears some resemblance to that of those foreigners; and their women, who seldom appear in their shops, are not drest like those of the Hindoos. Nevertheless the legislator Menu reckons the *Hulwyes* among the true Hindoos.

Commentary: Hālwāis (Hāluis) make and sell a variety of sweets using a flour base, characteristic of North India, in contrast to the more traditional Bengali sweets of milk and sugar prepared by the Mayarā.[1] Their name is derived from *halwā*, a sweet made of flour, *ghī* (clarified butter), sugar, and typically flavored with cardamom and almond paste. Often colored with saffron, it may contain raisins, or pistachio nuts. Solvyns is wrong regarding the Hālwāis' use of *ghī*, for it is an ingredient in most, if not all, *hālwās*, but they do not use oils in making their sweets.

The confections are prepared in a number of ways. The flour, for example, may be fried in *ghī*, then boiled in a solution of milk and sugar to the consistency of a thick jelly, and baked in small earthen pans.[2] Puddings, often with grated vegetables such a carrots, are a popular *halwā* variety, and a particularly delicate *halwā* uses cream and requires considerable skill in preparation.

The word *halwā* is from the Arabic, giving support to Solvyns's suggestion of the profession's Muslim connection, but although there are Muslim confectioners, those of the Hālwāi caste are Hindus of respectable śūdra status. Risley writes that "there is no caste in India which is too pure to eat what a confectioner has made. In marriage banquets it is he who supplies a large part of the feast, and at all times and seasons the sweetmeat is a favourite viand to a Hindu requiring temporary refreshment."[3]

1 The word *mayarā* is generally used today to refer to all sweet makers and sellers.

2 J. N. Bhattacharya, 191; Stocqueler, *The Oriental Interpreter*, 102.

3 Risley, *The Tribes and Castes of Bengal*, 1:312. Entry, 1:310-13.

II.40. Mayarā. Confectioner

Pl. II.40. Mayarā. Paris: I.6.4.

Calcutta: Sec. I, No. 30. A Myra, a maker of sweetmeats, with oil, ghee, and sugar without pastry.

Paris: I.6.4. MAYRAS CONFECTIONERS. This profession differs from the preceeding one, as we have already remarked, by their using *gui* [*ghī*] and oil. The oil which the *Mayras* use is extracted from mustard seed, and has a flavour which is agreeable even to Europeans. There is a great demand for this sort of pastry; it is served up at their feasts, and habitually at their breakfasts and collations. The children, who are very fond of it, eat it at every hour of the day; consequently there is no market, however inconsiderable without its *Mayras*. The print gives an idea of their way of exposing their goods for sale, as well as of their ovens and utensils.

The *Mayras* are not so cleanly as the *Hulwyes* [Hālwāi, Pl. II.39], either in their persons or their cloaths; which proceeds from the nature of their work. As they are constantly in the smoke of the frying-pan, the whole family are as it were impregnated with oil, which forms a very distinguishing mark of their profession.

Commentary: Traditional Bengali sweets, made by the Mayarā (or Mairā) caste,[1] are famous throughout India. Their basic ingredients are milk and sugar, epitomized by the *roshogollā* (H., *rasgullā*), a spongy cheese ball cooked in sugar syrup and flavored with rose water. Many preparations, like *pantuā* or *gulāb jāmun*, are made by frying in hot oils, as Solvyns notes.

The Bengali sweet tooth is proverbial. As William Ward, Solvyns's contemporary in Bengal, writes of confectioners, both Mayarā and Hālwāi, "They make and sell nearly a hundred different kinds of sweetmeats, principally composed of sugar, molasses, flour, and spices. The Bengalees, if their circumstances permit of such indulgence, eat large quantities of sweetmeats every day, and give them to their children. If a market place contains a hundred shops, twelve or fifteen of them will belong to confectioners."[2]

1 Risley, *The Tribes and Castes of Bengal*, 2:84-86.
2 *A View of . . . the Hindoos*, 1:124.

II.41. Gandha Bāniyā, Gandhabanik. Grocer

Pl. II.41. Gandha Bāniyā. Paris: I.6.5. **Calcutta: Sec. I, No. 31.** A Gund Bunnya or seller of gums and spices, with a view of his wares and shop.

Paris: I.6.5. GUND BUNNYAS. GROCERS: The Grocers form a division of the third original cast, that of the *Bayces* [Vaiśyas] or Merchants. They make but little shew, but are very well provided. They lay in their stock in proper season, and are in general well informed in every thing concerning their trade, which is very considerable, on account of the great demands for spices in Hindoostan. They are the retailers of all aromatic gums and dried herbs, as well as of opium, which they sell nearly for its weight in gold. The Hindoos seldom use it otherwise than in the tobacco which they smoke; but great quantities of it are consumed by the Musselmans, the Malais [Malays], the Mogols, the Chineese, and other foreigners who frequent Hindoostan. We shall have occasion hereafter to treat of this branch of commerce so lucrative to the English.

Commentary: Their name is derived from the word for perfume, but Gandhabaniks are the Bengali caste of merchants selling spices, drugs, and groceries. Although claiming vaiśya descent, they are regarded as middle class śūdras.[1] They are generally prosperous, but, as Solvyns notes, they have a reputation for frugality. Bhattacharya writes that, while they live in good houses, "they very seldom spend much of their wealth in any other kind of personal comfort [and] even the wealthiest among them generally live in a very shabby style."[2]

Solvyns identifies the Gandhabanik as an opium merchant, a trade which they continued over the nineteenth century. According to Risley, "The Gandhabanik retails charas, bhang, opium, and ganja, but some have scruples about selling the last, and employ a Mahomedan servant to do so."[3]

During the years Solvyns was in Calcutta, the opium trade was well established. Produced in Bihar and "upper India" under a monopoly of the British East India Company, principally for export, it was auctioned at Calcutta and shipped mainly to Southeast Asia and China.[4] As for Solvyns later discussing the opium trade, he may have had second thoughts, for it is not again mentioned.

1 Risley, *The Tribes and Castes of Bengal*, 1:265-67; J. N. Bhattacharya, 158; 160-61.
2 161.
3 Risley, *The Tribes and Castes of Bengal*, 1:267. Charas, bhāṅg, and gā̃ja (gānjā) are narcotic preparations of *Cannabis sativa*, Indian hemp or marijuana, and gā̃ja is particularly strong in its effect.
4 See Dharma Kumar, Vol. 2, passim; and the entry for "Opium" in Embree, 3:153-54.

II.42. Tili. Shop-Keeper

Paris: I.6.6. TILLYS. RETAILERS:
Although among the Hindoos every commodity has its appropriate merchant, there are nevertheless retailers for eatables and other articles of daily consumption, such as rice, gui, spices, oils, fruit, wood, grain of every kind, etc. They are also money-changers, so that they are of very great use, especially in the country, where they are most to be met with. They sometimes amass large fortunes; which will not appear surprising, when it is known, how well they calculate for their own profit, not unfrequently even at the expence of the simple and ignorant buyer who places too much confidence in their honesty. They are notwithstanding true Hindoos, and do not belong to any of the foreign classes which the prospect of gain has drawn to Hindoostan.

The plate represents a retailer sitting upon his little board, in the middle of his shop. The *Tillys* have a spoon which they use with great dexterity to take up the articles that called for. They wrap up the smaller objects in plantain leaves. One of these leaves also serves to write the accounts of their different sales.

Commentary: The Tili caste, rising in a comparatively short time to become one of the foremost mercantile communities, provides one of Bengal's most successful cases of social mobility.[1] Some time in the eighteenth century, perhaps even earlier, the Tilis emerged as a distinct sub-caste of the Teli caste, engaged traditionally in extracting oil (*til*) from the sesame seed. Tilis were shop-keepers, cloth and grain merchants, and money-lenders, and they distinguished themselves by taking the name Tili, claiming a derivation for the word that would separate them from their oil-presser origins.[2] In Solvyns's time, the two names were often used interchangeably for the merchants—although the oil-pressers, to whom Solvyns makes no reference here, were known only as Telis, or as Kalus, the name by which Solvyns identifies the caste.[3] Solvyns in the Calcutta edition titles the etching Tilly, but in the accompanying *Catalogue*, the entry is for Telly. In the Paris edition, the table of contents gives Tilly in French and Telly in English, but in both French and English texts to the plate, as well as in the title below the plate, the name Tilly is used.

Solvyns gives no indication of the controversy over the caste's name or origin, but even in the late nineteenth century, Risley expresses doubt that "the process of separation has yet gone so far" as to make the Tili a caste "wholly distinct" from the Teli.[4] Nripendra Kumar Dutta, in *Castes in Bengal* (1896), recognizes the Teli connection, but accepts the Tili as

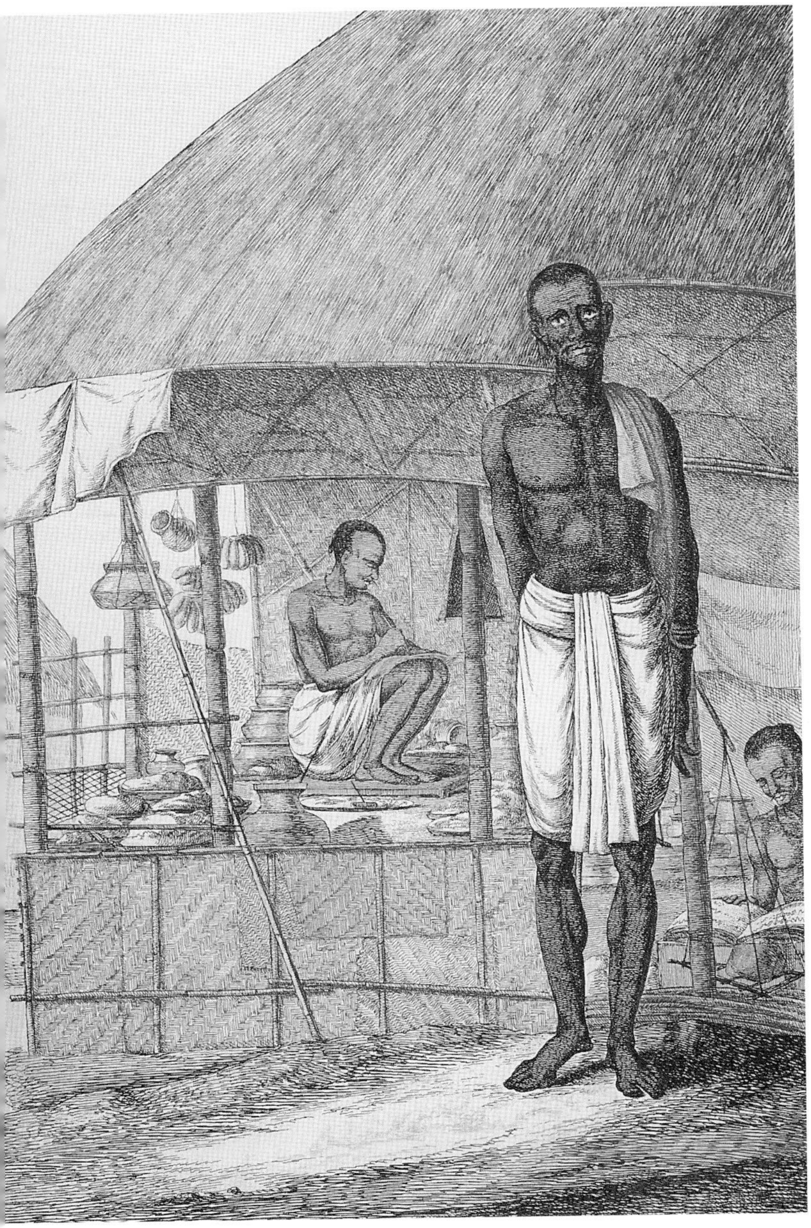

Pl. II.42. Tili. Paris: I.6.6.
Calcutta: Sec. I, No. 24. Telly, or Retailer of Fruit, Rice, Ghee, &c. with a View of his shop.

a distinct caste and writes, "If any Vaiśya order be recognized in the social organization of Bengal the Tilīs from their mode of living, their profession of trading and banking may well claim to belong to it."[5] It was not until 1931, however, that the Census of India listed the Tilis as a separate caste.

The Telis, as oil-pressers, occupy a position as "clean" or respectable śūdras, but the Tilis, who abandoned the oil trade to become bankers and shop-keepers, secured rank among the higher śūdra castes from whose hands a brahmin may take water.[6] By the late eighteenth century, a number of Tilis had become wealthy, some acquiring substantial land holdings. Among them, the most famous was Krisna Kanta Nandy, or "Cantoo Baboo" (c. 1720-1794), the banian of Warren Hastings. An influential merchant and zamīndār, Cantoo Baboo worked, with considerable success, to gain recognition for the Tilis as a distinct caste of high social status, and his descendants, the rājās of Kasimbazar (Cossimbazar), have been renowned for their charity and public spirit.[7]

1 See Hitesranjan Sanyal, "Continuities of Social Mobility in Traditional and Modern Society in India: Two Case Studies of Caste Mobility in Bengal," reprinted in Sanyal, *Social Mobility in Bengal*, with the study of the Tilis.
2 Tilis claim that the name comes from *tulu*, the balance scale used by shop-keepers, and in the 1770s, Krisna Kanta Nandy, a wealthy and influential Tili, successfully appealed to brahmin pundits in asserting the claim. Risley, *The Tribes and Castes of Bengal*, 2:309; Nandy, 1:22-23; 498. J. N. Bhattacharya, 209, disputes the claim.
3 See Koalhoos (Kalu), Pl. II.58.
4 Risley, *The Tribes and Castes of Bengal*, discusses the Tilis only under his entry for Teli, 2:305-10. Also see Wise, 389-91; J. N. Bhattacharya, 209; Asok Mitra, *The Castes and Tribes of West Bengal*, 33-34.
5 127.
6 Risley, *The Tribes and Castes of Bengal*, 2:309.
7 See Nandy. On the role of the banian, see the Commentary for Solvyns's portrayal of the banian, Pl. II.99 (who Nandy mistakenly takes to be a likeness of Cantoo Baboo). Somendra Chandra Nandy is a direct descendant of Cantoo Baboo and bears the title Maharajkumar of Cossimbazar. He is a prominent Calcutta industrialist and distinguished scholar. The two-volume work on Cantoo Baboo is the most detailed study of any eighteenth century banian.

Palanquin Bearers

Solvyns portrays palanquin bearers by caste in four Paris etchings, distinguishing their status and characteristics. He depicts another caste of palanquin bearers (Pl. II.76) in his Calcutta collection that he does not include in the Paris edition. In a separate section, Solvyns portrays the various kinds of palanquins (Pls. II.221-28).

In Calcutta, in Solvyns's time, most Europeans and Indians who could afford to do so had private palanquins and kept their own teams of bearers, using them in household employment when not engaged as carriers. But hired palanquins were readily available on short notice, and even for those who had their own palanquin, bearers could be hired as needed.[1] Public palanquins were subject to regulation by the East India Company,[2] and labor relations could sometimes be difficult, especially with the highly-organized Oriya bearers.

The number of carriers varied according to the bearers' caste, the type of palanquin used, the occasion, and as to whether it was within town or on extended travel in the countryside. Typically, the bearers would move at "a steady running walk," averaging about four miles an hour, including stops taken every quarter mile to shift positions so as to change the shoulder on which the pole rests.[3] In extended travel, the team would have enough carriers to permit alternation in bearing the palanquin, and at relay houses—"*dāk* stages"[4]—along the road a fresh team would be ready to take over.

Teams were usually matched by height, but "When their heights are unequal, they use a small quilted pad of linen, stuffed with rags or cotton, which is suspended from the palankeen pole, or bamboo, placed between it and the shoulder. . . ."[5]

---

1 Johnson, 1:43, quoted in Nair, *Calcutta in the 19th Century*, 827.

2 The East India Company, for example, in 1774, specified that a "set of bearers" should consist of six carriers and a headman. P. J. Marshall, "The Company and the Coolies," 24.

3 Johnson, 1:43-44, quoted in Nair, *Calcutta in the 19th Century*, 827.

4 "Dawk," *Hobson-Jobson*, 300.

5 Williamson, 1:300-310.

II.43. Palanquin Bearers of the Oriya Caste

Pl. II.43. Oriya Bearers. Paris: I.7.2.
Calcutta: Sec. I, No. 25. Ooria Bearers, commonly called Balasore Bearers,—they have regular meetings and clubs, with the President or surdars [*sardārs*], to regulate the duties the class shall perform in service.

Paris: I.7.2. PALANQUIN CARRIERS OF THE OORIAH CAST: We have already mentioned the Ooriahs in their quality of Brahmuns [Pl. II.17]. We are now to notice them as palanquin Carriers, and shall have occasion to speak of them hereafter in other capacities.

The inhabitants of Hindoostan, who are any way in easy circumstances, never go out on foot. They are carried in palanquins, a sort of chair of which the description will be given in its proper place. The number of Carriers, for those who do not go much abroad, is generally seven or eight, and never less than five. The Ooriahs prefer the service of foreigners, and especially of Europeans, to that of the natives. They are much cleaner about their persons than the other Carriers; but are inferior to them in their manner of serving. Whether from meer caprice or from their being subject to a number of minute ceremonies, they are much less ready and obliging. They are under *Serdars* [*sardārs*] or chiefs, who meet together, and establish rules, which a private Carrier does not dare to disobey. Whence it happens, that they often refuse to render services which do not appear to be at all out of their line.

While they have no objection, for example, to brushing cloaths, or even cleaning shoes, they will refuse to hand a glass of water. They will give you a light, provided it be of wax or oil; for they would by no means light a tallow candle. They never extinguish a light otherwise than by agitating the air with their hand or with their cloaths, and would loose their cast by blowing it out with their breath. An opportunity of describing a number of other singular habits of the Ooriahs, will occur in the article of domestics, in the fourth volume [Sardār, Pl. II.106].

Commentary: The Oriya (or Balasore) bearers were the most prominent of the palanquin carriers in Calcutta, and in private employment, like other carriers, their responsibilities embraced various household duties in addition to bearing the palanquin at such times as required. In his note to the drawing, Solvyns writes that although Europeans prefer Oriyas over other bearers for their cleanly appearance, "they are objected to by many for their scruples to do any household duties which their Brahmuns declare . . . against the tenants of their Religion."

Williamson described the Oriya bearers as able-bodied, capable, and neat in their person and dress. Their dress, he writes, consists merely of a *dhotī*, wrapped round the middle and tucked in, together with a cloth, usually folded and carried over the shoulder, to be thrown over them in inclement weather. They wear no turban and "preserve one lock of hair on the top of their heads"—a style, not evident in the Solvyns etching but distinctive among the Oriya bearers, that involved shaving the front of the scalp and pulling the hair at the back into a knot. (See Alefounder's etching of "A Balasore Bearer," Pl. I.19, p. 34.) They "touch their faces, arms, throats, and breasts with sandal-wood and vermilion." Some wear small beads, chiefly of turned wood, about their necks, and occasionally a stout silver bangle on each wrist, as seen in Solvyns's portrayal. "The *Ooreah* bearers never wear shoes and prefer clothes of an almond colour."[1]

Solvyns portrays the Oriya bearer as a man of considerable dignity, and gives prominence to his distinctive umbrella, or *chātā*, as does Colesworthy Grant in a later print of "Ooriah Bearers."[2] Most palanquin teams included a *chātā*-bearer, but for the Oriya bearers, the *chātā* was emblematic of their claim to high status—as, no doubt, was the lock, or "tuft," associated with brahmins, though most Oriya palanquin carriers came from the Goālā cowherd caste, also depicted by Solvyns with a *chātā* (Pl. II.47). Their status was asserted—and preserved—as well by their adherence to caste strictures.

The Oriya bearers were organized in what were effectively labor unions. In 1766, Thomas Motte—to whom Solvyns refers in his note to the drawing of the Oriya bearer—described them coming from Bhadrakh taluq, near Balasore, in Orissa. "Seven thousand of the stoutest young fellows go into Bengal, and are employed as chairmen, leaving their families behind." In Calcutta, they form a "Commonwealth"—"the most politic in the world"—with "president" and "councils" to determine their conditions of work. "They have gained their present ascendance by taking advantage of the heat of the climate and the indolence of the English," Motte writes, "for if a person incurs the displeasure of this Worshipful Society, he may walk till he dies of fever." Thus, "by their concord they have made themselves masters of the conquerors of Hindustan."[3]

An American merchant, Dudley Pickman, who visited Calcutta in 1803-1804, wrote in his journal that the Oriya bearers "are so leagued that any injury done to one of them is resented by the whole class and an European sometimes finds it difficult or impossible to get a new set of bearers till he has appeased the wrath of his former ones."[4] They were still a formidable force in 1827, when in protest against new regulations and taxes, they went on strike and threatened to march *en masse* back to Orissa.[5]

In the background of the etching is a chair pālki (Pl. II.228).

---

1 Williamson, 1:300-310.
2 *Sketches of Oriental Heads*, Pl. 34.
3 Motte, 54. Also see W. H. Carey, *Good Old Days*, 2:70; Pradip Sinha, *Calcutta in Urban History*, 249; and P. J. Marshall, "The Company and the Coolies," 24. On Motte's mission in Orissa, see Phillimore, 1:30.
4 "Journal of the *Derby*, 1803-1804," Phillips Library, Peabody Essex Museum, Salem, Massachusetts, quoted in Bean, *Yankee India*, 114.
5 *Calcutta Gazette*, May 28, 1827, and Colesworthy Grant, *Anglo-Indian Domestic Life*, 67-68.

II.44. Palanquin Bearers of the Rawāni Caste

Pl. II.44. Rawāni Bearers. Paris: I.7.3.
Calcutta: Sec. I, No. 26. Rowanny Bearers, often called Patna Bearers.
Orme: 5.

Paris: I.7.3. CARRIERS OF THE ROWANNY CAST: These are known chiefly in the north of Hindoostan, tho' some are seen at Calcutta, in the service mostly of the military. In their manner of serving they make fewer difficulties, and are of an abler frame of body than the Ooriahs, owing perhaps to the habit of drinking the strong liquors of the country, such as rum, arrack, tarry [*tāṛī*], a spirit extracted from the fruit of the cocoa-tree.[1] They do not even scruple to drink European wines, nor to eat meat coming from the table of foreigners. The author has often seen them eating even pork, without any fear of losing their cast.

The *Rowannys* are to be preferred for the service of the army, and altogether are better than the other Carriers. Their dress is such as it is represented in the plate. They wear commonly a *Paquie* [*pāg* or *pāgaṛi*], or very full turban, carry large whiskers, and let their beards grow even upon their cheeks. The Hindoos of Bengal frequently class them with the Musselmans, though many of them are strict observers of the law of Brahmah. Their wives and children almost always follow them. Their principal nourishment is wheat-flour kneaded with water into a cake [chapati, *capātī*].

Commentary: Rawāni is a subcaste of the Kahārs, a large cultivator and palanquin-bearing caste of Bihar, that had even into the eighteenth century been held in slavery. They came into Bengal principally as palanquin carriers and domestic servants for Indians and Europeans. They are traditionally ranked among the lower śūdra castes, despite their alleged propensity to drink and comparative laxity in dietary customs. Those in domestic service assert higher status than those in the more menial palanquin-bearing occupations, but employed in the households of those with private palanquins, Rawānis worked as domestic servants when not otherwise employed in carrying the master's palanquin.[2]

Wise described Rawānis as "the most docile and industrious of workmen [and] in much request throughout Bengal."[3] They served as a lower class of palanquin bearer, but worked as scullions, water-carriers, and personal attendants. "In every well-to-do family," J. N. Bhattacharya writes, "there is at least one Rawani to serve as the 'maid of all work.'"[4] They were particularly favored by Europeans, as Solvyns notes, because of their willingness to take, without caste compunction, almost any task. In his notes to the original drawing, Solvyns wrote that Rawānis are "generally employed by Gentlemen of the Army" because "they do not refuse menial duties, are well-clothed, . . . and of a strong athletic make."

The Orme text, accompanying the pirated depiction of Solvyns's "Rowanny Bearer," states that often the head palanquin bearer takes charge of his master's apparel and carry keys emblematic of his duties, while others are employed about the house and in the garden. "They are remarkably honest, and the utmost confidence is placed in them." In the Calcutta edition (and in Orme), Solvyns portrays the Rawāni with keys hanging from his cummerbund; they are absent in the Paris etching.

Mrs. Belnos portrays a team of Rawāni bearers, with a chair palanquin, waiting for a European gentleman to conclude his business with an Indian "baboo," for whom Oriya bearers wait with a long palanquin.[5] Belnos also sketched a team of six Rawāni bearers celebrating the Holī festival,[6] but in Bengal, Rawānis are especially devoted to Kālī, and their usual cry, in taking the palanquin on to and from their shoulders, was "*Jai Kālī Kalkattāwālī*," Long live Kālī of Calcutta.[7]

The Rawāni depicted by Solvyns stands before a thatched house—probably a *dāk* bungalow (a rest house for travelers)[8] or relay house for the palanquin bearers—and what appears to be a covered *colāpā* palanquin (Pl. II.221). The house is Solvyns's clearest depiction of the bungalow (*bāṅgālā*), a form adapted by Europeans in rural Bengal. The bungalow is a single-storied, rectangular house, with a sloping thatched or tile roof. A ceiling made of white cloth prevented thatch and vermin from falling on the bungalow's occupants. In the European versions, windows usually had venetians, as seen in the print. The entrance typically opened onto a veranda on which people might relax and enjoy the breeze. Captain Bellew, in his *Memoir of a Griffin*, noted that the veranda was often occupied by the master's palanquin, camp equipment, etc., and "there too the bearers lie and snore during the sultry hours. . . ."[9]

1 On *tāṛī* (toddy), see Pl. II.62.
2 Risley, *The Tribes and Castes of Bengal*, "Kahār," 1:370-75.
3 Quoted in Risley, *The Tribes and Castes of Bengal*, 1:374.
4 246.
5 *Twenty-Four Plates Illustrative of Hindoo and European Manners in Bengal*, Pl. 23.
6 Ibid., Pl. 11.
7 J. N. Bhattacharya, 246-47.
8 See *Hobson-Jobson*, 129.
9 Quoted in Sykes, 25. On the bungalow, see *Hobson-Jobson*, 128-29, and Williamson, *The East India Vade-Mecum*, 1:488-518; and on its architecture, King, *The Bungalow*, 14-64, 123-55; Nilsson, 186; and Buchanan, 2:922-24.

II.45. Dulīa. Palanquin Bearer

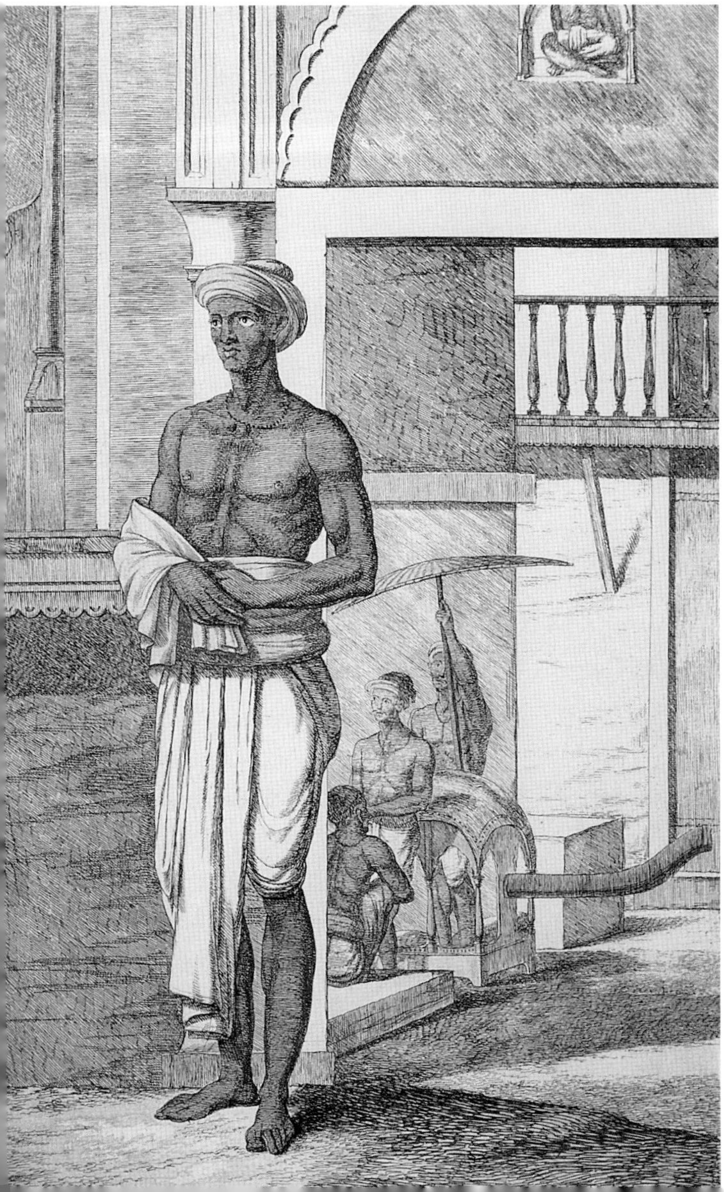

Paris: I.7.4: DOOLEES, OR CARRIERS OF THE CAST OF BENGALEES: These Carriers are appropriated to the service of the Hindoos, though some may be met with the houses of Europeans, and even of Musselmans. The *Baboos* [bābūs][1] or people of easy fortunes, the *Bannyans* [banians, Pl. II.99] or bankers, and the *Sircars* [Pl. II.100] or commissioners, are in the habit of employing them. They have lower wages than the others; but, being ill fed, they have also less strength: and from their dirtiness are unfit for any other domestic service, than meerly carrying the palanquin, and scarcely even that, except in the country. In a word, they are the lowest class of Carriers, and might without injustice be called *Pariahs*,[2] a disgrace which they are sure to incur when they take to drinking strong liquors to which they are very subject, though their ordinary drink ought to consist only of water. Their food is no other than herbs boiled up with coarse rice, and seldom extends to fish, which is the favourite food of the other Hindoos.

Pl. II.45. Dulīa. Paris: I.7.4.
Calcutta: Sec. I, No. 27. Doolee-a Bearers, who should confine themselves to carrying the Dooly.

Commentary: The term *duliā* (*dulīya* or *dule*), from *dulī*, a type of palanquin (Pl. II.224), means literally "bearer of a palanquin" and was often used to refer generally to palanquin carriers. Its more particular use, however, as in Solvyns's description, refers to the palanquin-bearing subcastes of the untouchable Bāgdi (Pl. II.79) and Bauri (Pl. II.76) communities.

The Duliā Bāgdi were more numerous and is likely the caste Solvyns portrays. In addition to carrying palanquins, Risley writes, Dulīas, in common with other Bāgdi subcastes, "earn their livelihood by fishing, making gunny-bags, weaving cotton, and preparing the red powder (*abir*) for the Holī festival."[3]

The palanquin depicted is a miyānā, portrayed by Solvyns in a separate etching (Pl. II.225).

1 Once a term of respect for Bengali gentlemen, but transformed by the British into one of "disparagement, as characterizing a superficially cultivated, but too often effeminate, Bengali." *Hobson-Jobson*, 44.

2 See Commentary, Pl. II.22.

3 *The Tribes and Castes of Bengal*, 1:42. Also see Mitra, *Tribes and Castes of West Bengal*, 70.

II.46. Jāliyā Bearers

Paris: I.7.5. JELLEES, OR CARRIERS OF THE CAST OF FISHERMEN: Their chief business is fishing, but very different from the rest of the Hindoos. They are of so active a disposition, that they become palanquin Carriers, when the lowness of the waters interrupts their former occupation. And even in this occasional employment, they turn to profit every moment of leisure which it leaves them. They carry their work with them, when they go out with the palanquin; and as often as they stop, they immediately begin to twist their thread or make their nets, which by these means are in readiness at the return of the fishing season. They have various ways of catching fish, unknown in Europe, which, as they are interesting at least to our curiosity, will not be neglected in the course of this work.

These Carriers too have but a mean appearance. They are ill dressed, and frequently dirty. Their turban is small, and their head is sometimes covered only with a stripe of yellow linnen. They are represented with great truth in the engraving; where it is needless to repeat that the outline and colouring are always taken from nature.

Pl. II.46. Jāliyā Bearers. Paris: I.7.5.

Calcutta: Sec. I, No. 28. Jellee-a Bearers: by cast Fishermen, which profession they occasionally follow—when they lay down the Palenqueen they employ themselves in making fishing nets.

Commentary: Solvyns portrays the Jāliyā (or Jele) as fishermen in a separate etching (Pl. II.57). The term applies generally to the fisher subcastes of a number of Bengali castes,[1] and here Solvyns affirms their enterprise in taking up the palanquin when not employed in their primary occupation.

1 Risley, *The Tribes and Castes of Bengal*, 1:340-42, and Mitra, *Tribes and Castes of West Bengal*, 73.

II.47. Goālā. Cow-Herd

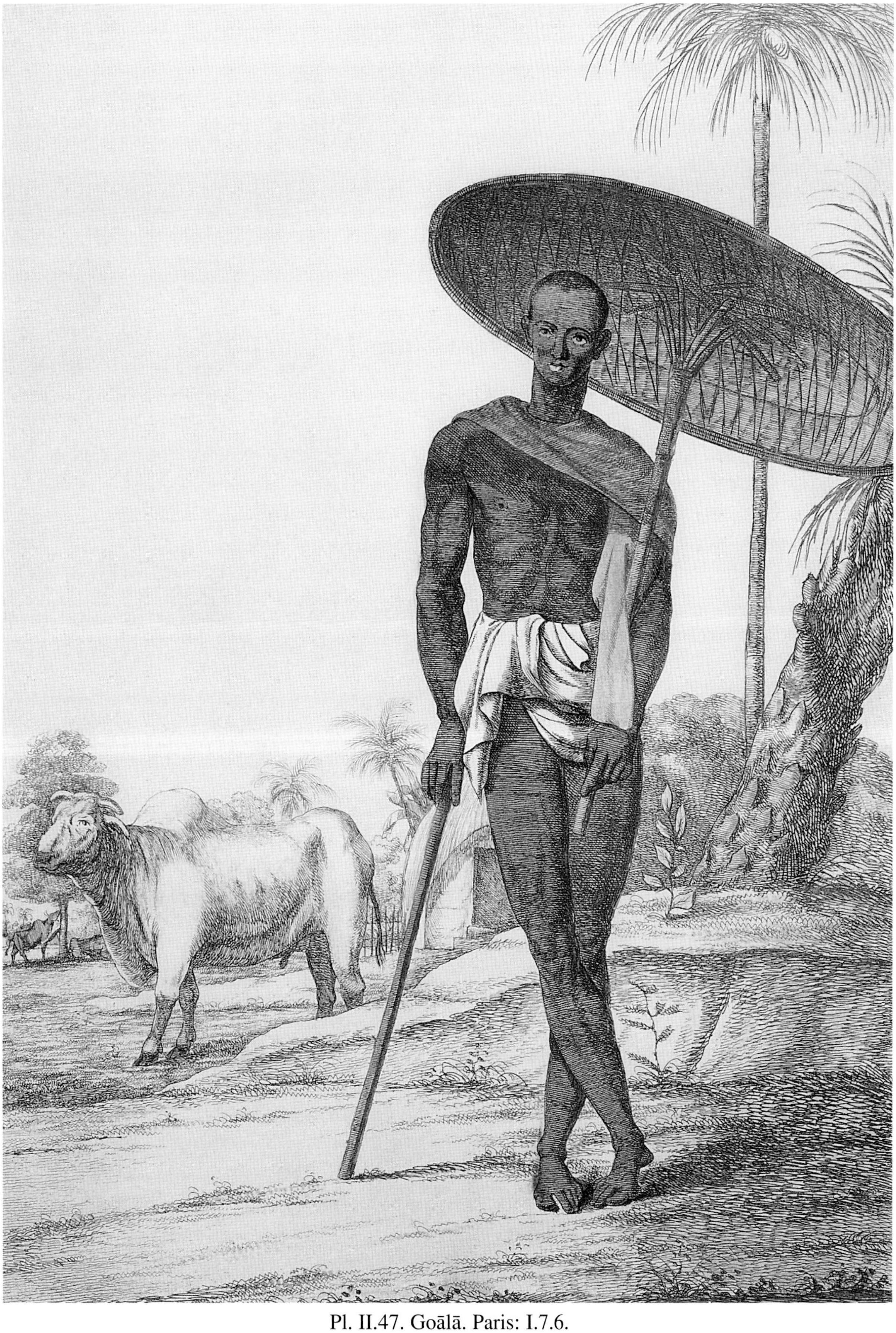

Pl. II.47. Goālā. Paris: I.7.6.

Calcutta: Sec. I, No. 36. A Gwalla, or Cowherd—the Cows are remarkable for the hump on their shoulders.

Paris: I.7.6. GWALLAHS. COW-HERDS: The Cow-herds being almost always Ouriahs [Oriyas], are often confounded with the Ouriah Carriers, so that it appeared proper to class them together.

While the *Gwallah* is tending his cows, he preserves everywhere the same attitude, leaning on a little stick, with a *chattah* [*chātā*] or umbrella in his hand. This umbrella too is of the same form for all the Cow-herds: it is one of those articles of domestic use which serve to denote the different casts of the Hindoos, each cast having one peculiar to itself. The same rule is applicable to many other things; the shoes, the sticks, the water-pots, the vases for boiling rice, etc. All the different forms of these had become so familiar to the author, that it was impossible for a Hindoo to conceal his cast from him.

The *Gwallah* women rub their bodies and those of their children, in the same way as they do their houses, with the dung and urine of their cows; which gives them a deep yellow tint. But as these animals are objects of veneration in the country, some degree of consideration derives to those whose business it is to attend them.

Commentary: The Goālā is the large caste of cow-herders, or *gopas*, in Bengal and Orissa and is related to the Āhir (Pl. II.28) of Bihar and North India.[1] Risley treats the two as regional names for the same pastoral caste, noting various usages and distinctions. The Bihari Āhirs, as Solvyns noted in his discussion, command a higher social status than the Bengali Goālās, but the Oriya Goālās assert superiority over the others by reason of their ritual purity and religious orthodoxy.[2]

The *chātā*, umbrella, which catches Solvyns's fancy, is made of palm leaves, and in Bengal, such a covering, without the pole, is also worn as a hat. The umbrella is traditionally associated with superior social position, and its use by Oriya Goālās reflects their assertion of dignity. The Oriya palanquin bearers, who come from the Goālā caste, also affect the umbrella, as we saw in Solvyns's depiction in Pl. II.43, but most palanquin teams, of whatever caste, included an attendant with an umbrella.

Solvyns depicts a Goālinī, woman of the Goālā caste, in Pl. II.90.

---

1 The Indian artist of the Fraser album (see Chapter Three, pp. 101-04) labels the print, in Bengali, as *Rākhāl*, meaning literally "a watch guard," but a term referring to cowherds.

2 *The Tribes and Castes of Bengal*, 1:282-90. Also see J. N. Bhattacharya, 238-39.

II.48. Rājput. Soldier

Pl. II. 48. Rājput. Paris: I.8.2.

Calcutta: Sec. I, No. 50. A Rajpoot: by profession they are generally soldiers:—here he is represented in an undress.

Paris: I.8.2: RAJPOOTS: These Hindoos, who bear the name of the country which they inhabit, form a military cast connected with that of the Khutterys [kṣatriya], of whom we have already spoken. They are a brave and robust people, and though strict observers of the religion of Brahma, they allow themselves some relaxation when from home. They serve as soldiers for pay, preferring those who offer most. For this reason probably they are so numerous in the English armies. More sedentary nevertheless than the other military hindoo tribes, they spread less abroad, especially in Bengal and the south of Hindoostan.

The tribe of Rajpoots, as well as those of which we are going to speak, consist of primitive Hindoos and were known before the invasion of Timur or Tamerlan. Since that time they are so much assimilated to the Musselmans, that it requires some attention to retrace their original character.

The Rajpoot represented in the engraving is leaning carelessly against a tree: his dress is not military, because we profess to treat only of the distinction of casts by Menu [Manu], the Hindoo legislator.

Commentary: The Rājputs are the warrior caste from Rajasthan in western India. Romanticized by the British in such chronicles as James Tod's *Annals and Antiquities of Rajasthan*[1] and described as one of the "martial races," they were recruited for service in the Indian Army under the Raj.[2]

In Solvyns's time in Bengal, Rājputs were sometimes termed "Tonkmen," a name derived from the Tonk region of Rajasthan. J. N. Bhattacharya writes, "The Rajputs are . . . true Ksatriyas. . . . The inferior Rajputs of Bengal are called Pukuria or 'Tonkmen.' They wear the sacred thread, but some of them are to be found employed as domestic servants and tillers of the soil."[3]

A copy of Solvyns's figure, with modifications in the position, appears among the color prints in Wahlen's *Moeurs, usages et costumes de tours les peuples du mond* (1843).[4]

---

1 Originally published, 1829-32.

2 On the "martial races," see Philip Mason, 341-61. For a discussion of Rājputs in Bengal, see Risley, *The Tribes and Castes of Bengal*, 2:184-92. For a description and portrayal of Rājput military, see Thapliyal, 15-16 and plate.

3 109.

4 Vol. I, *Asia*.

II.49. Rāwāt/Rāut. Soldier

Pl. II.49. Rāwāt/Rāut. Paris: I.8.3.

Calcutta: Sec. I, No. 51. Rauwut,—a soldier differing little from the Rajpoot.

Paris: I.8.3: RAUWUTS: This tribe, who inhabit a mountainous country, form also a military cast, and esteem themselves superior to the others, asserting that they, as well as the Ouriahs [Oriya], descend from the first inhabitants of Hindoostan, which adds not a little to their pride.

Their customs are the same as those of the other Hindoos, but from their mixing with the Musselmans they have in some degree taken the manners of the conquerors, whom notwithstanding they detest. Their dress consequently bears no resemblance to the other Hindoos.

Many of them are seen in the service of the grandees of the country, as well as of foreigners, to whom their fidelity and activity are a recommendation. They are well looking and have something of a military air; but are nevertheless seldom employed in the service of the house, as they would not easily bear the subjection of domestic attendance. They run before the palanquin, go on messages, carry letters, etc.

Commentary: The identity of Solvyns's "Rauwut" is not clear. It could be the Rāwāt, a small Rājput clan of alleged Āhir-Rājput descent and concentrated geographically in the districts of Fatehpur and Unnao in what is now central Uttar Pradesh. In Solvyns's time, the area lay within the kingdom of Awadh (Oudh), which might account for the Muslim manners Solvyns describes, but it is on the Gangetic plain and hardly "mountainous country."[1]

Perhaps more likely, "Rauwut" might be the Rautiā landholding and cultivating caste of Chota Nagpur, the rugged hill country of southeastern Bihar and western Orissa. Henry M. Elliott notes that the cognate term Rāut is used in some districts for inferior Rājputs,[2] and the Rājput association is reflected in the Rautiā tradition that military service was their original occupation.[3] Risley, in *The Tribes and Castes of Bengal*, describes them as ranking "fairly high" socially,[4] but makes no reference to the Muslim manners referred to by Solvyns. It is possible, however, that in military service under Muslim rulers, they acquired the Muslim dress and manners Solvyns observed among them in Calcutta.

Solvyns depicts the Rāut against a background of "mountainous country," perhaps Chota Nagpur, but this is a setting of the artist's imagination, for Solvyns nowhere indicates that he traveled beyond the environs of Calcutta.

1 Bahadur, 125.

2 *Encyclopaedia of Castes, Customs, Rites and Superstitions of the Races of Northern Indian*, 24.

3 Risley, *The Tribes and Castes of Bengal*, 2:207. Entry for Rautiā, 2:199-209.

4 Ibid., 2:207-08.

II.50. Brajbāsī. Guard

Pl. II.50. Brajbāsī, Guard. Paris: I.8.4.

Calcutta: Sec. I, No. 52. Brijbasi, employed by merchants and bankers to guard their effects, and are noted for their fidelity and courage.

Orme: 10

Paris: I.8.4: BRIJBASIS, A HINDOO TRIBE: It is needless to repeat what has been already said, in the article of the Brahmuns, of the bravery and fidelity of the Brijbasys, as well as of the sort of services in which they are employed, such as escorting merchandises from distant countries, etc.: the idea of which is recalled in the print. It is necessary only to add, that travellers never fail to engage them in their suite, when safety is an object; and that moreover their service is in every respect so much to be preferred, that they are to be met with in that of Hindoos, Musselmans and Europeans.

They paint, as may be seen in the print, their faces and their bodies, as well from a religious practise as to give themselves a martial appearance. They continue to carry the old arms of the country, and make use of match-locks. They have archers among them (*tirendars*) [Persian, *tīrandāz*] who draw their bow, sitting, with their feet, and shoot a dozen arrows together, many of which are poisoned, and all pointed so as to make a very dangerous wound. They have also hunters, (*cicarries*) [*shikārīs*, Pl. I.38]; but these are not in general numerous among the Hindoos: many assume the name, but they are in reality only to be met with among the military casts whom we are now describing.

The Brijbacy women are tall, well made, and of a lighter colour than the men: the children have this tint; but the boys become darker as they grow up, probably when they begin to lead the same life as their fathers.

Commentary: The Brajbāsī brahmins, as we saw in the discussion of the brahmins (Pl. II.16), are from Braj, the area in today's Uttar Pradesh that includes Mathura, Agra, and Etawah. Risley writes that "the warlike character of the Braj people has led to the term Brajbāsi being used to denote an armed attendant, one carrying arms, as a sword and shield, or sometimes a matchlock, and employed as a door-keeper, a guard, or an escort. . . ."[1] Various British glossaries of Indian terms include an entry for Brajbāsīs, as men, armed with swords and shields, employed by zamīndārs to guard their property against *dacoits* (robbers).[2]

All Europeans did not share Solvyns's judgment as to their "fidelity and courage." as the handwritten comment in a volume of the Calcutta etchings attests: "Note ought to have been for their infidelity and cowardice."[3]

The term *Brajbāsī* may be used to refer to anyone from Braj, and perhaps here Solvyns uses the name to include more than brahmins alone. But that brahmins were engaged as soldiers was not at all unusual. From the later eighteenth century, the Bengal Army recruited substantial numbers of brahmins as sepoys, principally from Bihar and Uttar Pradesh.[4] The painted marks on the face and chest of the Brajbāsī portrayed indicates that he is probably a Vaiṣṇavite "renouncer," of an order of warrior ascetics, here employed as an armed guard.

Solvyns portrays another Brajbāsī in military dress in the Calcutta edition (Pl. II.97), an etching not included in *Les Hindoûs*.

---

1 *The Tribes and Castes of Bengal*, 1:162.

2 See Charles Wilkins, *A Glossary of Oriental Terms*, 1493; Stocqueler, *The Oriental Interpreter*, 41; and *A Glossary of Indian Terms*, 35.

3 The comment, perhaps by J. Gillett, appears beside the handwritten *Catalogue* text copied in the volume of etchings owned originally by Gillett and now in the collection of the Wellcome Institute, London. The "J." is likely Jonathan, who with his brother Gabriel, were shipbuilders in Calcutta. Solvyns probably painted his "The Launching of Garbriel Gillett's Armed Merchantman in Calcutta Harbour" (Pl. I.11) for the family.

4 See Pl. II.95, Sepoys.

II.51. Sikh

Paris: I.8.5: SICS, A HINDOO TRIBE: These Hindoos form also a people with independent laws and customs. There are persons who hesitate to rank them among the Hindoos. But it is certain that their tribe was founded by Nanuck-Shah [Guru Nānak], a descendant of Timur's, who through expiations and money was allowed to become a Hindoo. The first volume of the Transactions of the Asiatic Society of Calcutta may be consulted upon this subject.[3]

The Sics never quit their families but for military service. They are brave, and acquit themselves well in battle; but all their force is in their first charge: if that is resisted, their defeat soon follows.

It is worthy of observation, that among them a family goes into mourning on the birth of a child, and rejoices and puts on white clothes when death carries off one of its members. This custom, which has been remarked among other nations, proceeds from an opinion perhaps too well founded, that this world is a vale of tears and misery, from which it is always a happiness to be delivered.

The Sic who forms the principal figure in this engraving, is in his ordinary costume, which is black, or oftener very dark blue. The back ground of the plate gives a view of the mountainous country which these Hindoos inhabit, with a group of their warriors near a tent, which is their ordinary abode.

Commentary: There were not many Sikhs in Bengal when Solvyns arrived in 1791, though, earlier in the century, the great Sikh banker and urban landlord Omichand was among Calcutta's most prominent residents.[4] But if comparatively few in number, Sikhs were distinguished by their dress and customs and drew Solvyns's attention as he prepared his collection of etchings. Solvyns provides the earliest published depictions of Sikhs in his two prints, "A Sic in his family dress," portrayed here, and "A Nanuk-Punthy" (Pl. II.139), in the series of etchings depicting "Faquirs and Holy Mendicants." The descriptive text of the 1799 *Catalogue* and that of the Paris edition reflect limited information and considerable confusion on Solvyns's part, and his portrayal and description of the Nānak Panthī is as baffling as it is interesting.[5]

The Sikhs emerged as a distinct religious community from among Punjabi Hindus who followed the teachings of Guru Nānak (1469-1539). Nānak—often Nanuck Shah in early European writings—was of a Hindu family, and one can only wonder where Solvyns heard that he was a descendent of Timur and a convert to Hinduism. There are no such references in Ghulam Hussain or in Wilkins nor, indeed, in any published work on the Sikhs.[6]

Solvyns refers to the Sikhs as "these Hindoos," as most understood themselves, but Khālsā Sikhs increasingly sought to shape a consciousness of their distinctive character, and it is evident from Solvyns's comments that by the late eighteenth century some observers regarded them as a separate religious body.[7] The British, who fought the Sikhs in two wars (1845-46 and 1848-49), later recruited them for the Indian Army as one of the "martial races."

Solvyns portrays the Sikhs, though without specification in the text, with some of the visible

Pl. II.51. Sikh. Paris: I.8.5.

Calcutta: Sec. I, No. 9. A Sic in his family dress—the back ground represents them armed as Soldiers.

The History and origin of this curious Tribe, are to be met with in Hadgee Mustafah's Translate of Golaum Housain Khaun's Seir Mutaquirean;[1] and an account of them by Mr. Wilkins, is inserted in 1st Volume of the Transactions of the Asiatic Society.[2]

attributes of membership in the Khālsā, the militant Sikh order established by Guru Gobind Singh in 1699. Prominent among the distinguishing features are the "Five Ks," items (each beginning with the letter "k") that males must wear: uncut hair, sword or dagger; steel bangle on the right wrist; distinctive military-style shorts; and the comb worn in the topknot of the hair (concealed beneath the turban and unseen in the print).[8]

Khālsā Sikhs also wear dark blue garments and turban—not black, as Solvyns describes. Guru Gobind Singh never required Sikhs to wear any particular color, but Ganda Singh, in an annotation to Browne's early account of the Sikhs, writes that the zealous Nihang sect "patronized the dark blue colour used by the Guru during his escape from Machhiwara. As the Nihangs exercised great influence in the community and occasionally led the expeditions of the Sikhs against their enemies, their dark blue dress acquired general popularity."[9]

Europeans, like Solvyns, often took the distinctively-dressed and militant Khālsā Sikhs as constituting the whole of the Sikh community, but the Panth, as the Sikh community is known, included a variety of other groups, such as the Nānak-panthī, who Solvyns depicts (Pl. II.139) in his series of religious mendicants, although apparently without recognizing them as Sikhs.

Solvyns's comment on Sikh military tactics—that "all their force is in their first charge; if that is resisted, their defeat soon follows"—is unsupported. Colonel Polier, in his 1787 presentation on the Sikhs before the Asiatic Society in Calcutta, held that "their military capacity . . . are far from being so formidable as they are generally represented, or as they might be," attributing this to "disorderly manner" in which they fight."[10] Such views may have been held by a few Europeans in Calcutta in Solvyns's time, but they contrast with the more general judgment of "remarkably good" Sikh military skill.[11] W. H. McLeod suggests that Solvyns (and others) may have been confused by a frequently used Sikh tactic "to feign flight and then pull up suddenly and strike their enemy who would be caught off balance."[12]

Solvyns's discussion of Sikh birth and death practices is similarly at odds with their tradition. McLeod relates that "The Sikhs (and Punjabis) in general) have been a world-affirming and life-affirming community, and such practices would seem to be in direct contradiction to their normal way of viewing such incidents."[13]

The differences between Solvyns's Calcutta and Paris prints are considerable. In the Calcutta etching, the central figure, a Kes-dhārī Sikh,[14] stands against a clouded sky and wears a black cloak and blue turban, tied as many Sikhs then bound their turban. In the background are three small armed figures, two standing and one sitting. In the Paris print, against a clear sky, the central figure is depicted with a more natural face, with finer features, and the cloak and turban are colored dark blue—despite the text reference in the Paris edition to the black costume. The small background figures have been replaced by two Sikhs, both armed, now standing in the foreground just behind the central figure. In both Calcutta and Paris editions, the shorts are shown as white, and in each, the principal figure of the Sikh is depicted without a sword or dagger. The shoes are of Punjabi style, save for the instep Solvyns depicts, but are not typical of those generally worn by the Sikhs.

Both plates depict a hilly background and in the text he refers to "the mountainous country which these Hindoos inhabit," but it was only during the seventeenth and early eighteenth centuries that Sikhs occupied the hills. By Solvyns's time, their land was principally the Punjabi plains.

---

1 Syed Gholam Hossein Khan [Ghulam Hussain Khan], *Sëir Mutaqherin: or View of Modern Times, Being a History of India*, published in Calcutta in 1789. The discussion of " Nanec-Shah" and the "Sycs" appears in 1:82-84. The translation is by M. Raymond, a French Creole, who had assumed the Muslim name Hajee Mustapha, but the published translation from Persian appeared under the pseudonym Nota Manus. A later translation, *Siyas-ul-Mutakherin*, was published in London in 1832.

2 Charles Wilkins, "Observations on the Seeks and their College" [1781], *Asiatick Researches* 1 (1788): 246-54. Colonel A. L. H. Polier read a paper on the "The Siques," at a meeting of the Asiatic Society in Calcutta in 1787, but it was not published until its inclusion in *Indian Studies: Past & Present* in 1962. For another early account in the transactions of the Asiatic Society, see Sir John Malcolm, "Sketch of the Sikhs." Also see Ward, "Account of the Sikhs, A Sect of Hindoos," in *Account of the . . . Hindoos*, 4:381-406, and Ward, *A View . . . of the Hindoos*," 3:448-66.

3 The brief Wilkins article, cited above, is the only discussion of the Sikhs in Vol. I of *Asiatick Researches*, and it makes no reference to Guru Nānak as a descendant of Timur.

4 Described as a Punjabi and by faith a Nānak Panthī in Buckland, *Dictionary of Indian Biography*, 322-23.

5 See Hardgrave, "An Early Portrayal of the Sikhs: Two Eighteenth Century Etchings by Baltazard Solvyns," for an

expanded discussion of Solvyns's depiction of the Sikhs and of portrayals of Sikhs by other artists in the nineteenth century.

6 Letter from W. H. McLeod to the author, December 16, 1994. For a discussion of early European writing on the Sikhs, see Grewal, *Guru Nanak in Western Scholarship*. On the Sikhs generally, see McLeod, *The Sikhs: History, Religion, and Society*, and his *Historical Dictionary of Sikhism*. For Sikh history, see Khushwant Singh, *A History of the Sikhs*, and Grewal, *The Sikhs of the Punjab*. Madra and Singh provide an account of the Sikh military tradition, with numerous illustrations, including Solvyns's etching, 29.

7 Oberoi, 24, emphasizes the fluidity of Sikh identity well into the nineteenth century, but notes the dramatic change in the eighteenth century as the Khālsā Sikhs pushed for "a distinct and separate religious culture." On the problem of Sikh identity, also see McLeod, *The Sikhs*, 16-47. Although a matter of controversy, McLeod argues that it was only with the Singh Sabha movement in the late nineteenth century that Sikhs asserted their separateness from the Hindus.

8 Five Ks, *Panj-Kakkas*, in Dogra and Mansukhani, 148-49, and McLeod, *The Sikhs*, 45, 71-72.

9 Ganda Singh, 17, fn. 4. Solvyns is apparently unaware of Major James Browne, "History of the Origin and Progress of the Sicks," the first treatise on the Sikhs by an Englishman, published as part of *India Tracts* in 1788.

10 60.

11 Browne, 17.

12 Letter, December 16, 1994.

13 Ibid.

14 An "orthodox" Khālsā Sikh with uncut hair. See McLeod, *The Sikhs*, 78-80.

II.52. Mārāṭha. Soldier

Pl. II.52. Mārāṭha. Paris: I.8.6.
Calcutta: Sec. I, No. 64. See Commentary below.

Paris: I.8.6: MAHRATTAS, A HINDOOS TRIBE: Although in general we have not better information about this *tribe* than about the others, they are in some respects better known, on account of the figure which they have made in the wars of the country, and because they alone have preserved a great degree of importance, by the large bodies of warlike troops which they maintain. The Mahrattas nevertheless, by nature and by their religion, are fond of peace, and even inclined to indolence. But they have been so harassed, that they are become warriors, and have assumed a military appearance. Their chief force is their cavalry, the first charge of which is formidable even to Europeans.

They have always been attached to the English; and it may be said that, without their aid, that nation never could have possessed themselves of the Carnatic, and made themselves masters, as they are this day, of the whole of Asia from Ceylon to Cachemir [Kashmir]. They particularly distinguished themselves in the war against Tippoo Saib, by following the English army with their bazars (or markets), and ensuring its subsistance.

Poonah is the capital of their country, and the residence of an English agent with a numerous suite.

They have many customs peculiar to themselves: for example, that of women burning themselves with the body of their husband. But we are not yet come to speak of this.

Commentary: The Mārāṭhas, beginning with their unification under Shivaji in the seventeenth century, in challenge to the Mughals expanded power from their native Maharashtra across central India.[1] By the mid-eighteenth century they had pushed into Orissa and western Bengal with raiding parties that terrorized and plundered the area. The Mārāṭha raiders, or "Bargis," as they were called, created such fear that thousands of people west of the Hugli River periodically poured into Calcutta as refugees, pressing the resources of the city. Calcutta itself was threatened, and in 1742, the British dug the deep, broad "Mahratta ditch" to protect the town from invasion. The danger subsided before the ditch was completed, and over the next fifty years it served as little more than a "receptacle for all the filth and garbage in Calcutta."[2] It was covered over in 1799, during Solvyns's residence in Calcutta, when Wellesley, the Governor-General, ordered the construction of the Circular Road.

Solvyns's history is muddled here, for the Mārāṭhas were not "attached to the English" in the manner he describes. Indeed, the British fought a series of wars against the Mārāṭhas, conducted even as Solvyns wrote the text for his "Mahrattas" etching, defeating them finally in 1818 and thereby securing their position as the dominant power over all India east of the Punjab and Sind.[3]

Solvyns's portrayal of the Mārāṭha soldier as scantily clad conforms generally to the 1757 description by Grose: "[A] roll of coarse muslin round their heads, to which they give the name of puckery, or turban, or perhaps a bit of cloth, or striped callico, or cuttance-cap; a lungee or clout, barely to cover their nakedness, and a pamree or loose mantle to throw over their shoulders, or to lye on upon the ground, composes the whole of their wardrobe."[4] Many, probably most, Mārāṭhas, however, wore distinctive military dress of half-length breeches, a quilted coat, waist-band, and a turban of circular shape.[5] Solvyns's Mārāṭha lacks not only the typical uniform, but is also without shield or musket. He is armed with a sword—the Mārāṭha's favored weapon, either curved or, as Solvyns's depicts, straight and double-edged.[6]

The etching of the Mārāṭha appears in the Calcutta edition, Sec. I, No. 64, but it is mislabeled in all copies as "A Shikaury" (shikārī). The drawing from which Solvyns prepared the etching carries his note, "A Shikaury. A Hunter by profession."[7] The 1799 *Catalogue* compounds the mistake with the descriptive entry for the etching, "Shikaury,—Hunters; with their arms, their method of taking their game, and shooting poisoned arrows at wild beasts." It is surely odd that Solvyns did not catch the mistake early on, as the description is so clearly at odds with what is portrayed, but for the Paris etchings, he correctly identifies the figure as a Mārāṭha. Solvyns did, in fact, do a drawing of a shikārī (Pl. I.37) that corresponds to the *Catalogue* description, but he never etched it.

---

1 See Gordon, *The Marathas, 1600-1818*, and *Marathas, Marauders, and State Formation in Eighteenth-Century India*.
2 Cotton, *Calcutta Old and New*, 31. On the ditch, also see Long, *Calcutta in Olden Times*, 49-50.
3 Philip Mason, *passim*.
4 Grose, 126.
5 Thapliyal, 16 and plate.
6 Grose describes Mārāṭha weapons, 124-25; see Surendra Nath Sen, 70.
7 Victoria and Albert Museum, London, Department of Prints, Drawings, and Paintings, accession number 8937.64.

II.53. Mālī. Flower-Seller

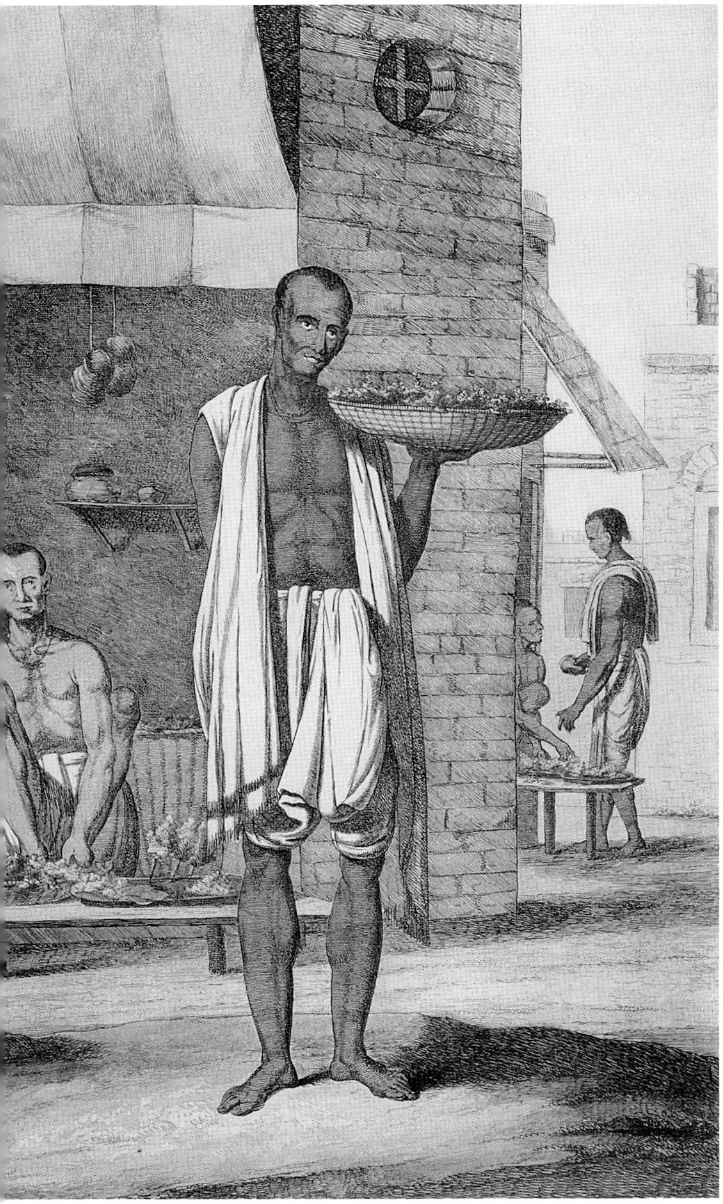

Pl. II.53. Mālī. Paris: I.9.2.

Calcutta: Sec. I, No. l8. A Mauly or Flower-man, whose business it is to make ornaments for Idols and to sell flowers—Europeans improperly call every servant employed in their Gardens a Mauly.

Paris: I.9.2: MAULYS, FLOWERMEN: It is a common error to confound the Maulys with the Chassah-Khyberts or gardeners [Pl. II.30], whereas these last [the Maulys] are merely retailers of flowers. They are to be met in all the bazars; and so great is the demand, that their business suffers little interruption. Flowers are used in the sacrifices which the Hindoos are constantly offering, not only as ornaments on these occasions for their gods, their brahmuns and the assistants; but they form also a part of the dress of persons of distinction, who wear them in their hair. Red flowers are preferred, but every species of flower is generally liked by the Hindoos; another proof of the simplicity of their taste and the mildness of their manners.

Although the Maulys look upon themselves as a high cast, they are nevertheless but a subdivision of the Byces [vaiśya] or merchants, or of the Sooders [śūdra] or servants. They are strict observers of primitive customs, and have preserved the outward appearance of the true Hindoo. Naturally attached by the interests, of their profession to the ceremonies of religion, they are well acquainted with all the festivals, and live in habits of frequent intercourse with the brahmuns.

Commentary: The Mālīs, or Malakars, of Bengal are garland-makers and flower-sellers, deriving their name from the Sanskrit *mālā*, meaning garland. The Bengali Mālī disdains gardening, the occupation with which Mālīs are traditionally associated in the rest of India.

Risley divides the caste into two main groups, the Phulkāta-Mālī, who make ornaments, toys, and the traditional Bengali wedding crown (*ṭopar*) from the pith of the sola (*Hedysarum lagenarium*), and the Dokāne-Mālī, who keep shops. In addition to making garlands and objects of pith, Bengali Mālīs manufacture the tinsel used in decorating the clay images and, as Bhattacharya notes, were suppliers of fireworks. Although Solvyns makes no reference to this, Mālīs in Bengal also had a vitally important sideline—treatment of small-pox and "eruptive fevers."[1]

1 Risley, *The Tribes and Castes of Bengal*, 2:60-63; J. N. Bhattacharya, 220-21; and Wise, 342-44.

II.54. Chutār. Carpenter

Pl. II.54. Chutār. Paris: I.9.3.

Calcutta: Sec. I, No. 35. A Chooter, or Carpenter; with their method of holding their work between their feet.

Paris: I.9.3: CHOOTERS, CARPENTERS: Although the tools which the Chooters use consist simply of a hatchet, a wooden mallet, a saw, a chisel, and rarely a plane, they find means to execute what we should deem the work of turners and joiners. If they are slower than our workmen, they are on the other hand no way inferior to them in neatness. But they are all liable to the common reproach of not working with much activity, when they are employed and paid by the day; while they are exceedingly laborious, when they work on their own account.

They work sitting, and hold with their feet the piece of wood they are about. The plate gives a view of their posture, and of their different ways of sawing up their timber. Those who are in the employment of Europeans have adopted the tools of the English workmen.

The Chooters are in general more dissolute than the other classes of workmen; this is principally observed at the public festivals. When not at work, they are commonly well dressed, and wear a *packy* [*pāg* or *pāgaṛi*] or very full turban. The younger Chooters let their hair grow till setting no farther value on this species of ornament and withdrawing as it were from a life of pleasure, they shave half their head, to conform to the habits of the true Hindoos and assume a more regular conduct.

Commentary: The Chutār, or more properly Sūtradhara, is the carpenter caste of Bengal and takes its name, "thread-holder, from the Sanskrit *sūtra*, thread, through which the course of the saw is marked."[1] There are numerous Sūtradhara subcastes, some local, but others are occupationally specialized, such that one may make boats or household furniture, while another makes wheels, ploughs, and agricultural implements. They occupy a traditional social rank among the lower śūdra castes, although it seems likely that they once may have enjoyed a higher status.

The etching depicts the Sūtradhara's different modes of sawing wood. In the background, to the left, two men are sawing planks in a manner that Solvyns portrays in the foreground of his view of a Bengali road in Black Town (Pl. II.6).

Sūtradhara craftsmen are not simply carpenters, but also carvers of wood, stone, horn, and ivory, and they were the traditional architects of Bengal. "Even today," Prabhas Sen writes, "some well-known Sūtradhar families have handwritten treatises, drawings and diagrams setting out old conventions, proportions, and traditional plans, etc., for temples, dwellings, *rath*, chariots, and boats."[2] They also make reinforced clay images, and wooden dolls, toys, and masks. Among their crafts, now abandoned, Sūtradharas made the terracotta panels and plaques attached to the brick walls of temples in Bengal, and they painted wooden images, walls, wooden book-covers, and playing cards, and, like the Paṭuā folk-painters (Pl. II.67), on cloth and paper scrolls. Crafts pursued by Sūtradhara women are principally, like the Paṭuā and Kumār (Pl. II.36) women, earthen dolls and toys made by mold-castings.[3]

1 Risley, *The Tribes and Castes of Bengal*, 2:287. The entry for Sūtradhar is 2:287-90. On the caste, its occupations, organization, and status, see S. K. Ray, "The Sutradharas (Architects and Architectural Wood-Carvers)." N. Bhattacharya has a brief entry for Sutar, 197-98.

2 Prabhas Sen, *Crafts of West Bengal*, 112. Sen describes the crafts, with color photographs, in "Wood and Stone," 110-21. On Sūtradhara architects, see S. K. Ray, "The Sutradharas (Architects and Architectural Wood-Carvers)," 321-24, and, specifically as temple architects, Santra.

3 S. K. Ray, "The Sutradharas (Architects and Architectural Wood-Carvers)," 321.

II.55. Dhobā. Washerman

Paris: I.9.4: DOBYS, WASHERMEN: Although, the business of the Dobys not being of general necessity among the Hindoos, who bathe at least twice a day, and consequently wash their own clothes, they do not occupy a considerable place, yet as they form a particular class, we have thought it necessary to speak of them. They are included in the domestic establishment; every household of any importance has one or more of them, who wash, smooth, and fold the linnen with great care and cleanliness. They are besides so active and intelligent in their way of serving, that Europeans and other foreigners keep them about their persons, so as even to take them in their retinue, if they go from home but for a few days.

He that is represented, is in his ordinary dress, and in the different distances may be acquired an idea of the Doby's manner of washing the linnen, as well as of their habitations which are always near a river or pond. They make their wash of ashes, and kali,[1] which is very abundant in Hindoostan. Their starch is rice water called *congy* [*kañji*].

Pl. II.55. Dhobā. Paris: I.9.4.

Calcutta: Sec. I, No. 48. A Doby or Washerman, with their mode of washing Cloth by beating it against a knotched board.

Commentary: The Dhobā (or Dhopā) is the washerman caste of Bengal and Orissa and is distinct from the Dhobī washerman caste of North India.[2] Europeans throughout India, however, used the Hindustani term *dhobī* generically to refer to all washermen.[3]

Hindus of the "clean" castes do not wash their own clothes—contrary to Solvyns's observation—and rely on the Dhobā as a matter of both ritual and practical necessity. But Solvyns was surely correct in identifying the Dhobā as essential for any European household and is portrayed again in Solvyns's section on servants (Pl. II.112).

Williamson, in his *East India Vade-Mecum*, provides a detailed account of the way the Dhobā washes clothes: He first boils the clothes in a large earthen vessel, mixing in plenty of soap, lye, ashes, or alkali. The clothes are then rinsed, either in a large tank or in a running stream, where they are again rubbed with soap and left to soak. After a few hours, the Dhobā washes the clothes again and folds them into bundles, which he forcibly beats on a board that is placed aslant in the water, as portrayed by Solvyns, or on a smooth stone. After dashing the bundle several times on the board, he opens it and rinses the clothes, bundles them again and repeats the dashing "as though he were beating the board with a flail, until every part of the linen appears to be duly cleansed." The clothing is then hung on a line or frame to dry. In every part of the process, Williamson writes, the Dhobā's wife assists.[4]

Neither Williamson nor Risley, who describes the Dhobā's mode of washing, make reference to the use of *kali*, but Risley says that indigo is used as a whitening agent and that Dhobās use rice starch before ironing the clothes.[5]

Because they wash soiled clothing, Dhobās are ranked ritually as "unclean," and the 1911 Census listed them among "castes which cause pollution by touch" and "are not allowed inside Hindu temples."[6]

The demand for their services ensures steady employment for the Dhobā, but Risley (drawing from Wiley) notes that some give up their traditional occupation to become clerks, messengers, and rent collectors, and it is "native tradition" that a Bengali Dhobā was the first interpreter for the English factory of Calcutta.[7] Raja Binaya Krishna Deb relates the story: On their arrival, the English requested the Basacks or Setts, leading families of the cloth trade, "to send a *dubas* or dhobhasia, which means one who knows two languages . . . . Without comprehending what they meant, the Basacks sent some washermen (dhobies) in their employ; and the washermen by frequent intercourse with the English learnt somewhat imperfectly their language, and they are said to have been the first who knew anything of the language. One Ratan Sarkar, a dhobie by caste, was the first Indian who was employed as an Interpreter by the English."[8]

1 *Kali*, or *kali cun*, is a powder of slaked lime prepared for white-washing. Sukumar Sen, 123.
2 See Risley's entry for Dhobā, *The Tribes and Castes of Bengal*, 1:229-233; for Dhobī, Bihar washerman caste, 1:233-36.
3 See *Hobson-Jobson*, 312-13.
4 1:245-57. Also see Stocqueler, *The Hand-Book of India*, 237; Henry Grant and Edward Colebrooke, 61; and Grierson, 81-82.
5 1:232. Also see Commentary for Pl. II.112 for Williamson's detailed description in *East India Vade-Mecam*, 1:245-47.
6 Asok Mitra, *The Castes and Tribes of West Bengal*, 20.
7 Risley, *The Tribes and Castes of Bengal*, 1:232; Wise, 263.
8 47-48.

II.56. Dāṇḍī. Boatman

Paris: I.9.5: DANDYS, BOATMEN: The Dandy must not be confounded with the fisherman: their classes are even essentially different. A boatman, for example, may be taken into service or hired even by the day; but no such engagement can be taken with a fisherman.

The Dandys eat large quantities of rice of a much coarser grain than what is generally used by the Hindoos. They may almost be compared to beasts of burthen, who work in proportion to the food they get, or feed in proportion to the labour they undergo.

They are bold and skilful, and swim remarkably well, but not in the way Europeans do. They move sideways working alternately the right leg and arm together. They often row with their feet to leave their hands free, to smoke the *hooka* more at their ease. The Indian oar is such as is represented in the engraving, but in some places the flat of the oar is formed by a piece of wood nearly oval, with a long bambou for a handle. Further details upon this subject will be given in the article of boats.

Commentary: Dāṇḍī (or dā̃ṛī), boatman or oarsman, is an occupational description (not a caste category) peculiar to the Gangetic rivers. The word is derived from the Arabic *dānḍ*, "staff, oar."[1] Captain Thomas Williamson, in *The East India Vade-Mecum*, details the work of the dāṇḍī as an oarsman or rower,[2] and he provides the descriptive text to D'Oyly's portrayal of Marquess Wellesley's dāṇḍī in *The European in India*.[3]

In the eighteenth and early nineteenth century, European travelers in Bengal frequently describe their river trips by budgerow (*bājrā*, Pl. II.232) and refer to "dandies" at the oars. Captain G. C. Mundy notes that "The crews are of either sect, Mussulman or Hindoo;

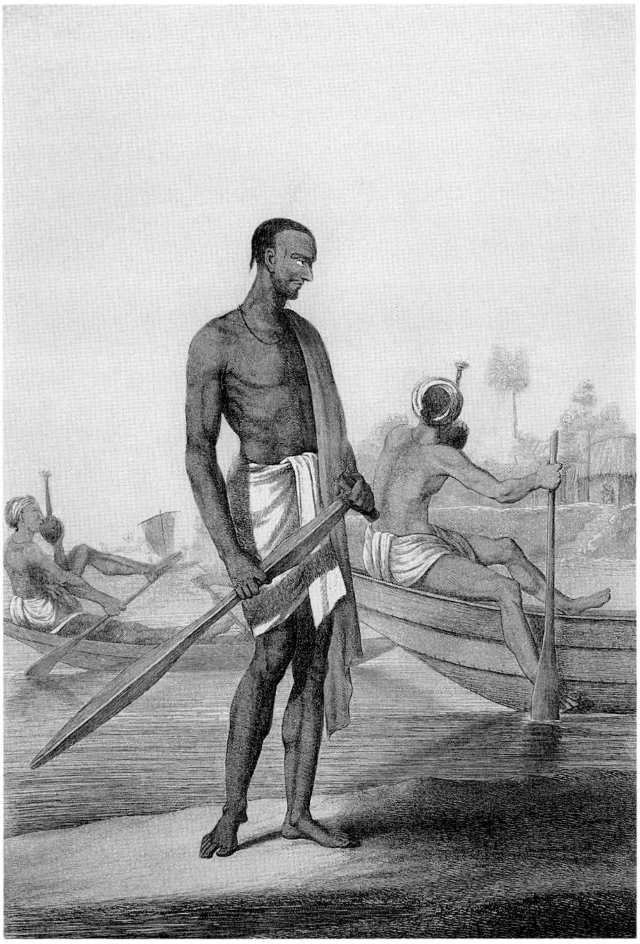

Pl. II.56. Dāṇḍī. Paris: I.9.5.
Calcutta: Sec. I, No. 45. A Dandy, or boatman.
Orme: 8.

the former are, perhaps, the more able-bodied seamen, and stauncher at the oar. . . . The dandies," he writes, "are generally fine, stout and sleek figures. In rowing they stand upright, advancing and retiring two or three steps at every stroke; and lightening their labour, as well as preserving the measure, by a song and chorus."[4]

---

1 *Hobson-Jobson*, 298; Lewis, 98.
2 283-88.
3 Pl. 12.
4 1:149-50; reprinted in Nair, *Calcutta in the 19th Century*, 486.

II.57. Jāliyā. Fisherman

Paris: I.9.6: JELLE-AS, FISHERMEN: This class of Hindoos offers nothing very remarkable. It might indeed be said that men who spend the greater part of their lives upon or even in the water, are a sort of amphibious animal. The women, who must not be confounded with the *polyes*[1] or fishsellers, are modest, and, notwithstanding poverty, very cleanly in their houses: unlike the others, who, here, as in many other countries, are illdrest, forward, and, talkative. The Jelle-as, like true Hindoos, lead a regular life. They unite many families together, forming what they call a *gunge* [*ganj*],[2] and have frequently a bazar near their abode.

It would be impracticable to place here a description of all their ways of fishing. One of the most common is that which is used for the *mangoo* or *topsi* [Pl. II.288],[3] a fish described in our books of Natural History, and consists in spreading a large net by means of strong bambous: they have earthen pots for bouys, and draw the net at every flow of the tide. For other fish they have a pocket-net kept open by a semicircle. The Fisherman, by means of an oar, keeps with one hand his boat motionless against the stream; the fish, which always ascends or descends with the tide, falls into the net: the slightest motion is felt by the fisherman, who drops from his other hand a small cord with a stone to it, which closes the net and shuts in the fish.

Pl. II.57. Jāliyā. Paris: I.9.6.
Calcutta: Sec. I, No. 57. A Jellee-a; or Fisherman.
Orme: 9.

Commentary: Risley writes that Jāliyā (or Jele) is a general name used in Bengal for "all classes of people who are engaged in boating and fishing" and is not, strictly speaking, a caste name.[4] There are, however, endogamous caste groups among those described as Jāliyā, such as the fishing Kaibarta. Fishermen are of low social status, and substantial numbers of the Kaibarta had by the late eighteenth century abandoned fishing for agriculture. They are depicted by Solvyns as "Chassah-Khyberts" (Cāṣākaibartas, Pl. II.30), gardeners. Solvyns also portrays Jāliyās in palanquin bearers (Pl. II.46), an occasional occupation which many assume in the dry season when fishing is poor.

Some authorities derive the name Jāliyā from *jāl*, net, and that is the principal means by which they catch fish, as Solvyns depicts. Risley details the characteristics of eight nets commonly used by fishermen in Bengal and notes, more generally, that "Nets are made of hemp, never of cotton, and they are steeped in gab (*Diospyrus glutinosa*) pounded and allowed to ferment, by which means the net is dyed a dark brown colour, becoming after immersion in water almost black. Floats are either made of sholā [*śolā*] or pieces of bamboo, but dried gourds are occasionally preferred. Sinkers are made of baked clay or iron."[5]

The text to Orme's pirated edition erroneously identifies the Jāliyā as a "sect of the lowest order of Mohammedans."

1 Solvyns may have mistakenly taken the name of the basket, *palui*, used by female fish vendors, to mean "fishwife," which in Bengali is *mechani*. See Pl. II.98.

2 A *ganj* (Anglo-Indian, gunge) is a market for a particular commodity. Jāliyās, as many other occupational castes in Calcutta, resided in a particular locality or quarter, Jāyiyāṭolā.

3 Tapsī or tapassī (Hindustani) is a flavorful and highly prized fish, appearing in the Calcutta markets with the onset of the hot season, when the mangoes ripen. *Hobson-Jobson*, 555; Lewis, 161, 238-39.

4 *The Tribes and Castes of Bengal*, 1:340. Also see Wise, 281-85.

5 Risley, *The Tribes and Castes of Bengal*, 1:340-42.

II.58. Kalu. Oil Man

Paris: I.10.2: KOALHOOS. OILMEN: The Koalhoos make the oil and sell it before the door of their houses. They extract it from different grains, but chiefly from mustard seed. This oil is an article of very extensive use among the Hindoos, they anoint their bodies with it at least once a day, employ no other in their aliments, and burn it for light.

Their mills and their mode of working them are very simple, and furnish another opportunity of remarking that if the Hindoos are behind hand in bringing the arts to perfection, it is perhaps because their first instinctive operations of necessity have always been very happy. A glance of the engraving will give a better idea of their oil mills than any description. They are made of a large trunk of a tree hollowed out in form of a vase at the top, in which a piece of wood in form of a pestle is put into a circular motion by a traverse to which oxen are yoked. Sometimes to add weight to the machine, or rather perhaps out of laziness, the workman seats himself upon the traverse, and quietly smokes his *houqah* [*hukā*]. The oil is received in a vessel through a small opening at the bottom of the bason.

The Koalho's appearance does not announce that his profession is very lucrative. The whole family inhabit the place where the mill is fixed, which is also the residence of the oxen, who are generally most excessively meager, and, like their masters, covered with a coat of oil.

Pl. II.58. Kalu. Paris: I.10.2

Calcutta: Sec. I, No. 38. Koalhoo, a maker and seller of oil and Bran—the Oil Mill as represented, is simply a log of wood, with a hollow space at the top, in which is turned the end of a pole by bullocks.

Commentary: The name Kalu is taken from *kolhū*, the Hindi word for oil mill[1] and is used broadly to refer to those, Hindu and Muslim, engaged in extraction of oil from all kinds of seeds. More specifically, Kalu is a sub-caste of the large Teli oil-pressing and trading caste of Bengal and Orissa, but the name is used interchangeably with Teli more generally.[2] Solvyns makes no reference to Telis as oil-pressers, but portrays the Tili (Pl. II.42), the appellation taken by Telis engaged in retail trade who sought to identify themselves as a distinct caste.

As a Teli sub-caste, the Kalus are distinguished by their use of a mill with a hole to let out the oil, to which Solvyns refers.[3] In contrast to the larger Teli community, their status, Risley writes, "is very low, and their separation from the main body of the Telis is so complete that many regard them as a separate caste."[4] In the Indian Census caste rankings, Kalus occupied over time a variable and ambiguous low status. The 1911 Census, for example, identified Kalu as a caste whose touch does not pollute, but who are denied entry into temples.[5]

The name Kalu is used today for those who actually press oil. The majority of Telis have become cultivators, and the more prosperous landowners among them, like the retail traders, have taken the name Tili.[6]

1 The Bengali word for oil mill is *ghāṇi*.
2 Risley, *The Tribes and Castes of Bengal*, 1:309, for the brief entry under Kalu; for the entry for Teli, 2:305-10.
3 On oils and oil-presses more generally, see Nirmal Kumar Bose, *Peasant Life in India*, 19-23.
4 *The Tribes and Castes of Bengal*, 2:307.
5 Asok Mitra, *The Tribes and Castes of West Bengal*, 15, 20-21.
6 Amiya Kumar Banerji, *West Bengal District Gazetteers: Bankura*, 176.

II.59. Kāpāli. Rope-Maker

Pl. II.59. Kāpāli. Paris: I.10.3.

Calcutta: Sec. I, No. 32. A Kapauly or Rope maker; representing their simple method of twisting and uniting the strands of the Rope made of Hemp, or Kyar [coir], the bark of the Cocoanut.

Paris: I.10.3: KAPAULYS. ROPE-MAKERS: Besides hemp they use in Hindoostan in the fabrication of ropes the rind of the cocoa, which they call *kyar*. Their manner of twisting it is not the same as in Europe. They do not make use of our sort of wheel. They drive into the ground two bambous, which they join by two double traverses: between these traverses are placed horizontally three small pieces of bambou, moving on their axis, and doubly interlaced by small cords forming a circle round them, which being put into a continued rotatory motion, by the young Hindoo who attends the business, communicates it to the little bambou in the middle, to the upper end of which is fixed the matter of which the rope is made, and the Kapauly twists it moving backwards.

The Kapaulys are drunken and dissolute, and their conduct rather than their profession has caused them to be looked upon as *parriahs*. Consequently their habitations are outside the towns and even outside of the simple villages, where they are confounded with the basest subdivisions of casts. For this reason they are placed in this work in the rank of subdivisions, which, not to deviate from the plan of *Menu* [Manu], ought to occupy the lowest degree.

Commentary: Although Solvyns identifies the Kāpāli as rope-makers, Wise, Risley, and Mitra describe them more broadly as a cultivating and weaving caste, principally concentrated in East Bengal. According to Wise, they chiefly cultivate jute, weaving the fiber into the coarse canvas, *tāt*, for gunny sacks, boat sails, floor-matting. Of the later, Wise writes that "Bamboo mats for floors are seldom used in Bengal, but canvas is laid down in every shop, and beneath bedding whenever the ground is slept on."[1] Oddly, no mention is made of robe-making at all, but it would be an expected extension of their work with jute.

Solvyns makes a point of their "dissolute" character, and Risley concludes his entry on the caste by noting that "They assert that they never taste spirits, but it is generally believed that they do. Gunja-smoking, however, is common among them."[2] Their traditional caste rank is low, but not nearly so degraded as Solvyns suggests. They were described in the 1931 Census as a "depressed class" and listed among the Scheduled Castes ("untouchables'), but they were subsequently omitted from the list.[3]

1 Wise, 305-06. Also see Risley, *The Tribes and Castes of Bengal*, 1:421-22.

2 Risley, *The Tribes and Castes of Bengal*, 1:422.

3 Asok Mitra, *The Tribes and Castes of West Bengal*, 5, 15, 21.

II.60. Cunāri. Lime-Worker

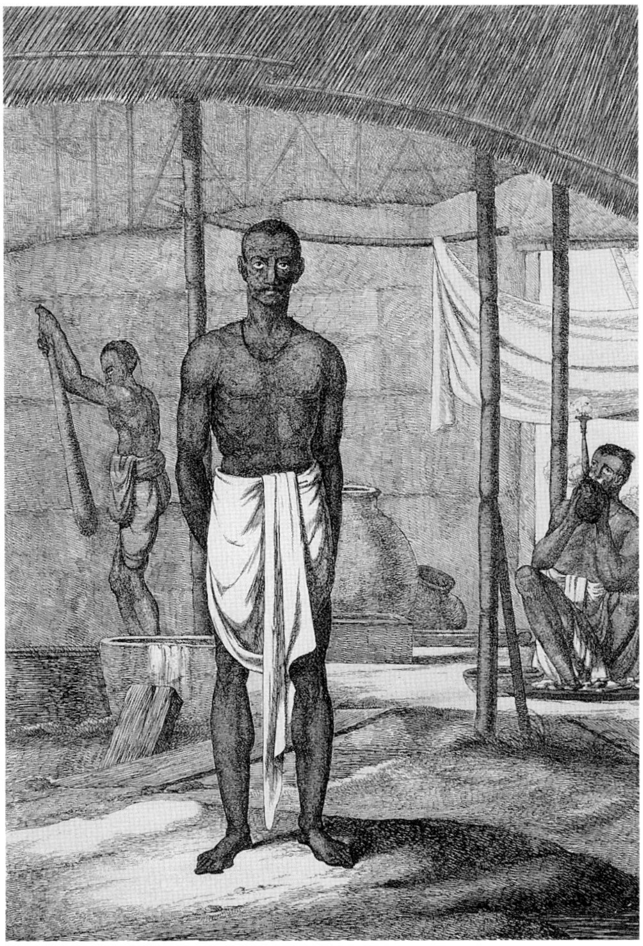

Pl. II.60. Cunāri. Paris: I.10.4.

Calcutta: Sec. I, No. 37. Chunhary—preparer of fine lime to be eaten with the pawn.

Paris: I.10.4: CHUNHARYS. PREPAIRERS OF FINE LIME: The lime prepared by the Chunharys is used chiefly to mix with *pawn* [*pān*, Pl. II.212], which the Hindoos are constantly chewing. It is made of shells calcined and then reduced to a fine powder in logs of wood scooped out like mortars; this powder is again pounded in the water, until it becomes as white as snow. It is then exposed to sale by the lime-burner, in plantain leaves, on a large plate of wood, in which consists the whole shew of the warehouse.

The sale is very considerable, for there is not an Hindoo, man or woman, who does not use great quantities of it. It blackens the teeth, and burns the inside of the mouth, but at the same time gives a fine red to the lips, a sort of beauty to which those whose object is to please, attach great consequence.

The grosser particles of this lime are used to whiten the inside walls of their houses. Sometimes mixed with the *sulky* [*surkhī*][1] or brick-dust pounded, it forms the *packa* [*pakkā*] or *solid*, material used in the construction of temples or other buildings. Hindoostan is as if it were covered with monuments of this sort, which have lasted for ages.

Commentary: The small Cunāri caste prepares lime (*cun*) as its traditional occupation. Risley identifies the caste as Bāiti or Bāoti, but writes that it is "usually called Chunari or Chuniya, from being engaged in the manufacture of lime from shells." They are also mat-makers,[2] weavers, dancers, and beggars, and occupy a low position in the caste hierarchy. They do not themselves gather the shells, but engage only in the preparation and sale of the lime. They sell unslaked lime to medicinal purposes, "while the finest and most expensive lime for chewing, pan-chun, is prepared with the ashes of tamarind wood."[3]

Solvyns describes the Cunāri's preparation of the lime for *pān*, and in his portrayals of the Bārai, betel-grower (Pl. II.32) and the Tāmulī̆, pan-seller (Pl. II.75), he discusses the betel nut preparation for *pān* and its use of lime. The reddened lips in chewing *pān*, described above by Solvyns, is the product of the betel nut, not of the lime.

Cunāris also supplied lime for *cūnā* (Anglo-Indian, *chunam*), the plaster (described in the Commnetary for Pl. II.1) that gave a polished brilliance to the walls of European buildings in Calcutta.

Solvyns describes the solid materials used in construction as *pakkā* (*pucka* or *pukka,* in Anglo-Indian usage). The word means ripe, cooked, but has a wide range of applications and broadly may be taken as superior, permanent, and is contrasted with the term *kachchā* (Anglo-Indian *cutcha*) for raw, uncooked, inferior. In construction, the term *pakkā* refers to a building of brick and mortar; *kachchā* to a thatched or mud hut.[4]

1 From *surkh*, meaning red brick colored. The Anglo-Indian spelling was usually "soorky." *Hobson-Jobson*, 854.

2 See Solvyns's portrayal of the Bāiti as mat-maker (Pl. II.77).

3 Risley, *The Tribes and Castes of Bengal*, 1:52-53. Also see Wise, 208-09.

4 *Hobson-Jobson*, 734. The widely used *pakkā* and *kachchā* are Hindi; the terms in Bengali are transliterated as *pākā* and *kā̆ca*.

II.61. Śũṛī. Distiller

Pl. II.61. Śũṛī. Paris: I.10.5.

Calcutta: Sec. I, No. 49. Soonree, Manufacturer and dealer in spirituous Liquors, with a view of the shop and Distillery.

Paris: I.10.5: SOONREES MANUFACTURERS AND DEALERS IN WINE: The Hindoos abhor drunkenness: none but the very lowest casts, or *parriahs* of other casts, are addicted to strong liquors. Hence the sellers of these liquors are not held in much higher estimation than their customers: though among the latter nevertheless, even brahmuns are sometimes to be met with: but they are soon looked upon as *parriahs*, a name of reprobation extending even to the liquors with which they are intoxicated.[1]

Commentary: Solvyns places the Śũṛīs (Śunṛīs) among the lower castes, degraded by their traditional occupation as distillers and sellers of spirits, but it is likely that by the late eighteenth century, many among this large caste had abandoned their original profession for broader mercantile pursuits. Risley, writing in 1891, notes that these merchants call themselves by the title Saha and often take the name Das to conceal their caste origin, disowning "all connexion with those who still follow the characteristic occupation of the caste." But "in spite of their wealth and enterprise," he writes, "ancient associations still hold them down," and Risley relates the mythological story from the Vaivarta Purana that "keeps alive the memory of their degradation."[2]

Although not mentioned by Solvyns, the Śũṛīs themselves, despite their occupation, abstain from liquor.[3]

Ward, Solvyns's contemporary in Bengal, describes the manufacturing process. Distillers "make several kinds of arrack, the principal ingredients in which are, rice, molasses, water and spices. . . . The distillers place eight pounds of rice, and the same quantity of molasses and spices, in a jar containing one hundred and sixty pounds of water; and close the mouth with clay, to prevent the entrance of the external air; in this state it continues in the hot weather, five or six days, and in the cold, eight or ten. It is then carried to the still, where, from the above mentioned quantity forty pounds of arrack is drawn off."[4]

1 For Solvyns's discussion of Pariah, see Pl. II.22, in connection with śūdras.

2 *The Tribes and Castes of Bengal*, 2:275. Risley's entry for Śunṛī, 2:275-80. Also see Wise, 373-76, and J. N. Bhattacharya, 203-05. For an account of the efforts of a similar caste in South India to rise from its traditional occupation, Hardgrave, *The Nadars of Tamilnad: The Political Culture of a Community in Change*.

3 J. N. Bhattacharya, 204.

4 Ward, *A View of . . . the Hindoos*, 1:137-38. Also see Keir. Shoberl, 4:81-91, discusses the Śũṛīs technique and the process of distillation in detail.

II.62. Śiuli. Toddy-Tapper

Pl. II.62. Śiuli. Paris: I.10.6.

Calcutta: Sec. I, No. 47. A Seuly, who collects Toddy from the Tree bearing that name—it is used in this country, instead of yeast in making bread, and when fermented, causes intoxication.

Paris: I.10.6: SEULYS. MAKERS OF TODDY: Toddy is a juice procured by incision from the fruit of a tree of that name. To obtain it they climb up the tree by means of a cord thrown over the branches, and make incisions in the fruit with a piece of crooked iron, having first placed small pots to receive the juice, which oozes out slowly drop by drop; when full, they are emptied into a larger vessel carried on the back of the person who gathers it. This operation lasts two or three days for each tree.

The liquor freshly gathered is rather pleasant; after fermentation it is very intoxicating and occasions sickness when drank to excess. Europeans use it instead of yert [yeast].

A liquor also called *tary*[*tāṛī*] is drawn from a mixture of several other sorts of fruits, which resembles toddy, and produces the same effects.

The retailers of these liquors lie under an imputation of bad morals: being frequented only by *parriahs* and not unfrequently by prostitutes.

The drawing represents a Seuly preparing to climb up the tree.

Commentary: Risley lists the Śiuli as a subcaste of the Hāṛi (Pl. II.71) and as "a title of Chandals, Doms, Haris and similar lower castes, as well as Mahomedans who extract juice from date-trees for manufacture of *gur*, molasses, or toddy."[1]

When the toddy (*tāṛī*) is collected in the early morning, it is sweet and cool, but if allowed to set it quickly ferments. Sweet, unfermented toddy may be made into the delicacy *nolen gur*, a liquid jaggery, with a lovely aroma, or boiled to make *gur*, molasses, or *jaggery*, a coarse brown sugar. Fermented, it is a palm wine and distilled becomes arrack.[2]

1 *The Tribes and Castes of Bengal*, 2:254. Asok Mitra, *The Tribes and Castes of West Bengal*, 72, similarly places the Śiuli as one of the many Hāṛi subcastes.

2 Colesworthy Grant describes tapping and toddy preparation in Bengal in *Anglo-Indian Domestic Life*, 136; Shoberl, 4:81-89, describes tapping techniques; and Hardgrave portrays toddy-tapping in South India in *The Nadars*, 24-29. Also see "Toddy," *Hobson-Jobson*, 927-28.

II.63. Nāi, Nāpit. Barber

Paris: I.11.2: NAUYS. SHAVING BARBERS: The *Nauy* in general, under cover of his parasol, has no other professional apparatus than a small cup of brass or of cast iron to contain water, and a plate of iron convex on the sharp edge, which serves him as a razor; and in the interior of the country they make use of a piece of glass, a bit of a broken looking-glass for example, or even of a broken bottle. We may imagine what sort of an operation the patient has to undergo, when we are told that the Hindoo barber uses no soap, and that it is not untill after he has long and violently rubbed the face with water, that he has recourse to the repeated application of his miserable razor.

Notwithstanding all this, the Hindoos, who are generally very cleanly, get themselves shaved frequently. It appears too that it is one of their religious rites, as well as one of their constant practices, not to suffer the hair to grow upon any part of their body: from their earliest youth they rub themselves with depilatory ointments, and take great pains to destroy whatever may have escaped this operation. The hair of the head only is excepted, which to make amends they hold in high estimation, the women especially; it is generally black, thick, and hard like horse hair: they give it a great lustre by rubbing it with coco or mustard oil.

Those only who are in easy circumstances have their barbers at home. Others go to the market, where they are always to be found. Sometimes, they are called in as they pass by and will then shave you wherever you happen to be, even on the roofs or terraces of the houses, as seen in the engraving, which also represents the posture in which this operation is performed.

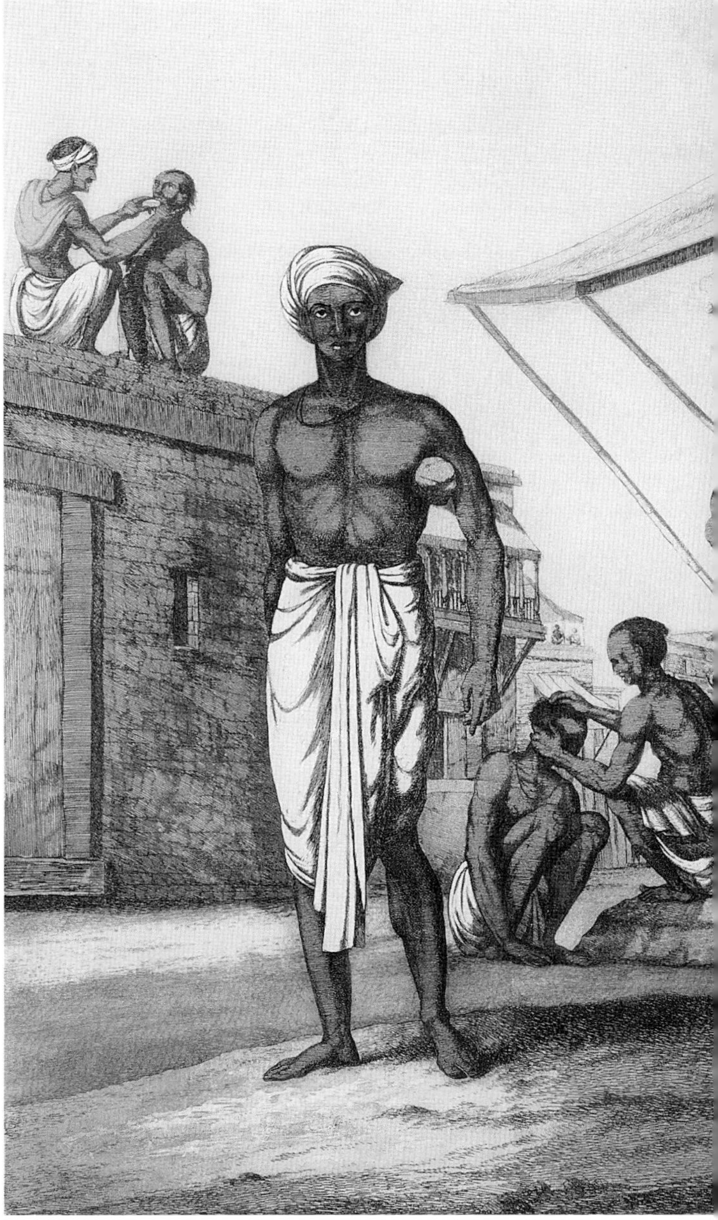

Pl. II.63. Nāi, Nāpit. Paris: I.11.2.
Calcutta: Sec. I, No. 17. Nauy or Shaving Barbers, representing their method of shaving with a short convex piece of Iron.

Commentary: Solvyns's term *Nauy* (Nāi) is the name by which "up country" Nāpits, the barber caste of Bengal, are known.[1] Nāpits are ritually pure, a requirement in their close physical contact with patrons, and enjoy high social standing among the śūdra castes.[2]

The barber is an indispensable member of the Hindu community, performing essential functions. Hindus, traditionally, do not shave themselves, but are shaved by Nāpits, the frequency of shaves varying considerably by wealth and social class. Walter Hamilton, who visited Calcutta in the early nineteenth century, noted that "farmers and labourers shave only once a month, and generally pay the barber in grain. Rich men often keep barbers who shave them, pick their ears, cut their nails, crack the joints, and knead their bodies, to which operation the natives are much attended."[3] The barber's wife or mother pares the nails of women and paints their feet and hands with red lac dye.[4]

The Nāpit also plays an important role in family domestic rituals, in marriage and at the birth of a child, and for some castes serves as a priest. "In addition to all these vocations, the barber, like his European namesake of the seventeenth century, practises surgery, opening boils and abscesses, inoculating for small-pox, and prescribing in all forms of venereal disease. Often he is also an exorciser of devils. . . ."[5]

In his note to the original drawing of the Nāpit, Solvyns writes that "they commonly perform in the streets. . . ," as he portrays them in the etching.

Europeans employed Nāpits as shaving barbers, calling them by the Hindustani term *hajām*, and Solvyns portrays them separately in his series of etchings depicting domestic servants (Pl. II.126).

1 Asok Mitra, *The Tribes and Castes of West Bengal*, 35.
2 Risley, *The Tribes and Castes of Bengal*, 2:124-29; Wise, 348-50; J. N. Bhattacharya, 243-44.
3 1:104.
4 Ward, *A View . . . of the Hindoos*. 1:122-23; J. N. Bhattacharya, 243.
5 Risley, *The Tribes and Castes of Bengal*, 2:128.

II.64. Kān. Singer

Pl. II.64. Kān. Paris: I.11.3.

Calcutta: Sec. I, No. 62. A Kawn or Dussahee, a hindoo singer on the public road, singing and accompanying his voice with the beat of the drum,—their women follow the same occupation.

Paris: I.11.3: KAWNS. HINDOO SINGERS: The *Kawns*, men, women and children, earn their subsistance, and spend their lives singing on the highways or before the doors of houses. They accompany themselves sometimes with the tambourin or with the *khole*, an instrument which will be described in its place [Pl. II.158], and sing, in a disagreeable tone and in a country jargon which few understand, the loves and exploits of the Gods.

The *Kawns* have some affinity to the Musselmans, but without being confounded with them. Though in their dress and in some other particulars, they differ from the other Hindoos, they never wear feathers nor other ornaments by which the Musselmans are distinguished.

The Hindoos of this class also are but little esteemed, either on account of the great number of dissolute persons among them, or of the intercourse which they keep up with other very inferior casts, such as shoe-makers, basket-makers, etc. Their habits of life offer otherwise nothing remarkable. They carry a sack in which they put the fruit that is given them, and tye up the different sorts of rice in the extremities of their garments.

Commentary: Risley identifies the Kān only as "a very low caste of musicians akin to the Doms,"[1] and the entry in *An Etymological Dictionary of Bengali*, gives Kān as "the caste name of professional singers."[2] Musicologist Deben Bhattacharya suggests that the word may be a corruption of *gāyan*, meaning singer, particularly the Vaiṣṇava singers who accompany themselves with the khol and khanjari during the *prabhat pheri*, "the morning circulation," singing songs in praise of Kṛṣṇa from door to door.[3] It may also be that Solvyns's ear failed him and that the word he heard was *gān*, "singer" in Bengali.[4] Solvyns's term "Dussahee" is elusive.

Solvyns depicts the Kān singing and accompanying himself on a khanjari, portrayed again in the etchings of musical instruments (Pl. II.170).

1 *The Tribes and Castes of Bengal*, 1:396. Also see Asok Mitra, *The Tribes and Castes of West Bengal*, 21, 78. Mitra, 4, includes the Kāns among several small castes that "may become extinct or absorbed within a short while." On Doms, see Solvyns's portrayal of the Murdāśo, Pl. II.72.

2 Sukumar Sen, 137.

3 Letter to the author, February 17, 1992.

4 Sukumar Sen, 221.

II.65. Māl. Snake-Catcher

Paris: I.11.4: MAULS. SNAKE-CATCHERS: This is the trade of a juggler, and consists in catching snakes, depriving them of their venom, and making them dance before the public: but above all in selling antidotes against their bite, the great efficacy of which the *Maul* does not fail to proclaim. Their specifics acquire a certain credit from the manner in which these mountebancks allow their snakes to wind round them and bite them, in presence of the people, who are not aware that they have been deprived of their power of doing mischief.

The *Mauls* have a particular talent for discovering the retreat of these animals. But what is still more extraordinary, is the manner in which they make themselves masters of them as if by enchantment. They begin by strolling about the house of garden, stop where the serpents are, make certain grimaces, sing or produce some musical sound generally from a small flute: the reptile is not long before he appears, and comes out as it were dancing; his motions follow the measure; he seems to obey the *Maul*, and even to understand him when he speaks. They seize him then between two pieces of bambou, or in any other safe way, pull out his venomous teeth, and soon make him tame.

It is not easy for Europeans to accustom themselves to the sight which so often occurs of these dangerous and frightful animals.

In the upper parts of Hindoostan, there are some of an enormous size and prodigious strength; but these are not the most to be feared. The Cobra-Capello[1] is one of the most venomous. The subtility of its poison causes death in a few minutes. But these animals have been sufficiently noticed by travellers and naturalists, to render it unnecessary for us to exceed any further the limits of our plan on this subject.

Commentary: Solvyns portrays "snake-catchers" in two plates, "Mauls" and "Sauperea," and in depicting *sāpuriyās*, snake-charmers, he identifies them as Māls. Solvyns again portrays Māls in his etching of Jhāpān (Pl. II.196), the festival of the snake goddess Manasā, to whom the Māls are devoted, and refers to them in his discussion of the tobrie, the snake-charmer's musical instrument (Pl. II.179).

The Māls, of disputed origin and diffuse character, are principally engaged in cultivation, but with varying occupations.[2] Risley identifies only one subcaste among them, Sāpuriyā (Sapuriā) or Bediyā (Bedya) Māls (Pl. II.78), engaged as snake-charmers. He writes that they live by "charming snakes, catching monkeys, hunting or conjuring. . . . Although they catch snakes, Sāpuriyā Māls hold the animal in the highest reverence, and will not kill it, or even pronounce its name, for which they use the synonym *latā*, 'a creeper.'"[3]

Wise, writing of East Bengal, identifies Sāpuriyā or Bediyā Māls with the Sāmperia, one of the seven divisions of the Bediyās, bands of vagrants, often associated with petty theft, "who correspond to the gipsies of Europe."[4] But Risley suggests that "it is equally possible that the Māl may be the parent group, and that the Bediyās may have separated from it by reason of their adhering to a wandering mode of life when the rest of the tribe had taken to comparatively settled pursuits." Nevertheless, he concludes that the evidence of Māl-Bediyā kinship is insufficient to identify the Sāpuriyā Māls with the Sāmperia Bediyās of Eastern Bengal. "Snake-charming is an occupation

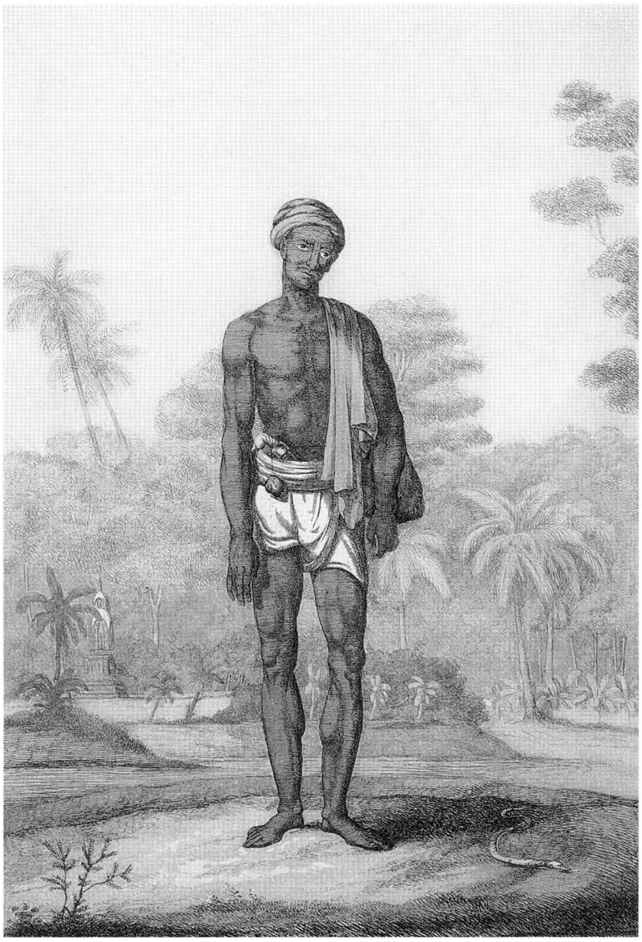

Pl. II.65. Māl. Paris: I.11.4.

Calcutta: Sec. I, No. 53. A Maul or Snake-catcher:—they use the pipe, tabour, drum, and other musical instruments to intice the serpent out of its hole, when they press it between two pieces of bamboos, previously laid on the sides of the hole for the purpose. They pretend to be possessed of a specific against the bite of all poisonous reptiles.

likely enough to be adopted by any caste of gipsy-like propensities, and there is no reason why both Māls and Bediyās should not have taken to it independently."[5]

Rajendralla Mitra, in an appendix on snake-charmers of Bengal for Fayrer's 1872 treatise on venomous snakes of India, draws a sharp distinction between Māls, "most expert" among those who catch and exhibit snakes, and the Bediyās, whom he disdains as "jugglers, bear and monkey dancers, sellers of simples, fortune-tellers, reputed adepts in curing rheumatism, gout, toothache, and other complaints; professors of witchcraft, experts in cupping, applying moxas and actual cautery, as well as snake-charmers." And they are, in contrast to the Māl, thieves "of the most inveterate type."[6]

Mitra also identifies another group, the "tobrie-wallahs," who, with the charm of their gourd pipes, "draw out snakes from holes and cracks—not unoften from the bedding—in the houses of the persons who employ them." More often than not, these snakes have been planted by the charmer, who is then paid to catch and take them away.[7]

Most commentators, as the general public, make little or no distinction between the various groups that deal with snakes. Ashok Mitra, in *The Tribes and Castes of West Bengal*, lists them as a Scheduled Caste under Bedia, but writes that in Bengal, the Bedia comprise "a number of vagrant gypsy-like groups who can hardly be considered to form a caste."[8]

Benoy Bhattacharya, in his book on the Paṭuā painters of Bengal (Pl. II.67), takes *bediyā* in its more generic sense as a wandering people and identifies the Māls as a Paṭuā subcaste. "The occupations associated with them are snake charming, cow-leaching (go-baidya), scroll painting and scroll exhibiting."[9] At Durgā Pūjā, in the Bengali month of Aswin (September-October), on the day the goddess is immersed, Paṭuās, particularly Māl Paṭuās, "go out for a ceremonial catching of snakes," and offerings are made to the snake goddess Manasā to ensure good luck in catching snakes throughout the year.[10]

The Rev. Ward, Solvyns's contemporary, describes the Māls as snake-catchers and quack doctors. "They carry snakes in baskets as a shew, and, having taken out their poisonous fangs, play with them before the spectators, receiving their bite on their arms, folding them round their necks, &c. at which times they use musical instruments; but there does not appear to be any instances of serpents being affected by music, though many Hindoos believe, [that] they can be drawn out of their holes by the power of charms or incantations."[11] Ward here is quite right regarding the effect of music on the snakes, for although not deaf, as commonly believed, their hearing is limited. A snake's response is to the movement, not the sound, of the tobrie, the charmer's pipe, and it is seemingly mesmerized through its focused attention on the instrument's swaying motion.

Edward Orme's pirated edition of the Solvyns etchings, *The Costume of Indostan*, includes the surmaṇḍal (Pl. II.169) among the musical instruments used by the Māl. Incorporating Solvyns's brief description from the 1799 *Catalogue*, the Orme text adds the following: These "pretended sorcerers" use musical instruments to entice serpents from their holes, and they then "press them with two piece of bamboo, previously laid on the side of the hole for the purpose; they pretend to be possessed of a specific against the bite of all venomous reptiles. Some of these people will put their hand into a bag of the most poisonous kind of serpents, and take one out, which they will teach to rear and move about to the sound of their music, and which they pretend is done by means of certain incantations. The fact, however, is, that they provoke the reptile in private, by every kind of irritation, so that when it is let out from the bag, it becomes exasperated against its tormentor. The serpents used in such exhibitions have been previously deprived of their sting; and those charmed from the holes, become stupefied by the din of the instruments, and suffer themselves to be put in a bag."[12]

1 The English name *cobra* is short for the Portuguese *cobra de capello*, "snake with a hood." See Pl. II.284.
2 Risley, *The Tribes and Castes of Bengal*, 2:45-50.
3 Ibid., 2:48.
4 Wise, 217. For Risley's entry on Bediyās, see *The Tribes and Castes of Bengal*, 1:83-85. Here he discusses the Sāmperia snake-charmers.
5 Risley, *The Tribes and Castes of Bengal*, 2:48. The ambiguity of Māl identity is further suggested by Sherring's listing them as one of the seven clans of Nats, "a tribe of vagrants who live by feats of dexterity, sleight of hand, fortune-telling, and the like." Sherring, 1:387. Also see Asutosh Bhattacharyya, "The Bengal Snake-Charmers," 3-6, on the Māl-Bediyā relationship.
6 Appendix IV, in Fayrer, 149.
7 Ibid.
8 70.
9 51.
10 Ibid., 95-96.
11 *A View of . . . the Hindoos*, 1:141.
12 Solvyns, *The Costume of Indostan*, Pl. 60.

II.66. Sāpuriyā. Snake-Charmers

Pl. II.66. Sāpuriyā. Paris: II.8.1. Double-plate.

Calcutta: Sec. XII, No. 20. Saupereah,—or Snake Catchers.

Paris: II.8.1. SAUPEREAH. SNAKE CATCHERS: We have seen in the preceding number [Jhāpān, Pl. II.196], that the fear which the Hindoos naturally felt of an animal so dangerous and so common as the serpent, had caused the institution of a feast in honour of these reptiles, or rather in honour of those who discovered the secret of depriving them of their venom. The *Mauls* [Māls, Pl. II.65], as we have remarked, act the principal part in this ceremony. By the address of these men in the perilous operation which we have already described, the Hindoos have forced the serpent to contribute to their amusement, and have made an object of diversion of what nature seems to have created for the terror of warm climates. The means which the *Mauls* employ to draw the serpents from their holes, and to divest them of all that is dangerous, are really so extraordinary in their effect, that they almost resemble enchantment. After taming them in this manner, and training them by frequent exercise, these people go about the towns and markets, carrying their serpents in baskets, and bringing them forward in the public places to dance to the sound of instruments. They are sometimes so large and heavy, that it requires several men to carry one serpent. Notwithstanding his prodigious bulk, the animal comes quietly out of his basket: his master first excites him to put him in train, taking care to cover his face whenever the serpent darts out his pointed tongue. The animal then begins to move in time, rolling and unrolling himself in a thousand different ways with as much docility as suppleness. The print represents this sight, which at first gives more fear than pleasure to an European. It requires some habit to make it as pleasing to him as it seems to be to the Hindoos.

The limits which I have prescribed to my undertaking do not allow me to enter upon the natural history of these serpents; a very satisfactory account of them may be seen in an English work enriched with engravings of all the varieties of this animal. I will confine myself to observing that the most numerous species of serpents in Asia are the *Covra Capella,* and the little black serpent which the Hindoos suppose to the be *Covra Manilla,* described by many European naturalists. Serpents of an enormous size are met with in the mountains of Hindoostan. I have seen some which weighed several hundreds; but those are not the most dangerous. They generally keep in the mountains, while the smaller kind prefer the flat and marshy country. The people of the country pretend that the more the skin is spotted or striped in black, the more, venomous the serpent. I do not know how much truth there may be in this remark.

Commentary: We have discussed snake-charming in the commentary on Māls (Pl. II.65), and it is addressed again on the worship of the snake goddess Manasā by sāpuriyās in Jhāpān (Pl. II.196). *Sāpuriyā* is the term for professional snake-catchers and snake-charmers, and, although they are principally Māls and Bediyās (Pl. II.73), they may come from various castes.[1]

James Wise describes snake-catching in Bengal:

> The snakes [usually cobras] are caught in the forest. When one is seen the samperia pursues and pin it to the ground with a forked stick. He then rapidly glides his hand along, and fixed his thumb over the first vertebra, the animal being rendered quite helpless. If the snake be a poisonous one, the fangs are barbarously torn out, but the poison "bag," the most profitable product of his dangerous trade, is carefully preserved. Snake poison is highly valued by Hindu physicians, being used in the treatment of diseases. . . .
>
> The samperia are in great request for the due performance of the Manasa Devi festival . . . .
>
> When snakes are exhibited the Samperia plays on a pipe, while his wife, or child, chaunts a monotonous Hindustani song and irritates the reptile to strike by threats and shouts.[2]

Solvyns portrays the sāpuriyās, with their baskets of cobras, in a street performance. A seated man blows the tobrie (Pl. II.179), the snake-charmer's pipe, and a standing figure plays the huḍuk, an hour-glass drum. Asutosh Bhattacharyya, in "The Bengal Snake-charmers and their Profession," refers to the etching and quotes Solvyns's text, noting that "the distinguished artist" gives "a very realistic description of an exhibition of this art . . . ."[3]

D'Oyly, in *The European in India*, portrays "A

Saumpareeah, or Snake-Catcher, Exhibiting Snakes Before Europeans," with an accompanying description by Williamson.[4]

The Indian cobra bears the scientific name *Naja naja*, from the Indian word *nāga*, for "snake"), and "cobra" is short for the Portuguese *cobra de capello*, "snake with a hood." Solvyns has a separate print for the *cobra de capello* (Pl. II.284) and describes its exceptionally wide hood and distinctive head markings. It is highly venomous and in India may kill several thousand people each year—sometimes including the sāpuriyās who catch them.

Solvyns writes of a "little black serpent which the Hindoos suppose to the be *Covra Manilla*." Pennant, in 1798, writes that "the *Cobra Manilla* is only a foot long, of a bluish color, haunting old walls. Its bite is as fatal as that of the *Cobra Capello*, which kills in he space of a quarter of an hour."[5] The term "Cobra Manilla" could refer to any number of snakes, and the serpent both Solvyns and Pennant refer to is almost surely the common krait, bluish black in color with piles of bricks and rubble as a favored habitat.[6]

In contrast to the cobra, with lengths of five to six feet, Solvyns refers to "serpents of enormous size," probably the Indian python or the larger reticulated python, the longest snake in existence, with a recorded length of 28 feet and weight of 250 pounds.[7]

---

1 Risley, in his entry for Bediyā, describes snake-catching. *The Tribes and Castes of Bengal*, 1:84-85.
2 218-19.
3 3-4.
4 Pl.11. On snakes, Williamson refers the reader to his *Oriental Field Sports*.
5 1:101.
6 Ewart, 19, Pl. 4; Whitaker, 49-50; Daniel, 107-08.
7 Daniel, 71-73.

II.67. Paṭuā. Painter

Pl. II.67. Paṭuā. Paris: I.11.5.
Calcutta: Sec. I, No. 63. Puttooa, a Painter of the Hindoo Idols.

Commentary: Paṭuās (also known as Chitrakāras) are folk painters, particularly noted for scroll painting. In the eighteenth and nineteenth centuries, *paṭ-citras* (scroll-paintings) were the most popular form of painting in Bengal. The word *paṭ* means "cloth," upon which the paintings, *paṭas*, were originally done. The paintings range from a simple square (of cloth or paper) with a single picture of a Hindu deity or mythological subject to a scroll (made of thick handmade paper) as long as 50 feet, with consecutive illustrations portraying a mythological story, with such popular subjects as Kṛṣṇa, Manasā, and Durgā, or tales of a popular folk deity. The exhibition of the scrolls, called *citrapradarśan vidyā*, is central to the profession of the Paṭuā, and as he slowly unrolls the scroll, the Paṭuā provides an explanatory narration in song, often with the accompaniment of instrumental music. The tradition continues today as in Solvyns's time.[1]

Paṭuās, as Solvyns indicates, are also "sculptors," but they are not to be confused with the Kumār potters (Pl. II.36), who model the large clay images of the gods that play so central a part in Bengali festivals. The Paṭuās have a more modest craft. The men, in addition to scroll-painting and exhibiting, make small sun-baked earthen images.

Paris: I.11.5: PUTTOOAS. PAINTERS: The Hindoo painters are also sculptors; they carve and colour the images of their Gods: and, as there is a great consumption of them, both because they are everywhere exposed to public view, and because some of their feasts terminate by throwing them into the water, the *Puttooas* never are in want of employment. They make also toys for children, of earth which they dry in the sun, and sell in the bazars, particularly on their feast days. Their varnishes are much superior to ours, and very well suited to their climate.

The *Puttooas* have no great talents, nor would such in fact be of much use to them, because they are obliged to give their idols exactly the same form that they had in the most remote periods. They are consecrated forms, not to be altered without profanation; so that the brahmuns watch with great severity over their preservation.

There are also *Puttooas* who make only pictures and drawings, but always upon the same subjects; M. Solvyns having never seen any other things represented than their deities. They have some good copiers, but that is the utmost extent of their art; if some original painters are to be met with in Hindoostan, they are Mahometans, Persians, Greeks, and other foreigners.

The *Puttooas* are degraded to the class of *parriahs*, because they handle grease and all sorts of colours. It might be added too that they seem to wish to merit that appellation by their dissolute conduct: consequently there are few true Hindoos among them.

They also decorate walls with paintings and engrave stucco walls. Paṭuā women, like Kumār women, make toys (depicted in Solvyns's etching on the porch) and dolls, fashioned of clay by hand or cast in terracotta molds, and paint on ceremonial pottery or wooden seats supplied to them by potters and carpenters.[2]

Risley, in *The Tribes and Castes of Bengal*, gives the Paṭuā only a brief entry, describing them as "a class of people, both Hindu and Mohamedan, whose profession is painting Hindu deities."[3] Elsewhere, under Bediyā, the generic name for a number of vagrant, "gypsy-like" groups, he identifies "Patwa" as "pedlars and mountebanks professing to be Mahomedans, but singing songs in praise of Rama and Lakshmana, and exhibiting painted scrolls representing the exploits of Hanumān."[4]

Solvyns gives no recognition of the peculiar social position—often described as half way between Hinduism and Islam—that Paṭuās occupy. They are folk painters who have assimilated a Muslim identity, but retain Hindu names, and observe Islamic rites, yet paint exclusively on Hindu mythological themes. Benoy Bhattacharya titled his study of the Paṭuā *Cultural Oscillation*, suggesting their movement back and forth between the two religious cultures.[5] Ratnabali Chatterjee writes that it is the "twilight zone" that Paṭuās inhabit that partly explains Solvyns's describing them as pariahs, but that it may have been their low Hindu status that drew them initially toward Islam.[6]

Bhattacharya's study focuses on the scroll-painters, the Chitrakar Paṭuā, but he identifies three hierarchically-ranked subcastes below them: Māl Paṭuā, snake charmers; Bede Paṭuā, a wandering people who perform magic shows and trained animal acts; and Maskata Paṭuā, the lowest Paṭuā subcaste, who cut the umbilical cord of newborn infants and perform abortions.[7]

---

1 On Paṭuā history and tradition, see Jyotindra Jain; S. K. Ray, "The Chitrakaras or Patuas (Painters)"; Sankar Sen Gupta, *The Patas and the Patuas of Bengal*; Guruswamy Dutt, 67-83; Ratnabali Chatterjee, 47-48; Prabhas Sen, *Crafts of West Bengal*, 168-72; Benoy Ghose, 75-84; Sarojit Datta; and Sumanta Banerjee, 130-37. Markel, 63, in writing of Kālīghaṭ painting, reproduces Solvyns's portrayal of the Paṭuā. On Kālīghaṭ *paṭuās*, see Pl. II.4, fn.15.

2 S. K. Ray, "The Chitrakaras or Patuas (Painters)," 307. Also see Benoy Ghose, 23-27.

3 *The Tribes and Castes of Bengal*, 2:172.

4 Ibid., 1:83.

5 *Cultural Oscillation (A Study of Patua Culture)*. Also see Siddiqui, "The Patuas of Calcutta: A Study in Identity Crisis."

6 50-51.

7 51-52.

II.68. Dom. Basket-Maker

Paris: I.11.6: DOAMS. BASKET-MAKERS: The *Doams* work with osier, bambou and reeds called rotins or ratans [rattan]; they make baskets, fans, mats, etc.; and build houses or huts of bambous and matting. Some of them work by the day, and are less scrupulous than the Hindoos of other casts with respect to the business they will perform. They are employed also to burn dead bodies, and to carry off carrion and the carcasses of animals; in which they resemble the *Moorda-Shos*, whom we shall soon have to describe [Pl. II.72]. They are accordingly looked upon as a mean class, in a great measure *parriahs*, which they deserve from being so much given to drinking.

These *Doams* form a sort of sect which affords a remarkable singularity. A particular rite of their worship is to adore *Rahoo* the evil spirit, especially during an eclipse, entreating him to appease his vengeance against the sun or the moon, who discovered him when he assumed the appearance of a good genius, to steal *Amratia* which floats upon the Ocean: by which is meant immortality. This allegory of the *Mohabaurut* is taken notice of in the notes of M. Wilkins on his translation of the Bhagat-Geeta.

Pl. II.68. Dom. Paris: I.11.6.

Calcutta: Sec. I, No. 43. A Doam, a maker of Baskets, Matts,—employed to burn the dead,—to remove carcases of animals, &c. This sect worship the evil spirit Rahoo [Rāhu],[1] and claim charity on an Eclipse, that their God, (in constant enmity with the sun and Moon, for having detected him in assuming the appearance of a good Genii, to obtain the Amratia [Amṛta][2] or immortality churned from the Ocean,) may desist in his vengeance against these luminaries. This beautiful allegory from the Mahabharat [*Mahābhārata*], is among the Notes of Mr. Wilkin's translate of the Bhagvat Geeta [*Bhagavad Gītā*].[3]

Commentary: The Dom, also known as Caṇḍal (Sk., Caṇḍāla), is an "untouchable" caste whose origins are probably among the aboriginal tribes of India. Their substantial numbers are distributed over a wide area of northern India, including Bengal. Most Doms engage in what Risley calls the "comparatively cleanly occupation of making baskets and mats," but the entire caste is degraded by functions which some of them perform as scavengers, hangmen, and as tenders of the dead. Some among them, the Bajaniā Doms, perform as musicians, usually drummers, at festivals and weddings.[4] As sweepers in some places, Doms remove nightsoil and dead bodies.[5] Among the many Dom subcastes, however, only two are engaged in removing corpses and tending the dead.[6] Parry, in *Death in Banaras*, writes that "The cremation ground Doms—who distinguish themselves as Gotakhor ('diver') Doms—insist that they are an entirely separate sub-caste from the Sweeper Doms of Banaras and other north Indian cities, and from the Basket-maker Doms of the rural areas."[7]

Risley writes that the Doms are "regarded by all Hindus with extreme repulsion,"[8] and, by Wise's account, "the Dom is regarded with both disgust and fear, not only on account of his habits being abhorrent and abominable, but also because he is believed to have no humane or kindly feelings. To those, however, who view him as a human being, the Dom appears as an improvident and dissolute man, addicted to sensuality and intemperance, but often an affectionate husband and indulgent father. As no Hindu can approach a Dom, his peculiar customs are unknown, and are therefore said to be wicked and accursed."[9]

Solvyns notes that in religion the Doms have particular affinity for Rāhu, but, according to Risley, "The religion of the Doms varies greatly in different parts of the country, and may be described generally as a chaotic mixture of survivals from the elemental or animistic cults characteristic of the aboriginal races, and of observances borrowed in a haphazard fashion from whatever Hindu sect happens to be dominant in a particular locality."[10] Risley makes no reference to Rāhu, the demon responsible for eclipses, but writes that "A curious custom followed by all castes throughout Bengal is associated with the Dom, and may perhaps be a survival from times when that caste were the recognized priests of the elemental deities worshipped by the non-Aryan races. Whenever an eclipse of the sun or moon occurs, every Hindu householder places at his door a few copper coins, which . . . were until recently regarded as the exclusive perquisite of the Dom."[11]

Solvyns's Dom is portrayed as a basket-maker, holding a cutter in his right hand and a bundle of split bamboo or reeds in his left.

---

1 Rāhu is the "seizer," a demon responsible for the eclipses of the sun and moon as he devours them. See Stutley, 242-43, and John Garrett, 496. He is identified as an "Asoor" (Asura), an evil spirit, in Wilkin's translation of the *Bhagavad Gītā*, 149.

2 Amṛta, the ambrosia of Vedic and Hindu mythology, is the nectar of immortality, produced by the churning of the oceans by the gods and demons. Stutley and Stutley, 11-12; Dowson, 12-14; John Garrett, 28-30.

3 Charles Wilkins, translator, *The Bhagvat-Geeta, or Dialogues of Kreeshna and Arjoon*, published under the patronage of Warren Hastings. The Orientalist Sir Charles Wilkins (1750-1836) was the first Englishman to acquire a thorough knowledge of Sanskrit. He joined Sir William Jones in founding the Asiatic Society in Calcutta in 1784, and on his return to London in 1786, he became the first librarian of the India House Library. See Buckland, *Dictionary of Indian Biography*, 451-52.

4 For a discussion of Doms as musicians, see Joorghaje, Pl. II.161.

5 Risley, *The Tribes and Castes of Bengal*, 1:240-51, and Vol. 2, Appendix I, 42; Wise, 365-68; Sherring, 1:400-02; and Asok Mitra, *The Tribes and Castes of West Bengal*, 72. Watson and Kaye, in their photographic portrayal of *The People of India*, Vol. I, photo 12, include the Doms. On the Dom's craft of basket-making, see Prabhas Sen, "Mats and Basketry," in *Crafts of West Bengal*. 40-51.

6 Risley, Vol. 2, Appendix I, 42. See Solvyns's Murdāśo, Pl. II.72.

7 90.

8 *The Tribes and Castes of Bengal*, 1:241.

9 266. The "abhorrent" habits to which Wise refers could well be the eating of carrion and "the flesh of diseased animals," described by Sherring, 1:401.

10 *The Tribes and Castes of Bengal*, 1:245.

11 Ibid., 1:246-47.

II.69. Pod. Laborer

Paris: I.12.2: POADS A LOW CLASS OF SERVANTS: The *Poads* may be considered as forming the first class of *Coolies* [*kuli*], who are commonly journeymen or some other sort of subaltern servants. They are employed in the meanest domestic offices, but have notwithstanding some remaining scruples; they will not for example touch every thing indifferently, as the *Baugdys* [Bāgdi, Pl. II.79] who are of another low class. Some of them even pique themselves upon observing all the precepts of their religion to the utmost of their power; with the pretension of being true *Soodders* [śūdras], and consequently part of the fourth original cast: but, according to *Menu* [Manu], they are in reality but an inferior subdivision.

The *Poads* are with all this, very useful in the European hospitals: the *Baugdys* are sometimes preferred only because their religious prohibitions do not interfere with their service.

It is not foreign to the subject to remark here, that such of the Hindoos as affect the rigorous profession of their precepts, and especially the Brahmuns, have so great an aversion for the meaner domestic functions, that they would have it believed that the lower classes of servants are not of their nation: and those who are destined to such services, never fail to throw them as much as they can upon the Musselmans, who have not the same objection.

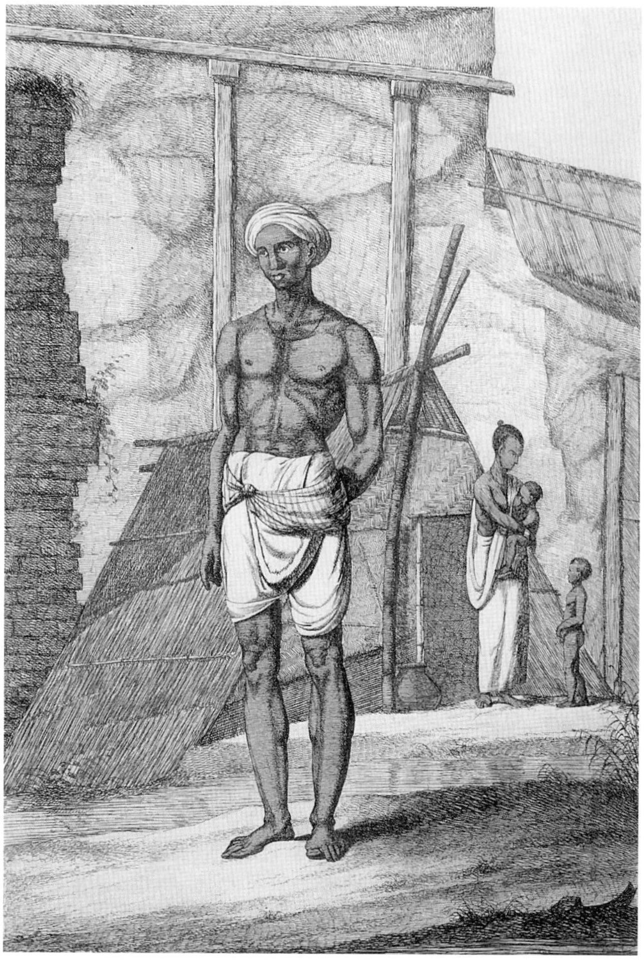

Pl. II.69. Pod. Paris: I.12.2.

Calcutta: Sec. I, No. 55. A Poad, the higher cast of Coolies or labourers.

Commentary: The Pods are a large caste of traditional cultivators concentrated in lower Bengal and particularly 24-Parganas District. Wise identifies the Pods as one of the eight classes of Caṇḍāls, a term of abuse used to describe despised "outcaste" or "untouchable" groups. While the majority were engaged in agriculture and fishing, they entered any number of occupations, as evidenced in Solvyns's discussion, and despite their low social status, their numbers included craftsmen, traders, and landowners.[1]

Land records of 1793, according to Pradip Sinha, in his *Calcutta in Urban History*, show the Pods to have made up a substantial portion of the population in the environs of Calcutta in Solvyns's time. New economic opportunities afforded by Calcutta may have been a factor in a split in the caste sometime in the later nineteenth century, but, Sinha writes, "Even in the late 18th century Solvyns. . . noticed a tendency towards upward social mobility among the Pods, especially in relation to the Bagdis."[2] The Pods were orthodox Hindus and were served by "degraded" brahmin priests. Solvyns noted their "pretension" of being true śūdras, but over the nineteenth century, more advanced members of the caste took the title Padmarajah and, harkening back to the *Mahābhārata*, claimed to be "Puṇḍra Kṣatriyas."[3]

1 Wise, 255-61; and Risley, *The Tribes and Castes of Bengal*, 2:176-77.

2 33-34 fn.

3 Ashok Mitra, *The Tribes and Castes of West Bengal*, 76; Risley, *The Tribes and Castes of Bengal*, 2:176.

II.70. Mucī. Leather-Worker

Pl. II.70. Mucī. Paris: I.12.3.

Calcutta: Sec. I, No. 59. A Moochee or Shoemaker, working in his shop,—he is likewise a Tanner, and often kills and skins in the morning the animal of whose hide he has a pair of shoes finished before night.

Paris: I.12.3: MOOCHEES TANNERS, SHOE-MAKERS: The *Moochees*, who are at the same time Tanners and Shoe-Makers, do also every other sort of work in leather. The skin of an animal killed in the morning, is salted and dried in the sun, and at two or three o'clock in the afternoon, the *Moochee* taking up his other trade makes shoes of it. He sits at his work as all the Hindoo workmen generally do, and holds it with his feet: instead of thread or cotton which he seldom uses, the seams are made with leather cut very thin. Some of them makes shoes for Europeans. The leather has a fine lustre, and they look very well, but can scarcely be used in rainy weather. A roupee, about half a crown, will purchase eight or ten pair.

The *Moochees*, as well as their women and children, are very dirty even in their dress. They nourish themselves ill, and spend the little money they earn in liquors of the country: which, added to their debauchery, procures them the name of *parriahs.*

Commentary: The Mucīs, the leather-working caste of Bengal, are probably associated with the Chamār leather-workers of North India, but, in Risley's words "claim to be a distinct caste of somewhat higher social position."[1] Whatever fine distinction Mucīs might make, however, their status, as Solvyns notes with the name "parriah," is traditionally that of the untouchable. Defiled by their contact with leather, they are considered by caste Hindus as unclean. And, nearly a century after Solvyns's described their "debauchery," Risley confirmed caste stereotype in a sweeping generalization that "all Muchis are great spirit-drinkers, and notorious for their indulgence in the more dangerous vice of gānja-smoking."[2]

Mucīs work as tanners and make shoes, saddles, drums, and rattan baskets. In addition to making drums, such as the tablā (Pl. II.160), Mucīs also perform as musicians at Hindu weddings and at festivals, playing various drums, notably the joorghaje (Pl. II.161), and stringed instruments (in which hides and gut are used in construction) as well as the oboe-like surnāī (Pl. II.178).[3]

1 Risley, *The Tribes and Castes of Bengal*, 2:95. Risley's entry for "Muchi" is 2:95-99. Risley accepts the Mucīs as distinct from Chamārs, although Wise, 251-56, and J. N. Bhattacharya, 212-13, use the names interchangeably. Also see Asok Mitra, *The Tribes and Castes of West Bengal*, 75.

2 *The Tribes and Castes of Bengal*, 2:98.

3 Ibid., 2:98-99, and Wise, 225.

II.71. Hāṛi. Scavenger

Paris: I.12.4: HAURYS. NIGHTMEN: It is not necessary to describe the occupations of the *Haurys*, nor to say that in their persons they are dirty and in general ill clad. Their earnings nevertheless are not inconsiderable, but they are soon absorbed in the tavern; which would immediately draw upon them the reproach of *parriahs*, if it were not already in some degree attached to the meanness of their employment and the relaxation of their morals.

Their marriages and domestic festivals are remarkable for a great profusion of strong liquors, which attracts a multitude of the lower classes of Hindoos.

Their wives generally serve in families as sweepers (*materannys*) [Methānī], which is nearly the same thing as embracing a state of prostitution. Some of them are very handsome.

The *Haurys* are more robust than the other Hindoos; which proceeds from their manner of living: for it is to be observed that, in proportion as the habitual occupations of the Hindoos are mean, they look upon themselves as exempt from the strict rules of abstinence in eating and drinking. So that the *Haurys*, who, as we have already said, are addicted to strong liquors, eat pork with as little repugnance as the other Hindoos do fish, which is the food prescribed by their religion.

Pl. II.71. Hāṛi. Paris: I.12.4.
Calcutta: Sec. I, No. 60. Haury; or Scavenger and Nightman.

Commentary: Risley describes the Hāṛi as "a menial and scavenger caste of Bengal," but among their subcastes the Methar (or Mihtar) alone are employed in removing nightsoil.[1] Solvyns portrays them by this name in his section on servants—"Mater" (Methar) for the male (Pl. II.129) and "Materanny" (Methrānī) for the female (Pl. II.134). Among other Hāṛi subcastes, Risley lists the Kāorā (hog-keepers) and Śiuli (toddy-tappers), both of which Solvyns portrays as separate castes (Pl. II.73 and Pl. II.62 respectively), as well as others employed as caukīdārs (Pl. II.122), palanquin-bearers, and musicians, as well as in cultivation.

Their social rank is of the lowest," Risley writes. "No one will eat with a Hāri or take water from his hands. . . . They are troubled by few scruples regarding diet [and] will even indulge in beef. Their partiality for strong drink is notorious."[2]

1 *The Tribes and Castes of Bengal*, 1:314-15.
2 Ibid., 316. Also see Asok Mitra, *The Tribes and Castes of West Bengal*, 72.

II.72. Murdāśo. Remover of Dead Bodies

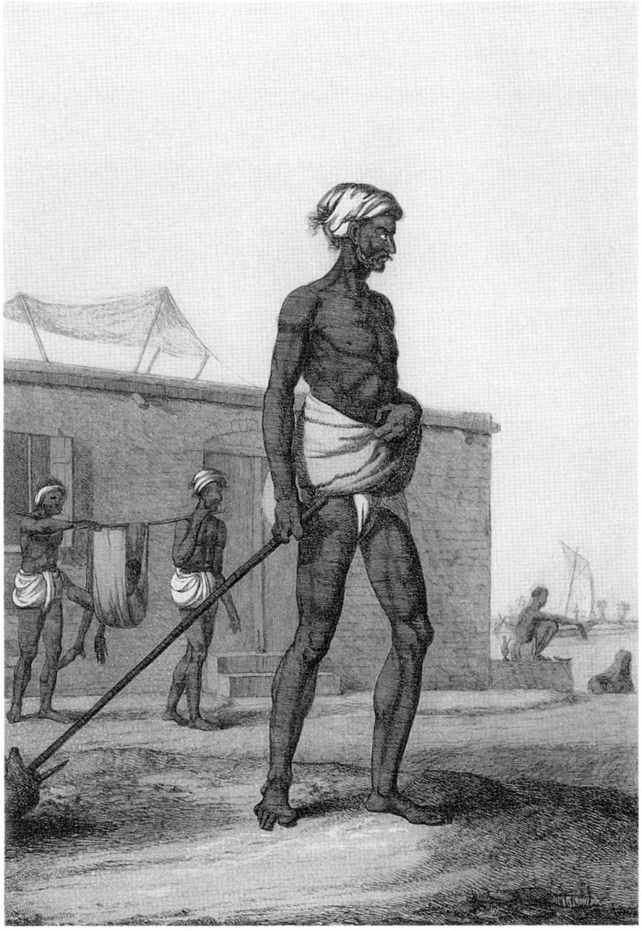

Pl. II.72. Murdāśo. Paris: I.12.5.
Calcutta: Sec. I, No. 65. A Moorda Sho, or Moorda Feraush, removing corpse and carcases of animals.

Paris: I.12.5: MOORDA-SHOS UNDERTAKERS, REMOVERS OF CORPSES: The *Moorda-Shos* burn the dead bodies, sweep all sorts of filth from the streets, and drag the carrion to the river. No urgent necessity nor increase of labour, in times of mortality, can procure them any assistance; for, except the *Doams* [Doms], who also burn the dead, no Hindoo will stoop to such vile offices. The *Moorda-Sho* consequently is in the last class of the Hindoo subdivisions: he may even be said to be inferior to the *parriahs* of every other cast, since he demeans himself so far as to become their servant.

The engraving represents the manner in which they drag or carry the dead bodies to the river, and gives also an idea of the gloominess and ferocity of their countenance, which seems to bear the stamp of their profession.

It would not be conveying an adequate knowledge of the Hindoos, to withhold the description even of the lowest subdivisions of this people, where simplicity is combined with pride, and mildness with austerity. But it may appear surprising that any among them should be destined to fonctions so derogatory as to exclude them in some sort from the national association. It must be observed that the absolute necessity of such occupations made some voluntarily descend to this mean rank; while on the other hand, misalliances, bad conduct and breach of their religious institutions caused others to be degraded to it by the superior casts of Hindoos. This loss of their cast is a sort of excommunication which condemns them and their posterity to the rank of *parriahs*: and we may here remark that this punishment is more dreaded by the Hindoos than death itself; and that there are few examples of their being reinstated even by the most costly offerings, the most rigorous abstinencies, or every other kind of expiation.

Commentary: Solvyns's term "Moorda-Shos"—*murdāśo* in Bengali—is from the Persian *murdahshūr*, meaning literally a person who washes corpses, and refers more generally to people who deal with dead bodies.[1] In his note to the original drawing, Solvyns writes, "A person whose occupation is to remove all dead bodies from the public Roads."

There are no entries for Murdāśo in the various glossaries of castes, and it seems likely that Solvyns took a descriptive word used in Bengal for the caste name and distinguished them from Doms, when in fact it is a Dom subcaste that he portrays. Risley, for example, has no entry for the term, but does list Murdafarash as "a sub-caste of Doms in Bengal who attend to cremation and disposal of dead bodies, or undertakers, each in charge of a burning ghāt."[2] Risley lists only one other Dom subcaste of Bengal, the Dhākāl Dhesiā (or Tapaspuriā), as engaged in the removal of dead bodies and notes that they also dig the trench which forms the base of the funeral pyre.[3] Colebrooke and Grant, in their *Anglo-Hindustanee Handbook*, describe Doms as "a set of people employed in Calcutta by the Police to sink dead bodies discovered floating in the river, to remove all carcasses, and kill all stray dogs found in the streets."[4] But, of great importance, the Dom—noted especially for their role at the burning ghāṭs of Banaras[5]—traditionally perform essential functions in Hindu cremations, supplying wood for the base of the pyre and the handful of lighted straw that will set the pyre ablaze.

The Doms are sometimes called Caṇḍāls and are thus associated with the caṇḍāla of classical Indian society, the class whose principal task was the carrying and cremation of corpses and who served, as well, as executioners of criminals. A. L. Basham, in *The Wonder That Was India*, writes that "According to the lawbooks the caṇḍāla should be dressed in the garments of the corpses he cremated, should eat his food from broken vessels, and should wear only iron ornaments. . . . By Gupta times caṇḍālas had become so strictly untouchable that, like lepers in Medieval Europe, they were forced to strike a wooden clapper on entering a town, to warn the Āryans of their polluting approach."[6]

The Doms are presumed to have tribal origins and occupy in traditional Hindu rankings the lowest rung of the caste hierarchy. They constitute a large and widespread community, employed in the most menial jobs, and are divided into numerous, usually occupationally-specific, subcastes. In addition to the two Bengali subcastes engaged in tending dead bodies, other subcastes work as scavengers, basket-makers, musicians, and in various pursuits.[7] Solvyns portrays a Dom subcaste of basket-makers (Pl. II.68).

---

1 I am grateful to Ali Jazayery for this clarification.
2 *The Tribes and Castes of Bengal*, 2:109. The term *murdāfarash* (*murdāpharāś* in Bengali) is a corruption of the Persian *murdahfurush*, a seller of corpses.
3 Ibid., 1:242. Here Risley relates the legend of their origin.
4 111.
5 See Sherring's description, 1:401.
6 146.
7 Risley, *The Tribes and Castes of Bengal*, Vol. 2, Appendix I, 42. Risley's entry for Dom appears in 1:240-51.

II.73. Kāorā. Swineherd

Paris: I.12.6: KAWRAS. HOG-KEEPERS: The *Kawras* are classed still lower than the *Moorda-Shos* [Murdāśo, Pl. II.72], and constitute the last of the subdivisions, and that meerly because their profession relates to an animal which the Hindoos hold in abhorrence, and carry it to such a degree, that M. Solvyns has seen market-places totally deserted when a hog has by chance got loose into them. The greatest affront that can be offered to an Hindoo, is to shew him a bit of pork; and when an European eats it, all his servants fly from the house. In general, care is taken to have only Mahometans in the kitchen; but the difficulty still exists for putting the pork on the table, an employment which the servants studiously avoid: so that the interposition of the master's authority, or at least that of the *Kaunsamaun* [Pl. II.104], the steward or butler, is absolutely necessary.

Researches have been made in vain to discover how the *Kawras* came to be first established in Hindoostan, and particularly whether they existed before the invasion of foreigners. Which seems to be proved by the mention made of them by the legislator *Menu* [Manu]: it is admitted moreover, that even at a more remote period there were wild boars in Hindoostan.

The bad qualities of the pork in India may moreover be a sufficient motive for this aversion, as well as the reason of the religious prohibition which extends to it. It is unwholesome, and hard of digestion: Europeans themselves make but little use of it, and sometimes feel its bad effects.

Commentary: The Kāorā are swineherds of Bengal. Risley has a brief entry in *The Tribes and Castes of Bengal* identifying Kāorā as a Hāṛi subcaste and writes, "They rear pigs and prepare *gur* or molasses from the juice of date-trees. Many of them also act as cooks for Europeans."[1] Under his entry for Hāṛi, Risley gives the subcaste as "Khore or Khoriyā," who he identifies as "keeping pigs," but says no more about them.[2] Risley complicates the matter, however, by listing "Kaurā" as a Dom subcaste who "breed pigs and act as scavengers."[3] The 1891 Census of India also gives Kāorā as a subcaste of the Dom, but Mitra

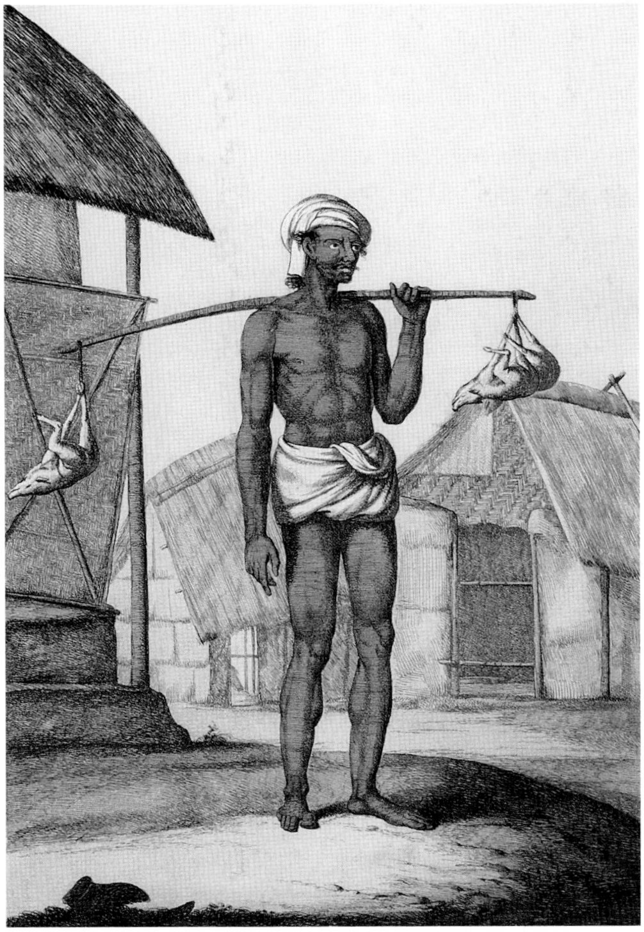

Pl. II.73. Kāorā. Paris: I.12.6.
Calcutta: Sec. I, No. 66. Kawra, or Hog-keepers, carrying pigs to Market.
Orme: 11

notes that they are also considered to be a subcaste of Hāṛi.[4]

The text to the plate in Orme's pirated edition of Solvyns states, "Hog's flesh is eaten only by Europeans, and the lowest tribes and outcasts of society."

Solvyns describes Hindu abhorrence of pigs and states that the "greatest affront" to a Hindu is to present him with pork, but however odious pork may be to Hindus, beef would be a far greater offense. Solvyns is correct in saying that Europeans generally employed Muslims as cooks, who, of course, could prepare beef without compunction, but Risley's note regarding Kāorās as cooks for Europeans suggests a likely pork dish.

1 *The Tribes and Castes of Bengal*, 1:420.
2 Ibid., 1:315. Also see 1:487, and Vol. 2, Appendix I, 59.
3 Ibid., Vol. 2, Appendix I, 42. In his entry for Dom, 1:240-51, Risley makes no reference to a swineherd subcaste.
4 Asok Mitra, *The Tribes and Castes of West Bengal*, 73.

Calcutta Etchings

II.74. Sadgop. Warehouse Keeper

Commentary: Sadgop is a small, primarily landowning, agricultural caste, but it still has some pastoral connection to its Goālā (Pl. II.47), cowherd, origins. Sadgops emerged as a distinct group in the eighteenth century, and are considered to be a superior and purified section of the Goālā caste. Their rise in social ranking is notable.[1] Solvyns makes no reference to their status, but from the order of the Sadgop portrayal in the series of caste professions in the Calcutta edition—reflecting his judgment of ranking—Solvyns considered them to command comparatively high social status.

Apparently, from the unpublished note Solvyns made to the drawing, Sadgops were regularly employed as sarkārs (Pl. II.100) in warehouses in Calcutta, and Solvyns identifies "warehouse keeper" as the "usual profession of his Cast." The term *sarkār* was used by Europeans for a variety of native employees—house stewards, accountants, purchasing agents, and, in Solvyns's portrayal here, managers. In the etching, the figure, standing before the door of the warehouse, is portrayed with a quill pen behind his ear.

The Sadgop is not included in the Paris edition, *Les Hindoûs*.

1 Risley, *The Tribes and Castes of Bengal*, 2:212-14; Jogendra Nath Bhattacharya, 225-26; Tara Krishna Basu, 24; and Hitesranjan Sanyal, *Social Mobility in Bengal*, 83-97.

Pl. II.74. Sadgop. Calcutta: Sec. I, No. 10.
Calcutta: Sec. I, No. 10. Sudgope, in the employment of a Godown or Ware-house Sircar.

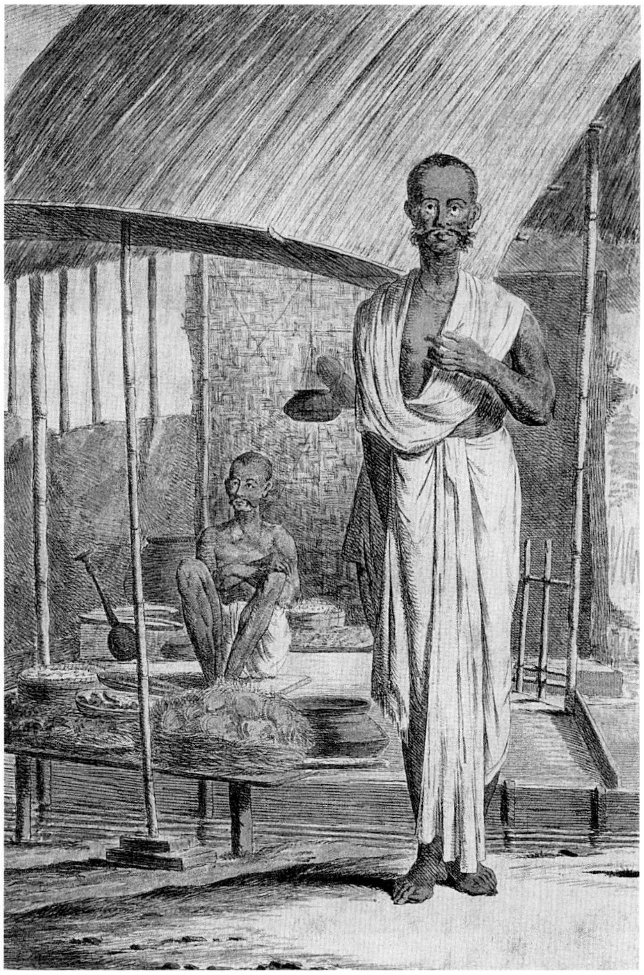

Pl. II.75. Tāmulī̆. Calcutta: Sec. I, No. 34.
Calcutta: Sec. I, No. 34. Tamooly or seller of the Pawn leaf, which made up with spices, &c. is called Donna, Bera, &c.

II.75. Tāmulī̆. Pān-seller

Commentary: The Tām(b)ulī̆, or Tāmbulibanik, is the seller of *pān*-leaves, betel-nut, and the *pān* preparations to which Solvyns refers in the text for Bārai, betel cultivator (Pl. II.32) in the Paris edition.[1] Tāmulī̆ is a caste name derived from *tāmul*, meaning betel. Sen's *Etymological Dictionary of Bengali* also gives Tāmbuliyā as "betel-seller."[2] Solvyns does not include the print of the "Tamooly" in the Paris edition.

The word *pān*, betel-leaf, is used for the mildly narcotic chewing preparation popular throughout India. In its preparation, the Tāmulī̆ smears the leaf with lime and fashioned as a small packet containing a mixture chipped areca-nut and such spices as coriander seeds, cardamom, mace, and cinnamon. Occasionally opium would be included. When filled, the leaves are folded and fastened with a clove.[3] Solvyns's word "Donna" is *donā*, a packet (or cup) made of leaves, here betel leaves; in the note to the original drawing, he calls it a "Khela Donna" (*khelā donā*), meaning "pleasure packet." "Bera" (*bāṛā*) refers to the betel garden .

Solvyns describes the enjoyment—and addiction—to *pān* in a separate print (Pl. II.212).

1 See Risley, *The Tribes and Castes of Bengal*, 2:292-95.
2 398-99.
3 Walker, 1:133; *Hobson-Jobson*, 89-90, 689; Stocqueler, *The Oriental Interpreter*, 183-84.

II.76. Bauri. Bearer and Grass-Cutter

Pl. II.76. Bauri. Calcutta: Sec. I, No. 29.

Calcutta: Sec. I, No. 29. A Bowry—alternately a Bearer and Grass-cutter.

Commentary: The Bauris, according to Risley, are "a cultivating, earth-working, and palanquin-bearing caste" of western Bengal. Although by the end of the nineteenth century, some among them had tenancy rights and a few had risen to be traders and money-lenders, the majority of Bauris were landless day-laborers. Of probable tribal origin, their caste rank is very low, and, Risley writes, "With few exceptions, they are entirely indifferent to the nice scruples regarding food, which have so important a bearing on the status of the average Hindu. . . ."[1]

In his note to the original drawing, Solvyns writes that Bauris "are seldom to be met with, but in the country" and that in his etching, "In the background they are represented carrying a Palanquin and one cutting grass." The Bauri is not included in the Paris edition, *Les Hindoûs*.

1 *The Tribes and Castes of Bengal*, 1:78-82.

II.77. Bāiti. Mat-Maker

Pl. II.77. Bāiti. Calcutta: Sec. I, No. 46.

Calcutta: Sec. I, No. 46. A Boyty:—a rush mat maker.

Commentary: Risley describes the Bāiti as "a small caste of Central and Eastern Bengal, usually called Chunāri or Chuniyā [Cunāri, Pl. II.60], from being engaged in the manufacture of lime from shells. They are," he writes, "also mat-makers, weavers, dancers, and beggars." They are among "the most impure of Bengali castes. . . ."[1] Mat-making, like basket-making is a "clean art," but the crafts are generally practiced among ritually polluted castes, such as the Bāiti.[2]

Solvyns portrays the Bāiti, as he writes in his note to the original drawing, in "their mode of making Rush Mats, used as a covering for the floor both by Europeans and Natives." The Bāiti is not included in the Paris edition, *Les Hindoûs*.

1 *The Tribes and Castes of Bengal*, 1:52-53.
2 Jogendra Nath Bhattacharya, 214.

II.78. Bediyā. Snake-Catcher

Pl. II.78. Bediyā. Calcutta: Sec. I, No. 54.

Calcutta: Sec. I, No. 54. A Buddee-a,—another class of snake-catcher, who also prescribe remedies for some species of disorders.

Commentary: The Bediyā snake-catchers are likely the Sāpuriyā or Bedya Māls discussed in Pl. II.65. Solvyns does not include the Bediyā portrayed here in the Paris edition, *Les Hindoûs*.

In addition to catching snakes, Bediyās performed as snake charmers and as "jugglers."[1] Risley, in his *Tribes and Castes of Bengal*, terms Bediyā "a generic name of a number of vagrant gipsy-like groups,"[2] and Hornell, in his account of "The Boats of the Ganges," identifies Bediyās as "nomadic dacoits" who once infested rivers in the deltaic region of Bengal.[3]

1 See "Jugglers," Pl. II.9.

2 1:83.

3 183-84. On the activities of these dacoits, see Commentary, Pl. II.241.

II.79. Bāgdi. Laborer

Pl. II.79. Bāgdi. Calcutta: Sec. I, No. 56.

Calcutta: Sec. I, No. 56. A Baugdy,—the lower class of Coolies, who perform offices that the rest refuse.

Commentary: The Bāgdi, among the largest of the "untouchable" castes of Bengal, is "a cultivating, fishing, and menial caste of Central and Western Bengal." Risley writes that "Some Bāgdis eat beef and pork, and all indulge freely in flesh of other kinds, and are greatly addicted to drink."[1]

The Duliā (or Dule) Bāgdi subcaste was traditionally engaged as palanquin-bearers (Pl. II.45), taking the name from the *dulī*, a type of palanquin (Pl. II.224).

Members of the Bāgdi caste are traditionally employed at Calcutta's Kālīghāṭ temple (Pl. II.4) to hold the animals for sacrificial slaughter. Bāgdi men were prominent celebrants of the Gājan festival, taking part in Jhā̃p (Pl. II.191), Nīla Pūjā (Pl. II.192), and Caṛak Pūjā (Pl. II.193), and today at Calcutta's Kālīghāt, only Bāgdis participant in Jhā̃p.[2]

Solvyns does not portray the Bāgdi in the Paris edition, and there only refers to the caste in his discussion of the Pods (Pl. II.69).

1 *The Tribes and Castes of Bengal*, 1:37, 1:43. Also see Satadal Dasgupta's monograph of the Bāgdi caste; Asok Mitra, *Tribes and Castes of West Bengal*, 4, 70; and Jogendra Nath Bhattacharya, 444.
2 Indrani Roy, 47.

II.80. Nikāri or Machhuā. Fishmonger

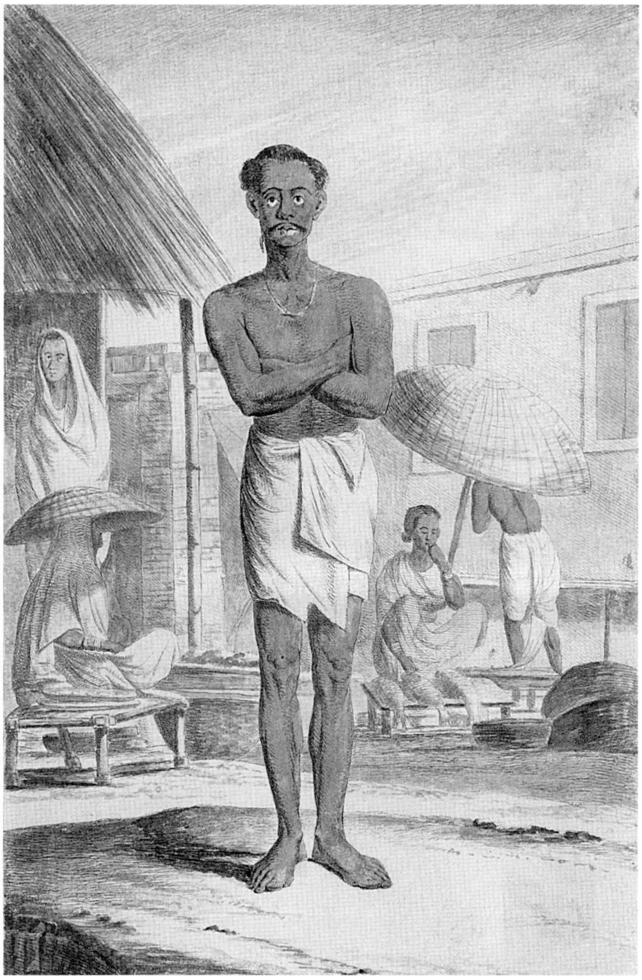

Pl. II.80. Nikāri or Machhuā. Calcutta: Sec. I, No. 58.
Calcutta: Sec. I, No. 58. A Nikaury or Machooah,—Fishmongers, with their women selling Fish in the Bazar or Market.

Commentary: Risley lists Nikāri as "Hindu fishmongers, who do not catch fish themselves, but obtain their supplies on a system of advances from the regular fishing castes."[1] More generically, Sen's *Etymological Dictionary of Bengali* defines *nikāri* as "a seller who does not produce."[2]

Contrasted with Nikāri, Risley writes that Muslim fishmongers are called "Mechuā,"[3] but for that entry, he spells it "Machhuā." There he describes it as a title for Māls and low class Muslims who sell fish, but he also gives it as a Bāgdi subcaste.[4] To make the matter all the more confusing, Sukumar Sen lists *māchuyā* (also *māchiyā*) simply as "a fisherman,"[5] and Bhattacharya, in *Hindu Castes and Sects*, states that "The Nikaris of Bengal, who are fishermen, are all Musalmans."[6]

The Nikāri is not included in the Paris edition, *Les Hindoûs*.

1 *The Tribes and Castes of Bengal*, 2:133.
2 490.
3 *The Tribes and Castes of Bengal*, 2:133.
4 2:26.
5 749.
6 Jogendra Nath Bhattacharya, 250.

II.81. Pākmāra. Bird-Catcher

Commentary: The bird-catcher, pākmārā (literally "bird-killer"), is surely one of the most fascinating of Solvyns's occupational portrayals, yet he chose inexplicably not to include the etching in the Paris edition.

In his note to the original drawing of the pākmārā, Solvyns writes that "The Drawing shows their mode of Bird Catching, which is done by fixing together pieces of Bamboo, small at the end like a fishing rod, where they put a species of Bird lime [*lāsa*, a sticky substance to catch birds]; they then introduce with caution the rod among the branches of trees, which secures the Bird the moment he touches it."

Bird-catchers may have come from various castes, but Solvyns's etching perhaps portrays members of the Baheliā caste of hunters and bird-catchers.[1] Solvyns depicts the North Indian Baheliā as a "Hindoo Soldier" (Pl. II.85), but Crooke identifies them with the bird-catching technique of the pākmārā who Solvyns portrays.[2] In his *Things Indian*, Crooke provides a detailed description: Bird-catchers, also called *mirsikārs*, "arrange a set of bamboo slips somewhat like the joints of a fishing-rod. The thinnest piece is smeared with bird-lime. This is passed up through the branches of a tree; joint after joint is added, till the first piece approaches the top, when it is deftly pressed against the feathers of the unhappy bird.

Pl. II.81. Pākmāra. Calcutta: Sec. I, No. 61.
Calcutta: Sec. I, No. 61. Puckmar, or Bird-catcher, presenting their method of taking birds, by means of gums put on sticks placed among the branches of a tree.
Orme: 12

The skill of the sportsman is shown in the care with which he avoids making any rustling of leaf or branch."[3]

Sherring, in *Hindu Tribes and Castes*, similarly identifies the Baheliā with the bird-lime technique, but describes, as well, another technique by which the bird is pierced: "A man is seated on the ground with a long pole in his hand, at one end of which is a sharp spike. He slowly introduces the pole among a number of birds carelessly hopping about picking up grain, giving it a zig-zag direction and imitating as much as possible the movement of a snake. Having brought the point near one of the birds, which is fascinated by its stealthy approach, he suddenly jerks it into its breast, and then, drawing it to him, releases the poor palpitating creature, putting it away in his bag, and recommences the same operation."[4]

The text to the Orme pirated edition of Solvyns adds another approach: "In taking water fowl they place a large earthen pot over their heads, and swim very slowly until they get among their destined victims, which they drag by their legs under the water, and by such means will secure many before an alarm be give."

Yet another bird-catching technique involves the use two kinds of nets, one for daytime, the other for catching birds at night.[5]

1 Risley, in *The Tribes and Castes of Bengal*, 1:45.
2 *Tribes and Castes of North Western India*, 1:110.
3 44. Grierson, 80, provides a similar account in *Bihar Peasant Life*, with the Hindi terms for the various instruments.
4 1:352
5 Grierson, 80.

Dresses of Hindu Men and of Hindu Women

In his Preliminary Discourse to the first volume of *Les Hindoûs*, Solvyns writes,

> If hitherto I have not spoken of the Hindoo women, the truth is, that the part which they act among that people is so little interesting, and they are so seldom to be met with in the public places of Hindoostan, that it is not to be wondered at that I have confined myself generally to the representation only of the men.
>
> In the code of Menu [Manu], in other respects replete with precepts of wisdom, it is declared with great harshness, that women are incapable of independence, and it even seems to be insinuated that they are beings of an inferior order, to whom on that account the texts of the Vedas or sacred books cannot be applied. Shut up in their separate apartments, the Hindoo women are seen only by their nearest relations, and when they appear in public, it is never without a veil upon their face. This, as may be supposed, does not extend to the lower classes, whose women appear in public and frequent assemblies without reserve. This distinction may be easily remarked in the plates which represent any feast or ceremony.
>
> Although the women of the higher casts are never exposed to the eyes of the public, they are here as in Europe and every where else, very fond of dress, but with this difference, that fancy and fashion make a great part of the value of the ornaments of an European woman, while those of the Hindoo woman have all their intrinsic worth, and join solidity to shew.[1]

In his Introduction to *Les Hindoûs*, Vol. II, Solvyns has an extended discussion of the position of women and the "cruel practice" of suttee. (See introduction to section on Satī, Pls. 199-202.)

---

1 1:28, reproduced in Chapter Four, p. 124.

II.82. A Man of Distinction in his Family Dress

Pl. II.82. A Man of Distinction. Paris: II.1.2.

Calcutta: Sec. III, No. 1. A Man of distinction in his Family Dress, consisting of a Dootee [*dhotī*] bound round his Loins, and a Doubgah thrown over his shoulders. In this habit he eats and performs his Devotions and domestic occupations,—the Jamah [*jāma*] or long Robe, so often introduced in other parts of the work, is the full Dress.

Orme: 29.

Paris: II.1.2. A HINDOO OF RANK IN HIS UNDRESS: The costumes of this people are my next object. Their dress is always simple and nearly alike in every class: it consists in two pieces of cotton cloth, one of which, called *dootee*, is tied round their loins, the other (*doubgah*) thrown over their shoulders. This is the dress of the Hindoo in his different occupations, at his meals, his devotions and sacrifices (*poojahs*). It is the same for the rich and the poor, except that the former aim at some distinction by the fineness of the stuff, and even in the manner in which it is folded round their bodies. In his visits to a grandee or a relation, the richer Hindoo takes a larger *dootee* with fuller plaits in the front. In his house he seldom wears shoes; for common use they have sandals such as we have already described. [Pl. II.33] They continually wet the *dootee*, and apply it to their faces as well for cleanliness as for coolness. When they are seated, they place the *doubgah* on their knees; at other times it is thrown over their shoulders, as we have said, or carried on their arm. The rest of their body is naked and generally shining, from the oil of mustard with which they rub themselves several times a day. They frequently also shave not only their chins but all the other parts of their body. Their beauty consists in having the skin free from any cicatrice or spot, shining, and of a yellowish tint. Plumpness and fat seem with them to be the distinctive attributes of dignity and riches: a distinction which nevertheless many of their Radjahs or princes are not able to attain.

The Hindoo represented in this print carries in his hand a chaplet [prayer beads], an instrument of devotion which he seldom lays aside when at home. The accessories in the print shew that he is in an interior court, planted as it generally is with bananas and other shrubs. Several small doors shew the staircases leading to the inner apartments, where he lives with his women and children, and to the platform which covers his house and where he goes to breathe a cooler air.

Commentary: The *dhotī* is an unstitched white cotton cloth, sometimes with a colored border, worn over the lower body by men of "all the respectable Hindu castes."[1] The manner in which it is tied and draped varies by region within India. In Bengal, as Solvyns depicts, it is wrapped round the waist, with the end passed between the legs, tucked behind, and left to drape down below the knee. Solvyns calls the shoulder cloth a *doubgah,* but neither the word or possible variants appear in any Bengali dictionary. It is perhaps related to *dupaṭṭā*, the cloth worn loosely as an "upper cloth" or light shawl by women. As suggested by the word's literal meaning, "two strips" (*du* + *paṭṭā*), the cloth was originally of two pieces joined together, but, though retaining the name, it came to be woven as a single piece.[2]

The figure depicted is a high caste Vaiṣṇava, as indicated by the *tilak* mark on his forehead.

Somendra Chandra Nandy identifies him as Krishna Kanta Nandy, Warren Hastings' s banian,[3] but as discussed in the commentary on Solvyns's portrayal of the banian (Pl. II.99), this seems improbable.

1 *Hobson-Jobson*, 314. On dress generally, see Goswamy; Ghurye, *Indian Costume*; Dar; and Tarlo.
2 *Hobson-Jobson*, 324.
3 2:viii.

II.83. A Man of Inferior Rank

Paris: II.1.3. A HINDOO OF INFERIOR RANK: The dress of the Hindoo here represented differs from the preceding one by being shorter, and the *dootee* having fewer plaits and less fulness. In this case, the *doubgah* [*dupaṭṭā*] is but a small piece of cotton cloth called *romal* [*rūmāl*],[1] and generally of a yellowish colour, because it stands better against the heat of the sun and the continual application of water.

The principal figure of this print is an inhabitant of the country, advanced in age, in easy circumstances, as is generally the case of the Hindoo who lives far from towns. Neither opulence nor poverty are remarked in his dress. His habitation in the background is suited to his style of life, and announces the simplicity and frugality of its master. It has a ruinous appearance, which is often the case of these country habitations, raised with bricks baked in the sun, and kept together with a little mud: this sort of construction, the least solid and lasting of any, is called *catia*[*kachchā*]. The more durable edifices are also constructed with bricks, but cemented with lime or (*chunam*).[2] A house built in this manner is called *paccah* [*pakkā*]. These two terms of *catia* and *paccah* are frequently used metaphorically in India, to signify solidity or frailty in general, ignorance and knowledge, in fine riches or poverty. I have represented an old man, to give an idea of the great age to which men here, as elsewhere, attain from early and strict habits of temperance. It is common here to see very old men who have never known sickness. Their skin, from the use of mustard oil, acquires a degree of thickness which renders it insensible to the effects of the sun: yet, in cases of deep wounds, it closes and heals with extraordinary quickness, as I have often witnessed. —The background is a Bengal landscape, the soil flat and planted with different trees, especially bananas and the cocoa plant, which are their favourite trees.

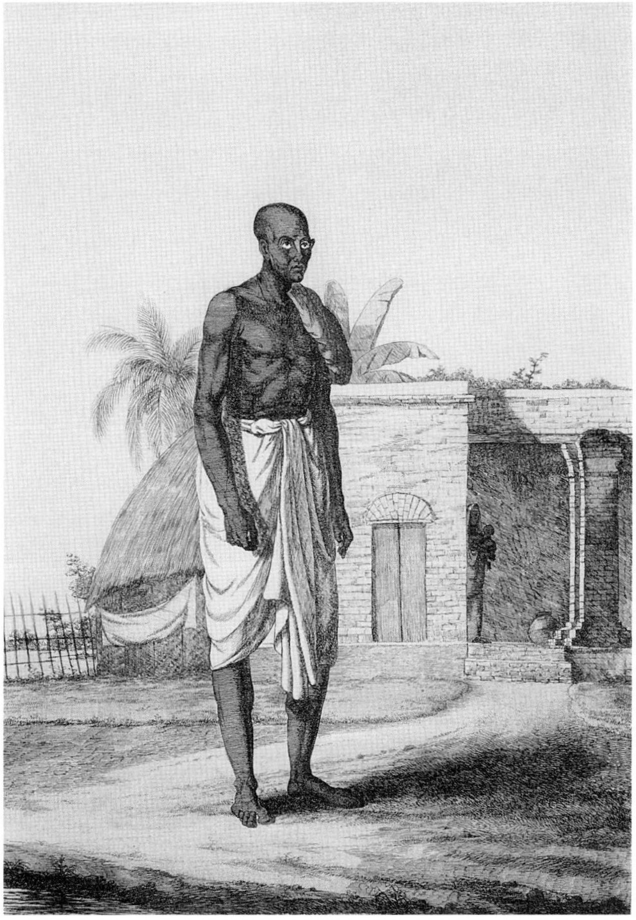

Pl. II.83. A Man of Inferior Rank. Paris: II.1.3. **Calcutta: Sec. III, No. 2.** A man of inferior Rank.

Commentary: Solvyns's text here is largely self-explanatory, but a note may be made on two widely used terms in India. The term *kachchā* (Anglo-Indian, kutcha or cutcha) means unripe, raw, or crude, and here applies to a house of mud or straw mats. In contrast, something that is *pakkā* (Anglo-Indian, pukka or pucka) is ripe, cooked, or superior, as in a building of brick and mortar or of stone.[3]

1 The *rūmāl* is a towel or handkerchief usually worn over one shoulder. See *Hobson-Jobson*, 769.
2 See Pl. II.60 for a discussion of the use of *chunam* (*cūnā*) in construction.
3 See *Hobson-Jobson*, pp. 287 and 734.

II.84. A Man of Low Rank

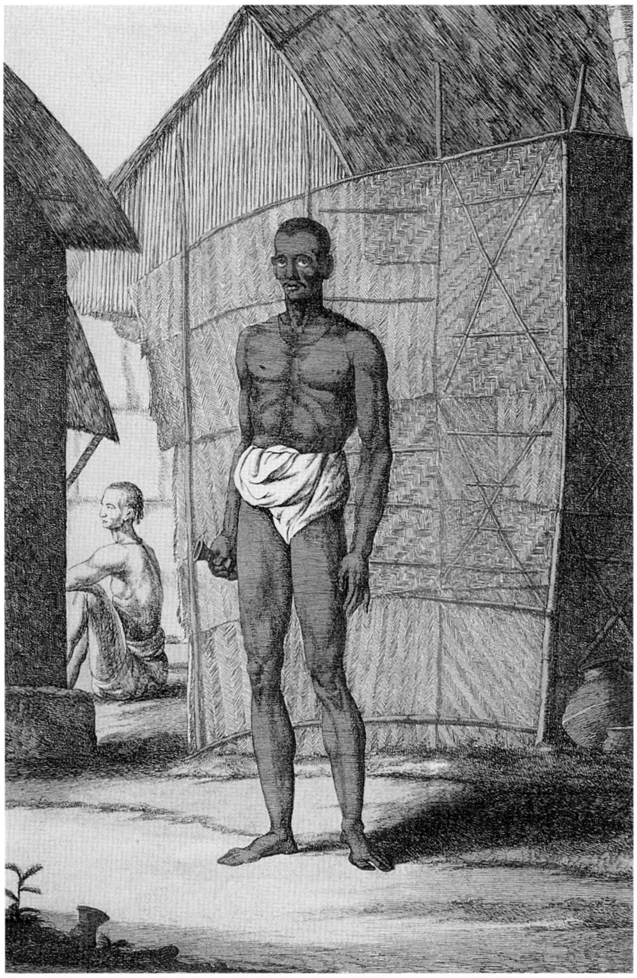

Commentary: The *langoṭī* is a narrow loin cloth passed between the legs and tucked in both front and back by a string around the waist and is, in the words of *Hobson-Jobson*, "the scantiest modicum of covering worn for decency by some of the lower classes when at work. . . ."[3] It is distinct from the *lungī*, a cloth wrapped simply once or twice around the hips and tucked in at the upper edge. Usually colored and generally of a checked pattern, the *lungī* is worn principally by Muslims.[4]

1 See Solvyns's portrayal of the *hukā*, Pls. II.203-210.

2 See Pl. II.61.

3 525. Also see Nirmal Kumar Bose, *Peasant Life in India*, 36-37.

4 *Hobson-Jobson*, 519.

Pl. II.84. A Man of Low Rank. Paris: II.1.4. **Calcutta: Sec. III, No. 3.** A Man of low rank.

Paris: II.1.4. A HINDOO OF THE LOWEST CLASSES: The dress of the lower classes of the people consists only in a piece of cotton cloth called *langoutie* [*langoṭī*], tied loosely round their loins, but preserving nevertheless something of the form of breeches: and much preferable to the large trowsers of the Mussulmen, which are well known to be the cause of particular infirmities or at least of great difformity.

Among the true Hindoos these three sorts of dress only which we have described, are known and are kept distinct. In their festivals their apparel is cleaner and more ample: the lower classes on these occasions, wrap up their heads in a sort of turban or piece of muslin. But their ranks can never be mistaken from their dress. Besides the costume and the manners, the colour also distinguishes the lower from the higher, the former being of a much deeper tint: this distinction is most perceptible on the borders of the sea and salt waters. These lower classes too at home, and when they bathe, have no other clothing but a small bit of cotton hung round them by a string, for meer decency.

The individual here represented is one of the *Coulies* [*kulī*] or working men; he is near his habitation made with mats and bambous. A *Coulie* may earn about three roupies, or half-crowns a month, and upon this little salary he keeps all his family, consisting generally of a wife and five or six children; which at once gives an idea of the population of the country, the abundance of food, and the frugality of the inhabitants. Rice, as is well known, is the principal food of the Hindoo, but luxury has added to it almost as articles of necessity the betel which they chew, the *houka*[*hukā*][1] which they smoke, and the liquors known under the name of *tarry* [*tāṛī*] and *arrack*,[2] which they drink with great avidity. These objects are become of common use among the people of Hindoostan, who, when they can get them and the liquors we have just mentioned, are satisfied for their food with a little rice dry or toasted.

II.85. Baheliā. Soldier

Pl. II.85. Baheliā. Paris: II.1.5.

Calcutta: Sec. III, No. 6. A Behaleea or Hindoo Soldier, dressed in cotton quilted Armour, with his Match-lock Gun.

Orme: 32.

Paris: II.1.5. BEHALEE-A, THE PRIMITIVE HINDOO SOLDIER: A soldier in the complete military accoutrement of the ancient times of Hindoostan is very rarely to be met with: no part of the country has preserved it, and perhaps I should never have seen it, had it not been for a Rajah or Indian prince, who shewed me one of several which he said he had in his palace. It consists in a vest of cotton cloth quilted to the thickness of about two fingers. I have been assured that the credulity of the ancient Hindoos went so far as to persuade them that these quilted vests could resist a musket ball. The Behalee-a used match-locks, such as are still seen in some parts of India: a horn was their powder pouch, and their sabres were more or less curved: they wore long trowsers, very heavy shoes, and in general the whole dress was heavy and cumbersome. Since the invasion of the Mussulmen this military costume has disappeared; all the Hindoo armies have now adopted the dress of the seapoys, which will be described in its proper place. The Behalee-a lived under tents and fed as the Hindoo soldier of our days upon rice and water. The bullock is employed in India for the transport of baggage and military equipage: the elephant and camel are reserved for officers of distinction. The seapoys maintain the ancient reputation of bravery of the Hindoo soldier. What chiefly tends to inspire a contempt of death among the Hindoos is their belief in the transmigration of souls, that fundamental dogma of all Indian religion, which contains an imperfect idea of the immortality of the soul.

The domestic dress of the soldier, when he is not on service, and in his family, is the same as that of the other Hindoos who are not warriors, but with the distinctive marks of the cast in which he was born: for there are at present in all the Indian armies, even those in the service of Mahometans or Europeans, soldiers of all the casts, not even excepting Brahmuns.

Commentary: The Baheliā (Baheliya) are a North Indian caste of wandering hunters and fowlers,[1] and they long provided an important source for military recruitment. Akbar garrisoned the fort of Chunar on the Ganges above Banaras with Baheliās, and they remained there, led by the *hāzarī*, the Baheliā commander, until their surrender to the British in 1772. Dirk H. Kolff relates that after the surrender, the Baheliās "fell into obscurity" and, in the 1890s, the descendent of the last *hāzarī* of Chunar was a "runner" in government service. But the Baheliās were not restricted to Chunar. Kolff, who describes them as "spurious Rajput infantrymen," notes that "during the seventeenth century, Baheliyas were conspicuous as footsoldiers fighting under Mughal commanders." And they were later employed as sepoys by native nobility and gentry in the region of Banaras and, by Solvyns's report, into Bengal as well.[2]

In his note to the original drawing, Solvyns writes that "The background exhibits a soldier's tent, with soldiers preparing their victuals, and a distant view of a hill fort."

Solvyns is probably wrong in thinking that the padded coat could not stop a musket ball, at least for longer distances, but improved muskets and more efficient firing in the late eighteenth century, at about Solvyns's time, did reduce the effectiveness of such coats in deflecting volleys.[3]

---

1 Sherring gives their name also as Badhak, 1:352; Russell places them among the Pārdhi, 4:359; and Crooke, *Tribes and Castes of North Western India*, 1:104-11, includes a photograph of a Baheliā hunter and details their bird-catching techniques, a procedure very similar to that described by Solvyns in his portrayal of the Pākmārā, bird-catcher, Pl. II.81.

2 117-19.

3 Stewart Gordon, personal communication, August 17, 1994.

II.86. A Sarkār Dressed in a Kurtā

Pl. II.86. A Sarkār Dressed in a Kurtā. Paris: II.1.6

Calcutta: Sec. III, No. 4. A Sircar [*sarkār*] dressed in a Courta [*kurtā*]; and an Eklie [*eklāi*] over his shoulders,—this dress is of Mahometan origin, but much used at present by the Hindoos—A Hindoo may be distinguished in this dress, the Ungha [*aṇga* or *aṇgarkhā*], Ulkaluck [*alkalaq*], &c. by having the opening on the right breast, while the Mahometans wear it on the left.

Orme: 30.

Paris: II.1.6. THE COURTI, ANOTHER SORT OF DRESS: This dress at first sight appears to be that of the Mussulmen: but it differs from it essentially; it is much shorter than their *jamna* [*jāma*] and open[s] on the left side of the breast, as theirs is on the right. The sort of turban which is worn with it, is flatter in the front and fuller behind than that of the followers of Mahomet in India. In fine, the form of the costume is not exactly the same.

The *courti* is not looked upon as a very suitable dress among the Hindoos; and is therefore never seen in any of their ceremonies. It is little worn unless by young men and (*loutias*) people of a suspicious character, who use it in their private visits to women. The fullness and fineness of the stuff are in this, as in the other costumes, the distinction of the rich. The turban and sash are seldom of any other colour than white. My opinion is, that this dress is not originally of Hindoostan; for which reason I have placed it after the primitive forms in this number.

The strict observers of the law of Brahma never wear shoes, they are even expressly forbidden by their religion, and this prohibition was formerly universally adhered to. But now the use of shoes is pretty general in Hindoostan. They resemble our slippers, leaving the heel bare, and scarcely covering the toes, with sharp and turned up points.

When the Hindoos wear the *courti,* they do not paint themselves, except in upper Hindoostan where the *courti* is in more general use.

Commentary: In the entry in the *Catalogue* for the 1799 edition, Solvyns identifies the figure in this print as a sarkār, a steward, here depicted in the role of house servant,[1] and describes him as dressed in a *kurtā*, with an *eklāi*, a mantle of a single woven width of cloth, draped over his shoulders.[2] The *kurtā* is a "loose-fitting garment for outerwear, often with a round neck, of knee-length or even longer, with side slips at the helm and generally flared skirt."[3] Often of fine muslin, it became popular in the eighteenth century. In the Paris text, Solvyns expresses doubt that the dress is "originally of Hindoostan." In the 1799 *Catalogue*, he more confidently asserts that it "is of Mahometan origin, but much used at present by the Hindoos." Probably of Persian origin, the *kurtā* was associated in Bengal with the Punjab and was sometimes known as a "Punjabi." The *kurtī* is a shortened version of the *kurtā* and is worn mostly by women.[4]

The *jāma*, of Central Asian origin and a popular Mughal style worn well into the nineteenth century, is a full-length gown, tied in the middle with a sash, with the fullness of a skirt below.[5] In the *Catalogue* entry, Solvyns does not mention the *jāma*, but refers to the "Ungha" [*aṇga* or *aṇgarkhā*],[6] a long gown similar to the *jāma*, and "Ulkaluck" [*alkalaq*], a long loose-fitting robe, the name derived from the Turkish. He notes that Hindus and Muslims are distinguished by the side on which the garment is tied across the chest, but in the 1799 *Catalogue*, Solvyns mistakenly reverses it, correcting himself in the Paris edition: Muslims, as familiar in Mughal miniatures, tie the *jāma* (or *aṇgarkhā*) to the left, while Hindus tie it across the right, fastening it under the left shoulder.[7]

In the Paris text, Solvyns refers to people of "suspicious character" as "loutias," as he does elsewhere (Pls. II.151, II.152, and II.160) in describing those given over to debauchery. The Anglo-Indian word listed in *Hobson-Jobson* is *loocher* (from the Hindi *luchchā*; Bengali, *lochchā*), meaning "a blackguard libertine, a lewd loafer."[8]

1 Solvyns depicts the sarkār in his series on servants, Pl. II.100.
2 Williamson, *East India Vade-Mecum*, 1:206, provides a detailed description of the sarkār's dress.
3 Goswamy, 390.
4 Ibid., 136-37, 390.
5 Ibid., 390. Also see *Hobson-Jobson*, 449. See Solvyns's Pl. II.19.
6 Ibid., 389; Lewis, 50. The *jāma* and *aṇgarkhā* are depicted in Dar, Pls. 11, 12, and 13.
7 On this difference in fastening, see Ghurye, *Indian Costume*, 114-15.
8 519.

II.87. A Woman of Distinction

Commentary: Walter Hamilton, in his *Description of Hindostan*, writes that "Sometimes men amuse themselves singing hymns or love songs, accompanied by small drums; but it is considered disgraceful for a modest woman to sing or play on any musical instrument."[1] Respectable women (as Solvyns's "Woman in Full Dress," Pl. II.92) did sometimes sing to their own accompaniment, but the woman Solvyns depicts is "the Mistress of an Opulent Hindoo."[2]

Ghurye, *Indian Costume*, reproduces Orme's portrayal after Solvyns and notes that "as in the illustration. . . the only covering for the bosom consisted of the portion of the 'sāri' passing over it. No special breast-garment was donned. So much was this considered to be the decent mode of dress that the word 'coli' [blouse] and the piece of apparel denoted by it are . . . foreign to Bengal."[3] Nirad Chaudhuri, in an essay on Indian dress, writes that in Bengal, well into the nineteenth century, Hindu women "of even the highest castes and wealthiest families" wore the sari as the sole garment covering their bodies. They wrapped the sari around the lower body like a skirt, with the remaining half thrown "over their shoulders and bust, leaving the back virtually exposed."[4] Among the higher classes, the sari was of the sheerest fabric—almost to be transparent.[5]

Europeans and Hindu reformers of the Brahmo Samaj regarded such dress as immodest, but, as Solvyns depicts, the Bengali woman (as those of North India generally) drew a portion of the sari in modesty to cover her head. The blouse or closely-fitted bodice (*colī*), worn by Hindu women in North India, was not in Solvyns's time part of the Bengali woman's attire. This was so for women of distinction as it was, described by Solvyns, for women of "inferior rank" (Pl. II.88).

Behind the woman portrayed is a *hukā*, and on the cushion beside her is a tray with various boxes for

Pl. II.87. A Woman of Distinction. Paris: II.2.2.
Calcutta: Sec. IV, No. 1. A Woman of Distinction.—were she married she could not with propriety wear shoes or smoke the Hooka [*hukā*].
Orme: 36.

the preparation of *pān* (Pl. II.212), the betel-leaf "packet" chewed by Indians as a mild narcotic. An 1809 British print, copied from Solvyns's Calcutta etching, places "the woman of distinction" at "A Smoking Party in the Province of Bengal" (Pl. I. 55), with two men smoking the *hukā* as they sit below her.

1 1:104
2 Solvyns's note to the original drawing.
3 169, Pl. 355.
4 *Culture in a Vanity Bag,* 15.
5 Ibid., 62-63.

Paris: II.2.2. A WOMAN OF DISTINCTION: The richness of this lady's dress is striking, but the ornaments with which it is overloaded shew that it is not an original costume of the Hindoo country, whose simplicity has in the course of this work been so often and so justly the subject of my praise. In reality the dress here represented is not worn by the Hindoos who conform strictly to the law of Menu. It is that of public women, in the line of kept mistresses or concubines. Nevertheless, the upper garment, or *sari,* is used by other women, as well as the jewels which ornament the nose, the ears, the neck, the hands and the feet of this figure; but by women of character they are worn only in great festivals: on any other occasion such a dress would be ill received by the husband, for the Hindoos have the simplicity to imagine that a woman ought not to adorn her person for strangers, more than she does in common for her husband. Children and young girls wear indiscriminately all these ornaments, with the difference that their *sari* is of red silk with worked borders, whereas that of the women is generally of a very fine stuff sometimes striped.

It has been already remarked that all these jewels of the Hindoo women have the merit of an intrinsic value, and a solidity which sometimes gives them a massive and heavy appearance. We may judge by this of the value of such a dress as is here represented, rendered not unfrequently still more precious, by the profusion of pearls with which they cover their heads and even their shoes.—The attitude is that which a woman of this rank preserves during the greater part of the day: seated on an elevation richly ornamented, and preserved by transparent curtains from the annoyance of the musquitos which infest this climate, her whole time is spent in eating, drinking, smoking, and sleeping: sometimes indeed, at intervals only, she will relieve the monotony of this existence by music, which she performs upon the *dole* [ḍhol, Pl. II.157] or the *tom-tom* accompanied by her voice. Accessible only to the person who keeps her, no other visitor is admitted; which makes it very difficult for Europeans to penetrate to the interior of her apartments.

II.88. A Woman of Inferior Rank

Pl. II.88. A Woman of Inferior Rank. Paris: II.2.3. **Calcutta: Sec. IV, No. 2.** A Woman of Inferior Rank.—a Widow cannot wear coloured boarders to her cloaths or any ornaments, excepting a Necklace of wooden beads.
Orme: 38.

Paris: II.2.3. A WOMAN OF INFERIOR RANK: This is the true costume of the women of the middle classes; it consists meerly in a drapery or *sari* of cotton, tied round the loins and past over the head. This simple dress covers their whole body sufficiently to preserve the idea of decency, in which they are by no means deficient; but modesty with them requires that the head should be covered at the approach of a man, and this condition fulfilled, they feel no impropriety in leaving the rest of their forms exposed to view. They never besides appear abroad but going to bathe in the river. By a law of their religion they carry always a little black mark, in the form of a star, upon their chin, on one side of the nose, and between their eyebrows: they have also a small ring of gold in one of their nostrils, gold rings in their ears, and (*sunks*) [*śaṅkha*] or bracelets of shell, round their wrists. Their *sari* has a border of blue or red or any other colour: only when they are widows the coloured *sari* is not allowed. The colour of the Hindoo women is yellowish bordering upon copper colour. The situation of a married woman among them is rather that of a slave than of a wife: the husband, who is the sole chief and master of the family, requires from them the most humbling demonstrations of duty. Obliged to prepare his meat and drink, she is not allowed to partake of it in his company, nor even to smoke the *hooka* [*hukā*] in his presence. The whole concerns of the family, the care of the husband and of the children rest upon her; and notwithstanding all these painful duties, she is sure to meet with very little consideration from the person to whom she is united for life.

I speak particularly of the women of Bengal, Behar and Orissah, because I chiefly describe the inhabitants of those provinces, which are the residence of the primitive Hindoos. The Brahmuns even pretend that Brahma himself came down from heaven into this country to people the earth; a further proof too, that this was the cradle of the Hindoo people, appears in the colleges and public schools, which still exist, and where the ancient Hindoostan language [Sanskrit] is still taught.

Commentary: The conch shell (*śaṅkha*) bangles to which Solvyns refers are traditionally worn by Bengali women of "respectable castes" as a sign of marriage and are broken on the death of her husband.[1] Solvyns's reference to the little black marks remain something of a puzzle. They are likely "beauty marks" without religious significance, probably made with *kājal*, the oily black soot from butter lamps that is used as an eye-liner and, among infants, to ward off the evil-eye. Cosmetics vary by caste and local tradition, and many forms that may have been common in Solvyns's day are now lost. The most distinctive cosmetic ornamentation worn by Hindu women is the "dot" on the forehead just above the eyes. Called a *ṭīkā* or (more commonly today) *bindī* in Hindi and *ṭip* in Bengali, its color is traditionally red for married women.

1 See Commentary, Pl. II.34.

II.89. A Woman of Low Rank

Paris: II.2.4. A WOMAN OF LOW RANK: The bad condition of this dress indicates the low rank of its owner. The *sari* has been mended in several places, and is thrown carelessly over the shoulders: the border without any ornament shews that she is a widow; her face too has several marks upon it. Her hair is plaited like that of all the Hindoo women; it is only when they bathe that it is allowed to flow loosely. Before they go into the river, they rub all their body with mustard oil, a custom which I have remarked in the preceding number. The skin hardened and blackened by this practice, and by the heat of the sun, gives them very early a look of old age and decrepitude; so that the beauty of a Hindoo woman is past, before that of an European is in its prime. At twenty they are looked upon as matrons in the decline of life.

In the north of Hindoostan the lower classes of women sometimes wear another small garment under the *sari*; which last is also frequently of a fuller stuff.

The children are left naked till the age of five or six years, and often longer: but they begin then to dress them in different coloured silks, and to cover them with every sort of ornaments and jewels. A curious observation that I had an opportunity of making during my residence in Hindoostan is, that the women in general shew the most decided preference for their male children: they are the objects of their particular care, while the females are treated with a sort of contempt. This conduct is evidently a result of the prejudices in which all the Hindoos are brought up, and which influence the whole course of their lives.

The food which they give their children is very simple, boiled rice only, and a little water: they are very little subject to sickness, and their mothers suckle them longer than is the custom in Europe: for this reason the Hindoo children are fat and healthy; and being little exposed to the sun during their first years, their skin is generally of a lighter tint than that of their fathers and mothers.

Pl. II.89. A Woman of Low Rank. Paris: II.2.4.
Calcutta: Sec. IV, No. 3. A Woman of Low Rank

Commentary: Solvyns remarks on the preference for male children and treatment of females with "a sort of contempt"—prejudices (alas, still evident today) "which influence the whole course of their lives." His judgment, enlightened for a European of his time, is reflected as well in his earlier comments, Pl. II.88, on the status of the wife as little more than a "slave."

II.90. Goālinī. Milkmaid

Paris: II.2.5. GWALLIN. MILK-WOMAN: The women who follow this trade, are mostly born in the country of Orissah, and married to palanqueen carriers or cow-keepers. Their dress is distinguished from that of other women of their class by the breadth of the borders of their saries, who are sometimes also embroidered. These women are generally of a yellower tint, from their disgusting habit of rubbing their skin with cow dung, also their drapery. The milk women's ornaments consist of a chaplet or *malla* [*mālā*] hung round their neck, and made sometimes of red coral, a small ring through the lower part of the nose, and large rings of brass round their wrists and arms: such is the solidity of these articles, that their weight amounts not unfrequently to fifteen or twenty pounds. Under such an incumbrance it would not be easy for these poor women to follow their business, if they were not endowed with more bodily strength and spirit than the rest of the Hindoo women. It is not uncommon to see these qualities exerted against each other in very obstinate battles, where their decorations are used for arms with a success deeply marked on the bodies of their antagonists. These women, with their robust frame of body, make use of the same frugal diet as the other women of Hindoostan. They are easily known at first sight by the broad borders of their drapery, which I have just noticed, and the deeper yellow tint of their complexion.

Pl. II.90. Goālinī. Paris: II.2.5.

Calcutta: Sec. IV, No. 4. A Gwallin, or Milk Woman,—the brass bracelets are often very weighty, and serve occasionally for defence as well as ornament.

Orme: 37.

Commentary: The Goālinī, milkmaid, is the woman of the Goālā (cowherder) caste, described in Pl. II.47.

The text with the Orme plate reads;

> Their cows are remarkable for having a hump on their shoulders: their mode of making butter is by half curdling the milk, and then agitating it with a machine made of bamboos, placed in an earthen jar, whirled about by means of a string. The milk is commonly boiled preparatory to the making of butter, and the butter of India therefore tastes of smoke: that which is used by Europeans of distinction is different, being made in their own houses, and as nearly as possible in the European manner. The butter so produced is not much inferior to the best in England.

II.91. Aghori. Female Ascetic

Pl. II.91. Aghori. Paris: II.2.6.
Calcutta: Sec. IV, No. 8. Agoree,—this low class eat dead bodies, and use the skull as a cup to drink out of.

Commentary: Solvyns encountered one of the comparatively rare women of the Tantric Aghorapanthī sect, but oddly makes no reference to the men, either here or in his discussion of fakirs and ascetics. He depicts the woman sympathetically, giving her (as often in his portraits) a melancholy expression. There is nothing to suggest the disgust with which Aghoris were generally viewed by Europeans nor the mixture of fear and awe in which they were held by Hindus.

In the Paris text, Solvyns identifies the Aghori as a woman who, on the death of her husband, refuses suttee[1] and rejects the more traditional alternatives of widowhood to take "exile and solitude" as a wandering ascetic. The Aghori sect was open to all classes and castes and such an option, however extreme, would surely have been available, but nowhere in the literature on satī or on the Aghoris is there reference to such a practice.

Aghoris, followers of the goddess Śakti, all-powerful embodiment of Energy, are associated with death and darkness. They live in cremation grounds, and by virtue of their terrible austerities, are "held to acquire the capacity to defy the ordinary laws" that govern the world.[2] "In proof of their indifference to worldly objects," Horace H. Wilson wrote in 1828, the Aghoris "eat and drink whatever is given to them, even ordure and carrion. They smear their bodies also with excrement, and carry it about with them in a wooden cup, or skull, either to swallow it, if by doing so they can get a few pice; or to throw it upon the persons, or into the houses of those who refuse to comply with their demands."[3] Solvyns makes no reference in the text of the Paris edition to such extreme practices, although in the 1799 Calcutta *Catalogue*, he states that Aghoris "eat dead bodies." And in other sources, Aghoris were reported to feed on human corpses at the burning ghāṭs in Calcutta.[4]

These practices—today largely suppressed—are an expression of the unity of opposites, of a conquest of the distinction between purity and pollution. "If everything in existence is only a manifestation of the universal soul, nothing can be unclean!"[5]

Usually identified with the skull-carrying Kāpālika sect, described in Sanskrit texts, and surely resembling them in their appearance and manner, the Aghori eats his food "out of a human skull which is his constant companion and alms-bowl."[6] Solvyns portrays the skull bowl on the ground to the woman's left, but of the ornate bowl Solvyns describes, Balfour, in his "Life History of an Aghori Fakir," writes, "This was presumably an exceptional instance, and the gold mounting of the skull bowl of this reclaimed Aghori woman reminds me of the elaborately decorated skull vessels of the Mongolian Buddhists rather than of the rough uncleansed skulls used by the ordinary Aghori wanderers. The skull bowl is characteristic in not

Paris: II.2.6. AGOOREE. A PROSCRIBED WOMAN: This is one of those particular classes of women whose mode of life differs so much from that of the other Hindoos, that I thought it necessary to enter into some details concerning them. This name of *Agooree* is given by the Hindoos to those women who, though they are of the religion of Brahma, would not consent to be burnt with the body of their deceased husband, and who, instead of consenting to the penalties prescribed by their law, such as to become slaves in their own house, or to degrade themselves to the class of public women, as is ordered by the Brahmuns in such cases, prefer a life of exile and solitude in the woods and deserts. There the law gives them entire liberty to act according to their own inclination, and to follow their own taste in their food, with this one restriction, that their drink must be only water, and that always drank in a human scull. For this reason this plate represents a scull and some human bones from whence it was taken near this unhappy *Agooree.* It is extraordinary that the existence of these women should be so little known even in the interior of Hindoostan: many celebrated pundits or learned men, though they acknowledged that the legislator Menu grants even to the *Agoorees* a life of greater happiness hereafter, provided that they conform to the commandment of never drinking but in a human scull, still maintained that no such women did exist, and might perhaps have persuaded me, if I had not myself met several of them in the same attitude, and with all the circumstances expressed in the print. I was even acquainted with one of them, who lived with a rich European, and who had adopted the manners and habits of Europe, but who never drank but in a cup formed of a human scull set in gold, and on a base beautifully worked. What these pundits asserted of the *Agoorees,* they also wished to support with respect to the lower classes of the last cast, such as the *mourdashos* [Murdāśo, Pl. II.72] or undertakers, the *haurys* [Hāṛi, Pl. II.71] or nightmen, the *kaurahs* [Kāorā, Pl. II.73] or porkmen, etc.; as they would insinuate these vile employments were never exercised by Hindoos: it is true that they are often performed by Mussulmen; but they are also frequently practised by Hindoos, as must necessarily be the case in those districts which are exclusively inhabited by the natives.

being embellished in any way, the mere vault of a human skull, not even trimmed or smoothed at the edges for convenience in use."[7]

---

1 See Solvyns's portrayal of satī, Pls. II.199-202.

2 Parry, 252. Parry, an anthropologist who studied the Aghoris who live at the burning ghāṭs in Banaras, describes the sect, 251-71. On the Aghoris, see R. V. Russell, 2:13-17; Barrow; Briggs; Ghurya, *Indian Sadhus,* 116-36; Bedi and Bedi, 96-109; Hartsuiker, 35-37; and B. D. Tripathi, 72-74. J. P. Losty discusses Aghoris in the context of Company School paintings depicting "The Sheep-eater of Fatehgarh." Watson and Kaye, include a photograph of an Aghori with his skull in *The People of India*, Vol. 2, photo 94.

3 "A Sketch of the Religious Sects of the Hindus" (1828), in *Essays and Lectures*, 1:234. Also see Ward, *A View of the History, Literature, and Mythology of the Hindoos* (1822), 3: 407-08, and Ward, *Account of the . . . Hindoos,* 3:432-33..

4 Long, *Calcutta in the Olden Times: Its Localities & Its Peoples*, 134. Walker, in his entry on "Necrophilia" in *Hindu World*, 2:130-31, writes that "the Aghori sect openly practiced cannibalism till the end of the nineteenth century." Also see Jogendra Nath Bhattacharya, 308-11.

5 Oman, *The Mystics, Ascetics, and Saints of India,* 164-67.

6 Parry, 253. He notes, 252, that although perhaps historically linked to the Kāpālikas, Aghoris trace their origin to a mid-eighteenth century ascetic, Kina Ram, whom they claim as an incarnation of Śiva. On Kāpālikas, see John Garrett, 315-16.

7 Henry Balfour, Jr., 246-47. Balfour's article principally concerns the skull cup and discusses similar forms in other cultures.

II.92. A Woman in Full Dress

Pl. II.92. A Woman in Full Dress. Paris: II.3.2.

Commentary: As in his discussions of women of "distinction" (Pl. II.87) and of "inferior rank" (Pl. II.88), Solvyns here describes the woman's isolation as a virtual prisoner of her class and status. She sits attended by two *ayahs*, maid servants [Pl. II.132], one of whom offers her *pān* [Pl. II.121] to chew, the mild betel nut narcotic that may make her boredom more tolerable. The box with the ingredients for making *pān* is beside the servant's foot. The perfumes are on a tray to the woman's left with another tray containing flowers. The other *ayah* fans her with a hand *pankhā* (Anglo-Indian, *punkah*).[1] In the background, the *hukā*-bearer (*hukābardār*, Pl. II.108) prepares the tobacco and coals in the *chilam*, or bowl, for the "snake" *hukā* for her smoke.[2]

The cosmetic beauty marks to which Solvyns refers are discussed in the Commentary for "A Woman of Inferior Rank" (Pl. II.88).

The etching, "A Woman in Full Dress," is not included in the Calcutta edition.

Paris: II.3.2. A WOMAN IN FULL DRESS: The magnificence displayed in the dress and the apartment of this lady are sufficient proofs that she does not conform strictly to the wise laws of Menu, but has adopted the manners of that part of Hindoostan which has been least the residence of true Hindoos. Few Hindoo women indeed would use so splendid a dress, unless on the day of some great festival. The lady here represented is seated on a rich carpet; her legs and arms are supported by cushions of embroidered silk; near her is the box which contains the betel, and golden vases for perfumes. An *Ayah* or waiting maid refreshes the air round her face, by means of a *punka*: another is presenting her *pawn* [*pān*]; and behind her, they are preparing the *houka* [*hukā*] which she is to smoke. Her hair, which is rendered shining by the use of cocoa oil, is plaited behind and separated on the forehead by a bunch of pearls or precious stones, the largest of which is in the middle. In conformity to the general mode of the Hindoo women, she has on the bottom of the chin, the left side of the nose, and between the eyebrows, a mark in the form of a little star.

The apartment of a woman of this rank is extremely rich and on a level with the gardens, into which they open by a door half closed with a cloth curtain. Here the life of women of the higher orders is spent, absolutely useless to their fellow creatures; strangers alike to the useful occupations of the labouring class and to the charms of society, they are meerly as it were in a state of vegetation. The utmost extent of their refinement in the pleasing arts is to play on the *tom-tom*, an instrument on which they sometimes attain some degree of perfection. They are hardly ever seen by strangers, and this secluded state of apathy and idleness seems to be their natural destination, for, happily for them, their minds are of too dull a texture to suffer much under it.

1 The hand *pankhā* is generally made from the palmyra palm leaf. *Hobson-Jobson*, 742. The ceiling *pankhā* is described in Solvyns's Pl. II.3.

2 See Solvyns's series on the variety of *hukās*, Pls. II.203-210.

II.93. Rāmjanī. Dancing Girl

Paris: II.3.3. RAMJANNY, DANCING GIRL: In the description which I gave in the beginning of the last number [Pl. II.195], of the original dance which the Hindoos call the *Nautch,* I said that the women who perform it go by the name of *Ramjanny;* but as I did not then take any notice of their costume, I shall here enter into some particulars concerning it.

The dress of the *Ramjannys* is in general very rich and splendid, consisting of precious stuffs embroidered in gold and silver. The under garment is very ample, and generally of coloured silk with lace or embroidery: after turning round several times with great velocity, this sort of petticoat swells out in the form of a sphere, the folds disappear, and the effect is very striking when they let themselves fall and sink as it were into this extended drapery. The richness of their ornaments extends to their toes, which being covered with little bells and moved as they choose, give a pleasing sound and mark the measure of their steps.

I have already observed that formerly the *Ramjannys* were in the service and formed part of the retinue of the Hindoo princes: these young women who were then kept together, under the inspection of a mistress of a more advanced age, were wholly taken up with the study of their profession, and were treated with great respect: but they are now wholly assimilated to the *Bayaderes,* though they still pretend to some preeminence over them: but it is not by their moral conduct that they seek this distinction, for I have often seen them mixed with troops of *Bays* and leading as dissolute a life as any other women of that class. This degeneracy seems to be one of the many effects of the invasion of the Mahometans who spread their luxury and their vices among the conquered people.

Pl. II.93. Rāmjanī. Paris: II.3.3.

Calcutta: Sec. IV, No. 5. A Ramjanny, or Dancing Girl.

Orme: 40.

Commentary: Solvyns's Ramjanny (*rāmjanī*), was not widely used among Europeans as a term for nautch girls and rarely appears in descriptions of the nautch. The origins of the word are disputed. For "Rum-Johnny," obsolete by the late nineteenth century, *Hobson-Jobson*, the glossary of Anglo-Indian words and phrases, gives two meanings. The first applied to the touts who solicited employment from newcomers to Calcutta. The second, "among soldiers and sailors, 'a prostitute,'" is derived from Sanskrit, "*rāmā-janī*, 'a pleasing woman,' 'a dancing-girl.'"[1] Pran Nevile gives a formal meaning to *rāmjanī* as those women who know the god Rāmā, but notes that in its usage, mainly in Bihar, it refers to Hindu dancers or courtesans.[2] Sen's *Etymological Dictionary of Bengali*, on the other hand, provides a very different compound origin. For Rām(a)jǟni, "a prostitute, courtesan," the origin is from Hindi, *rambhā* (courtesan) plus Perso-Arabian, *zāniya* (prostitute).[3]

Sherring, in his compendium of Hindu castes, lists "Ramjana, or Rāmjanī," as professional musicians. "They wear the sacred cord, and call themselves Kshatriyas. . . . They also, like the Kathaks, give instruction in singing and dancing to women intending to be professional performers. The caste is devoted to prostitution. The female children born in the caste are brought up to immorality and vice; the sons, however, are trained as musicians, and sometimes engage in trade or other occupations. . . . The Ramjana is a distinct and acknowledged caste, yet it differs from others in admitting women from various casts into the order."[4] Risley provides a brief entry for "Ramjani" in his *Tribes and Castes of Bengal*: "A caste of dancers, singers, and prostitutes" and identifies them as synonymous with the Gandhār, a small caste of musicians, said to be connected with Māls.[5]

Solvyns laments that the distinction between the *rāmjanī* and the "Bayaderes"—dancers he identifies disparagingly with the Muslim courtesan tradition—had largely disappeared by the late eighteenth century. *Bayadere* is, of course, a French word, from the Portuguese *bailadeira*, dancer, but was often used "as if it were a genuine Indian word" by Europeans in India for dancing girls generally.[6] Francis Buchanan, writing in 1810-11, noted the distinction between Muslim dancing girls called *bai* and the Hindu "rumzani" (*rāmjanī*) in the Bhagalpur district of Bengal.[7] In North India, various names were used for dancers. Muslim dancers, as distinct from the Hindu *rāmjanī*, were often known as *kanchanī*,[8] and the Census distinguished dancers as Paturiya (Hindus) and Tawaif (Muslims).[9]

In his discussion of both the nautch and *rāmjanī*, Solvyns refers to the princes and "grandees" who formerly maintained troupes of dancing girls. Abu'l-Fazl 'Allāmī, the Mughal emperor Akbar's secretary and historian, describes the "akhārā," "an entertainment held at night by the nobles of this country," and the bands of "natwās" retained in service of the courts.[10]

"Dancing girls," as the Europeans termed them generally, had long been associated with the courtesans of Muslim courts and, however talented as artists, with prostitution, and the musicians associated with them—and the very instruments they played—carried the taint of the profession.[11] Thus, for example, respectable Hindus held the tābla (Pl. II.160) and the sāraṅgī (Pl. II.152), used in accompaniment to dance, as vulgar or, as Willard described them, "licentious" instruments.[12]

---

1 773-74. Whitworth, 264, gives the same derivation.

2 Interview, New Delhi, January 1995. Nevile does not refer to the term in his *Nautch Girls of India*.

3 Sukumar Sen, *An Etymological Dictionary of Bengali*, 804.

4 Sherring, 1:274.

5 "Ramjani," 2:195, and "Gandhār," 1:267. Solvyns, Pl. II.65, portrays the Māls as snake-catchers, but the term is used to include various "gypsy-like" wandering groups.

6 *Hobson-Jobson*, p. 75. There is no reference to Solvyns's abbreviation, "Bay," but his use suggests its currency in the Calcutta of his time. Shoberl, 3:53-60, describes the *bayaderes* in dress and dance. His earlier description of the *rāmjanī*, 43-44, paraphrases Solvyns without attribution.

7 Quoted by Bor, "The Voice of the Sarangi," 95-96.

8 Anglo-Indian, *cunchunee*. *Hobson-Jobson*, 280, and under "Dancing Girl," 295-96.

9 Crooke, *Tribes and Castes*, 4:364-65.

10 273.

11 Bor, "The Voice of the Sarangi," 81-87.

12 95.

II.94. Hijrā. Eunuch

Pl. II.94. Hijrā. Paris: II.3.4.
Calcutta: Sec. IV, No. 6. A Hidgra, or Hermaphrodite.
Orme: 39.

Commentary: Solvyns presents the earliest European account of hijrās that is anything more than a brief reference,[1] and he does so in terms that conform generally with their character even today. Hijrās present themselves on the occasion of the birth of a male child, at weddings, and at various festivals, where, gaudily dressed as women, they sing and dance in raucous parody. They are by tradition to be paid, and failure to do so, as Solvyns relates, will incur their wrath. Many engage in prostitution. Drawn from all backgrounds, they function as a caste, live in organized groups and, as a religious cult, worship the mother goddess in the form of Bahuchara Mata.[2]

Various definitions are given for the term *hijrā*, but it is most frequently "eunuch," as in the *Etymological Dictionary of Bengali*. There Sen gives the origin of *hijiṛā* from the Persian *hiz*, "an infamous boy."[3] In popular belief and among some Europeans, hijrās were thought to be hermaphrodites. The text for print in the Orme pirated edition, for example, in a wonderfully naive description, accepts their condition as natural: "These extraordinary beings are frequently met with in India; they inherit, from the sport of nature in her most capricious humour, the capacity of plural enjoyments; but it does not appear that any of them are endowed with procreative faculties."

Solvyns—though he labels the hijrā an "hermaphrodite"—is correct in rejecting their physical condition as from birth. True hermaphroditism is comparatively rare, and nearly all hijrās are "created" eunuchs by removal of the male sexual organs. Some, perhaps those we would today describe as "transsexual" or "transgendered," alienated from their own community, undergo the transformation voluntarily. Others may have been taken as children and made hijrā by genital mutilation, but more in "recruitment" by hijrā bands—as feared today as in the past—than, as Solvyns suggests, to find a means of subsistence.[4] And there are a few who, without castration and removal of the sexual organs, dress as women and join hijrā "family."

In one of the few early references to hijrās (though not by name), the Abbé Dubois, Solvyns's contemporary, wrote of their "unnatural" and "disgusting practices," noting that these "degraded beings . . . dress like women, let their hair grow in the same way, pluck out the hair on their faces, and copy the walk, gestures, manner of speaking, tone of voice, demeanour, and affectations of prostitutes."[5]

Solvyns refers to hijrās as prostitutes, but also as entertainers, as he does in his discussion of the nautch (Pl. II.195), weddings (Pl. II.197), and in their use of musical instruments (Pl. II.174). James Wise, in his ethnographic notes on Bengal, wrongly identifies them as Muslim musicians, although hijrās come from Muslim as well as Hindu backgrounds: "The most despicable class of Muhammadan players . . . are

Paris: II.3.4. HIDGRA, AN HERMAPHRODITE: It is doing justice to this vile class of beings, to place them as I do here among the commonest women, whose dress even they affect to adopt. Nothing, I think, can inspire a stronger aversion for idolatry in its moral effects, than the picture of the wretches whom I am going to describe. Could it be believed, that there is a country in the world which tolerates a set of men, whose whole life is an outrage to morality and common decency, by the ostentatious display which they continually make of the privation of the marks of their sex? This is the case in Hindoostan. Some Hindoos believe that they are really born in this state; but it is very certain that it is inflicted on themselves, as a means of subsistance for them and their children: for these *Hidgras* (so these mutilated men are called) infest as vagabonds the streets and bazars, soliciting the charity of the passengers: and when they meet an European, they never fail to discover this claim to his commiseration. When they hear of the birth of a child in a family, they come and sing at the door, for which they expect their pay: if it is refused they endeavour to be revenged, and in a singular way; they climb to the roof of the house, and make water upon it. Not a Hindoo but is persuaded that this vengeance is never without its effect, that is, the speedy death of the new born child. This vindictive spirit has made them feared in some places: but their abominable depravity has caused them to be every where despised. Their debauchery is carried to that degree, that they meet together and offer themselves in the public houses of prostitution.

When I was making this collection of drawings I sent for a *Hidgra* to my house as a model which this plate represents: the following days he came of his own accord and continued his attendance at the door of my house; I at last enquired from my *jemindar* (servant) [jamādār, Pl. II.101] the reason of this importunity, who informed me of the vile practices of these scandals to mankind: and it was only by means of money and threats, that I could at last get rid of the intrusion of this *Hidgra*.

The dress of this class of men is, as the print shows, the same as that of the common class of women in Hindoostan.

Hijrā, who personate women in their dress, and are generally believed, as their name imports, to be hermaphrodites. Their obscene songs, and lascivious movements are regulated by a beating of a 'dholak,' by morris-bells (ghungrū) attached to the ankles of one of the performers, by cymbals, and by clapping of the hands. . . ."[6]

---

1 The paucity of European references to Hijrās seems odd given the fascination for the exotic, but perhaps omission is by lack of awareness or, for some, embarrassment.

2 On Hijrās generally, see Nanda, Preston, and Jaffrey.

3 Sukumar Sen, 928. Also see Risley, *The Tribes and Castes of Bengal*, 1:319.

4 The Indian press periodically reports instances of such kidnappings. The danger is surely exaggerated, but for every confirmed case, there are no doubt many more where the victim is silenced by the "shame" of his experience.

5 312.

6 39.

II.95. Sepoys. Soldiers

Pl. II.95. Sepoys. Paris: II.3.5.

Calcutta: Sec. III, No. 7. Seapoys, a Native Soldier,—the Dress introduced by Europeans, will be readily distinguished from the original country attire. **Orme: 33 & 34.**[1]

Commentary: The Anglo-Indian "sepoy" or "seapoy" (*siphāi* in Bengali), for Indian native soldier, is from the Persian *sipahi*, belonging to an army.[2] In 1857, in Calcutta, Clive raised the first unit armed, clothed, and dressed in the European fashion—the 1st Regiment of the Bengal Native Infantry, popularly called the Lal Paltan ("Red Platoon").[3] The British government in Madras had already decided to dress the sepoys in red broadcloth "partly to give them a better appearance and partly to get rid of surplus cloth. . . . The basic idea of dressing the Sepoys and European troops alike was to create an impression on the enemy that the entire Line was of European troops."[4] The red coat was the standard dress, but styles varied to preserve regimental distinction.[5]

In Solvyns's portrayal of sepoys, the central figure is a Jamādār (2nd Lieutenant),[6] of the Bengal

Paris: II.3.5. SEAPOYS. SOLDIERS: This print represents several soldiers under arms: in the foreground are some *havildars* and *jemidars* [*jamādār*], the terms by which they distinguish their commanders: among these one is in the European service; he is easily known by his scarlet uniform; the simple *Seapoys* besides do not wear as he does white trowsers and halfboots: but the ornaments on the side of the casque and round the neck and wrists are worn in common by all the Indian soldiers. Although the Hindoos in general bear the character of being timid and unfit for war, a reputation but too well confirmed in all the invasions which foreigners have made on their country, it is nevertheless acknowledged that their soldiers or *Seapoys* are full of courage and enterprise when they are well commanded and regularly paid. In the chief possessions of the English in India, they employ the *Seapoys* to great advantage: it is true, that they take care to have them always commanded by European officers: the highest rank to which they allow the *Seapoys* to rise is that of serjeants or other non commissioned officers.

I have represented next to the *Seapoy* in the foreground one of these Hindoo under-officers or *Havildars* in his native dress with his sabre and matchlock; behind him are his colours; in the background some private *Seapoys* are exercising in the European manner. There are among these soldiers many very robust and well made men: they support with extraordinary patience the greatest heat of their climate, but on the other hand they are sensibly affected and lose their courage under the slightest degree of cold.

The law of Menu [Manu] orders those who are born in the Brahmun cast, not to enter into the military state, and forbids all Hindoos in general to quit their country. In these times many Hindoos openly transgress these injunctions; in all the European armies in India there are numbers of Brahmuns, and other Hindoos, who make no scruple of following them into foreign countries. In the late war especially they embarked, and made a great part of the English army, even in Egypt.

Native Infantry, in pantaloons and halfboots, similar to the Subadar (Major) described by Mallo, in *The Indian Army*, and depicted in a watercolor by a Company School artist, c. 1805. A companion painting by the same artist depicts a sepoy private, again attired very much like those portrayed by Solvyns. In both, officer and sepoy wear the "sundial" hat distinctive to the Bengal regiment.[7] The uniform and hat are portrayed in other Company School paintings depicting Bengal sepoys,[8] in a European watercolor, c. 1790, by "Green," in the British royal collection,[9] and in an oil painting by William Hodges (1744-1797) depicting five native officers dressed almost identically to Solvyns's Jamādār.[10]

The "sundial" hat, built on an iron frame, rose from the head to a wide brim, with a dome of varied shape and, in front, the sharp triangle that gave the hat its nickname. The hats were black or dark blue, with embellishments for rank and regiment, and were worn by the Bengal Native Infantry until about 1810, when they were replaced by a turban of compact shape.[11]

Mollo describes the dress of the Bengal Native Infantry: "Coats were red with collar and cuffs of facing colour [here blue]. They were worn open until the turn of the century, by officers, and beyond that date by the sepoys. . . ." For native officers, "The shoulder-belt plates were either gilt or silver according to the regimental lace colour, and were oval or rectangular, with regimental number. The sword was suspended from a black or buff leather shoulder belt. Waistcoat and trousers were made of white linen for hot weather and of white cloth for other times. . . ." For officers and infantrymen alike, "Beneath the coat was a white shirt with a cummerbund over the lower part allowing only an inch or two of the shirt to show below. The cummerbund was of dark blue linen and was fastened in place by white linen strips, giving the appearance of a saltire cross. Below [sepoys wore] janghirs or shorts, white with a pattern of blue triangles and lines around the lower edge. White pantaloons were worn by native officers at all times, and by sepoys in cold weather." Equipment was carried on belts, with cross-belt. Mollo also draws attention to "the propensity of the native ranks for wearing necklaces and other jewelry,"[12] as Solvyns portrays in his etching.

In contrast to the European-style of the Bengal Native Infantry uniform, Solvyns portrays a *havildār* (sergeant)[13] in traditional Indian military dress. The Orme text identifies him as "a Seapoy of Bengal under the Mogul government." He is very likely a *najib*, or "irregular" swordsman/rifleman, and, as suggested by his beard, a Muslim. *Najibs* were often Muslims from Rohilkhand and Awadh (Oudh) in north central India. A copy of Solvyns's figure of the *havildār* is included among the color prints in Wahlen's *Moeurs, usages et costumes de tours les peuples du mond* (1843).[14]

Solvyns refers to the recruitment of brahmins as sepoys. The Bengal army by the late eighteenth century was predominantly brahmin (in contrast to the Madras and Bombay armies), recruited principally from the region of eastern Awadh, the area of Banaras, and Bihar. This was not by any official policy, but as brahmins were recruited, they were effectively able to exclude lower castes from service as sepoys.[15] The British employed sepoys out of India for the first time in 1762 against Spain in the Philippines, and they served in Egypt in 1801.[16] But brahmins cited caste strictures against crossing "dark waters," and the issue of overseas service provoked mutiny at Barrackpore, near Calcutta, in 1824—an unheeded warning of the great sepoy Mutiny of 1857.[17]

---

1 The Orme edition portrays Solvyns's sepoys in two prints, one (Pl. 33) of "a Seapoy under the Mogul government." The other (Pl. 34) depicts a sepoy of the Company.

2 *Hobson-Jobson*, 809-11.

3 Mollo, 13.

4 Longer, 28. On the Lal Paltan, also see Revet-Carnac, 181. On the sepoys more generally, see Alavi.

5 Thapliyal, 17. In contrast to the style of the Bengal sepoy depicted by Solvyns, Thapliyal includes a plate, opposite p. 18, depicting "The Red Coat Soldier" of the Madras Army.

6 The term *jamādār* means variously the head servant of a domestic establishment, as in Solvyns's portrayal (Pl. II.101); a head constable of police; the head of any body of men; or, as here, the lowest rank of native officer in a sepoy regiment. See *Hobson-Jobson*, 458; Lewis, 135-36; Kolff, Glossary, xiii.

7 Mollo, 42, Pl. 25. Also see Mollo's Pl. 4, p. 15, of a Company watercolor, c. 1785, depicting a golandar of the Bengal Artillery, a sepoy of the Bengal Native Infantry, and a subadar of the Governor-General's Bodyguard. The subadar's coat is richly decorated and the cummerbund is red. Captain Williams, in his 1817 history of the Bengal Native Infantry, includes four color plates depicting sepoys, but the uniforms do not correspond to those depicted by Solvyns, nor do the sepoys wear the "sundial" hat.

8 Archer, in *Company Drawings in the India Office Library*, includes a painting of a "Subadar of the Bengal Native Infantry," Calcutta, c. 1805, by a Calcutta artist, probably from Murshidabad. The single figure wears the sundial hat and the same uniform as Solvyns depicts, although it is not a copy of Solvyns. Pp. 86-87, Pl. 27. Carman, Vol. 2, Pl.17, depicts a 13th Bengal Native Infantry officer and sepoy, c. 1797, with

sundial hats. Carman refers to Solvyns's etching but does not reproduce the print.

A Company School painting, c. 1780, portrays an Indian officer and two sepoys of the Bengal Native Cavalry, each with the "sundial" hat. Guy and Boyden, Pl. 34, p. 209. Also see Guy and Boyden for Company School portrayals of uniformed sepoys of Bombay, 1773 (Pl. 33, p. 208), and Madras, 1810 (Pl. 103, p. 237).

9 The watercolor (Cat. No. 253), "Soldiers, Bengal Infantry," by an artist identified only as "Green," depicts the sepoys (as Solvyns portrayed them) wearing red jackets with blue borders, cross-belts over the shoulders, white shirt, blue cummerbund, shorts, and the sundial hat. They wear beads around their neck. Miller and Dawnay, Vol. 1, Pls. 189 and (detail) 188. The scene depicted in the painting is "posting reliefs, that is, changing over sentries." 2:253.

10 The painting, "A Camp of a thousand Men formed by Augustus Cleveland three miles from Bhagalpur, with his mansion in the distance," oil on canvas, 122 x 160 cm., is illustrated as Lot 132 in the auction catalog, *Visions of India*, p. 102-03, for the Christie's sale of June 5, 1996.

11 Carman, 2:98, Mollo, 22. By the time Capt. James portrayed the Bengal sepoys in various military exercises, 1814, the sundial hat was no longer worn.

12 Mollo, 22-29. Carmen provides a detailed description of the uniform, 2:97-99, noting that there seemed to be a series of government orders in 1796, just after Solvyns completed his drawings, to "tidy-up" the uniform. On Bengal sepoy uniforms, also see Barat, 51-52, 166, and Hopkins.

13 The word is from the Persian *hawāldār*, meaning a charge holder, one holding an office or trust. In the military, the havildār was a non-commissioned sepoy officer corresponding to a sergeant. *Hobson-Jobson*, 412-13; Lewis, 125; Madan Paul Singh, 16, fns. 36 and 38.

14 Vol. I, *Asia*.

15 Philip Mason, 125-26; Madan Paul Singh, 157; Cardew, 54; Bayly, *Indian Society and the Making of the British Empire*, 84-85

16 Longer, 42.

17 Philip Mason, 242-46.

II.96. Bālak. Dancing Boy

Paris: II.3.6. BAULUK, DANCING BOY: I have already shewn the functions of the *Bauluks* in my description of the feast of the *Joolun-Jatrah,* fifth number, plate the first [Jhulan Yātrā, Pl. II.186]. I have now to describe their dress, which is very singular.

All the dancing boys, or *Bauluks* have their faces painted in several places, particularly about the eyebrows, the foreheads and the ears: their heads are adorned with red flowers, peacock's feathers in the form of a fan, or some other ornamental object. A large plate of metal, of gold, covers their breasts, and is inscribed with the names of the gods and goddesses, or some other sacred form: their back is covered with a small mantle of a bright colour, such as blue , yellow, or red: round their thighs are tied different pieces of muslin : their feet are covered with a variety of ornaments fancifully arranged and full of little bells which follow the slightest motion of the dancer, and produce the degree of sound they choose to impart. Their dance, like that of the *Ramjannies*, consists in graceful attitudes and difficult steps: they carry in dancing a small stick painted red, which they move round on every side, and which gives them an opportunity of displaying all the graces of their forms.

Few *Bauluks* are to be met with except among the true Hindoos; at least I have not seen them with the other nations of Hindoostan; whence we may conclude that their costume and danse take their origine from the remotest antiquity.

Commentary: Solvyns, in his portrayal of Jhulan Yātrā, depicts three dancing boys (*bālak* meaning "boy")—each dressed as Kṛṣṇa. Here Solvyns provides a detailed depiction and description of the costume.[1] Dancing boys were often included in nautch performances (Pl. II.195) along with dancing girls (Rāmjanīs, Pl. II.93)

Risley discusses such dancing boys in his description of the Naṛ, a caste of dancers and musicians in eastern Bengal: When young the Naṛ boys, then called Bhagtiyās, are taught dancing, but on reaching manhood they become musicians. . . and attend on dancing girls (Bāī), who are usually Muhamadans."[2] Mrs. Belnos, in a colored lithograph of 1832, depicts two dancing boys ("*Ba-yéés*"), attired in Muslim dress, before a group of Europeans.[3] A copy of Solvyns's bālak is included among the color prints in Wahlen's *Moeurs, usages et costumes de tours les peuples du mond* (1843).[4]

1 Shoberl, 3:44-45, without attribution to Solvyns, includes a copy of this etching as "A Hindoo Dancer called Balok" (Pl. 35) and paraphrases Solvyns's description.

2 *The Tribes and Castes of Bengal*, 2:130.

3 *Twenty-Four Plates Illustrative of Hindoo and European Manners in Bengal,* Pl. 15.

4 Vol. I, *Asia*.

Pl. II.96. Bālak. Paris: II.3.6.
Calcutta: Sec. III, No. 5. Bauluck, or Dancing Boy
Orme: 31.

II.97. Brajbāsī in Military Accoutrement

Pl. II.97. Brajbāsī in Military Accoutrement. Calcutta: Sec. III, No. 8.

Calcutta: Sec. III, No. 8. A Brijbasi, in his Military accoutrements.

Orme: 35.

Commentary: Solvyns portrays the Brajbāsi in three etchings, first as representative of the brahmin caste (Pl. II.16); then as an armed guard (Pl. II.53); and here—not included in the Paris edition—as a soldier, dressed and armed with matchlock and powder horn, sword, dagger, and shield. The text for the plate in Orme's pirated edition of Solvyns reads: "In his military accoutrements, in which he travels, and which is particularly requisite in the upper provinces of Bengal. . . . They are in some parts of India called Gollars,[1] and employed as well to guard houses and offices as to carry specie from one province to another; and such is their honourable fidelity, that they will resign their trust only with their lives."

As discussed in the Commentary for Solvyns's portrayal of the Brajbāsī as guard, men from the area of Braj were regarded as having "warlike character" and were traditionally recruited as soldiers.

---

1 The reference is unclear. Perhaps it is to *ghol* (Anglo-Indian, gole), a Hindustani military term, but this refers to a body of troops and not to individual soldiers. *Hobson-Jobson*, 383.

II.98. Fisherwoman

Pl. II.98. Fisherwoman. Calcutta: Sec. IV, No. 7.

Calcutta: Sec. IV, No. 7. A Polye, or Fisherwoman.

Orme: 41.

Commentary: Solvyns's word for fisherwoman, "polye," is likely a misunderstanding, for the Bengali word he assumed referred to the woman is probably *palui*, a kind of basket for catching fish.[1] The women he portrays carry baskets of fish on their heads. The Bengali artist of the Fraser album, painting over Solvyns's etching, labels it "*Mechanī*,[2] the Bengali word for "fish-wife" or female fish vendor. Solvyns portrays the male fish-monger, the Nakāri or Machhuā, in a separate etching (Pl. II.80), but includes neither the Nikāri nor the fisherwoman in the Paris edition, *Les Hindoûs*.

---

1 Sukumar Sen, 533. Solvyns also mistakenly uses the term "polye" in Pl. II.57, to refer to female fish-sellers.

2 Vol. I, No. 15. See Chapter Three, pp. 101-04, on the Fraser collection.

Servants of the European Household in Calcutta

The vast number of servants required to maintain a substantial household in Bengal—European or Indian—was a source of continuing amazement to newcomers and visitors, and eighteenth and early nineteenth century European accounts of travels in India almost invariably discuss it, often at some length.[1] Indian artists of the Company School included servants in their sets of paintings prepared for Europeans,[2] and servants were a frequent subject for European artists, most famously Charles D'Oyly in the early nineteenth century,[3] and, later, George Atkinson, whose satirical prints in *Curry & Rice*, enjoyed enormous popularity through many editions.[4]

Books especially written for those coming to India for the first time, such as Williamson's richly informative *East India Vade-Mecum* (1810),[5] provide detailed accounts of the various servants, their duties and foibles, and the wages their employer might be expected to pay. Calcutta newspapers also provided updates on going monthly wages for household servants.[6]

"The number of servants necessary in a private family exceeds all moderation," the Rev. William Tennant wrote in 1799. For some time after arriving in Calcutta, he lived with a private family, "where the servants of all descriptions amounted to an hundred and five. What is more remarkable, they were to a man all necessary. This surely is no small inconvenience to Europeans; but it is an evil for which there is no remedy as long as the superstition of the natives shall deter them from performing service beyond one specific kind of work".[7]

What Tennant takes as "superstition" relates, of course, to Hindu concern for ritual pollution and to caste-specific occupations, and it accounts for the employment of Muslims in various service roles in European households. Indeed, in his notes to the original drawings, Solvyns writes that this is "the only Section in which MAHOMETANS are introduced."

The number of servants was thus, in part, a product the religious and caste strictures that created a division of labor, but it was also a matter of status. Officials of the East India Company emulated "Mughal grandees in the parade of servants. Thus a member of the Fort William Council never appeared in the street with a train of less than twenty fellows or walked from one room to another in his house unless preceded by four silver-stick bearers." And as an official rose in rank, the number of servants in his retinue increased to match his enhanced status.[8]

By Solvyns's time, some of the ostentation and pomp had declined, though the sheer numbers of servants had not. In his 1799 *Catalogue* to the Calcutta etchings, Solvyns writes:

> Europeans in India, holding the higher offices, as the members of government, and those of the boards of trade and revenue, and the judges,—and in the military line, all above the rank of major, till of late years, were attended with the silver stick-bearers, and by branch lights at night, but at present most of these marks of distinction are dispensed with.
>
> [Nevertheless,] A monthly Clerk in Calcutta, has often more servants, than are entertained by the first of the nobility in England; the cause may be partly attributed to the religious prejudices and natural indolence of the Natives, but more to the indulgent customs prevalent among the Europeans . . . ."[9]

Alexander Macrabie, Sheriff of Calcutta, described the entourage of 110 servants required to maintain the household of Philip Francis, where he resided with Francis, a member of the Supreme Council, and two other Company officials in 1775. Following his listing, he wrote,

> Please to observe that these are only Mr Francis' train, and a very moderate one. I have, as a private man, fourteen, officially about eight more. If you add to these about thirty belonging to two gentlemen, who are our family, and four European servants, you

have our whole suite. Count them up, if you please. When I see them all together, they appear innumerable, a legion, an army, and all thieves.

For the due superintendence of these devils. . . we have an endless tribe of *banians*, chief and subordinate, together with their train of clerks, who fill a large room and control, or rather connive, at each others accounts. We are cheated in every article, whether of the house, the garden, the stable, or our own private expenses. . . . I do most cordially esteem them the greatest rogues on earth.[10]

Macrabie's judgment of banians as "rogues" was widely shared,[11] and Europeans often viewed servants as untrustworthy.[12] Servants were usually seen in terms of stereotypes, each category (as with castes) with its own particular character, virtues and vulnerabilities. The themes are recurrent, almost canonized, in European descriptions and references to servants in India, and they are evident in Solvyns's textual descriptions of the servants he portrays. The sarkār (Pl. II.100), for example, is deemed "cunning and rapacious" and must be scrupulously watched, but the jamādār (Pl. II.101) is respected, worthy of trust and confidence; some servants are seen as given to "eastern indolence" or debauchery, others to hard work and high standards of personal decency.

Solvyns portrays the servants of a European household, as indicated by the title for the section of the Calcutta edition: "35 Prints, of the Servants employed in the domestic Concerns of European Families: and the only Section in which Mahometans are introduced." In the Introduction to *Les Hindoûs*, Vol. IV, Solvyns discusses domestic servants more generally, including the numbers employed by wealthy Hindus, but the employment of Muslims and "black Portuguese"[13] in the household was confined, with few exceptions, to Europeans and was the product of Hindu caste restrictions. Of his portrayal of servants, Solvyns writes,

Here, more than any where else, we perceive the singularity of hindoo manners. Had we to describe to a distant nation the ways of european life, we should have but a few words to say of the class of domestics, who with us are less numerous and uninteresting, compared with the other branches of society; but it is quite otherwise in India, where asiatic effeminacy has given rise to this species of menial luxury so foreign to our taste. A rich Hindoo would make but an unbecoming figure if he allowed himself to be seen without a great train of attendants, his house must swarm as it were with servants. Each branch of his service must have its appropriate agents, for the hindoo institutions require that each servant should confine himself to his particular fonction, without ever interfering in any manner with those of his companions: almost every articles besides of economy is made at home, which lays them under the necessity of keeping men of every trade; pastrycooks, bakers, taylors, washers, etc., etc. All these male and female domestics, who have fallen under my observations, will be found represented in the thirty-six following plates, from the head or superintendant of the establishment to the sweeper: not forgeting either him whose business is to whip the others, nor him whose occupation is to drive away the flies, nor the purveyer of each horse, nor his attendant and leader, nor infine the man who goes his rounds to protect the house by night. All these particulars having never been attentively considered by any traveller, I flatter myself that I shall be allowed some share of merit for having entered into so minute a discription of them; as the greater part of the objects which I notice in the text are unknown in Europe, and many of them appear new, even to those who have travelled in India. I may be permitted also to observe that it required much time and trouble to collect them.

It is necessary in the first place to inform the reader that among the servants of Hindoostan the greater number are not Hindoos but Mussulmans, who would have made naturally but a very secondary appearance in this work, if they did not, from the habits of the country, form as it were the most striking feature of the domestic life of the rich Hindoos, who from the facility with which servants of this discription are procured, have indulged to such an excess in the luxury of a numerous retinue. Ancient prejudices besides, handed down by long tradition, have attached such a degree of contempt to certain services that no true Hindoo will consent to perform them, so derogatory do they appear to him, so contrary to the pure doctrine of Brahma. The learned men of their nation go so far even as to pretend that no Hindoo has ever been known to perform these degrading offices, an assertion to which daily experience furnishes a sufficient contradiction, though it is true that far the greater part of servants in Hindoostan is composed of foreigners, Moguls, black Portuguese, Malays, Chinese, but chiefly of Mussulmans. The Hindoos seem better adapted to military than to domestic service; in the latter situation they are incapable of attachement, distitute of feeling and of gratitude, quit their masters or see them dye with the utmost indifference, as if he was a stranger, after living twenty or thirty years with him: they are besides much addicted to stealing, cowardly in the extreme, and sure to abandon their master if he should happen to be attacked by an European, of whom they are particularly affraid, and before one of whom I may venture to affirm that a hundred of them would fly. The mussulman servants on the other hand, though they are not without their faults, do their duty with great alacrity and exactness, so that masters in general in India have no complaint to make on that head: they have but to express their wishes and they are instantly complied with, without any sort of scruple. As to their moralty the most vile commissions are performed with an obsequious coolness and gravity, which astonish an European on his first arrival. The female servants are not in any degree more backward, and frequently even anticipate the desires of their masters. Slavery has been abolished in India by the persevering efforts of the english government. The black Portuguese and the Dutch who endeavoured to maintain it have been obliged at last to give it up: some vestiges however of this degrading state remain, and it is not uncommon for masters to beat their servants, in which they are tolerated though not authorised by the laws. Some Europeans too, who on their first coming were loudest against this inhumain practice have been known in a short time to follow the example of the hindoo grandees. Europeans are very seldom seen in the service of the rich natives, and are sure to be treated on that account with contempt by their countrymen and excluded from their society. It is not common either for Europeans to live in intimacy with Hindoos, though they seem to have less objection to the society of the Mussulmans, Moguls, Armenians and other foreigners. The stile of the rich Europeans in Hindoostan is modelled upon that of the Rajahs and Nabobs of the country: they get up at about six o'clock in the morning, take an airing on horseback, bathe, change linnen, breakfast and attend to their business. About one o'clock they make a second breakfast of meat, repose, give a little further attention to their affairs, and dress to go out in their carriage, return only for dinner which, with the wine that follows, lasts till night, when after taking tea the company breaks up. Society is not promiscuous here as in Europe, the English do not frequent the house of the portuguese or armenian merchants, and even among themselves the servants of the company do not live in much intimacy with the merchants and bankers.[14]

On the title page to the Paris edition, *Les Hindoûs*, Vol. IV, portrays himself attended by his personal servants (Frontispiece, Pl. I.1).

1 See, for example, Mrs. Kindersley's published letter of 1768, 282-88, quoted in Nair, *Calcutta in the 18th Century*, 148-51, and in Losty, *Calcutta: City of Palaces*, 41-42. Fanny Parks, in describing her visit to Calcutta, 1:209-10, makes frequent reference to servants and provides a list of those employed by "a private family" and their wages. Descriptions of the retinue of servants and household operations are also to be found in Colesworthy Grant, *Anglo-Indian Domestic Life*; W. H. Carey, *Good Old Days*, 2:57-71; H. E. A. Cotton, *Calcutta Old and New*, 76-79; Blechynden, 107-08; Spear, *The Nabobs*, 51-53; and Rudrangshu Mukherjee.

2 See Mildred Archer, *Company Drawings in the India Office Library*.

3 See especially *The European in India* (1813).

4 The 40 plates depict British social life in the imaginary "station" of Kabob. *Curry & Rice* was first published in 1859.

5 Much of the first volume, 1:188-342, is devoted to servants. Stocqueler's *Hand-Book of India* (1844), provides a similar account, 229-41, and, like his later *Oriental Interpreter*, is largely taken verbatim from Williamson, updated as appropriate. Stocqueler also sets out a list of the monthly wages for servants in "Calcutta As It Is," 136-37. Nair, *British Social Life in Ancient Calcutta*, in note 36 to Stocqueler, provides a comparative list for wages paid in various years, including 1801, when Solvyns was in Calcutta, and he quotes, 233-36, a lengthy description of the Bengal establishment from the *Asiatic Journal* (1833). On wages, also see Long, *Calcutta in the Olden Time*, 95-97. For a list of the servants employed in the home of a wealthy Hindu, Krishna Kanta Nandy, in the late eighteenth century, see Somendra Chandra Nandy, 2:519-26.

6 See, for example, the list for March 31, 1785, in Seaton-Karr, *Selections from Calcutta Gazettes*, 1:96-97.

7 1:63.

8 Suresh Chandra Ghosh, 109-110.

9 12.

10 A letter to friends in Fulham, dated January 1775, in Asher, 34; also in Busteed, 114. Mackrabie also recorded a detailed description of the various servants attending the household in his journal, now in the India Office Library, and quoted in Suresh Chandra Ghosh, 110-11. An ironic footnote may be added to this account. A satirically biting description of the retinue of servants attending their master was penned by William Mackintosh in 1779 as an indictment of Anglo-Indian indolence. Letter 55 (Calcutta, Dec. 23, 1779), 2:214-19, in Nair, *Calcutta in the 18th Century*, 184-86, and Spear, *The Nabobs*, 53-55. Mackintosh's account of his travels, published anonymously, was underwritten and promoted by Francis, leader of the camp seeking the impeachment of the Governor-General, Warren Hastings. See Nair, *Calcutta in the 18th Century*, 180-81, and Teltsher, 160-63.

11 See Pl. II.99.

12 Teltsher, 146-50, from a postmodern perspective, sees this, insofar as true, as a disguised form of resistance.

13 References to "black Portuguese" are to the mixed Indo-Portuguese and to Indian Roman Catholics. See Commentary for Pl. II.6.

14 4:7-8.

II.99. Banian. Chief Servant, Comptroller

Pl. II.99. Banian. Paris. IV.1.1.

Calcutta: Sec. II, No. 1. A Bannyan,—chief servant in the employ of an European, and often the comptroller of the household; of late years their influence has been much curtailed, and their service dispensed with,—these are the persons who accommodate their masters with the loan of cash, in the hopes of profitting in their employ,—the profession is confined to no particular rank or cast, but every Hindoo who has accumulated property, aspires to the dignity of Baboo. When employed in the public offices, they are nominated, in common with Mahometans, Dewans, &c.

Paris: IV.1.1. BANNYANt: The *Bannyan* is the chief of the domestics, a sort of superintendant or steward of the household, who gives out what is necessary to the other servants, places them, is answerable for their conduct; and transacts in short all the business of his master. The *Bannyans* are in general dangerous persons, on account of the great expence in which they involve their employers, who let them too easily into their confidence, and whom they very soon contrive to ruin, without ever forgetting to secure their own private interests. Europeans who land for the first time in India, cannot be cautioned too much against the *Bannyans*. However great their fortunes may be it will soon be squandered if they listen to the insinuations of these faithless stewards, who carry the appearance of disinterestedness so far as to make considerable advances to their masters, but never without all possible security. Unfortunately there is a great deal of business which cannot well be transacted, without the intervention of these agents, which gives them a certain degree of importance. There are many *Bannyans* in the service of government, and then they take the distinguished title of *Baboo*.

The *Bannyan* whom I have represented is sitting, to indicate their exclusive privilege of being seated before their masters: any Hindoo of property easily obtains an employment of this sort.

Commentary: The term "banian" (or "banyan")[1] is, via the Portuguese, an Anglicized form of *bāniyā* (trader) that was specifically applied in the eighteenth and early nineteenth centuries to native brokers and interpreters employed by European gentlemen in Calcutta to act on their behalf in transacting private business or who as commercial agents were attached to European business houses.

The banian, as here portrayed by Solvyns, was, in the words of P. J. Marshall, "the personal factotum of his European 'master'. He managed his household, kept his accounts, provided both the capital and the local knowledge for his commercial transactions, and in general was his link to the Indian world. He was a combination of steward, secretary and business partner."[2] Banians, in short, made themselves generally indispensable, and many built great personal fortunes in trade, finance, and real estate.[3]

Banians, however, "were not simply creatures of the British."[4] Many, like Krishna Kanta Nandy (1720-1794), banian to Warren Hastings, already had substantial wealth before taking direct European employment. Interestingly, Krishna Kanta's biographer identifies the subject of Solvyns's "Bannyan" portrait as Krishna Kanta himself, but this seems highly improbable, for Solvyns first announced his project in the year that Krishna Kanta died, 1794. Moreover, a person of such wealth and influence would surely not have posed for an anonymous genre portrait nor would Solvyns have failed to identify him by name.[5]

Early banians were drawn from the Seth and Basak families of wealthy cloth merchants, but from the mid-eighteenth century, they were largely displaced by literate and managerially-skilled Vaidyas (Pl. II.25), Kāyasthas (Pl. II.26), and brahmins. Banians came to positions of substantial wealth, influence, and respect in Calcutta, but their reputation was not unmixed, as suggested by the warning in Solvyns's text. In his *East India Vade-Mecum* of 1810, Thomas Williamson wrote that banians in general possess "very large property, with most extensive credit and influence. So much is this the case, that Calcutta was, some twenty years ago, absolutely under the control of about twenty or thirty *banians*, who managed every concern, in which they could find means to make a profit. . . ."[6] They were often seen as rapacious, eager to extend credit to newly-arrived Europeans and thereby secure the avenue to their own further enrichment.[7]

Solvyns writes that banians "take the distinguished title of *Baboo*." A term of respect in the late eighteenth century, "baboo" (*bābū*) came later to be used by Europeans as an expression of disparagement, even contempt, "as characterizing a superficially cultivated, but too often effeminate, Bengali."[8]

---

1 *Hobson-Jobson*, 63-64.
2 Foreword to Somendra Chandra Nandy's *Life and Times of Cantoo Baboo*, 1:viii.
3 On banians, see, among others, D. Basu; Marshall, *East Indian Fortunes*; Marshall, "Masters and Banians in Eighteenth Century Calcutta"; Kindersley, 130-31, in Nair, *Calcutta in the 18th Century*, 143; Long, *Calcutta in the Olden Time*, 83; Pradip Sinha, "Social Change," 390; Chitra Deb; N. K. Sinha, *Economic History of Bengal*, 1:85-86; 101-03; Sumanta Banerjee, 21-23; Spear, *The Nabobs*, 51-52.
4 Bayly, *Indian Society in the Making of the British Empire*, 55.
5 Somendra Chandra Nandy, in his richly documented biography of Krishna Kanta Nandy, or "Cantoo Baboo," 2:viii, also identifies Solvyns's subject for the etching of "A Man of Distinction" (Pl. II.82) as "Kantababu." "The reason for the presumption," Nandy writes, "is that the description of Kantababu resembles the pictures." Nandy reproduces both etchings from Solvyns's Paris edition (1810, 1812), but the date he gives, 1790, presumably for the original drawings, precedes Solvyns's arrival in Calcutta.
6 1:188.
7 On the procedure by which this was done, see Valentia, in Nair, *Calcutta in the 19th Century*, 26; N. K. Sinha, *Economic History of Bengal*, 1:101, and Ranjit Sen, 1:41-43.
8 *Hobson-Jobson*, 44. Such a view is epitomized in the lampoon by F. Anstey, *Baboo Jabberjee, B.A.*, originally appearing in *Punch*.

II.100. Sarkār. Steward

Paris: IV.1.2. SIRCAR: Immediately under the Bannyan, is the *Sircar* or general house-steward, whose province is the household expenditure; he buys the provisions, pays the wages of servants and workmen, and in mercantile houses buys and sells all the commodities. On every article whatsoever of this sort of expence, even the servants wages, he has a certain perquisite called *dustore;* besides this, which is general throughout India, he has other petty profits by his advances to servants and workmen upon what is due to them. This class of men are in general cunning and rapacious, and their own interest in the *dustore,* makes them very attentive to the family's disbursements. A servant who should presume to buy any thing for the house without their knowledge, would be instantly discharged. They remain almost constantly at home, and wait upon their master every morning to take his orders for the day. In great houses there are several *Sircars,* those in the service of Europeans generally speak several languages.

The *Sircar* represented in the print is drest in a *courti* [*kurtā*], and is supposed to serve an European: otherwise his dress would be a *dootee* [*dhotī*] without a turban and with a piece of cloth called *doubgah* over his shoulders or in his hand, according to the costume represented in the 2nd vol. [Pl. II.82].[1]

Commentary: The term *sarkār* is Persian in origin, meaning "head agent," and in Bengal was applied to the chief servant, or steward, in European households responsible for making purchases and keeping account of expenditures. In larger households, he would serve under the banian, but, as Solvyns indicated in his note to the original drawing, for most families, he functioned in place of the banian—both in duties and, as the banian so often did, especially in the eighteenth century, in extending credit to a hard-pressed employer. And, like the banian, he often took the title "baboo" (*bābū*) to denote his status.[2]

Pl. II.100. Sarkār. Paris: IV.1.2.

Calcutta: Sec. II, No. 2. Sircar,—an underling to the Bannyan; his business is to purchase the necessaries of house keeping, or in the service of merchants and tradesmen, employed to buy and sell merchandize. The general custom is, for the sircar to enjoy the wages, paid him by his master, and all gain, dustore [*dastūr*] or customary draw-back, profits, pilferings, &c. to go to the Bannyan.

Orme: 13.

Sarkār was also used to designate Hindu "writers," accountants or purchasing agents employed by merchants or in government offices.[3]

The sarkār was, as Stanhope wrote in 1774, the European's "cash-bearer," for "in this country no gentleman takes the trouble of keeping his own money."[4] Sarkārs were almost always honest, in the sense of never absconding with their employer's money,[5] but they had a reputation for being, in Solvyns's words, "cunning and rapacious," and they never failed to take their *dastūr*. The *dastūr* (Anglo-Indian, "dustoor") was the customary commission or percentage taken on every cash transaction, purchase or disbursement.[6] The amount was typically one or two annas on the rupee, with 16 annas to the rupee, though the sarkār might exact a higher percentage for his service.[7]

Solvyns here portrays the sarkār, as in an earlier print (Pl. II.86) illustrating native dress, as wearing a *kurtā* and a shawl identified as an *eklāi*.

A sarkār is also depicted as a warehouse, or godown, manager in Solvyns's portrayal of the Sadgop (Pl. II.74).

---

1 See commentaries for Pl. II.82 and Pl. II.86 (portraying a Sarkār). Williamson, *The East India Vade-Mecum*, 1:206, provides a detailed description of the sarkār's dress.

2 Stocqueler, *The Oriental Interpreter*, 210; also see Stocqueler, *The Hand-Book of India*, 235-36. D'Oyly, Pl. 9, *The European in India*, portrays "a gentleman with his sircar, or money-servant," with Williamson's accompanying text.

3 On the different meanings of the term, *Hobson-Jobson*, 840-41.

4 *Genuine Memoirs of Asiaticus*, 47-48; in Nair, *Calcutta in the 18th Century*, 168-69.

5 Stocqueler, "Calcutta As It Is," 145-46

6 See *Hobson-Jobson*, 333-34.

7 Parks, in writing of Calcutta in 1822, describes the sarkār and his profit, 1:22; in Nair, *Calcutta in the 19th Century*, 247-48; also see Stocqueler, "Calcutta As It Is," 247.

II.101. Jamādār. Head Servant

Paris: IV.1.3. JUMMADAR: The *Jummadar* has the office of *valet-de-chambre,* and is generally an old and confidential servant. He accompanies his master wherever he goes in or out of the house, and does not even quit him when he retires to rest. His dress is the *Jumma* [*jāma*], with a poi[g]nard [dagger] or crest with its ornament, in his girdle: and the importance of his appearance is sometimes heightened (as in the print), by a white beard. The *Jummadar* transmits the orders of the master of the house to the *Chobdār* [cobdār, Pl. II.102], of whom we shall speak presently, who in his turn communicates them to the *Soonta Burdar* [soṭābardār, Pl. II.103]. The *Jummadar* is the most respected of all the subaltern servants.

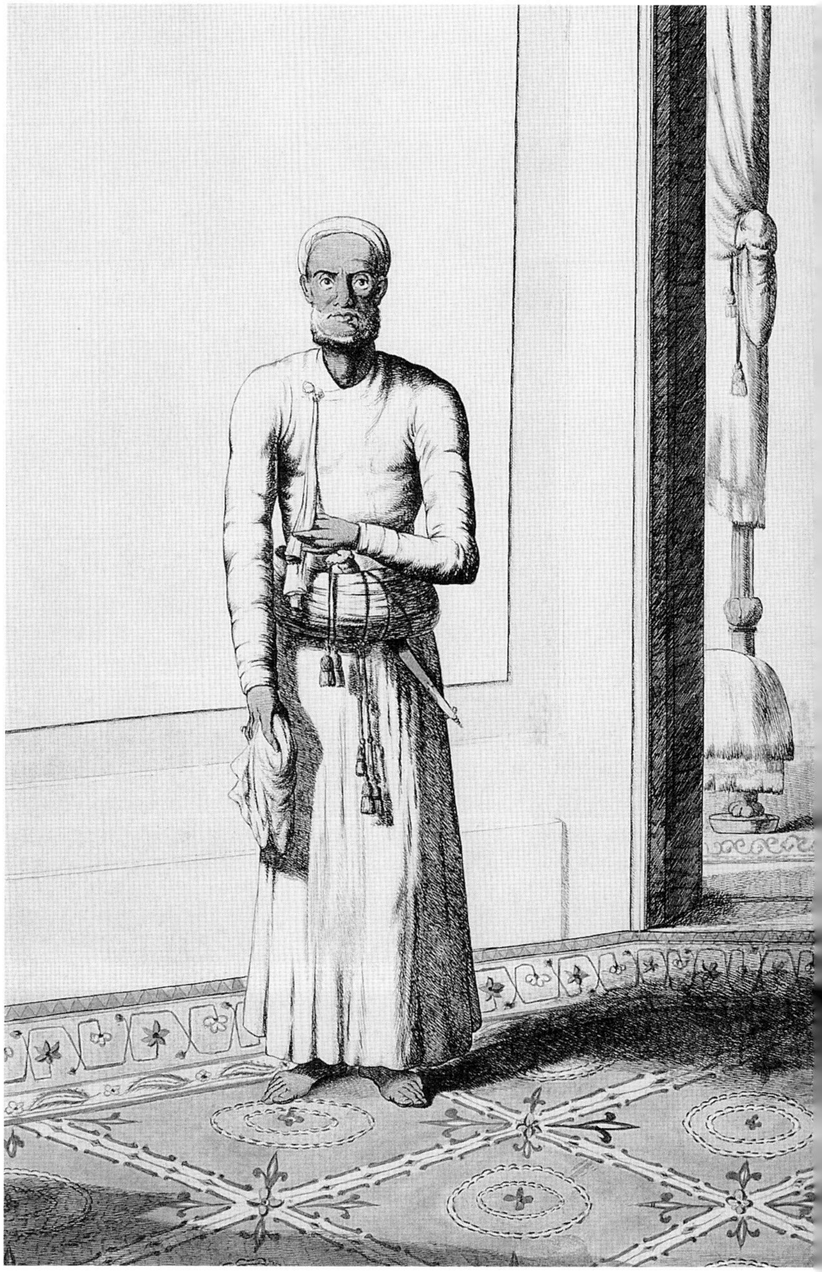

Pl. II.101. Jamādār. Paris: IV.1.3.

Calcutta: Sec. II, No. 3. A Jummadar, the head servant in waiting on Europeans and Natives of distinction.

Orme: 14

Commentary: The term *jamādār* (Anglo-Indian, "jemadar') is Hindustani, from the Arabic and Persian, meaning the head of a body of men.[1] Solvyns uses the term to refer to the head servant in a large household.[2] This trusted servant served as a chamberlain or domestic overseer and was the gentleman's closest confident among the retinue of servants. Solvyns portrays him wearing the *jāma*, long gown, with a cummerbund and dagger, symbol of his office, ornamented with gold and tassels.[3]

Jamādār was also the title both of second rank native officers (lieutenants) in sepoy regiments of the Indian army and of native head police constables. In public offices and large commercial establishments, the head of the peyādās (Pl. II.124)—peons or foot-messengers—was called the jamādār and, as the household servant, was distinguished by wearing the ornamental dagger.[4]

---

1 The word, though similar, is distinct from *jamidār*, the Bengali for zamīndār, "landholder." Europeans often pronounced and wrote the words in the same way. *Hobson-Jobson*, 980; *A Glossary of Indian Terms*, 107.

2 *Hobson-Jobson* notes that jamādār was also an honorific title often used by the other household servants in addressing the bhīstī, water-carrier, (pl.II.111)458-59.

3 Williamson, *The East India Vade-Mecum*, 1:195, writes that the jamādār is often distinguished by the ornamental dagger. Also see Henry Grant and Colebrooke, *The Anglo-Hindoostanee Hand-Book*, 63, and Colesworthy Grant, *An Anglo-Indian Domestic Sketch*, 125.

4 Stocqueler, *Oriental Interpreter*, 111.

II.102. Chobdār or Āṣā-soṭābardār. Mace-bearer

Pl. II.102. Chobdār. Paris: IV.1.4.

Calcutta: Sec. II, No. 4. A Chaubdar or Assahburdar, with a long silver stick, the badge of his office,—he derives his name from chaub club.

Orme: 15.

Paris: IV.1.4. CHAUBDAR: The *Chaubdar* or *Assahburdar* comes after the Jummadar [jamādār], and has also some share of consideration. His business is to transmit his masters orders to the inferior servants; his station is at the foot of the stairs of the apartments, to announce or rather introduce visitors whom he accompanies on their return as far as their palanquin. The distinctive mark of his office is a long silver stick. His costume (as appears in the print), differs from that of the true Hindoos. A very respectable English author pretends that the fonctions of the *Chaubdar* are limited meerly to causing silence to be observed, and founds his opinion on the etymology of the word *Chaubdar* from *Chaub* to impose silence: but I have been assured by Hindoos that the same word also signifies a stick, from which he may take his name.

Commentary: The chobdār (or, less frequently, āṣā-soṭābardār) is the mace-bearer and was retained only by European gentlemen of the highest rank—government officials, judges, and military officers above the rank of major. The mace (*chob* or *āṣā-soṭā*) was about four-and-one-half feet long, secured with ferrules of iron and tapering down from the top, about four inches in diameter, to the base. Covered with silver and richly decorated, the staff was often—though not in Solvyns's portrayal—topped with a figure, such as a tiger's head.[1]

Chobdārs—usually two, sometimes even four—attended their employers both at home and outside. In the home or office, the chobdār stood by the door of the receiving apartments, announced visitors and conducted them into the presence of his master. Accompanying their employer outside, chobdārs ran before the palanquin or sat beside the coachman in carriages. They might also carry messages or notes on formal occasions to persons of high status.[2]

Solvyns makes no reference to the limited use of such servants, and by his time, even gentlemen of high office increasingly dispensed with these "marks of distinction."[3]

In the text to the Paris edition, Solvyns takes issue with a "respectable English author" over the etymology of *chobdār*. In his note to the original drawing, in the Victoria and Albert Museum, Solvyns identifies the gentleman as "Major Dirom." Dirom had written an account of the war with Tipu Sultan in 1792, and there had wrongly defined *chobdār* as "literally, one who commands silence."[4] Solvyns, ever scrupulous to accuracy, respectfully corrects him.

1 Henry Grant and Colebrooke, *The Anglo-Hindoostanee Hand-Book*, 59-60; and *Bengal Past & Present*, "Life in Old Calcutta," 139.

2 Ibid., and Stocqueler, *Oriental Interpreter*, 60.

3 As noted in the text accompanying the print, Number 15, in the Orme pirated edition of Solvyns, *The Costume of Indostan* .

4 Dirom, 293.

II.103. Soṭābardār. Staff-Carrier

Pl. II.103. Soṭābardār. Paris: IV.1.5.
Calcutta: Sec. II, No. 5. Soonta-burdar, next in rank to a Chaubdar, with a short silver stick.

Paris: IV.1.5. SOONTA BURDAR: This servant also carries a short silver stick, but his is called *Soonta* and not *Chaub* like the former. Of an inferior rank to the domestics of whom we have already spoken, the *Soonta Burdar* does not enjoy the privilege of running by the side of his master, but must precede him: it is his office to cry out the name of his employer in the streets, and to proclaim that of his visitors in the house. Europeans except the governor general, have at most two of these servants, but the Indian Radjahs have four, eight or even twelve.

Commentary: The soṭābardār[1] (Anglo-Indian, soonta-burdar), staff-carrier, had duties similar to those of the chobdār, but had lower standing in the hierarchy of domestic service and was retained by officials of second or third rank who did not have a chobdār. The highest officials, however, might have both chobdārs and soṭābardārs in their service.[2] D'Oyly, in *The European in India* (1813), depicts a soṭābardār attending a gentlemen.[3]

The soṭābardār carried a short silver baton over the shoulder, as Solvyns's portrays. The *soṭā*, or baton, was about 30 inches in length, with a somewhat larger, curved upper end that was capped typically by a tiger's face or similar design.[4]

1 Bengali transliteration, Sukumar Sen, 902.
2 Stocqueler, *Oriental Interpreter*, 214.
3 Pl. 6.
4 *Bengal Past & Present*, "Life in Old Calcutta," 139.

II.104. Khānsāma. House Steward

Paris: IV.1.6. KHAUNSAMAUN: The functions of this servant are nearly those of the house steward, they extend however particularly also to the table and kitchen. He is dependant on the *Sircar,* to whom he gives in his accounts. He is generally an old servant of the family, and besides his wages, he has also a *dustore* [*dastūr*] upon the purchase of all the eatables: this employment was formerly of more importance, and there are still persons who place an unlimited confidence in their *Khaunsamaun,* who consequently often leads them into immence expence. A good *Khaunsamaun* is a great object in a rich family, and as all the table concerns come within his department, his merits are under the judgement of all the guests: every morning his master tells him how many are expected, and they agree together upon the wines to be served. During the repast he never quits his post at the sideboard, where he keeps a watchful eye over the other servants of the house, and those whom the visitors have brought with them, and has a right to have them searched before they go, which is often done to prevent thefts.

The *Khaunsamaun* has a particular manner of knotting his girdle and his turban, by which he is known even out of doors when he is not in service.

Pl. II.104. Khānsāma. Paris: IV.1.6.
Calcutta: Sec. II, No. 6. A Khaunsamaun or house Steward.

Commentary: The khānsāma (from the Persian, literally, "master of household goods") was house steward and was the chief table-servant and purchaser of food.[1] As the case for many servants associated with the kitchen and table in European homes, the khānsāma was almost always a Muslim.[2] Foods consumed by most Europeans were "unclean" for both Hindus and Muslims, beef and pork, respectively, being offensive to each. The kitchen nevertheless triumphed over dietary restriction to produce magnificent dishes that the khānsāma and cook might never have tasted.

Though typically described as a steward or butler, the khānsāma's duties went beyond those of his British counterpart. He did the marketing, prepared the pastries and main dishes—though leaving the actual cooking to others—and supervised kitchen operations generally. At table, he served the wine and supervised the bearers in their service.

In households without a sarkār (Pl. II.100) or jamādār (Pl. II.101), the khānsāma, as chief servant, was typically entrusted to hire other servants and pay them their monthly wages, and he, in turn, was responsible for their conduct.[3]

Stocqueler writes that khānsāmas "are always intelligent, respectful, and well-mannered men . . . and have much influence in the house, being treated very similarly (within perfectly becoming bounds) by their masters and mistresses, of whose interests they are usually watchful against all depredations but themselves."[4] Solvyns refers to the risks of expense the khānsāma might impose on his employer, and, though honest, the khānsāma was viewed as something of a "rogue" in taking a "small profit" on every market purchase. Like the sarkār, he was entitled to *dastūr*, a percentage on the transaction, usually one-half anna for every rupee. In addition, it was customary for the khānsāma to round the rupee and keep the small change.[5]

In the background, below the dining room's pankhā (ceiling fan),[6] two bearers, khidmatgārs (Pl. II.107) prepare the table. In the Paris print, Solvyns gives to these two servants a very different turban style from that depicted in the Calcutta print. In a yellow color matching their cummerbunds, their turbans are of the typically Bengali form called *śāmlā,* with a wide brim made of *śolā* (pith) and covered with minute folds of muslin.

1 *Hobson-Jobson*, 247.
2 See Nair's note, 38, to Stocqueler, in *British Social Life in Ancient Calcutta*, 236-37.
3 Johnson, in Nair, *India in the 19th Century*, 824-25.
4 Stocqueler, "Calcutta As It Is," 139-40; also see Stocqueler, *Oriental Interpreter*, 125, and Stocqueler, *The Hand-Book of India*, 231-32.
5 Ibid.
6 The *pankhā* (Anglo-Indian, punkah) is described in the Commentary for Pl. II.3.

II.105. Dwārbān. Porter

Paris: IV.2.1. DURWAN: *Durwan* is the general name for the porter in the houses both of natives and Europeans. They are mostly advanced in age and of very sedentary habits, never stirring out but to procure what is necessary for their subsistance. Their wages are very low, receiving only from four to five roupes a month. The *Durwan* in the print is represented in a negligent dress, and standing before the door of his lodge in the house.

The *Durwans* often affect importance, and refuse entrance to such as will not pay them a *dustore* [*dastūr*], their fellow servants even of the house, are not exempt from this tribute to their avarice. Their lodge is the place of rendez-vous, and the scene of exhibition of the *Bhauts* [Bhāt]. (See an account of this extraordinary caste in the 1st vol. [Pl. II.24]). The *Durwan* presents the hooka to all those who come upon commissions, and the tobacco is furnished by the *Khaunsamaun* [khānsāma, Pl. II.104] or *Kherchburdar* [kharacbardār, Pl. II.109]. The rich Hindoos and Mussulmans have not only a *Durwan,* but a number of *Brijbasis* [Brajbāsī, Pl. II.50], *Rawhuts* [Rāwāt, Pl. II.49], *Seapoys* [Pl. II.95], *Hircaras* [harkarā, Pl. II.123], etc. to keep their door.

In some Indian houses the *Durwan* announces the arrival of strangers by the sound of the *Caunsy* [*kā̃si*, Pl. II.172], but the Europeans use the *Ghaunta* [*ghaṇṭā*, Pl. II.146] for this purpose.

Pl. II.105. Dwārbān. Paris: IV.2.1.
Calcutta: Sec. II, No. 9. A Durwan,—a Door keeper or Porter.

Commentary: The dwārbān (Anglo-Indian, durwan), the porter, was stationed at the entrance door of the house or gate of the compound. He might have a small lodge near the door or often a raised recess in the wall where he could sit or sleep.[1] Solvyns describes them as demanding a small gratuity, for which he uses the term *dastūr*,[2] of the visitor (or servant) to gain entrance, a supplement to his meager pay to exclude all but those welcome to the household.

Solvyns writes that the dwārbān at Indian houses announces the arrival of a stranger with a gong (*kā̃si*) and in European households by ringing a bell (*ghaṇṭā*). Roberteau, in 1805, wrote that the dwārbān cried out in Bengali, "'There is a stranger arrived, go and give information,' on which an *Hircarrah* [message-bearer, Pl. II.123] runs to the Gate, learns the name of the Party and informs his master."[3]

Mrs. Fenton relates that the dwārbān, at the end of a "*burra-khanna*," dinner party, searched the guests' servants as they left to make sure that the spoons and forks did not disappear with them.[4]

Although often described as a "guard," Solvyns's disheveled fellow is "armed" only with his *hukā* (Pl. II.206), and the typically aged dwārbān rarely offered more protection than a cry of warning. Households seeking greater protection might employ a Brajbāsī as an armed guard,[5] and a caukīdār (Pl. II.122), night-watchman, might also be hired. Moreover, as Solvyns writes, wealthy natives—and no doubt some Europeans—often had various armed attendants at their door.

1 *Hobson-Jobson*, 333; Williamson, *East India Vade-Mecum*, 1:298-99. Also see Johnson, in Nair, *Calcutta in the 19th Century*, 827.
2 See Commentary, Pl. II.100.
3 In Nair, *Calcutta in the 19th Century*, 56-57.
4 Quoted in Cotton, *Calcutta Old and New*, 118.
5 Pradip Sinha, *Calcutta in Urban History*, 255.

II.106. Sardār. Valet

Paris: IV.2.2. SERDAR: We have already spoken of the several classes of *Serdars* and bearers, (in the 7th number of the first volume);[1] we shall consider them here only in their capacity of house servants. In riche families the *Serdar* is not himself a palanquin bearer: his service is confined to that of a valet-de-chambre, to dress and undress his master, and take care of his linnen; which requires some activity in a climate like that of Bengal, where they bathe and change linnen many times in the day. He performs his masters private commissions, and has the keys of the apartements. It is his business to take care that the rooms are lighted up with waxcandles, not with tallow, as it would be a dishonour to his caste to touch it; but coco or mustard oil brings no derogation. The *Serdars* are very tenatious to the usages of their caste, and are the most cleanly of the bearers. In houses where there are no *Jammadars,* the *Serdars* transmit the orders of the master to the other servants.

The print represents a *Serdar* with his keys on his shoulders, in one of his masters rooms.

Pl. II.106. Sardār. Paris: IV.2.2.
Calcutta: Sec. II, No. 8. A Serdar or head Bearer,—employed by Europeans in charge of their wardrobe, household-furniture, &c.

Commentary: The term *sardār* (Anglo-Indian, *sirdar*), from the Persian, had various usages in late eighteenth century India, referring to a chief or military commander, the head of a set of palanquin-bearers [See Pl. II.43] and, in Bengal, to a valet or body-servant.[2] It is in this later sense that Solvyns here portrays the sardār.

As valet, the sardār assisted his master in dressing and cared for the wardrobe. With the help of subordinate bearers, he made the beds and kept the furniture in its place, properly dusted and polished to "brightness with cocoanut shell and wax-cloth."[3] In large households, separate bearers were employed for the preparation and care of the lights, but in most cases, the sardār and, if married, his wife had responsibility for the evening lights, candles and oil-lamps. But Solvyns, with the Oriya bearer in mind, emphasizes that caste restrictions forbade any contact with animal fats. In fact, as Solvyns wrote in his note to his drawing of the Oriya bearer, many Europeans objected to them "for their scruples to do any household duties which their Brahmuns declare . . . against the tenants of their Religion."[4]

The sardārs were typically high caste Oriyas, valued for their cleanliness and sobriety; Rawānis from Bihar, "the least sober, but the most trustworthy, active, and intelligent" of bearers;[5] or Bengalis, usually of low caste and thought less reliable.

Solvyns portrays the sardār with keys fastened to the shawl over his shoulders, thought the keys were perhaps more often worn at the waist. Stocqueler writes that the sardār "carries an immense bunch of keys at his girdle, and whether his master have boxes enough to demand a large bunch or not, such bunch there is to be sure, for the dignity of the office."[6]

1 Solvyns portrays five classes of palanquin bearers, Pls. II.43-46 and Pl. II.76.
2 *Hobson-Jobson*, 841.
3 Stocqueler, "Calcutta As It Is," 142; Stocqueler, *Oriental Interpreter*, 211; also see Johnson, in Nair, *Calcutta in the 19th Century*, 826.
4 See Commentary on the Oriya bearers, Pl. II.43. On Oriyas in domestic service in Bengal, see Pradip Sinha, *Calcutta in Urban History*, 250-51.
5 Colesworthy Grant, *An Anglo-Indian Domestic Sketch*, 108. See Solvyns's discussion of the Rawāni bearers, Pl. II.44.
6 "Calcutta As It Is," 142-43.

II.107. Khidmatgār. Table Servant

Paris: IV.2.3. KIDMUDGAR: The servants called *Kidmudgars* are solely for the service of the table. In great houses there are always several behind their masters chair, and oftentimes a dinner of six persons is attended by fifteen or twenty. Nothing is more singular than their manner of serving at a great repast: at a signal given by the *Khaunsamaun* [khānsāma] or head butler by orders of the master, they sally forth from the kitchen each his dish in his hands, and as it is always at a great distance to avoid the smoke, they form a sort of procession moving one by one; and the scene is enlivened by the variety of colours in their turbans and sashes. As soon as dinner is over they depart, and have nothing more to do for the rest of the day: this want of occupasion leads them into debauchery, especially in the towns.

They are generally children of the servants of the house, and have but little wages; unless they are at the same time in some other employment, which does not happen in great families.

The *Kidmudgars* are mussulmans like the great part of the other servants. When a dish of pork is to be taken away, they slip aside not to be obliged to carry it, and the butler is forced to do it himself; but experience has prouved that though they refuse to carry it in public, they consent to eat it very freely of it in private.

The print represents a *Kidmudgar* in his ordinary dress behind his master, with a plate, and a knife and fork in his hand: further on are two other *Kidmudgars*, bringing from the sideboard the things which have been called for.

Pl. II.107. Khidmatgār. Paris: IV.2.3.
Calcutta: Sec. II, No. 7. A Kidmudgar,—who attends at table, and is under the Khaunsamaun.

Commentary: *Khidmatgār*, from the Persian, means literally "one who renders service," but its Anglo-Indian use was peculiar to Bengal, where the word applied to Muslim table servants.[1] An ambitious khidmatgār might aspire to become the khānsāma (Pl. II.104), or house steward.

It was customary for each person to have at least one table servant, and dinner guests would bring their own khidmatgārs, who would stand behind their chairs and make themselves useful in setting the plates and serving the food—all under the watchful eye of the khānsāma. Gentlemen at table were often attended by as many as three khidmatgārs, one of whom kept away the flies with a small fan or whisk.[2]

A European of modest means, if a bachelor, kept only one khidmatgār, who served generally as his master's valet.[3] "Strictly speaking, the duty of these men [was] merely to attend at meals," but, if need be, they could cook and, where economy required, would act as the abdār (Pl. II.127), who cools the wine, or as the hukābardār (Pl. II.108), who prepares the pipe—though normally separate servants were retained for these purposes.[4]

Khidmatgārs dress, as Solvyns portrays, in tight-fitting trousers, *churidār*, and *jāma* (gown) of white muslin, with cummerbund and turban, which may be of the same bright colored cloth, as seen on the servants at the sideboard in the background. Solvyns changed the turban style for the khidmatgārs in the Paris edition, giving them the wide-brimmed Bengali *śāmlā*, a form that was typically worn by table-bearers.[5]

1 *Hobson-Jobson*, "Kitmutgar," 486-87.

2 Stocqueler, "Calcutta As It Is," 140; *Bengal Past & Present*, "Life in Old Calcutta," 139; Roberdeau, in Nair, *Calcutta in the 19th Century*, 81. D'Oyly , Pl. 7, *The European in India*, portrays a khidmatgār preparing the table, and Williamson's accompanying text describes the servants role.

3 Colesworthy Grant, *An Anglo-Indian Domestic Sketch*, 105-06.

4 Nair's note, 36, to Stocqueler, in *British Social Life in Ancient Calcutta*, 235.

5 See Commentary for Pl. II.104, regarding the khidmatgār's dress. Honoria Lawrence, 43, writing in 1837, describes khidmatgārs as wearing the *śāmlā;* in Nair, *Calcutta in the 19th Century*, 610.

II.108. Hukābardār. Hukā-bearer

Paris: IV.2.4. HOOKA-BURDAR: This is the pipe carrier, and is charged with the care of all that concerns it, which is no trifling occupation among the Europeans. He accompanies his master wherever he goes, for the desire of smoking never quits him: on foot or in his palanquin, in his garden or only grassing from one room to another, this servant with all that is necessary for his employ, follows him step for step. One would imagine that this immoderate use of tobacco would be attended with fatal consequences in such a burning climate as that of Hindoostan, but it seems that custom has rendered it innocent. I have even known European ladies contract this habit and smoke from morning till night, without any inconvenience. The wages of the *Hooka-Burdar* are pretty high.

The one represented in the print is in the mohametan costume, carrying the Hooka to his master, while another is preparing the *chillum*.

Pl. II.108. Hukābardār. Paris: IV.2.4.

Calcutta: Sec. II, No. 12. A Hooka-burdar carrying the Hooka.

Orme: 18

Commentary: Solvyns depicts *hukās* of various forms in a series of separate etchings,[1] but it was the snake *hukā* that was most popular among Europeans in Bengal and is here portrayed in the hands of the hukābardār, or *hukā*-bearer. Seated on the floor, another hukābardār prepares the *chilim,* the small bowl that holds the hot charcoal ball and the tobacco mixture.[2]

The Commentary on the snake *hukā* (Pl. II.208) describes, in detail, its use and the role of the hukābardār. Accounts of Calcutta in the late eighteenth century make frequent reference to the hukābardār as a virtual shadow to his master, wherever he might go, and the addiction of some Europeans to the *hukā* was such that often two hukābardārs were retained, one for day, another for night. As guests at dinner parties, Europeans usually took several personal servants, including their own table-bearers, khidmatgārs (Pl. II.107), and the hukābardār. But that the hukābardār at least was regarded as indispensable is suggested by an invitation to a concert and supper in 1779 by the Governor-General and his wife. The card read: "Mr. . . . is requested to bring no servants except his huccabadar."[3]

In prints depicting Europeans smoking the *hukā*, the hukābardār is usually in attendance, as in that by Sir Charles D'Oyly,[4] and, of course, in Solvyns's portrayal of himself for the title page of fourth volume of *Les Hindoûs*. The hukābardār himself was portrayed by George Chinnery[5] as well as by Solvyns, and the servant was also the subject of paintings by Indian artists of the Company School.[6]

1 On the *hukā*, see the introduction to the section on "Modes of Smoking, &c.," pp. 435-36, and commentaries for the following prints, Pls. II.203-10.
2 See Pl. II.207.
3 Mackintosh, 2:216, in Nair, *Calcutta in the 18th Century*, 185.
4 Pl. 10, *The European in India*, with Williamson's accompanying text.
5 Pl. 271, "Hookkaburdar." Etching (1807) after a drawing by George Chinnery, Madras, 1807," in Mildred Archer, *India and British Portraiture*, 364.
6 See Mildred Archer, *Company Drawings in the India Office Library*, Pl. 25, "Hookah-bearer. Calcutta, c. 1798-1804." Here the Indian artist may well have been influenced by Solvyns.

II.109. Kharacbardār. Marketing Servant

Pl. II.109. Kharacbardār. Paris: IV.2.5.

Calcutta: Sec. II, No. 10. A Kherch-burdar or house Purveyor, coming from Market, —in the style of eastern indolence, he must have an attendant to carry the articles he has purchased.

Orme: 16.

Paris: IV.2.5. KHERCH-BURDAR: This servant is found only in great houses, his business is to buy the provisions under the orders of the steward, who does this himself in great families, and if there is no steward, the place is supplied by the Kidmudgar: his wages are higher than those of the Kidmudgar, and he has nearly half the day to himself, unless he is sent out to a distance to collect provisions for the next day, which is often the case in the country, where it is frequently difficult to find a piece of butchers meat without killing an ox or sheep, but fish and poultry are tollerably plenty.

The *Kerchburdars* are generally mussulmans, but I have seen in some houses Hindoos in this situation. The one in the print is carelessly dressed and returning from market, and in the stile of eastern indolence too lazy to carry any thing himself, he is followed by a little boy who carries the provisions he has just bought.

Commentary: The kharacbardār,[1] in large households, did the marketing. In the print, he is accompanied by a bearer—described as "a little boy"—who carries the provisions. Solvyns reference to "eastern indolence" is supercilious (an attitude from which he was generally free) and unwarranted. Comparable servants in households of Europe of the time would surely have been accompanied by such attendants on shopping expeditions.

1 *Kharac*, alone, is "expenditure," Sukumar Sen, 181.

II.110. Chauṅrībardār. Whisk-Bearer

Pl. II.110. Chauṅrībardār. Paris: IV.2.6.

Calcutta: Sec. II, No. 14. A Chowry-burdar,—an attendant to drive away insects. Europeans at present, seldom have the Chowry used except at their meals,—formerly with them, as by the Natives, they were considered as an insignia of rank, and employed on all occasions of state.

Paris: IV.2.6. CHOWRY-BURDAR: This is quite a servant of grandeur, and is only seen with the princes of the country, though he was formerly in all great houses. His employ is to drive off the flies and knats. This, which appears to us very superfluous, is exceedingly useful in India where these insects are one of the great plagues of the inhabitants, and fall particularly upon the Europeans on their first arrival. Their sting produces red spots on the skin, and sometimes inflamation; but after some stay in the country they are less supportable.

I have represented a *Chowry-Burdar* in the service of an European, for which reason he does not wear the Jumma [*jāma*, long gown] as if he belonged to a *Radjah.* His dress is that of all the mussulmans servants, he is known nevertheless by the loose manner in which the ends of his sash hang. His *Chowry* is made of split feathers, but for the princes it is composed of peacocks feathers entire, fixed in a silver handle nicely worked. See the 8th number of the 1st volume [Pl. II.19].

The movements of the *Chowry-Burdar* with his instrument are performed with great lightness. At great dinners the Europeans frequently employ several of them.

Commentary: The *chauṅrī*, a whisk originally made of yak's tail or, later, of peacock feathers, was a symbol of exalted status.[1] Chauṅrībardārs (Anglo-Indian, "chowryburdar"), as separate servants, were an exceptional luxury in European households, but in his note to the original drawing, Solvyns wrote that "Formerly they were considered a necessary attendant on a Man of Rank, were always in waiting with the Palanquin, and are still kept by the Natives." Europeans, no less than rājās, however, were bothered by insects, and at meals, or as required, khidmatgārs (Pl. II.107) or *chātā* (umbrella) bearers might be used to keep away the flies with whisks or fans of palm leaves, and they would surely be in attendance at dinner parties.

---

1 See *Hobson-Jobson*, 214-15.

II.111. Bhīstī. Water-Carrier

Pl. II.111. Bhīstī. Paris: IV.3.1.

Calcutta: Sec. II, No. 11. A B'heesty or Waterman, carrying water in his Musuck or leathern Bag,—his business is to supply the house with water; and during the hot season to water the Tatees, (a grating of bamboos filled with the Kuskus Root or a small prickly shrub called Jewassee) which are placed against the openings of a habitation, to cool the wind in its passage to the apartments.

Orme: 17.

Paris: IV.3.1. B'HEESTY, WATERMAN: The B'heesty is the man who carries water to the house, which is the whole extent of his service within doors; but during the summer it is his business to throw water upon the *taties* before the windows of the apartments, which are a sort of basketwork of bambou filled with the *Kuskus* or an other root called *Jewassiee*. The *taties* are placed before the doors and windows, where by constantly throwing water upon them they contribute very much to cool the apartments.

The *B'heestys* are of the lower class of Mussulmans; there are few Hindoos among them, and those carry water in vases like that we have represented in the 19th plate of the 1st volume for the milkman [Pl. II.28], and would look upon it as dishonorable to use the *mussuk* or leathern dog skin bag, as the others do. The print gives an idea of the manner of carrying the *mussuk* when it is full of water, with its leather mug which is indispensible, as the *B'heetsy* is not allowed to draw water by any other means. The view represents the railing which encloses the square of the great tanck at Calcutta. At a distance are the writers buildings. The *B'heetsys* are ennured to fatigue and hardship, but are much addicted to liquor and toddy. They are in no estimation in the family, where their wives often serve in the capacity of *Dyes* [dāi, Pl. II.133] or *Materanies* [methrānī, Pl. II.134].

Commentary: *Bhīstī* (Anglo-Indian, bheesty) is the Hindustani word for water-carrier, portrayed by Solvyns with his goatskin bag, *mashak*, filled with water. As contact with leather was polluting for higher caste Hindus, the bhīstī was almost always Muslim.[1]

Solvyns's bhīstī walks beside "the Tank," which supplied residents of Calcutta with drinking water from its springs. Under Governor-General Warren Hastings, an embankment was built around the tank, and the new Tank Square was lined with handsome buildings, with the Writers' Buildings, built in 1777 to accommodate junior clerks ("writers") of the East India Company, along the north side.[2]

A young writer, Thomas Twining, recorded his observations of bhīstīs at the Great Tank in 1792. They had, he wrote, leather bags "slung at their backs, which, when filled, had rather a ludicrous appearance, exhibiting the form of the animals from which they were taken. The skin being submerged in the water, was filled at a small aperture left unsewed at the end of the neck, and when full this opening was tied up with a piece of leather, which being loosened to the degree necessary, the water spirted out, in a greater or smaller stream, according to the pressure of the man's hand. . . . All this was done, from the filling to the emptying, without unslinging the skin, the carrier merely bearing it forward over his side when discharging the water. . . ."[3]

In addition to supplying the household with water, in the hot season, the bhīstī also attended the *ṭaṭṭīs*, screens of fragrant *khaskhas* or *jawās*,[4] within a split bamboo frame, that were placed before open doors and windows and kept wet to cool and freshen the air of a room.[5] Palanquins were also often provided with cuscus *ṭaṭṭīs* that hung over the sides and when wetted by the attendant bhīstī kept the inside pleasantly cool.[6]

Solvyns writes that bhīstīs, given to drink, were held in no esteem in the households they served, but *Hobson-Jobson* takes strong exception to such a view: "No class of men (as all Anglo-Indians will agree) is so diligent, so faithful, so unobtrusive, and uncomplaining as that of the *bihistīs*."[7] This was especially noteworthy in their service in the Indian army, where often in battle they showed "courage and fidelity in supplying water to the wounded in the face of much personal danger."[8] Kipling, in his *Barrack-room Ballads*, wrote,

> Of all them black-faced crew,
> The finest man I knew
> Was our regimental bhisti, Ganga Din.

---

1 *Hobson-Jobson*, 92; Lewis, 65.

2 See Losty, *Calcutta: City of Palaces*, 49-51. The railing around the Tank is seen in Thomas Daniell's 1786 etching from his *Views of Calcutta*, reproduced in Losty, Fig. 25, and in Mildred Archer, *Early Views of India*, Pl. 6.

3 Twining, son of a Director of the Company, arrived in Calcutta in 1792 at the age of fourteen to take up service as a Writer. In his description, he wrongly identifies the *mashak* as a pigskin. *Travels in India,* 75, in Nair, *Calcutta in the 19th Century*, 278.

4 *Khaskhas* (Anglo-Indian, "cuscuss") is the aromatic fibrous root of a grass. *Hobson-Jobson*, 283-84. In Bengal, the grass (*Andropogon muricata*) is called beṇā. Gupte, 102; Sukumar Sen, 684. Solvyns's prickly shrub, "Jewassee" is *jawās* (*Hedysarum alhagi*).

5 *Hobson-Jobson*, 903; Lewis, 233; *OED*. The *ṭaṭṭī* (Hindi), or *ṭāṭī* (Bengali), was not used solely for cooling. The term refers generally to a screen or mat made of khas, bamboo strips, or palm leaves, and it served as a door flap in huts or as material for a thatched hut. Sukumar Sen, 353.
On the construction of the *ṭaṭṭī,* see Williamson, *East India Vade-Mecum*, 1:234-36. On their use, see Heber, 1:101-02, in Nair, *Calcutta in the 19th Century*, 391; Spear, *The Nabobs*, 50; and Suresh Chandra Ghosh, 103.

6 Colesworthy Grant, *An Anglo-Indian Domestic Sketch,* 27-28.

7 92.

8 Ibid.

II.112. Dhobī, Dhobā. Washerman

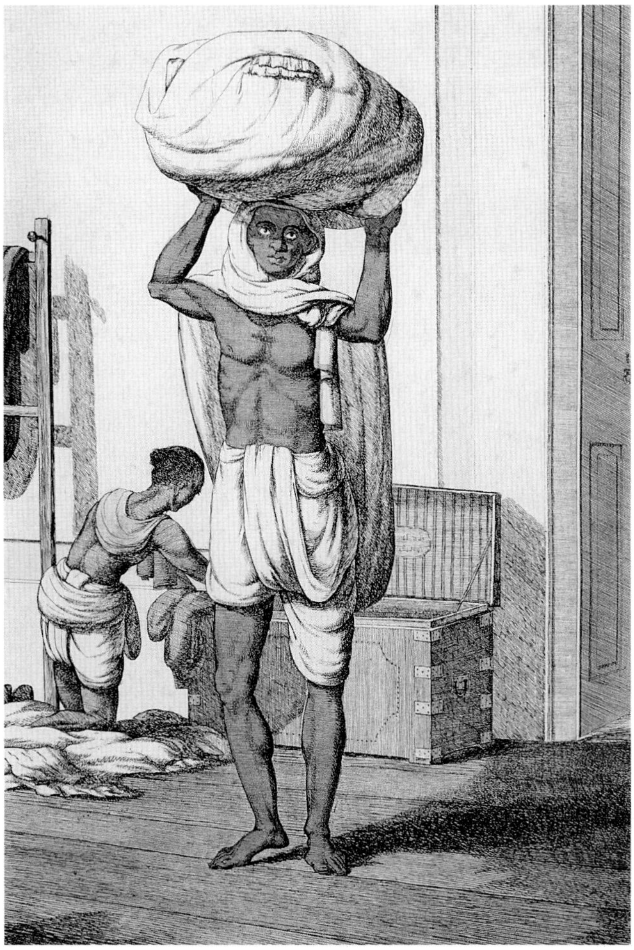

Paris: IV.3.2. DOBY, WASHERMAN: We have already mentioned the *Doby* in the first volume [Pl. II.55] with relation to his caste, here we are to consider him as one of the servants of the house, where his business is to wash all the linnen of the family, and given an account of it to the *Serdar-bearer* [sardār, Pl. II.106] or chief of the carriers. The *Doby* and his family accompany the master of the house on all his excursions, this is a necessary custom in a climate which requires such frequent change of linnen. The *Doby* washes also the servants' linnen. His wages are pretty high and paid monthly. He generally lives with his family and at a little distance from the house. There are some rogues among them who change the linnen and imitate perfectly their masters mark.

The print represents a *Doby* carrying his bundle of linnen on his head. Except a slight drapery they have no clothes.

Pl. II.112. Dhobī. Paris: IV.3.2.
Calcutta: Sec. II, No. 13. A Doby or Washerman.

Commentary: The distinct Hindu washerman caste in Bengal is Dhobā, portrayed in Solvyns's series of etchings on caste occupations (Pl. II.55). The British throughout India, however, used the Hindustani term *dhobī* (the name specific to the washerman caste of North India) as generic for all washermen.[1] The manner by which they wash clothes is described in the text and commentary to Dhobā print.

1 See *Hobson-Jobson*, 312-13.

II.113. Mākhanwālā. Butter-Man

Pl. II.113. Mākhanwālā. Paris: IV.3.3

Calcutta: Sec. II, No. 15. A Maukkun-walla, or Butter-man, with his mode of making butter, which is done by half curding the milk, and then agitating it with a machine made of bamboos, placed in a shallow earthen pan.

Paris: IV.3.3. MAUKKUN-WALLA: This servant makes the butter. Every great establishment has its *Maukkun-walla* who has fresh butter ready at every hour of the day, as the heat prevents it from keeping. The manner of making it has been mentioned in the first volume.[1] He must always have a supply of good milk ready. Latterly this servant is only necessary in the country, for in all the towns where there are Europeans, there are dairies and buttershops well supplied. There are several other servants as well as this whose employment has become unnecessary since the european industry has been known in India.

The *Maukkun-walla* in the print is a Hindoo, and the manner in which he carries his pot of butter is remarkable. It is surprising to see what heavy burdens the Hindoos carry in this manner.

Commentary: Fresh butter might have been favored by Europeans, but *ghī* (Anglo-Indian, "ghee"), clarified butter, was typically used in cooking and could be kept almost indefinitely without becoming rancid.

1 In his text for the Āhir, milkman (Pl. II.28), refers to *ghī* as a "butter which never corrupts," but he does not describe the manner for making either butter or *ghī*.

II.114. Rotīwālā. Bread-Maker

Pl. II.114. Rotīwālā. Paris: IV.3.4.
Calcutta: Sec. II, No. 16. A Rooty-walla, or Baker.

Paris: IV.3.4. ROOTY-WALLA: This is the baker of the house, who is generally a mussulman and confines himself mearly to making bread, they are mostly Portuguese who turn flower to the other uses of cakes tarts etc. There is nothing remarkable in the way they work, instead of levain [leaven] they use a fermenting liquor [*tāṛī*] produced by a species of palmtree.[1] The bread in India is excellent, and can bear a comparison with the best in Europe. The *Rooty-walla* is in the same predicament as the *Maukkun-walla* [mākhanwālā, Pl. II.113], being only necessary at present in the country, as there are good bakers in all the towns. Some of the country bakers have even large establishments for the use of the navy in the different ports.

The print shows the manner in which the *Rooty-walla* carries his bread. Further off are the persons who work the paste, which occupation they accompany with particular songs.

Commentary: *Rotī* (Hindustani) is an unleavened Indian bread, but for Europeans in Bengal, the rotīwālā, almost always a Muslim, "made bread according to the English method," using *tāṛī* (toddy) as a ferment instead of yeast.[2] According to Wise, the rotīwālā also made pie crust and *samōsās*, a three-cornered pastry stuffed with minced meat or vegetables,[3] but Solvyns has the pastries made by a "Portuguese," a loose term, probably referring here to Eurasian Indo-Portuguese, who were often employed in the kitchens of European households.[4]

In towns, rotīwālās typically sold their bread house to house rather than from a shop.

1 See Pl. II.62 on the making of *tāṛī*, or toddy.
2 Wise, 96-97.
3 Ibid.
4 See discussion of the "black Portuguese," see Commentary for Pl. II.6.

II.115. Darzī. Tailor

Pl. II.115. Darzī. Paris: IV.3.5.
Calcutta: Sec. II, No. 17. A Durzee, or Taylor.
Orme: 19.

Paris: IV.3.5. DURZEE, TAYLOR: The taylor is also a servant of the house, and is called *Dunzee*. He is generally very clever and astonishingly expeditious, working for the women as well as the men of the family. He uses Chinese needles, differing from ours by their round eyes and tops, neither is their manner of sowing the same as that of our taylors.

The *Durzees* scarcely quit their work during the day; they eat before they begin, and then seldom rise but to drink water or smoke the Hooka at the porters [dwārbān, Pl. II.105], without any other nourishment. They are well and deservedly paid, for their great application. There are houses which employ several at a time. They sit in an attitude which I have endeavoured faithfully to give. The *Durzee* represented is sitting on a mat, and his turban shews him to be a mussulman. The masters generally give their servants turbans and sashes leaving the colour to their own choice: the greater part prefer white, and as good cloth is not dear in India, they are mostly well dressed.

Commentary: The darzī,[1] tailor, enjoyed an esteemed position among the servants of the European household, making clothes for the entire family. He is portrayed at work in a print by D'Oyly, "An European Lady Giving Instructions to her Durzee, or Native Tailor," in *The European in India*.[2] The darzī was "an indispensable adjunct, his business being to mend the clothes as fast as the dhobee (dhobī, washerman, Pl. II.112) tears them . . . ."[3]

Darzīs were ordinarily Muslims, as traditionally Hindus did not wear sewn garments, wearing instead lengths of cloth draped and fastened around the body. Although sewing was not unknown in ancient India, as sometimes asserted, stitched garments were not widely worn and came to be associated with Muslim, and later European, style.[4]

1 Hindustani, from the Persian; Bengali, *darji*; Anglo-Indian, "dirzee" or "durzee," *Hobson-Jobson*, 319.
2 Pl. 13. Williamson describes the work of the darzī in the accompanying text.
3 Stocqueler, "Calcutta As It Is," 143. Also see Williamson, *East India Vade Mecum*, 242-46.
4 See Basham, *The Wonder That Was India*, 212-13. "Many [Hindus] . . . have adopted the Mussulmanne vest and trowsers, and, therefore, tailors have sprung up amidst the followers of Brahma. . . ." *Asiatic Journal*, August, 1836, in Nair's note, 45, to Stocqueler, in *British Social Life in Ancient Calcutta*, 235

II.116. Khālāsi. Sailor, Workman

Pl. II.116. Khālāsi. Paris: IV.3.6.

Calcutta: Sec. II, No. 22. A Clashy,—as Sailor, employed to manage the sails of the Yatchs used in the inland Navigation,—Natives employed in the artillery also have this name.

Paris: IV.3.6. CLASHY: These servants are only in great houses, their business is to oversee all the workmen, such as masons, gardeners etc. and to guide the boats which people of fortune are never without. The East-India company employ a great many *Clashys* in their land armies, for transporting baggage provisions etc. They serve also sometimes in the artillery, and the officers have them in their private service, the rich make them run before their palanquins; and infine they are employed in many different ways and are very useful.

The *Clashy* of the print is in the companies uniform; persons only of high rank in the service are allowed to give this dress to their servants, but notwithstanding this order, there are officers who employ *Seapoys* or soldiers to do their commissions, and even to run before their palanquins.

Commentary: *Khālāsi* (Anglo-Indian, classy, clashy) was a term applied to various roles—tent-pitcher, a surveyor's chain- or staff- man, artillery-man, dock-worker, and, most commonly, native sailor.[1] In his *Catalogue* for the Calcutta edition, Solvyns identifies the khālāsi as sailor and artillery-man, but, oddly, not in the role portrayed in the etching. In his note to the original drawing, however, he writes, "The Clashy is occasionally employed as a Sailor; on land as an overseer or workmen, as represented in the Drawing, and often as a Hircara [harkarā, Pl. II.123] or Peada [peyādā, Pl. II.124]."

Solvyns portrays the khālāsi supervising work on the construction of a house, but as a domestic servant, he performed a variety of services, such as pulling the *pankhā*, the fan suspended from the ceiling;[2] running errands, and assisting the sardār (Pl. II.106) with the furniture.[3]

In the employ of a high official of the East India Company, Solvyns's khālāsi is dressed in Company uniform—a red-bordered blue jacket and matching blue cummerbund. His turban, however, is colored red. Williamson, Solvyns's contemporary in Bengal, writes that "the whole of *Kalashies* wear blue turbans, of rather a flat form, having on their edge a red tape, about three fourths of an inch in breadth. . . ."[4] As if corrected, in the Paris edition, Solvyns's gives the khālāsi a flattened blue turban, though without the red border.

1 *Hobson-Jobson*, 223. *Hobson-Jobson* gives its equivalent as "Lascar," 507-09. Also see Lewis, 89.

2 On the *pankhā*, see Commentary, Pl. II.3. D'Oyly, Pl. 8, *The European in India*, portrays "an English family at table, under a punkah, or fan, kept in motion by a khelassy."

3 Williamson, *East India Vade-Mecum*, 281-83; also see Stocqueler, *Oriental Interpreter*, 115, and *Bengal Past & Present*, "Life in Old Calcutta," 140.

4 *East India Vade-Mecum*, 283.

II.117. Coachman

Pl. II.117. Coachman. Paris: IV.4.1.
Calcutta: Sec. II, No. 23. A native Coachman.
Orme: 23.

Paris: IV.4.1. COACHMAN: Notwithstanding the general use of palanquins, there are a great many coaches kept in Calcutta; a fashion which the Europeans have introduced, and there are few houses in which there is not at least a two wheel carriage. The horses for this purpose come from upper Hindoostan or from Arabia. On their first landing from Bombay they are lean and have but a mean appearance, but after a little rest they become beautiful. They are used more for the saddle than for draught, though some persons use no other in their carriages. This race of horses is remarkable for their obstinacy; for when they find the road too long, or refuse to get up or down a hill or over a ditch, nothing can get the better of them. I have often seen them rather overturn the carriage or overthrow their rider than to advance.

The coachmen in India are almost all mussulmans, and wear the turban and girdle of the same colours as those of the other servants of the house. The costume in the print is that generally worn. Besides the coachman each horse has a servant called a *syce* [sāis, Pl. II.118].

Commentary: The coachman stands besides a carriage, perhaps manufactured by Steuart & Co., by whom Solvyns had been employed in painting decorations on coaches and palanquins.[1]

In Solvyns's time in Calcutta, with unmetalled roads that were alternately dusty or muddy, the palanquin remained the principal means of conveyance, but the European quarter increasingly abounded with carriages, with great rivalry in their decorations and fine appointments. It was especially fashionable to take the carriage out for an evening ride on the Course, a triangular drive laid out on the Esplanade south of Fort William.[2]

The coachman would be dressed in turban, cummerbund, and coat, usually in matching colors, as in Solvyns's etching, and the carriage would be accompanied by running footmen (Pl. II.118), with great fly-whisks (*chauṅrīs*), mounted on silver handles, slung across their shoulders, and, at night, the maśālcī (Pl. II.120), or torch-bearer, would lead the way.[3]

1 On Solvyns's association with Steuart & Co., see pp. 30-31.
2 On the Course, see p. 137. Also, Losty, *Calcutta: City of Palaces*, 38, 40.
3 Blenchyden, 115-16; H. E. A. Cotton, 119; Roberdeau, 123, in Nair, *Calcutta in the 19th Century*, 51-53; and *Sketches of India: Written by an Officer*, 113-19, in Nair, *Calcutta in the 19th Century*, 201-04.

II.118. Sāis. Groom

Pl. II.118. Sāis. Paris: IV.4.2.

Calcutta: Sec. II, No. 24. A Syce or Groom,—each horse has one who attends, runs by his side, when used either in a carriage or the saddle.

Orme: 24.

Paris: IV.4.2. SYCE, GROOM: The *Syce* runs always by the side of the horse entrusted to his care, or when his master goes in his carriage, and is sure to keep pace with him, and return less fatigued than he, whatever may be the rate of going or length of the road. This servant is of an inferior class and very poor, generally debauched and in very low estimation: they are mussulmans, and notwithstanding their laborious life attain a great age. The print represents a *Syce* running before his master, with a *chowry* [*chauṅrī*] and a rope in his hand in case of need. In the back ground is an old *Syce* sitting before the stable near his horse and smoking the Hooka [*hukā*]. The domestic occupation of the *Syce* is to feed his horse who eats on the ground, as there are no recks.[1] In some parts they have a singular method of nourishing their horses: they boil the oats or *gram,* and make it into little balls, which they thrust into their mouths one at each side, but these are bad habits. The *Syce* inhabits the Stable, and frequently the whole family lies alongside the horse.

Commentary: The sāis (Hindustani, from the Arabic; Anglo-Indian, syce),[2] as groom, attended a single horse, caring for it and running by its side when taken out, mounted or with carriage. By the mid-nineteenth century, the sāis' running with the horse was apparently no longer general practice in towns, and "in the case of the vehicle, which is almost confined to city life, . . . the syce is generally seen sitting on the foot board, or at the back of the buggy or carriage, but upon approaching a crowd or dangerous turning, he alights, and holding by the shaft or other available projection, runs by the side of the horse, and by an admonishing cry gives warning to all before him of the approaching danger."[3]

The sāis was assisted by a ghāsyārā, grass-cutter (Pl. II.119), who supplied the horse with fodder and often helped clean out the stables. The ghāsyārā accompanied the sāis when the horse was taken out of town. "While the ghusyārā has been sent on at three in the morning with the cleaning, tethering, and feeding paraphernalia, the syce remains behind to saddle the horse and accompany his master on foot,—which, despite trotting and cantering to boot, he contrives with bear feet and girded loins, to do during a stage of probably twelve miles."[4]

Solvyns portrays the sāis with a rope to tether the horse and a horsehair whisk, or *chauṅrī*, to keep it free of flies.

Solvyns identifies the sāis as Muslim, but there were also Hindu sāis, perhaps employed mainly by other Hindus. One of the "characteristic occupations" of the low-caste Hāṛi (Pl. II.71), for example, was as a sāis.[5]

---

1 A board frame placed between two posts that could serve as a trough. Obs. *OED*.

2 *Hobson-Jobson*, 885-86. The Bengali is *sahis*. On the sāis, see Williamson, *East India Vade-Mecum*, 254-57.

3 Colesworthy Grant, *An Anglo-Indian Domestic Sketch,* 77-78. Also see Johnson, in Nair, *Calcutta in the 19th Century*, 828.

4 Colesworthy Grant, *An Anglo-Indian Domestic Sketch,* 77.

5 Risley, *The Tribes and Castes of Bengal*, 1:316.

II.119. Ghāsyārā. Grass-Cutter

Paris: IV.4.3. GASSYARA: The Syce is not enough for the care of a horse, each one must have his *Gassyaru*; whose business it is to furnish the necessary grass. He goes out early in the morning to the fields and pulls up the grass by the roots, cleans it, by beating it with small sticks, bundles it and carries it to the stable, as is shown in the print. In the foreground is a *Gassyara* with a bundle of grass on his head, and at a distance others cutting it. Though the *Gassyaru* goes out early in the morning, he never returns till night, the rest of the day is employed in rest or drinking, which accounts for their ordinary bad appearance. They are of a low class, very poor and addicted to debauchery: being constantly exposed to the sun they are blacker than the other servants, and their skin is very shining. We have already remarked in the 1st volume that in the interior of Hindoostan the *Gassyaras* are also palanquin bearers.[1]

Commentary: The ghāsyārās, grass-cutter,[2] worked closely with the sāis (Pl. II.118) in the care of a single horse, and, like the sāis, attended the horse in travel of any distance. The ghāsyārā, as seen in the squatting figure in the background of the etching, cuts the grass with a paring instrument about half an inch under the surface of the soil, "the upper part of the root being considered extremely nourishing."[3]

Ghāsyārās were usually from the "untouchable" castes, some of which, like the Dom (Pl. II.68), had distinct ghāsyārā subcastes.[4]

Pl. II.119. Ghāsyārā. Paris: IV.4.3.

Calcutta: Sec. II, No. 25. A Gassyara or Grass-cutter,—horses, bullocks, &c. are fed in this country with grass cut fresh every day.

---

1 Solvyns perhaps refers to the Rawāni bearers (Pl. II.44) from Bihar, but in his text, there is no mention of ghāsyārās.
2 *Hobson-Jobson*, 393-94.
3 Williamson, *East India Vade-Mecum*, 1:257-58.
4 Risley, *The Tribes and Castes of Bengal*, Appendix I, 2:42. Also see Wise.

II.120. Maśālcī. Torch-Bearer

Paris: IV.4.4. MUSHAULJEE, LINCKBOY: The *Mushauljee* is the torch bearer, if that name may be given to a bundle of rags tied to a copper handle, and steeped in oil, it gives however a great light, which is kept up by pouring oil upon it from time to time, for which purpose the *Mushauljee* always carries a pot of oil with a very narrow spout, that the oil may fall drop by drop. He runs at night by the side of the carriage, and is not less active than the other runners scarcely lifting his legs as he goes, while the motion of his feet is almost imperceptible. In the interior of the house he is sometimes employed as a scullion or helper to the cook.

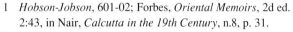

Pl. II.120. Maśālcī. Paris: IV.4.4.
Calcutta: Sec. II, No. 26. A Mushauljee or Link-boy.

Commentary: The maśālcī (Anglo-Indian, "mussaulchee") is the torch-bearer or "link-boy" who ran along side the palanquin or carriage at night. His torch (Hindustani, *maśāl*) as Solvyns portrays, was usually made of rags wrapped around a rod and kept alight with oil that he added at intervals from a brass vessel (as in the print) or earthen pot.[1] The maśālcī might also carry a lantern, as seen with the palanquin in the background of the etching, or, for great personages, what was called a "branch light," something like a candelabra with five or seven small torches and held aloft by a long central stem.[2]

In addition to serving as a torch-bearer, the maśālcī worked as a scullion under the khidmatgār (Pl. II.107), cleaning dishes, glassware, knives, and cutlery. By the early nineteenth century, with tigers and bandits less a threat when venturing out at night in Calcutta, his work was almost wholly that of scullion and domestic menial, polishing boots and shoes, tending house lamps, or whatever he may be called upon to do.[3]

1 *Hobson-Jobson*, 601-02; Forbes, *Oriental Memoirs*, 2d ed. 2:43, in Nair, *Calcutta in the 19th Century*, n.8, p. 31.

2 Williamson, *East India Vade-Mecum*, 1:220.

3 Stocqueler, "Calcutta As It Was," 141; Colesworthy Grant, *An Anglo-Indian Domestic Sketch*, 107; Dewar, *In the Days of the Company*, 30.

II.121. Ḍoriyā. Dog-Keeper

Pl. II.121. Ḍoriyā. Paris: IV.4.5.
Calcutta: Sec. II, No. 30. A Doorea-a, or Dog-keeper.
Orme: 27.

Paris: IV.4.5. DOOREA: We have already seen that every horse in India has two servants to attend him [sāis, Pl. II.118, and ghāsyārā, Pl. II.119], the dogs too have theirs who are called *Doorea,* to keep them clean and feed them. They are lodged in small bambou houses raised something above the ground and covered with mats. The greatest cleanness is indispensible for all those domestic animals, in a country where the heat is so excessive, and all sorts of vermine so abundant. It is moreover necessary that the dogs should have a person to take care of them, as the government kills all who are found in the streets, not only such as are without a master who go under the contemptable name of *pariahs,*[1] but even those who belong to the inhabitants. It is also forbidden to have dogs aboard the ships, but notwithstanding this order they are continually imported from Europe, and the prohibition of the company only serves to enhance their price to an enormous amount. I have seen fifty and even a hundred pounds given for a dog, and in the interior the English hunt with european hounds.

Commentary: The ḍoriyā (Hindustani, from *ḍor*, "a cord or leash")[2] was in charge of the dogs and usually resided at the kennel. Solvyns depicts him holding his characteristic short whip, a rawhide thong fastened to a short bamboo.[3]

1 A stray or mongrel, portrayed by Solvyns, Pl. II.282, was termed a pariah or, more typically, by contraction, "pi-dog." On the use of pariah for the worst of almost everything, see Commentary, Pl. II.22. Also see Lewis, "Pi-(dog)," 189.
2 *Hobson-Jobson*, 325.
3 See Williamson, *East India Vade-Mecum*, 1:279-81.

II.122. Caukīdār. Watchman

Paris: IV.4.6. CHOKEEDAR: The business of the *Chokeedar* is to watch the house at night. His accoutrements are most formidable: sabres, guns, pistols, an enormous cap and his face hideously painted, to judge by his weapons and appearance, ten robbers would not intimidate him, but notwithstanding all this he is often such a coward that he runs away at the slightest noise. Their cowardice renders them quite useless, and except the company no Europeans employ them. The rich Hindoos have several who patrol round their house, and keep guard during the whole night.

The government have formed a regular establishment of *Chokeedars* in the interior of the country, whose duty it is conjointly with the *Jummadar* [jamādār, Pl. II.101][1] to inspect the high roads and communications. The houses of these guards called *Tanna* [*thānā*] have been noticed in the third volume of this work.[2]

Pl. II.122. Caukīdār. Paris: IV.4.6.
Calcutta: Sec. II, No. 31. A Chokedar or Watchman,—employed by Government in the police, and by individuals to guard their habitations at night;—in the northern parts of Hindostan, it is almost impossible for an European in a private station, to enjoy security, without taking into his pay as Chokedars some persons from a gang of Robbers.

Commentary: In rural areas, the caukīdār (Anglo-Indian, chokidar) was a policeman, and in private service for both Indians and Europeans, he was the watchman, stationed in his guardhouse (*thānā*) at the gate of the compound or by the door. Caukīdārs usually came from low castes, such as the Hāṛi (with its own caukīdār subcaste),[3] and, as *Hobson-Jobson* notes, confirming Solvyns, "in some parts of India he is generally of a thieving tribe, and his employment may be regarded as a sort of blackmail to ensure one's property."[4]

Williamson shares Solvyns's judgment on the caukīdār's effectiveness: "at night parading about with his spear, shield, and sword, and assuming a most terrific aspect, until all the family are asleep; when HE GOES TO SLEEP TOO."[5]

1 Solvyns here does not refer to the jamādār as household servant, but as native head police constable.
2 Here he may refer to the outbuildings depicted beside European houses in the background of his etchings of palanquins. Solvyns refers earlier to a *thānā* in Pl. II.20.
3 Risley, *The Tribes and Castes of Bengal*, 1:315, and Asok Mitra, *The Tribes and Castes of West Bengal*, 3, 72.
4 205.
5 *East India Vade-Mecum*, 1:295.

II.123. Harkārā. Messenger

Paris: IV.5.1. HIRCARAH: The *Hircarah* is the message bearer, he runs before the palanquin with a sabre or a stick, or more generally with a pike as represented in the print. The *Hircarahs* affect a martial appearance, for which they paint their face in various ways, and mark it with the characters or signs peculiar to some sect. These servants are mostly from the north of India, and are *Sics* [Sikh, Pl. II.51], *Brijbasis* [Brijbāsī, Pl. II.50] or *Rawhuts* [Rāwāt/Rāut, Pl. II.49], they go also by the name of *Chauprasis* [chaprāsī]. They are dressed like Mussulmans and wear heavy shoes, notwithstanding which they run as lightly as the others, and scarcely seem to lift their feet. The india families of distinction keep several of them, and there are always great numbers at the doors of princes and persons of great fortunes, to announce strangers. They are dependant on the *Jummadar* [jamādār, Pl. II.101] from whom they receive their orders.

In the background of the print are *Hircarahs* running before the palanquin.

Commentary: *Harkārā* (Anglo-Indian, Hurcarra, Hircarah, etc.) is the Hindustani term for "messenger" or "courier" and was taken as the title of a Calcutta newspaper, *Bengal Hircarrah*, published from 1795 to 1828.[1] The harkārā's responsibilities as messenger normally involved lengthy journeys,[2] while letters or messages within the locality were usually carried by a peyādā, or footman (Pl. II.124).[3] Harkārās (like peyādās) also served as running footmen, preceding the palanquin, as depicted by Solvyns in the background of the etching.[4] And they were employed as spies, both by government and private parties.

Harkārās, though "of all sects," were typically from the same classes from which the army recruited, and the army, of course, had its own harkārās, frequently employed as spies. The text to Orme's pirated Solvyns edition notes that "those employed in the army are principally [Brijbāsī] Brahmuns, who are the most intelligent, and can best insinuate themselves into the sources of information. . . . ."

Harkārās dressed in Muslim fashion, with turbans and cummerbunds of the same color, and "when in the employ of great merchants, agents, and especially under the principal officers of the government, wear belts of colored broad-cloth, with metal breast plates [*chaprās*]; bearing either the initials, or arms, of their employers. . . ." Over the shoulder, they typically carried a pike, adorned with a tassel, by which they were distinguished from the inferior peyādā.[5] Often, however, the harkārā and peyādā were not clearly distinguished, and each might be referred to as a "peon" or as a chaprāsī, a name taken from the *chaprās*, metal badge, depicted by Solvyns in his portrayal of the peyādā.

The British artist Ozias Humphry, resident in India 1785 to 1787, portrayed a harkārā, without pike or *chaprās*, in a wash drawing.[6]

Pl. II.123. Harkārā. Paris: IV.5.1.

Calcutta: Sec. II, No. 20. A Hircarrah,—to carry messages, letters, &c. run in procession, and wait attendance under the Jummadar [jamādār].

Orme: 21.

---

1 *Hobson-Jobson*, 430. On the newspaper, see Shaw, 229-30.

2 With the letter perhaps concealed in the folds of their turban, harkārās were often dispatched distances of several hundred miles, and their expeditions, as Mrs. Kindersley observed in 1767, might be quite "extraordinary." 183-84, and in Nair, *Calcutta in the 18th Century*, 143-44.

3 Stocqueler, *The Oriental Interpreter*, 103.

4 They run before a European long palanquin of the type Solvyns portrays in III.9.4.

5 Williamson, *East India Vade-Mecum*, 1:274.

6 Pl. 121, in Mildred Archer, *India and British Portraiture*, 196.

II.124. Peyādā. Footman

Pl. II.124. Peyādā. Paris: IV.5.2.

Calcutta: Sec. II, No. 21. A Peada,—literally Footman—differing from the Hircarrah [harkārā, Pl. II.123], as the name is more generally applied to those who are hired on the occasion,—the Badge or Chaup [*chaprās*] in his Cumberbund, constitutes him a Chauprassee properly confined to the offices of Government.

Orme: 22.

Paris: IV.5.2. PEADAH: This is another running footman, but he is not always in constant service, and only hired on extraordinary occasions, such as feasts, marriages, etc. He carries on his girdle a plate of brass or silver, with the name, the cypher, or the armies of his master. I have represented him in the print with a sabre which he generally carries. In one hand he has a letter, in the other a *romal* [*rūmāl*] or piece of wet cloth to refresh his face after the manner of the Hindoos and Mussulmans. People of extensive connections in India cannot do without several *Peadahs,* to carry their numerous lettes and notes, which sometimes amount to the number of two or three hundred in a day, of which the contents are in general very trifling. When the *Peadah* accompanies the palanquin he runs before the *Hircarah*, who thinks himself of greater consequence, and avoids as a dishonour to be confounded with him.

Commentary: The peyādā (Anglo-Indian, peadah), footman, was often described as a "peon," a term that entered usage in India from the Portuguese.[1] His principal duty was to deliver letters, "chits" (notes),[2] bills, and small parcels within the locality, but he also attended his employer in running before or along side the palanquin or carriage and in performing any variety of odd jobs that might come to him.

The peyādā portrayed is armed with a sword, serving more as a symbol of his service than as a weapon, and wears a *chaprās*, metal badge-plate, on his cummerbund, that bears the initials of his employer—here, the artist's own "B. S." The badge, which, in place of initials, might carry the name or insignia of the office or firm to which the peyādā is attached, was also worn on a belt across the breast. From this badge, he (like the harkārā) took the name "chaprāsī."[3]

---

1 *Hobson-Jobson*, 696-97.

2 *Hobson-Jobson*, 303.

3 Colesworthy Grant, *An Anglo-Indian Domestic Sketch*, 124; Henry Grant and Edward Colebrooke, *The Anglo-Hindoostanee Hand-Book*, 60.

II.125. Baulber. Barber

Pl. II.125. Baulber. Paris: IV.5.3.
Calcutta: Sec. II, No. 18. A Baulber, corruption of Barber.
Orme: 20.

Paris: IV.5.3. BAULBER: This is the domestique hairdresser, attached to the family like the other servants: he is always a Mussulman, because a Hindoo would lose his caste by touching the grease of the pomatum, and would find it difficult and expensive to be restored to it by expiations. This trade requires more activity than in Europe, for in India the hair is dressed several times a day, so that each master must have his particular hairdresser. The *Baulber* in the print is waiting for his master in the room where the *Serdar* [sardār, Pl. II.106] has prepared the carpet, the chair and all that is necessary for his master: he carries his irons and combs wrapped up in a cloth in his girdle, and in this manner you meet him constantly walking about the house, thinking himself of no small importance, and not condescending to do any other service.

Commentary: The text for the Orme pirated edition of Solvyns reads:

"The hairdresser of India, like his brethren of Europe, propagate the lie of the day, and are inclined to embellishments that border upon fable.

"In his Jamma [*jāma*, gown] which he converts into an apron, are seen the implements of his trade, the comb and curling tongs, and near him the powder box and pomatum; his dress and appearance bespeak him a Mahommedan.

"Shaving is a distinct profession; the man who shaves cannot dress hair, and he who dresses hair will not shave." Solvyns portrays the shaving barber, or hajām, in the next print (Pl. II.126).

II.126. Hajām. Barber

Paris: IV.5.4. HAJAUM: In India another servant is required for shaving: this is the *Hajaum,* whose trade has already been the subject of a separate article in the first volume [Pl. II.63], under the name of *Napit,* which is applied indistinctly to all barbers in general, while the domestique one is called *Hajaum.* They are generally of Hindoo origin and so dexterious in their trade, that you scarcely feel the razor: they clean the ears and cut the nails of the hands and feet with same perfection, for which reason the Europeans are fond of having them in their service.

The *Hajaum* represented in the print, carries his razors and the other implements of his art in a sack under his arm; his head is covered, and he wears a piece of cloth over his shoulders out of respect for his master, before whom he will not appear naked, as the Hindoos who are not in the service of Europeans do.

Commentary: The word *hajām* is Hindustani, from the Arabic, and, in specific application, referred to Muslim barbers, who also acted as surgeons and performed circumcisions. Their wives served as midwives and nurses.[1]

Europeans apparently used the term loosely to include Hindus, and Solvyns writes that for Europeans, the shaving barber was usually a Hindu, as here portrayed in Hindu dress, and, in Bengal, a member of the Nāpit barber caste (Pl. II.63).

D'Oyly, in *The European in India* (1813), depicts "a gentleman attended by his hajaum, or native barber."[2] In the accompanying text, Williamson describes the procedure and adds, "It is . . . considered a part of the Hajaum's duty to supple the joints by pulling, twisting, and other modes not very acceptable to Europeans, but much relished by the natives."

1 Wise, 69; Whitworth, 115.
2 Pl. 5.

Pl. II.126. Hajām. Paris: IV.5.4.
Calcutta: Sec. II, No. 19. A Hajaum, or shaving Barber.

II.127. Ābdār. Cooler of Drinks

Commentary: The ābdār (Hindustani, from the Persian, literally "keeper of water") was the domestic servant who cooled the water and wine before "the Americans afforded the delightful luxury of ice." With the import of ice from New England into Calcutta from 1833, the ābḍar became the manager of ice, but only wealthy households retained such servants.[1]

As a cooler of drinks, the ābdār was indispensable to the European gentleman in Bengal, and, like the hukābardār (Pl. II.108), would accompany his employer to dinner parties, such that during the meal, the compound "would sometimes be half-filled with noisy *Abdars* . . . cooling master's *shrab* ["wine"][2] by the aid of saltpetre, after the approved, and not altogether inefficient manner of the time."[3]

Pl. II.127. Ābdār. Paris: IV.5.5.
Calcutta: Sec. II, No. 28. An Aubdar, or Cooler of water and wines, by the means of saltpetre.
Orme: 25.

Paris: IV.5.5. AUBDAR: The sole business of the *Aubdar* is to cool the liquors, and this is not as it may seem to an European a trifling charge. The heat of the climate renders it absolutely necessary, and every person of any fortune keeps a servant purposely to cool the water and the wine. During the whole day the *Aubdar* is occupied in answering the calls of his master and family; and if there is company at dinner, his business becomes still more urgent. For this purpose he has a vase or basin of lead, in which are leaden bottles with long and narrow necks, the basin is filled with saltpeter, into which he plunges the bottles with the wine or water and keeps them in constant motion, for it has been observed that the more they are stirred, the greater degree of cold they acquire.

This process is very exactly represented in the engraving. There is another more ancient and more simple manner of cooling liquors, which is to put them into vases of a black earth, with very narrow mouths, which they cover all over with wet cloths and expose them to the wind.

The text to Orme's pirated edition of Solvyns provides a succinct description of the process: The cooling, which is done outside the house, "is effected by placing a vessel containing either water or wine into a small [pewter] tub filled with the purist water, and into which is thrown a certain quantity of salt-petre; the immersed vessel is then turned round slowly until the salt-petre dissolves; when the cold air contained in its particles explodes, and communicates its quality to the contents of the vessel."[4]

---

1 Stocqueler, "Calcutta As It Is," 145; Stocqueler, *The Hand-Book of India,* 239. On the ābdār, also see Dewar, *In the Days of the Company*, 45-52. On the ice trade, see Susan S. Bean, "Cold Mine," *American Heritage* 42 (July/August 1991): 71-76, and David G. Dikason, "The Nineteenth Century Indo-American Ice Trade: An Hyperborean Epic," *Modern Asian Studies* 25 (February 1991): 53-89.

2 *Shrāb*, Hindustani for "wine," *Hobson-Jobson*, 831.

3 Hart, *Old Calcutta*, 23.

4 Williamson, *East India Vade-Mecum*, provides a detailed description of the process. Also see Abdar, in Henry Grant and Edward Colebrooke, *The Anglo-Hindoostanee Hand-Book*; and Roberdeau, 114, in Nair, *Calcutta in the 19th Century*, 41.

II.128. Bāwarchī. Cook

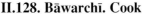

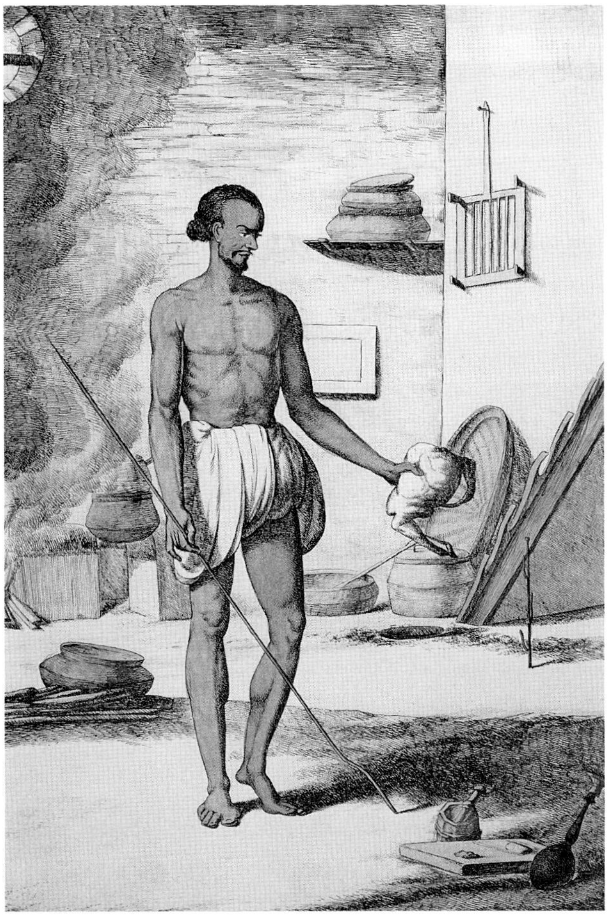

Paris: IV.5.6. BAWERCHEE, COOK: This is the servant of the house who has the most business, his employment of cook is the most painful and fatiguing, on account of the variety and nice preparation which the tables of the rich require in India, to which may be added the heat of the climate and the bad construction of the kitchens, in which there is mearly an opening to let out the smoke. The drawing gives the interior of a kitchen with a *Bawerchee* putting a piece of meat on the spit: at his feet is a stone for brusing pepper, and a morter for pounding spices, two utensils indispensible in indian cookery: there is also a machine for cleaning rice and *cudjeric* [*khicuṛī*] pots for boiling it. It gives also an idea of the manner of placing the fire, the stewholes, and such like objects.

The *Bawerchee* has frequently several assistants under him. They are addicted to drinking, and lead very dissolute lives.

Pl. II.128. Bāwarchī. Paris: IV.5.6.
Calcutta: Sec. II, No. 27. A Bawerchee or Cook.

Commentary: The bāwarchī (Anglo-Indian, "bobachee")[1] was the cook in European households in Bengal. Usually a Muslim, he prepared, in Williamson's words, "the most sumptuous dinners," though never tasted what he cooked.[2] Cooks might also be "Portuguese"[3] or Maghs, Arakanese, who after Solvyns's time came to be renowned among Europeans as "the best class of native cooks."[4] Hindus were less frequently employed as cooks in European households. From whatever background, however, the cook commanded a much superior status among household servants than suggested by the order in which Solvyns presents him.

The *bāwarchī-khāna* (Anglo-Indian, "bobachee connah") was the cook-house, or kitchen, detached from the residence in European households, with a covered walkway typically connecting the two.[5]

1 The Hindustani term is probably of Turkic origin. See *Hobson-Jobson*, 100.

2 *East India Vade-Mecum*, 1:236. Also, Stocqueler, "Calcutta As It Is," 141, and Stocqueler, *The Hand-Book of India*, 234-35.

3 Although including Indo-Portuguese Eurasians, the term "Portuguese" was loosely used to include native Christians. On the use of this term, see the Commentary for Pl. II.6.

4 *Hobson-Jobson*, 594. Also see Colesworthy Grant, *An Anglo-Indian Domestic Sketch*, 106. On Maghs (or "Mugs"), see Pl. II.251.

5 *Hobson-Jobson*, 101; Lewis, 67. Williamson, *East India Vade-Mecum*, 235-42, provides a detailed description of the kitchen.

II.129. Methar. Male Sweeper

Pl. II.129. Methar. Paris: IV.6.1.

Calcutta: Sec. II, No. 35. A Mater—male Sweeper or Nightman.

Paris: IV.6.1. MATER: The employment of the *Mater* is the meanest in the house, it is to sweep and keep the necessaries clean. He is in such contempt, that the name of *pariah*[1] is applied to him, and the other servants, except the very lowest, such as the *Mushauljees* [maśālcī, Pl. II.120] *and Materannys,* will not deign to coverse with him. It is remarkable that they are ordinarily of a very robust frame, which proceeds probably from their good food, as they do not scruple to eat without distinction of whatever comes in their way. Besides the particular service of the house to which they belong, they are sometimes employed for the public, which makes their condition better than that of the other servants. I have seen some of them at the marriage of their children give very brilliant feasts, and dress them in shalls and other precious stuffs.

Commentary: The methar, male "sweeper" or scavenger, occupies the lowest rung in the hierarchy of domestic servants in Bengal. The methrānī (Pl. II.134) is the female sweeper and most frequently wife of the methar. The word *methar*, from the Persian for "prince," has been, according to *Hobson-Jobson*, "applied to the class . . . in irony, or rather in consolation. . . ,"[2] for they are "paraiahs." They are of the "untouchable" Hāṛi caste of Bengal (Pl. II.71) and constitute a specific Methar (or Mihtar) subcaste, which alone among the Hāṛi is employed in removing nightsoil. The equivalent sweeper caste in northern and western India is the Bhangī.

Solvyns's methar holds the basket and broom that are the implements of his occupation and the badge of his degradation. The broom, called a *jhāṛu* and much the same as that used by sweepers in India today, was in Bengal made of "the fibrous parts of the cocoanut and toddy tree leaves."[3] Williamson described them as also "made of bamboo, split to the size of a wheat straw, about thirty inches long, and tied together very firmly for about six or eight inches at one end. . . ."[4]

1 On Solvyns's use of the term, see Pl. II.22.
2 566. Also see Stocqueler, "Calcutta As It Is," 143.
3 Solvyns's 1799 *Catalogue* description for Methrānī (Pl. II.134). Also see Henry Grant and Edward Colebrooke, 65.
4 *East India Vade-Mecum*, 277.

II.130. Koṛābardār. Lash-Bearer

Paris: IV.6.2. CORAH-BURDAR: This servant is now seldom met with, many years may be past in India without seeing a single one. *Corah* in indian signifies a bulls nerve; the *Corah-Burdar* is a man hired to flog the servants. This punishment is very cruel, and seldom inflicted without causing almost immediate death. The hands and feet are tied to a long bambou, as in the print: at each stroke, the *Corah,* which is very long, passes through or four times round the body. The English government has suppressed this cruel instrument, and substituted to it, in the *Tannas* [*thānā*, police station] or courts of justice, the cat. It is only with the great men in India, and Europeans at a great distance from the courts of justice, that the *Corah-Burdar* is still among the servants of the household. During my long stay in India, I saw very seldom the *Corah* inflicted, and that only in parts where the mahometan laws were still in vigour.

Commentary: A *koṛā* is a whip or lash, and in his note to the original drawing, Solvyns describes it as "made of thread and leather." His reference to the word's meaning "bull's nerve" is unclear.

Pl. II.130. Koṛābardār. Paris: IV.6.2.

Calcutta: Sec. II, No. 29. A Corah-burdar, whose office it is to inflict punishment with the corah according to the Mahometan law,—but the principal figure is delineated with a cat, (which has been substituted by Government for the corah,) in his hand. **Orme: 26.**

II.131. Ayah. Nursery Maid

Paris: IV.6.3. AYAH: We shall now speak of the female servants. The first is the *Ayah,* that is the nursery maid. This servant is in every house of any fortune: she takes care of the children, and dresses the young ladies of the family. Her costume is the mussulmans, and consists of a peticoat, a jacket, and a drapery for the head; which she wears while in presence of her mistress, and to which there is sometimes a border of coloured silk. She wears, like all the indian women, a ring in her nose, and is constantly chewing bettel.[1] She is generally the wife of some servant of the house, and resembles them all in performing no other service than her own particular one, and being incapable of any attachment to her masters, whatever benefits she may have received from them.

Pl. II.131. Ayah, Nursery Maid. Paris: IV.6.3. **Calcutta: Sec. II, No. 32.** An Ayah or Waiting-woman, to European and Native Ladies.

Commentary: The Anglo-Indian term *ayah,* for native lady's-maid or (as here portrayed by Solvyns) nursery maid, is from the Portuguese *aia*, via its adoption in Indian vernaculars as *āyā*. In the European household in Bengal, with few women servants, she was usually the wife of one of the Muslim servants, often that of the khidmatgār (Pl. II.107), but she might also be Indo-Portuguese.[2] For the children of the European household in India, the ayah was the ever-present and caring attendant, as illustrated by D'Oyly, in *The European in India*.[3]

1 Betel (areca-nut) is chewed in a preparation called *pān*, described by Solvyns in Pl. II. 212.

2 Stocqueler, "Calcutta As It Is," 145. On the Indo-Portuguese, see Commentary for Pl. II.6. Williamson, Solvyns's contemporary in Calcutta, shared the disparaging judgment of the "Portuguese" generally held among Europeans: "Many Portuguese *ayahs* affect to be in possession of genealogies whereby it should appear they are lineally descended from most illustrious characters. . . ; she retains all the offensive hauteur of her progenitors, which being grafted upon the most obnoxious qualities of the Hindu and Mussulman characters, makes a *tout ensemble* as ridiculous as it is despicable!" Williamson, *East India Vade-Mecum*, 1:339-40.

3 Pl. 17, "An European Lady and her Family, Attended by an Ayah, or Nurse."

II.132. Ayah. Ladies' Maid

Paris: IV.6.4. ANOTHER AYAH: There are other females who fill the place of ladies' maid: they are the confidants of their mistresses, and attach vast importance to their employment. Some of them acquire such an ascendancy over them, that they become absolutely indispensible. It is true that they are in general very discreet, but their secrecy is always in proportion to the money and presents which they receive. They are mostly from upper Hindoostan, and are not so cleanly as those we have just mentioned. The one I have drawn has the mussulmans costume, wide drawers down to her feet, and a fuller drapery than the preceding *Ayah.*

Commentary: Solvyns portrayed the ayah in the Calcutta edition only as nurse-maid, but for the Paris edition he included "another ayah" as ladies' maid. The ayah often had a relationship of intimacy with the European women she served, but she was also frequently disparaged. "The ayah, or lady's maid, has no innate taste for dressing," wrote Stocqueler in the 1830s, "but can usually plait hair well, and contrives to fasten a hook, and to stick in a pin so that it will come out again."[1]

1 "Calcutta As It Is," 145. An even more disparaging view may be found in the *Asiatic Journal* of 1833, in Nair, *British Social Life in Ancient Calcutta*, note 53, "Ayah," 244-45.

Pl. II.132. Ayah, Ladies' Maid. Paris: IV.6.4.

II.133. Dāi. Wet-Nurse

Paris: IV.6.5. DYE, NURSE: This is the name of the nurse. The *Dyes* wear a particular dress, consisting of a red or blue drapery tied round the loins in form of a petitcoat. They are very indolent, and incapable of any other service. Though their food is much simpler than that of european nurses, they are very strong. In rich families every child has several servants under the orders of the *Dye*. The engraving represents the nursery in Hindoostan: in the second distance a *Dye* is sitting on a *moorah* [*moṛā*] or stool, made of bambou and joined with cordes; near her is a bed or rather a sofa with four pieces of wood, to bear the musquito curtain: with another little one for the child in the day time. The european ladies seldom suckle their children in India, and generally quit the country soon after their lying in, on account of the climate which is very unfavorable. I have however seen some european ladies enjoy excellent health there, after having had several children very healthy.

Pl. II.133. Dāi. Paris: IV.6.5.

Calcutta: Sec. II, No. 33. A Dye or Nurse.

Commentary: Solvyns makes no reference to the social class from which the dāi, or wet-nurse, was drawn, but they were generally of low status. Indo-Portuguese women were preferred, according to an account in the *Asiatic Journal* in 1836, but they were difficult to find, and the Muslim women who sought such service were of low class. Methrānīs (Pl. II.134) were sometimes employed, but this was deemed "very objectionable" because of their "pariah" caste.[1] Dāis also served as midwives.

1 In Nair, *British Social Life in Ancient Calcutta*, note 54, "Mehtaranee," 245-46. Risley, *The Tribes and Castes of Bengal*, Vol. II, Appendix I, 42, lists Dāi-Dom ("the men are day-labourers and the women serve as midwives") as a subcaste of the Dom (Pl. II.68).

II.134. Methrānī. Female Sweeper

Paris: IV.6.6. MATERANNY: The *Materanny* is the lowest servant in the house, and ranks with the *Mater* [methar], having nearly the same employment, to sweep morning and evening the appartments, courts, etc. Their caste is so base, that they are termed *pariahs,* and consequently do not think themselves obliged to observe all the formalities to which the Hindoos of higher castes adhere so strictly to in their way of living: they smoke the Hooka [*hukā*] with every body, drink water with the other servants, and eat without distinction of whatever comes from their masters table. There are some pretty women among the *Materannys,* and notwithstanding the extreme modicity of their wages they are tollerably well dressed; but it is often at the expence of their virtue, some of them being addicted to thiefing, and others in clandestine intrigues with the other servants of the house, which makes many persons prefer the service of a man in this station.

The brooms are made of filaments of the cocao or palm leaf. In some european houses, where cleanliness is a great object, there are in the apartments *picdannies* [*pikdāni*][1] or vases of copper or china, for loose papers or other dirt.

Pl. II.134. Methrānī. Paris: IV.6.6.

Calcutta: Sec. II, No. 34. A Matranny or female Sweeper, &c.—The Broom is made of the fibrous parts of the cocoanut and toddy tree leaves.

Commentary: The methrānī is the female sweeper or wife of the methar (Pl. II.129), and typically households employed both husband and wife in sweeping and in removing dirt and nightsoil. The methrānī attended particularly to the women's quarters, and traditionally they served as midwives[2] and sometimes as wet-nurses (dāi, Pl. II.133).[3]

1 The Bengali term refers specifically to a spittoon used for the betel juice spit out while chewing *pān* (Pl. II.212).

2 Risley, *The Tribes and Castes of Bengal*, 1:316.

3 On the methrānī's "pariah" status, see Nair, *British Social Life in Ancient Calcutta*, note 54, "Mehtaranee," 245-46.

Fakirs or Religious Mendicants

In the Calcutta edition, Solvyns includes ten etchings depicting "Faquirs." For the Paris edition, he places one of his subjects, the "Ooddoobahoo," in a scene with "other Faquirs" in a large format print and adds a new etching—"a faquir at his prayers." Two Solvyns drawings of religious mendicants that were never completed as etchings are illustrated in Chapter Three (Pls. I.35 and I.36).

Solvyns uses the term "faquir" (fakir), as was customary in his time, to mean Hindu holy mendicants. The word is from the Arabic *faqīr*, meaning "poor," and properly refers to a Muslim religious mendicant, but, as noted in *Hobson-Jobson*, in "the most ordinary Anglo-Indian use," it was "loosely and inaccurately" extended "to Hindu devotees and naked ascetics."[1]

Hindu ascetics were known to the Greeks as "gymnosophists" ("naked" sophists),[2] and the term had currency in the eighteenth century accounts of India. Another term in Anglo-Indian parlance was *gosāīn* (in various transliterations), meaning literally "lord of cows," but used to mean one who has subdued passion and renounced the world.[3] "Fakir," however, was the most commonly used term among Europeans in Solvyns's time and well into the twentieth century, as Churchill's abusive reference to Gandhi as a half-naked fakir reminds us.[4]

The inclusive term most widely used today for Hindu religious ascetics or holy men is *sādhu*, although *sannyāsī* and sometimes *yogī* (Anglo-Indian, jogee) are used to mean Hindu ascetics generally. "In their pursuit of the 'inner light', the liberation from all earthly bonds, the 'knowledge' of the Absolute, [sādhus] have chosen the way of asceticism and yoga. This implies a systematic 'reprogramming' of body and mind by various methods, such as celibacy, renunciation, religious discipline, meditation and austerities. The general term with which these methods are designated is *sādhāna*, literally 'the means of achieving a particular goal'"[5] The term, like *sādhu* itself, is derived from the Sanskrit root *sādh*, meaning to go straight, to the goal, to succeed.

Europeans from their first contacts with India were fascinated by these holy men (and sometimes women), and early accounts, often illustrated by engravings, are replete with descriptions of their austerities and character. The title page of the discourse on Hinduism by Dutch missionary Abraham Roger (d. 1649), for example, depicts vignettes of holy men undergoing austerities.[6] Jean Baptiste Tavernier (1605-1689), in his *Travels in India,* described an "infinite multitude" of fakirs in India, and an engraving depicts Hindu "penitents" under a banyan tree in self-inflicted tortures.[7] Tavernier's work, through many editions and translations, was among the most popular books of the seventeenth century.[8] The French engraver Bernard Picart (1673-1733), in 1729, published a print of a gathering of sādhus based on Tavernier's print and description, expanding the original scene to include a variety of other ascetics.[9] (See Pl. I.42.) François Bernier (1620-1688), in India from 1656 to 1668, describes, in his *Travels in the Mogul Empire*, the austerities of "an endless variety of *Fakires*."[10] Eighteenth century travelers Captain Alexander Hamilton,[11] Pierre Sonnerat,[12] and Thomas Pennant,[13] among others, describe fakirs in varying detail. Pennant includes engravings of two sādhus as the frontispiece to *The View of Hindoostan*, Vol. I, and refers to the Tavernier print in his accompanying description of the plate. In 1794, Thomas Maurice, in his *Indian Antiquities*, details "the horrible penances of the Indian devotees" and includes an engraving, "Hindoos in various attitudes of penance under the great banian tree of India," a copy of the Tavernier print.[14]

Indian artists of the Company School, principally from Murshidabad, had in the late eighteenth century included Hindu ascetics in their depiction of occupations and "types" in Bengal,[15] but Solvyns was the first artist—European or Indian—to attempt some systematic portrayal of the different types of sādhus, identifying them by name and, for the Paris edition, with descriptive text. In the nineteenth century, sādhus continued to attract European artists and later photographers, as they do today.[16] Indian artists, some influenced by Solvyns, catered to European interest with paintings depicting Hindu ascetics of all sorts.[17]

The Introduction to *Les Hindoûs*, Vol. II, provides a general discussion of Hindu ascetics. The text, drawing from European sources rather than from the artist's first-hand observation, is almost surely by Depping rather than by Solvyns.[18]

> A great part of the preceding volume [Vol. I] has been taken up with the Hindoo religion and the casts particularly devoted to the cares of worship, under the name of Brahmuns; but these, as it is well known, are not the only class of religious votaries; there exists in Hindoostan another sect, distinguished for ages past by the rigor of their devotion and the absurdity of their religious practices. These are the Faquirs, of whom the ancients speak under the appellation of *gymnosophists*. A description of this singular species of men will be found in the sixteenth and seventeenth numbers of this volume [Vol. II, portrayed below]; I will at present only say a few words upon the origin of their sect.
>
> Like the greater part of human institutions, that of the Faquirs may be traced to a pure origin, corrupted as it passed through the hands of men whose interest it was to alter its primitive customs, and fashion them to their own dispositions. In the ancient writings of the Hindoos we may learn what the Faquirs, *Jougies* [*yogīs*] or *Soonassees* [*sannyāsīs*] (for these three names are given to them) originally were. Among others, there are passages [6.1-8; 6.10-13] of the poem intitled *Phaquat geeta* [*Bhagavadgītā*],[19] which are sufficient to prove that it was by corrupting the precepts of the ancient sages that the Faquirs arrived at that strange sort of life by which they affect to distinguish themselves from the other Hindoos. "He is in reality a *Jougie* or a *Soonassee,*["] says the Brahmun author of that work, ["]who performs his duty without any interested motive, not he who lives inactive without the fire of sacrifice. Learn, son of *Pandas* [Pāṇḍu], that what men call *Soonassee,* or the renonciation of the world, is the same thing as *Jougie,* or the practice of devotion. He can not be a *Jougie* who in his actions is not free from all views of interest: actions are the means by which men who aspire to devotion may arrive at it; and repose is the means for the man who has attained devotion. When the contemplative *Soonassee* is not occupied by the objects of the senses, nor in action, he is then said to have arrived at devotion. His elevation should proceed from himself, and he should not suffer his soul to be depressed. He is himself his own friend as he is also his own enemy. He is the friend of him whom subdues his inclinations, and he delights in the hatred of him who has no soul.—The soul of the tranquil man whose inclinations are subdued, is the same in heat and in cold, in pleasure and in pain, in honour and in disgrace. The man whose mind is filled with divine wisdom and knowledge, who has raised himself to the summit of perfection, and who has subdued his passions, merits the appellation of devout or *Jougie*. He looks with the same eyes on gold and silver as on stone.—The mind of the *Jougie* is continually exercised in retreat: as he is abstracted from the world, his mind and his heart are in a state of calm; he is free from hope and free from outward perceptions. His seat is solidly fixed in a spot which is not sullied; neither too high nor too low; he sits on the sacred sod called *Cusa* [*kuśa*],[20] covered with a skin and a cloth. Such should be the seat of him whose aim is to subdue his passions: then fixing his mind upon one single object, he may give himself up to the practice of devotion for the purification of his soul, keeping his head, his neck, and all his body motionless, his eyes fixed upon the end of his nose, without ever looking round him."

It is evident that the precepts of the sacred writings, though enveloped in superstitious rites, are of a very moral tendency, and that the Faquirs have attached themselves meerly to these latter practices without paying much attention to the real sense of their moralists; they have taken up the letter and not the spirit of the law, and they imagine, or at least would make others believe, that their merit is in proportion to the pious extravagancies which they commit.

The most innocent of these follies is the profound meditation in which they are plunged without relaxation for whole hours together, the body without motion, the muscles stretched, the eyes immovably fixed on the end of the nose, to the very letter of what the sacred books prescribe. This tension of the mind is sometimes carried to such a height, that they become insensible to all that passes around them, and all their faculties are as it were absorbed in meditation upon the grand attributes of the Divinity or the beauties of the creation. Others keep their eyes closed during their long meditations; and the contorsions of their limbs and features betray the difficulty which they find to detach their mind from any other subject than that upon which they intend to meditate. They pretend that during these abstractions of the mind they fall into a sort of extasy or ravishment which renders them insensible to every terrestrial object, and during which they enjoy a pleasure which no mortal tongue can tell. Some Faquirs have attained such a degree of perfection in this sort of exaltation, that they pretend to have it in their power to procure themselves this delight whenever they please.

But the superstition of the Faquirs is not confined to these simple and absurd practices, which are innocent in comparison to the torments and macerations of which some of them make a merit in the eyes of the people. Former travellers have mentioned several sorts of voluntary pennance which these Faquirs inflict upon themselves; but no work upon this subject has as yet been complete: there still remained to be made known the differences between the several classes of the devotees, the attributions as well as the follies of each in particular, by classing them according to their sects, and taking care not to omit any of their principal divisions. I think I may presume to assert that I am the first who has given an accurate and full idea of this system of the Faquirs, which will be found consecutively in the sixteenth and seventeenth numbers of this volume, but so that each sect may be easily separated and distinguished from all the others.

On seeing such crowds of senseless fanatics, it may well be asked how it happens that so many persons in India embrace a mode of life so full of pains and hardships, and so contrary to sense and reason. But a little reflection will suggest that credulity, so natural to mankind, especially in these climates, and the great consideration of the populous every where for what is extraordinary, must attract great numbers, and that, moreover, the excessive indolence of the Hindoos must engage them to adopt any mode of life which promises them subsistance without labour. But there is another cause to which we may attribute the great prevalence of the Faquir sects throughout India: which is the permission granted by the law of the *Yajurreda* [*Yajurveda*][21] to every Hindoo who feels himself unhappy in his family to abandon it and divest himself of all domestic cares, provided however that he becomes a Faquir: and here again it is by an abuse of the letter of the law, that the Hindoos imagine that they may violate the most sacred rights. These are the words of the text of the *Yajurreda*;[22] "Restrain, o ignorant man, says Menou [Manu], the thirst of wealth, comprehend that there are no true riches but those of good actions proceeding from a pure soul.—What is thy wife? What is thy son? What is there great or wonderful in this world? Whence comest thou, and where art thou going?—Reflect, my brother, upon these subjects, and act according to thy reflections.—Cease to attach thyself to these illusions; they are the work of *Meya* [Māyā].—Place thy heart at the feet of Brahma, and thou wilst soon arrive at his divine knowledge.—Cease to be affected by the passions of love or hatred, by the fate of thy son or of thy parents, by war or by peace; view all these objects with the same calm and tranquillity of soul. If thou canst reach this state, thou wilst soon attain to the resemblance of a Vichnou [Viṣṇu]."

It is possible that the superstition which influenced the writings of Menou may have altered in this instance the general purity of his intentions; but it is certain that this law does not authorise the excesses into which the Hindoos have fallen in this respect, and which they even wish to have considered as meritorious in the eyes of the divinity. They have put upon the law their own interpretation, and it has become predominant. In this manner many customs unknown to antiquity are found established among the Hindoos.

The pennances of the Faquirs, however ancient they may be, do not appear to have been in their primitive institution either as frequent, or as cruel as they have since become. In the drama of *Sacoutala* [*Śakuntalā*],[23] where the author has introduced almost all the different conditions of human life, there is a pious Hindou devoted to the service of the divinity; but how different is this virtuous recluse from the fanatics who take the name of Faquirs? *Canna* [Kaṇva], the pious hermit, passes his days in the midst of a secluded forest, but he does not think himself exempt from the duty of being useful to his fellow-creatures. He practises towards them the most liberal hospitality; he takes care of animals and of plants: unbounded benevolence towards all that lives or vegetates is his predominant virtue: the most timid animals enter the dwelling of the benignant *Canna,* and partake without fear of the food which the good hermit offers them. *Sacoutala,* his adoptive daughter, and her companions raise the most beautiful flowers which they can find, and exercise a sort of sensibility in protecting their tender progress. Several disciples share his solitude and learn from the holy sage the principles and the practice of religion and morality. *Canna* calls them his sons, and *Sacoutala* is their sister; the greatest harmony reigns in this amiable family. All the travellers who visit it meet with a most friendly reception; their feet are washed, and they are regaled with flowers and fruits. *Canna* and the friends who reside with him follow the simple dictates of nature in their mode of life. Alas! why do not the Faquirs endeavour to imitate this model of mildness, piety and humanity, instead of subjecting themselves merely to the absurd practices prescribed in their books of devotion, such as exposing themselves to the rays of the sun, to storms, and to the excess of cold, seeking the most painful ways of moving, macerating their bodies, and undergoing all those voluntary torments of which the description is given in this volume? Is it not because they are sensible that a life so retired and such tranquil virtues are not so likely to draw the attention and raise the admiration of the crowd, and that, perhaps too, their weak minds are flattered with the hope of enjoying an eternal happiness superior to that of the vulgar? It is superstition and vanity that people India with its crowd of Faquirs, and that will probably long prevent the extinction of this senseless institution.

---

1 "Fakeer," *Hobson-Jobson*, 347.
2 *OED*; Dubois, 426.
3 *Hobson-Jobson*, 389.
4 Said on the occasion of the First Round Table Conference in London, 1930. See Fischer, 277.
5 Hartsuiker, 11. Also see Bedi and Bedi, 13-14. On sādhus generally, see Walker, 2:322-26; Ghurye; and Gross.
6 Roger's title page is reproduced in Lach and Van Kley, Vol. 3, Bk. 2, Pl. 196, with details in Pls. 199 and 200. Mitter also includes the title page, Pl. 23, and discusses the illustrations, 60-61. Picart, after Roger's vignettes, depicts "brahmin" austerities in *Ceremonies and Religious Customs* (1731), 3:357.
7 Among the various editions, there are at least two versions of the print. In some French editions (e.g., 1703, 2:422), it corresponds fully to the description in text. The print in the 1676 French edition (reproduced in Lach and Van Kley, Vol. 3, Bk. 2, Pl. 127) and 1678 English edition, however, omits the tiny "hut" in which a fakir has entombed himself for days without food or water and into which three Europeans (including Tavernier) peer. In the 1678 English edition, the description appears in Pt. 2, pp. 165-66; the print is opposite p. 166. Pennant, in the description of the frontispiece for Vol. 1, refers to the Tavernier print in the English edition, but later, 2: 306, mistakenly attributes it to Linschoten. Tavernier's descriptive text, alas without the engravings, is readily accessible as *Travels in India* (1889; 1977), 2:153-58. Also "Concerning Fakirs," 2:139-41.
8 Lach and Van Kley, Vol. 3, Bk. 1, p. 416.
9 The Picart engraving is reproduced in Mitter, *Much Maligned Monsters*, Pl. 35, Okada and Isacco, 58-59, and Hartsuiker, 18-19, with a description of the scene. In Hartsuiker, also see prints of the mortification of "keeping two arms raised," 11, and the "austerity of fire," 14. The Picart print, in *Ceremonies et coutumes religieuses* exists in several editions. Picart depicts other "penitents," *Ceremonies and Religious Customs* (1731), 3:357 and 3:430, and discusses their austerities, 3:430-34.
10 316. For his descriptions, 316-23. Lach and Van Kley describe Bernier's *Travels* as "probably the most original and popular account of India" in the 17th century. Vol. 3, Bk. 1, p. 414.
11 1:91-92.
12 *A Voyage to the East-Indies and China*, 1:164-177.
13 2:306-09.
14 Maurice, 5:72. The copy, without acknowledgment, is based on the engraving from the French edition.
15 See Mildred Archer, *Company Drawings in the India Office Library*, 59-72.
16 The six-volume photographic collection, *People of India* (1868), by Watson, includes portraits of sādhus. The best modern photographic essays on sādhus are Hartsuiker, and Bedi and Bedi.
17 Mildred Archer, *Company Drawings in the India Office Library*, "Ascetics" indexed, 288-89; Mildred Archer, *Company Paintings: Indian Paintings of the British Period*, "Ascetics" indexed, 236, "Fakirs," 237.
18 2:13-15. On Depping's role in the authorship of the introductions, see Chapter Two, pp. 65-67.
19 The *Bhagavadgītā* is an episode of the great Hindu epic, the *Mahābhārata*, recounting the dynastic war between the Pāṇḍavas and Kauravas. The first translation into English was by Charles Wilkins, *The Bhăgvăt-Gēētā, or Dialogues of Krēēshnă and Arjŏŏn* (1785). Wilkins (1749/50-1836) was among the first Europeans to acquire a knowledge of Sanskrit, and his translation of the *Gītā* was under the patronage of Warren Hastings, Governor of Bengal. Wilkins joined Jones in founding the Asiatic Society in 1784, and on his return to London, he became the first librarian of the India House Library. On Wilkins see Lloyd; Marshall, *The British Discovery of Hinduism*, 12-13; Buckland, *Dictionary of Indian Biography*, 451-52; and Kejariwal, 21-22.
The quotation corresponds to Wilkins's translation of Kṛṣṇa's lecture "On the Exercise of the Soul," 62-64, but it is not Wilkins, as indicated by the transliteration of such words as "Jougie" (Yogēē in Wilkins). As earlier with quotations from Jones and Colebrooke, Depping, the likely author here, may have translated Wilkins's text into French, with Solvyns's wife then translating it back into English. Depping, however, may have used the Abbé Parraud's, *La Bhagaut-Geeta, ou dialogues de Kreeshna et d'Arjoon*, the 1787 French translation of Wilkins's work. The French letterpress in Solvyns's Introduction corresponds, word for word, to portions of the Parraud translation, although there are differences in the spellings of some proper names as well as in the title itself.
20 The most sacred of Indian grasses, *kuśa* (*Por cynosuroides*), commonly called by the more general name *darbha*, is required in various Hindu rituals. See Dubois, 651-52, and B. A. Gupte, xxxv. That Depping worked from the French translation of Wilkins's *Gītā*, then translated back into English, is suggested by Wilkins's text, 63: The Yogēē "sitteth upon the sacred grass which is called *kŏŏs*, covered with a skin and a cloth."
21 One of the four Vedas, it is principally concerned with sacrificial ritual.
22 The quotations are not from the *Yajurveda*, but are perhaps from a later text attached to it.
23 The play *Śakuntalā*, by the greatest of Sanskrit poets, Kālidāsa (5th c.), was among the most important and influential European "discoveries" of India. Sir William Jones's first published translation from Sanskrit was *Sacontala; or the Fatal Ring* (1789).

II.135. Paramhaṃsa

Pl. II.135. Paramhaṃsa. Paris: II.4.2.

Calcutta: Sec. VII, No. 1. A Purum Hungse,—said to be descended from Heaven, to live without food, and to survive under water or earth, to the age of thousands of years. It is surprising with what credulity the monstrous absurdities related of him are believed by the Hindoos.

Commentary: The Paramhaṃsa is the highest of the four classes of ascetics devoted to the attainment of perfection and final liberation.[1] He "is believed to have attained such a stage of self-knowledge that routine distinctions and observances of the mundane world are not binding on him. He is believed to be so perfect in self-control that nothing can disturb him. He is so pure that nothing can contaminate him."[2] They are thought to be "indifferent to pleasure or pain, insensible of heat or cold, and incapable of satiety or want."[3] As Solvyns relates, they often appear not to eat at all—and, when they do, eat anything given to them.

They live under trees, as depicted by Solvyns, or in graveyards. In their meditation, they make no

Paris: II.4.2. PURRUM-HUNGSE, PENITENT.: In this and the following prints of this number, my intention is to describe a class of men very singular, and frequently met in the countries inhabited by the Hindoos. It is that of the Faquirs, a set of fanatics who exist without either property or attachment of any sort in the world : totally given up to devotion, living every where at other people's expense, and in general with a degree of respect bordering upon the most submissive veneration.

We shall begin by the species of Faquirs called *Purrum-Hungse,* who, in the belief of the superstitious Hindoo, is a man described from heaven, who lives thousands of years without taking the smallest nourishment, and who, thrown into the water or the fire, suffers no fatal effect from either. The truth of these ridiculous stories is, that a *Purrrum-Hungse* is never seen eating or drinking. I myself having seen one day a Faquir of this kind (the same I have represented here), sitting under a tree in the garden of a Hindoo famous for his piety, had the curiosity to observe him during the greater part of the day: he remained always in the same attitude, and almost without motion. Being obliged to retire, I ordered my servants, to continue observing him, and many hours after, they came and told me, that he was still in the same position. I do not know what took place during the night; but the day after, and the following days, I saw him in the same attitude and still as it were motionless. It was not till after five or six days that I was told that the *Purrum-Hungse* was no longer under the tree. Some Hindoos who were present assured me with great seriousness, that he was probably gone up again to heaven, from whence he had descended to visit this pious Hindoo. It is here too be remarked, that the reputation of a Hindoo is established from the moment a *Purrum-Hungse* condescends to enter his abode, and that he and his family are thenceforth in odour of sanctity throughout all the country. These Faquirs are therefore sure of being always received with the most profound respect. The people especially perform all sorts of mummeries around them, and there is no end to all the ridiculous ceremonies by which they compliment the holiness of their origin.

distinctions among worldly things, pure or impure, and may be either naked or, as here, clothed.[4]

A copy of Solvyns's portrayal of the Paramhaṃsa is shown in relief on one side of a small silver match case manufactured in the early nineteenth century in China for the Anglo-Indian market.[5]

1 Stutley, 219.
2 Ghurye, *Indian Sadhus*, 73. See Ward, *Account of . . . the Hindoos*, 3:415-19.
3 Horace H. Wilson, "Hindu Sects," quoted in Jogendra Nath Bhattacharya, 305. Also see Ward, *A View of . . . the Hindoos*, 3:410.
4 Stutley, 219; Ray and Gidwani, 3:196.
5 On the match case, see Chapter Three, p. 110.

II.136. Daṇḍī

Paris: II.4.3. DUNDEE. ANOTHER SORT OF FAQUIR: The name of *Dundee* which some Faquirs bear is derived from the Hindoo word *Dund*, which signifies a stick, or rather a switch, because they always have one with them. Walking, they carry it in their hand, and sitting, lay it at their feet, at the end of the mat or *cusa* [*kuśa*]. To the extremity of this *Dund* is fastened a small piece of red cloth. The *Dundee* is distinguished from the other Faquirs by his pretensions to an immediate communication with the divinity and his not offering any worship to the images or symbolical representations of their gods: which is the reason that they do not appear with the little string which all the other Brahmuns are obliged to carry.

The *Dundees* have a great reputation of sanctity, which procures them great honours wherever they are seen. They travel in bands of twenty, thirty, or even more; and generally make their establishment in the gardens of the rich Hindoos. As they do not pique themselves upon living without food, like the *Purrum-Hungses,* the garden is not long without feeling the effects of their visit. But the proprietors, so far from shewing any resentment, think themselves highly honoured by furnishing them any thing which they may require.

The head of these *Dundees* is generally a man of very great knowledge, especially in matters of divinity: when he takes his seat under a tree upon a little mat, with his *poytahs* [*pothī*] before him, crowds of Brahmuns gather round him and treasure up his instructions on the difficult or doubtful points of their religion. I also had recourse to one of the chiefs of the *Dundees* for information upon different objects in the religion and morals of the Hindoos: his answers were always satisfactory, and I must acknowledge that to him I owe a great many of the particulars contained in this work. The same *Dundee* had also in my presence many conversations with the celebrated Sir William Jones, who spoke of him as one of the wisest and best informed *pundits* he had met with. Whenever he came to pay me a visit, I was obliged to prepare a new cabbin (*Bungalou*) to receive him, a new palanqueen to convey him: in short it was necessary that every thing which he used during this visit should be new and have never served any other person. This is a dogma of their sect to which they adhere with great strictness.

Commentary: The Daṇḍī—literally one who carries a staff (*daṇḍa*)—is of one of the Śaivite Daśanāmi orders, followers of the philosopher Śaṅkarācārya, although the term is often used for any *sannyāsī* who carries the *daṇḍa*, symbolizing both spiritual power and restraint. Carried only by brahmins, it is both weapon and wand. The Śaivite *daṇḍa* is a single bamboo cane, while that carried by Vaiṣṇava ascetics is made of three bamboo sticks bound together.[1]

Solvyns depicts the Daṇḍī sitting on a mat of sacred *kuśa* grass.[2] To his right is a palm leaf book (*pothī*), what appears to be unbound leaves of sacred text, and what may be the small pillow that Daṇḍīs carry with them. In front are his pegged wooden sandals (*pādukā*) and, to one side, the water pot (*kamaṇḍalu*) and *daṇḍa*. Solvyns states that he lays the *daṇḍa* at his feet, as shown, but a later source states that it should be "stuck erect in the ground" or "suspended from a tree."[3]

The Daṇḍī wears a red-ocher colored *dhotī* and, following the rules of the order, his head and face are shaven. Only brahmins are permitted to become Daṇḍīs, but with initiation, they (as *sanyāsīs* more generally) discard the sacred thread of the "twice-born" in renunciation of worldly distinctions of caste.[4] According to Horace H. Wilson, the small red-ocher

Pl. II.136. Daṇḍī. Paris: II.4.3.

Calcutta: Sec. VII, No. 2. A Dundee,—a Brahmun who having cast off his thread and laid aside all regard to the personified attributes and symbolical representations of the Deity, worships him in spirit and unity,—the name is derived from Dund, a staff, which he always carries in his hands.

cloth attached to the *daṇḍa* contains the discarded thread,[5] but normally the thread is not retained, and the red cloth is used to strain and purify water.

In his note to the original drawing, Solvyns writes that the Daṇḍī "can not remain two days in the same place, or eat two days from the gifts of the same person, who should be a Brahmun, neither can he make use of anything that has been used by another." In the Paris text, Solvyns's reference to the garden should not be taken to mean that Daṇḍīs help themselves to the vegetables and prepare their own food. They are, in fact, forbidden from cooking their own food, but take it prepared once a day from brahmin households.

The prohibition on the use of fire extends to cremation, and Daṇḍīs, as most other sādhus, bury their dead or commit the body to a sacred river.[6]

1 Ghurye, *Indian Sadhus*, 71-72; Ray and Gidwani, 2: 12, 2: 20-21; Sherring, 1:258; Jogendra Nath Bhattacharya, 300-02; and Hartsuiker, 55, 89. The Rev. Ward, describes the Daṇḍī very much as does Solvyns, his contemporary in Bengal, but identifies them as Vaiṣṇavas. *A View . . . of the Hindoos*, 3:408-09. Also see Ward, *Account of . . . the Hindoos*, 3:419-24. Although traditionally of bamboo, Śaivite *daṇḍas* may also be of wood.

2 On *kuśa*, see fn. 20 in the introduction to the section on Faquirs and Religious Mendicants, p. 313.

3 Oman, *The Mystics, Ascetics, and Saints of India*, 160-62.

4 On discarding the sacred thread, see Hartsuiker, 90.

5 "A Sketch of the Religious Sects of the Hindus," in *Essays and Lectures*, 1:193. Also see Garrett, 154-55.

6 Horace H. Wilson, "A Sketch of the Religious Sects of the Hindus," in *Essays and Lectures*, 196.

II.137. Sannyāsī

Commentary: The term *sannyāsī* ("renouncer") broadly refers to religious ascetics—who in Solvyns's time were also frequently called *gosāins*, "those who have control over their senses." In the context of the four stages of life (*āśrama*), however, *sannyāsīs* are those persons who, having fulfilled the duties of the householder, enter the fourth and last stage of life as a wandering religious mendicant.[2] More specifically still, the term applies to the Śaivite ascetics of the Daśnāmi ("ten name") orders that include the Daṇḍīs, Brahmacārīs, and Nāgas,[3] and Solvyns focuses on one class of these, the Nāga warriors.

The Nāgas, also known as *astradhārī* (fighting) Daśanāmi *sannyāsīs*, first arose in the middle ages as the defenders of the faith. Organized in brigades, with gymnasiums (*akhādās*) as centers of military training, they were at the forefront of Hindu resistance to Muslim invaders, even as some among them hired out as mercenaries for the other side. Sometime between 1650 and 1700, Vaiṣṇavas joined the resistance with their own "Nāga" brigades, battling Śaivite rivals as well as Mughal armies.[4]

In the later half of the eighteenth century, with Mughal rule in decline and British administration not yet fully established, these warrior ascetics, principally the Śaivite Nāgas, formed the nucleus for marauding

Paris: II.4.4. SOONASSEE: This also is a class of Faquirs, but more dangerous than the former: the *Soonassees* are not satisfied, like the Dondees, with the spoils of a garden: but, like true banditti, they march in numerous troops, attack the lonely proprietors in the country, steal, pillage, and commit every sort of violence and devastation. These vagabonds are always armed: they paint half their face and some parts of their body, and let their beard and hair grow without ever combing them. Their thick locks flowing disorderly, and covered besides with mud or coloured earth, give them a dark and savage appearance. They carry in their hands a stick and a *tillie*[1] or little brazen pot, to supply themselves with water.

The Hindoo religion prescribes to the *Soonassees* never to sleep but under the shade of a palm-tree: and this is the only precept which they observe strictly; all the others they dispense with at will. They affect celibacy under a pretext of sanctity; but it is no curb to their libertinism and debauchery.

Wherever they appear, rice and other provisions are offered to them voluntarily, as means of escaping from their violence, which is the more to be feared as they are generally of an uncommon strength and size. In times of anarchy, the little Rajahs have been known to take bands of *Soonassees* into pay, and they have often attacked and pillaged whole districts. But the vigilance of the existing government prevents their meeting and disturbing the public peace. The *Soonassees* therefore become every day more rare, to the great satisfaction of the inhabitants of the country.

Pl. II.137. Sannyāsī. Paris: II.4.4.
Calcutta: Sec. VII, No. 6. A Soonassee,—these people travel armed in large bodies, and commit horrid depredations.

bands that ravaged the Bengal countryside and engaged the British in what came to be known as the "sannayāsī rebellion."

Large groups of mendicants, Hindu *sannyāsīs* and Muslim fakirs, had long wandered as pilgrims to visit shrines in Bengal. "Piety was mixed with trade and money lending, and the ascetics evidently expected to receive support from the countryside through which they passed. . . . To the British they were plunderers who must be prevented from pillaging Bengal, [and] Company servants acted on their beliefs, using force to block the passage of the *sannyasis* and break up their parties."[5] Nāga brigades led resistance, and with recruits from the lower castes, they first fought the combined forces of the British and zamīndārs in 1761, and in the following years, the "fakir raiders," as they were often called, periodically attacked British trading centers. It was the great Bengal famine of 1769-70 that brought uprooted peasants, both Hindu and Muslim, to the uprising. They were joined as well by "impecunious Zamindars deprived of their property and disbanded soldiers."[6]

In 1773, the Company Council at Calcutta reported to London that "A set of lawless banditti, known under the name of Sannyasis or Faquirs, have long infested these countries, and under the pretence of religious pilgrimage, have been accustomed to traverse the chief part of Bengal, begging and plundering wherever they go. . . ."[7] Another dispatch related that following the famine, "their bands were swollen by a crowd of starving peasants who had neither seed nor implements to recommense cultivation . . . ."[8] What had become fundamentally a peasant uprising, for the most part suppressed by 1802, remained officially a "sannyāsī rebellion."

The figure of the *sannyāsī* Solvyns portrays bears the sectarian *tilak* markings across the face and on the arms. Usually made of a mixture of white clay or sandalwood paste and sacred ash, the horizontal lines identify him as a Śaivite.[9] He wears a small cloth over the genitals, but Nāgas are often entirely naked, thus giving the order its name, for the word *nāga* (corruption of the Sanskrit *nagna*) itself means "naked." The *sannyāsī* is unshaven and has the long and matted hair (*jaṭā*) of the god Śiva.[10] Solvyns depicts another Nāga, identified as such, in Pl. II.144.

---

1 Possibly *patīlī*, meaning "pot."

2 Basham, *The Wonder That Was India*, 159-60, and Ghurye, *Indian Sadhus*, 70. On the four stages of life, see Olivelle.

3 Hartsuiker, 31; Jogendra Nath Bhattacharya, 302-04; and B. D. Tripathi, 68-76.

4 Bedi and Bedi, 74-79; Atis K. Dasgupta, 10-19. See Judanath Sarkar, *A History of Dasnami Naga Sannyasis*.

5 P. J. Marshall, *Bengal: the British Bridgehead*, 96.

6 R. C. Majumdar, *History of Modern Bengal*, 1:19. A. M. Chandra offers perhaps the best treatment of the Sannyāsī Rebellion as an agrarian uprising. As with most other modern historians, Chandra views the *sannyāsīs* as rebels against existing authority rather than as bandits plundering the land. Also see Atis Dasgupta, Jamani Mohan Ghosh, and Lorenzen.

7 Letter from the President and Council (Secret Department), Calcutta, to the Court of Directors, London, January 15, 1773, quoted in Atis Dasgupta, 59-60. The word *banditti*, which Solvyns also uses, was the common term used by the English to refer to all men who took to violence. Ranjit Sen, *Social Banditry in Bengal*, 17.

8 Letter from the President and Council, Calcutta, to the Court of Directors, March 1, 1773, quoted in Atis Dasgupta, 60.

9 Bedi and Bedi, 14.

10 Solvyns also portrays the *jatā* in Pl. II.143. The matted strands of hair, the *jaṭā*, are symbolic of the strength of Śiva, but Vaiṣṇava as well as Śaivite sādhus wear the *jaṭā* as a distinctive emblem of ascetic power. Hartsuiker, 84-85. On *jaṭā*, see Olivelle, "Hair and Society," 23-26. Ward describes the hair and the characteristics of the *sannyāsī* more generally in his *Account of . . . the Hindoos*, 3:429-32.

II.138. Baiṣṇab, Vaiṣṇava

Paris: II.4.5. BEESHNUB. A DEVOTEE: Beeshnub is the name given by the Hindoos to individuals who, after having renounced all the pleasures of life, the riches and good things of the earth, devote themselves to the worship of Vishnou, and consecrate the remainder of their days to the uninterrupted adoration of that divinity. Young people are seldom seen in this class of devotees: but it is frequently embraced by men of maturer age. It is not uncommon for fathers of families, after having amassed an immense fortune, and brought their house to the highest degree of prosperity, to renounce all of a sudden the whole of their possessions, and exile themselves voluntarily from their homes, to avoid the intrusion of temporal affairs upon preparations for a future life. Before they set out, they call together their children and nearest relations, and communicate to them the resolution which they have taken to take no more concern in the affairs of this world. They then cover their heads with a blue and red cap, clothe their bodies with a piece of linnen, take up a staff and a chaplet, and abandon all that was dearest to them. From opulent merchants, they become wandering pilgrims, without any sort of property, strolling from temple to temple, and existing upon the alms which common charity affords them. It is a just subject of surprise, that the followers of a religion such as that of the Hindoos should find in its dogmas motives sufficiently powerful to break all those strong ties which attach mankind so forcibly to this world. To Christians alone such sacrifices should appear possible. But we must recollect that the only dogma which can have an influence upon the Hindoos is doubtless that principle so conspicuous also in the Christian religion, the immortality of the soul and the hope of a better life. This is the doctrine of consolation which the devout Hindoo never loses sight of in devoting himself for ever to the worship of Vishnou. This salutary persuasion elevates his soul to a nobler and more sublime object, and makes him a model of resignation, of piety and of sanctity.

Commentary: The term Vaiṣṇava (or Baiṣṇab) broadly includes all Hindus who worship Viṣṇu, the Preserver, in his many forms and incarnations, such as Kṛṣṇa and Rāma. But it also refers to members of the ascetic Vaiṣṇava sect, commonly known by the name Bairāgī," meaning "detached."[1]

Solvyns's respect for the Baiṣṇab is evident both in the text and in his portrayal. In Bengal,

Vaiṣṇavas are most commonly devotees of Kṛṣṇa. They wear white, as Solvyns depicts, in contrast to the Śaivite ocher, and are identified readily by the vertical marks of the *tilak* on the forehead.[2] The Baiṣṇab fingers the "rosary" beads of a *japamālā*, which for Vaiṣṇava are of *tulsī* wood, sacred to Viṣṇu. With each bead, usually in a string of 108, a holy number,[3] but as many as a thousand, he recites a *mantra* or repeats the name of the deity. It is through *japa*, muttered prayer, often involving the endless repetition of the god's name, that salvation is attained.[4]

The Orme text relates that "At some of their religious ceremonies, they recite the history of their God and his family. Their musical instruments, the Baunk [bā̃k, Pl. II.177], Mirden [mṛdaṅga, Pl. II.158], and Kirtaul [kartāl, Pl. II.171], are played on at intervals; and the audience, according to the subject, are exalted with joy or depressed with grief, and weep, prostrating themselves on the ground, embracing the reciting Vishnoo, and depositing money at his feet."

1 Risley, *The Tribes and Castes of Bengal*, 2:340-45, and Hartsuiker, 55. On Vaiṣṇavism in Bengal, see Ramakanta Chakravarti.

2 On the Vaiṣṇava *tilak*, see Bedi and Bedi, 14-19.

3 108 is a "mystical number comprising the seven planets and the two phases of the moon, i.e., 9, multiplied by the 12 signs of the zodiac, and symbolizing the whole heavens. There are said to be 108 shrines of special sanctity, 108 Upanishads, 108 beads in the Śaivite rosary." Walker, 2:137.

4 Hartsuiker, 89-90.

Pl. II.138. Baiṣṇab, Vaiṣṇava. Paris: II.4.5.
Calcutta: Sec. VII, No. 7. Beeshnub, worshipper of Vistno [Viṣṇu], the preserving attribute of the Deity.
Orme: 42.

II.139. Nānak Panthī

Commentary: In the broadest sense, Nānak Panthī refers to the followers of Guru Nānak—the Sikhs. But Solvyns here describes an order of mendicants, and although he notes the respect in which they are held by Sikhs, he does not identify them as Sikhs.
According to historian H. W. McLeod, the term Nānak-panthī was used principally for non-Khālsā Sikhs, and there were many of them in various sects in the late eighteenth century. McLeod suggests that the Nānak-panthī depicted by Solvyns may have been a member of one of the Udāsī orders. The name Udāsī is from the Sanskrit *udāsīna*, detachment, and was taken by the followers of Srī Chānd (by tradition, 1494-1612), eldest son of Guru Nānak. These ascetics were distinguished from the militant Khālsā Sikhs (depicted by Solvyns, Pl. II.51) by their renunciation of the world, their celibacy and rejection of such practices as keeping their hair and beard uncut. Among the Udāsī orders, numbering more than a dozen, there was neither uniformity in doctrine nor organization.[1] But Solvyns's description does not correspond with any of the groups known to McLeod. The representation of the "Nanuk-Punthy" as having only half a mustache and one shoe is baffling, as is the reference to the turban being covered with "a sort of network of wire" and the two silver bells hanging from the turban above the left ear. McLeod concludes that Solvyns must have "encountered a rather peculiar kind—and the practice of striking sticks together further supports this."[2]

A possible explanation for the Nānak-panthī's wearing only one shoe, however, may be in connection to a story related by the Rev. William Ward, Solvyns's

Paris: II.4.6. NANUK-PUNTHY: The Faquirs who go by the name of *Nanuk-Punthys* are very different, and much more peaceable than those of which we have just been speaking. Their outward appearance offers something striking, not to be met with among any of the other Faquirs; which is caused by their wearing only one whisker and one shoe. The origin of so strange a custom still remains unknown to me, notwithstanding all my endeavours to discover it. Every Faquir of this class has his turban covered with a sort of network of wire, of which also he wears a kind of cord as a collar round his neck. To the left side of the turban, above the ear, are fastened two little bells of silver. The *Nanuk-Punthy* carries besides in each hand a stick which he is continually striking together, reciting at the same time, with a most extraordinary volubility of tongue, a *Durnah* or text of the Hindoo legend. There is a pretty ample description of this *Durnah* or text in the third volume of the Memoirs of the Society of Calcutta. These Faquirs are persuaded that this pious trick gives them an incontestable claim upon the charity and beneficence of all those upon whom they intrude their endless declamations; to which, as often as they are disappointed, curses and reproaches succeed with equal volubility. They pretend to have a warrant for this in the precepts of their sect; and we must remember that the Hindoos feel more hurt by reviling language than by any other sort of ill treatment.

Some of the *Nanuk-Punthys* choose the markets and public places for the theatre of their perpetual harangues: others go from house to house, from shop to shop, striking their sticks together and pouring forth their declamations, untired and incessant, excess in the well filled intervals of scolding. This is their trade, the profession they have embraced for life. They are in other respects quiet in their demeanour, and are even treated with some degree of respect, especially among the Sics and the Mahrattas.

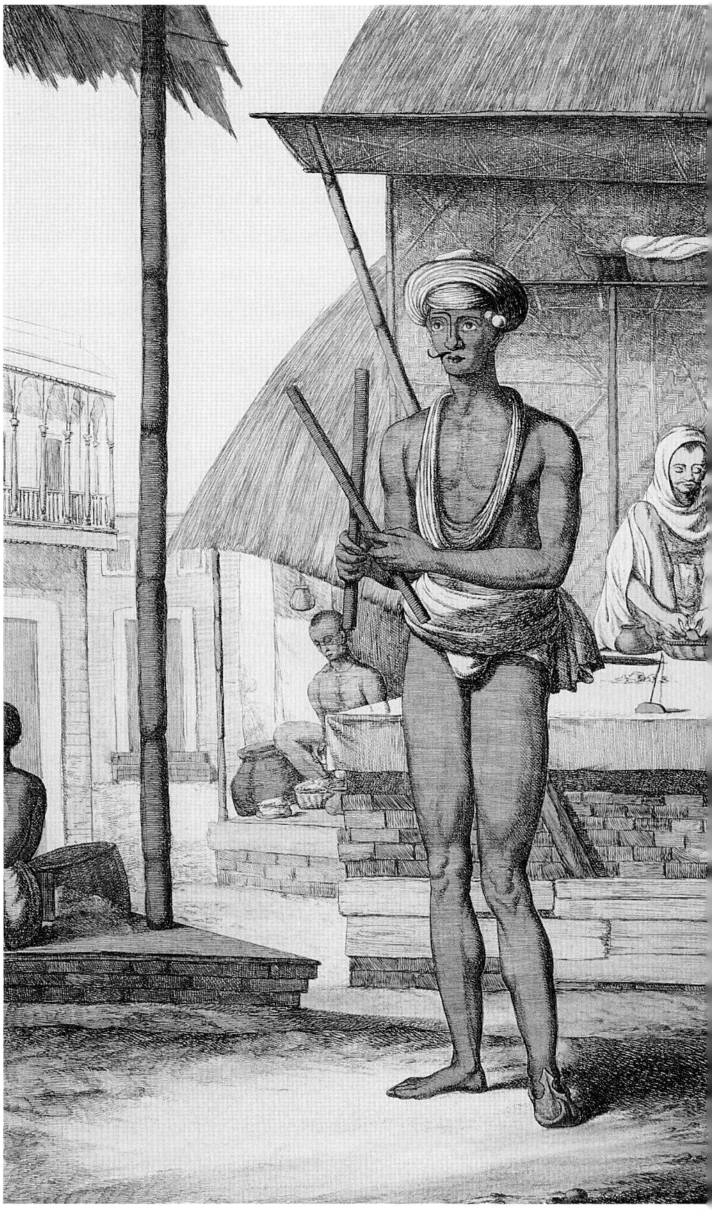

Pl. II.139. Nānak Panthī. Paris: II.4.6.

Calcutta: Sec. VII, No. 8. A Nanuk-Punthy,—a sectary formed by Nanuk, and are remarkable for wearing one shoe only and shaving one mustache,—he is represented setting in Durnah [*dharnā*], a religious fraud, an account of which is given in the 3d volume of the Asiatic Researches, in Article 22, on some extraordinary Facts, Customs, and Practices of the Hindoos.

contemporary in Bengal. In writing of the sect, Ward describes its founder, "a Sikh named Soot'hara," as having protested the Mughal government's ban on the wearing of religious marks on the forehead by having two pair of shoes, ten feet long, made and placing one of them at the shrine of a Muslim saint. The keeper of the shrine declared the shoe to have fallen from heaven and took it to the emperor, who blessed it as a precious relic. "Soot'hara hung the other shoe up on a pole, and went all over the neighbouring country, declaring he had lost his shoe." The emperor came to hear of this and summoned the devotee and inquired how he came to own such a shoe. When Soot'hara's foot miraculously enlarged to fill the shoe, "The astonish emperor, full of admiration at Soot'hara, desired him to ask any favour he chose. The devotee asked permission, that his Hindoo countrymen might wear the marks of their religion on their foreheads, and that his disciples [Nānak-panthīs] might be permitted to obtain a half-penny from each shopkeeper where they went to beg. The emperor granted his requests." Ward then makes reference to the sticks. "Some of these devotees carry two round sticks along with them, and sing to the sound of these two sticks the praises of Nanuku."[3]

Solvyns's reference to "durnah" is most curious. He writes of the "Nanuk-Punthy" reciting "a *Durnah* or text of the Hindoo religion," but then refers to a description in the journal of the Asiatic Society. The reference is more specific in Solvyns's brief entry for the 1799 *Catalogue* accompanying the Calcutta edition of the etchings. There, he describes the figure as "represented setting in Durnah, a religious fraud, an account of which is given in the 3d volume of the Asiatic Researches, in Article 22, on some extraordinary Facts, Customs, and Practices of the Hindoos." The article appeared, not in the third volume, but in the fourth, 1795, and describes Solvyns's "fraud" as a form of extortion where the supplicant "sets down in *Dherna*" before a person's house and there threatens suicide or engages in fast and "completely arrests him . . . until the institutor of the *Dherna* obtains satisfaction."[4] The article makes no reference to "Nanuk-Punthy."

Writing in 1843 of his years in Calcutta, an Englishman observed that "The practice of squatting down *dhurna*, till the favour solicited is obtained has long fallen into desuetude, and is indeed, declared illegal by a government regulation. . . ."[5] *Dharnā*, however, is used today as a political weapon: demonstrators sit before the home or office of an offending party and may threaten "fast unto death" to secure their demands.[6]

Solvyns's text description of the turban as covered by a "network of wire" is not evident in the etching, and it is surely unlike the turban of the zealous Akāli Nihangs, who wear a large, conical blue turban encircled by razor-edged steel quoits.[7]

Altogether, Solvyns's portrayal of the Nānak Panthī is very odd—one whisker and one shoe, the peculiar turban, the striking of sticks, and the "pious trick" of *dharnā*. What sort of Nānak Panthī could Solvyns have been describing, or was this person a Sikh at all?[8]

---

1 McLeod, *Historical Dictionary of Sikhism*, 214-15. Also see Oberoi, 78-80, and John Clark Archer, *The Sikhs*, 227-28.

2 Letter to the author, December 16, 1994. Published descriptions of Sikh ascetics provide nothing to verify Solvyns's portrayal. Horace Rose's description of the Udāsī, for example, bears no resemblance to Solvyns's account. Moreover, Rose describes Udāsī ascetics as wearing red or going entirely naked, at odds with Solvyns's depiction in the etching, although there may well have been considerable variation in appearance among the various Udāsī orders. 3:479-81. There is a faint resemblance in Solvyns's description to the Suthrā Shāhi order of Sikh devotees. Some among them carry a *daṇḍa* (staff) with which they strike their iron bracelets. They claim to be Udāsīs and live by begging, but, although possible, it would seem unlikely that Solvyns would have encountered someone from so small an order. See Dogra and Mansukhani, 457.

3 *Account of the . . . Hindoos,* 3:437-39.

4 Shore, 4:330-31. The author again discusses the practice, with the spelling "Dhurna," in a note at the end of the article, 4:346-48. On *dharnā*, see *Hobson-Jobson*, 315, and Lewis, 101.

5 George Johnson, 1:127-28.

6 See Hardgrave and Kochanek, 218.

7 The quoits, *chakkars*, are described by Dogra and Mansukhani, 344 and 378. The Akālis are vividly portrayed in two similar Company School paintings, c. 1860, in Welch, pl. 57, pp. 128-29, and in Mildred Archer, *Company Paintings: Indian Paintings of the British Period*, pl. 162, p. 173. The Akāli Nihangs are also portrayed in Kang, 118-34.

8 For an expanded discussion of Solvyns's Nānak Panthī and Khālsā Sikhs (Pl. II.51) and portrayal of Sikhs by European artists in the nineteenth century, see Hardgrave, "An Early Portrayal of the Sikhs: Two Eighteenth Century Etchings by Baltazard Solvyns."

II.140. Udbāhu, Ūrdhvabāhu

Pl. II.140a. Udbāhu. Calcutta: Sec. VII, No. 10.

Pl. II.140b. Udbāhu and Other Faquirs. Paris: II.5.1. **Calcutta: Sec. VII, No. 10** [depicting the Ooddoobahoo only]. An Ooddoobahoo, who inflicts himself with pain and intolerable austerities, under the idea of its being acceptable to the Deity,—some keep their limbs in particular positions, until the sinews and joints become immovable, others chain themselves to trees, sleep on a bed of pointed iron spikes, and subject themselves to other almost incredible torments.—An account of two of these Faquirs, by the present Governor of Bombay, is inserted in the 5th Volume of the Asiatic Researches.
Orme: 43.

Commentary: In the Calcutta edition, the udbāhu is depicted as a separate figure, while for the Paris edition, Solvyns places the same figure among other sādhus practicing their various austerities (*tapasya*) outside the compound of a temple complex.

Udbāhu (also *ūrdhvabāhu*) means literally one with upraised arm or arms, and the term is used for ascetics—also called *ek-bāhu* ("one-arm") *bābās*—who vow to keep the right up for twelve years or more, the longer the greater the merit. Initially, during the night, the arm may be tied to a bamboo support until it grows rigid and can no longer be lowered to its natural position. Uplifted, the arm atrophies to become no more than a useless stick, and the nails grow long and twisted, sometimes, in a closed fist, pushing into and through the hand. On fulfillment of the vow, according to Ward, an udbāhu "anoints the joints with clarified butter, and in about two months, by degrees, the arm obtains its former position, and in time becomes as strong as before."[1]

Tavernier, in 1676, was among the first Europeans to describe the udbāhus—"penitents who, till death, keep their arms elevated in the air, so that the joints become so stiff that they are never able to lower them again. Their hair grows below their waist, and their nails equal their fingers in length. Night and day, winter and summer, they remain stark naked in this position, exposed to the rain and heat, and to the stings of mosquitoes, without being able to use their hands to drive them away."[2]

In the original drawing for the Calcutta etching and in the expanded scene in the Paris edition, the udbāhu is portrayed with his left, ritually "unclean," arm raised, The Calcutta etching, in its mirror image, depicts the ascetic with his right aloft.

Solvyns portrays the udbāhu in both the Calcutta and Paris prints with a shawl of ocher color,

Paris: II.5.1. OODDOOBAHOOS AND OTHER FAQUIRS: One cannot behold without astonishment the ingenuity of the superstitious Hindoos in refining upon the ways of torturing themselves, and rendering their lives painful; and all that, to please the divinity. In the foregoing number, we past in review some classes of Faquirs; but they were reasonable people in comparison of those whose extravagancies are to form the subject of this plate. In the foreground are two Faquirs called *Ooddoobahoos:* one of them holds up his arm continually extended in the air; the other keeps his two hands joined over his head without ever separating them, so that the nails of his fingers grow till they enter into the flesh of his arms. Still unsatisfied with this horrid punishment, the same Faquir is also under a vow to hold for ever his legs across: to nourish himself in this inconvenient position, he must have the food put into his mouth.

It would really seem that there was a sort of rivality among them, to invent new tortures and punishments for themselves. The same plate represents a third, who is travelling from one temple to another, a distance frequently of some hundred miles, not on foot, but lying on his back, and making a little way, by rolling his body round. Not less extravagant than his companion, he at his right hand has made a vow to traverse a like distance, but in going constantly two steps backward for three that he goes forward. Farther on, is a Faquir who has caused himself to be chained to a tree, that he may continue in that painful attitude till his death. Near him is another, who has made it his duty to fix his eyes steadfastly all the remaining days of his life upon the sun, without ever taking them off during its whole course from rising to setting. At a little distance again from him are two others, one of whom lyes continually upon a bed stuck all over with iron points; the other passes his whole life reciting prayers, without one instant of interruption.

I could represent many other voluntary punishments of this kind, if I was not afraid of tiring the sensibility of my readers: for, who can see without indignation the cold and premeditated cruelties which this people, so mild in their natural dispositions, inflict upon themselves? Still in hopes of obtaining the favour of their gods and a life of happiness in the next world, as a recompense for their gratuitous sufferings in this, doubtless this is one of the most fatal effects of their doctrine of the transmigration of souls, or at least of the arbitrary sense in which they interpret them.

which would suggest that he is Śaivite, although he wears no *tilak* to identify his sect. Wilson writes that although many udbāhus go naked, some wear a wrap "stained with ochre" and "usually assume the Śaiva marks. . . ."[3] But Ward, as does Sherring later, identifies the austerity with Vaiṣṇava asceticism, and Fanny Park, seeing udbāhus at the Caṛak Pūjā in Calcutta in 1823, writes that "To fulfil some vow to Vishnoo this agony is endured, not as a penance for sin, but as an act of extraordinary merit."[4] It would thus seem that the austerity is practiced among both Śaivites and Vaiṣṇavas.

Udbāhus, as sādhus more generally, drew the interest of Indian painters of the Company School[5] and numerous European artists. The article in *Asiatick Researches* that Solvyns mentions in his 1799 Calcutta *Catalogue* is accompanied by a drawing of "Praun Poory Oordhbahu," described as "a *Sunyassy*, distinguished by the epithet of *Oordhbahu*, from his arms and hands being in a fixed position above his head. . . ."[6] Charles Gold, an English artist in Madras between 1791 and 1798, included among his *Oriental Drawings* a portrait of "A Female Devotee, of the Gentoo cast, doing penance by keeping her arm in an erect posture." His accompanying text describes in grisly detail the effects of her twelve-year vow on the woman's arm and nails.[7] Charles D'Oyly depicts an "Ordbhawn or Hindoo Fakeer," in a colored lithograph, c. 1830,[8] that Losty rightly describes as a "semi-caricatured" portrayal in contrast to the dignified "*urddhvabahu* ascetic" drawn by Jai Ram Das, one of D'Oyly's Indian assistants.[9] Colesworthy Grant, c. 1846, also includes an udbāhu among his lithographic portraits.[10] Modern portrayals of udbāhus are included in photographic collections on sādhus of India.[11]

Solvyns's Paris etching depicts a gathering of sādhus in various austerities reminiscent of the Tavernier/Picart engravings (Pl. I.42),[12] and it is likely that Solvyns may have seen these—or perhaps the version in Maurice, for Solvyns/Depping quotes from *Indian Antiquities* in his Introduction to the Paris edition. That the gathering of sādhus is included only in the Paris edition, however, suggests that, if Tavernier/Picart was the inspiration, he may have seen the print only after completing the Calcutta etchings.

Solvyns, of course, might have seen such a gathering at Sagur Island, at the mouth of the Hugli River, where his contemporary, the Rev. William Ward, observed a variety of Hindu ascetics, including an udbāhu, who had come together to practice their austerities.[13] Without attribution, a crude copy of Solvyns's Paris etching is included in the 1824 abridgment of Ward's *A View of the History, Literature, and Religion of the Hindoos* to illustrate these religious austerities.[14] Earlier, Ferrario included a copy of Solvyns's etching in his *Il Costume antico e moderno* (1816).[15]

An original watercolor of the "Ooddoobahoo" by Solvyns was included in the album of 40 drawings assembled by his widow, Mary Ann Greenwood.[16] The collection was broken in the 1980s, and William K. Ehrenfeld acquired the udbāhu. It is handsomely reproduced, with notes, in *Interaction of Cultures: Indian and Western Painting, 1780-1910: The Ehrenfeld Collection*.[17]

1 Ward, *A View . . . of the Hindoos*, 3:411, 3:409fn. Also see Ward, *Account of . . . the Hindoos*, 3:425-26; Oman, *The Mystics, Ascetics, and Saints of India*, 46; and Hartsuiker, 114.
2 *Travels in India*, 2:157.
3 Horace H. Wilson, "A Sketch of the Religious Sects of the Hindus," in *Essays and Lectures*, 1:234-35. In the photograph in Hartsuiker, 116, the udbāhu wears an ocher-colored shirt.
4 Ward, *A View . . . of the Hindoos*, 3:411; Sherring, 1:266; and Park, in Nair, *Calcutta in the 19th Century*, 256.
5 For example, Mildred Archer lists four paintings of "urdhvabahus" in *Company Drawings in the India Office Library*, 63, 69, 80, 161.
6 Duncan, 37.
7 Pl. 7.
8 From D'Oyly's *Costumes of India*, Patna, 1830, in Losty, "Sir Charles D'Oyly's Lithographic Press and his Indian Assistants," Fig. 23, p. 158.
9 Losty, "Sir Charles D'Oyly's Lithographic Press and his Indian Assistants," Fig. 22, p. 156. See 151, 157. A copy of D'Oyly's print by an Indian artist, probably Bani Lal, Patna, c. 1880, is illustrated in Mildred Archer, *Company Paintings: Indian Paintings of the British Period*, No. 67, p. 94.
10 *Sketches of Oriental Heads*, Pl. 50, "Sunyassee."
11 Hartsuiker, 116; and Bedi and Bedi, 44-45.
12 On the Tavernier and Picart prints, see the introduction to the section on Faquirs or Religious Mendicants," p. 309.
13 *A View . . . of the Hindoos* (1822), 3:401-16.
14 Ward, *A View of the History, Literature, and Religion of the Hindoos*, 370.
15 *Asia*, Vol. II, No. 28.
16 On the album of drawings, see Chapter Three, pp. 83-85.
17 Bautze, 52-55, Pl. 3.

II.141. Avadhūta

Commentary: *Avadhūta* means one who has "shaken off" worldly attachment, and the name is used to describe ascetics who are "beyond all restriction" or who have "dispelled all imperfections."[1] They include both householders (*kulāvadhūta*) and recluses. Ghurye writes that "they may be stark naked or may use a small strip of cloth to cover their privities. But they wear matted hair and are not shaved." As Tantric ascetics, "Their indifference to rules of observance may carry them to the extreme of taking intoxicating drink and eating meat."[2] In Bengal, Rāmānandīs and Nāgas are known by the name, and, although a distinct group, bāuls are sometimes called "avadhūtas."[3]

Of various orders, avadhūtas are distinguished by their appearance, as Solvyns portrays in this etching and in an earlier watercolor in the collection of the India Office Library.[4] Solvyns's figure holds a back-scratcher and a cloth bag, perhaps a *gomukhā*[5] for his rosary beads. He wears a Vaiṣṇava sect mark on his forehead, but instead of tulsī beads, sacred to Viṣṇu, the necklace he wears appears to be *rudrākṣa*[6] sacred to Śiva, and another strand encircles his turban.

The central figure of the avadhūta in the Calcutta etching wears a loin cloth, while that of the Paris edition stands naked. More intriguing in the difference between the two etchings is Solvyns's addition to the background of the Paris etching, where he portrays a group of five women gathered around a naked avadhūta. The "indecent" manner by which the women pay homage to him—and which delicacy forbids Solvyns to describe—is depicted, with a woman kissing the advadhūta's penis as he blesses her with his hand upon her head. Similarly, Picart in his 1729 engraving (Pl. I.42) depicts a gathering of ascetics in which a kneeling woman is shown kissing the penis of a naked sādhu.[7]

1 Monier-Williams, 100; Sherring, 1:266; Narendra Nath Bhattacharyya, 30; and Ghurye, *Indian Sadhus*, 77.
2 Ghurye, *Indian Sadhus*, 77.

Paris: II.5.2. AB'DHOOT, A PENITENT NAKED: I have still to describe many singular sorts of Faquirs or devotees, to which I shall give up the remainder of this number; beginning with the *Ab'dhoot,* who attracts notice by the frightfulness of his exteriour appearance, as the engraving shews. A horrible air seems to be the great object of all the Faquirs, or to make at least an impression upon the multitude by any means. The *Ab'dhoots* obtain this end by painting their faces and their bodies in the strangest manner, but always differently from any other Faquirs; for every class of them has its peculiar mode of painting, of arranging the turban, the beard and the several parts of their adjustment. An *Ab'dhoot* is particularly careful not to resemble in his outward appearance to a *Soonassee,* as this last would not on any account resemble him or any other Faquir.

The *Ab'dhoots* generally go together in bands, and are cleanly and well made. The one I have drawn has in his hand a little stick, one end of which is carved into the shape of a hand: this serves him to scratch the different parts of his body. The *Ab'dhoots* are remarkable for the great veneration and blind confidence with which they inspire the women, who implore them that their marriages should not prove sterile: but the manner in which this hommage is paid is so disgusting and indecent, that delicacy forbids to describe it. I must however say that the *Ab'dhoot* remains insensible to all these marks of extravagant adoration, and distributes quietly his benedictions among the women, without ever abusing of their excessive confidence. They are generally married, and have many children.

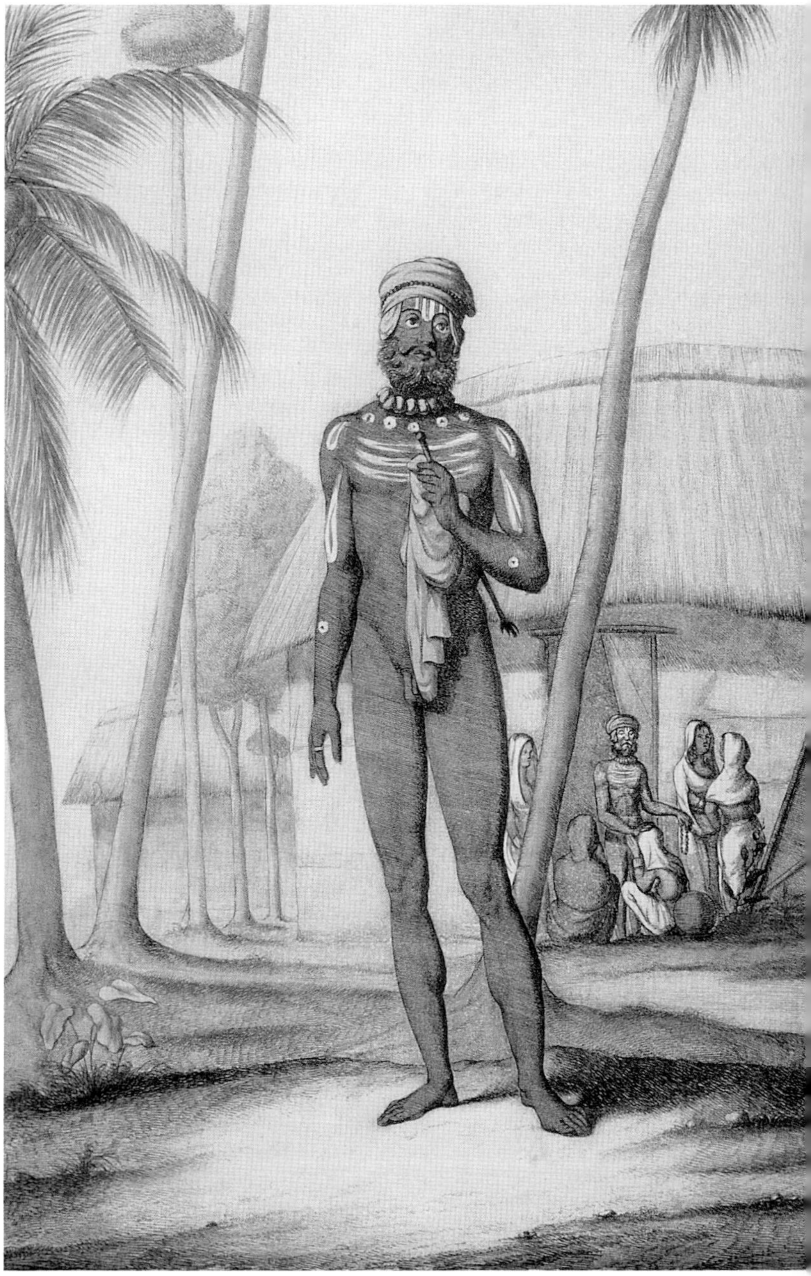

Pl. II.141. Avadhūta. Paris: II.5.2

Calcutta: Sec. VII, No. 5. An Ab'dhoot,—a sect of Faquirs, that sometimes go intirely without cloaths.

3 Bedi and Bedi, 70; Ray and Gidwani, 1:154. Garg describes various types of avadhūta, 3:823.

4 The pencil and watercolor drawing, c. 1795, is from an album of drawings assembled by the artists widow and is illustrated in the India Office Library and Records, *Annual Report 1985-86*, p. 31. It is one of four drawings from the album purchased by the India Office Library in 1986, Acquisition number WD 4123. Kattenborn, 294. On the album, see discussion of Solvyns' life and work pp. 83-85.

5 See Commentary for Pl. II.18

6 Ibid.

7 Although the scene is modestly portrayed, the copy of the engraving for the later, English edition removes the woman, leaving the scene otherwise unchanged.

II.142. Rāmānandī

Pl. II.142. Rāmānandī. Paris: II.5.3.
Calcutta: Sec. VII, No. 3. A Ramanundy,—or Worshipper of Ram the creating attribute of the Deity.

Paris: II.5.3. RAMANUNDY. A DEVOTEE OF THE GOD RAM: The Hindoos give the name of Ram to the divinity who has the creative power, and the Faquirs devoted to him are called *Ramanundys*. They are distinguished from other Faquirs by some exteriour peculiarities, such as wearing their hair exceedingly long and thick, and covering with a reddish powder mixed with earth or mud. But it is impossible to suppose that the natural growth of their hair can furnish the immense mass which surrounds their head, and we cannot help believing that they employ other hair besides their own, to give themselves a terrible and striking appearance. They allow besides a lock to grow in the middle of their beard, which touches the ground even when they are standing.

The *Ramanundys* commonly carry in their hands a bundle of dry leaves, in the middle of which is some ashes: this they distribute with a mysterious air to the devout Hindoos who flock round them wherever they appear. These Faquirs are oftener met with in the country than in the town: in the flat countries of Hindoostan, particularly in Bengal, they seem to prefer the winter to the summer for making their appearance; but, like all the other Faquirs, they do not wear more clothes in the cold than in the greatest heat.

The *Ramanundys* have three marks; one on their forehead, the hollow of the breast, and the upper part of the arm. They frequently too cover their whole bodies with a white earth or ashes, which, especially under their enormous load of hair, gives them really a most hideous look. They have under their arm a bit of cloth constantly wet, with which they refresh their face and rub their bodies.

Commentary: Rāmānandīs (also termed Ramats) are followers of Rāmānanda, a Vaiṣṇava saint of the late fourteenth, early fifteenth century and a major figure of the *bhakti*, or devotional, movement. As the largest sect of Vaiṣṇava sādhus, they were active in spreading the popularity of Lord Rāma, incarnation of Viṣṇu, in northern India.[1]

Known as *bairāgī*, "detached," or as *avadhūta*, the Rāmānandī wears on his forehead a Vaiṣṇava sect mark called the *ūrdhvapuṇḍra*, consisting of three vertical lines. Solvyns depicts the lines as a pale ocher in color (yellow in the Paris edition), but among Rāmānandīs, the center line is typically red and those on each side are white, or, less characteristic, all three lines are white. His necklace and rosary beads are of *tulsī* wood, sacred to Viṣṇu. His uncut and matted hair, *jaṭā*, is tied in a twisted bundle on his head—to be "opened" only in ritual and on special occasions—its size an emblem of status and strength of yogic power.[2] His body—naked or, as Solvyns depicts him, with only a small cloth (made of bark or sacred grass) over the genitals—is rubbed with the sacred ash of cow-dung to seal his body from influences of the transient world. The Rāmānandī is portrayed with a cloth under his left arm (shown as right in the Calcutta etching, reversed from the original drawing), and he holds a palm leaf book. Though not shown in the etching, Solvyns writes that Rāmānandīs carry "a bundle of dry leaves" (fashioned as a cup) holding ash that they give to devotees as a holy gift (*prasād*). And also not shown in the print, Rāmānandīs carry a gourd water pot and perhaps a deer skin to sit upon.[3]

The figure stands with his right hand in the gesture of the tyāga-mudrā, the "position of renunciation." The thumb (the soul) is over the index-finger (the ego), symbolic of the desired ascetic state of ego subjugation. The *mudrā*, although widely used in worship, suggests that he may be a member of the Tyāgī (renouncer) Rāmānandī subsect.[4]

Solvyns writes that Rāmānandīs allow a long lock of hair to grow in the middle of their beard, but the figure depicted here has no such lock, unless it is knotted below his chin. Solvyns's "A Fakir at his Prayer" (Pl. II.145), however, portrays a sādhu with the lock of beard hanging to the ground.

---

1 See Burghart, "The Founding of the Ramanandi Sect," and "Wandering Ascetics of the Rāmānandī Sect"; Ward, *A View. . . of the Hindoos*, 3:4;05-06; Wilson, "A Sketch of the Religious Sects of the Hindus," 36-52; Jogendra Nath Bhattacharya, 350-52; Oman, *The Mystics, Ascetics, and Saints of India*, 188-89; Bedi and Bedi, 70; and B. D. Tripathi, 34-37.

2 On *jaṭā*, see Pl. II.137, fn. 10.

3 Burghart analyzes the ornaments of the Rāmānandīs as insignia and icons of their path of renunciation in "Ornaments of the 'Great Renouncers' of the Ramanandi Sect."

4 See Hartsuiker, 52-53, 82-83.

II.143. Brahmacārī

Paris: II.5.4. BERMACHARRY. ANOTHER SORT OF DEVOTEE: The *Bermacharrys,* another species of Faquirs, make themselves remarkable for their chastity, a virtue which in reality they seem to practise with great vigour. They are very devout, and are for ever praying with a chaplet in their hand. Like many of the other Faquirs, they pass before the houses of the Hindoos, but without asking alms. They accept indeed the food which is offered to them, consisting of rice, fruits, and milk; but they cannot take more than the quantity necessary for the subsistance of the day. Without adding any thing more to what I have said of the Faquirs, it will be remarked that, the life of these superstitious devotees is a state of continual laziness, and that, the keep of these idlers is a heavy charge upon the labouring part of the community, who do not affect such extravagant demonstrations of devotion, but who employ more wisely the faculties that nature has given them in providing subsistance for themselves and families. It were natural to imagine that the people must be soon tired of supplying the wants of these indolent beings who live at their expence; but we must reflect that these men have the art of drawing the attention of feeling souls, and exciting their pity, by the extraordinary pennance which they inflict upon themselves, and can never fail obtaining all they want from the piety of the Hindoos, who look upon it as a very meritorious act to take care of a Faquir. There are tradesmen even, who think themselves honoured when a Faquir condescends to choose whatever he may want in their shop, and look upon it as a blessing to their trade. Thus, as we see, one class of men hopes to gain heaven by doing nothing, and the other by nourishing the first by the fruits of their labour.

Commentary: The Brahmacārī, in the broadest sense, is a student of the Vedas. In the Hindu ideal, on investiture with the sacred thread, a young male leaves his childhood to become a *brahmacārī*, a religious student, entering the first of the four stages of life (*āśramas*), the period of celibate and austere study under a spiritual master.[1] On mastering the Vedas, he then enters the second stage as a householder. As a practical matter, many twice-born Hindus never formally become Brahmacārīs, and among those who do, a few renounce the world to continue in life-long celibacy and ascetic discipline.

These life-long Brahmacārīs are found among various *sannyāsī* orders but are also identifiable as distinct groups of brahmin ascetics.[2] As Śaivites, they wear ocher-colored clothing and *rudrākṣa* beads, and typically let their hair and beard grow long. Solvyns's Brahmacārī—perhaps in the stage of studenthood

rather than in life-long commitment—wears a white *dhotī* and his hair and beard appear to be trimmed. In his hand, he holds a rosary of *rudraksa* beads. Brahmacārīs usually retain the sacred thread, but Solvyns's figure does not wear it—perhaps, as with most *sannyāsīs*, symbolic of his renunciation of worldly attachments.

1 See Basham, *The Wonder That Was India,* 159-60.
2 Ghurye, *Indian Sadhus*, 79-81.

Pl. II.143. Brahmacārī. Paris: II.5.4.
Calcutta: Sec. VII, No. 4. A Bermacharry, whose excellence consists in purity.

II.144. Nāga

Paris: II.5.5. NAUGUS. ANOTHER KIND OF FAQUIRS: By casting a look over the different species of Faquirs which I have already represented, it will be observed that they form two very distinct classes: one leads the most peaceable life possible, satisfied with a meer subsistance procured by their superstitious and strange practices: the others are objects of terror from the outrages which they commit, and which they think warranted by the sacred name they bear. The *Naugus* and the Soonassees, whom we described in the foregoing number, are of this last description. We have taken notice that they appear in greater numbers in the flat countries, and in winter, from December to March, more than in any other season: during the great heats they remain at home in the midst of the mountains. They are easily known by their vulgar and disagreeable countenances. The terror which these pious robbers spread among the Hindoo people has given rise to a number of absurd tales concerning them, which, as I have never witnessed any confirmation of them, I think too ill founded to deserve a particular description. But what is certain is, that in these times many Mahometans, who probably find it convenient to live at other people's expence, have taken up the trade of *Naugus,* and pass themselves off for true Faquirs. The Hindoos nevertheless soon discover them, and look upon them in a very bad light. What leads to a discovery of these impostors, is their frequently asking alms, contrary to the usage of the true Faquirs, who are either satisfied with what is offered them, or take it by force, like the *Naugus* and Soonassees. The Faquirs moreover are not subject to taxation, and look upon themselves as exempt from paying the hire of carriages, the passage of rivers, or any other public charge. They assist in numerous bodies at extraordinary ceremonies, such as the marriage of rich people, cavalcades, processions, etc., where their presence is amply paid; happy if the feast ends without some specimen of their usual violence.

Pl. II.144. Nāga. Paris: II.5.5.
Calcutta: Sec. VII, No. 9. Naugus,—rather a Banditti than Beggars.

Commentary: As Solvyns's description of the *sannyāsī* (Pl. II.137) relates principally to the Nāga warriors, we have already discussed the Nāga at some length, but here Solvyns identifies his subject as such. The word, as earlier indicated, means "naked," and these armed sādhus were frequently described as "naked and fighting."[1] They hired on as mercenaries in the armies of Indian princes, and during the late eighteenth century were at the center of the so-called *sannyāsī* rebellions. In the pages of *Asiatic Researches*, some years after the rebellion ended, Wilson—perhaps alluding to the presence of Muslims among their numbers, to which Solvyns refers—wrote that the Nāgas are "unquestionably the most worthless and profligate members of their respective religions. A striking proof of their propensities is their use of arms. They always travel with weapons, usually a matchlock and sword and shield, and that these implements are not carried in vain has been shewn on various occasions [in] the sanguinary conflicts of opposite sects of Hindu mendicants. . . ."[2]

Although Nāgas were often wholly unclothed, Solvyns's Nāga covers his genitals with a strip of cloth and wears an ocher cloth, a "shroud," over the shoulders and tied around his waist. He is unconventionally clean-shaven, but his hair is long and matted, twisted into *jaṭā* "crown" upon his head. He holds an earthen pot under his left arm and, with his right, brandishes a stick as if to threaten Solvyns himself.

1 Ghurye, *Indian Sadhus*, 77, 98-113, and Jamini Mohan Ghosh, 14-15.
2 "A Sketch of the Religious Sects of the Hindus," 16:135-36. Wilson, a missionary, was generally disdainful of sādhus, describing them as "mountebanks" and given to "the performance of low mummeries or juggling tricks." *Asiatic Researches*, 17:186.

II.145. A Fakir at his Prayers

Commentary: The sādhu depicted in this print from the Paris edition does not appear in the earlier Calcutta edition. Solvyns likens him to the Rāmānandī (Pl. II.142) by the long lock of hair from the middle of his beard. The figure is seated in *pūjā* before a *liṅga*, representation of the god Śiva, here in a flower-decked "formless mass" that Solvyns refers to as "that bit of earth."[3] In worship, the *liṅga* here directs the devotee to the deity's formless omnipresence.

The "sacred fire" (*dhūnī*) is a central part of the ritual life of many sādhus, particular among Śaivites. The *dhūnī* and its sacred ashes are associated with Śiva, the fiery god, and with the ash-covered sādhu. "The *dhūnī* is thus a prime symbol of ascetic status, indicating self-sacrifice—the burning of one's karma—transformation in the fire of wisdom, and rebirth from the ashes. As an object—or rather 'subject'—of worship, the fire is saluted with gestures of respect and the uttering of *mantras*."[4] The sādhu shown here with his left hand in the gesture of the *tyāga-mudrā*, the position of renunciation.[5]

There is an anomaly here in that the figure is represented in worship of Śiva, but he has on his forehead the Vaiṣṇava *ūrdhvapuṇḍra* of the

Pl. II.145. A Fakir at his Prayers. Paris: II.5.6.

Rāmānandī sect, and the three white lines are similar to those worn by the Rāmānandī of the *tyāgi* (renouncer) subsect in a photograph in Hartsuiker's *Sādhus: Holy Men of India*. The Rāmānandī similarly gestures in the *tyāga-mudrā*.[6]

1 A small brass pot usually used for water.

2 Solvyns portrays the śaṅkha and ghaṇṭā in Pl. II.146.

3 The word *liṅga* means "sign" and refers to Śiva. Although most frequently embodied in phallic form, it is manifest in various representations, including the "formless mass." See Daniélou, 222-31.

4 Hartsuiker, 97, and, more generally, 95-100.

5 Ibid., 82-83.

6 Ibid., 52-53.

Paris: II.5.6. A FAQUIR AT HIS PRAYERS: The Faquir who is represented in this engraving, is one of the class who adore fire, and who recite their prayers or *Muntars* [mantras] almost without interruption. He is seated on the skin of a royal tiger of Bengal, and in his outward appearance bears a strong resemblance to the Ramanundy of whom I have spoken in this number. While he is praying, his hair is let to flow loosely round his head; and as it is also very long and thick, it forms an immense mass round his shoulders. The first time I saw these Faquirs, I could not persuade myself that all this was their own hair: I afterwards examined them more closely, without being able to discover any indication of its being false, and yet I can scarcely conceive how so much hair can grow upon the head of one man: they too, like the Ramanundy, let a lock of their beard grow till it reaches to the ground. When they are not praying, they knot up this lock close to their chin, and wind their hair round their heads so as to form a sort of turban. But this, in their opinion, is not sufficiently hideous; they rub their skin besides with a whitish earth, and paint their face so as to make themselves really horrible.

He that is here represented, has in his hand some of this earth in a *louta* [*loṭā*],[1] with which he rubs his body: before him is a *sunk* [śaṅkha] or shell, and a *guntha* [ghaṇṭā] or little bell,[2] instruments which he use in praying. Seated near a fire, the object of his adoration, he is decking with flowers the God *Sieb* [Śiva], whom the credulous Hindoo conceives to be present as much in that bit of earth, as in all other matter. He performs this sacrifice before the house of some pious Hindoo, who employs him to obtain the happy issue of some pending affair, such as the delivery of his wife, or an abundant harvest of rice, indigo, sugar: these sacrifices are often repeated till the arrival of the desired event; which turns to the profit of the Faquir, who is generally well rewarded for his trouble.

Musical Instruments[1]

Commentary Co-Authored with
Stephen M. Slawek

To the European in India in the eighteenth century, Indian music was surely strange and exotic, and to many it was little more than noise, cacophonous and irritating. Captain Donald Campbell, in his *Journey Over Land to India* (1781-1784), described it as "inelegant, harsh and dissonant."[2] Pierre Sonnerat, in the account of his voyage, wrote of Indian musical instruments, "That which makes the greatest noise is to them the most harmonious and pleasing."[3] The Abbé J. A. Dubois, an astute observer of India in the late eighteenth and early nineteenth century, wrote that "what they [the Hindus] like is plenty of noise and plenty of shrill piercing sounds";[4] and Walter Hamilton, writing in 1820, described Indian music as "disagreeable" and "insufferable."[5] James R. Martin, in 1837, complained from Calcutta, "It is impossible to speak of Bengalee music with any feeling short of disgust, or to compare it to any thing but the noise made by cows in distress, with an admixture of the caterwauling of a feline congregation and the occasional scream of a affrighted elephant."[6] But for many officers, merchants, and administrators of the British East India Company who had been influenced by the tastes and habits of the Indian gentry and for those "adventurers" who had settled into Indian life, "country musick" might be heard with pleasure. The nautch (Pl. II.195) especially enjoyed a vogue among Europeans in India. Percival Spear notes that "it became the recognized form of entertainment for an Indian merchant to provide for his English guests," and the tradition continued into the nineteenth century long after the European taste for nautch had disappeared.[7]

Indian music for most Europeans was, at best, a diversion, but for the members of the Asiatic Society in Calcutta, it was a matter of scholarly inquiry. Sir William Jones, the great Orientalist and doyen of the Society, wrote "On the Musical Modes of the Hindus," published in 1792 in the third volume of *Asiatick Researches*.[8] Another scholar-administrator in service of the East India Company, Francis Fowke, provided a detailed description of the bīn, or vīṇā, with an engraving depicting the instrument.[9] But it is to Solvyns that we owe the first systematic portrayal of Indian musical instruments and the manner in which they were played.[10]

In the Preliminary Discourse for *Les Hindoûs*, Volume I, Solvyns writes,

> Drawings . . . of their several musical instruments have been published, but in a very imperfect manner; in the first place, they do no more than represent the instrument, without giving an idea of the manner in which it is played, which is not easy to conceive without having it under the eye: the figures too are so small, that it is not possible to guess the parts of which they are composed, and still less to make one of them. The manner in which I have drawn these different instruments in my collection is not, if I am not mistaken, liable to any of these objections.[11]

In the text accompanying the plates of the Paris edition, Solvyns describes the musicians as largely from the lower castes—scavengers, leather workers, palanquin carriers—and often the disreputable and dissolute among them, whom he terms *loutchias* and *Pariahs* (see Commentary for Pl. II.151). Solvyns identifies a few instruments, notably string (such as the bīn or vīṇā, Pl. II.149), with brahmins, but drums, most wind instruments, and many stringed instruments are the preserve of the "untouchable" Hindu castes and of Muslims. Drums or stringed instruments with gut or skins, such as the sāraṅgī (Pl. II.152), are a source of ritual pollution. And the tradition—to which Solvyns alludes in his discussion of the flute (bā̃śi, Pl. II.180)—is that the high castes are prohibited from playing wind instruments because of, as Abbé Dubois explains, "the defilement which the players contact by putting such instruments in their mouths after they have been touched by saliva . . . . There is by no means the same feeling with regard to stringed instruments. In fact, you may often hear Brahmins singing and accompanying themselves on a sort of lute which is known by the name *vina*. . . . It has always been a favourite amongst the better classes."[12] Sir William Jones noted that in India music is "known and practiced . . . not by mercenary performers only, but even by *Mussalmans* and *Hindoos* of eminent rank and learning."[13]

Solvyns emphasizes that he portrays the Hindus, as distinct from Muslims, for whom he expresses disdain, and in the text on musical instruments, he seeks, as elsewhere, to distinguish that which is *Hindu* from contaminating Muslim influences.[14] That was surely not easy in late eighteenth century Bengali society, especially among professional musicians. Persian, the court language of the Mughals, was still the language of administration—as it remained in British India until 1835. Upper class Hindus—or at least those who sought jobs or influence in government, whether under the Mughals or the British—were educated in Persian, Hindustani (Urdu), and often Arabic, in addition to Sanskrit and their native Bengali. Many cultivated Muslim culture. Nabakrishna Deb, Clive's Persian translator and political adviser, was a Hindu. Ram Mohan Roy mastered Persian and Arabic before he learned English. Hindu musicians of the Hindustani tradition, as distinct from the Bengali folk idiom, surely knew Persian and Urdu and then, as today, probably wore Muslim costume.

In *Les Hindoûs*, Vol. I, Solvyns writes that "Music is very generally cultivated among the Hindoos, especially as it is subservient to dancing, one of their favourite diversions," and he notes that "we may form a judgment of the character of this art in Hindoostan" from publications by Sir William Jones, William Hamilton Bird, and Baron d'Alberg.[15]

Solvyns rejects the use of secondary sources in his descriptions of the instruments he portrays, relying solely, he tells us, on his own observation, but in his Introduction to *Les Hindoûs*, Vol. II, Solvyns draws upon Jones's "On Musical Modes of the Hindus,"

> where the author endeavours to explain the whole theory of Hindoo music, as it is taught in some of their sacred books of great antiquity, particularly the *Upaveda*,[16] which describes all the accords of music known to the primitive Hindoos. What may be collected from that work, is that the Hindoos believe their music to be a present of the divinity, and, with the rest of the fine arts, of celestial origin. That part of their mythology which concerns music is justly represented by Sir William Jones as a delightful and graceful allegory: Brahma himself bestowed music upon mankind, through the mediation of his active power, called the divinity who presides over language, and whose son *Nereda* [Nārada][17] invented the *Vina*, the finest instrument of their ancient music. There are four musical systems, which have a sensible relation to the four seasons of the year, each of which has its analogous mode. The melancholy is well adapted to the cold and gloomy season of the latter end of autumn; one more gay and lively suits the season where nature seems to revive; the heats of summer require more languid tones; the autumn, in fine, has a brilliant mode congenial to the feelings, where the rains give new life to the drooping vegetation, and create a sort of second spring.
>
> Each of these modes in the Hindoo music is a celestial spirit, a grand Harwa [Gandhava; *rāga*];[18] and each of these aerial musicians is allied or married to five nymphs or Rageni [*rāgiṇī*],[19] and the father of eight little genii. From the marriage of these grand *Harwas* proceeds what mortals call harmony; and melody is nothing more than the succession of generations issuing from these alliances. Music then in their sacred writings is but the figurative system of accords between celestial beings, and of the harmonic alliance between the aerial spirits called *Tones*.

> Sir William Jones tells us, that he had given himself much useless trouble to discover some piece of ancient music which might have been preserved, as he supposed among the Brahmuns. We have to regret with this learned gentleman, that nothing remains except the theory of their music, and that we can form but a very imperfect judgment of the effect of their musical compositions, to which they themselves attribute the power of raising and of calming the human passions, of enchanting the most savage animals and subduing their ferocity. In music, especially combined with dancing and singing, they suppose these supernatural powers: Among the Hindoos these three arts were formerly closely connected; it is remarkable that the metre of their poetry is always in conformity with the sentiment which it wishes to inspire, and that it varies like music with the nature of the subject. This attention of their poets gave the greatest effect to their words when they were sung and accompanied by music and pantomime perfectly adapted to them. But there is nothing like regularity or systematic arrangement in the actual music of the Hindoos. My work gives only a description of their instruments; but it is accompanied with remarks which will, I believe, be sufficient to give an idea of what their music is at present, and must have been for ages past: for . . . it may be seen that changes do not take place in India with as much facility as in the nations of Europe where the arts are always influenced by the genius of the times.[20]

Throughout *Les Hindoûs*, Solvyns refers to music and instruments in association with festivals and in relation to particular castes or occupations, and he includes instruments in etchings of various festivals and of the nautch. Thirty-five plates in *Les Hindoûs*, Volume II, depict musical instruments. Because of the organization of the Paris edition, Solvyns omitted an additional instrument—the "Burung"—portrayed in the Calcutta edition. It is, of course, included here (Pl. II.181).

As we have noted, Solvyns's portrayal of the Hindus received little recognition in scholarly literature on Indian culture and society, but the Dutch ethnomusicologist Jaap Kunst, in a 1945 article, might be said to have "rediscovered" the Solvyns etchings depicting musical instruments.[21] Mantle Hood, in 1963, brought Solvyns again to light with a discussion of his portrayal of instruments. "Historically," Hood writes, "*Les Hindous* is especially valuable for the fine engravings . . . showing in many instances the playing positions of a number of Indian instruments no longer in use today. Without this reference the actual method of playing many instruments would be largely speculative."[22] More recently, the Dutch ethnomusicologist Joep Bor, in "The Voice of the Sarangi: An Illustrated History of Bowing in India," refers extensively to Solvyns and reproduces five Solvyns etchings.[23]

A Note on the Annotations for Musical Instruments

There are a vast number of musical instruments in India.[24] The single most comprehensive source for information on Indian instruments is *The New Grove Dictionary of Musical Instruments* (NGMI), and it is needless in the Commentaries on Solvyns's portrayals to duplicate what is available in NGMI and in other recent sources on Indian musical instruments.

There is considerable regional variation in the names of instruments, and each may be variously transliterated. For instrument names, we use the Roman transliteration following NGMI or, for distinct Bengali forms, that closest to Solvyns's term. When possible, our first citation to the instrument portrayed is to the volume and page number of NGMI where it is discussed.

1 This section on Solvyns's portrayal of musical instruments appeared in earlier versions as Hardgrave and Slawek, "Instruments and Music Culture in Eighteenth Century India: The Solvyns Portraits," in the journal *Asian Music*, and as a book, *Musical Instruments of North India: Eighteenth Century Portraits by Baltazard Solvyns.*

2 3:124, quoted in Spear, 34.

3 *A Voyage of the East-Indies and China*, 2:124.

4 64.

5 1:103.

6 51-52.

7 Spear, 35. From the end of the eighteenth century, as social contact between Indians and Europeans became both less frequent and less intimate, "the English taste [for nautch] gradually changed from a slightly guilty appreciation or naive enjoyment to frank incomprehension, boredom and finally disgust." Spear, 35. Kencaid, 105, also notes this change in European attitudes in the late eighteenth century, as Indian music, once enjoyed, becomes "horrid screeching" and "disgusting caterwauling."

8 The article, originally written in 1784, was published in an expanded version in *Asiatick Researches* 3: 55-87. In an earlier article, "On the Gods of *Greece*, *Italy*, and *India*," *Asiatick Researches* 1: 264-65, Jones briefly discusses Indian music and, in a plate, includes a copy of an Indian miniature painting depicting the god Nārada with the bīn (vīṇā), the instrument, according to tradition, he invented.

9 "On the *Veena*, or *Indian* Lyre" (1788), 1:250-54. Reprinted in Tagore, 191-97.

10 Charles Gold, Solvyns's South Indian counterpart in the 1790s, depicted musical instruments, numbered and identified, in his *Oriental Drawings* (1806), Pl. 22. On Gold, see Chapter Three, pp. 80-81.

11 1:26-27, reprinted in Chapter Four, pp. 122-123.

12 64-65.

13 Jones, "On the Musical Modes of the Hindus," 62, in Tagore, 133.

14 On Solvyns's antipathy to Muslims, see Chapter Three, pp. 99-100.

15 1:26, in Chapter Four, Preliminary Discourse, p. 115. Bird's *The Oriental Miscellany: Being a Collection of the Most Favourite Airs of Hindoostan* was published in 1789. D'Alberg's *Ueber die Musik der Indier* (1802) is a German translation of Jones's "On the Musical Modes of the Hindus," and includes plates depicting musical instruments. For a detailed discussion of early European accounts of Indian music, see Bor, "The Rise of Ethnomusicology."

16 Treatises on music belong to the category of texts called *Upaveda*, i. e., subsidiary texts attached to the four Vedas, referred to by Jones, 3:67.

17 Nārada, a *mahārṣi*, or great spirit, messenger of the gods, and one of the heavenly musicians.

18 Gandhavas are semi-divine singers and musicians in Indra's heaven.

19 A *rāginī* is a muse of a particular musical mode, or rāga. There are six chief rāgas, personified as handsome youths, each married to five beautiful rāginīs. As their union results in additional musical modes, new rāgas and rāginīs are created.

20 2:15-16.

21 "Een vergeten musicologische bron: De instrumentafbeeldingen in 'Les Hindous' van F. Baltazard Solvyns."

22 220. Hood reproduces Solvyns's plates for the Surnāī (Pl. II.178) and the Nautch (Pl. II.195).

23 1-183. Bor also discusses Solvyns in "The Rise of Ethnomusicology."

24 A useful visual overview may be found in the chapter on "Indian Musical Instruments," with 200 line drawings, in Shirali. Many instruments from Bengal are illustrated with photographs in Meerwarth. On Indian music more generally, see Arnold.

Opposite page:

Pl. II.146. Śaṅkh and Ghaṇṭā. Paris: II.6.2.

Calcutta: Sec. XI, No. l. A Sunk and G'unta,—used by the Brahmuns at their religious ceremonies.

Orme: 46.

II.146. Śaṅkh[1] and Ghaṇṭā[2]

Paris: II.6.2. SUNK AND G'UNTA, MUSICAL INSTRUMENTS: The instruments which they [the Hindus] use are either for the purposes of religion or of amusement; we will begin by the former. The simplest of the instruments which the Brahmuns use in their temples, is the *sunk,* which is meerly a shell into which they blow with all their strength to call the faithful together. They employ also the *G'unta* for the same purpose: this is a sort of bell of brass, with a head and two wings by way of ornament; they sound it morning and evening, before the sacrifices begin, in the first court of the temple, where there are always some of the images of their divinities, but not always the same: they change them generally every month, and this period is exclusively devoted to their worship, though their festival in reality lasts but eight or ten days, and is celebrated and concluded with the ceremonies which we have already described. After this, each family employs the remainder of the month in devotions to their domestic deities.

The plate represents a Brahmun standing before the divinity of the month, blowing into the shell, and striking the *G'unta* or bell with his other hand. Other idols are seen, placed on a wooden bench. The figures prostrated on the steps of the altar, in an act of devotion, are also Brahmuns who fulfil this duty before they give themselves up to their private business; for this prayer must of necessity precede all the occupations of the day. That the idea of the Divinity may be ever before their eyes, the Brahmuns are commanded never to write on any occasion whatsoever, without having previously written the name of God upon their paper.

The *sunk* or shell is sometimes heard in the bazars or markets; where the Faquirs employ it to announce their arrival.

It is worth remarking that this is the shell of which the *Sunkhaurys* [Ś͂ākhāri], whose business we have already described in the first volume, make the bracelets of the Hindoo women. The sacred function in which the matter that they employ has been used, gives them a rank in the subdivision of a cast above common artisans.

Commentary: The śaṅkh, or conch shell, obtained from the gastropod *Turbinella pyrum*, is used today in precisely the same manner as Solvyns describes. Charles R. Day notes that the conch shell "is said to have been first used by the god Krishna and is mentioned in . . . the Ramayana, where it is called Devadatta. We also find it under the name of Goshringa, both in the Ramayana and Mahabharata."[3]

Frederic Shoberl, in his account of *Hindoostan* in *The World in Miniature*, provides descriptions of musical instruments, drawing principally from Solvyns, with occasional acknowledgment to the artist as his source. On the "sunk," he notes that the shell is "tipped at each end with copper, into which the Brahmins blow for all their might to summon the people to the temples."[4] Copper is deemed to be ritually non-polluting, and the śaṅkh is a notable exception to the general brahminical prohibition against use of wind instruments.

Ś͂ākhāri (Sankahakara) is the caste of shell-workers, described by Solvyns, Pl. II.34, who make conch shell bangles. The craft includes decorating the intact conch shell used as a horn. Ashok Mitra, Census Commissioner for West Bengal, states that the craft and the occupational caste is "peculiar to and characteristic of Bengal and Bengali society."[5]

The word *ghaṇṭā* refers to several types of bells, as the sort Solvyns depicts, but it also refers to a plate gong, either hand held or suspended from a support, that is commonly used in temples and sounded in various rituals, especially during *ārtī*, honoring the deity with lighted oil lamps. The gong is used in secular contexts to mark the passing of the hour.

1 Dick, "Śaṅkh," *NGMI*, 3:289-90.
2 Dick, "Ghaṇṭā," *NGMI*, 2:39-40.
3 103-04.
4 27.
5 *The Tribes and Castes of West Bengal*, 340-41. Also see Risley, 2:221-23.

II.147. Kã̃sar[1]

Pl. II.147. Kãsar. Paris: II.6.3.
Calcutta: Sec. XI, No. 2. A Kunser,—beat at stated times by the servants of Priests.

Paris: II.6.3. KUNSER. AN OTHER INSTRUMENT: This instrument is used for the same purposes as the two others, and is not less simple: it is nothing more than a piece of brass suspended by a cord; a servant of the temple, even a Brahmun, holds the instrument in one hand, strikes it with a stick sometimes in a quick and sometimes a slow measure, to call together the Hindoos to their sacrifices and other acts of devotion: sounding his *Kunser* till it becomes tiresome. Sometimes the instrument is of a red colour and has a number of small ornaments covered with that beautiful varnish of which the Indians alone possess the secret.

On days of public festivity or *poudjahs* [*pūjās*] the ears are incessantly stunned with the monotonous sound of the *Kunser;* but this instrument is never used at private feasts or rejoicings, nor to celebrate the arrival of a prince or rich Hindoo, as some travellers whose researches have not been very exact upon the countries they traversed, have believed: the Hindoo laws expressly forbid the use of it, except on religious occasions. But the *Kunser* is often confounded with another instrument, the *Kaunsy* [kãsi, Pl. II.172], from the resemblance of the name; a description of which will be given hereafter.

The three instruments which I have just described are consecrated solely to religious purposes: some add also the *khole* [khol, Pl. II.158] and the *surmungla* [surmaṇḍal, Pl. II.169], but without reason. — We now pass to the description of those which are used for the amusement of private persons, and are infinitely more curious, being more complicated, and some even of a very ingenious invention. As to the *Sunk,* the *G'unta* and the *Kunser,* their noisy sounds scarcely deserve to be honored with the name of music.

Commentary: The more frequently used temple plate gong in Bengal is the ghaṇṭā, which is of consistent thickness, whereas the Bengali kãsar (kansar) is slightly thicker in the center than towards the rim. The instrument takes its name from the material from which it is made, *kãsar*, meaning "bell-metal."

Solvyns makes a distinction between kãsar, a temple gong, and a similar instrument used on secular occasions that he calls a "kaunsy" (kãsi, Pl. II.172). Today there is little structural or functional difference between the two instruments. This either indicates a loss of specificity in the terms since Solvyns's time or possibly that Solvyns has described usages of the terms restricted to a limited region.

1 Dick, "Kãsar," *NGMI*, 2:362.

II.148. Tambūrā[1]

Pl. II.148. Tambūrā. Paris: II.6.4.

Calcutta: Sec. XI, No. 3. A Tumboora,—played on by the higher orders for their amusements.

Orme: 47.

Commentary: Solvyns's misunderstanding of Indian music is nowhere more in evidence than in these comments concerning the tambūrā, the ubiquitous drone instrument of Indian classical music. Looking beyond his disdainful remarks, we find an interesting comment indicating that the tambūrā was looked upon by upper class Hindus as a symbol of wealth. This is most probably related to the patronage of musicians by zamīndārs in Bengal, thus leading to the association of music with the wealthy class and, by extension, the association of the tambūrā with financial well being.

Of the instrument depicted, the presence of a wide bridge of the type used on instruments such as the bīn (Pl. II.149), sitār (Pl. II.151), and the modern tambūrā is notable. The system of anchoring the wires and what appears to be a bone decorative guard plate at the base of the sound board, indicating probable use of tuning beads, are similar to those used today and suggest remarkable continuity in construction of the instrument over the past two hundred years.

Paris: II.6.4. TUMBOORA: A great deal has been said upon the music of the Hindoos. The Transactions of the Society of Calcutta among others, contain many treatises upon this subject,[2] which is notwithstanding but very imperfectly known in Europe, for this simple reason, that the instruments which they use have never been described with sufficient precision, which ought to have been the principal object, for they are much more remarkable than the music itself. Their instruments have been carried successively to a surprising degree of perfection; but those improvements have not reached their music, which still remains in its infancy. It is impossible not to make this remark in seeing a Hindoo play upon the *Tumboora*; in his hands is a magnificent instrument, covered with paintings and gilding, ornamented to an excess of luxury, and we are naturally led to imagine that he is to draw from it the most enchanting sounds; but on the contrary he remains for hours together in the same attitude, singing a monotonous air, and touching from time to time one of the four chords [strings] which compose this instrument. This is the only use he makes of it, the only pleasure which he seeks from it. And for him even this is a great deal: seated on a carpet or a piece of white cloth, he gives himself up to the pleasing sensations which the vibrations of a single chord produce, and probably he would give up even this enjoyment, if it required the smallest exertion. Every thing about him must be proportioned to his natural taste for laziness and indolence.

The *Tumboora* with the rich Hindoos is an object of luxury which they expose frequently in their best rooms, as one of their most precious effects, to attract the eyes of strangers. As to the form of the instrument itself, no description of it is necessary, as I am persuaded that the drawing will give a very sufficient idea of it.

1 Dick, "Tambūrā," *NGMI*, 3:514-15.

2 Solvyns here refers to *Asiatick Researches*, the transactions of the Asiatic Society, that included in the third volume Sir William Jones's article, "On the Musical Modes of the Hindus."

II.149. Kuplyans or Bīn[1]

Pl. II.149. Kuplyans or Bīn. Paris: II.6.5. **Calcutta: Sec. XI, No. 7.** A Kuplyaus, or Been,—described in the 1st volume of the Asiatic Researches.

Commentary: Hindu mythology relates that the sage Nārada, son of Brahmā and leader of the celestial musicians, invented the vīṇā,[3] and Sarasvatī, goddess of learning and patroness of music, plays the vīṇā, one of her iconographical attributes as she is represented in painting, sculpture, and sacred images.

The vīṇā is the first Indian musical instrument to receive detailed discussion by European travelers and scholars. Pietro Della Valle (1586-1652) describes the instrument in the account of his travels to India, and Marin Mersenne includes the vīṇā in his seventeenth century treatise on music, *Harmonie Universelle*.[4] The most extensive early European description (referred to above by Solvyns) is Francis Fowke's "On the Vina, or Indian Lyre," published in the first volume of *Asiatick Researches* in 1788, with an engraving depicting the instrument itself and another as it is played.[5] In that same volume, Sir William Jones, in writing "On the Gods of *Greece*,

Paris: II.6.5. KUPLYANS, OR BEEN: In order to judge whether the following description is more exact, and consequently more deserving of credit, than that which is inserted in the first volume of the Transactions of the Asiatic Society,[2] it is necessary to inform the reader that I was in possession, while in India, of the instrument in question, and heared it played by the Hindou from whom I purchased it, meaning to bring it over with the rest of my collection, to make it known in Europe: unfortunately it was destroyed by insects so as to frustrate my intentions: but the drawing at least remained such as it is seen in the engraving. The *been* is an instrument composed of two pumpkins of unequal size, dried and cut through the middle, united by a long tube of wood, upon which are stretched several chords of spun cotton gummed, and two of wire; the two pumpkins are joined to the tube which conveys the sound, by other pieces of wood also hollowed out. The instrument is tuned as ours with strings, by turning the pegs fixed in the wood, but the chords are not supported by a bridge, as in the drawing of the Asiatic Society, nor are they so numerous: mine had but four. The musician who played upon it, a Brahmun, of *Mursadabad* in Bengal, had very strong nails and of a great length: with one hand he pinched with his nails the chords below, and with the other he pressed them above, striking them also at times with a little stick. I can affirm that the sounds produced by this singular instrument, are very sweet and harmonious, especially in the higher notes. I am even persuaded that this musician would have been heard with pleasure in an European concert: it is true that he had in the country the reputation of excelling on this instrument, and was consequently capable of giving me all the information which I might require.

None of the *beens* which I had an opportunity of seeing during my residence in Asia, resembled that given by the Asiatic Society, and I was always careful to compare them. The instrument is nevertheless of true Hindoo origin, and is properly played only in the countries inhabited by primitive Hindoos, I cannot therefore conceive why in the drawing of the Society it is in the hands of a Mussulman.

Italy, and *India*," includes an engraving of Nārada playing the vīṇā and quotes from the poem *Magha* [6]: "*Nāred* [Nārada] sat watching from time to time his large *Vīnā*, which by impulse of the breeze, yielded notes that pierced successively the regions of his ear, and proceeded by musical intervals."[7]

Solvyns refers to Nārada's invention of the vīṇā in his Introduction to *Les Hindoûs*, Vol. II,[8] but makes no mention of the instrument's association with Sarasvatī. His concern in the descriptive text accompanying the plate here is with the instrument itself. Another early European artist, Charles Gold, working in South India at the time Solvyns was in Bengal, also portrayed the instrument in a drawing, published later as a print.[9]

The name *kuplyans*, used by Solvyns, is limited to Bengal and, as far as we are aware, appears nowhere else in reference to a stick zither type instrument. It is notable that Solvyns was unaware of the fretted variety of stick zither, also known as bīn, that was popular in the Mughal courts. It is possible that the fretted bīn had entered its period of decline by the time of Solvyns's visit to India, but the instrument seems to have been available to later writers. Perhaps it was less known in Bengal than in the heartland.

Concerning Solvyns's description of the instrument, in which he gives the number of strings as four (two of wire, two of gummed cotton), the print indicates that two strings were approximately half the length of the others. It is probable that these served a drone function in the same manner as the *cikārī* strings of the modern vīṇā and sitār. It is also to be noted that the instrument pictured lacks any bridge. The strings are simply anchored to small posts projecting from the carved end of the stick body. This part is carved in the shape of a swan head, possibly indicating some connection with the goddess Sarasvatī, whose vehicle is the swan. However, what is most interesting about Solvyns's bīn is that the instrument is played both with a wooden slide and by pressing with the fingers of the left hand. These methods of pitch production existed on the ekatantrī vīṇā (a one-stringed stick zither with a gourd resonator) described in the *Saṅgitaratnākara* by the thirteenth century musicologist Śaṛṅgadeva.[10] A stick zither called sar-vīṇā, possibly played in a similar manner, is mentioned in the *Ā'īn-i-Akbarī* of Abu'l-Fazl 'Allāmī, court chronicler of Akbar.[11] Mention of this playing technique in the late eighteenth century gives us evidence that the modern vicitrā vīṇā, or baṭṭu vīṇā, which is thought to have been "invented" in the nineteenth century, is a direct lineal descendent of an earlier indigenous instrument. In essence, the Solvyns bīn provides us with a missing link that suggests the continuous existence of a fretless stick zither played with a slide on the Indian subcontinent since the thirteenth century.

In the print, the musician's strapless sandals, *pādukās*, are set to one side.[12]

---

1 The instrument is described in *NGMI* under the name by which it is most widely known, vīṇā: Dick, Geekie, and Widdess, "Vīṇā," 3:728-35.

2 Fowke, "On the *Vina*, or *Indian* Lyre" (1788). Perhaps the earliest European description is by Pietro Della Valle (1586-1652) in his *Travels*, 1:117-18.

3 Daniélou, 187.

4 For a discussion of these early descriptions of the vīṇā, see Bor, "The Rise of Ethnomusicology," 52-53.

5 Fowke. The plate appears opposite p. 252.

6 Jones refers to the *Sisupalavadha* (*Maghakavya*) by the seventh century poet Magha.

7 1:227.

8 See Solvyns's reference to Nārada in the introduction to the section on "Musical Instruments," p. 332.

9 *Oriental Drawings*, Pl. 22, "A Satadevan, accompanied by his son dancing." The figure is portrayed playing a vīṇā.

10 3:233-38.

11 Abu'l-Fazl 'Allāmī, 269.

12 They are worn, as depicted in Pl. II.33, by grabbing a peg between the toes.

II.150. Pināk[1]

Paris: II.6.6. PENNAUCK: This is also a very singular instrument, and very different from those which we use in Europe. The form of the *Pennauck* is not unlike that of the *been* of which we have just been speaking, being likewise composed of two pumpkins; but they are joined by an iron rod, and one of them is much larger, and forms consequently a wider aperture than the other: the smaller is at the bottom, the larger at top. The essential difference between this instrument and the *been* is that, in the place of chords it has but one string of wire, strongly stretched. To draw out the sound, a bow like that of a base is prest upon this chord, at the same time that another part of it is struck or rubbed with a little stick. I confess that this strange music is far from being agreeable, and can be pleasing only to the ear of an Hindoo.

The *Pennauck* is now as seldom heard in India as in the other provinces of Asia; it is not even easy to find a musician who knows how to play upon it. The same may be said of the *been.* In former times both these instruments were much in vogue, and I have been assured that those who excelled in playing them where held in a certain degree of consideration, which has lasted even to our times. The masters of the *been* and the *Pennauck* being very few, are treated with great respect, and people flock round them to hear their singular music as a curiosity. They are to be heard only with the rich, as they never play for money before the public. I take it for granted that it is not necessary to repeat here, that I profess to treat only of true Hindoos: it is no concern of mine if the Mussulmen have, or have not appropriated to themselves these instruments, and use them as means of earning their bread. My purpose is to make known only what relates to the Hindoo people exclusively: I must therefore be careful to distinguish their customs from those of their oppressors.

Pl. II.150. Pināk. Paris: II.6.6.

Calcutta: Sec. XI, No. 8. Pennauck,—the shell of a large Pumkin, and half the shell of a small one joined together by an iron wire.

Orme: 50.[2]

Commentary: The word *pinākī* means "bow" and is associated with the god Śiva. As Solvyns portrays the instrument, it is essentially a bowed bīn. The pināk, most widely known as the pinākī vīṇa, is described in detail in the *Saṅgitaratnākara*[3] and is mentioned as the pināk in the *Ā'īn-i-Akbarī*.[4] Solvyns informs us that this instrument and the preceding bīn were objects of great prestige and status among Hindus, that the musicians who specialized on these instruments were non-professionals, and that the instruments themselves were nearing extinction in Hindu culture at the time of his writing. The pinākī vīṇā appears to have disappeared completely from Hindustani music culture in the early nineteenth century. It is not mentioned by Willard,[5] nor is it mentioned by later nineteenth century writers. Indeed, as Joep Bor writes, Solvyns provides us with what is probably the last description of the instrument.[6]

A copy of Solvyns's portrayal of the pināk is included among the color prints in Wahlen's *Moeurs, usages et costumes de tours les peuples du mond* (1843).[7]

1 Dick, "Pināk," *NGMI,* 3:113; also see under "Vīṇā," *NGMI,* 3:731.

2 The Orme plate's title, "Pennauck, or Been," recognizes no distinction between the two instruments, and the confusion is evidenced by the plate's slightly modified copy of Solvyns's one-stringed, fretless pināk, while the text describes a seven-stringed bīn. In contrast to Solvyns's portrayal and description of the pināk's lower gourd as smaller, the two gourds depicted in the Orme plate are of roughly equal size, and the accompanying text gives their dimensions as the same. The Orme text, without attribution, is drawn from Francis Fowke's description of the bīn in the first volume of *Asiatick Researches* (1788).

3 3:314-17.

4 Abu'l-Fazl 'Allāmī, 269.

5 "A Treatise on the Music of Hindoostan" (1834).

6 "The Voice of the Sarangi," 41. Among the numerous illustrations in this volume, Bor includes Solvyns's depictions of five bowed instruments, including the pināk, and writes, "Despite his [Solvyns's] lack of understanding of the music. . . his descriptions reveal information which is to be found nowhere else, and particularly so in those cases where the instruments have become obsolete." 71.

7 Vol. I, *Asia.*

II.151. Sitār[1]

Pl. I.151. Sitār. Paris: II.7.2.

Calcutta: Sec. XI, No. 4. A Sittar, or Guittar.

Orme: 48.

Commentary: Alastair Dick traces the history of the Indian sitār to the tanbūr of the early Muslim sultanates in India, postulating that the Indian sitār and the Uzbek dutar share a common ancestor. He bases his argument on structural similarities exhibited by the

Paris: II.7.2. SITTAR, OR GUITTAR: To resume the subject of the preceding number, the instrument called *Sittar* or *Guittar,* resembles very much our guitar as well in its form as in its name. I am even uncertain whether it is originally Hindoo: I have been assured of the contrary, but the assertion remains without proof. An European would make much more of this instrument than the Hindoo musicians, who are satisfied with touching the chords meerly from time to time; and as they are much more charmed with the noise than with the melody of their music, they frequently, to create a variety in their dull and monotonous sounds, place an iron ring in each chord of the *Sittar,* which being put in motion by the vibration, and striking against each other, produces a singular noise which delights the ear of the Hindoos, and appears to them the supreme degree of perfection.

The *Sittar* is now seldom used in India; perhaps the better sort of Hindoos have taken it in aversion since the *Loutchias,* or people of dissolute manners, have taken to playing it for money, and have chosen this music to accompany their obscene songs and other immoral practices. At their feasts, the *Nautch,* a dance which we have described in the second number of this volume [Pl. II.195], is sometimes performed to the sound of the *Sittar,* and some tolerable musicians, or rather meer players upon it, may be heard.

The Mussulmen have taken up this instrument as they have the others, and if a traveller by chance hears the *Sittar,* he may be pretty certain that it is played by one of them.

two instruments. The tanbūr eventually was known as tanbūrah. From various references in court chronicles, we know that the tanburah was a popular instrument in the Mughal courts and was adopted by Hindu musicians of the highest rank (Kalavant) by the seventeenth century.[2] How or why this instrument came to be known as the sitār, if indeed that was the case, remains obscured. Dick suggests that there might have been a three-stringed tanbūr known as sihtār-tanbūr (*sihtār* indicating three strings) whose name was eventually shortened to sihtār and then sitār. We do not hear of specialists on the sitār until the mid-eighteenth century, when Masit Khan established the style of playing on the instrument known today as the *masīkhānī bāj*. According to some authorities, it was Masit Khan who added two strings to an earlier three-stringed instrument to invent the sitār. Another popular story attributes the invention of the instrument to Amir Khusrau Khan, a musician in the Delhi court of Muhammad Shah, the Mughal emperor, who ruled from 1719 to 1748. Willard's reference in 1834 to the sitār as a modern instrument (but invented by Umeer Khosro [Amir Khusro] of Delhi) gives somewhat contradictory evidence that at least the use of the term *sitār* to designate this instrument was still relatively new.[3]

Solvyns's comments about the sitār indicate that the instrument was used in at least two different social and musical contexts: as an accompanying instrument in courtesan dancing and as a solo instrument of professional Muslim musicians, presumably of the courts. It appears also to have been an instrument known to unskilled amateur musicians in urban society who dawdled upon it, trying new ways (such as placing iron rings on the strings) to produce amusing sounds. In his note to the original drawing, Solvyns wrote that the sitār was "used by the lower order of Natives, and itinerant musicians."

It is known that the number of strings on the sitār was increased during the course of its evolution. The instrument pictured here had six strings. Twelve frets can be discerned in close examination of the etching, but it is not possible to determine if these were of the raised, arched type used today or were simply tied gut frets as found on Middle Eastern lutes. The joint connecting the gourd (*tumbā*) to the wooden "shoulder," which in turn connects to the neck, is clearly visible in the etching. The noticeable absence of the wide bridge used on modern instruments supports the assertion that the Indian sitār was developed from an imported instrument by overlaying features of the bīn. On the other hand, the presence of a double-nut and added tuning beads (could Solvyns have mistaken these as the source of jangling?), along with the considerable size of the instrument and the relatively wide neck, clearly indicates that many features of the modern sitār are at least two hundred years old.

If the sitār developed from the tanbūr of the Mughal courts, it remains unexplained how the instrument entered the society of the "loutchias" (Bengali, *loccā*; Hindi, *luccā*, meaning a vile, wanton person)[4] mentioned by Solvyns and subsequently acquired much of the social stigma among Hindus of the time that attached to other instruments used by these people. One possibility might be that many of these people were illegitimate offspring of the court dancing girls who, forced to leave the court because of economic decline, gravitated to the brothel districts of urban centers and took with them remnants of the court life they had experienced in their youth.

It is not clear if Solvyns uses *loutchia* as a term for a specific group or simply as a descriptive noun applicable to any dissolute individual no matter what his origins may be. *Hobson-Jobson* states that the term *loocher* is often used in Anglo-Indian colloquial as "a blackguard libertine, a lewd loafter." No caste or community identity is inferred.[5] Be that as it may, Solvyns's "loutchias" appear to have been a musician group in close association with the courtesans. They were drawn from both Hindu and Muslim sectors of the society and, in addition to the sitār, played the tablā (Pl. II.160) and the sāraṅgī (Pl. II.152).

Solvyns notes that the Hindu musicians had adopted some of the sartorial tastes of the Muslims, possibly a vestige of life during Muslim court patronage. The sitār's low status among the *bīnkār* (musicians specializing on the bīn) of the Mughal courts can be explained if we assume that the instrument entered court life in the hands of low class accompanists of dancers, or possibly as an instrument that accompanied the songs of vocalists of lesser rank than the Kalavant singers of *dhrupad*, the most important genre of North Indian classical music of that period. As the *bīnkār* improved upon the instrument by adding to it various features of the bīn, the sitār became more popular and more versatile as a solo instrument. A tremendous transformation in the instrument's popularity ensued during the nineteenth century. Willard, who was "in the service" of the Nawab of Banda, a court in what is now Madhya Pradesh renowned for the famous *bīnkār* and *sitāriyā* musicians who were in its employ during the nineteenth century, indicates that the instrument was admired by professionals and amateurs alike.[6] Charles R. Day, writing nearly a century after Solvyns, states that the "sitar is called also Sundari, and is perhaps the commonest of all the stringed instruments in India, being much admired."[7] Apparently, the instrument had acquired such high cultural esteem through its association with the *bīnkār* musicians that its intermediate history as an instrument of the "louchias" was soon forgotten.

---

1 Dick, "Sitar, "NGMI, 3:392-400. On the history of the instrument, see Miner, *Sitar and Sarod in the 18th and 19th Centuries*, and "The Sitār: An Overview of Change," 27-57. In both the book and article, Miner refers to Solvyns and reproduces the etching.
2 Dick, "Sitar," 292-93.
3 Willard, 98.
4 Sen, 826, derives the word from the Persian *lucha*. The English *lout*, an ill-mannered fellow, is obviously similar, but *OED* makes no etymological connection. The word also suggests the French/English *louche*, seedy or of questionable taste or morality.
5 519.
6 98.
7 Day, 117.

II.152. Sāraṅgī[1]

Pl. II.152. Sāraṅgī. Paris: II.7.3.
Calcutta: Sec. XI, No. 16. Saringee,—played at Nautches, &c.
Orme: 51.

Commentary: In his descriptive note on the sāraṅgī in the 1799 *Catalogue*, Solvyns writes simply that it is played at nautchs, and in his print portraying the dance (Pl. II.195), Solvyns includes a sāraṇgī among the instruments.

The sāraṇgī is believed to have originated as a folk instrument. This view is supported by the widespread use of it, in a variety of forms, in folk cultures of different regions of South Asia. Its suitability as a melodic accompanying instrument for voice promoted its popularity among singers of the classical *khayāl* in the princely courts. That popularity greatly diminished, however, partly because of the instrument's association with courtesan life. This association seems to have been well-established by the end of the eighteenth century, as is evidenced by Solvyns's assertion that the "*loutchias* are the most frequent performers on the instrument." Day, a century later, writes that the sāraṅgī "is considered to be rather vulgar, and hence musicians, though they admire and like it very much, will usually employ either a low caste Hindu or a Mussulman to play it."[2]

Solvyns makes frequent reference to the low status of most musicians, both Hindu and Muslim, and to the disrepute in which they are held. "Musicians are regarded all over India as a debased race," ethnographer James Wise wrote in 1883, "and in Eastern Bengal Muhammadan musicians are either barbers (hajjām), or the husbands of midwives (dāi), classes ranked among the vilest of the population."[3]

Paris: II.7.3. SARINGEE: This instrument, which is frequently met with in every part of Hindoostan, is very like the violoncello, though it is smaller and has more chords. The sounds which it produces are soft and melodious, and susceptible of greater variety than those of the other instruments. Of all the different kinds of Hindoo music in general, the *Saringee* comes nearest to that of Europe. The chords are of spun cotton; the pieces of wood which form the instrument are united by a very fine white skin glued over the joints. The sweet sounds of the *Saringee* are well adapted to accompany the voice; it is used in all the dances both of men and women.

The *louchias* too are the most frequent performers on this instrument; for which reason in the back-ground of the print I have represented a house of bad fame, and a woman of the vilest class, because such is the general resort of the *louchias,* where they give themselves up to every excess of debauchery. They are sunk to such a degree of degradation, that they respect neither their national manners nor dress. Some of them, though of Hindoo origin, dress like Mussulmen, or rather like the Mogols of the north of India, others, though by birth they are Mussulmen, pass their lives with the most corrupt of the Hindoos.

These *louchias* are much more despised in Hindoostan, than the female prostitutes with whom they constantly consort. In general, the irregularities of women meet with less contempt here than in Europe; the heat of the climate is supposed to operate as an incitement to vice, and by encreasing the number of its votaries, seems to exempt it from that degree of horror which it inspires when it is confined to a few miserable wretches. Many Hindoo women are destined from their infancy to this abominable trade, and carry it on without having an idea of its immorality.

1 Sorrell and Helffer, "Sāraṅgī," *NGMI,* 3:294-96. For a rich portrayal of the instrument and its traditions, see Bor, "The Voice of the Sarangi." Bor draws extensively on Indian painting and includes, in addition to various European depictions of the sāraṅgī as a part of nautch performances, Solvyns's sāraṅgī etching. He provides, as well, references to the instrument by European travelers as early as the seventeenth century.

2 125.

3 In the entry under "Bājunia," a class of Muslims, 38.

II.153. Sārindā[1]

Paris: II.7.4. SARINDA: As the *Tumboora* and the *Been* are the instruments of the richer class of Hindoos, so that which we are going to speak of under the name of *Sarinda* belongs almost exclusively to the poor: in so much, that most of the common people, particularly the palanquin bearers, have one of them of their own making: this does not require much genius, being no more than a bit of wood hollowed out, over which are stretched some chords of spun cotton: and the sound is produced by drawing over them a bow, as represented in the print. The music is proportioned to the rudeness of the instrument, and can be pleasing only to its Hindoo inventers. Few of those who play upon the *Sarinda* have any knowledge of music; they meerly follow their fancy, continuing sometimes in a lower tone with deep expression, at others rising suddenly from the lowest to the highest notes in reiterated cadences, but always without taste, measure or harmony.

I have just observed that the *Sarinda* is the ordinary amusement of the palanquin bearers: the person I have represented is one of them: he stands on a little platform before the door of his employer; this the place generally allowed to these servants; the houka [*hukā*] alone which he has by him is a sufficient indication of his condition.[2]

If his amusements are ill suited to our European taste, we must however acknowledge that they cannot be more innocent, and that the diversions of persons of the same rank among us are neither so harmless nor so easily attained.

Commentary: The sārindā continues to exist in the same form today as pictured in Solvyns's etching. It is, Solvyns wrote in his note to the original drawing, "a kind of violin cello, used by the lower orders, particularly ballad singers and bearers. It is remarkable the strings are only a kind of hempen cords." An instrument of identical shape is pictured by Day, who writes that it "is common in Bengal. . . . The Sarinda is not a very high-class instrument, but is very popular with the lower classes."[3] In *The Costume of Indoostan,*

Orme's pirated edition of the Solvyns etchings, the text for the plate describes the sārindā as "the most common musical instrument in Hindostan. Its effect is neither unpleasant, nor captivating; and it is in general performed on by those who have little ear, or less taste, and may class with the blind fidlers at country wakes."[4]

Palanquin bearers in Bengal, associated with the instrument, were drawn from various castes, typically lower, often "untouchable," castes, and especially from the various Jāliyā (Pl. II.46) fishermen castes. The Duliā (Pl. II.45), a subcaste of the Bāgdi fishermen caste, are traditionally palanquin bearers, but neither Solvyns nor Risley, in his *Tribes and Castes of Bengal*,[5] refer to music in association with these groups.

1 Baily and Dick, "Sārindā," *NGMI*, 3:297-98. Also see Bor, "The Voice of the Sarangi," 13-17, and with reference to Solvyns, 71.
2 Solvyns portrays various *hukās*, Pls. II.203-10. The *hukā* shown here, with its coiled "snake" or tube, is of the better sort and would be indicative of lower social status only by its unadorned simplicity.
3 125.
4 Pl. 49.
5 1:37-41.

Pl. II.153. Sārindā. Paris: II.7.4.
Calcutta: Sec. XI, No. 5. A Sarinda or Violin,—the most common Hindostanee musical instrument.
Orme: 49.

II.154. Amr̥ti (Omerti)[1]

Paris: II.7.5. OMORTI. This is also an instruments with strings; but what renders it more curious, and proves it of Hindoo origin is, that the body of the instrument is made of a cocoa-nut, cut down to about one third, and covered over with a very fine skin. To this species of tymbal, is joined a wooden handle with strings stretched from one end of the instrument to the other; there is the whole secret of this truely Hindoo invention. The man who plays it, is seated, holds it between his knees, and endeavours to draw musical sounds from the shell of his cocoa-nut. At a distance it would be difficult to form a guess at what he is about, and still harder to conceive that it is an amusement. The sound of the *Omerti* is not unlike that of the *Sarinda* and the *Saringee,* but something sweeter and less grating to the ear of an European. One is not a little surprised to hear a tolerably harmonious music from a cocoa-shell.

The praises which I heard a skilful Brahmun bestow on a concert of *Omertis* of different sizes, made me curious to assemble one in order to judge of the truth of his assertions; the more so, as the Brahmun himself was really an excellent performer, and I imagined that a reunion of several such as he, might have rather a fine effect: but this instrument being very rare, I could with difficulty find but three, and those very indifferent and far inferior to him; so that my hope was deceived.

This instrument is unknown to many Hindoos, though some among the higher classes, play on it for their amusement.

Pl. II.154. Amr̥ti. Paris: II.7.5.
Calcutta: Sec. XI, No. 9. Omerti,—kind of Fiddle.

Commentary: The amr̥ti—"omerti" to Solvyns's ear—was already in decline in the late eighteenth century, and Joep Bor suggests that it "must have vanished" soon after Solvyns portrayed it.[2] References to the amr̥ti are few, but the *Ā'īn-i-Akbarī* briefly describes the instrument as having one gourd and a single iron string[3]—clearly different from the amr̥ti Solvyns portrays. Solvyns's reference to its use by "higher classes. . . for their amusement" indicates that the amr̥ti might be a predecessor of the esrāj, a hybrid instrument combining the fretted neck of the sitār with the waisted, skin-covered resonator of the Bengali dotār and the bow of the Western cello.[4] As pictured, the amr̥ti appears to have had at least four strings, indicating a potential pitch range of two or more octaves. The bow appears to be similar to that used for the sāraṇgī and other indigenous bowed instruments.

Amr̥ti is used today as a term for the rāvaṇhatthā, a spike fiddle,[5] and Bor notes a similarity in the instrument Solvyns portrays to the "ravanastron" (rāvaṇhatthā) depicted by Pierre Sonnerat in 1782.[6]

Deben Bhattacharya writes that Solvyns's description and illustration suggest similarity to the keñkariyā from Bundelkhand in central India. "The term 'Kenkār' means the cry of the swan and also the noise of scraping metal with other objects. The fiddle 'Keñkariyā' has a belly of split coconut covered with skin and a long wooden neck bearing one melody string made of a strand of horsetail hair and seven sympathetic strings of metal. It is played with a hunter's bow (as in the picture) which is also made of horsetail hair."[7]

1 *NGMI*, 1:56. Solvyns's titles it "Omorti" in the Paris edition, but in the text (as in the Calcutta edition) spells it "Omerti."
2 "The Voice of the Sarangi," 73. Bor notes that the last reference he found to the amr̥ti was by S. N. Tagore in 1877, and "it is doubtful if he ever saw any such instrument."
3 See Dick, "Sirbīṇ," *NGMI*, 3:390, and Bor, "The Voice of the Sarangi," 75.
4 Dick, "Esrāj," *NGMI*, 1:719.
5 See Dick and Sorrell, "Rāvaṇhatthā," *NGMI*, 3:198-99.
6 Bor, "The Voice of the Sarangi," 75. The instrument is illustrated in Pl. 40, in Bor, 46. See Sonnerat, *Voyage aux Indes Orientales et a la Chine*, 1:178-81. A plate in the original, French edition depicts various musical instruments, but the plates are not included with the English translation.
7 Letter to author, February 17, 1992.

II.155. Oorni

Paris: II.7.6. OORNI: The *Oorni* scarcely deserves the name of a musical instrument, and I should not have noticed it, but that it is common all through India, especially on the coast of Coromandel: but in the great towns, such as Calcutta, Madras, Bombay, it is seldom seen but in the hands of *Says* (stable-boys) *Haurrys,* (nightmen), and others of the lowest ranks. The print suffices to shew that the *Oorni* is nothing more than an open cocoa-nut to which a hollow stick of bambou is applied, and one chord which they scrape with a bow often loaded with ornaments. The sound of this music, if it may be called by that name, cannot be compared to any thing better than to the crying of a cat or of a wild beast; the same note is heard for several minutes, and is followed by another higher or lower, but always as shrill and as monotonous. This does not prevent the lower classes of Hindoos from entertaining a high opinion of their *Oorni,* and even imagining that nothing can be more charming to the ear of Europeans. With this idea they frequently come and play it under the windows of their houses, and to render the concert more complete, mingle with it the no less harsh and discordant sound of their own voices. I have been sometimes so stunned with it, that I have been obliged to send out my servants to drive off these execrable musicians.

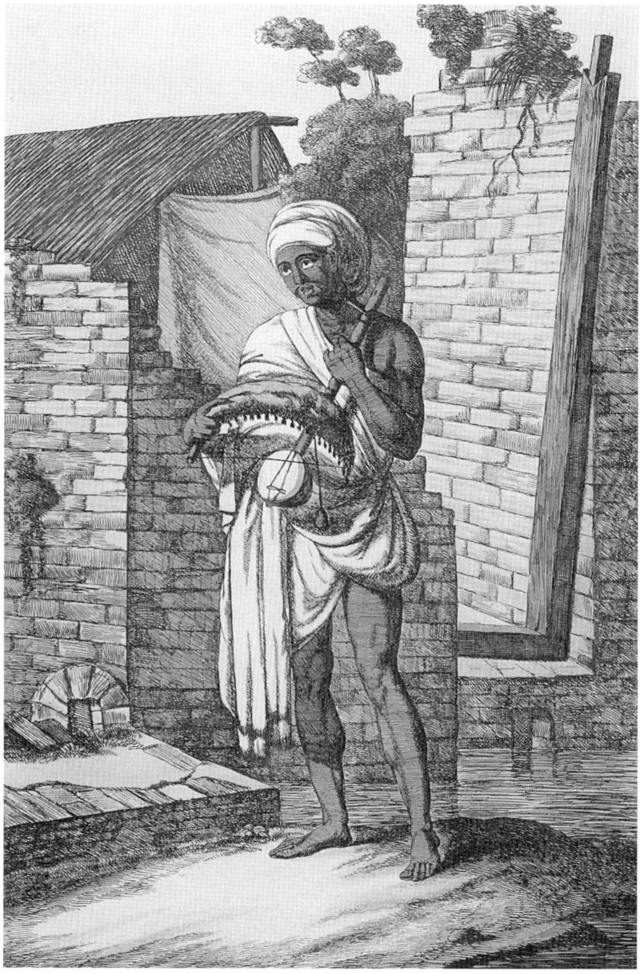

Pl. II.155. Oorni. Paris: II.7.6.
Calcutta: Sec. XI, No. 35. An Oorni, from the Coromandel Coast.
Orme: 28.[1]

Commentary: While the amr̥ti was an instrument associated with the higher classes, the oorni seems to have been restricted to the lower castes. Such one-stringed bowed lutes can be found throughout North Indian folk cultures under various names, but the term *oorni* may be either specious or obsolete. In the area of Bengal, the bena of the Rajbansi people closely resembles Solvyns's description of the oorni.[2] The bow depicted in the Solvyns portrait appears to have a set of bells (ghuṅgrū) attached to it. Such bows are still common in folk cultures of North India.

The oorni also appears similar to the ektāra,[3] a one-stringed instrument made from a gourd or of wood, with one side open. It is widely used in Bengal, notably among the Bauls, wandering minstrels, in accompanying their devotional songs.[4]

Shoberl writes that "The oorni yields but two sounds, one of which is described as resembling the mewing of a cat, and the other the lowing of deer."[5]

Solvyns's "Says" (sāis, Pl. II.118) is the syce, or groom. "Hurry" is Hār̥i (Pl. II.71), which Risley describes as "a menial and scavenger caste of Bengal" and whose various occupations include "playing of instruments at weddings and festivals."[6]

1 The Orme text accompanying the plate depicting the oorni mistakenly identifies it as the "Bansee" (bā̃śi, Pl. II.180) and follows the description from the Solvyns 1799 *Catalog*ue for the bamboo flute.
2 Sanyal.
3 Dick, Babiracki, and Helffer, "Ektār," *NGMI*, 1:649-50.
4 On the Bauls, see Capwell.
5 3:30.
6 1:316.

II.156. Ḍhāk[1]

Pl. II.156. Ḍhāk. Paris: II.8.2.

Calcutta: Sec. XI, No. 21. D'Hauk,—used at Marriages and Religious ceremonies.

Orme: 55.

Commentary: The term *ḍhāk* has been used since medieval times in reference to various types of Indian drums. The Bengali ḍhāk, depicted by Solvyns, is a large drum, often decorated with feathers, that continues to be played in association with Śaiva-Śākta religious festivals.[2] Solvyns refers to their use in such festivals as Durgā Pūjā (Pl. II.194) and Kālī Pūjā (Pl. II.190). (His "Calkee" is clearly meant to be Kālī, as Kalki, the last and yet-to-come avatar of Viṣṇu, is not celebrated in festival.) In his etching of Jhā̃p (Pl. II.191), part of the Gājan festival dedicated to Śiva, Solvyns prominently portrays several ḍhāks. Caṛak Pūjā (Pl. II.193), the hook-swinging that is also part of Gājan, attracted large crowds and drew the particular interest of Europeans before the British suppressed the practice in the nineteenth century. Here too ḍhāks added to the excitement, though Solvyns includes none in his portrayal of the scene.

Paris: II.8.2. D'HAUCK: I have yet many musical instruments to describe: this engraving represents the *D'Hauck,* an enormous drum which a single man finds it difficult to carry. The Hindoo who plays upon it has two sticks with which he strikes the skin of the drum quicker or slower, as he fancies, and sometimes with astonishing velocity. It must be observed that the *D'Hauck* is a privileged instrument; that is to say, that it cannot be played without an autorisation from the *Jummadar* [*jamādār*] of the place: this permission is not obtained without a certain retribution, and only on great festivals, marriages, etc. The *D'Hauck* is particularly suited to the Hindoo people, who are extremely fond of noisy instruments; they are delighted with its hollow sounds, and think that nothing can surpass them.

On days of great ceremony, such as the *Durgah* [Durgā Pūjā], *Calkee* [Kālī Pūjā], *J'haump* [Jhāmp], *Churrack* [Caṛak Pūjā], they ornament the *D'Hauck* with plumes and horsehair, which encreases its preposterous size.

It is with this instrument that they who give the feast of the *Churrack* assemble the persons who choose to perform the swinging which we have described in the twelfth number of the first volume. Some days before the ceremony, they are led in procession through their quarter, to the sound of the *D'Hauck.* It sometimes happens that the courage of these devotees not being equal to their piety, they begin by following the drum slowly and trembling; but soon its noisy sounds and the fumes of intoxicating liquors, animate them, and exalt their imagination to a degree of intrepidity which allows them to see only the glory which is to attend this fanatical undertaking.

Today ḍhāks are seen most prominently in Bengal at Durgā Pūjā and are typically accompanied by a kā̃sar (Pl. II.147; or kā̃sī, Pl. II.172), or gong. The *ḍhākis*, as the players are known, are usually from the low Bauri (Pl. II.76) and Bayen castes, and they often dance to the rhythmic beat of their drums.[3] Traditionally, though no longer today, the master *ḍhāki* would be "sumptuously remunerated" during Durgā Pūjā.[4]

The term *jamādār*, from the Persian, refers to the head of any body of men and in Bengal, in Solvyns's time, had various meanings depending on context. Here Solvyns probably refers to the *zamīndār*, the commonly used Persian word for landholder. In Bengal in the late eighteenth century, the two words seem to have been conflated. *Hobson-Jobson* notes that at that time the prevailing pronunciation of *zamīndār* (*jamidār* in Bengali) was indistinguishable from *jamādār*.[5]

1 Dick, Babiracki, and Dournon, "Ḍhāk," *NGMI*, 1:559.
2 Ray, *Folk-Music of Eastern India*, 41.
3 Prabhas Sen, 128. A large color photograph, 128-29, depicts the *ḍhākis* with their plumed drums.
4 Ray, *Music of Eastern India*. 105.
5 980. On the zamīndār, see Pl. II.20.

II.157. Ḍhol[1]

Pl. II.157. Ḍhol. Paris: II.8.3.

Calcutta: Sec. XI, No. 25. A D'Hola,—beaten on one side by the hand, and on the other by a stick.

Paris: II.8.3. D'HOLA: This also is a sort of drum, but smaller than the *D'Hauck* [*ḍhāk*]. It is beaten on the upper skin with the hand, and on the lower with a stick; the sound is dead, and serves only for accompanying: it is used at all their feasts and with every sort of music; so that it is universally known among the Hindoos.

It may easily be supposed that it does not require much art to play upon it; for which reason many of the lower classes abandon their trades, by which they earned a moderate but competent subsistance, to become *D'Hola* players; a profession which suits their indolent disposition, promises them an easy life and all the pleasures that accord with the grossness of their taste. The liquors and portions of *pawn* [*pān*][2] which those who give feasts are in the habit of distributing to them must necessarily ruin the health of these unhappy people by continual and immoderate use. Their wives and children too, by partaking of the profusion of these donations, contract habits of debauchery. As these feasts always take place in the night, they can sleep but in the day. This continual fatigue and sitting up, and still more the excessive use of strong liquors by which they think to recruit their strength, gives them a pale and livid complexion, and renders them for ever indisposed and unfit for labour. The greater part of these unfortunate beings sink into a state of absolute stupidity, and are soon branded by their countrymen with the contemptuous appellation of *Pariahs*.

The form of the *D'Hola* is the same all through Hindoostan, and differs only in its ornaments: they generally cover this instrument, as they do all the others, with a red cloath, to preserve it from the damp and the dust.

Commentary: Although correctly identified in the Calcutta edition, Solvyns mislabels and reverses the plates for the ḍhol and the ḍholak (Pl. II.159) in the Paris edition. The ḍhol, depicted here, is usually larger than the ḍholak and has a ratio of length to head diameter in the range of 5:4. The drummer hangs the drum from his neck, and it is commonly played, as Solvyns notes, with a combination hand and stick technique, with the left hand striking the higher pitched head (usually above or to the right) and, in the right hand, the stick striking or scraping the lower pitched head (below or to the left). The stick is traditionally of bamboo, with a curved or hooked head.[3]

Contrary to what Solvyns asserts, the ḍhol is not the same throughout India. Alastair Dick establishes two lineages of ḍhol in South Asia: a shallow barrel type stemming from West Asian influence with a head to body length ratio of 1:1 or less, and larger barrel drums stemming from the paṭaha, a drum of ancient and medieval India. Examples of the first type include the Rajasthani ḍhol and the ḍhol of Garhwal, Uttar Pradesh.[4] The Bengali ḍhol is an example of the second type.

Drummers and musicians more generally were often from "untouchable" castes, such as, in Bengal, Mucī (Pl. II.70), Haṛī (Pl. II.71), and Dom (Pl. II.68). The term *pariah* derives from the untouchable Paraiyar caste of South India. The Tamil *parai* means drum, and members of the caste traditionally drummed at festivals, but Solvyns's use of *pariah* conveys no such association. Rather, he uses the term to mean simply the lowest or worst of anything.[5]

Drumming in the late eighteenth century, however, was not confined to the low castes. In his discussion of "A Woman of Distinction" (Pl. II.87), Solvyns writes that "sometimes . . . , at intervals only, she will relieve the monotony of this existence by music, which she performs upon the *dole* [ḍhol] or the *tom-tom* [ḍholak] accompanied by her voice." Again, in describing women of rank and wealth (Pl. II.92), he writes that "the utmost extent of their refinement in the pleasing arts is to play on a *tom-tom*, an instrument on which they sometimes attain some degree of perfection."

Sukumar Ray, writing of the folk music of Bengal, notes that the ḍhol "was taken up by the people of upper society in Calcutta,"[6] and that "connoisseurs of music used to take a fancy to expert DHOL-playing in their parlours."[7]

1 Dick and Dournon, "Ḍhol," *NGMI*, 1:560-62. Also see Ray, *Folk-Music of Eastern India*, 42.
2 *Pān* is a mildly narcotic preparation of betel, acrea nut, lime, etc. wrapped in a betel leaf and chewed. See Pl. II.212.
3 Musicologist Deben Bhattacharya notes that in playing the ḍhol, the drummer uses a friction or scraping technique with the stick. Letter to the author, February 17, 1992.
4 Dick and Dournon, "Ḍhol," 561. Also see Dick, "Paṭaha," *NGMI*, 3:21-22.
5 On Solvyns's use of the term *pariah*, see Pl. II.22.
6 *Folk-Music of Eastern India*, 42.
7 *Music of Eastern India*, 105.

II.158. Khol[1]

Paris: II.8.4. KHOLE, OR MIRDEN: Although many people look upon this instrument as sacred, and that it is often seen, especially in their religious festivals, in the hands of the devout Hindoos, such as Faquirs[2] and Beeshnubs [Baiṣṇab], it is not less true that the people make use of it also at their feasts. The form of the *Khole* is exactly such as I have represented it in this engraving; it is sufficient to look at it, to have a perfect idea of this instrument, which consists meerly in a piece of earthen ware covered at the two ends with a skin stretched like our drums, except that the lower end is wider and produces a deeper sound than the upper. It is not necessary to remark that the music of the *Khole* is as monotonous as that of the other instruments which I have been describing. But the Hindoos, on the contrary, find in it an extraordinary charm, and pretend that, accompanied by the voice, this instrument is capable of expressing all the emotions of the soul, from the most violent to the most tender.

At their great festivals a number of these *Kholes* are generally seen contending with each other in noise and uproar. (See number 2 and 3 of the first vol.)[3] I have been assured that, in former times, all Hindous were not indiscriminately allowed to play upon it, and even now those who make most use of it are, as I have already mentioned, almost always of the devout class.

The accessories of the print represent, as in all the other plates of Hindoo instruments, the places in which they are generally heard.

Commentary: The khol is a classical Indian double-headed drum of eastern India. The body is made from clay in an asymmetrical barrel shape. The tapering toward the right end of the khol's body is more sharply

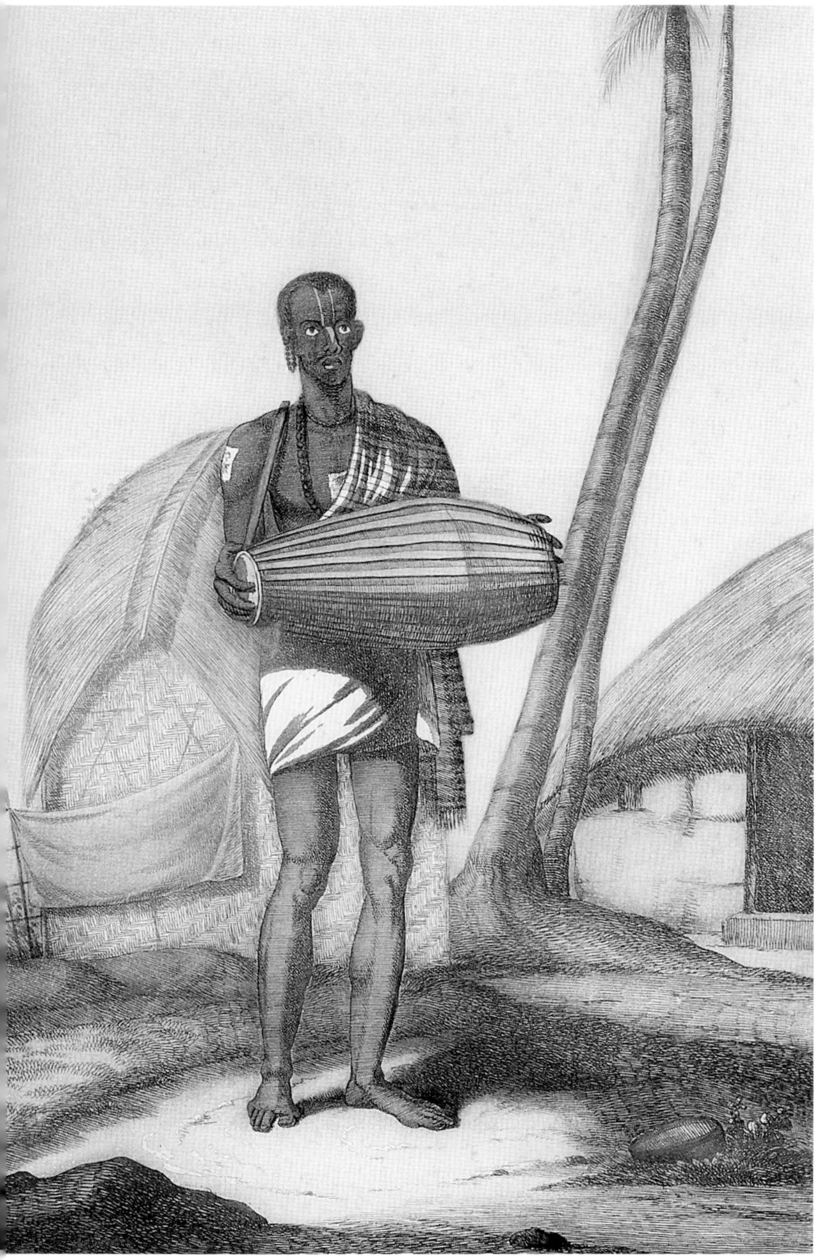

Pl. II.158. Khol. Paris: II.8.4.
Calcutta: Sec. XI, No. 10. A Khole or Mirden,—the Tube of the Drum is of earthen ware.

accentuated than that of the classical pakhāvaj (Pl. II.163) associated with the *dhrupad* tradition of North Indian music. Like the pakhāvaj, the khol has a treble right head tuned to a specific pitch and a lower-pitched bass left head. However, the khol is tuned higher than the pakhāvaj and has a metallic timbre.

The khol is closely associated with *kīrtan* (devotional singing) of the Vaiṣṇava tradition of Śrī Caitanya Māhaprabhū, the late sixteenth century *bhakti* poet-saint of Bengal. The instrument continues to be looked upon as sacred by Vaiṣṇava devotees of this sect, and its worship, along with that of the kartāl cymbals, still forms part of the ritual practices of the *kīrtan* event. Solvyns depicts the use of the khol—which he refers to as "mirdun" (mr̥daṅga)—along with the bā̃k and kartāl in his portrayal of Hari Saṅkīrtan (Pl. II.184), a congregational singing of devotional songs praising Hari (an epithet of Viṣṇu). The practice is believed to have been begun by Caitanya.

The "Beeshnubs" (Baiṣṇabs) mentioned by Solvyns are Vaiṣṇava. Solvyns portrays a Baiṣṇab in one of the etchings depicting Hindu ascetics (Pl. II.138), and writes that they are "individuals who, after having renounced all the pleasures of life, the riches and good things of the earth, devote themselves to the worship of Vishnou." The figure depicted in the etching wears the mark of Viṣṇu on his forehead. The "faquirs" mentioned might have been Bauls, who are known to have adopted the khol from the Vaiṣṇava tradition.[4]

The khol is used in religious contexts of sects other than the Caitanya Vaiṣṇava now as it was in Solvyns's time. In discussing Rāmāyan Gāyan (Pl. II.183), "singing the exploits of Rāmā," Solvyns notes that the recital is generally accompanied by such musical instruments as mr̥daṅga, khol, and kartāl. Here he seems to distinguish the khol and mr̥daṅga, but in the title to the khol etching, Solvyns gives its name as "Khole or Mirden," and from his Hari Saṅkīrtan, the two names would seem to refer to the same instrument. Sukumar Ray, in *Folk-Music of Eastern India*, writes that the khol is often called the "*Mridanga* of Bengal,"[5] and Bandyopadhyaya, in *Musical Instruments of India*, says that the khol, widely used in Bengal, is also known as "mr̥daṅga."[6] The mr̥daṅga (meaning "clay-bodied") was the ancient clay drum of the *dhrupad* singers, who replaced it with the wooden barrel pakhāvaj.

1 Dick, "Khol," *NGMI*, 2:423-24. Also see Ray, *Folk-Music of Eastern India*, 42-43.

2 Solvyns uses the term *faquir* (fakir) to refer to Hindu religious ascetics and mendicants.

3 Solvyns refers to Pls. II.183, Rāmāyan Gāyan, and II.184, Hari Saṅkīrtan.

4 Capwell, 108.

5 42.

6 71. It should be noted that the Bengali mr̥daṅga differs from the South Indian mr̥daṅgam both in shape and sound.

II.159. Ḍholak[1]

Paris: II.8.5. D'HOLUK: Simply to say that the *D'Holuk* is also called *Tomtom,* is giving a very true idea of a sound of this instrument, which may be looked upon as national in Hindoostan; for, of all their musical instruments, this is the most common as well among the natives as among the Mussulmen, the Armenians, the Portuguese, and other foreigners. The *Tomtom* is to be met with in every house and in every body's hands: it is the amusement and delight of them all, men and women, young and old. The *D'Holuk* is also a sort of drum, as the print represents it: the manner of playing upon it is as simple as its form; nothing more is required than to strike with the fingers the two skins which cover the ends of the wood, one of which, being less than the other, gives a sharper sound. Although an European finds this music very monotonous, the Hindoos nevertheless have various means of varying the tone of it by the different degrees of force with which they strike it. There are some who play it with astonishing rapidity. The public women and kept mistresses are never without a *Tomtom,* with which they endeavour to relieve the languor and insipidity of their unhappy situation, using it sometimes to accompany their voice, which has frequently a very pleasing effect.

The music of the *D'Holuk* not being loud, it is seldomer found in the open air than in their houses, where good players are sometimes heard with great pleasure.

Pl. II.159. Ḍholak. Paris: II.8.5.

Calcutta: Sec. XI, No. 18. A D'holuk,—small drum.

Orme: 53.

Commentary: The ḍholak is played by the hands at each end. Known to have been an instrument of the Mughal courts, the ḍholak was by Solvyns's time, as it remains today, common throughout North India and played by members of all classes of society. It is apparent that the practice of modulating the pitch of the bass head by sliding either the thumb or the heel of the left hand along the skin, as is also done on the modern tablā, was a ḍholak technique known to players in the eighteenth century.

The ḍholak is frequently described as a small ḍhol, and in contrast to the ḍhol, this popular instrument is widely used in indoor performance as Solvyns portrays it.

Solvyns describes the ḍholak as a "tomtom," a word sometimes used generically for a small drum and, in the quaint phrasing of *The Oxford English Dictionary*, "extended to the drums of barbarous people generally." *Hobson-Jobson* gives the origin as Hindustani *ṭamṭam*, an onomatopoeia for the beat of the drum.[2] Whitworth, in his *Anglo-Indian Dictionary*, gives the Bengali form as *ṭanṭan*, "a small drum."[3]

As noted in the discussion of the ḍhol, Solvyns mistakenly reversed the labeling on the ḍhol (Pl. II.157) and ḍholak (Pl. II.159) prints in the Paris edition.

1 Dick, Babiracki, and Webber, "Ḍholak," *NGMI*, 1:562-63.
2 929-30.
3 320.

II.160. Tablā[1]

Pl. II.160. Tablā. Paris: II.8.6.
Calcutta: Sec. XI, No. 17. A Tubla,—wooden Drums.
Orme: 52.

Paris: II.8.6. TUBLA: The *Tubla* is composed of two tymbals, one of earthen ware, the other of wood, both of them covered with a skin upon which the musician strikes with his fingers. Each tymbal gives a different sound, the mixture of which produces tolerable music. The engraving shews the attitude of the performer and the manner of treating the instrument.

I have already more than once observed that the amusements of the Hindoos are adapted to the manners and way of living of the different classes: the better sort are distinguished, even in their modes of diversion, from those who are without principles of honour. Several musical instruments are in use only among this latter sort: of this number is the *Tubla,* which in general is played only by *Loutchias,*[2] people of dissolute manners, and by public prostitutes, who have it played in their houses by those who frequent them and share in their debaucheries. The dress of the musician represented in the engraving, differs from the national costume of the Hindoos, because men of this class, in contempt of the laws of their country, affect in their appearance a resemblance with the Mussulmen. He is seated on a carpet or piece of cotton cloth. A wooden box, a pitcher, a candlestick with a *charrack,*[3] or a little lamp, forms the whole of his household furniture. In the background is another musician carrying a *Sarinda.*

Commentary: The assertion that the tablā was played only by "loutchias" is probably incorrect. Willard describes the tablā as an instrument of great popularity at the court of the Nawab of Banda, and it can be assumed that the instrument was part of the instrumentarium at other Mughal courts. It is notable that the musician pictured is holding the tablā in the same manner as is done in *qawwālī* ensembles,[4] with the bass drum (bāyā̃) in the lap of the performer. The right hand's position is the same as in modern tablā performance.

Earthenware bāyā̃ continue to be made, especially for beginning students. Metal bāyā̃ were not necessarily unknown in Solvyns's time. Copper bāyā̃ are mentioned by writers in the late nineteenth century,[5] and wooden ones are not unknown even today.

Risley writes that "The tabla-wala, or drum-maker, is always a Muchi [Mucī, Pl. II.70]," the Bengali leather-working caste. "Goats' skins are used for the covering, while cows' hides supply the strings for tightening the parchment. On every native drum, at one or both ends, black circles (*khiran*) are painted to improve the pitch. The Muchi prepares a paste of iron filings and rice, with which he stains the parchment." Risley also notes that "At all Hindu weddings, they [Mucīs] are employed as musicians, and engaged in bands, along with Muhamadans."[6]

1 Dick and Sen, "Tablā," *NGMI*, 3:492-97.

2 For a discussion of "loutchia," see commentaries in Pls. II.86 and II.151.

3 What Solvyns refers to here is unclear. The Anglo-Indian *charrack*, a corruption of the Persian *charkh*, is the word for wheel.

4 *Qawwalī* are the songs of the Muslim sūfī assembly.

5 See, for example, French, "Catalogue of Indian Musical Instruments," in Tagore, 261, and Day, 138.

6 Risley, 2:99. See Solvyns, Mucī, Pl. II.70. For a discussion of the Mucī as musician, see commentary under Joorghaje, Pl. II.161.

II.161. Joorghaje

Pl. II.161. Joorghaje. Paris: II.9.2.
Calcutta: Sec. XI, No. 24. A Joorg-haje,—two Drums of different sizes.

Paris: II.9.2. JOORGHAJE, A MUSICAL INSTRUMENT: Although we have already seen a variety of musical instruments in the foregoing numbers, there remains a still greater number to be described in the remainder of this and the following, which are to complete the second volume. It is, as we must have already remarked, their most noisy instruments that the Hindoos have endeavoured to vary. Noise being always more pleasing to their ears than harmony, of which they are very little sensible, or have rather no idea whatsoever, they have been studious to encrease the pleasures suited to their taste, by giving to their music at least the charm of variety. The merit of invention is not what is most striking in the construction of these instruments; but still we cannot help being surprised that a people so evidently without the genius of music, should have been so anxious to multiply the means of this amusement, and have carried the number of their instruments much beyond what we have done in Europe.

I have already represented many which bear a strong resemblance to our drums, and are used to beat the time and mark the cadence and movement of the steps in their religious processions and feasts. This is the use they make of the *Joorghaje* which this print represents: this instrument consists of two long cases of an unequal size, the skin on the under part is beaten with the fingers, that on the upper side with a stick: the sounds follow sometimes in a quicker, sometimes in a slower measure, as in the other instruments. The performers are generally men of the lowest classes, *Doams* [Dom] or *Moochees* [Mucī].

Commentary: The name seems to indicate a pair (*joṛ*) of *ghaje*—Hindi for "elephant." Drums having names sounding similar to *ghaje* exist in eastern India. The ghasā is a barrel drum with raised hoops that is struck on one side with a cane and rubbed on the other side with a crook-stick. It is played by the Pāṇa musicians of southern Orissa. Dick relates this to the medieval ghadasa, a barrel drum played partly by friction.[1] A drum pair of similar construction to this joorghaje is the pambai of South India.[2] It is not possible, however, to establish a connection between the joorghaje and any of these other instruments on the basis of Solvyns's description.

Of the Doms (Pl. II.68), also known as Caṇḍal, *Hobson-Jobson* describes them as "a very low caste. . . . In many places they perform such offices as carrying dead bodies, removing carrion, &c. They are often musicians. . . ."[3] Risley identifies them as in charge of the burning *ghāṭs* at Banaras and associated generally with the disposal of the dead. But, while a degraded position is forced upon all Dom by reason of this role, most Dom, Risley states, follow "the comparatively clean occupation of making baskets and mats."[4] Risley cites Carnegy, *Notes on the Races of Avadh (Oudh)*, that "it is not uncommon for men of this class to rise to high office under kings by whom they were employed as musicians."[5] In Bengal, Risley writes, "the Bajunia [Dom] subcaste are employed to make highly discordant music at marriages and festivals. His women-folk, however, only perform as musicians at the weddings of their own people, it being considered highly derogatory for them to do so for outsiders."[6]

The Mucī (Pl. II.70) are variously identified as a branch of or identical with the Chamār caste. Mucī are the leather workers of Bengal, engaged as "tanners, shoe-makers, saddlers, musicians, and basket-makers."[7] "At all Hindu weddings they are employed as musicians, and engaged in bands, as among Muhamadans. Their favourite instruments are drums of various shapes and sizes, the violin, and the pipe."[8] Jogendra Nath Bhattacharya states that "for the Muchi and Mohamedan musicians who are a necessity on festive occasions, there is generally special accommodation in the mansions of the rich and in the big temples. . . . [T]he Muchi bands entertain the bye-standers from the Nat-Mandir or dancing hall in front of the puja *dalan* or chapel."[9]

1 Dick, "Ghaḍasa," *NGMI*, 2:39.
2 Deva, 85.
3 322.
4 1:249.
5 1:240.
6 1:250.
7 Risley, 2:98.
8 Ibid., 2:99.
9 213.

II.162. Ṭikārā[1]

Pl. II.162. Ṭikārā. Paris: II.9.3.

Calcutta: Sec. XI, No. 31. A Tickora,—played at Nautches [II.2.1], Feasts, &c.

Paris: II.9.3. TICHORA, A MUSICAL INSTRUMENT: Here is another instrument of the same nature as the foregoing, as well in its form as in the manner of playing upon it. The *Tichora,* as is shown in the print, is also composed of two tymbals, one of which is rather smaller than the other. The performer is generally seated on the ground behind his instrument; but in the public ceremonies, marriages, cavalcades of persons of high rank, or on the arrival of a Radjah [rājā], the instrument is carried on the camels of the retinue, where the *Tichora* becomes a mark of honor, and adds to the solemnity of the feast or procession. It will easily be perceived that I could not represent this ceremony without losing the exact form of the instrument which I wished to give: for this reason I have preferred a drawing of a performer on the *Tichora* sitting before the house of a person who, according to the Hindoo custom, hires musicians with the permission of the *Jemindar* [*zamīndār*][2] of the district. Although the *Tichora* is originally of Hindoostan, it is seldom played but by Mussulmen. At the Radjahs nevertheless and in the Nautches, it is sometimes used by Hindoos of inferior casts, but not so low as the tanners, nightmen, or undertakers.

Commentary: According to Dick, the ṭikārā of Bengal is a single kettledrum, while that of Orissa is a "paired, earthenware kettledrum with the skins braced with ropes and tuning paste applied to the lower drum."[3] Solvyns, however, depicts the instrument as paired kettledrums. Shoberl, in his description of the "tikora," follows Solvyns, and adds that it is frequently seen in the train of Mārāṭha, carried on a camel that follows the elephant upon which the prince rides.[4] But Shoberl also describes a "double drum, used on occasion of festivals and processions" as a "nagur."[5] The ceremonial use of the instrument described by Solvyns and its use primarily by Muslim performers would seem to indicate that the drums referred to were what would be most widely recognized as nagārā (Pl. II.164).

1 Dick, "Ṭikārā," *NGMI*, 3:584.
2 See commentary on Ḍhāk, Pl. II.156.
3 Dick, "Ṭikārā," *NGMI*, 3:584.
4 3:20.
5 3:21.

II.163. Pakhāvaj[1]

Pl. II.163. Pakhāvaj. Paris: II.9.4.

Calcutta: Sec. XI, No. 32. A Pukwauz,—used as the foregoing [i.e., "at Nautches, Feasts, &c."]

Orme: 58.

Paris: II.9.4. PUCWAUZ: Those who remember my former description of the *Khole* [Pl. II.158] will find some resemblance between that instrument and the *Pucwauz* which this plate represents: but it must be observed, that it is not like it made of baked earth, but of wood covered at the two ends with a skin; little bits of wood moveable at pleasure at one of the ends join these skins together. The *Pucwauz* is seldom heard at the feasts or ceremonies of religion, but is in frequent use at private entertainments, especially in Nautches, where it often serves for accompanying. On these occasions performers rather of an higher cast are hired. It is also an amusement for several casts of Hindoos, who play upon it for hours together in their houses, and appear exceedingly delighted with the sounds which they produce by striking the skins in a variety of motion with their hands. The Hindoo in the print is an inhabitant of the country, seated before his house, and giving himself up to the enjoyment of the freshness of the air and the sounds of his instrument. He is drest in blue and white cloth, which shews that he is of the northern parts of Hindoostan, or that he follows the doctrine of *Bichno* [Viṣṇu], whose sectaries affect those colours.

Commentary: The pakhāvaj, also called mr̥daṅg, is known today as the primary percussion accompaniment in musical genres belonging to the *dhrupad* style. In previous times it was associated with some traditions of *kīrtan* singing, especially that of the Vallabhā *Sampradāya*, a Vaiṣṇava sect of western India, and with court dance. It is the most classical of the North Indian drums and apparently has enjoyed such high esteem throughout its long history that it has been acceptable for use by members of the highest Hindu castes. Exponents of the pakhāvaj have steadily decreased in number with the decline of the *dhrupad* tradition, beginning in the eighteenth century. The resurgence of interest in *dhrupad* singing during the last two decades has helped to promote the rediscovery of the pakhāvaj, but has not yet secured the survival of the tradition.

1 See discussion of the "northern mr̥daṅg or pakhāvaj" by Dick in "Mr̥daṅga," *NGMI*, 2:696-699; and Bandyopadhyaya, "Pakhāwaja," 72-74. The Bengali form is pākhwāj.

II.164. Nagāṛā[1]

Paris: II.9.5. NAGRA: This print represents one of those couriers who in India perform the functions of the postrunning on foot, from town to town, with letters and commissions in a leather sack. They are called *Dauks* [*dāk*] in the Hindoo language, and are remarkable for their fidelity and extraordinary dispatch.

The reader will not immediately perceive how these circumstances are connected with the musical instrument which I am going to describe. It is necessary then to inform him that it is confirmed by long experience, that the sound of the *Nagra* has the effect of driving away the dangerous animals, such as tygers and serpents, which, to the great terror of the traveller, infest the high roads of Hindoostan. As the instrument, which resembles a small drum, is very portable, all those who have to traverse any unfrequented country are preceded by a *Kouli* [*kulī*, or coolie] constantly beating the *Nagra,* whether they travel in a palanquin or on foot. Even servants have a *Nagra*-beater to accompany them when they are sent on commissions by their masters to any distance. The couriers or *Dauks* have always one before them, which they transmit with their packets to those of the next station, who forward them as rapidly and in the same manner. During the night they have besides two *Koulies* with *machals* [*maśāl*] or torches to light them.

So simple is the mode of communication among the Hindoos. As to the *Nagra,* to which sometime the *Kaura* is added, I have given a sufficient idea of this noisy instrument by describing its use. I have only to add that it is also heard at public festivals and in all great ceremonies.

Pl. II.164. Nagāṛā. Paris: II.9.5.

Calcutta: Sec. XI, No. 27. A Nagra,—played on by two sticks.

Orme: 56.

Commentary: The shape of the instrument in Solvyns's portrait is obscured by a decorative skirt. Nagāṛā generally refers to kettledrum in South Asia. Its uses have been diverse, ranging from an instrument of the court, shrine or temple ceremonial band (*naubat*) to an accompanying instrument for tribal dances in eastern Bihar and Bengal. Modern writers do not mention use of the nagāṛā as a noise-making device to drive away wild animals, but the use of the drums is still a part of game hunting in India. The *dākwālā* (postman) or *kulī* (hired laborer or burden-carrier) no longer beats nagāṛā in the context of their occupations.

The figure Solvyns's depicts is a *dāk*, or mail carrier. The term *dāk* (Anglo-Indian, *dawk* or *dauk*) was used both for post and postman, but its more precise and broader meaning refers to transport by relays of men and horses, stationed at intervals—an institution in India dating at least from the fourteenth century. As well as for the post, a relay system was used for carrying passengers in palanquins.[2]

In British India, a postal system, apparently introduced by Clive in 1766,[3] used the *dāk.* As Lady Nugent described it in her Calcutta journal in 1814, "There are three men; one carries the bangy, or basket, which holds the letters—I should say rather, baskets for there is one for letters and another for packages—these are equally balanced, and swung, by a light bamboo, over the man's shoulders. The other carries a torch, for they always set off at night, and travel night and day. The third man has a tomtom [Solvyns's nagāṛā] on which he beats incessantly, to keep off tigers and other wild beasts. They all three run very fast, keeping close to each other, for the light is as necessary as the music, and the dauk, or postman, is always between the two others."[4]

In his ethnographic notes of 1883 on eastern Bengal, Wise writes that "Formerly the naqārah [nagāṛā] players were Chamārs [leather workers], but of late years the lower grade of Muhammadans . . . are exclusively employed, and are known as Bājunia."[5]

1 Dick and Babiracki, "Nagāṛā," *NGMI*, 2:739-41.
2 "Dawk" in *Hobson-Jobson*, 299-300; "dak" in *OED*.
3 Ivie, 130-31, cited in Nair, ed., *British Social Life in Ancient Calcutta*, 46-47.
4 2:254, quoted in Nair, Calcutta *in the 19th Century*, 171-72.
5 Entry under "Bajhunia," 39. Wise notes that a nagāṛā band "plays at each 'pahar,' or watch of the day."

II.165. Kāṛā[1]

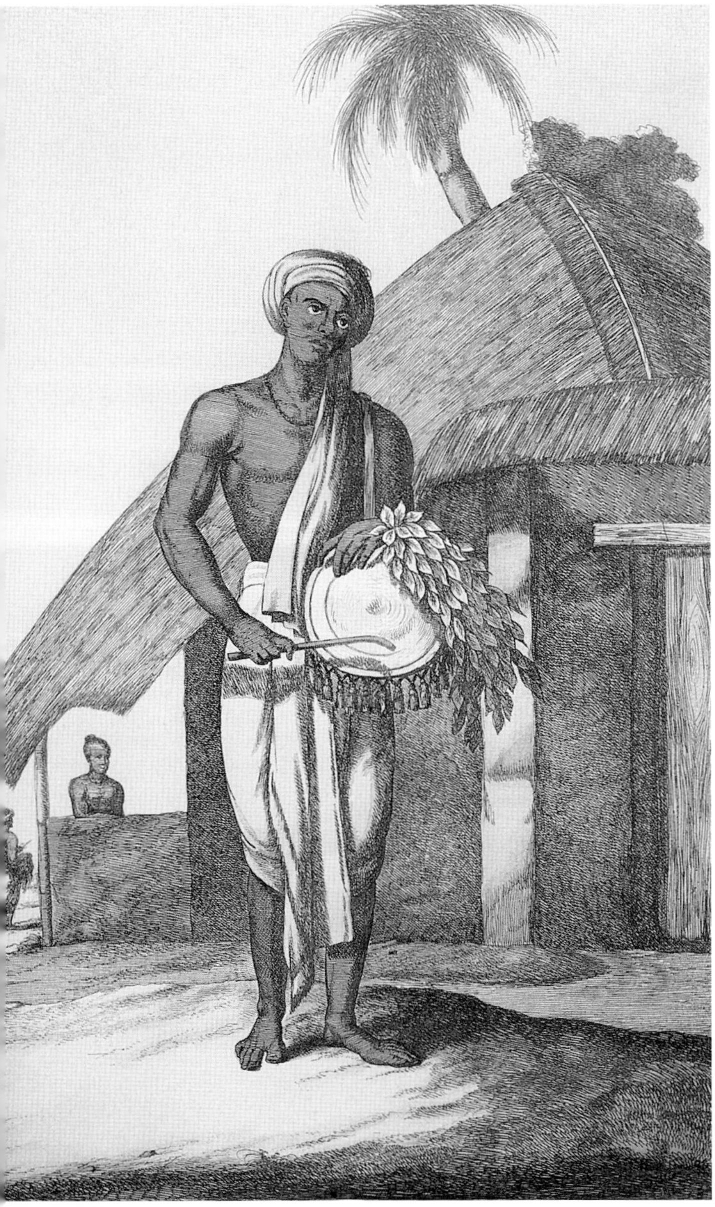

Pl. II.165. Kāṛā. Paris: II.9.6.

Calcutta: Sec. XI, No. 28. A Kaura,—beaten with a stick.

Orme: 57.

Paris: II.9.6. KAURA: The only difference between this instrument and the *Nagra* represented in the preceding print is, that the former is beaten with one stick only, whereas two are used for this. The feathers and tassels which surround this sort of drum are meerly ornaments with which the Hindoos are fond of decorating every object of luxury or festivity. Besides its use on journeys, which I have noticed in speaking of the *Nagra,* this instrument serves also in opulent houses to announce the arrival of ceremonious visitors. Among people of distinction *Kauras* are placed at certain distances, from the entrance to the audience chamber. He who is nearest to the first door proclaims the arrival of strangers by a signal, and pronounces their names in a loud voice. A *Kaura* is always seen hanging at the door of great houses with the bucklers of the *Chokidars* [*caukīdār*] or guards, of whom we have spoken in the first volume.[2]

It is also with the sound of the *Kaura* that the *bazars* or markets are opened. The *Jemindar* [*zamīndār*][3] of the district makes known by this signal that every Hindoo may bring his wares for sale, and find safety and protection for his goods and person while the market lasts.

Commentary: Solvyns once again provides a contradiction between what is described and depicted. The nagāṛā is shown being played with two sticks and the kāṛā with one, yet he states that the main distinction between the two drums is that the former is played with one stick and the latter with two. It seems likely that Solvyns intended to emphasize that the nagāṛā is played with two sticks, as he notes in the 1799 *Catalogue*, but here inadvertently reversed his reference.

Dick states that the kāṛā is similar to the smaller ṭikārā kettledrum of Bengal.[4] Babiracki, however, describes the "karah" as a "double-headed drum with a truncated-conical wooden body and laced-on skin heads" of Bengal. The term also occurs among tribal groups of southern Bihar in reference to a specific function (filling in syncopated patterns with even groups of beats and rolls) provided by a member of the percussion section in an instrumental ensemble.[5]

From Solvyns we learn that several musical instruments fulfilled conventional functions in the zamīndār society of Bengal in the eighteenth century that were apparently lost with the implementation of land reform.

1 Dick, "Kāṛā," *NGMI*, 3:360. Babiracki, NGMI, 2:360, describes the "Karah," a distinct instrument with a similar name.
2 The specific reference to Vol. I is unclear, and perhaps Solvyns refers to the Brajbāsī guard (Pl. II.50). For caukīdār, see Pl. II.122.
3 Landholder. See commentary on Dhāk, Pl. II.156.
4 Solvyns's Ṭikārā (Pl. II.162) . See Dick, "Ṭikārā," *NGMI*, 3:584.
5 Babiracki, "Karah," NGMI, 2:360.

II.166. Ḍamphā[1]

Pl. II.166. Ḍamphā. Paris: II.10.2.
Calcutta: Sec. XI, No. 12. A Dump. Species of Tabors.

Paris: II.10.2. DUMP: The instruments which I am going to describe in this number are common only in certain parts of Hindoostan, and are scarcely known in others. That which is represented in this print, called *Dump,* is a large drum differing from ours, only in its octagon form and its being beaten only with the right hand; whence it may be supposed that it can serve but to accompany a band, and is therefore must used in religious festivals. The dress of the musician is not bengale. The cottage which he inhabits is seen in the back-ground; it is composed of bambous and mats. This is the most general mode of construction in the north of Hindoostan, where the earth has not sufficient consistence to be employed in raising cabins. It is near a stream, for the Hindoos always seek the vicinity of water for their dwelling. The country, of which a part is seen, represents the mountainous parts of Hindoostan.

Commentary: The ḍamphā of Bengal is an octagonal frame drum belonging to a class of drums most widely known in India as ḍaph. Although frame drums existed in India before the Muslim invasions, as evidenced in sculpture, ḍaph drums, including the ḍamphā and the doira of the following print (Pl. II.167), were introduced into northern India from the Middle East in the twelfth century.[2] With the exception of the South Indian kanjira, frame drums are to be found today primarily among folk and tribal cultures in South Asia.

The ḍaph is played typically with the fingers of the right hand, while intermittent strokes are executed with a stick held in the left forefinger and manipulated by the middle finger. As Solvyns portrays the ḍamphā and notes in the text, however, the player supports the base of the instrument with his left hand and beats the drum with his right hand. Dick states that "This type [of ḍaph] has earlier been recorded for other parts of India under the name *ḍamphā* (e.g., in Bengal, where it is hand-played), but does not appear common nowadays."[3] According to Solvyns's description, the ḍamphā was not common in Bengal, although S. Bandyopadhyaya, in *Musical Instruments of India*, with particular focus on Bengal, writes that it is played on various festivals and processions and invariably at Holī[4]—and Solvyns himself prominently portrays it in his depiction of the Dol Yātrā, as Holī is celebrated in Bengal (Pl. II.189).

The octagonal variety of frame drum portrayed by Solvyns is known in Rajasthan today as the gherā (a term that, paradoxically, derives from a word meaning "circular").[5]

Solvyns's reference to the mountainous part of the country is unclear, for it is not depicted in the print.

1 "Ḍamphā," *NGMI*, 1:540; Dick, "Ḍaph," *NGMI*, 1:545-46.
2 Dick,"Ḍaph," *NGMI*, 1:545.
3 Ibid.
4 77-78.
5 Dick, "Ḍaph," *NGMI*, 1:545.

II.167. Doira[1]

Pl. II.167. Doira. Paris: II.10.3.

Calcutta: Sec. XI, No. 13. A Doyra. Species of Tabors.

Paris: II.10.3. DOYRA: It would be a great mistake for Europeans who have resided at Calcutta, or in the other towns of Bengal, to pretend that the *Doyra* is not an Hindoo instrument, because they have never heard it played. For, notwithstanding the *Doyra* is not used in Bengal, it has nevertheless been known for time immemorial in different parts of India. In general, many of the customs which are the subject of this work may appear foreign, without affording any reason to infer from thence, that they do not belong to the Hindoos; for, what is well known in one province, is frequently unknown in another at a very small distance from it. To bring together and describe all these different customs, is the chief aim of this collection, and I hope that I have not omitted any thing which relates to the Hindoo nation.

The *Doyra* is an instrument like our tambourine, surrounded with copper rings which the musician shakes with one hand, while he strikes with the other the interior skin. There is nothing particular in the manner of playing it.

Commentary: Contrary to Solvyns's assertion, this type of frame drum, belonging to the ḍaph class, most probably entered India with the Muslims beginning in the twelfth century. The name for the drum in India, *doira*, and its many variants, comes from the Persian *dāirā* ("circle"), and the drum itself is related to the Arabic duff.[2] Similar drums with related names are to be found throughout West Asia and southeastern Europe and are, of course, familiar (as Solvyns recognizes) as a tambourine.

1 Atanassov, "Daire," *NGMI*, 1:536.
2 Ibid. Also see Dick, "Ḍaph," *NGMI*, 1:545-46.

II.168. Jagajhampa

Paris: II.10.4. JUGO, JHUMPO: This instrument is still less known than the two former, and I have remarked that the Hindoos themselves, when they have heard it played, have asked with surprise whence the music came that was so foreign to their ears. As the Hindoos never travel, we must not be surprised at their admiration of every thing which comes from a country beyond that where they were born. The sound of this instrument has moreover something particular in it. It is a humming sound produced by rubbing a long stick at the end of which is a clew of packthread upon a skin stretched over a cylinder of earthen ware. This cylinder is composed of two parts which join and are covered over with a skin which may be loosened or made tighter at pleasure, by means of a band which goes round the instrument. The musician, at the same time that he draws his long stick over one of the skins, strikes it with a second stick which he holds with his other hand.

Pl. II.168. Jagajhampa. Paris: II.10.4.
Calcutta: Sec. XI, No. 33. A Jugo, Jhumpo,—one side is beaten while the other is rubbed.
Orme: 59.

Commentary: A search of available literature on Indian music failed to yield these terms or the exact instrument witnessed by Solvyns, although in rural areas of Bengal and Bangladesh, the instrument portrayed is still known as either jugojhamp or jugol.[1] Sen's *An Etymological Dictionary of Bengali* gives "jagajhampa" as "a kind of drum and drum beating"; the first element, *jaga*, is onomatopoeic, and the second, *jhampa*, means to leap or jump.[2] The word *jagajhampa* perhaps from the sound of the drum, means "cacophony" in modern Bengali.

T. C. Gupta, in *Aspects of Bengali Society*, describes the jagajhampa as a kind of kettle-drum "which is suspended with a cord from the neck of the man who played on it with a pair of cane-sticks. Feathers of birds were used to decorate [it]."[3] But the instrument Solvyns portrays is no kettle-drum, and what Gupta describes fits Solvyns's nagāṛā.

In his note to the original drawing, Solvyns writes that the drum is "beaten on the one end by a small stick, with a constant friction, on the other with a curved cane." The earthenware body of the jagajhampa and the suggestion of a waisted cylindrical structure that is presented by the portrait indicate that this drum might be a form of the mādar of eastern India. The mādar exists in various forms, but most of these have a baked clay body resembling the waisted cylindrical form of the jagajhampa. The friction technique of playing described by Solvyns is not mentioned in descriptions of the mādar[4] and is not common in Indian drumming, but can be found in the playing of the ghasā (ghaḍasa) barrel drum of the Pāṇa musicians of southern Orissa.[5]

According to Deben Bhattacharya, this scraping technique is also used for the Bengali ḍhol. He notes, as well, the similarity of the drum Solvyns depicts to the timila from Kerala.[6] He writes that "although the 'timila' is shaped from wood and is played by hands, it too employs the 'ghasā' or the rubbing technique along with squeezing the waist strap of the drum for pitch variations." Bhattacharya suggests that the jagajhampa may have been played by a similar technique, combining varied sounds produced by beating the drumhead, scraping the skin, and by varying the pitch by tightening and loosening the skin strap placed on the waisted center of the drum.[7]

1 As related by Bengali students at the University of Texas at Austin.

2 306.

3 81. Gupta says that it is a favorite instrument of Muslims.

4 See, for example, Babiracki, "Mādar," *NGMI*, 2:590-91.

5 Dick, "Ghaḍasa," *NGMI*, 2:39.

6 Pitoëss, "Timila," *NGMI*, 3:586.

7 Deben Bhattacharya, letter to the author, February 17, 1992.

II.169. Surmaṇḍal[1]

Pl. II.169. Surmaṇḍal. Paris: II.10.5.

Calcutta: Sec. XI, No. 34. A Surmungla,—formed of reeds and played on by the hand.

Orme: 60.

Paris: II.10.5. SURMUNGLA: It will be remarked without difficulty that this instrument is of true Hindoo origin, and that it could have been invented no where but in India; and in reality it is one of the most singular which we have as yet had to describe. The sound of the *Surmungla* is very sweet and grateful to the ear, and produces altogether a very good effect; and yet of what does the music of this instrument consist? The musician does no more than pass his fingers over some pieces of bambou split at the two ends, and kept together by thin traverses: all the rest is represented in the print.

An European cannot help being surprised at hearing such sweet sounds from so simple an instrument; he never could have thought that so much could be made of it.

The *Surmungla* is little known in the flat countries, but it is in great repute in the mountainous parts of Hindoostan. At Calcutta it is seen only among traders, and sometimes with palanquin bearers and other servants, who come originally from the mountains.

The performer here represented is surrounded by a crowd of curious people who are listening to him with great attention, and are never tired of this music.

Commentary: In his note to the original drawing, Solvyns describes the surmaṇḍal as "made of reeds split of different thicknesses to vary the tones; it is played on with both hands, & on both sides." As pictured, it appears to be the idiochord raft zither known as dendung[2] in Assam. It was apparently known in a wider geographical area in the eighteenth century than it is today. The term *surmaṇḍal* has been applied since Mughal times to a plucked board zither in North India. Hindu musicologists link the surmaṇḍal to the mattakokilā vīṇā, mentioned in the *Saṅgitaratnākara* through later textual references. However, it is more likely that the term was coined to name the Middle Eastern qanun brought to India by invading Muslim armies and mentioned in court records of the Delhi Sultanate.

Solvyns writes that the musician he portrays is surrounded by listeners, although none is depicted in the etching.

1 Dick, "Surmaṇḍal," *NGMI*, 3:477.

2 Dick, "Dendung," *NGMI*, 1:556.

II.170. Khanjari[1]

Pl. II.170. Khanjari. Paris: II.10.6.
Calcutta: Sec. XI, No. 14. A Khunjery. Species of Tabors.

Paris: II.10.6. K'HUNJERY: The *K'hunjery,* a sort of little drum, serves to accompany the voice; it is most used by the Faquirs, the *Beeshnubs* [Baiṣṇab][2] and the *Kawns*, those professional singers of whom I have spoken in the eleventh number of the first volume: this instrument therefore is known in all the countries of Hindoostan.

The musician in the print is an Hindoo whose whole life is spent in singing the praises, the incarnation and the loves of some divinity of the country, going from house to house, and existing upon the alms which he receives. To draw the attention of passengers, and still more to excite their pity, he paints his face, his breast and arms even more than the Faquirs; and while he is playing, makes the most horrible grimaces and contorsions, so as to make it believed that it is not without the greatest pain that he can draw the sounds from his *K'hunjery*.

The back-ground represents some of those buildings which are common in the Indian country.

Commentary: The *khanjari* is a variety of frame drum, distinguished from other types by its small size and deep, heavy frame. Some are tambourine-like, with metal discs fastened in slots cut into the wooden frame. In Bengal, the head is made from the skin of the iguana; in other parts of the subcontinent, leather or snake skin might be used. According to Deva, crocodile skin or iguana skin is used for the head of the related South Indian kanjira.[3] This variety of the drum is smaller than its northern counterparts. There it has long been used in the accompaniment of devotional songs of the *bhajana* tradition. Day mentions that it is also used by "Nautch girls."[4]

Kothari identifies the khanjari as played by snake-charmers, along with the pūngī[5]—Solvyns's "tobrie" (Pl. II.179).

The "Kawns" to whom Solvyns refers are the professional singers of the Kān (Pl. II.64) caste, which Risley identifies as "a very low caste of musicians akin to the Doms [Pl. II.68]."[6] Deben Bhattacharya suggests that the name may be a corruption of *gāyan*, meaning singer, particularly the Vaiṣṇava singers who accompany themselves with the khol and khanjari during the *prabhāt pheri*, "the morning circulation," singing songs in praise of Kṛṣṇa from door to door.[7] Solvyns portrays a Kān, with khanjari, in the series of etching of caste occupations.

1 Dick and Dournon, "Khanjari," *NGMI*, 2:422.
2 See commentary on Khol, Pl. II.158.
3 142.
4 Ibid.
5 22. In his portrayal of the Sāpuriyā snake-catchers (Pl. II.66), Solvyns depicts their use of the hour-glass drum, huḍuk, rather than the khanjari. For the huḍuk, see Dick, *NGMI*: 2:257-58.
6 1:396. Sukumar Sen, 137, gives *kān* as "the caste name of professional singers."
7 Letter to the author, February 17, 1992.

II.171. Kartāl[1]

Pl. II.171. Kartāl. Paris: II.11.2.
Calcutta: Sec. XI, No. 11. Kurtaul or Symbols.

Paris: II.11.2. KURTAUL: There is nothing to be said upon the form of this instrument. It is easy to see that it is no more than a small tymbal carried in the hand. Its antiquity only entitles it to a place here, as it is one of the earliest instruments which the Hindoos possessed. It appears to have been formerly used in religious ceremonies, as a great number of their ancient idols are represented with it. It is now sometimes seen in the hands of people who affect piety, who sing in the streets and markets, and accompany their voice with the *Kurtaul*:they stop generally before the shops in hopes of obtaining the fruit of their labour.

Many of the Hindoo instruments are not much more deserving of notice than the *Kurtaul*; I shall not have admitted them into my collection, had it not been my intention, as I have already mentioned, to give a complete description of the music of this people.

Commentary: The term *kartāl*—literally handclapping—generally denotes wooden clappers that may or may not incorporate jingles. In Bengal, the term is applied to hand-held cymbals, and they are typically used in conjunction with the khol (Pl. II.158) as favored instruments in Vaiṣṇava *kīrtan*.[2]

The kartāl is known elsewhere throughout North India either as manjīrā or, in its larger size, jhānjh.[3] In Bengal, the manjīrā, which Solvyns portrays in another etching (Pl. II.174), is smaller and of a somewhat different shape.[4]

---

1 Dick, "Kartāl," *NGMI*, 2:361-62. On the kartāl and idiophonic Indian instruments more generally, see Ray, *Folk-Music of Eastern India*, 44-45.

2 Das Gupta, 85.

3 "Jhānjh," *NGMI*, 2:328.

4 Ibid. Das Gupta terms it "mandira."

II.172. Kā̃si[1]

Paris: II.11.3. KAUNSY: No feast is celebrated in Hindoostan without having a *Kaunsy* in the music; and in private entertainments it is also one of the commonest instruments. However poor the Hindoo, the *Kaunsy* must be heard in his house on his wedding day. The sound of it is overcoming, especially when many of them are played together. In rich houses strangers are sometimes announced by the *Kaunsy:* in this case, the stick with which it is beaten is larger.

The performers are persons of the lower casts, such as the musician represented in the print.

Commentary: Solvyns appears to make a distinction between the kā̃sar, the temple gong, and the kā̃si (kansi), apparently the same instrument used in a secular context. These instruments have been discussed under kā̃sar (Pl. II.147).

---

1 See Dick, "Kā̃sar," *NGMI*, 2:362.

Pl. II.172. Kā̃si. Paris: II.11.3.
Calcutta: Sec. XI, No. 26. A Kaunsy,—a plate of brass beaten by a stick.

II.173. Jaltaraṅg[1]

Paris: II:11.4. JULTRUNG: Though the name of this instrument does not promise much harmony, it produces very agreeable sounds: The *Jultrung* is not unlike the Harmonica, one of our sweetest instruments, but is more simple, consisting meerly in seven *piallas* [*pīelā*, cup], or earthen vases in a progression of different sizes on the same line, and unequally filled with water, which causes the diversity of tone required. The performer strikes the edges of the vases with a little stick, and draws out a very soft and melodious music. Having remarked that the Hindoos preferred China vases, I asked the reason, but the only answer I could get was that China *piallas* had always been used, though they have in their own country a very fine earth of which they make an excellent ware. The *Jultrung* is not common in Bengal, and is therefore but little known to Europeans. It is to be met with mostly in the northern districts of Hindoostan.

Commentary: The history of the jaltaraṅg is unclear. Textual references to the term do not occur before the seventeenth century, although Bandyopadhyaya, in *Musical Instruments of India,* writes that in the medieval period, metal cups were used for the instrument before the comparatively recent introduction of porcelain cups. He gives the literal meaning of the word as "waves of water," and indicates that instead of seven cups, "sixteen to twenty cups are used in its performance to cover a range of two octaves."[2]

Today the instrument is used primarily by Hindustani musicians, but is not at all common. However, those who do play the jaltaraṅg continue to favor porcelain bowls made in China. The repertory of the jaltaraṅg when played solo is modelled on the *gat*

repertory of the sitār and other plucked string instruments. Because of its limited capacity for producing embellishments (*gamak*), the jaltaraṅg is more often used in ensemble performance.

1 "Jaltaraṅg," *NGMI*, 2:321.
2 84-85.

Pl. II.173. Jaltaraṅg. Paris: II.11.4.
Calcutta: Sec. XI, No. 19. A Jultrung, earthen or China Cups.—fitted to the different notes of music, and played on with two sticks or pieces of iron.
Orme: 54.

II.174. Manjīrā[1]

Paris: II.11.5. MUNJERRAH: The *Munjeerah* bears some resemblance to our *castagnettes,* but in India the use of it is not confined, as in Europe, to the lower classes; it is the delight of the richer Hindoos. Seated on a carpet with their legs across, whole hours are spent in singing to the sound of their *Munjeerah* an air as monotonous as their music. Such is the occupation of their day, which is interrupted only by smoking and sleeping. Their diet, as I have already observed, is so frugal and simple, that very little time is spent at their meals. The indolence to which they are so entirely given up does not even allow them to seek for any refinement in their pleasures. Repose and idleness are the prerogatives of the Hindoo of rank and fortune. The *Munjeerah* is frequently used in the natches, and is also a favorite instrument of the Hidgras [Hijrās].[2]

Pl. II.174. Manjīrā. Paris: II.11.5.
Calcutta: Sec. XI, No. 20. Munjeera,—two brass cups beaten together.

Commentary: In most parts of North India, manjīrā are paired cup cymbals, often joined together by a cord, and distinguished from the kartāl by their smaller size. They are commonly used to keep rhythm in devotional singing, but may also be used to accompany dance or other instruments. A diversity of tones and timbres is obtained from the instrument by striking the two parts together at various angles and through the mixture of damped and non-damped strokes. Small cymbal playing has been developed to virtuoso levels in some areas of India. Deva has written that "the virtuosity sometimes exhibited is really staggering. For instance, the *kamsale* dancers of Mysore form groups of two men, each person holding a pair of small *tala*-s [small cymbals equivalent to manjīrā]. Dancing with exuberance, they clash the cymbals producing rhythmic patterns of great beauty."[3]

1 Dick, "Manjīrā," *NGMI*, 2:609.

2 As noted in the commentary on the Nautch (Pl. II.195), Hijrās are eunuchs dressed as women who sing and dance in often lewd parody of women. Solvyns portrays them separately, though without reference to music or dance, in Pl. II.94.

3 55.

II.175. Jhā̃jhari[1]

Paris: II.11.6. J'HAUNJREE: The *J'haunjree* is also very like our *castagnettes;* it consists of two hollow rings of copper enclosing little balls of the same metal, which the performer puts in motion with his fingers. The pleasure which the Hindoos experience in playing on this little instrument, if it deserves to be called one, is extreme. They appear almost transported with joy at the noise which they produce with their *J'haunjree*.

The accessories of the drawing and the dress of the Hindoo represented, announce a person of a superior cast; though the furniture consists only of a mat that serves as a bed, a box filled with *pawn* [*pān*, Pl. II.212], the little altars of his domestic gods, and two sticks painted blue and red, fastened to the wall, to hang the clothes upon. All the articles which to us appear indispensable, such as a table, a chair, a bed, are wanting: the Hindoos find it very easy to do without them; and Europeans themselves, after some years residence in India, begin to look upon them as superfluous.

Contrary to the custom of true Hindoos, the man whom I have drawn wears slippers instead of wooden sandals: in this respect his costume differs from that which we have described in the first volume.[2]

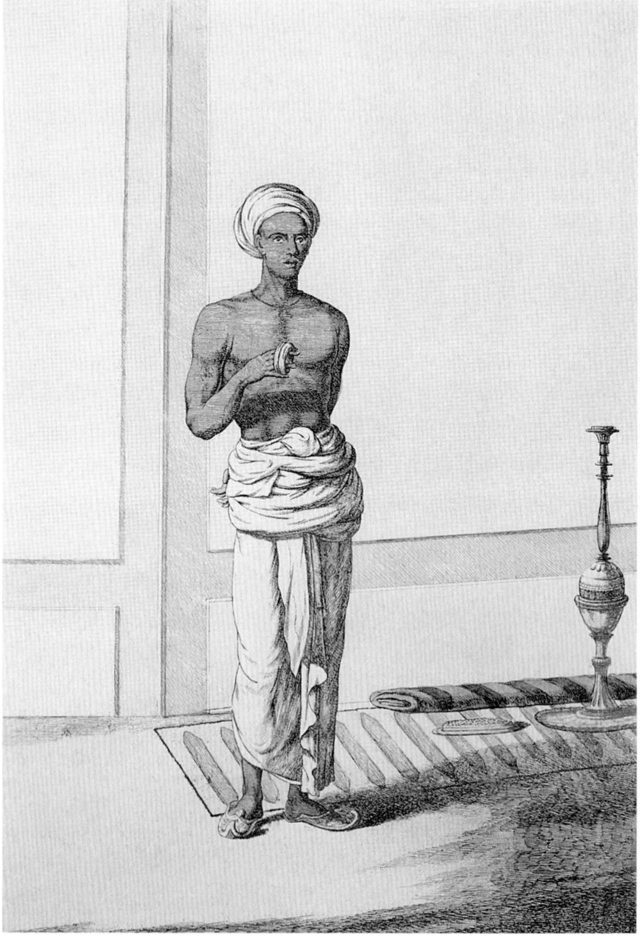

Pl. II.175. Jhā̃jhari. Paris: II.11.6.

Calcutta: Sec. XI, No. 15. A J'haunjree,—two hollow brass rings, containing small Balls, played on by a quick movement of the hand.

Commentary: Carey has defined the term *jhā̃jhari* as "a kind of metal ring with small bells fixed on its periphery, which all ring together when it is properly shaken."[3] An instrument similar to what Solvyns portrays is used today by the Bauls of Bengal. This is the *nūpur*, "a slit tubular anklet filled with shot."[4] However, *nūpur* might also refer to tiny bells attached to decorative jewelry such as anklets (*pāyal*).[5] The term *jhā̃jhari*—with something of the sound of "jhanjhari" to the European ear, as reflected in

Solvyns's transliteration—is onomatopoeic, indicating (from the Bengali) a jingling (*jhā̃j*) cascade (*jharaṇi*). Other instruments of this type in India occur under the names silampu (Tamil Nadu) and gaggara (Karnataka).

1 Among variants, Sukumar Sen, 340, gives jhājhuri.
2 Reference to the Paris edition. Solvyns, in fact, portrays both the kṣatriya (Pl. II.20) and vaiśya (Pl. II.21) with slippers and the brahmins barefoot. He does describe the "remarkable" sandals in Pl. II.33, where they are worn by a Tā̃ti, or weaver. "They are of wood, and he holds them by a sort of button with his toes. . . ." Solvyns also depicts the wooden sandals in the etching of the kuplyans or bīn, Pl. II.149.
3 2:310.
4 Capwell, 100.
5 Deva, 52.

II.176. Rāmśiṅgā[1]

Pl. II.176. Rāmśiṅgā. Paris: II.12.2.

Calcutta: Sec. XI, No. 30. A Ramsinga,—resembling a Serpent.

Paris: II.12.2. RAMSINGA: We shall conclude in this number the description of the musical instruments; those which remain are wind instruments; the *Ramsinga* is the most remarkable of them. It consists of four pipes of very thin metal which fit one within the other, and are generally covered with a fine red varnish; it is played in the same manner as our large trumpet. It requires very strong lungs to draw from it a continuation of sounds, for which reason it is seldom heard except among the inhabitants of the mountains: the Hindoos of the flat country are too weak and of too delicate a frame to make use of such an instrument. The sound of the *Ramsinga,* is strong and rather agreeable when heard at a distance. There are Faquirs who play on it tolerably well.

In the higher Hindoostan the *Ramsinga* serves to open and close the great markets. The musicians who are sometimes heard with this instrument in the villages are sure to attract a great crowd.

Commentary: Sukumar Sen's *Etymological Dictionary of Bengali* derives the name "rāmśiṅgā" from *rām*, Bengali for "big" and *śiṅgā*, "horn," as an animal's horn, from which the instrument was originally made.[2] It is today most widely known as narsīgā or raṇsīga vaik, Hindi for "crooked war-horn." Das Gupta, in *Aspects of Bengali Society*, writes that the rānśiṅgā was used in ancient times by commanders to issue directions to troops in the battlefield.[3]

According to Lalmani Misra, the instrument is fashioned from either copper or brass and produces two tones the interval of a fifth apart.[4] The S-shaped horn is most common in Himachal Pradesh and Bihar. It is played in Bihar in combination with the śahnāī and drums, such as the ḍhāk and ḍhol at weddings and in martial dances.[5]

1 Babiracki and Helffer, "Narsīgā," *NGMI*, 2:749.
2 803
3 83.
4 108.
5 Babiracki and Helffer, "Narsīgā," *NGMI*, 2:749.

II.177. Bā̃k[1]

Paris: II.12.3. BAUNCK: The *Bаunck* may be very well compared to our trumpet both for the form and the sound. As it is common among the Hindoos that almost every body plays it, they endeavour to surpass each other, not in skill, but in noise: at their feasts the contest is whose *Baunck* shall be the loudest, and this strange rivality produces a confusion to which an European ear does not find it easy to get accustomed. The *Baunck* is painted red like the *Ramsinga*.

The middle distance of the drawing represents the habitation of a man of the country; it is built of earth and has a mat hung from a stick instead of a door. The master of the house is seated before this entrance; his costume is the dress of the cold season: farther on is another house of the same description: both of them are surrounded with cocoa-trees, bananas, mango-trees and palm-trees, with which all the country of Hindoostan is covered.

Pl. II.177. Bā̃k. Paris: II.12.3.
Calcutta: Sec. XI, No. 23. A Baunk, or Trumpet.

Commentary: The brass bā̃k [baṅk], which derives its name from its twisted shape,[2] appears not to enjoy the same popularity today as it did in the late eighteenth century. A similarly shaped end-blown trumpet is known as bānkīyā in Rajasthan. There it is played by the professional musician Sargura caste at marriages and other festive occasions.[3] In southern Bihar, the term *bā̃k* is applied to an S-shaped trumpet by the Oraon tribal people.[4]

Shoberl notes that it was used in processions and was employed by the Mārāṭhas as a military instrument for both cavalry and infantry.[5]

1 "Bā̃k," NGMI, 1:112.
2 From the Bengali *bā̃k(a)*, meaning curved, crooked, twisted. Sukumar Sen, 652.
3 Dournon, "Bankiya," *NGMI*, 1:155. Also see Kothari, 44, and Blowmik, 141.
4 "Bā̃k," *NGMI*, 1:112.
5 3:25.

II.178. Surnāī[1]

Paris: II.12.4. SOORNA: The *Soorna* is our hautboy; but the Hindoos play it so ill, that they can draw from it only shrill and disagreeable sounds; the European the most accustomed to the stunning of Hindoo music can not stand a concert of several *Soornas* accompanied with some of their other noisy instruments. Every *Soorna* exerts his whole strength and entirely after his own fancy, without any respect to measure or harmony: at a distance one would imagine that it was the roaring of a number of wild beasts. The musician whom I have represented is before his house, and not in a very easy attitude.

The *Soorna* players are men of bad morals, and pass the greater part of the day in the shops of the retailers of *toddy* [*tāṛī*] and other spirits. There they recite at great length to those who will listen to them, the very shameful adventures of their lives, without omitting the most trifling circumstances of their gluttony and debauchery, with an exact amount of all the feasts where they assisted, and the quantity of victuals and of betel which they received.

Commentary: This is the double reed oboe-type aerophone common throughout Asia, the Middle East, and part of Africa affected by Islamic influence. The surnāī of Indian folk traditions differs from the classical śahnāī in that it includes a metal lip-disc, allowing the entire reed to be placed inside the mouth, while the reed of the śahnāī is lip-held.

Both Risley and Bhattacharya refer to low caste Mucīs (Pl. II.70) and Muslims who play drums and surnāī together in bands at weddings and festive occasions. "Those who play on the kettledrum and the pipe called *sanai*, and who are generally Mahomedans, are perched on the top of the main entrance. . . ."[2]

1 Dick, "Surnāī," *NGMI*, 3:478. Also see Flora, "Śahnāī," *NGMI*, 3:283-84.

2 Bhattacharya, 213. Also see Risley, 2:99.

Pl. II.178. Surnāī. Paris: II.12.4.
Calcutta: Sec. XI, No. 22. A Soorna, or Hautboy.

II.179. Tobrie[1]

Paris: II.12.5. TOBRIE: The *Tobrie* is not unlike our bagpipe: they make this instrument out of a dried fruit hollowed out so as to admit three pipes of bambou, one above and two below, in which last there are several holes as in our clarinets; the performer blows into the upper pipe, and modifies the sound by stopping one or more of the holes in the lower ones.

The *Tobrie* is very common on the coast of Coromandel and in several provinces of Hindoostan: it is more rare upon the borders of the Ganges and of the Barampouter [Brahmaputra].

In the Carnatic, the Mauls [Māl, Pl. II.65],[2] or serpentmen, make use of the *Tobrie,* as they do of the Tomtom in the other provinces, to attract the serpents from their holes.

There is nevertheless nothing very enchanting in the sound of this instrument; the only thing in it which can give any pleasure to an European, is the expression which the Hindoos give to their sounds, and the variations which they take care to produce by the mixture of the *forte,* the *piano,* and the *crescendo.*

Pl. II.179. Tobrie. Paris: II.12.5.
Calcutta: Sec. XI, No. 6. A Tobrie,—resembling the Bagpipe.

Commentary: The instrument described here is the common snake-charmer's pipe of India. The term Solvyns uses to designate the instrument is uncommon, and it is most widely known as the pūngī. In some parts of North India, this instrument is called tumbā, tumbī, or tomrā (all meaning "gourd"), and *An Etymological Dictionary of Bengali* gives *tumaṛi*, as the snake-charmers flute.[3] "Tobrie" might be a corruption of one of these. The instrument is made of a curved gourd about eighteen inches long, with an opening at the narrow end.[4]

Shoberl writes that "this instrument is played by barbers; it is used in all the pagodas, and likewise accompanies the dances of the *bayaderes* and *devedassees*."[5]

---

1 Dick, "Pūngī," *NGMI,* 3:159.
2 Solvyns portrays the Māl, Pl. II.65, without the tobrie, but in his etching of the Sāpuriyā snake-charmers, Pl. II.66, he depicts both the tobrie and huḍuk, an hourglass drum. The Māls are a cultivating caste among whom only a few "with gipsy habits" live by catching snakes. Risley, 2:48.
3 Sukumar Sen, 405.
4 Bandyopadhyaya, 23.
5 3:26.

II.180. Bā̃śi[1]

Commentary: The Bengali word for flute, *bā̃śi*, which Solvyns gives as "bunsee," is from the word for bamboo, *bā̃ś(a)*.[2] Originally of a particular species of bamboo, it was by the twentieth century more frequently of metal, wood, or ivory. Its length varies from about four to eighteen inches, with an opening to blow in, and six other openings for the fingers to play. In its association with Kr̥ṣṇa, it is usually known as murali.[3]

C. R. Day writes that wind instruments are "looked upon as of secondary importance. Possibly this may have some reason in the fact that Brahmins are not allowed by their religious laws to use them, excepting only the flute blown by the nostrils, and one or two others of the horn or trumpet kind. And so men of low caste are employed as players of wind instruments."[4] Abbé J. A. Dubois, a contemporary of Solvyns in India, as we noted in the introduction to the section on musical instruments, also remarked on the pollution associated with wind instruments, the

Paris: II.12.6. BUNSEE: The *Bunsee,* made of bambou, a very sonorous wood and consequently very fit for musical instruments, is the same as our common flute; but the Hindoos play it very differently, for, instead of putting it between their lips, they put it into their nose. Nothing is more comical than to see the flute merchants in the bazars surrounded by a group of amateurs with their flutes in their noses, trying the sound of the instruments with the most extraordinary grimaces. This strange custom has its origin in the religious opinion that a Hindoo of a superior cast is contaminated if his mouth should touch any thing which has approached the mouth of an inferior. It is this scrupulous religious repugnance which makes them prefer playing the flute with their noses. It is sometimes carried to a very great excess: a woman of the lowest class thinks herself dishonoured, if a stranger should even see her mouth: when she meets one, her first care is to cover this part, though she should leave all the rest of her body exposed.

defilement arising from "the players contact by putting such instruments to their mouths after they have once been touched by saliva, . . . the one excretion from the human body for which Hindus display invincible horror."[5]

However, lip-blown transverse flutes are well-documented in ancient and medieval iconographic and textual sources in South Asia. End-blown flutes played by blowing air through the nose are not unknown in South Asia, but the transverse type seems to have been better known since antiquity, except during a period of decline during Muslim rule in North India, suggesting the possibility of a prohibition against the instrument by Muslim rulers because of its strong symbolic association with Kr̥ṣṇa, the divine cow-herd. Today, the end-blown flute is more commonly found in the westernmost parts of India, where it is known as the nar̥. The Indian nar̥ is thought to be related to the Central and West Asian nāy.[6] The flute depicted here is apparently of the fipple type. Such instruments are most popular today among amateur players and folk musicians.

Pl. II.180. Bā̃śi. Paris: II.12.6.

Calcutta: Sec. XI, No. 36. A Bunsee,—a Bomboo Flute as often played on through the nose as the mouth.

1 Dournon and Helffer, "Bā̃suri," *NGMI*, 1:192.
2 See Sukumar Sen, 653-54.
3 Das Gupta, 84; and Bandyopadhyaya, 20-22.
4 103.
5 64.
6 Dick, "Nar̥," *NGMI*, 2:749.

II.181. Bhoraṅga[1]

Pl. II.181. Bhoraṅga. Calcutta: Sec. XI, No. 29.
Calcutta: Sec. XI, No. 29. A Burung,—used at the Hindoo Festivals.

Commentary: The bhoraṅga (Solvyns's "Burung") is a long trumpet-like aerophone and seems to be what is most frequently known as the turya or turhī, with variants. The war trumpet of the *Mahābhārata* was the turya. In the Himalayan regions, the tubular karnal once signaled danger to neighbors across the hills, but today, as for all such horns, they are used, together with drums, principally for folk dance accompaniment. Each region of India has such a straight trumpet, and they are variously named.[2]

Shoberl, who follows Solvyns's text in the Paris edition for most of his descriptions, includes the instrument in his account of the music of Hindustan, but while Solvyns depicts the bhoraṅga in the Calcutta collection, it is omitted from the Paris edition. The instrument Shoberl depicts in his accompanying plate is very similar to Solvyns's "burung" and is described as "a long pipe called *tare*. . . , more particularly employed for the purpose of announcing the death of a person, or the offerings made by his relatives on his funeral pile. The dull, mournful tunes of this instrument render it very suitable for this office."[3]

Das Gupta, in *Aspects of Bengali Society*, describes the "bhoraṅg" as "a kind of pipe," consisting "of double tubes, one inner and the other outer. Clever manipulation of the instrument produced notes of different pitches. This is now practically out of use."[4] Such instruments, made from thin brass or copper sheets, produce what Bandyopadhyaya describes as a very harsh and loud sound that "cannot be considered to be musical, yet they were in great use in bygone age in various ceremonial occasions of the Hindus, [blown at the beginning of functions] like religious festivals, marriage and in war."[5]

---

1 Sukumar Sen, 727, lists bhoraṅga as "a kind of bugle." Solvyns's contemporary in Bengal, the Rev. William Ward, 1:259, refers to a "Bhorungu, a straight trumpet."
2 NGMI, 3:682, gives "turhī" as the "alternative term for the Narsīgā of southern Bihar." Also see Deva, 111-12.
3 3:24-25.
4 83.
5 23.

Festivals and Ceremonies

Solvyns's portrayals of the festivals of Bengal are the most complex and compelling of all his etchings. In the Calcutta edition, most are grouped together in the final section of the *Collection*. For *Les Hindoûs*, they are distributed through the first three volumes in the large format, double-plates that open each section (*livraison*). Oddly, given the attention Solvyns devotes to the subject, he provides no general discussion of festivals and ceremonies in the Preliminary Discourse or introductory essays.

II.182. Mahābhārata Sabhā

Pl. II.182. Mahābhārata Sabhā. Paris: I.1.1. Double-plate.

Calcutta: Sec. XII, No. 3. Mohabaurut-er-Shobah [Mahābhārata Sabhā],—or an assembly to hear the text and comments on the mohabaurut [*Mahābhārata*].—The reader sits on an elevated chair, decorated with flowers, the Salgrum [*śālagrāma*] stone,[1] sunk [*śaṅkh*] shell,[2] &c.—In the morning, he reads the text, which is very little attended, from few understanding the Schanscrit [Sanskrit] language; but in the evening, which is here represented, when the explanation in the Bengalee language is delivered, together with the comments of the officiating Priest, the meeting is exceedingly crowded.

Paris: I.1.1: MOHABAURUT-ER-SHOBHA, OR THE EXPLAINING OF THE TEXT AND COMMENTARIES OF THE MOHABAURUT BY A BRAHMUN: The Brahmun, adorned with red flowers, is seated on an eminence or little hill of earth, holding in his hands the *poitahs* [*pothiī*] or leaves of trees[3] upon which is engraved the text of the *Mohabaurut*, one of the sacred books of the Hindoos. Upon a stool before him are other *poitahs*, and opposite to him the *salgram* stone, the *sunk* or shell, and the *guntah* [*ghaṇṭā*] or bell.[4]

In the morning, the Brahmun reads the sacred text to the public, with a loud voice, in the shanscrit tongue; but as this learned language is understood by few, there is hardly any one at this first reading. In the afternoon, or late in the evening, a numerous audience attends an other explanation of the *Mohabaurut* in the *bengalee* language, or in some other common idiom of the country. This is the reading which this plate represents.

This sort of religious ceremony is always performed before the front or in the first court of their houses. Separate places are reserved for the rich, and the higher ranks of the women of the family can neither see nor be seen but through a grating made of bamboos crossed. The print represents these different arrangements. The original drawing as well as all those which compose this collection was taken on the spot from nature by M. Solvyns.

Commentary: A Mahābhārata Sabhā is, as Solvyns relates, an assembly to hear an exposition on the *Mahābhārata*, the great Sanskrit epic that is both a chronicle of war and a rich commentary on ancient Indian culture, philosophy, and religion. In its length of more than 90,000 stanzas, it is the longest poem in the world. Such gatherings as Solvyns depicts were typically held under the patronage of a wealthy Hindu, who demonstrates his religious devotion and thereby gains merit. Recitations, from memory or read, and commentaries of the sacred texts were (and remain) an important part of Hindu religious life, and such oral performances might extend over several days.[5]

The most famous part of part of the epic is the *Bhāgavadgītā*, the great text of Hindu ethics, in which the god Kṛṣṇa, as charioteer to the hero Arjuna, develops a doctrine of duty and order. The first English translation from the Sanskrit, by Charles Wilkins, appeared in 1785,[6] and was known to Solvyns.

The Mahābhārata Sabhā portrayed by Solvyns is at the home of a wealthy Hindu patron. The great houses of "opulent" Hindus were usually constructed with a large inner courtyard where religious festivities, *yātrās* (religious dramas),[7] and musical and nautch[8] performances were held. Although sometimes held outside the house (as presented in the Calcutta etching), Solvyns's depiction in the Paris etching suggests that the recitation takes place in the courtyard, in which temporary bamboo and thatch shelters provide shade for those assembled in the open. The more distinguished guests sit in the columned hall open to the courtyard, and unseen women watch through woven bamboo screens.

In several etchings (Pls. II.183, II.184, II.185, II.186, II.194, and II.195), Solvyns portrays Hindu festivities and ceremonies taking place in the courtyard of great houses. Among wealthy Hindus, Raja Nabakrishna Deb (1733-1797) was especially celebrated in hosting such occasions.[9] Raja Nabakrishna (or Nubkissen) had served as Lord Clive's Persian teacher and banian (broker, Pl. II.99) and, by the time of Solvyns's arrival in Calcutta, he had long been the city's most influential Bengali. Europeans were regularly invited to his house in Sobhabazar, off Chitpur Road (see map, p. 18), for nautch parties (Pl. II.195) or for Durgā Pūjā (Pl. II.194), as they were to the houses of other wealthy Hindus.[10]

The houses, two or three stories high and with flat roofs, were constructed in the form of a hollow square. On the ground floor, arcades on three sides faced into the large, central courtyard, while the interior rooms were given over to offices and stores. At the northern end of the court and open to it, as an elevated marble stage, was the *ṭhākur-dālān*, the hall of the deity,[11] where the images of the household deities were installed—save for the period of Durgā Pūjā, when the goddess Durgā was worshipped.[12] The upper floors contained the living apartments, and, supported by the arcades below, verandahs faced inward to the court. These were closed in by venetian blinds, narrow windows, or screens through which the women of the house could view festivities in the court below. When used for such an occasion, with as many as several hundred people in attendance, the ground of the court might be covered by temporary matting, with cloth or carpets, while an immense cloth above provided shelter from the sun or rain. A profusion of oil lamps gave illumination at night.[13]

The Rev. William Ward, Solvyns's contemporary in Bengal, described the scene, very much as Solvyns portrays in the etching. "At the times when great poojas [*pūjā*, worship] are performed, an awning is thrown over the top of this court, into which the common spectators are admitted. The brahmuns, or respectable people, sit on the two side verandahs, while the women are able to peep out from small crevices of windows above."[14]

---

1 The stone, a black fossilized ammonite, is worshipped as a representation of Viṣṇu.

2 A conch shell, blown by the priest at the beginning of a *pūjā* or religious performance, as also before battle, as in those chronicled in the *Mahābhārata*. On the *śaṅkh*, see Pl. II.146.

3 Solvyns uses both *poitah* and *poltar* (Pl. II.18) for the Sanskrit *pothī*, the leaves of a book, also the book itself. Sacred texts were frequently written on palm leaves, dried and cut into strips, which were usually bound together with cords at one end. The text may be written in India ink or, as Solvyns indicates, engraved into the leaf with a stylus. See Basham, *The Wonder That Was India*, 400.

4 The *ghaṇṭā* is used in *pūjā*, portrayed in Pl. II.146.

5 Philip Lutgendorf portrays the character and role of such performances in an incisive study of the *Rāmāyaṇa* tradition in *The Life of a Text: Performing the* Rāmcaritmānas *of Tulsidas*. On performances in Calcutta, see Sumanta Banerjee, 170-71.

6 *The Bhăgvăt-Gēētā, or Dialogues of Krēēshnă and Arjŏŏn* See the Introduction to *Les Hindoûs*, 2:13-14, quoted in the introduction to the sections on Fakirs and Religious Mendicants, p. 310 and fn 19, p.313.

7 See Commentary on Rās Yātrā, Pl. II.185.

8 The nautch performances at Durgā Pūjā in these great houses are described in Pl. II.195.

9 On Raja Nabakrishna Deb, see Pradip Sinha, *Calcutta in Urban History*, 66-70, 88, and Nagendra Nath Ghosh for a full biography. As discussed in the Commentaries for Pls. II.194 and II.195, Nabakrishna was especially notable in promoting Durgā Pūjā. Also see references to Nabakrishna in Commentaries for Pls. II.4, II.17, and II.26.

10 The grandson of Nabakrishna described the house in his will, dated 1867, in Pradip Sinha, *Calcutta in Urban History*, 160-62.

11 *Ṭhākur* refers to master, or lord, and here to the deity; *dālān* means hall.

12 Pradip Sinha, *Calcutta in Urban History*, 77-78, portrays such courtyards in three sketches.

13 On the character of this construction, see James R. Martin, 20; Colesworthy Grant, *An Anglo-Indian Domestic Sketch*, 7; H. E. A. Cotton, 217; Nisith Ranjan Ray, *Calcutta: The Profile of a City, 68-70*; McCutchion, "Temples of Calcutta, 46; R. P. Gupta, "Baboo, Bibi & Bhadramahila," 17-18; and, on the great houses more generally, Chitra Deb.

14 *Account of . . . the Hindoos*, 1:102-03. Walter Hamilton, *A Geographical, Statistical, and Historical Description of Hindoostan*, 1:98-99, borrows Ward's description without acknowledgment. Mrs. Heber, wife of the bishop, provided a similar account in 1823, when she described her visit to a nautch given by a wealthy Hindu, quoted in Heber, 1:47.

II.183. Rāmāyan Gāyan

Paris: I.2.1: RHAUMIEN-GAUYIN BRAHMUNS CHANTING THE EXPLOITS OF RHAUM: This Brahmun is singing the exploits of the god Rhaum-Outar during his incarnation. He holds with a silver stick a *choury* [*chauṅrī*][2] of black horse hair, which he is constantly waving. He is richly dressed in shawls and precious stuffs, and always adorned with red flowers. The assistants who keep behind him repeat the same exploits in different tones. The audience listen with admiration, and as the subject varies are transported with grief or joy.

This religious ceremony is celebrated before the house of the pious Hindoo who chooses to be at the expence of it. It takes place generally, like that of the *Mohabaurut* [Mahābhārata Sabhā, Pl. II.182] in the first court. The masters of the house are seated on an eminence. The women can see or be seen only through a grating of bambou. Those who are in the varanda, or gallery, are the women of an inferiour class, who are more free to shew themselves in public.

The *Rhaumien* is also celebrated in the bazars or markets, and in the villages. In the evening especially this ceremony attracts a numerous audience. The recital is generally accompanied by musical instruments, as the *mirdun* [mṛdaṅga],[3] the *kole* [khol] or *kurtaul* [kartāl][4] which we shall describe hereafter.

This plate gives an idea of the interior architecture of the Hindoo houses.

Commentary: The epic *Rāmāyaṇa* is the chronicle of Rāma, king of Ayodhyā and incarnation (*avatāra*) of the god Viṣṇu, who in this form saves the world from the demon Rāvana. Lord Rāma is the embodiment of righteousness, as his consort, Sītā, is the faithful wife.[5] The Sanskrit epic, consisting of 24,000 verses, dates

Pl. II.183. Rāmāyan Gāyan. Paris: I.2.1. Double-plate.

Calcutta: Sec. XII, No. 2. Rhaumien Gauyin,—A Brahmun with his Assistants singing the exploits of Rhaum [Rām] in the incarnation of the Deity, called the Rhaum Outar [Avatāra].[1]

from perhaps as early as the 4th century BCE, and is attributed to the sage Vālmīki. Solvyns's contemporaries in Bengal, the Serempore missionaries William Carey and Joshua Marshman, under sponsorship of the Asiatic Society, made the first English translation, publishing the first part of the poem in 1806.[6]

Recitations of the *Rāmāyaṇa*, expositions, singing, and the elaborately-costumed *Rāmlīlā* folk pageants are all a part of a vibrant Hindu tradition. Numerous vernacular versions brought the story of Rāma to the common people as a part of the *bhakti* (devotional) movement, in which singing, often in groups, is a central form of religious expression.[7] The performance in song, *gāyan*, by a Rāmāyaṇi, as Solvyns depicts, may vary in duration, extending to a twenty-four hour marathon or over several days.

In his note to the original drawing, Solvyns identifies the scene simply as "A Gauyin. Hindoos singing the praises of their favourite Deities, in which they occasionally introduce complements to great Men."

1 "Outar" is an Anglicization of *avatāra*, incarnation of a god, especially Viṣṇu, but meaning literally "one who comes down" or "descends." Rāma is one of the ten *avatāras* of Viṣṇu. Basham, *The Wonder That Was India*, 304-09.

2 A fly whisk, originally made from the bushy tail of the Tibetan yak. *Hobson-Jobson*, 214-15. Others are made of peacock feathers and the cheapest from leaves of the date palm.

3 Also called khol. See Pl. II.158.

4 See Pl. II.172.

5 See Daniélou, 172-75.

6 *The Ramayuna of Valmeeki*.

7 Lutgendorf, in *The Life of a Text: Performing the* Rāmcaritmānas *of Tulsidas*, provides a rich portrayal of these oral performances in Hindi-speaking North India.

II.184. Hari Saṅkīrtan

Pl. II.184. Hari Saṅkīrtan. Paris: I.3.1. Double-plate. **Calcutta: Sec. XII, No. 1.** A Hurry Sung Kertun [Hari Saṅkīrtan],—recitation of the History and life of the birth of Hurry [Hari] or Vestno [Viṣṇu], the preserving attribute of the Deity:—a Vestnub [Vaiṣṇavite] assisted by others of his Sect is relating the history and amours of the God and his family,—their musical instruments the Baunk [bā̃k], Mirden [mṛdaṅga] , and Kirtaul [kartāl], are played on at intervals, and the audience, according to the subject, are exalted with joy, or weep, prostrating themselves on the ground, embracing the reciting Vistnub, and laying down money at his feet.

Paris: I.3.1. HURRY-SUNG-KERTUN. Recitation of the history and life of Hurry or Vestn: Hurry is the name given to Vestno incarnate for the conservation of the human race. Hurry-Sung-Kertun is that of a religious festival celebrated in honour of the god.

A Vestnub Brahmun recites the incarnation and the life of Hurry, whose loves are also the subject of his song. What relates to this latter part is repeated by other Vestnubs, to the sound of various instruments, the *baunt*, the *mirdun* and the *kurtaul.*

The Brahmun, who accompanies himself with the castagnettes, sings or declaims with vast expression: while, as his subject varies, the audience are rapt into extasy, dissolved in tears, or convulsed with laughter.

This festival, which is among those that attract the most followers, is celebrated towards the close of day, and sometimes later.

It is attended with great expence to the person who gives it; because during the fifteen days which it generally lasts, he is obliged to furnish the Vestnubs with every necessary which they may require.

Nor does this prevent the assistants from offering considerable sums of money to the Brahmun, which they come and lay at his feet; embracing him afterwards.

The dress of the Vestnub, which consists of jewels, shawls and precious stuffs, is very rich, and may not unfrequently be valued at some thousand roupees.

Their turban is of wire, as well as several collars which hang upon their breast. This decoration, as well as the wire of which it is composed, is indispensable.

Commentary: Hari Saṅkīrtan is "singing the praises of Hari." Viṣṇu embodies the principle of duration and is the preserver of the universe, and Hari is the name for Viṣṇu as "Remover of Sorrow."[1] *Saṅkīrtan*, or *kīrtan* "consists of services of sacred song, either at a meeting or in a procession, often led by professional singers and accompanied by music, the assembled worshippers joining in chorus to glorify the god of their adoration and to chant his praises." In emotional rapture, such devotional singing may last the whole night.[2] In *kīrtan*, celebrants often display ecstatic behavior, raising their arms in the air, as several persons do in Solvyns's portrayal.

The tradition is associated with Caitanya (1485-1533), a Bengali saint who enjoined his followers to use *kīrtan*—the repetitious singing of the names of god (Hari, Rām, Kṛṣṇa)—in expression of their devotion.[3]

The pattern or structure of "harikirtan consists of a series of cycles, each beginning at a slow tempo and modern volume and accelerating to the verge of frenzy, when . . . the climax is abruptly terminated and the singing and playing resumed at a slower tempo and lower volume, to begin the cycle anew."[4]

In Bengal, O'Malley writes, "there are Vaishnava associations called *Hari Sabhas*, of which the object is spiritual development by means of *bhakti* or fervent love of God. Meetings are held once a week either in a building erected for the purpose or at the house of one of the members. Here the conception of a divine personality is brought home to the assembled people both by the reading of sacred books and the singing of sacred songs. A Pandit is engaged to read and explain sacred books, and parties of singers are hired to sing hymns in honour of Vishnu in one or other of his incarnations. The worship is very different from that of temple services, where the priest is the sole celebrant and the people merely look on. It is also different from domestic worship, which is confined to the members of a family, for the meeting-house is a place where all may join in devotional exercises, and the worship is not that of separate individuals or families but of a united congregation."[5]

There is no one Hari Saṅkīrtan festival. Rather, these celebrations are held irregularly and in scattered localities, where they are patronized by merchants or landowners. The duration of the Hari Saṅkīrtan varies and may last for as long as a month.

In Solvyns's portrayal, the *kīrtan* takes place under a *paṇḍāl*, or tent, erected outside the house of a Hindu patron. The singer is accompanied by musical instruments—the bā̃k, a trumpet (Pl. II.177); two mṛdaṅga, drums (Pl. II.158); and kartāl (Pl. II.171). The castanets to which Solvyns refers is the jhā̃jhari (Pl. II.175). Such musicians often wandered the streets singing devotional songs.

Solvyns portrays the Vaiṣṇavite singer wearing a closely bound turban that, as described in the original French text, is wrapped with strands of wire, the ends of which hang down to his chest.[6] (The English text's reference to a "turban of wire" and to "several collars" is a mistranslation.) The turban, called a *cūḍā* in Bengali, is worn by a *pāṭhak*, a narrator (or singer) of Hindu sacred texts—stories from the Purāṇas or Vaishnava holy books—to lay listeners. As a ceremonial headdress, the *cūḍā* is adorned with fine silver or gold threads (*jhālar*—Solvyns's "wire"), some of which hang down as tassels. Why Solvyns describes the *cūḍā* as "indispensable" remains a puzzle, for the *cūḍā* was more popular in north and west India, and in Bengal, shaven-headed *pāṭhaks* did not generally wear them.[7]

---

1 Daniélou, 151. Hari is said to be incarnate in countless gods and, as "supreme lord of all, comprises all that is perishable and imperishable." Stutley, 109.

2 O'Malley, *Popular Hinduism,* 111.

3 Hawley, *At Play with Krishna*, 312-13, and Kennedy, 20-23, 201-205. On the *kīrtan* traditions associated with Caitanya, see especially Ramakanta Chakravarti, 453-75.

4 Henry, 155, quoted in Lutgendorf, 98, fn. 51.

5 O'Malley, *Popular Hinduism,* 112.

6 The French reads: Leur turban est entortille de fils d'archal, dont plusiers filets tombent sur leur poitrine.

7 I am grateful to Ramakanta Chakravarty (Chakravarti) for the identification of the "turban" as the *cūḍā* worn by a *pāṭhak*.

II.185. Rās Yātrā

Commentary: Kṛṣṇa is one of the most celebrated deities of the Hindu pantheon, and his love for Rādhā, the beautiful cowmaid (*gopī*), is the inspiration of devotional (*bhakti*) movements.[1] This love is a favored theme of the mystical and erotic poetry of medieval India and is richly portrayed in Indian miniature painting.[2] Various festivals celebrate Kṛṣṇa's love for Rādhā and the cowmaids, and the *rās līlā*—one of the plays on the life of Kṛṣṇa—portrays in musical drama Kṛṣṇa's circle dance with the *gopīs*.[3] In Solvyns's time, *yātrās* on the life of Kṛṣṇa were especially popular in Bengal, drawing greater crowds than those on the exploits of Rāma or even Durgā.[4]

In Bengal, held over three nights of the full moon in the month of Kārttika (October-November), Rās Yātrā celebrates the frolic and loves of Kṛṣṇa with Rādhā and the *gopīs* in the gardens of Vṛndāvan. Each of the *gopīs* desired to dance with the handsome god, "but as all could not hold Kṛṣṇa's hand as they danced, he multiplied himself into as many forms as there were women, each woman believing she held the hand of the true Kṛṣṇa."[5] In the celebration of Rās Yātrā,

Paris: I.4.1. RAUSH-JATRAH CELEBRATION OF THE LOVES OF KISTNA: Every year, a feast is celebrated in commemoration of the loves of the god Kistna with his numerous mistresses, the chief of whom was called *Radica*.

This feast takes place in the open air, generally before the house of some rich Hindoo. The chosen spot is overhung with nets, and the principal ornaments of this species of temple consist of flowers, leaves, representations of birds, flags, and lanterns. Each person brings his gods to this public exhibition.

The ceremonies are performed in the night: it may be to avoid the excessive heats, but more probably to conceal the disorder which accompanies them. To paint this would be disgusting, and perhaps possible only to the imagination which can conceive every thing most licencious in debauchery. If many nations of antiquity did not furnish the remembrance of such excesses, it would be difficult of belief that such rites were paid to the divinity by the Hindoos.

It will no doubt appear extraordinary that among the actors of these scenes there reigns such a spirit of emulation, that they endeavour by every means to surpass each other, and that those who have really distinguished themselves in this contest obtain the veneration of their companions, and even lay claim to some degree of consequence in the world.

This feast is so far protected by the police, that games of hazard are then permitted, which at other times are so strictly forbidden to the Hindoos. This makes it the general rendezvous of gamesters, and the ruin of many. Here the sircars [sarkār, Pl. II.100] and servants come to lose the money of which they have robbed their masters, in order to celebrate the pleasures of Kistna.

After this it needs scarcely be added that few attend this feast out of devotion, and that the enlightened and distinguished part of the nation do not think it necessary to participate in it.

Pl. II.185. Rās Yātrā. Paris: I.4.1. Double-plate. **Calcutta: Sec. XII, No. 6.** Raush Jatrah,—the celebration of the amours of Kistna [Kṛṣṇa] with Radica [Rādhā], and his other loves,—in this Pooja [*pūjā*], nets are hung, and leaves, flowers, birds, &c. are placed over the open apertures, to represent nature, sympathising in the sports of the libidinous God.

"Each night, after the usual ceremonies in the pagoda, the image of Krishna, accompanied with songs and music, is removed to the interior of a distant building, open on all sides and decorated and illuminated for the occasion."[6] Sixteen clay images of Kṛṣṇa are required, and at the conclusion of the festival they are thrown into the river. A tiny seventeenth image, made of gold, is the object of special adoration and is afterward given to the officiating brahmin.

In the Rās Yātrā, Horace H. Wilson writes, "vast crowds, clad in their best attire," collect to celebrate the event "with music, singing, and dramatic representations of Krishna's sports. . . ."[7] In the streets around the building, booths are erected for the sale of sweets and the baubles of a fair. But, "as usual at all festivals kept in honour of this impure god," writes another European observer, "most licentious songs are sung and indecent dances take place."[8]

Solvyns, generally sympathetic to the Hindus, here succumbs to the more usual European judgment of condemnation of Hindu festivals and joins other accounts of Rās Yātrā in Bengal in alluding, without specificity, to "excesses."

The word *yātrā* (or *jātrā*) has two basic meanings: the first is "to travel"; the second, derivatively, is a pilgrimage, religious procession, or festival and, in Bengal, a musical drama on the occasion of a religious festival or theatrical performance on mythological and religious themes. Deeply influenced by Bengali Viṣṇava (Baiṣṇab) tradition, *yātrās* celebrated Kṛṣṇa in song and dramatically portrayed his life and loves.[9] Wealthy Hindus acted as patrons of *yātrā* performances, and they were typically staged in the inner courtyard of their great houses (described in Pl. II.182) or outside the house under *paṇḍāls* (tents) erected for the occasion. As in the European miracle plays to which *yātrās* have been likened, men and boys take all roles. The performance takes place in front of the image of the god—as much for the delight of the god as for the amusement and edification of the people—and they normally begin about 11:00 at night and may go on until sunrise.[10]

1 For a very good brief summary on the god, see Walker, 1:559-67.

2 See W. G. Archer, *The Loves of Krishna in Indian Painting and Poetry*, and P. Banerjee, *The Life of Krishna in Indian Art*. On Rādhā, see Wulff.

3 "The Great Circle Dance," in Hawley, *At Play with Krishna: Pilgrimage Dramas from Brindavan*, 155-226. The Sanskrit word *līlā* means "sport" or "play" and conveys the notion that god is animated by "a free and joyous creativity." Hein, 13.

4 William Ward, *Account of the Writings, Religion and Manners of the Hindoos*, 2:496.

5 *An Alphabetical List of Feasts and Holidays of the Hindus and Muhammadans*, 67-68.

6 Grant and Colebrooke, 307-08.

7 A Sketch of the Religious Sects of the Hindus," originally in *Asiatic Researches*, in *Essays and Lectures Chiefly on the Religion of the Hindus*, 1:130. On the *yātrā*, see Horace H. Wilson, *Select Specimens of the Theatre of the Hindus*, 2:383-415.

8 Murdoch, 70.

9 Sushil Kumar De, 401-12; Narendra Nath Bhattacharyya, 173; Lewis, 135. On Kṛṣṇa as subject of the Bengali *yātrā*, also see Keith. Sumanta Banerjee, 103-04, discusses the form of the *yātrā*. Nisikanta Chattopadhyaya's *The Yātrās or the Popular Dramas of Bengal* deals mainly with the Kṛṣṇā yātrās composed by Krishnakamal Gosvami (1810-1888).

10 William Wilkins, 224-25.

II.186. Jhulan Yātrā

Paris: I.5.1. D'JOLEN JATRAH. SWINGING OF KISTNA: The object of this feast is to celebrate the Incarnation of Kistna. The God is represented in the fore ground of the engraving; attended by his companions, and his favourite *Radica*. His mother, *Jussudhah,* is placed behind him, holding a lamp with five branches, as a spell to preserve her son from the enchantments of his numerous mistresses.

The mysteries or allegories of this religious commemoration are under the direction of the Brahmuns. At times the companions of Kistna retire to change their costume and their dress, and reappear representing even the mistresses of the God.

In the background over a little altar is represented the swinging of Kistna with Radica. Here the people come to offer up their prayers and sacrifices or poujahs [*pūjā*] to which the morning is consecrated, as is the evening to the dances: which are followed by immense crowds to whom the sight of the dancers gives great delight. The feast continues thro' the night and is lighted by *machals* [*maśāls*] (lanterns) carried by servants called *coulies* [*kulī*].[2]

The first court of the rich Hindoos is never without a pagoda, in which the feast is celebrated. Overhead the court is hung with cloath, and the ground is overspread with carpets of more or less value, or in preference with white coton cloath. Betel, essence of roses, and all sorts of refreshments are served up, which makes the feast very expensive.

Further details will be given with the description of the most solemn and most frequented of all the Hindoo feast, the *Durgah Poujah* [Durgā Pūjā, Pl. II.194].

Commentary: The Jhulan Yātrā is the "swinging festival" of Bengal held in the month of Śravana (July-August) for either three or five nights, depending on family tradition. It celebrates Kṛṣṇa's love for Rādhā and his "frolics" with the *gopīs* (milkmaids) and takes its name from the swing, or *jhūlā*, on which the images of Kṛṣṇa and Rādhā are placed. The portrayal of Rādhā and Kṛṣṇa seated on a swing is a familiar

Pl. II.186. Jhulan Yātrā. Paris: I.5.1. Double-plate. **Calcutta: Sec. XII, No. 5.** Joolun Jatra,—or the celebration of the swinging of Kistna [Kṛṣṇa], an incarnation of the Diety, with his favourite Radica [Rādhā].—In the fore ground appears the representations of Kistna, Bularam [Balarāma], Sedam [Śrīdamā], and Subul [Subal], the brothers [sic] and companions of Kistna;—occasionally some of them disappear and change their dress, to personify Radica, Laletah [Lalitā], Bisakah [Viśākhā], and Chundrahbullie [Candrāvali], the loves of Kistna.—On the left sits a man dressed to represent Jussudah [Yaśodā],[1] the mother of Kistna, holding in his hand a lamp of five lights,—with which is performed the charm to guard Kistna from Evil Spirits,—on the left [right] in the back ground is the Swing, &c

---

theme in Indian miniature painting, and Edward Moor, in his 1810 *Hindu Pantheon*, takes such a painting for his depiction of the lovers.[3]

Many of the ceremonies of Jhulan Yātrā, including the swing, are similar to those of Dol Yātrā (Pl. II.189), the North Indian Holī festival, but colored powders are not thrown. Wealthy Hindus hosted the festivities in their homes, in the central courtyard described in the commentary to Mahābhārata Sabhā (Pl. II.182).

Grant and Colebrooke, in their *Anglo-Hindoostanee Handbook*, describe the festival:

"During the early part of each of these nights the images of Krishna and Radha are removed from their usual place to a chair or throne suspended from the ceiling of an adjoining room in the pagoda, and there swung, by the officiating Brahmuns till 10 o'clock; the images are then returned to their former seats when various forms of worship are repeated amidst offerings of flowers, incense, sweetmeats, fruit, &c., accompanied by singing, dancing, and music by people outside. At midnight the owner of the pagoda or image generally feasts a company of Brahmuns, after which the whole assembly of people are entertained, till day-light, with dramatic entertainments usually illustrative of the lives and amours of Krishna and Radha."[4]

The Rev. William Ward, Solvyns's contemporary in Bengal, offers a disparaging portrayal: "During the celebration of worship in the house, the crowd out of doors sing, dance and make a horrid noise with barbarous instruments of music, connecting with the whole every indecency. At twelve o'clock, the owner of the image entertains a great multitude of bramhuns. After eating and drinking, they literally 'rise up to play;' youths dressed so as to represent Krishnu and his mistress Radha, dance together; and the festivities are thus continued till this crowd retire at day-light."[5]

In the 1799 *Catalogue,* Solvyns oddly refers to four performers in the foreground of the print—Kṛṣṇa, his brother Balarāma, and Kṛṣṇa's cowherd companion Śrīdamā and friend Subal—but only three dancing boys[6] are portrayed. In the course of the performance, as Solvyns indicates, the dancers portray various characters, including Rādhā and the milkmaids Lalitā (Rādhā's closest friend), Viśākhā, and Candrāvali (Rādhā's arch rival).

In the *Catalogue*, Solvyns also identifies a man dressed to represent Kṛṣṇa's foster-mother, Yaśodā, holding an oil lamp of five lights (the devotional *pañcapradīp*), but in the Calcutta print, the torch-bearer conceals the lamp from the viewer. In the Paris etching, Solvyns widens the space between the torch-bearer and the "mother" to reveal her holding the lamp described.

Solvyns's etching depicts the dancers, with musical accompaniment by the khol (Pl. II.158), manjīrā (Pl. II.174), and, only partially visible, what appears to be a ḍholak (Pl. II.159).

1 Yośodā and her husband Nanda are the cowherd foster parents of Kṛṣṇa. The mother of Kṛṣṇa is Devakī. See P. Banerjee, 15-16.

2 The Anglo-Indian *coolie* or *cooly*, a hired laborer, entered English and other European languages in the sixteenth century. The word, of disputed origin, is *kulī* in Bengali.

3 See, for example, W. G. Archer, *The Loves of Krishna in Indian Painting and Poetry*, Pl. 33. Moor, Pl. 67.

4 301-02. Also see *An Alphabetical List of Feasts and Holidays of the Hindus and Muhammadans*, 37.

5 *A View of . . . the Hindoos* , 3:150. Also see Murdock, 60, who describes the "dances and dramatic exhibitions" as "of the most indelicate and obscene kind."

6 Solvyns provides an individual portrait of the dancing boy, or *bālak*, Pl. II.96.

II.187. Snān Yātrā

Pl. II.187. Snān Yātrā. Paris: I.7.1. Double-plate.

Calcutta: Sec. XII, No. 8. Chaun Jatra or Ausnaun Jatra,[1]—the celebration of the washing of Juggernaut:—He is said to travel in one night from Cuttack to the Mundar [*mandir*, or temple], here represented near the Danish Settlement of Serampore.—He is bathed on the first day of his arrival—but afterwards is kept warm on account of a fever, proceeding from a cold he catches—until his return to Juggernaut.—As the Public have not any satisfactory interpretation of this symbol of Juggernaut, it is to be lamented that the Gentleman who has so very ingeniously decyphered it, from the initial letters of the Hindoo Triad, to be the emblem of Brehim [Brahmā] the one Supreme Being, witholds from the world his opinions on the subject;[2]—and it is a matter of greater regret, that the encomiums and entreaties of his Friends, have not yet prevailed on him to favour the Public with his many other discoveries and philosophical remarks on the Fables of Eastern Mythology—and the harmony melody, and brilliancy of his Numbers.—It being most strictly forbidden the Hindoos to make any representation of the Almighty—the command, it seems, is evaded by forming the image without hands and feet; in short anything rather than not have a God that they can see and feel.

Paris: I.7.1. CHAUN-JATRAH. CELEBRATION OF THE BATH OF JUGGERNAUT: The Hindoos believe that the god *Juggernaut* [Jagannātha] transports himself, in one night, from his pagoda at Cattach [Cuttack], in Oorissah [Orissa], to the spot where the ceremony of the bath is performed near Serampore, on the banks of the Ganges. Upon the day of his arrival, they wash and bathe him, and take great care to keep him warm on account of the fever which the cold has given him. After this he does not stir out until his return, which takes place after about three months, at the end of the rainy season. It does not appear that the public have ever had any satisfactory explanation of this allegorical festival.

The representation of *Juggernaut* consists only of an head and part of the arms. To this unfinished form is attached the sublime idea, that it is not for man to represent the divinity under material forms, lowering as it were the dignity and omnipotence of the godhead by supposing it in human shape. The Hindoos therefore are persuaded that no mortal can ever finish this statue, and that, of those who have made the attempt, some have been struck dead before the end of their work, or that by a power unseen the chisel has dropt from their hands, nay even that some parts in the instant they were finished fell spontaneously from the body.

Thousands of Hindoos contemplate with transport the Brahmun, who, several times a day, throws a vase of water from the Ganges on the unformed idol. But many are not satisfied with the enjoyment of this religious sight; for this too is one of the feasts which cover the most unrestrained debauchery. The husband has no power to prevent his wife, nor the father his daughter, from attending it, under the pretext of devotion. Not unfrequently the bride who had never beheld the face of man except her husband's, the virgin who for the first time had ventured beyond the paternal roof, become victims of the brutality of those whom the licenciousness of the festivity had attracted.

Commentary: Jagannātha, Lord of the Universe, is a form of Kṛṣṇa, the worship of whom is centered at Purī, in Orissa, where he is enshrined with his brother Balabhadra (Balarāma) and sister Subhadrā.[3] Various accounts explain the "unfinished form" of the god,[4] but few are as elegant as that suggested by Solvyns.

The Snān Yātrā is the festival of the ritual bath of Lord Jagannātha conducted on the day of the full moon in the Bengali month of Jaiṣṭha (May-June).[5] Seventeen days later, with slight variations depending on the lunar calendar—not three months, as Solvyns mistakenly writes[6]—Jagannātha is honored in the Rath Yātrā (Pl. II.188), the chariot festival. The greatest of these festivals is held at Purī, chief abode of the god, but both festivals are celebrated as well in various places in Bengal, most notably at the village of Māhesh, one mile south of Serampore (the old Danish enclave famed for its Christian mission) and some 12 miles from Calcutta. It was in Māhesh that Solvyns observed both the Snān and Rath Yātrās.[7]

The image of Jagannātha in Māhesh is some 600 years old and, at odds with Solvyns's more realistic portrayal of a human head, has the same amorphous, mask-like appearance as the god in Purī. The size of the image is roughly as Solvyns portrays it, but at Māhesh, the accompanying images of his brother and sister are much smaller, whereas in Purī, they are close to the same size.

Legend recounts that Jagannātha stopped and bathed at Māhesh on his way to Purī, and a shrine was constructed there to honor the god. The Māhesh Jagannātha temple, seen in the etching, is in the curvilinear form of the Orissan style and was built by a wealthy Calcutta Hindu in 1755.[8]

The Rev. William Ward, Solvyns's contemporary in Bengal, observed the Snān Yātrā at Māhesh. Jagannātha, wrapped in cloth, is carried out and placed on a large platform near the temple, portrayed by Solvyns very much as it appears today. "Here the brahmuns, surrounded by an immense concourse of spectators, bathe the god by pouring water over his head, during the reading of incantations."[9] Those who behold the spectacle are blessed, believing that the sight of Jagannātha will take away their sins. When the bathing is complete, the god is reclothed and returned to the temple for worship. There then follows a fair, with sales stalls, shows, and various amusements.

George Johnson, who lived in Calcutta in the early 1840s, cast a disparaging eye: "*Chanjattra* . . . is the time of the annual ablution of the god Juggernauth. It is not celebrated with such pomp and solemnity in

Calcutta as at Mahesh. . . . Under the plausible pretence of witnessing the holy ablution, tens of thousands of natives pour thither in budgerows, pinnaces, and dinghys, decorated with festoons of flowers, but, in reality, freely to indulge in debauchery. Smoking, carousing, and rioting are the inseparable accompaniments of the rites. The most obscene exhibitions are presented; songs of indecency are continually sung, and prostitutes are expressly encouraged to add to the licentiousness of the scene."[10]

Gangooly, in his *Life and Religion of the Hindoos*, describes the Snān Yātrā at Māhesh as "the next exciting scene to that of Orisa, but excels the other in its licentious shows and amusements."[11] Johnson and Gangooly, as did Solvyns earlier, refer to the "debauchery" of the accompanying fair, but there is nothing licentious in the religious ceremonies. Indeed, William J. Wilkins, writing in 1887, described the bathing festival at Māhesh as "the most impressive ceremony I have seen connected with Hinduism."[12]

The descriptions by Ward and Wilkins, as later by O'Malley and Chakravarty in the Hooghly District gazetteer, refer to the bathing of a single god, Jagannātha, and Solvyns depicts Jagannātha alone on the platform as priests pour holy water over him. If correct, this is in contrast to the Snān Yātrā as performed at Purī, where Jagannātha is placed, together with his brother Balabhadra and their sister Subhadrā, on the platform atop the great temple wall, and the three deities are bathed.[13] In Māhesh today, all three gods are similarly bathed.

Tradition has it that on the occasion of his bath, Jagannātha catches cold and suffers from a fever. He is secluded for a period of fifteen days, during which time the image is repainted and decorated in preparation for the Rath Yātrā. On the sixteenth day, when the image is ready, its eyes are ritually opened, and it may again be properly worshipped. Having recovered from his indisposition, on the seventeenth day after Snān Yātrā, Jagannātha then undertakes his chariot procession.

1 Solvyns gives the colloquial Bengali *Cān* and, less common, *Asnān* for Snān (Sk., Snānā) Yātrā, the bathing festival.
2 Solvyns's "Gentleman" remains elusive.
3 On Jagannātha and the cult more generally, see Eschmann, Kulke, and Tripathi; Starza; H. C. Patnaik; and K. C. Mishra.
4 See, for example, K. C. Mishra, 110-12; John Garrett, *A Classical Dictionary of India*, 270; and Stutley, 122-23.
5 For the Snān Yātrā at Purī, see Mohapatra, 84-87; K. C. Mishra, 1128-29; Ward, *A View . . . of the Hindus,* 3:162; Brijendra Nath Sharma, 23; and O'Malley, "The Worship of Jagannath," *Bengal District Gazetteers: Puri*, 104.
6 In referring to three months' time, Solvyns may be confused with a four month period, from Āṣāṛha (June/July) to Kārtik (October/November), when Jagannātha is asleep. This is during the rainy season, deemed inauspicious. Reflecting variation in the lunar calendar, sources differ in the number of days between the Snān and Rath Yātrās. Seventeen is the usual number, but it may sometimes be 15 or 16 days. The time elapsed may, however, be longer, as in 1996, when the Rath Yātrā took place six weeks after Snān Yātrā because of the rules of the Hindu almanac relating to an inauspicious period.
7 I am grateful to Falguni Sakha Bose (Basu) of Calcutta for information on the Jagannātha tradition in Māhesh and for specific information relating to both the Snān and Rath Yātrās.
8 Michel, 51; O'Malley and Chakravarti, 318; and Amiya Kumar Banerji, *West Bengal District Gazetteer: Hooghly*, 721.
9 *A View . . . of the Hindoos,* 3:336. Also see Hunter, *A Statistical Account of Bengal,* 3:323-24, for an account of the Snān Yātrā at Māhesh.
10 1:136-37.
11 108-09.
12 220-21
13 See Eschmann, Kulke, and Tripathi.

II.188. Rath Yātrā

Commentary: The Rath Yātrā is the car or chariot festival of Jagannātha, held in Āsāṛh (June-July). Its most important enactment is at Purī, principal abode of the god,[1] but it is celebrated at various places in Bengal, notably Māhesh, where Solvyns made his observations. The Rath Yātrā there is second in importance to that of Purī, drawing vast crowds, and the chariot, *rath*, is almost as ponderous as those of Purī.[2] On the morning of the Rath Yātrā, thousands of people are fed and the procession is formed. Men carrying flags walk in rows, and musicians with drums, flutes, cymbals accompany singers in praise of Kṛṣṇa.

In describing the Rath Yātrā, Solvyns makes no reference to Jagannātha, but to Kṛṣṇa and Rādhā, perhaps reflecting the Vaiṣṇava syncretism of the festival as celebrated at Māhesh. Solvyns's contemporary, William Ward, a missionary at the Serampore mission, described the Rath Yātrā honoring Jagannātha as a festival "intended to celebrate the

Pl. II.188. Rath Yātrā. Paris: I.6.1. Double-plate.

Calcutta: Sec. XII, No. 7. Ruth-Jatrah,—the riding of the Gods in their Carriage, drawn by thousands of fanatics,—some of whom throw themselves under the cart, with the persuasion that their death will secure them immediate bliss in heaven.

Paris: I.6.1. ROUTH-JATRAH.
PROCESSION OF THE GODS IN THEIR CAR:
This festival, one of the most solemn among the Hindoos, is celebrated once every year in the month of *assar* [Āṣāṛh] which answers to our month of june. The object is to celebrate the travels of Kistna [Kṛṣṇa] with Radica [Rādhā]; and it consists in dragging with great pomp, the God, his mistress, and his companions, in a sort of edifice or pagoda constructed in wood, and adorned with tolerable sculpture. These relievos, and its hieroglyphic paintings are too obscene to admit of representation. With this exception the engraving gives an exact idea of this species of building, which is called *Routh* [*rath*]. Two horses of wood painted blue appear to draw, and a Brahmun to guide, it, while the machine placed upon a number of small, but very solid wheels, is moved in reality by two cords which are grasped by the most zealous among the thousands of attendants of both sexes and of every age and sect: a Brahmun receives the offerings which are always made in great abundance.

This feast never takes place without some fanatics throwing themselves under the wheels on purpose to be crushed, in the persuasion that such a death ensures to them the immediate enjoyment of perfect felicity. The author himself has seen as many as thirty individuals sacrifising their lives in this manner under a single Routh.

The gods and their moving temple are left upon the spot which terminates their career until the eighth day, when they are brought back to the place of their departure; but their return is attended with much less pomp. The following day the machine is divested of all its ornaments, and remains deposited under a straw shed until the next year, when the feast recommences with the same ceremonies, a car perfectly similar, and new victims of fanaticism.

diversions of Krishna and the milk-maids, with whom he used to ride out in his chariot."[2]

According to tradition, the Rath Yātrā at Māhesh dates back some 600 years, but since the mid-eighteenth century, it has been celebrated under the patronage of the Basu family of Shyambazar in Calcutta.[3] In 1757, Krishna Ram Basu, Dewan of Hooghly, commissioned the construction of the *rath* that Solvyns portrays. The *rath*, as shown by Solvyns and confirmed by Basu family records, was made of wood, with three stories and five pinnacles, rising to a height of some 50 feet. The two life-size wooden horses, painted blue, are "driven" by a wooden brahmin charioteer who stands 5 feet, four inches. In the early nineteenth century, the *rath* was destroyed by fire.

The chariot used today in the Māhesh festival, constructed in 1885, is made of iron. It is of the same general style as that depicted by Solvyns, but more elaborate, with four stories and nine pinnacles. Its 125 ton weight is drawn on 12 wheels, each ten feet in diameter, enclosed within the outer frame of the *rath*, as in Solvyns's depiction of the earlier car. Its horses are today of brass, one blue and the other white, though the wooden charioteer of the earlier *rath* is still used. The Māhesh *rath* now in use carries a pantheon of Vaiṣṇavite imagery: On the first level are scenes of the Vaiṣṇavite saint Chaitanya; on the second level, images of Kṛṣṇa and Rādhā; on the third, Rāma; and on the fourth, Lord Jagannātha.[3] In contrast to the celebrations at Purī, the Rath Yātrā at Māhesh clearly honors Kṛṣṇa and Rādhā as well as Jagannātha, perhaps accounting for Solvyns's failure to identify Jagannātha, but the omission remains an anomaly.

Ward, Solvyns's contemporary, describes the festival at Māhesh: "About seventeen days after the Shanu-yatra [Snān Yātrā] . . . the Ru'thu or car festival is held. . . . The car belonging to the image near Serampore is in the form of a tapering tower, between thirty and forty cubits high [some 40-60 feet]. It has sixteen wheels, two horses, and one coachman, all of wood. Jugunnat'hu, his brother Baluramu [Balarāma], and their sister Soobhudra [Subhadrā] are drawn up by ropes tied round their necks, and seated on benches in an elevated part of the carriage, where a servant on each side waves a tail of the cow of Tartary, called a chamuru [*chaunrī*]. The crowd draw the carriage by means of a hawser [rope]; . . . . Being arrived at the appointed spot, the bramhuns take out the images, and carry them to the temple of some other god, or to a place prepared for them, where they remain eight days. At Serampore, Jugunnat'hu, and his brother and sister, visit the god Radhu-Vullubhu [Rādhāballah, a form of Kṛṣṇa]; . . . . ." At the end of eight days, the gods are returned to their home.[4]

Hunter, in the 1870s, describes the Rath Yātrā at Māhesh as celebrated "with great pomp, and attended by a large concourse of people." "Sixteen days after the bathing festival, the *rath-jātrā* or car festival takes place. The god is again brought out of his temple at Mahesh, placed on a huge car, and dragged for a distance of a mile to the village of Ballabhpur, where he is placed in the temple of another god, Radhaballabh. After a lapse of eight days, the *ultā-jātrā*, or return journey takes place and the god is escorted back to his temple in the same way as he was brought out." During the course of the festival, great fairs are held at Māhesh and Ballabhpur.[5]

The temple at Ballabhpur, a neighborhood of Serampore, was built in 1764 and honors Kṛṣṇa in the form of the mendicant Rādhāballabh, and the images of Kṛṣṇa, as Rādhāballabh, and Rādhā are housed in the sanctum sanctorum. In Solvyns's time, a side chamber housed Jagannātha, Balabhadra, and Subhadrā in their visit from Māhesh on the occasion of the Rath Yātrā—the principal festival of the temple. (In 1850, a dispute between priests of the two temples ended the visits. The Rādhāballabh temple installed its own set of Jagannātha images, and thereafter the Māhesh gods took their eight days rest at Jagannātha's garden house.)[6]

Perhaps no festival so fascinated Europeans as the Rath Yātrā. Another contemporary of Solvyns, the Rev. William Tennant, describes the great festival at Purī and—sharing Solvyns's modesty—refers to the sculptures on the car, as those in Hindu temples, as "images of fecundity and of creative power too gross for description." "The *Ruth Jatra*," he writes, "is a ceremony at once cruel and indecent. The carriages on which their deities are . . . placed, are of immense height and supported on sixteen wheels; the whole drawn along by thousands of fanatics, some of whom fall down before these wheels, and being instantly crushed are, as they believe, put in possession of immortal bliss."[7] European travelers and especially missionaries often illustrated their accounts of India with prints depicting the Rath Yātrā. Sonnerat, in 1782, for example, includes an engraving with a rather fanciful *rath*, with the wheels of the car rolling over the body of a devotee.[8]

Ward relates that "many recent instances might be recalled of persons, diseased or in distress, casting themselves under the wheels of this ponderous car, and being crushed to death,"[9] and Calcutta newspapers annually reported the deaths of Jagannātha celebrants. Gangooly denies that devotees throw themselves under the wheels, asserting that the deaths are by accident.[10] O'Malley states that the more zealous devotees rush in front of the cars, before which they prostrate themselves with the object of touching the car and thereby obtaining merit. It is believed that one who sees Jagannātha at this time will be saved from the misery of future rebirths. "The accidents which have occurred in this way," O'Malley writes, "have given rise to the belief that self-immolation is practiced at the festival."[11] Solvyns describes having seen at least thirty people throw themselves under the wheels of the *rath*. We need not question his veracity, but he could have seen such accidents as described by O'Malley and, having heard accounts of ecstatic suicide, assumed that was indeed what he had witnessed. European descriptions of worshippers throwing themselves under the wheels of the car of Jagannātha, however, are numerous, dating from the fourteenth century, and cannot be wholly discounted, but they were surely exaggerated.[12]

Solvyns portrays the *rath* at rest before the procession begins, and the ropes, not yet taken by the celebrants, lie coiled before the car. An 1816 Italian copy of the etching (Pl. I.56) embellishes Solvyns's portrayal with a throng of people pulling the *rath* as one of its wheels crushes a devotee.

The word *juggernaut*, a corruption of Jagannātha, came into English as a metaphor for an overwhelming force before which everything is crushed, or for an institution or belief that demands blind and destructive devotion or to which people are ruthlessly sacrificed.

---

1 See Kulke, "Rathas and Rajas: The Car Festival at Puri"; Mohapatra, 87-103; K. C. Mishra, 130-35; O'Malley, *Bengal District Gazetteers: Puri*, 104; H. S. Patnaik, 114-26; Mohanty, 50-66; Starza, 16-17; and Mahapatria.

2 In Māhesh, there is a single *rath* upon which Jagannātha and his brother and sister ride, while in Purī, each of the three deities has a separate *rath*.

2 Ward, *A View. . . of the Hindoos,* 3:163-64. Also see Grant and Colebrooke, 300-01.

3 I am grateful to a leading member of that family, Falguni Sakha Bose [Basu], for providing me detailed information on the Rath Yātrā at Māhesh. He has been responsible for organizing the Rath Yātrā and maintaining the Māhesh *rath* since 1972. Mr. Bose situates Solvyns's portrayal of Māhesh very much as it is today, though he suggests that Solvyns apparently reduced the distance between the main temple wall, to the right, and, in the background, the Dol Māñcā, the pavilion where Jagannātha is worshipped on the occasion of Dol Yātrā (see Pl. II.189).

3 A photograph, "Ceremonial drawing of the Wooden chariot of Jagannathdeva at Mehesh," depicts the *rath* now in use. Amiya Kumar Banerji, *West Bengal District Gazetteers: Hooghly.*

4 Ward, *A View. . . of the Hindoos*, 3:163-64.

5 *A Statistical Account of Bengal*, 3:306, 3: 324. Also in O'Malley and Chakravarti, 105-06.

6 O'Malley and Chakravarti, 318. Amiya Kumar Banerji, *West Bengal District Gazetteers: Hooghly*, 720-21.

7 Tenant, 3:258. Among the numerous accounts of the festival at Purī, see O'Malley, "The Worship of Jagannath," in *Bengal District Gazetteers: Puri*, 87-124.

8 French ed., Vol. 2, opp. p. 61. European portrayals of Rath Yātrā did not always focus on the macabre. Shakti M. Gupta, 86-87, reproduces a large, unidentified early nineteenth century European etching depicting the Rath Yātrā at Puri. The scene is one of benign, joyous celebration.

9 Ward, *A View . . . of the Hindoos,* 3:163-64.

10 Gangooly, 132-33.

11 O'Malley, *Bengal District Gazetteers: Puri* , 107.

12 *Hobson-Jobson*, 466-68.

II.189. Dol Yātrā

Commentary: Dol Yātrā is the name used in Bengal for Holī, the festival of colors celebrating the loves of Kṛṣṇa that probably originated as a wheat harvest festival in North India. Held over several days, it culminates on the day of the full moon in Phālguna (February-March), when celebrants throw red powder and colored water, as in myth Kṛṣṇa did in his sport with Rādhā and the *gopīs* (milkmaids). At Holī, there is bawdy song, dancing, and exchange invectives and obscenities —not in anger, but in a ribald sport of competition.

Holī takes its name from Kṛṣṇa's victory over Holikā, a demoness who devoured children, and in much of North India, on the night before the full moon, an effigy of Holikā is burned. The festival ends the next day in revelry. In Bengal, the festival is known as Dol Yātrā, from the word *dolā*, "swing." Movement of the swing "symbolizes bliss and the cessation of care."[1] In worship, an image of Kṛṣṇa, frequently with Rādhā, is placed on a swing and gently rocked at dawn, noon, and at sunset. During the day,

Paris: I.8.1: DOLE-JATRAH. CELEBRATION OF THE ORGIES OF KISTNA: This festival is believed to be a celebration of the orgies of Kistna with his mistresses and companions. As there is a religious tradition that they cast a red powder on each other, the Hindoos, upon this occasion, fling upon one another a fine earth of the same colour: the same that is used for painting, and which is found in great abundance in Hindoostan. They mix it with very fine sand to which it gives its tint. Some dilute it in water and sprinkle the passengers with it from syringes: happy if their eyes escape, where it causes great pain.

It would be difficult, as may be imagined, to give an explanation of this singular ceremony; but what is not less extraordinary, it takes place nearly at the same time as the Ash-wednesday of the Christians, and precedes also the Lent or expiatory season of the Hindoos; the Christians too, as well as the Musselmans, meet to partake, at least as a diversion, in the sprinkling of the red earth.

The festival indeed has nothing of sad solemnity in it; but offers on the contrary a ceremonious pretext for invitations and visits, in which the Hindoos pass several days of reciprocal entertainments and great repasts, which bear a relation to its name. Here also pawn [*pān*, Pl. II.212], bettel [betel], and perfumes are profusely distributed, and even presents of shawls, handkerchiefs, etc.

It takes place likes all the others before the house of some rich Hindoo, and in sight of a temple where the Brahmuns from time to time throw a little red earth, which they call *holie* [Holī] upon their gods. Outside are musicians, who, with different instruments and very great noise, proclaim and celebrate the feast.

Pl. II.189. Dol Yātrā. Paris: I.8.1. Double-plate. **Calcutta: Sec. XII, No. 9.** Dole Jutrah, or the Hoolee, in celebration of the Orgies of Kistna.

---

the household receives a host of visitors, who scatter color over one another as musicians chant the name of Kr̥ṣṇa and sing of his youthful frolics with Rādhā and the milkmaids, while more raucous antics take place outside in the streets.[2]

In his portrayal of the Dol Yātrā, Solvyns depicts musicians, with a standing figure playing the ḍamphā (Pl. II.166), an instrument associated with Holī. The musicians have blotches of red powder on their clothing, and to the sides, both adults and children throw color at each. To the left and rear, we see brahmin priests in worship before two images—sketchily rendered, but presumably Kr̥ṣṇa and Rādhā—placed on a swing. Holī was often depicted in Indian miniatures,[3] and a Company School painting, c. 1790, depicting the Nawab of Murshidabad celebrating Holī is presumed to be based on a painting by George Farington.[4] Among other European artists, in addition to Solvyns, Mrs. S. C. Belnos portrays "The Hooly Festival" among her *Twenty-Four Plates Illustrative of Hindoo and European Manners in Bengal*.[5]

---

1 Walker, 2:470. The image of Kr̥ṣṇa is also placed on a swing at Jhulan Yātrā, Pl. II.186.

2 For accounts of Bengal's Dol Yātrā, see Ward, *A View of . . . the Hindoos,* 3:152-53; Horace H. Wilson, "The Religious Festivals of the Hindus," in *Works,* 2:222-43; Grant and Colebrooke, 291-92; *An Alphabetical List of Feasts and Holidays of the Hindus and Muhammadans,* 18-20, and (on Holī) 38-39; Murdock, 34-42; John Garrett, *Classical Dictionary of India*, 34; B. A. Gupta, 89; and Sivananda, 40-41. For a description, from the *Calcutta Gazette*, 1826, of the Dol Yātrā given at a private Bengali home, see Anil Chandra Das Gupta, 134-35.

3 See, for example, the Rajput painting of Holī on the cover of *Art Journal*, 49 (Winter 1990).

4 In Mildred Archer, *India and British Portraiture, 1770-1825*, Plate 78, p. 126.

5 The plate represents Rawāni bearers dancing in the street, their clothes covered with red powder. An accompanying text describes the festival. Murdock, 37, notes that in Bengal much of the revelry is associated with the palanquin bearers.

II.190. Bisarjan

Pl. II.190. Bisarjan. Paris: I.9.1. Double-plate.

Calcutta: Sec. XII, No. 10. Busio Jun, or Callee Pooja, throwing the Image of their Gods and Goddesses into the water,—the Ceremony represented in the plate is of Durgah, or Caleeh, &c.

Commentary: In Bengal, at the conclusion of many Hindu festivals, the terracotta images made for the occasion are immersed in water, pathway of the gods. In the use of clay images, "After the offerings have been made, and the prescribed time for the deity's stay upon the earth has expired, it is . . . respectfully asked by the priest to go back to its heavenly abode. The idol is then a lump of clay, like the body of a living organism after life has departed from it. It is then consigned into water."[2] *Bisarjan* (Sk., *visarjana*) literally means "dismissal" or "the act of giving up" and here refers to the immersion of the image. Solvyns recognizes that *bisarjan* symbolizes the essential oneness of the immanent and many-faceted Hindu divinity.

The worship of clay images and their immersion would seem to have ancient roots, but one authority dates the tradition only from the seventeenth century. According to Prabhas Sen, Maharajah

Paris: I.9.1: BUSSO-JUN. THE THROWING THE IMAGES OF THE GODS INTO THE RIVER: To judge by the multiplicity of their festivals, the variety of the names and images of their gods, we should be led to suppose that unlimited polytheism was the creed of the Hindoos. Nevertheless there can be no doubt, but that the unity of the divinity is one of the fundamental dogmas of their faith, and that, under various allegories and denominations, they celebrate only the diverse attributes of one eternal, infinite, almighty God: and attach to the existence of their different subaltern deities an idea not very different from that which Christians entertain of the angels. If they appear to worship the elements, the rivers, the mountains, it proceeds from their opinion that God is the soul of the universe, pervading every particle of nature, animating every atom by his presence; and we must acknowledge that the infinity of the supreme Being can scarcely enter into the minds of the vulgar without being accompanied with some such error.

The religious festivals of the Hindoos consist in worshipping the images of the gods, offering up sacrifices (*poojahs*) and spending the remainder of the day in entertainments, dances and other amusements; but they do not all end in the same manner.

In that which we are now describing, after having carried the gods in procession during several days, they convey their images to the river, and place them on the edge of two boats drawn alongside each other. There, their adoration is followed by the grossest invectives, and the most violent imprecations. The brahmuns theirselves vie with each other in their abuse; and he who distinguishes himself most in this way, acquires a sort of veneration which lasts until the next celebration of the feast. To terminate this strange and inexplicable demeanour, the two boats are separated, and the images of the gods precipitated into the river amidst the acclamations of the multitude.

The engraving represents this moment. In the foreground is a sideview of the boats and of the position of the gods as well as of the brahmuns, the musicians, and principal actors in the ceremony. In another distance the boats are represented in front to give an idea of their separation; on the right are the assistants and spectators.

The principal figure is that of the goddess *Calkee* [Kālī],[1] wife of *Shieb* [Śiva], the genius of evil, or allegorically the destructive power: for the Hindoos distinguish in the deity three principal powers, creation, preservation and destruction. She has about her all her symbolical ornaments; which it would not be possible to explain so as to conciliate all the different ideas which have been entertained of them. Her feet are upon the body of *Shieb* as it were to restrain him: and many are of opinion that she puts out her tongue in shame of the persecutions which he inflicts upon mankind. This would be in conformity to the custom of the Hindoo women who make that grimace where any thing affects them disagreeably and even when they do or say any thing improper.

Krishnachandra of Nadia (1710-1783) early in his reign introduced into Bengal both the use of clay images in worship and their immersion in *bisarjan*.

> He had brought a couple of talented clay modellers to Bhurni, a suburb of his capital, Krishnagar, and supplied them with iconographic details of different deities which had been codified by the scholars of his court. Earlier, the worshippers had venerated either a symbolically decorated clay pot, a *ghat*, or a painting, a *pat* by a folk painter. Krishnachandra was also the originator of the tradition of *bisharjan*, the immersion of the images, after the annual worship, thus necessitating the making of fresh images each year. This was done to sustain and nurture the crafts associated with image-making, which thrived as clay-image worship rapidly gained popularity.[3]

Solvyns here depicts the *bisarjan* at the end of Kālī Pūjā, held in the month of Kārttika (October-November). During Solvyns's time, Kālī Pūjā was a more important public festival in Bengal than it is today, when Durgā Pūjā (Pl. II.194) is the major festival and its *bisarjan* is celebrated with great exuberance.[4] Indeed, it was from roughly Solvyns's time in Calcutta that, under the patronage of newly wealthy Hindu families, the goddess Durgā gained increasing prominence and over the course of the nineteenth century became the principal deity of Bengal.

The mother goddess, consort of Śiva and embodiment of divine energy, *sakti*, has many manifestations in Bengal. As Durgā, she is benign protector, and as Kālī, destroyer of evil and personification of supreme power. The iconic representation of Kālī that Solvyns's portrays is that of Dakṣiṇā or Śyāmā Kālī, the most popular form of the goddess in Bengal. Kālī is represented in horrific aspect. As depicted by Solvyns, she is black, with protruding tongue and disheveled hair reaching to her feet, and is naked but for a garland of heads. (More typical in iconic representation is a necklace of skulls and a girdle of human hands, which Solvyns does not depict. She frequently wears dead bodies of children as ear-rings, and her face and breasts are smeared with blood.) Kālī has four arms. In the upper left, she holds a sword, representing the power of destruction, and in the lower arm, the severed head of the demon she has killed; her upper right arm is raised as a sign of protection, removing fear, while the lower, giving hand is extended to bestow blessing.[5]

Various traditions relate to the body of Śiva upon which she stands and to her protruding tongue. The most popular is recounted by Ākos Östör: "Kālī, the destroyer of all evil, begins a mad dance of victory after her triumph. The whole world is threatened with destruction, for the earth cannot withstand the joy of the goddess. The gods approach Śiva in terror; only he can intercede with Kālī, the power of destruction. Śiva throws himself at the feet of the whirling goddess, but it takes her some time to realize that Śiva is under her feet, and stopping suddenly she puts her tongue out in shame."[6]

Grant and Colebrooke, in *The Anglo-Hindustanee Hand-Book*, describe the two days of Kālī Pūjā: "The first day ends with singing, dancing and feasting; the lower orders of the people, in and near Calcutta especially, indulging in the most shameless excesses of lewdness and intoxication—the raw *spirits* (uruk) [arrack] drank on the occasion, being consecrated, by previous solemn presentation, to the idol goddess. On the second morning the images made of the occasion of this festival, after various brahminical rites and ceremonies, are carried, in procession, to the river, and there, from boats, cast into the stream; at the conclusion of which ceremony the festival ends."[7]

The spirit of *bisarjan* and the activities portrayed by Solvyns are captured more fully in two descriptions of Durgā Pūjā, the first by Solvyns's contemporary, the Rev. William Ward of the Serampore Mission near Calcutta: At the conclusion of the Durgā Pūjā festival, men assemble "with their bodies daubed with turmeric, oil, and sour milk, and bringing out the image, place it on a stage, to which they fasten it with cords, and carry it on their shoulders to the water. It is here placed in the centre of two boats lashed together, and filled with people, among whom are dancers, musicians, singers, &c. At this time, in many instances, men dance stark naked on the boat before many thousands assembled, who only laugh at the gross indecency. Perhaps in one place on the river twenty or thirty images are exhibited at once, while the banks are crowded with spectators rich and poor, old and young, all intoxicated by the scene. The last ceremony is that of letting down the image into the river."[8]

Ghosha, in *Durga-Puja*, describes the same event: As the Pūjā ends, the idol is taken from the house "and carefully tied on a frame of bamboos and carried on the shoulders of bearers to the riverside with great pomp, drums beating, fools dancing antics, all kinds of music playing, flags flying &c. The idol is then taken on a couple of boats and after cruising a little is thrown overboard [with recitation of mantras] . . . , after which a variety of sports and auspicious rites with the beating of drums, and loud clamours, together with the blowing of conch-shells, transports, and percussion of mrudagas [mṛdaṅga], patahas and all sorts of drum instruments; and throwing of dust and mud, and pastimes, frolics, and other pantominnic games."[9]

Such ribaldry at the climax of many Hindu festivals and ceremonies is by no means unique to India, but as a holiday from conventional morals marks festivals around the world. In the European tradition, it can be seen from the Roman Bacchanalia and Saturnalia through numerous medieval revelries to Carnival or Mardi Gras of our own day. But what specifically is involved in the scene Solvyns describes?

At *bisarjan*, whether for Kālī or Durgā, celebrants—groups (*dals*) from a particular neighborhood or families who have taken their image to the river for immersion—often indulge in a competition of obscenities. On the way to the river, to the beating of drums, young men perform a dance of jerky, sometimes lewd, movements, colloquially called *khemṭā*, and there is an atmosphere of exhilaration and excitement. Suchitra Samanta explains that the advent of the goddess at her annual festival marks a period of sacred time (as distinct from secular time), accompanied by appropriate social action, but the brief interval from the time when the goddess "leaves" the clay image until the immersion "is marked by behavior *not* sanctioned under the normal and regular rules of society." With the immersion, secular time returns with an affirmation of social ties as men and women imbibe a mixture of marijuana, yogurt, sugar, and bananas, those of the same age embrace each other, and the young touch the feet of their elders in respect.[10]

Hindu texts may prescribe the lewd or "immoral" behavior that so shocked—and fascinated—Europeans. The *Kālīkapurāṇa*, a fourteenth century text on the myths and rituals of the goddesses Kālī and Durgā, states that "People should be engaged in amorous play . . . amidst the sounds of horns and instruments, . . . with songs on the male and female organs . . . until they have enough of it." And the exchange of invectives is similarly prescribed: "If one is not derided by others, if one does not deride others, the Goddess will be angry with him and utter a very dreadful curse."[11]

In Solvyns's etchings, we have noted variations between the Calcutta and Paris editions, sometimes in detail and background or, more significantly, in the closer presence of the central subject in many of the Calcutta prints. In the Paris portrayal of Bisarjan, with greater artifice and refinement of detail over all, Solvyns has added a throng of people to the far bank and has changed one of the figures in the boat to have him looking out at us, a European convention to draw the viewer into the picture. The effect of the Paris etching gives a greater sense of spectacle, emphasizing the festival's cultural importance, but it loses the immediacy of the "cruder" Calcutta print.

Solvyns's portrayal of the Kālī Pūjā *bisarjan* was copied, usually without attribution, for several engravings illustrating nineteenth century accounts of India,[12] but the most intriguing "borrowing" is an engraving by James Moffat (1775-1815), who was in Calcutta during Solvyns's time there. One of a series of prints, it is entitled "View of Benares, with a representation of the Callee Poojah, a Hindoo Holiday. Exhibiting the ceremony attending the throwing of the image of their Gods and Goddesses into the water." "Drawn & Engraved by J. Moffat, Calcutta," in 1802, the scene is a direct copy of Solvyns's Bisarjan and placed against a backdrop of the ghāṭs of Banaras (Pl. I.54).[13]

William Prinsep, in his own view of *bisarjan*, portrayed the "Water Procession of the Image of Doorga Previous to her Immersion at Sunset" in a 1825 watercolor.[14]

---

1 Solvyns here means Kālī, but mistakenly uses the name of Kalki, the Fulfiller, the avatar of Viṣṇu yet to come. On Kalki, see Daniélou, 181.

2 T. N. Mukharji, 60.

3 Prabhas Sen, *Crafts of West Bengal*, 164. Sen's discussion of "Festival Crafts" includes color photographs of the clay images, 160-73.

4 See commentary on Durgā Pūjā, Pl. II.194.

5 On Kālī and her image, see, *inter alia*, Kinsley, 116-31; Daniélou, 271-73; and S. C. Banjerji, 178-86. Harding discusses Kālī generally, including Kālī Pūjā, 125-43.

6 21.

7 306. Also see *An Alphabetical List of Feasts and Holidays of the Hindus and Muhammadans*, 42-45.

8 *A View of . . . Hindoos*. 3:88. Also see Ward's *Account of the . . . Hindoos*, 3:135-36, for the description of the Durgā bisarjan and 3:187-89 for the Kālī bisarjan.

9 Ghosha, 81-82. Ghosha describes the ritual in detail, at every stage, with specifics as to construction of the images, prayers at the separate *pūjās*, and descriptions of the ritual implements. The paṭaha referred to is an elongated barrel drum and is not portrayed by Solvyns in his series of musical instruments. See Dick, "Pataha," 3:21-22.

10 Letter to the author, March 12, 1993. Such "intervals" are discussed by Turner, and, with reference to the goddess in Bengal, by Östör.

11 Kooij, 121. On the obscenities that accompany *bisarjan* on Durgā Pūjā, see commentary, Pl. II.194.

12 The *Missionary Papers* of the Church Missionary Society, 33 (Lady Day, 1824), for example, copies Solvyns, without acknowledgment, in "Water Procession of the Image of Kalee, or the Black Goddess of the Hindoos." The same engraving is included in *The First Ten Years' Quarterly Papers of the Church Missionary Society*. Shoberl, *Hindoostan*, Vol. 2, Pl. 27, "Ceremony of throwing the colossal statute of the goddess into the water," the opp. p. 252, cites Solvyns in the text description. A copy, Pl. XVII, 1, "Procession sur l'eau de la Kaly Déesse" appears in Dumont d'Urville, opp. 1:131.

13 The print is reproduced in the context of a discussion of copies made after Solvyns by Moffat and others. See Chapter Three, pp. 106-07.

14 Reproduced in color in Pal and Dehejia, Pl. 9.

II.191. Jhā̃p

Pl. II.191. Jhā̃p. Paris: I.10.1. Double-plate.

Calcutta: Sec. XII, No. 11. A J'Haump—Sannassies and other Devotees throwing themselves from a height on beds of nails, knives, swords, pikes, &c. supported by a number of men—It is necessary they say, to prepare themselves by abstinence and mortifications to render themselves invulnerable.—It can hardly be expected, that credit will be given to the relation of the severe Penance performed by the Hindoos, by those who have not the testimony of their own eyes:—Through instances of this fanaticism are to be met with in the history of the superstitions of all nations, and lately of the Romish Saints; one of whom, Bellarmine[1] encouraged vermin to prey on him, saying—"we shall have Heaven to reward us for our sufferings, but these poor creatures have only the enjoyment of the present life."

Commentary: Solvyns vividly portrays Jhā̃p (frequently transliterated as Jhāmp or Jhāp), a rite of expiation in which devotees jump from high scaffolds onto spikes and other sharp objects.[3] It is part of the Gājan festival dedicated to Śiva and held at the end of Caitra (March-April), the last month of the Hindu calendar.[4] It is during the last four days of Gājan that celebrants, as "temporary *sannyāsīs*," undergo self-inflicted "tortures" in expression of their devotion. The festival was known among Europeans as Caṛak, taking the name from the "hook-swinging," Caṛak Pūjā, performed on the last day. Grant and Colebrooke, in their *Anglo-Hindoostanee Handbook*, relate the festival's origin to Raja Vanoo (Vana), a member of an austere sect, who to propitiate the favor of Śiva swung on a revolving swing by hooks from his back; pierced his tongue and sides; danced on fire; and threw himself upon spikes.[5]

The word *gājan*, Östör suggests, "probably comes from the Sanskrit *garjana*, meaning cry or shout. During the festival, bhaktas [devotees] call Śiva, hoping to draw his attention to the acts of

Paris: I.10.1: J'HAUMP. HINDOOS TROWING THEMSELVES ON KNIVES AND SWORDS: The Hindoos, like many other people, think that the anger of the gods can be disarmed by expiatory punishments, and that self-inflicted pains in this world, are so much deducted from those we may have deserved in the next. Penetrated with this idea, they put themselves to tortures not easy to be imagined, and which are rendered still more horrible by the tricks of mountebanks. We shall give a representation of the most remarkable, and refer to another place for a description of the different classes of fanatics who are here the principal actors.[2]

The plate represents Hindoos who from scaffolds several stories high, and from different elevations proportioned to the degree of their zeal, cast themselves upon a sort of straw or cotton mattress in which are inserted several edged or pointed instruments. They are Brahmuns who hold the mattresses to receive the patients. They have generally the address to accommodate themselves to the shock, and prevent too great wounds. For the essential point is not that the injury should be considerable; it suffices that the effusion of blood should be so.

Those who devote themselves to this species of sacrifice are obliged to prepare themselves for it during several days, by fasting and abstinence: they conceive that by so doing they become less vulnerable. This preparation also conceals the design of those who direct the scene, to render wounds easier to heal.

The victims of both sexes, for women do not think themselves exempt, are led before the act through the town or village, to the sound of different instruments. They are adorned with red flowers, and carry fruits which they throw to the spectators, who pick them up with a religious avidity. When their blood flows, they are the object of a new procession where they are carried by Brahmuns amidst the acclamations of the people.

Night opens another scene of the same sort, which shall have its separate engraving [Nīla Pūjā, Pl. II.192].

devotion they perform. . . . Their sole purpose is to gain his favor by various ascetic practices."[6]

During the Gājan festival, devotees, primarily from among the lower castes, wear the sacred thread of the "twice born" and assume the profession and dress of *sannyāsīs* in preparation for the expiations they will undertake. In the days before their expiations begin, they wander in groups through the streets, accompanied by musicians on horns and drums. Murdock notes that "respectable" śūdras "often hire individuals from the dregs of the population to act on their behalf, and to inflict the usual cruelties on themselves; but reserving of course for their own benefit the merit accruing from these practices. The Sudras who perform those penances *on their own account*, do it generally to fulfill a vow . . . ."[7]

That part of Gājan known as Jhā̃p takes place during the last days of the festival, the precise day—as the length of the festival—varying according to local traditions. The Rev. William Ward, Solvyns's contemporary in Bengal, termed the festival "abominable" and, with morbid fascination, detailed the course of its activities: On the first day of the festival, having prepared themselves over the previous month through purification ceremonies and by abstinence from certain gratification, *sannayāsīs* ascend a bamboo stage with three levels, the highest about twenty feet from the ground. From this height, they cast themselves onto iron spikes and knives stuck in bags of straw. The spikes, Ward notes, are generally in a reclining position, and when the person falls upon them, they are generally pressed down by his weight rather than entering his body. "There are instances, however, of persons being killed and others wounded, but they are very rare." At the festival, several such stages may be erected, and "as many as two or three hundred people cast themselves on these spikes, in one day, in the presence of great crowds of people."[8]

> Captain Thomas Williamson, in his *Vade Mecum* (1810), writes that preceding the Jhā̃p, the first expiation is that of suspension, which is performed by two posts being erected, on top of which is placed a strong bar, from which the *Sunnyasee*, or worshipper, is suspended by his feet over a fire kindled beneath him, into which rosin is occasionally cast. . . . On the following day the *Sunnyasees* dance and roll themselves on downy beds of various descriptions of prickly plants. Their next ceremony is called the *Jamp Sanya*, or jumping on a couch of pointed steel. . . . A bamboo scaffolding of three or four stages is

erected, on which the *Sunnyassees* stand, tier above tier, the principal and most expert occupying the upper row, which is sometimes between twenty and thirty feet high. A kind of bedding, supported by ropes, is stretched beneath the scaffolding by a number of men. Upon the mattresses are attached several bars of wood, to which are fixed very loosely, and in a position sloping forward, semicircular knives, upon which the *Sunnyasees* throw themselves in succession. In general the effect of the fall is to turn the knives flat upon the bedding, in which case they do no harm; but occasionally severe wounds, and even death are the consequences of this rite. Before they take their leap, the performers cast fruits, as cocoanuts, bels, plantains, etc., among the crowd, in which there is a great scramble for them, as they are supposed to possess much virtue. Women anxious for progeny are very anxious to get these donations; and those of the first families send persons to obtain them and bring them for their private eating."[9]

Bishop Reginald Heber and his wife Amelia witnessed the festival in Calcutta in 1824 and describe the scaffold very much as Solvyns depicts it. Heber quotes from his wife's journal: "Near the river a crowd was assembled round a stage of bamboos, 15 feet high, composed of two upright and three horizontal poles, which last were placed at about five feet asunder. On this kind of ladder several men mounted, with large bags, out of which they threw down various articles to the by-standers, who caught them with great eagerness. . . . They then one by one raised their joined hands over their heads, and threw themselves down with a force which must have proved fatal had not their fall been broken by some means or other. . . , but it is certain they were unhurt, as they immediately re-ascended, and performed the same ceremonies many times."[10] The crowd was too dense for her to see that they had, in fact, thrown themselves onto mattresses into which knives were stuck.

Solvyns depicts the devotee in jumping with hands raised, as Mrs. Heber describes, and two figures on the highest level of the scaffold hold out fruit to throw down to those below. Solvyns shows the mattresses with sharp instruments to be held at about waist level by those attending immediately below, thus providing substantial cushion to the fall. The plumed drums depicted are ḍhāks, which Solvyns portrays in a separate etching (Pl. II.156). In his descriptive text for the ḍhāk, Solvyns writes of its use in the Caṛak Pūjā: "Some days before the ceremony, they [the celebrants] are led in procession through their quarter, to the sound of the *D'Hauck* [ḍhāk]. It sometimes happens that the courage of these devotees not being equal to their piety, they begin by following the drum slowly and trembling; but soon its noisy sounds and the fumes of intoxicating liquors, animate them, and exalt their imagination to a degree of intrepidity which allows them to see only the glory which is to attend this fanatical undertaking."

Frederic Shoberl, in his volumes for *Hindoostan* (1822) in *The World in Miniature*, reproduces a part of Solvyns's etching of Jhā̃p in a depiction of Hindu expiations.[11]

Jhā̃p is still practiced in Bengal today as an important part of the Gājan festival at the Kālīghāṭ temple in Calcutta. Described by Indrani Basu Roy, participation in the "jump" itself at Kālīghāṭ is limited to males of the Bāgdi caste (Pl. II.79) who are employed by the temple to hold the sacrificial animals at the time of ritual slaughter. From the beginning of the month, just as in Solvyns's time, those who will take part prepare themselves by temporarily assuming the life of a religious mendicant and ascetic as a *sannyāsī*.[12]

Jhā̃p is performed twice at Kālīghāṭ during Gājan. Each begins as the Bāgdi celebrants bathe in the Ganges tributary that flows along side the temple complex. Then, wearing only a white *dhotī* around the waist, they place flowers on the head of the image of Kālī and dance to the accompaniment of drums. The first Jhā̃p takes place at the riverside, where two bamboo posts are erected to support a platform from which the *sannyāsīs* jump onto thorns of the date palm spread below. Just as in the jhā̃p of Solvyns's time, the *sannyāsīs*, climbing onto the platform, throw fruit to those below. Roy writes that "local faith is that if one such thrown fruit is eaten by a barren woman, she must bear a child." The *sannyāsī* then jumps from the scaffold onto the thorns below. "They remain unhurt by the grace of Siva."[13]

The second Jhā̃p is held the following day before the Nakuleswar temple, dedicated to Śiva, located about one hundred yards from the main Kālīghāṭ temple. Those who jumped the day before again climb the scaffold, this time to fall upon sharp blades set in a framework held by a large number of people. After this act of expiation, the *sannyāsīs* bathe in the Ganges and their period of asceticism is over.

Östör describes a variation of the rite as practiced today—*jhāpbhanga* (thorn-breaking)—in which the devotee falls down on spike-like thorns.[14]

1 Robert Bellarmine (1542-1621), an Italian Jesuit, was a leading defender of the church in the sixteenth century. He was canonized as a saint in 1930.

2 See Solvyns's etchings of "Fakirs and Religious Mendicants," Pls. 135-45.

3 The expiation takes its name from the word *jhāp*, which, with its variations, means "jump." See Sukumar Sen, 338, 342, 344.

4 Accounts of the Gājan festival vary in the number of days and order of events. Ram Comul Sen, in a paper read before the Asiatic Society in 1829, stated that the festival and its austerities have been reduced from thirty days to as few as four, two, or even one, and he laments that "The ceremony which was called an act of piety, is converted into an occasion of dissipation, drinking, gamblings, and acts of immorality." 610.

5 295. Also see William J. Wilkins and *An Alphabetical List of Feasts and Holidays of the Hindus and Muhammadans*, 13-14. The Rev. Duff, 264-82, describes the various expiations associated with the festival in the 1830s.

6 *The Play of the Gods*, 28. Östör on Gājan in myth and legend, 28-32, and on the festival, 98-148.

7 48. Also see entry for "Churuk Pooja" by Williamson, quoted in Stocqueler, *The Oriental Interpreter*.

8 *A View of . . . the Hindoos*, 3:16.

9 Quoted by Stocqueler, *The Oriental Interpreter*, in his entry for Churuk Pooja.

10 Mrs. Reginald Heber, April 9, 1824, in Heber, 1:98; reprinted in Nair, *Calcutta in the 19th Century*, 389. The narrative may be consulted in numerous editions of Heber's journal.

11 Vol. III, Pl. 29, "Hindoos throwing themselves on mattresses covered with sharp instruments." Although the plate does not cite Solvyns as its source, Shoberl's description of Jhāp is taken from Solvyns and is so acknowledged on p. 2.

12 Indrani Basu Roy, 83.

13 Ibid.

14 Östör, *The Play of the Gods*, 124. He defines *jhāp* as meaning "thorn," but states it may also refer to iron nails.

II.192. Nīla Pūjā

Pl. II.192. Nīla Pūjā. Paris: I.11.1. Double-plate.

Calcutta: Sec. XII, No. 12. Nila-Payah [Nīla Pūjā],—at which the Bigots run sharp pointed iron rods through their tongues; through the muscular part of the breast, the back, the arm, the skin, of the forehead, &c. and dance with stretched cords passed through the integuments of the sides, in the manner of Setons;[1]—in the evening the Payah is performed to Nila, or Mahadeva Seib [Śiva], &c.

Commentary: In the last days of the Gājan (or Caṛak) festival, ending the Bengali year, celebrants, as "temporary" *sannyāsīs*, undergo such physical tortures as rolling on thorns, walking on burning coals, and piercing of the body and tongue in expiation of sin or in fulfillment of a vow.[2] These acts of devotion to Śiva, which Solvyns identifies as Nīla Pūjā, precede the Caṛak Pūjā, or "hook-swinging," which terminates the festival on the fourth day.

The name Nīla Pūjā has various Śaivite

Paris: I.11.1: NILA-POOJA.VARIOUS EXPIATIONS OF THE HINDOOS: At night, when the j'haump, of which we have already spoken, is over, the most zealous performers of expiations ressort in crowds to the *munders* [*mandir*] or pagodas. There, some of them pierce their tongues with long irons, and even with a sort of cutlass or other large instrument; some get their fingers bored, and suffer iron spikes of a considerable size to remain in them; others have one hundred and twenty wounds of the same size inflicted on their foreheads, their breasts or their backs: this number, of which the mysterious amount remains unknown to us, is rigorously enjoined. Some, in fine, there are, who cause their loins to be pierced, and pass cords, the pipes of the *hooka*, and reeds, through the aperture, in the form of a seton.

In this manner they go in procession the whole of the following day, stopping to dance before the doors of such as pay them; for the rich profit of these expiations through their money, and redeem their sins by the sufferings of the poor: which, in the creed of the Hindoos, is not less efficacious, nor less agreeable to God. Their march is accompanied with the sound of instruments and the acclamations of the crowd; perfumes are burned in the hands of certain Hindoos, which being probably prepared to resist the effect of the fire give something of a miraculous appearance to the feast.

The tongue is pierced to expiate lying, the fingers for theft: the wounds on the forehead are for bad thoughts or illicit looks: those on the breast for having drank wine or other strong liquors. In fine, the object of those who perforate their loins, is to expiate the unlawful commerce of the unmarried with women, with prostitutes, and above all adultery.

We should be astonished at the quick cure of all these pious wounds, especially comparing them with those received on any other occasion. Milk is used to cure the tongue, and simples for the rest.

The feast which is celebrated with the greatest solemnity of expiatory ceremonies and tortures is that of the god *Callee* [Kālī]. At three miles distance from Calcutta, the author was present at it. In the interior of the temple the feet waded in blood.

associations,[3] but here refers to Nīler Upabās, the fast held during the Gājan festival on the next-to-last day of Caitra (March-April). At this time, women fast for the welfare of their sons, either—depending on the tradition—in worship of Śiva, of Ṣaṣṭhī, protective goddess of children, or of the goddess Nīlavatī, wife of Śiva.[4] In Calcutta, the women devotees go to the Śiva temple in the Kālīghāṭ complex and there, in *pūjā*, pour sacred water over the *liṅga*, the phallic representation of Śiva, in the form of a natural stone.[5] Their fast is broken after a lamp is lighted for each son before the image of the deity.

It is on this day of women's worship and fasting that male devotees go in processions, singing and dancing, from various parts of Calcutta to converge at the Kālīghāṭ temple and undergo the piercings of the body described by Solvyns and other witnesses.[6]

An American merchant, Dudley L. Pickman, witnessed the expiations of Nīla Pūjā in Calcutta in 1803-04, and recorded the event in his journal:

> Some [of the celebrants] cut two gashes in each side of their bodies, about two inches long, through which on each side they pass a rattan or several strings, twenty or twenty-five feet long. The ends of these are supported by two persons who stop, or move slowly on, while the performer runs backward and forward, the rattans or strings passing through, dancing and exhibiting much self-satisfaction. Others pass a rattan or iron bar, of the size of a large rattan, through their tongues, constantly moving it up and down, passing through the streets. They are all attended by music. A gentleman attached to the Police Office told me that the last year one of the natives substituted for the iron bar a large venomous snake, holding his head in his hand. While passing through the streets probably much exhausted, the snake cleared his head from the grasp, entwined himself around the neck of the miserable creature and drew out his tongue. He expired shortly after. . . . Some of those I saw with strings through their sides were boys of fourteen and fifteen years old. They all dress gaily, are of the lowest classes, and generally wrought up by opium.[7]

The Rev. Ward, in his account of the Gājan festival in 1806, describes, in detail, the piercings of the tongue and body he witnessed in the village where the temple to the great goddess Kālī is situated[8]—in all likelihood Kālīghāṭ, where Solvyns witnessed Nīla Pūjā.

In 1822, Fanny Park took in the sight at Kālīghāṭ, writing that "had not the novelty of the scene excited my curiosity, disgust would have made me sick. . . ."[9] Two years later, in 1824, Bishop Reginald Heber and his wife Amelia witnessed the expiations. These took place on the day following Jhā̃p as part of the festival culminating in Caṛak Pūjā. They were awakened before daybreak by the "discordant sound of native musical instruments" and immediately mounted their horses and rode to Calcutta's Maidan. As the morning advanced, an immense crowd came down Chowringhee, the main road leading from Kālīghāṭ. "In the midst of this crowd," Mrs. Heber wrote, "walked and danced the miserable fanatics, torturing themselves in the most horrible manner. . . . The noise of music continued till about noon, when the devotees retired to heal their wounds. . . . One of our servants, a 'Musalchee', or torch-bearer, of the lowest caste . . . ran around the house with a small spear through his tongue. . . ; this man appeared stupified with opium, which I am told is generally taken by these poor wretches, to deaden their feelings; and the parts through the spears are thrust are said to be previously rubbed for a considerable time, till numbness ensues."[10]

The bishop, without expression of horror or condemnation, added his own description of the "picturesque" crowd at the Maidan:

> The music consisted chiefly of large double drums, ornamented with plumes of black feathers like those of a hearse, which rose considerably higher than the heads of persons who played on them; large crooked trumpets. . . , and small gongs suspended from a bamboo, which rested on the shoulders of two men, the last of whom played on it with a large thick, and heavy drum-stick, or cudgel. All the persons who walked in the procession, and a large majority of the spectators, had their faces, bodies, and white cotton clothes daubed all over with vermilion. . . . They were also crowned with splendid garlands of flowers, with girdles and baldrics of the same. Many trophies and pageants of different kinds were paraded up and down, on stages drawn by horses, or bullocks. Some were mythological, others were imitations of different European figures, soldiers, ships, etc. and in particular, there was one very large model of a steam-boat. The devotees went about with small spears through their tongues and arms, and still more with hot irons pressed against their sides. All were naked to the waist, covered with flowers, and plentifully raddled with vermilion, while their long, black, wet hair hung down their backs, almost to their loins. From time to time, as they passed us, they laboured to seem to dance, but in general their step was slow, their countenances expressive of resigned and patient suffering, and there was no appearance, that I saw, of anything like frenzy or intoxication. The peaceableness of the multitude was also as remarkable as its number; no troops were visible, except for two sentries, who at all times kept guard on two large tanks in the Meidan. . . . A similar crowd in England would have shewn three boxing-matches in half an hour, and in Italy there would have been half a dozen assassinations before night.

That evening, Bishop Heber made his way to a neighborhood of native Calcutta to see the "hook-swinging," Caṛak Pūjā.[11]

Solvyns portrays the procession in front of the Kālīghāṭ temple, and he depicts its celebrants with tongues pierced by spears and sides, dripping blood, by metal instruments. The lead figure, holding a fan, bears the 120 wounds, referred to in the text, on his forehead and around his upper chest and back.[12] Three men walk with their right arms up, their hands holding what Solvyns identifies as burning perfumes. In the center, three other figures are linked by a single cord running through both sides of their bodies. Heber's description of their countenances as "expressive of resigned and patient suffering" aptly characterizes Solvyns's portrayal. The musical instruments included in the etching are the plumed drum (ḍhāk, Pl. II.156), the "large crooked trumpet" (rāmśiṅgā, Pl. II.176), and, in the background, rising above the heads of the people, a trumpet (bā̃k, Pl. II.177).

The amateur artist Mrs. S. C. Belnos sketched scenes of the festival in Calcutta, probably sometime in the 1820s, that were published in two lithographs entitled "Feast of the Churruck Poojah." The first plate depicts celebrants with "their tongues, sides and different parts of their body, bored with spits, ropes, canes, etc." She writes that "these tortures are inflicted by those who have made vows to the goddess Callee, on rising from a dangerous illness or returning safe from a perilous voyage or journey, etc." Of the second plate depicting what she witnessed in this "abominable festival," she writes:

> In the group was a man dressed in red silk, decked with female ornaments, and bells to his feet, dancing with a water snake alive thrust through his tongue, and hissing. Another man . . . held in his hand an iron shovel with two pointed handles which were thrust through both his sides, the shovel contained red hot coals on which from time to time he threw some kind of powder that blazed up into a flame, which he continued to keep up while dancing about wildly, to the sound of large drums ornamented with plumes and feathers. Another group shortly after passed, one of the men had a bamboo, nearly three inches in circumference bored through his tongue, which he held in an horizontal position, varying the movement as he continued to dance. Another had two thick ropes through the sides, the four ends of which were held by two men, one before, the other behind, while he danced backwards and forwards, with as much unconcern as if the ropes were merely run through his garments. A man dressed as a female with another man in a most ludicrous masquerade danced together. These ceremonies are called *Vanaphora* [*bāṇphuṛā* (colloquial, *bāṇphoṛā*)—piercing], the object of which is that *Shiva*, may bestow on them some blessing, in this life or the next.[13]

Sir Charles D'Oyly, about 1835, did a considerably more romantic and picturesque rendering of the "Procession of the Churruckpooja."[14]

---

1 A thread or tape drawn through the skin to maintain an opening for discharges. *OED*.

2 These practices continue today as a part of the Gājan festival. See Östör, *The Play of the Gods*, 128-30. Also see Satindra Narayan Roy for a 1928 account of "penances" practiced in North Balasore.

3 The word *nīl* means "blue," and Nīla is "the blue one," who Stella Kramrisch, 478, identifies as "a demon in elephant shape, killed by Śiva, whose skin Śiva wears." Sukumar Sen, 506, identifies Nīla as "an amorphous deity connected with the cult of Dharma but now identified with Siva." On the association of Nīla Pūjā with the Tantric Dharma cult, see Shashibhusan Das Gupta, 279-80. The word *nīl* also relates to Śiva as Nīlakaṇṭha, the "blue-throated" god. The name was applied to Śiva when at Brahmā's request he swallowed a poison that came from the churning of the ocean. Stutley and Stutley, 209.
Tara Krishna Basu, 148-49, in an account of religious rites in a Bengali village, relates Nīla Pūjā, as celebrated on the next-to-last day of the Bengali year, to the anniversary of the marriage of the goddess Durgā with Nīlakaṇṭa. The goddess Ṣaṣṭhī is also worshipped on this day for the protection of children. There are a number of Ṣaṣṭhīs, goddesses of fertility and protection, worshipped throughout the year.

4 The fast is termed "Nīlavatī Pūjā" in *An Alphabetical List of Feasts and Holidays of the Hindus and Muhammadans*, 62. It is identified with the piercings by male celebrants.

5 S. G. Bagchi, 163; H. E. A. Cotton, *Calcutta: Old and New*, 794-95. Cotton terms this "Nil Shashthi" rather than Nīla Pūjā.

6 Ram Comul Sen, 611-12, identifies "Nila Sanyāsa" as the day during Gājan for worship of Nīlavati, a wife of Śiva, and describes the piercings of the body that take place on this occasion. He provides a detailed description of ten instruments of self-torture used during Gājan that were deposited in the Calcutta Museum. Benoy Kumar Sarkar makes reference to the evening worship by women of the goddess Nīlavati at the Śiva temple, 87, but also describes Nīla Pūjā as a day of fasting in which male celebrants at the Kālīghāṭ temple engage in various expiatory activities that include piercings of the body, jhā̃p (involving jumping onto both scythes and thorns), and swinging over fire. 80-81. Sarkar also describes the various instruments used to pierce the body and how the piercing is done, 103-08.
The missionary Alexander Duff, 275-82, in the 1830s, describes, in breathless prose, the processions of pierced devotees converging on Kālīghāṭ

7 From "The Journal of the *Derby*, 1803-1804," Phillips Library, Peabody Essex Museum, Salem, Mass., quoted in Bean, *Yankee India,* 115-16. Bean, 115 (Fig. 7.5), reproduces Solvyns's Calcutta etching of Nīla Pūjā.

8 *A View of . . . the Hindoos*, 3:17-20.

9 1:27; reprinted in Nair, *Calcutta in the 19th Century*, 252.

10 Mrs. Reginald Heber, April 9, 1824, in Heber, 1:99; reprinted in Nair, *Calcutta in the 19th Century*, 389-90.

11 Heber, 1:100-101; reprinted in Nair, *Calcutta in the 19th Century*, 390-91.

12 Although Solvyns states that 120 as the number of wounds is "rigorously enjoined," the number has no power or significance in standard Hindu numerology, although it may possibly relate to local tradition.

13 *Twenty-four Plates Illustrative of Hindoo and European Manners of Bengal*, Pls. 6 and 7.

14 Pl. 10, colored lithograph, in *Views of Calcutta and its Environs*. The plate is reproduced in Losty, *Calcutta: City of Palaces*, 119.

II.193. Caṛak Pūjā

Pl. II.193. Caṛak Pūjā. Paris: I.12.1. Double-plate.

Calcutta: Double plate preceding Sec. XI. The Churrack Pooja—Hindoos swinging in expiation of their sins:—the rich hire the poor to perform penance in their stead, and which is believed to answer fully the purpose for obtaining absolution.

Commentary: Few Hindu festivals drew greater European fascination than Caṛak Pūjā, "hook-swinging," the culmination of the Gājan festival. Sukumar Sen derives the name from the Bengali *caṛak*, meaning "hanging down," referring to the devotee's suspension by hooks passed through the muscles over his bladebones as he is whirled round,[1] but another derivation takes it from *car(a)ka* or *cakra*, "wheel," and relates it to the rotations made by the devotee.[2] Although hook-swinging was prevalent over much of India, with variation in form among regions,[3] it was fervently performed in Bengal until its abolition in 1865. European travel accounts of India in the eighteenth and early nineteenth century would be remiss in failing to describe it,[4] and it was a favored subject among European and Company School Indian artists portraying India in its more "exotic" character.

Perhaps the earliest European depictions of hook-swinging are in Roger's 1651 work on Hinduism[5] and in Olfert Dapper's *Asia*, published in

Paris: I.12.1: CHURRACK-POOJA. HINDOOS SWINGING IN EXPIATION OF THEIR SINS: The expiatory tortures finish by the *Churrack-Pooja,* of which, as well as of all the others, the patient makes a sort of trade, and undergoes oftener for the sins of those who pay him than for his own. It consists in getting the flesh bored under the bladebone by two iron hooks fastened by a rope to a lever poised on the top of a sort of mast. By applying a weight to the other branch of the lever, the patient is elevated to the height of about thirty feet, and whirled round as many times as his zeal prompts him, or his strengths permits him to bear. The firmness of some lasts for a long quarter of an hour, without giving any signs of pain. As they swing round, they throw cocoa-nuts and other fruits to the crowd who pick them up with great eagerness, or loose pidgeons which the spectators pursue, as all these objects are looked upon as sanctified. The flesh sometimes gives way; but to prevent this accident, especially in young timid beginners, a girdle or sash is wound very tight round the body above the insertion of the iron hooks.

This strange and cruel ceremony is performed in the public places of the towns and villages, to the sound of instruments, and amidst the acclamations of the people. The scene represented in the engraving is taken from the most frequented spot in the town of Calcutta; it was filled by a prodigious concourse of spectators of all nations, who by the splendor of their appearance and especially of their equipages, carriages, palanquins, elephants, etc., gave great magnificence to the feast.

As soon as the expiations are over, the populace give themselves up to a degree of joy which approaches madness, and as on other occasions to an excess of licenciousness which will not bear describing. Even those whose flesh was perforated and mangled but the day before, do not fail to take part in it; you see them mixed with people in masks, running through the streets, all animated as it were the demon of the feast.

1681.[6] A later engraving accompanies Capt. Alexander Hamilton's description of the hook-swinging he witnessed in the early 1700s on the southern coast.[7] Charles Gold made two drawings in 1793 at a hook-swinging at Nagaputtinam in South India, and provides descriptive text with the published prints.[8] Among other European portrayals, James Moffatt depicted the festival in an 1805 aquatint;[9] Charles D'Oyly did a lithograph of "Churruck poojah," c. 1828;[10] and James Atkinson (1780-1852), who had described the hook-swinging in his 1824 poem of Calcutta, "City of Palaces," painted "Charakpuja, the Hook-Swinging Festival" in 1831.[11] In addition to European artists, Indian painters of the Company School, some directly influenced by Solvyns, catered to European appetite in depicting hook-swinging, among other Indian subjects, in works on paper and on mica. A Murshidabad artist (with no Solvyns influence), for example, provides, c. 1798-1804, a rich portrayal of hook-swinging and various austerities of Gājan.[12]

Solvyns's depiction of Caṛak Pūjā served as the model for a relief on an early nineteenth century silver snuff box (Pl. I.60), with the other side portraying Solvyns's scene of suttee "A Woman Leaping into the Flames to the Corpse of her Husband" (Pl. II.201).[13]

European descriptions of Caṛak Pūjā were often vivid and highly detailed, as in the Rev. William Ward's account of the festival in the area of Calcutta in 1806:

> The man who is to swing prostrates himself before the tree [that is, the swinging pole],[14] and a person, with his dusty fingers, makes a mark where the hooks are to be put. Another person immediately gives him a smart slap on the back, and pinches up the skin hard with his thumb and fingers; while another thrusts the hook through, taking hold of about an inch of the skin; the other hook is then in like manner put through the skin of the other side of his neck, and the man gets up on his feet. As he is rising, some water is thrown in his face. He then mounts on a man's back, or is elevated in some other way, and the strings which are attached to the hooks on his back are tied to the rope at one end of the horizontal, and the rope at the other end is held by several men, who drawing it down, raise up the end of which the man swings, and by their running around with the rope the machine is turned.
>
> In swinging, the man describes a circle about thirty feet diameter. Some swing only a few minutes, half an hour or more. I have

heard of men swinging for hours. In the southern parts of Bengal a piece of cloth is wrapped round the body underneath the hooks, lest the flesh should tear and the wretch fall and be dashed to pieces, but the whole weight of the body rests on the hooks. . . . [About] the year 1800 five women swung in this manner, with hooks through their backs and thighs, at Kidurpooru [Kidderpore] near Calcutta.[15]

Fanny Parks witnessed hook-swinging, taking place at the same time as the expiations of Nīla Pūjā (Pl. II.191), at Kālīghāṭ in 1822. There "three swinging posts" had been erected, each some thirty feet high and

> crossed at the top by a horizontal bamboo, from one end of which a man was swinging, suspended by a rope, from the other end another rope was fastened to a horizontal pole below, which was turned by men running round like horses in a mill. The man swung in a circle of perhaps thirty feet diameter, supported by four iron hooks, two through the flesh of his back, and two in that of his chest, which, by a small bit of cloth across the breast, he was entirely supported: he carried a bag in one hand, from which he threw sweetmeats and flowers to the populace below. Some men swing with four hooks on the back and four on the chest without any cloth, eight hooks being considered sufficient to support the body. The man I saw swinging looked very wild, from the quantity of opium and bengh he had taken to deaden the sense of pain. Bengh is an intoxicating liquor, which is prepared with the leaves of the Ganja plant (Cannabis Indica). . . . Sometimes four men swing together for half an hour; some in penance for their sins; some for those of others, richer men, who reward their deputies and thus do penance by proxy.[16]

Bishop and Mrs. Reginald Heber described the Caṛak Pūjā they witnessed in Calcutta in 1824. Having recounted the events of Jhā̃p (Pl. II.191) and Nīla Pūjā, Mrs. Heber recorded in her journal that on the evening of the second day of the festival, following the procession of penitents earlier that day, the bishop went into the native quarter of the city to Boitaconnah [Boytaconnah; Bhaitak-khanah] where the swinging was to take place. "He arrived in time to be a spectator of the whole ceremony," she wrote. "The victim was led, covered with flowers, and without any apparent reluctance, to the foot of the tree [the term she uses for the poll erected for the swing]: hooks were then thrust through the muscles of his sides, which he endured without shrinking, and a broad bandage was fastened round his waist, to prevent the hooks from being torn through by the weight of his body. He was then raised up, and whirled round; at first the motion was slow, but by degrees was increased to considerable rapidity." To convey a better impression of what he saw, Bishop Heber includes a "rude" sketch of the Caṛak Pūjā.[17]

As those who undertook the mortifications of Jhā̃p and Nīla Pūjā, hook-swingers in Bengal were largely from the lowest castes—those who, in words of the Rev. William Carey, Ward's colleague at the Serampore Mission, "are hunters, bird-catchers, tanners, shoe-makers, etc. and are esteemed execrable by other casts."[18] And palanquin-bearers were especially conspicuous, at least in Calcutta, among the swingers, who, as noted, were often "proxies" for those of higher caste.[19]

Caṛak Pūjā, typically under the patronage of a wealthy Hindu, was conducted at various places in Calcutta. Fanny Parks witnessed it at Kālīghāṭ, Heber in Boytaconnah in North Calcutta. S. C. Nandy places the probable location of Solvyns's Caṛak Pūjā near Chhatu Babu's house, Rambagan, which he identifies in the left background. This was in an area called Bhitar Shimulia (or "Shimley" by the British), at the western end of Beadon Street in today's North Calcutta.[20]

Solvyns's etching of Caṛak Pūjā gives full flavor of the festival's attraction. In the center, standing along side a sedan chair (Pl. II.228), are three European men. To the right, another European stands next to an Armenian, with the distinctive peaked hat, and in the distant crowd, a European may be seen raised high for better viewing. To the left, by the elephant, are two Chinese figures, one with a straw "coolie" hat and both wearing the distinctive queue. Especially notable in Solvyns's depiction is that the middle swinging figure is a woman, more clearly identifiable as such in the Paris edition.

The "cruelties" of Caṛak Pūjā had long been described in European accounts, but hook-swinging became a public issue in British India in 1856-57, when the Calcutta Missionary Conference petitioned the government for its suppression. Sir Frederick Halliday, Lieutenant-Governor of Bengal, took the matter under consideration and concluded that, "as the case was one of pain voluntarily undergone, the remedy must be left to the missionary and school-master and that, as stated by the Council of Directors, all such cruel ceremonies must be discouraged by influence rather than by authority."[21] The pressure continued, however, and in 1864-65, Caṛak Pūjā was again before the government. "After consulting the British Indian Association and obtaining from them a recommendation that all cruel practices should be suppressed, so long as no religious observances were interfered with, [Lieutenant-Governor] Sir Cecil Beadon issued a Resolution on the subject on 15 March 1865. It directed all Magistrates of Districts in the Lower Provinces to prevent any person from the act of hook-swinging or other self-torture, in public, and from the abetment thereof. Persons disobeying any such injunction were to be prosecuted and punished according to law."[22]

Caṛak Pūjā was effectively suppressed, and its practice today is usually simulated with belts fastened around the body rather than with hooks through the skin.[23] But although the Gājan festival is celebrated today in West Bengal "without the harrowing physical torture," Jhā̃p is still practiced, as are the various piercings of the tongue and body.[24]

---

1 260.

2 See, for example, Ram Comul Sen, 609.

3 For a detailed account of hook-swinging in colonial India, see Oddie.

4 See, for example, Ives, 27; Pennant, 2:306; Sonnerat, 1:149; Dubois, 598; and Maurice, 5:306-07.

5 Title page of the original Dutch edition, reproduced in Lach and Van Fley, Vol. 3, Bk. 2, Pl. 196. Thomas Bowrey included a sketch of hook-swinging in his account of Bengal, 1669-1679, but it was not published until 1905, p.12; reproduced in Oddie, 5.

6 Reproduced in Lach and Van Fley, Vol. 3, Bk. 2, Pls. 130 and 131.

7 1:152-53. Powell discusses various early accounts of hook-swinging in South India.

8 Gold, Pl. 35, "Barbarous Ceremony, in honour of Mariatale, Goddess of the small-pox, at Negapatnam," and, especially dramatic in its presentation, Pl. 36, "The same subject; a single figure suspended by hooks." The volume contains 50 colored plates of South Indian scenes, half of which depict figures in costume.

9 "View on the Banks of the Ganges with Representation of the Churruck Poojah—A Hindoo Holiday," Calcutta," reproduced (Fig. 7.6) in Bean, *Yankee India*, 116.

10 149, Pl. 9.

11 The oil painting is reproduced in Bayly, *The Raj*, Pl. 284, p. 223, and in Mildred Archer, *The India Office Collection of Paintings and Sculpture*, entry 81, Pl. 16.

12 Mildred Archer, *Company Paintings*, 72; also in Welch, 54-55, Pl. 16. The artist Sewak Ram of Patna depicts "Charak Pooja-Penance," c. 1805, in pencil, gouache, and watercolor, with gold, on handmade paper. The painting, from the collection of the Second Earl of Caledon, is handsomely reproduced in Rousslet, *India of the Rajahs*, 148-49. A Company School lithograph, signed by Jai Ram Das, c. 1830, depicts Caṛak Pūjā, in Losty, "Sir Charles D'Olyly's Lithographic Press," 147, Pl. 7. Company School depictions of hook-swinging on mica are reproduced in Pal and Dehejia, 163, Pl. 167, and in Bean, "Yankee Traders and Indian Merchants, 1785-1865," 135.

13 On the stuff box, see Chapter Three, p. 109.

14 Ward uses "tree" to refer to the swinging pole, as does Mrs. Heber in her description.

15 Ward, *A View of. . . the Hindoos*, 3:20-21. Captain Thomas Williamson provides a generally similar account from the same period in his *East India Vade-Mecum* (1810), quoted in Stocqueler's entry for Churuk Pooja in *The Oriental Interpreter*, 61-63. Also see Duff's account, 264-82, from the 1830s.

16 1:27-28. Pl. 6, facing p. 27, depicts the Caṛak Pūjā she describes.

17 Heber, 1:99-100; reprinted in Nair, *Calcutta in the 19th Century*, 390.

18 Extracts from Carey's diary, *Periodical Accounts*, 1:197, quoted in Oddie, 30.

19 Oddie, 30. On proxy payments, see Oddie, 69-81.

20 Letter from Somendra Chandra Nandy to the author, March 21, 1995. In his *Life and Times of Cantoo Baboo: The Banian of Warren Hastings*, Nandy reproduces the Solvyns etching of Caṛak Pūjā (Vol. II, Pl. 28) and identifies the site as near Chhatu Babu's house in North Calcutta.

21 R. C. Majumdar, *Glimpses of Bengal in the Nineteenth Century*, 69-70.

22 Ibid., 70. On the abolition, see Oddie, 88-92, and Buckland, *Bengal Under the Lieutenant-Governors*, 1:32, 177, 312-14, 438-39.

23 As in the festival celebrated in a Mindapur village described by Gauranga Chattopadhyay, 156.

24 R. C. Majumdar, *History of Modern Bengal, Pt. 1 (1765-1905)*, 234-35.

II.194. Durgā Pūjā

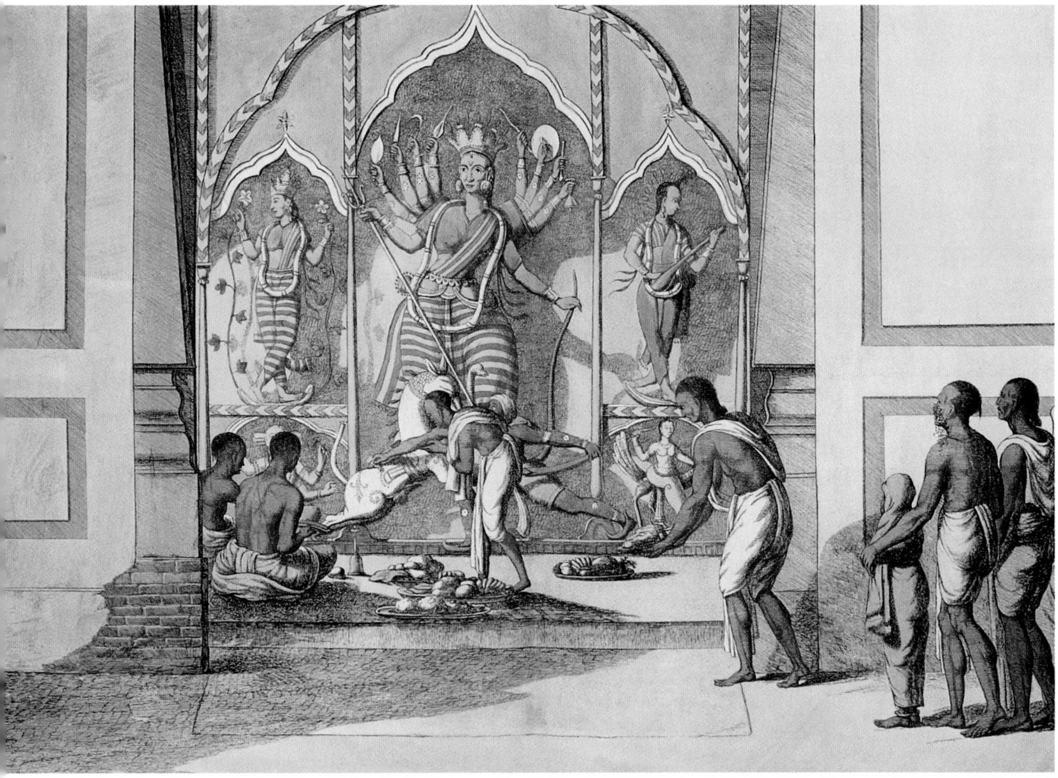

Pl. II.194. Durgā Pūjā. Paris: II.3.1. Double-plate. **Calcutta: Sec. XII, No. 4.** The Durgah Pooja.—The plate represents in the middle, Durgah [Durgā], wife to Mahadeb [Mahādeva], the destroying or transforming attribute of the Deity; the animal she is mounted on, is called a Sing [*siṁha*] (Unicorn,) at her feet, is Myhassor [Mahiṣa], an Evil Genii, which she destroys; on the right and left, are Lutchme [Lakṣmī] and Sursutee [Sarasvatī], the wifes of Vistno [Viṣṇu], and below them, Guneesa [Gaṇeśa] and Cartic [Kārttikeya], Gods of Wisdom and War, the sons of Durgah.—This festival is well known to Europeans, who, in common, with the professors of all religions, are invited by the opulent Hindoos to partake of the sight, and are regaled with refreshments and dances.

Commentary: The goddess Durgā is one of the most venerated Hindu deities among Bengalis, and Durgā Pūjā is the most richly celebrated of all festivals in Bengal.

Before considering Durgā Pūjā, it is essential to identify the deities to which Solvyns refers and to clarify his discussion. Durgā is the wife of Śiva—the great or transcendent god, Mahādeva—his *śakti*, or the personification of the energetic aspect of the god. She is the supreme Mother Goddess in Bengal, but in other forms, she is known by various names—the benevolent Pārvatī or horrific Kālī, among others. As Durgā, the warrior, she is generally depicted with ten arms, each bearing a weapon. Riding the lion, *siṁha* (*singha*) or a tiger (not a unicorn, as Solvyns oddly states), Durgā, as Mahiṣāsuramardinī, battles the demon genie Mahiṣa, who took various shapes to fight her, finally that of a buffalo, symbol of death. One of the most popular iconographic representations is of Durgā holding the buffalo demon down with her foot and trident, as she cuts off the head of Mahiṣa emerging in human form from the carcass of the animal. Evil has been destroyed and order restored to the cosmos.[1]

Solvyns portrays Durgā, not in her more familiar representation, but as thrusting her spear into the body of the genie in human form—partially obscured by the figure of the priest in *pūjā* before the image. Solvyns depicts what he identifies as a "unicorn" at the feet of the goddess—though without a horn, it appears more like a horse—and describes it as her mount. It is traditional that Durgā arrives for the Pūjā season by a different animal vehicle each year—sometimes a horse. What Solvyns portrays is not a horse, however, but a highly stylized lion, *siṁha*.[2]

In Solvyns's portrayal—and following iconographic form—Durgā is flanked by her "children." To her left is Lakṣmī, wife of Viṣṇu and goddess of fortune, standing on a white lotus and holding in each hand a lotus blossom. Below her (behind the seated priests) is the image of the elephant-headed Gaṇeśa. On the right is Sarasvatī, wife of Brahmā (not Viṣṇu, as Solvyns states) and goddess of learning, shown standing on a lotus with her vīṇā. And below her is Kārttikeya, the god of war.[3]

In the print, four priests are shown in *pūjā* before the images, and the standing priest to the right holds a tray with the head of a goat in offering to Durgā. In the Paris print, the foreground is widened to

Paris: II.3.1. DURGAH-POOJAH: We have already seen in the foregoing numbers several religious ceremonies and acts of Hindoo worship. This is an exact representation of their devotion to the goddess Durgah; the wife of Mahahdeb.

The idol of this goddess, to whom the power of destruction and of transformation is attributed by the Hindoos, is seen in their pagodas mounted upon an animal resembling an unicorn, which they call *sing*; at her feet is *Myhassor,* an evil spirit whom she has overthrown; to the right and left of the idol two female figures are remarked; these are *Lutchme* and *Sursutee,* wives of Vishnoo : the small statues in the niches under the idol, are those of *Guneesa* and *Cartic,* sons of the goddess *Durgah,* one of whom is the god of wisdom and the other the god of war. As in the feasts of the other divinities, the Brahmuns begin the rites of the *Durgah-Poojah* by reciting in the morning a number of *munters* [mantras] or forms of prayer. After this they receive the offerings brought by the faithful, which consist of rice, fruits and pastry. All these pious gifts fall to the share of the priests, and form a considerable part of their revenue. The Hindoos on this occasion sacrifice animals also, such as buffalos, bulls, but more commonly goats. The head only of the victims is offered to the idol on a brazen plate.

The feast of the goddess *Durgah* is one of the most solemn and most pompous of those which the Hindoos celebrate in honour of their divinities. No person of what rank soever, but goes to some expense in contributing to the grandeur of this solemnity. Those especially who have more means, contend in magnificence on this occasion, often giving eight days together exhibitions of the dance of the Nautch, and offering to all the company a profusion of refreshments and perfumes. The Europeans generally take part in this festivity, and the Hindoos take a pleasure in procuring them this enjoyment. This magnificence sometimes costs a rich Hindoo more than a hundred thousand roupees.

In the ceremonies of the *Durgah-Poojah* the same order is observed as in the other feasts : the sacrifices are performed in the morning, and the dances in the evening; and after a few days the solemnity closes by a procession after which they cast the idol into the water, as I have described in the ninth number of the first volume [Pl. II.190].

include a group of persons peering into the sanctuary to watch the *pūjā*. The setting is probably the *ṭhākur-dālān*, the hall of the deity (described in Pl. II.182), in the house of a wealthy Hindu, as Durgā is worshipped in the home in seasonal observance, and there are very few permanent temples to Durgā.[4] There is, however, an account of what is described as a Durgā temple in Calcutta where, during Durgā Pūjā, hundreds of goats are sacrificed, their heads stacked in piles before the image of the Goddess.[5] This is likely a reference to the famous Kālīghāṭ temple, where Durgā Pūjā is "the most elaborate and complicated" occasion.[6]

Durgā Pūjā is celebrated in the month of Āśvina (September-October) and takes place over a period of nine days, giving its name Navarātrī, "nine nights," as the festival is known outside Bengal. Coinciding with the autumn harvest, the festival—and the goddess herself—is associated in origin with agriculture and crop fertility, but it is in the city of Calcutta that Durgā Pujā is most enthusiastically and richly celebrated.[7]

In the weeks before Durgā Pūjā begins, the clay-modelers of Kumartuli, the potters' quarter in Calcutta, shape the images of the goddess to be used in the festival.[8] In the first days of the festival, recitations from the *Purāṇas* recount exploits of the goddess, and on the sixth day, the clay image of Durgā is installed and "awakened" in a ceremony by which the goddess becomes manifest. It is in these last four days that the major festivities of Durgā Pūjā take place. Various activities are prescribed for each day, with *pūjās* at fixed times, visits among friends and family, and games. At night, feasts and entertainments, such as *yātrās* (musical performances) and, in Solvyns's time, nautch parties [Pl. II.195], go into the early hours of the morning. Buffalos and goats, animals representing evil forces, are sacrificed to the goddess.

On the tenth day, no *pūjā* is performed. In the morning, the priests ritually "dismiss" the Goddess and request her presence to depart from the image. In the afternoon, in great celebration and dancing to the sounds of drums and horns, the clay images, some as tall as twelve feet, are carried to the river where they are immersed. Maria Graham, in 1810, provides a vivid description of the Durgā procession to the Hugli river: "The figures were placed under canopies, which were gilt and decked with many gaudy colours, and carried upon men's heads. Several of these moving temples went together, preceded by musical instruments, banners, and bare-headed Brahmins, repeating *muntras* (forms of prayer). The gods were followed by cars, drawn by oxen or horses, gaily caparisoned, bearing the sacrificial utensils, accompanied by other Brahmins, and the procession was closed by an innumerable multitude of people of all castes."[9]

As we saw in Solvyns's portrayal of Bisarjan (Pl. II.190), the immersion is accompanied with shouts and profanities, described vividly by eighteenth century travelers Stavorinus and Grandpré in their accounts of Durgā Pūjā,[10] but about which Mrs. Graham is discretely silent. It is a time, wrote one observer, when "licentiousness and obscenity prevail."[11] Kinsley, in his study of the Hindu goddess, relates this behavior to the agricultural roots of the festival. "Promotion of the fertility of the crops by stimulating Durgā's powers of fecundity . . . underlie the practice of publicly making obscene gestures and comments during Durgā Pūjā. Various scriptures say that Durgā is pleased by such behavior at her autumnal festival, and such behavior is suggested in the wild, boisterous activities that accompany the disposal of the image of Durgā in a river or pool."[12]

For immersion, at least ideally, the image is taken out into the river, lashed between two boats (as seen in Solvyns's Bisarjan) and is consigned to the water as the boats separate. As her image is immersed, the priests supplicate Durgā to bring life, health, and affluence, and then urge her to go to her abode and return at some future time.[13] The artist Charles D'Oyly portrayed the scene in a watercolor, c. 1820, with Durgā in the same iconographic form as in Solvyns's etching.[14]

Following the immersion of the goddess, the people return to their homes where they receive the *śāntī jal*, a sprinkling of the "water of peace," signifying "the end of the battle over evil and the descent of peace among people." In the days that follow, celebrating victory, friends and relatives visit each other. Approximately three weeks after Durgā Pūjā, Kālī Pūjā marks the end of the autumn festivals.[15]

Durgā Pūjā probably dates back to the late sixteenth or early seventeenth centuries, but Maharajah Krishnachandra (1710-1783), ruler of Nadia, is usually credited with the promotion of the festival,[16] and it was Krishnachandra who introduced the worship of clay images, central to the festival as it developed.[17] By Solvyns's time in Bengal, Durgā Pūjā was celebrated in the palatial homes of zamīndārs and wealthy urban Hindus with increasing pomp, splendor, and expense, as rich families competed for recognition. "Immense sums" were spent, and the Rev. Ward, Solvyns's contemporary, "supposed, upon a moderate calculation, that half a million sterling is expended annually on the festival."[18]

In the late eighteenth century, in Calcutta, the festival began to shift from the elite patronage of zamīndārs to sponsorship by groups of friends. It was not until 1926, however, that Durgā Pūjā took on the community character it has today, as neighborhoods vie with each other in street celebrations and in the construction of elaborate Durgā images.[19]

It was Raja Nabakrishna Deb, Clive's *munshī* and *banian*, who set the trend in making Durgā Pūjā a social event. In 1757, at his palace in North Calcutta, he hosted a celebration of both Durgā's victory over Mahiṣa and Clive's victory at the battle of Plassey, inviting Clive among other British dignitaries.[20] In 1766, Holwell wrote that Durgā Pūjā "is the grand general feast of the *Gentoos*, usually visited by all *Europeans*, (by invitation) who are treated by the proprietor of the feast with the fruits and flowers in season, and are entertained every evening whilst the feast lasts, with bands of singers and dancers."[21] Europeans were regularly invited to attend Durgā Pūjā festivities at the magnificently illuminated houses of "opulent" Hindus, and many late eighteenth or early nineteenth century accounts of Calcutta include descriptions such as those related in the following Commentary on the Nautch (Pl. II.195).

---

1 Kinsley, 95-115; Ghosha, 5-7; Daniélou, 288; and Vijayankanta Mishra.

2 The same image of Durgā and the stylized lion appears in a photograph in Dye, 43.

3 Ghosa describes these attending deities, in the same arrangement, in his account of Durgā Pūjā, 5-6. On these and deities more generally, see Daniélou and standard references on Hinduism, such as Stutley.

4 Solvyns, in his text for Kālīghāṭ, Pl. II.4, refers to having portrayed the interior of "the sanctuary of a Pagoda consecrated to the goddess Dourgah," though this could be a sanctuary within a home rather than a Durgā temple as such.

5 Stutley, 84, from a quotation incorrectly attributed to Gait.

6 Indrani Roy, 79. She describes the rituals at the temple during Durgā Pūjā, 79-82.

7 Early descriptions of Durgā Pūjā include Ward, *Account of the*

. . . *Hindoos*, 3:121-37, and Ward, *A View. . . of the Hindoos*, 3:78-90, and, briefly, Stocqueler, *Oriental Interpreter*, 78. Kale discusses its scriptural context in the *Dharmaśāstra*, 5:154-89, and Ghosha provides virtually a manual of instruction, liv-lix, 60-66. Shib Chunder Bose, with disdain for Hindu "superstition," describes Durgā Pūjā, 95-135, as does Duff, 242-64, in a missionary perspective from the 1830s. Also see William J. Wilkins, 227-31, and *An Alphabetical List of Feasts and Holidays of the Hindus and Muhammadans*, 20-26. Nandini Roy, 17-20, provides a detailed, yet succinct, description of Durgā Pūjā today, and for a history of the festival, Chaliha and Gupta, "Durga Puja in Calcutta." See Östör on the "Puja of Durga in Myth and Legend," l6-28, and on the festival, 33-97. Nirad Chaudhuri, *The Autobiobraphy of an Unknown Indian*, 63-71, describes from his rich memory the Durgā Pūjā of his youth in his ancestral Bengal village.

8 On the image, see Östör, *The Play of the Gods*, 38-42. Pranab Bandhyopadyay, *Mother Goddess Durga*, 108-16, describes the making of the Durgā image. The clay images are depicted in color photographs in Prabhas Sen, *Crafts of West Bengal*, 164-65, 167.

9 Letter of October 25, 1810, in *Letters on India*, 134.

10 Grandpré, 2:64-65; Stavorinus, 1:418.

11 Stocqueler, *Oriental Interpreter*, 78.

12 106.

13 Stocqueler, *Oriental Interpreter*, 78.

14 Losty, "A Career in Art: Sir Charles D'Oyly," Pl. 1, p. 83. The immersion of the image is vividly portrayed today in photographs of the festival. See, for example, those by Raghubir Singh, *Ganga: Sacred River of India*, 143, and dust-jacket, and Robert Arnett, *India Unveiled*, 49.

15 Nandini Roy, 20.

16 Biswas, 406, and Chaliha and Gupta, "Durga Puja in Calcutta," 2:331.

17 See discussion of the modelers, Pl. II.36, on the Maharaja of Nadia, Pl. II.18, and on his introduction of clay images, Pl. II.190.

18 *A View . . . of the Hindoos*, 3:79fn. On the competition, see Chitra Deb, 1:58-60, and Chaliha and Gupta, "Durga Puja in Calcutta," 2:333-36.

19 Pranab Bandhyopadyay, 121; Chaliha and Gupta, "Durga Puja in Calcutta," 2:332; and Rachel McDermott, personal communication.

20 Chaliha and Gupta, "Durga Puja in Calcutta," 2:332-33. On Raja Nabakrishna Deb, see Pl. II.182.

21 Entry dated 1766, *Interesting Historical Events*, 2:128.

II.195. Nautch

Commentary: The nautch (*nāc* in Bengali, from the Sanskrit *nṛtya*, "to dance") was a form of entertainment by "dancing girls" that became popular among affluent Hindus in Bengal, especially in celebration of Durgā Pūjā (Pl. II.194), in the late eighteenth and early nineteenth centuries. Its character was similar to katthak, the dance tradition associated with Muslim courtesans of North India.

In early accounts of life and travels in India, Europeans almost invariably included a description of the nautch,[1] and both professional and amateur artists—Tilly Kettle, Thomas Hickey, Thomas Daniell, and Charles D'Oyly, for example—portrayed the nautch in all its sensuous grace.[2] Solvyns was the first European to depict the nautch in a print, and in visual representations of Indian life in publications that followed, as well as in the many paintings produced for Europeans by the Indian Company School artists, the nautch continued to fascinate well into the nineteenth century.[3] By the 1830s, however, Europeans, once "addicted" to the nautch, were less inclined to attend such functions, and the nautch as an after-supper entertainment in European households, the fashion when few European women graced Calcutta society, gave way to the increasingly frequent round of both private and public balls.[4]

A nautch might be attended by as many as seven or eight hundred people, and wealthy Hindus in Calcutta frequently invited Europeans—usually by printed invitation. "When a black man has a mind to compliment a European," Mrs. Nathaniel Kindersley wrote in 1767, "he treats him to a nautch."[5] In his *European in India*, D'Oyly portrayed a nautch in the house of "a rich Native of Calcutta, named Sookma Roy, a person remarkable for many excellent qualities, especially for his attachment and hospitality toward Europeans."[6] It was at his house that, in 1792, a "novelty" was introduced at the natuch, "namely, a combination of English airs with the Hindostanee songs."[7]

The weekly *Calcutta Chronicle*, on September 18, 1792, carried an item headlined, "Doorgah Pooja," listing the principal houses where the customary festivities were to take place, and noted, "The scarcity of amusements in Calcutta, and the silence of the nights will, no doubt, cause this spectacle to attract, as usual, numbers of Europeans, though to far the greatest part of them, it must want novelty."

Most Europeans—at least those new to Calcutta—were captivated by the nautch, but some were clearly bored, as was the Rev. William Tennant in 1797: "Though the Notches are intended to do

Pl. II.195. Nautch. Paris: II.2.1. Double-plate.
Calcutta: Plate before Section IV. A Nautch or Hindostany Dance.

honor to some deity, who presides over the festival; yet they seem of all institutions the least calculated to excite religious ideas. Part of the ceremony consists of listening to the music of the singing girls, who drawl out their monotonous ditties with a nonchalance and dulness, which can only be equalled by the sluggish dance, and the inanimate gestures with which they are accomplished. Of all entertainments, an Hindostanee Notch is the most insipid. . . . Yet such invitations are given from politeness, it is proper that they should be accepted, with at least an appearance of satisfaction."[8]

Mrs. Kindersley, in 1767, found the nautch "very delightful," but noted the dancers' "languishing glances, wanton smiles, and attitudes" were "not quite consistent with decency. . . ."[9] Other Europeans, especially later in the nineteenth century, were less charmed. The Reverend William Ward expressed the "greatest horror" at the "filthy songs" and "indecent" dancing of the nautch,[10] and Mrs. Fenton found it quite "odious,"[11] but Mrs. Reginald Heber, wife of the Bishop of Calcutta, wrote in her diary of the nautch girls that she "never saw public dancing in England so free from every thing approaching to indecency. Their dress was modesty itself, but their faces, feet, and hands exposed to view."[12]

Although the nautch was usually associated with religious festivals, it was sometimes staged specifically for European guests. William Hickey's *Bengal Gazette*, August 18-25, 1781, provides an account of "a nautch and magnificent entertainment" given by Nabakrishna Deb, banian to the East Indian Company and credited with introducing the nautch into Calcutta society.[13] That the nautch often took the character of a variety show is evident in various descriptions of not only dancers, but "bands of music, both European and native, tumblers, jugglers, actors, and pantomimes. . . ." All of this was then followed by "a sumptuous supper, where champagne circulated like water, and the richest ices were melted in the most costly liquors." But of such suppers, the Hindus did not partake.[14]

Rajkrishna Deb (Raja Rajkissen), described as "an opulent and respectable Hindoo," continued the tradition of his father Nabakrishna, hosting nautches

Paris: II.2.1. NAUTCH A HINDOO DANCE: It is to be observed that the dance represented in this plate has nothing in common with that which is performed all over India, by women known by the name of *Bayaderes, Baladeres* or *Bays*; a description of which is found in the works of many travellers. As this amusement is foreign to the true Hindoos, and known only among the other Indians, the Mussulmen, Portuguese, etc., it could not form a part of this collection. But here is a short description of an original Hindoo dance called *Nautch*.

This dance is generally executed by three female dancers or *Ramjannys,* who are courtesans as well as the *Bayaderes*. It is opened by a single dancer, who is joined successively by the two others in a great variety of motions, and of very graceful and often very lascivious attitudes. An European accustomed to look upon the dances of his own country as the perfection of the art, would be surprised to see the languid case, the natural grace, the voluptuous suppleness, displayed in every movement of the accomplished *Ramjanny*. We must not wonder if this beautiful dance is but little known even to those who have resided some time in India; it is of late seldom performed by Hindoos, and is more in vogue among the Mussulmen and in the north of Hindoostan than in the south. It is besides now frequently danced by the *Bayaderes* who have corrupted it by so much obscene actions and attitudes, that its original character is no longer to be known. What has caused this diversion to degenerate still more, is it being sometimes danced by *Hidgras* [*hijrā*] (hermaphrodites), or by dissolute young men who accompany all their motions with the most libidinous and immoral songs.

The instruments to which the *Ramjannys* dance the *Nautch* are the *been* [bīn], the *sitar* and others with cords; whereas the Mussulmen use only the *sarinda,* the *tubla* [tablā] and the *d'hola* [ḍhol], each of which shall have its particular description in the course of the present volume.

Formerly the princes and grandees of the country, kept troops of dancing girls in their pay, who attended them every where as a part of their suite. This practice has now totally ceased. It is only at feasts that these women, who are generally prostitutes, are hired for money, so that no great beauty nor freshness can be expected in these miserable victims of debauchery.

At great festivals, such as the marriage of some rich person, or a *poojah* [*pūjā*] or *durgah* [Durgā Pūjā], twenty or thirty of these dancing girls, and from thirty to fifty musicians are hired. The *Ramjannys* move in groups three by three, and perform the *Nautch* in every part of their vast halls, often varying the spot, and following the company to the sound of the instruments.

I shall have occasion to describe the dress of these dancers in this number [Pl. II.93].

over three nights during Durgā Pūjā. Maria Graham, an astute and sympathetic observer and perhaps the first woman Orientalist, provides a detailed account of the nautch—her first—on the occasion of Durgā Pūjā, in October 1810, at the home of Rajkrishna. Mrs. Graham describes the house—in Sobhabazar, off Chitpore Road, in North Calcutta—as "fine," and writes,

> The room into which we were ushered was a large square court, covered in for the occasion with red cloth, to which a profusion of white artificial flowers was fastened. Three sides of the court are occupied by the dwelling-house, the walls of which are adorned by a double row of pillars in couplets, and between each couplet is a window. The fourth side is occupied by the family temple, of a very pretty architecture . . . A flight of steps leads to the veranda of the temple, where Vishnu [more likely Durgā] sat in state, with a blaze of light before him, in magnificent chandeliers. When we entered there were some hundreds of people assembled, and there seemed to be room for as many more. The dancing was begun, but as soon as our host perceived us he led us to the most commodious seats, stationed boys behind us with round fans of red silk, with gold fringe, and then presented us with bouquets of the mogree [jasmine] and the rose, tied up with a green leaf, ornamented with silver fringe. A small gold vase being brought, the Maha Rajah, with a golden spoon, perfumed us with ottur [attar], and sprinkled us with rose-water, after which we were allowed to sit and look on. The first dancers were men [possibly *hijrās*], whom by their dresses I took for women, though I was

surprised at the assurance of their gestures, which had nothing else remarkable in them. These gave way to some Cashmerian [Kashmiri] singers, whose voices were very pleasing. They were accompanied by an old man, whose long white beard and hair, and fair skin, spoke a more northern country than Bengal. His instrument was a particularly sweet-toned guitar, which he touched with skill and taste to some of the odes of Hafiz and some Hindostanee songs. I was sorry when he finished, to make way for a kind of pantomime, in which men personated elephants, bears, and monkeys. After this some women danced; but though they were pretty, and their motions rather graceful, I was disappointed, after hearing so much of the nautch-girls of India. One of them, while dancing in a circle, twisted a piece of striped muslin into flowers, keeping each stripe for a different coloured flower. The last amusement we staid to partake of, was the exhibition of a ventriloquist (the best I have ever heard), although the Maha Rajah pressed us to remain, saying he had different sets of dancers, enough to exhibit during the whole night. I was pleased with the attention the Rajah paid to his guests, whether Hindoos, Christians, or Mussulmans; there was not one to whom he did not speak kindly, or pay some compliment on their entrance; and he walked round the assembly repeatedly, to see that all were properly accommodated.

I am sorry I could not go to his nautch the next night, where I hear there was a masquerade, when several Portuguese and Pariahs appeared as Europeans, and imitated our dances, music, and manners.[15]

Another European visitor to the house of Rajkrishna, sometime between 1811 and 1814, described the "room" where the nautch was held as "supported by twelve pillars of the Corinthian order, round which were entwined fine silk and wreaths of flowers; in the middle was spread a carpet, for the European part of the company, and on each side was ranged in rows and seats on pillows, the most respectable natives."[16]

In the great mansions of wealthy Hindus like Rajkrishna, the nautch was typically held in the courtyard at the center of the house, covered over for the occasion by a scarlet canopy, just as Maria Graham and the anonymous visitor described it. The artist William Prinsep portrays such a pillared courtyard with its canopy, with the family temple open to one side, in his watercolor, "Entertainment during the Durga puja," c. 1840.[17]

For these entertainments, European women joined the men, but the Hindu women remained secluded in their upper floor apartments, peering down into the courtyard through louvered blinds or latticework at the activities below. "European ladies, on the evening of the Doorga poojah, are asked to visit the female part of the family, whom they have always found apparently happy and full of curiosity."[18]

Among the entertainers at the house of Rajkrishna, described by the anonymous guest, was "a beautiful girl, and very superior singer, Neekhee. . . . She was about fourteen years of age, and possessed a form and face moulded by the graces; her black eyes, full and piercing, reflected the pleasurable sensations of her heart; her mouth, around which a smile was ever playing, enclosed teeth, regular, perfect, and white as ivory; her voice was feeble; but inexpressibly sweet; and . . . I must own myself much gratified, and confess, that the twelve hundred rupees (one hundred and fifty pounds), and two pair of shawls of the same value, the price of Neekhee's attendance for three nights, was only commensurate with her singular accomplishments."[19] The celebrated Nicki (spellings vary) reigned supreme for many years. Mrs. Heber heard her—"a songstress of great reputation"—at a nautch in 1823,[20] and that same year, Fanny Parks heard her at the home of the great reformer Ramohan Roy.[21] Emma Roberts, writing in 1835, described her as "*prima donna* of the East."[22]

Solvyns distinguishes the dancers of the true nautch—*Ramjannys* [*rāmjanī*], as he identified them—from the *Bayaderes*, who had, in his judgment, corrupted the nautch as it was most widely performed—especially as it took the form of a variety show—and as typically described by Europeans. And he deplores the degradation of the nautch by *hijrās*, eunuchs dressed as women who sing and dance in often lewd parody. Solvyns depicts the Rāmjanī (Pl. II.93) and the Hijrā (Pl. II.94) in separate etchings.

Dancers were not limited to nautch performances. In his portrayal of Hindu marriage

(Pl. II.197), Solvyns refers to chariots in the wedding procession "filled with Ramjannys (dancers) and even Hidjeras (singers), who with bands of music and other objects add to the festivity and pomp."

Dancers and musicians in Bengal came from a variety of low Hindu castes and, especially dancers, from among Muslims, although Herbert H. Risley notes that "no Hindu will have a Muhamadan musician in his house if he can possibly avoid it."[23] The Nar, or Nat, of eastern Bengal is a dancing and musician caste,[24] and a number of low castes have specific sub-castes that are musicians by occupation.

James Wise, in his ethnographic notes on predominantly Muslim East Bengal, terms the musical group accompanying the nautch "Taifa-dar,"[25] and writes, "This is the musical party which attends nautch girls, who are always Muhammadans. It consists of two players on the violin (sārangī), two men who beat drums (tablā), and a player on the cymbals (manjīrā,)."[26] Joep Bor, from miniature paintings and European prints, as well as from European accounts, identifies various instruments used in accompanying the nautch—the sāraṅgī, sitār, tablā, and manjīrā.[27] In portraying the nautch, Solvyns depicts a group of eight musicians playing the bīn (Pl. II.149), manjīrā (Pl. II.174), jhā̃jharī (Pl. II.175), sāraṅgī (Pl. II.152), pakhāvaj (Pl. II.163), tablā (Pl. II.160), and ḍholak (Pl. II.159).

---

1 See "Some Examples of Impressions of Indian Dancing and Music," Dyson, 336-56.

2 Nevile, in his richly illustrated *Nautch Girls of India*, reproduces an array of works by European and Indian artists. Also see his "The Nautch Girl and the Sahib." Kettle's 1772 oil painting, "Colonel Antoine Louis Henri Polier Watching a Nautch," is now lost, but a superb gouache copy was done by a Mughal artist, c. 1780. It depicts Polier, engineer and Orientalist, dressed in Indian clothing and reclining on cushions as he watches a nautch performed for his personal enjoyment. Welch, 88-89. Kettle also painted nautch girls c. 1770 and in 1772, in Archer, *India and British Portraiture*, Pl. 26, pp. 70-72, and Pl. 31, p. 79; and Thomas Hickey painted the dancers c. 1805, Archer, Pl. 126, p. 204. Thomas Daniell, from a sketch done in India, painted "The Nautch" in 1810, reproduced in Shellim, 70.

3 Among early prints depicting the nautch, the three by Mrs. S. C. Belnos, in her *Twenty-Four Plates Illustrative of Hindoo and European Manners in Bengal,* are noteworthy. Among the last prints depicting the nautch was that by the Russian artist Prince Alexis Soltykoff, in his lithographic collection, *Indian Scenes and Characters,* published in 1858, a year after the Sepoy Mutiny. It depicts European guests with their wealthy Hindu host at a nautch in the "Festival of the Goddess Durga at Calcutta," reproduced in Pal and Dehejia, Pl. 63, p. 72. Numerous Company School paintings depict dancing girls or nautch performances. See, for example, Archer, *Company Paintings:,* 93, 156-57, 160, and 164-65, and Rousselet, 158-59. European fascination with the nautch continued into the age of photography, as seen in "Nautch Girl," c. 1875, in Pal and Dehejia, Pl. 217, p. 208. Okada and Isacco, 102-11, reproduce a number of prints and early photographs depicting nautch.

4 Nayak, 114, 119.

5 *Letters . . .*, 230. Mrs. Kindersley provides one of the earliest descriptions of a nautch—and surely the earliest by a European woman—in a letter dated Ahmedabad, October 1767, pp. 229-33.

6 Pl. 14, "A Dancing Woman of Bengal, Exhibiting Before an European Family." Pl. 15 depicts "A Dancing Woman" of Lucknow.

7 Carey, *Good Old Days of the Honorable John Company*, abridged ed., 76.

8 *Indian Recreation,* 1: 55-56. Bayly, in *Indian Society and the Making of the British Empire*, 39, describes Tennant as "supercilious" and as someone who condemned "the domestic economy of Hindus for corruption and superstition."

9 231.

10 *A View of the History, Literature, and Mythology , of the Hindoos*, 3:86. Also see Ward, *Account of the . . . Hindoos*, 3:133-35.

11 *The Journal of Mrs. Fenton*, 241-46, quoted in Nair, *Calcutta in the 19th Century*, 468-69.

12 Quoted in Heber, 1:47.

13 See Nagendra Nath Ghose, 183-84. See Solvyns's Pl. II.194 for a discussion of Nanakrishna's role in promoting Durgā Pūjā as a social event. On the patronage of nautch by Hindu elites, see Sumanta Banerjee. See Solvyns's Pl. II.182 for Nabakrishna Deb.

14 Wallace, 264-65, quoted in Nair, *Calcutta in the 19th Century,* 322. Fanny Parks, attending a Durgā Pūjā at the house of wealthy Hindu in 1823, describes a "handsome supper . . . where ices and French wines were in plenty for the European guests." 1:30, reprinted in Nair, *Calcutta in the 19th Century*, 258-59. On the often "lavish hospitality and the entertainment of sahibs," see Chitra Deb, 1:59-60.

15 From her letter of October 25, 1810, in *Letters on India*, 134-36. Maria Graham was also known as Lady (Maria) Callcott. For a life of Graham, see Gotch. Her reference to "Portuguese" appearing in the nautch is to the Indo-Portuguese Eurasian community resident in Calcutta, discussed in the Commentary for Pl. II.6.

16 *Sketches of India* , 211, quoted in Nair, *Calcutta in the 19th Century*, 191.

17 Pl. 25, in Losty, *Calcutta: City of Palaces.*

18 Wallace, 265, quoted in Nair, *Calcutta in the 19th Century*, 323.

19 *Sketches of India*, 212-13, quoted in Nair, *Calcutta in the 19h Century*, 192.

20 Quoted in Heber, 1:47.

21 *Wanderings of a Pilgrim,* 1:30.

22 *Scenes and Characteristics of Hindostan*, 1:248-53, quoted in Dyson, 347.

23 *Tribes and Castes of Bengal*, 2:130.

24 Risley, 2:129-30.

25 *Tawāyaf + dār*, one who accompanies a courtesan.

26 In the entry under "Bājunia," a class of Muslims, 38-39.

27 "The Voice of the Sarangi," 87-96. Bor includes Solvyns's depiction of the nautch.

II.196. Jhāpān

Pl. II.196. Jhāpān. Paris: II.7.1. Double-plate.

Calcutta: Sec. XII, No. 19. Jaupaun,—The child seated on the stage, plays with snakes, while his father and other kindred repeat munters or incantations to prevent their injuring him—this is a Ceremony of the Monsah Pooja, when Carpenters and other artificers worship their Tools.

Commentary: Jhāpān is the festival of the snake-charmers held in the Bengali month of Śravaṇa (July-August) as part of Manasā Pūjā, the worship of the snake goddess Manasā. In temples, her image is in female form, with snakes coiled around her neck and hands, but, reflecting her fertility cult origins, when worshipped outside or under a tree, she is represented by a twig of the *sīj* tree (*Euphorbia lingularum*).[1] Manasā is also represented by a vessel of worship called a *ghaṭ* or *bāri*, "a pot surmounted by three hooded snakes made of clay."[2] The goddess has special power to counteract the poison of snakes, and she is worshipped to obtain preservation from their bite. The festivals honoring Manasā begin with the onset of the monsoon in May, as the rains drive snakes from their holes, and continue into September.[3] Manasā is especially popular in Bengal among the lower castes, such as the Doms (Pl. II.68), for whom, in addition to the Māl snake-charmers (Pl. II.65), Manasā Pūjā is their principal festival.[4]

Paris: II.7.1. JAUPAUN, OR MUNSAH POOJAH: The *Jaupaun* is the feast of serpents; the lower classes call it also the carpenters feast, because it is celebrated particularly by carpenters, joiners and those in general who work in wood. On the day of the *Jaupaun* all the Hindoos of these trades get their tools blest, and as the feast is in honour of the serpents, every true Hindoo of whatsoever rank, as long as the feast lasts, leaves at his dinner a little rice in his plate, or in the banana leaf which serves him in place of it, and deposits it after his meal behind the house, in hopes to attract the serpents by this regale, and that such a voluntary offering will preserve him during the year from these venimous reptiles, whose bite is often mortal.

When the *Jaupaun* or *Munsah Poojah* [Man(a)sā Pūjā] is to be celebrated, several *Mauls* [Māls, Pl. II.65], (of whom it will be remembered we have spoken in the first volume) are hired for the purpose, and one of the children is drest up in the best manner possible; after which they seat him upon bambous, and the other *Mauls* carry him in procession, escorted by an immense concourse of people and many musicians. The *Mauls,* though in general dirty and slovenly in their persons, are on this occasion remarkably well drest. They have often magnificent shawls which they borrow from their neighbours. To shew that it is the feast of serpents, every member of the procession carries one in his hand; the child whom they escort has them even round his neck, his arms and his body, as may be remarked in the print.

This ceremony in reality is not so disgusting as at first sight it may appear, for the serpent in India, deprived of his venom, and tamed by men who understand this art, is looked upon quite as a domestic animal, on account of its suppleness and mild disposition. I have already made some mention of this subject in the first volume, in describing the *Mauls,* and shall have occasion to recur to it hereafter in another place [Pl. II.66].

It is easily conceived, that this feast is founded in the fear which the serpent in its natural state inspires. Perhaps it may also be to perpetuate the glory and the art of those that tame them, that these animals are carried in a sort of triumph.

The word *jhāpān* means "palanquin" and refers here to the bamboo platform upon which the boy rides in the Solvyns print. Jhāpān brings snake-charmers (sāpuriyā, Pl. II.66) of a particular area together, and in processions with music, they play with snakes and, repeating mantras, demonstrate their resistance to the poison of the serpent's bite. These processions are conducted all over town in two consecutive afternoons. With stops along the way at Manasā temples for the performance of *sāpkhelā* ("playing with snakes"), the processions converge on "the place of Jhāpān," where the snake-charmers "rival each other in the mastery of snakes and in the recitation of verses and mantras . . . concerning the Goddess and her creatures."[5]

Among the most popular of the season's Manasā festivals in Bengal is Nāgapañcamī, held on the fifth day of Śravaṇa, celebrating Kṛṣṇa's victory over the serpent Kāliya, the five-headed serpent king. On this day, live cobras, or their images, are worshipped with offerings of milk.[6]

In the background to Solvyns's portrayal of the festival is a flat-roofed temple, capped with a four curved cornice superstructure of the "hut" or *chālā* Bengali style.[7]

Solvyns made a watercolor copy of his *Jhāpān* print that is among the unbound Calcutta etchings in the Peabody Essex Museum. (See p. 86.) An Indian artist, c. 1800, painted another watercolor copy of the etching (Pl. I.51, pp. 104-05).

---

1 Amiya Kumar Banerji, *West Bengal District Gazetteers: Hooghly*, 201.

2 Östör, *Culture and Power*, 40.

3 Ibid., 40-90. Also see "Manasā Pūjā" in *An Alphabetical List of Feasts and Holidays of the Hindus and Muhammadans*, 57-58.

4 P. N. Bose, 54.

5 Östör, *Culture and Power*, 58. Also see Ward, *A View . . . of the Hindoos*, 3:136-37; Asutosh Bhattacharya, 222; and William J. Wilkins, 225-26.

6 Gupte, *Hindu Holidays*, 176-78; *An Alphabetical List of Feasts and Holidays of the Hindus and Muhammadans*, 58-59; Vogel, 275-80; Gnanambal, 9; and B. N. Sharma, 24-25. On Nāgapañcamī and "snakes in Indian culture," see Deoras, 10-23. Shakti M. Gupta, 94, reproduces an unidentified nineteenth century etching depicting "Naga Panchami, the festival of snake worship."

7 On the architectural style, see Pl. II.15.

II.197. Bibāha. Marriage

Paris: II.6.1. BEHAHO, OR MARRIAGE: Many different ceremonies are practised in the celebration of a Hindoo marriage, but as it is not possible to give an idea of them all in a single print, I have given the preference to what appeared to me most interesting to an European, the wedding itself; which closes all the ceremonies, and takes place during the night, under a tent, in the first court of the house of the bridegroom's family. The nearest relations and a number of Brahmuns form various groupes round the young couple, on whom their eyes are fixed. The bridegroom is richly drest; an immense cap of a conical form is absolutely necessary to the solemnity. He receives the hand of his bride, whose arm is supported by her father or nearest relation. On her forehead is an ornament of which the print gives an exact representation; she is but from seven to nine years of age, at which period the Hindoo laws admit of marriage: between twelve and fourteen is the age prescribed for males, who are allowed to have several wives. The hands of the young couple are joined over the brazen vase filled with water and covered with *pawn* and *mangoe* leaves, and *plantin* fruit, while a Brahmun recites his munters [*mantras*], and in a solemn tone reads over the genealogy of the parties. After the performance of these necessary formalities, the family of the bride delivers the portion [dowry] which was before stipulated, consisting among other things of brazen vases, earthen pots, cows, etc. Refreshments are then offered to the company, abundance of bethel, tobacco, aromatics, and perfumes, if, the two families are of a higher rank. After this the assembly proceeds to the bride's house: in this procession great luxury is displayed, palkees [palanquins], and even sometimes elephants are seen; chariots ornamented and filled with *Ramjannys* (dancers) [Pl. II.93], and even *Hidjeras* (singers) [*hijrā*, eunuch, Pl. II.94] , who with bands of music and other objects add to the festivity and pomp.

The bridegroom is not allowed to see his future bride publicly before the marriage; if he does, it must be furtively. Even after the ceremony which I have described, he does not live with his wife; he sees her, remains some days with her, and receives her at his own house, in his turn; their time is spent in the innocent playfulness of their age, till nature prompts them to consummate the marriage, from which time he is allowed to cohabit with her.

I must not omit mentioning that many Hindoos pretend, that the matrimonial ceremony is null if it can be proved that a stranger was present at it. I could not therefore have represented it, if I had not found means of seeing it unperceived, and taking an exact sketch of this mysterious solemnity.

Commentary: The marriage ceremony in Bengal, the *bibāha* (*vivāha* in Sanskrit), varies in its specific form and ritual among castes and subcastes.[1] Among the rich, it is celebrated with hundreds of guests and at great expense. That portrayed by Solvyns is a high caste marriage at the house of a wealthy family, where a *paṇḍāl* (a tent-like structure) has been erected as a "marriage-booth" for the ceremony in the open courtyard. Solvyns, surely with the knowledge and cooperation of at least the bride's family, secretly watched, perhaps through the louvered windows that in such grand Hindu houses of Calcutta looked out onto the courtyard. Solvyns's contemporary in Bengal, the Rev. Ward, had no such good fortune, and relied on others to provide a description for him.[2]

On the evening of the ceremony, the bridegroom goes in procession with his relations, friends, and neighbors to the house of the bride, and there the wedding takes place at the auspicious moment fixed by the astrologers. In the Calcutta *Catalogue*, Solvyns states correctly that the wedding ceremony is conducted at the house of the bride's family, but the Paris text mistakenly locates it at the house of the bridegroom's family. And the groom's procession, of course, takes place *before* the wedding, as he proceeds to the house of the bride's family—not after the ceremony, as the Paris text confusingly relates.

In the light of two oil lamps, the groom is shown seated across from his bride on a low wooden seat or possibly a mat made of sacred *kuśa* grass. He holds her right hand above a brass water-pot that Solvyns describes as covered with betel (*pān*) and mango leaves and a plantain.[3]

The groom wears a special silk *dhotī* and on his head a *ṭopar*, the distinctive Bengali wedding crown made of pith and mica.[4] The bride, as Solvyns

Pl. II.197. Bibāha. Paris: II.6.1. Double-plate.
Calcutta: Sec. XII, No. 17. Behaho or Marriage;—shewing the final Ceremony of uniting the parties,—the Bridegroom receives the hand of the Bride over a brass pot filled with water, and covered with pawn [*pān*, betel] or Mangoe leaves, having on them a Plantain—the Father, or a Relation of the Bride, then declares, the Marriage of the parties, reciting the Genealogies of their families, and concludes the whole by the delivery of the Bride's portion; after this the Bridegroom must remain for sometime at the house of the Parents of his Bride, where he goes in procession to be married. Previous to this celebration the parents agree among themselves, and the Husband cannot see his intended, but by stealth—the parity of ages is not always consulted, but the most proper is deemed, the male between 12 and 14, and the girl from 7 to 9,—the number of Wives is not limited.

---

portrays, wears a sari of red silk. Her face is covered until a specific point in the ritual, but Solvyns's "exact representation" of the ornament on her forehead is by no means clear. The bride often wears a *ṭikli*, a small pendant that is held on her forehead by a single fine chain that comes down the part of the hair and is attached to the bun in back. In other ritual traditions, she may wear a larger pendant held by a *pātimor*, a kind of tiara.[5]

Solvyns, in his text for the Paris edition, places the wedding in the "first court" of the house (described in Pl. II.182), but in the Paris etching, the ceremony is portrayed as taking place under a canopy outside the house, as indicated by the view on the left of the thatched roof of a neighboring hut and the palm rising behind it. The Calcutta etching (reversed) has a different composition for those gathered to watch, and, although we see the same wall of the house with the two windows from which the women watch, the view beyond is not portrayed.

---

1 See Buddhadev Roy, *Marriage Rituals and Songs of Bengal.* Risley describes the brahmin marriage ceremony in *The Tribes and Castes of Bengal*, 1:146-52. Also see Henry Thomas Colebrooke, "Religious Ceremonies of the Hindus," 7:288-311. On the orthodox Bengali ceremony, see R. C. Majumdar, *The History of Bengal*, 1:603-06. Shib Chunder Bose provides a detailed, if idiosyncratic, account of the ceremonies of high caste Bengalis, 41-89. A detailed description of a Bengali village marriage is provided in Lal Behari Day's *Bengal Peasant Life*, a closely observed "novel," 85-94, and, for a modern account of marriage in Day's village, Tara Krishna Basu, 95-105.

2 See Ward, *A View of . . . the Hindoos*, 1:163-85, and Ward, *Account of the . . . Hindoos*, 4:137-58

3 There is great variation in ritual practice, as evident in Buddhadev Roy, and the specifics of what Solvyns's portrays and describes may not be taken as "typical."

4 The *ṭopar* is made by Mālīs (Pl. II.53) of pith from *śolā,* a marshy plant.

5 Buddhadev Roy, 2.

II.198. Gaṅga Yātrā

Pl. II.198. Gaṅga Yātrā. Paris: III.6.1. Double-plate.

Calcutta: Sec. XII, No. 18. Gungah Jutra or Mello Pray,—when a patient is thought past recovery, he is carried in a bed to the river side, and when near his last gasp, he is placed half into the water, a portion of which is forced down his throat—the Corpse is afterwards burnt, if the family can pay the expenses, and the ashes or the body thrown into the river.

Commentary: Death practices in India vary among regions and communities and may even differ among those of the same caste, but there are general practices relating to the process of dying that represent cultural ideals. *Gaṅga yātrā* is the Bengali term for the custom where a dying man is brought with much ceremony to the banks of the holy Ganges and there, partially submerged, awaits an auspicious death.[1] By some accounts, there is a formal distinction between Gaṅgā yātrā, the practice of taking a dying person to the riverside, and what is termed *antarjali*, the immersion of the lower half of the body in the water.[2] Solvyns's term "Mullo Pray" is unclear. It might be either of two Sanskrit words, one meaning a ritual procedure (*mūlaprāga*); the other, a place of sacrifice, as in the confluence of two holy rivers (*mūlaprayoga*).[3]

Among Hindus, "a 'good' death occurs at the right time and at the right place—ideally in Banaras on the banks of the Ganges with the lower limbs in the water. Failing Banaras or some other place of pilgrimage, one should die at home on purified ground and in the open air, and not on a bed or under a roof."[4] "It is imperative," writes Bayly, "to give the spirit access to the pure elements and preferable to a sacred river by which it could begin its journey to the realms of Yama, Lord of the Dead. Moving the dying onto the ground, outside the house, or even to a riverside burning place (burning *ghāṭ*) minimized the pollution of death in the household and also helped ensure that the entrapped spirit did not become a malignant ghost."[5]

Solvyns's contemporary, the Rev. William Ward, provides a detailed description of Gaṅgā yātrā,

Paris: III.6.1. GUNGA-JATRA, OR MULLO-PRAY. HINDOOS DYING: A singular article of religious belief, universally received through Hindoostan, has furnished the subject of this engraving. A Hindoo is persuaded that he sullies the house in which he dies, and that, to avoid this inconvenience, he must endeavour to expire on the banks of the sacred river, the Ganges. A family would be dishonoured, even in its descendants, and its house must be burnt, if any of its members happened to die in it. Consequently, when one of them falls sick, the relations transport him to the banks of the river, where they wait for the tide, pushing him forwards as it advances, so that he is frequently drowned in a few minutes. The body is then drawn out to be burnt, or thrown into the middle of the river if the family can not supply the expences of a funeral. For persons of high rank, tents are pitched to receive them on the banks of the river. The print represents a Hindoo dying, surrounded by his family and by Brahmuns who are giving him the water of the Ganges to drink, and exhorting him to die with the sentiments of a true Hindoo. To the left, in front of a small pagoda, is a sick person, who, being without relations, and destitute of means to get himself carried, has dragged his body painfully to the river side, to expire there as the others do. Another Hindoo is represented in the river. We cannot reflect without a painful emotion, that a great part of those poor Hindoos are labouring perhaps only under some slight indisposition, which becomes mortal meerly by their immersion in the river, or drinking cold water in a fit of the fever. I have often witnessed the fatal effects of this treatment. I remember seeing the Rajah of Kisnagur carried to the river to order to die in due form. Fortunately an European physician was passing by, who undertook to cure him, provided he should be carried back to his house. I since heard that the doctor had succeeded, and had been very generously recompensated by the prince.

with considerable disapproval for the discomfort to which the dying are subjected in bringing them to the riverside.

> As death approaches, the relations exhort the sick man, if he is a regular Hindoo, to repeat the name of . . . his guardian deity, and those of other gods. . . . If the doctor is present, and should declare that the patient is on the point of expiring, he tells them to let him down into the water up to the middle. When there is no doctor, his friends attend to this according to their own judgment. Just before or after being thus immersed, they spread the mud of the river on the breast &c of the dying man, and with one of their fingers write on this mud the name of some deity; they also pour water down his throat; shout the names of different deities in his ears, and, by this anxiety after his future happiness, hurry him into eternity. . .[6]
>
> If a Hindoo should die in his house, and not within sight of the river, it is considered as a great misfortune, and his memory is sure to be stigmatized for it after death.[7]

Paraphrasing Ward in accompanying text, Mrs. Belnos portrayed the scene in "The Dying Hindoo Brought to the Ganges," one of her *Twenty-four Plates Illustrative of Hindoo and European Manners in Bengal*.[8] She depicts a man in a sitting position in the water, attended by his wife and four brahmin priests, one of whom pours "water mixed with the sediment of the Ganges" into his mouth.

In Gaṅgā yātrā, those brought to the riverside *ghāṭs* to await death were not always terminally ill, and missionaries recounted instances where they had nursed a "victim" back to health. And Solvyns relates seeing the Nadia rājā, Ishwar Chandra of Krishnagar,[9] carried to the river to die, only to be saved by the intervention of a passing European physician. Sometimes those awaiting death were neglected and, lacking food and water, may have been hastened into the realms of Yama by relatives eager for an inheritance.[10] Ward's colleague at the Baptist Mission in Serampore, the Rev. William Carey, in 1802, argued for outlawing the practice of Gaṅgā yātrā,[11] and by the 1820s, the Baptist missionaries had launched a major public attack on what they terms "*ghāṭ*-murders." By their efforts, legislation was enacted to police the *ghāṭs* and to forbid the exposure there of those supposed to be dying.[12]

The Church Missionary Society, without attribution, included an engraved copy of the Solvyns's print in its *Missionary Papers* in 1823,[13] and a rather free and slightly modified version of the print appeared as one of the 24 colored lithographs in *L'Inde française* (1827-1835).[14] The Solvyns etching was also reproduced in an engraving in *India's Cries to British Humanity* (1830), the Rev. J. Peggs's extended tract against "ghaut murders," suttee, and other Hindu practices.[15]

In Solvyns's Paris etching, the dying Hindu, to the right, is given sacred water from the Ganges. Further back, in the center, another Hindu is taken on his cot into the water, and to the left, behind the small temple, a funeral pyre is tended by two figures. In the Paris etching, Solvyns widens the vista from the earlier Calcutta print and changes the composition slightly by adding both the dying man in the water and the pyre.

In his Introduction to *Les Hindoûs*, Volume III, Solvyns refers to the etching as "shewing the religious custom of desposing the sick on its banks." He then writes,

> It is well known that to all the Hindoos the waters of the Ganges are sacred, as proceeding from the foot of Brahma, and are supposed to possess the virtue of washing away the sins of those who bathe in them. This superstitious veneration is entitled to some indulgence, when we consider the benefits which this noble river confers upon the beautiful countries through which it flows. Wider and deeper than the Nile, it is open to navigation, for an extent of five hundred leagues, during which it receives many large rivers, and opens a communication with the finest provinces of Hindoostan; not to mention the salubrity of its waters, the abundance of its fisheries, its periodical inundations by which the plains are fertilized, which have attracted the notice of every traveller, and entitled it to the name of Ganges or the river by excellence.[16]

---

1 On the authority of the *Purāṇas*, it is prescribed that the dying man should be taken, if possible, to a holy place, preferably the Ganges. By dying in the waters of the Ganges, a man attains *mokṣa*, final release. Kale, 4:186-87.

2 Buckland, *Bengal Under the Lieutenant-Governors*, 1:323.

3 I am grateful to Patrick Olivelle and to Klaus Peter Zoller, respectively, for these suggestions.

4 Parry, 160. On the death ceremonies of the Hindus more generally, see Chapter 5, "The Last Sacrifice," 151-90. Basanta Coomar Bose, 85, states that immersion in the sacred water of the Ganges is taken as the equivalent of dying in Banaras itself, and he is emphatic that if the dying person cannot be taken to the river, "in all cases he must be removed from his room and placed under the sky."

5 "From Ritual to Ceremony," 158-59.

6 *A View of the History, Literature, and Mythology, of the Hindoos*, 269. Also see Ward, *Account of the . . . Hindoos*, 4:181-86.

7 Ibid., 270.

8 Pl. 4.

9 Solvyns depicts the rājā in an etching, Pl. II.18.

10 Bayly, "From Ritual to Ceremony," 172.

11 Potts, 143.

12 Bayly, "From Ritual to Ceremony," 172. Baptist missionary J. Peggs, for example, published a number of tracts against "ghaut murders." See his discussion in *India's Cries to British Humanity*, 303-62. The Rev. Duff, 233-40, decries these "inhuman practices" in his account of "the abandonment of the dying."

13 "Death of Hindoos on the Banks of the River Ganges," 29 (Lady Day, 1823). The print is also included in *The First Ten Years' Quarterly Papers of the Church Missionary Society*.

14 Burnouf and Jacquet, Pl. 21.

15 Peggs, 303.

16 3:2.

Satī[1]

When Solvyns arrived in Calcutta in 1791, the debate over satī was just beginning as missionaries, among others, condemned official toleration of the "dreadful practice" and called for its suppression. Of all Hindu customs, none more fascinated—or appalled—the Europeans than "suttee," the practice of widow-burning. The term *satī* is Sanskrit for "virtuous woman," but is used principally to refer to the faithful wife who "becomes satī" through self-immolation on the funeral pyre of her husband. Europeans erroneously took the word to mean the practice itself, and *suttee*, the European corruption, has become the conventional term for the wife's self-immolation. Solvyns uses neither *suttee* nor *satī* as terms in his description, but rather the Sanskrit word he spells phonetically from Bengali pronunciation. The practice by which the wife joins her husband in the flames and becomes satī is termed *sahamarana*, "dying together," also known as *sahagamaṇa*—Solvyns's Shoho-Gomon—meaning "going together."[2]

The practice was prevalent in Bengal in the eighteenth and early nineteenth centuries. Benoy Bhusan Roy, in *Socioeconomic Impact of Sati in Bengal,* writes that suttee was most frequent among brahmins, but that the practice was found among the families of lower castes that had distinctive positions in wealth or property. Indeed, the possible increased frequency of suttee may have reflected aspiration to higher social status among upwardly mobile śūdra families.[3] But, as official records in the early nineteenth century reveal, suttee was not limited to the more affluent. The practice was to be found among many castes and at every social level.[4]

Among European travelers in India during the late eighteenth and early nineteenth centuries, no description was complete without reference to suttee—preferably with at least one eye-witness account. Pierre Sonnerat, who traveled in India in the 1770s, describes the practice and provides an engraving of an Indian woman going to be burned with the body of her husband.[5] Another French traveler, Grandpré, writing of his experience in Bengal in 1789 and 1790, relates his own unsuccessful effort to rescue a beautiful young woman who was to become satī, and notes that the practice of suttee was particularly "horrible" in Bengal.[6] Failed intervention was a frequent theme in European accounts, as in Thomas Twining's description of his thwarted effort to prevent a suttee some 60 miles outside Calcutta in 1792.[7] Confirming accounts of restraints to prevent the woman's escape, Edward Thompson writes in *Suttee* that "Especially in Bengal, [the woman] was often bound to the corpse with cords, or both bodies were fastened down with long bamboo poles curving over them like a wooden coverlet, or weighted down by logs."[8]

Most instances of suttee were described as "voluntary" acts of courage and devotion. But there were surely cases involving the use of force, drugs, or restraints. In "An Account of a Woman burning herself, By an Officer," appearing in the *Calcutta Gazette* in 1785, one of various instances of suttee reported periodically in Calcutta newspapers, the observer describes the woman as likely under the influence of bhang or opium but otherwise "unruffled." After she was lifted upon the pyre, she "laid herself down by her deceased husband, with her arms about his neck. Two people immediately passed a rope twice across the bodies, and fastened it so tight to the stakes that it would have effectually prevented her from rising had she attempted."[9]

The Reverend William Ward, a Baptist missionary at Serampore, near Calcutta, and a contemporary of Solvyns, recounts his own witness of the practice (which he terms *suhu-murunu*), as well as reported instances in the area of Calcutta. William Carey, the famed author of the *Dictionary of the Bengali Language* and Ward's colleague at the Serampore Mission, undertook a census in 1803 of suttees and counted 438 that had reportedly taken place that year within a thirty mile radius of Calcutta.[10]

In contrast to the expressions of horror in most accounts, an American merchant,

Benjamin Crowninshield, described the suttee he witnessed while in Calcutta in 1789 with "extraordinary detail" and "great sensitivity."[11] In his ship's log, he concluded his sober account: "Whether it is right or wrong, I leave it for other people to determine. . . . [I]t appeared very solemn to me. I did not think it was in the power of a human person to meet death in such a manner."[12] Similarly, Maria Graham, in her *Letters on India*, published in 1814, wrote sympathetically and without judgment of the practice—particularly remarkable at a time when European missionaries and Indian reformers were mounting their campaign against suttee.[13]

Within the city of Calcutta, under jurisdiction of British law, suttee had been prohibited since 1798, but outside Calcutta, the "dreadful practice" flourished in Bengal—indeed, some said, in epidemic proportions. As the debate over widow-burning intensified, officials took steps to suppress the practice in 1812, with a distinction between "legal" (voluntary) and "illegal" (involuntary) suttee.[14] Its complete abolition came under Lord William Bentinck through Regulation XVII of the Bengal Code, December 4, 1829, declaring the practice of suttee, whether voluntary or not, illegal and punishable by the criminal courts.[15]

The European fascination with suttee, expressed through travelers' accounts and in the debates over official policy, was mirrored in visual representations by both amateur and professional artists. Among the earliest portrayals of suttee is an engraving, 1598, to illustrate the account of the Dutch traveler, Jan Huygen van Linschoten (1563-l611), who lived in India from 1583 to 1588. The print shows a widow, with arms raised, stepping off into a pit in which her husband is consumed in flames.[16] The Hindu widow again leaps onto the pyre in the 1670 frontispiece engraving for the book by the Dutch missionary Abraham Roger.[17] An engraving gave visual form to Eyles Irwin's 1776 poem on satī, *Bedukah or the Self-Devoted*.[18] The early portrayals of suttee in prints were based on travelers' descriptions, such as those by Linschoten and Roger, and are often highly fanciful, but by the late eighteenth century European artists in India were drawn to the subject and its powerful imagery. Tilly Kettle painted the serene young widow bidding farewell to her relatives.[19] Johann Zoffany, in one of at least three paintings he devoted to the subject, depicted suttee as a "heroic act," as Giles Tillotson notes. "The widow here is not a sentimental figure inviting pity, but a moral exemplar to be admired."[20] The paintings by Kettle and Zoffany are idealized, and it is unlikely that they were based on first-hand observation, but in the early 1780s, William Hodges witnessed a suttee near Banaras and made a drawing at the scene. He subsequently completed a painting, "Procession of a Hindoo Woman to the Funeral Pile of her Husband," that served as the basis for the engraving accompanying his description in *Travels in India*.[21] There is in Hodges's depiction a somber atmosphere of sadness, but it too is idealized and draws Solvyns's criticism as not being "correct."[22] A later painting, 1831, by James Atkinson (1780-1852), is also romantic and conveys in its portrayal of the beautiful young widow an overtone of the erotic that was so often associated with the depiction of suttee. Archer and Lightbrown suggest that Atkinson "probably intended to express sympathy with the plight of young Indian womanhood condemned by inexorable custom to premature death."[23] Many European portrayals of suttee, as in written accounts, reflect ambivalence—admiration for the courage of the virtuous woman and sympathy for the victim of a heathen rite—but satirist Thomas Rowlandson uses his 1815 engraving, "The Burning System," as an attack upon the government for its complicity in permitting "voluntary" suttee.[24] And over the course of the nineteenth century, with imagery of horror, missionary tracts and journals frequently depict suttee as the symbol of benighted India and Hindu "superstition."[25]

Solvyns, in his portrayal of suttee, seeks to record faithfully and accurately as an observer what he witnessed "in order to give fullness, truth and spirit to the resemblance." But Solvyns, no less than his contemporaries, brings a mixture of admiration and sympathy and condemnation. In 1799, in his *Catalogue* for the 250 etchings of the Calcutta edition, he writes that suttee—what he terms "Shoho Gomon"—has been "often described and is so generally known" that he need not provide a separate account of the ceremony itself. But perhaps with a larger, less knowledgeable audience in mind for the Paris edition in 1810, Solvyns felt compelled to offer a description of the suttee to which he was eye-witness.

In the Introduction to Volume II of *Les Hindoûs*,[26] Solvyns writes:

> It has been said in the preliminary discourse [Vol. I], that women among the Hindoos appear but in a secondary light, and for that reason can occupy but a small place in a description of their manners; it may consequently have been remarked that scarce any mention has been made of them in the foregoing numbers; in the present volume only, this interesting half of the human race will appear such as it is found in that singular people of which we treat. The state of the women in Hindoostan is not undeserving of a part of the reader's attention.
>
> The laws of Menu [Manu] are sufficient to persuade us, that, by the Hindoo religion, women are condemned to perpetual dependence and subordination, and although Mr. *Robertson*[27] advances that in more ancient times their lot was less severe than at present, we have every reason to believe that in the most remote periods, they did not enjoy a milder fate than they do at present in all the regions of the East.
>
> > "A woman (says Menu) must be in the dependance of her father during her childhood, of her husband while she is married, of his sons when her husband dies, of his father's nearest relations if he has no sons, and in fine of the sovereign if there are no such relations. A woman never should wish to make herself independant nor to separate from her father, her husband or his sons; for, by removing from them, she exposes herself to the contempt of the two families." [Manu 5.148-149; also see 9.3.][28]
>
> Menu then speaks of the duties of the husband towards his wife, which are numerous. "A father is deserving of blame if he does not marry his daughter at the age prescribed; a husband, if he does not approach his wife at the proper times; and a son, if he does not protect his mother after the death of her master. Above all, a woman must be prevented from forming illegal connections, least she should become the cause of affliction to the two families." [Manu 9.4-5]
>
> These laws enacted by a legislator to whom the appellation of wise cannot be refused, give a sufficient idea of the female sex in India. But I think it right also to lay before the reader a very remarkable passage of his code, where he treats of the respect due to married women, and which will serve to prove, that, though Menu prescribes very narrow bounds to female liberty, it never was his intention that the rights of a wife and of a mother should be overlooked. "Wives (says the great legislator) must be honored by their fathers and their brothers, by their husband and his brothers, if they have the happiness of the family at heart: the gods are pleased wherever the wife is treated with respect; but where she is despised, religion is of no avail. [Manu 3.55-56] For this reason, men who wish to become rich, should never allow their wives to want for dress, ornaments or nourishment on days of festivity and rejoicing [3.59]; for, surely, if the woman is not careful in her dress, she cannot exhilarate her husband; and if he is not in good humour, they will be without children." [3.61]
>
> Who would have expected such delicate attentions, approaching even to gallantry, in the severe code of the Hindoo legislator. Unfortunately, as soon as the husband expires, the unhappy Hindoo widow becomes the victim of the most cruel superstition: that

moment puts a period to all the happiness she may have enjoyed, and all the respect she has met with during her marriage; all is ended; a new and dismal scene opens for her; no longer is she considered as a being of any consequence: she has lost all, when she loses her husband; no choice is left her in her dress or diet; the laws prescribe the strictest abstinence; the remainder of her days must be spent in prayers and fasting; her lot is humiliation or suffering, as I shall explain it in several numbers of this volume. ["]Woe to the woman who forgets the laws of her religion so far as to contract a second marriage! She draws shame upon herself in this life,["] says Menu, ["]and in the next passes into the body of *Jackal*, where she becomes a prey to the elephantiasis and other dreadful disorders, the just punishment of criminals.["] [Manu 5.164]

Intimidated by the threats of her religion and by the sad prospect of the humiliations which await her in the widowed state, the unhappy woman who loses her husband can look only to the sacred writings of the Brahmuns for hope or consolation. There, instead of the mortifications which she is to expect as a widow, she meets the promises of happiness and consideration if she has the courage to accompany her husband to the grave. "The woman (says one of these books)[29] who gives herself to the flames with the body of her husband, shall equal *Arundhati*[30] and shall reside in *Swerga* [Svarga].[31]—She who accompanies her husband (says another), shall reside in *Swerga* as many years as there are hair on the human body, that is thirty-five millions.—By dying with her husband (says a third), she sanctifies her paternal and maternal ancestors and those of the man to whom she has given her virginity: the woman who gives this proof of affection to her deceased husband shall be eternally admired, praised by the celestial choirs of the great *Harwas* [Gandhavas],[32] and shall enjoy with him the delights of heaven during the reign of fourteen *Indras*."[33]

How could such promises fail to move the weak and superstitious mind of a woman intimidated besides by the fate which she sees prepared for the remainder of her life? Is it astonishing that in such a sad alternative she should make a choice, dreadful indeed in itself, but which frees her from a life of calamity and contempt, and procures her inexpressible and eternal happiness which the Brahmuns never fail to paint to her in the most lively and seducing colours? No positive law commands the widow to follow her husband to the tomb: but the passages which we have just quoted speak of it as a most glorious act, and as the only one which can, not only maintain, but encrease the consideration which a woman enjoyed during the life of her husband. The greater number of widows under these impressions take the courageous resolution of burning themselves, or, what is perhaps still more dreadful, of burying themselves alive with the remains of their husbands. This cruel practice will be represented in the large prints of the four last numbers of this volume [Pl.s II.199, II.200, II.201, and II.202]. In the text will be found a description of all the ceremonies used on these occasions, and neither will contain any thing to which I myself have not been an eye-witness.

A custom so absurd and so barbarous cannot be defended in opposition to good sense and humanity. Nevertheless, upon reflection, we shall find that the motives upon which it was founded were not so cruel as at first sight they appear. "Although the voluntary suicide of the Hindoo widows,["] says Mr. Forster,[34] ["]is very contrary to all the notions of humanity received in Europe, yet, as the intention is to strengthen by it the ties of interior and domestic affection, we must not inconsiderately condemn it nor attribute it to ideas of cruelty or injustice."

1 An earlier version of this discussion was published in *Bengal Past and Present* in 1998.

2 Hawley, "Introduction," in *Sati, the Blessing and the Curse*, 12-13; Thompson, 15; V. N. Datta, 1; Narasimhan, 19. On the woman's duty to die with her husband, see Lesie, 291-98. On suttee more generally, there is an extensive literature. See especially Ajit Kumar Ray, Hawley, Datta, and Mani. Amal Chatterjee, 111-24, focuses on the representation of suttee in British poetry, plays, and novels.

3 43-48.

4 From 1815 until its abolition in 1829, the government kept records of reported suttees in Bengal. The practice may well have been most frequent among brahmins, but the various śūdra castes together (principally those of higher status) accounted for the majority of instances of suttee. Amitabha Mukherjee, 244-50. Considerable controversy attends the discussion of the increased reports of suttee in Bengal in the late eighteenth and early nineteenth centuries. See, for example, Embree, "Widows as Cultural Symbols," and Ashis Nandy.

5 Sonnerat, *A Voyage to the East Indies and China*, 1:112-19. The engraving appears only in the original French edition, *Voyage aux Orientales et à la Chine*, Vol. I, Pl. 15 (opp. p. 95).

6 2:69-74.

7 463-67; in Kaul, 92-96.

8 Thompson, 40-41.

9 February 10, 1785, reprinted in Seton-Karr, 1:89-91. Also reproduced in Blechynden, 190-93.

10 *A View of the History, Literature, and Mythology of the Hindoos*, 3:308-30. Also see Ward, *Account of the Writings, Religion, and Manners of the Hindoos*, 2:544-66. On missionary efforts to suppress suttee, see Potts, 144-57.

1 1Bean, *Yankee India*, 41.

12 From "Log of the 'Henry,' Nov. 28, 1789." Phillips Library, Peabody Essex Museum, Salem, Massachusetts. Quoted in Bean, *Yankee India*, 43.

13 303-06. Maria Graham, also known as Lady Callcott, was surely a remarkable woman for her time in India. These letters—discourses on Indian religion, art, and manners—reveal her as perhaps the first woman Orientalist.

14 The distinction reflected the view held by most eighteenth century Orientalists that the practice was sanctioned in Hindu religious texts. See Rocher, "British Orientalism in the Eighteenth Century," 230.
Under regulations adopted in 1812, authorities were to preclude, as far as possible, instances of "illegal" suttee, deemed by the government repugnant to Hindu law, such as those involving the use of drugs or compulsion. These and subsequent regulations before the final abolition of suttee are examined in "Suttee," *Calcutta Review* 92 (1867): 221-61. See especially 227-29. The article is based on a series of parliamentary (House of Commons) papers, running to several hundred pages, published between 1821 and 1825. For a listing of the papers see *Hansard's Catalogue and Breviate of Parliamentary Papers* [1699-1824], 98.
On movement to suppress suttee, see Amitabha Mukherjee, 238-85, and on the official debates, Mani.

15 V. N. Datta, 105. The text of the Regulation is in Datta, Appendix II, 251-53.

16 Linschoten's *Itineraro*, first published in Dutch in Amsterdam in 1596, was the most important Dutch book on Asia in this period and went through 15 reprints and translations in the seventeenth century. The engraving, Pl. 20, "A Suttee," appears in the English translation of 1598, but is not included in the Hakluyt Society reprint edition. On Linschoten, see Lach and Van Kley, Vol. 3, Bk, 2, 435-36-549. A copy of the engraving was included in Bry's *India orientalis* (1599), Pl. IX, and was reprinted in various Bry editons. The Bry engraving is reproduced in Lach, following p. 356.

17 *Theatre de l'idolatrie ou la porte ouverte*. The original edition, published in Leiden in 1651, does not have the engraving. The print is reproduced in Lach and Van Kley, Vol. 3, Bk.2, Pl. 197. For Roger's description "of those women who are burnt or buried with their Husbands," see "A Dissertation on the Religion and Manners of the Brahmins," in Picart, 3:334-6. Mannesson-Mallet's 1683 *Description de l'univers* includes a print portraying suttee, 2:111, Pl. XLIX. Okada and Isacco, 89-93, include early depictions of suttee among a number of European prints reproduced.

18 Frontispiece to the three canto poem.

19 The painting is in the Oriental Club, London, and is reproduced in Mildred Archer and Lightbown, *India Observed*, Pl. 2, p. 33, and in Mildred Archer, *India and British Portraiture*, Pl. 27, p. 71.

20 The painting is reproduced, with Tillotson's commentary, in Bayly, *The Raj*, Pl. 278, p. 221. Zoffany's fascination with suttee is further evidenced by his inclusion of paintings of suttee in the backgrounds of two group portraits.

21 The engraving (opp. p. 84) is by W. Shelton. See 79-84 for his description of the suttee. Tillotson, *The Artificial Empire*, 93-95, and Leoshko and Charlesworth, 77-80, discuss Hodges's portrayal.

22 See Pl. II.199 for discussion of the Hodges print .

23 Mildred Archer and Ronald Lightbown, 133. The painting is reproduced Pl. 131, p. 132.

24 Reproduced in Bayly, *The Raj*, Pl. 279, p. 222.

25 Courtright discusses changes in the visual representation of suttee in *The Goddess and the Dreadful Practice* and in "The Iconographies of Sati."

26 2:11-13. Although Solvyns acknowledges no assistance in the authorship of the introductions to the four volumes of *Les Hindoûs*, the sections, as here, which draw from European accounts of India or from translations of Hindu texts are probably by Depping. See Chapter Two, pp. 65-67, on Depping's role.

27 William Robertson (1721-1793), *An Historical Disquisition Concerning the Knowledge which the Ancients had of India* (1791).

28 The quotations from Manu, identified by verse in brackets, are not directly from Jones's translation. Solvyns (or here, more likely, Depping) apparently translated the passages from Jones's *Institutes of Hindu Law* for the French text of the Introduction to *Les Hindoûs*, and Solvyns's wife, Mary Anne Greenwood, then translated them back into English. A similar procedure is evident in quotations from Colebrooke (fn. 29) and in other quoted material in the introductions to the four volumes. (A German translation of Jones's *Institutes* was published in 1797, but a French translation of Manu—direct from Sanskrit—did not appear until 1830.)

29 These quotations are from Vijñāneśvara's commentary on *Yājñavalkya Smṛti*, 1.86. See Kane, 2:631. Solvyns's source is Henry T. Colebrooke (1765-1837), "On the Duties of a Faithful Hindu Widow," 4:208. Solvyns translated Colebrooke's text into French, and his wife translated it back into English. In 1810, Colebrooke published a translation from Vijñāneśvara's commentary in *Two Treatises on the Hindu Law of Inheritance*.

30 "Fidelity," the goddess Arundhatī is the model of wifely excellence.

31 Svarga is "heaven."

32 Gandhavas are semi-divine singers and musicians in Indra's heaven.

33 Indra is the celebrated war god of the *Ṛgveda*, associated with storm and thunder. During the life of Brahmā, there are 14 cycles of Manu, each having one Manu and one Indra. Thus, during one world age, there are 14 Indras.

34 George Forster, *A Journey from Bengal to England*, 1:59. The quotation, from Forster's letter from Banaras, 30 September 1782, is not as Forster wrote it. It is either Solvyns's (probably Depping's) translation into French, translated back into English by his wife, or it is a translation from Langlès's French translation of Forster. Forster wrote: "Though the issue of such a resolution [self-destruction by the widow] forcibly affects those feelings of humanity cherished amongst European nations, yet as the usage appears to originate in a cause tending to strengthen domestic policy, it ought not to be condemned, or imputed altogether to the dictates of cruelty or injustice." On Forster, see Preliminary Discourse, fn. 28, in Chapter Four.

II.199. Sahagamana

Pl. II.199. Sahagamana. Paris: II.9.1. Double-plate.

Calcutta: Sec. XII, No. 13. Shoho Gomon,—Women burning themselves with the Corpse of their Husband.—This ceremony has been so often described and is so generally known, that an account of it would be superfluous.

Commentary: Solvyns here portrays the ritual events leading to the sacrificial self- immolation he terms "Shoho-Gomon," *sahagamana*, by which the widow "goes together" with her dead husband on the cremation pyre. While Solvyns assures his readers that he relies for his descriptions only on what he can

Paris: II.9.1. SHOHO-GOMON.A WOMAN BURNING HERSELF WITH THE CORPSE OF HER HUSBAND: This ceremony, which is closely connected with one of the most singular dogmas of the Hindoo religion, appeared to me of sufficient importance to require several plates in order to represent it with all its circumstances and most minute details, notwithstanding that it has been already described in several works. The Asiatic society has given to the public many different Memoirs upon this subject,[1] and Mr. Hodges has represented it in an engraving,[2] but not very correctly. The truest description is that which Mr. Shakespeare, one of the directors of the East-India company, has published in a small pamphlet printed in England about the year 1790.[3] For my part, I shall only say what I myself have been an eye-witness of: the principal functions of this melancholy ceremony are prescribed in the sacred writings of the Hindoos. The woman who has made the vow of burning herself with the dead body of her husband, begins by bathing; after which she dresses herself in entirely *new* apparel; the priests then paint her face with *minium*[4] or red oker, with which I have been assured they mix gunpowder and sulphur, no doubt to shorten the sufferings of the unfortunate victim of their superstition. When this is done, she takes in one hand an evergreen herb called *Cusa* [*kuśa*],[5] and some water in the other; and while the Brahmuns are repeating the word *Om, Om,* she distributes *minium* among her relations, and her jewels among the priests. To those who assist at the ceremony, she throws some grains of rice as she proceeds three times around the pile on which the corpse of her husband has been deposed wrapt up in a white sheet. Two Brahmuns accompany her repeating texts of the sacred writings, and representing to her the inexpressible pleasures which await her in the next world. Even the whole family of the widow are to participate of the happiness which, according to their opinions, is to be the result of this sublime action; for the Brahmuns assert that all those who lead the widow to the pile will enjoy for every step they take many years of felicity. I must refer my readers to the Memoirs of the society of Calcutta, for the religious forms and sacred sentences which are employed throughout the ceremony.

This print represents the procession round the pile: on one side are seen the banks of the river and a little temple, for the scene generally takes place in the vicinity of a pagoda. What follows will be the subject of the first print of the next number.

verify, he appears here and in the next description of suttee, to have drawn for detail upon Colebrooke's essay in *Asiatick Researches*, "On the Duties of a Faithful Hindu Widow." There Colebrooke quotes from a Sanskrit source as to the ritual preparation in terms very similar to that of Solvyns: "Having first bathed, the widow dressed in two clean garments, and holding some *cūsā* grass, sips water from the palm of her hand. Bearing *cūsā* and *tila* [sesame], she looks toward the east or north, while the *Brāhmana* utters the mystic word *Om*."[6] Again, after quoting various Sanskrit texts, Colebrooke ends with a description by an unidentified witness that bears close resemblance to Solvyns's account: "Adorned with all jewels, decked with *minium* and other customary ornaments, with the box of *minium* in her hand, having made *pūjā*, or adoration to the *Dévātās* [gods], thus reflecting that *this life is nought: my lord and master to be was all,*— she walks round the burning pile; she bestows jewels on the *Brāhmanas*, comforts her relations, and shows her friends the attention of civility, while calling the Sun and elements to witness, she distributes *minium* at pleasure; and having repeated the *Sancalpa* [*saṃkalpa*],[7] proceeds into the flames; there embracing the corpse, she abandons herself to the fire, calling *Satya! Satya! Satya!* "[8]

The print depicts the woman, soon to become satī, escorted toward the pyre by two brahmins. She wears a white sari draped over her left shoulder, revealing bare breasts. Paul B. Courtright, who has written on the representation of satī, wonders whether Solvyns might here have succumbed to the romance of Orientalism. "In European art of the period, . . . semi-nude portrayals of women were commonplace, especially in representations of 'natives' from exotic parts of the world."[9] In Solvyns's time, however, Bengali women, even of the highest castes, wore the sari as their sole garment. The bodice, or *colī*, was adopted later as a result of reform efforts by the Brahmo Samaj and Christian missionary concern that women dress modestly.[10]

The attending priests are Vaiṣṇavites, as

indicated by the faintly etched *tilak* (sectarian mark) on the forehead, seen most clearly in the Paris edition, where it is colored in vivid ocher.

Many of Solvyns's etchings were reproduced, as was this print, usually without attribution, in various books on India published during the nineteenth century.[11] Indeed, reproduction of Solvyns's representations of suttee may have played an important role in shaping the visual image of the practice in the European mind.

---

1 See particularly Henry. T. Colebrooke, "On the Duties of a Faithful Hindu Widow." The essay was presented to the Asiatic Society Calcutta, in 1794.

2 Hodges, in *Travels in India* , 79-84, describes a suttee he witnessed near Banaras, with an accompanying engraving, "Procession of a Hindoo Woman to the Funeral Pile of Her Husband" (opp. p. 84). The plate is reproduced as the frontispiece in Hawley and as the cover for the paperback edition. In Hodges's print, the woman is escorted forward by a brahmin priest. The shrouded husband is being picked up, and in the background is a straw structure, the pyre, before which a man stands with a torch. Hodges's satī, age 24 or 25, is of the "Bhyse (merchant)" caste (Vaiśya, Pl. II.21). He describes her as with "composure and without the least trepidation." She wears a "loose robe of white flowing drapery. . . ." Hodges refers to descriptions of satī in forms different than he observed. Solvyns does not specify what he finds "not very correctly" portrayed in the Hodges print.

3 The pamphlet is not in the India Office Library or other libraries consulted nor is it cited in the bibliographies of the many books on suttee. The name "Shakespeare" does not appear in C. H. Philips's "List of Directors" in *The East India Company 1784-1834* , 335-37. Too early to be John Shakespear (1774-1858), author of an 1812 Hindustani grammar, perhaps Solvyns's author is Colin Shakespear, who designed the bridge over Tolly's Nullah in Calcutta and served as Postmaster General. Arthur W. Devis painted his portrait, c. 1790, reproduced in Nayak, 64.

4 Latin, native cinnabar; a red, or vermilion, mercuric sulfide used as a pigment. A color sacred to the Greeks as well as Hindus.

5 *Kuśa* (*Poa cynosuroides*), also known as *darbha*, is a sacred grass that is required at various Hindu rituals.

6 Henry T. Colebrooke, "On the Duties of a Faithful Hindu Widow," 206.

7 *Saṃkalpa*, meaning, in this context, a vow or declaration of the widow to burn herself with her deceased husband. Monier-Williams, 1126.

8 Henry T. Colebrooke, "On the Duties of a Faithful Hindu Widow," 214-15. The word *satya* is Sanskrit for "truth." For detailed descriptions of the ceremonial preparations for suttee, see Ahmed, 157-58, and Amitabha Mukhopadhyay, 104.

9 Personal communication, June 4, 1993. See his "The Iconographies of Sati," and *The Goddess and the Dreadful Practice*.

10 On Bengali women's dress, see Pls. II.89 and 90.

11 Engravings or lithographs after this Solvyns print appeared as "Gentoo Widow Going to be Burnt with her Dead Husband," in Ward, *A View of the History, Literature, and Religion of the Hindoos*, Vol. 1, opp. p. 375; "Ceremony of Burning a Hindu Widow with the Body of her Late Husband," acknowledged as "Painted by B. Solwyn [sic]," in Corner, litho plate opp. p. 252; and in Shoberl, Vol. 3, Pl. 40, opp. p. 99. An anonymous colored etching from 1811(V41910) in the collection of the Wellcome Institute, London, depicts Solvyns's central figures, the widow and her two brahmin attendants, in a composition with a scene of the pyre by another artist.

II.200. Anumaraṇa, Anumṛtā

Commentary: If the husband dies at some distance and is cremated there or if the suttee is postponed for some reason, the immolation of the widow is known as *anumaraṇa* , "dying after," or *anugamana*, "going after" or "to follow," as here in death. *Anumṛtā* is "one who has followed her husband in death." Solvyns uses the terms "Onnoo-gomon" and "Onnoo-mutah."

In his account of suttee, Thompson writes that *anumaraṇa* "was the term used when her lord died and was burned at a distance from her—during a campaign perhaps, or when her own death was postponed because she was pregnant; she was then burned with something that belonged to and represented her husband—his shoes or turban or some piece of clothing."[5] Various factors might result in the postponed suttee, and there are cases of widows going to the pyre as long as fifteen years after their husbands' death.[6]

Even as the British government in India reaffirmed its policy against interference in matters of the Hindu religion, suttee came under increasing official scrutiny in the early nineteenth century. In 1817, the government ruled that Hindu law did not permit brahmin widows "to ascend any other pile than that of their husbands" and that, consequently, they "could not be allowed to perform the rite of *anumarana*, or of burning after their husband's death and at a different time and place, but that they could only be allowed to perform the rite known as *sahamarana,* or burning on the same funeral pile."[7]

In the print, Solvyns depicts two attendants holding down bamboo poles as restraints in the manner described in the 1785 account "By an Officer" of the suttee he witnessed: After the wife had been secured on the pyre and "everything was ready, her eldest son came and set fire to the under part of the

Pl. II.200. Anumaraṇa, Anumr̥tā. Paris: II.10.1. Double-plate.

Calcutta: Sec. XII, No. 14. Onnoo-Gomon, or Onno-Mutah,—this represents the Wife burning herself with some apparel or property of her husband, when he had died in a distant country, or in the instance of her being prevented [from] devoting herself at the time of her husband's Corpse being burnt, by his decease happening during her pregnancy, or at the period of sexual indisposition.—The great advantage of this sacrifice is supposed to be, that it liberates both parties from Hell, and entitles them to millions of years of bliss in Heaven.—Priestcraft, in gaining its ends, looks with indifference on the sacrifice of the lives of the ignorant; and private calamities and nations deluged in blood, as tending to establish its power, must be regarded with equal unconcern, if not satisfaction:—but religious frenzy will now perhaps give way to political fanaticism.

straw: in a moment all was in a blaze. Two men kept a very long bamboo closely pressed upon the bodies . . . ."[8] In 1799, the missionary William Carey, on witnessing a suttee for the first time, wrote: "She in the most calm manner mounted the pile. . . . She lay down on the corpse, and put one arm under its neck and the other over it, when a quantity of dry cocoa-leaves and other substances were heaped over them to a considerable height, and then Ghee or melted preserved putter, poured over the top. Two bamboos were then put over them and held fast down, and the fire put to the pile. . . ."[9]

1 Thompson, in writing of suttee, 40-44, notes that "She was by no means always left free [on the pyre]. Especially in Bengal, she was often bound to the corpse with cords, or both bodies were fastened down with long bamboo poles curving over them like a wooden coverlet or weighted down by logs." In a footnote, he refers to Ram Mohan Roy in 1818 saying this custom was a recent innovation and confined to Bengal.

2 Aghoris, mendicants who are "without terror" of the impure. See discussion for Pl. II.91.

3 In a compendium of official accounts of suttee reported by the East India Company, from Fort William in Calcutta, the British House of Commons paper relating to "Hindoo Widows and Voluntary Immolations" relates instances of official intervention. *Great Britain, Parliamentary (House of Commons) Sessional Papers,* 18 (1821): 295-565. This was sometimes undertaken unofficially, as in Grandpré's unsuccessful attempt to prevent a suttee. A story long associated with Job Charnock, who founded Calcutta in 1690, is that he rescued a beautiful 15-year-old girl from her husband's pyre, took her under his protection, and married her. See Alexander Hamilson, 2:5; and Nair, *Job Charnock*, 27-28.

4 In 1799, in a village near Nadia, not far from Calcutta, 37

Paris: II.10.1: ONNOO-GOMON, OR ONNOO-MUTAH. THE WIFE BURNING HERSELF WITH SOME OF HER HUSBAND'S PROPERTY: After walking thrice round the pile, the widow ascends it with courage, places herself by the side of her dead husband and cries out three times *satiah* [*satya*]. At the same instant fire is set to the wood which is always raised a little above the ground. Dried leaves, oil, melted butter *gue* [*ghī*], (a kind of) and all sorts of combustible matters are thrown upon the pile, to put a speedier period to her sufferings. Her body is kept from moving by two bambous;[1] the flames reach it instantaneously, and in a few minutes she is consumed.

In general, this dreadful act is performed a few hours after the decease of her husband: but if he dies in distant country, it is differred on the contrary for some months, which puts the widow to a much severer trial, since during all that time she has constantly before her eyes the horrid fate which awaits her. Until the fatal period arrives, she has constantly upon her some part of the apparel, a sandal, or some other object which her husband used to wear. In all other respects, the ceremony is exactly the same as that which we have described. It must however be remarked that every country in India has some particular custom of its own, beyond what is sanctioned by the law; but the essential points are everywhere the same.

By the sacred writings this voluntary death is forbidden to women giving suck, to those who are under periodical indisposition, or who are with child, or may be supposed to be so. Except in these cases, every widow is obliged to burn herself, unless she prefers to live as a slave in her own house, to perform the meanest offices, or to become a prostitute in the public places, an outcast from all respectable society, and abandoned by her family. They have but one way to escape the infamy of such a situation, which is to become exiles in the desert, and lead the life of those *Agoorees* [Pl. II.91][2] of whom I have given a description in the second number of this volume.

It is believed in Europe, upon the word of some travellers, that the horrid ceremony represented in this print is totally out of use. It is true that examples of it are less frequent than formerly; but whoever travels at all in the Hindoo country, may still be witness of it. The English government wished to abolish this cruel custom, and the execution of it has frequently been prevented by military interference:[3] but these measures, dictated by humanity, have only rendered the Hindoos more circumspect, and they perform in secret what they are not allowed to do publicly. The widows still burn themselves with their husbands, and the death of an Hindoo is sometimes followed by the voluntary suicide even of all the women whom he kept.[4]

women became satī on the pyre of a kulīn brahmin. "At the first kindling of the fire only three of his wives were present; so the fire was kept burning for three consecutive days, while relays of widows were fetched from a distance." Amitabha Mukherjee, 241. (Kulīn polygamy involved the practice of high caste brahmins, in effect, selling themselves as husbands to a large number of women, whom they then visited in rotation. Amitabha Mukherjee, 242.)

5 *Suttee*, 15. Also see, V. N. Datta, 1, and Narasimham, 19.
6 Amitabha Mukhopadhyay, 102.
7 "Suttee," *Calcutta Review*, 228.
8 *Calcutta Gazette* , February 10, 1785. Seton-Karr, 1:91.
9 Quoted in George Smith, 108.

II.201. Sahagamana

Commentary: In the 1799 Calcutta edition, the woman leaping into the flames appears older, both in facial features and with somewhat drooping breasts. In the Paris edition, 1810, she is shown to be young, with small, firm breasts, and the accompanying text describes her as "in the first bloom of youth." Whether the difference lies in the comparatively crude etching of the Calcutta print, such that a young woman appears older, or in a conscious decision by Solvyns to change the figure to that of a young woman is not evident, but Solvyns drew the scene from life, and he repeatedly emphasizes his commitment to a faithful representation of what he observes. In "A Woman Burning Herself with the Corpse of her Husband" (Pl. II.199), the satī is seen as young in the etchings of both the Calcutta and Paris edition.

Paul Courtright, in reflecting on the images of the Solvyns prints, notes that the erotic display of bare breasts runs through many representations of suttee by European artists. Moreover, he argues, "in both Hindu myths . . . and European genre of eye-witness testimony, the wife is frequently represented as young, nubile,

Pl. II.201. Sahagamana. Paris: II.11.1. Double-plate.

Calcutta: Sec. XII, No. 15. Shoho-Gomon,—representing the Woman leaping into the fire to the Corpse of her Husband, or to some relict of the deceased,—this is allowed equally with the other modes, but seldom practiced in Bengal.

---

and virginal. Within the Hindu framework youth and innocence underscore the purity and effectiveness of the sacrifice; while for the European representations the innocence of the young wife, at the mercy of relatives, priests, and superstition, serves to stress the theme of victimization and heightens the role of the colonial as the heroic rescuer of the damsel in distress."[1]

Although European accounts of suttee typically related the sacrifice of a beautiful young woman, the practice, in reality, included women of all ages, with reported instances ranging from a girl as young as four to a 100-year-old widow, with the larger number, not surprisingly, aged 40 or above.[2]

Solvyns's vivid depiction of suttee as the woman leaps into the flames was reproduced in various publications (without attribution to the artist),[3] and it served as the model for the relief on a silver snuff box (Pl. I.59).[4] Perhaps this portrayal was favored by missionaries in their campaign against suttee because it might appear from the print alone that she is pushed by her brahmin attendant. The text makes clear, however, that she was "full of courage and resolution" and "jumped without the smallest signs of fear."

---

1 Personal communication, June 4, 1993.

2 Amitabha Mukherjee, 251. Walter Hamilton, *East India Gazetteer*, 1:205-06, provides statistics on age for the year 1823: Of 575 women who performed suttee in Bengal, 32 were below the age of 20; 208 between 20 and 40; 266 between 40 and 60; and 109 over 60.

3 Engravings of this Solvyns plate appear in Ward, *A View of the History, Literature, and Religion of the Hindoos,* Vol. 1, opp. p. 392; in Church Missionary Society, *Missionary Papers*, No. 34 (1824); in Church Missionary Society, *First Ten Years'*

Paris: II.11.1: SHOHO-GOMON. A WOMAN LEAPING INTO THE FLAMES TO THE CORPSE OF HER HUSBAND: This is a custom which seldom takes place in the countries of Hindoostan where I have chosen the greater part of the subjects of my prints. But as I was myself once present at it, I had an opportunity of making a drawing of this ceremony with all its circumstances. It seemed to me more cruel than what I have described in two foregoing numbers, and indeed it is most in vogue among the warlike tribes of the Mahrattas [Pl. II.52] and Seics [Sikhs, Pl. II.51].

The widow whom I saw burn herself, was in the first bloom of youth: she appeared nevertheless full of courage and resolution: the attending Brahmuns entertained her with their pious addresses as they led her to the pile where she jumped without the smallest signs of fear, and while she was yet crying out three times *salya* [*satya*] the flames surrounded her: her friends and relations then threw upon her different combustible matters, and in five or six minutes her body was entirely consumed; some few bones remained which were gathered up and reduced to ashes. When the dreadful ceremony was over, the Brahmuns returned with the family of the unhappy widow, and received as they went the compliments of the public for having performed an act of devotion from which they derive the highest consideration in the eyes of this fanatick people.

The women, especially the wives of the Brahmuns, are instigated by their blind superstition to choose this mode of death: they look upon it as a duty to evince in the midst of torture their superiority over other women whom they look upon as much beneath them. And yet it often happens that there is very little affection between the Brahmuns and their wives, to whom they are sometimes married almost against their consent. I shall mention a strange practice w[h]ich I had an opportunity of observing during my stay in India. When a father of a family has a daughter of an age to be married and has not the means of making a suitable provision for her, he invites under some pretext a Brahmun of his acquaintance to his house: as soon as he appears the father presents him his daughter; she, out of respect, offers him her hand, which the Brahmun takes without any suspicion; immediately the father begins to repeat the genealogy of the family: this simple ceremony is sufficient; the marriage can not be dissolved. It not unfrequently happens that the Brahmun is unable to support his young wife; be that as it may, the father has saved her from the reproach of remaining a maid, and his daughter enjoys the honors due to the wife of a Brahmun.

Quarterly Papers of the Church Missionary Society; and in Dumont d'Urville, Pl. XVII, 3, opp. 1:134. Paul Thomas, *Hindu Religion, Custom and Manners*, Pl. 93, reproduces the Solvyns print from the Paris edition.

4 The other side of the box portrays Solvyns's scene of Caṛak Pūjā, "hook-swinging," Pl. II.193. On the snuff box, see pp. 109-10.

II.202. Sahagamana

Commentary: Few European accounts of suttee make reference to the burial of the widow with her husband, and Solvyns provides a comparatively rare description[2] and one of the few visual depictions of the rite.[3] In his portrayal, the widow stands with her palms together in an attitude of devotion as she prepares to join her husband. In the Calcutta etching, she is bare-headed, but in the Paris print, depicted here, Solvyns, in conformity with his descriptive text, places a *khicuṛī* pot upon her head. He depicts a grave that is circular and a ladder by which the widow will descend.[4] The musicians are seen to the left in the print, and a European—perhaps a Company official—stands shaded by an umbrella and attended by several guards as he watches the ceremony.

Ward, as does Solvyns, notes that widows of the Jugi ("Yogee" for Ward) community—a caste of weavers—were sometimes buried alive with their deceased husbands. "If the person have died near the Ganges, the grave is dug by the side of the river; at the bottom of which they spread a new cloth, and on it lay the dead body. The widow then bathes, puts on new clothes and paints her feet, and after various ceremonies, descends into the pit that is to swallow her up; in this living tomb she sits down, and places the head of her deceased husband on her knee, having

Pl. II.202. Sahagamana. Paris: II.12.1. Double-plate.
Calcutta: Sec. XII, No. 16. Shoho-Gomon,—the Wife of the Joggee buried alive with the Corpse of her Husband,—after her descending into the Pit, it is instantly filled up with earth by her relations and other attendants.—The Joggee, and the race of Facquirs, called Visnubs [Baiṣṇabs, Vaiṣṇavas], are the only classes of the Hindoos, whose bodies are buried.

a lamp near her. The priest (not a brahmun) sits by the side of the grave, and repeats certain ceremonies, while the friends of the deceased walk round the grave several times [repeating incantations. The friends cast various offering into the grave.] The son also casts a new garment into the grave, with flowers, sandal wood &c. after which earth is carefully thrown all round the widow, till it is has risen as high as her shoulders, when the relations throw earth as fast as possible, till they have raised a mound of earth on the grave, when they treat it down with their feet, and thus bury this miserable wretch alive . . . ."[5]

Most Hindus are cremated, but burial is used among some caste communities, most notably in South India, and for certain classes of individuals—religious ascetics (*yogīs*, *sādhus*, and *sannyāsīs*), young children, and those who die by violence or with such diseases as cholera or small-pox.[6] The Jugis, however, seem to have been alone—at least in Bengal—in suttee burial. Mythically, the Jugi weavers claim descent from an ascetic, who on his death was buried, following the custom for yogis. Risley, in *The Tribes and Castes of Bengal*, writes that "On the burial of their dead all Jugīs observe the same ceremonies. The grave . . . is circular, about eight feet deep, and at the bottom a niche is cut for the reception of the corpse. The body, after being washed with water from seven earthen jars, is wrapped in new cloth, the lips touched with fire to distinguish the funeral from that of a *sannyāsi* or ascetic and a Mahomedan. . . . The body being lowered into the grave, and placed in the niche with the face towards the north-east [sacred to Śiva], the grave is filled in . . . ."[7] By the time of Risley's account in 1891, suttee among the Jugis (to which he makes no reference) had long been suppressed.

In 1813, there was an official inquiry into the

Paris: II.12.1: SHOHO-GOMON. THE WIFE OF AN HINDOO BURIED ALIVE: Besides the Faquirs and *Beeshnubs* [Baiṣṇabs, Vaiṣṇavas], the *Joogees* [Jugis, Pl. II.27], dealers in cloth and weavers, are the only people among the Hindoos who bury their dead: the cruel custom therefore of widows burying themselves alive with the bodies of their husbands, exists only in this division of the working cast, and is confined moreover to the country of Orissah and that of the Marattas. Travellers who visit only Bengal and Behar have very seldom an opportunity of witnessing these fanatic ceremonies, which I shall describe exactly as I saw them. When the widow of a *Joogee* has signified her intention to bury herself with her deceased husband, her family dig a grave from six to eight feet deep, into which the body of the husband is let down, and placed sitting with the hands joined. The widow then approaches the grave, escorted as in the ceremonies which we have already described by a solemn procession. She bathes before the public without giving occasion to the slightest scandal, being already considered, from the sanctity of the death she has chosen, as a supernatural being. At the edge of the grave she listens to the pious exhortations of the Brahmuns who accompany her, gives them her jewels, and after placing upon her head a *cudjery* [*khicuṛī*][1] or pot filled with rice, plantains, betel and water, makes her farewell salutations to the assistants with her hands joined. She descends into the grave by a ladder of bambou which is instantly drawn up again. She seats herself by the side of her husband; at that moment all the instruments hired for the ceremony are heard, and the relations throw such quantities of earth upon the unfortunate widow, that she is soon suffocated and interred. The preparations for this ceremony are horrid, but it does not appear that the sufferings of the unhappy victim are of long duration.

The print is an exact copy of what I observed; even the little eminence is there, from which I witnessed this scene: but the pencil can not convey the dreadful sensations it gave rise to. We can not refuse our pity to the poor Hindoo women who are sacrificed to this ancient and barbarous custom; but their courage, firmness, and resignation, entitles them to some share of admiration. While their husband lives they are slaves, when he dies they must be ready to resign in the most cruel manner a life of which they never tasted the enjoyments. In no part of the universe are women born to so dismal a prospect.

Jugi practice of burial suttee. The case involved a Jugi woman who, "at her own request," asked to be buried with her husband. British officials, consulting Pundits on their reading of the *Dharma Śāstra*, Hindu legal text, determined that "the practice was in conformity with the Shasters" and that it was not to be enjoined.[8] But with mounting pressure for reform, in 1829, the Governor-General, Lord Bentinck, outlawed "the practice of suttee; or of burning or burying alive the widows of the Hindoos. . . ."

---

1 Solvyns uses the Bengali term for a one pot dish of rice, dhal, and vegetables that is often used as a ritual offering. *Hobson-Jobson*, 477, lists *kedgeree-pot* as a vulgar Anglo-Indian expression for a pipkin, or small earthenware cooking pot, with Solvyns as a reference in usage.

2 Shoberl, 3:127-29, acknowledging his source, follows Solvyns's description almost word for word, but, oddly, adds that burial suttee "is followed only is Orissah and the Mahratta country, by widows of cloth-dealers and weavers."

3 Picart provides an earlier portrayal based on written reports of burial, reproduced in Okada and Isacco, 90. Solvyns's print is copied, without acknowledgment, in an engraving in Church Missionary Society, *Missionary Papers*, 32 (1823), and is reproduced in *First Ten Years' Quarterly Papers of the Church Missionary Society.*

4 Solvyns's depiction of a circular grave is confirmed by later descriptions and confirms the link of the Jugi weavers to the *yogī* mendicants, who also bury their dead in circular graves, described by Briggs, 40. Johan Splinter Stavorinus, a Dutch admiral, however, after describing a widow-burning he witnessed in Bengal in about 1770, provides an account of a suttee burial in which the woman "jumps" into a pit that is six foot square. 1:451.

5 Ward, 3:323. Perhaps the most detailed account of a Jugi suttee burial is by Captain Kemp in 1813, related in a compilation of accounts of "Widows and others Buried Alive," in Johns, 67-68. Suttee among Jugis is also described in Ambitabha Mukhopadhyay, 104-05.

6 Burial among ascetics is based on the theory that they have renounced their household fires and thus have no fire for cremation, but there is also a popular perception that they are not truly dead. See Briggs, 39-43. With variation in practice among regions and castes, children below the age of three are buried rather than cremated because they are not yet fully "persons." See Parry, 184-88, and Kane, 4:227-31.

7 Risley, *The Tribes and Castes of Bengal*, 1:359.

8 See *Great Britain. Parliamentary (House of Commons) Sessions Papers*, 18, (1821): 332-33.

Modes of Smoking, &c.

Tobacco was introduced into India by the Portuguese in the early seventeenth century. The first Englishman to mention it was Edward Terry, who served nearly three years in western India (1616-1619) as chaplain to Sir Thomas Roe, and he was the first to describe the *hukā* (hookah).[1] By the eighteenth century, the cultivation and use of tobacco was widespread in India, and smoking was a means of relaxation and, among friends, of socializing enjoyed by men of virtually all classes and, as Solvyns portrays, by women as well.

In his observations on India in 1805, Roberdeau, a civil officer in Bengal, wrote, "The Natives universally and invariably smoke, from Childhood to old age, from the Beggar to the prince: tobacco, opium, and other intoxicating Drugs."[2] "The Tobacco," he wrote, "undergoes great preparation. It is first soaked and beat to pieces till it becomes of the consistence of a paste. It is then mixt up with Rose-water, Musk, Raisins, the fruit of the plantain, persian apples, or whatever pleases your palate best. Afterwards it is put into a large Earthen pot well covered up and buried some feet under Ground where it must remain a month or two and will then be fit for use. It is the pleasantest thing in the World & the tobacco thus prepared diffuses a very fragrant smell throughout the Room. . . . It is certainly the most elegant way of using Tobacco."[3]

In these preparations, tobacco was sometimes only a small component, and opium was frequently included. Ladies liked a "mixture of sweet-scented Persian tobacco, sweet herbs, coarse sugar, spice, etc." as ingredients for their *hukā*.[4] In his etching, "A Woman of Distinction" (Pl. II.87), Solvyns depicts a *hukā*, and his image of the woman was copied by another artist for inclusion in an 1809 print, "A Smoking Party in the Province of Bengal" (Pl. I.55).

In nine etchings, Solvyns portrays the various modes of smoking peculiar to social rank or income, from the meanest *chilim* or *nārikel* to the most elegant *hukā*, and in another print, depicts the enjoyment of pān. In the Preliminary Discourse to *Les Hindoûs*, Vol. I, he writes,

> Quiet is the happiest state of life to the peaceable Hindoo: as soon consequently as his business is done, and that he can gave himself up to his natural indolence and smoke his houka in repose, he enjoys his utmost notion of happiness, and remains hours together without stirring from his place or changing his attitude, which to us Europeans would be a very uneasy one. The postures of the Hindoo at rest and smoking are indisputably very original, and I thought myself under an obligation to bring them into the pictoresque description of this people. Their very mode of smoking differs materially from that of Europeans. As it has never been faithfully represented in the prints yet published, it appeared to me to require great exactness in the drawings that I took, which give even the most minute circumstances.[5]

In the Introduction to *Les Hindoûs*, Vol. III, Solvyns writes that he seeks to provide

> a notion of a custom common to all the nations who inhabit India, and which has grown into an imperious want among the greater part of them, particularly among the Hindoos; I mean the use of tobacco and of Betel. If at first it should seem extraordinary that I should employ two whole numbers [ten prints] for a practice which appears to us so insignificant, we must enter into the details with which I have accompanied them. It will then be seen that the Hooka [*hukā*] or tobacco pipe, constitutes the greatest enjoyment of the Hindoo, that to it he gives up the greater part of the day, and would with pleasure sacrifise his meat and drink if it were necessary. He gives but little time to his dress and meals, but in return he thinks he cannot devote too much to his dear Hooka: in it is all his society, his all that

makes life agreeable. From the richest Radjah [rājā] to the most miserable Palanquin bearer, the Hindoo knows no greater pleasure than to smoke his Hooka, and enjoy for hours together the sort of charm which the vapour of the tobacco produces: keep the Hooka going, and the labouring class will never refuse the hardest labour, or complain of the most violent fatigue. It will be seen in the text, that the enjoyments of the Hooka begin at the earliest age, and grow insensibly into a habit. This favorite instrument of all the castes, varies in its appearance with the fortune of its employer. The rich man displays his luxury in decking his Hooka with ornaments of gold and silver, while a simple Cocoa nut is the Hooka of the poor. All these variations are given in the tenth and eleventh numbers [the following prints].[6]

---

1 Laufer, 11-12.

2 122, in Nair, *Calcutta in the 19th Century*, 50.

3 121-22, in Nair, *Calcutta in the 19th Century*, 50. On the preparation, also see Gilchrist, 117-22; Stocqueler, *Oriental Interpreter*, 101; and Gold, text for Pl. 44, "Smoking the Hooka."

4 *Price's Tracks*, 1782, in *Hobson-Jobson*, 424.

5 1:26, and in Chapter Four, p.122.

6 3:3.

II.203. Nārikel

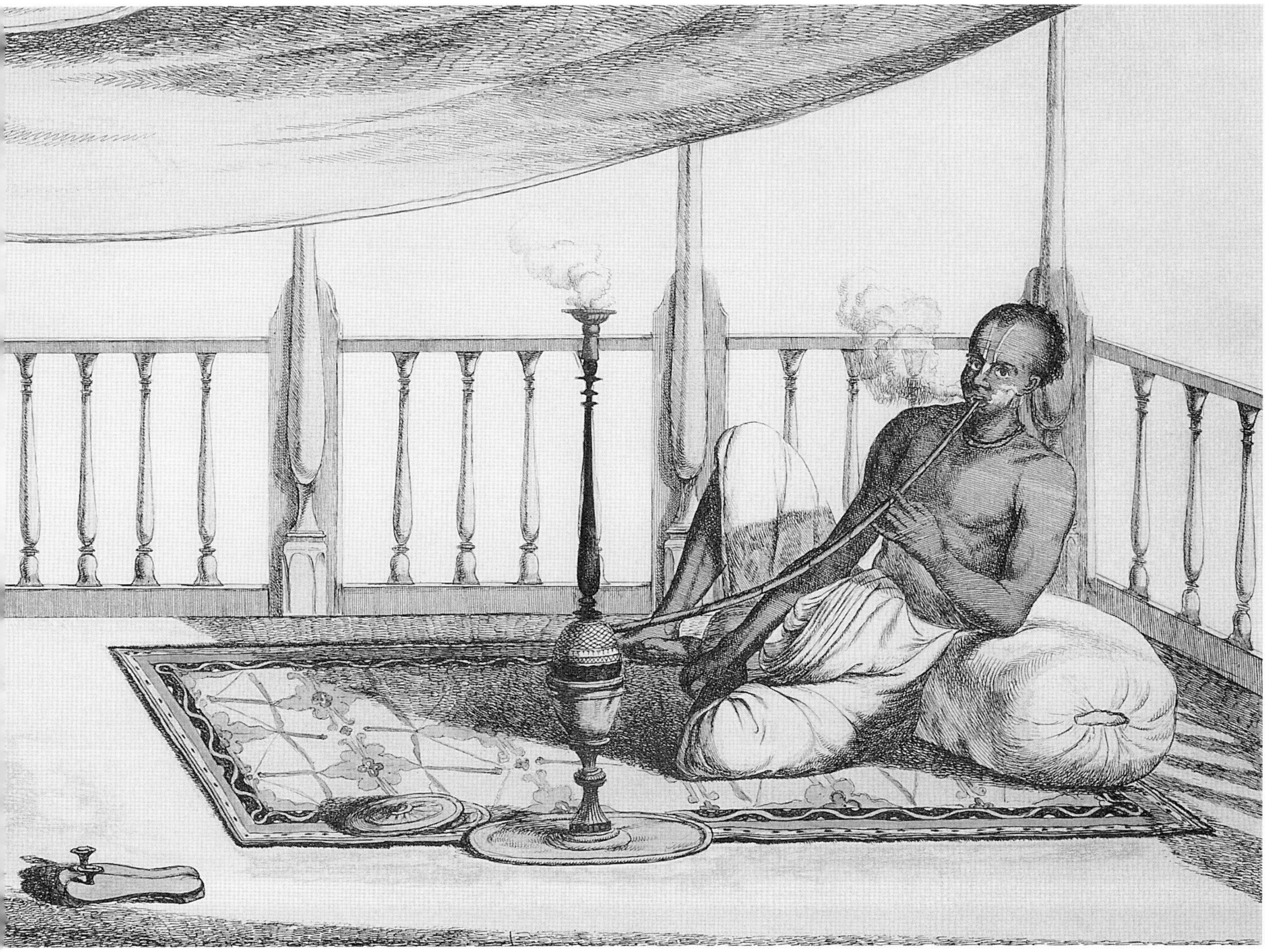

Pl. II.203. Nārikel. Paris: III.10.2.

Calcutta: Sec. X, No. 1. Narial, or Cocoanut Shell Hookas,—the first, represents the method of smoking through a Tube made of Plantain leaf.

Orme: 44.

Paris: III.10.2. NARIAL HOOKA: I shall now notice the different manners of smoking among the Hindoos. Their pipes are of various sorts. That by which I begin is made of a cocoa nut, or *Narial*, and placed in a copper vase. A banana leaf rolled up is put into the hole of the nut to cool the smoke which comes through the *Houka*. The *Narial* is ornamented in silver, tin, or copper, and sometimes nicely worked, so as to become an object of luxury. The Hindoo does not like to lend his *Houka*, and never allows another to smoke through the same pipe as he. This custom is religiously observed amongst all casts.

Commentary: The Anglo-Indian "narial" (also "nargeela," or "narghile") and Bengali *nārikel* is from the Persian *nārgīleh*, a water pipe made from a coconut (*nārgiī*) shell.[1] It is the simplest form of the *hukā*, also a term of Persian derivation.

In the *nārikel* portrayed by Solvyns, a pipe stem inserted through a hole in the top of the coconut holds the *chilim*, the small terracotta bowl for the hot coals and tobacco. The coconut is half-filled with water and the pipe reaches into the water. Through a hole on the upper side of the coconut, above the water, a rolled banana leaf (or reed), from ten inches to two or three feet in length, is inserted. When the smoker draws on the tube, the smoke is pulled down through the water, with a bubbling sound, and thus cooled.

Solvyns here depicts a *nārikel* that in his note to the original drawing he associates with "the superior orders." The coconut, itself ornamented, rests in a vase-like receptacle made of copper (or of other fine metals).

The pegged wooden sandals (*pādukā*), in the left foreground of the print, are worn by gripping the peg between the toes.

Solvyns's reference to the Hindu's refusal to share his pipe relates to concern for ritual pollution, for contact with the saliva of another person is highly polluting. In fact, as his own saliva is polluting, the most scrupulous observance requires the smoker to avoid direct contact with the tube or mouthpiece by closing his fist around it and placing his lips only against his own hand.

1 Balfour, 2:99, uses the term "narial"; *Hobson-Jobson*, 618, uses "nargeela" or "nargileh"; and the *OED* and *American Heritage Dictionary* both give "narghile."

II.204. Nārikel

Pl. II.204a. Nārikel. Calcutta: Sec. X, No. 2.

Calcutta: Sec. X, No. 2. Narial, or Cocoanut Shell Hookas,—through a Bamboo.

Pl. II.204b. Nārikel. Paris: III.10.3.

Commentary: The *nārikel* depicted in this print is without the metal base and is fitted with a bamboo rather than rolled banana leaf, but with its ornamented shell is otherwise similar to that Solvyns portrays earlier.

Beside the woman are what appear to be a small brass pot and covered pan, likely used for the tobacco mixture.

In the Paris edition, Solvyns portrays the two figures included in the Calcutta etching (Pl. II.204a) in separate prints (II.204b and II.205).

Paris: III:10.3. NARIAL HOOKA: This species of *Houka* is also made of a cocoanut, but instead of being placed in a copper vaser is set on the ground. The vapour is drawn out, as in the preceding one, through a bambou pipe. The person whom I have represented smoking, is a woman setting on a piece of wood. There does indeed exist a law of Menu [Manu] which forbids the Hindoo women to smoke, but of all his laws this is the least observed. Through all Hindoostan women make no scruple of smoking publicly; they take the same delight in it as the men, and shew the same repugnance to allow another person to make use of their *Houka*. The Mahometans who are established in India, and who have adopted so many of their customs, imitate them also in this scrupulous delicacy without perhaps knowing the cause of it.

II.205. Nārikel

Paris: III.10.4. NARIAL HOOKA: This differs from the two former by the absence of all ornament, and is used frequently by the working classes. The one who is standing before his door, enjoys the luxury of smoking with all the indolence of the richest and idlest Hindoo.

The substance smoked is always the same, but is suited to the luxury and appetites of the smokers. Sometimes it consists of tobacco mixed with *Gaur* [*gur*] (sugar)[1] or aromatics, sometimes of different preparations. The plant of betel is in great favour with the ladies, who not only smoke it, but have it constantly in their mouth; which produces an effect disagreeable to Europeans who are not accustomed to it. The cocoanut of the *Houka* is kept always half full of water, so that the vapour is rendered more agreeable by passing through the water before it reaches the lips.

Pl. II.205. Nārikel. Paris: III.10.4
Calcutta: Sec. X, No. 2. Narial, or Cocoanut Shell Hookas,—through a Bamboo.

Commentary: In his note to the original drawing, upon which the Calcutta print (Pl. II.204a) was based, Solvyns described his portrayal as the "mode of smoking by the lower class, thro a small plantain leaf or a long hollow cane." The class association is suggested by the man's simple coconut rather than the woman's ornamented *nārikel*, and this is perhaps why Solvyns chose to separate the two figures for portrayal in the Paris edition. Both the man and the woman, however, appear to be of "clean" caste, and Solvyns portrays the lowest castes with a different modes of smoking.

Solvyns makes several comments on the popularity of *pān*—the betel leaf preparation—among both men and women and describes its preparation in a separate print (Pl. II.212).

1 Gur is a coarse sugar or molasses made from sugarcane.

II.206. Nārikel

Paris: III.10.5. NARIAL HOOKA: The Hindoos frequently smoke the *Narial Hooka*, without using a pipe to draw the vapour, by approaching the opening of the nut to their mouth, and haling it through the palm of their hand. This way of smoking is very common in Hindoostan, as well among the richer as the lower classes: they call it *Hubbel* of *Bubbel*. The attitude in which they place themselves is very singular; the print only can give an idea of it: it is by no means uneasy for a people so lightly clad, or whose body is as it were only draped; it would be very different for Europeans. The Hindoos pique themselves upon the beauty of the cocoa nut of their pipes, and rub them with cocoa or mustard oil to give them a fine black colour. They frequently also renew the water in the vase, and pretend that, from the smell it has contracted, it keeps serpents from the spot where it is thrown. I have found this opinion confirmed by my own experience.

Commentary: Dispensing with the tube, here the smoker places his mouth (or fist to avoid direct contact) to the hole on the side of the coconut and draws the smoke. This is the simplest *nārikel*, and in his note to the original drawing, Solvyns writes that it is "used by the lowest class of Natives." Perhaps on second thought, however, in the Paris text, he describes it as common among the richer as well as lower classes.

In this rudimentary form, the pipe was known among Europeans as the "hubble bubble," an onomatopoeia for its gurgling.[1] The term came to be used more generally for any small *hukā*.

Solvyns takes the occasion of this print to comment on the squatting position, favored by Indians, that Europeans found so hard upon both the trousers and the knees.

Pl. II.206. Nārikel. Paris: III.10.5.
Calcutta: Sec. X, No. 3. Narial, or Cocoanut Shell Hookas,—the common way through the hand, is called the Hubbul-Bubbul.

1 *Hobson-Jobson*, 428.

II.207. Chilim

Pl. II.207. Chilim. Paris: III.10.6.

Calcutta: Sec. X, No. 7. Smoking the Chillum by the lower order.

Paris: III.10.6. CHILLUM: The Hindoos give this name to the part of the Hooka which contains the tobacco and the fire. Those who have not the means to procure a Narial must be satisfied with a *Chillum*, which they hold in one hand while they inhale the vapour through the hollow of either of their hands. They have not the same scruples for the *Chillum*, as for the rest of the Hooka, and it is often lent even among people of rank; whereas the very proposition for the Hooka gives rise frequently to the most ridiculous quarrels, in which each party endeavours to debase his adversary, and to prove to him that he is not of so high a cast as his vanity would have it thought.

Commentary: The *chilim* is the small bowl, usually of terracotta, that holds the hot charcoal ball (the *gul*) and the tobacco mixture. In popular parlance, the term refers collectively to the bowl, coal, and smoking ingredients, and is also applied to the replenishment of the bowl, as one might ask for "another glass."[1] In the *nārikel* and *hukā,* the *chilim* is attached to the pipe stem, but among the poor, it is smoked in the manner Solvyns describes. That it may be shared without pollution comes from the way in which it is held, with the mouth having no direct contact with the *chilim.*

The need for charcoal comes from the nature of the smoking mixture. Among the masses, for example, the tobacco is cut finely cut and kneaded with molasses and a little water into a pulp. "Hence actual contact with glowing charcoal is need to keep it alight."[2]

1 *Hobson-Jobson*, 195.
2 *Hobson-Jobson*, 195. Also see Lal Behari Day, 20.

II.208. Snake Hukā

Paris: III.11.2. SNAKE HOOKA: This is the *Hooka* of the richer classes, and that which the Europeans have adopted. The foot rests upon a rich carpet, or a matt, as represented in the print; it is half filled with cold water as all others, with which two pipes of bambou communicate, one contains the tobacco in a paste, with a burning coal: by the other which is longer and more flexible the vapour is inhaled. This pipe is made of wire surrounded with dried leaves, and covered with a rich stuff enlaced with gold or silver wire, the foot is of gold, gilded, plain silver, or some other precious matter. This instrument which frequently costs several hundred pounds, becomes an object of great expence.

Commentary: The term *hukā* is from the Arabic *ḥuqqah*, the water bottle through which the tobacco smoke passes to cool and, by way of Persia, came to refer the whole apparatus.

European accounts of India in the late eighteenth and early nineteenth centuries frequently had detailed descriptions of this "Oriental smoking machine."[1] The conical- or bell-shaped bottom, some

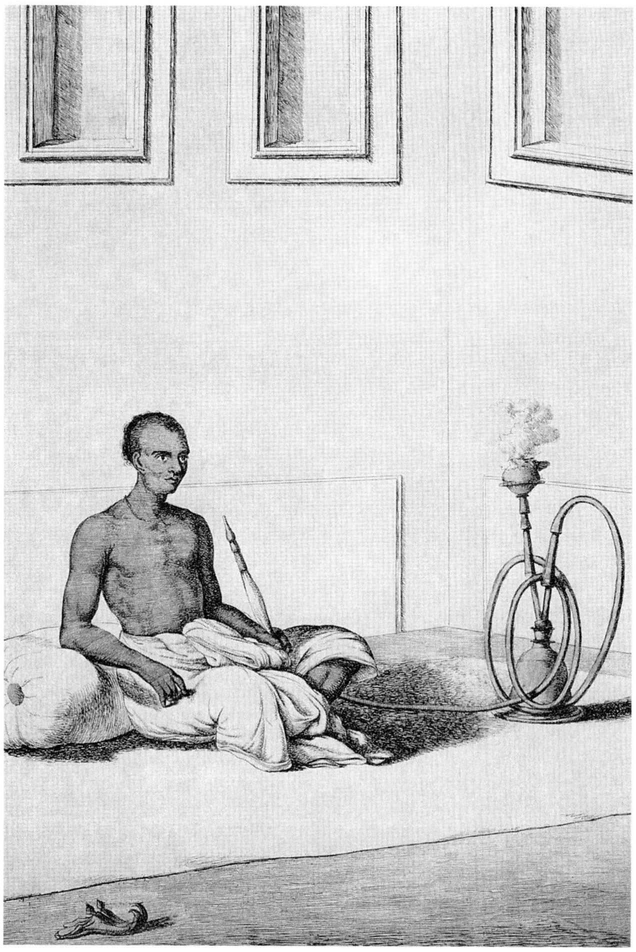

Pl.II.208. Snake Hukā. Paris: III.11.2.
Calcutta: Sec. X, No. 4. A Hooka Snake, formed of twisted wire, leaves, bark and cloth.

ten inches high, is typically made of metal—silver, gold, or more frequently the black pewter alloy *bidrī*[2]—or of imported European glass, and is filled half to two-thirds with cold water (often rose-water). A vertical bamboo tube is inserted into the "bottom" so that it is immersed in the water about three inches. The tube, a foot or more in height, is topped by the *chilim*, the terracotta (sometimes china) bowl or "receiver." This supports an earthen tile under which the tobacco mixture is affixed as a paste. Three or four charcoal fire balls (*gul*), prepared from burnt rice, are placed, red hot, on the tile, causing smoke to arise from the tobacco preparation below. A silver (or gold) cover is placed over the *chilim* so that the smoke may be more readily be drawn down through the water for the smoker's pleasure.

The "snake" or flexible smoking tube is the most distinctive feature of the *hukā*. The snake is made by coiling wire around a rope three-quarters of an inch in diameter and covering it with the paper-thin bark of a tree resembling birch. This in turn is covered with white cloth and then with black or purple silk or with silver or gold thread. The rope is removed to produce a tube of typically eight to ten feet in length. The snake must be cleaned daily with a horse-hair rope, and it will last only some three months, as it becomes foul with continual use and the wire corrodes. The mouth-piece of the snake is about five inches long and may be made of amber, agate, *bidrī*, silver, or gold, some even set with diamonds and other precious stones. The snake is inserted into the upper part of *hukā* "bottom," into the chamber above the water level, and as the smoker inhales, the sweet smoke is drawn down from the *chilim* and through the cooling water.

Among eighteenth and early nineteenth century European travelers in India, the *hukā* drew comment, especially on its adoption by European residents. Its use by Europeans is first recorded in an inventory of 1675, and a century later the *hukā* had "come into fashion with increasing wealth and ostentation."[3] Stanhope, in a letter from Calcutta in 1774, wrote, "Most of the gentlemen, who have resided any length of time in India, are much addicted to the Hooka, a most curious machine for smoking tobacco through water, the smoke being conveyed by a tube of amazing length, which is called a snake, and is washed with rose-water. Even the writers [clerks], whose salary and perquisites scarce amount to two hundred pounds a year, contrive to be attended wherever they go by their Hooka-burdaar [hukābardār, Pl. II.108], or servant, whose duty it is to replenish the Hooka with the necessary ingredients, and to keep up the fire with his breath."[4] In extending invitations to friends for a concert and supper in 1779, the Governor-General Warren Hastings and his wife requested that no servants be brought "except a *houccabardar*."[5]

According to Grandprè, who visited India just before Solvyns's arrival, "It is chiefly in Bengal, where smoking after meals is customary, that the *hooka* is in use. Every *hooka-brodar* prepares separately that of his master in an adjoining apartment, and, entering all together with the desert, they range around the table. . . . It is scarcely possible to see through the cloud of smoke which fills the apartment. . . . The rage of smoking extends even to the ladies; and the highest compliment they can pay a man is to give him preference by smoking his hooka. In this case it is a point of politeness to take off the mouth-piece he is using, and substitute a fresh one, which he presents to the lady with his hooka, who soon returns it. . . . Tobacco forms but a small part of the ingredients that are burnt in this instrument: dried fruits, sugar, and many other things are made use of, which added to the rose-water with which the tube of the instrument is wetted, give a taste and fragrance to the smoke that are extremely agreeable; and the smoke too, by passing through the water before it reaches the mouth, acquires a coolness that renders it still more pleasant."[6]

Roberdeau, in Calcutta in 1805, provides a detailed description: "Soon after the second course has been placed on the Table the Gentlemen's *Hookahs* are brought in by the respective Hookahburdars. A handsome Carpet is first spread behind the Chair to prevent the 'Snake' being soiled, the Hookahburdar then puts the Snake under the arm of the Chair . . . into the Gentleman's hand and he begins puffing away."[7] It was regarded as a "dire offense" to step over another person's small *hukā* carpet or snake, and men who did so intentionally were "called out."[8] Having enjoyed the "first houkah" at table, "inveterate smokers have their houkahs transferred to the drawing-room,"[9] where "Nicotine in fairest form held smoothing sway."[10]

"Imagine," Lady Nugent recorded in her journal in 1812, "half of the men of a large company, puffing and blowing, and the hookahs making an extraordinary noise—some a deep bass, others, a bubbling treble—the variety of cadence depends, I believe, on the length of the snake, and the quantity of rose-water poured into the receptacle for it."[11]

The *hukā*, however, like the Anglo-Indian taste for the nautch (Pl. II.195), was beginning to fall out of favor, in part, no doubt because of the enormous expense involved in its use. As early as 1792, it was excluded from assembly rooms, and by Lady Nugent's time, its use had been banned at Government House, but even into the 1840s and later, the *hukā's* soft gurgle could still be heard in the houses of the old Nabobs.[12] The new generation of officers and merchants preferred after dinner to retire for "segars" and brandy.

As in European descriptions of life in India, the *hukā* was frequently included in European portrayals of the Indian scene. Solvyns, on the title page of *Les Hindoûs*, Volume IV, portrays himself with a snake *hukā* (Pl. I.1, frontispiece). Charles Gold, Solvyns's South Indian counterpart, in a drawing from the 1790s, depicts a European and an Indian smoking *hukās* as they play chess;[13] Charles D'Oyly includes a comic print, "A Gentleman with his Hookah-Burdar," in *The European in India*;[14] and Mrs. Belnos illustrates a European gentleman at home with his *hukā*, as he and his wife examine the wares of a silk merchant.[15] Emily Eden did a watercolor of her nephew relaxing with his *hukā* and attended by the hukābardār and "punkahwalla" with fan,[16] and James Moffat portrays a similar scene in the Writer's Building.[17] An unsigned colored engraving accompanying an anonymous poem, "Calcutta," celebrates the *hukā* with the inscription, "But give me, Gods, to catch, in spacious tent,/My Hookah's breathe & Chillum's grateful scent."[18]

Francesco Renaldi, in 1787, painted a Muslim lady holding the stem of her snake *hukā*,[19] and Thomas Daniell, in his oil painting, "A Zenana Scene," c. 1804, portrays a Muslim woman of rank with her *hukā*.[20] An 1809 print, "A Smoking Party in the Province of Bengal" (Pl. I.55), combines Solvyns's image of "A Woman of Distinction" (Pl. II.87) with two reclining Indian men and, as its centerpiece, a coiled snake *hukā*.

Solvyns portrays the snake *hukā* carried by the hukābardār (Pl. II.108), as does Orme, in the pirated edition of Solvyns's Calcutta etchings.[21]

---

1 The following description is drawn from Roberdeau, 121, in Nair, *Calcutta in the 19th Century*, 49-50; Williamson's text to Charles D'Oyly's comic print, "A Gentleman with his Hookah-Burdar," in *The European in India*, Pl. X; Nair's note to Horne ("Naufragus"), in *Calcutta in the 19th Century*, n. 9, p. 441; Mundy, 298, in Nair, *Calcutta in the 19th Century*, 481; Gold, text to Pl. 44; and Orme, *Costumes of Indostan*, text for Pl. 18.

2 *Bidrī* takes its name from Bidar in the Deccan, where the metal-ware is chiefly made. "The ground of the work is pewter alloyed with one-fourth copper: this is inlaid (or damascened) with patterns in silver; and then the pewter ground is blackened." *Hobson-Jobson*, 93. Solvyns refers to this "black compound" in his description of the *gaṛgarā* (Pl. II.209).

3 Spear, *The Nabobs*, 36.

4 50-51, in Nair, *Calcutta in the 19th Century*, 170.

5 H. E. A. Cotton, *Calcutta Old and New*, 77.

6 2:12-13. Also see Dewar, *In the Days of the Company*, 53-63; Charles R. Wilson and W. H. Carey, 174; Goldsborne, 16, and notes, 295-96.

7 121, in Nair, *Calcutta in the 19th Century*, 49.

8 Major-General R. H. Keating, quoted in *Hobson-Jobson*, 424.

9 Mundy, 298-99, in Nair, *Calcutta in the 19th Century*, 481.

10 Blechynden, 108.

11 1:107.

12 *Hobson-Jobson*, 423-24; Suresh Chandra Ghosh, 146; and Blechynden, note 3, p. 198.
13 "Smoking the Hooka," Pl. 44.
14 Pl. 10, with Williamson's accompanying text. The print is reproduced as the frontispiece, "The Nabob at Home," in Spear.
15 *Twenty-Four Plates Illustrative of Hindoo and European Manners in Bengal*, Pl. 13, "Cloth and Silk Merchant."
16 Reproduced in Mahajan, 34, and in Rudrangshu Mukherjee, 50.
17 Reproduced in Rudrangshu Mukherjee, 51.
18 *Calcutta: A Poem* (1811). See Abbey, 452, Entry No. 493.
19 Reproduced in Mildred Archer and Lightbown, *India Observed*, 38, and Nayak, 90.
20 Mildred Archer and Lightbown, *India Observed*, Pl. IV and p. 43.
21 Pl. 18.

II.209. Gaṛgarā

Paris: III.11.3. GOURGOURY HOOKA: Though of Hindoo origin this species of *Hooka* is not at present most used in Hindoostan, except by women of foreign extraction, such as Musulmans, Moguls, Persians and Portuguese,[1] especially the latter who use no other. It is common in the grand Bazars. These *Hookas* are made of copper, or tin, or more frequently of a black composition [*bidrī*],[2] which is prefered, because it keeps the water cooler, and the part of the pipe which is put in the mouth is of the same substance. It is inlaid with gold and silver, and sometimes ornamented in a tollerably good taste. The Hindoo woman whom I represent here smoking the Gougoury is of an inferior cast in upper Hindoostan, where the custom is somewhat different from that of Bengal. The dress is frequently of various colours, and surrounded by very large borders. They wear a sort of jacket, loose pantalons and shoes. It seems that the further we go from Bengal, the less we meet the original customs of the nation.

Pl. II.209. Gaṛgarā. Paris: III.11.3.

Commentary: Solvyns associates the *gaṛgarā* (a word of Turkish origin) with "foreign" women. Williamson describes it as a small *hukā* used by Europeans in palanquins and in being carried about the house: The smoker holds the vase-shaped bottom by its neck and draws the smoke through "a stiff, instead of a pliant pipe, formed of a reed, arched into such a shape as should conduct its end conveniently to the mouth."[3]

Solvyns's depicts the woman beside a spinning wheel, with a curious—and improbable—image in a small temple in the background. Despite Solvyns's commitment to portray only what he saw, the image depicted here seems more likely a product of his imagination—or, perhaps, his memory of the popular Tavernier/Picart engraving of Hindu "penitents" that portrays a similar head filling a small temple (Pl. I.42).[4]

1 On the Indo-Portuguese, see Commentary for Pl. II.6.
2 See Pl. II.208, fn. 2.
3 *The East India Vade-Mecum*, 1:227. Williamson again describes the *gaṛgarā* and discusses its use in the text accompanying D'Oyly's print of "A Native Gentleman Smoking a Goorgoory," Pl. 19, *The European in India*.
4 For a discussion of the engraving, also see introduction to Solvyns's series of etchings of "Fakirs or Religious Mendicants," p. 309.

II.210. Kaliyūm

Pl. II.210. Kaliyūm. Paris: III.11.4.
Calcutta: Sec. X, No. 5. A Persian Cullyaun.

Paris: III.11.4. CULLYAUN HOOKA: We must not confound the *Cullyaun* of the Hindoos with the Persian *Cullyaun,* to which as many pipes are adopted as there are persons in company, and which are used frequently by twenty individuals at a time. The Indian *Cullyaun* is a species of the Gourgoury which we have just described: differing in size and in the form of the pipe as appears in the engraving. The *Cullyaun* comes from upper Hindoostan, and is seldom met with elsewhere. The Hindoo whom I have represented is a merchant of that country: he is indolently laying before his shop inhaling voluptuously the sweet vapour of his tobacco, to which he knows no enjoyment to be compared.

Commentary: In the Paris text, Solvyns warns against confusing the Indian *kaliyūm* (or *qalyān*) with a communal Persian pipe of the same name, yet in his 1799 *Catalogue* for the Calcutta etchings, he labels it "Persian Cullyuan." *Hobson-Jobson*, under the spellings "caleeoon or calyoon," gives it as a Persian form of the *hukā*,[1] as does the *Oxford English Dictionary* under "kalian." Williamson, in his *The East India Vade-Mecum,* describes it as a small *hukā* and, noting its Persian origin, places its use principally on the west coast of India.[2]

The terms in North India for the various water-pipes—*nārikel, hukā,* and *kaliyūm*—have Persian origins, and the water-pipe may well have been invented in Persia. The first European illustrations of the water-pipe are in an early book on tobacco, *The Tabacologia*, written in Latin by the physician J. Neander and printed in Leiden in 1626. They correspond to the Persian *kaliyūm* and reflect considerable sophistication, suggesting perhaps that such pipes may have been used for smoking hemp before the introduction of tobacco at the beginning of the seventeenth century. But Laufter, in his account of tobacco in Asia, finds is no evidence for the smoking of hemp in Persia or India before the introduction of tobacco, and it remains a matter of conjecture.[3]

1 147.
2 1:226.
3 Laufer, 26-27.

II.211. Cheroot

Pl. II.211. Cheroot. Paris: III.11.5.
Calcutta: Sec. X, No. 8. Smoking the Cheroot, or Seegar.

Paris: III.11.5. CHEROOT: It is sufficient to say that the *Cheroot* is the seegar, all the lower classes of Hindoos who can not afford a *Hooka* must be content with a *Cheroot* which they themselves make. The Ouriahs [Oriyas], particularly the bearers, use a longer and thicker *Cheroot*. When they interrupt their smoking, they put the *Cheroot* behind their ear, as we sometimes do our pens. It must be observed that the *Cheroots* are not equal to our seegars, and that in general the Indian tobacco is not as good as the American, probably owing more to the mode of cultivation, than the quality of the soil. Besides, the immense consumption of this plant in India obliges the cultivators to attend more to the quantity than to the quality: tobacco consequently is cheap, and within the reach of all classes of society.

Commentary: Cheroots in Solvyns's time were generally used only by the lowest classes of Indians and Europeans, presumably those, Spear suggests, who could not afford a *hukā*.[1] They were associated as well with sailors, as Solvyns writes in his note to the original drawing, and most of the officers of country-ships smoked *cheroots*.[2]

According to Williamson, "The natives smoke *cheroots* without any precaution whatever to guard the lips and teeth from the highly acidulated fumes derived from the burning tobacco. Yet when, as sometimes has been the case, *cheroots* were brought into fashion, through but for a while, it was found expedient to use small silver or earthen sockets to receive the end of the cheroot; thereby avoiding contact with the tobacco."[3]

Cheroots and more refined cigars did come into fashion among Europeans and over the course of the early nineteenth largely displaced the *hukā*, with all its accouterment and expense.

1 *The Nabobs*, 99.
2 Williamson, as digested by Gilchrist, 230-31.
3 Ibid.

II.212. Pān

Paris: III.11.6. PAWN: This is the place to speak of the habit of chewing *Pawn,* the cultivation of which has already been the subject of another article [Pl. II.32], it is used in the following manner. They take several green leaves of *Pawn* rubbed with quick lime and wrap up in them bits of betel nut, of tobacco, and different aromatics: those rolled up all together are put into the mouth, and chewed for hours. This custom so justly repugnant to Europeans is so prevelant among the Hindoos, that their very children are brought up to it, with an idea that it helps digestion: there are women who never cease chewing betel but at their meals, and even in lying down to sleep fill their mouths, and frequently call up their servants to supply them with it: to such a pitch, that the interior of their mouths is burned up, and all their teeth spoiled. Many Hindoos would rather suffer a privation of rice or any other food than of *Pawn,* and could live many days following, upon these leaves.

It is customary for the opulent Hindoos to carry a box of *Pawn* in which are other smaller boxes or cups for the betel, the aromatics, etc. Much luxury is frequently exhibited in these boxes: the *Pawn* leaves are kept continually damp to preserve their freshness. The engraving represents a Hindoo seated with his *Pawn* prepared, and ready to be carried to his mouth: the idea of the pleasure he is going to receive, already appears in his countenance, and gives him an air of happyness.

Pl. II.212. Pān. Paris: III.11.6.

Calcutta: Sec. X, No. 6. The Hindoo method of eating the Paun, described in No. 15, of Section I.

Orme: 45.

Commentary: Solvyns earlier portrayed the Bārai, the *pān*-leaf cultivator (Pl. II.32) and the Tāmuli, the *pān*-seller (Pl. II.75), where, in the Commentary, the *pān* packet of lime, betel (areca) nut, and spices is described, and a number of etchings depict the ubiquitous *pān* box.

Orme, in the pirated edition of Solvyns, relates that "From early habit, the use of this article has become with the natives almost a necessity of life: it is wonderful how long they can endure the privation of food, when allowed the free use of the Paun and Suparee [*supāri*, Hindi for betel nut]. The leaf is aromatic, the nut has an astringent taste, and the lime, which serves to extract the juice from both, is as hot as pepper, but without its pungency. Either of these ingredients when taken separately is rather insipid, but when blended together, the composition is quite pleasant."[1]

Traditionally, according to *Hobson-Jobson*, *pān* is offered to guests to intimate the termination of the visit.[2]

1 Text for Pl. 45.

2 689.

Modes of Conveyance

Of the various modes of conveyance in Bengal, Solvyns writes in the Introduction to *Les Hindoûs*, Vol. III, that

> In general the people of Asia do not make much use of carriages; they have few horses fit for draught, the oxen which they use are exceedingly slow, and perhaps the climate too is ill suited to this way of moving; the Hindoos therefore have a more commodious and expeditious method of travelling in their palanquins: in the eighth and ninth numbers, it will be seen by the text, that the easiest postchaise is not to be preferred for expedition, and that this sort of conveyence has attained the utmost perfection. Palanquins have been in use among them from time immemorial, and have been the constant object of the industry of their artisans, so that we have not to wonder at the various forms which they have assumed, from the coast of Malabar to the frontiers of China; not at the way of carrying which is often varied. Had I spoken of every particular species of palanquins. I should have made a very voluminous and very useless collection: I have therefore confined my descriptions to those which are used in the capital and the environs, which alone are deserving of notice.[1]

1 3:2.

II.213. Elephants and Camels

Pl. II.213. Elephants and Camels. Paris: III.7.1. Double-plate.

Calcutta: Before Sec. V. Elephants and Camels, with the method of using them.

Paris: III.7.1. ELEPHANTS AND CAMELS: These animals are very common in several parts of India. The elephant is used, as is well known, for hunting the tiger and for war. The camel carries great burdens, and also follows the armies. The Indians set an extraordinary value upon the elephants who have a bunch of hair at the end of their tails, and take great pains to preserve it entire; which is very difficult, on account of the continual motion in which it is kept, in brushing off the insects. The elephants in the print are represented eating the leaves and the bark of some shrubs of which they break the branches with their trunk; they have all of them one of their legs pinched with a piece of wood, w[h]ich prevents their making their escape. At a distance are some camels following a corps of troops. The landscape is a pass in the Carnatic, the only entrance is by narrow roads, through very steep rocks, which in the rainy season are rendered impracticable by the torrents, and from the natural defence of this mountainous country.

It would be useless to say more of the nature and habits of the elephant, which are amply described in different works of natural history.

Commentary: There is no evidence that Solvyns ventured beyond the environs of Calcutta, and his portrayal of the Carnatic landscape may be based upon descriptions or sketches by others.

II.214. Lādū Bail

Pl. II.214. Lādū Bail. Paris: III.8.6.

Calcutta: Sec. V, No. 6. A Ladoo Byle, or Carrier's Bullock.

Paris: III.8.6. LADOO-BYLE:The *Ladoo-Byle,* or ox, is an animal of the greatest use to the Hindoos, answering all the purposes of the ass in Europe, and as it is stronger, carrying immense loads. Its mildness and docility is such, that it kneels at the command of its master, bows down to the earth, receives the load he pleases to impose, and rises with it. The print represents a market-place with some grain merchants before their *gollas,* or magazines, loading oxen with enormous sacks of wheat or rice. The oxen of India are almost all white, with a hump on their backs, the flesh of which the Europeans reckon delicious. They lead them by a string passed through their nostrils. It is astonishing that the Hindoos have so little feeling for an animal which they look upon as in a manner sacred, and whose form they all wish to bear in their transformation. It is not easy to find a reason for such an inconsistency.

Commentary: *Lādū*, from *lād*, "load," is Hindustani for "beast of burden," and *bail* is the word for bullock. The Bengali for a bull or ox is *balad*, and Wise writes that pack-bullocks, which he terms "balads," are used where there are no cart roads.[1]

Solvyns portrays the pack-bullocks before thatched granaries, which he identifies as *golās*, but should be termed "godowns," warehouses. The word *golā* means a round-shaped receptacle for grain, and it typically consists of a circular mud wall with a conical roof.[2]

1 39-40.
2 Sukumar Sen, 239; *Hobson-Jobson*, 383; and Whitworth, 108.

II.215. Horse and Ṭaṭu

Pl. II.215. Horse and Ṭaṭu. Paris: III.9.2.
Calcutta: Sec. V, No. 7. A Horse richly caparisoned in the Hindostany manner. **No. 8.** A Tatoo,—a small common horse.

Paris: III. 9.2. HORSE RICHLY CAPARISONED, AND A TATTOU: The custom of bestowing so much ornament on their horses, as here represented, is really Hindoo, though it is now not often meet with; and it was not without some trouble that I had an opportunity of making this drawing. The rider must be a riche Hindoo, and the horse is an Arab, the race most esteemed in Hindoostan, of which considerable numbers are constantly imported. On their arrival the Arabian horses make at first but a very poor appearance, from the fatigue of the passage; but they soon get into condition, and become very fine parade horses. The horse near the Arabian is a *Tattou*, or one of the Hindoo race. For size and beauty he bears no comparison with the other, but is superior to him for use: he seems particularly adapted to the climate, of which he supports admirably all the vicissitudes. But his chief value with the Hindoos poorer is his great temperance, his whole food consisting in a few herbs which he finds in spots dried up and burned by the sun, so as to cost his master little or nothing for keep.

Commentary: For the Paris edition, Solvyns combined the two separate Calcutta etchings of the horse and *ṭaṭu*, the Bengali term for the Indian-bred pony.

In his note to the original drawing, Solvyns writes that "The Tattoo is a species of Horse, the peculiar production of India and particularly described in Buffon's Natural History[1] and in Capt. Pigett's treatise on the Horse in India." John Pigott was a

Lieutenant of Cavalry and his "Treatise on the Horses of India," published in Calcutta in 1794, described the "Tattoo as the peculiar production of India . . . . The general and most laborious uses to which these animals are applied, evince their utility, insomuch that through the most arduous campaigns performed in India, the necessities of the soldiers, followers, and even their families, are conveyed principally by their means; the patient endurance with which they perform their tasks, through almost incredible hardship, and under very heavy burdens, excite in the beholders no less admiration, than compassion. . . ."[2]

1 Solvyns might have had access in Calcutta to the 1785 English edition, 3:373.

2 45-46.

II.216. Rath

Paris: III.7.2. RUTH, OR CHARIOT: After having described the boats of the Hindoos in the foregoing numbers, we will now take notice of their carriages.

To begin by the *Ruth*: it is a carriage of Hindoo origin, though the Mahometans use it as well as the natives. The *Ruth* is roomy, and in general highly ornamented: it has *pordas* [*pardā*], or gratings of very thin and coloured bambous, to secrete the person who sits in it from the eyes of the public. But, being without any sort of braces, it is exceedingly incommodious, and almost insupportable to an European who is not accustomed to it. It is commonly drawn by two large fat oxen, in adorning which the Hindoos are fond of making a shew of their riches. Rings of gold and silver are fastened to the nose and the horns of these animals; their hoofs and tail are painted red, and their harness is magnificent. For the form of the *Ruth* the reader may be safely referred to the print.

Pl. II.216. Rath. Paris: III.7.2.
Calcutta: Sec. V, No. 1. A Ruth or country Chariot.

Commentary: The *rath* is a four-wheeled carriage normally drawn by bullocks,[1] although in his note to drawing, Solvyns describes it as occasionally drawn by horses. Used primarily by women, as portrayed and described, the *rath* has a bamboo screen, a *pardā*, to conceal the occupant. The term *pardā*—Anglo-Indian "purdah"—is from the Persian for "curtain," especially that used to screen women from the eyes of men, and came to refer generally to the seclusion of women, a practice extended from Muslim society to many higher caste Hindus in North India.

Wallace, in 1823, although terming the cart a "hackery" (Pl. II.220), referred to these "native carriages of the opulent Hindoos, drawn by bullocks richly caparisoned with silk, and jingling bells of silver, in which their wives are concealed from the eye of man when they visit their female friends."[2]

The word *rath* is also used for the car on which a temple idol is carried, as in Solvyns's portrayal of the Rath Yātrā (Pl. II.188).

1 Anglo-Indian "rut" or "ruth," *Hobson-Jobson*, 776. For the structural components of the *rath*, see Grierson, 38-39.

2 70-71; quoted in Nair, *Calcutta in the 19th Century*, 310.

II.217. Gāṛi

Pl. II.217. Gāṛi. Paris: III.7.3.
Calcutta: Sec. V, No. 2. A Gary,—sometimes with four wheels as the Ruth.

Paris: III.7.3. GARY: The *Gary* is the Hindoo hackney-coach. In the towns and frequented bazars there are always *Garies* ready to carry people, for a trifle, to all parts in the neighbourhood. These carriages are drawn by horses, but are hard, inconvenient, and liable to many objections. They carry many persons; and it is not uncommon to meet them on the highroads, on their return from some festival or party of pleasure, loaded with passengers inside and out, expressing their joy by loud cries, while the drivers, drunk and overcome by fatigue, are scarcely able to guide their horses. I shall only repeat here cursorily, that none but the lowest ranks of the people among the Hindoos are ever seen drunk in public. The lassitude brought on by the heat of the day, followed by the cold nights, seems to excite a taste for drinking, more particularly in the labouring classes.

Commentary: Solvyns portrays a common two-wheeled, horse-drawn *gāṛi*, but the term is generic for cart or carriage and its particular form is often specified by a descriptive prefix.[1] Though occasionally used by Europeans, it was primarily an Indian vehicle. "It is a very comfortable carriage for travelling in at night or in bad weather;" wrote George Johnson in the 1840s, "but, it is too close and hot for purpose of evening exercise."[2]

1 *Hobson-Jobson*, 365.
2 1:46; quoted in Nair, *Calcutta in the 19th Century*, 829.

II.218. Ekkā

Pl. II.218. Ekkā. Paris: III.7.4.
Calcutta: Sec. V, No. 3. An Ekka, or one horse chaise.

Paris: III.7.4. EKKA: This is perhaps the simplest carriage that can be imagined, being nothing more than a chair covered with red cloth, and fixed upon an axle-tree between two small wheels. The *Ekka* is drawn by one horse, who has no other harness than a girt to which the shaft of the carriage is fastened, as is represented in the print. The drivers are of the lowest class, and belong to no cast: they are despised, and stigmatised with the name of *parriahs,*[1] by the Hindoos. At present there are many Mussulmans in this trade, as we have already seen there are in all the other low employments; which gives rise to an assertion founded only on the national pride of the Hindoos, that none of the followers of Brahma ever defiled themselves by exercising a trade reputed dishonourable. There are notwithstanding in the *Soodder* [śūdrā] cast many Hindoos who, in defiance of the laws of their religion, live indiscriminately with all nations, and adopt their manners and their vices.

Commentary: The carriage takes its name from the one (*ek*) horse that draws it. Whitworth, in his *Anglo-Indian Dictionary*, provides a succinct description: "A small light two-wheeled carriage made chiefly of bambu; it is drawn by a single horse or pony, the shafts meeting on the animal's back; it has no seat in the European sense, and is used only by natives."[2] The carriage was fitted so that little or no weight fell on the horse's shoulders, and it can easily go 30 to 40 miles a day, especially, writes Crooke, if the horse is "kept up to the mark by stimulants, of which hemp and treacle are the chief constituents."[3]

The red cloth over the seat must have been traditional, for Stoqueler refers to the "crimson cloth cushions. . . on which natives of India (who alone use them) sit cross-legged."[4]

1 For Solvyns's discussion of the pariah, see Pl. II.22.
2 94. Grierson gives a detailed description, with two pictures, 40-42.
3 *Things Indian*, 82.
4 *Oriental Interpreter*, 80.

II.219. "Rahhoo"

Pl. II.219. "Rahhoo." Paris: III.7.5.
Calcutta: Sec. V, No. 4. A Rahhoo,—an inferior kind of Carriage.

Paris: III.7.5. RAHHOO: The *Rahhoo* holds but a single person: it is a very light and very simple carriage, consisting meerly of a pole with a traverse of timber, and two wheels. On this piece of wood a mat and a bit of white cloth and sometimes a cushion, is spread. It is drawn by two oxen of the small pieces: these animals, of which the greatest care is taken, are very swift and safe in their gaits, continuing always at the same rate, in every sort of road. The passenger in the *Rahhoo* runs no sort of risk. The driver is seated before him, with his feet on the pole, which is generally very wide and covered with a cloth highly ornamented. There are a great many of these carriages in Hindoostan, particularly in the service of the Jemidars [jamidār] and persons in office. In great establishments, especially in the country, the head-servants have a *Rahhoo* at their orders.

Commentary: Solvyns's term "rahhoo" is perhaps derived from the Hindustani *rāhū*, meaning "road."

Grierson portrays a variation of this "light country cart," which he identifies as a "saggar" and contrasts with the chhakrā (hackery, Pl. II.220).[1]

1 Picture, opp. p. 33; description, 37-38.

II.220. Hackery

Pl. II.220. Hackery. Paris: III.7.6.

Calcutta: Sec. V, No. 5. A Hackery, or Cart.

Paris: III.7.6. HACKERY: The *Hackery* is a cart consisting meerly in an axle traversed by two large bambous, and is used for conveying merchandise: the whole is made of wood, without any piece of iron. They are common in many of the towns of Hindoostan, particularly in the bazars. The Hindoo carters are without mercy for the oxen yoked in the *Hackeries:* they sit on the pole, and twist the tails of these poor animals in the most cruel manner, goading them at the same time with sticks pointed with iron. Many of the oxen die under this cruel treatment. An European can not at first suppress his indignation at the barbarity of these Hindoo carters; but habit little by little reconciles him to it.

Commentary: The word *hackery* is Anglo-Indian and is almost surely a corruption of the Hindi *chhakrā*, two-wheeled cart.[1] Though sometimes used to refer to a horse-drawn cart, the word more typically is used for a bullock cart—a *garur gāṛi*, as commonly termed in Bengali.

Hobson-Jobson notes that "In the Bengal Presidency this word [hackery] is now applied only to the common native bullock-car used in the slow draught of goods and materials. But formerly in Bengal, as still in Western India and Ceylon, the word was applied to lighter carriages (drawn by bullocks) for personal transport."[2] Solvyns portrays the hackery in *Hobson-Jobson*'s "modern" Bengal sense, and pictures of the cart in Grierson's *Bihar Peasant Life* identifies the structural components of the cart.[3]

Roberdeau, in 1805, describes the hackery as "a mere Bamboo frame fixed on a pair of Wheels and drawn by oxen. They are 'dreadful harmony' for the wheels having neither iron, or grease, make a most horrid creaking."[4]

---

1 *OED*, and *Hobson-Jobson*, 407-08.

2 407.

3 Opposite pp. 24 and 25, with detailed descriptions, 27-37 .

4 125; quoted in Nair, *Calcutta in the 19th Century*, 54. Also see Williamson, in Gilchrist, 181-83.

Palanquins

Early European accounts of India make frequent reference to the use of palanquins, or *pālkis*, and they often provide detailed descriptions.[1] Solvyns portrays eight types or variations. Six are litters, sometimes generically called *mīyānas* (Pl. II.225), in which the rider may sit with legs extended and his (or her) back supported by a board and pillows. Europeans generally assumed this recumbent position, while Indians were likely to sit cross-legged. Two are chair *pālkis*, similar to the European sedan, in which the rider sits upright on a seat. Notably different from European palanquins, supported by side poles, Indian palanquins have a single, thick pole, usually of bamboo, from which the litter is suspended or two such poles, each some four feet long, secured to the front and back of the palanquin by iron rods.[2] The poles may be straight or curved, and the ends are often capped in metal animal heads.

Borne by a team of carriers, the palanquin often proceeded with an extensive entourage. With an important personage, such as a high Company official, *peyādās*, running footmen (Pl. II.124), followed by two *harkarās* (Pl. II.123), typically bearing spears, led the way for the palanquin. During the day, to protect the occupant from the sun, a member of the palanquin team carried a *chātā*—an umbrella, usually called a "roundel" or "kittysol" in Anglo-Indian usage.[3] At night *maṣālcis*, or torch-bearers (Pl. II.120) led the way. In travel, the palanquin bearers would, like boatmen, often keep time by singing, frequently making up the words as they went along.[4]

The teams were composed of carriers from particular castes or subcastes, described separately by Solvyns. The Oriya bearers (Pl. II.45) were the highest in status and best-paid, and they were well-organized. Of lower status were the Rawāni (Pl. II.46), Duliā (Pl. II.47), and Jāliyā (Pl. II.48) bearers. Each caste, according to its traditions, followed particular rules regarding the number of bearers for each team and the various responsibilities bearers would assume.

The teams also varied in number of bearers, ranging from eight to a minimum of four, "according to the rank, occupation, or circumstances of their employer." In private employment, palanquin bearers had household responsibilities. The head bearer (*sardār*) served as his master's valet, and normally remained within the house. The others, when not bearing the palanquin, made themselves useful in cleaning the furniture, preparing the candles and oil lamps, and in various odd jobs.[5]

While high officials used the palanquin with much pomp, Company officials in Calcutta in the eighteenth century banned the use of this "piece of Eastern luxury" by junior clerks. Sumptuary laws also forbade these young gentleman from hiring roundel-boys to carry umbrellas to protect them from the sun.[6] By Solvyns's time, such bans, if still on the books, were probably ignored, at least in the use of palanquins, by all who could afford the expense to do so.

Palanquins were used both in the city and for extended travel. Lord Valentia, in 1803, undertook a trip by palanquin of some 800 miles upcountry. Orders were placed ahead at the different towns to supply bearers at stages about ten miles apart, and with a teams of eight carriers for each palanquin, three maṣālcis, and three bearers for luggage, they traveled during the night, stretched out full length and asleep.[7]

Valentia's ten mile intervals were frequently stretched to as far as 16 miles between "*dāk* stages," and at each point a fresh team of eight or more men would be ready, and with four carrying the palanquin, they relieved each other every quarter mile. Their speed averaged about four miles per hour.[8] In running about Calcutta, as few as four men might be employed, although the team usually consisted of a *chātā* carrier and a relief man in addition to the four bearers.

Among European artists in India, Solvyns was not alone in illustrating the palanquin, though he alone sought to do so systematically in terms of their types. Thomas Daniell includes various styles of palanquins in his *Views of Calcutta*. Gold, Solvyns's contemporary in South India, portrays palanquins in his *Oriental Drawings*,[9] and Mrs. Belnos, in her *Twenty-four Plates Illustrative of Hindoo and European Manners in Bengal*, depicts both the chair and long palanquins with their respective teams of Rawāni and Oriya bearers.[10]

1 For reference to the earliest European descriptions, see *Hobson-Jobson*, 659-61. For detailed descriptions, see, for example, Tavernier, *Travels*, 1:45-46; Williamson's handbook for Europeans coming to India, *East India Vade-Mecum*, 1:315-324; and Shoberl, 4:173-189, with three colored engravings. On the use of palanquins in Calcutta, see Dewar, *In the Days of the Company*, 75-90. The English word *palanquin* is from the Portuguese, and it in turn is derived from the Sanskrit for "bed." *Hobson-Jobson*, 659.

2 The distinction is noted by Orme in the text for Pl. 5.

3 "Chatta," *Hobson-Jobson*, 185. "Roundel," an English word for a variety of round objects had specific Anglo-Indian usage as an umbrella. *Hobson-Jobson*, 770-71. "Kittysol," a word used especially for the Chinese style made of bamboo and oiled paper, is a corruption of the Portuguese *quitasol*, meaning "to take the sun away." *Hobson-Jobson*, 487; Lewis, 148. The use of an umbrella in India was traditionally associated with high status, and was used in processions as a mark of royal or of great dignity. Europeans adopted the custom both as an assertion of status and for practical reasons of comfort. A roundel (or kittysol) boy was a servant who carried the umbrella over his master's head. See Solvyns's portrayal, Pl. II.7.

4 Acland, 40-41.

5 Grant and Colebrooke, *The Anglo-Hindoostanee Hand-Book*, 64-65.

6 Nisith Ranjan Ray, *Calcutta: The Profile of a City*, 54; *Hobson-Jobson*, "Roundel," 771.

7 Valentia, 1:70-71, and Hodges, 16-17.

8 Bacon, quoted in Nair, *Calcutta in the 19th Century*, 536.

9 Pl. 43. The accompanying text describes traveling by palanquin.

10 Pl. 23, "Civilian Going Out."

II.221. Copālā Pālki

Pl. II.221. Copālā Pālki. Paris: III.8.2.

Calcutta: Sec. VI, No. 1. A Chowpaul Palkee, chiefly used at marriages and other processions.

Paris: III.8.2. CHOWPAUL: The preceding number was taken up with wheel carriages; in this we shall treat of those which are carried, and known under the general name of palanquins.

Of these the *Chowpaul* is the most ancient, and, as it were, the original from which all the other forms of palanquins may be traced: on this account it is used in all great ceremonies, marriages, processions, etc. The *Chowpaul* is simply a very light bed or sopha, over which a large bambou forms an arch. But as this is not a sufficient defence against the sun, it is always attended by a servant carrying a *chata* or parasol. I have been careful to represent with this palanquin its appropriate class of bearers and the dwelling of those who are in the habit of using it; which attention shall be continued through all the prints of this number.

Commentary: The copālā (or caupāla) pālki is an open palanquin, and its single bamboo poll is carried by four bearers.[1] The seventeenth century French traveller Tavernier described the Indian palanquin very much as Solvyns here portrays the copālā pālki, but with the addition of a covering. It is, Tavernier wrote, "a kind of bed of six or seven feet long, and three feet wide with a small rail all around. A sort of cane, called bamboo, which they bend when young in order to cause it to take the form of a bow, in the middle sustains the cover of the *pallankeen*, which is of satin or brocade; and when the sun shines on one side, an attendant, who walks near the *pallankeen*, takes care to lower the covering."[2] Tavernier also refers to an attendant with an umbrella, but rather than the circular *chātā* depicted here by Solvyns, he describes something more like what Solvyns portrays with the Jhālidār Pālki (Pl. II.222).

1 Sukumar Sen, 287.

2 *Travels in India*, 1:45-46. A palanquin of similar style is depicted by a Company School artist of Madras, c. 1787, in Mildred Archer, *Company Drawings in the India Office Library*, Pl. 1.

II.222. Jhālidār Pālki

Pl. II.222. Jhālidār Pālki. Paris: III.8.3.

Calcutta: Sec. VI, No. 2. J'halledar Palkee, used in state by the Natives; as it formerly was by Europeans.

Commentary: The jhālidār pālki is covered by a fine cloth stretched over a bamboo framework, and in the note to his original drawing, Solvyns writes, "They are now used by Natives of Distinction as a State Palanquin and often richly ornamented."

The accompanying servants to which Solvyns refers are the hukābardār (Pl. II.108); chauṅrībardār (Pl. II.110), with the fly-whisk; soṭābardār (Pl. II.103), mace-carrier; harkarā (Pl. II.123), message carrier; peyādā (Pl. II.124), footman or peon; and, of course, the *chātā*-bearer. The *chātā* depicted here is not the round umbrella seen in other Solvyns etchings, but is of a style described by Tavernier in the 1640s—a "kind of basket-work shield," covered in beautiful silk or brocade and carried at the end of a stick.[1]

1 *Travels in India*, 1:45-46.

Paris: III.8.3. J'HALLEDAR: The *J'halledar* differs from the *Chowpaul* only by its ornaments: it is the palanquin of radjas and rich noblemen, and is generally covered with rich stuffs embroidered in silk or gold, which extend over the bambou. The end of this bambou sometimes represent the head and the tail of a tiger, or some other animal, whose feet form the ornament of the bottom of the bed. The bearers of the *J'halledar* wear over their ordinary dress, as a sort of uniform, a coloured jacket, with a red, blue, or yellow turban. The *chata,* or parasol, which one of them carries, is of a rich stuff surrounded with fringe; the handle is frequently of silver, sculptured with great art. Besides the bearers, it is attended with never less than five other servants, one of whom carries the houka, or pipe, while two others keep off the flies. The rest are *soonta-burdars, hircarahs,* etc. The palanquin is sometimes also escorted by a crowd of *peadahs.*

II.223. Mahāpā

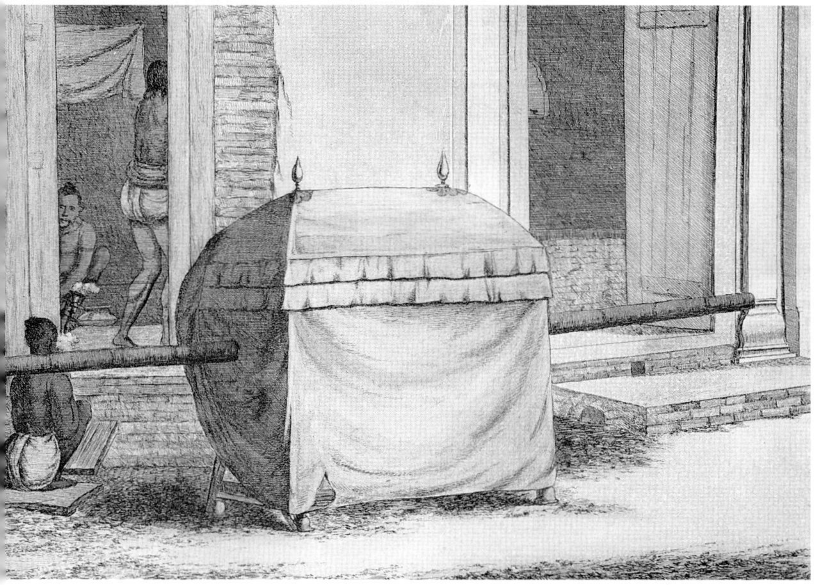

Pl. II.223. Mahāpā. Paris: III.8.4.
Calcutta: Sec. VI, No. 7. A Mohafa;—a carriage for women

Paris: III.8.4. MOHAFA: This is the palanquin of rich females, who use it to go to festivals, and on visits to their relations: it is entirely covered with a red hanging, and has no other ornament than a ball of copper at the top of the bambou. The lady is seated in these palanquins as if she was in her chamber, her back supported by a large round cushion, and smaller flat ones for her knees, her feet, and her elbows. The *Mohafa* is carried by four servants, and attended by a number proportioned to the rank of the lady. When she is of the first class, the train is very considerable; some carrying betel, others the houka, or perfumes. Sometimes maids walk by the side of the palanquin, to be ready to receive the orders of their mistress. Nevertheless the women who conform strictly to the precepts of their religion, are attended but by four bearers, however great their fortune.

Commentary: The mahāpā (or mohafa)[1] provides, as Solvyns portrays, concealment for women behind the rich cloth covering the palanquin. Francis Buchanan refers to a particular kind of palanquin as "mahāpā" or "mīyāna" (Pl. II.225), and states that "In some places, these terms are considered as synonymous, in others the *Miyana* is open at the sides, while the *Mahapa*, intended for women, is surrounded with curtains."[2]

A mahāpā was included in a panorama of Calcutta exhibited in London in 1830. The catalogue described the palanquin as "used by native ladies only, frequently carrying two. . . ." Entirely covered with cloth, "a small opening on the side allows persons in the interior to look out without being seen. . . ."[3]

1 See *A Glossary of Indian Terms*, 156, for variations of the term.
2 From Montgomery Martin, *The History, Antiquities, Topography, and Statistics of Eastern India*, 2:426, quoted in *Hobson-Jobson*; 565.
3 Burford, 9.

224. Dulī

Paris: III.8.5. DOOLY: The contrast of this palanquin with those which we have described is striking: it is a sort of frame of bambou, to which girts are adapted. Two men only are required to carry it; but there is generally a third, who follows behind, to relieve him who is tired. Though they run with incredible swiftness, the motion is scarcely felt. Upon these the sick are carried to the river. The bearers lean upon a stick as they run, to avoid stumbling. The appropriate class of carriers is also called Doolys; though men of other classes sometimes follow this trade. They are to be hired in all the villages and bazars.

Commentary: The dulī is a covered litter consisting of a cot or frame suspended by the four corners from a bamboo pole and carried by two or four men.[1] In his note to the original drawing, Solvyns wrote, "The Dooly is a vehicle used by the inferior class of Natives as a conveyance for the sick, and in the northern part of Hindoostan to travel expeditiously with only two or three Bearers." The rider he portrays could be an ill man, but is perhaps a woman. Although Solvyns says nothing of it, the dulī was used principally by women—and, in contrast to the mahāpā, by those of the lower classes.

Stocqueler provides a detailed description of the dulī: "Its usual construction is extremely simple;

consisting of a small *charpoy* [*chārpaī*, cot], a very slight frame of bamboo work, equal in size to the frame of the litter, is placed over it horizontally, serving as a roof for the support of a double cover . . . , which lies over the roof, and falls all around, so as to enclose the whole space between the roof and the bedstead. There is seldom any bedding but what is provided by the party carried in the *dooly*; unless it be one appertaining to some family, by whom it is frequently used; in such case, the interior is made very comfortable, and the cover ornamented with borders, fringes &c. This last kind, being almost exclusively appropriated to the *zananah*, is on a very small scale, rarely exceeding three feet by little more than two."[2]

Solvyns writes of the dulī's use for carrying the sick and dying, and Williamson writes that in the army of the East India Company the dulī, no doubt because of its speed and smoothness, afforded "excellent means of transporting sick and wounded men, either to hospitals, or on a march."[3]

The dulī bearers—called duliās or (Anglo-Indian) "doolees"—were drawn from the lower castes, and those so engaged typically formed a distinct subcaste, such as the Duliā Bāgdi, a subcaste of large Bāgdi community portrayed by Solvyns (Pl. II.79). Solvyns depicts the dulīa in a separate etching (Pl. II.45), although the palanquin in the scene is a mīyāna pālki (Pl. II.225), not a dulī.

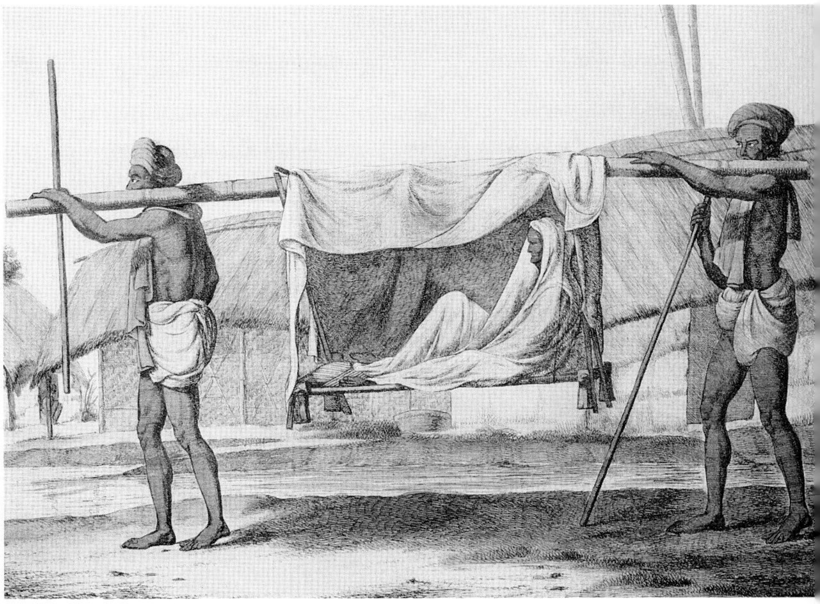

Pl. II.224. Dulī. Paris: III.8.5.
Calcutta: Sec. VI, No. 8. A Dooly, used by the inferior ranks; and for the purpose of travelling with speed.

1 *Hobson-Jobson*, 313. The word is *dulī* in Bengali, *ḍolī* in Hindi, and *dhooly* or *doolie* in Anglo-Indian usage. For a detailed description of its construction, see Grierson, 45-46. Spear, 100, identifies the dulī as "the original palanquin," from which the more elaborate palanquins developed.

2 *Oriental Interpreter*, 77-78.

3 Gilchrist, 174. On its use as an army ambulance, also see *Hobson-Jobson*, 313.

II.225. Mīyāna

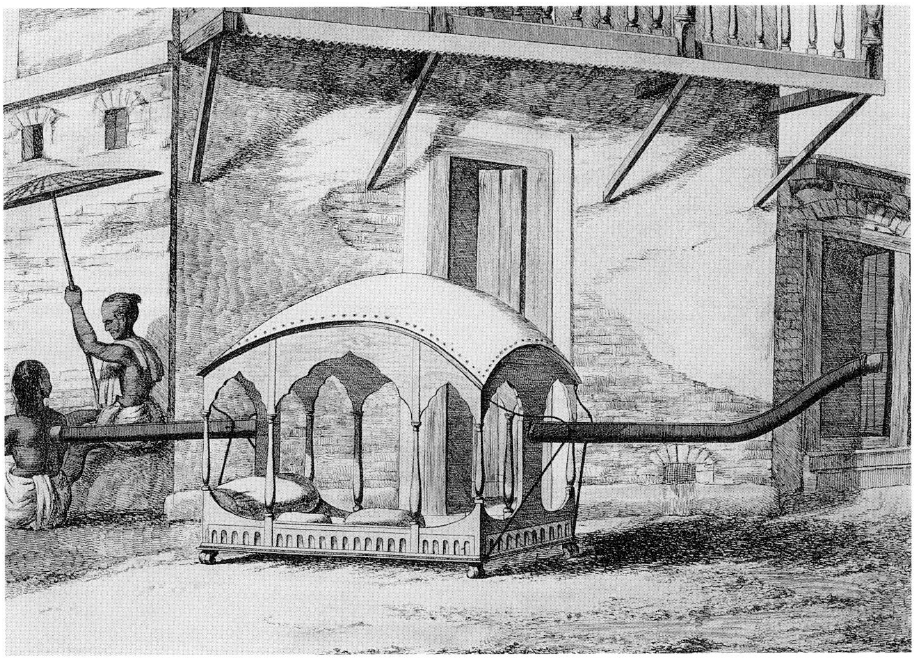

Pl. II.225. Mīyāna. Paris: III.9.3.
Calcutta: Sec. VI, No. 3. The original Meanna Palkee.

Paris: III.9.3. MEJANAH: The palanquin called *Mejanah* differs from those which we have described, by being built of wood, joined with iron, and covered with leather, and not like them of bambous tied together. It is not a shew carriage, and is often even not painted. Within is a bed and cushions of white cotton. Although the *Mejanah* is certainly an invention of the country, it is not much used by the natives. Those Hindoos only who adhere to the customs of their ancestors, prefer it, such as the *Banyans* [banians, Pl. II.99] and *Sercars* [sarkārs, Pl. II.100], when they attend the levees of the great Europeans in the morning, to receive their orders. This mark of dependance will be noticed in the fourth volume when we come to treat of the state of domesticity among the Hindoos. I shall only remark here, that the custom formerly was, when a Hindoo in his palanquin met an European, he alighted and made him long protestations of submission. This custom is altered, and it is now not uncommon to see Europeans bowing before rich Hindoos, and offering to them the same marks of submission which they had formerly received from them.

The *Mejanah* is almost always carried by Bengalies or *Doulias*. The back-ground represents a Hindoo house of very simple structure, though belonging to a rich master.

Commentary: In his note to the drawing, Solvyns describes this as "the original Mianna or long Palanquin, used by natives." *Hobson-Jobson* derives the Anglo-Indian "meeana" from the Hindustani-Persian *mīyāna*, meaning "middle-sized" and was "the kind out of which the palankin used by the Europeans has been developed, and which has been generally adopted in India for the last century."[1] The term *mīyāna*, however, was often used to refer generally to long palanquins, and Williamson, in his *East-India Vade Mecum*, provides a detailed description of what Solvyns identifies simply as a "long palanquin" (Pl. II.226).

Steuart & Co. was Calcutta's leading maker of coaches and palanquins. In 1795, the *Calcutta Gazette* noted that "Two very elegant Mehannah Palanquins are just finished by Mr. Steuart who has shown great skill in the design and execution of them; they are commissioned by the Rajah of Tanjore."[2] The Tanjore mīyānas, probably "long palanquins," were described by William Baillie in a letter to fellow artist Ozias Humphry in London as having venetians and linings, bedding, and pillows of velvet, and a cost said to be near 10,000 rupees each. Baillie's reference to the palanquins comes in his discussion of Solvyns's employment by Steuart & Co., and it is possible that Solvyns was involved in decorating the two mīyānas.[3]

In his portrayal of the Duliā (Pl. II.45), Solvyns depicts a *mīyāna*.

---

1 565.

2 August 20, 1795.

3 Letter dated October 4, 1795, Ozias Humphrey Papers, HU/4/112-117, Royal Academy of Arts, London. The letter is reproduced in part, in Evan Cotton, "A Famous Firm. The Story of Steuart & Co.," 70. On Solvyns's association with Steuart & Co., see pp. 30-31.

II.226. Long Palanquin

Paris: III.9.4. LONG PALANQUIN: This species of palanquin was brought into India by the Europeans, and is much used in all the towns where they have settled, such as Calcutta, Madras, Bombay, etc. . . . It is of a good construction, and has lanterns, with four bearers, as is seen in the print, and is preceded by *Hircarahs* [harkārā, runner, Pl. II.123] and *Peadas* [peyādā, footman, Pl. II.124]. The movements of the bearers are so easy that they are scarcely felt by the person in the palanquin, though they are at the same time very rapid, and get over a great deal of ground in a short time. They change sides with astonishing promptness, still running on, and without interrupting their song or their conversation. Throughout all Hindoostan there are changes of bearers, as there are of posthorses in Europe; so that you may cross the country in a palanquin almost as quick as in a postchaise. The sumptuousness of the palanquin we are describing has been carried to a very great height: during my stay at Calcutta some were made at the price of eight to twelve hundred pounds; but the ordinary cost is no more than from twenty to forty.—The back-ground represents the house of an European.

Pl. II.226. Long Palanquin. Paris: III.9.4.

Calcutta: Sec. VI, No. 4. A long Palkee, introduced by Europeans.

Commentary: Solvyns's note to the drawing reads, "A long Palanquin or Miana, as introduced and used by Europeans." But oddly, in the drawing and the Calcutta etching, the figure riding inside is in Indian dress. For the Paris edition, he changes the figure to a European.

This print is of special interest in its setting, for Solvyns here depicts the gated entrance to Steuart & Co., Coachmakers, with whom the artist had been employed in decorating palanquins and carriages. The building is portrayed in a 1795 painting once attributed to Solvyns.[1]

In the print, to the right, the legs of the harkarās and the tops of their spears may be seen as the palanquin passes the building. In portraying the harkārā in the series of European servants (Pl. II.123), Solvyns depicts in the background a long palanquin preceded by two spear-carrying runners and accompanied—as in his portrayal here—by a servant bearing a *chātā* (umbrella).

Europeans frequently used the term "mahannah" (*mīyāna*) for the long palanquin, as did Williamson in a detailed description of what Solvyns clearly portrays:

> The *mahannah* resembles an immense chest, standing on four feet, raising it nearly a foot from the ground. About two-fifths of each side is open, serving for a door; the residue being closed up, either with very thin pannels, or with canvas, leather, &c. The doors are sometimes made to close, by means of two Venetian frames. . . .
>
> The roof is made of very thin pannelling board, laid longitudinally over slight battens a little cambered; though some are quite flat: over the boards a stout, but think, canvas is well stretched, and beaded down at the edges: this is usually painted white. The fore and back, parts are in general closed, with the exception of two small Venetian, or perhaps glass, windows near the top; to allow a draught of air. The exterior is painted according to the fancy of the proprietor, often very handsomely, and well

varnished. The front and hind poles attach at about three-fifths up the body of the vehicle; being riveted to iron ribs, firmly screwed by means of diverging claws to the main pieces. They are further steadied by iron stays, proceeding from the top and bottom corners of each end respectively to the pole; to which they are bolted at about eighteen inches from the body. The poles are always covered in leather.

The body of a *mahannah* is generally about six feet, or six feet two inches long, and from 26 to 30 inches in width; the height is sufficient to allow a tall person's sitting upright, without a hat. The beddings of most are covered with chintz of neat patterns; while a small piece of carpet, tiger's skin, or morocco-leather, or some such article, is spread at the feet, to prevent its being soiled.

In most *mahannahs* there are racks, which serve to support the back; others are provided with two small, or one large pillow, also covered with chintz. Above the doors it is common to screw in flat brass knobs, whereon to button either canvas or leather curtains, that will roll up occasionally, ...[2]

Stocqueler likened the palanquin "to a wooden box, opening at the sides by sliding doors. It is about six feet long and four in height. . . . Usually painted a dark green, with sometimes the crest of the owner painted on the pannels, and furnished inside with a long cushion, covered with morocco leather, silk, or chintz, and a pillow of some material for the support of the head or back. . . . At the opposite end of the palkee is a flat wooden resting-place for the feet, and above that a shelf and a small drawer for reception of light articles, papers, &c. some people take great pride in these vehicles, causing the upper part of the sides to be provided with Venetian blinds, and throwing over the whole, in very warm weather, a covering of fragrant *cuscuss*."[3] *Khās* (Anglo-Indian "cuscuss") is a fragrant root used to make screens (*ṭaṭṭīs*) that when dampened provided a pleasant coolness as the palanquin was speeded to its destination.[4]

Acland, in 1843 describes his palanquin: "The top is covered with a white cement to prevent its leaking, and is slightly curved, so that the rain may run off. The bottom is often wicker-work, on which is laid a mattress and other cushions, covered generally with thin leather. The sides, top, &c., are lined, often with crimson silk."[5]

Such palanquins were often quite elegant, and Solvyns mentions their expense, with a cost as high as 1200 pounds. Solvyns could speak with authority on the price of palanquins, for in his employment by Steuart & Co. he gained substantial remuneration and considerable attention for his work on the magnificent long palanquin that Cornwallis ordered for the conveyance of the hostage princes of Tipu Sultan.[6]

Along with the chair pālki, the long palanquin was widely used by Europeans in India, and St. John's Church, constructed in 1787, had a special slope at the entrance to accommodate these palanquins.[7]

In illustrating street scenes of urban India, European artists often included the long palanquin, and, in an 1828 painting, a native artist of the Company School provides a fine portrait of a British officer carried in a palanquin.[8]

---

1 For a discussion of Solvyns's employment with Steuart & Co. and of the painting, see pp. 30-34.

2 *East-India Vade Mecum*, 1: 319-21. Grierson identifies the structural components of the long palanquin, which he calls a "bardari," 46, and includes a picture. The Peabody Essex Museum in Salem, MA, has a long palanquin from Calcutta, c. 1800, and a model of a palanquin, with Western passenger and native bearers, c. 1870, in its collection. Both are illustrated in Bean, *Yankee India*, 80 (Fig. 4.18) and 236 (Fig. 16.5).

3 *Oriental Interpreter*, 180.

4 See Pl. II.111, fn. 5; *Hobson-Jobson*, 283-84; 903.

5 85.

6 See pp. 30-31.

7 Nisith Ranjan Ray, *Calcutta: The Profile of a City*, 54-55.

8 "Palanquin with British Officer," by a Tanjore artist working in Vellore, in Mildred Archer, *Company Drawings in the India Office Library*, Pl. 7.

II.227. Bochā

Pl. II.227. Bochā. Paris: III.9.5.

Calcutta: Sec. VI, No. 5. A Bocha, or original chair Palkee, at present chiefly used by the Portuguese.

Paris: III.9.5. BOUTCHA: This is a palanquin of Hindoo invention, and known in the country time out of mind. It resembles our sedan chairs, and is ornamented with copper like all the old furniture of the Hindoos. Copper is their favourite metal; the use of it is prescribed in their religious institutions, which gives it a preference in their eyes above gold and silver. But after all, the *Boutcha* has no pretensions to magnificence; it is without any sort of painting: they are satisfied with a simple coat of oil on the wood, which gives it all the lustre of a varnish.

It is to be remarked that the *Boutcha* is much used by the Portuguese. It is well known that under this name are comprised the descendants of the Portuguese who settled in these countries some centuries back, who are now as black as the Caffries of the Mosambic [Mozambique], and spread all through India, where they are not much respected. Almost every house inhabited by this race of men has its *Boutcha*; and if they are in any sort of affluence, they seldom appear abroad without it.

Commentary: The term *bochā* applied to the original, native form of the chair palanquin portrayed here and to the European chair palki (Pl. II.228).

Solvyns makes much of the use of the Indian style *bochā* by "Portuguese," the term used to include Indian Roman Catholics as well as Eurasians of Portuguese-Indian ancestry.[1] The "Caffrees" to whom Solvyns refers are black Africans, seen in Calcutta as servant slaves in European households.[2]

A variation of this chair pālki was the open "tonjon," a portable chair suspended from a single pole and carried four bearers.[3]

1 On the Eurasian "Portuguese," see Commentary for Pl. II.6.
2 See discussion and note in Commentary for Pl. II.6.
3 *Hobson-Jobson*, 931.

II.228. Chair Palanquin

Paris: III.9.6. ANOTHER SORT OF PALANQUIN: This palanquin, introduced by the Europeans, is not so light, but more elegant in its form, than those of the country. It is mostly used by women. The accuracy of the print dispenses with farther description. At Calcutta, which is the town of most luxury, great numbers of these palanquins are built. Many Europeans have made great fortunes in this capital, by building carriages and palanquins. The Indians endeavour to copy, and can afford to undersell them; but these attempts, though they are admired by their countrymen, are far from satisfying the taste of an European. A Hindoo seldom succeeds in this sort of work, unless he is under the direction and immediate inspection of an European.

Commentary: Solvyns here portrays a European version of the chair palanquin, used by both Europeans and Calcutta's Indian elite, and its widespread use in the city is suggested by Solvyns including it in two other prints. In one, it is depicted with the team of bearers beside a European woman who has come with several men to view the hook-swinging of Caṛak Pūjā (Pl. II.193). In the other, the team of four carriers and the *chātā*-bearer, with the ubiquitous umbrella, relax beside the palanquin, with a vista of Calcutta in the background (Pl. II.2).

The Indian term *bochā* was apparently used

Pl. II.228. Chair Palanquin. Paris: III.9.6.

Calcutta: Sec. VI, No. 6. A Chair Palkee, introduced by Europeans.

for chair palanquins of both Indian and European styles, for Williamson, in *East-India Vade Mecum*, 1810, writes that European "Ladies are usually conveyed about Calcutta [in a] *boçhah*. This has its poles fixed much in the same manner as in the *mahannah* [*mīyāna*, long palanquin] , but its body is of a very different form; being a compound of our sedan chair with the body of a chariot. [It has] two doors, one on each side, with one window in the front, as well as a small one behind, all furnished with Venetians and glasses. . . ."

Williamson adds that "most of the gentlemen residing in Calcutta, ride in *boçhahs*; which afford a better look-out, are more portable, and can turn about in narrow places, where a *mahannah* could not: besides they are far lighter. The *boçhah* made expressly for a lady, is fitted up in some style, and always has four large tassels, commonly of white silk, hanging at the four upper corners. There are usually pockets in front, and to the doors. . . ."[1] In his note to the original drawing, though not depicted in the palanquin portrayed, Solvyns refers to the ladies' chair palanquins as having "small silver vases on the corners of the top, from which are suspended large silk tassels."

In his Paris text, Solvyns's reference to the great fortunes made by Europeans in building palanquins and carries comes from first-hand knowledge, for Solvyns in the first years after his arrival in Calcutta was employed as a decorator by the most distinguished of coachmakers in the city, Steuart & Co.[2]

1 1:322.
2 See pp. 30-31.

Boats of Bengal[1]

There are a great variety of distinctive boats in Bengal and many variations of the same type, reflecting local traditions, adaptations to navigational requirements, and user demands. Moreover, "the same name might often designate different boats and, conversely, a single type of boat might be referred to in different areas by different names."[2] "Different names can also be given to the same boat to give expression to the purpose for which it is used."[3] Solvyns's names for the various boats generally conform to Anglo-Indian usage, but in some instances, his ear may have failed him or he mistook for a name an informant's response to his question as to what kind of boat it is.

In its riverine character, Bengal in Solvyns's time afforded little use of carriages or carts beyond Calcutta. "Almost all journeys are by boat," Grandpré wrote of his travels in 1789-1790. "Bengal is so intersected with rivers and canals that you can go to any part of it in a boat."[4]

Boats were also for pleasure and provided a refreshing alternative to an evening carriage ride over Calcutta's dusty roads, but a boating expedition on the Hugli river, say to suburban Garden Reach, for all the charm of its elegant country houses and cool breezes, might well meet with "unsavory smells and the sight of animal or even human carcasses on the banks."[5] Wealthy Europeans and opulent Hindus kept their own, often richly ornamented, boats—pinnaces (Pl. II.229), bājrās (Pl. II.232), and magnificent "snake boats" (Pls. II.230 and II.231). For these outings, crews were handsomely dressed, and the passengers might be entertained by musicians. European artists, such as the Daniells, often included these boats in their views of India.

Among the boats portrayed by Solvyns are those that carry cargo or passengers for longer river voyages. These "Ganges boats" are "generally broad in beam to avoid awkward squalls, and draw little water so as to escape the numerous shoals."[6] Indeed, flat-bottomed boats are used widely in Bengal because of the many sandbars in the rivers.

Depending on the depth of water, currents, and weather conditions, boatmen row, paddle, pole, and tow their boats, and, with favorable winds, raise the sail. Colesworthy Grant, in *Rural Life in Bengal*, writes that most "Indian boats, though built, adapted, and provided for rowing, are *sailing* boats; and being round, or flat at the bottom, having no keels, are of course very liable, if caught in a squall, or through carelessness falling into the trough of rough water, to be overturned. Hence, in a great measure, the frightful extent of casualties on the river during some of our sudden squalls or terrible nor'-west gales."[7]

Many of Solvyns's boats are portrayed without a mast, though in the text there is reference to sail. The masts may be taken down and are frequently shown in the etchings laid horizontally, usually from the support to which it is hinged.[8] To raise the mast, it is "stepped" into a box-like support (called a "tabernacle") in which the heel of the mast is fixed.

Most often, writes William Crooke, "There is a single mast carrying a rude sail, a marvel of rents and patches, of dull brown colour. . . . Going downstream, [the boat] is propelled by a long bamboo pole, and guided by a large rudder of the most clumsy construction." But going upriver, boats such as the bājrā, must usually be tracked "by ropes fastened to the top of the mast, and each tracker has a separate rope, so that the watchful eye of the skipper may detect if any man is shirking in his work."[9]

In a number of the etchings, Solvyns follows the convention among marine artists by portraying the boat broadside in the center foreground with (or, alternatively, without) the mast set, while the same boat is depicted in the background in a stern and/or bow view and/or at a different point of sail. Thus, for example, where Solvyns portrays the pānsi (Pl. II.235) with mast down, in the background, the boat is shown with the mast stepped and sail unfurled.

Historian Radha Kumud Mookerji concludes his 1912 study of Indian shipping with reference to Solvyns's "very interesting account, together with very fine sketches, of the typical Indian (Hindu) ships that were in use in the earlier part of the 19th century." He then quotes selectively from Solvyns's descriptions of various boats, illustrating the vessels with seven drawings made after Solvyns's etchings. In a footnote, he writes of *Les Hindoûs*, "This rare work is to be found in the splendid library of Mr. Abanindranath Tagore, the renowned Bengali artist. . . ."[10]

In the Preliminary Discourse to *Les Hindoûs*, Volume I, Solvyns writes that

> In ancient times the Indians excelled in the art of constructing vessels, and the present Hindoos can in this respect still offer models to Europe; so much so that the English, attentive to every thing which relates to naval architecture, have borrowed from the Hindoos many improvements which they have adapted with success to their own shipping. This was a very particular object of my attention during my residence in India, and I dare hope that the drawings which I give . . . will be looked upon as what is most complete upon that subject. On examining them it will without difficulty be agreed that the Indian vessels unite elegance and utility, and that they are models of patience and fine workmanship.[11]

In the Calcutta edition of the etchings, Solvyns divided his portrayal of boats into two sections—Section XIII, 13 prints of "pleasure boats," and Section XIV, 17 prints of "boats and vessels of burden." Two additional prints depicting boats, the Bore and the Northwester, precede Sections VIII and IX. In the 1799 *Catalogue*, he writes:

> The different kinds of boats of Hindostan are admirably adapted to the navigation of the various parts in which they are used;—the rivers of the northern provinces require flat broad vessels, with little draft of water; while the southern navigation admits of a construction of greater depth, for security against the high waves of the larger branches of the Berampoter [Brahmaputra] and Ganges.[12]

For the Paris edition, *Les Hindoûs*, Vol. III, Solvyns presents the boats in six sections (or *livraisons*, as he terms them), each beginning with a large, double-size etching. In his Introduction, he assures the reader that his portrayals are based on his own observations and with concern for "truth and exactness of detail." This is surely true for the 32 etchings appearing in the Calcutta edition, for which the original drawings exist. The four etchings in the Paris edition that were not included in the earlier collection are problematic, particularly the two etchings that bring several ships together in composite portrayals, "View of Ballasore Roads" (Pl. II.262) and "Vessels of all Sorts" (Pl. II.263). Here, at least with respect to some of the ships portrayed, Solvyns appears to have copied another artist's print or painting to illustrate a particular kind of vessel.

The Introduction to the third volume of *Les Hindoûs* lays out the plan for the presentation of the prints. Thirty-six etchings portray boats of Bengal, the number, in Solvyns's judgment, "necessary to give a competent idea of their [the Hindus'] navigation."

> Many travellers have bestowed general praises upon the naval arts of the Hindoos, but as none of them have entered into any detail, the subject notwithstanding their elogiums, remained unknown in Europe. This may be deemed therefore the first attempt which has been made, to give a complete description of all the different vessels used in those countries.

My taste as well as my reflections, led me to give a particular attention to this subject, and I believe that my drawings are not liable to any reproach, with respect to their truth and exactness of detail. The multitude of vessels which fill the six first numbers of this volume, may at first sight occasion some surprise, but we must consider, that the greater part of them are meer boats; and it is natural enough that the Hindoos being debarred from maritime expeditions by their religion, which enjoins them not to quit their country, should turn all their attention to inland navigation, and bring it to as great a degree of perfection as the genious of their nation could attain, to which a free scope was given, by the great number of navigable rivers by which Hindoostan is traversed, whose annual inundations, force the neighbouring inhabitants to have recourse to this mode of communication. Hence that variety of boats and barges for the purposes of pleasure or commerce. The first offer an easy and expeditious mode of travelling; by the second, the communications between the country and great towns are kept up, and the wants of their vast population supplied. The forms of both are decided by the local circumstances: in the north of Hindoostan for example, where the waters are subject to little agitation, they are generally flat bottomed; while near the coast, on the contrary they have sharp keels, to resist and cut the waves. Though not a single nail of iron enters into their structure, it is exceedingly solid. This manner of building boats without iron, is very ancient in India. Procopius[13] takes notice of it in his history of the Persian wars, and says that it was known also to the Ethiopians. The engravings in the six first numbers, represent faithfully the forms of all these vessels, and the text enters into every detail of their construction and use, as well as the advantages and disadvantages which attend them. I have sometimes had recourse to a larger scale, to give a clearer idea of the manner of adapting and managing the oars, and of some of the minuter parts of the tackle. I think it necessary to repeat here my assertion, that I never on any occasion whatsoever exceed the bounds of my own observations, which may quit the doubts of those readers, who are always ready to suspect the veracity of a traveller when he relates customs in opposition to those received in Europe, or ventures to contradict what has been related by other respectable travellers. In this manner doubts have been entertained about what I have said of the Pariahs; founded upon their opposition to the prior reports of other creditable authors. I am nevertheless obliged to repeat what I advanced in the first volume, that there never existed in India a particular caste of Pariahs,[14] that the word is generally applied to all that is mean, bad and contemptable; so that my subject may naturally lead me to speak perhaps of a Pariah ship, a term familiar to every sailor who has frequented the Indian seas.

The larger ingravings of the six first numbers of this volume, relate more or less to the navigation of Hindoostan: the two first represents a phenomena well known and dreaded by Indian mariners, the North Wester [Pl. II.260] and the Maerce [*macrée,* or bore, Pl. II.261]. I have endeavoured to retrace their effects with as much truth as such a subject will admit, where the fury of the sea and of the heavens are combined in all their horror. The text will furnish a minute description of these singular phenomena, which appear with more or less violence on all the coasts of India, and not without reason struck Alexander with astonishment as he entered the mouth of the Indus. The third large print [Pl. II.264] is a view of the island of Penang, much frequented by the Indian and Malayan shipping; especially the latter, which renders this island interesting, by affording an opportunity of comparing the naval craft of these two nations; and to give the reader an opportunity of carrying these comparisons still further, I have brought together in the sixth print of the last number [Pl. II.263], all the different species of shipping, which are habitually seen in the Indian seas.

The fourth large print of this volume [Pl. II.262], represents the road of Balasore, in which is the principal entrance of the river Ougly [Hugli], and where a number of vessels constantly stop, some to take in, others to discharge their pilots.

The fifth large engraving [Gudārā, Pl. 258], represents the manner of passing the Ganges. . . .

In making the collection and description of Hindoo shipping, I thought it necessary here and there to make some remarks upon the class of men whose particular destination it is to work them; for the patience and perseverance of the Hindoo boatmen, are very deserving of attention. Occupied day and night in a work which is frequently very laborious, they never lose courage nor shrink from the most formidable obstacles: if they have to struggle with a rapid current, they row without intermission, and though their efforts produce a progress scarcely perceptible they never relax, till they gain the term of their voyage, which frequently lasts for whole months together; this laborious perseverance, is a marked feature in the Hindoo character, and we have already observed how well adapted they are, to all works of patience.[15]

---

1 An earlier version of this section was published as a book, Hardgrave, *Boats of Bengal: Eighteenth Century Portraits by Balthazar Solvyns*.

2 Deloche, 2:156, fn. 44. Prinsep, in 1830, in Appendix A4, devotes seven pages to 29 etchings illustrative of his "remarks concerning country boats" of Bengal, 48-49. The variety of boats are portrayed in some 150 color photographs in Jansen, *Sailing Against the Wind*. On the boats of Bengal, see Greenhill and, more particularly, on boat types and construction, Jansen, *The Country Boats of Bangladesh,* 70-105, and Tamonash C. Das Gupta, 13-40. Also see Hornell's discussion of "Boats of the Ganges," in *Water Transport*, 241-53. A compendium of Hindustani terms relating to country boats of Bihar (many similar to those used in Bengal) is included in Grierson, 42-45. Of great scholarly value is Deloche's work on "modes water transport" in India, 2:127-222, which draws on Solvyns's portrayals, with sketches from the etchings to depict various boats of Bengal, 2:156-64.

3 Jansen, *The Country Boats of Bangladesh,* 74.

4 2:17.

5 Suresh Chandra Ghosh, 140.

6 Crooke, *Things Indian*, 428.

7 6. Grant here refers to "all boats," but later, 26, modifies his sweeping generalization.

8 This is clearly depicted in a photograph in Jansen, *Sailing Against the Wind*, 52-53.

9 *Things Indian*, 428. On tracking, see Deloche, 2:172-74; Greenhill, *Boats and Boatmen of Pakistan*, 45-46; and Bernstein, 16-20. See the description of tracking in the Commentary on the bājrā (PL. II.232).

10 250. The drawings, copies of Solvyns, are inscribed "Seyne." In the preface, x, Mookerji writes, "To the kindness of some of my artist friends I owe the sketches of several representations of ships. . . ."

11 1:28; reproduced in Chapter Four, p. 124.

12 19.

13 Byzantine historian (c.499-565).

14 Solvyns makes this assertion in *Les Hindoûs*, Pl. II.22. I note there in the Commentary that there is surely a "Pariah" (Paraiyan) caste in South India, though in Calcutta, Solvyns would not have encountered it. The term "pariah," however, was widely used among Europeans in India to refer to the worst of almost anything, including "pariah ships."

15 3:1-2.

II.229. Pinnace

Pl. II.229. Pinnace. Paris: III.1.2.
Calcutta: Sec. VIII, No. 1. A Pinnace or Yatch [obs., yacht] for the inland Navigation.

Paris: III.1.2. A PINNACE OR YATCH: These yatchs which are made use of by Europeans are very commodious and generally employed for the voyage from Calcutta to Banares, Lucknow, etc. There are others which belong to private people, and sail down the river to its mouth; but these are real ships and could stand the open sea. I speak here only of the public pinnace. They carry sail, and are generally strongly masted: each one is divided into two or three apartments, one for company, another for the beds, and a third as a cabinet, besides a place called *varandah* forwards for the servants. The yatch has several attendant boats to carry provisions and serve for kitchen and other offices, which keep to leeward not to incommode their masters with the smoke. They have in general as many conveniencies as a small house. The sailors, called *Dandys* [*dāṇḍī*], labour day and night to stem the strongest currents. The assiduity with which these people work is the more surprising, as their wages are very moderate, and their nourishment exceedingly frugal, a little fish and rice, with water. They are continually smoking the *hooka*.

Commentary: The pinnace (*pinās* in Bengali) takes its name from the French word for the long, narrow boat with a sharp stern used in the Bay of Biscay.[1] The boat was introduced in Bengal and was the "largest and handsomest boats" used principally by Europeans.[2] The pinnace is generally schooner-rigged and has two masts, though sometimes one. It is typically 40 to 50 feet in length, with a burden of 12 to 20 tons. Its crew, under a captain, usually called the *mājhī* [3] or *serang*,[4] ranges from 12 to 16 *dāṇḍīs* (Pl. II.56)—or *māllās*, another word for the boatmen—who row, pole, or tug when the wind is insufficient to use the sails.[5] In his note to the original drawing of the pinnace, Solvyns writes that "they draw little water, and are therefore well calculated for inland navigation."

In Solvyns's time and well into the nineteenth century, the pinnace was used to transfer passengers to Calcutta from Diamond Harbor, 41 miles down river, the usual anchorage for Indiamen, or from Kijari (Kedgeree), 68 miles below Calcutta near the mouth of the Hugli, where the larger ships used to anchor.[6]

Pinnaces were usually owned privately by wealthy officials and merchants, but Governor-General Wellesley had, as the East India Company's state yacht, a pinnace, the "Soonamooky" (having the "appearance of gold"), that Sir Charles D'Oyly depicted in a print.[7] Williamson, in the accompanying text, describes the boat, originally built for Warren Hastings, as "a strong mixture of European and Oriental architecture." Taking about 30 oars, it was constructed "of teak, sheathed with copper, and fitted up in a style suited to the dignity of a Viceroy." In the print, the pinnace is accompanied by a fīlcehrā (Pl. II.230).

Pinnaces could be hired in Calcutta for pleasure trips or short journeys, but, because they were expensive to hire, they were used less frequently for lengthy journeys.[8] They did, however, provide superior accommodation to the more widely used, but cumbersome bājrā (Pl. II.232), and, as Tennant noted in 1797, "from its resembling the structure of European craft, both in the hull and rigging, it is better fitted for encountering a gale in the great river."[9] Thomas and William Daniell enjoyed the comfort of a pinnace for their journey "up the country" and included the boat in one of the plates in *Oriental Scenery*.[10]

For extended travel upriver into the interior, the pinnace was typically accompanied by several smaller service vessels. In 1823, Fanny Parks described the boats for a three to four month trip from Calcutta to Lucknow taken by friends: "a very fine sixteen-oared pinnace, containing two excellent cabins, fitted up with glazed and Venetian windows, pankhas [fans], and two shower-baths;" "a dinghee for the cook, and provisions"; an immense baggage boat, containing all their furniture"; "a vessel for the washerman, his wife, and the dogs"; and two large boats with the horses. "What a number of boats for one family!" she declared, "An absolute fleet."[11] The pinnace and its supporting boats could well have a total crew of more than one hundred plus an equal number of servants to attend to the passengers' every need.[12]

About two-thirds of the boat is given to often luxurious accommodation. In the front, several steps down from the fore deck, is an open veranda, as Solvyns describes. This opens into a comfortable living and dining area, behind which are two, sometimes three, spacious cabins, a bathroom and storage closets. The rooms are well-ventilated and cooled by the sway of *pankhās* or by mats that are sprinkled with water over the venetianed windows.[13]

Captain Thomas Williamson, in his *East India Vade-Mecum*, 1810, describes the windows used on both the pinnace and the bājrā: "The sides [of the interior cabins] are furnished, for their whole length, with Venetian blinds, in frames which lift up by means of hinges at their tops; and a long curtain, made either of tarpaulin, or of painted, or of white canvas, is nailed on the outside; letting down at pleasure, to keep out wind, rain, dust, &c."[14]

"The roofs of these boats are usually flat; and some have side rails to prevent luggage, or those who sleep there, from falling overboard. . . . Baggage may be put under the deck; but that part is generally occupied by the dandies, (or rowers,) if permitted to sleep there. . . ."[15]

In the Calcutta edition, the pinnace is portrayed alone, filling the etching. For the Paris edition, Solvyns depicts other boats at sail in the background—a brig (Pl. II.249) and what may be a bhur (Pl. II.256)—and, in the foreground, two rowers take a ḍiṅgi out with supplies for the pinnace.

---

1 Kerchove, 534. Also see Kemp. In his description of the pinnace, Kemp reproduces Solvyns's Calcutta etching, but makes no reference to the boat in India.

2 Colesworthy Grant, *Rural Life in Bengal*, 4-5, with a small engraving.

3 The *mājhī* (Bengali) is the master or steersman of any native river-craft. The commonly used Anglo-Indian name *mangee* is from the Hindi *mānjhī*. *Hobson-Jobson*, 558.

4 Boatswain or skipper of a small native vessel; from the Persian *sarhang*, overseer. *Hobson-Jobson*, 812.

5 Hunter, *A Statistical Account of Bengal*, 1:33; Grant and Colebrooke, 116-17. A common Anglo-Indian word for the native sailor was *lascar*. See Clashy (Pl. II.116).

6 See Pls. II.262 and II.254.

7 "Marquis Wellesley's Dandy, or Boatman, in his Livery," Pl. 12, *The European in India*.

8 Grant, *Rural Life in Bengal*, 4.

9 1:46-47.

10 "Ramnugur near Benares on the Ganges" (I:14), reproduced in Mildred Archer, *Early Views of India*, Pl. 23, with detail of the boat, p. 40. Sutton, 29, refers to the Daniell's pinnace as "roomy and convenient," "from which they could paint at their ease. . . ."

11 1:31.

12 *Admiral Paris' Native Boats*, 34-35.

13 Ibid. For descriptions, see also Lawrence, 51, reprinted in Nair, *Calcutta in the 19th Century*, 616, and London Missionary, *Travels in India* (1852), in Nair, *Calcutta in the 19th Century*, 948.

14 1:129-30.

15 Ibid.

II.230. Fīlcehrā

Pl. II.230. Fīlcehrā. Paris: III.1.3.

Calcutta: Sec. VIII, No. 2. A Feal Chara, named from the elephant's head;—used by the Princes and Nobility, for state and pleasure.

Paris: III.1.3. FEAL-CHARA: The word *Feal-chara* means elephant's head: and the boat represented in the print take this name from their prow. They are become so scarce, that I met with but two or three of them during my stay in India, and these were used but in parties of pleasure. The Radjahs only, and rich people of the country, make use of them. Some old Hindoos, who had been in the service of great men, have assured me that they had formerly *Feal-charas* an hundred feet long by six. They have oars and sails. That which I have represented here was but fifty feet in length by four in breadth. This disproportion will be less striking when the reader becomes acquainted with what I shall say here after upon the naval construction of the Hindoos.

The *Feal-charas* are richly ornamented within and without; they move with a number of oars, one of which, of a larger size, is fixed in front, and in some sort steers this lengthly bark. The master or most distinguished personnage is seated before the rowers.

Commentary: The boat, as Solvyns states, takes its name from the elephant's head on the bow (prow)—in Hindustani, *fīl* (elephant, from the Persian) + *cehrā* (face). The fīlcehrā, like the morpaṅkhī (Pl. II.231), was one of a genre of long and narrow pleasure boats known generally as "snake boats," but the fīlcehrā must have been comparatively rare, belonging only to the exalted few.

In a letter of 1784, Warren Hastings wrote, "I intend to finish my voyage [to Calcutta] to-morrow in the feelchehra." Busteed footnotes Hasting's use of the word as "A large native boat; so called from the prow being commonly decorated with the figure of an elephant's head."[1]

Bishop Heber, in an 1823 entry in his diary, described the "Feel Churra" belonging to the Governor of Bengal, Lord Amherst. The name, he relates, means "elephant bark, from having its head adorned with that of an elephant, with silver tusks. It is a large, light, and beautiful canoe, paddled by twenty men, who sit with their faces toward the head, with one leg hanging over the side of the boat, and the great toe through a ring fastened to its side. They keep time with their paddles, and join occasionally in chorus with a man who stands in the middle, singing. . . . In the fore-part of the boat is a small cabin, very rich ornamented, like the awnings in English barges, but enclosed with Venetian blinds; and between this and the head the mace-bearers of the Governor stand. the Union Jack is hoisted at the head and stern of the boat, and the Company's flag in the centre."[2] With sails and its slim elegance, it must have been an impressive boat.

1 Hasting's letter in Busteed, 291. Hastings's fīlcehrā was later wrecked off Nayaserai. Suresh Chandra Ghosh, 140.

2 1:51-52. In his note to the drawing of the Morpaṅkhī (Pl. II.231), Solvyns writes that the fīlcehrā, as the morpaṅkhī, is rowed to the song of a *jamadār* (leader).

II.231. Morpaṅkhi

Pl. II.231. Morpaṅkhī. Paris: III.1.4.
Calcutta: Sec. VIII, No. 4. A Moorpunkee,—a Pleasure Boat used by the Natives.

Commentary: The morpaṅkhī (or mayūrpaṅkhī) takes its name from the boat's peacock (*mor*) bow. In Solvyns's portrayal of the morpaṅkhī, there are some differences between the Calcutta and Paris etchings. In each, the hull of the boat is the same, but the canopy constructions are quite distinct. Also, in the Paris etching, the oarsmen wear red jackets; in the Calcutta etching, blue.

The morpaṅkhī and boats of similar character drew the attention of artist William Hodges, who noted their curious construction: "These [boats] are very long and narrow, sometimes extending upwards of an hundred feet in length, and not more than eight feet in breadth; they are always paddled, sometimes by forty men, and are steered by a large paddle from the

Paris: III.1.4. MOOR-PUNKEE: Moor-punkee means peacock's head. This boat is now in much more general use, and its construction is nearly the same as that of the *Feal-charra*. But the rowers use paddles, and are seated, with their faces to the prow. It is less expensive, though it is also richly ornamented. They are both very light and deserving of the attention of Europeans from the ingenuity of their construction. The prow and poop might be easily mistaken one for the other. The prince or leading person of the *Moor-punkee* is seated smoking his hooka under a particular canopy, in front of all the others. The grandees and servants of his retinue are under another awning. At the head of the rowers is a *Jemidar* [*jamadār*][1] who, by his voice and his motions, regulates the measure like the leader of an orchestra, and keeps the paddles to a regular movement. The comparison is apter from the little bells fastened to the paddles, which, shaken together, produce a sort of music. The *Magee* [*mājhī*] or pilot of the bark has a long oar with which he steers it.

stern, which rises either in the shape of a peacock, a snake, or some other animal. The persons employed to paddle are directed by a man who stands up, and sometimes he makes use of a branch or a plant to direct their motions. In one part of the stern is a canopy supported by pillars, in which are seated the owner and his friends, who partake together of the refreshing breezes of the evening. These boats are very expensive, owing to the beautiful decorations of painted and gilt ornaments, which are highly varnished and exhibit a very considerable degree of taste."[2]

Solvyns provides a rich illustration for Hodge's account, with the standing *jamadār*—leader[3]—with a *chauṅrī* (whisk) in his hand, directing the oarsmen as if conducting an orchestra. And, indeed, these pleasure boats often took musicians for entertainment, with one observer describing "the oars beating time to the notes of the clarionet." [4] In his note to the original drawing, Solvyns writes that the morpaṅkhī is paddled to the song of the *jamidār*.

In the note, Solvyns describes the morpaṅkhī as "A pleasure boat for princes and people of consequence in Hindostan." In Calcutta, the boats were especially popular for an evening's relaxation by European gentlemen and such wealthy Hindus as Kantababu, who owned one.[5]

One gentleman, the Marquess of Hastings, however, was not wholly enchanted. His diary for July 1814 carries the following entry: "A most splendid boat. . . a morpankha (peacock's feather) really elegant, but very inconvenient. The howdah or seat, near the bows, according to the fashion of those boats, was an extensive canopy of silver brocade divided into three domes, which were supported by silvered pillars. The body of the boat was painted with flowers on a yellow ground like a chintz. The effect was equally light and rich, but the howdah afforded little shelter from the sun. The boat must be from fourscore to ninety feet long. Her head and stern were so high out of the water, that the man who managed the oar with which she was steered, easily communicated (by dancing) a springing motion to those who sat in the howdah."[6]

Both the morpaṅkhī and fīlcehrā were of a genre of pleasure boats termed "snake boats" for their length and quick daring motion. These boats, described by a British officer in 1819, "are very narrow, and have large crews, who use short, broad paddles, with which they strike the water in a quick-measured cadence, which tells loudly, as it falls on the boat's gunwale. Here the owners are seated on cloths or carpets, with, or often without awnings; have their hookahs, and sherbet; a musician or two, or a story-teller: and the crews, too, sing accustomed airs with a wild chorus, led by their coxswain, who stands at the very stern, in a bold graceful attitude, as their boat darts on the bosom of the stream with fearful velocity."[7]

Lord Valentia, on his arrival in Bengal in 1803, described Governor Wellesley's "state barge"—apparently a snake boat—that transported him from his anchored ship upriver to Calcutta as something from a fairy tale: "It was very long in proportion to its width, richly ornamented with green and gold; its head, a spread eagle gilt; its stern, a tiger's head and body. The centre would contain twenty people with ease and was covered with an awning and side curtains: forward were seated twenty natives dressed in scarlet habits with rose-coloured turbans who paddled away with great velocity."[8]

Lady Nugent, in 1812, described perhaps the very same snake boat built by Wellesley. The boatmen, dressed in short pantaloons, scarlet jackets and turbans and sitting cross-legged, paddle in time with song or to the waving of "chowries" (*chauṅrī*)—"white cow's tails, set in silver handles"—by a man (very much as Solvyns depicts) standing in the center of the boat.[9]

Solvyns was surely not the only artist to portray the snake boats. Thomas Daniell, for example, in *Views of Calcutta*, includes a morpaṅkhī in his etching of country boats on the Hugli.[10] The *jamadār* stands, whisk in hand, very much as in Solvyns's portrayal. William Daniell did a watercolor of the state barge of Lucknow, "a moah-punkee,"[11] and a drawing of the same boat for an engraving in *The Oriental Annual*.[12]

By the time Yule and Burnell compiled *Hobson-Jobson* in 1886, these "state pleasure-boats on the Gangetic rivers" survived "only (if at all) at Murshīdābād."[13]

1 *Jamadār* is the head of a group of men. See "Jemadar," in *Hobson-Jobson*, 458-59. (*Jamidār* is Bengali for *zamīndār*, landholder.)

2 *Travels in India*, 40. This description appears, without acknowledgment to Hodges, as a footnote by the translator of Stravorinus's *Voyages to the East Indies* , 1:467-68. The Rev. James Long, *Calcutta in the Olden Time*, 111, quotes it, attributing it to Stavorinus in 1770, as does W. H. Carey (in Wilson and Carey, *Glimpses of the Olden Times*, 155), perhaps simply borrowing from Long. Raja Binaya Krishna Deb, 205, also follows Long.

3 In his note to the original drawing, Solvyns identifies the leader as a "Sareewalla," surely a mistake, for he correctly uses the term *jamidār* in the Paris text.

4 Quoted in Long, *Calcutta in the Olden Times*, 13.

5 Long, *Calcutta in the Olden Times*, 111. Nandy, 1:521. Nandy describes the boat as "peacock faced."

6 1:80-81.

7 *Sketches of India: Written by an Officer*, 166-67, quoted in Nair, *Calcutta in the 19th Century*, 219. Williamson, Pl. 12, *The European in India*, writes that fīlcherās and morpaṅkhīs usually had from 30 to 50 oars and could proceed at 10 to 12 miles per hour, but could not compete with longer "snakes" that "absolutely dart through the water."

8 1:60, in Nair, *Calcutta in the 19th Century*, 2. In his note to the original drawing, Solvyns writes that the boat is paddled "to the song of a Sareewalla who with a chowry in his hand [who] displays the most ridiculous attitudes." Solvyns makes no such disparaging judgment in the 1799 *Catalogue* or in the Paris text, and his "Sareewalla" is probably a mistake for what should be *chauṅrīwala*, whisk-man.

9 78-80.

10 Pl. 8, "Calcutta from the River Hoogly" (1788), reproduced in Mildred Archer, *Early Views of India*, Pl. 11. The Daniells portray the morpaṅkhī in other prints as well, as in the view of Ramnagar on the Ganges, *Oriental Scenery* (I:14), reproduced in Archer, Pl. 23.

11 Spink, 9, color reproduction.

12 Pl. opp. p. 128, *The Oriental Annual, 1835*.

13 584.

II.232. Bājrā

Paris: III.1.5. BUDGEROW: This, like the yatch [yacht] we have described [Pinnace, Pl. II.229], is a boat hired for voyages on the rivers of Hindoostan: it is much higher in the poop and not so swift, so that it is eighteen of twenty days on a voyage which the other performs in fifteen. In other respects the *Budgerow* is extremely commodious, and with plenty of provisions, nothing is wanting in this sort of floating house. The kitchen and offices, as we have already mentioned, are in the attendant boats. We have but few such convenient barges in Europe, and travelling by water is in no part of the world so pleasant as in India. It is true that these voyages become very expensive from the quantity of things it is necessary to provide even for a few days: neither cloaths nor food must be forgotten, nor servants of every description, even washingmen and bakers. Each rower in Bengal has three roupees per month: the *Magee* [*mājhī*] or pilot the double; but they find themselves in cloaths and diet. The hire of a *Budgerow* may come to from three to five roupees a day. Among the *Magees* and *Dandys* [*dāṇḍī*] there are at present many Mussulmans who find employment even among the Hindoos, although the true followers of Brahma consider it as it duty to employ none but those of their own religion.

Commentary: Valued for its utility, the bājrā—Anglo-Indian budgerow or, less commonly, bazara[1]—was used by Europeans and prosperous Indians for traveling on the Ganges and its tributaries. Its early use by Europeans in Bengal is recorded by the seventeenth century traveler Thomas Bowrey: "A Budaroo Or Pleasure boat, wherein the English and Dutch Chiefe and Councill goe in State Upon the water, in Use alsoe by the Moors Grandees of Governours."[2]

Of all the boats of Bengal, the bājrā was most widely used by Europeans. In his "reminiscences of the good old days," William H. Carey, in 1882, wrote that

Pl. II.232. Bājrā. Paris: III.1.5.
Calcutta: Sec. VIII, No. 3. A Budgerow or Bengalee Barge.

"Budgerows are now extinct. Steamers nearly drove them off the river, and the railroad has extinguished them. But in days previous to steam navigation, they were the principal conveyance for officers, and others proceeding to the north-western provinces."[3]

Flat-bottomed and drawing little water—a foot or a little more—the bājrā was sometimes described as a keelless barge. Bājrās were "large and commodious, but generally cumbrous and sluggish."[4] They varied in size, ranging from 25 to 60 feet or more in length, with a high stern that rose as much as 12 feet above the water. The stern apparently varied from the sharp point seen in Solvyns's etching to spoon or sometimes square shapes, and the prow might be ornamented with a figurehead such as that described by Carey: "a hideous attempt at an European, with a black hat, a bright blue coat, and a yellow waistcoat."[5] In Solvyns's portrayal, the bow is fitted with the head of what appears to be a crocodile with gaping mouth.

The bājrā, though less luxurious than the pinnace, provided considerable comfort. Some two-thirds of the aft portion were given to cabins, with venetianed windows that could be lifted along each side. A veranda in front opened at the same level into the sitting and dining room, with a ceiling height of some seven to nine feet. Toward the stern and rising one or two steps were either one or two sleeping cabins, each usually with a small toilet closet, or head. Toward the fore, the bājrā was decked and equipped with two covered hatchways.[6] The roof was flat and was used by passengers as a promenade deck in the evening and as a place for the crew and servants to sleep at night.

With a crew under the *mājhī*, bājrās typically had ten to twenty oars. In Solvyns's portrayal, the bājrā is manned by twelve oarsmen, *dānḍīs*. The oars are long poles with a small oval board affixed at the end. Stavorinus, from his travels, 1768-1771, notes that "they do not strike the water cross ways, but obliquely backwards."[7] The *mājhī*, at the helm on the upper deck, steered the boat by a large rudder extending from the stern. With the danger of the boat's running aground, a "*goleer*" (also *golea*, *golia*) at the bow determines the depth of the water by means of a long oar or bamboo pole.[8]

Although Solvyns's bājrā is not shown with the mast raised, to take advantage of any winds, bājrās were equipped with a single square-rigged mast. Hornell describes the mast as fixed and stepped amidships, with a slender topmast usually added. "The mainsail is square with a bamboo yard along the upper margin; in fine weather a square topsail is hoisted above the mainsail."[9] With a crosswind, the boat, without a keel, would move forward transversely.[10]

As flat-bottomed boats, bājrās did not sail well and were dangerous in the wind and, top-heavy, could be easily overturned.[11] But the artist William Hodges writes in 1781 that "the English gentlemen have made great improvements on the budgerow in Bengal, by introducing a broad flat floor, square sterns, and broad bows. These boats are much safer, sail near and keep their wind, and there is no danger attending their taking the ground; they are besides, calculated for carrying a greater quantity of sail."[12]

But the bājrā's progress upriver was usually by neither sail nor oar. Rather it was towed, "tracked," along the edge of the shore by a line some 80 to 100 yards long, with the crew laboring in relays throughout the day.[13]

Mrs. Kindersley, in a letter from Patna in 1766, described her bājrā journey:

> The progress up the Ganges is so exceedingly slow, that the voyage from Calcutta to Allahabad takes nearly three months to perform it in; at the same time that it is common to go from Allahabad to Calcutta in twenty days. . . .

[I]n the passage up the river they most tow; but when they [*dānḍīs*] come to a creek, of which there are many very broad, they fasten the rope round their wastes, and, throwing themselves from the land, which is often very high, swim across, dragging the *budgeroo* after them.

When the squalls of wind and rain come on, if they can find no place to lay by, they jump into the river, and hang with their hands upon the edge of the boat, to keep it steady, with just their mouth above the water . . . . The work of towing, or as it is called, tracking, is sometimes exceedingly laborious; for the banks, which, when the river is lowered, are the height of a house at least above the water, are so softened by the rains, that *dandies* sink midleg at every step they take; frequently large pieces of the banks give way, and by their fall boats are sunk or overset.

Sometimes they row; then it is they seem to enjoy themselves, singing all together, with great vehemence, some songs peculiar to their employment.

A family has frequently two *budgeroos*, besides boats; one of the boats is for cookery, the others for servants, provisions, furniture, and other necessities; for whenever people remove from one place to another, they are obliged to carry all these things with them, even *palenqueens*, carriages, and horses; so that the troop of attendants of every kind amounts to a great number of people.

When once chooses to dine, &c. the *budgeroo* is stopped, and the boats which are wanted come round it, and dinner is served with as much order as on shore. . . .

Except in the squalls, which are frequent in the season, it is a most easy method of traveling, and, when a party of *budgeroos* go together, very agreeable.

When the *budgeroos* stop at night, the *dandies* make their fires on shore, each *cast* by themselves. . . .[14]

With one or two bājrās and their attendant boats, the river convoy included, at a minimum, a palwār (Pl. II.252) as a kitchen boat and a smaller, more maneuverable pānsi (Pl. II.235), used to convey bājrā passengers to shore and back.[15] For longer trips and those with heavy or substantial freight, one or more separate baggage boats accompanied the bājrā, providing both storage for goods and chattel and accommodation for an overflow of servants.

The stock for a long voyage upriver would consist of "groceries of all kinds, wine, beer, and brandy, salt provisions, tongues, hams, tamarind-fish (fish cured with the acid of the tamarind), flour, biscuits, and charcoal; a dozen or two of live fowl and ducks, and a couple of milch goats."[16]

Atop the bājrā, in Solvyns's portrayal, is a long palanquin, covered by a tarpaulin and awaiting use on land by the European party.

---

1 *Hobson-Jobson*, 120.

2 228.

3 "Sidelights and Reminiscences of the Good Old Days," 1882, in Wilson and Carey, 184.

4 Colesworthy Grant, *Rural Life in Bengal*, 5, with a small engraving.

5 "Sidelights and Reminiscences of the Good Old Days," 1882, in Wilson and Carey, 184.

6 Williamson, *East India Vade-Mecum*, 377.

7 465-66.

8 "Sketches of Indian Society: No. VI, Travelling--the Buderow," *Asiatic Journal*, 12 (September-December 1833), 13-14, quoted in Nair, *British Social Life*, 60-61. Solvyns's "goleer" for bowman is probably from the Bengali *golui*, bow. On the perils of running aground, see Bernstein, 18-19.

9 *Water Transport*, 246. Also see Hornell, "The Boats of the Ganges," 185-87.

10 Stavorinus, 465-66; Hodges, *Travels*, 39; and Grant and Colebrooke, 115.

11 Bacon, quoted in Nair, *Calcutta in the 19th Century*, 561-62.

12 *Travels*, 40.

13 Carey, "Sidelights and Reminiscences of the Good Old Days," 1882, in Wilson and Carey, 185.

14 Kindersley, 93-97; reprinted in Nair, *Calcutta in the 18th Century*, 141-42. Kindersley provides one of the earliest accounts of travel by bājrā, but descriptions of the bājrā are frequent in subsequent accounts of European life in Bengal. See, for example, Nugent, 2:371-72; *Sketches of India*, in Nair, *Calcutta in the 19th Century*, 192-93; Fenton, 29-30, in Nair, *Calcutta in the 19th Century*, 457-58; Mundy, 2:147-51, in Nair, *Calcutta in the 19th Century, 485-86;* Roberts, 2nd ed., 1:261-93; and Dewar, *In the Days of the Company*, 64-74. Thomas Williamson and Gilchrist, 450-471, in manuals for Europeans coming to India for the first time, provide detailed instructions for outfitting these bājrā flotillas.

15 Hodges, *Travels*, 39.

16 "Sketches of Indian Society: No. VI, Travelling—the Budgerow," *Asiatic Journal*, 12 (September-December 1833), 13-14, quoted in Nair, *British Social Life*, 60-61.

II.233. Bhāuliyā

Pl. II.233. Bhāuliyā. Paris: III.1.6.
Calcutta: Sec. VIII, No. 5. A Baawalee-a, a large narrow Boat for expedition.

Paris: III.1.6.
BAAWALEE-A: This species of boat is the swiftest we know. The extreme lightness of its construction gives it incredible speed. An example among others is cited of a governor general, who in his *Baawalee-a* performed in eight days the voyage from Lucknow to Calcutta, a distance of four hundred marine leagues. This fact is attested by several persons: it is true the governor took care to have frequent changes of rowers at proper distances.

Though the number of rowers seem to increase the speed, experience has proved that too many impede it. The middle-sized *Baawalee-as* have but six or eight, and they are the best: they go against wind and tide. They differ from the *Moor-punkee* [Pl. II.231] by the height of the poop above the prow, and by not having so many conveniences. The master is seated behind the rowers, near the Magee [*mājhī*]. No one can change his place without giving a shock to the whole boat; it is so light and so narrow.

Commentary: The bhāuliyā (bhāule in modern Bengali)[1] is a long, narrow Bengali river boat with generally four to eight oars. Hornell contrasts the smaller and more manageable bhāuliyā with the leisurely, if sometimes cumbersome bājrā: "with a lusty crew rowing cheerfully to a rhythmic chant it carries its passengers swiftly along, even against the stream."[2] Most descriptions give it one small cabin, but Solvyns depicts what *Hobson-Jobson* refers to as "only a small kiosque at the stern."[3] Grant, in *Rural Life in Bengal*, includes an illustration of the bhāuliyā with not only a cabin but a mast.[4] The mast in the better bhāuliyās is hinged in a tabernacle; others rely simply on a pole that is taken aboard as needed.[5]

Buchanan, in the early 1800s, writes that the bhāuliyā, like the pānsi (Pl. II.235), is a passenger boat. "It is sharp at both ends, rises at the ends less than the *Pansi*, and its tilt is placed in the middle, the rowers standing both before and behind the place of accommodation of passengers." But reflecting the variation of names for boats in eastern India, Buchanan notes, "On the Kosi [river in northeastern Bihar], the *Bhauliya* is a large fishing-boat, carrying six or seven men."[6]

1 Sukumar Sen, 704; *Hobson-Jobson*, "boliah," 102.
2 Hornell, "The Boats of the Ganges," 187.
3 102.
4 3.
5 Hornell, "The Boats of the Ganges," 188.
6 As related in Montgomery Martin, 3:345.

II.234. Paṭuā

Pl. II.234. Paṭuā. Paris: III.2.2.
Calcutta: Sec. IX, No. 5. A Pettooa,—a Balasore Boat.

Paris: III.2.2. PETTOO-A: This is the name given to some boats which come from Balassora or the coast of Palmira [in Orissa, Pl. II.262]. The *Pettoo-as* differ from other vessels by their being clincherbuilt [clinker-built]: the boards are one upon the other, contrary to our European construction of that kind: they are fastened by little pieces of iron in the form of cramps. The anchors are often of wood, but they are not at present much in use. The yard is always without sail, and the sails are hoisted and lowered by blocks. The *Pettoo-as* are very crank, and cannot keep close to the wind: for which reason they always wait for the fine monsoon to sail: they seldom go alone. On their return upon their ballast they appear always on the point of turning over, from their excessive lightness: the weight of a single man on either side is sufficient to make them dip several feet. They are generally manned with *Ourihas* [Oriyas]: when they arrive, they run them a-shore on the sand, and haul them up dry with the paras[1] so much used in the Mediterranean, waiting prudently for the fine weather to return. The *Pettoo-as* are provided with large *jars* to hold their water. The cordage called *cariar* [coir], is generally made of the filaments of the cocoa-nut. The engraving will give a sufficient idea of the form of the *Pettoo-a*.

Commentary: The paṭuā is a sea-going boat of Orissa, but rather unstable ("crank") and liable to capsize in rough water. Solvyns describes its hull in terms that suggest reverse clinker construction. In this ancient form, depicted in two carvings of boats from eleventh-twelfth century Orissa, "the overlaps are reversed, that is, the upper edge of the lower plank is outside the lower edge of the upper plank."[2]

In the etching, following convention, the boats in the distance are likely pātuās at sail.

1 The French word *para* refers to a construction to hoist a boat onto land. Fennis, 3:1346.

2 Deloche, 2:170.

II.235. Pānsi

Commentary: The pānsi (Anglo-Indian, paunchway or, less commonly, pansway) is a light river boat of Bengal, rather like a large ḍiṅgi (Pl. II.237). It is typically 20 to 30 feet in length, with a roof of matting or thatch, a mast that may be stepped in front, and with three to six oars.[1] Grant and Colebrooke suggest that the name "seems to import that it should carry 500 muns [maunds], but in practice this boat varies much in size; it is of light draught, and outstrips a Pinnace before the wind."[2]

According to *Admiral Paris' Native Boats*, "There are a great variety in the line and size of this name; they have no keel, are longer and less flat than 'dinghis', and are easier to sail. They have a framework, and their planking is joined by cramp-irons, and pierced by the beams. Almost all carry a cabin made of planks and matting, with a thatched roof. 'Pansways' carry an upper platform towards the rear only, and only if their rudder is vertical (usually they use an oar attached to a structure of posts.)."[3]

Pl. II.235. Pānsi. Paris: III.2.3.
Calcutta: Sec. VIII, No. 6. A Punsway, a small convenient passage Boat.

Paris: III.2.3. PANSWAY: The *Pansway* is a passage-boat very convenient for inland navigation. At Calcutta *Pansways* of different sizes are to be met with in all the *gauts* or wharfs, which convey passengers to the towns upon the rivers: in general they have but four oars and a *Magie* [*mājhī*] or pilot, and are hired for about a *roupee* or half-crown a day.

The *Pansways* are convenient only for a short passage: the seat under the awning is not easy; there is no kitchen: so that the dinner must be prepared on shore.

There are others which carry six oars, and are better equipped: those go down the river to take passengers to and from the ships. Others of a still larger size are used to carry rice and provisions to a great distance up the rivers. These are generally manned by Hindoos, as the others are by Mussulmans and men of all casts. The *Pansways* appropriated to passengers are painted with a bad sort of colours. There are some also of this kind which carry sail pretty well: but they cannot go close to the wind.

The pānsi, described by Kerchove, is "a double-ended open boat with long overhangs covered at the afterend with a bamboo and mat thatch. It is employed for transportation of goods and passengers on the Estuary of the Ganges River, Bengal. Iron wood is used for the bottom planking, teak for the sides and sal wood for the upper works and beams."[4]

As related in various accounts of the bājrā (Pl. II.232), a pānsi typically accompanied the larger boat to convey passengers back and forth to shore. The pānsi has the same general construction as the bājrā, with the difference, artist William Hodges relates, "that the greatest breadth is somewhat further aft, and the stern lower."[5]

It was by pānsi that William Hickey arrived in Calcutta from anchorage at Sagar Island, some 100 miles down river at the mouth of the Hugli. "This mode of traveling did not exactly meet our approbation, paunceways being so constructed that you have not room to sit upright under the roof or covering of mat to protect those within from sun or rain, nor is there any place to let your legs hang down in, passengers sitting upon a platform like tailors on their shopboard."[6]

Bishop Heber, in 1823, also arrived in Calcutta from Sagar by pānsi. In his diary, he recorded that

> a "Panchway," or passage boat, . . . was a very characteristic and interesting vessel, large and broad, shaped like a snuffer dish; a deck fore and aft, and the middle covered with a roof of palm branches, over which again was lashed a coarse cloth, the whole forming an excellent shade from the sun; but, as I should apprehend, intolerably close. The "serang," or master, stood on the little after-deck, steering with a long oar; another man, a little before him, had a similar oar on the starboard quarter; six rowers were seated cross-legged on the deck upon the tilt, and plied their short paddles with much dexterity; not however as paddles usually are plied, but in the manner of oars, resting them instead of rullocks, on bamboos, which rose upright from the sides. A large long sail of thin transparent sackcloth in three pieces, very loosely tacked to each other, completed the equipment.[7]

The etching provides a good illustration of the convention in marine painting of varied views of the boat, with the pānsi in the background with mast stepped and sails unfurled.

1 *Hobson-Jobson*, 688; Deloche, 2:162; and Hornell, "The Boats of the Ganges," 181.
2 116.
3 37-39
4 517.
5 40; also see Stavorinus, 1:467fn.
6 Hickey, 2:117-118.
7 1:5-6. An engraving illustrates a "Calcutta Panchway."

II.236. Khelā or Lāl Ḍiṅgi

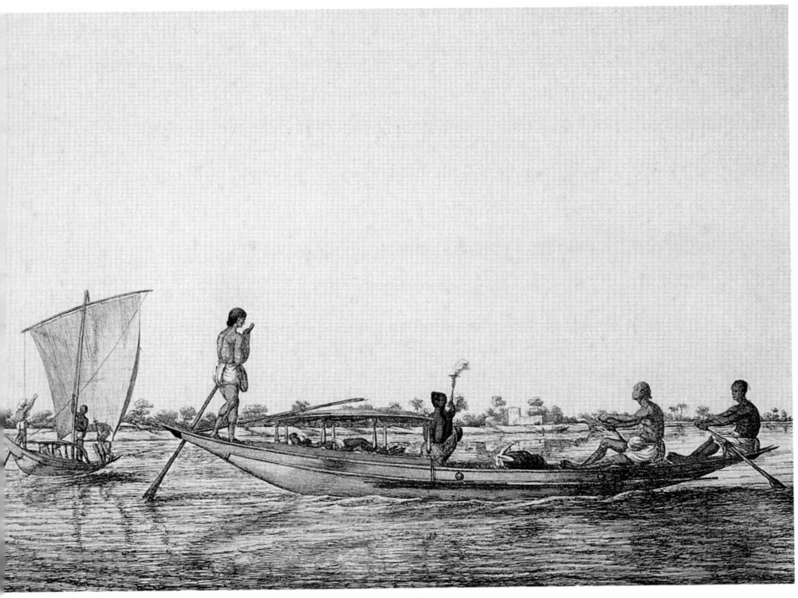

Pl. II.236. Khelā or Lāl Ḍiṅgi. Paris: III.2.4. **Calcutta: Sec. VIII, No. 9.** A Khela or Loll Dingee,—the common pleasure Boat of the Natives, and used by Europeans for expedition.

Paris. III.2.4. KHELA OR LOLL DINGEE: These are boats of a very slight construction, generally used by persons who live near the river. The *Circars* [sarkār, steward or broker, Pl. II.100] come to town for their business in a *Khela* on which they bestow more or less ornament. The *Khela-Dingee* represented in the engraving is of the plainer sort: it is worked by two rowers: the master is stretched out indolently, while his companions are smoking the hooka.

The Hindoo oar consists of a cross-grained board tied to a bambou: to put it in motion they use another smaller bambou fastened to the first with a hempen cord.

The rowers of these little boats are far from being as dexterous as the other Hindoo workmen; there is always something wanting in their tackle: and when any accident happens, they are quite at a loss, and are satisfied with calling God to their assistance, without endeavouring to help themselves.

Commentary: The boat is a variety of ḍiṅgi, the word *khelā* meaning pleasure or sport. "Loll" carries no suggestion of nautical meaning, but it is likely *lāl*, "red," as one might well imagine Solvyns asking the boatman, "What do you call this boat?" and the man replies, "lāl ḍiṅgi, sahib." Solvyns, however, does not portray a "red" boat. In the Calcutta etching, the fore rail is blue and there is a red gunwale; in the Paris etching, these colors are reversed.

The boat in the background is a khelā ḍiṅgi with sail.

II.237. Ḍiṅgi

Paris: III.2.5. DINGEE: Although the word *Dingee* means a boat in general, it is more particularly applied to a sort of boat used to keep up the communication between the ships and the different ports and landing-places. Vast numbers of these *Dingees* ply all along the port of Calcutta, and for a meer trifle you may be carried aboard the ships. While a vessel is at anchor before the town, the *Dingees* perform a regular service in carrying provisions, and supplying the crews with whatever they may want. In this case they are hired by the month.

Some *Dingees* have one or even two rowers, but in general they are managed by a single man with one oar in the poop. This will not appear extraordinary to those who know that in some countries, as in China for example, vessels of some hundred tons are worked by the motion of a single oar in the stern.

Commentary: Ḍiṅgi, in Bengali, means "small boat"—the diminutive of *ḍiṅgā*, "boat"[1]—and, with a variety of shapes and sizes, it resembles a canoe or wherry.[2] The word entered English as "dinghy" to refer to a small boat carried as a tender, lifeboat, or pleasure craft on a larger boat, and also to a small rowboat.[3] With a brig in the background of the etching, Solvyns suggests such use here.

In North India, the term is used to mean a dugout, hollowed from a tree trunk, but in Bengal, the word generally refers to half-decked, round-bottomed boats build of planks, fastened with nails or

Pl. II.237. Ḍiṅgi. Paris: III.2.5.
Calcutta: Sec. VIII, No. 8. A Dingee,—a general name for every small boat.

boatbuilders stables, or, as perhaps here in Solvyns's portrayal, sewn together. Manned usually by two rowers toward the front and a steersman at the stern, the ḍiṅgi is "of slight construction, spoon-bottomed, with a circular awning of bamboo-work, under which a person can sit. . . ."[4]

Ḍiṅgis were used for river passage of short duration, as in ferry-crossings from Calcutta to the opposite shore, for fishing, and in transport back and forth from ship to shore, as Solvyns here portrays.

1 Sukumar Sen, 375.
2 Hornell, *Water Transport*, illustrates four types of ḍiṅgis, 242-44.
3 *American Heritage Dictionary*. Also see *Hobson-Jobson*, 318.
4 Stocqueler, *Hand-Book of British India*, 185. Also see Grant and Colebrooke, 115; and Deloche, 2:158.

II.238. Magarcehrā

Paris: III.2.6. MUGA-CHARA: This species of boat is seldom seen at Calcutta, but is much used in upper Hindoostan, especially in Dacca. In this country, which is traversed by rivers and canals, passengers are conveyed by the *Muga-charas,* and sometimes in great multitudes, as at feasts and marriages. I have here given the representation of a wedding travelling in one of these boats. The palanqueen, the musicians, and all that characterises this solemnity, are seen in the engraving. On such occasions several boats are necessary; and it is not uncommon therefore to see *Muga-charas* accompanied by *Pulwars* [Palwār, Pl. 252], *Pansways* [Pānsi, Pl. II.235], and other vessels. The fore-part or prow of the *Muga-chara* is higher than the poop, and is ornamented with a head and other figures, like the *Feal-chara* [Fīlcherā, Pl. II.230] and *Moor-Punkee* [Morpañkhī, Pl. II.231]. It is covered with double or triple mats, which, though extremely light, are a sufficient protection against the rain.

Pl. II.238. Magarcehrā. Paris: III.2.6.
Calcutta: Sec. VIII, No. 12. A Muga Chara,—a Dacca Boat, commonly hired by the lower class to celebrate their marriages, festivals and parties of pleasure.

Commentary: As with the fīlcehrā, the name refers to the "face" on the bow of the boat. Here, Solvyns's "muga" (Anglo-Indian, muggur or muggar) is *magar*, the broad-snouted marsh crocodile of the Ganges.[1] Solvyns's portrays what at first glance appears more like an elephant with a curving trunk, but the sharp teeth reveal what is a rather peculiar crocodile. No reference to a boat of this name appears in the literature consulted.

The boat is fitted with a *chāunri*, a thatched shelter, typically (as here) of woven bamboo that is bent over to make a tunnel-like covering for crew and passengers.[2]

The wedding party, to which Solvyns refers, is shown in a magarcehrā along the shore. A palanquin, for the bride, is aboard, as are musicians with a rāmśiṅgā (Pl. II.176) and bā̃k (Pl. II.177), more clearly evident in the Paris than the Calcutta etching.

1 *Hobson-Jobson*, 595. For a description of the magar (*Crocodylus palustris*), see Daniel, 10-12.
2 Greenhill, *Boats and Boatmen of Pakistan*, 28.

II.239. Donī

Pl. II.239. Donī. Paris: III.3.2.
Calcutta: Sec. IX, No. 4. A Dony,—a clumsy Craft, from the Coromandel Coast.

Paris: III.3.2. DONY: This is the name of a very unwieldy boat with one mast, resembling a sloop: its deck consists of a few planks fastened on each side: it is badly rigged, and sails but in the favorable monsoon. It comes from the coast of Coromandel, with a few men only, generally of Hindoo origin. The *Donys* profit of the south-west monsoon to make a yearly voyage to Calcutta, with their sails set from the moment of their departure till their arrival. They set out again with the north-east monsoon. Without these precautions they never could keep the sea, from the great ignorance of their sailors and the clumsiness of their vessels. These sailors too are unable to stand damp weather; it enervates them to such a degree, that even the Mussulmans, who are tolerable seamen in the hot climates, sink under it, and become unfit for service.

Commentary: The donī (Tamil, *toṅi*; Telugu, *doni*) is a common boat on South India's Coromandel coast and in Sri Lanka and is variously described as both small and large. *Hobson-Jobson* identifies it as "a small native vessel" that, as both early accounts and etymology suggests, evolved from a dugout.[1] In the first volume of *The Journal of the Royal Asiatic Society of Great Britain and Ireland*, Edye, formerly His Majesty's Master Shipwright in Ceylon, describes it as "a huge vessel of ark-like form, about seventy feet long, twenty feet broad, and twelve feet deep; with a flat bottom or keep part, which at the broadest place is seven feet" and, confirming Solvyns's judgment, "the whole equipment of these rude vessels, as well as their construction, is the most coarse and un-seaworthy that I have ever seen."[2] Solvyns's donī is considerably smaller, however. In a preliminary drawing, from the album assembled by his widow, Solvyns penciled in its dimensions as 36 feet in length, 12 feet in breadth.[3]

In his note to the original drawing, in the Victoria and Albert Museum, Solvyns described the donī as "A vessel with two or three masts, but commonly with one, [as] represented in the drawing.[4] The Dony appears an ill constructed clumsy vessel; they are employed generally in carrying salt from Balasore and the coast."

European influence is evident in many donīs, as that portrayed here by Solvyns, and boats of this type, confined to coastal navigation between Bengal and the Coromandel, were disparaged as "pariahs" by French sailors. These boats, Deloche writes, "had a square stern with a high poop, a rigging of European influence with a large mast bearing a fore-and-aft sail, topsail and sometimes a top gallant," and were built at Coringa (Korangi) on the Godavari coast of what is today Andhra Pradesh. "Almost all of these boats had a bad reputation among European sailors, who considered them to be badly built, weak and lacking in stability because of their light water draft. Their rigging was judged inefficient, not allowing the boats to venture any great distance from the coast, for fear of being carried off to open seas by the south-westernly winds."[5]

1 323.

2 Edye, 13. Kerchove, in the *International Maritime Dictionary*, 213, identifies the "doney" as a coaster on the east coast of India, with a length of 70 to 100 feet, a breadth of 20 to 21 feet, and depth of 12 to 14 feet. It has a keelless flat bottom and a fore- and afterbody of similar form.

3 On the album, see pp. 83-85.

4 Admiral Smyth, 257, states that these "unshapely" vessels have only one mast, but according to Kerchove, 213, the rig consists of one, two, or three masts, with lateen or gaff sails. Headsails are carried on a bowsprit with huge jibboom.

5 Deloche, 2: 185-86.

II.240. Jāliyā Ḍiṅgi

Pl. II.240. Jāliyā Ḍiṅgi. Paris: III.3.3. **Calcutta: Sec. VIII, No. 7.** A Jell-a Dingee, or Fishing Boat.

Paris: III.3.3. JELLEE-A DINGEE: This is a very light and well-built boat, used for fishing. The pilot of the *Jellee-a* sits high at the top of his boat, and steers it with an oar which he frequently manages with his feet, while his hands are employed with the hooka which he is constantly smoking. They are of different size according to the nature of the fishery; the topsy (mango fish, described in the New Dictionary of natural history),[1] the shad. For this latter, which is so abundant that five and twenty or thirty are sometimes to be had for a roupee, there are a vast number of boats of an extraordinary length, which carry five or six fishermen. These boats take also large quantities of prawns, which are eaten by the people with great avidity. The Mugs[2] and Malays keep them till they are putrid, and blend them with salt into a paste, which has a very strong smell, and is put up in jars and small pots for use. Some fishermen remain often four months together in their boats without leaving them. It seems that the *Jellee-a* has served as a model for all the other boats which are used in Hindoostan.

Commentary: Hornell provides a similar description for the jāliyā (or jeli) ḍiṅgi to that of Solvyns, noting that "they differ considerably in detail and proportion and have their special local names, often given however not because of difference in form but merely because of the kind of net used from them. . . ."[3]

"In form and construction all varieties of the *jalia dinghi* are admirable and exactly suited to contend with the strong currents and tides of the Ganges and its branches within tidal influence. Its rounded bottom, the high sheer of stem and stern and narrow build make it easy to handle in a tide way; they are lively craft and require considerable skill in handling."[4] Reflecting a variety of traditions in boat-building technology, used simultaneously, as in many boats of Bengal, ḍiṅgi construction is eclectic.

Fishermen in the jaliyā ḍiṅgi in the background hoist the net.

1 On the tapsī fish, see Pls. II.288 and Pl. II.57, fn. 3. The volume to which Solvyns refers is William Frederick Martyn, *A New Dictionary of Natural History*, 2 vols. London: Harrison & Co., 1785.

2 Maghs, see Pl. II.251.

3 "The Boats of the Ganges," 182.

4 Ibid., 183.

II.241. Saraṅgā

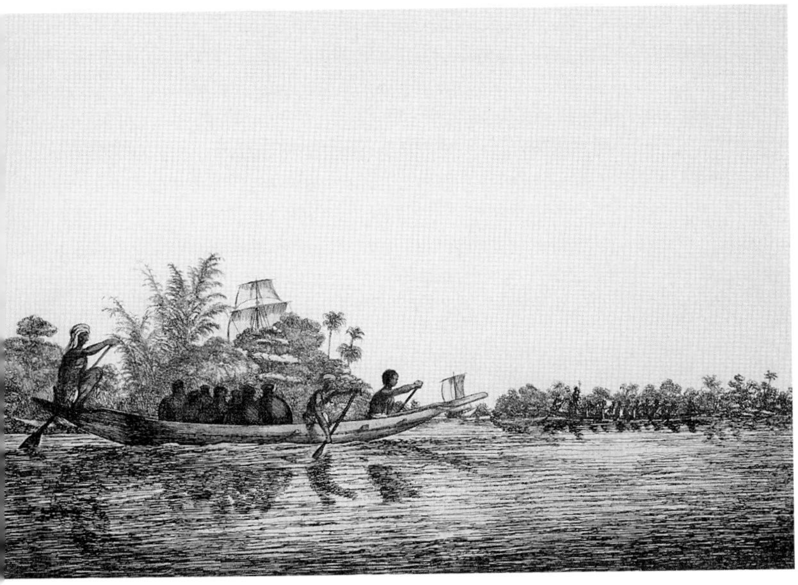

Pl. II.241. Saraṅgā. Paris: III.3.4.

Calcutta: Sec. IX, No. 10. A Scringee,—being an Ek-gachee [ekṭhā, Pl. II.242] with the addition of some Planks on each side.

Paris: III.3.4. SERINGEE: The *Seringee* resembles the last boat which we have described, and differs from it only by having a few more planks. Some of them are of a great length, and these are generally used in the *sunderbunds*, or very close woods, which are infested by tigers and other ferocious animals. This species of *Seringee* is manned by *banbuyties*, a sort of banditti, who accost the vessels they meet in the evening, under pretext of asking to light their fire. Three of four only of their crew appear; the remainder are hid under the sails and mats. If they perceive that the vessel is too strongly manned to be attacked, they follow their course; if on the contrary they feel sufficiently strong, they board it and carry off all the cargo, and not unfrequently throw the passenger into the river. The *Chaukys*, a sort of boat very well manned, give chase to these river pirates, and punish them severely as often as they catch them. The *Seringee* represented in the engraving is of the smaller sort, and has paddles instead of oars. It follows a larger vessel, and is laden with leather jars filled with fish oil. That in the distance is one of the *banbuyties*. The view represents one of the *sunderbunds* which we have just mentioned.

Commentary: The saraṅgā is the general term for cargo-carrying dugouts in eastern Bengal, and similar dugouts, sometimes with variations in size and form, are found throughout the region, each with distinct names, such as ekṭhā (Pl. II.242), ḍoṅga (Pl. II.243) and śālti. Greenhill writes that saraṅgās "are cut from single logs, hollowed out until only the equivalent of a thin planking . . . is left" and then built up on the sides with planks, which are secured to the dugout by split bamboo stitches. The seam is caulked.[1] Jansen, in *Country Boats of Bangladesh*, describes the "sharonga" as "a sea-going boat. . . , both small and medium-sized, used in fishing as well as transport."[2] In his note to the original drawing, Solvyns indicates that "some are as large as 200 or 300 maunds." They are, he writes, used with paddles, as portrayed in the etching.

That spellings and pronunciations vary for the names of boats in Bengal—not to mention transliterations—is surely evident in the words for this boat. Solvyns gives three different transliterations, and it appears elsewhere, without diacritical marks, as saranga (Greenhill), sharonga (Jansen), and in sources cited by Jansen as sarangi and haranga.[3]

Solvyns refers to *banbuyties*, who he describes as "a sort of banditti."[4] Bandits—"dacoits" in common Indian parlance—were widespread in Bengal, especially in the Sundarbans, the area of intersecting channels, swampy islands, and jungles of the lower Ganges delta.[5] In the early days of British rule, these "night-hawks of the river" operated at night in long and narrow many-oared boats "to plunder inland villages or, gaining one of the main rivers, would attack the slow-moving heavy cargo boats and merchant vessels, robbing and slaying with impunity, disappearing again, as swiftly as they had come, to their lairs in the riverine labyrinth of the delta."[6]

Perhaps Solvyns here portrays the Sundarbans channel that Europeans in the seventeenth and eighteenth centuries called "Rogues's River." "It was so called from being frequented by the Arakan Rovers, sometimes Portuguese vagabonds, sometimes native Muggs,[7] whose vessels lay in this creek watching their opportunity to plunder craft going up and down the Hoogly [Hugli]."[8]

Solvyns identifies the saraṅgā in the distance of his portrayal as manned by "banbuyties." In the Calcutta etching, the boat is only sketchily evident, but for the Paris edition, Solvyns changes the composition by shifting the boat of the foreground to one side and, in the background, detailing the pirate saraṅgā with a dozen boatmen. A large, square-rigged merchantman, the sails of which are seen above the trees, may represent its prey.

Solvyns's "chauky" is probably a guard boat, taking its name from *caukī,* Hindustani for "guard station."

1 111-13. Also see Hornell, "The Boats of the Ganges," 179-80; and Deloche, 2:156-58.
2 80.
3 Ibid.
4 A report from the Justices of the Peace, Calcutta, to the Governor-General, January 31, 1800, listed various classes of criminals in Bengal. Among them are "Bumbutteas, or river thieves." Quoted in Sterndale, 57.
5 *Hobson-Jobson*, "Dacoit," 290. See Marshall, *Bengal: The British Bridgehead*, 98, on dacoity in Bengal in the late eighteenth and early nineteenth centuries. On the Sundarbans ("Sunderbunds"), see *Hobson-Jobson*, 869; Deloche, 2:122-23.
6 Hornell, "The Boats of Bengal," 183-84.
7 On the Maghs, see Pl. II.251.
8 *Hobson-Jobson*, 765.

II.242. Ekṭhā

Pl. II.242. Ekṭhā. Paris: III.3.5.

Calcutta: Sec. IX, No. 9. An Ek-gachee,—a Canoe made from the trunk of a tree.

Paris: III.3.5. EKGACHEE: The *Ekgachees*, like the *Seringees*, are a sort of canoe, that is to say, a bark cut out of the trunk of a tree. They serve as lumber-boats, and follow larger vessels which carry commodities, particularly rice, to the bazars. The oar of the *Ekgachee* is a long bambou fastened to a small board. At some distance from it I have represented another little bark belonging also to a larger vessel. This is flatbottomed, its planks are joined by *rattans*, or small bambous. The *Ekgachee* generally carry three *Dandys*, two of whom work while the other rests and smokes; they make three meals a day of coarse rice, their ordinary food, to which they sometimes add vegetables and fish. They are constantly smoking a bad sort of tobacco, and at night, after their last meal, they sit round the *Magie* [*mājjī*] or pilot, and amuse themselves by telling stories till they fall asleep. They lie in the open air, with a bit of cloth for their only covering: in winter they get under the sail: one of them is obliged to keep watch. They sometimes, as a pastime, play on the *sittar* [Pl. II.151] or some other of the instruments which we have already described.

Commentary: According to Hornell, the dugout canoe, called ḍoṅga (Pl. II.243) in Bengal, is known as ekṭhā in Bihar, "a name evidently given in reference to this kind of boat being formed out of a simple log or tree trunk." Such boats, he writes, are usually from 10 to 15 feet in length, with a breadth of two feet or more, and with about the same depth[1]—a description that corresponds to Solvyns's portrayal, but the ekṭhā depicted is clearly distinct in form from the ḍoṅga and bears greater similarity, as Solvyns notes, to the saraṅgā (Pl. II.241).

The word "ekgachee" (*ekgāchi*) appears in no dictionary (nor does the "agacha" of Solvyns's note to the drawing), but seems descriptive of the dugout—*ek* (one) + *gāch* (tree).

In the Calcutta etching, the boat is centered in the foreground and fills the print, but for the Paris etching, Solvyns moves the ekṭhā to the right and widens the perspective, adding a small dugout and a pāṭeli (Pl. II.246) in the background to the left.

1 "The Boats of the Ganges," 177, 179. Also see Deloche, 2:256-58.

II.243. Ḍoṅga

Pl. II.243. Ḍoṅga. Paris: III.3.6.

Calcutta: Sec. VIII, No. 10. A Gunga,—a small bark made out of a toddy tree [palmyra], and used for fishing, &c.

Paris: III.3.6. GUNGA: This is a very small boat hollowed out from the trunk of a tree, and takes its name of *Gunga*, or shell, from its form. It is used on the lakes and tanks, for spreading fishing-nets and other purposes. Many different sorts of *Gungas* are represented in the print. The view is a saltwater lake, about a league from Calcutta. This lake is surrounded by *sunderbands*, where the Hindoos sometimes go to cut wood, but never without great risk, from the quantity of tigers with which these close woods are infested. Allured by the prospect of a trifling gain, to brave this danger, they approach the borders of the woods in large boats, offer up sacrifices on their landing, and light fires with a great deal of noise to frighten off the tigers. They are sometimes successful, and cut wood enough to lade all their boats, which they sell for a tolerable profit at Calcutta; but it frequently happens that they never return, and it is then certain that they have been devoured by the wild beasts. As a memorial of such misfortunes, they plant in the earth an oar bearing a *cudgeri* [*khicuṛi*] or earthen pot.[1] Many of these monuments are seen at a little distance from each other: a melancholy proof of the frequency of these accidents.

Commentary: Solvyns's "gunga " (*ghonghā*, "shell" in Hindustani) may be a local term, but, more likely, his ear failed him, for the boat Solvyns depicts is, in Bengali, called a ḍoṅga, defined in the *Etymological Dictionary of Bengali* as a "trough-like bark."[2]

James Hornell writes that "Dug-out canoes, called *donga* in Bengal, and *ekhta* in Bihar, are seen everywhere in the shallow tributaries of the Ganges. . . . Commonest of all [illustrated by Hornell and portrayed by Solvyns] is the little dug-out made from the lower end of the stem of the Palmyra palm. . . . The entire butt end of the tree is used together with 8 or 10 feet of the cylindrical stem above. The butt end of this palm is unusually bulbous, and when hollowed out gives a wide roomy cavity where a considerable quantity of goods can be stored, or several passengers accommodated if they sit close together at the bottom."[3] The trunk end of the ḍoṅga "is sealed with a mud wall or a fragment of the palm's soft interior. . . ."[4]

These dugouts "were commonly employed over a large part of the watercourses by the peasants to go from village to village, to cross inundated paddies, or to transport their produce to neighbouring markets."[5]

In the print, the single boatman poles the ḍoṅga with a long bamboo. Most boats in Bengal carry such poles for use when unable to row or sail.

1 See note, Pl. II.33, fn. 1.
2 Sukumar Sen, 377. The word *ḍoṅga* is also used for a ḍiṅgi fashioned of the shell-like bark of the banana tree.
3 "The Boats of the Ganges," 177. Also see Hornell, *Water Transport*, 190.
4 Greenhill, *Boats and Boatmen of Pakistan*, 111.
5 Deloche, 2:156-58.

II.244. Grab

Pl. II.244. Grab. Paris: III.4.2.
Calcutta: Sec. IX, No. 1. A Grab:—a method of building peculiar to Bombay.

Paris: III. 4.2. GRAB: This is a ship with three masts, a pointed prow, and a bowsprit, as is represented in the print: its crew consists of a *Nicodar* [*nākhodā*][1] or captain, and a few *Clashies* [*khālasī*] or Moorish sailors, generally of a very robust frame. The *Grabs* are built at Bombay, where it appears that navigation was brought to some degree of perfection at a very early period. In this part of India too the teck [teak] is found, a resinous tree on which they say that the sea-worm has no effect. This is used for the sides and ribs; but the keel, and in general all that is under water, is made of saul [sāl],[2] very heavy wood which the Hindoos look upon as incorruptible; and in effect this timber remains sometimes for ages uninjured, but at other rots almost as soon as it is cut. In their most ancient temples there are beams of this wood as solid and as fresh as if they had been but just put up.

The pointed prow which distinguishes the *Grab* belongs to the Hindoo construction, and is not met with in any other country. The Portugese have imitated it in their India ships. Sometimes also the poops of the Hindoo vessels are very high, as they were formerly in our European seas.

Commentary: "Grab" is an Anglo-Indian word (near obsolete by the late nineteenth century) from the Arabic *ghurāb*, literally "raven," applied to a kind of galley used along the coasts of the Indian Ocean. The grab draws little water, is broad in proportion to its length, and varies in size from 150 to 500 tons burden. It has two, sometimes three masts that are square-rigged, and it has an elongated bow. Various descriptions specify that it does not have a bowsprit,[3] but Solvyns's grab does have a bowsprit as well as the less common three masts. The masts, with European rigging, carry a lower sail and top sail, with a flag atop. There is a spanker, or gaff-headed sail, at the stern.[4] Solvyns's portrayal presents an interesting amalgamation of sophisticated Western rigging on an Eastern hull of specialized local design.

In his note to the original drawing, Solvyns writes that the "mode of building" seen in the grab has been long used in India. They are, he continues, "commonly 250 to 300 tons burden rigged as a brig; or snow,[5] but some have three masts [as he portrays here] and are of 800 tons."

Many grabs sailed out of Arabia and the Persian Gulf and others from the western coast of India could well have had "Moorish" crews, but "clashy" (*khālāsi*) is a general term applied to native sailors and a variety of servants or workmen, as Solvyns portrays in a separate etching (Pl. II.116).

1 Persian for a "skipper," corrupted as *nākhodā*, *nacoda*, etc. *OED*; *Hobson-Jobson*, 612; Lewis, 173. See Bulley, 228-39, for an extended discussion of "nacodas and lascars."

2 Sāl, a hardwood resistent both to water and sun, is especially suitable for ship construction under Indian conditions, and it was judged by Europeans the equal of the best oak. See "saul-wood," *Hobson-Jobson*, 798.

3 *Hobson-Jobson*, 391-92; *OED*. Bulley, 40-42, discusses the grab.

4 See Deloche, 2:193.

5 A snow is a small brig-like sailing ship, carrying a main and fore mast and a supplementary trysail mast close behind the main mast. *OED*.

II.245. Bangles

Pl. II.245a. Bangles. Calcutta: Sec. IX, No. 11.

Calcutta: Sec. IX, No. 11. A Bangles,—a large rice boat of from 2 to 4000 maunds.

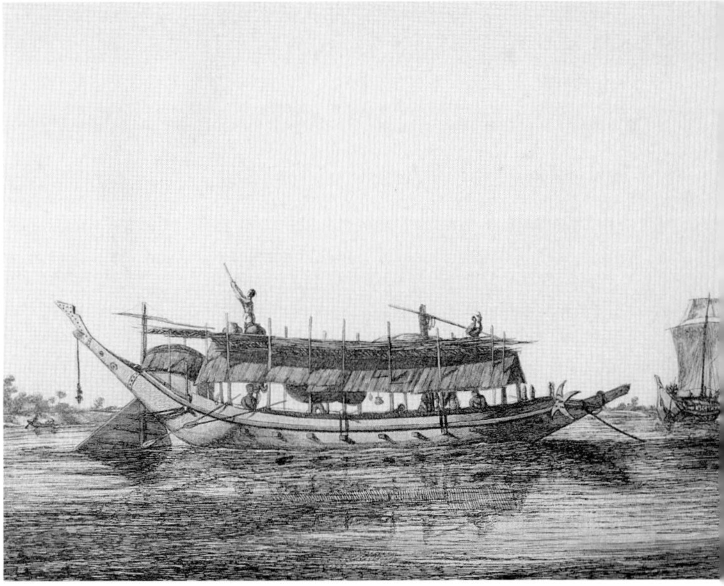

Pl. II.245b. Bangles. Paris: III.4.3.

Commentary: Solvyns's term "Bangles" does not appear as a boat in dictionaries and would seem to derive from a generic *Bāṅgāli*, "belonging to Bengal."[1]

Solvyns states that the boats have a mast of enormous size, as portrayed in the Calcutta etching. For the Paris etching, however, Solvyns took down the mast, although the "Bangles" in the distance are depicted with mast raised and at sail. Although anchored, the boat in the foreground of the etching is shown with a wooden grapnel anchor on the side.

1 Sukumar Sen, 628.

Paris: III.4.3. BANGLES: The *Bangles* are incontestably the largest boats in the rivers of Hindoostan: some of them carry four or even five thousand *maunds* of rice; a *maund* is worth 75 pounds. They have a roof of thatch [*chāuni*] to protect the *Magie* [*mājhī*, captain] and the sailors or *Dandies,* who are almost always Hindoos. The merchant has a sort of cabin in the aft of the vessel. The masts of the *Bangles* are of an enormous size, and consist of several bambous fastened together. The *Bangles* in the print is placed so as to shew the whole of its form. At a distance are seen several boats of this kind under sail. The poop is generally covered with ornaments in brass and wreaths of flowers, like all the Hindoo vessels. The owners of these boats make but one trip in the year, setting out in the rainy season, and returning home before the great droughts. The sailors make cordage and other necessary articles, during the passage.

II.246. Pāṭeli

Paris: III.4.4. PATAILY: This is the name of a boat very common in the provinces of Behar and Benares, but seldom seen in the other parts of Hindoostan. It is flat, except at the two ends, which are a little raised. It is the worst of all Hindoo vessels, and made of planks laid over each other without being worked up or planed: the outside is gross and without ornament. Instead of masts, the *Pataily* frequently has but a *bambou,* and some *gonies* [*gonī*, gunny] for sails. It has a covering of thatch like the other lumber-boats, but is in general so ill constructed that it is five or six times longer getting up the river, and it is even surprising to see so poor a vessel undertake long voyages. Its general lading is rice, for it is seldom trusted with a more valuable cargo, though I have sometimes seen it freighted with other merchandise.

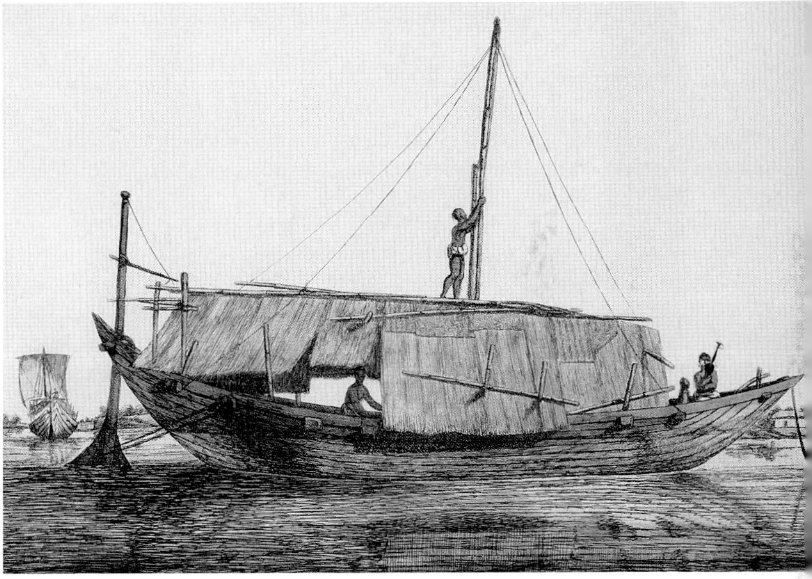

Pl. II.246. Pāṭeli. Paris: III.4.4.

Calcutta: Sec. IX, No. 7. A Pataily,—a flat clinker built boat from the Provinces of Behar and Benares.

Commentary: The pāṭeli is a large flat-bottomed boat of the Ganges. Upcountry, it is known as a katrā, and Solvyns provides a separate print (Pl. II.247) for the boat under that name. Solvyns expresses little confidence in the vessel, but a hundred years earlier, Thomas Bowrey thought these boats, which carried saltpeter and grain, of "Exeeding Strength." "They are built very Strong, by reason of the most impetuous Eddies they meet with in some places, that force them many times Upon one Shoale or Other . . . ."[1]

Prinsep, in 1830, describes the pāṭeli as a "baggage boat." It is clinker-built, that is, with overlapping planks, and "its great breadth gives it a very light draught of water, and renders it fittest for the cotton and other up-country products, which require little better than a dray and secure raft to float them down the stream."[2] Pāṭelis vary in size, usually in the range of 35 tons burden, but occasionally double that size, and they carry grain, salt, cotton, and other produce.[3] The boat, writes Colesworthy Grant, is an "unwieldy-looking piece of rusticity" and is used by some Europeans as a baggage boat. "Families in middling or narrow circumstances journeying to the upper provinces, avail themselves of boats of this description. . . ."[4]

The pāṭeli "is manned by ten or twelve boatmen,—each man—when there is no wind to bring the sail into use—standing up on the bamboo platform or roof, and labouring at an enormous bamboo oar, full eighteen feet in length, with a broad round blade at its extremity, like a baker's peel, with which it is impossible for more than one stroke to be made in about two minutes!"[5]

Admiral Paris' Native Boats, 1841, provides a detailed description:

> The transportation of produce from the upper regions of Bengal requires strong boats. The largest of this type of vessel is the "patilé". Some are planked and nailed, while others are clinker-built, with wooden pins joining the planks to the framework. Some have a flat, vertical rear, a very slanting front, flattened out at the bottom, and lateral planks pinned to the sides. The upper part of the side, which is made from several pinned planks, is covered with a large projecting plank, on which a man can stand to punt. Sometimes, other planks are positioned on the ends of the beams for the same purpose. The rudder, which is positioned at the side, is triangular.
>
> These boats vary in length from 12 to 20 meters. They all carry a large cabin made from reeds tied with twine, and covered with a coconut palm thatch. Through this go posts, which support cross-beams laid with such a haphazard assortment of planks and poles that only Indians can walk across them.
>
> The sails, supported by bamboo poles, are very small.
>
> Some of the large "patilés" from Calcutta, which have their planking held together by cramp-irons, have rounder lines, very similar to those of "bauléas" [bhāuliyā, Pl. II.233]. Their rear, which is pointed and very high, is made from a single piece of wood, which is stronger than planking. They have a framework, and projecting beams, but never any decking. They carry enormous cabins, which are covered by a platform which is as long as the boat itself. The lightness of their construction, and their flat lines allow them to carry sizable loads, and they are especially suited to the transportation of cotton.[6]

Solvyns portrays the pāṭeli broadside, with a background view of the boat head-on with sail.

1 Bowrey, 225. Also see 229.
2 48, with illustration in Appendix A4.
3 *Hobson-Jobson*, 687-88; Hunter, *A Statistical Account of Bengal*, 1:33; and Deloche, 2:161.
4 *Rural Life in Bengal*, 6, with a small engraving of a "putelee."
5 Ibid., 25. The "great steering paddle" on the cargo boats is described by Hornell in "The Origins and Ethnological Significance of Indian Boat Designs," 189, and in "The Boats of the Ganges," 192-93.
6 35-37.

II.247. Katrā

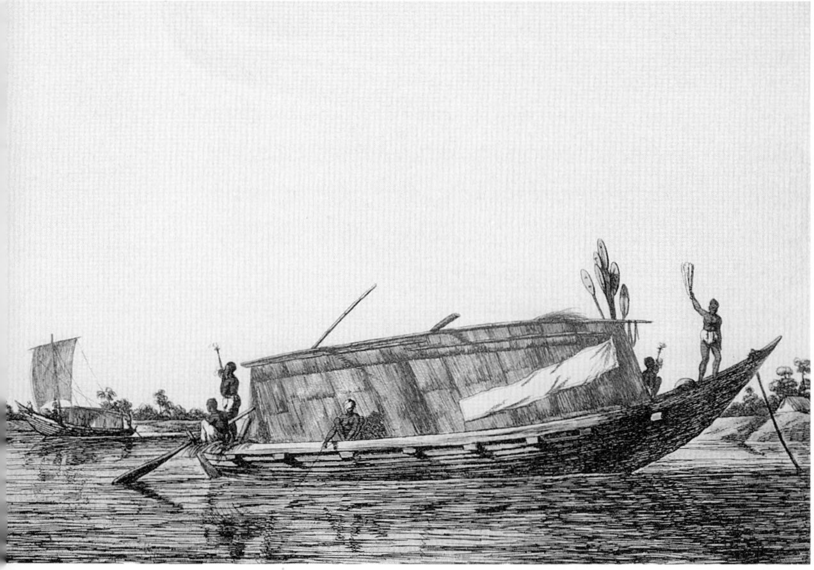

Pl. II.247. Katrā. Paris: III.4.5.

Calcutta: Sec. IX, No. 8. A Kautry,—from the Northern Provinces of Hindostan, differing little from a Pataily with the head and stern reversed.

Commentary: Solvyns notes a slight difference in construction between the katrā and the pāṭeli, but both are flat-bottomed and clinker-built. The difference is essentially in name. The boat is known as a katrā in the upper Ganges area and as pāṭeli in the mid-Ganges region of Bihar and eastern Uttar Pradesh. Individual boats varied, but perhaps the difference Solvyns noted may have been due to the distribution of weight.[1]

Following convention, Solvyns portrays the katrā at sail in the background.

1 See Deloche, 2:161.

Paris: III.4.5. KAUTRY: The *Kautry* is higher in the prow and lower astern than the *Pataily* [pāṭeli, Pl. II.246] from which it is distinguished by this difference of construction. The northern countries of Hindoostan employ a great number of *Kautrys* in conveying their produce to Calcutta, from whence they frequently return with the troops which are to be cantoned in the upper districts, or attend the *Pinnaces* [Pl. II.229] and *Budgerows* [bājrā, Pl. II.232] going to Lucknow or elsewhere, as baggage boats, with the kitchen and provisions. The Hindoos who come with the *Kautrys* are more robust than those of Bengal, speak a language of their own, and sometimes the true Hindoo tongue [Sanskrit]. They are three or four months getting up the river, during which time their patience must be equal to their exertions. There can be no relaxation in their efforts to overcome the force of the currents, against which they have to hawl up a very heavy boat, and escape the danger of the squalls in which, notwithstanding all their labour and perseverance, many of them perish.

II.248. Bālām

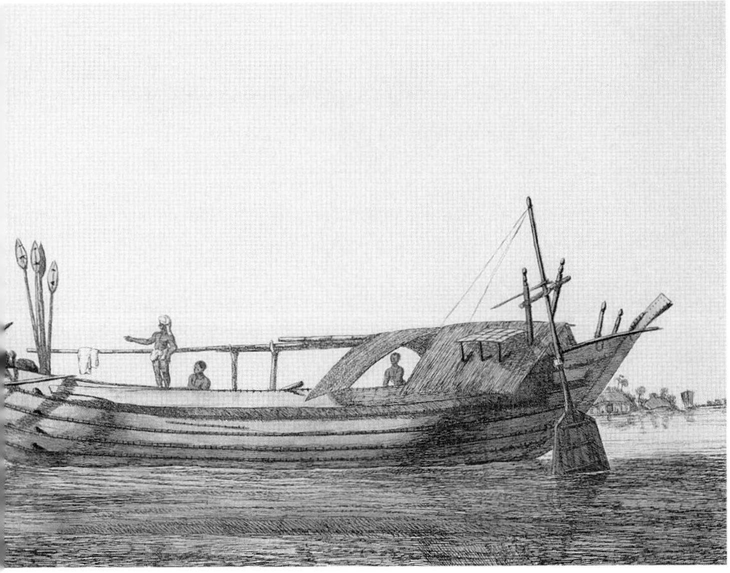

Pl. II.248. Bālām. Paris: III.4.6.

Calcutta: Sec. IX, No. 14. A Chittagong Balaum, built on a Scringee [saraṅgā], having the Planks sown together with Cane or Hemp.

Paris: III.4.6. BALAUM: This is the simplest of all boats and consists meerly of the trunk of a tree hollowed out, to the extremities of which pieces of wood are applied to represent a stern and a prow: the two sides, are boards joined by rottins [rattan] or small bambous without nails: no iron whatsoever enters into their construction: even the anchor is of wood.

The *Balaums* are used in the district of Chittagong: they sometimes come to Calcutta, where they are broken up for the timber. How clumsy soever these boats may be, their construction is superior to that of the northern countries: it is true they are exposed to greater dangers in the arms of the sea which they have to pass, and are built higher in the sides than the river boats, to keep out the waves.

Commentary: Solvyns identifies the bālām—Anglo-Indian "baloon"[1]—with Chittagong, as does *The Anglo-Hindoostanee Hand-Book* in identifying it as a "Mug Boat," referring to the people of Chittagong and Arakan known as Maghs.[2] The *Hand-Book* describes the boat as "having a floor of a single hollowed piece of timber, and raised sides, neatly attached by rattan sewing, with strips of bamboo over the seams."[3]

Bālāms are, in Greenhill's words, "no more than greatly enlarged versions of the simple canoe."[4] In the 1799 *Catalogue*, Solvyns refers to the base of the boat as a "Scringee," *saraṅgā*, the general term for cargo-carrying dugouts, portrayed by Solvyns in Pl. II.241. This base is hollowed out to leave only thin sides, perhaps no more than one inch in thickness, and on the edges of this keel-like bottom "the sides are raised by means of three and six planks flaring outward and sewn together by means of rattan and coir. Not a single nail is used in these boats," and "the nature of their construction confers upon them a considerable degree of elasticity and so enables them to bump over a river bar with comparative impunity."[5]

The bow and stern boards, unseen in Solvyns's depiction, are richly decorated in complex designs in vivid color. Greenhill's *Boats and Boatmen of Pakistan*, with extensive discussion of these "powerful" and "impressive" vessels, includes photographs of large sea-going bālāms over 60 feet long, 7 feet deep, and 12 or 14 feet in the beam.[6]

These large cargo boats carry crews with up to 30 when rowing. Solvyns does not show the bālām with its mast raised, but although equipped with oars, shown vertically in the print, it is a sailing boat, with the heel of the mast usually stepped (or placed) in a tabernacle made of a heavy log with a deep notch. With stout rigging, the mast carries a square sail.[7] The anchor depicted aboard the bālām is a wooden grapnel.

Hornell suggests resemblance both in name and construction to boats in South India,[8] and Kerchove, in the *International Maritime Dictionary*, places the "ballam" on the Malabar coast and describes it as a large dugout generally used in hook and line fisheries. He notes that Arabs have copied the design in a planked boat of larger dimensions capable of carrying mast and sail.[9]

1 *Hobson-Jobson*, 53.
2 On Maghs, see Pl. II.251.
3 Grant and Colebrooke, 115.
4 *Boats and Boatmen of Pakistan*, 114. Also see Deloche, 2:179.
5 Hornell, "The Boats of the Ganges," 194.
6 114-17; photographs, 105. Also see Jansen, *The Country Boats of Bangladesh*, 72-73.
7 Greenhill, *Boats and Boatmen of Pakistan*, 115, and Hornell, "The Boats of the Ganges," 194.
8 "The Boats of the Ganges," 194.
9 33.

II.249. Brig

Pl. II.249. Brig. Paris: III.5.2.
Calcutta: Sec. IX, No. 2. A Bengal pariar Brig.

Paris: III.5.2. BRIG: The slightest view of the engraving is sufficient to give an idea of the meanness of this sort of vessel, which is consequently, in all the Indian seas, stigmatized with the appellation of *pariah,* which is given indistinctly, as I have already had occasion to remark in the beginning of the first volume, to all that is bad.

These *Brigs* come from the coast of Coromandel and of Malabar, and bring to Calcutta the produce of those countries. It appears surprising that such indifferent vessels should attempt so long a voyage, till we reflect that they perform it but once in the year, and wait the favourable monsoon to come and return. With this precaution, the Indian seas are without danger for the frailest vessels; but without it, the stoutest ships run great risks. The frigates and company ships, which venture out of the bay of Calcutta in the bad season, frequently put in again dismasted. The passage from Madras to Calcutta requires but five or six days in the good season, and several months in the bad, though the distance between these two towns is but a few degrees.

Commentary: A brig is a two-masted ship and is the smallest seagoing vessel that is square rigged. It is some 90 to 100 feet in length and 24 to 34 feet in breadth, with a burden of 200 to 500 tons.[1] The terms "brig" or "brigantine," however, were often used loosely and were "variously applied by the mariners of different European nations to a peculiar sort of vessel of their own marine."[2] Solvyns depicts a country-made version of this European-style ship and terms it a "pariah," a caste name used to refer to the worst of anything.[3] In his portrayal, as evident in the bow, these are brigs built to handle volume and not for speed.

In his note to the original drawing, Solvyns writes that the "Bengalee Paria (common) Brig" conveys "a pretty correct idea of the naval architecture of the Natives; they are remarkably sparing of iron in building, the chair plates &c are of wood, as also the anchor, or more properly the drag, which is filled with stones." The anchor Solvyns refers to is a cross-armed Indian grapnel, more clearly depicted on the ulāk (Pl. II.250).

In the Paris etching, though not in the Calcutta print, a grab (Pl. II.244) is portrayed in the background.

1 Kerchove, 92.
2 Falconer, *Marine Dictionary* (1787), in Smyth, 134-35.
3 See Commentary, Pl. II.22.

II.250. Ulāk

Pl. II.250. Ulāk. Paris: III.5.3.
Calcutta: Sec. IX, No. 12. A Wolack,—a large boat for merchandize.

Paris: III.5.3. WOLACK: The *Wolack* resembles the *Bangles* [Pl. II.245]. I have represented it on a larger scale, to give a more complete idea of the construction of this boat, and of the different parts which compose it. At a distance is another *Wolack* under sail. The back-ground, as in most of the other prints, is the banks of the river. The *Wolacks* bring rice to Calcutta, where great magazines of it are formed, as well for exportation as for consumption. The covering of the *Wolacks* can be raised or lowered at pleasure. With the wind abaft [toward the stern], they sail tolerably well: but if it blows any way against them, they are very hard to manage, and can not stand the wind and waves. Another inconvenience of the *Wolack* and of many other Hindoo boats, is, that they are so ill calked, that the water easily penetrates them. The insects too are exceedingly troublesome, and, if it were not for the constant smoking, they would be quite insupportable.

Commentary: The ulāk (Anglo-Indian, wollock) is a "bulky baggage boat of Bengal" that Colesworthy Grant likens to the pāṭeli (Pl. II.246) in its substantial size. But in contrast to the clinker-built pāṭeli, the side planking of the ulāk is laid edge-to-edge and fastened with iron clamps, giving it the appearance of being stitched.[1] With a sharp bow, smooth sides and rounded bottom, the ulāk was generally used to carry grain. Williamson, in his 1810 *East India Vade-Mecum*, wrote that "some of the woolacks used by the more opulent native merchants are capable of bearing from fifteen hundred to three thousand maunds (eighty to a hundred tons), but their medium may be taken at from four to eight hundred maunds."[2] Prinsep notes that "this boat is the best for tracking and sailing before the wind, and is tolerably manageable with the oar in smooth water."[3]

The enormous rudder—similar to that portrayed on the "Bangles" (Pl. II.245) and pāṭeli—"is constructed of a triangular frame on which are nailed vertical planks strengthened with three or four cross battens."[4]

The etching provides a view of the "cross-armed Indian grapnel anchor," constructed of wood and weighted with stones.[5]

Solvyns slips in the Paris text in referring to another ulāk in the distance. The boat is depicted at sail in the Calcutta etching, but is not shown in the Paris print.

1 *Rural Life in Bengal*, 25, with small engraving. On the ulāk, see Deloche, 2:161.
2 383.
3 48. Prinsep illustrates the "oolak" in Appendix A4.
4 Hornell, *Water Transport*, 250.
5 Van Nouhuys, 2-23. Van Nouhuys reproduces Solvyns's etching to illustrate the anchor, 22. Solvyns also portrays the grapnel anchor aboard a kośā, Pl. II.251.

II.251. Kośā

Pl. II.251. Kośā. Paris: III.5.4.

Calcutta: Sec. IX, No. 16. A Kose,—peculiar to Chittagong and Luckipore [Lakhipur, on the Brahmputra River in Assam.]

Paris: III.5.4. KOSE: This species of boat, much in use in the province of Chittagong, carries sail very well, and can navigate without danger in all the rivers of Hindoostan. The wind has but little power over it, on account of the lowness of its covering. The *Kose* can even stand the sea. Its crew is generally composed of *Mugs,* a dirty and disgusting people, but strong and skilful. They are somewhat of the Malayan race, and will be mentioned hereafter [Pl. II.7]. The *Mugs* are perfectly acquainted with all the passes of the Indian coasts, where the navigation is impeded by a number of small islands. They are frequently obliged to wait for the tide, and can not approach the land without the greatest danger from the tigers, the wild buffaloes, the crocodiles, and other ferocious animals, with which the coasts are infested. The tiger especially are dreaded on account of their audacity: they sometimes even swim to the boats, dart into them with incredible velocity, choose out the plumpest man of the crew, and carry him off to their den. To avoid being surprised by night, the boats are surrounded with netting.

Commentary: The kośā is a small to medium-sized boat of eastern Bengal. They are "more expeditious" than their form promises, Solvyns writes in his note to the original drawing, and they "are said to be strong and safe."

The kośā is flat-bottomed, narrow, and as long as 20 feet. Greenhill describes a "korsha" as "double ended, often without sheer, but some with the flat bottom steeply canted up at either end, giving the boat a marked sheer. . . ." He writes that he was told that "the name comes from a Bengali word for a small votive vessel used in Hindu temples which is of similar shape to these little boats."[1] The votive vessel is a *kośā*, portrayed by Solvyns in his etching of the Śrotriya Brahmin (Pl. II.13). Its shape is like the long petal of a plantain flower, and the boat of the same name is sometimes described as shaped like a spoon—though that is suggested neither by Solvyns's portrayal nor Greenhill's description.

The kośā, according to Greenhill, is of "chine" construction, with wide planks, fastened by staples, coming up on the sides from the flat bottom.[2] By contrast, Montgomery Martin, in his compilation of survey material on Eastern India by Francis Buchanan, describes the kośā as "clinker-built of Sal."[3] Solvyns makes no reference to clinker construction nor in his depiction does the boat appear to be of that character. Martin writes that "both ends [of the kośā] are nearly the same shape ending in a sharp point, and rise very little above the water. . . . Their bottoms are perfectly flat without any keel [and are] rather unsafe; but, drawing very little water, are exceedingly convenient [in shallow] waters."[4]

Solvyns refers to the kośā's capacity to carry sail, but as depicted in the print, the mast is down (with the sail apparently wrapped around it), and it is fitted with three oars on each side.

Kośās are used for fishing and ferrying and, fitted with a thatched covering (*chāuni*), as in Solvyns's portrayal, serve as small cargo carriers.[5] Jansen, in *Country Boats of Bangladesh*, notes that it carries a wide range of goods, but "small size and special shape make it well-suited for the transport of such bulk commodities as stone, bricks, and sand. It is particularly well-suited for small timber hauls."[6] The boat is fitted with a wooden grapnel anchor similar to that shown in Solvyns's portrayal of the ulāk (Pl. II.250)

Solvyns identifies the boat with the "Mugs"—Maghs—a common name for the Arakanese, ethnically Burman, Buddhist inhabitants of the coast south of Chittagong.[7] They describe themselves by various names, and "Magh" may well be "a foreign epithet, unknown to the Arakanese themselves."[8] The derivation of the name "Magh" is disputed, but from whatever source, the word in Bengali, *mag* or *magh*, as applied to Arakanese raiders, was extended to mean "pirate."[9]

Walter Hamilton, in his 1820 *Description of Hindostan*, writes that "Under the name of Mughs, the Aracaners infested and devastated the lower districts of Bengal, carrying off the inhabitants into slavery."[10] In the seventeenth century, the Portuguese purchased slaves from them for resale. These raids extended well into the eighteenth century, and Rennell's map of 1771 shows wide areas of the Sundarbans—the tiger-infested islands referred to by Solvyns—"depopulated by the Maghs"[11] "So great was the dread of the Mugs" that about 1770 a chain was run across the Hugli river "to protect the port of Calcutta against pirates."[12]

As a result of the Burmese invasions of Arakan in 1782-84, a major portion of the "Mugs" fled north toward Chittagong and into the hills. Although raids continued intermittently, by Solvyns's time, many Arakanese had established peaceable residence in Chittagong, and some ventured to Calcutta, where they soon came to be renowned among Europeans as "the best class of native cooks."[13] Solvyns includes a "Mug" in his portrayal "of the nations most known in Hindoostan" (Pl. II.7).

Today in Bangladesh, the Arakanese, generally termed "Marma," are concentrated in the area of Cox's Bazar and, as a distinct group (the Jūmiā Maghs or Khyoungthā, "children of the river"), in the Chittagong Hill Tracks.[14]

Solvyns's etching of the kośā in the Calcutta edition portrays the boat along the bank of the river, with a squatting man at the water's side for his morning ablution. An original watercolor drawing of the kośā, from the album assembled by Solvyns's widow, is reproduced, with notes, in *Interaction of Cultures: Indian and Western Painting, 1780-1910: The Ehrenfeld Collection*.[15]

---

1 *Boats and Boatmen of Pakistan*, 110.
2 Ibid., 110.
3 4:343.
4 4:343-44.
5 Greenhill, *Boats and Boatmen of Pakistan*, 110.
6 77.
7 Risley, *Tribes and Castes of Bengal*, 2:28-37; *Hobson-Jobson*, 594; O'Malley, *Bengal District Gazetteers: Chittagong*, 60-62; and Rizvi, 60-92, 114-15.
8 Risley, *Tribes and Castes of Bengal*, 2:28-29.
9 Sukumar Sen, 730, gives *mag* as "pirate" and makes no mention of the Arakanese. There is no entry for *magh*. On Magh pirates, see Pl. II.241.
10 *A Geographical, Statistical, and Historical Description of Hindostan and Adjacent Countries*, 1:175.
11 Jamini Mohan Ghosh, *Magh Raiders in Bengal*, 6.

12 Long, *Calcutta in the Olden Times*, 124.

13 *Hobson-Jobson*, 594. Colesworthy Grant, in *An Anglo-Indian Domestic Sketch*, 106, wrote that "Mugs" are "esteemed by us in the culinary department, being heaven-born cooks from the Burmese quarter."

14 Hunter, *A Statistical Account of Bengal*, 6:39-43, 6:142-43. Hutchinson gives the term Jumiya Magh to the Maghs of the Hill Tracks, and says that they are divided into the "Marama or those who come from Burma, and the Kyongsa or those who live on the river." 29. He discusses Maghs, 28-35.

15 Bautze, 304-05, Pl. 80.

II.252. Palwār

Pl. II.152. Palwār. Paris: III.5.5.

Calcutta: Sec. IX, No. 15. A Dacca pulwar,—a commodious and expeditious boat.

Paris: III.5.5. PULWAR: Of all the Hindoo boats the *Pulwar* is the best built and fittest for inland navigation. In consequence of which the East-India company, it is said, have ordered that no other boat should be employed to transport precious goods, such as silver, muslins, opium, indigo, etc. The *Pulwars* are very light, and carry sail well: of a middle size, and with able rowers, they are sure to pass any other species of boat. Both of its ends are of an equal height; it carries a small mast with a square sail which extends beyond its sides, and sometimes a topsail. The Hindoos call them *Dacca Pulwar,* from the great number which are built in the town of Dacca, where almost all their boats have that form. Since this town, formerly so commercial, has come under the dominion of a Mussulman prince, the *Magies* [*mājhī*, captain] and *Dandys* [*dānḍī*, sailor] of the *Pulwars* are Mussulmans, and there are few Hindoos among their crews.

Commentary: The palwār (Anglo-Indian pulwar), "light, maneuverable and secure,"[1] is a broad, keelless boat, some 60 feet long and capable to carrying 12 to 15 tons.[2] It is the typical cargo river boat of the Dhaka region, "a craft built to carry heavy loads at the lowest possible cost." It is carvel-built, that is, with its hull planks edge to edge rather than overlapping, permitting easy repair. "The single mast is stepped fairly well forward and carries a square sail,"[3] as seen on the boat in the background of Solvyns's portrayal. The palwār Solvyns presents for closer view is anchored and its mast is down.

In his note to the original drawing, Solvyns wrote, "They are remarkable among the Country Boats for safety and expedition," and Europeans generally shared Solvyns's high regard for the palwār. Prinsep described it as "the fastest and most handy boat in use for general traffic."[4]

The palwār provides a good example of variable boats with the same name. In eastern Bengal, the Dhaka palwār, as it is known, is "a good, well-constructed barge," but in upper Bengal and Bihar, the name refers to "a small craft sometimes used by a single person" or that was used as a kitchen boat and for accommodation of servants in the flotilla accompanying a bājrā (Pl. II.232) or pinnace (Pl. II.229) on extended trips. And in parts of Bihar, "palwār" was used for a pilot-boat, of whatever form, that guided others through difficult passages.[5]

1 Deloche, 2:162.

2 *Hobson-Jobson*, 737. Greenhill, *Boats and Boatmen of Pakistan*, 85, states that although widely recognized by the name "pulwar," the accurate word for this "big, beamy, full-ended cargo boat" is "pallar." Greenhill illustrates various features of the palwār in drawings, 92-96. But, to make any sorting out of the various names more difficult, Jansen, *Sailing Against the Wind*, 70, gives it as "palowary."

3 Hornell, "The Boats of the Ganges," 190-91.

4 48, illustrated Appendix A4.

5 Deloche, 2:162, fn. 64; Hodges, 39; Colesworthy Grant, *Rural Life in Bengal*, 7, with engraving.

II.253. Holā

Pl. II.253. Holā. Paris:III.5.6. **Calcutta: Sec. IX, No. 13.** A Hola,—a flat square boat employed to transport Salt from Ingelee [Hijili][1] and Tomlook [Tumluk][2] to Calcutta.

Commentary: The *Anglo-Hindoostanee Hand-Book* describes the holā as having "a circular bow and stern, and great proportionate beam: it is used for heavy freight, such as coals, bricks, kunkur [gravel], &c."[3] Solvyns describes the holā as "square at both ends," but, if so, it is surely not evident in his portrayal.

"The *hola*," Hornell writes, "is the humble coal and brick carrier, dirtiest and most unkempt of Hoogly craft. Built on the same lines as the larger bhar [Pl. II.256], its mast is usually a single pole placed rather further forward and carries only a single square sail. The rudder is of the sweep type, suspended from the quarter and worked by the steersman from the usual little bamboo platform. . . . When the *hola* is loaded, the crew of four or six men pull their long paddles, sitting at the fore end; when it is light, they pull standing."[4]

1 Also Hidgelee, Ingellie, etc., a town at the mouth of the Hugli. See Deloche, 2:162-64.
2 Corrupted as Tumlook and Tomberlee, Tumluk is an ancient port on the west side of the Hugli near its mouth.
3 Henry Grant and Colebrooke, 115.
4 *Water Transport*, 251, fig. 252. Also see Hornell, "The Boats of the Ganges," 194.

Paris: III.5.6. HOLA: The *Hola* resembles entirely a pontoon, being square at both ends, and very unlike any other boat. It is the only flat-bottomed boat which goes to the mouth of the Ougli [Hugli], where there is so much danger for other boats. It is used to convey to Calcutta, and to a greater distance, the salt of Ingelee, Tomlouck, and its environs. To ship the salt, several *creeks* and *nullahs* [ravines] come out of the little streams, and meet in the river near the sandbanks and shallows, where the salt abounds. These boats are always careful to shelter themselves in some bay at nightfall, or on the appearance of foul weather, and always anchor under the land.

The *Holas* are well masted, and carry good sails, which are in general remarkably white; their cables and anchors too are excellent; notwithstanding all which it still is surprising that they can sail in the Ougli and the Ganges without danger. The *Dandys* [*dāndī*] who are in general of Hindoo origin, live wholly upon rice. Their complexion is darker than that of the other *Dandys*. It is a general remark, that the inhabitants of the mouths of the rivers, where the water is salt, are much blacker than those of the north of Hindoostan, as the inhabitants of Bengal have not so clear a skin as the Hindoos of Behar.

II.254. Sloop

Pl. II.254. Sloop. Paris: III.6.2.

Calcutta: Sec. IX, No. 3. A Sloop, employed for the Coast trade, and to carry down the River the Cargo for large ships.

Paris: III.6.2. SLOOP: The *Sloops* are used to carry goods to and from the merchant-ships which are laded or unladed. They are employed particularly at Cutgerie, at Engelee, at Diamonds harbour, and near Culpee. The East-India company have many in its service. They have five or six men on board, who are well acquainted with all the dangers of the river. They carry masts and sails, are strong and well built, but not swift sailors. With an European crew, they could stand the open sea. Some of them now have cordage and anchors, like European vessels. They print gives a sufficient idea of their form.

Commentary: The sloop is a small European style vessel with one mast, fore-and-aft rigged (and often, as in Solvyns's portrayal, a square topsail), a short standing bowsprit, and a jib set on a stay. Kerchove states that they usually have one headsail, the foresail and jib forming one sail.[1] In his note to the original drawing of the sloop, Solvyns writes that "altho from their appearance they may be considered unsafe, from a proper attention to the season for sailing, few accidents happen."

In a signed watercolor drawing of the sloop, from the album assembled by Solvyns's widow, Solvyns notes the length as 60 feet and breadth as 18 feet.[2] The sloop is included in a waterfront scene that one of Solvyns's Indian assistants produced as a composite of Solvyns's individual portrayals (Pl. I.52.).[3]

Solvyns describes the sloop as used where Indiamen, unable to proceed further upriver, found safe anchorage. In the days of sail, accounts of travel to Bengal[4] almost always make reference to these anchorages, for here, passengers and goods were transferred to smaller ships, like the sloop or pinnace (Pl. II.229), for transport upriver to Calcutta. Diamond Harbor, 41 miles below Calcutta on the east bank of the Hugli, was the highest point that could be reached by the larger Indiamen. The village itself was on the edge of swamps and was regarded as "exceedingly unhealthy."[5] Kulpi (Culpee, Coulpy), just below Diamond Harbor, also provided good anchorage, but was less favored.

Kijari (Cutgerie or Kedgeree), at the mouth of the Hugli, provided a healthier situation than Diamond Harbor and was a usual anchorage for larger Indiamen.[6] Walter Hamilton advised that "ships of war, unless compelled by strong reasons, should never go higher up the river. . . ."[7] Indiamen also anchored at Hijili (Engelee, Ingelee, or Hidgelee), on west side of the Hugli esturary, as well as Balasore and Sagar Island.

1 688.

2 On the album, see Chapter Three, pp. 83-85. The drawing, "A Sloop," c. 1795, is now in the collection of the Indian Office Library (WD 4124) and is reproduced in India Office Library and Records, *Annual Report, 1985-1986*, 27, with details about the acquisition, 31; in Losty, "The Belgian Artist F. B. Solvyns," 8; in Kattenborn, 3:294, Pl. 48.

3 The composite drawing is discussed in Chapter Three, pp. 105-06.

4 See, for example, the entries in Nair, *Calcutta in 19th Century*.

5 Walter Hamilton, *A Geographical, Statistical, and Historical Description of Hindostan and Adjacent Countries*, 1:141. Also see his *East India Gazetteer*, 1:510, and Heber, 1:11; Long, *Calcutta in the Olden Time, 10*-11; *Hobson-Jobson*, 317.

6 *Hobson-Jobson*, 477.

7 *A Geographical, Statistical, and Historical Description of Hindostan and Adjacent Countries*, 1:141, and *East India Gazetteer,* 2:80.

II.255. Towboat

Pl. II.255. Towboat. Paris: III.6.3.

Calcutta: Sec. VIII, No. 11. A Tow Boat, to assist ships, &c. in the dangerous navigation of the Houghly River.

Paris: III.6.3. TOWBOAT: These are boats which help the ships coming from sea to enter the Ganges and the Ougly [Hugli], and are of very great service in this navigation, which is full of difficulties. They are of a pointed form, with their broadest surface above the water; and so light that the least motion makes them incline from side to side. They carry eight or ten sailors, generally boys, with small oars, except the *Magie* [*mājhī*, captain]. They spend their lives aboard their boats, and sleep under the sails. They are ill fed and ill paid, and are satisfied with a little rice and tobacco. Their constant living on the water, and drinking frequently brackish water, gives their skin a deeper tint than that of the other *Dandys* [*dāṇḍī*, sailor].

Commentary: Solvyns does not here use the Bengali word for towboat, and in the French text for the Paris edition, he uses the term *chaloupe de remorque*. A *chaloupe* (shallop in English), with considerable diversity, is usually an open boat with no deck, powered by oars and/or the sail of a single mast.

II.256. Bhur

Paris: III.6.4. BURR: The *Burr* is an open boat, with three or four men, used to lade and unlade the ships in the road. There are a certain number of them at Calcutta; their crews are generally composed of the refuse of the *Dandys* [*dāṇḍī*, sailor]. The *Burrs* are often without cordage, anchors, or oars; and yet their construction is well enough adapted to the service for which they are intended. Like the rest of the Calcutta boats, the *Burr* is lower before than behind, in order probably to stand the swell at high tides. When the phenomenon whose dreadful effects I have already described ["North-Wester," Pl. II.260] takes place, all the vessels which have not been able to take shelter in time, take care to present their poop to the wave.

Commentary: The bhur (also bhurā, bharā, bhār) is a cargo river boat,[1] the name derived from the Bengali word *bharā*, meaning cargo or load.[2] *Hobson-Jobson* gives the Anglo-Indian word as "bora."[3] The seventeenth century traveler Thomas Bowrey wrote that "The boora . . . being a very floaty light boat, rowinge with 20 to 30 Owars, these carry Salt peeter and Other Goods (from Hugly) downewards, and some trade to Dacca with Salt; they also Serve for tow boats for the Ships bound up or downe the River."[4]

The bhur has an open hold and a small matted shelter astern for the crew.[5] Stavorinus, in his *Voyages to the East-Indies,* 1768-71, provides a detailed description of a boat that his translator identifies as a "bur" of Bengal: "The vessels which are used for inland navigation, on the *Ganges*, are very lightly built of thin deals, without either keel or side-timbers. The edges of the planks are fastened together with staples, and the seams are stopped up with moss, and payed with grease. The largest width of them is about one-third of their whole length. . . ; they are very sharp forwards, and are not very high above the water. Although they are of different sizes, they are all the same shape and construction; and some of them can

Pl. II.256. Bhur. Paris: III.6.4.
Calcutta: Sec. IX, No. 6. A Burr,—used for the inland rice trade and to load and unload ships.

load fifty thousand pounds of weight of merchandize, and more."[6]

The translator's note, in identifying the boat as a bhur, quotes (without attribution) the artist William Hodges's description: Bhurs, Hodges writes in his *Travels*, "are large rude barks, the sides of which are raised very high, and sewed together with the fibres of the cocoanut tree. They have only a single mast, with a large square sail, and the bottoms of them are nearly flat. They take in a great quantity of water from their sides and bottoms, which compels the crew to employ some people continually in bailing. They are used for the carriage of cotton, and other very bulky materials, the weight of which cannot bear any proportion to their size."[7]

Hornell describes the bhur as the principal jute carrier of Bengal:

> Of great beam, with low bows, bluff and rounded, and a stern but slightly elevated, it is undecked except for a short distance aft, where a thatched cabin is erected; behind this, right at the stern, is a small raised platform nearly level with the cabin roof, for the accommodation of the helmsman.
>
> The cargo is packed in the open waist, and rises high above the gunwales, kept in place by a temporary loose framework of bamboos on each side and protected from the weather by tarpaulins, or mats.
>
> The mast, made up of two lengths spliced roughly together, is stepped amidships. A huge squaresail, often much tattered, carries this clumsy vessel along at a fair speed when favoured with a good wind. A topsail is added whenever possible. Without a good wind progress is slow. . . . When there is need to row, the men work long sweeps from on top of the cargo. Against the stream these boats have to tracked laboriously along the bank by the crew.[8]

In a preliminary drawing, from the album assembled by his widow, Solvyns penciled in the dimensions of the bhur he portrays as 40 feet in length, 12 feet in breadth.[9]

1 Sukumar Sen, 720.
2 Ibid., 702.
3 *Hobson-Jobson*, 105. Also see Deloche, 2:162, fn.66.
4 229
5 Henry Grant and Colebrooke, 115.
6 1:465.
7 38.
8 *Water Transport*, 251. Also see "The Boats of the Ganges," 193-94.
9 On the album, see pp. 83-85.

II.257. Iṭā Ḍiṅgi

Pl. II.257. Iṭā Ḍiṅgi. Paris: III.6.6.
Calcutta: Sec. IX, No. 17. A Yet-Dingee,—boat for carrying bricks.

Paris: III.6.6. YET DINGEE: Here we have another species of boat, called a *Dingee,* and used for carrying bricks: the print represents this boat on shore, a situation which I chose purposely to give an idea of the construction of the Hindoo boats in general. In the building of a boat the Hindoos begin by choosing a large piece of timber, which they bend as they please. To the two ends of this they attach another piece thicker than it, and cover this simple frame with planks: but they have a particular manner of joining these planks to each other, by flat cramps with two points, which enter the boards to be joined, and use common nails only to join the planks to the knee. For the sides of the boat they have pieces of wood, which outpass the planks. This method is as solid as it is simple: and the mode of uniting the planks is not unworthy of the imitation of Europeans.

Commentary: Solvyns's "yet" is *iṭā*, meaning "brick," and ḍiṅgi (Pl. II.237) is a small boat. The scene depicts the boat being loaded with bricks at the site of a kiln.

II.258. Gudārā

Pl. II.258. Gudārā. Paris: III.5.1. Double-plate.
Calcutta: Sec. VIII, No. 13. A Gudwaree, or Ferry Boat

Paris: III.5.1. FERRY, OR PASSAGE ON THE GANGES: In different parts, particularly in the neighbourhood of the bazars or markets, there are boats on the Ganges. I have represented one of these, with the company going over, which is composed of women of the lower classes and their children, of *Coulies* or day labourers, Faquirs, Jemidars [*jamidār*],[1] etc. These boats are at times so overloaded, that they get over with the greatest difficulty: they sometimes even sink, and disappear for ever with all the passengers. I have more than once witnessed these accidents; and, what is most remarkable, the Hindoos do not make the slightest effort to save themselves from perishing in the Ganges: they are persuaded that, whatever accident may happen to them in passing that river, proceeds immediately from the express will of God, and that, entire resignation to their fate will ensure them happiness in the next world. Far from lamenting therefore the lot of those who are drowned in this manner, it is a subject of rejoicing to their families, and the memory of it is transmitted with a sort of exaltation to their descendants.

The price of the passage is a meer trifle, either in a boat or a pontoon; but a permission from the Jemidar, or officer of the district, is necessary.

Commentary: In the Calcutta edition, this etching is titled "A Gudwaree," gudārā, Bengali for ferry boat. The gudārā is again portrayed in the Paris edition (Pl. II.259)—though not in the Calcutta collection—with a depiction of ferry boats in passage over rough water.

Here the ferry is loading at the ghāṭ. In mid-river, another gudārā is shown with sail.

1 Bengali for the Persian word *zamīndār*, landholder. See commentary for Ḍhāk, Pl. II.156.

II.259. Gudārā

Pl. II.259. Gudārā. Paris: III.6.5.

Paris: III.6.5. GUDWAREE: In the preceding number [Pl. II.258] I spoke in general terms of the *Ferries* on the river; I shall now say a few words of the boats which are employed. They are called *Gudwarees* in the Hindoo language, and are of the same species as all the others. The boatmen are so skilful, that, though there may be a great swell in the river, and that they carry but one small sail, they make their passage very expeditiously, with a considerable number of passengers. No European boat, however well built, can be better managed than the *Gudwarees*. Nevertheless Europeans are frequently afraid of passing in these ferryboats, and prefer a *Pansway* [pānsi, Pl. II.235] or a *Dingee* [ḍiṅgi, Pl. II.237]. Only those of an inferior class use the *Gudwarees*.

Commentary: The Bengali for ferry is *gudārā* or *kheyā*. Here gudārās are depicted in crossing what is probably the Hugli in rough water. The etching is not included in the Calcutta edition, although the gudārā is depicted in an etching corresponding to the Paris edition (Pl. II.258).

II.260. North-Wester

Pl. II.260. North-Wester.
Paris: III.1.1. Double-plate.
Calcutta: Before Sec. IX.
A North-Wester off Calcutta

Paris: III.1.1. NORTH-WESTER: The phenomenon which I am going to describe borrows its name from the wind by which it is occasioned: it takes place in the gulf of Bengal and the rivers of Hindoostan, more particularly in the south-east monsoon. The print represents a view to the north-west of Calcutta. In the morning a south wind, warmer than usual, reigns upon the river; from sunrise the sky is clear till about noon, when some clouds, which appear to come from the high mountains, meet on the horizon to the north, and soon accumulate so as to cover nearly the whole of the sky: the south wind ceases and a dead calm succeeds for a few minutes. On a sudden this momentary silence of nature is followed by a dreadful noise which seems to announce the confusion of all the elements. The clouds thicken, and are torn by continual flashes of lightning, the thunder roars, and torrents of rain often deluge the country: the atmosphere becomes a few degrees cooler. The river then assumes the appearance of a boisterous sea, and sometimes overwhelms the vessels which have not had the produce to fly for shelter to the creeks or canals. These disasters are but too frequent, and I myself have seen ships at anchor with their topmasts lowered veer round and disappear under the waves: these accidents are often too sudden to be prevented. I shall have occasion frequently, in the course of this volume, to mention again the dismal effects of these periodical tempests.

Commentary: Bengal's North-Wester, or Nor'-wester in Anglo-Indian parlance, is a sudden and violent storm, with winds that may reach more than 100 miles per hour. Arising in the "hot season," April through June, Bengalis call them *kāl baisākī*, "disasters of May." They are typically preceded by a dust storm and followed by hail and as much as 20 inches of rain in a single storm.[1] They are, as Mrs. Kindersley wrote from Calcutta in 1766, "altogether tremendous."[2]

In the etching, Solvyns takes the scene of an an earlier oil painting (Pl. I.6) and portrays the North-Wester on the Hugli River with the buildings of Calcutta seen on the distant shore. Oarsmen on a bhur (Pl. II.256), center, struggle in the wind.

1 *Hobson-Jobson*, 630, and Greenhill, *Boats and Boatmen of Pakistan*, 24.

2 83.

II.261. Bore

Pl. II.261. Bore. Paris: III.2.1. Double-plate. **Calcutta: Before Sec. VIII.** A View of the coming in of the Bhaun [*bān*] or Boar, in Garden Reach.

Paris: III.2.1. THE COMING IN OF THE BHAUN OR BOAR: This number begins, like the preceding one, with the representation of a phenomenon of nature, the *Macree*, or tide at the mouth of the river Ougly [Hugli]. It is well known that the tide in general is strongest where it meets with least resistance. In the Indian seas its force is uncontrouled by any obstacle; which is probably the cause of its extraordinary violence in the Ougly: in less than five minutes, it rises to the height of fifteen of twenty feet and is impelled with such impetuosity that it carries off immense banks of sand, and forces the river out of its natural bounds, and as it were from its very foundations. Woe to the vessels which have not had the prudence to quit it at this time: the tide is most violent where the water is less deep: the waves at times glide along the sides, raise up the sand-banks, and dash through the river to the other side where the current is strongest. The noise is dreadful and heard at a great distance, especially in the night. I have endeavoured to give a representation of all the terrible scenes which the *Macree* produces, but I must confess that they are much more faithfully preserved in the imagination than by the graver. The view is in the environs of Calcutta; the horizon is bounded by magnificent private gardens, the botanical garden, etc.

The *Macree* is most to be feared in the months of march and april, particularly with a southerly wind: it is also very violent in the quadratures and oppositions of the moon.

Commentary: A bore—*bān* in Bengali—is "a sudden and abrupt influx of the tide into a river or narrow strait."[1] Solvyns uses *macrée* as French for bore. The word, according to *Hobson-Jobson*, is associated with *macareo*, "a term applied by old voyagers to the phenomenon of the *bore* . . . [and] used by them as if it were an Oriental word."[2]

Milbourn, in *Oriental Commerce*, describes the bore on the Hugli: "So quick is its motion, that it hardly employs four hours in traveling" some 70 miles upriver. "At Calcutta, it sometimes occasions an instantaneous rise of five feet; and both here and in every part of its track, the boats on its approach immediately quite the shore, and make for safety to the middle of the river."[3] This spring tidal rush passes rapidly and involves a "tremendous noise"—a sound, Bishop Heber wrote, that resembled a steam-boat, but "infinitely louder."[4]

William Daniell portrayed "The Bore Rushing Up the Hoogley" in a dramatic engraving for the *Oriental Annual* of 1837.[5]

In Solvyns's etching, a pānsi (Pl. II.235) struggles against the bore, as a Jāliyā, fisherman (Pl. II.57), with his nets, walks along the river bank. The view is from Garden Reach, a suburb just south of Calcutta on the east bank of the Hugli. Here East India Company officials built grand "garden houses" in large compounds to which they would retreat in the hot weather.[6] On the opposite shore in Shibpur was the Company's Botanic Garden, established in 1786. The mansion across the river in Solvyns's etching is likely Botanic Garden House, later portrayed in an aquatint by James Baillie Fraser (1783-1856) in his *Views of Calcutta and its Environs*.[7]

1 Milbourn, 251.
2 527.
3 251. Also see Williamson, *East India Vade-Mecam*, 2:231-37.
4 1:74.
5 Engraving by R. Brandard, after the drawing by Daniell. Opp. 224.
6 On Garden Reach, see the discussion of Solvyns's paintings of the Farquharson house (Pls. I.14 and I.15), Chapter One, pp. 27-29.
7 On the Botanic Garden, see H. E. A. Cotton, 785-91. See Losty, *Calcutta: A City of Palaces*, for a discussion of the house. Fraser's aquatint, "A View of the Botanic Garden House and Reach, 1819," is illustrated in Losty, Pl. 19.

II.262. Balasore Roads

Paris: III.4.1. VIEW OF BALLASORE ROADS: Ballasore is an open road, and offers nothing but the sea to the view: the weather must be very clear to discover the distant point of Palmyre, the highlands of Piply, or the roof of some pagoda. It is frequented by different sorts of vessels, and particularly by large ships from Bombay, Surate, and other parts of the western coast, with moorish crews. There are also several vessels from the Ganges, called *Schooners,* very well fitted out, and able to make a voyage to Europe: their pilots are very skilfull. The anchorage in the road is good; but these vessels prefer remaining under sail, to keep a better look-out for ships, which it is their business to pilot into the entrance of the *Ougly* [Hugli], and for which they are constantly plying in the roads of Ballasore. This entrance is full of danger: and, to avoid it, an experienced pilot is absolutely necessary. Besides the man who takes charge of the ship, another is employed constantly in throwing the lead, and crying out the depth of water and quality of the bottom, while a pilot vessel precedes the ship at a little distance, and makes signals to him who steers it.

The print represents several different sorts of vessels, with a pilot schooner stationed in the road.

Pl. II.262. Balasore Roads. Paris: III.4.1. Double-plate.

Commentary: On the north coast of Orissa, Balasore (Baleshwar), 125 miles south of Calcutta, provided sheltered anchorage for Indiamen awaiting favorable winds—and an experienced pilot—to take them up the Hugli river or for the transfer of goods and passengers from the larger ships to sloops (Pl. II.254) or other boats for the trip upriver.

Solvyns writes that the pilot vessels were "called *Schooners*" and that in the etching he represents "a pilot schooner stationed in the road," but the print depicts no schooner-rigged vessels. Schooners, built in India, had earlier been used by the Bengal Pilot Service, though it is unlikely that they were in service in Solvyns's time.[1] Pilot boats, typically brigs from the late eighteenth century, apparently continued to be called "schooners," and, indeed, the term was often used loosely to apply to any small fast vessel suitable for the river, but Solvyns, trained in Europe as a marine painter, would surely have been familiar with the schooner proper.

The term "schooner" was first applied to a fore-and-aft rigged, two-masted vessel in New England in the early eighteenth century, though other craft of similar rigging dated from 1600 in Holland.[2]

The print is not included in the Calcutta edition, and, as in his depiction of "Vessels of All Sorts" (Pl. II.263), Solvyns presents a composite, using his own drawings from India, as with the grab, but also taking images from other sources. What then does Solvyns portray in his "View of Ballasore Roads"? Daniel Finamore, curator of marine painting at Salem's Peabody Essex Museum, identifies the central ship as a grab (Pl. II.244), with a square-rigged foremast and square sail main top, fore-and-aft spanker, thus making it a standard brig rig. It has a very sharp bow and an unconventional construction at the stern, perhaps a passenger compartment.

On the left is a full-rigged ship of standard European type, though hardly graceful in design. It is old-fashioned for Solvyns's time, as indicated by its early eighteenth century spritsail yard, and Finamore suggests it likely that Solvyns copied the image from an older European print or painting. To the center right is a full-rigged European ship, and on the far right is a standard brig of the 1790-1810 era.

Balasore had been an early European commercial center, with an English factory established in 1633,[3] but with the rise of Calcutta, it came to be the center for pilot services. River pilots boarded the smaller ships to steer them upstream through the treacherous sandbars of the Hugli to safe harbor at Diamond Harbor, 41 miles south of Calcutta, or on to Calcutta itself.[4] For the Indiamen able to proceed upriver, pilot boats typically led the way into the Hugli, between the "sandheads"—shoals that stretched out from the mouth of the river like fingers—but, as decreed by the East India Company Board of Directors in 1700, ships of more than 400 tons burden were to anchor in Balasore Roads or at Kijari (Kedgeree), at the mouth of the Hugli, and their passengers and goods were to be transferred to smaller boats for transport to Calcutta.[5]

Often the last leg of the trip for passengers, from Diamond Point or Kulpi (Anglo-Indian "Culpee," a few miles below it on the Hugli) to Calcutta, was by bājrā (Pl. II.232) or, more grandly, by fīlcehrā (Pl. II.230).[6]

Palmyras Point, to which Solvyns refers, is a promontory below Balasore that served as a landmark for vessels from the south, and it was just past this headland that ships encountered the pilots that would lead them into the shifting channels of Hugli.[7] Pipli, north of Balasore, had been a center of Portuguese, Dutch, and English trade in the mid-seventeenth century, but by Solvyns's time, much of the coastal town had washed away.[8]

1 Maritime historian Anne Bulley records that several schooners were built in the Bombay dockyard for the Bengal Pilot Service between 1753 and 1776, but they were apparently not altogether satisfactory, and in the 1780s and 1790s, four brigs and a snow were built for the Pilot Service—but no schooners. Personal communication, January 22, 1998. See Bulley, *The Bombay Country Ships 1790-1833*.

2 MacGregor, 13. Early schooners were two-masted, and by Solvyns's time, some carried three masts. From the mid-nineteenth century, schooners ranged from two to six masts. Also see Kerchove, 629-30.

3 On the history of Balasore, see Hunter, *A Statistical Account of Bengal*, 18:280-83; Walter Hamilton, *A Geographical, Statistical, and Historical Description of Hindostan and Adjacent Countries*, 2:37; Deloche, 2:116; and Tripati, 156-57.

4 See, for example, the description by Father Matteo Ripa in 1709, quoted Nair, *Calcutta in the 18th Century*, 19. The various points of the river are described in "Early Charts and Topography of the Hugli River," Note by Henry Yule, in Hedges, 3:197-220. On Diamond Harbor, see Pl. II.254.

5 Marshman, in Alok Ray, 181. Deloche, in his account of water transport in India, 2:117-23, provides detailed information on the Hugli estuary and coastal fluvial navigation of the region. For a map of the area, from Palmyras Point up the Hugli to Calcutta, see Jean Sutton, 117, and description, 118. On the pilot service, also see Nilmani Mukherjee, 4-6, 26, 30.

6 Firminger's note on "Culpee," Stanhope, 29, vi.

7 Walter Hamilton, *East India Gazetteer*, 2:407.

8 See Walter Hamilton, *A Geographical, Statistical, and Historical Description of Hindostan and Adjacent Countries*, 1:152; Milbourn, 250; Deloche, 2:116; and Tripati, 157-58.

II.263. Vessels of All Sorts

Paris: III.12.6. VESSELS OF ALL SORTS.: Six numbers of this volume have been employed for the navigation of the Hindoos; but it did not enter into my plan, to describe the private boats, nor the foreign Indian vessels. I have endeavoured to unite in this print every object of this kind. Here are the high vessels of the Red Sea and Persian gulph, the Grabs [Pl. II.244], the ships of the Maldive isles, made of bambous and coconut trees, masts cordage and anchors. The boats employed in the pearl fishery on the coast of Ceylan, the Vliegers of Batavia, the Proues of Malacca, remarked for their swiftness: the Catamarans of Madras, and infine the Chinese Jonques. Among all this imperfect shipping though well adapted to the seas and climates they frequent, I have placed an European frigate, and a boat, as a sufficient proof of the superiority of our naval architecture over that of the Indian nations, and particularly the Hindoos.

Commentary: In Solvyns's composite depiction, on the far right, split by the frame, is the Chinese junk, with its distinctive sail. Just to the left of it, is the frigate, in broadside—portrayed as it would look in a treatise on naval architecture, with every sail that she carries set. She would never have looked like this at sea, especially near shore. Solvyns uses the term "frigate" correctly and shows a full-rigged three masted ship, with a single gun deck. The ship to the far left, stern view, is of seventeenth century design, and Solvyns almost surely copied the image from a painting rather than from drawings he may have made while in India.[1]

Other boats are not clearly distinguished, but Solvyns refers to various vessels that might be encountered, including a catamaran of Madras, though

Pl. II.263. Vessels of All Sorts. Paris: III.12.6.

it is nowhere evident in the etching. The catamaran is a raft of logs (usually three) lashed together, navigated typically by two men. The Tamil word is *kaṭṭumaram*, literally *kaṭṭu* (to tie) + *maram* (tree or log). Solvyns distinguishes the boats used in the pearl fisheries off Ceylon, but these were usually kaṭṭumaram.[2]

The "proue" of Malacca is the Malay *prāū*, a particular kind of galley used in the Straits and referred to by Solvyns in his portrayal of Penang (Pl. II.264).

Solvyns's reference to "Vliegers of Batavia" is mystifying. There was a Dutch marine artist named Simon Jocobsz de Vlieger (c. 1600-1653), but no identifiable type of boat by that name. Five Dutch vessels bore the name of the artist, but this hardly seems what Solvyns intends to convey.[3]

1 I am grateful to marine painting specialist Daniel Finamore, Curator, Peabody Essex Museum, Salem, Massachusetts, for his help in identifying the ships depicted in the etching.

2 See Deloche, 2:179-81; Edye, 4; Hornell, *Water Transport*, 61-67; and Hornell, "The Origins and Ethnological Significance of Indian Boat Designs," 169-72.

3 Although no boats styled "Vliegers" can be found, the Nederlands Scheepvaartmuseum, Amsterdam, lists five vessels named "Vlieger," one of which was an East Indiaman of 1669. None would fit Solvyns's description. Personal communication, January 6, 1998.

II.264. Penang

Pl. II.264. Penang. Paris: III.3.1. Double-plate.

Paris: III.3.1. POULO PENANG: The island of *Penang,* now called prince of Wales's, island, is situated to the north of the straits of Malacca; this view of it is taken on the side of the fort. It is one of the most beautiful and fertile islands on the Indian coast, and belongs to England, under the administration of a governor. Fish, fruits and grain are found here in the greatest abundance; the mangastan [mangosteen] especially (the *garcinia* of Linneus) is delicious.

The inhabitants are mostly of Malayan origin; there are also a number of Chinese, who have their temples, their playhouses, and a great many gaming houses, on which the governor levies a considerable tax: these houses, which are always open on the side of the street, are much frequented, and particularly by the class of workmen who often quit their work to game.

There are in the island several distilleries of arrak belonging to the Chinese, which pay also considerable duties to the governor, and are deserving of the attention of Europeans.

The island of *Penang* is frequented by a great number of boats of different sizes from the neighbouring islands, whose productions they bring to its magnificent bazar. One species of these vessels, the *proues,* is used by the Malays in their piratical expeditions in the straits but more to the south of Malacca these pirates are frequently in great force, and are not intidated by strong armed ships: they take advantage of the night or of a calm to endeavour to board them; they use poisoned *crests* [*krīs*].[1] And massacre the crews. These boats, of which several are represented in the engraving are excellent sailors, light and well manned, they carry square sails, and some of them one, two, or three masts; their construction is neat and light.

Commentary: The print does not appear in the Calcutta edition, and it is likely that Solvyns visited Penang only in 1803, on his return voyage to Europe. The route from Calcutta typically crossed the Bay of Bengal to stop at Penang and from there to Madras and on around the tip of India.

Solvyns's "Poulo" is the Malay *pulau,* "island," and *pinang* is the word for areca-nut or -tree.[2] The British took possession of the island in 1786, naming it "Prince of Wales Island," but this gave way to the Malay name.

Solvyns's "proue" is the Malay *prāū*, or *prāhū* (proa in English; *prao* in Portuguese), a particular kind of galley used in the Straits and the archipelago, but the term is used generally for any Malay native craft, though usually small craft.[3]

1 A Malay dagger: "creese " in *OED*, "crease" in *Hobson-Jobson*, 274, from the Malay *krīs*.

2 *Hobson-Jobson*, 695, and Walter Hamilton, *East India Gazetteer*, 2:418.

3 *Hobson-Jobson*, 733, and Noel.

Natural History: Plants and Animals

Solvyns did not include specific etchings of plants and animals in the Calcutta edition, and the early "Prospectus" for *Les Hindoûs* that announced the publication of 252 plates made no mention of these subjects. Soon after he began work on the Paris etchings, however, Solvyns decided to expand their number to 288, with the additional prints portraying plants and animals and distinct types of Indian heads. In the Introduction to *Les Hindoûs*, Vol. IV, Solvyns described his plan in including a section of "the natural history of India."

> I thought my readers would not be displeased to find at the end of the work a faithful representation of the vegetables and animals, which I had so frequent occasion to mention in the text: not that my intention is to give any thing like a complete treatise of the natural history of the countries where I have resided, that I am very sensible would require more knowledge than I can flatter myself to possess. Many learned naturalists besides have published works which contain a classefication and scientific discription of the productions of India. My only wish was to give a description and representation of such objects of natural history as occur most frequently during a residence in Hindoostan; the most common vegetables and the animals most known to the Hindoos: so far this was not foreign to my plan, since it afforded frequent opportunities of making known many of the habits of this people; the culture of indigo, of rice, of coton, of the sugar cane and many other productions led me naturally to describe the simplicity of their process in manufacturing them. I could not speak of their animals without remarking the use which they made of them, and the dangers which they had to avoid. We are inclined in Europe to imagine that India is the most fortunate country of the earth, and to envy those who are happy enough to visit it; but we make no account of the many serious inconveniences to which this happy region is exposed; we are ignorant that besides the heat of the climate the European especially has a constant combat to maintain against multitudes of dangerous or disgusting animals who intrude upon his hours of pleasure and repose, and are a terrible drawback upon the enjoyments of this delicious residence. Swarms of insects seize upon him on his arrival, pursue him into his house, devour many of the objects he may have brought from Europe, and often destroy even the merchandise upon which he has built the hopes of his fortune.
>
> I shall have occasion also to mention some particularities which seem to have escaped the notice of the naturalists, or which at least are not to be met with in their works. Here I might have taken a greater scope, but prudence recalled me to the bounds and the plan of my work. One number only has been given to the shrubs, one to the trees, one to quadrupedes and amphibious animals; the most remarkable birds have been comprised in another, and the insects and fishes occupy no more.
>
> It may perhaps not be unnecessary to repeat once more that every one of these drawings were taken from nature, and that along with the vegetables and animals are represented the accessaries which were upon the spot on which I saw them: infine that the text contains strictly no more than what I myself was witness to. This is an advantage which I may flatter myself to possess over the writers of natural history who have not travelled. All that I have read in Europe since my return from India, is a proof to me that the natural history of this country is still but little known, and that those who have written upon it are often ill informed.[1]

---

1 4:8-9.

II.265. Tamarind

Pl. II.265. Tamarind. Paris: IV.7.1

Paris: IV.7.1. THE TAMARINE TREE. *(TAMARINDUS INDICA):* Tamarine trees are very common in Hindoostan. They grow sometimes to a prodigious height, and offer an excellent shelter from the heat of the sun. The fruit and leaves are described in all the works of natural history; it remains only for me to say that the fruit gives a very refreshing juice and is used in the way of lemons. The natives mix it with their *carrys* [curries], and the Europeans make with it cooling draughts and sweetmeats which are often sent to Europe. All the markets of Hindoostan are full of it, though it is not always of an easy sale, as every one who will take the trouble of gathering it may supply himself, but from November to March it is not quite so plenty, and in upper Hindoostan it is sometimes hard to be got fresh. This tree has nothing valuable but its fruit, the wood is good for nothing.

Serpents of an enormous size sometimes wind themselves round it and dart their venom at those who approch to get the fruit. I was near being the victime of one of these reptiles of about an inch diameter and upwards of forty feet long; a servant had but just time to warn me of my danger.

II.266. Mango

Paris: IV.7.2. THE MANGO TREE. (MANGIFERA INDICA, LINN.): The Hindoos are fond of cultivating this tree. Its beauty appears sufficiently in the print. The fruit cuts like a peach. The aukward manner in which the Europeans, on their first arrival, attempt to eat it is a subject of mirth, not knowing how to cut it. It is eaten raw, often preserved or dried by the black Portuguese's[1] and Europeans; and the Hindoos put it in their *carry* [curry]. The quality and species are as various as our pears and apples. Some are excellent, others very bad with a tast of turpentine, but the best of them do not come near the fruit of the *mangestan* [mangosteen], a tree unknown in Hindoostan. The timber is but indifferent, yet the natives, who are not so nice, employ it for doors and windows and such like works.

1 Indo-Portuguese. See Commentary for Pl. II.6.

Pl. II.266. Mango. Paris: IV.7.2.

II.267. Jackfruit

Paris: IV.7.3. THE JAC TREE. (ARTO CARPUS JACQUA, Fauster.): The *Jac* tree differs essentially from all our trees by not bearing its fruits at the end of its branches as we are used to see our apples and pears, but projecting directly from its trunk, and weighing from twenty to thirty pounds, so that a single one is a sufficient meal for a whole family who eat it with salt when it is very ripe. It is of a deep yellow colour, and of so strong a smell that it is perceived in the house several days after it has been eaten, of an insipid taste to which Europeans are long before they get accustomed, but generally end by liking it. The timber is solid, of a deep yellow, and excellent for shafts and wheel work. The *Jac* is found only in the hindoo gardens, and oftener in the lower than upper Hindoostan. Its appearance in landskape is singular and very new to Europeans.

Pl. II.267. Jackfruit. Paris: IV.7.3.

II.268. Coconut and Other Palms

Commentary: The palms in the background on the right are wild dates (*Phoenix sylvestris*), khājur in Bengali. The most common palm in India, its juice is boiled for sugar (*jaggery*). The palm on the left appears to be a rather straggly palmyra (*Borassus flabellifer*), tāl in both Bengali and Sanskrit, the palm of a proverbially thousand uses.

1 See Solvyns's portrayal of the *nārikel*, coconut shell *hukā*, Pl. II.203-6.

Pl. II.268. Coconut and Other Palms. Paris: IV.7.4.

Paris: IV.7.4. THE COCO, AND OTHER PALM TREES. (COCOS NUCIFERA, Linn.): The vegitable reign offers to the Hindoo, and in general to the inhabitants of tropical climates, no plant so useful as the Coco-nut tree, whose size and majestic forms are moreover very ornamental to the scenery of their country. It is seldom indeed met with so beautiful as that I have represented, in which nevertheless all the truth of nature is scrupulously preserved, and the more so, because I had never seen a faithful drawing of this remarkable tree. It seldom grows single or at a distance from the water. Coco-nuts are in great use in India, the bazars are full of them, and they are even imported by sea. They produce an excellent drink, a very nourishing food, and an oil for various uses: of part of the inside excellent pastry is made, the shell becomes a Houka [*hukā*] or smoking case;[1] the filaments which surround it make cordage and cables, preferable to ours for sliding tackle on account of their superior suppleness; the trunk finishes a mast to their ships, and the branches fuel, so that no part of this plant is useless.

Near the Coco-tree I have drawn some other species of palms which generally grow in India.

II.269. Banana

Pl. 269. Banana. Paris: IV.7.5.

Paris: IV.7.5. THE BANANA TREE. (*BANANIERA, MUSA PARADISIACA,* Linn.): The *Banana* is among all other trees the most esteemed by the Hindoos, as well for the delicious taste of its fruit, as for the shade which it affords in the great heats; for which reason there are generally some of them planted near their houses. Their aspect has at first nothing striking for an European, but the taste of their fruit soon justifies their reputation. It is remarkable in this tree that it dies as soon as it has born its fruit. The inside of the trunk is so soft that it is easily cut to pieces and eaten. The leaves serve for plates and for paper. Few fruits are more agreable to the taste, neither natives nor foreigners are ever tired of it. The finest bananas are produced in the environs of Dacca, they excell all others in taste, flavour and size. Serpents and many insects are very fond of this fruit and conceal themselves in the branches which offer them a cool retreat. The Banana which I have represented, is the finest which I ever met with, and I have not left out the Hindoo who was reposing under its shade while I was sketching it, to shew the height of the tree.

II.270. Bamboo

Paris: IV.7.6. THE BAMBOU TREE. *(ARUNDO BAMBOS,* Linn.): The Bambou is another very useful tree. Though it does not attain in Hindoostan the height which it does in other places, as for example in the island of Java its groupes and masses of foliage have a striking effect on the eyes of foreigners. The Bambou alleys, as long as the sight can reach, are not more agreable to the eye than to the feelings, by their delightful coolness, but they are not without danger from serpents and insects which they shelter. When agitated by the wind they produce a loud but not unpleasing sound. Scaffoldings of buildings are made of Bambous. A few of them joined together bear any weight, split they make lattice, matting and all nice works. It is surprising to see the same tree turned into so many uses, which compensates for its want of fruit. It bears transplanting and grows well wherever there is moisture, either single or in groupes.

Pl. II.270. Bamboo. Paris: IV.7.6.

II.271. Rice

Paris: IV.8.1. RICE.*(ORIZA SATIVA,* Linn.): The Rice is a plant well known in Europe, I could not however omit mentioning it in a work upon the Hindoos whose chief nourrishment it is, and whose very existence, in a great measure, depends upon it, as a scarcity of this production never fails to cause the death of thousands. This print gives but a part of the process of its culture, the rest having been noticed in the first volume. In front is a rice ground in maturity. When it is about a foot above the soil they take care to keep it well watered by letting in streams through little trenches. In the harvest every workman has his particular occupation as I have mentioned elsewhere; he who ploughs does not thresh, nor he who sheaves winnow. There are many sorts of rice in India, the most esteemed is a very white small grain from Patna; the common people prefer the large yellowish grain which is courser, cheaper, and they pretend more nourrishing. With butter, rice sugar they make excellent pastry; but eat it even dry and raw, or with herbs, fruits, shrimps, pimanto, onions, ginger, etc. this is called a *curry.* There is something remarquable in the way they eat it, rolling it up in little balls between their fingers and swallowing it without chewing; it comes from them nearly in the same state, so that the rice seems only to pass through their intestines; this fact is worthy of the attention of naturalists.

Pl. II.271. Rice. Paris: IV.8.1.

II.272. Sugar Cane

Paris: IV.8.2. THE SUGAR CANE. *(SACCHARUM OFFICINARUM,* Linn.): Of this production also there are several species, some very high and thick, but these do not pass for the best. In most parts of Hindoostan sugar is so abundant that they frequently don't know what to do with it. They mix it with milk and butter, and make different sorts of sweetmeats with it, as I have observed in the first volume [Pl. II.40]. They strip the cane also of its bark and present it to strangers in pieces, of which the juice unprepared is very refreshing. The form of the plant is well known. All the simplicity of this nation appears in their mode of manufacturing it. The mill or press consists of three pieces of timber between which a man passes the cane, the juice of which is received in a *cudgeric* [*khicuṛī*] pot below, and is afterwards purified by the fire. The cane fields and mill are generally close to the house, as is represented in the print.

Pl. II.272. **Sugar Cane.** Paris: IV.8.2.

II.273. Mustard

Paris: IV.8.3. MUSTARD. *(SYNAPIS INGRA,* Linn): Mustard is cultivated in most countries, but in none so frequently used as in India, especially in oil, for extracting which almost everywhere is a *koaloo* [Kalu, Pl. II.58], every oilman has his mill. The fields under this culture have a pretty effect in indian landskape by the different yellow shades of the flower. One of these plants forms alone the foreground of the print: the grain is generally black, some white and yellow but scarce. In some parts they have two crops in the year, and the consumption of it is immense. The oil is used every day in their curries and in frying, leaves a very agreeable taste to Europeans. I have already taken notice of their practice of rubbing their bodies with it, which continued for some time produces an effect like tanning, and gives the skin the hardness and consistency of leather, which enables the Hindoo to support the burning heat of the sun.

Pl. II.273. Mustard. Paris: IV.8.3.

II.274. Cotton

Paris: IV.8.4. COTTON. *(GOSSYPIUM BERBACEUM,* Linn.): If the cotton which India produces is in high repute, the stuffs which the Hindoos make of it are still more so: which gives a double degree of interest to their mode of manufacturing it. I could represent but a part in this print, where the spinning, carding, and preparing for the loom are seen; the weavers have been described in the first volume [Jugi, Pl. II.27; Tā̃ti, Pl. II.33]. In all this their native simplicity may be observed. In the background is the plant growing. This shrub sometimes rises to ten or twelve feet. The countries most fertile in Cotton are Surate [Surat] and Guzurate [Gujarat]; which export immense quantities to China. Men, women and children of all ages and sexes of the Hindoos find occupation in preparing the Cotton and fabricating those stuffs, fine and strong at the same time, which notwithstanding all our arts we have never been able to equal in Europe.

Pl. II.274. Cotton. Paris: IV.8.4.

II.275. Indigo

Pl. II.275. Indigo. Paris: IV.8.5.

Paris: IV.8.5. INDIGO. *(INDIGOFERA TINCTORIA*, Linn.): While the European erects sumptious buildings with expensive machinery and apparatus to extend the fabrication of Indigo, and often ruins himself in speculating, the Hindoo is generally more successful in following the cheap and simple process of his forefathers, and though he is satisfied with smaller profits he is exposed to fewer dangers. When the plant is come to maturity the Hindoo steeps it during fifteen hours in water to ferment. When the liquor is in this state, which is known by the sinking of a piece of money, it is beaten up strongly with a switch and mixed with more water in which a powder of shells has been dissolved; which precipitates the feculence of the Indigo: it is then put into pointed bags, about two or three feet in length and one in diameter, and put under the press to draw of the water from the pulp. When it is of a proper consistence it is spread out on a board and cut with a copper knife into squares, which are finally transported to the drying house where care must be taken to keep them separate, and protect them from the wind and flies.

The print represents parts of this process: in the front is an Indigo plant six feet high; in Bengal they grow to nine or ten: the leaf is oblong, green and satiny, the under side rather whitish. From the interior of the leaf is extracted that fine blue which retains the name of Indigo.

Commentary: Indigo, for the production of its dark blue dye, was a major plantation crop and source of export income for the East India Company in Bengal in Solvyns's time. European travelers to India commented on indigo,[1] and eighteenth century accounts and treatises described its cultivation and manufacture.[2]

1 See *Hobson-Jobson*, 437-38.

2 See Charpentier-Cossigny de Palma (1789) and de Berauvais-Raseau (1794). Also see Claude Martin in *Asiatic Researches*. In the considerable literature on indigo, Colesworthy Grant, *Rural Life in Bengal*, 86-94, 114-136, provides succinct account of its cultivation and manufacture for the general reader.

II.276. Cochineal

Pl. II.276. Cochineal. Paris: IV.8.6.

Paris: IV.8.6. COCHINEAL. *(CACTUS COCCINELLIFER,* Linn.)[1]: The plant upon which the Cochineal insect dines is represented in the foreground; it grows abundantly in all the gardens of Hindoostan. The insect propagates upon it to such a degree that it requires but a few days to fill a whole field, all the plants are soon consumed, and it is not without difficulty that they can kill them. I have seen but little fine Cochineal in Hindoostan, the scarlet is generally mixed with a large proportion of white. But if India cannot boast of the perfection of this animal production, it possesses, as an indemnity, the most beautiful mineral colours: among others a very fine red, yellow and other coloured earth, found near Moursadabad [Murshidabad] a few days journey from Calcutta, the country itself is known by the name of *Rongamatty* [Rangamati] or the coloured earth.

Commentary: The cochineal is a tiny red scale insect (*Dactylopius coccus*) used for making carmine and scarlet dyes, made from the dried and pulverized body of the female. The insect feeds on prickly pear, cacti of the genus *Opuntia*, as depicted here—identified by Solvyns as *Cactus coccinellifer Linn*, a scientific name no longer used.[2] Cochineal insects are gathered by brushing them from the cactus into bags, and they are then killed by immersion in hot water or through the heat of the sun or in an oven. It takes 70,000 insects to make one pound of the cochineal dye.[3]

The insects were introduced into India in the late eighteenth century, and their propagation was encouraged by James Anderson (1738-1809), a botanist and Physician General of the Madras medical service.[4]

1 Obsolete scientific name for the *Opuntia* cactus depicted, not for cochineal.
2 The Linnaean genus *Cactus* is now subdivided into many genera. The *Opuntia* was introduced into India from Mexico.
3 *Enclyclopaedia Britannica*, 15th ed., *Micropaedia*, 2:1026-27.
4 Anderson, who wrote *An Account of the Importation of American Cochineal Insects into Hindostan* (1795), engaged in published correspondence with Sir Arthur Banks, President of the Royal Society, regarding the cochineal in India. Pennant refers to the introduction of both cochineal and cactus into India, 2:97. Also see W. H. Carey, *The Good Old Days of the Honorable John Company*, 2:931-92.

II.277. Buffalo

Paris: IV.9.1. THE BUFFALO: We may say of the animals of India, as of the plants, that their names and outward forms are very well known in Europe but that we have only very vague ideas of their qualities, which have been more closely observed by the natives who have them constantly under their eyes, being as it were brought up among them.

The *wild Buffalo*, for example, is much more feared in India than the tiger, and is untameable. The chase of the latter is often taken as an amusement, but no one ever attempts to hunt the former, who when he is attacked, even by an army, never turns to run, but defends himself to the last drop of his blood. The *wild Buffalo* is square built and of prodigious strength: his horns are finely shaped and weigh together from a hundred and ten to a hundred and twenty pounds. He likes water and mud, and takes great delight in rolling in marshy grounds. They are sometimes seen on the banks of rivers in herds of twenty to fifty, and from the boats great numbers of them may be perceived in the midst of the *Sunderbunds*. The *tame Buffalo* is not so strong, his milk is more nourishing than that of the cow, as I have proved by long experience. The Hindoos also use it, and would prefer it, were it not for the veneration which the laws of *Menu* [Manu] have attached to the cow.

Pl. II.277. Buffalo. Paris: IV.9.1.

II.278. Tiger

Commentary: Solvyns's portrayal of the tiger in the etching is comical and rather odd for someone who, claiming to have dissected tigers, should be familiar with its anatomy—unless he intends satirically to give the tiger the human face of a personal adversary. Even more odd is Solvyns's reference to the tiger's stealth in hiding its head under a rice pot (*khicuṛī*) when swimming up to a boat. In the print, without explanation, the tiger lies beside what appears to be a *khicuṛī,* upside down, over a bamboo paddle stuck in the ground.

Pl. II.278. Tiger. Paris: IV.9.2.

Paris: IV.9.2. THE TIGER: Next to the buffalo the *Tiger* is the animal most feared by the Hindoos, especially the *Royal* or *Bengal Tiger*. With great strength, and more suppleness and cunning than the other, he frequently commits dreadful depredations in the neighbourhood of their habitations. Not a year passes but some of the hindoo labourers, whom the Company employs in their salt works, are carried off and devoured by the *Tigers:* a fate the more deplorable as they are forced into this service and consequently exposed unwillingly to this dreadful danger. The *Tiger* seises his prey in the same manner as the cat, with whom he has a striking resemblance. He conceals himself, watches and darts upon it when it comes within his reach: if he misses it, he flies off and returns at another time. I have been followed by one of them in my boat from morning till night. When pressed by hunger they will swim to a boat at anchor, taking care to hide their heads under a *cudjery* [*khicuṛī*] or the large floating leaves, the boatsmen to avoid being taken by surprise by them are often obliged to hang networks round their boats; if unfortunately the *Tiger* gets aboard they may be sure he will leap into the water with the fatest man among them and drag him ashore. Travellers or hunters are warned of their approach by the horse or elephant which they ride, and sometimes by their scent. I have often dissected *Tigers,* and the stench which they exhaled was almost insupportable. It may be remembered that I have spoken in the former volumes of the use which the Brahmans [Pl. II.18] and Faquirs [Pl. II.145] make of *Tigers* skins for dress and for seats.

II.279. Hoolock Gibbon (?)

Pl. II.279. Hoolock Gibbon (?). Paris: IV.9.3.

Paris: IV.9.3. OURANG-OUTANG: Among the different species of monkeys the *Ourang-Outang* most resembles a man. I will relate an instance of their remarkable instinct, of which I was witness. On my arrival in India I inhabited a country house near the river Ougly [Hugli], when I was informed that a large *Ourang-Outang* came, for many years past, frequently to the kitchen door in the morning, to take the leavings of the day before. I was curious to observe this animal and went out with the cook early the next morning. At a little distance from the house he made me remark the traces of a tiger, and while we were following them we perceive the *Ourang-Outang* at a little distance, running sometimes on four legs sometimes on two: he was between six and seven feet high, and when he got near us stood erect, with the help of a stick, and began to cry out and make signs as it were to ask for his usual pittance: he was let into the kitchen where they gave him a plate of rice and some scraps of meat, which he eat sitting, without any signs of fear, muttering with a sort of satisfaction between his teeth. When he had done he walked about the kitchen and was going off when the cook called him back to give him some fruit and two coco-nuts, which he carried away. I saw him several times repeat this singular visit, but I was assured that he came only during part of the winter, not regularly every day, and always at sun rise.

Commentary: How Solvyns could have applied the name of the great ape of Borneo and Sumatra to an Indian species is curious, for there were surely no orangutans in India—unless Governor-General Wellesley had a caged one in the menagerie at his country residence at Barrackpore, 14 miles north of Calcutta. For all his commitment to fidelity, Solvyns here seems to have succumbed to exaggeration.[1] This "man of the jungle" (the literal meaning of the Malay *orangutan*), if not wholly a figment of Solvyns's imagination, is possibly a hoolock gibbon (*Hylobates hoolock*), a small ape, with a head and body length for the male of usually no more than 63 cm. They live in hilly forests of eastern Bengal and India's northeast and are almost entirely arboreal, but they can be trained to be good pets.[2] Whether the gibbon was Solvyns's "ourang-outang," however, must remain a matter of conjecture.

1 Desmond, in a discussion of natural history painting in India, reproduces the "Ourang-outang" etching (Pl. 4) and questions both Solvyns's veracity and ability as an artist, but he writes that "Although his drawings are undoubtedly naive, the work is still a *tour de force*. . . ." 166.

2 Roonwal and Mohnot, 315-18.

II.280. Hanuman Langur

Pl. II.280. Hanuman Langur. Paris: IV.9.4.

Paris: IV.9.4. THE GUENOU: This is another species of monkey for whom the Hindoos have a sort of veneration; they think themselves honored by their presence and prepare food for them as for a human being. There are countries reputed sacred because their forests are inhabited by *Guenous*. What is most remarkable is, that these animals seem capable of a sort of party spirit like associations and corporate bodies among mankind. The monkeys of one part of a forest frequently attack those of another, or of a different country. Of this I have seen a striking example: near a village of Brahmuns there was a lofty wood inhabited by a large troop of monkeys; another body formed a plan to dislodge them and detached six or eight of their party to attack them with stones. The old inhabitants sent out a detachment to drive the agressors from the plain. The battle soon became general, and the females were seen in great dismay leaping through the branches from side to side. At night fall both parties retired: but in the morning, for many days following, the same sort of warfare was renewed; and every day many monkeys were found killed or dangerously wounded. At length victory declared for the old foresters who repulsed the assailants. The Hindoos of the village took great interest in this success which they looked upon as a good omen for themselves.

In India no one ever kills a *Guenou*, and they pretend that if an European does, the whole body falls upon him; but I can contradict this assertion, for I have killed many without perceiving any symptom of revenge in their companions.

Commentary: The guenon, genus *Ceropithecus*, is a monkey of Africa, not Asia. No doubt some Europeans in India were rather casual in giving familiar names to unfamiliar animals, though this would not seem in character for Solvyns. In any case, the monkey is likely a Hanuman langur (*Prebytis entellus*), held sacred by Hindus as the living representation of the monkey god Hanuman.[1] The Hanuman langur, also called gray langur, is of fairly substantial size, a maximum body length of about 108 cm. and weight of 21 kg. for males.[2]

Another monkey, more tolerated than held sacred, is the rhesus macaque (*Macaca mulatta*), about half the size of the langur and the most common monkey in India. Commensal with humans, they are an urban nuisance and are notorious for thieving. "The close interaction of these macaques with the people of India forms perhaps the most intense relationship between human and nonhuman primates anywhere in the world. The rhesus macaque can be easily tamed and taught various tricks . . . , but is never fully domesticated. . . ."[3]

1 On the Hindu view of monkeys, see Crooke, *Things Indian*, 329-33.

2 Roonwal and Mohnot, 234-70.

3 Ibid., 99. On the rhesus macque generally, 97-174.

II.281. Jackal

Paris: IV.9.5. THE JACHAL: The *Jachal* is a dog of the middle species, in his gait and hind parts perfectly resembling a wolf. They are very common in India because the natives never seek to destroy them: perhaps too they may be of some use by their devouring dead bodies, which they seek out with great avidity and often fight for with the birds of prey. They hide themselves during the day under ground, and rove during the night in packs. Their howling is frightful. Hunting the *Jachal* is become a general amusement among the Europeans and dogs are imported from Europe solely for this purpose. Representations of this chase have been published in London in 1807, from sketches by capt. *Thomas Williamson,* and the drawings of *Samuel Howett.*[1] The *Jachal* is hard to kill and takes frequently many shots. His sense of smelling is very accute, and he never misses his prey how deep soever it may be buried. His bite is venemous, and it is altogether a dangerous animal especially when prest with hunger. Its skin is turned to several uses.

1 *Oriental Field Sports.*

Pl. II.281. Jackal. Paris: IV.9.5.

II.282. Bengali Dog

Paris: IV.9.6. THE BENGAL DOG: This is a different species in its form and habits. The *Bengal Dog* is large: he can raise his ears but half way up. He feeds upon carrion and other disgusting matter, is dirty, subject to the mange, no ways attached to man, and upon the whole a very useless animal. The Hindoos express the baseness of his nature by the apellation of a *Pariah Dog.*[1] They breed at Calcutta to such a degree that the police is frequently obliged to have them killed; sometimes to the number of two or three hundred in a day. It is the only Dog who goes alone in the streets, the others are always attended by a servant. The *Bengal Dog* seems to have an aversion for Europeans, and always barks when he meets them. His skin tanned furnishes a tolerably good leather. A black one of this species is seldom seen.

I was never able to meet in Bengal with the Dog known, in M. Buffons natural history, by the name of *Bengalee Brae.*

Pl. II.282. Bengali Dog. Paris: IV.9.6.

Commentary: Solvyns's view of dogs in Bengal conforms to Pennant's judgment that "The dogs of *India* are generally of the currish kind. . . ."[2] It is not surprising that Solvyns did not encounter the dog Buffon termed *Bengalee Brae* ("harrier of Bengal" in the English translation) and identified as a Dalmatian.[3] Pennant writes that Buffon did "a great mischief" in giving the beautiful spotted dog to Bengal, for none is to be found there.[4]

1 *Hobson-Jobson*, 681, describes the "pariah-dog" as "The common ownerless yellow dog, that frequents all inhabited places in the East, is universally so called by Europeans, no doubt from being a low-bred casteless animal. . . ." The mongrel is often called, by contraction, "pi-dog." Lewis, 189.
2 2:253.
3 4:21.
4 2:255.

II.283. Crocodile

Pl. II.283. Crocodile. Paris: IV.10.1.

Paris: IV.10.1. CROCODILE: There are in Bengal many species of *Crocodiles,* some of a monstrous size; they are often seen with their young ones running by their sides. This is a very dangerous animal for mariners, especially in the *sunderbunds.* The violence of their motion is capable of oversetting a boat, of which I was myself once near being an unfortunate proof. We were at daybreak coasting a little island where a huge *Crocodile* lay stretched upon the strand: we had scarce passed him, when upon perceiving us, he plunged into the river where he caused so violent an agitation that it was with great difficulty our boat surmounted it, which would have been impossible if we had not gained a little distance, and we should have been infalibly the prey of the monster. The *Crocodiles* hover round ships at anchor to catch the offals which are thrown overboard. One day I was aboard a *budgerow* [bājrā, Pl. II.232] when I saw a *Crocodile* dart forward and seise by the legs one of our *dandys* [*dāndī*, boatman, Pl. II.56], who was washing himself, hanging by two ropes to a pole as is their custom, (see the third volume)[1] the poor man raised a piteous cry, and his camerades dragged him up, but the animal would not quit his hold, and carried of[f] the two legs of the *dandy* who died a few minutes later.

Strange stories are told in India of a secret which some people, especially of the island of Java, have to allure *cayman* out of the water and make them loose their prey: but having never seen any thing of the kind I will not presume to say any thing about it.

Commentary: There are three species of crocodiles in India, the muggar or marsh crocodile, which lives in rivers and lakes; the estuarine or salt-water crocodile (the largest of present day reptiles), found in coastal river estuaries; and the gharial, the long-snouted crocodile, of the great river systems, where they favor midstream islands and sand banks for basting. Solvyns portrays the gharial, which takes its name from the word *gharā* (pot), referring to the pot-like mass of cartilage at the tip of its snout.[2]

Solvyns has his name wrong in identifying an Asian crocodile as a "cayman," for the caiman is limited in habitat to the Americas.

1 Solvyns makes frequent reference to *dāṇḍīs* in his portrayal of boats.
2 Daniel, 8-16.

II.284. Cobra

Pl. II.284. Cobra. Paris: IV.10.2.

Paris: IV.10.2. SERPENT: Serpents have already been mentioned in different parts of this work [Pls. II.65, II.66, and II.196], but I have not hitherto had an opportunity of representing them in their proper proportions. I hope that this and the following print will give an exact idea of the form of the two species of this reptile, which appeared to me most remarkable. The first is the *Cobra de capello,* described in several works on natural history, and more particularly in one published in London in 1796 by M. Patrick Russell. M. D. F. R. S.

The *Cobra de capello* is a very dangerous serpent, its bite is followed by death almost instantaneous, though I have seen people dye of it after dreadful sufferings and a sort of rage. It is not true that the *Cobra de capello* darts his poison only when he is attacked, he is himself frequently the aggressor. When he prepares to resist danger he rears himself up and his head swells to a prodigious size. This is the attitude which I have chosen for my drawing.

Music has a sort of magical effect upon these serpents. Playing on the flute one evening with a friend in the country, the room had been left open, I saw a large serpent come in leaping, turning round, standing erect and seeming to imitate the movements of the air we played: he seemed disarmed by the sound and quitted us without attempting any injury.

Commentary: The cobra has held a special fascination and is, for the European, inextricably associated with India. Patrick Russell (1727-1805), in his *Account of Indian Serpents* (1796), was among the first naturalists to provide detailed scientific descriptions of the cobra.[1]

The word "cobra," as noted in the Commentary on the Sāpuriyā snake-charmers (Pl. II.66), is from the Portuguese *cobra de capello*, "snake with a hood." The Indian cobra takes its scientific name, *Naja naja,* from *nāga*, the Indian word for snake. The cobra in Solvyns's etching is the "speculated" or binocellate cobra, found throughout India. Its distinctive feature is the hood design of a connected pair of rings.[2]

Snakes are surrounded by myths, tall-tales, and great misinformation—and the cobra has been among the most abused in this respect. The cobra is highly venomous, but its poison works slowly, bringing a paralysis of the respiratory system, and death is not "almost instantaneous," as Solvyns suggests, nor is it always fatal. Solvyns's reference to the cobra's "darting" his poison is likely to the venom ejected as a spray when the snake makes a forceful lunge at his prey but misses. The cobra's head does not "swell," as Solvyns writes, but when alarmed, the cobra will rise to its famous posture, spreading its hood in a dilation of the ribs.[3]

The Indian cobra is not usually aggressive, and Solvyns's experience in escaping injury would not be unusual. But it hardly seems likely that the snake was "disarmed" by the music, for as discussed in the Commentary on the Māl snake-catchers (Pl. II.65), the cobra's response to the charmer is to the swaying movement of the pipe, not to the sound.

1 1:7-10. Later, in the nineteenth century, the cobra was portrayed in lavish illustrations in Gunther, Fayrer, and Ewart.
2 Daniel, 112-14; Whitaker, 55-57.
3 Daniel, 112-13. I am grateful to herpetologist Carl Gans for leading me to a correction of Solvyns's mistaken description of the cobra.

II.285. Tryphlops, a Serpent

Pl. II.285. Tryphlops, a Serpent. Paris: IV.10.3.

Paris: IV.10.3. ANOTHER SPECIES OF SERPENT: The Serpent here represented appears to be unknown to naturalists. The Hindoos distinguish him by the appellation of the *Serpent with two heads,* because at the end of his tail is something that gives at first sight the appearance of a head at both ends of the body. His colour is black, and he is not unlike a worm; he slides under the mats and penetrates frequently into the magazines or *godowns,* sometimes into the apartments, and prefers damp places. His bite is venimous, and, if not mortal, is always attended with dangerous inflamation and acute pain. I had a servant bit by one in the leg, the reptile stuck to it like a leech and would not quit its hold till it was cut in pieces. The leg and thigh of the patient remained for more than a month in a dangerous state.

Commentary: The snake Solvyns portrays is almost surely the tryphlops, sometimes called a worm snake or, because its eyes are indistinct, a blind snake. Its bluntly rounded head and tail are similar in appearance. They feed on termites and are, as Solvyns writes, frequently found in warehouses (godowns) and in houses. They are not in any way poisonous. The species *Typhlina diardi* is common in Bengal.[1]

1 I am grateful to Carl Gans for identifying the snake. See Daniel, 64-65, and Whitaker, 2-4.

II.286. Centipede

Paris: IV.10.4. SCOLOPENDER, CENTIPEDE: The *Centipede* is known in many other countries but is of a large size in Bengal, where I have seen some fourteen inches long, of a reddish colour with very strong claws and scales upon their back, the belly whitish and the paws ending in a double claw. They are sometimes seen in the houses, but in general keep in the earth. The sting of this insect is nearly as dangerous as that of the *Scorpion.*

Bengal is full of dangerous animals: besides those I have already mentioned there are many sorts of *Scorpions* and other venimous insects which often destroy the pleasure which the country or public walks might give. Another great inconvenience to Europeans on their arrival are the *Musquetous* [mosquitoes], which annoy them to such a degree that their faces are soon covered with red blotches and their legs swelled so as to confine them to the house for weeks, at last they get accustomed to this plague, the sting has no longer the same effect and is only troublesome. The flying bugs are another annoyance from the bad smell which they diffuse in the rooms, happily they are known only in the neighborhood of Dacca. Among the spiders of India some are of a great size, and hideous by the length of their legs. The Hindoos from custom see them without disgust.

Pl. II.286. Centipede. Paris: IV.10.4.

II.287. Muskrat

Pl. II.287. Muskrat. Paris: IV.10.5.

Paris: IV.10.5. MUSK RAT: The *Musk Rat* is of the small species, longer and whiter than the common ones; he exhales, as he moves, a very strong smell of musk, which penetrates even the best inclosures. If, for example, one of these animals passes over a row of bottles, the liquor they contain will be so strongly scented with musk that it cannot be drunk. I have known tons of wine touched by them so strongly infected, that it was with the greatest difficulty, and by a variety of process, that they could be purged of this smell. This rat is a great plague to the country, and, if once they get into a celler or magazine, is very hard to destroy. Cats will not venture to attack them, for fear probably of being suffocated by the smell: nor will the european tarrier hurt them.

Commentary: In India, muskrat is the popular name for the *Sorex caerulescen.* The belief that their musk affected the contents of bottles must have been widely held, for two major nineteenth century works on Indian mammals specifically reject it as fanciful.[1]

1 *Hobson-Jobson*, 599-600.

II.288. Tapsī Māch

Pl. II.288. Tapsī Māch. Paris: IV.10.6.

Paris: IV.10.6. TOPSY MATCHI: This is a fish well known to those who have inhabited the banks of the Ganges; it seems that it comes from the sea and ascends the rivers but to a certain distance, seldom more than three leagues above Calcutta: it appears in great abundance only during the two or three hottest months of the year. The fins of the *Mango* are longer than the rest of the body. It is a very delicate fish, highly esteemed and preferred by all others in the epicures of Calcutta, but must be eaten quite fresh. Hindoos of the higher and middle casts dress it in a *curri,* Europeans eat it boiled or broiled, and dry it to send to Europe.

This fishery takes place about a month of may; it is caught in nets which occupy the whole breadth of the river, and resist the rapidity of the current, even at high water, although they are supported only by bambous. It is taken sometimes in immense qualities, and the fishermen never fail to send to Calcutta about dinner time.

The strick observers of the laws of Menu [Manu] among the Hindoos prefer the *Singli matchi* or prawn. In general shell fish is very much liked and is very abundant in India. They have a great variety of prawns; I have seen some four or five feet long, covered with a short hair which had the appearance of velvet.

Commentary: Tapsī, or tapassī, is the Hindustani name for a fish (*māccha* or *māch*), about the size of a trout, that inhabits the Hugli estuaries. Flavorful and highly prized as a delicacy, it appears in Calcutta markets with the onset of the hot season, when the mangoes ripen. Thus, it is often called a "mango fish."[1] Fanny Parks praised the fish,[2] and Lt. Wallace, recounting his life in Calcutta in 1823, declared "the mangoe fish is worth coming to India for."[3]

Solvyns refers to the tapsī and the manner by which it is caught in his description of the Jāliyā fisher caste (Pl. II.57).[4]

Prawn is *ciṅgṛi* in Bengali, but anything of the four or five foot length Solvyns refers to is surely fanciful. His description of "short hair" and velvety appearance suggests the "giant" fresh-water prawn (*Macrobrachium*), which is fished extensively. It has a body length of about 12 inches, and its long front claws, sometimes covered with short "hair," can extend another foot.[5]

1 *Polynemus paradiseus* or *P. risua*. The Hindustani *tapsī* means "ascetic" or "penitent," and the fish is so-termed, conjecturally, because they have long hairs like some Hindu ascetics. Lewis, 161, 238-39; *Hobson-Jobson*, 555; and Pennant, 2:317.

2 2:389; reprinted in Nair, *Calcutta in the 19th Century*, 295.

3 125, reprinted in Nair, *Calcutta in the 19th Century*, 313.

4 Also see Pl. II.240.

5 I am grateful to Brian Kensley and R. B. Manning of the Smithsonian Institution for the identification.

II.289. Adjutant Stork

Paris: IV.11.1. THE OLD MAN, A BIRD OF PREY: This bird of prey is not unknown in Europe, and may be seen in the Botanical garden in Paris. It is very common in Hindoostan, and is of some use by devouring carrion and dead bodies. It is remarkable voracious and capable of swallowing a chicken or a leg of mutton, etc. whole: when its stomach is full, the breast swells to a considerable size; and it perches on the tops of houses where it remains motionless for several days, probably till the digestion is completed. The Hindoos look upon the *Old man,* as it is called by Europeans, as a bird of ill omen; for my part, I think he is rather a sign of good cheer in the house on which he rests, for he is allured by the smell of the kitchen and preys upon the offals which are thrown out. In the field he fights sometimes with the *Jacal* [Pl. II.281] and *pariah dog* [Pl. II.282], as well as with other birds of prey. The inside of his beck is indented like a saw, which renderes his bite dangerous. In very hot weather he sometimes rises in the air so as to be lost to the eye, in search, as it is said, of a cooler atmosphere. He exhales a disagreable odour on his passage. There is something of pride and gravity in his motions.

Pl. II.289. Adjutant Stork. Paris: IV.11.1.

Commentary: The "old man"[1] is the Greater Adjutant stork (*Leptoptilos dubius*), the principal scavenger of Calcutta in the past but today an endangered species. Thomas Daniell, who included the stork in his 1788 *Views of Calcutta*, wrote, "Amidst the promiscuous concourse of people and equipages, stalks a tall meagre crane, nicknamed the adjutant. . . . The bird is remarkable for the slowness of its movements, and often stands on some roof, drooping its head with ludicrous solemnity, and looking as abstracted as a Fakir at devotions."[2] "The adjutant," Lt. Bacon wrote in 1831, "excites the notice and curiosity of all new arrivals [in Calcutta] . . . . [T]he action and walk of these large birds is ludicrously like the measure gait of a decrepit old man, as he may be seen sauntering about with his hands under his tail coat pockets, and his bowed head turned inquisitively first on one side then the other." [3] It takes the name "adjutant" from "its deliberate high-stepping military gait as it paces up and down in quest of food."[4]

Linnaeus gave it the name *Leptoptilus argala*, derived from the Hindustani *hḁrgīlā*, the name by which it was commonly known in India, and meaning, by some sources, "bone-swallower."[5] And the adjutant was a scavenger par excellence, feeding on carrion and offal. Perhaps as a sardonic comment on municipal services, the old emblem of the Calcutta Corporation showed two adjutant storks with serpents in their mouths.[6] That the city was well-served is evident in the numbers of adjutants shown in the sky and perched statuesque on buildings in James Baillie Fraser's 1824 aquatints, *Views of Calcutta and its Environs*.[7] Lady Sarah Amherst, included them in a drawing of Government House, and she wrote, describing the bird's greed, that "there is a story . . . that to satisfy Lord Hastings' own eyes, a calf's leg with an iron shoe on the hoof was thrown out and immediately swallowed whole by an Adjutant. . . . ."[8]

Forbes described the bird as "sometimes near six feet high, and from twelve to fifteen from the extremity of each wing." It is," he wrote, "one of the ugliest [birds] in Indian ornithology,"[9] but, for all its looks, the adjutant was highly prized for the plumes—commercially called "Commercolly feathers"—that grow in a tuft under its tail. Though the birds, once numerous, were protected by law in Calcutta, the demand for feathers in England and France hastened their decline.[10] By the end of the century, the Adjutant Stork, once so common in Calcutta, was "only a memory" and did not even have an entry in *The Birds of Calcutta*.[11]

---

1 *Solitaire* in the label below the etching and in Solvyns's French text.

2 Quoted in Nisith Ranjan Ray, *City of Job Carnock*, 32.

3 1:142, in Nair, *Calcutta in the 19th Century*, 544.

4 Ali and Futehally, 6. Also see *Hobson-Jobson*, 7. Taylor, *Thirty-eight Years in India*, 1:59, attributed the name to their frequent practice of lining up in rows "with the exactitude of military discipline."

5 *Hobson-Jobson*, 7.

6 The emblem, shown in Nair, "Civic and Public Services in Old Calcutta," 232, was replaced only in 1961. Nair, 228, also includes an engraving of a Hindu cremation attended by adjutant storks and vultures.

7 Fraser, Pls. 3, 4, 6, 11, and 14, reproduced in Losty, *Calcutta: City of Palaces*, Pls. 15, 16, 19, Figs. 46 and 53. An oil by Fraser, "Old Court House Street", portrays adjutants feeding in the foreground, reproduced in Losty, Pl. 20.

8 Quoted in Losty, *Calcutta: City of Palaces*, 97-98; her drawing is reproduced in Losty, Fig. 57.

9 *Oriental Memoirs*, 1:403-04, in Nair, *Calcutta in the 19th Century*, 31-32. Also see Heber's description, 1:26, in Nair, *Calcutta in the 19th Century*, 351.

10 Roberts, 2:42-43, in Nair, *Calcutta in the 19th Century*, 600-01.

11 Finn, 61.

II.290. Vulture

Pl. II.290. Vulture. Paris: IV.11.2.

Paris: IV.11.2. VULTURE: This species of bird is very common in Hindoostan, where it is of the same use as that last described. Their bite is looked upon as venimous: they are hard to kill flying, are little intimidated by the report of a gun, and scarcely move as the ball passes near them. When they have taken possession of a dead body no one dares approach them, but if another of them, who is said is their king, appears, they all quit the body, and keep at a distance till he has eaten sufficiently, and then return to their repast. Human bodies are frequently seen floating, to a very considerable distance, down the rivers with *Vultures* attached to them, till they meet a more abundant prey. The *Vulture* of Hindoostan contracts his neck when he flies; his breast is very white, and in some parts without feathers. His sense of smelling is very accute, and he scents dead bodies at a distance of some leagues.

Commentary: Solvyns portrays the Bengal vulture, *Gyps bengalensis*.

II.291. Black Kite

Pl. II.291. Black Kite. Paris: IV.11.3.

Paris: IV.11.3. MIOPE: What this bird of prey wants of the strength and size of the two former, makes up for it in activity and address: it is not without reason that he has got the surname of the *robber,* for his dexterity in stealing meat, his favorite food, is very remarkable. Frequently as the servants are carrying the dishes from the kitchen to the house, which, as we have already mentioned, are always separate, they snatch up the meat and carry it off with a rapidity almost imperceptible. This is a fact which I have often witnessed. There is something melancholly in the cry of this bird. There are also quantities of crows in Hindoostan who also contribute to clear the country of the odours which would otherwise be infectious in so warm a climate. The boldness of these birds is astonishing, they fly into the apartments and carry off whatever they can lay hold of; especially brilliant objects such as watches, pearls, trinkets, etc. It is frequently necessary to be more on your guard against these birds than against robbers.

Commentary: The black kite (*Milvus migrans*)—or common pariah kite, as it is known in India—is dark brown and distinguished by its forked tail, evident particularly in overhead flight. Commensal with humans, it is a scavenger in urban areas and, "remarkably adroit on the wing," will swoop down to seize a scrap of meat, carrion from the road or what was to have been someone's next meal.[1]

The Bengali name for the kite is *cil*. Solvyns's name "miope" appears in no standard book on Indian birds.[2]

---

1 Ali, 71.

2 The closest is the genus *Myiophoneus*, but it is a thrush.

II.292. Flying Fox

Paris: IV.11.4. THE FOX-BAT: This animal, which takes its name from its resemblance to a fox, is of the large species of *Bats,* and like them flies only by night. The Hindoos spread nets to catch them, and the Portuguese, in India, eat their flesh, which they say is tough and stringy, like that of many birds which we find delicious in Europe. The flesh of the *Pelican,* for example, is very ill tasted in some parts in India, but the *Ortolan,* on the contrary, is generally fat and exquisite, and in some parts as common as sparrows are with us. *Parrots* and *Parroquettes,* in all their varieties, are very common in India and used also for food. As these birds are very well known in Europe, it would be superfluous to enter into any description of them.

Commentary: The "flying fox," or fox-bat, is the popular name for the great bat *Pteropus giganteus.*[1]

1 See *Hobson-Jobson*, 356

Pl. II.292. Flying Fox. Paris: IV.11.4.

II.293. Cockroach

Paris: IV.11.5. KANKALAT: The *Kankalat* is a great inconvenience to seafaring men; it resembles our beetle or cockcheafer, but is flatter and larger. Besides its disagreeable smell, it spoils the objects on which it fastens, bores the bales and packages where it propagates with astonishing rapidity. In Hindoostan they sometimes get into the rice granaries, and do great mischief by the disgusting smell which they communicate to the grain. I sailed once in a dutch vessel which was annoyed by these *Kankalats* to such a degree that the sailors, passengers, officers and the captain himself had their hands, feet and face very painfully affected by their bite during the night: some of them were in a frightfull state, the matresses were bored through, and though mended over night were found in the same state the next morning.

Pl. II.293. Cockroach. Paris: IV.11.5.

Commentary: This is almost assuredly a cockroach (*Blattidae*), commonly called *ārsala* in Bengali. Solvyns's "kankalat" finds no Bengali recognition as a cockroach, and he may have mistakenly used the word for a kind of lizard.

II.294. White Ant, Termite

Pl. II.294. White Ant, Termite. Paris: IV.11.6.

Paris: IV.11.6. CARIAR: The *Cariar,* or white Ant, like in shape to the common *pismire,* is the most destructive insect known in Hindoostan, the viscous matter which falls from it, wherever it goes, corrodes every thing and eats even into metals. books, furniture, and even houses are reduced to dust and destroyed by this pernicious excrement. The passage of the *Cariar* on walls or upon iron or copper is marked by veins or a sort of furrow; beams are eaten through till they give way and bring down the roof. We can have no idea in Europe of the rapid and frightful ravages of so small an insect. It has been known that an agent of the Company has become unable to fullfil his engagements from the *Cariars* having destroyed a great part of his chests. Furniture is preserved by putting the feet in vases of water. There are specifics for destroying the *Cariar,* but in a short time they lose their efficacy, and the insects reappear as abundantly as ever. It is remarkable that there are beams in the houses which they never touch. I have often had occasion to make the same remark upon the *saul* [*sāl*] timber used in building in India, some of the beams are decayed and consumed while others resist for ages both the air and the insects

Commentary: Solvyns has clearly found his enemy in what he terms the *cariar,*[1] or "white ant," as it was popularly called in English. The insect, of course, is not an ant at all, but a termite. Their capacity to destroy is so great that Thomas Pennant, in 1798, suggested that these *termes fatale* might have been the creatures Herodotus described fancifully as used in India to mine gold.[2] Fanny Parks found them "the vilest little animals, . . . most marvelously troublesome."[3]

Solvyns describes placing the legs of furniture in vases of water or quick-lime for protection and portrays it in one etching (Pl. II.285). Though this defense against insects is still used today, Colesworthy Grant found it insufficient against termites. Indeed, he noted that the sparsity of furniture in European households in Calcutta reflected concern for harboring the insects.[4]

1 Solvyns's term does not appear in standard references to insects. Perhaps he heard the Bengali *cārā*, meaning "insect" and *rui-cārā*" is termite or "white ant." Sukumar Sen, 273.

2 1:18-19.

3 1:313.

4 *An Anglo-Indian Domestic Sketch*, 16, 19-20.

Indian Heads

In the 1799 *Catalogue* to accompany the etchings in the Calcutta edition, Solvyns writes that "It has been asserted that each of the many classes of the Hindoos, may be distinguished by their peculiarity of features, if this distinction does really exist amidst the present almost promiscuous intercourse of the casts, the lines of distinction must, I presume, be exceedingly obscure. That appearance of features, habits, and character strongly mark the inhabitants of different provinces, and some of the original casts cannot be denied, but it is impossible to reduce it to a system in a work of this kind."[1]

Nevertheless, in 1795, Solvyns had advertised a proposed "collection of heads," 300 etchings "exhibiting the native and various other inhabitants of India."[2] The collection was never realized. Moreover, no "heads" are included among the 250 etchings of the Calcutta edition. The twelve heads in the Paris edition, reproduced here, may well be from drawings Solvyns made for the proposed collection.

In the late eighteenth century, principally through the work of Johann Caspar Lavater,[3] physiognomy came into vogue in Europe, and Solvyns in *Les Hindoûs* succumbs to this pseudoscience. Physiognomy—which Solvyns sometimes spells "phisionomy"—purports to be the science of judging human personality and character from facial features. It takes racist form when a person's physiognomy (facial features) is categorized in terms of ethnic stereotypes, such that the face reflects character and traits attributed to the group, as Solvyns does in portraying heads of Hindu castes and of Muslims.

In the Introduction to *Les Hindoûs*, Vol. IV, Solvyns writes,

> In the last number of this volume I will acquit myself of the promise which I made in the beginning of my work of giving a representation of different hindoo heads. It is now well known that the study of the physiognomy and of the form and construction of the head of the individuals of a nation is of great importance in the science of geography, and that it often leads us to a discovery of the origin and country, the alliances and mixtures of different populations. I do not mean to investigate the origin of the Hindoos, that would exceed the limits of my power as well as of my plan: I have besides the testimony of the celebrated Sir William Jones, whose deep enquiries into all that concerns India are so well known, and it is from himself that I heard it, that the origin of the Hindoos is burried in abscurity, that the farther he penetrated into their history the less hopes he conceived of drawing any satisfactory notions from the chaos of which it is composed. The reason of this is not difficult to conceive. Repeated foreign invasion has had a considerable influence upon the morals, manners and languages of India, so that, as I have already observed in my first preliminary discourse, the number of true Hindoos is at present very inconsiderable, and in the great mass of the inhabitants of India we perceive the mixture of foreign nations who at different periods have overrun this country: but above all others the Mussulmans and black Portuguese have in latter times contributed to this alteration in the primitive features of the hindoo nation. I might have found ample matter for a very large collection if I had chosen to trace the countenances of all the different inhabitan[t]s of India: but I prefered keeping within the bounds of my original plan, and chosing as my sole object the inhabitants of Hindoostan, where the hindoo blood has undergone less mixture than in any other province of India, and even here a distinction must be made between upper and lower Hindoostan. In the former, which was probably first subdued, the Mussulmans have left much more perceptible traces of their residence than in the latter. I have represented those tribes which appeared to me to have retained

most of their native physionomy: I say most, because I have not entirely excluded those heads of Hindoostan which offer the hindoo features with something of a foreign mixture. These two, for example, in the plate before the last have something of the mussulman expression, and in the two mogul countenances there is an arabian cast of feature.

These observa[ti]ons are undoutedly curious; but those which I have had an opportunity of making upon the true Hindoos will appear still more so. Each of their casts has its appropriate physionomy, its characteristic features which it is not possible to mistake. They were so strongly impressed upon me, during my long stay among that people, that a look was sufficient for me to decide to what cast any one of them belonged, and I could frequently even guess in what subdivision of his cast fortune had placed him: as it is known that every Hindoo follows the state of life of his father, and is not allowed to take up any other. I do not wish to make any merit of a sagacity which is not so great as it may seem, for the features which distinguish the hindoo casts are in reality so striking that the difficulty would rather be to mistake them. The *Brahmun* has a mild and pious air; the *Kuttery* [kṣatriya] is haughty and bold in his appearance: cunning and mercantile caution is marked on the countenance of the *Byce* [vaiśya]. If none of these characteristics are perceived in the physionomy of an *Hindoo* we may safely pronounce that he is of the *sooder* [śūdra] cast, and if we carry our spirit of observation a little farther we shall soon be able to ascertain with tollerable accuracy what is the nature of his occupation in that cast.

There is nevertheless among the Hindoos a set of men among whom the features of all the four casts may be perceived; these are the *Pariahs*.[4] As these are people rejected by the four only casts which Menu instituted, they must naturally have preserved something of the air of the cast to which they originaly belonged, and which they forfeited by their misconduct. This remark, suggested by long observation, is I should think a new proof in favour of the opinion which I advanced in the first volume, and to which no solid argument has been opposed, that the *Pariahs* are but the outcast of the four other casts, and do not form a particular one, as some other authors have asserted.

The countenance of the Hindoo women offers nothing interesting to the observer. In countries where women exercise an empire over men, the cause or the effect of this power may be discerned in their air and features: beauty, sprightliness, gaiety, wit and grace, the consciousness of superiority leave a strong impression. Nothing of all this appears in the hindoo women, their physionomy announces that they are not formed by nature to govern, and their pretentions never rose so high; it is the countenance of slavery which has never been enlivened by a ray of hope.[5]

---

1 8.

2 See Chapter One, pp. 40-41.

3 Lavater (Swiss, 1741-1801) enjoyed great influence in promoting physiognomy as a science, and before the end of the century his *Physiognomische Fragmente* (1775-78) had been translated into French and English and published in numerous editions. Its first English translation, *Essays on Physiognomy*, appeared in 1789. If Solvyns did not read the work itself, he was surely influenced by it.

4 See discussion of Pariah in the Commentary for Pl. II.22.

5 4:9-10.

II.295. Brahmins

Pl. II.295. Brahmins. Paris: IV.12.1.

Paris: IV.12.1. HINDOOS OF THE FIRST CAST: I begin my collection of hindoo heads by the first cast, that of *Brahmuns* or priests.[1] The engraving represents the head of a man and his wife, both drawn from nature among the bengalee *Srouterys* [Śrotriya, Pl. II.13] because in my opinion and in that of the greater number of *Pundits,* Bengal is, if not the cradle of the hindoo people, at least a country where the primitive habits of the nation, and the laws of their founder *Menu* [Manu] are best preserved. It is obvious that the countenance of the *Brahmun* whose portrait I have given expresses, like that of the generality of his cast, the sweetness and tranquillity of their disposition and situation in life. Malice and suspicion are unknown to the servant of *Brahma.* Observe afterwards the head of the woman; her features are absolutely without expression, her whole phisionomy is that of a passive being who does not conceive that she was created to act, whose prevailing quality is apathy, who needs not to be taught by her husband that the utmost end of her destination is to breed children for him and to serve him: her own ideas extend no farther, and the nullity of her existence is to her neither a subject of satisfaction nor of regret.

1 Solvyns portrays brahmins in five etching that begin his series on castes and occupations, Pls. II.13-17.

II.296. Kṣatriyas

Paris: IV.12.2. HINDOOS OF THE SECOND CAST: These two heads are taken from the second cast among the *Khuttrys* [kṣatriya, Pl. II.20] The warlike occupations of this cast give a different character to these portraits. The martial air, the large prominent eye, the larger size of the nose, the lips more strongly pronounced are all indications of the warrior. The woman has something of the expression and features of her husband, her phisionomy is more striking than that of women of the other casts, her nose is sometimes a little aquiline. The *Khuttrys* have recourse to different expedients to render their countenance still more expressive of their profession; they let their whiskers grow, and wear a turban; the women blacken the edges of the eye, their lips are of a bright red, produced by the betel which they chew. The skin of the *Khuttrys* is yellower and more shining than that of the other Hindoos, either from a finer oil with which they rub themselves, or because they expose themselves less to the sun.

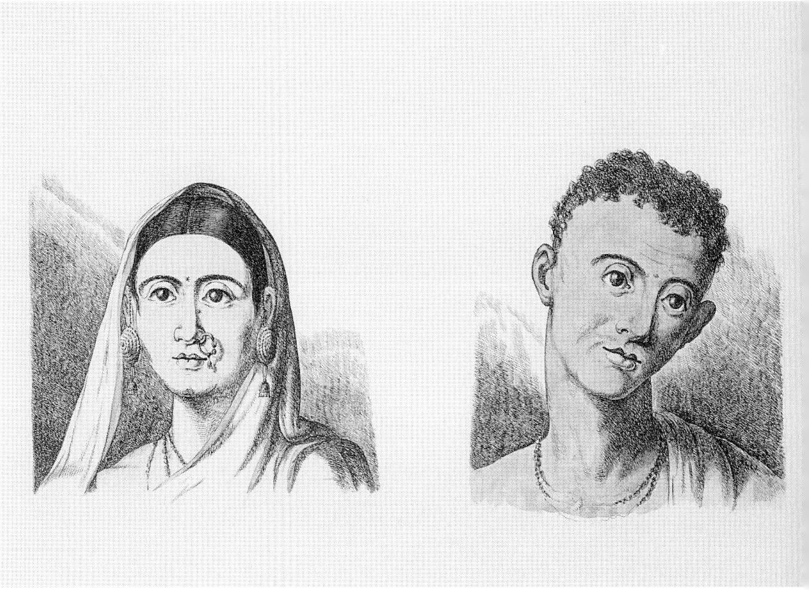

Pl. II.296. Kṣatriyas. Paris: IV.12.2.

II.297. Vaiśyas

Paris: IV.12.3. HINDOOS OF THE THIRD CAST: We may recollect that the their cast consists of the *Byces* [vaiśya, Pl. II.21] or merchants. The *Byce* is a being totally indifferent to every thing that does not concern his own immediate interests, cunning full of deceit and calculation, dispositions which seem to me to be impressed on the countenance of the one whom I have represented. As the *Byces* do not live together, like the *Brahmuns* and *Khuttrys* [kṣatriya], but frequently travel in opposition to the laws of their religion, there is not that sameness or analogy in their countenance which we have remarked in the preceding casts. The features of the female *Byce* bear more resemblance to those of the *Khuttery* than to those of the *Brahmun,* which proceeds probably from the greater degree of affluence in which she generally lives, as well as the *Khuttery,* and not being subject to all the minute religious practices which are prescribed to the *Brahmun* women, which influence her way of living, and her moral and physical character.

Pl. II.297. Vaiśyas. Paris: IV.12.3.

II.298. Śūdras

Paris: IV.12.4. HINDOOS OF THE FOURTH CAST: As the fourth cast comprehends different ranks and occupations in society, such as tradesmen, manufacturers, workmen, servants etc., we must not wonder at the difference which we perceive in the features of the *Soodders* [śūdras, Pl. II.22] of which it is composed. Some analogy may still be observed in the physionomy of such of the same nation who are of the same occupation, which is a natural consequence of its being transmitted from father to son, and of their always intermarrying in a similar line; a pastrycook will marry but the daughter of a pastrycook, a smith looks for a wife in the same profession. The general characteristic traits of the *Soodders* physionomy are application, meanness and stupid resignation. The portrait which I give was taken from one in a middle station, neither in the first nor in the last subdivision. The other head is that of a simple peasant woman, in a remote country where there is no mixture of Mussulmans or Portuguese, which might alter the original character of the countenance.

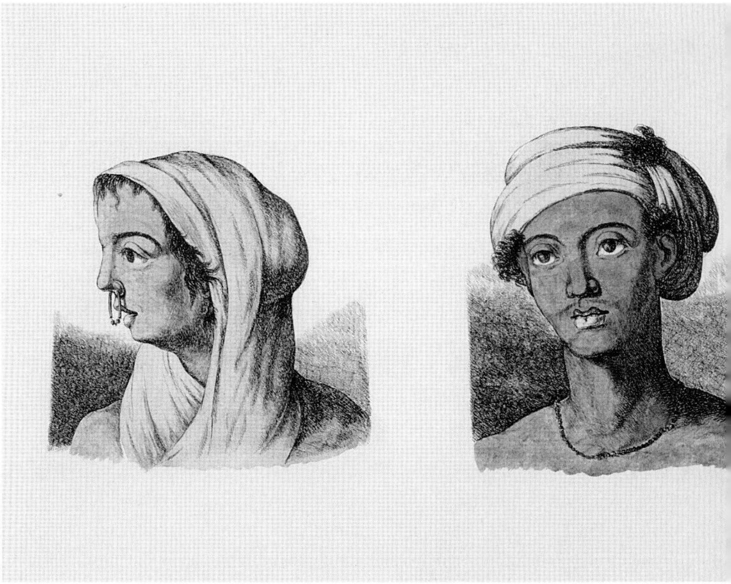

Pl. II.298. Śūdras. Paris: IV.12.4.

II.299. Hindus of Upper India

Pl. II.298. Hindus of Upper India. Paris: IV.12.5.

Paris: IV.12.5. INHABITANTS OF UPPER HINDOOSTAN: It has been observed, in the preliminary discourse of this volume, that upper Hindoostan offers a greater mixture of the hindoo and mussulman race, than the lower country: and observation has confirmed the inferrence which might naturally be drawn from it. The characteristic traits of both these people are discorn [discerned] in its inhabitants. In their dress and manners they have a resemblance to Mussulmans. They are for the most part servants in great houses, as we have remarked in the beginning of this volume.[1]

The same remarks extend to the countenances of the women, and it is also deserving of notice that this mixture of the two nations has had an influence not only on the features, but on the shape of the head.

1 Servants of the European Household in Calcutta, Pls. II.99-134.

II.300. Mughals

Pl. II.300. Mughals. Paris: IV.12.6.

Paris: IV.12.6. A MOGUL, MAN AND WOMAN: Of all the inhabitants of Hindoostan the true *Mogul* has, beyond dispute, the finest head and the best countenance. There is an elevation and nobleness in their air which are very pleasing. The features of the *Mogul* woman are remarkably regular; her eyes are full of vivacity, her mouth little, her shape small and delicate. The men are large and strong, their complexion not darker than that of Europeans settled in India, but the woman are very white. I have already observed that the *Moguls* appear to be descended from the Arabes: their turban is something different from that of the other easterns; but the headdress of the woman ressembles that of the Mussulmans, and is minutely represented in the print.

Appendix
Solvyns in Libraries

Copies of Solvyns's etchings are in the collections of the libraries listed below. The list is derived from a number of sources and is not exhausive. A number of libraries in continental Europe specifically may have copies of *Les Hindoûs*, but their catalogs are not online. European holdings are listed first, followed by India, Australia, Canada, and (by state) the United States.

A Collection of Two Hundred and Fifty Coloured Etchings: Descriptive of the Manners, Customs and Dresses of the Hindoos. Calcutta, 1796.

FR Bibliothèque nationale du France, Richelieu—Estampes et photographie, Paris.
FR Bibliothèque Universitaire de Haute-Alsace, Mulhouse.
UK Brighton Reference Library. Some 50 plates missing.
NY Buffalo and Erie County Public Library, Grosvenor Rare Book Room. Without title page, but corresponds closely in format to other copies of the 1796 imprint. Section and plate numbers and titles are written in by hand; 3 plates missing.
TX University of Texas at Austin, Harry Ransom Humanities Research Center. Poor condition; many plates uncolored; 9 plates missing.
VA Mariners' Museum Library, Newport News.

1799 imprint.

BL Stadsbibliotheek, Antwerp. The volume was presented to the library by William Solvyns, great-nephew of the the artist; no date. Exceptionally fine copy, with some prints uncolored. The large type *Catalogue* description is pasted opposite each plate on the back of the preceding page.
FR Bibliothèque nationale de France, Richelieu—Estampes et photographie, Paris. From the collection of Louis Matthieu Langlès.
FR Musée Guimet, Paris.
UK British Library, London. The King's Library. Bound in original leather, in one volume; many plates uncolored.
UK British Library, Oriental and India Office Collections, London.
UK British Museum, London.
UK National Art Library, Victoria and Albert Museum, London.
UK School of Oriental and African Studies Library, University of London. Incomplete, with 239 prints only.
UK Soane Museum and Library, London. Original leather binding; exceptionally fine copy.
UK Wellcome Institute, Library, London. The volume is signed by the name of the original owner, J. Gillett, presumably Jonathan Gillett of the Calcutta mercantile family that commissioned the Solvyns painting, "The Launching of Gabriel Gillett's Armed Merchantman in Calcutta Harbour." See p. 25-26. The text of Solvyns's 1799 *Catalogue* was copied by hand opposite most plates on the back of the preceding page.
UK Royal Asiatic Society Library, London.
UK Brighton Reference Library.
UK St. David's University College Library, Lampeter, Wales.
UK National Library of Wales, Department of Pictures and Maps, Aberystwyth, Wales.
IND National Library, Asutosh Collection, Calcutta.
CA Achenbach Foundation for Graphic Arts, California Palace of the Legion of Honor, Fine Arts Museums of San Francisco.
CT Yale Center for British Art, New Haven. From the library of J. R. Abbey.
DC Library of Congress, Washington, D. C. Two volumes, incomplete, with 248 plates.
IL University of Chicago Library, Special Collections, Rare Books. 113 plates missing.
MA Boston College, Burns Rare Books Library, Max and Peter Allen Collection.
MA Peabody Essex Museum, Salem. No title page; unbound, incomplete, and apparently never bound. Boxes 100, 100A, 100B.
MD National Library of Medicine, HMD Collections, Bethesda.
MN University of Minnesota, Ames Library.
NC University of North Carolina, Rare Books Collection, Chapel Hill.
NY New York Public Library, Arents Collection. The title page carries the name of the engraver, "F. Dormieux, Scripsit." Some of the plates, and most double-plates, are uncolored. The large type *Catalogue* description is pasted opposite each plate on the back of the preceding page.
NY Buffalo and Erie County Public Library, Grosvenor Rare Book Room. The title page carries the name of the engraver, "F. Dormieux, Scripsit," and the large type *Catalogue* description accompanies each plate, as in the NYPL copy.
PA University of Pennsylvania, Special Collections, Rare Books and Manuscripts Library. In two volumes.
TX University of Texas at Austin, Harry Ransom Humanities Research Center, Theatre Arts Collection. Disbound, incomplete, with some misnumbering.

A Catalogue of 250 Coloured Etchings; Descriptive of the Manners, Customs, Character, Dress, and Religious Ceremonies of the Hindoos. Calcutta: Mirror Press, 1799.

DK Kongelige Biblioteck, Copenhagen.
FR Bibliothèque nationale de France, Richelieu—Estampes et photographie, Paris. From the collection of Louis Matthieu Langlès.
UK British Library, Oriental and India Office Collections, London.
UK National Art Library, Victoria and Albert Museum, London.

UK	Soane Museum and Library, London. Original leather binding; superb condition.
UK	Brighton Reference Library.
UK	St. David's University College Library, Lampeter, Wales.
IND	National Library of India, Calcutta.
CA	Achenbach Foundation for Graphic Arts, California Palace of the Legion of Honor, Fine Arts Museums of San Francisco.
CT	Yale Center for British Art, New Haven. From the library of J. R. Abbey.
DC	Library of Congress, Washington, D.C.
MA	Boston College, Burns Rare Books Library, Max and Peter Allen Collection.
TX	University of Texas at Austin, Harry Ransom Humanities Research Center.

The Costume of Indostan [pirated edition]. London: Edward Orme [1804-05].

FR	Bibliothèque nationale de France, Tolbiac—Rez-de-jardin, Paris.
UK	National Art Library, Victoria and Albert Museum, London.
UK	Brighton Reference Library.
UK	Wellcome Institute, Library, London.
UK	British Library, London.
UK	British Library, Oriental and India Office Collections, London.
UK	National Library of Wales, Aberystwyth, Wales.
UK	John Rylands University Library of Manchester, UK.
IND	National Library, Rare Room, Calcutta.
IND	Goethals Indian Library and Research Centre, St. Xavier's College, Calcutta.
CA	University of California, Los Angeles, Library.
CA	University of California, Irvine, Library.
CA	California State Library, Sacramento.
CT	Yale University, Beinecke Library, New Haven.
DC	Library of Congress, Washington, D.C.
IA	Iowa State University, Parks Library Special Collections, Ames.
IL	University of Chicago Library, Special Collections, Rare Books.
KS	University of Missouri, Kansas City, Library.
MD	Johns Hopkins University, Garrett Library, Baltimore.
MA	Harvard University, Houghton Library.
MA	Boston Athenaeum.
MA	Boston College, Burns Rare Books Library, Max and Peter Allen Collection.
MI	University of Michigan Library, Speical Collections, Ann Arbor.
MI	Detroit Public Library.
MN	Minneapolis Public Library.
NJ	Newark Public Library.
NY	New York Public Library.
NY	Hunter College Main Special Collections, CUNY.
NY	State University of New York at Albany Library.
NY	Columbia University, Avery Memorial Architectural Library.
OH	Cleveland Public Library.
PA	Allegheny College, Pelletier Library, Meadville.
PA	Free Library of Philadelphia.
RI	Brown University Library, Providence.
TX	Dallas Public Library.
WA	University of Washington Library, Special Collections, Seattle.

1807 imprint, retitled *The Costume of Hindostan.*

BL	Bibliothèque royale Albert I, Brussels.
FR	Bibliothèque nationale de France, Richelieu—Estampes et photographie, Paris.
UK	University of London Library.
UK	Royal College of Art Library, London.
UK	Glasgow School of Art.
UK	Glasgow University Library.
IND	National Library, Asutosh Collection, Calcutta.
IND	Victoria Memorial, Calcutta.
IND	National Archives, New Delhi.
AUS	National Library of Australia, Canberra.
CAN	University of British Columbia, Fine Arts Library, Vancouver.
CT	Yale Center for British Art, New Haven. From the library of J. R. Abbey.
CT	Yale University, Beinecke Library, New Haven.
DC	Library of Congress, Washington, D. C.
LA	Louisiana State University, Hill Rare Books Collection, Baton Rouge.
MA	Harvard University, Houghton Library.
MA	Peabody Essex Museum, Salem, Massachusetts.
MI	Cranbrook Academy of Art Library, Bloomfield Hills.
MN	University of Minnesota, Ames Library.
NJ	Morris Country Library, Special Collections, Morristown.
NY	New York Public Library.
NY	City College Special Collections, CUNY.
OH	Public Library of Cincinnati and Hamilton County.
OH	Toledo-Lucas Country Public Library.
PA	University of Pittsburgh Library.
TX	University of Texas at Austin, Harry Ransom Humanities Research Center.
WA	University of Washington Library, Seattle.
WA	Spokane Public Library.

Les Hindoûs. 4 vols. Paris: Chez L'Auteur, 1808-1812.

BL	Stadsbibliotheek, Antwerp. The volumes were presented to the city of Antwerp by the children of the artist, March 6, 1829.
BL	Bibliothèque royale Albert I, Brussels. Richly bound in tooled, red Morocco, with gilded page edges. These handsome volumes were presented to the Brussels library by King William I in 1814.
FR	Bibliothèque nationale de France, Tolbiac—Rez-de-jardin, Paris.
FR	Bibliothèque de l'Arsenal, Paris.
FR	Bibliothèque du Musèum d' Histoire Naturelle, Paris.
FR	Bibliothèque du Musée de l'Homme, Paris.

FR	Bibliothèque centrale du Muséum national d'histoire naturelle, Paris.
FR	Bibliothèque d'Art et d'Archeologie, Paris.
FR	Bibliothèque municipale d'etudes et de conservation de Besancon (DOUBS).
UK	The British Library, Oriental and India Office Collections, London.
UK	National Art Library, Victoria and Albert Museum, London.
UK	Bodeleian Library, Oxford.
UK	John Rylands University Library of Manchester.
IND	Victoria Memorial, Calcutta. The volumes, badly foxed, were presented to the Victoria Memorial in the George Lylle Collection in 1932. Each volume notes that it was "presented to W. Browne Mast. . . . [indistinguishable] by the author's widow."
IND	National Library, Calcutta, Asutosh Collection.
IND	Asiatic Society, Calcutta.
IND	Goethals Indian Library and Research Centre, St. Xavier's College, Calcutta.
CAN	University of Alberta Library, Edmonton, Alberta, Canada.
CA	University of California, Los Angeles, Library.
CA	Huntington Library, San Marino.
CA	Achenbach Foundation for Graphic Arts, California Palace of the Legion of Honor, Fine Arts Museums of San Francisco. Vol. III (1811) only.
DC	Library of Congress, Washington, D.C.
IL	University of Chicago Library, Special Collections, Rare Books.
MD	Johns Hopkins University, George Peabody Library, Baltimore.
MA	Amherst College Archives and Special Collections.
NJ	Princeton University Library.
NY	New York Public Library. The volumes were originally in the Astor Library, one of the major consolidating collections in the founding of the New York Public Library.
NY	Metropolitan Museum of Art, Library, New York.
NY	Cornell University Library, Kroch Library Rare & Manuscripts, Ithaca.
NY	City College Special Collections, CUNY.
OR	Multnomah County Library, Portland.
TX	University of Texas at Austin, Harry Ransom Humanities Research Center.
TX	Texas Tech University, Special Collections, Lubbock.
VA	Mariners' Museum Library, Newport News.

Les Hindoûs. Quarto edition. Paris: Frères Mame,1808. [42 plates only; see discussion of the edition, pp. 59-60.]

FR	Bibliothèque nationale de France, Richelieu—Estampes et photographie, Paris.

Microform

Costume of Hindostan (1807). Microfilm. Research Publications, Woodbridge, CT, 1979 (Goldsmiths'-Kress Library of Economic Literature, No. 19551.11).

A Catalogue of 250 Coloured Etchings; Descriptive of the Manners, Customs, Character, Dress, and Religious Ceremonies of the Hindoos (1799).
Research Publications, Inc., Woodbridge, CT, 1986. 1 reel; 35mm. (The Eighteenth Century; reel 4293, no. 03).

Bibliography

Abbey, John Roland. *Travel in Aquatint and Lithography, 1770-1860, From the Library of J. R. Abbey. A Bibliographical Catalogue*. 2 vols. London: Curwen Press, 1956-57.

Abu'l-Fazl 'Allami. *Ā'in-i-Akbarī* (Book III of *Akbar Nāma* , 1597). Translated by H. S. Jarrett, revised and annotated by Jadu-Nath Sarkar in "Sangīta," *Bibliotheca Indica*, Royal Asiatic Society of Bengal (Calcutta), 270 (1948), 260-73.

Ackermann, Rudolph. *Instruction for Painting Transparencies*. London: R. Ackermann [1820].

Acland, Charles (Rev.). *A Popular Account of the Manners and Customs of India*. London: Charles Murray, 1847.

Admiral Paris' Native Boats of Asia and the Pacific, 1841: The catalog of an exhibition and sale of hand-coloured original lihtographs of native craft of Asia and the Pacific executed in 1841 by François-Edmond Paris in his Essai sur la construction navale des peuples extra-européens. Singapore: Antiques of the Orient, 1989.

Ahmed, Zakiuddin. "Sati in Eighteenth Century Bengal." *Journal of the Asiatic Society of Pakistan* 13 (August 1968): 147-64.

Alavi, Seema. *The Sepoys and the Company: Tradition and Transition in Northern India 1770-1830*. New Delhi: Oxford University Press, 1995.

Ali, Salim. *The Book of Indian Birds*. 7th ed. Bombay: Bombay Natural History Society, 1964.

———, and Laeeq Futehally. *Common Indian Birds*. New Delhi: National Book Trust, 1968.

Alexander, Neil. "'The Economy of Human Life': Arthur William Devis and the Agriculture, Arts and Manufactures of Bengal." *The Connoisseur* 202 (October 1979): 120-23.

Alphabetical List of Feasts and Holidays of the Hindus and Muhammadans. Calcutta: Imperial Record Department, 1914.

American Heritage Dictionary. 3d ed. Boston: Houghton Mifflin, 1992.

Anderson, James. *An Account of the Importation of American Cochineal Insects into Hindostan*. Madras: William Urquhart, 1795.

Andrews, Malcolm. *The Search for the Picturesque: Landscape Aesthetics and Tourism in Britain, 1760-1800*. Aldershot, UK: Scholar Press, 1989.

Anglo-Hindoostanee Hand-Book. See Grant, Henry, and Edward Colebrooke.

Annual Register, or a View of the History, Politics, and Literature for the Year 1824. London: Baldwin, Chadock, and Joy, 1825.

Anquetil-Duperron [du Perron], Abraham Hyacinthe. *L'Inde en rapport avec l'Europe*. 2 vols. Paris: Lesguilles, 1798.

———. *Recherches historique et chronologiques sur l'Inde*. Vol. 2 of *Description historique et geographique de l'Inde*, edited by Jean Bernoulli. Berlin: P. Bordeaux, 1788.

———, tr. *Oupenek'hat, Id Est, Secretum Tegendrum* [*Upanishads*]. 2 vols. Strasbourg: 1801-02.

Anstey, F. [pseud.] *Baboo Jabberjee, B.A.* London: J. M. Dent & Sons, 1897.

Archer, John Clark. *The Sikhs*. Princeton: Princeton University Press, 1946.

Archer, Mildred. "Baltazard Solvyns and the Indian Picturesque." *The Connoisseur* 170 (January 1969): 12-18.

———. *British Drawings in the India Office Library*. Vol. I, *Amateur Artists*. Vol. II, *Official and Professional Artists*. London: Her Majesty's Stationery Office, 1969.

———. "British Painters of the Indian Scene, 1770-1825." In *European Artists and India 1700-1900*, edited by Hiren Chakrabarti, 1-6. Calcutta: Victoria Memorial, 1987.

———. *Company Drawings in the India Office Library*. London: Her Majesty's Stationary Office, 1972.

———. *Company Paintings: Indian Paintings of the British Period*. London: Victoria & Albert Museum/Ahmedabad: Mapin Publishing, 1992.

———. *India and British Portraiture, 1770-1825*. London: Sotheby Parke Bernet, 1979.

———. *The India Office Collection of Paintings and Sculpture*. London: British Library, 1986.

———. "India and the Illustrated Book." Introductory essay for *A Journey to Hindoostan: Graphic Art of British India, 1780-1860* [Catalogue to the exhibition of prints from the Max Allen and Peter Allen Collection], by Thomas P. Bruhn, 7-5. Storrs, CT: The William Benton Museum of Art, The University of Connecticut, 1987.

Archer, Mildred, and William G. Archer. "Francois Baltazard Solvyns: Early Painter of Calcutta Life." In *Science, Philosophy and Culture: Essays Presented in Honour of Huymayun Kabir's Sixty-Second Birthday*, edited by Frank Moraes et al., 1-10. Bombay: Asia Publishing House, 1968.

———. *Indian Painting for the British 1770-1880*. Oxford: Oxford University Press, 1955.

Archer, Mildred, and Ronald Lightbown. *India Observed: India as Viewed by British Artists, 1760-1860*. London: Victoria and Albert Museum, 1982.

Archer, William. G. *Kalighat Paintings: A Catalogue and Introduction*. London: Her Majesty's Stationary Office, 1971.

———. *The Loves of Krishna in Indian Painting and Poetry*. New York: Grove Press, 1957.

Archibald, E. H. H. *Dictionary of Sea Painters*. Woodbridge, Suffolk: Antique Collector's Club, 1980.

Arnett, Robert. *India Unveiled*. Columbus, Georgia: Atman Press, 1996.

Arnold, Alison, ed. *The Garland Encyclopedia of World Music*, Vol. 5, *South Asia: The Indian Subcontinent*. New York/London: Garland, 2000.

Art Journal

Asiatic Annual Register. . . for the Year 1801. London: J. Debrett, 1802.

Asiatic Annual Register, for the Year 1802. London: J. Debrett, 1803.

Asiatic Researches. Journal of the Asiatic Society of Bengal, Calcutta. Early volumes were also published in London and, in French translation (see under *Recherches asiatiques*), in Paris. In the Calcutta edition, the title *Asiatick* was used through Vol. 14 (1822). Vol. 1-20 (1788-1834) have been reprinted by Cosmo, New Delhi.

"Asiaticus." See Stanhope.

Atanassov, Vergilij. "Daire." NGMI, 1:536.

Atkinson, George F. *Curry & Rice (on Forty Plates): The Ingredients of Social Life at "Our" Station in India*. London: Day, 1859.

Babiracki, Carol M. "Karah." NGMI, 2:360.

———. "Mādar." NGMI, 2:590-91.

Babiracki, Carol M., and Mireille Helffer. "Narsīgā." NGMI, 2:749.

Bacon, Thomas. *First Impressions and Studies from Nature in Hindostan: Embracing an outline of the voyage to Calcutta, and five years' Residence in Bengal and the Doab from 1831 to 1836.* 2 vols. London: Wm. H. Allen, 1837.

———. *The Oriental Portfolio: Picturesque Illustrations of the Scenery and Architecture of India.* Edited by H. H. Wilson. London: Smith, Elder, 1841.

Bagchi, P. C. *Calcutta Past and Present.* Calcutta: Calcutta University Press, 1939.

Bagchi, Subhendu Gopal. "The Rituals of the Pitha of Kalighata." In *Religion and Society in Ancient India.*, edited by Pranabananda Jash, 257-67. Calcutta: Roy & Chowdhury, 1984.

Bahadur, Krishna Prakash, ed. *Caste, Tribes and Culture of Rajputs.* Delhi: Ess Ess, 1978. [Edited and revised version of Alfred H. Bingley, *Rajputs*, 1898.]

Baillie, William. *Twelve Views of Calcutta.* Calcutta: William Baillie, 1794.

Bailly, Jean Sylvain. *Traite de l'astronomie indienne et orientale.* Paris: Debure l'aine, 1787.

Baily, John, and Alastair Dick. "Sārindā." NGMI, 3:297-98.

Balayé, Simone. *La Bibliothèque nationale des origines à 1800.* Geneva: Broz, 1988.

Baldaeus, Phillipus. *Naauwkeurige beschryvinge van Malabar en Choromandel, der zelver aangrenzende ryken, en het machtige eyland Ceylon.* 3 pts. Amsterdam: J. Janssonius van Waasberge & J. van Someren, 1672.

Balfour, Edward, *Cyclopaedia of India.* 3 vols. London: Bernard Quaritch, 1885.

Balfour, Henry, Jr. "Life History of an Aghori Fakir." *Journal of the Anthropological Institute of Great Britain and Ireland,* 26 (1897): 340-56.

Bandhyopadhyay, Brajendranath. *Saṃvādapatre Selāler Kathā.* 3 vols. Calcutta: 1930-35.

Bandhyopadhyay, Pranab. *Mother Goddess Durga.* Calcutta: United Writers, 1993.

Bandhyopadhyay, Raghab. "Calcutta's Markets." In *Calcutta: The Living City*, edited by Sukanta Chaudhuri, 2:117-22. Calcutta: Oxford University Press, 1990.

Bandyopadhyaya, S. *Musical Instruments of India.* Varanasi: Chaukhambha Orientalia, 1980.

Bandhyopadhyay, Sekhar, et al., eds. *Bengal: Communities, Development and States.* New Delhi: Manohar, 1994.

Banerjee, P. *The Life of Krishna in Indian Art.* New Delhi: National Museum, 1978.

Banerjee, Sumanta. *The Parlour and the Streets: Elite and Popular Culture in Nineteenth Century Calcutta.* Calcutta: Seagull, 1989.

Banerji, Amiya Kumar. "Temples in Calcutta and its Neighbourhood." *Bengal Past and Present* 87 (1968): 99-105.

———. *West Bengal District Gazetteers: Bankura.* Calcutta: Government of West Bengal, 1968.

———. *West Bengal District Gazetteers: Hooghly.* Calcutta: Government of West Bengal, 1972.

Banerji, S. C. *Tantra in Bengal: A Study of its Origin, Development and Influence.* 2d ed. New Delhi: Manohar, 1992.

Barat, Amiya. *The Bengal Native Infantry: Its Organization and Discipline, 1796-1852.* Calcutta: Firma K. L. Mukhopadhyay, 1962.

Barrow, H. W. "On the Aghoris and Aghorapanthis (Bengal)." *Journal of the Anthropological Society of Bombay*, 3 (1893-94): 197-256.

Basham, A. L. *The Wonder That Was India* . Rev. ed. New York: Hawthorn Books, 1963.

Basu, D. "The Banian and the British in Calcutta, 1800-50." *Bengal Past and Present,* 92 (1973): 159-70.

———. "The Early Banians of Calcutta." *Bengal Past and Present,* 90 (Jan.-June 1971): 30-45.

Basu, Tara Krishna. *The Bengal Peasant from Time to Time.* Indian Statistical Series No.15. Bombay: Asia Publishing House; Calcutta: Statistical Publishing Society, 1962.

Bateson, Charles. *Convict Ships.* Glasgow: Brown, Son & Fereguson, 1959.

Bautze, Joachim K., ed. *Interaction of Cultures: Indian and Western Painting, 1780-1910. The Ehrenfeld Collection.* Alexandria, VA: Art Services International, 1998.

Bayly, Christopher A. "From Ritual to Ceremony: Death Ritual in Hindu North India Since 1600." In *Mirrors of Mortality: Studies in the Social History of Death*, edited by Joachim Whaley, 154-86. New York: St. Martin's 1981.

———. *Indian Society and the Making of the British Empire.* New Cambridge History of India, II.1. Cambridge: Cambridge University Press, 1988.

———. *Rulers, Townsmen, and Bazaars: North Indian Society in the Age of British Expansion, 1770-1870.* Cambridge: Cambridge University Press, 1983.

———. ed. *The Raj: India and the British 1600-1947.* London: National Portrait Gallery, 1990.

Beames, John. See Henry M. Elliot, *Memoirs . . . .*

Bean, Susan S. "Cold Mine." *American Heritage* 42 (July/August 1991): 71-76.

———. *Yankee India: American Commercial and Cultural Encounters with India in the Age of Sail, 1784-1860.* Salem, MA, and Ahmedabad: Peabody Essex Museum and Mapin Publishing, 2001.

Beauvais-Rasaeau, de. *A Treatise on Indigo.* Translated from the French by Richard Nowland. Calcutta: James White, 1794.

Bedi, Rajesh, and Ramesh Bedi. *Sadhus: The Holy Men of India.* New Delhi: Brijbasi, 1991.

Bellew, Captain (Francis John). *Memoirs of a Griffin.* London: W. H. Allen, 1843.

Belnos, Mrs. S. C. *Twenty-Four Plates Illustrative of Bengal.* Calcutta: Riddhi-India, 1979 [1832].

Bénézit, Emmanuel. *Dictionnaire Critique et Documentaire des Peintres, Sculpteurs, Dessinateurs et Graveurs.* Paris: Gründ, 1911-1923.

Bengal Almanack. Calcutta: C. L. Vogel [annual, late 18th century].

Bengal Directory and Almanak. Compiled by Henry M'Kenly. Calcutta: Telegraph Press [annual, late 18th-early 19th centuries].

Bengal Kalendar and Reister. Calcutta: Mirror Press [annual, late 18th-early 19th centuries].

Bengal Past and Present. "Life in Old Calcutta." 28 (July-December 1924): 129-41. Reprinted from "Englishman" [no date].

Bentley, John. "On the Antiquity of the Surya Sidhanta, and the formation of the Astronomical Cycles therein Contained." *Asiatick Researches.* New Delhi: Cosmo, 1979 [1799], 6:540-593.

———. "On the Hindu Systems of Astronomy, and their connection with History in ancient and modern times." *Asiatic Researches*. New Delhi: Cosmo, 1979 [1805], 8:195-244.

Bernier, François. *Travels in the Mogul Empire*. Translated by Archibald Constable, 2d ed. London: Oxford University Press, 1914.

Bergmans, Paul. "Praet." In *Biographie nationale . . . de Belgique*, 18:154-63.

Berko, Patrick, and Vivian Berko. *Dictionnaire des peintres Belges nés entre 1750 et 1875*. Brussels: Laconti, 1981.

———. eds. *Marines van Belgische schilders geboren tussen 1750 en 1875* [Marine Paintings by Belgian Artists Born Between 1750 and 1875], Tr. of 1981 French edition. Brussels: Editions Laconti, 1984.

Bernoulli, Jean, ed. and tr. *Description historique et geographique de l'Inde*. 3 vols. Berlin: S. C. Spener/P. Bourdeaux, 1786-89.

Bernstein, Henry T. *Steamboats on the Ganges*. Bombay: Orient Longmans, 1960.

Bertuch, Fredrich Justin. *Bilderbuch für Kinder*. 12 vols. Weimar: Im Verlage des Landes-Industrie-Comptoirs1792-1830. *Porte-feuille des enfans*. 7 vols. Weimar: Bureau d'Industrie, 1798, 1810.

Beterams, Frans G. C. *The High Society, Belge-Luxembourgeoise . . . au Début du Gouvernment de Guillaume Ier, Roi des Pays-Bas (1814-1815)*. Wetteren, Belgium: Cultura, 1973.

Bhagavadgītā: *The Bhăgvăt-Gēētā, or Dialogues of Krēēshnă and Arjŏŏn*. Translated by Charles Wilkins from the Sanskrit. London: C. Nourse, 1785. French translation, *La Bhaguat-Geeta, ou dialogues de Kreeshna et d'Arjoon; contenant un précis de la religion et de la morale des Indiens. Traduit du Sanscrit en Anglois par C. Wilkins; et de l'Anglois et François par M. Parraud*. London and Paris: Buisson, 1787.

Bhattacharya, Benoy. *Cultural Oscillation (A Study of Patua Culture)*. Calcutta: Naya Prokash, 1980.

Bhattacharya, Jogendra Nath. *Hindu Castes and Sects*. Calcutta: Editions Indian, 1973 [1896].

Bhattacharyya, Asutosh. "Dharma and Serpent Worship in Bankura District." In *West Bengal District Gazetteers: Bankura*, edited by Amiya Kumar Banerji, 207-22. Calcutta: Government of West Bengal, 1968.

———. "The Bengal Snake-charmers and their Profession." *Indian Folk-lore* (Jan-March 1958): 3-10.

Bhattacharyya, Narendra Nath. *A Glossary of Indian Religious Terms and Concepts*. New Delhi: Manohar, 1990.

Bibliographie de l'Empire Français. Vol. 2 [For the years 1811-12]. Paris: Pillet, 1813. Reprint: Nendeln, Liechtenstein: Kraus Reprints, 1960.

Bingley, Alfred H. See Bahadur.

Biographie Nationale Publiée par l"Académie Royale des Sciences, Des Lettres et des Beaux-Arts de Belgique. 28 vols. Brussels: Émile Bruylant, 1866-1944.

Biographie nouvelle des contemporains. "SOLVYNS (F. Balthazar)," 19:243-44. Paris: Librairie Historique, 1825.

Bird, William Hamilton. *The Oriental Miscellany: Being a Collection of the Most Favourite Airs of Hindoostan, Compiled and Adapted for the Harpsicord, &c*. Calcutta: Joph. Cooper, 1789.

Biswas, Oneil. *Calcutta and Culcuttans: From Dehi to Megalopolis*. Calcutta: Firma KLM, 1992.

Blagdon, Francis William. *A Brief History of Ancient and Modern India*. London: Edward Orme, [1802], 1805.

Blechynden, Kathleen. *Calcutta Past and Present*. Edited by N. R. Ray. Calcutta: General, 1978 [1905].

Blowmik, S. K., ed. *The Heritage of Musical Instrumentents (A Catalogue of Musical Instruments in Museums of Gujarat)*. Vadodara, Gujarat: Department of Museums, Government of Gujarat, 1990.

Boarse, Federick. *Modern English Biography*. 6 vols. Truro: Netherton and Worth, 1892-1921.

Boerner, C. G. *Etchings by Giovanni David* [gallery catalogue]. Düsseldorf: C. G. Boerner, 2000.

Bohn, Henry C. *A Catalog of Books*. London: 1841.

———. *Catalog of Books*. London: 1847.

Bolstad. See Jansen, *Sailing Against the Wind*.

Bonnaire, Marcel. *Procès-verbaux de l'Académie des beaux-arts*. Vol. 3, *La Classe des beaux-arts de l'Institut (suite), 1806-1810*. Paris: A. Colin, 1943.

Bor, Joep. "The Rise of Ethnomusicology: Sources on Indian Music c. 1780-c.1890." *Yearbook for Traditional Music* 20 (1988): 51-73.

———. "The Voice of the Sarangi: An Illustrated History of Bowing in India." *National Centre for the Performing Arts Quarterly Journal* (Bombay) 15-16 (1986-87): 1-183.

Borchgrave, Baron de. "SOLVYNS (François-Balthazar)." In *Biographie Nationale Publiée par l"Académie Royale des Sciences, Des Lettres et des Beaux-Arts de Belgique*. Brussels: Émile Bruylant, 1921-1924. 23:134-38.

Bose, Basanta Coomar. *Hindu Customs in Bengal*. Calcutta: Book Company, 1930.

Bose, Nirmal Kumar, Ed. *Peasant Life in India: A Study in Indian Unity & Diversity*. Memoir No. 8. Calcutta: Anthropological Survey of India, 1961.

Bose, Pranindra Nath. "Snake-Worship in Bengal." *Man in India* 7 (January-March 1927): 53-56.

Bose, Shib Chunder [Sivachander]. *The Hindoos as They Are*. Calcutta: W. W. Newman, 1881; London: Edward Stanford, 1881.

Bouchardon, Edmé. *Etudes prìses dans le ba Peuple ou les Cris de Paris*. Paris: Joullain, 1737-46.

Boumans, René. *Het Antwerpse stadsbestuur voor en tijdens de Franse overheersing* Bruges: De Tempel, 1965.

Bowrey, Thomas. *A Geographical Account of Countries Round the Bay of Bengal, 1669-1769*. 2d Series, No. 12. Cambridge: Hakluty Society, 1905.

Bowring, Lewin. *Haidar Ali and Tipu Sultan*. Oxford: Clarendon Press, 1893.

Briggs, George W. *Gorakhnāth and the Kānphata Yogīs*. Delhi: Motilal Banarsidass, 1973 [1938].

Brown, W. Norman. *India and Indology: Selected Articles*. Edited by Rosane Rocher. Delhi: Motilal Banarisidass, 1978.

Browne, Major James. "History of the Origin and Progress of the Sicks." In *India Tracts*. London: East India Company, 1788. Reprinted, with annotations, in *Indian Studies: Past & Present*, 2 (1961): 535-42, 549-83; and in *Early European Accounts of the Sikhs*, edited by Ganda Singh, 9-19, Calcutta: Indian Studies: Past & Present, 1962.

Bruhn, Thomas P. *A Journey to Hindoostan: Graphic Art of British India, 1780-1860* [Catalogue to the exhibition of prints from the Max Allen and Peter Allen Collection]. Storrs, CT: The William Benton Museum of Art, The University of Connecticut, 1987.

Brunet, Jacques-Charles. *Manuel du libraire et de l'amateur de livres*. 5th ed. 5 vols. Paris: G. P. Maisonneuve & Larose, 1860-1865.

Brussels Museum d'Ixelles. "François Baltasar Solvyns," in *Autour du Neo-Classicism en Belgigue, 1770-1830*, 304. [Catalogue of an exhibition, 14 November 1985-5 February1986.] Brussels: Crédit Communal, 1985.

Bruyn, Cornelis de. *Reizen van Cornelis de Bruyn, door de vermaardste deelen van Klein Asia*. Delft: Henrick van Kroneveld, 1698. English translation: *A Voyage to the Levant*. London: Jacob Tonson; Thomas Bennett, 1702.

———. *Voyages de Corneille Le Brun par la Moscovie, en Perse, et aux Indes Orientales*. 2 vols. Amsterdam, Freres Wetstein, 1718. English translation: *Travels into Muscovy, Persia, and Parts of the East-Indies*. 2 vols. London: A. Bettesworth, 1737.

Bry, Theodor de. *Discovering the New World; based on the works of Theodore de Bry*. Edited by Michael Alexander. London: London Editions, 1976.

———. *India orientalis*. 4 pts. Frankfurt: 1599-1601.

———. *Petit voyages*. Frankfurt: 1598-1628.

Bryan, Michael. *Biographical and Critical Dictionary of Painters and Engravers*. 2 vols. London: Carpenter & Son, 1816. For revised edition, see under George C. Williamson.

Buchanan, Francis. *The History, Antiquities, Topography, and Statistics of Eastern India*. Compiled and edited by Montgomery Martin. 4 vols. London: Wm. H. Allen, 1838. See Montgomery Martin.

Buckland, Charles E. *Bengal Under the Lieutenant-Governors*. New Delhi: Deep, 1976 [1902].

———. *Dictionary of Indian Biography*. New York: Haskell House, 1968 [1906].

Buddle, Anne. *The Tiger and the Thistle: Tipu Sultan and the Scots in India 1760-1800*. Edinburgh: National Gallery of Scotland, 1999.

———. "The Tipu Mania: Narrative Sketches of the Conquest of Mysore." In *India: A Pagent of Prints*, edited by Pauline Rohatgi and Pheroza Godrej, 53-70. Bombay: Marg Publications, 1989.

Buffon, Comte de. *Natural History*. Translated from the French by William Smellie. 2d ed. 9 vols. London: W. Strahan and T. Cadell, 1785.

Bulley, Anne. *The Bombay Country Ships 1790-1833*. Richmond, Surrey, UK: Curzon Press, 2000.

Burbure, Albert de. "Le Gotha de nos argonauts." *Revue de la Ligue maritime belge* (Brussels) 31 (March 1931): 45-47.

Burford, Robert. *Description of a View of the City of Calcutta; now exhibiting at the Panorama, Leicester Square*. [Panorama taken from drawings for that purpose by Capt. Robert Smith.] London: J. and C. Adlard, 1830.

Burghart, Richard. "The Founding of the Ramanandi Sect," *Ethnohistory* 25 (Spring 1978): 121-39.

———. "Ornaments of the "Great Renouncers' of the Ramanandi Sect." In *The Cultural Heritage of the Indian Village*, edited by Brian Durrans and T. Richard Blurton, 107-118. London: British Museum, 1991.

———. Wandering Ascetics of the Rāmānandī Sect," *History of Religions* 22 (1983): 361-80. Reprinted in Richard Burghart, *The Conditions of Listening: Essays on Religion, History and Politics in South Asia*, edited by C. J. Fuller and Jonathan Spencer, 113-35. Delhi: Oxford University Press, 1996.

Burnouf, Eugène, and E. Jacquet. *L'Inde française, ou Collection de dessins représentant les divinités, temples, meubles, ornements, armes, ustensiles, cérémonies religieuses et scènes de la vie privée, faisant connaître les costumes et les diverses professions des peuples hindous qui habitent les possessions françaises de l'Inde . . . dessinée et publiée par MM. Géringer et Chabrelie, et accompagnée d'un texte explicatif rédigé par M. E. Burnouf . . . et M. E. Jacquet*. Paris: Aruthus Bertand [1827-1835].

Büsching, Anton Freidrich (a.k.a. Anthony F. Busching). *A New System of Geography*. English tr., 6 vols. London: A. Millar, 1762.

Bushby, Frank E. "Old-Time Conveyances in Calcutta." *Bengal Past and Present* 41 (1931): 138-40.

Busteed, H. E., *Echoes from Old Calcutta*. 3d ed. Calcutta: Thacker, Spink, 1897.

Bysack, Gaur Das. "Kalighat and Calcutta," *Calcutta Review* 92 (April 1891): 305-27. Reprinted in *Calcutta Keepsake*, edited by Alok Ray, 7-35. Calcutta: Rddhi-India, 1978.

Calcutta: A Poem. [Anonymous]. London: J. J. Stockdale, 1811.

Calcutta Chronicle (weekly, published in the 1790s).

Calcutta Gazette (1784-1832; thereafter as a solely official publication). Also see Seton-Karr.

Calcutta Monthly Register (published 1790-91).

Calcutta Review. "The Astronomy of the Hindus." 1 (1844): 20, in 1867): 221-61.

_____. "The Territorial Aristocracy of Bengal. No. II—The Nadiya' Ra'j." 109 (1872):85-118.

Callcott, Lady (Maria). See Maria Graham.

Campbell, Capt. Donald. *Journey Over Land to India*. London: Cullen, 1795.

Cannon, Garland. *The Life and Mind of Oriental Jones: Sir William Jones, the Father of Modern Linguistics*. Cambridge: Cambridge University Press, 1990.

Capwell, Charles. *The Music of the Bauls of Bengal*. Kent, Ohio: Kent State University Press, 1986.

Cardew, Lieut. F. G. *A Sketch of the Services of the Bengal Native Army to the Year 1895*. New Delhi: Today and Tomorrow's, 1971 [1903].

Carey, W. H. *Good Old Days of the Honorable John Company*. 2 vols. Calcutta: R. Cambray, 1906 [1882]. Abridged edition, edited by Amarendra Nath Mookerji, Calcutta; Quins, 1964.

Carey, William. *A Dictionary of Bengal Language (Bengali-English)*. 2 vols. New Delhi: Asian Educational Service, 1981 [1825].

Carman, W. Y. *Indian Army Uniforms Under the British from the 18th Century to 1947*. Vol. 1, *Calvalry*. London: Leonard Hill, 1961. Vol. 2, *Artillery, Engineers, and Infantry*. London: Morgan-Grampian, 1969.

Chaliha, Jaya, and Bunny Gupta. "The Armenians of Calcutta." In *Calcutta: The Living City*, edited by Sukanta Chaudhuri, 1:54-55. Calcutta: Oxford University Press, 1990.

———. "Durga Puja in Calcutta." In *Calcutta: The Living City*, edited by Sukanta Chaudhuri, 2:330-36. Calcutta: Oxford University Press, 1990.

Chakrabarti, Hiren, ed. *European Artists and India 1700-1900*. Calcutta: Victoria Memorial, 1987.

Chakrabarti, K. "British Artists in India--Early 18th and 19th Centuries," *Bulletin of the Victoria Memorial Hall* 3-4 (1969-70):16-24.

Chakravarti [Chakrabarty], Ramakanta. *Vaiṣṇavism in Bengal 1486-1900*. Calcutta: Sanskrit Pustak Bhandar, 1985.
Chandra, A. M. *The Sannyasi Rebellion*. Calcutta: Ratna Prakashan, 1977.
Charpentier-Cossigny de Palma, Joseph François. *Memoir Containing an Abridged Treatise, on the Cultivation and Manufacture of Indigo*. Calcutta: Manuel Cantopher, 1789.
Chatterjee, Amal. *Representations of India, 1740-1840: The Creation of India in the Colonial Imagination*. London: Macmillan, 1998.
Chatterjee, Ratnabali. *From Karkhana to the Studio: Changing Roles of Patron and Artist in Bengal*. New Delhi: Books & Books, 1990.
Chatterton, E. Keble. *The Old East Indiamen*. London: Rich & Cowan, 1933 [1914].
Chattopadhyay, A.. K. *Slavery in the Bengal Presidency 1772-1843*. London: Golden Eagle, 1977.
Chattopadhyay, Gauranga. "Carak Festival in a Village in West Benghal: Its Socio-Religious Implications." In *Aspects of Religion in Indian Society*, edited by L. P. Vidyarthi, 151-65. Meerut: Kedar Nath Ram Nath, 1961.
Chattopadhyaya, Nisikanta. *The Yātrās or the Popular Dramas of Bengal*. London: Trübner, 1882. Reprinted, Calcutta: Rddhi, 1976.
Chaudhuri, K. N. *Asia Before Europe: Economy and Civilization of the Indian Ocean from the Rise of Islam to 1750*. Cambridge: Cambridge University Press, 1990.
———, ed. *Economic Development of India Under the East India Company, 1814-58: A Selection of Contemporary Writings*. London: Cambridge University Press, 1971.
Chaudhuri, Nirad C. *The Autobiography of an Unknown Indian*. London: Macmillan, 1951.
———. Chaudhuri, Nirad C. *Culture in a Vanity Bag*. Bombay: Jaico, 1976.
Chaudhuri, Sibadas, ed. *Proceedings of the Asiatic Society*, Vol. I, 1784-1800. Calcutta: Asiatic Society, 1980.
Chaudhuri, Sukanta, ed. *Calcutta: The Living City*. 2 vols. Calcutta: Oxford University Press, 1990.
Chaudhury, Sushil. *From Prosperity to Decline: Eighteenth Century Bengal*. New Delhi: Manohar, 1995.
Chitra, Jaya, and Bunny Gupta, "Durga Puja in Calcutta." In *Calcutta: The Living City*, edited by Sukanta Chaudhuri, 2:331-36. Calcutta: Oxford University Press, 1990.
Choudhury, Dhriti K. L. "Trends in Calcutta Architecture 1690-1903." In *Calcutta: The Living City*, edited by Sukanta Chaudhuri, 1:156-175. Calcutta: Oxford University Press, 1990.
Choudhury, Ranabir Ray. *Calcutta A Hundred Years Ago*. Calcutta: Nachiketa [1986].
Chowdhury, Pritha, and Joyoti Chaliha. "The Jews of Calcutta." In *Calcutta: The Living City*, edited by Sukanta Chaudhuri, 1:52-53. Calcutta: Oxford University Press, 1990.
Christie's. *Exploration and Travel with Visions of India* (catalog for the auction of 21 September 2000). London: Christie's, 2000.
———. *Important English Pictures* (catalog for the auction of 22 June 1979). London: Christie's, 1979.
———. *Visions of India* (catalog for the auction of 5 June 1996). London: Christie's, 1996.
———. *Visions of India* (catalog for the auction of 10 June 1997). London: Christie's, 1997.
———. *Visions of India* (catalog for the auction of 5 October 1999). London: Christie's, 1999.
Church Missionary Society [London]. *First Ten Years' Quarterly Papers of the Church Missionary Society*. London: Seeley & Son, 1826.
———. *Missionary Papers*.
Claeys, Prosper. *Les Expositions d'art à Gand,1792-1892*. Ghent: Société Royal pur l'Encouragement des Beaux Arts, 1892.
Coekelberghs, Denis, and Pierre Loze, eds. *1770-1830: Autour du neo-classicisme en Belgique* [Catalog of an exhibition held at the Musee Communal des Beaux-Arts d'Ixelles, Brussels, Nov. 14, 1985-Feb. 8, 1986]. Brussels: Crédit Communal, 1985.
Colas, René. *Bibliographie générale du costume et de la mode*. 2 vols. New York: Hacker Art Books, 1963 [1933]. "Solvyns," 2:982-85.
Colebrooke, Henry Thomas. "On the Duties of a Faithful Hindu Widow." *Asiatick Researches*. New Delhi: Cosmo, 1979 [1795], 4:205-15.
———. "Religious Ceremonies of the Hindus, and the Bra'hmens Especially." Essay I. *Asiatic Researches*. New Delhi: Cosmo, 1979 [1798], 5:345-68.
———. "Religious Ceremonies of the Hindus, and the Bra'mens Especially." Essay II. *Asiatic Researches*. New Delhi: Cosmo, 1979 [1801], 7:232-311.
———, tr. *Two Treatises on the Hindu Law of Inheritance* [*The Law of Inheritance, from the Mitāksharā. A Commentary by Vijñāneśvara on the Institutes ofYājñavalkya.*] Translated from the Sanskrit. Calcutta: A. H. Hubbard, 1810.
Colebrooke, Lt. Robert H. "On the Andaman Islands." *Asiatick Researches*. New Delhi: Cosmo, 1979 [1795], 4:385-94.
———. *Twelve Views of Places in the Kingdom of Mysore*. London: 1794.
Conner, Patrick. *George Chinnery, 1774-1852: Artist of India and the China Coast*. Woodbridge, Suffolk: Antique Collectors' Club, 1993.
Copley, Stephen, and Peter Garside, eds. *The Politics of the Picturesque: Literature, Landscape, and Aesthetics Since 1770*. Cambridge: Cambridge University Press, 1994.
Corner, Miss [Julia]. *The History of China & India, Pictorial & Descriptive*. London: Henry Washbourne, 1846.
———. *India: Pictorial, Descriptive, and Historical*. Bohn's Illustrated Library. London: G. Bohn, 1854.
Cornwallis, Lord. *Correspondence of Charles, First Marquis Cornwallis*. Edited by Charles Ross. 3 vols. London: John Murray, 1859.
Cotton, Sir Evan. "A Calcutta Painter" [John Alefounder]. *Bengal Past and Present* 34 (1927), 116-19.
———. *East Indiamen: The East India Company's Maritime Service*. Edited by Sir Charles Fawcett. London: Batchworth Press, 1949.
———. "A Famous Calcutta Firm. The Story of Steuart & Co." *Bengal Past and Present* 46 (1933): 63-73. Also see "The Editor's Notebook," *Bengal Past and Present* 49 (1935): 142.
———. "Letters from Bengal: 1788-1795: Unpublished Papers from the Correspondence of Ozias Humphry, R. A." *Bengal Past and Present* 35 (1928): 107-34.
Cotton, H. E. A. *Calcutta Old and New*. Edited by N. R. Ray. Calcutta: General, 1980 [1909].
Courtright, Paul B. *The Goddess and the Dreadful Practice: The Immolation of Wives in the Hindu Tradition and its Western Interpretations*. New York: Oxford University Press, forthcoming.

———. "The Iconographies of Sati." In *Sati, the Blessing and the Curse:The Burning of Wives in India*, edited by John S. Hawley, 27-53. New York: Oxford University Press, 1994.
Craufurd, Quintin. *Sketches Chiefly Relating to the History, Religion, Learning, and Manners of the Hindoos*. London: T. Cadell, 1790. 2d ed., enlarged. 2 vols. London: T. Cadell, 1792.
Crill, Rosemary. *Hats From India*. London: Victoria and Albert Museum, 1985.
Crooke, William. *Things Indian, being notes on various subjects*. London: John Murray, 1906. Reprinted, New Delhi: Oriental Books Reprint Corporation, 1972.
———. *Tribes and Castes of North Western India*. 4 vols. Delhi: Cosmo, 1974 [1896].
Cuzin, Jean-Pierre. "Vincent, François-André." In *The Dictionary of Art*, 32:584-85.

D'Alberg (Dalberg), Baron Johan Friedrich Hugo von. *Ueber die musik der Indier. Eine abhandlung des Sir William Jones. Aus dem Englischen übersetzt mit erläuternden anmekungen und zusätzen begleitet von F. H. v. Dalberg*. Erfurt: Beyer und Maring, 1802.
Dalvimart, Octavian. *The Costume of Turkey*. London: William Miller, 1804.
Daniel, J. C. *The Book of Indian Reptiles*. Bombay: Bombay Natural History Society, 1983.
Daniell, Thomas. *Views of Calcutta* [12 colored aquatints]. Calcutta: 1786-1788.
———, and William Daniell. *Oriental Scenery*. 6 pts. London: 1795-1808.
———. *A Picturesque Voyage to India by the Way of China*. London: 1810.
Daniélou, Alain. *Hindu Polytheism*. New York: Pantheon, 1964.
Dar, S. N. *Costumes of India and Pakistan: A Historical and Cultural Study*. Bombay: Taraporevala, 1969.
Dasgupta, Atis K. *The Fakir and Sannyasi Uprisings*. Calcutta: K. P. Batgchi, 1992.
Dasgupta, Satadal. *Caste, Kinship and Community: Social System of a Bengal Caste*. Madras: University Press, 1986.
Dasgupta, Shashibhusan. *Obscure Religious Cults*. 2d ed. Calcutta: Firma K. L. Mukhopadhyay, 1962.
Das Gupta, Anil Chandra, ed. *The Days of John Company, Selections from Calcutta Gazette, 1824-1832*. Calcutta: West Bengal Government Press, 1959.
Das Gupta, Tamonash C. *Aspects of Bengali Society from Old Bengali Literature*. Calcutta: Univesity of Calcutta, 1935.
Datta, Sarojit. *Folk Paintings of Bengal*. New Delhi: Khama, 1993.
Datta, V. N. *Sati: A Historical, Social and Philosophical Enquiry into the Human Rite of Widow Burning*. New Delhi: Manohar, 1988.
Davenport, Millia. *The Book of Costume*. 2 vols. New York: Crown, 1948.
Davis, Samuel. "On the Astronomical Computations of the Hindus." *Asiatick Researches*. New Delhi: Cosmo, 1979 [1790], 2:175-226.
Day, Charles R. *The Music and Musical Instruments of Southern India and the Deccan*. Delhi; B. R. Publishing Corp., 1974 [1891].
Day, Rev. Lal Behari. *Bengal Peasant Life*. London: Macmillan, 1878.
De, Sushil Kumar. *Bengali Literature in the Nineteenth Century*. 2d ed. Calcutta: Firma K. L. Mukhopadhyay, 1961.
Deb, Chitra. "The 'Great Houses' of Old Calcutta." In *Calcutta: The Living City*, edited by Sukanta Chaudhuri, 1:56-63. Calcutta: Oxford University Press, 1990.
Deb, Raja Binaya Krishna. *The Early History and Growth of Calcutta*. Edited by Subir Ray Choudhuri. Calcutta: Rddhi, 1977 [1905].
De Bry. See Bry, Theodor de.
Della Valle, Pietro. *The Travels of Pietro Della Valle in India*. 2 vols. London: Haklvyt Society, 1892.
Deloche, Jean. *Transport and Communications in India Prior to Steam Locomotion*. Translated from the French by James Walker. Vol. 1, *Land Transportation*, Delhi: Oxford University Press, 1993; Vol. 2, *Water Transportation*. Delhi: Oxford University Press, 1994.
Delvenne, Mathieu Guillaume, ed. *Biographie du royoume Des Pays-Bas* [Biography of the Kingdom of the Low-Countries]. Mons: M. J. LeRoux, 1829.
De Marchi, Neil. "The Role of Dutch Auctions and Lotteries in Shaping the Art Market(s) of 17th Century Holland." *Journal of Economic Behavior and Organization* 28 (1995): 203-221.
Deoras, Purushottam J. *Snakes of India*. New Delhi: National Book Trust, 1965.
De Paepe, P. "Biographie Belge: Balthazard Solvyns, D'Anvers." *La Revue Belge* 6 (September 1837): 83-92.
Depping, Georges-Bernard [George Bernhard]. *Erinnerungen aus dem Leben eines Deutschen in Paris* [Reminiscences from the Life of a German in Paris]. Leipzig: Brodhaus, 1832.
———. "SOLVYNS (François-Balthazar). In *Biographie universelle, ancienne et moderne*, 43:62-63. Paris: L. G. Michaud, 1825. Reprinted (without acknowledgement) in *Biographie du royoume Des Pays-Bas*, edited by Mathieu Guillaume Delvenne, 417-18. Mons: M. J. LeRoux, 1829. Reprinted in *Biographie universelle ancienne et moderne*, 39:592-93. Rev. ed. Paris: Delegrave, 1870.
Desmond, Ray. "A Bountiful Arc." In *India: A Pagent of Prints*, edited by Pauline Rohatgi and Pheroza Godrej, 161-76. Bombay: Marg Publications, 1989.
De Seyn, Eugène. *Dictionnairie biographique des sciences, des lettres et des arts en Belgique*. 2 vols. Brussels: Editions l'Avenir, 1935.
Deva, B. Chaitanya. *The Musical Instruments of India: Their History and Development*. Calcutta: Firma KLM, 1978.
Dewar, Douglas. *Bygone Days in India*. London: Bodley Head, 1922.
———. *In the Days of the Company*. Calcutta: Thacker, Spink & Co., 1920. Reprinted, Calcutta: Bibhash Gupta, 1987.
Dick, Alastair. "Dendung." NGMI, 1:556.
———. "Ḍaph." NGMI, 1:545-46.
———. "Ektar." NGMI, 1-649-50.
———. "Esrāj." NGMI, 1:719.
———. "Ghaḍasa." NGMI, 2:39.
———. "Ghaṇṭā." NGMI, 2:39-40.
———. "Huḍukkā." NGMI, 2:257-58.
———. "Kāṛā." NGMI, 3:360.
———. "Kartāl." NGMI, 2:361-62.
———. "Kā̃sar." NGMI, 2:362.
———. "Khol." NGMI, 2:423-24.
———. "Manjīrā," NGMI, 2:609.
———. "Mṛdaṅga." NGMI, 2:696-699.
———. "Naṛ." NGMI, 2:749.
———. "Paṭaha." NGMI, 3:21-22.
———. "Pināk." NGMI, 3:113.

———. "Pūngī." NGMI, 3:159.
———. "Śaṅkh." NGMI, 3:289-90.
———. "Sirbīṇ." NGMI, 3:390
———. "Sitār." NGMI, 3:392-400.
———. "Surmaṇḍal." NGMI, 3:477.
———. "Surnāī." NGMI, 3:478.
———. "Tambūrā." NGMI, 3:514-15.
———. "Ṭikārā." NGMI, 3:584.
Dick, Alastair, and Carol M. Babiracki. "Nagāṛā." NGMI, 2:739-41.
Dick, Alastair, Carol M. Babiracki, and Genèvieve Dournon. "Ḍhāk." NGMI, 1:559.
Dick, Alastair, Carol M. Babiracki, and Mireille Heffer. "Ektār," NGMI: 1:649-50.
Dick, Alastair, Carol M. Babiracki, and Natalie Webber. "Ḍholak." NGMI, 1:562-63.
Dick, Alastair, and Geneviève Dournon. "Ḍhol." NGMI, 1:560-62.
———. "Khanjari." NGMI, 2:422.
Dick, Alastair, Gordon Geekie, and Richard Widdess. "Vīṇā." NGMI, 3:728-35.
Dick, Alastair, and Devdan Sen. "Tablā." NGMI, 3:492-97.
Dick, Alastair, and Neil Sorrell. "Rāvaṇhatthā." NGMI, 3:728-35.
Dictionnaire de biographie française. Paris, Letouzey et Ane, 1933-
Dictionary of Art. Edited by Jane Turner. 34 vols. New York: Grove/London: Macmillan, 1996.
Dictionary of National Biography. Edited by Leslie Stephen and Sidney Lee. Oxford: Oxford University Press, 1921-1922.
Dikason, David G. "The Nineteenth Century Indo-American Ice Trade: An Hyperborean Epic." *Modern Asian Studies* 25 (February 1991): 53-89.
Dirks, Nicholas B. "Guiltless Spoilations: Picturesque Beauty, Colonial Knowledge, and Colin Mackenzie's Survey of India." In *Perceptions of South Asia's Visual Past*, edited by Catherine B. Asher and Thomas R. Metcalf, 211-32. Delhi: AIIS/Oxford & IBH, 1994.
Dirom, Major Alexander. *A Narative of the Campaign in India which Terminated in the War with Tippoo Sultan in 1792*. London: Bulmer, 1793.
Dogra, Ramesh Chander, and Gobind Singh Mansukhani. *Encyclopaedia of Skih Religion and Culture*. New Delhi: Vikas, 1995.
Dournon, Geneviève. "Bankiya." NGMI, 1:155.
Dournon, Geneviève, and Mireille Helffer. "Bā̃suri." NGMI, 1:192.
Dow, Alexander. *History of Hindostan*. 3 vols. London: T. Becket and P. A. De Hondt, 1768-1772
Dowson, John. *A Classical Dictionary of Hindu Mythology and Religion*. 11th ed. London: Routledge & Kegan Paul, 1968.
D'Oyly, Sir Charles. *Tom Raw, The Griffin: A Burlesque Poem in Twelve Cantos*. London: 1828.
———. *Views of Calcutta and its Environs*. London: 1848.
———, and Thomas Williamson. *The European in India; from a Collection of Drawings, by Charles Doyley, Esq. Engraved by J. H. Clark and C. Dubourg; with a Preface and Copious Descriptions, by Captain Thomas Williamson*. London: Edward Orme, 1813.
Dubois, Abbé J. A. *Hindu Manners, Customs and Ceremonies*. 3rd ed. Oxford: Clarendon Press, 1959 [1816].
Duff, Alexander. *India and India Missions: Including Sketches of the Gigantic System of Hinduism both in Theory and Practice*. 2d ed. Edinburgh: J. Johnstone, 1840. Reprinted Delhi: Swati, 1988.
Duflos, Pierre Le Jeune. *Recueil d'Estampes, représentant le grades les rangs et les dignités, suivant le costume de toutes les nations existantes; avec des explications historiques, et la vie abrégée des grands hommes qui ont illustré les dignités dont ils-étoient décorés*. 2 vols. Paris: Chez Duflos, 1780.
Dumont d'Urville, Jules-Sebastian-Cesar. *Voyage pittoresque autour du monde: resumé général des voyages de découvertes*. 2 vols. Paris: L. Tenré et Henri Dupuy, 1834-35.
Duncan, Jonathan. "An Account of Two Fakeers, with their Portraits." *Asiatick Researches*. New Delhi: Cosmo, 1979 [1798], 5:37-48.
Dutt, Guruswamy. *Folk Arts & Crafts of Bengal*. Calcutta: Seagull, 1990.
Dutt, Nripendra Kumar. *Origin and Growth of Caste in India*, Vol. II, *Castes in Bengal*. Calcutta: Firma K. L. Mukhopadhyay, 1965 [1896].
Dutta, Abhijit. *European Social Life in 19th Century Calcutta*. Calcutta: Minerva, 1994.
Dutta, Kalyani. "Kalighat." In *Calcutta: The Living City*, edited by Sukanta Chaudhuri, 1:24-26. Calcutta: Oxford University Press, 1990.
Dye, Joseph M. *Ways to Shiva: Life and Ritual in Hindu India*. Philadelphia: Philadelphia Museum of Art, 1980.
Dyson, Ketaki K. *A Various Universe: A Study of the Journals and Memoirs of British Men and Women in the Indian Subcontinent, 1765-1856*. Delhi: Oxford University Press, 1978.

East India Kalendar. London: J. Debrett [annual in the 1790s].
Ebert, Friedrich Adolphus. *A General Bibliographical Dictionary*. Translated from the Germany, *Allegemeines Bibliographisches Lexikon* [1821-30], by A. Brown. 4 vols. Oxford: University Press, 1837.
Edney, Matthew H. *Mapping an Empire: The Geographical Construction of India, 1765-1843*. Chicago: University of Chicago Press, 1997.
Edye, John. "Description of the Various Classes of Vessels Constructed and Employed by the Natives of the Coasts of Coromandel." *Journal of the Royal Asiatic Society of Great Britain and Ireland* 1(1834): 1-14.
Elliot, Henry M. *Memoirs on the History, Folk-lore, and Distribution of the Races of the North Western Provinces of India*. Original 1844 edition revised and edited by John Beames. 2 vols. London: Trubner, 1869-70. Reprinted as *History, Folk-lore and Culture of the Races of North Western Provinces of India*. Vol. 1. Delhi: Sumit, 1978 [1869]; and *Encyclopaedia of Castes, Customs, Rites and Superstitutions of the Races of Northern India*. Vol. 2. Delhi: Sumit, 1985 [1870]. The *Encyclopaedia* is sometimes listed as *Supplemental Glossary*, and, running only through the letter 'k," it was never completed.
Embree, Ainslie T. "Widows as Cultural Symbols." In *Sati, the Blessing and the Curse: The Burning of Wives in India*, edited by John S. Hawley, 149-59. New York: Oxford University Press, 1994.
———, ed., *Encyclopedia of Asian History*. 4 vols. New York: Scribner's, 1988.
Encyclopaedia Britannica, 15th ed.
Eschmann, Anncharlott, Hermann Kulke, and Gaya Charan Tripathi. *The Cult of Jagannath and the Regional Tradition of Orissa*. New Delhi: Manohar, 1978.

Ewart, Joseph. *The Poisonous Snakes of India*. London: J. & A. Churchill, 1878. Reprinted, New Delhi: Himalayan Books, 1985.

Eyre, Giles, and Charles Greig. *Landscape Paintings in the Victoria Memorial Collection*. Calcutta: Victoria Memorial, 1991.

Falkener, Edward. *Games Ancient and Oriental and How to Play Them*. New York: Dover, 1961 [1892].

Farrington, Anthony. *Catalogue of East India Company Ships' Journals and Logs, 1600-1834*. London: British Library, 1999.

Fay, Mrs. Eliza. *Original Letters from India (1779-1815)*. London: Hogarth Press, 1925, 1986 [1817].

Fayer, J. *Thanatophidia of India, Being a Description of the Venomous Snakes of the Indian Peninsula*. London: J. & A. Churchill, 1872.

Featherstone, Rupert. "New Insights through Restoration: Oil Paintings of India by European Masters *circa* 1760-1830." In *The Victoria Memorial Hall, Calcutta: Conception, Collections, Conservations*, edited by Philippa Vaughan, 66-80. Mumbai: Marg Publications, 1997.

Fennis, Jan. *Trésor du langage des galères*. 3 vols. Tübingen: Niemeyer, 1995.

Fenton, Mrs. E. *Journal of Mrs. Fenton—A Narrative of her life in India, the Isle of France (Mauritius), and Tasmania During the years 1826-1830*. Edited by H. W. Lawrence. London: Edward Arnold, 1901.

Ferrario, Giulio. *Il costume antico e moderno, . . . : Asia*, Vol. II. Milan: 1816. French trans., *Le Costume ancien et moderne, . . . par le Dr Jules Ferrario*, Vol. XIV, *Asie*. Milan: 1827.

Ferriol, Charles de (Marquis). See Le Hay.

Fiorillo, Johann Dominik. *Geschichte der zeichnenden Künste von ihrer Wiederaufebung bis auf die nuestenzeiten*. [History of the drawing arts from their renewal to recent times] 5 vols. Göttingen: Johann Friedrich Rower, 1798-1808. Vol. 5, 1808.

Finn, Frank. *The Birds of Calcutta*. Calcutta: Caledonian Steam Printing Works, 1901.

Fischer, Louis. *The Life of Mahatma Gandhi*. New York: Harper & Bros., 1950.

Flora, Reis. "Śahnāī." NGMI, 3:283-84.

Forbes, James. *Oriental Memoirs*. 4 vols. London: White, Cochrane, 1813. [Reprint: Delhi: Gian, 1988.] Second edition: 2 vols. London: R. Bentley, 1834.

Ford, John. *Ackermann 1793-1983: The Business of Art*. London: Ackermann, 1983.

Forster, George. *A Journey from Bengal to England*. 2 vols. London: R. Faulder, 1798. French translation by Louis Langlès, *Voyage du Bengale à Pétersbourg*. 3 vols. Paris: 1802.

———. *Sketches of the Mythology and Customs of the Hindoos*. London: [East India Co.?] 1785.

Foster, William. "British Artists in India, 1760-1820." *The Walpole Society* 19 (1930-31): 1-88. Reprinted, *British Artists in India, 1760-1820*. London: 1931.

———. "Additional Notes to British Artists in India, 1760-1802." *The Walpole Society* 21 (1932-33): 108-09.

———. "Some Foreign European Artists in India." *Bengal Past and Present* 40 (1930): 79-98.

Fowke, Francis. "'On the *Veena*, or *Indian* Lyre,' An Extract of a Letter from Francis Fowke, Esq. to the President." *Asiatick Researches*. New Delhi: Cosmo, 1979 [1788], 1:250-54. Reprinted, with plate, in Tagore, 191-97.

Fraser, Charles Fraser. See Unpublished, Solvyns, *Portraits of East Indians*.

Fraser, James Baillie. *Views of Calcutta and its Environs*. London: 1824-26.

La France littéraire. See Quèrard.

French, Colonel P. T. "Catalogue of Indian Musical Instruments." In *Hindu Music from Various Authors*, edited by Sourindro Mohun Tagore. Chowkhamba Sanskrit Studies, 49. Varanasi: Chowkhamba Sanskrit Series Office, 1965 [1882] , 243-73.

Frison, Theo. "De Antwerpse havenkapiteins: Max Solvijns was der eerste" ["Harbor Captains of Antwerp: Max Solijns was the First"]. *Sirense* [Quarterly Shipping Review, Duerne, Belgium] 106 (December 1976/January 1977):19123.

Furber, Holden. *John Company at Work: A Study of European Expansion in India in the Late Eighteenth Century*. Cambridge: Harvard University Press, 1948.

Füssli, Hans Heinrich [Johann Rudolf Fuessli]. "SOLVYNS, F. Balthasar." *Allegemeines künstlerlexikon*. 2:1675. Zurich: Orell, Füssli & Co., 1814.

Gait, E. A. "Human Sacrifice (Indian)." In *Encyclopaedia of Religion and Ethics*, edited by James Hastings, 6:849-53. New York: Charles Scribner's Sons, 1961 [1914].

Gangooly, Joguth Chunder. *Life and Religion of the Hindoos*. Boston: Crosby, Nichols, Lee & Co., 1860.

Garg, Ganga Ram, ed. *Encyclopedia of the Hindu World*. 20 vols. projected. New Delhi: Concept, 1992–.

Garrett, J. H. E. *Bengal District Gazetters: Nadia*, Vol. 14. Calcutta: Bengal Secretariat Book Depot, 1910.

Garrett, John. *A Classical Dictionary of India*. Madras: Higginbotham, 1871.

Gazette nationale, ou, Le Moniteur universel. (Paris).

Génard, Pierre. *Anvers a travers les ages*. 2 vols. Bruxelles: Bruylant-Christophe & Cie., 1888.

Géringer. See Burnouf.

Ghose, Arun. "British Artists in India," n. p., in *Up the Country: Exhibition of Upper Indian Views, 18th & 19th Centuries, from Victoria Memorial, Calcutta*. Exhibition catalog. Calcutta: Victoria Memorial, 1981.

Ghose, Benoy. *Traditional Arts & Crafts of West Bengal: A Sociological Survey*. Calcutta: Papyrus, 1981.

Ghose, Nagendra Nath. *Memoirs of Maharaja Nubkissen Bahadur*. Calcutta: K. B. Basu, 1901. Calcutta: Bookland, 1960.

Ghosh, Benoy. "Some Old Family Founders in Eighteenth Century Calcutta." *Bengal Past and Present* 79 (1960): 42-55.

Ghosh, Jamini Mohan. *Magh Raiders in Bengal*. Calcutta: Bookland, 1960.

———. ed. *Sannyasi and Fakir Raiders in Bengal*. Calcutta: Bengal Secretariat Depot, 1930.

Ghosh, Nagendra Nath. *Memoirs of Maharaja Nubkissen Bahadur*. Calcutta: K. B. Basu, 1901.

Ghosh, Suresh Chandra. *The Social Condition of the British Community in Bengal 1757-1800*. Leiden: Brill, 1970.

Ghosha, Pratapachandra. *Durga-Puja*. Calcutta: Hindu Patriot, 1871.

Ghurye, Govind S. *Indian Costume*. 2d ed. Bombay: Popular Prakashan, 1966.

———. *Indian Sadhus*. 2d ed. Bombay: Popular Prakashan, 1964.

Gilchrist, J. B. *The General East India Guide and Vade Mecum (Being a Digest of the work of the late Capt. Williamson)*. London: Kingsbury, Parbury, & Allen, 1815.

Gilpin, William. *Three Essays on Picturesque Beauty; on Picturesque Travel; and on Sketching Landscape*. London: R. Blaire. 1792.
Glassie, Henry. *Art and Life in Bangladesh*. Bloomington: Indiana University Press, 1997.
A Glossary of Indian Terms. Madras: Central Press, 1877.
Gnanambal, K. *Festivals of India*. Calcutta: Anthropological Survey of India, 1969.
Godrej, Pheroza, and Pauline Rohatgi. *Scenic Splendors: India Through the Printed Image*. London: British Library, 1989.
———. Also see under Rohatgi.
Gold, Charles. *Oriental Drawings, Sketched Between 1791 and 1798*. London: G. & W. Nicoll, 1806.
Goldsborne, Sophia [pseud.]. *Hartley House, Calcutta*. Notes by H. E. A. Cotton. Calcutta: Stamp Digest, 1984 [1789, 1908].
Gordon, Stewart. *The Marathas, 1600-1818*. Cambridge: Cambridge University Press, 1993.
———. *Marathas, Marauders, and State Formation in Eighteenth-Century India*. Delhi: Oxford University Press, 1994.
Gorton, John. *A General Biographical Dictionary*. London: Hunt and Clark, 1828.
Goswamy, B. N. *Indian Costumes in the Collection at the Calico Museum of Textiles*, Vol. 5, *Historic Textiles of India at the Calico Museum*. Ahmedabad: Calico Museum, 1993.
Gotch, Rosamund Brunel. *Maria, Lady Callcott* [A life of Maria Graham]. London: John Murray, 1937.
Gough, Richard. *A Comparative View of the Antient Monuments of India*. London: 1785.
Graham, Maria [Lady (Maria) Calcott]. *Letters on India* . London: Longman, 1814.
Grandpré, L. De. *A Voyage in the Indian Ocean and to Bengal, Undertaken in the Year 1789 and 1790*. Translation of the 1801 French edition. London: G. & J. Robinson, 1803.
Grant, Colesworthy. *Anglo-Indian Domestic Life*. 2d ed. [revising *An Anglo-Indian Domestic Sketch*] Calcutta: Thacker, Spink & Co., 1862. Reprint: Calcutta: Subarnarekha, 1984.
———. *An Anglo-Indian Domestic Sketch*. Calcutta: W. Thacker, 1849.
———. *Rural Life in Bengal*. Calcutta: Stamp Digest, 1984 [1866].
———. *Sketches of Oriental Heads, being a Series of Lithographic portraits drawn from Life, intended to illustrate the Physiognomic characteristics of the various People and Tribes of India*. Calcutta: Thacker, Spink & Co., c1844.
Grant, Henry, and Edward Colebrooke. *The Anglo-Hindoostanee Hand-Book; or Stranger's Self-Interpreter and Guide to Colloquial and General Intercourse with the Natives of India*. Calcutta: W. Thacker; London: Smith, Elder & Co., 1850.
Great Britain. Parliament. House of Commons. *Hansard's Catalogue and Breviate of Parliamentary Papers, 1699-1834*. Oxford: Blackwell, 1953 [1836].
———. *Parliamentary (House of Commons) Sessional Papers*.
———. *Parliamentary Papers (Misc.)*.
Greenhill, Basil. *Boats and Boatmen of Pakistan*. Newton Abbot, Devon: David & Charles, 1971.
———. "River Boats of Bangladesh." *Classic Boat* 54 (December 1992): 14-19.
Grierson, George A. *Bīhār Peasant Life, Being a Discursive Catalogue of the Surroundings of the People of that Province*. Delhi: Cosmo, 1975 [1885].
Grewal, J. S. *Guru Nanak in Western Scholarship*. Shimla: Indian Institute of Advanced Study; New Delhi: Manohar, 1992.
———. *The Sikhs of the Punjab*. The New Cambridge History of India, II.3. Cambridge: Cambridge University Press, 1990.
Grindlay, Robert M. *Scenery, Costumes and Architecture, Chiefly on the Western Side of India*. 2 vols. London: R. Ackerman, 1830.
Grose, John-Henry. *A Voyage to the East-Indies*. London: S. Hooper & A. Morley, 1757.
Gross, Robert L. *The Sadhus of India: A Study of Hindu Asceticism*. Jaipur: Rawat, 1992.
Guillain, Simon. *Diverse figure al numero di ottanta, disegnate di penna, nell'hore di ricreatione*. Rome: Lodovico Grigniani, 1646.
Günter, Albert C. L. G. *The Reptiles of British India*. London: The Ray Society, 1864.
Gupta, Bunny, and Jaya Chaliha. "Barabazar." In *Calcutta: The Living City*, edited by Sukanta Chaudhuri, 2:113-16. Calcutta: Oxford University Press, 1990.
Gupta, R. P. "Art in Old Calcutta: Indian Style." In *Calcutta: The Living City*, edited by Sukanta Chaudhuri, 1:137-45. Calcutta: Oxford University Press, 1990.
———. "Baboo, Bibi & Bhadramahila: Women in a Man's World." In *Naari: A Tribute to the Women of Calcutta 1690-1990*, edited by Tilottama Tharoor, 13-19. Calcutta: Ladies Study Group, c1990.
———. "Craftsmen at Work." In *Arts of Bengal and Eastern India*, edited by R. P. Gupta. Calcutta: Crafts Council of West Bengal, 1982.
———. "Some British & European Painters in India 1760-1850." In *Art Mosaic: In Celebration of Calcutta's Tercentenary*, n. p. Calcutta: Purmima, 1990.
Gupta, Shakti M. *Festivals, Fairs and Fasts of India*. 2d ed. Delhi: Clarion, 1996.
Gupte, B.A. *Hindu Holidays and Ceremonies*. Calcutta: Thacker, Spink & Co., 1919.
Guy, Alan, and Peter Boyden, eds. *Soldiers of the Raj: The Indian Army 1600-1947*. London: National Army Museum, 1997.

Halhed, Nathaniel B. *A Code of Gentoo Laws, or, Ordinations of the Pundits, from a Persian Translation, Made from the Original, Written in the Shanscrit Language*. London: [East India Company] 1776.
Hall, Barbara. *A Desperate Set of Villains: The Convicts of the Marquis Cornwallis, Ireland to Botany Bay, 1796*. Sydney: Barbara Hall, 2000.
Hamilton, Capt. Alexander. *A New Account of the East-Indies*. 2 vols. Edinburgh, 1727; London: 1744. Reprint, edited by William Foster. London: Argonaut Press, 1930.
Hamilton, Walter. *East India Gazetteer*. 2d ed. 2 vols. London: Parbury, Allen & Co., 1828.
———. *A Geographical, Statistical, and Historical Description of Hindostan and Adjacent Countries*. 2 vols. Delhi: Oriental Publishers, 1971 [1820].
Hansard's Catalogue and Breviate of Parliamentary Papers, 1699-1834. Oxford: Blackwell, 1953 [1836].
Hardgrave, Robert L., Jr. "An Early Portrayal of the Sikhs: Two Eighteenth Century Etchings by Baltazard Solvyns." *International Journal of Punjab Studies* 3 (July-December 1996): 213-27.
———. *Boats of Bengal: Eighteenth Century Portraits by Balthazar Solvyns*. New Delhi: Manohar, 2001.
———. *The Nadars of Tamilnad: The Political Culture of a Community in Change*. Berkeley: University of California Press, 1969.

———. "A Portrait of Black Town: Baltazard Solvyns in Calcutta, 1791-1804." In *Changing Visions, Lasting Images: Calcutta Through 300 Years,* edited by Pratapaditya Pal, 31-46. Bombay: Marg, 1990.

———. "The Representation of Satī: Four Eighteenth-Century Etchings by Baltazarad Solvyns." *Bengal Past and Present* 117 (1998): 57-80.

Hardgrave, Robert L., Jr., and Stanley A. Kochanek. *India: Government and Politics in a Developing Nation.* 6th ed. Fort Worth: Harcourt College Publishers, 2000.

Hardgrave, Robert L., Jr., and Stephen M. Slawek. "Instruments and Music Culture in Eighteenth Century India: The Solvyns Portraits." *Asian Music* 20 (Fall/Winter 1988-89): 1-92.

———. *Musical Instruments of North India: Eighteenth Century Portraits by Baltazard Solvyns.* New Delhi: Manohar, 1997.

Hardie, Martin, *English Coloured Books.* London: Methuen, 1906.

Harding, Elizabeth V. *Kali: The Black Goddess of Dakshineswar.* York Beach, Maine: Nicolas-Hays, 1993.

Hardy, Charles. *A Register of Ships, Employed in the Service of the East India Company.* 4th ed. London: Parbury, Allen, 1835.

Hart, William H. *Old Calcutta: Its Places and People A Hundred Years Ago.* Calcutta: Christian Literature Society, 1895.

Harrold, Pauline. See Rohatgi.

Hastings, James, ed. *Encyclopaedia of Religion and Ethics.* New York: Charles Scribner's Sons, 1961 [1914].

Hastings, Marquess of [Frances Rawdon-Hastings]. *The Private Journal of the Marquess of Hastings* [1813-18]. Edited by his daughter. 2 vols. London: Saunders and Otley, 1858.

Hartsuiker, Dolf. *Sādhus: Holy Men of India.* London: Thames and Hudson, 1993.

Hawley, John S. *At Play with Krishna: Pilgrimage Dramas from Brindavan.* Princeton: Princeton University Press, 1981.

———, ed. *Sati, the Blessing and the Curse: The Burning of Wives in India.* New York: Oxford University Press, 1994.

———, and Donna M. Wulff, eds. *Devī: Goddesses of India* Berkeley: University of California Press, 1996.

Hawkesworth, John. *Asiaticus,* Pt. I. Calcutta: Telegraph Press, 1803.

Heber, Reginald. *Narrative of a Journey Through the Upper Provinces of India, From Calcutta to Bombay, 1824-1825.* 2d ed. 3 vols. London: John Murray, 1828.

Hedges, William [1681-1687]. *Diary of Hedges.* Notes by Henry Yule. 3 vols. London: Hakluyt Society, 1887-1889.

Hédou, Jules. *Jean Le Prince et son oeuvre.* Paris: Chez J. Baur, 1879.

Hein, Norvin. "Līlā." In *The Gods at Play: Lila in South Asia.,* edited by William S. Sax, 13-34. New York: Oxford University Press, 1995.

Hesse, Carla. *Publishers and Cultural Politics in Revolutionary Paris 1789-1810.* Berkeley: University of California Press, 1991.

Hickey, William [1749-1809]. *Memoirs.* Edited by Alfred Spencer. 4 vols. New York: Knopf, 1913-1925.

Hobson-Jobson: A Glossary of Colloquial Anglo-Indian Words and Phrases. By Henry Yule and A. C. Burnell. 2d ed., edited by William Crooke. Sittingbourne, Kent: Linguasia, 1994 [1886, 1903].

Hodges, William. *Select Views of India.* London: J. Edwards, 1785-1788.

———. *Travels in India, during the years 1780, 1781, 1782 & 1783.* London: J. Edwards, 1793. French translation by Louis Langlès, *Voyage Pittoresque de l'Inde fait dans les années 1780-1783.* 2 vols. Paris: 1805.

Hodson, V. C. P. *List of the Officers of the Bengal Army, 1758-1834.* 4 pts. London: Constable & Co., 1927-47.

Holwell, John Zephaniah. *India Tracts.* 3d ed. London: T. Becket, 1774.

———. *Interesting Historical Events, Relative to the Province of Bengal and the Empire of Indostan.* 2 vols. London: T. Becket and P. A. de Hondt, 1765, 1767.

Home, Robert. *A Description of Seringapatam.* London: Robert Bowyer, 1796.

———. *Select Views in Mysore, the Country of Tipoo Sultan; from Drawings Taken on the Spot by Mr. Home.* London: Robert Bowyer, 1794.

Hood, Mantle. "Music, the Unknown." In *Musicology,* edited by Frank Harrison et al., 215-316. Englewood Cliffs, NJ: Prentice-Hall, 1963.

Hopkins, Sylvia. "A Compromise in Clothing: Uniform of the East India Company and Indian Armies, c. 1700-1947." In *Soldiers of the Raj: The Indian Army 1600-1947,* edited by Alan Guy and Peter Boyden, 118-37. London: National Army Museum, 1997.

Horne, Moffat James (under the pseudonym "Naufragus"). *The Adventures of Naufragus, written by himself.* London: Smith, Elder & Co., 1827.

Hornell, James. "The Boats of the Ganges." *Memoirs of the Asiatic Society of Bengal* (1924), 8: 171-198.

———. "The Fishing Methods of the Ganges." *Memoirs of the Asiatic Society of Bengal* (1924), 8:199-237.

———. "The Origins and Ethnological Significance of Indian Boat Designs." *Memoirs of the Asiatic Society of Bengal* (1920), 7:139-256.

———. *Water Transport: Origins and Evolution.* Cambridge: Cambridge Univesity Press, 1946.

Hossain, Hameeda. *The Company Weavers of Bengal.* Delhi: Oxford University Press, 1988.

Hostyn, Norbert. "De Zee en de Kunst: Frans-Balthasar Solvijns" [The Sea and Art]. *Neptunus* (Ostend), July 1980, 46-47.

———. "Frans-Balthasar Solvyns." *Het Visserijblad* (Ostend), August 6, 1982, 19-20.

———. "Omtrent een gezicht op de haven van de stad Oostende" [About a View of the Harbor of the City of Ostend]. *Bulletin des musées royaux d'art d'history* (Brussels), 1984, 114-18.

———. "Schilders van de zee," *Openbaar kunstbezit in Vlaanderen* 1 (1984), n.p.

———. "Solvyns, François-Balthazar." In *Marines van Belgische schilders geboren tussen 1750 en 1875* [Marine Paintings by Belgian Artists Born Between 1750 and 1875], edited by Patrick Berko and Vivian Berko, 150-53. Tr. of 1981 French edition. Brussels: Editions Laconti, 1984.

———. "Solvyns, Frans-Balthasar." In *National Biographish Woordenbook* [National Biographical Dictionary], 10: 594-99. Brussels: Pleisder Acadeiën, 1983.

Hughes, Robert. *The Fatal Shore: The Epic of Australia's Founding.* New York: Alfred A. Knopf, 1987.

Hunt, John Dixon. "Picturesque." In *The Dictionary of Art,* edited by Jane Turner. 24:740-43. New York: Grove/London: Macmillan, 1996.

Hunter, William Wilson. *A Statistical Account of Bengal.* 20 vols. London: Trübner, 1875-77.

Hutchinson, Robert Henry Sneyd. *Chittagong Hill Tracts.* Allahabad: Pioneer Press, 1909. Reprinted, Delhi: Virek, 1978.
Hymans, Henri. "Lens." In *Biographie nationale . . . de Belgique,* 11:810-16.
———. "Quertenmont." In *Biographie nationale . . . de Belgique,* 18:462-68.

Immerzeel, Johannes. *De Levens en werken der Hollandsche en Vlaamsche kunstschilders, beeldhouwers, graveurs en Bouwmeesters* [The Lives and Works of Dutch and Flemish Painters, Sculptors, Engravers and Architects]. 3 vols. Amsterdam: J. C. Van Kestern, 1842-1843.
India Office Library and Records. *Annual Report 1985-86.* London: British Library, 1987.
Ishaq, Muhammad, ed. *Bangladesh District Gazetteers: Chittagong Hill Tracks.* Dacca: Bangladesh Government Press, 1972.
Ironside, Col. Gilbert. "Account of Feats of Strength, Activity, and Legerdemain, in Hindustan." "Miscelleneous Tracts," 27-33. In *The Asiatic Annual Register. . . for the Year 1801.* London: J. Debrett, 1802.
Ives, Edward. *A Voyage from England to India, in the Year 1754.* London: J. Asperne, 1805.
Ivie, G. I. Hamilton. *An Outline of Postal History and Practice, with a History of the Post Office in India.* Calcutta: 1910.

Jacobs, Alain. "Lens, A(ndries) C(ornelis)." In *The Dictionary of Art,* 19:165-66.
Jadin, A. "Feletz." In *Nouvelle biographie générale,* 17:270-71. Paris: Didot Frères, 1856.
Jain, Jyotindra. *Kalighat Painting: Images from a Changing World.* Ahmedabad: Mapin Publishing, 1999.
Jaffey, Zia. *The Invisibles: A Tale of the Eunuch of India.* New York: Pantheon, 1996.
James, Captain. *Military Costumes of India.* London: T. Goddard Military Library, 1814.
Jansen, Eirik G. *Sailing Against the Wind: Boats and Boatmen of Bangladesh.* Photographs by Trygve Bolstad. Dhaka: University Press Ltd., 1992.
———, et al. *The Country Boats of Bangladesh.* Dhaka: University Press, 1989.
Jefferys, Thomas. *A Collection of the Dresses of Different Nations, Antient and Modern.* 4 vols. London: T. Jefferys, 1755-1772.
Johns, William. *A Collection of Facts and Opinions Relative to the Burning of Widows with the Dead Bodies of their Husbands and to other Destructive Customs Prevalent in British India.* Birmingham: W. H. Perarce, 1816.
Johnson, Daniel. *Sketches of Field Sports as followed by the Natives of India.* London: Torrington, 1822.
Johnson, George W. *The Stranger in India; or Three Years in Calcutta.* 2 vols. London: Henry Colburn, 1843.
Jones, Sir William. *A Discourse on the Institution of a Society for Inquiring into the History, Civil and Natural, the Antiquities, Arts, and Sciences, and Literature of Asia.* London: T. Payne and Son, 1784.
———. "On the Musical Modes of the Hindus." *Asiatick Researches.* New Delhi: Cosmo, 1979 [1792], 3:55-87. Reprinted in Tagore, 125-60.
———. "On the Gods of *Greece, Italy,* and *India.*" *Asiatick Researches.* New Delhi: Cosmo, 1979 [1788], 1:188-215.
———. *The Works of Sir William Jones.* 6 vols. London: G. G. and J. Robinson, 1799. Supplement. 2 vols. London: G. G. and J. Robinson, 1801.
———, tr. *Institutes of Hindu Law; or, the ordinances of Menu, according to the Gloss of Cullúca, Comprising the Indian System of Duties, Religious and Civil: Verbally Translated from the Original Sanscrit, with a Preface, by Sir William Jones.* Calcutta: Honourable Company's Press, 1794. Calcutta: Printed by order of the government; London: Reprinted for J. Sewell and J. Debret, 1796.
———, tr. *Sacontala; or the Fatal Ring.* Calcutta: 1789.
Joppien, Rudiger, and Bernard Smith. *The Art of Captain Cook's Voyages.* 3 vols. New Haven: Published for the Paul Mellon Centre for Studies in British Art by Yale University Press, 1985.
Journal de l'empire (Paris).

Kale, P. V. *History of Dharmaśāstra.* 6 vols. Poona: Bhandarkar Oriental Research Institute, 1930-1974.
Kang, Kanwarjit Singh. *Punjab Art and Culture.* Delhi: Atma Ram, 1988.
Kattenhorn, Patricia. *British Drawings in the India Office Library.* Vol. 3. London: The British Library, 1995.
Kaul, H. K., ed. *Travelers' India: An Anthology.* Delhi: Oxford, 1979.
Keir, Archibald. "Of the Method of Distilling" (1786). *Asiatick Researches.* New Delhi: Cosmo, 1979 [1788], 1:262-70.
Keith, Arthur B. *The Sanskrit Drama in its Origin, Development, Theory and Development.* London: Oxford University Press, 1924.
Kejariwal, O. J. *The Asiatic Society of Bengal and the Discovery of India's Past.* Delhi: Oxford University Press, 1988.
Kemp, Peter. *The Oxford Companion to Ships and the Sea.* Oxford: Oxford University Press, 1976.
———, and Richard Ormond. *The Great Age of Sail: Maritime Art and Photography.* Oxford: Phaidon, 1986.
Kencaid, Dennis. *British Social Life in India, 1608-1937.* London: George Routledge & Sons, 1938.
Kennedy, Melville T. *The Chaitanya Movement: A Study of the Vaishṇavism of Bengal.* Calcutta: Association Press, 1925.
Kerchove, René de. *International Maritime Dictionary.* New York: Van Nostrand, 1948.
Khan, Syed Gholam Hossein [Ghulam Hussain Khan]. *Seir Mutaqherin: or View of Modern Times, Being a History of India.* 4 vols. Calcutta: 1789. Reprinted Lahore: Sheikh Muharak Ali, 1975.
Kieffer, Jean-Luc. *Anquetil-Duperron, l'Inde en France au xviiie siècle.* Paris: Less Belles Lettres, 1983.
Kindersley, Mrs. Nathaniel. *Letters from the Island of Tenerisse, Brazil, the Cape of Good Hope, and the East Indies.* London: J. Nourse, 1777.
King, Anthony D. *The Bungalow: The Production of a Global Culture.* London: Routledge & Kegan Paul, 1984.
———. *Colonial Urban Development: Culture, Social Power and Environment.* London: Routledge & Kegan Paul, 1976.
Kinsley, David. *Hindu Goddesses: Visions of the Devine Feminine in the Hindu Religious Tradition.* Berkeley: University of California Press, 1986.
Knight, Charles. *The Hindoos.* 2 vols. Illustrations by William Westall. London: Charles Knight, 1834. Reprinted as William Westall, *The Hindoos.* 2 vols. London: Nattali and Bond [1847].
Knox, Robert. *An Historical Relation of the Island Ceylon, in the East-Indies.* London: Richard Chriswell, 1681. Facimilie reprint, New Delhi: Navrang Booksellers & Publishers, 1995.

Kolff, Dirk H. *Naukar, Rajput and Sepoy: The Ethnohistory of the Military Labour Market in Hinduston, 1450-1850.* Cambridge: Cambridge University Press, 1990.

Kooij, K. R. van, tr. *Worship of the Goddess According to the Kālikāpurāṇa.* Pt. 1. Leiden: E. J. Brill, 1972.

Kopf, David. "European Enlightenment, Hindu Renaissance and the Enrichment of the Human Spirit: A History of Historical Writings on British Orientalism." In *Orientalism, Evangelicalism and the Military Cantonment in Early Nineteenth-Century India: A Historical Overview,* edited by Nancy G. Cassels, 19-53. Lewiston, NY: Edwin Mellan, 1991.

Kossmann, E. H. *The Low Countries, 1780-1940.* Oxford: Clarendon Press, 1978.

Kothari, Komal. *Folk Musical Instruments of Rajasthan: A Folio.* Borunda, India: Rupayan Sansthan, Rajasthan Institute of Folklore, 1977.

Kramm, Christiaan. *De levens en werken der Hollandsche en Vlaamsche kunstschilders, beeldhouwers, graveurs en bruwmeesters* [The Lives and Works of Dutch and Flemish Painters, Sculptors, Engravers and Architects]. 6 vols. Amsterdam: Gebroeders Diederichs, 1856-1864.

Kramrisch, Stella. *The Presence of Śiva.* Princeton: Princeton University Press, 1981.

Krill, John. *English Artists Paper.* London: Trefoil, 1987.

Kulke, Hermann. "Rathas and Rajas: The Car Festival at Puri." In *The Cult and Culture of Lord Jagannath,* edited by Daityari Panda and Sarat Chandra Panigrahi, 181-98. Cuttack: Rashtrabhasha Samavaya Prakashan, 1984.

Kumar, Dharma. *The Cambridge Economic History of India.* 2 vols. Cambridge: Cambridge University Press, 1982.

Kunst, Jaap. "Een vergeten musicologische bron: De instrumentafbeeldingen in 'Les Hindous' van F. Baltazard Solvyns." *Cultureel Indië.* Leiden. 7 (1945): 197-200.

Lach, Donald F. *Asia in the Making of Europe.* Vol. 1, Bk. 1. Chicago: University of Chicago Press, 1965.

——, and Edwin J. Van Kley. *Asia in the Making of Europe.* Vol. 3, Bks. 1 and 2. Chicago: University of Chicago Press, 1993.

Lang, David M. *The Armenians.* London: Allen & Unwin, 1981.

Langlès, Louis Matthieu. *Catalogue des Livres, imprimés et manuscripts, composant la bibliothèque de feu m. Louis-Mathieu Langlès.* Compiled by J. S. and R. Merlin. Paris: Chez: J.-S. Merlin, 1825.

——. "*Les Hindoûs,* by Balthasar Solvyns." [Review of Vol. I] *Gazette nationale, ou, Le Moniteur universel.* November 5, 1809:1224-26, and April 26, 1811: 448-50.

——. *Monuments anciens et modernes de l'Hindoustan.* 2 vols. Paris:1812, 1821.

——. tr. Willaim Hodges, *Voyage pittoresque de l'Inde fait dans les années 1780-1783.* Translated from English and with notes by Louis Langlès. 2 vols. Paris: 1805.

Lawrence, Honoria. *The Journals of Honoria Lawrence: India Observed 1837-1854.* Edited by John Lawrence and Audrey Woodiwiss. London: Hodder & Stroughton, 1980.

Laufer, Berthold. *Tobacco and its Uses in Asia.* Chicago: Field Museum of Natural History, 1924.

Lavater, Johann Caspar (Kaspar). *Essays on Physiognomy.* Translation of *Physiognomische Fragmente* (1775-78) by Thomas Holcroft. 3 vols. London: G. G. J. and J. Robinson, 1789.

Le Gentil de la Galaisière, Guillaume Joseph H. J. P. *Voyage dans les mers de l'Inde.* 2 vols. Paris: L'Imprimerie Royale, 1779, 1781.

Le Hay, Jacques. *Recueil de cent estampes représentant différentes nations du Levant tirées sur les tableaux peints d'après nature* [by Jean-Baptiste Vanmour] *en 1707 et 1708 par les ordres de M. de Ferriol, ambassadeur du roi à la Porte. Et gravées en 1712 et 1713 par les soins de Mr Le Hay.* Paris: Jacques Collombat, 1714. Published with *Explication des cent estampes qui represent differentes nations du Levant.* Paris: Jacques Collombat, 1715.

Leoshko, Janice, and Michael Charlesworth. "Strangers in a Strange Land: Selected Views of India in British Printed Books, 1780-1827." *The Library Chronicle* 27, 3 (1997): 68-101.

Lesbroussart, Philibert. "Notice Biographique sur François-Balthazar Solvyns, auteur des Hindous." In *Messager des sciences et des arts, recueil* [Published by the Royal Society of Fine Arts and Lettters and by the Society of Agriculture and Botany], 68-76. Ghent: P. F. de Goesin-Verhaghe, 1826. [Brussels, 1824.]

Leslie, I. Julia. *The Perfect Wife: The Orthodox Hindu Woman according to the* Strīdharmapaddhati *of Tryambakayajvan.* Delhi: Oxford University Press, 1989.

Lewis, Ivor. *Sahibs, Nabobs, and Boxwallahs: A Dictionary of the Words of Anglo-India.* Bombay: Oxford University Press, 1991.

Lingat, Robert. *The Classical Law of India.* Berkeley: University of California Press, 1973.

Linschoten, Jan Huygen van. *His Discours of Voyages into ye Easte and West Indies.* Translated from the Dutch by William Phillip. London: John Wolfe, 1598. Reprinted as *The Voyage of John Huyghen van Linschoten to the East Indies,* edited by Arthur C. Burnell and P. A. Tiele, 2 vols. London: Hakluyt Society, 1885; New Delhi: Asian Educational Services, 1988.

Lloyd, Mary. "Sir Charles Wilkins, 1749-1836." In *India Office Library and Records Report for the Year 1978,* 8-39. London: British Library, 1979.

Lloyd's List 1803 & 1804. Westmead, Frarnsborough, Hants., England: Gregg International, 1969.

Long, Rev. James. *Calcutta in the Olden Time: Its Localities & Its People.* Calcutta: Sanskrit Pustak Bhandar, 1974. First published in *Calcutta Review* 18 (Dec. 1852): 275-320, and 35 (Sept. 1860):164-217.

——. "Peeps into Social Life in Calcutta a Century Ago," In *British Social Life in Ancient Calcutta,* edited by P. Thankappan Nair, 12-109. Calcutta: Sanskrit Pustak Bhandar, 1983. Originally published Calcutta: Bengal Social Science Assocation, 1868.

Longer, V. *Red Coats to Olive Green: A History of the Indian Army 1600-1974.* Bombay: Allied Publishers, 1974.

Lorenzen, David. "Warrior Ascetics in Indian History." *Journal of the American Oriental Society* 98 (1978): 61-75.

Losty, J. P. "The Belgian Artist F. B. Solvyns and his Influence on Company Painting." *The British Libary, India Office Library and Records, Oriental Manuscripts and Printed Books Newsletter.* Nos. 37-38 (March 1987), 6-9.

——. *Calcutta: City of Palaces: A Survey of the City in the Days of the East India Company, 1690-1858.* London: British Library/Arnold, 1990.

——. "A Career in Art: Sir Charles D'Oyly." In *Under the Indian Sun: British Landscape Artists,* edited by Pauline Rohatgi

and Pheroza Godrej, 81-106. Bombay: Marg Publications, 1995.
———. "The Sheep-eater of Fategarh." *South Asian Studies* 4 (1988): 1-12.
———. "Sir Charles D'Oyly's Lithographic Press and his Indian Assistants." In *India: A Pageant of Prints*, edited by Pauline Rohatgi and Pheroza Godrej, 135-60. Bombay: Marg, 1989.
Loze, Pierre. "André Corneille Lens." In *1770-1830: autour du néo-classicisme en Belgique*, edited by Denis Coekelberghs and Pierre, 67-89. Brussels: Crédit Communal, 1985.
Lutgendorf, Philip. *The Life of a Text: Performing the* Ramcaritmanas *of Tulsidas*. Berkeley: University of California Press, 1991.
Ly-Tio-Fane, Madeleine. *Pierre Sonnerat 1748-1814: An Account of his Life and Work*. Mauritius: By the author, 1976.

Mabon, Robert. *Sketches Illustrative of Oriental Manners and Customs*. Calcutta: 1797.
MacGregor, David R. *The Schooner: Its Design and Development from 1600 to the Present*. Annapolis: Naval Institute Press, 1997.
MacKenzie, John M. *Orientalism: History, Theory and Arts*. Manchester: Manchester University Press, 1995.
Mackintosh, William. *Travels in Euorpe, Asia, and Africa*. 2 vols. London: J. Murray, 1782.
Madra, Amandeep Singh, and Parmij Singh. *Warrior Saints: Three Centuries of the Sikh Military Tradition*. London: I. B. Tauris/New York: The Sikh Foundation, 1999.
Mahajan, Jagmohan. *The Ganga Trail: Foreign Accounts and Sketches of the River Scene*. New Delhi: Clarion Books, 1984.
———. *The Grand Indian Tour: Travels and Sketches of Emily Eden*. New Delhi: Manohar, 1996.
———. *Picturesque India: Sketches and Travels of Thomas and William Daniell*. New Delhi: Lustre Press, 1983.
———. *The Raj Landscape: British Views of Indian Cities*. New Delhi: Spantech Publishers, 1988.
Mahapatria, Sarat Chandra, ed. *Car Festival of Lord Jagannath Puri*. Puri: Sri Jagannath Research Centre, 1994.
Majumdar, Ramesh Chander. *Glimpses of Bengal in the Nineteenth Century*. Calcutta: Firma K. L. Mukhopadhyay, 1960.
———. *History of Modern Bengal*. 2 vols. Calcutta: G. Bharadwaj, Vol. 1, 1978; Vol. 2, 1981.
———. *History of Modern Bengal, Pt. 1(1765-1905)*. Calcutta: G. Bharadwaj, 1978.
Malcolm, Sir John. "Sketch of the Sikhs." *Asiatic Researches*. New Delhi: Cosmo, 1979 [1810], 11:197-292.
Manesson-Mallet, Allain. *Description de l'univers: contenant les differents systems du monde*. 3 vols. Paris: D. Thierry, 1683.
Mani, Lata. *Contentious Traditions: The Debate on* Sati *in Colonial India*. Berkeley: University of California Press, 1998.
Manu. See Sir William Jones, tr., *Institutes of Hindu Law; or, the ordinances of Menu*.
Markel, Stephen. "Images from a Changing World: Kalighat Paintings of Calcutta." *Arts of Asia* 29 (July-August 1999): 58-71.
Marshall, Peter J. *Bengal: The British Bridgehead, Eastern India 1740-1828*. The New Cambridge History of India, II.2. Cambridge: Cambridge University Press, 1987.
———. "The Company and the Coolies: Labour in Early Calcutta." In *The Urban Experience—Calcutta: Essays in Honour of Professor Nisith R. Ray*, edited by Pradip Sinha, 23-38. Calcutta: Riddhi-India, 1987.
———. "Masters and Banians in Eighteenth Century Calcutta." In *The Age of Partnership: Europeans in Asia before Dominion*, edited by B. B. Kling and M. N. Pearson, 191-213. Honolulu: University of Hawaii Press, 1979.
———, ed. *The British Discovery of Hinduism in the Eighteenth Century*. Cambridge: Cambridge University Press, 1970.
Marshman, John Clark. *The Life and Times of Carey, Marshman, and Ward, embracing the History of the Serampore Mission*. 2 vols. London: Longman et al., 1859.
———. "Notes on the Left or Calcutta Bank of the Hooghly." *Calcutta Review* 3 (January 1845). In *Calcutta Keepsake*, edited by Alok Ray, 181-82. Calcutta: Rddhi-India, 1978.
Martin, Lt. Col. Claude. "On the Manufacture of Indigo at Ambore." *Asiatic Researches*. New Delhi: Cosmo, 1979 [1799]. 3:475-76.
Martin, James Ranald. *Notes on the Medical Topography of Calcutta*. Calcutta: Bengal Military Orphen Press, 1837.
Martin, Montgomery. *The History, Antiquities, Topography, and Statistics of Eastern India*. 4 vols. London: Wm. H. Allen, 1838. Principally a compilation of survey materials by Francis Buchanan.
———, ed. *The Dispatches, Minutes, and Correspondence of the Marquess Wellesley, K. G.* 5 vols. London: Wm. H. Allen, 1837.
Martinelli, Antonio, and George Michell. *India Yesterday and Today: Two Hundred Years of Architecture and Topographical Heritage in India. Aquatints by Thomas and William Daniell, Modern Photographs by Antonio Martinelli, Text by George Michell*. Shrewsbury, England: Swan Hill Press, 1998.
Martyn, William Frederick. *A New Dictionary of Natural History*, 2 vols. London: Harrison & Co., 1785.
Mason, George Henry. *The Costume of China*. London: William Miller, 1800.
Mason, Philip. *A Matter of Honour: An Account of the Indian Army, its Officers and Men*. London: Jonathan Cape, 1974.
Mayor, A. Hyatt. *Prints and People: A Social History of Printed Pictures*. New York: The Metropolitan Museum of Art, 1971.
Maurice, Thomas. *The History of Hindostan*. 2 vols. London: Printed for the author, by W. Bulmer, 1795, 1798.
———. *Indian Antiquities*. 7 vols. London: Printed for the author, by H. L. Galabin, 1794-1801.
———. *Memoirs of an Author of Indian Antiquities*. London: Printed for the author, 1819-20.
McCutchion, David J. *Late Mediaeval Temples of Bengal: Origins and Classification*. Asiatic Society Monograph Series, Vol. 20. Calcutta: Asiatic Society, 1972.
———. "The Temples of Calcutta." *Bengal Past and Present* 87 (1968): 45-58.
———. See Michell, George, ed., *Brick Temples of Bengal*.
McLeod, W. H. *Historical Dictionary of Sikhism*. Lanham, Md: Scarescrow Press, 1995.
———. *The Sikhs: History, Religion, and Society*. New York: Columbia University Press, 1989.
Meerwarth, A. M. *A Guide to the Collection of Musical Instruments Exhibited in the Ethnographic Gallery of the Indian Museum, Calcutta*. Calcutta: Zoological Survey of India, 1917.
Meister, Michael. See Renou, Louis.
Mercure de France (Paris).

Michell, George, ed. *Brick Temples of Bengal: From the Archives of David McCutchion*. Princeton: Princeton University Press, 1983.
Milbourn, William. *Oriental Commerce*. New edition. London: Kinbgsbury, Parbury, and Allen, 1825. [First edition, 2 vols, London: 1813]
Miller, A. E. Haswell, and N. P. Dawnay. *Military Drawings and Paintings in the Collection of Her Majesty the Queen*. 2 vols. London: Phaidon, vol. 1, plates, 1966; vol. 2, text, 1970.
Miller, Russell. *The East Indiamen*. Alexandria, VA: Time-Life Books, 1980.
Milner, James D. "Tilly Kettle, 1735-1786." *The Walpole Society* 15 (1927): 47-103.
Miner, Allyn. "The Sitar: An Overview of Change." *The World of Music* 32 (1990), 27-57.
———· *Sitar and Sarod in the 18th and 19th Centuries*. Intercultural Music Studies 5. Wilhelmshaven, Germany: Florian Noetzel Verlag, 1993.
Mishra, K. C. *The Cult of Jagannatha*. Calcutta: Firma K. L. Mukhopadhyay, 1971.
Mishra, Vijayakanta. *Mahishamardini*. New Delhi: Rajesh, 1984.
Misra, Lalmani. *Bharatiya Sangit Vadya*. New Delhi: Bharatiya Jnanpith, 1973.
Mitra, Asok. *The Tribes and Castes of West Bengal, Census 1951, West Bengal*. Calcutta: West Bengal Government Press, 1953.
Mitra, Debrenda Bijoy. *The Cotton Weavers of Bengal, 1757-1833*. Calcutta: Firma KLM, 1978.
Mohanty, Surendra. *Lord Jagannatha*. Bhubaneswar: Orissa Sahitya Akademi, 1982.
Mohapatra, Gopinath. *The Land of Viṣṇu (A Study on Jagannātha Cult)*. Delhi: B. R. Publishing Corp., 1979.
Mollo, Boris. *The Indian Army*. Poole, Dorset: Blandford, 1981.
Monglond, André. *La France révolutionaire et impériale. Annales de bibliographie méthodique et description des livres illustrés*. 10 vols. Paris: Imprimerie Nationale, 1953-1963.
Moniteur universel. See *Gazette nationale, ou, Le Moniteur universel*.
Monier-Williams, Sir Monier. *A Sanskrit-English Dictionary*. Oxford: Clarendon Press, 1899.
Mookerjee, Ajitcoomar. *The Folk Art of Bengal*. Calcutta: University of Calcutta, 1939.
Mookerji, Radha Kumud. *Indian Shipping: A History of Seaborne Trade and Maritime Activity of the Indians from Earliest Times*. London: Longmans, Green and Co., 1912. Reprinted, Allahabad: Kitab Mahal, 1962.
Moor, Edward. *The Hindu Pantheon*. London: J. Johnson, 1810. Reprint, New York: Garland, 1984.
Motte, Thomas. "A Narrative of a Journey to the Diamond Mines at Sumbhulpoor, in the Province of Orissa." *Asiatic Annual Register . . . , for the year 1799*. 2d. ed. London J. Deyrett, 1801. *Miscellaneous Tracts*, 48-84.
Mukherjee [Mukhopadhyay], Amitabha. *Reform and Regeneration in Bengal, 1774-1823*. Calcutta: Rabindra Bharati University, 1968.
Mukherjee, Meera. *Metal Craftsmen of India*. Calcutta: Anthropological Survey of India, 1978.
Mukherjee, Nilmani. *The Port of Calcutta: A Short History*. Calcutta: Commissioners for the Port of Calcutta, 1968.
Mukherjee, Rudrangshu. "'Forever England': British life in Old Calcutta." In *Calcutta: The Living City*, edited by Sukanta Chaudhuri, 1:43-51. Calcutta: Oxford University Press, 1990.
Mukherjee, S. N. *Calcutta: Myths and History*. Calcutta: Subarnarekha, 1977.
———· *Sir William Jones: A Study in Eighteenth Century British Attitudes to India*. Bombay: Orient Longman, 1987.
Mukharji, T. N. *Art-Manufactures of India*. New Delhi: Navrang, 1974 [1888].
Mukhopadhyay [Mukherjee], Amitabha. "Sati as a Social Institution in Bengal." *Bengal Past and Present* 76 (1975): 99-115.
Mundy, Captain G. C. *Pen and Pencil Sketches, Being a Journal of a Tour of India*. 2 vols. London: John Murray, 1832.
Murdoch, John. *Hindu and Muhammadan Festivals*. New Delhi: Asian Educational Services, 1991 [1904].
Murray, H. J. R. *A History of Board-Games Other Than Chess*. Oxford: Clarendon Press, 1952.
Murray, Hugh, et al. *Historical and Descriptive Account of British India*. Edinburgh: Oliver & Boyd, 1832.

Nagler, G. K. *Neues allgemeines künstler-lexikon*. Munich: von E. A. Fleishmann, 1847.
Nair, P. Thankappan, ed. *British Social Life in Ancient Calcutta (1750 to 1850)*. Calcutta: Sanskrit Pustak Bhandar, 1983.
———, ed. *Calcutta in the 17th Century*. Calcutta: Firma KLM, 1986
———, ed. *Calcutta in the 18th Century*. Calcutta: Firma KLM, 1984.
———, ed. *Calcutta in the 19th Century*. Calcutta: Firma KLM, 1989.
———· "Civic and Public Services in Old Calcutta." In *Calcutta: The Living City*, edited by Sukanta Chaudhuri, 1:224-37. Calcutta: Oxford University Press, 1990.
———· "The Growth and Development of Old Calcutta." In *Calcutta: The Living City*, edited by Sukanta Chaudhuri, 1:10-23. Calcutta: Oxford University Press, 1990.
———, *Job Charnock: The Founder of Calcutta*. Calcutta: Engineering Times, 1977.
NGMI, *The New Grove Dictionary of Musical Instruments*. See Sadie.
Nanda, Serena. *Neither Man Nor Woman: The Hijras of India*. Belmont, CA: Wadsworth, 1990.
Nandy, Ashis. "Sati: A Nineteenth-Century Tale of Women, Violence and Protest." In *At the Edge of Psychology: Essays in Politics and Culture*, 1-31. Delhi: Oxford University Press, 1980.
Nandy, Somendra Chandra. *Life and Times of Cantoo Baboo: The Banian of Warren Hastings*. 2 vols. Vol. 1: Bombay: Allied, 1978; Vol. 2: Calcutta: Dev-All, 1981.
Narasimhan, Sakuntala. *Sati: A Study of Widow-Burning*. New Delhi: Viking, 1990.
Narrative Sketches of the Conquest of Mysore. 2d ed. London: 1800.
National Archives of India. *Fort William-India House Correspondence*. 21 vols. Delhi: Manager of Publications, 1958-1961.
National Maritime Museum. *Concise Catalog of Oil Paintings in the National Maritime Museum*. Woodbridge, Suffolk: Antique Collector's Club, 1988.
Naufragus. See Moffat James Horne.
Navari, Leonara. *Greece and the Levant: The Catalogue of the Henry Myon Blackmer Collection of Books and Manuscripts*. London: Maggs, 1989.
Nayak, Narendra Kumar, ed. *Calcutta 200 Years: A Tollygunge Club Perspective*. Calcutta: Tollygunge Club, 1981.

Nevile, Pran. "The Nautch Girl and the Sahib." *India Magazine* (January 1990): 42-52.
———. *Nautch Girls of India: Dancers, Singers, Playmates*. New Delhi: Ravi Kumar, 1996.
Nicolay, Nicholas de. *Les Navigations, pèrègrinations et voyages faits en la Turquie*. Antwerp: G. Sillvius, 1576. English translation: *The Navigations, Peregrinations, and Voyages, made into Turkie*. London: Thomas Dawson, 1585. [Facsimile edition, New York: Da Capo Press, 1968.]
Nieuhof, Johannes. "Mr. John Nieuhoff's Remarkable Voyages and Travels into the East Indies. *A Collection of Voyages and Travels, some now printed from original manuscripts. . . ,* edited by Awnsham Churchill and John Churchill, 2:181-369. 4 vols. London: 1704. [2nd ed., 6 vols. London: 1732. 3d ed. 6 vols. London: 1744.]
Nilsson, Sten. *European Architecture in India, 1750-1850*. London: Faber & Faber, 1968.
Noel, John V. *The VNR Dictionary of Ships and the Sea*. New York: Van Nostrand Reinhold, 1981.
Nouvelle biographie générale. 46 vols. Paris: Didot Frères, 1853-1866.
Nugent, Lady Maria. *A Journal From the Year 1811 till the Year 1815*. 2 vols. London: 1839.

OED. *Oxford English Dictionary*.
Oberoi, Harjot. *The Construction of Religious Boundaries: Culture, Identity, and Diversity in the Sikh Tradition*. Chicago: University of Chicago Press, 1994.
Oddie, Geoffrey A. *Popular Religion, Elites and Reform: Hook-Swinging and its Prohibition in Colonial India, 1800-1894*. New Delhi: Manohar, 1995.
Okada, Amina, and Enrico Isacco. *L'Inde du XIXe siècle: voyage aux sources de l'imaginaire*. Marseille: AGEP, 1991.
Olivelle, Patrick. *The Āśrama System: The History and Hermeneutics of a Religious Institution*. New York: Oxford University Press, 1993.
———. "Hair and Society: Social Significance of Hair in South Asian Traditions." In *Hair: Its Power and Meaning in Asian Cultures*, edited by Alf Hiltebeitel and Barbara Miller, 11-49. New York: State University of New York Press, 1998.
O'Malley, L. S. S. *Bengal District Gazetteers: Balasore*. Calcutta: Bengal Secretariat Book Depot, 1907.
———. *Bengal District Gazetteers: Chittagong*. Calcutta: Bengal Secretariat Depot, 1908.
———. *Bengal District Gazetteers: Puri*. New Delhi: Usha, 1984 [1908].
———. "The Insignia of Hindu Sects," *Census Report of Bengal, 1911*, 252-55. In *The Tribes and Castes of West Bengal, Census 1951, West Bengal*. Calcutta: West Bengal Government Press, 1953, 272-74.
———. *Popular Hinduism, the Religion of the Masses*. Cambridge: Cambridge University Press, 1935.
O'Malley, L. S. S., and Monmohan Chakravarti. *Bengal District Gazetteers: Hooghly*. Calcutta: Bengal Secretariat Book Depot, 1912. Reprinted New Delhi: Logos Press, 1985.
Oman, John C. *The Mystics, Ascetics, and Saints of India*. 2d ed. London: T. Fisher Unwin, 1905.
———. *Cults, Customs and Superstitions in India*. 2d ed. Delhi: Indian Bibliographies Bureau, 1991 [1908].
Oriental Annual, 1835. London: Bull and Churton, 1835.
Oriental Annual, 1837. London: Charles Tilt, 1837.
Oriental Miscellany. Calcutta: 1798.
Orme, Edward. *An Essay on Transparent Prints, and on Transparencies in General*. London: Edward Orme, 1807.
———. See Solvyns, *The Costume of Indoostan*.
Orme, Robert. *A History of Military Transactions of the British Nation in Indostan from the Year 1745*. 3 vols. London: J. Nourse, 1663-1778.
Orme, William. *Twenty-four Views in Hindostan, Drawn by William Orme From the Original Pictures Painted by Mr. Daniell & Colonel Ward*. London: Edward Orme, 1805.
———. See Solvyns, *The Costume of Indoostan*.
Östör, Ákos. *Culture and Power: Legend, Ritual, Bazaar and Rebellion in Bengali Society*. New Delhi: Sage, 1984.
———. *The Play of the Gods: Locality, Ideology, Structure, and Time in the Festivals of a Bengali Town*. Chicago: University of Chicago Press, 1980.

Paepe, P. de. See De Paepe.
Pal, K. B. *Handicrafts Survey Monograph on Cutlery of Jhalda, Census of India 1961, West Bengal & Sikkim*, Vol. XVI, Pt. VII-A(12). Calcutta: Government of India Press, 1967.
Pal, Pratapaditya. "Indian Artists and British Patrons in Calcutta." In *Changing Visions, Lasting Images: Calcutta through 300 Years*, edited by Pratapaditya Pal, 125-42. Bombay: Marg Publications, 1990. Reprinted in *Marg*, 41, 4 (1990), 17-34.
———. "Kali, Calcutta, and Kalighat Pictures." In *Changing Visions, Lasting Images: Calcutta through 300 Years*, edited by Pratapaditya Pal, 109-24. Bombay: Marg Publications, 1990.
Pal, Pratapaditya, and Vidya Dehejia. *From Merchants to Emperors: British Artists and India, 1757-1930*. Ithaca: Cornell University Press, 1986.
Panda, Daityari, and Sarat Chandra Panigrahi. *The Cult and Culture of Lord Jagannath*. Cuttack: Rashtrabhasha Samavaya Prakashan, 1984.
Parks, Fanny. *Wanderings of a Pilgrim, in Search of the Picturesque*. 2 vols. Karachi: Oxford University Press, 1975 [1850].
Parraud, Abbé. See Wilkins, *The Bhăgvăt-Gēētā*.
Parry, Jonathan. *Death in Banaras*. Cambridge: Cambridge University Press, 1994.
Patnaik, Himanshu S. *Lord Jagannath: His Temple, Cult, Festivals*. New Delhi: Aryan Books, 1994.
Paulinus (Paolino) a S. Bartholomaeo. *Dissertation on the Sanskrit Language*. A reprint of the original Latin text of 1790, together with an introductory article, a complete English translation, and index of sources by Ludo Rocher. Amsterdam: John Benjamins, 1977.
———. *Systema Brahmanicum*. Rome: A. Fulgonium, 1791.
———. *Viaggio alle Indie Oriental*. Rome: A. Fulgoni, 1796.
———. *A Voyage to the East Indies*. Translated from German by William Johnson, with notes and illustrations by John Reinhold Foster. London: Vernor and Hood, 1799. Reprinted London: J. Davis, 1800.
Pavière, Sydney H. *The Devis Family of Painters*. Leigh-on-Sea: F. Lewis, 1950.
Peggs, Rev. J. *India's Cries to British Humanitiy, relative to the suttee, infanticide, British connexion with idoloary, ghaut murders, and slavery in India*. 2nd rev. ed. London: Seeley & Son, 1830.
Pearson, Roger. *Eastern Interlude: A Social History of the European Community in Calcutta*. Calcutta: Thacker & Spink, 1954.

Pennant, Thomas. *The View of Hindoostan*. 2 vols. London: Henry Hughs, 1798.
Persoons, Guido. *Schone Kunsten in Antwerpen* [Fine Arts in Antwerp]. Antwerp: Nationaal Hoger Insitutut en Koninklijke Academie voor Schone Kunsten, 1976.
Phillimore, R. H. *Historical Records of the Survey of India*. 2 vols. Dehra Dun: Survey of India, 1945, 1950.
Philips, C. H. *The East India Company 1784-1834*. Manchester: Manchester University Press, 1961.
Phillips, Sir Richard. *Geography, on a Popular Plan, designed for the use of schools, and young persons: illustrated with sixty copper-plates., . . . by Rev. J. Goldsmith* [pseud.]. 5th ed. London: Richard Phillips, 1808.
Phipps, John. *A Collection of Papers, Relative to Ship Building in India*. Calcutta: Scott and Co., 1840.
Picart, Bernard, ed. *Cérémonies et coutumes religieuses des tous les peuples du monde*. 9 vols. Amsterdam: Chez J. F. Bernard, 1723-1743. Tr. *The Religious Ceremonies and Customs of the Several Nations of the Known World*. 6 vols. London: 1731. Compiled from the works of various writers, including Abraham Roger.
Pigott, John P. *A Treatise on the Horses of India*. Calcutta: James White, 1794.
Pitoëss, Pribislav. "Timila." NGMI, 3:586.
Playfair, John. "Questions and Remarks on the Astronomy of the Hindus." *Asiatick Researches*. New Delhi: Cosmo, 1979 [1795], 4:151-55.
Polier, A. L. H. "The Siques" [1787]. *Indian Studies: Past & Present* 3 (1962): 181-243. Reprinted in *Early European Accounts of the Sikhs*, edited by Ganda Singh, 53-69. Calcutta: Indian Studies: Past & Present, 1962.
Popham, Hugh. *"A Damned Cunning Fellow": The Full Life & Adventures of Rear-Admiral Sir Home Popham*. Tywardreath, Cornwall: Old Ferry Press, 1991.
Portman, M. V. *A History of Our Relations with the Andamanese*. Calcutta: Office of the Superintendent of Government Printing, 1899.
Potts, E. Daniel. *British Baptist Missionaries in India, 1793-1837: The History of Serampore and its Missions*. Cambridge: Cambridge University Press, 1967.
Powell, J. H. "Hook-Swinging in India." *Folk-lore* 25 (June 1914): 147-97.
Preston, Laurence W. "A Right to Exist: Eunuch and the State in Nineteenth-Century India." *Modern Asian Studies* 21 (1987), 371-87.
Price, Uvedale. *An Essay on the Picturesque*. London: J. Robson, 1794.
Prideaux, S. T. *Aqautint Engraving: A Chapter in the History of Book Illustration*. London: W. & G. Foyle, 1968 [1909].
Prims, Floris. *Antwerpiensia 1929. Losse bijdragen tot de Antwerpsche geschiedenis*. Antwerp: De Vlijt, 1930.
———. "Max en Jean-Pierre Solvyns." In *Antwerpiensia 1933. Losse bijdragen tot de Antwerpsche geschiedenis*, 310-18. Antwerp: De Vlijt, 1934.
———. "Pierre Jean Solvyns." In *Biographies Anversoises illustrées*. Antwerp: Editions de Papegay, 1941.
Prinsep, G. A. *An Account of Steam Vessels and of Proceedings Connected with Steam Navigation in British India*. Calcutta: Government Gazette Press, 1830.
Quèrard, Joseph-Marie, ed. *La France littéraire, ou Dictionnaire bibliographique des savants, historiens et gens de lettres de la France*. 12 vols. Paris: G. Firmin Didot Fréres, 1827-1864.

Rahman, M. Akhlaqur. *The Country Boats of East Pakistan: An Economic Analysis*. Dhaka: East Pakistan Inland Water Transport Authority, 1963.
Rainey, H. James. *A Historical and Topographical Sketch of Calcutta*. Edited by P. Thankappan Nair. Calcutta: Sanskrit Pustak Bhandar, 1986 [1876].
Rāmāyaṇa. Translated by William Carey and Joshua Marshman under the title *The Ramayuna of Valmeeki*. Serampore: Mission Press, 1806-10.
Ray, A. K. *A Short History of Calcutta: Town and Suburbs* [Census of India, 1901, Vol. VII, Pt. I]. Calcutta: Rddhi-India, 1982 [1902].
Ray, Ajit Kumar. *Widows are not for Burning*. New Delhi: ABC Publishing House, 1985.
Ray, Alok, ed. *Calcutta Keepsake*. Calcutta: Rddhi-India, 1978.
Ray, Ashim Kumar, and N. N. Gidwani, eds. *Dictionary of Indology*. 4 vols. New Delhi: Oxford & IBH, 1983.
Ray, Gordon N. *The Art of the French Illustrated Book, 1700-1914*. 2 vols. New York: The Pierpont Morgan Library/Ithaca: Cornell University Press, 1982.
Ray, Nisith Ranjan. *Calcutta: The Profile of a City*. Calcutta: K. B. Bagchi, 1986.
———. "Calcutta Houses and Streets in 1789." *Bulletin of the Victoria Memorial* 8 (1974): 41-50.
———. *The City of Job Charnock*. Calcutta: Victoria Memorial, 1979.
———. "George Lyell Collection in the Victoria Memorial, Calcutta." *Bulletin of the Victoria Memorial* 5 (1971): 55-72.
Ray, Sudhansu Kumar. "The Chitrakaras or Patuas (Painters)." In *The Tribes and Castes of West Bengal*, edited by Asok Mitra, 307-14.
———. "The Kangsakaras (Makers of kangsa or kansha, an alloy)." In *The Tribes and Castes of West Bengal*, edited by Asok Mitra, 333-36.
———. "The Karmakaras (Ironsmiths)." In *The Tribes and Castes of West Bengal*, edited by Asok Mitra, 329-31.
———. "The Kumbhakaras (Potters and Clay-Modelers)." In *The Tribes and Castes of West Bengal*, edited by Asok Mitra, 315-20.
———. "The Sankhakaras or Sankharis (Makers of Conch-Shell Bangles." In *Castes and Tribes of West Bengal*, edited by Asok Mitra, 340-41.
———. "The Sutradharas (Architects and Architectural Wood-Carvers)." In *The Tribes and Castes of West Bengal*, edited by Asok Mitra, 321-28.
———. "The Tantubayas or Tantis (weavers)." In *Castes and Tribes of West Bengal*, edited by Asok Mitra, 342-43.
Ray, Sukumar. *Folk-Music of Eastern India, with Special Reference to Bengal*. Shimla: Indian Institute of Advanced Studies/Calcutta: Naya Prakash, 1988.
———. *Music of Eastern India*. Calcutta: Firma K. L. Mukhopadhyay, 1973.
Raychaudhuri, Tapan. "Norms of Family Life and Personal Morality Among the Bengali Hindu Elite, 1600-1850." In *Aspects of Bengali History and Society*, Asian Studies at Hawaii, No. 12, edited by Rachael Van M. Baumer. Honolulu: University Press of Hawaii, 1975.

Raychaudhuri, Tarak Ch., and Bikash Raychaudhuri. *The Brahmans of Bengal*. Calcutta: Anthropological Survey of India, 1981.

Recherches asiatiques; au, Mémoires de la société établie au Bengale [Annotated French translation of vols. 1-2 of *Asiatick Researches*]. 2 vols. Paris: l'Imprimerie Impériale, 1805

Redouté, Pierre-Joseph. *Les roses*. 3 vols. Paris: Imprimerie de Firmin Didot, 1817-1824.

Rennell, James. *A Bengal Atlas*. London: East India Co., 1781.

———. *Memoir of a Map of Hindoostan*. London: 1779. Various editions.

Renou, Louis. "The Vedic Hut." Preface and translation by Michael W. Meister. *Res, Anthropology and Aesthetics* 34 (Winter 1998):141-61.

Revet-Carnac, S. *Presidential Armies of India*. London: W. H. Allen, 1890.

Revue Belge (Liège). "Baux-Arts." 23 (January-April 1843): 90-91.

Risley, Herbert H. *The People of India*. 2d ed. Delhi: Oriental Books Reprint Corp., 1969 [1915].

———. *The Tribes and Castes of Bengal*. 2 vols. Calcutta: Bengal Secretariat Press, 1891.

Rizvi, S. N. H. *East Pakistan District Gazetteers: Chittagong*. Dacca: East Pakistan Government Press, 1970.

Roberdeau, I. H. T. "A Young Civilian in Bengal in 1805." *Bengal Past and Present* 29: 110-47. In *Calcutta in the 19th Century*, edited by Nair, 36-85.

Roberts, Emma. *Scenes and Characteristics of Hindostan, with Sketches of Anglo-Indian Society*. 3 vols. London: W. H. Allen, 1835. 2d ed. 2 vols. London: W. H. Allen, 1837.

Robertson, William. *An Historical Disquisition Concerning the Knowledge which the Ancients had of India*. London: A. Strahan and T. Cadell, 1791.

Rocher, Rosane. *Alexander Hamilson (1762-1824): A Chapter in the Early History of Sanskrit Philology*. New Haven: American Oriental Society, 1968.

———. "British Orientalism in the Eighteenth Century: The Dialectics of Knowledge and Government." In *Orientalism and the Postcolonial Predicament: Perspectives on South Asia*, edited by Carol A. Breckenridge and Peter van der Veer, 215-49. Philadelphia: University of Pennsylvania Press, 1993.

———. *Orientalism, Poetry, and the Millennium: The Checkered Life of Nathaniel Brassey Halhed, 1751-1830*. Delhi: Motilal Banarsidass, 1983.

Roger [Rogerius], Abraham. *De open-deure tot het verborgen heydendom* [The Open Door to Occult Paganism]. Leyden: Francoys Hackes, 1651.

———. *Théatre de l'idolatrie ou la porte ouverte, pour parvenir à la connoissance du paganisme caché*. French translation of *De open-deure,* from the Dutch by T. LaGrue. Amsterdam: Chez Jean Schipper, 1670.

———. See Picart.

Rohatgi, Pauline. "The Growth of Georgian Calcutta Seen through the Eyes of British Artists." In *European Artists and India 1700-1900*, edited by Hiren Chakrabarti, 7-13. Calcutta: Victoria Memorial, 1987.

———. "The India Office Library's Prints of Calcutta." In *India Office Library & Records Report 1 April 1972 to 31 Decembere 1973*, 7-24. London: 1975.

———. *Portraits in the India Office Library and Records*. London: British Library, 1983.

———, and Pheroza Godrej, eds. *India: A Pageant of Prints*. Bombay: Marg Publications, 1989.

———, eds. *Under the Indian Sun: British Landscape Artists*. Bombay: Marg Publications, 1995.

———, and Graham Parlett. *The British Artist in India: A Catalogue of the Collections at the Victoria & Albert Museum*. London: Victoria and Albert Museum, forthcoming.

———. Also see under Godrej.

Roonwal, M. L., and S. M. Mohnot. *Primates of South Asia*. Cambridge: Harvard University Press, 1977.

Rose, Horace A. *A Glossary of the Tribes and Castes of the Punjab and North Western Frontier Province*. 3 vols. Delhi: Languages Department, Punjab, 1970 [1919].

Rosenfeld, Sybil. *Georgian Scene Painting*. Cambridge: Cambridge University Press, 1981.

Rosenthal, Donald. *Orientalism: The Near East in French Painting 1800-1880*. Rochester: Memorial Art Gallery of the University of Rochester, 1982.

Rousslet, Louis. *India of the Rajahs*. Milan: Franco Maria Ricci, 1985 [1882].

Roux, Marcel. *Inventaire du fonds français; graveurs du XIIIe siècle*. 14 vols. Paris: Bibliothèque nationale, 1949.

Roy, Benoy Bhusan. *Socioeconomic Impact of Sati in Bengal*. Calcutta: Naya Prakash, 1987.

Roy, Buddhadev. *Marriage Rituals and Songs of Bengal*. Calcutta: Firma KLM, 1984.

Roy, Indrani Basu. *Kalighat: Its Impact on Socio-Cultural Life of Hindus*. New Delhi: Gyan, 1993.

Roy, Nandini. "Durga Puja." In *Festivals of India*, 11-22. New Delhi: Ministry of Education and Social Welfare, Government of India, 1977.

Roy, Satindra Narayan. "The Festivities in Honour of Siva in the Month of Chaitra." *Journal of the Anthropological Society of Bombay* 14 (1927): 181-85.

Russell, Patrick. *An Account of Indian Serpents, Collected on the Coast of Coromandel*. 2 vols. London: George Nicol, 1796, 1801.

Russell, R. V. *The Tribes and Castes of the Central Provinces of India*. 4 vols. London: Macmillan, 1916. Reprinted Delhi: Cosmo, 1975.

Russell, Ronald. *Guide to British Topographical Prints*. North Pomfret, VT: David & Charles, c1979.

Sadie, Stanley, ed. *The New Grove Dictionary of Musical Instruments* [NGMI]. 3 vols. London: Macmillan, 1984.

Said, Edward W. *Orientalism*. New York: Random House, 1978.

Saint Génois, Jules de. *Les voyagers Belges du XVIIe et du XIXe siècle*. 2 vols. Brussels: A. Jamar [1847].

Sandby, Paul. *Twelve Views in Aquatinta from Drawings Taken on the Spot in South-Wales*. London: J. Boydell, 1775.

Santra, Tarapada. "Architects and Builders." In *Brick Temples of Bengal*, edited by George Michell, 53-62. Princeton: Princeton University Press, 1983.

Sanyal, Charu Chandra. *The Rajbansis of North Bengal*. The Asiatic Monograph Series, Vol. 11. Calcutta: The Asiatic Society, 1965.

Sanyal, Hitesranjan. "Continuities of Social Mobility in Traditional and Modern Society in India: Two Case Studies of Caste Mobility in Bengal." *Journal of Asian Studies* 30 (Fall 1971): 315-40. Reprinted in Sanyal, *Social Mobility in Bengal*.

———. *Social Mobility in Bengal*. Calcutta: Papyrus, 1981.

Saraswati, Baidyanath, and N. K. Behura. *Pottery Techniques in Peasant India*, Memoir No. 13. Calcutta: Anthropological Survey of India, 1966.

Sarkar, Benoy Kumar. *The Folk-Element in Hindu Culture.* New Delhi: Oriental Book Reprint Corp., 1972 [1917].

Sarkar, Judunath. *A History of Dāsnāmi Nāgā Sanyāsīs.* Allahabad: Sri Panchayata Akhara Mahanirvani, 1958.

Sarkar, Nikhil. "Printing and the Spirit of Calcutta." In *Calcutta: The Living City*, edited by Sukanta Chaudhuri, 1:128-36. Calcutta: Oxford University Press, 1990.

Sarkar, Smriti Kumar. "Caste, Occupation and Social Mobility: A Study of the Kansaris in Colonial Bengal." In *Bengal: Communities, Development and States*, edited by Sekhar Bandyopadhyay, 65-98. New Delhi: Manohar, 1994.

Śarṅgadeva. *Saṅgitaratnākara.* Edited by Pandit S. Subrahmanya Sastri. Madras: Adyar Library, 1951.

Sax, William S., ed. *The Gods at Play: Lila in South Asia.* New York: Oxford University Press, 1995.

Schnapper, Antoine, and Aarlette Serullaz, eds. *Jacques Louis David, 1748-1825.* Paris: Eds. de la Reunion des musses nationalux, 1989.

Schwab, Raymond. *The Oriental Renaissance: Europe's Rediscovery of India and the East, 1680-1800.* Translated by Gene Patterson-Black and Victor Reinking. New York: Columbia University Press, 1984.

Sen, Prabhas. *Crafts of West Bengal.* Ahmedabad: Mapin Publishing, 1994.

———. "Potters and Pottery of West Bengal. " In *Arts of Bengal and Eastern India*, edited by R. P. Gupta. Calcutta: Crafts Council of West Bengal, 1982.

Sen, Ram Comal. "Charak Puja Ceremonies." *Journal of the Asiatic Society of Bengal*, 2 (1833): 609-12. Reprinted in Oddie, 151-56.

Sen, Ranjit. *Calcutta in the Eighteenth Century.* Vol. 1. Calcutta: OPS Publishers, 1985.

———. *New Elite and New Collaborations: A Study of Social Transformations in Bengal in the Eighteenth Century.* Calcutta: Papyrus, 1985.

———. *Social Banditry in Bengal: A Study in Primary Resistence, 1757-1793.* Calcutta: Ratna Prakashan, 1988.

Sen, Sukumar. *An Etymological Dictionary of Bengali: c. 1000-1800 A.D.* Calcutta: Eastern, 1971.

Sen, Surendra Nath. *The Military System of the Marathas.* 2d ed. Calcutta: Bagchi, 1979 [1958].

Sen Gupta, Sankar. "A Note on Soma and Bel-tree and their Presiding Deities—Chandra and Siva." In *Popular Festivals of India*, edited by Sunil Kumar Nag, 105-06. Calcutta: Golden Books, 1983.

———, ed. *The Patas and the Patuas of Bengal.* Calcutta: Indian Publications, 1973.

Seton-Karr, W. S. *Selections from Calcutta Gazettes. . . . showing the political and social condition of the English in India.* Micrographic ed. 9 vols. Calcutta: Bibhash Gupta, 1987. Volumes 1-5 by W.S. Seton-Karr; vols. 6-9 by Hugh David Sandeman and Anil Chandra. Originally published Calcutta: Military Orphans Press, 1864-1869. Contents: v. 1. 1784-1788; v. 2. 1789-1792; v. 3. 1793-1797; v. 4. 1798-1801; v. 5. 1803-1805; v. 6-7. 1806-1815; v. 8-9. 1816-1823.

Sharma, Brijendra Nath. *Festivals of India.* New Delhi: Abhinav, 1978.

Shaw, Graham. *Printing in Calcutta to 1800.* London: Bibliographical Society, 1981.

Shellim, Maurice. *India and the Daniells.* London: Inchcape/Spink & Son, 1979.

Sherring, Mathew A. *Hindu Tribes and Castes.* 3 vols. Delhi: Cosmo, 1974 [1872-1881].

Shirali, Vishnudass. *Sargam: An Introduction to Indian Music.* New Delhi: Abhinav/Marg, 1977.

Shrivastav, P. N. *Madhya Pradesh District Gazetters: Indore.* Bhopal: Government of Madhya Pradesh, 1971.

Shoberl, Frederic, ed. *The World in Miniature: Hindoostan.* 6 vols. London: R. Ackermann [1822].

Shore, Sir John. "On Some Extraordinary Facts, Customs, and Practices of the Hindus." *Asiatick Researches.* New Delhi: Cosmo, 1979 [1795], 4:329-48.

Siddiqui, M. K. A. *Aspects of Society and Culture in Calcutta.* Calcutta: Anthropological Survey of India, 1982.

———. "The Patuas of Calcutta: A Study in Indentity Crisis." In *Aspects of Society and Culture in Calcutta*, 49-66.

Siddiqui, M. K. A., and Pranab Jyoti De. "The Image-Makers of Kumartoli." In *Aspects of Society and Culture in Calcutta*, 101-18.

Siddons, Joachim H. See Stocqueler, J. H.

Singh, Madan Paul. *Indian Army Under the East India Company.* New Delhi: Sterling, 1976.

Singh, Ganda, ed. *Early European Accounts of the Sikhs.* Calcutta: Indian Studies: Past & Present, 1962.

Singh, Khushwant. *A History of the Sikhs.* 2 vols. Princeton: Princeton University Press, 1963.

Singh, Raghubir. *Ganga: Sacred River of India.* Hong Kong: Perennial Press, 1974.

Sinha, N. K. *The Economic History of Bengal, 1793-1848.* 3 vols. Calcutta: Firma K. L. Mukhopadhyay, 1970.

———, ed. *The History of Bengal (1757-1905).* Calcutta: University of Calcutta, 1967.

Sinha, Pradip. *Calcutta in Urban History.* Calcutta: Firma KLM, 1978.

———. "Printed Sources for 18th and 19th Century Studies." In *Primary Printed and Manuscript Sources for Sixteenth to Nineteenth Century Studies Available in Bengal, Orissa and Bihar Libraries*, edited by Katherine S. Diehl. Calcutta: American Institute of Indian Studies, 1971.

———. "Social Change." In *The History of Bengal (1757-1905)*, edited by N. K. Sinha. Calcutta: University of Calcutta, 1967.

Sinha, Sukumar. *Handicrafts Survey Monograph on Conch Shell Products, Census of India 1961*, Vol. 16, *West Bengal & Sikkim*, Pt. VII-A(i). Calcutta: Government of India Press, 1965.

Sircar, Jawhar. "The Chinese of Calcutta." In *Calcutta: The Living City*, edited by Sukanta Chaudhuri, 2:64-66. Calcutta: Oxford University Press, 1990.

Siret, Adolphe. *Dictionnaire historique des peintres.* Brussels: Périchon, 1848.

Sivananda, Swami. *Hindu Fasts and Festivals.* Shivanandanagar: Divine Life Society, 1947.

Sketches of India; or Observations Descriptive of the Scenery, &c, in Bengal. London: Black, Parbury, and Allen, 1816.

Sketches of India: Written by an Officer for Fire-side Travellers at Home. London: Longman et al., 1821.

Smith, Bernard. *Imagining the Pacific: In the Wake of the Cook Voyages.* New Haven: Yale University Press, 1992.

———. See Joppien and Smith.

Smith, George. *The Life of William Carey.* London: John Murray, 1885.

Smith, Jerome I. "An Eighteenth-century Turkish Delight." *The Connoisseur* 156 (July 1964): 215-19.

Smith, Philip Chadwick Foster. *More Marine Paintings and Drawings in the Peabody Museum*. Salem, MA: Peabody Museum, 1979.

Smyth, Adm. William Henry. *The Sailor's Word-Book: An Alphabetical Digest of Nautical Terms*. London: Blackie and Son, 1867.

Solvyns, François Balthazar [Baltazard]. *A Catalogue of 250 Coloured Etchings; Descriptive of the Manners, Customs, Character, Dress, and Religious Ceremonies of the Hindoos*. Calcutta: Mirror Press, 1799.

———. *A Collection of Two Hundred and Fifty Coloured Etchings: Descriptive of the Manners, Customs and Dresses of the Hindoos*. Calcutta, 1796, 1799.

———. *The Costume of Indostan* [pirated edition]. London: Edward Orme [1804-05], 1807.

———. *Les Hindoûs*. 4 vols. Paris: Chez L'Auteur, 1808-1812.

———. See Unpublished.

Sonnerat, Pierre. *Voyage aux Indes Orientales et à la Chine*. 3 vols. Paris:L'auteur, 1782.

———. *A Voyage of the East-Indies and China*. Translated from the French by Francis Magnus. 3 vols. Calcutta: Stuart and Cooper, 1788, 1789.

Sorrell, Neil, and Mireille Helffer. "Sāraṅgī." NGMI, 3:294-96.

Spear, Percival. *The Nabobs: A Study of the Social Life of the English in Eighteenth Century India*. London: Oxford University Press, 1963.

Spink. *A Journey Through India: Pictures of India by British Artists* (catalog of the sale, October 9-November 1, 1996). London: Spink, 1996.

Spooner, Shearjashub. *A Biographical and Critical Dictionary of Painters, Engravers, Sculptors, and Architects, From Ancient to Modern Times*. New York: G. P. Putnam, 1853.

Sreemani, Soumitra. *Anatomy of a Colonial Town: Calcutta, 1756-1794*. Calcutta: Firma KLM, 1994.

Srinivas, M. N. *Caste in Modern India and Other Essays*. Bombay: Asia Publishing House, 1962.

Staes, Josef. *Antwerpsche reizigers* [Antwerp Travelers]. Antwerp: Lodwijk Janseens, [c.1884].

Stanhope, Philip Dormer ["Asiaticus"]. *Genuine Memoirs of Asiaticus*. 2d ed. Reprint by the Calcutta Historical Society. Introduction and notes by Walter Kelly Firminger. Hugli: L. Chowdhury, 1909 [1785].

Starza, O. M. *The Jagannatha Temple at Puri: Its Architecture, Art and Cult*. Leiden: E. J. Brill, 1993.

Stavorinus, Johan Splinter. *Voyages to the East-Indies* [1768-71]. Translated from the Dutch by Samuel H. Wilcocke. 3 vols. London: G. G. and J. Robinson, 1798.

Sterndale, Riginald C. *An Historical Account of 'The Calcutta Collectorate'*. Calcutta: West Bengal Government Press, 1958 [1885].

Stocqueler, J. H. [Joachim H. Siddons]. "Calcutta As It Is." In *British Social Life in Ancient Calcutta*, edited by P. Thankappan Nair, 110-252. Calcutta: Sanskrit Pustak Bhandar, 1983. Originally published the *Asiatic Journal*, 1843-44.

———. *The Hand-Book of India*. London: W. H. Allen, 1844.

———. *The Oriental Interpreter*. London: James Madden, 1848.

Stuebe, Isabel C. *Life and Work of William Hodges*. New York: Garland, 1979.

Stutley, Margaret, and James Stutley. *Harper's Dictionary of Hinduism*. New York: Harper & Row, 1977.

Sutton, Jean. *Lords of the East: The East India Company and its Ships*. London: Conway Maritime Press, 1981.

Sutton, Thomas. *The Daniells: Artists and Travelers*. London: Bodley Head, 1954.

Suykens, F., et al., eds. *Antwerp: A Port for all Seasons*. Antwerp: MIM, 1986.

Sweetman, John. *The Oriental Obsession: Islamic Inspiration in British and American Art and Architecture, 1500-1920*. Cambridge: Cambridge University Press, 1988.

Sykes, Laura, ed. *Calcutta Through British Eyes, 1690-1990*. New Delhi: Oxford University Press, 1992.

Symes, Lt. Col. "An Account of the Andaman Islands." In *Asiatic Annual Register, for the year 1800*, "Miscellaneous Tracts, 89-95. London: J. Debrett, 1801.

Tagore, Sourindro Mohun, ed. *Hindu Music From Various Authors*. Chowkhamba Sanskrit Studies, 49. Varanasi: Chowkhamba Sanskrit Series Office, 1965 [1882].

Tarlo, Emma. *Clothing Matters: Dress and Identity in India*. London: Hurst & Co., 1996.

Tayler, William. *Sketches Illustrating the Manners and Customs of the Indians and Anglo-Indians*. London: Thomasa McLean, 1842.

———. *Thirty-eight Years in India*. 2 vols. London: W. H. Allen, 1881, 1882.

Tavernier, Jean-Baptiste. *Les Six Voyages de Jean-Baptiste Tavernier*. 3 vols. Paris: 1703 [1676] . English ed., *The Six Voyages of John Baptista Tavernier*. London: John Starkey, 1678.

———. *Travels in India by Jean Baptiste Travernier*. Translated from the original l676 French edition by V. A. Ball, 2d ed., edited by William Crooke. 2 vols. New Delhi: Oriental Books Reprint Corp., 1977 [1889].

Teltscher, Kate. *India Inscribed: European and British Writing on India 1600-1800*. Delhi: Oxford University Press, 1995.

Tennant, Rev. William. *Indian Recreations; consisting chiefly of strictures on the domestic and rural economy of the Mohomedans & Hindoos*. 2d ed. 3 vols. London: Longman, Hurst, Rees & Orwe, 1804-08.

Ter Bruggen, Edouard. *Historie de la gravure d'Anvers. Catalogue de la collection Ter Bruggen, eaux-fortes & gravures de maîtres Anvrsois det des peintres & graveurs. . . . Propiété de la ville d'Anvrs par Ed. Ter Bruggen*. Antwerp: 1874-1875.

Thapliyal, U. P., ed. *Military Costumes of India*. New Delhi: Government of India, Ministry of Defence, Historical Section, 1991.

Tharoor, Tilottama, ed. *Naari: A Tribute to the Women of Calcutta 1690-1990*. Calcutta: Ladies Study Group, c. 1990.

Thieme, Ulrich, and Felix Becker. "Solvyns." In *Allgemeines Lexikon der bildenden Künstler* [Thieme-Becker *Künstler-Lexikon*], 37:260. Leipzig: E. A. Seeman [1937].

Thomas, Paul. *Hindu Religion, Custom and Manners*. Bombay: D. B. Taraporevala Sons, 1960.

Tief(f)enthaler, Joseph. *Erdbeschreibung von Indien und Hindustan*. Berlin: Gotha, 1785. *La geographie de l'Indoustan*. Vol. 1 of *Description historique et geographique de l'nde*, edited and translated by Jean Bernoulli. Berlin: C. S. Spener, 1786.

Tillotson, Giles H. R. *The Artificial Empire: The Indian Landscapes of William Hodges*. Richmond, Surrey, UK: Curzon, 2000.

———. "The Indian Picturesque: Images of India in British Landscape Painting, 1780-1880." In *The Raj: India and the British 1600-1947*, edited by C. A. Bayly, 141-51. London: National Portrait Gallery, 1990.

Timberg, Thomas. *The Marwaris: From Traders to Industrialists.* New Delhi: Vikas, 1978.

Tod, James. *Annals and Antiquities of Rajasthan.* 2 vols. New Delhi: K.M.N., 1971 [1829-32].

Thompson, Edward. *Suttee.* London: George Allen & Unwin, 1928.

Tijs, Rutger J. *R. R. Rubens en J. Joraens barok in eigen huis.* Antwerp: Stichting Mercator-Plantjin, 1984.

Tooley, R. V. *English Books with Colourd Plates, 1790 to 1860.* Rev. Ed. Folkestone, Kent: Dawson, 1979.

Tripathi, Bansi Dhar. *Sadhus of India: A Sociological View.* Bombay: Popular Prakashan, 1978.

Tripati, Sila. "Ports and Maritime Activities in Orissa (16th to 19th Centuries)." In *Ship-building and Navigation in the Indian Ocean, AD 1400-1800*, 155-64. New Delhi: Munshiram Manoharlal, 1997.

Tübingen Morgenblatt (Tübingen, Germany).

Turner, Victor. *The Ritual Process.* Chicago: Aldine, 1969.

Twining, Thomas. *Travels in India, a Hundred Years Ago.* London: James R. Osgood, 1893.

Valentia, Viscount George. *Voyages and Travels to India.* 4 vols. London: F. C., and J. Rivington, 1811.

Van den Branden, Frans Joseph. *Geschiedenis der Antwerpsche schilderschool.* [History of the Antwerp School of Painting]. 3 vols. Antwerp: Buschmann, 1883.

Vanmour, Jean-Baptiste. See Le Hay.

Van Nouhuys, F. W. "The Anchor." *The Mariner's Mirror: The Journal of the Society for Nautical Research* (1951): 17-47.

Vatin, Michel. *Calcutta.* Insight City Guides. Singapore: APA Publications, 1991.

Vaughan, Philippa, ed. *The Victoria Memorial Hall, Calcutta: Conception, Collections, Conservation.* Mumbai: Marg Publications, 1997.

Veraghtert, Karel. "From Inland Port to International Port, 1790-1914." In *Antwerp: A Port for all Seasons*, edited by F. Suykens, et al., 278-418. Antwerp: MIM, 1986.

Verbanck, Richard. "Twee Figuren Kruisende Paden: Popham/Solvyns." In *Jaarboek 1973*, 1-8. Bredene, Belgium: Heemkring Ter Cuere, 1973.

Victoria Memorial. *Up the Country: Exhibition of Upper Indian Views, 18th & 19th Centuries, from Victoria Memorial, Calcutta.* Exhibition catalog. Calcutta: Victoria Memorial, 1981.

Vinet, Ernest. *Bibliographie méthodique et raisonnée des beaux-arts.* 2 vols. Paris: Firmin-Didot, 1874, 1877. Reprinted Hildesheim: George Olms, 1967.

Vögel, J. *Indian Serpent-lore.* London: Arthur Probstain, 1926.

Wahl, Samuel Friedrich Guenther. *Erdbeschreibung von Ostindien . . . in Nachträgen zu der von M. C. Spengel angefangenen Fortsetzung von D. A. F. Busching's Erdbeschreibung Asiens.* Hamburg:1805.

Wahlen, August. *Moeurs, usages et costumes de tours les peuples du mond.* 4 vols. Vol. I, *Asia.* Brussels: Librarie historique-artistique, 1843-44. Italian translation: *Usi e costumi sociali, politici et religiosi di tutti i popli del mondo.* 4 vols. Turin: Stabilimento tipografico Fontana, 1844-47.

Waley, Arthur. "Anquetil du Perron and Sir William Jones." *History Today* 2 (January 1952): 23-33.

Walker, Benjamin. *Hindu World: An Encyclopedic Survey of Hinduism.* 2 vols. London: George Allen & Unwin, 1968.

Wallace, Lt. R. G. *Fifteen Years in India: Or Sketches of a Soldier's Life*, 2d ed. London: Longman, Hurst, Rees, Orme, and Brown, 1823.

Ward, Rev. William. *Account of the Writings, Religion, and Manners of the Hindoos.* 4 vols. Serampore: Baptist Mission Press, 1811.

———. *A View of the History, Literature, and Mythology, of the Hindoos.* Rev. ed. 3 vols. London: Black, Kingsbury, Parbury & Allen, 1822. Reprinted Port Washington, NY: Kennikat Press, 1970.

———. *A View of the History, Literature, and Religion of the Hindoos. From the Second Edition, carefully abridged, and greatly improved.* Hartford: H. Huntington, 1824.

Watson, J. Forbes, and J. W. Kaye. *The People of India: A Series of Photographic Illustrations, with Descriptive Letterpress, of the Races and Tribes of Hindustan.* 6 vols. London: India Museum: 1868-75. Reprinted 1987.

Welch, Stuart Cary. *Room for Wonder: Indian Painting during the British Period, 1760-1880.* New York: American Federation of Arts, 1978.

Westall, William. See under Knight, Charles.

Wheatley, Francis. *Cries of London.* London: J. Newberry, 1775. London: J. Harris, 1804.

Whitaker, Romulus. *Common Indian Snakes: A Field Guide.* Delhi: Macmillan, 1978.

Whitworth, George C. *An Anglo-Indian Dictionary.* London: Kegan, Paul, Trench, 1885.

Wild, Antony. *The East India Company: Trade and Conquest from 1600.* London: HarperCollins, 1999.

Wilenski, R. H. *Flemish Painters, 1430-1830.* 2 vols. London: Faber & Faber, 1960.

Wilkins, Charles. *A Glossary of Oriental Terms.* London: Government Press, 1830.

———. "Observations on the Seeks and their College" [1781]. *Asiatick Researches.* New Delhi: Cosmo, 1979 [1788], 1:246-49.

———, tr. *The Bhăgvăt-Gēētā, or Dialogues of Krēēshnă and Arjŏŏn.* London: C. Nourse, 1785. French translation, *La Bhaguat-Geeta, ou dialogues de Kreeshna et d'Arjoon; contenant un précis de la religion et de la morale des Indiens. Traduit du Sanscrit en Anglois par C. Wilkins; et de l'Anglois et François par M. Parraud.* London and Paris: Buisson, 1787.

Wilkins, William J. *Modern Hinduism.* London: T. Fisher Unwin, 1887.

Wilkinson, Wynyard R. T. *The Makers of Indian Colonial Silver.* London: By the Author, 1987.

Willard, Capt. N. Augustus. "A Treatise on the Music of Hindoostan" (1834). In *Hindu Music from Various Authors*, edited by Sourindro Mohun Tagore. Chowkhamba Sanskrit Studies, 49. Varanasi: Chowkhamba Sanskrit Series Office, 1965 [1882], 1-122.

Williams, Captain John. *An Historical Acount of the Rise and Progress of the Bengal Native Infantry, From its First Formation in 1757, to 1796.* London: John Murray, 1817. Reprint facsimile edition: London: Fredrick Muller, 1970.

Williamson, George C. *Bryan's Dictionary of Painters and Engravers.* New edition, revised and enlarged by George C. Williamson. Port Washington, NY: Kennikat Press, 1964 [1903]. Original edition by Michael Bryan, *Biographical and Critical Dictionary of Painters and Engravers*, 1816.

Williamson, Captain Thomas. *The East India Vade-Mecum: or, Complete Guide to Gentlemen Intended for the Civil, Military, or Naval Service of the Hon. East India Company*. 2 vols. London: Black, Parry & Kingbury, 1810. Digested by J. B. Gilchrist, 1825.

———, and Sir Charles D'Oyly. *The European in India; from a Collection of Drawings by Charles Doyley, Esq., Engraved by J. H. Clark and C. Dubourg*. London: Edward Orme, 1813.

———, and Samuel Howett. *Oriental Field Sports; being a complete description of the Wild Sports of the East . . . drawings by Samuel Howett*. London: Edward Orme, 1807.

Wilson, Charles Robert. *The Early Annals of the English in Bengal*. 3 vols. New Delhi: Bimla, 1983 [1895].

———, and W. H. Carey. *Glimpses of the Olden Times: India Under East India Company*. Edited by Amarendranath Mookerji. Calcutta: Eastlight Book House, 1968.

Wilson, Horace Hayman. *Essays and Lectures Chiefly on the Religion of the Hindus*. Edited by Reinhold Rost. 12 vols. London: Trübner, 1862-71.

———. "The Religious Festivals of the Hindus." *Journal of the Royal Asiatic Society* 9 (1846): 60-110. Reprinted in Vol. 2, *Works*, edited by Reinhold Rost et al. 10 vols. London: Trübner & Co., 1862-70.

———. *Select Specimens of the Theatre of the Hindus*. 2 vols. London: Parbury, Allen, 1835.

———. "A Sketch of the Religious Sects of the Hindus." *Asiatic Researches*. New Delhi: Cosmo, 1979 [1828], 16:1-136, and [1832], 17:169-313.

———. *Religious Sects of the Hindus. Based on the "Sketch" by H. H. Wilson, with additions from later sources or information*. London; Christian Literature Society for India, 1904.

———. *The Oriental Portfolio*. See Bacon.

Wilson, John. *Indian Caste*. 2 vols. Bombay: Times of India, 1877.

Wilton-Ely, John. "Neo-classicism." In *The Dictionary of Art*, 22:734-42.

Wise, James. *Notes on the Races, Castes, and Trades of Eastern Bengal*. London: Harrison & Sons, 1883.

Woodcock, George. *The Greeks in India*. London: Faber and Faber, 1966.

World, The. Calcutta weekly, 1791-1793.

Woussen, Martine. "Frans Balthasar Solvyns." In *1770-1830: autour du néo-classicisme en Belgique*, edited by Denis Coekelberghs and Pierre, 304. Brussels: Crédit Communal, 1985.

Wulff, Donna M. "Rādhā: Consort and Conqueror of Krishna." In *Devī: Goddesses of India*, edited by John S. Hawley and Donna M. Wulff, 109-34. Berkeley: University of California Press, 1996.

Wurzbach, Alfred von. *Niederlèndisches Künstler-Lexikon*. 3 vols. Vienna/Leipzig; von Halm and Goldmann, 1904-1911.

Yule, Henry, and A. C. Burnell. See *Hobson-Jobson*.

Unpublished

Bisschops, "Solvyns," genealogical notes, Stadsarchief, City of Antwerp.

Donnet, "Solvyns," genealogical notes, Stadsarchief, City of Antwerp.

Finnegan, Malia Elizabeth. "Francois-Balthazar Solvyns: Artist and Ethnographer of India Between the Years 1790-1812." Master's thesis, University of Maryland, 1991.

"Généalogie de la famille baronniale Solvyns originaire de la principauté de Steenhuyse au Comté de Flandre, MCDL-MCMX," unpublished family record, Brussels.

Henry, Edward O. "The Meanings of Music in a North Indian Village". Unpublished Ph.D. dissertation, Michigan State University, 1973.

India Office Record. "Shipping and Ship Building in India", 1736-1839. London: 1995.

Sagala, Marie-José. "Solvyns Franz Balthazar, 1760-1824". Mémoire de Maîtrise d'Historie de l'Art Moderne, Universite Paul-Valery, Montpellier III, U.F.R.III. [1990.]

Solvyns, François Balthazar [Baltazard]. "A Collection of Two Hundred and Fifty Drawings Descriptive of the Manners Customs and Dresses of the Hindoos by Balt. Solvyns. Calcutta." [Original drawings for the Calcutta edition, 248 drawings in actual number.] Department of Prints and Drawings, Victoria and Albert Museum. Press Mark: S-20 (Reg. No. 8937.1-98; 8937.98a-247).

———. *Portraits of East Indians by C. C. Fraser after the plan and manner of Solvyns*. Folio, 2 vols. Calcutta, 1805. [Paintings by an Indian artist over the Solvyns etchings from the Calcutta edition, in the collection of Charles Collins Fraser.] Harvard University, Houghton Library, HEW 14.7.1.

Styles, Michael H. *Captain Hogan: Sailor, Merchant and Diplomat on Six Continents*.

Archival Materials

Bibliothèque nationale de France, Paris.

Solvyns, F. Balthazard. *Les Hindoûs*, 29th livraison. Od.32a. tomes 1 et 2. Fol.

Index & Glossary

Selective index, with glossary, to principal subjects treated and to leading personalities. References are to both pages and plates. Page numbers for each Solvyns etchings (text and commentary) are in bold type. References to Hindu deities and sects are repleat throughout the book and are listed below only when a subject of Solvyns's major concern.

D